SCHIZOPHRENIA AND OTHER PSYCHOTIC DISORDERS

Schizophrenia

Paranoid type
Disorganized type
Catatonic type
Undifferentiated type
Residual type

Schizophreniform disorder
Schizoaffective disorder
Delusional disorder
Brief psychotic disorder
Shared psychotic disorder
Psychotic disorder due to . . . *(indicate the general medical condition)*
Substance-induced psychotic disorder
Psychotic disorder NOS

MOOD DISORDERS

Depressive Disorders

Major depressive disorder
Dysthymic disorder
Depressive disorder NOS

Bipolar Disorders

Bipolar I disorder
Bipolar II disorder
Cyclothymic disorder
Bipolar disorder NOS
Mood disorder due to . . . *(indicate the general medical condition)*
Substance-induced mood disorder
Mood disorder NOS

ANXIETY DISORDERS

Panic disorder without agoraphobia
Panic disorder with agoraphobia
Agoraphobia without history of panic disorder
Specific phobia
Social phobia
Obsessive-compulsive disorder
Post-traumatic stress disorder
Acute stress disorder
Generalized anxiety disorder
Anxiety disorder due to . . . *(indicate the general medical condition)*
Substance-induced anxiety disorder
Anxiety disorder NOS

SOMATOFORM DISORDERS

Somatization disorder
Undifferentiated somatoform disorder
Conversion disorder
Pain disorder
Hypochondriasis
Body dysmorphic disorder
Somatoform disorder NOS

FACTITIOUS DISORDERS

Factitious disorder
Factitious disorder NOS

DISSOCIATIVE DISORDERS

Dissociative amnesia
Dissociative fugue
Dissociative identity disorder
Depersonalization disorder
Dissociative disorder NOS

SEXUAL AND GENDER IDENTITY DISORDERS

Sexual Dysfunctions

Sexual Desire Disorders
Sexual Arousal Disorders
Orgasmic Disorders
Sexual Pain Disorders
Sexual Dysfunction Due to a General Medical Condition

Paraphilias

Exhibitionism
Fetishism
Frotteurism
Pedophilia
Sexual Masochism
Sexual Sadism
Transvestic Fetishism
Voyeurism
Paraphilia NOS

Gender Identity Disorders

Gender identity disorder
Gender identity disorder NOS
Sexual disorder NOS

EATING DISORDERS

Anorexia nervosa
Bulimia nervosa
Eating disorder NOS

SLEEP DISORDERS

Primary Sleep Disorders

Dyssomnias
Parasomnias

Sleep Disorders Related to Another Mental Disorder

Other Sleep Disorders

IMPULSE-CONTROL DISORDERS NOT ELSEWHERE CLASSIFIED

Intermittent explosive disorder
Kleptomania
Pyromania
Pathological gambling
Trichotillomania
Impulse-control disorder NOS

ADJUSTMENT DISORDERS

PERSONALITY DISORDERS (AXIS II)

Paranoid personality disorder
Schizoid personality disorder
Schizotypal personality disorder
Antisocial personality disorder
Borderline personality disorder
Histrionic personality disorder
Narcissistic personality disorder
Avoidant personality disorder
Dependent personality disorder
Obsessive-compulsive personality disorder
Personality disorder NOS

OTHER CONDITIONS THAT MAY BE A FOCUS OF CLINICAL ATTENTION

Psychological Factors Affecting Medical Condition

Medication-Induced Movement Disorders

Other Medication-Induced Disorder

Relational Problems

Relational problem related to a mental disorder or general medical condition
Parent-child relational problem
Partner relational problem
Sibling relational problem
Relational problem NOS

Problems Related to Abuse or Neglect

Physical abuse of child
Sexual abuse of child
Neglect of child
Physical abuse of adult
Sexual abuse of adult

Additional Conditions That May Be a Focus of Clinical Attention

Noncompliance with treatment
Malingering
Adult antisocial behavior
Child or adolescent antisocial behavior
Borderline intellectual functioning
Age-related cognitive decline
Bereavement
Academic problem
Occupational problem
Identity problem
Religious or spiritual problem
Acculturation problem
Phase of life problem

Abnormal Psychology

Martin E. P. Seligman

UNIVERSITY OF PENNSYLVANIA

Elaine F. Walker

EMORY UNIVERSITY

David L. Rosenhan

STANFORD UNIVERSITY

Abnormal Psychology

FOURTH EDITION

W · W · NORTON & COMPANY
NEW YORK · LONDON

The text of this book is composed in Bembo, with the display type set in Matrix Script.
Composition by TSI Graphics. Manufacturing by R. R. Donnelley.

Editor: Jon Durbin
Developmental Editor: Sandy Lifland
Associate Managing Editor: Jane Carter
Production Manager: Roy Tedoff
Editorial Assistants: Robert Whiteside, Aaron Javsicas
Text and Cover Design: Rubina Yeh
Illustrations: Franklin Boyd Forney

Library of Congress Cataloging-in-Publication Data

Seligman, Martin E. P.
    Abnormal psychology / Martin E. P. Seligman, Elaine F. Walker, David L. Rosenhan.—4th ed.
        p. cm.
    Rev. ed. of: Abnormal psychology / David L. Rosenhan. 3rd ed. 1995.
    Includes bibliographical references and index.
    ISBN 0-393-97417-0
    1. Psychology, Pathological. 2. Psychotherapy—Case studies. I. Walker, Elaine F. II. Rosenhan,
David L. III. Rosenhan, David L. Abnormal psychology. IV. Title.

RC454 .S394 2001
616.89—dc21
                                                                                    00-067861

Cover illustration: Josef Forster, *Untitled* (after 1916). Collection Prinzhorn-Sammlung,
University of Heidelberg.

The artwork on this book's cover was created by Josef Forster and belongs to the world-renowned
Prinzhorn Collection, located in the Psychiatric Clinic of the University of Heidelberg. The evoca-
tive style and emotional expressiveness of Forster's painting is characteristic of the art of the mentally ill. Originally coined "Art Brut" by Jean Dubuffet and often referred to as "Outsider Art" in
America, this term is popularly applied to work by an individual from any of a variety of marginal-
ized groups, including the mentally ill, convicts, and eccentrics. We have sought to include Outsider
Art throughout the text whenever appropriate. Nearly all of the chapter openers feature works from
the Prinzhorn Collection, the Art Brut Gallery in Lausanne, Switzerland, Hospital Audiences, Inc.,
in New York City, the Henry Boxer Gallery in London, and others as credited in the book. The
authors and editors of this book hope that these works will enhance the reader's interest in the study
of psychology and underscore the shared humanity of the sick and the sound.

Acknowledgments and copyrights appear on pages A109-A114, which constitute a continuation of
the copyright page.

W. W. Norton & Company, Inc., 500 Fifth Avenue, New York, NY 10110
www.wwnorton.com
W. W. Norton & Company, Ltd., Castle House, 75/76 Wells Street, London W1T 3QT

4 5 6 7 8 9 0

About the Authors

Martin E. P. Seligman, Ph.D., is Robert A. Fox Leadership Professor of Psychology in the Department of Psychology at the University of Pennsylvania, where for fourteen years he also served as the director of the clinical training program. He teaches and conducts research on topics in positive psychology, learned helplessness, depression, and on optimism and pessimism. He is well-known in academic and clinical circles, a best-selling author, and former president of the American Psychological Association.

Dr. Seligman's publications include fifteen books and 150 articles on motivation and personality. Among his books are *Learned Optimism* (Knopf, 1991), *What You Can Change & What You Can't* (Knopf, 1994), *The Optimistic Child* (Houghton Mifflin, 1995), and *Helplessness: On Depression, Development, and Death* (Freeman, 1975, 1993). He is the recipient of two Distinguished Scientific Contribution Awards from the American Psychological Association, the Laurel Award of the American Association for Applied Psychology and Prevention, and the Lifetime Achievement Award of the Society for Research in Psychopathology. Dr. Seligman received both the American Psychological Society's William James Fellow Award (for contribution to basic science) and the James McKeen Cattell Fellow Award (for the application of psychological knowledge). He was also named "Distinguished Practitioner" by the National Academies of Practice.

Elaine F. Walker is Samuel Candler Dobbs Professor of Psychology and Neuroscience at Emory University. She teaches and conducts research on the causes of serious mental disorders. Much of her research focuses on the developmental course of schizophrenia, especially childhood precursors. Along with colleagues and a group of highly talented graduate students, Dr. Walker has studied the earliest signs of vulnerability to schizophrenia. More recently, her research has focused on the biological effects of stress on mental disorders, and the development of adolescents at risk for schizophrenia.

Dr. Walker has published over 100 books and articles. She is the recipient of several awards, including the James McKeen Cattell Award, the W. T. Grant Foundation Faculty Scholar Award, the Gralnick Award for Research on Schizophrenia, the Emory University Scholar-Teacher Award, the Zubin Memorial Research Award, an Established Investigator Award from the National Alliance for Research on Schizophrenia and Depression, and the Research Scientist Development Award from the National Institute of Mental Health. She is the former director of the clinical program at Emory University and is currently the president of the Society for Research in Psychopathology.

David L. Rosenhan is Professsor Emeritus of Psychology and Law at Stanford University. Over the years, he has been a major proponent of the legal rights of mental patients, and an investigator of basic personality and social processes. He has published widely in the leading professional journals. His 1973 "pseudopatients" study remains a landmark in the field.

Contents in Brief

Contents

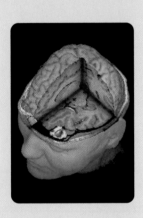

Preface

Dramatic changes have occurred in the years since the publication of *Abnormal Psychology,* third edition. A sheep has been cloned, new drugs have been synthesized that have helped patients to live longer and more productively, the human genome has been sequenced, and the Worldwide Web and the Internet have revolutionized the analysis and dissemination of knowledge. These revolutionary events in science and technology have captured international headlines, and this fourth edition tries to keep pace with these developments.

There is no doubt that we now know much more about biological processes than we did when the last edition was published. By comparison, our progress in understanding psychological processes, especially abnormal processes, has not been as dramatic. There haven't been any international headlines about major breakthroughs on the causes of depression, anxiety, or schizophrenia. But that does not mean that there have not been significant advances in our understanding of how mental functions can go awry. We certainly know more now than we did when the third edition was published. For example, we know more about the effectiveness of various psychological and biological treatments for mental disorders. This means that patients suffering from problems like depression, anxiety, or obsessive-compulsive disorder can be fairly confident that there are proven treatments available for them. We also know more about the risk factors, both psychological and biological, associated with mental disorders. Finally, we know a great deal more about the how the brain works. This knowledge is, in part, a consequence of technology— the development of sophisticated devices for observing brain structure and function in living people.

The most important change in the field of abnormal psychology has come at the intersection of biology and psychology. New findings in neuroscience have produced a revolution in the way researchers think about the mutual influence of biological and psychological processes. New and often more successful ways of treating patients have also modified our views of the interacting causes of many mental disorders. Researchers have found numerous examples of how "top-down" psychological experiences can affect biological and psychological processes, and how "bottom-up" biological factors can affect psychological and biological processes. Indeed, the effects are profound. In fact, many scientists are convinced that we are on the brink of important new discoveries about the interactions between psychology and biology. Many believe that it is no longer "nature versus nurture," but rather the interplay between mind and body, between experience and brain function.

This new edition of *Abnormal Psychology* reflects the changes in the field. We challenge the student to consider experience (beginning as early as the prenatal period) together with biological processes. The journey takes the reader through all the levels of our existence—from cellular activity, to the impact of genes, hormones, and brain chemistry, to the role of the social environment. We explore the new horizons charted by behavioral neuroscientists as they seek to unravel the mystery of how the interactions of human beings with their physical and social environments mold the expression of the thousands of genes that contain the blueprint for the human brain. Using a "levels of analysis approach," we draw on the best behavioral and neuroscience research of the past decade. We show how these research findings can shed light on psychological disorders like depression, schizophrenia, anxiety, obsessive-compulsive disorders, sexual disorders, and drug addictions.

Another major theme of this edition is development. Like all other mammals, human beings undergo changes in their physical and mental abilities as they age. Developmental psychologists have documented the amazing changes that occur as human beings traverse the path from infancy to old age. Throughout childhood and adolescence, new physical, social and cognitive abilities are acquired. Then, with advanced age, certain abilities diminish. Elaine Walker, the new coauthor of *Abnormal Psychology,* has been in the forefront of the field of developmental psychopathology. She has emphasized the critical role that developmental change plays in the emergence of mental disorders. Indeed, researchers have found that developmental changes are associated with marked changes in the risk for psychological disorders. Certain disorders, like autism, always arise in early childhood, whereas others, like dementia, usually occur with advanced age. In contrast, the risk for disorders such as depression and schizophrenia increases with age through adolescence and young adulthood, then decreases throughout the rest of life. There is no doubt that these differences hold some

important clues about the causes of psychological disorders. The fourth edition of *Abnormal Psychology* leads the field in acknowledging the importance of a developmental perspective on psychopathology.

The treatment of mental disorders is also undergoing rapid change. When the first edition of this book was conceived, most people who were diagnosed with serious mental illnesses were in state hospitals. In fact, the original authors, Martin Seligman and David Rosenhan, came up with the idea for the textbook while they were together in a mental hospital! At that time, David Rosenhan was conducting a landmark study in which a diverse group of normal people were admitted to mental hospitals pretending to have a single symptom: They heard voices that said "empty," "meaningless," and "thud." From the moment they were admitted, these "pseudopatients" stopped exhibiting that symptom and acted the way "normal" people do. Nonetheless, they were still labeled as "mentally ill" and treated that way. This study had a major impact on the field, because it demonstrated how the judgment of mental health workers could be influenced by initial impressions about a person's mental status. The results of the study also sensitized people to the plight of those in mental hospitals.

Since the time of the classic "pseudopatient" study of David Rosenhan, however, the tide has turned. Many psychiatric hospitals have closed, and too many patients who need treatment are not getting it. We are now in an era in which the mentally ill are as likely to be walking the streets homeless, as they are to be hospitalized. Today, there is increasing concern about inadequate mental health care, and the limits on patients' access to hospitalization. The way to test the outcome of treatments has been shifting from laboratory efficacy studies to field-based effectiveness studies, and Martin Seligman as president of the American Psychological Association has been at the forefront of some of the latest developments. In this edition of *Abnormal Psychology,* we describe these changes, and the factors that have brought them about. We discuss the effect of deinstitutionalization and managed health care on mental health treatment. We also describe the field of positive psychology, a major interest of Martin Seligman, and the need for a shift in the paradigm, such that psychologists not only treat people with disorders but also help people to develop strengths that prevent them from succumbing to mental disorders in the first place.

In some very important ways, the fourth edition of *Abnormal Psychology* also maintains certain traditions established by the previous editions. First, we continue to emphasize the scientific basis of clinical psychology. This scientific perspective provides the framework for understanding the causes and treatments of mental disorders. The text highlights the fact that science is the most important source of information guiding the work of psychologists in clinical practice.

At the same time, we are keenly aware of the fact that each person suffering from a mental disorder is unique, and that there are not always clear-cut answers to many of the challenges faced by mental health workers and the people they serve. This new edition of *Abnormal Psychology* addresses in detail the ethical and social considerations that surround the treatment of people with mental illness. It explores the plight of families who have a loved one with mental illness. Like no other text in the field, it addresses the harsh realities of limited access to treatment in the American mental health care system.

Another tradition maintained in the fourth edition of *Abnormal Psychology* is a commitment to the foundations of the field. We continue to cover the classic theories and research findings that influenced the course of scientific progress in abnormal psychology. We take the reader from ancient Greek theories of brain function, to Freud, to revolutionary new ideas in neuroscience.

Finally, following the approach taken in the previous editions, we stress the diagnosis and treatment of mental disorders. We describe the various techniques, and then illustrate, often with case examples, how psychologists use them to diagnose and treat patients. The text provides diagnostic criteria boxes for each major disorder from the fourth edition of the Diagnostic and Statistical Manual of Mental Disorders (DSM-IV). At the same time, we do not blindly adhere to the classifications adopted by DSM-IV, and we directly examine limitations of the DSM. We also include treatment tables that compare the various treatments for most of the disorders discussed in the text.

In summary, this new edition of *Abnormal Psychology* tries to retain all the strengths of the previous editions and combines them with exciting new findings and perspectives that bring it to the cutting edge of the field. It is our goal that the text should represent a unique synthesis of the biological, psychological, and social levels of analysis. In doing so, it brings the study of abnormal psychology into the new millennium.

Supplementary Materials

The new fourth edition of *Abnormal Psychology* comes with an exciting array of support materials:

- **Clinical Guide to Abnormal Psychology:** This new video cassette was created specifically for use with the fourth edition of *Abnormal Psychology* and is exclusive to W. W. Norton. It features fourteen brief interviews with individuals who have been diagnosed with a mental disorder. These are patients, not actors, and their remarks provide valuable insight into the experience of living with a mental disorder.

- **Student Website (http://www.wwnorton.com/abnormal):** This thought-provoking student resource features an online casebook that pairs streamed audio and video excerpts from the Clinical Guide to Abnormal Psychology videocassette with case profiles, DSM-IV criteria boxes, links to outside resources, and assignable Levels of Analysis thought questions. Other site resources include biweekly Psychology in the News postings about current developments in mental health research, Society and Mental Health essays, and online study tools, including chapter overviews with key terms and definitions, new and improved interactive multiple-choice quizzes, and crossword puzzles.

- **Student CD-ROM:** The contents of the Student Website are also available on a CD-ROM that will be packaged with the textbook upon request.

- **Abnormal Psychology: Essential Cases and Readings** by Tom Bradbury and Cindy Yee-Bradbury (UCLA): This new casebook has fifteen chapters covering all major facets of the field. It is designed to provide students with deeper analyses of topics typically mentioned only briefly in abnormal psychology textbooks. Each chapter includes four readings that have been culled from diverse sources to address a wide array of classic and contemporary topics in psychopathology. Each reading has been edited carefully to provide students with succinct coverage of key ideas, and each is introduced by the editors and supplemented with suggested readings.

- **Norton Media Library for Instructors:** A CD-ROM (dual platform with Powerpoint slides) offers instructors the resources and software necessary to present multimedia materials in lecture. This CD-ROM includes selected art from the text, patient videotape segments, Powerpoint viewers, and Powerpoint presentations.

• **Study Guide** by Kieran Sullivan (Santa Clara University): Completely revised for the new edition, this highly useful study aide includes a general guide to the reading, objectives, multiple-choice and fill-in-the blank questions, and an examination of key chapter themes.

• **Instructor's Manual and Computerized Test-Item File:** Completely revised for the new edition, this highly useful teaching tool includes chapter overviews, sample lecture topics, demonstrations, suggested readings, suggested films, and over 1,000 test items in both print and computerized format. The Norton Testmaker uses Microtest III software developed by the Chariot Software Group.

Acknowledgments

We would like to gratefully acknowledge the highly talented scholars and teachers that have provided invaluable advice on creating this new edition of *Abnormal Psychology*. We would first like to thank those colleagues who attended our initial planning meeting in Philadelphia:

Mary Dozier, *University of Delaware*
Angela Gillem, *Beaver College*
Steven Krauss, *Villanova University*
Leslie Rescorla, *Bryn Mawr College*

We would also like to recognize the following colleagues who provided detailed reviews of draft chapters:

Paul Abramson, *University of California at Los Angeles*
Tom Bradbury. *University of California at Los Angeles*
Ty Cannon, *University of California at Los Angeles*
Lee Ann Clark, *University of Iowa*
Jane Costello, *Duke University*
Alan Fridlund, *University of California at Santa Barbara*
Marc Henley, *Delaware County Community College*
Jill Hooley, *Harvard University*
Erick Janssen, *The Kinsey Institute*

Suzanne Bennet Johnson, *University of Florida*
Tom Joiner, *Florida State University*
Ann E. Kelley, *University of Wisconsin at Madison*
Bruce McEwen, *Rockefeller University*
Brad Pearce, *Emory University*
James Pennebaker, *University of Texas at Austin*
Al Porterfield, *Oberlin College*
Barbara Rothbaum, *Emory University*
Kieran Sullivan, *Santa Clara College*

We would also like to give special thanks to Alan Fridlund (University of California at Santa Barbara) who commented on a significant number of chapters. Certainly his keen insights and contributions have helped make this an even better book.

So much of what we know about the nature and origins of mental disorders is a result of the efforts of people who have suffered from them. Many patients and their families have contributed substantial time and energy to research on psychopathology. They have participated in scientific studies, and contributed to the work of advocacy groups that fund research and educate the public about mental health and illness. We thank them for being so generous.

We owe a debt of gratitude to the research assistants who helped with this revision of the text: Kerry Haffey, Felicia Reynolds, and Annie Bollini. Their hard work made this a much better textbook. The fourth edition of this book also benefitted enormously from the diligent and careful labors of Terry Kang, Jay Reid, and Rachel Elwork. Jane Gillham, Linda Petock, Derek Isaacowitz, Mandy Seligman, Peter Schulman, and Karen Shore provided valuable assistance along the way.

We would especially like to thank all of the students who have inspired us and collaborated with us in pursuing difficult research questions about the origins of psychopathology. Without the contagious enthusiasm of students, the research process would not be nearly as rewarding. Also of critical importance are the many faculty colleagues with whom we have worked over the years. Their scholarly insights, collegial support, and personal friendships have enriched our work as behavioral scientists, teachers, and authors.

Our biggest vote of thanks goes to four Norton folk: to Jon Durbin, who shepherded the project from start to finish; to Drake McFeely and Roby Harrington, who encouraged and enabled it; and above all to Sandy Lifland. Sandy was our guide, our cheerleader, and our most valuable critic. We also would like to thank Rubina Yeh, who created the beautiful design for this new edition; Rob Whiteside, who searched for the wonderful photos that appear in the book; Roy Tedoff, who managed the production of the book; and Jane Carter, Jan Hoeper, and Aaron Javsicas, all of whom helped with many essential editorial and production details.

Martin E. P. Seligman
Elaine F. Walker
David L. Rosenhan

Abnormal Psychology

1

Abnormality: Past and Present

August Natterer, *The Miraculous Shepherd (II).*

Learning Objectives

→ Become familiar with the concept of exploring abnormal behavior at both biological and psychological levels of analysis.

→ Be able to discuss the contributions of both science and practice to the understanding and treatment of abnormality.

→ Learn how developmental changes can affect the onset of abnormal behaviors.

→ Describe how psychologists can determine whether treatments are effective, and what specific treatments might be the treatment of choice for particular disorders.

→ Learn how different historical approaches to abnormality led to differences in perceived causes and methods of treatment of mental disorder.

→ Familiarize yourself with the elements of abnormality and the "family resemblance" approach to defining abnormality.

→ Be aware of the hazards of self-diagnosis and of the problems of strictly adhering to only one model of abnormality.

At the approach of the millennium, as religious pilgrims descended on Jerusalem, some making this journey were diagnosed with a new condition called the "Jerusalem Syndrome." Those who were so afflicted believed they were figures from the Bible or in contact with biblical figures. One of them was Lars, a second-grade teacher from Copenhagen, Denmark:

On the second day of his trip to Jerusalem, Lars began to feel very uneasy. An inexplicable sense of dread came over him. He had arrived with a group of Danish tourists, but he was now overwhelmed with a need to get away from them and be alone. A loud voice from inside his head instructed him to "cleanse himself and go to the Mosque of Omar and meet the Messiah." He bathed in scalding water in his room, and then he ran, clad only in a long white shirt and white under-shorts, to the Old City. When he entered the courtyard of the Mosque, he was struck with the realization that here at last he could talk face-to-face with Jesus. He had yearned for such an encounter all his life, and indeed his peculiar religious visions had landed him in trouble back at home with more than one arrest for disturbing the peace outside his local church on the Sabbath.

Lars was sure that he saw Jesus sitting on the roof of the Mosque, looking directly at Lars and beckoning to him. Lars began to shout to Jesus at the top of his lungs. He then saw Jesus joined on the roof by the Virgin Mary. His agitation increased. When the police who guard the Temple Mount arrived, Lars was writhing on the ground and shouting devotions. A brawl ensued when the guards tried to calm him, and Lars was taken to Kfar Shaul Psychiatric Hospital. (Adapted from Abramowitz, 1996)

Lars was one of 470 tourists afflicted with the Jerusalem Syndrome and taken to Kfar Shaul in the final years of the millennium. The syndrome often begins with ritual cleansing, with the patient then dressing in white robes and proclaiming himself to be some prominent figure from the Old or New Testament. Two-thirds of those diagnosed with this syndrome are Jews, and one-third are Christians. Some have definite religious goals, like one Californian who was seeking the purifying red heifer from Numbers 19. Others have political goals, like those of the Australian, Dennis Rohan, who burned the El Aksa

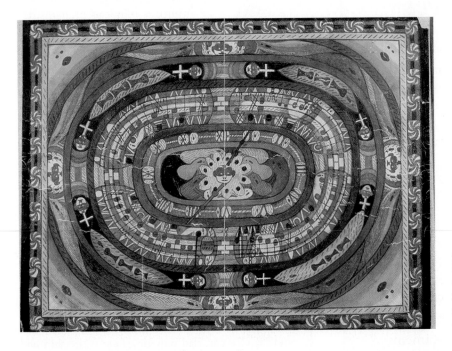

Adolf Wölfli's art is a manifestation of his disturbed mental state. Wölfli was arrested several times before he was finally diagnosed with schizophrenia and committed to the Waldau Asylum, where he was confined until his death.

Mosque, or David Koresh, who wandered Jerusalem before the tragedy in Waco, Texas. Most are harmless and draw curious stares from people in Jerusalem. Nonetheless, the most severely disturbed, like Lars, can end up disintegrating and being hospitalized.

Although newly named, the Jerusalem Syndrome is actually ancient, just one dramatic manifestation of a condition as old as humanity itself—abnormality. Mental illness, the common modern term for such abnormality, is legion. In the last month of 1999, the surgeon general of the United States issued an authoritative report on mental illness (Satcher, 1999). Among its findings, the report included statistics showing how widespread and costly mental disorders are in American society today:

- Twenty percent of Americans—more than 44 million people—have at least one mental illness in any given year, with one-third of these problems persisting for more than one year.
- Six percent of Americans—more than 15 million people—have an addictive disorder.
- Between 5 and 9 percent of children aged nine to seventeen have a "serious emotional disturbance," and at the other end of the age spectrum a full 20 percent of adults over age fifty-five have a mental disorder.
- The direct cost of these disorders in treatment and rehabilitation in 1996 (the last year for which figures are available) was $100 billion—and the majority of these disorders are not treated at all, and so

are not included. The indirect cost in lost productivity at work and school was another $80 billion.
- The disease "burden," the measure of years lost to disability and premature death from mental illness is second only to heart disease, with cancer ranked third. Unipolar depression alone accounts for more disease burden than cardiovascular disease.

Nonetheless, all the news is not so grim. Over the last century, a science of abnormal psychology has grown up to fight these disorders. A taxonomy that yields reliable diagnosis now exists. Abnormal conditions like depression, schizophrenia, and alcoholism, which seemed too fuzzy to be measured fifty years ago, can now be measured and diagnosed with rigor. How these disorders are caused both biologically and environmentally has now been illuminated by experiments and by longitudinal studies of many individuals across their life span. And most importantly, at least fourteen of these disorders are now highly treatable, and often curable.

Themes and Challenges

As the science of abnormal psychology enters its second century, it confronts four burning issues. These four issues are the main challenges and opportunities the field faces at the start of the new century, and so they form the four main themes of this textbook.

Biological and Psychological Levels of Analysis

Until the 1990s, there were two grand traditions in abnormality that worked at different levels of analysis. By and large, each went its own separate way, and each worked in isolation at its own level of analysis. One tradition is *biological* and medical. Its basic tenets are that psychopathology is a disease of the body that can be cured by changing the body. Its investigators work with genes, hormones, neurons, and brain chemistry. Adherents to this tradition reside largely in medical schools, and most of them are called "biological psychiatrists." What aspect of "nature" or "biology" or "medicine" they work on varies with their specialty, be it genetics or neurochemistry or anatomy. But what they have in common is the belief that unlocking the secrets of mental illness depends on scientific progress at the level of biology.

The other grand tradition is *psychological*. Its basic tenets are that psychopathology is caused by disordered habits and by a disordered mental life, and that mental illness can be cured by changing behavior, emotion, and thought. These "clinical psychologists" research and do therapy on automatic thoughts, maladaptive habits, unconscious conflicts, and negative emotional states. They attempt to understand interpersonal conflict and work out issues of responsibility and control with their patients. For the most part, exponents of this tradition reside in psychology departments. What aspect of psychology they emphasize varies with their specialty: conscious thought or unconscious conflict, emotion, or behavior. But what they have in common is the belief that unlocking the secrets of abnormality depends on scientific progress at the level of mind, conflict, and behavior.

We illustrate the main themes of our book by the liberal use of case histories integrated throughout every chapter. We will use these cases to lead into the scientific principles that illuminate cause and cure, and then return to the cases, like Celia's below, to exemplify the principles in action.

The first time Celia had a panic attack, she was working at McDonald's. It was two days before her twentieth birthday. As she was handing a customer a Big Mac, she had the worst experience of her life. The earth seemed to open up beneath her. Her heart began to pound, she felt she was smothering, she broke into a flop sweat, and she was sure she was going to have a heart attack and die. After about twenty minutes of terror, the panic subsided.

Trembling, she got into her car and raced home. To her mother's despair, Celia did not leave the house for the next three months. Since that time, Celia has had about three attacks a month. She does not know when they are coming.

A closer look at Celia's symptoms reveals two gross clusters. First, there is what she is thinking and what she is feeling. During an attack, she feels dread, dizziness, and shakiness. She sometimes thinks this is all not real and that she is going crazy. She always thinks she is going to die. Second, there are dramatic bodily symptoms. Her heart rate doubles, her blood pressure soars, and she breaks into a flop sweat. She has searing chest pain, and she feels she is smothering.

The biological level of analysis focuses on Celia's bodily symptoms: the heart palpitations and chest pain. The psychological level of analysis focuses on Celia's cognitive symptoms: her belief that she is having a heart attack. Yet, psychologists are finding that neither kind of symptom works in isolation. Rather, each affects the other

Work on the two levels of analysis used to go on mostly in isolation or with lip service paid to the other level of analysis. The two levels were often set in opposition to each other: nature versus nurture (Is panic caused by genes or by learning?) or mind versus body (Is panic caused by thoughts of an impending heart attack or by chemicals in the brain?). The setting of the research itself fed this either/or mentality. So, for example, biological psychiatrists measured chemicals in the brain called neurotransmitters and found that patients with low neurotransmitter activity often were diagnosed with depression. The measurement of cognition, behavior, and emotional conflict in these patients was not part of such research programs. Alternatively, clinical psychologists working on obsessions and compulsions found that they could often get rid of a patient's hand-washing compulsion by putting dirt all over her and getting her to agree not to wash it off. Brain activity in the neural centers related to the behavior went unmeasured in such research.

Many biological psychiatrists once were "reductionists" and claimed that all psychological phenomena—thought, emotion, and will, for example—would be fully explained by underlying biological phenomena such as neurotransmitters and immune activity. They believed that mental illness was just a disease of the body and that its cure came about by changing the body. Most clinicians, on the other hand, once believed that only thoughts, emotions, and behavior mattered, and that biology didn't affect psychological state. They believed that progress in the understanding and relief of abnormality would come from measuring and manipulating higher processes and that the so-called "underlying" biological processes were merely "slave processes."

But the whole picture is now changing. And what has caused the change is great progress in answering a very old question: what is the relation of the biological to the psychological—of genes to environment, of thought to neurotransmitters, of emotion to the immune system—in abnormality? This question has been asked since the time of Descartes. But before the advent of the huge technological leaps in the measurement of biological states (see Chapter 4), the answers were just philosophical speculation, not matters of empirical fact. Once these technical advances came

about in the last decade, the wall between the two levels of analysis began to crumble. Clinical psychologists and biological psychiatrists began to work side by side to unravel some of the secrets of exactly how the body influences the mind, and more astonishingly, how the mind influences the body. Within the context of our theme of biology and psychology, we will discuss how these secrets were unlocked and what they tell us about how mental illness is caused and how it can be relieved, cured, or prevented for all the disorders covered in this book (see Box 1–1 for a discussion of sociocultural contributions to mental disorders).

The discoveries fall into two categories: *bottom-up causation* and *top-down causation*. Taken separately, each provides evidence for one kind of explanation. Appreciated together, however, the two kinds of discoveries tell us that the cause and cure of the disorders are both psychological and biological. The

Society and Mental Health

Box 1—1

Moderating Influence or Level of Analysis?

There are many ways in which culture and society influence the perception of abnormality. In some cultures and at some times, practices we now think of as normal were considered disorders: masturbation in nineteenth-century America was considered a hallmark of insanity, whereas today we recognize it to be almost universal in males and very common in females. Conversely, the Jerusalem Syndrome is now a clear disorder that warrants hospitalization, whereas in biblical times hearing divine voices and obeying their commands was considered not only acceptable, but sacred.

Societal variables, like poverty, race, class, nationality, and gender have well-documented and powerful influences on mental illness. So, for example:

- Poor people in America have much more schizophrenia than wealthier people (Hollingshead and Redlich, 1958).
- White Americans have markedly higher rates of depression than African Americans (Kessler et al., 1994).
- Women have the clear majority of anxiety disorders, while men have the clear majority of substance-abuse disorders (Robins et al., 1984).
- Koro, a disorder in which a man fears that his penis will retract into his abdomen and that he may die, is reported in Malaysia and other parts of Southeast Asia, but not elsewhere (Rubin,1982).
- Jamaican children have more disorders of undercontrol than overcontrol, but American children show the reverse pattern (Lambert et al., 1992).

- Anorexia and bulimia only occur in cultures (like modern urban societies) that have a thin ideal for women, but not in cultures (like native tribal societies) that do not have a thin ideal for women (McCarthy, 1990).
- Depression in China is characterized by bodily symptoms, but depression in America is characterized mostly by sadness and pessimism about the future (Kleinman, 1986).

Given the pervasiveness of sociocultural influences on mental illness, some authors (Nolen-Hoeksema,1998) have postulated a *bio-psycho-social* model, in which biology, psychology, and society are each thought of as parallel influences, each interacting with the others. We take a more differentiated view of these three kinds of influence. We see biology and psychology as different *levels of analysis* of abnormality, but we see society and culture as only a *moderator* of abnormality. A level of analysis is a comprehensive approach to all of mental illness—its symptoms, cause, and treatment. Biological and psychological approaches are comprehensive in just this way. In contrast, sociocultural approaches are more modest. They do not put forward a complete theory of what causes or how to treat mental illness and its symptoms. Rather, they merely show that sociocultural variables influence the symptoms, cause, and treatment of mental illness, and admonish us to pay careful attention to such factors when we try to understand the causes and suggest the treatments for abnormality in psychological and biological terms.

"bottom-up" explanations take the form of a biological state causing a psychological state; in Celia's case, they would say that a fast heart rate and difficulty breathing would lead to her belief that she was experiencing a heart attack. "Top-down" explanations say that a psychological state causes changes in the biological state; in Celia's case, they would say that her belief that she was having a heart attack caused her heart to beat faster, her pulse to race, and her breathing to become labored. In fact, Celia's bodily and cognitive symptoms influence each other, leading to a state of spiraling out-of-control panic.

Both bottom-up and top-down causation have also been found for depression. An example of bottom-up causation is shown when there is brain damage due to stroke (oxygen starvation in part of the brain). When such damage is to the left hemisphere, it results in a dominance of right brain activity, and it is more often followed by depression than when there is damage to the right hemisphere (Sackeim et al., 1982). After such strokes, formerly cheerful individuals often feel hopeless and cry much of the time. In contrast, equivalently devastating damage to the right hemisphere does not produce depression. In fact, such damage often produces unwarranted and unexpected good cheer. So we know that it is not brain damage alone that produces depression, but the site of the brain damage as well. This is unequivocal evidence that the change in an anatomical state causes changes in emotion.

On the other hand, we also know that cognitive states will affect the brain itself. In one study, researchers monitored brain activity in healthy people as they read very sad excerpts from autobiographical scripts they had written. The scripts were so sad that most subjects started to cry. Marked and systematic brain changes ensued: limbic sites became more active, while the back part of the right cortex became less active (Mayberg et al., 1999). This demonstrated unequivocally that sad thoughts and sad emotion could cause brain activity, and that such brain changes were just the opposite of the brain changes that happened when patients were recovering from depression.

Appreciating bottom-up and top-down causal demonstrations together has profound implications for the study of abnormal psychology. What can no longer be denied is that sometimes biological changes cause psychological states and influence psychological disorders, but also that sometimes psychological changes cause biological states and influence

biological disorders. As the Surgeon General's Report summarizes, "The pendulum now is coming to rest with the recognition that behavior is the product of both nature and nurture. . . . Each contributes to the development of mental health and mental illness. Nature and nurture are not necessarily independent forces but can interact with one another: nature can influence nurture, and nurture can influence nature" (Satcher, 1999).

Scientific progress in understanding and treating abnormality may depend on breaking down the barriers that have existed between the biological and psychological approaches. Tensions and funding differences and cultural differences still abound between biological psychiatrists and clinical psychologists. But happily, much important, integrative research in this field now involves these two kinds of scientists working side by side. We will highlight such research throughout the book. Most importantly, it also implies that questions that have for four hundred years been couched as "nature versus nurture," "mind versus body," and "biology versus psychology" should be reformulated. We will re-pose these questions as "biology *and* psychology" and as "nature *and* nurture" and "mind *and* body" to capture the many new findings that show bidirectional cause and cure. The mutual influence of the biological and psychological levels of analysis is the first main theme of this book.

Three questions from this theme will arise repeatedly as we examine the disorders:

- What biological, psychological, and social factors contribute to particular disorders?
- What are some bottom-up influences on psychological states and what are some top-down influences on biological states?
- How does the interplay of biological, psychological, and social factors illuminate the causes and treatments of particular disorders?

Science and Practice

We call our second theme "science and practice." Like each of the other three themes, it has many facets, but in essence the science/practice issue is about two strikingly different views of approaching psychological disorders. The practitioner's first aim is to help—to treat—a particular person who presents with a problem. The therapist will first call upon her rich store of knowledge about the patient, his loves and friendships, his childhood, his particular strengths and vulnerabilities, his therapy so far. The therapist's intuitions about the patient's particular and complex biography will shape the treatment. Often, however, in the press of a crisis, she will have little time for reflection, and no possibility of trying out alternate approaches to see which one works best, as can be seen in Celia's case:

> After the three worst months of her life, Celia, in desperation, sought out therapy. Her closest friend recommended Miles, a psychologist from a nearby health maintenance organization (HMO). Miles spent all of the first three meetings taking a detailed history as well as a full description of Celia's panic attacks. Celia's panic symptoms were classic and a diagnosis of panic disorder was clear. Miles also had the strong sense that Celia's attacks were somehow related to her recurrent fear of abandonment after her father left her mother, to her angry breakup with her boyfriend a month before the first attack, and to her ambivalence about working rather than going back to junior college. Miles knew that cognitive therapy was a good treatment for panic disorder. He liked this treatment, not only because the research said it worked more than 80 percent of the time, but because it took advantage of one of Celia's strong points: Celia was proud of her rationality, her ability to think clearly under stress. "These attacks bug me so, because they make me so irrational." Just as Miles was about to begin a brief course of this treatment, however, Celia's mother, along with Celia, suddenly moved across the state to Pittsburgh. The reason that her mother moved them across the state was so that they could live with Celia's aunt, who agreed to replace Celia as her mother's outside helper.
>
> When Celia and her mother arrived in Pittsburgh, Celia's attacks became more frequent and more severe. Her aunt recommended that Celia go to the famous psychiatric clinic at the university hospital. Celia did and was put on high doses of Xanax, a potent tranquilizer. This worked, sort of. Her panic attacks became less frequent, one a month rather than one a week, and they were a little less intense. But she was so drowsy most of the time that she couldn't read a magazine or follow the plot of television shows. "I was like a zombie," she said. "I decided that this was even worse than the panic attacks, and I stopped taking the stuff." But then the attacks returned.

The scientist's first aim, in contrast to the clinician's goal, is to test causes and treatments for any number of similar people with similar problems. She will first call on the rich store of theory and evidence about a diagnosis. She will look to the research literature for the likely cause and for the best-documented treatments. At the core of this approach are the general laws that arise from experiments, epidemiology, and outcome studies of groups of individuals having different treatments. Understanding comes from the ways in which the research literature illuminates the individual case.

For some, this issue is science *versus* practice, and some psychologists work only at one pole. But many more psychologists use both science *and* practice in their work, sometimes thinking about their patients from the science perspective and sometimes from the practice perspective. We emphasize the contributions of each approach, not as antagonists, but in service of each other and of the troubled patient. This textbook presents our integration of practice *and* science.

Three questions will arise repeatedly in our discussion of each of the disorders:

- What has research revealed so far about the causes of particular disorders that the practitioner can use in treating patients?
- What treatments do practitioners find effective for helping patients to learn to cope with their disorders.
- What areas are currently at the frontiers of research that have implications for treatment?

Development

Our third theme is that developmental changes are very important in understanding abnormality. Researchers have known this for some time. Yet, it is only in the past two decades that they have focused attention on the clues that developmental changes offer to how psychological disorders come about. This burgeoning new field is called "developmental psychopathology." Mental health and mental disorder change across the life span, with different stages of life often associated with vulnerability to very different disorders. Developmental psychopathology studies what is constant and what changes across the life span, and how genes and their expression change as a person grows older and as she encounters different environments. We now return to the case of Celia to illustrate the possible contributions of genes and development to the onset of a disorder:

When you know Celia's mother better, you know that Celia's anxiety attacks did not come completely out of the blue. Celia's mother also had panic attacks just like these. As a consequence, her mother avoided going out as much as she could, afraid that she might get sick in the street or in the supermarket and that no one would help her. In fact, Celia was her window to the world, until Celia succumbed to the same malady.

As a child, Celia was acutely aware of her mother's fears. Anxiety was the emotion that pervaded daily life. Celia was far from a placid child, and she frequently had nightmares about being abandoned by her mother and lost in a strange city. But despite her fears, once she became a teenager, she was able to take over the shopping and otherwise orchestrate dealing with the outside world on behalf of her mother. Taking a job at McDonald's presented no problem for such an organized and reliable young adult until the day of her first panic attack.

Was Celia vulnerable to panic attacks because she had her mother's genes, or because she was raised in a household whose emotional backdrop was pervasive anxiety and whose major events were her mother's panic attacks? If she modeled her panic attacks on her mother's panic attacks, why did Celia's symptoms not appear until early adulthood? Was her fear of abandonment by her mother a harbinger? Was it possibly even a cause of her panic attacks?

The changes that occur with age in the human body are the most obvious signs of development. Humans progress from physical immaturity and complete dependency during infancy, to greater size and physical ability through young adulthood, then, with advanced age, through a period of gradual decline in physical capacities. At the same time, less obvious, but no less important, changes occur in lockstep in the brain. The structures and microscopic organization of the brain undergo dramatic changes as the infant passes through childhood, adolescence, young adulthood, middle age, and old age.

Moving from the biological to the psychological level of analysis, we see that the metamorphosis is just as dramatic. As humans mature, their mental abilities, motivations, fears, and beliefs change. Vulnerability to various kinds of psychological problems also changes with the person's developmental stage (Cicchetti and Rogosch, 1999; Rende, 1999). For example:

- Debilitating fear about separation from parents is a daily challenge for many young children like Celia, but it rarely occurs among adults.

- Preoccupation with weight gain is commonplace in teenagers, and in extreme cases it leads to eating disorders. But very few elderly people are seriously concerned about their weight, and eating disorders are virtually nonexistent after age sixty.
- Between 1 and 2 percent of those in the age range of twenty to forty have experienced a visual or auditory hallucination. But among children, hallucinations rarely occur.
- Depression is just as frequent in boys as in girls before puberty. But after puberty, twice as many young women suffer depression as do young men.

There are several reasons why our vulnerability to various kinds of psychological problems changes across the life span. First, at each stage of development, we are confronted with different expectations, expectations that stem from the demands of our social world. Toddlers are not expected to sit in a classroom and pay attention to a teacher for an extended period of time, but seven-year-olds are. In Western cultures, there are no pressures on children to pursue heterosexual relationships prior to adolescence. In high school, however, many adolescents experience intense peer pressure to date the "right" person.

Turning to the biological level, another reason why vulnerability to different psychological disorders changes with age is because the brain undergoes developmental changes throughout life. For example, adolescence is a critical period for the onset of many psychological disorders, including depression. In Chapter 7, you will read about what is considered a modern epidemic of depression, which begins at puberty. Sex hormones surge at puberty and change the way the brain functions. They are believed to drive the changes in mood that explode in adolescence.

The sheer cumulative effects of experience also play a role in the development of vulnerability to psychological problems. With experience and parental guidance, most children gradually acquire more self-confidence and self-control. At the same time, irrational childhood fears of natural events (for example, thunder) and objects (for example, spiders) gradually diminish. By adolescence, concerns about thunder and spiders have been replaced by worries about social status. But trauma may disrupt this developmental path. When a child is exposed to a traumatic event, normal childhood fears may be amplified into a full-blown phobia. A youngster whose classmate is killed in a school shooting may develop a fear of thunderstorms that will persist into adulthood and require treatment.

Finally, both nature and nurture play a joint role in the path of human development. Newborns differ in their biological constitutions, and this has implications for how the environment affects them. What amounts to a mild jolt for one child may be a trauma for another. The interplay between biological and psychological factors continually shapes the developmental course. As stated in the Surgeon General's Report on Mental Health:

> Understanding the process of development requires knowledge, ranging from the most fundamental level—that of gene expression and interactions between molecules and cells—all the way up to the highest levels of cognition, memory, emotion, and language. The challenge requires integration of concepts from many different disciplines. A fuller understanding of development is not only important in its own right, but it is expected to pave the way for our ultimate understanding of mental health and mental illness and how different factors shape their expression at different stages of the life span. (Satcher, 1999)

As the surgeon general urges, we take a developmental approach to understanding abnormality. Doing so means that three key questions will arise repeatedly in our discussions of the disorders:

- At what developmental stage do the clinical signs of the disorder usually emerge?
- Are there more subtle harbingers of vulnerability before the major symptoms are observed?
- Do the developmental changes offer clues about the cause of the disorder?

Treatment of Choice

The fourth great issue psychologists confront in the new century is discovering the treatment of choice for each disorder. This issue is the treatment corollary of the level of analysis theme. The treatment of psychological disorders has seen enormous progress in the last half-century. Before 1950, there were virtually no disorders that could be treated reliably—in fact, there was not even an agreed-upon classification of what disorders there were. There is now a reliable nosology, or system of classification, that you will read about in Chapter 2. Even better, there are now fourteen disorders that can be treated successfully—with outcomes ranging from moderate relief all the way to cure. In Celia's case, it became clear that cognitive therapy was indeed the treatment of choice:

> Celia's story has a happy ending. Celia decided to call Miles. Miles convinced Celia and her aunt to fly back to Philadelphia for three sessions of cognitive therapy. During these sessions, Celia learned about the symptoms of panic and how they differ from the symptoms of a heart attack. Celia had been misinterpreting her heart racing and shortness of breath as the symptoms of a heart attack. Afraid she was having a heart attack and was going to die, Celia felt her heart speed up even more, and she found it even harder to breathe. She then saw these spiraling symptoms as even stronger evidence of an impending heart attack. Miles taught Celia that her heart racing and her shortness of breath were actually just symptoms of mounting anxiety, nothing more harmful. Miles taught Celia the skill of whole-body relaxation and then demonstrated compellingly the harmlessness of Celia's symptoms right in his office. Celia breathed rapidly into a paper bag. Miles pointed out that although her heart was racing and she felt she was suffocating, these were normal manifestations of overbreathing. Celia now tried whole-body relaxation in the presence of these symptoms and found that they gradually subsided. After two more practice sessions, Celia had mastered her panic attacks. Celia has now gone for two years without a single panic attack.
>
> Miles used the findings in the research literature to identify the underlying pathology, Celia's misinterpretation of her bodily symptoms, and to identify the treatment of choice for Celia. He also used his experience as a therapist, however, to identify Celia's main strengths as a person—her rationality and her pride in seeing the world clearly. He was then able to amplify these strengths by showing her how to use them to overcome the worst situation in her life.

In some cases, as for Celia, specific forms of psychotherapy work best; in other cases, medications work best. For many disorders, it has become common clinical practice to give both medication and psychotherapy at the same time. But surprisingly, the combination of drugs and psychotherapy does not usually work noticeably better than either one alone.

A lot is now known about treatment. Some abnormal conditions change readily in therapy or with medications, but others resist change mightily. Here is a sampling of what can be treated successfully:

- Panic can be easily unlearned in psychotherapy, but drugs do not cure it.
- The sexual "dysfunctions"—frigidity, impotence, premature ejaculation—are quite easily treated.
- Our moods, which can wreak havoc with our physical health, are readily controlled by both psychotherapy and medications.
- Depression can be relieved by changes in conscious thinking and by drugs, but not by insight into childhood.

And here are some facts about what resists change:

- Dieting almost never works lastingly.
- No treatment is known to improve significantly on the natural course of recovery from alcoholism.
- Reliving childhood trauma does not undo adult personality problems.

Sometimes the aim of treatment is merely symptom relief. This is almost always the aim with medication and one of the unspoken shortcomings of biological psychiatry as currently practiced. The universal outcome of the psychoactive medications is that once the patient stops taking it, he is back to square one. Other times the aim of treatment is cure—not just relief of symptoms, but also the prevention of recurrence—and this is more often—but not always—the aim of psychotherapy.

This textbook not only discusses the diagnosis, theories, and etiology of disorders, but it also attempts to provide an accurate and factual guide to which treatments work and which ones do not (see Chapters 5 through 14). We will present summary tables for each disorder, comparing the major treatments' overall effects as well as degree of relief, relapse, side effects, expense, and duration.

Not only has there been real progress in finding effective treatments but the method of deciding which treatments work has become more sophisticated. There is now an authoritative way of deciding which treatments work and which do not: *outcome studies,* which evaluate treatments—both biological and psychological. Rather than relying on word of mouth about psychotherapeutic treatments or the slick advertising of the pharmaceutical companies about their drugs, you should rely on the much better evidence of outcome studies to make important decisions about treatment.

Outcome studies come in two varieties: *efficacy studies,* which test a treatment under controlled laboratory conditions, and *effectiveness studies,* which test a treatment as it is actually delivered in the field.

When these two kinds of evidence agree, we can feel most confident that the treatment works. In this text, we will rely heavily on the available evidence from outcome studies when we review which treatments work for each disorder, and we will ask three questions about each disorder:

- What treatments work for each disorder, and how effective are they?
- What new treatments are now being researched?
- What interventions may prevent disorders from occurring in the first place?

Early Approaches to Abnormality

While our four themes capture the essence of abnormal psychology as we know it today, in times past very different issues dominated the field. Throughout human history, there have been many different notions about what behaviors could be defined as abnormal. Behaviors that have been revered in one time or place have been defined as clear examples of madness in others. The ancient Hebrews and the ancient Greeks held in awe those who claimed to be prophets and had "the gift of tongues." Yet, in the modern world, those who claim to see into the future generate suspicion, and those who speak in unknown words and rhythms are usually classified as suffering from schizophrenia.

> One effect of the illness was that I heard voices—numerous voices—chatting, arguing, and quarreling with me, telling me I should hurt myself or kill myself. I felt as if I was being put on a heavenly trial for misdeeds that I had done and was being held accountable by God. Other times I felt as if I was being pursued by the government for acts of disloyalty.
>
> I thought the voices I heard were being transmitted through the walls of my apartment and through the washer and dryer, and that these machines were talking and telling me things. I felt that the government agencies had planted transmitters and receivers in my apartment so that I could hear what they were saying and they could hear what I was saying. I also felt as if the government had bugged my clothing, so that whenever I went outside my apartment I felt like I was being pursued. I felt like I was being followed and watched twenty-four hours a day.

I would like to point out that these were my feelings then, and in hindsight I hold nothing against these government agencies. I now know that this constant monitoring was either punishment at the hands of God's servants for deeds I committed earlier in my life . . . or alternatively, but less likely, that I just imagined these things." (Anonymous, 1996)

Much as there have been remarkable differences in the ways in which such things as "hearing voices" have been interpreted, so have there also been vastly contradictory theories about the causes of such behaviors. William Shakespeare portrayed Ophelia as driven "mad" by Hamlet's cruel rejection, implying to his Elizabethan audiences that Ophelia's withdrawal and eventual suicide were products of the social influences in her immediate environment. Yet, during the same period in history, other "mad" women were accused of having willfully made pacts with Satan. Clearly, a society's definitions of madness and perceptions of its causes have influenced whether the mad were revered, feared, pitied, or simply accepted. In turn, these perceptions have determined the ways in which those who were viewed as mad were treated: whether they were honored for their unique powers or incarcerated, abandoned or given therapy for their madness.

There is very little about abnormality that tells what causes it, or that even provides clues about where to look for causes. Yet, because choice of treatment depends upon perceived cause, people find it difficult to resist attributing causes to abnormality. Thus, there were times when abnormality was attributed to the wrath of the gods or to possession by demons. At other times and in other places, earthquakes and tides, germs and illness, interpersonal conflict and bad blood were separately and together used to explain the origins of abnormality. Notions about abnormality arise from the culture's worldview. If the culture believes that animistic spirits cause events and behavior, abnormality will be viewed in animistic terms. If it believes in scientific and materialistic causes, abnormality will be viewed in scientific terms.

Animistic Origins: Possession

In pre-modern societies, the belief in *animism*—that everyone and everything has a "soul"—was widespread, and mental disturbance was often ascribed to animistic causes. One of the most common explana-

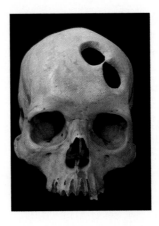

Paleolithic cave dwellers are believed to have made holes, or trephines, in skulls to free those who were "possessed" by evil spirits.

tions of madness was that evil spirits had taken possession of an individual and controlled that person's behavior. Much as a parasitic tapeworm lives in and weakens the body, so could a parasitic spirit inhabit and weaken the mind. Some skulls of Paleolithic cave dwellers have characteristic holes, called *trephines,* which appear to have been chipped out by stone instruments. It is thought that trephining was performed to provide an exit for demons or evil spirits trapped within the skull.

People could be possessed by many different kinds of spirits. The spirits of ancestors, animals, gods, and heroes, and of victims whose wrongs had not been redressed, were among those that could wreak madness. These spirits could enter a person through their own cunning, through the work of an evildoer with magical powers, or through a lack of faith on the part of the possessed individual. Not surprisingly, because possession was a result of invisible forces, freeing the possessed individual from these spirits required special techniques. Across time and place, there has been the widespread belief in the power of some individuals to use magic both to induce evil and expel it; shamans, witch doctors, sorcerers, priests, and witches were all believed to be able to influence animistic forces (Douglas, 1970). In medieval Europe, for example, individuals from all levels of society resorted to sorcerers and witches for spells, potents, and prophecies.

By the middle of the fifteenth century, however, tolerance for bizarre behavior became strained. The perception of witches and the response to them changed radically—from respect to fear. As a result, thousands of suspected witches were put to death, both in Europe and later in America; this was believed to be the only fail-safe "cure" for their abnormality (see Box 1–2).

Evidence at the Salem Witch Trials

The viable explanations of insanity have changed across the centuries. In seventeenth-century North America, a religious level of analysis—possession by the devil—was a viable explanation. The notorious Salem Witch Trials illustrate this.

The famous Salem Witch Trials, and the witchcraft mania that grew up in that town, evidently arose from the antics of children. A group of young girls played imaginary games at the village minister's house. Ghosts, devils, witches, and the whole invisible world were the subjects of their games, borrowed in the manner that children today borrow space explorations from the adult world that surrounds them. Their games of imagination, however, came to the attention of the village elders who solemnly concluded that these children were "bewitched." The children, perhaps stimulated by the attention they were receiving and the excitement they had caused, became more involved in their imaginings, feeding the concern of the elders.

Pressed by the elders to name those who had been casting evil spells over them, they named one person, then another, then still others, until it appeared that nearly half of the people in the village had signed their souls over to the devil. Neighbors hurled wild accusations against each other. These accusations resulted in the arrest and trial of 250 persons in one year (1691–1692), of whom 50 were condemned, 19 executed, 2 died in prison, and 1 of torture. Similarly, tens of thousands of innocents had been tried as witches throughout Europe in the late Middle Ages, and many were executed most cruelly.

It is important to remember that the elders of the community were "sane," sober, and intelligent people. Cotton Mather was a leading colonial figure, son of the president of Harvard University, and a founder of Yale. Deeply religious, he wanted to protect the community against dangers that, for him, were real. And precisely because he and other elders were so deeply convinced of the dangers, they were remarkably credulous in weighing the evidence. An example of their gullibility is seen in the interrogation of Sarah Carrier, age eight, whose mother, Martha, was subsequently hanged as a witch.

"How long hast thou been a witch?"

"Ever since I was six years old."

"How old are you now?"

"Nearly eight years old."

"Who made you a witch?"

"My mother. She made me set my hand to the book."

"You said you saw a cat once. What did the cat say to you?"

"It said it would tear me to pieces if I would not set my hand to the book."

[Sarah is speaking here of the Devil's Book.]

"How did you know that it was your mother?"

"The cat told me so, that she was my mother."

Viewed from a twenty-first century perspective, this tragic episode is no longer explained from a religious level of analysis, but instead either from a biological one, as the result of ergot poisoning, a hallucinogenic condition caused by a fungus, or as mass hysteria, a contagious psychological condition.

SOURCE: Upham, 1867, cited in Deutsch, 1949, p. 35.

As a result of the witchcraft mania and fear of satanic forces, 250 people were tried as witches in colonial Salem, Massachusetts.

Physical Causes

While animistic causes served to explain psychological distress for centuries, the approach to abnormality that is the forerunner of the biological level of analysis can also be traced back to the ancient world. This is the belief that abnormality has *physical* causes. In fact, it is possible that the prehistoric peoples who practiced trephining were employing a primitive surgical technique to relieve the pain of severe headaches. One of the first psychological disorders thought to have arisen from physical causes was **hysteria.**

Papyri from early Egypt, as well as the writings of Greek physicians, record a remarkable disorder that was found mainly among women who were virgins or widows. Its symptoms included such complaints as epileptic-like fits, pains of all sorts in various parts of the body, aphonia (loss of speaking voice), headaches, dizziness, paralysis, blindness, lameness, listlessness, and melancholia. The Greeks believed that all of these arose from a single source: a wandering uterus, which had somehow dislodged itself from its normal place to rove around the body, perhaps in search of water and nourishment, but often enough, for no good reason, and which would attach itself here or there and create havoc. The Greek word for uterus is *hystera*, and the Greeks believed so deeply that the uterus was responsible for these difficulties that they named the entire disorder after it—hysteria (Veith, 1965).

This view of hysteria prevailed until the second century A.D., when physicians such as Galen, who recognized that the uterus was not a living animal, challenged it. They believed that the hystera was a malfunctioning sexual organ. And they thought that there might be a similar organ in men which, when malfunctioning, could cause men to have similar symptoms. Galen observed that both men and women suffer similar symptoms following periods of sexual abstinence, and therefore he argued that hysteria has a sexual basis, a view that was widely accepted until only a decade or two ago.

Attributing psychological distress to physical causes took a peculiar twist hundreds of years later with the belief in **animalism.** This belief asserted that there were remarkable similarities between animals and mad people. Like animals, the mad could not control themselves and therefore needed to be severely controlled. Like animals, the insane were capable of violence, often suddenly and without provocation. Like animals, they could live without protest in miserable conditions, conditions under which normal people simply could not exist. One proponent of this view pointed to

> the ease with which certain of the insane of both sexes bear the most rigorous and prolonged cold. . . . On certain days when the thermometer indicated . . . as many as 16 degrees below freezing, a madman . . . could not endure his wool blanket, and remained sitting on the icy floor of his cell. In the morning, one no sooner opened his door than he ran in his shirt into the inner court, taking ice and snow by the fistful, applying it to his breast and letting it melt with a sort of delectation." (Foucault, 1965, pp. 74–75)

This 1530 painting by Jan Sanders van Hemessen shows physicians trying to remove the "Stone of Folly" from a bound patient possessed with madness. However gruesome this procedure, the theory and treatment of mental illness as a disorder of the body has survived; we now know that tumors in the brain sometimes bring about abnormality.

Much of the treatment of the insane followed from this view until the late eighteenth century, when changes you will read about below occurred.

These primitive notions of physical cause that are captured in the early Greek views of hysteria, or in animalism, gradually yielded to more sophisticated, medical approaches. With the development of modern medicine, many physicians came to consider madness to be a form of illness amenable to the same kinds of treatment as physical illness. Purges, bleeding, and forced vomiting were choice medical remedies of the seventeenth and eighteenth centuries, and these were administered to the infirm and the insane alike. Gradually, these views and treatments were replaced by approaches that characterize present-day medicine: surgery and pharmacology. This approach has now been subsumed under neuroscience, the branch of biology and psychology that studies the central nervous system. You will read about its discoveries and its techniques in Chapter 4.

Psychogenic Origins

The quest for understanding psychological abnormality was pursued down still another path by the ancient Greeks and Romans. This **psychogenic** (originating in the soul) path is the forerunner of the psychological level of analysis. Galen, in addition to his observations about hysteria, contributed important insights into the psychological causes of abnormality. In a particularly striking instance, Galen examined a woman who complained of sleeplessness, listlessness, and general malaise. He could find no direct evidence of physical illness and ultimately narrowed his inferences to two possibilities. Either she was suffering from melancholy, which was a biological disorder of one of the four body "humors," or fluids, "or else she was troubled about something she was unwilling to confess," a psychological explanation. He concluded:

> After I had diagnosed that there was no bodily trouble, and that the woman was suffering from some mental uneasiness, it happened that at the very time I was examining her, this was confirmed. Somebody came from the theatre and said he had seen Pylades dancing. Then both her expression and the colour of her face changed. Seeing this, I applied my hand to her wrist, and noticed that her pulse had suddenly become extremely irregular. This kind of pulse indi-

cates that the mind is disturbed; thus it occurs also in people who are disputing over any subject. So on the next day I said to one of my followers that, when I paid my visit to the woman, he was to come a little later and announce to me, "Morphus is dancing today." When he said this, I found that the pulse was unaffected. Similarly also on the next day, when I had an announcement made about the third member of the troupe, the pulse remained unchanged as before. On the fourth evening I kept very careful watch when it was announced that Pylades was dancing, and noticed that the pulse was very much disturbed. Thus I found out that the woman was in love with Pylades, and by careful watch on the succeeding days my discovery was confirmed. (Galen, cited in Veith, 1965, p. 36)

Galen's assessment of possible cause is the hallmark of the scientific method that was eventually to advance our understanding and treatment of psychological disorders. Rather than leaping to a conclusion, Galen tested two alternative hypotheses and decided which was correct according to the evidence. In this case, the evidence favored the hypothesis that stressed psychological experience rather than biology.

Galen's observations on the psychological origins of abnormality were forgotten for centuries. Thus, until the middle of the eighteenth century,

The Greek physician Galen (circa 130–201 A.D.) was one of the first to believe that some apparently physical disorders were psychological in origin.

hysteria was believed to be a female neurological disorder that had its origins in genital illness. The recognition that mental disorders were psychological in origin and could be treated by psychological means did not arise again until the middle of the eighteenth century.

MESMERISM

To understand how the psychological view of abnormality returned in the eighteenth century, we first need to look at one of the most colorful people in the history of Abnormal Psychology, Franz Anton Mesmer. Mesmer is not only one of the most colorful, but surely one of the most maligned, characters in the history of Abnormal Psychology. Variously called a genius and a charlatan, he proposed that many diseases, from epilepsy to hysteria, develop from the obstruction of the flow of an invisible and impalpable entity that he first called "universal magnetic fluid" and later, *animal magnetism*. Very much a man of the Enlightenment, Mesmer was influenced by contemporary discoveries in electricity. He proposed the existence of a physical magnetic fluid which, when unequally distributed, causes disease in the body. He theorized that the lunar cycle, the tides, the planets, and the stars influenced magnetic fluid. Mesmer believed that using certain techniques that induced "crises" in the body could restore health. These crises would be provoked again and again, but each time would be experienced as less severe, until they disappeared, and the body was back in equilibrium.

Mesmer went to Paris from Vienna in 1778. He opened a clinic where patients suffering from the various symptoms of hysteria were seen in groups. In a heavily curtained room, patients were arranged around a large wooden tub, or *baquet*, which was filled with water and magnetized iron filings. Iron rods protruded from the tub and were pointed by the patients to their ailing parts. The baquet was supposed to concentrate the magnetic fluid and induce the patient's crisis. Mesmer, dressed in a lavender cape, would pass among the patients to the accompaniment of gentle music, fixing his eye on them, and touching each with his iron wand. One patient would experience strange sensations, including trembling and convulsions. After the first succumbed, others experienced similar symptoms, though there were always a few who were unaffected (Pattie, 1967).

Mesmer had departed from Vienna under a cloud: he had been accused of charlatanry. And, despite his therapeutic successes, it was not long before similar accusations were leveled against him in Paris. So heated and acrimonious were the charges and countercharges, that in 1783, Louis XVI appointed a Royal Commission to investigate animal magnetism. The Commission, which included such luminaries as Benjamin Franklin, heard evidence and concluded that there was no such thing as animal magnetism and that Mesmer's cures were entirely due to "imagination." Crushingly defeated, Mesmer, a proud man, vanished into obscurity. But the reality of his "cures" remained. Animal magnetism, soon called *mesmerism,* continued to be practiced and in some cases succeeded in restoring people to health. It took the next generation of investigators to examine mesmerism and to conclude that it was not magnetized iron filings but rather "suggestion" and "suggestibility" that led to cures.

FROM MESMER TO FREUD

Cures derived from mesmerism continued to excite interest. The process now focused on the role of suggestion and came to be known as *hypnotism.* A major figure in the scientific study of hypnosis was Jean-Martin Charcot, medical director of one of the largest sections at La Salpêtrière, where insane patients were treated in Paris. Charcot was widely regarded as a first-rate scientist, the most eminent neurologist of the nineteenth century, and an awesome and much-feared teacher. While Charcot was at La Salpêtrière, one of the wards in his charge housed women patients who suffered from convulsions. Using hypnosis, Charcot sought to distinguish hysterical convulsions from those brought on by epilepsy. If, for example, a patient who suffered a paralyzed arm was able to move her arm under hypnosis, then the diagnosis of hysteria could be given; otherwise, the appropriate diagnosis was a neurological disorder. Charcot also extended his study to male patients, demonstrating that the symptoms of traumatic paralysis in men were the same as those of hysterical paralysis (Ellenberger, 1970).

Hypnosis fascinated Charcot, and he quickly generated a neurological theory about it. His students, ever eager to please their teacher, tested his views and brought back confirmatory evidence. But

Jean-Martin Charcot (1825–1893) demonstrating hypnosis to a class of medical students.

Charcot himself never hypnotized his patients. Rather, his students "worked them up" and taught them how to perform, after which Charcot unwittingly used them as demonstration subjects. Other scientists, particularly Hyppolyte Bernheim in Nancy, were unable to replicate Charcot's findings, and they quickly located the source of the error.

Despite some initial setbacks, psychogenic theories about abnormal behavior began to gain credence. The emphasis turned to two explanations: first, that psychological distress could be a biological illness, not different in kind from any physical illnesses; and second, that mental disorder could be psychological, and very different in kind from physical illness.

Much of the excitement that was generated by the psychogenic viewpoint came about through the study of hysteria. With its paralyses, anesthesias, and convulsions, its loss of voice, sight, or hearing, and occasional loss of consciousness, hysteria seemed patently a physical disorder. Charcot used hypnosis to distinguish between symptoms that had an organic cause and symptoms that were hysterical in nature. Subsequent theorists proposed that the therapeutic effects of hypnosis resulted from psychological "suggestion" (Bernheim, 1886, cited in Gordon, 1967).

By the end of the nineteenth century, hypnosis was widely used in Europe and in the United States for treating hysterical disorders. It formed the basis for the development of modern forms of psychotherapy and was a significant milestone in the psychogenic approach to mental disorders.

One of the people who used hypnosis in his treatment of patients was Josef Breuer, a distinguished Viennese internist whose practice included a large number of hysterical patients. Breuer's treatment often consisted of inducing these patients to talk about their problems and fantasies under hypnosis. Frequently patients would become emotional under hypnosis, reliving painful experiences, undergoing a deep *catharsis,* or emotional release, and emerging from the hypnotic trance feeling much better. The patients, of course, were unaware of a relationship between what they discussed under hypnosis, how emotional they had become, and how they felt subsequently. But Breuer believed that, because his patients had experienced a catharsis under hypnosis, their symptoms disappeared.

Just as Breuer was making these discoveries, Sigmund Freud, a Viennese neurologist who had just completed his studies with Charcot, began to work with Breuer. Together they utilized Breuer's cathartic method, in which patients reported their experiences and fantasies under hypnosis. Freud, however, noticed that similar therapeutic effects could be obtained without hypnosis, as long as the patient reported everything that came to mind and experienced emotional catharsis. It was this discovery that led Freud to the theory and therapeutic technique called *psychoanalysis,* which is described in detail in Chapter 3. Freud's psychoanalytic theory made even more plausible the notion that abnormal behavior has a psychogenic origin. Although many of Freud's specific theories have subsequently been questioned and fallen into disrepute, the basic notion that the mind is at work influencing perceptions and behavior continues to hold great strength.

Treatment of the Insane

The beginning of the modern psychological era dates from the establishment of the psychiatric hospital. Both the medical hospital and the psychiatric hospital evolved from seventeenth-century institutions that were created to house and confine the poor, the homeless, the unemployed, and among them, the insane. In 1656, the Hôpital Général of

Paris was founded for the poor "of both sexes, of all ages, and from all localities, of whatever breeding and birth, in whatever state they may be, able-bodied or invalid, sick or convalescent, curable or incurable" (Edict of 1656, cited in Foucault, 1965). From a strictly humane point of view, the Hôpital Général was surely an improvement over the conditions that preceded it. For the first time in France, the government took responsibility for feeding and housing its "undesirables." But in return, those social undesirables—the poor, the homeless, and the mad—gave up their personal liberty.

Segregating the Insane

Although governments did not distinguish the insane from other unfortunates, within the hospital such distinctions were quickly made and were ultimately institutionalized. Compared to other residents, the insane were given much worse care, including brutal physical abuse. One eighteenth-century visitor to La Salpêtrière, a division of the Hôpital Général, commented that what made the place more miserable, and often fatal, was that in winter, "when the waters of the Seine rose, those cells situated at the level of the sewers became not only more unhealthy, but worse still, a refuge for a swarm of huge rats, which during the night attacked the unfortunates confined there and bit them wherever they could reach them; mad-women have been found with feet, hands, and face torn by bites which are often dangerous and from which several have died" (Desportes, cited in Foucault, 1965).

Paris was not unique. In St. Mary's of Bethlehem (which soon became known as Bedlam) in London, patients were chained to the walls or kept on long leashes. The United States established its first hospital, the Pennsylvania Hospital, in 1756. At the urging of Benjamin Franklin, the government set aside a section for "lunatics." They were consigned to the cellar and "their scalps were shaved and blistered; they were bled to a point of syncope (unconsciousness), purged until the alimentary canal failed to yield anything but mucus, and in the intervals, they were chained by the waist or ankle to the cell wall. . . . It was not considered unusual or improper for the keeper to carry a whip and use it freely" (Morton, 1897, cited in Deutsch, 1949).

Clearly, to the modern mind, such treatment is cruel and inhumane. That judgment arises because, in the modern view, the insane are entitled to compassion and kindness. But it is not the case that our predecessors were less concerned with the treatment of the insane, or necessarily, morally obtuse. Rather, they had a different theory of insanity; they believed that madness resulted from animalism, that the insane had lost the one capacity that distinguished humans from beasts: reason. Because they had lost that capacity, their behavior was disordered, unruly, and wild. The first mandate of treatment, then, was to restore reason. Fear was believed to be the emotion that was best suited to restoring the disordered mind.

The eminent physician William Cullen wrote that it was "necessary to employ a very constant impression of fear . . . awe and dread." Such emotions should be aroused by "all restraints that may occasionally be proper . . . even by stripes and blows" (Cullen, 1808, cited in Scull, 1981). Clearly, some unscrupulous madhouse operators took advantage of this view to abuse those in their care. But even the most eminent patients received similar treatment. King George III of England was a clear case in point. As Countess Harcourt later described his situation, "the unhappy patient . . . was no longer treated as a human being. His body was immediately encased in a machine that left it no liberty of motion. He was sometimes chained to a stake. He was frequently beaten and starved, and at best he was kept in subjection by menacing and violent language" (Jones, 1955, cited in Bynum, 1981). In addition, he was bled, blistered, given emetics and various other drugs of the day. Again, such treatment arose from the belief that the insane did not have the physical sensitivities of human beings but rather were like animals in their lack of sensitivity to pain, temperature, and other external stimuli.

The Growth of Humane Treatment

By the end of the eighteenth century, the idea that the insane should be treated as animals was under attack. From a variety of respected sources, protest grew over the conditions of confinement, and especially over the shackles, the chains, the dungeons, and the whippings.

Hospitals began to unshackle their insane patients. The first hospital to remove the chains from psychiatric patients was St. Boniface in Florence,

Italy. There, in 1774, Vincenzo Chiarugi introduced a radical reform in patient care: allowing patients freedom of movement. Later, in 1787, Joseph Dacquin initiated similar reforms in the Insane Department of the hospital at Chambery, France. Despite political opposition, Philippe Pinel, the newly appointed director of La Bicêtre, part of the Hôpital Général of Paris, unshackled the chains of the mental patients housed there in 1792, moved them from their cellar dungeons into sunny and airy rooms, and allowed them freedom on the hospital grounds. Pinel still believed in the need for control and coercion in psychiatric care, but he insisted that for coercion to be effective, it needed to be psychological rather than physical.

New models of treatment now were sought. One such model was found at Gheel, a religious Belgian community that had been accepting the insane for quite some time. There, consistent with a religious ethos, "cure" was achieved through prayer and in the "laying on of the hands." Those who prayed were treated in a special, and for the time, unusual way. The deeply troubled were shown habitual kindness, courtesy, and gentleness. The insane lived in a community, and apart from being forbidden alcohol, suffered few restrictions. Gheel was not a hospital, but rather a refuge for those who were fortunate enough to make their way there. Similarly, in England, reforms developed from religious concerns. Following the suspicious death of one Hannah Mills, a Quaker, who had been admitted to the Lunatick Asylum in 1791, William Tuke urged the Yorkshire Society of Friends to establish a humanitarian institution for the insane. Despite stiff political opposition, the Retreat of York was established in 1796. The Retreat's cornerstones were kindness, consideration, courtesy, and dignity. Also, consistent with the Quaker philosophy, was the emphasis on the value of work and the personal esteem that the patients, called "guests," derived from it.

The ideas that led to the unshackling of the insane in Europe and to the founding and success of the community at Gheel and of Tuke's Retreat also spread quickly to the United States. This new form of treatment, called **moral treatment,** formed the basis of the Friends Asylum at Frankford, Pennsylvania, in 1817, and also of the Bloomingdale Asylum, established in 1821 in New York City by Quaker businessman Thomas Eddy. Although not yet especially effective, treatment became increasingly humane.

Defining Abnormality Today

How our understanding of abnormality is articulated depends on the beliefs that dominate in a culture and epoch. Historically, people have used animistic, physical, and psychogenic theories to explain disordered behavior. Today, biological and psychological levels of analysis are the two most viable approaches that continue to be offered to understand abnormality. But in our complex society, a more fundamental question has also been raised: What does it mean to say that someone is abnormal? In the past, hearing voices was a sign of divine inspiration. Today, it is a sign of madness. How do we know that a person's behavior is abnormal? How did it become that way? How can it be changed? The answers to these questions have implications for understanding the causes of mental distress and for organizing society's institutions for treating people with mental disorders.

The Elements of Abnormality

Abnormality is recognized everywhere, in every culture, by nearly everyone. Sometimes the impression of abnormality comes through clearly and unambiguously. At other times, reasonable people— even diagnosticians—will disagree as to whether a particular person, action, or thought is or is not abnormal. The following clinical vignettes make this clear:

- Don is viewed by nearly everyone as a quiet, mild-mannered executive. But one day, gripped by a sudden seizure in the temporal lobe of the brain, he picks up his sales manager, chair and all, and hurls her to her death through a plate glass window on the eleventh floor of their office building.
- Vanessa, a teenage girl, eats nothing at all for three days, then gorges herself on eight hot-fudge sundaes within two hours, vomits explosively, and then eats nothing more for three days.
- Carla's religious principles prohibit her from wearing makeup or drinking liquor. Her college friends do both. She is continually anxious when she is with them.

Are Don, Vanessa, and Carla all abnormal? Of these three cases, two things can be said immediately.

First, they involve behaviors that arise from sources as diverse as brain pathology and religious belief. And second, while some people will be quite confident that all of these instances represent abnormality, not everyone will agree. Everyone will judge the first person abnormal. Nearly everyone will judge the second person abnormal. But there will be heated debate about the third.

The act of defining the word "abnormal" suggests that there is some single property that these three cases of abnormality, and all others, *must* share. Such a shared, defining property is called a *necessary condition* for abnormality. But there is no common element among these three cases, for what is it that temporal lobe seizures, gorging oneself on hot-fudge sundaes, and conflict between religious conviction and social acceptance have in common?

Moreover, a precise definition of "abnormal" requires that there be at least one distinguishing element that only cases of abnormality share and that no cases of "normality" share. This is called a *sufficient condition* of abnormality. But is there any one feature that separates all cases of abnormality from all those that we would call normal? Not any that we can find. In fact, as we will shortly see, there is no single element that defines all cases of abnormality

In short, the word "abnormal" cannot be defined precisely. Indeed, few of the words we commonly use, and especially those that are used socially, are precisely defined, for the use of language often depends on flexible meanings. But the fact that abnormality cannot be defined "tightly" does not mean that abnormality does not exist or that it can-

not be recognized at all. Diagnosing whether a behavior is abnormal is made by spelling out the various elements that count toward a behavior being seen as abnormal.

We will look at seven properties or elements that count toward deciding whether an action or a person is abnormal. Our analysis describes the way ordinary people and well-trained psychologists actually use the word. These elements of abnormality are:

- Suffering
- Maladaptiveness
- Irrationality
- Unpredictability and loss of control
- Rareness and unconventionality
- Observer discomfort
- Violation of standards

The more of these elements that are present, and the more clearly each can be seen, the more certain we are that the behavior or person is abnormal. At least one of these elements must be present for abnormality to exist. But no one particular element must always be present, and almost never will all of the elements be present. Let us examine these elements in greater detail.

SUFFERING

Abnormality hurts. A depressed student feels miserable. For her, the prospect of going through another day seems unbearable. We are likely to call people abnormal if they are suffering psychologically, and

One of these images is by a commercial artist, one by a mental patient. Just as no single feature of the drawings sets them apart from each other, no single symptom or behavior is necessary or sufficient to define abnormality.

Jennie Maruki's outsider art clearly depicts suffering, but whether her suffering is an indication of abnormality would depend on whether other elements of abnormality were also present.

the more they suffer, the more certain we are. But suffering is not a necessary condition of abnormality: it does not have to be present for us to label a behavior as abnormal. Someone who phones the president in the middle of the night, certain that the chief executive wants to hear all about his plan for ending schoolyard shootings, may feel exuberant, cheerful, and full of hope. Nevertheless, such a person is viewed as abnormal, since the other elements of abnormality override the absence of suffering and convince us that his behavior is abnormal.

Suffering, moreover, is not a sufficient condition for abnormality because suffering is commonplace in the normal course of life. A child will grieve for a dead pet, for example, much as all of us mourn the loss of loved ones. If no other elements of abnormality are present, however, grief and suffering will not be judged as abnormal.

Suffering, then, is an element that counts toward the perception of abnormality. But it is neither necessary nor sufficient. The context in which the suffering occurs counts heavily toward whether it is seen as abnormal.

MALADAPTIVENESS

Whether a behavior is functional and adaptive—how well it enables the individual to achieve certain goals—is a fundamental element in deciding whether the behavior is normal or abnormal. Behaviors that strong-

ly interfere with individual well-being are maladaptive and count as factors in assessing abnormality.

By individual well-being, we mean the ability to work and the ability to conduct satisfying relationships with other people. Depression and anxiety interfere with love and work and, almost always, with an individual's sense of well-being. A fear of going out (agoraphobia) can be so strong that it keeps the sufferer locked inside an apartment, unable to fulfill any of his goals. Such a fear grossly interferes with the enjoyment of life, the ability to work, and relationships with others. The more there is such *harmful dysfunction,* the clearer the abnormality (Klein, 1999; Lilienfeld and Marino, 1999; Wakefield, 1999).

IRRATIONALITY

When a person's behavior seems to have no rational meaning, we are inclined to call that behavior and that person abnormal. One kind of irrationality that counts very strongly for the designation of abnormality is thought disorder, a major symptom of schizophrenia. Beliefs that are patently absurd and bizarre, perceptions that have no basis in objective reality, and mental processes that ramble from one unrelated idea to another constitute thought disorders. A classic example of such thought disorganization occurred during a formal experiment. The patient's task consisted of sorting colored blocks of various shapes and colors into a number of groups. The patient was cooperative and earnest. But he also exhibited an irresistible tendency to sort objects on the desk and on the experimenter's person, as well as parts of the room, things he pulled from his pockets, and even the experimenter himself, whom the patient recommended be remade of wood and cut into blocks. Here is what he said:

> I've got to pick it out of the whole room, I can't confine myself to this game . . . Three blues (test blocks) . . . now, how about that green blotter? Put it there too. Green peas you eat. You can't eat them unless you write on it (pointing to green blotter). Like that wristwatch (on the experimenter's wrist, a foot from the subject)—don't see three meals coming off that watch. . . . To do this trick you'd have to be made of wood. You've got a white shirt on—and the white blocks. You have to have them cut out of you! You've got a white shirt on—this (white hexagonal

block) will hold you and never let you go. I've got a blue shirt on, but it can't be a blue shirt and still go together. And the room's got to be the same. . . . (Excerpted from Cameron, 1947, p. 59)

UNPREDICTABILITY AND LOSS OF CONTROL

We expect people to be consistent from time to time, predictable from one occasion to the next, and very much in control of themselves. To be loved by someone one day but hated by the same person the next day is troubling. One hardly knows how to respond or what to expect. In a predictable world, we can maintain a sense of control. In an unpredictable one, we feel vulnerable and threatened. Don, the mild-mannered executive, adores his wife on Monday, but pummels her brutally on Tuesday. He is frightening in much the same way that Dr. Jekyll's alter ego, Mr. Hyde, is; both are unpredictable and out of control.

The judgment that behavior is out of control will be made under two conditions. The first occurs when the ordinary guides of behavior suddenly break down. Don's outbursts of violence exemplify this judgment. The second condition occurs when we do not know what causes an action. Imagine coming upon someone who is angry—raging and screaming in the streets. There may be good and socially acceptable reasons for such anger. But if we do not know those reasons and are unable to elicit them at the time, we are likely to consider that the person is out of control and to designate those actions as abnormal.

RARENESS AND UNCONVENTIONALITY

Generally, people recognize as acceptable and conventional those actions that they themselves are willing to do. Those who accede to a request to walk around campus wearing a sandwich board that reads "JOIN PHI DELTA KAPPA" are likely to estimate that a healthy majority of their peers would make the same choice. On the other hand, those who are unwilling to wear such a sign estimate that relatively few people would be willing. Thus, with the exception of behaviors that require great skill or daring, we tend to judge the abnormality of others' behavior by our own. Would you wear a sign around campus? If you would, you would judge such behavior as conventional and normal. If you wouldn't, such behav-

ior would stand out as unconventional and abnormal (Ross, Greene, and House, 1977).

Behaviors that are rare and undesirable are often considered abnormal. It hardly matters whether the behavior actually is rare, so long as it is perceived to be rare. Thus, there are many varieties of sexual and aggressive fantasies that are quite common but that are perceived to be rare and therefore abnormal. Nor is rareness itself a necessary condition for abnormality. Depression is a common disorder, as are anxiety states, and both are considered to be abnormal. But behavior that is both rare and socially undesirable is often seen as abnormal.

OBSERVER DISCOMFORT

People who are very dependent on others, ingratiating, or hostile, create discomfort in observers. Their behaviors often enable them to feel more comfortable, but the psychological conflicts they create are painful for others. We are most likely to experience vague observer discomfort when someone violates his or her culture's unwritten rules of behavior (Scheff, 1966). Violation of those rules creates the kind of discomfort that leads to the designation "abnormal."

For example, in some cultures, there is an unwritten rule that states that, except when angry or making love, one's face should be at least ten inches away from that of one's partner. Should that invisible boundary be overstepped, a rule will be violated, and the partner will feel uncomfortable. Similarly, there are unwritten rules about clothing one's genital area which, when violated, contribute to the impression that the person is abnormal.

Behavior we consider unusual and unconventional—when measured against our own—may be considered abnormal.

In the film *Twelve Monkeys,* most of the psychiatrists believe that the character played by Bruce Willis is abnormal. It is ambiguous, however, whether or not his behavior really is abnormal.

VIOLATION OF STANDARDS

There are times when behavior is assessed, not against our judgments of what is common and conventional, but against moral standards and idealized norms that are believed to characterize all right-thinking and right-acting people. This view starts with the notion that people ought to behave in a certain way, whether they really do or not, and it concludes with the view that it is normal to behave in the way one ought, and abnormal to fail to behave properly. Thus, it is normal to work, and abnormal not to do so—unless wealth, the unavailability of job openings, or illness exonerates one. It is normal to love, to be loyal, and to be supportive, and abnormal not to—regardless of the fact that evidence for these dispositions is not universally found in modern society. It is abnormal to be too aggressive or too restrained, too shy or too forward, too ambitious or not sufficiently ambitious.

The Family Resemblance Approach to Defining Abnormality

Family members resemble one another across a fixed number of dimensions, such as height, hair and eye color, and shape of nose, mouth, and ears. How do we know, for example, that Ed Smith is the biological offspring of Bill and Jane Smith? Well, he looks like them. He has Bill's blue eyes and sandy hair, and Jane's upturned nose and easy smile. Even though Ed is six inches taller than his father and has a rounder face than his mother, we sense a family resemblance among them because they have many significant elements in common. (But careful now: Ed might just be the *adopted* son of Bill and Jane Smith. Such are the hazards of family resemblances!)

Abnormality is recognized in the same way, by determining whether the behavior, thought, or person bears a family resemblance to the clearest examples—the "paradigm" cases—of behaviors, thoughts, and people we would all recognize as abnormal. Abnormality is assessed according to the match between an individual's characteristics and the seven elements of abnormality (Lilienfeld and Marino, 1999).

Examine the following case study with a view toward determining the "family resemblance" between the individual and the elements of abnormality:

Ralph, the seventeen-year-old son of a physician and a pharmacist, moved with his family from a small farming town to a large suburban community during the middle of his junior year in high school. The move was sudden: both his parents were offered jobs that were simply too good to turn down. The abruptness of the move generated no complaint from Ralph, nor did he acknowledge any difficulty. Nevertheless, he seemed to withdraw. At the outset, his family hardly noticed, but once the family settled down, his distant behavior became apparent. He made no friends in his new school, and when the summer came, he seemed to withdraw even further. He spent a good deal of the summer in his room, emerging only to take extended walks around the house. He often seemed preoccupied, and occasionally seemed to be listening to sounds that only he could hear.

Autumn approached and with it the time for Ralph to return to his senior year of high school. Ralph became even more withdrawn. He had difficulty sleeping, and he paced inside and outside the house. Shortly after he returned to school, his behavior deteriorated further. Sometimes, he seemed not to hear when called upon in class, while at other times his answers bore no relation to the questions. Both behaviors generated a good deal of mocking laughter in his classes, and his classmates actively avoided him. One day, he marched into class, stood up, and began to speak absolute gibberish. School authorities notified his parents, who came immediately to pick him up. When he saw them, he grimaced and began to roll a lock of hair between his fingers. He said nothing as he was brought to a psychiatric clinic. (Adapted from DSM-III Training Guide, 1981)

Is Ralph abnormal according to the preceding criteria? Even this brief vignette, which fails to describe fully the richness of Ralph's problem, leaves us convinced that Ralph is suffering some kind of psychological abnormality. It is a clear-cut case. Let us return to the elements of abnormality, and examine the extent to which Ralph's actions reflect those elements.

- **Suffering.** We have no information about whether, or to what degree, Ralph is suffering. His withdrawal from his family might reflect subjective distress. But then again, it might not.
- **Maladaptiveness.** Ralph's behavior is highly dysfunctional. Not only does he needlessly draw negative attention to himself, but also he obviously fails to respond to the demands of school. Such behavior neither serves his own needs nor those of society.
- **Irrationality.** There can be little doubt that Ralph's behavior is incomprehensible to observers, and that his verbalizations seem irrational to them.
- **Unpredictability and loss of control.** There is little evidence for loss of control in the vignette, but Ralph's parents would presumably find his behavior unpredictable. So too might his schoolmates.
- **Rareness and unconventionality.** Ralph's behavior is quite unusual. His silent withdrawal stands out noticeably and his speeches in class make him the center of undesirable attention.
- **Observer discomfort.** It is not clear from the vignette whether all observers are made uncomfortable by Ralph's behavior, but it is a fair guess that his schoolmates are avoiding him because they feel uncomfortable.
- **Violation of standards.** There is no evidence that Ralph's behavior violates widely held moral standards, but it is far from meeting idealized standards.

In the main, then, Ralph's behavior is maladaptive and irrational. These two elements alone would have qualified his behavior as abnormal in most people's judgment. Additionally, some evidence suggests that his behavior is unpredictable, unconventional, creates discomfort in observers, and violates ideal standards. The likelihood that these elements are present lends additional strength to the judgment that his behavior is abnormal.

What is the source of Ralph's abnormality? His behavior is abnormal. His thought is abnormal. And because these problems of behavior and thought last for such a long time and occur across so many different situations, many would call Ralph himself abnormal. This is the convention; it invites us to generalize from the actions and thoughts of an individual to the individual himself. This linguistic convention is costly, however, for we can easily be misled into believing that a particular pattern of behavior or thought is much more stable and pervasive than it really is. It is tragic enough that Ralph has the problems he is afflicted with. But it adds considerably to his tragedy to somehow infer that Ralph himself is flawed, rather than merely realizing that only at some times and only in some situations are Ralph's behaviors and thoughts abnormal.

The Hazards of Defining Abnormality

The main virtue of a family resemblance approach to abnormality is that it describes the way the term is actually used. The facts are that there is no single way in which all sons resemble all fathers, neither is there a single way in which all abnormal behaviors resemble one another. The notion that all abnormality must involve psychological suffering, or vividness, or observer discomfort is simply false, as we have seen. No single element exists that binds the behaviors of, say, a person who is deeply depressed, a person who is afraid to be alone, and a person who gorges herself and then vomits. Yet, we regard each of these people as suffering an abnormality because their behaviors are members of the family of characteristics that we have come to regard as abnormal.

But there are some hazards to the family resemblance approach to abnormality. The hazards all arise from the fact that this is a "descriptive" approach—describing actual usage, and not a "normative" approach—dictating how the term ought to be used in an ideal world. Let's look at three of these hazards: society's error, disagreement among observers, and disagreement between actor and observer.

SOCIETY MAY ERR

Unlike the judgment of temperature, the judgment of abnormality is a social one. Look again at some of the elements: observer discomfort, maladaptiveness, unconventionality, and violation of standards. These all require a social judgment. Social judgments change in time and, worse, they can easily be abused. Because the judgment of abnormality is so heavily social, it is even more susceptible to social abuse.

The notion of abnormality can easily and erroneously be applied to all manner of behavior that society presently finds objectionable. The very poor, who look so different from the rest of us, the deeply religious, whose values may seem idiosyncratic, these people march to their own drummers, and they create discomfort in the observers who disagree with them. Similarly, those who violate the ideal standards of others in the course of maintaining their own ideal standards risk being termed abnormal.

OBSERVERS DISAGREE

A family resemblance approach to abnormality is bound to generate some disagreements about whether or not a behavior qualifies as abnormal. Two observers might disagree that any given element was present. Moreover, they might disagree about whether enough elements were present, or whether they were present with sufficient intensity to constitute a clear case of abnormality. This is why some observers will see Carla's behavior as abnormal and others will not.

Such an approach generates disagreement for the further reason that the elements of abnormality are neither so precise nor so quantifiable that everyone will agree that a behavior or person fits the category. The more dramatic the behaviors and the longer they are sustained, the more agreement there will be among observers. The problem of observer disagreement is a serious one. As we shall see in Chapter 2, the problem is dealt with, to some extent, by stipulating as clearly as one can, the kinds of behaviors that are associated with each element of abnormality. When this is done, wider agreement occurs.

OBSERVERS AND ACTORS DISAGREE

There will occasionally be different opinions as to whether a behavior or person should be judged as abnormal, according to who is doing the judging:

La Chaise Electrique was one of many drawings done by Guillaume Pujolle, who was diagnosed with chronic persecution mania, with hallucinations and episodes of hyper excitation. The painting does not clearly indicate abnormality, however, and observers might well disagree as to his diagnosis.

the individuals who are generating the behaviors in question—we call them actors—or those who observe the behaviors. Generally, actors will be less inclined to judge their own behaviors as abnormal for three reasons: First, they have much more information available to them than do observers. What seems unpredictable or incomprehensible to an observer may seem quite predictable and comprehensible to an actor, and what generates discomfort in an observer may, as we indicated, generate none in the actor. Second, people who are psychologically distressed are not distressed all the time. Distress comes and goes. People, therefore, may be "crazy" at one time, but not crazy at another. Actors are uniquely positioned to recognize changes in themselves. Observers, however, often assume a continuity of psychological state that does not exist. Third, people generally are inclined to see themselves in a more favorable light than observers see them. As a result, actors will tend to see themselves and their behaviors more favorably, and hence more normally, than observers.

Thus, the family resemblance approach to abnormality is not perfect; it has its pitfalls, some of which are worse than others. We might wish that this were not the case and that abnormality were a more objective judgment. But our present wishes are beside the point, though eventually abnormality may be assessed with considerably greater objectivity. We are not endorsing the way abnormality is presently judged. Nor are we prescribing how the word "abnormal" should be used in an ideal world. Rather, we are merely describing how the word is actually used by laymen and professionals alike, with the hope that such a description will help in both diagnosis and treatment.

The Hazards of Self-Diagnosis

There is almost no one who has not harbored secret doubts about his or her normality. "Am I too afraid of speaking up in class?" "Do other people occasionally have fantasies about their parents dying in violent accidents?" "Why am I so down all the time?" A number of students show up in college counseling centers with such feelings.

After hearing and reading about various kinds of mental disorders in an abnormal psychology course, some students may find themselves prone to a phenomenon called "interns' syndrome." In the course of early training many years ago, a fledgling medical student reported finding in himself symptoms of almost every disease he studied.

> I remember going to the British Museum one day to read up on the treatment for some slight ailment of which I had a touch—hay fever, I fancy it was. I got down the book, and read all I came to read; and then, in an unthinking moment, I idly turned the leaves, and began to indolently study diseases, generally. I forgot which was the first distemper I plunged into—some fearful, devastating scourge, I know—and, before I had glanced half down the list of "premonitory symptoms," it was borne in upon me that I had fairly got it.
>
> I sat for a while frozen with horror, and then in the listlessness of despair, I again turned over the pages. I came to typhoid fever—read the symptoms—discovered that I had typhoid fever, must have had it for months without knowing it—wondered what else I had got; turned up St. Vitus's Dance—found, as I expected, that I had that too—began to get interested in my case, and determined to sift it to the bottom, and so started alphabetically—looked up ague, and learnt that I was sickening for it, and that the acute stage would commence in about another fortnight. Bright's disease, I was relieved to find, I had only in a modified form, and, so far as that was concerned, I might live for years. Cholera I had, with severe com-

plications; and diphtheria I seemed to have been born with. I plodded conscientiously through the twenty-six letters, and the only malady I could conclude I had not got was housemaid's knee.

> I felt rather hurt about this at first; it seemed somehow to be a sort of slight. Why hadn't I got housemaid's knee? Why this invidious reservation? After a while, however, less grasping feelings prevailed. I reflected that I had every other known malady in the pharmacology, and I grew less selfish, and determined to do without housemaid's knee. Gout, in its most malignant stage, it would appear, had seized me without my being aware of it; and zymosis I had evidently been suffering with from boyhood. There were no more diseases after zymosis, so I concluded there was nothing else the matter with me. . . . I had walked into that reading-room a happy healthy man, I crawled out a decrepit wreck. (Jerome, 1880)

This description makes clear the hazards of self-diagnosis. As you read this book, you may encounter symptoms in yourself that may make you think that you have each disorder in turn. Be forewarned: It is a very unpleasant experience and one about which neither authors nor readers can really do much. In part, it arises from the privacy that surrounds our lives. Many of our thoughts, and some of our actions, strike us as private, if not secret—things about which no one should know. If they did know, people, even (perhaps particularly) friends, might think less of us, or be offended, or both. One consequence of this privacy is the development of an exaggerated sense of the uniqueness of our forbidden thoughts and behaviors. Seeing them suddenly alluded to on these pages and associated with certain syndromes (commonly in contexts that are quite different from the contexts of our own behaviors—but we don't notice that) might make us believe that we have fallen prey to that problem too.

There are two things that can be done to combat the distress you may experience from reading this book and going to lectures. First, read carefully. You may, for example, be concerned when you read about depression: "Yes, I'm blue. I cry now more than I used to." But as you inquire deeply into the symptoms of depression, you will find that your lack of suicidal thoughts, your continued interest in sex or sports, your optimism about the future, all count against the diagnosis of depression.

Second, talk with your friends. Sometimes, merely mentioning that "when I read Chapter so-and-so, I got the feeling they're talking about me. Do you ever get that feeling?" will bring forth a chorus of "you bets," and relief for all.

Putting It All Together

Even when observers can agree that a behavior is abnormal, they are not always able to agree as to what causes that behavior or what can be done to change that behavior. Reasoning about causes and treatment varies, based on time and culture. Most of us in the twenty-first century United States believe that we can improve in almost every way if we just identify what needs to be improved and work at changing ourselves. This includes the belief that we can change abnormal behavior. Yet, in fact, there are some things about ourselves that we can change and other things that we cannot change or that we can only change with extreme difficulty. We need to readdress the central questions about self-improvement and human plasticity and ask: What can we succeed in changing about ourselves? What can't we change about ourselves? When can we overcome our biology? When is our biology our destiny?

A great deal is now known about change. Much of this knowledge exists only in the technical literature and has often been obfuscated by vested commercial, therapeutic, and cultural interests. The behaviorists long ago told the world that everything can change—intelligence, sexuality, mood, masculinity, femininity. The psychoanalysts still claim that, with enough insight, all your conflicts can be "worked through." The "cultural construct" movements, such as the feminist movement, and the self-help industry voiced their agreement. In contrast, many drug companies, DNA mappers, and biological psychiatrists believe that our character is fixed and that we are prisoners of our genes and the chemicals in our bodies.

Both the "everything can change" view and the "nothing can change" view are ideologically driven statements. In fact, some psychological problems change readily in therapy or with medications, and others resist change mightily. Moreover, biology and psychology interact, with each affecting the other. Our biological makeup can be changed to a certain

extent, as can our psychological makeup. It is important to remember, however, that the mind cannot be divorced from the body, that each has effects on the other. Development also affects biology and vulnerability to abnormality, as do genes, brain structures, thoughts, and emotions. This intermingling of the biological and psychological causes of mental disorders necessitates that treatments of choice take into consideration what will work in particular situations for particular individuals. Sorting out the causation and course of treatment means that scientists and practitioners need to work together by taking insights from each other.

While the surgeon general has found that one out of five Americans suffers from a mental disorder in every year, most of them never seek treatment for their disorder, be it out of embarrassment, belief that they cannot change, fear of discrimination because of the stigma of mental disorder, lack of money, or the unavailability of nearby therapists to go to. The surgeon general believes that to ensure the mental health of all Americans, we need to continue to do research on the brain and behavior, to reduce the stigma attached to mental health problems, and to educate the public about effective treatments. Moreover, he stresses the need to ensure that there are sufficient mental health services and providers and state-of-the-art and affordable treatments available for all who need them. He also emphasizes the importance of tailoring treatments to individuals based on their age, gender, race, and culture. This is a humane, grand, and expensive agenda, but one that is well worth pursuing.

As you read about the various approaches, assessments, and disorders, you may recognize yourself, your parents, your children, or those with whom you work or go to school. The findings and treatments you read about may thus have implications for you, not just for the people whose cases are discussed in this book. But keep in mind that as much as is now known, much more still needs to be discovered.

We believe that understanding and cure for mental disorders will not come from just one level of analysis or from any one school of thought. For example, a psychoanalytically inclined investigator might believe that early childhood trauma is the primary influence on adult psychopathology. He could spend years studying his patient's past history and never relieve his manic-depression, for it turns out that manic-depression is caused by a biological disruption and is well relieved by a drug. His strict adherence to a particular model would have blinded him to this other possibility—in this case, a neuroscience explanation of manic-depression. In sum, there is danger inherent in following any particular model of abnormality slavishly. Rather, we must find both the psychological and biological factors that can lead to abnormality. We need to realize that the effects are more than simply additive. Rather, biology and psychology have mutual effects on each other. Finding the way to integrate the psychological and biological perspectives and to use treatments that work and find others that might work is the hope and promise of those who study Abnormal Psychology in the twenty-first century.

Summary

1. The first theme of the book is the two main levels of analysis of abnormality: biological and psychological. The *biological level* uses the techniques and discoveries of neuroscience, while the *psychological approach* uses the sciences of mental life and behavior. Cause and cure turn out to be both *bottom-up,* with biological events controlling psychological events, and *top-down,* with psychological events controlling biological events.

2. The second theme of the book is *science and practice.* The practitioner is faced with immediate problems of diagnosis and treatment. She is concerned with a particular person, and she relies on the case history. The scientist is concerned with the underlying cause and the discovery of new treatments, which relies on *experiment, epidemiology,* and *outcome studies.*

3. The third theme of the book is *development.* Mental disorders change across the life span, with different stages of life associated with very different disorders. Developmental psychopathology studies what is constant and what changes across the life span, and how genes and their expression change as a person grows older and encounters different environments.

4. The fourth theme of the book is the evaluation of the *treatments of choice* for each disorder. In some cases, such as panic disorder, the treatment of choice turns out to be psychological. In other cases, such as erectile dysfunction, the treatment of choice turns out to be a medication. Sophisti-

cated *outcome studies* of both the *efficacy* (laboratory) and *effectiveness* (field) variety allow objective appraisal of which treatments work best.

5. Time and place determine how abnormality is perceived. When the world is perceived in *animistic* terms, abnormality is likely to be viewed as a supernatural phenomenon. Prehistoric people attributed abnormality to *animism,* or possession by spirits trapped in the head, and chipped *trephines* in the skull to let the spirits out.

6. Some Greeks and Romans attributed abnormality to *physical causes.* For example, they believed that hysteria was caused by a wandering uterus that created discomfort wherever it settled. They treated it by trying to draw the uterus back to its proper place. Galen challenged this idea and said that hysteria was caused by a malfunctioning sexual organ. Furthermore, Galen also contributed important insights into psychological causes of abnormality.

7. In the middle of the eighteenth century, it gradually was recognized that mental disorders were *psychological* in origin and could be treated by psychological means. Mesmer tried to induce crises to restore the flow of animal magnetism. Charcot treated mental disorders by *hypnosis,* after distinguishing hysterical convulsions from symptoms with an organic cause. Both Breuer and Freud used hypnosis to induce *catharsis* in hysterical patients.

9. There are no hard and fast definitions of normality and abnormality, for there is no single element that all instances of abnormality share, nor any single property that distinguishes normality from abnormality.

10. There are seven properties or elements that count toward deciding whether a person or an action is abnormal: *suffering, maladaptiveness, irrationality, unpredictability and loss of control, rareness, and unconventionality, observer discomfort,* and *violation of standards.* The more of these elements that are present, and the more visible each element is, the more likely are we to judge the person or the action as abnormal.

11. Abnormality is recognized the way members of a family are recognized: because they share a *family resemblance,* they have many significant elements in common.

12. Because the judgment of abnormality is a social judgment, there is sometimes disagreement about who is abnormal, and about which thoughts and

actions qualify as being considered abnormal. Society occasionally errs about whom it calls abnormal, as sometimes do observers, even observers who are qualified diagnosticians. But the absence of complete agreement should not be taken to mean that abnormality is always or frequently a matter of dispute.

13. Satisfactory understanding of the cause and cure of the panoply of abnormality will not arise from adhering to one particular level of analysis or one particular school of thought. Rather, we believe that the *integration* of biology and of psychology holds the most promising future for the field of Abnormal Psychology.

2

Assessment, Diagnosis, and Research Methods

Chapter Outline

Gaston Duf, *Pültlhinéle Günsthérs Vitrés'-he.*

- Familiarize yourself with how clinical interviews, observation, and psychological testing can help psychologists determine whether a person is suffering from a mental disorder.

- Learn about neuropsychological assessment and neuroimaging so that you can understand how technical advances have helped psychologists to assess brain abnormalities that may be contributing to abnormal behavior.

- Understand the difference between categorical and dimensional approaches to diagnosis, and how disorders are classified in DSM-IV.

- Be able to describe some factors that may influence the reliability and validity of diagnoses and become familiar with conditions that may bias diagnoses.

- Learn about the value and limitations of the clinical case history.

- Become familiar with the experimental method (including laboratory models that use animals, as well as experiments conducted with humans) and how it can be used to determine causation of psychological disorders.

- Learn about the value and contributions of various nonexperimental methods of investigating abnormality, including experiments of nature, comparative studies, correlational studies, and epidemiological studies.

The main goal of clinical psychologists is to better understand the nature and origins of a person's symptoms and problems so that they can make a diagnosis and treat the troubled person. Like good detectives, psychologists use a variety of sources of information, including self-reports, observations, and psychological tests to evaluate, or assess, what is wrong. If the evaluation only involves observations, the conclusions may differ from those that are also based on psychological testing. When psychologists look at the entire body of evidence, they can make a more accurate evaluation. The process generally begins when there are behavioral problems or other symptoms that interfere with a person's life and interpersonal relations, as in the following case:

Brent, the youngest of six children, was nine years old when he was first referred for a psychological evaluation. Brent's mother described him as having a "long history" of behavior problems, and she was not sure how to manage him. She said he was constantly moving and seemed to ignore her attempts to discipline him. Brent was failing most of his classes at school, and the teachers believed he might be retarded. He scored far below grade level on standardized achievement tests. The principal was considering placing Brent in a special school.

Brent's family lived in a trailer park in an isolated rural area and, although both parents worked part-time as laborers at a local paper mill, they had little money. They both had only eighth-grade educations, and neither had previous experience with mental health professionals. Nonetheless, both parents were very concerned about their son and wanted to find out why he was "such a problem." Brent was interviewed by a child psychologist. The same psychologist made a school visit to observe Brent in the classroom, and she asked his teachers to fill out some behavior rating forms. In addition, another member of the assessment team administered a comprehensive battery of psychological tests, including a test of intelligence.

Within the first five minutes of the interview, there was little doubt that Brent's verbal skills were quite limited. He had a slight lisp and spoke in short sentences. His was also quite fidgety and appeared somewhat anxious. Based solely on these observations, the psychologist tentatively concluded that there was a basis for concern about Brent's cognitive abilities. But the results of the psychological tests painted a very different picture. Brent scored substantially above average on those portions of the test that did not involve language. In fact, his scores on a test of spatial memory and reasoning were in the superior range, placing him at the level of the average sixteen-year-old. In contrast, his score on a measure of vocabulary was comparable to that of the average six-year-old.

The school observation and teacher reports were quite consistent. Brent had a very hard time sitting still in the classroom. His attention seemed to wander. Brent rarely spoke at inappropriate times, but he was a source of distraction for the other students because he was constantly moving about. He was also very conspicuous because of the way he looked. Most of the other students were from the town and came from middle-class homes. They were well-dressed and sophisticated. Brent was one of only a handful of children from the trailer park outside of town. His clothes fit poorly and were worn and out of style. He had little exposure to popular "child culture" because his family did not have a working television set. The teachers and most of the other children did not enjoy having Brent in the classroom. Brent did have friends, however. In fact, he was the leader among the group of nine elementary-school-aged boys who rode the bus with him from the trailer park. Putting all of the results together, the mental health team concluded that Brent was definitely not retarded, although he did have serious delays in the development of expressive language skills that were partially environmentally determined. He also showed signs of attention problems and hyperactivity. The team concluded that a diagnosis of attention deficit disorder with hyperactivity was most appropriate. In addition, developmental language delay was present. With these diagnoses, Brent was eligible for special services within the regular school setting. The child psychologist developed a treatment plan for Brent that involved interventions aimed at helping him control his behavior in the classroom. Medication was considered to be a possibility for the future.

Just as the teacher and psychologists had to assess Brent, so do we all assess or "size up" other people's psychological characteristics on a daily basis. Although our assessments do not lead to diagnoses and treatment, as do the assessments of psychologists, they do have implications for our interactions with others. Throughout the course of our everyday lives, we interact with a variety of people: family members, friends, co-workers, classmates, clerks, and others. In order for these interactions to run smoothly,

we must be capable of assessing other peoples' moods and attitudes. For example, if we are in a restaurant being served by a waitress who has a serious facial expression and speaks few words of greeting, we are likely to infer that she is either in a bad mood or simply an unfriendly person. Either way, we will probably be less inclined to ask her for advice about the menu or to request extra service. Our assessment of her will lead us to certain conclusions, and we will behave accordingly. We may also be less inclined to offer her a generous tip.

Of course, we have a great deal of experience interacting with members of our own species, so these everyday "assessments" become automatic. They are usually not systematic or objective, but instead, are based on hunches. Sometimes they occur unconsciously. If we are honest with ourselves, we must admit that our evaluations of others are not always correct. We might assess a person as being shy and introverted the first time we meet her, only to find out later that she is really very outgoing. Our intuition might tell us that someone is not trustworthy, but we might later discover that he is a person of great integrity. Most of the time these mistakes do not have a major impact on the other person or on us. Our impression of the individual changes, for better or worse, and we act accordingly.

When psychologists and other mental health workers are called upon to conduct an evaluation of someone, however, the accuracy of their assessment is more important. Fleeting impressions and hunches are not sufficient. The results of the psychological evaluation or assessment may determine whether or not the person receives a diagnosis, gets hospitalized, or is prescribed a drug to alter his mood. The results may even determine whether a person is deemed dangerous to others and confined in a mental institution against his will, or whether he is judged to be no threat and released into society. Because the stakes can be so high, psychological assessment procedures should be as thorough, systematic, and objective as possible. The good clinician knows, of course, that her own personal biases may come into play and influence her conclusions. But she tries to minimize the impact of such biases.

In the same way, the clinical researcher is seeking accurate information. She wants to add to our understanding of the causes and best treatments for mental disorders. Health-care consumers also want to have confidence in research findings. They would like to believe that the research was conducted care-

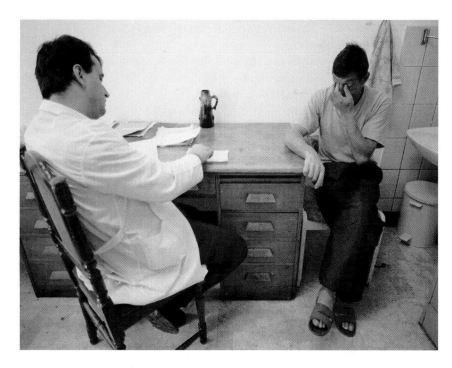

When a psychologist makes a psychological evaluation, he notes the patient's words, manner, posture, tone of voice, and degree of eye contact. This former front-line soldier weeps as he relates his war-related nightmares to a therapist at a psychiatric hospital in Tuzla, Bosnia.

fully and has produced useful information on which they can base rational decisions. In order to insure that this is the case, the researcher, like the clinician, utilizes a systematic approach and tries to minimize biases. Thus, a systematic approach is the hallmark of psychological assessment and the cornerstone of the scientific method. In this way, the *scientific method* provides the framework for both the clinician and the researcher.

In this chapter, we will concern ourselves with modern psychological assessment, diagnosis, and research methodology. We will explore the psychological assessment techniques that help us to understand mental functions. We will describe the major diagnostic system for mental illness, the Diagnostic and Statistical Manual of Mental Disorders (currently DSM-IV), which psychologists use to diagnose whether or not a person has a mental disorder and what that disorder might be. DSM-IV is comprised of categories that permit us to group people according to their similarities. We will ask what diagnostic categories seem most promising for understanding and treating psychological distress, and how to assess whether a diagnostic category is useful and reliable. Finally, we will examine the various scientific research methods that provide clues about the causes and best treatments for mental disorders. These research methods are the foundation of clinical psychology, and they have

yielded numerous findings that have altered the way we live our lives.

Before embarking on our discussion of psychological assessment, we should mention that we address both its strengths and weaknesses. As clinical scientists, we have been trained to take a balanced, yet critical, approach. It is important, however, to keep the weaknesses of psychological assessment in proper perspective. All of us have had the experience of going to the doctor with a physical ailment and undergoing an examination, only to hear that it could be any number of things: a virus, a bacterial infection, food poisoning, or maybe an allergy. The diagnosis of physical illnesses is imprecise. So is the diagnosis of psychological disorders. Acknowledging the limitations of psychological assessment does not mean we fail to see its benefits.

Assessment

A **psychological assessment** is an evaluation of a person's mental functions and psychological health. Psychologists seek to understand individuals through a variety of procedures. They talk to people, administer psychological tests, and observe their behavior in real-life situations. These procedures are the tools used by psychologists to achieve a more in-depth understanding of the client. That understanding may result in a diagnosis, but it commonly also results in much more. Assessment can yield an understanding of a person's individuality, the forces that generate his or her uniqueness. Often, the assessment will give us some clues about why a person is experiencing difficulty, and about how the difficulty can be resolved.

In order for an assessment device to generate meaningful information about people, it must possess two characteristics. First, it must be *reliable,* that is, it must generate the same findings with repeated use. Imagine a physical universe in which yardsticks are made of rubber. Each time you measured something, you would come up with different answers simply because of the stretchy nature of the measuring instrument. Such an instrument would be unreliable, which is to say you could not depend on it to come up with the same measurement each time it was used. One of the chief criteria for a psychological test is that it be reliable, producing similar results each time it is administered.

Second, an assessment device must be *valid.* It must actually measure what it is intended to measure. Even a high-tech digital thermometer is useless for measuring the size of a room. A psychological test can be useful for one purpose and thoroughly invalid for others. If the test is intended to measure attentional problems, but instead it seems to be more sensitive to individual differences in mood, it is not a valid test.

Psychological assessment techniques can be divided into three general categories: interviewing, observing, and testing. When the findings from all three are combined, the clinician gains a richer and more accurate picture of the individual's psychological functioning. After discussing the various approaches to assessment, we will return to the issues of reliability and validity later in this chapter.

When a person seeks help for psychological problems, his physical health is also a matter of concern. This is because many physical illnesses affect mental functions. Thus, a physical examination may be conducted to determine whether the person is suffering from a specific physical condition that is impairing mental health. When the results of a physical examination are combined with the findings from a psychological assessment, the clinician can get a broader picture of the client's health. Each approach can offer a specific vantage point on the client's problems and provide very useful information.

The Physical Examination

It is not unusual for people who are experiencing stress or feelings of depression to go to their family physician with complaints of physical symptoms. They might tell their general practitioner that they are experiencing back pain, heart palpitations, sleeping difficulties, or a loss of appetite. After conducting an examination, the physician may conclude that there is no identifiable physical reason for the symptom. If the doctor begins to suspect that the core problems are actually psychological, perhaps a consequence of undue stress, she may then refer the patient to a psychologist or psychiatrist. In these cases, the physical symptoms are a consequence of, or *secondary* to, the psychological problems.

The causal pathway can also be in the opposite direction; psychological problems can be secondary to physical conditions. For example, symptoms of anxiety and depression can arise from undetected strokes, anemia, thyroid hormone deficiency, and abnormalities in sex hormone levels. Psychotic symptoms are not uncommon in patients with seizure disorders, brain tumors, exposure to toxic chemicals, or traumatic brain injury produced by a blow to the head. Prescription drugs used to treat physical health problems, such as heart conditions, can have psychological side effects. And, of course, abuse of alcohol or illegal drugs can lead to disturbances in mood or thought processes. In these kinds of cases, it is important to identify and treat the physical condition in order to eliminate the psychological symptoms.

When a psychologist or psychiatrist conducts an initial interview with a client, he will inquire about the person's medical history. If it appears that the person has not undergone an adequate physical examination in the recent past, the psychologist is likely to recommend that he receive one. This is especially true if the symptom pattern is similar to one that tends to be associated with a physical illness. For example, if the client reports feelings of severe depression, along with dizziness and weight loss, thyroid disorder may be suspected.

There are several physical tests that are particularly helpful in the assessment of people with psychological symptoms. The laboratory tests used to measure hormone levels in the person's blood can reveal unusually high or low levels, which may affect mood or behavior. Electroencephalograms (EEGs) measure brain electrical activity through the placement of electrodes on the patient's scalp. Researchers have studied the electrical waves produced by the brain, so they can distinguish normal from abnormal patterns. EEGs can provide important information about the presence of abnormal brain electrical activity that might be indicative of seizures. The administration of a neurological examination can help to identify abnormalities in motor functions or sensory systems that result from damage to the nervous system.

If a thorough physical assessment does not show any evidence of a specific medical condition, the focus shifts to a detailed psychological assessment. The first step is to ask the client to provide information about his or her past experiences and current symptoms. This calls upon the clinician's skills as an interviewer.

The Clinical Interview

The **clinical interview** is the most commonly used approach to assessment. It is used by clinical psychologists, psychiatrists, and other mental health professionals, reflecting the widespread view that we can get an understanding of a person by talking to him. But it takes skill and experience to be a good interviewer. Clinicians who are skilled at interviewing can get information, not only from what people say, but also from how they say it: their manner, tone of voice, body posture, and degree of eye contact (Beutler, 1996; Hersen and Turner, 1994; Nowicki and Duke, 1994). Of course, in order to get this information, there must be a good rapport between the client and the interviewer. One cannot expect people to be honest if they feel that their statements are going to incriminate them or lead to punitive decisions about their future. For an interview to be maximally informative, the client needs to perceive the interviewer as being nonthreatening, supportive, and encouraging of self-disclosure (Jourard, 1974).

UNSTRUCTURED INTERVIEWS

Clinical interviews vary in structure. Some are completely unstructured interactions. This approach is not systematic. Instead, the clinician may allow the client to verbalize his concerns as he chooses, or she may explore a particular topic based on something the client has said. When this approach is used to gather information about a client, the clinician's personal and professional experiences play a big role in the outcome. The clinician's hunches, based on past experience, guide the process. The unstructured interview, therefore, is very flexible, but it "pays a price" for that flexibility. Because they are unstructured, no two of these interviews are the same. They elicit different information, which may reduce the reliability and validity of the interview (Fisher, Epstein, and Harris, 1967).

Paul Meehl, a famous clinical psychologist, has written extensively on the problems associated with unstructured clinical interviews and diagnosis (Meehl, 1996). Over the years, he has been a vocal advocate of using structured and objective procedures, based on statistical prediction, to diagnose people suffering from mental disorders. He points out numerous studies that have shown that standardized assessment procedures are far better than "clinical judgment" in predicting the prognosis for psychological disorders. Furthermore, experts have criticized unstructured clinical interviews because suggestive techniques used by some clinicians may lead clients to say things that are inaccurate. This was illustrated in the McMartin Preschool case, in which allegations of ritual abuse of children in day care drew national attention from 1983 to the early 1990s. Seven teachers at the McMartin Preschool in a Los Angeles suburb were accused of sexually abusing hundreds of children over a ten-year period. As evidence, the prosecution presented several hundred videotaped interviews with the children. Some psychologists criticized these interviews, on the grounds that they contained suggestive and leading questions. Though none of the accused were ever convicted of the crime, the case raised concerns regarding interviewing techniques that may cause children to make false reports. Several researchers have suggested that techniques such as suggestive questioning, social influence, reinforcement, and removal of the child from familiar surroundings may elicit false allegations by children and adults (Garven, Wood, Malpass, and Shaw, 1998). In light of the potential consequences of unstructured interviews, Meehl and others advocate the use of more structured procedures for gathering clinical data.

STRUCTURED INTERVIEWS

In recent years, clinical interviews have become much more structured. The structured clinical interview involves *standardized* questions; in other words, the psychologist asks the same questions in more or less the same order. The amount of clinical judgment required in these interviews is substantially reduced. The answers to the specific questions lead automatically to the scoring of the symptoms, and the results can be processed by a computer. The structured interview is now routinely used in research to overcome the reliability and validity problems that arise from unstructured interviews (Ventura, Liberman, Green, Shaner, and Mintz, 1998). This is important for two reasons. First, because other researchers must be able to *replicate* the results. Second, because clinicians want to know whether the results of the research are likely to apply to other patients. For example, when a researcher publishes a study of patients with "major depression," the findings are only of use to the clinician if the researcher's procedures for diagnosing major depression are clearly stated.

One of the most widely used structured interviews is the Structured Clinical Interview for DSM, or the "SCID" (First, Spitzer, Gibbons, and Williams, 1995). Training manuals and videotapes are available to prepare clinicians to administer the SCID. The SCID begins with general questions about the person's current life, such as, "What kind of work do you do?" The interviewer then informs the client that she will begin asking about mental health problems: "I am going to be asking you about problems or difficulties you may have had, and I'll be making some notes as we go along." Then she proceeds with queries about specific symptoms and syndromes: "Now I am going to ask you some questions about your mood. In the past month has there been a time when you were feeling depressed or down most of the day nearly every day?" The client's responses are recorded by the interviewer and guide the line of questioning.

It is obvious that clinicians must use different kinds of questions when interviewing children. For diagnosing childhood disorders, the Diagnostic Interview Schedule for Children (DISC), is now one of the most widely used structured interviews. It was designed to assess children, ages six to seventeen. When compared to the SCID, the DISC questions are posed with simpler vocabulary and address different issues. The DISC contains a series of interview questions aimed at both the child (DISC-C) and the parent (DISC-P). The questions focus on the child's level of functioning in areas such as school, peer relationships, family relationships, and community involvement. When the DISC is readministered at another time (referred to as "test-retest"), the results tend to be stable. This suggests that the DISC yields reliable symptom scores and DSM diagnoses (Bellack and Hersen, 1998).

We can expect to see more innovation in clinical interviewing in the future. For example, researchers are exploring the possibilities for interviewing via live telecommunication (Ruskin et al., 1998). This could include a video image of the client, so that a clinician at another location would also be able to observe nonverbal behaviors that might provide diagnostic clues. Telecommunication interviews may be very beneficial in rural communities where mental health professionals are not readily available. A clinical psychologist from another area could conduct a routine diagnostic assessment and communicate the results to a local treatment provider. One important question that researchers will need to address about this approach is whether it affects the way people respond: Are they as inclined to give honest answers in a telecommunication interview?

Observation

Sometimes clinical psychologists find that the information clients provide in interviews doesn't seem to fit with their own observations. For example, a parent might bring in her child for a psychological evaluation, saying, "He just can't sit still. He is always moving." Yet, the child is able to sit right there, perfectly still, in the psychologist's office for an extended period of time. How can this be? Why is the parent's description inconsistent with the psychologist's observation of the child's behavior? One source of such inconsistency is bias in the observer's perceptions: the parent's personal attitudes and expectancies may be influencing how she views the child. Another factor is that behavioral styles differ in different situations. The child's activity level may be way above average at home, but not in other contexts, or his activity level may be excessive at school, but not at home. One of the best ways to get an accurate picture is to observe the individual's behavior directly in different settings.

BEHAVIORAL ASSESSMENT

Behavioral assessment consists of keeping an accurate record of the behaviors or thoughts that are the focus of research or treatment (Bellack and Hersen, 1998). The researcher or clinician wants to know when the behaviors occur, how often they occur, how long they last (duration), and where possible, how intense they are. In the psychological assessment of children, behavioral assessment can be very important. Often clinicians conduct school visits to observe the child in the classroom and record the number of problematic behaviors. These behaviors might be physical aggression, inattentiveness, or motor tics.

Sometimes the clinician structures the behavioral observation. A client might report, for example, that she becomes nervous when she has to speak in public. If the clinician wants a fairly precise measure of how nervous the client becomes, she might ask the client to deliver a speech (Paul, 1966). The clinician can then record, in detail, what form the anxiety took (for example, trembling knees, rigid arms, lack of eye contact, quivering voice, flushed or pale face) and how often the signs of anxiety occurred. In some situations, family members may participate in the behavioral assessment. For example, in order to develop an effective pain management strategy for a patient with recurring pain, family members might be asked to record the patient's verbal and physical expressions of pain (Fernandez and McDowell, 1995).

Behavioral assessment can also be done by clients themselves. People who desire to give up smoking are commonly asked to begin by recording when and under what conditions they smoke each cigarette. People who desire to lose weight are asked to record when, where, how much, and under what conditions they eat. Assessments by clients are not only useful for overt behaviors, but for private thoughts and physical sensations as well. Mahoney (1971), for example, asked a client to record each time that she had a self-critical thought. Her recorded self-observations became the basis for evaluating whether subsequent interventions had any effect.

Behavioral assessment is commonly used in conjunction with treatment (Rachman, 1997). It can help to define the problem, to provide a record of what needs to be changed, and subsequently, of what progress has been made. The assessment does not stand apart from the treatment, nor is it an evaluation of the client for the therapist's use only. It is rather part of the treatment, a procedure of interest to both client and therapist, and one in which they fully share.

Sometimes behavioral assessment reveals causes for distress of which the respondent was unaware (Mariotto, Paul, and Licht, 1995). Metcalfe (1956; cited in Mischel, 1976) asked a patient who was voluntarily hospitalized for asthma to keep a careful record of the incidence, duration, and the events surrounding her asthma attacks. Attacks occurred on fifteen of the eighty-five days during which records were kept. Nine of the attacks occurred after contact with her mother. Moreover, on 80 percent of the days in which she had no asthma attacks, she also had had no contact with her mother. But while "contact with mother" seemed to be a source of the attacks, attempts to induce an attack by discussing her mother during an interview, or by presenting cards portraying mother figures, were unsuccessful. Because words, as symbols of experience, sometimes do not elicit the behaviors that the direct experiences themselves produce, interviews that rely heavily on words often fail to be fully diagnostic.

While behavioral assessment has clear advantages, it cannot be used with every psychological problem. Sometimes, tracking behavior in the required detail is simply too costly or time-consuming. Often, when the tracking is done by the client alone, the assessment fails for lack of motivation or precision. Finally, there are situations in which behavioral assessment may not work well: covert behaviors such as thoughts and feelings are not as amenable to reliable assessments as are overt behaviors.

PSYCHOPHYSIOLOGICAL ASSESSMENT

Anxiety, fear, and tension often have physiological correlates. When people are anxious, stressed or fearful, they may experience changes in muscle tension, blood circulation, body temperature, breathing pattern, or rate of perspiration. Also, the pattern of electrical activity (as measured by an electroencephalogram, or EEG) in their brain may change. *Psychophysiological assessment* involves the measurement of one or more of the physiological processes that reflect autonomic nervous system activity (see Chapter 4 for more on the nervous system). Included among these processes are heart rate, skin conductance (that is, sweat gland activity), muscle activity, brain electrical activity, pulse and body temperature. Psychophysiological assessment not only confirms whether there is a physiological component to the emotional reaction, but how intense that component is, and whether treatment affects it (Sturgis and Gramling, 1998).

As you might expect, people are not necessarily consciously aware of their physiological responses. For example, they can have a skin conductance

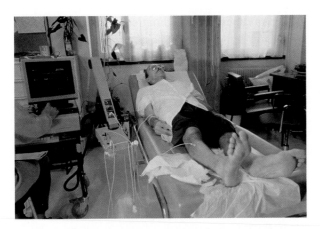

This client is being tested for psychophysiological changes through the use of an electromyagraph.

response to an angry face that is presented so briefly they are not even conscious of having seen it (Esteves, Parra, Dimberg, and Oehman, 1994). Similarly, patients who have experienced traumatic stressful events are not necessarily aware of the intensity of their level of physiological arousal (Laor et al., 1999).

Psychophysiological assessment has a variety of clinical applications. For example, it can be used to measure the heart rate response to the stress of examinations (Hazlett, Falkin, Lawhorn, Friedman, and Haynes, 1997), or the presentation of traumatic stimuli to patients suffering from post-traumatic shock disorder. (Keane et al., 1998). Very recently, psychologists have developed procedures for measuring psychophysiological response in persons who are engaged in everyday activities. Referred to as ambulatory psychophysiology, these procedures are useful in assessing anxiety or phobic reactions in natural settings, such as reactions to air travel in persons who have a phobic reaction to flying (Wilhelm and Roth, 1998). Heart rate, skin conductance, or respiration patterns can be measured with ambulatory psychophysiology. The case below provides an example of the use of psychophysiology in clinical assessment:

> Tammy, a sixteen-year-old female, was referred by her mother to the Behavioral Medicine Clinic of a large medical center in a noncoastal state. Tammy's mother was concerned about the degree to which her daughter's fears interfered with her daily functioning. Tammy was in agreement with the referral.
>
> Tammy and her mother related a complicated and confusing account of her fears that centered on

sharks and certain large objects (e.g., billboards). These fears had begun following Tammy's repeated viewing of a popular adventure/horror film involving sharks, approximately six years prior to our evaluation. After viewing the film, Tammy began to "see" images of the sharks swimming towards her whenever she was in water (e.g., swimming, taking showers). These images resulted in anxiety which had increased significantly over the two-year period before the evaluation. Presenting problems included an inability to swim alone in pools, screaming and feeling panicked when presented with images of sharks (e.g., seeing sharks on television), and an inability to shower with the shower curtain closed. The last problem was the most distressing to Tammy as it resulted in excessive amounts of water on the bathroom floor and feelings of helplessness. An additional problem which had developed over the past few years and which Tammy felt was related to her fear of sharks, was her discomfort in standing near large statues, billboards, or theatrical back drops. This was a concern because Tammy was a dancer who occasionally practiced and performed on stage. (Harris and Goetsch, 1990, pp. 147–65)

Before the psychologist began treating Tammy, a psychophysiological assessment was conducted to examine her heart rate and skin conductance responses to various mental images. When Tammy was instructed to imagine showering, there was an increase in her heart rate and a more pronounced skin conductance response. This did not occur when she was asked to imagine other situations, especially relaxing images. This assessment provided further evidence of the nature and intensity of Tammy's fear. After treatment, the same psychophysiological assessment procedures were used to determine whether the treatment had the desired effect. The results confirmed that Tammy's fear of water was significantly reduced.

In a treatment process called *biofeedback,* a client can be made attentive to small psychophysiological changes, and to the psychological states that bring them about. The typical approach in biofeedback is to have the client directly observe the changes that occur in a physical indicator of a biological variable, such as heart rate, blood pressure, pulse, electrical activity in the brain or muscle tension. For example, migraine headaches often arise from changes in muscle tension. During biofeedback, these changes can be directly measured and communicated to the client. As the client is trained to relax, he can immediately see the effects of that relaxation on the indicator of muscle tension. Gradually he can reduce the frequency and intensity of headaches by using the techniques he has learned to control muscle tension (Allen and Shriver, 1998; Hermann, Blanchard, and Flor, 1997).

NEUROIMAGING

There is no doubt that the development of **neuroimaging,** techniques for imaging the living human brain, has set the stage for a new era in both clinical treatment and research. The introduction of **computerized-axial tomography (*CAT* or *CT*)** was a watershed in the era of neuroimaging. CAT scanning is an extension of the much older X-ray technique, supplemented by modern computing power. The X-ray itself is based on the principle that abnormal tissue absorbs X-rays to a different degree than bone or normal brain tissue. From a series of X-rays of the brain taken at different angles, the

computer constructs a three-dimensional representation of the brain, and abnormal tissue can be located (Figure 2–1). CAT scanning can aid in the diagnosis of brain tumors, injuries, and abnormalities in the shape of various brain regions. Furthermore, it is not very invasive and does not require much time, only fifteen to thirty minutes. But it does involve exposure to X-rays, and this can cause damage to cells.

Magnetic resonance imaging (MRI) is another technique that is more sensitive and accurate than the CAT scan. It gives a clearer image of the brain. In MRI, a magnetic field surrounds the head, and radio frequency signals are transmitted through the skull and brain tissue. The MRI scanner then detects the changes in the position of protons in the hydrogen atoms in the tissue. It does this by measuring the resonant frequency throughout the brain. The results are reconstructed by a computer as an image representing the different parts of the brain. Damaged or abnormal brain tissue can be seen on the image because it differs in darkness (see Figure 2–1). In contrast to the CAT scan, which reveals the density of tissue, the MRI can actually provide information about the composition of cells and their surroundings. MRI also has an advantage over the CAT scan in that it does not involve X-rays. However, it is much more expensive and more invasive. The patient must hold her head still inside a very narrow tube for fifteen to forty-five minutes, and the sound of the MRI machine can be quite loud. People who are claustrophobic or sensitive to loud noises may find the procedure very uncomfortable. For this reason, the person is sometimes given an alarm button to push, just in case she is not able to tolerate the discomfort.

Both the CAT scan and the MRI provide images of static brain structures. This kind of brain imaging is called *structural* neuroimaging. Some of the newer techniques are capable of measuring the metabolic activity of the brain. These techniques are called *functional* neuroimaging. Based on the same principles as MRI, a technique called **functional MRI (fMRI)** records images of the brain at a much faster rate than the regular MRI. By recording changes in the tissue that occur within milliseconds, the actual metabolic functioning of the brain can be measured. Using fMRI, researchers can study the changes that occur in the brain when a person is processing sensory information, such as sounds or visual stimuli. They can also observe changes in brain activity when the

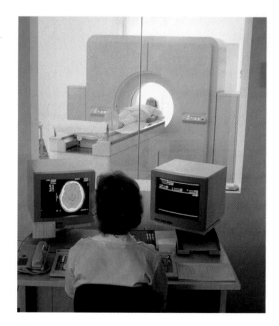

This patient is undergoing a CAT scan in which X-rays are moved in an arc around the head and detectors analyze the amount of radiation that has passed through the head; a technician monitors the computer, which is making a composite picture based on many X-ray views taken from different angles. MRI scans are more detailed than CAT scans and are produced by the use of magnetic energy rather than X-rays.

Figure 2–1

NEUROIMAGING TECHNIQUES

The figure shows direct methods of viewing the brain, including (A) the CAT (CT) scan technique; (B) a CAT scan image; (C) the PET scan technique; (D) a PET scan image; (E) the MRI technique; and (F) an MRI image. (Source: Rosenzweig and Leiman, 1989; scans courtesy of Dr. Marcus E. Raichle)

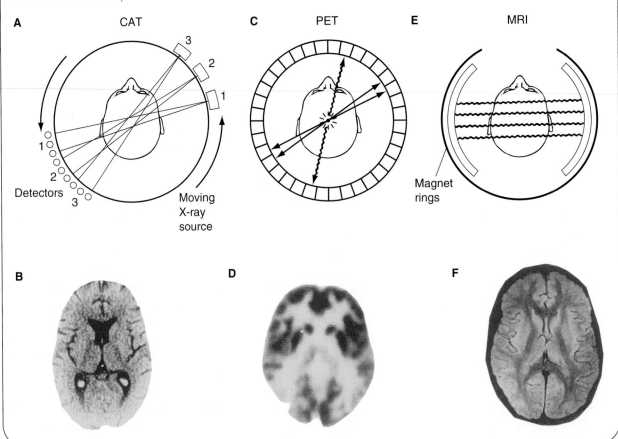

person is performing a mental task, like trying to remember specific words or imagine certain experiences. Like MRI, fMRI is very expensive and invasive. At the present time it is primarily used for research, although it is likely to play a greater role in diagnosis in the future.

Another neuroimaging procedure, ***positron emission tomography (PET) scans,*** is based on the measurement of cerebral blood flow and metabolic activity. In the PET scan procedure, a substance—often glucose—is made radioactive, injected into a person, and its rate of delivery and uptake to various brain regions is measured. The technique can reveal the increase in blood flow, oxygen, or glucose to more active brain areas (see Figure 2–1). The PET scan is also used to study the distribution of various receptors for neurotransmitters in

the brain. This is done through the injection of radioactively labeled substances that are known to bind to certain receptors. When PET images are combined with MRI images, more precise localization of the brain activity is possible. One major drawback to PET is that it involves the injection of a substance labeled with radioactivity. As a result, there are many guidelines to assure the safety of the procedure. Also, PET is quite costly and not widely available.

A relatively new technique is ***magnetoencephalography (MEG)*** (Bigler, Lowry, and Porter, 1997). MEG is based on the detection of the weak magnetic fields produced by brain electrical activity. Differences among brain regions in level of activity are inferred from differences in the strength of the magnetic field. This procedure is noninvasive and

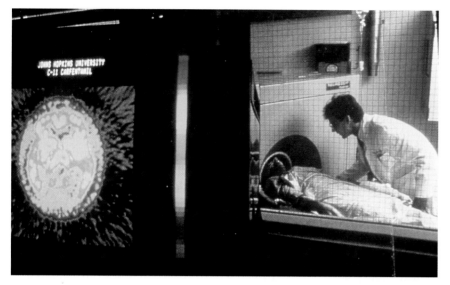

A patient who is depressed is undergoing a PET scan, which is used to measure levels of metabolic activity in the brain. Radioactive chemicals are injected into the blood vessels and travel to the brain; computers then analyze the difference in the uptake of the chemicals in different brain regions. There are observable differences in the metabolic activity of patients who are depressed and those who are not.

involves no radiation. Because it is so new, it has only been used in research, but it is likely that clinical applications will be identified in the near future.

Neuroimaging, especially MRI and PET scans, have been used in basic research on cognition and emotion, as well as in studies of patients with neurological and mental disorders. Some view the advent of neuroimaging as a watershed in behavioral neuroscience and assessment (Tulving, Markowitsch, Craik, Habib, and Houle, 1996). Others are more skeptical, however. These scientists urge caution in the use of functional neuroimaging (Sargent, 1994). They point out that we have only a limited understanding of the biological processes that give rise to the changes measured with functional neuroimaging. They also believe that enthusiasm about the potential of neuroimaging has caused some investigators to overlook its limitations. Thus, some of the initial conclusions drawn from studies using these techniques may not be correct. Time will tell whether this skepticism is justified.

Psychological Testing

Another source of information about the nature of an individual's problems and disabilities is psychological testing. There are literally thousands of psychological tests available for use. They vary in two main ways: *focus* and *format*. Some tests are narrow in focus, in that they are designed to illuminate a specific personality attribute, such as anxiety or de-

pression, or a particular kind of mental ability. Others tests are broader in focus and measure several aspects of an individual's personality or mental functions.

The format of a psychological test is the manner in which it is administered. Some tests are administered by an examiner who presents each question or item to the client. In contrast, some tests involve minimal interaction with the examiner; these are self-report inventories that are completed independently by the client. The format may also vary with respect to the structure of the test items. At one end of the continuum is a test like the "Draw-a-Person," which simply requires that the client draw a human figure as he chooses. There are, by intention, no rules about the content of the drawing. An example of a test on the other end of the continuum is the arithmetic subtest of the Wechsler Intelligence Scale. In this subtest, the examiner reads an arithmetic problem verbatim, and there is a specific time limit and a specific correct answer for each item.

In the following discussion, we will describe three general categories of tests: psychological inventories, "projective" tests, and intelligence tests. As you might suspect, there are guidelines about revealing the content of certain psychological tests. The companies that produce and sell them want to make sure that the validity of the results is not biased by someone's advance knowledge about the test. Therefore, we will not provide actual samples of the test contents.

PSYCHOLOGICAL INVENTORIES

Nearly everyone has taken an objective *psychological inventory* at one time or another. It may have been for vocational guidance, or personal counseling, or in connection with a job. These tests are highly structured and contain a variety of statements that can be answered in a limited number of ways, usually "true" or "false," or "yes" or "no." The client is asked to indicate whether or not each statement applies to her. Inventories have enormous advantages, the foremost being that they tend to be highly reliable.

By far, the most widely used and studied personality inventory in clinical assessment is the *Minnesota Multiphasic Personality Inventory (MMPI)* (Hathaway and McKinley, 1943). It is used in clinical settings and for research on personality and psychopathology. It consists of items that inquire into a wide array of behaviors, thoughts, and feelings. The person taking the test is asked to read each item and check "true" or "false," depending on whether it describes him. The meaning and purpose of most of the items are not obvious: Those taking the test have

to respond to such items as: "I often have the sensation that I am floating in air," or "I usually feel fine." The test was originally developed by administering hundreds of possible test questions to very large samples of people from all sectors of society. Some of the people were psychiatric patients who varied in diagnosis. Others included prisoners, students, and homemakers. The psychologists who developed the MMPI then used statistics to identify the questions that were best at differentiating among the various groups. An item was considered a good one if a particular group, such as depressed patients, tended to answer it one way, whereas other respondents gave a different answer. The end results were sets of items, or *scales,* that tended to be answered in a particular way by a specific group of people. The MMPI yields scores for scales that measure ten dimensions of personality or psychopathology. These are listed in Table 2–1. These categories have been validated against diagnostic judgments that arose from psychiatric interviews and other tests (Wrobel and Lochar, 1982).

TABLE 2–1

PERSONALITY CHARACTERISTICS ASSOCIATED WITH ELEVATIONS ON THE BASIC MMPI SCALES

Scale	Characteristics
1 (HS), Hypochondriasis	High scorers are described as cynical, defeatist, preoccupied with self, complaining, hostile, and presenting numerous physical problems.
2 (D), Depression	High scorers are described as moody, shy, despondent, pessimistic, and distressed. This scale is one of the most frequently elevated in clinical patients.
3 (HY), Hysteria	High scorers tend to be repressed, dependent, naive, outgoing, and to have multiple physical complaints. They express psychological conflict through vague and unbased physical complaints.
4 (Pd), Psychopathic Deviate	High scorers often are rebellious, impulsive, hedonistic, and antisocial. They often have difficulty in marital or family relationships and trouble with the law or authority in general.
5 (MF), Masculinity-Feminity	High-scoring males are described as sensitive, aesthetic, passive, or feminine. High-scoring females are described as aggressive, rebellious, and unrealistic.
6 (Pa), Paranoia	Elevations on this scale are often associated with being suspicious, aloof, shrewd, guarded, worrisome, and overly sensitive. High scorers may project or externalize blame.
7 (Pt), Psychasthenia	High scorers are tense, anxious, ruminative, preoccupied, obsessional, phobic, and rigid. They frequently are self-condemning and feel inferior and inadequate.
8 (Sc), Schizophrenia	High scorers are often withdrawn, shy, unusual, or strange and have peculiar thoughts or ideas. They may have poor reality contact and in severe cases bizarre sensory experiences—delusions and hallucinations.
9 (Ma), Mania	High scorers are called sociable, outgoing, impulsive, overly energetic, optimistic, and in some cases amoral, flighty, confused, disoriented.
10 (Si), Social Introversion-Extroversion	High scorers tend to be modest, shy, withdrawn, self-effacing, and inhibited. Low scorers are outgoing, spontaneous, sociable, and confident.

SOURCE: Butcher, 1969.

Figure 2—2

THE MINNESOTA MULTIPHASIC PERSONALITY INVENTORY

(A) An example of an MMPI profile. (B) An "automated" interpretation provided by a computer. The computer prints out statements that have been found to have some validity for other individuals with similar profiles. (Sources: Gleitman, 1981; NCS Interpretive Scoring Systems)

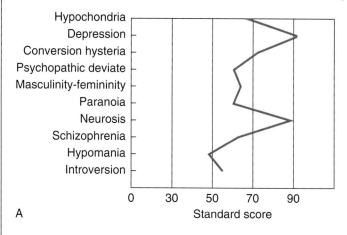

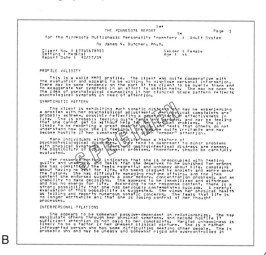

Countless research studies have used the MMPI and have found it to have excellent reliability and validity. The scores on the MMPI scales are relatively stable over long periods of time. Further, the results of the MMPI administered to adolescents and young adults can predict who is more likely to develop a psychotic disorder ten to twenty-five years later, in middle adulthood (Carter, Parnas, Cannon, Schulsinger, and Mednick, 1999).

Any psychological test can be subject to a variety of distortions, however, and the MMPI is no exception. A person can lie or simply be evasive. Some people try to put themselves in the best possible social light. People can do these things intentionally or unintentionally. However, the MMPI contains four "validity" scales that are designed to alert the diagnostician to such distortions. So, if a person were to respond "true" to the following items: "I never tell lies," and "I read the newspaper editorials every day," it might be reasonable to surmise that the test-taker is trying to present herself as favorably as she can—since it is a rare person who never tells lies and who reads the editorials daily. Notice that these judgments about social desirability and lying are not absolutely foolproof.

Rather they are "best guesses." Most (but not all) people who respond positively to the above items will be, wittingly or unwittingly, trying to improve their image. For all we know, however, there may well be some people who read every editorial every day and who never tell lies!

The results of the MMPI are recorded in the form of a profile (Figure 2–2A). The profile tells a clinician more than the individual scores would. By utilizing a sourcebook of MMPI profiles (Butcher, 1999; Greene, 1991), the clinician can compare the profile of a particular person with similar profiles obtained from individuals about whom a great deal is known (Figure 2–2B). Of course, the final personality assessment is more than the sum of the individual's MMPI scores. The MMPI results are interpreted in combination with other sources of information, with the goal of noting consistencies and reconciling inconsistencies (Korchin, 1976).

The MMPI is more than fifty years old. Times change. Language changes. And tests need to change to accommodate to new circumstances and new ways of describing people. The most recent version of the test, the MMPI-2, was designed to do precisely that

(Butcher, Dahlstrom, Graham, Tellegen, and Kraemer, 1994; Butcher and Rouse, 1996). It modernized language, changing such phrases as "acid stomach" to "upset stomach." And it attempted to assess modern psychological concerns, such as vulnerability to drug abuse and eating disorders, as well as poor adaptation to work.

Opinions regarding the MMPI-2 are divided. Many clinicians appreciate the modernization, as well as the fact that it was standardized on a larger and more representative sample than was the MMPI (Butcher, Dahlstrom, Graham, Tellegen, and Kraemer, 1994). But others prefer to use the original version, often due to the simple fact that the clinician is more familiar with the original test (Adler, 1989). Finally, there are some clinicians who do not favor either version of the test (Helmes and Reddon, 1993). This point of view is based on concerns that there is too much overlap on the scales and that the norming sample is not appropriate. Also, the cross-cultural validity of the test has not been established. While it is true that the test is primarily used in the United States, efforts to explore its usefulness in other cultures are underway (Butcher et al., 1996).

Although the MMPI is the most widely used inventory for assessing personality and psychopathology, there are several other well-known inventories that are used in psychological assessment (Cohen, Swerdlik, and Smith, 1992). One of these, the California Psychological Inventory (CPI) was first published in 1956 by Gough. Many of its scales are derived from the MMPI; however, the CPI was developed to focus on the more desirable aspects of personality rather than dimensions of psychopathology (as measured on the MMPI). For example, the CPI gives scores on "self-control," "well-being," and "tolerance," characteristics not measured on the MMPI. In 1987, the CPI was revised, and it now consists of twenty scales in contrast to the original eighteen.

Another inventory, the Symptom Checklist-90-Revised (SCL-90-R), is a relatively brief measure of clinical symptoms. It focuses more on psychopathology than on personality. The SCL-90-R was developed by Leonard Derogatis in 1977. The questionnaire asks the client to rate the severity of his or her symptoms over the past week on a five-point scale. The test consists of ninety items that yield scores on nine symptom scales: somatization, obsessive-compulsiveness, interpersonal sensitivity, depression, anxiety, hostility, phobic anxiety, paranoid ideation, and psychoticism. The SCL-90-R is typically used during "intake" in clinical settings to obtain some basic information about the person's psychological profile.

Many self-report measures have been designed to assess very specific aspects of personality or psychopathology. The most widely used measure of depression is the Beck Depression Inventory (BDI). It was originally published in 1961 and revised in 1978. The test consists of twenty-one items, each of which focuses on a specific symptom or attitude (for example, sense of failure, indecisiveness, and appetite loss). Each item is rated on a scale of 0 to 3, with a rating of 3 reflecting the greatest intensity of feeling. The test-taker is instructed to base the self-ratings on the way she has been feeling over the past week. A total score of 16 or higher suggests the presence of depression.

The assessment of personality and psychopathology in children requires specialized approaches and measures. One reason for this is that the symptoms of behavioral disorders are expressed differently in children and adults. For example, children's occupational functioning cannot be used as an index of adjustment, but school performance can. Moreover, self-report measures for children require simpler language. For these reasons, researchers have designed a variety of measures for assessing youth. Many of these measures are child-focused versions of adult measures. An example is the Children's Depression Inventory (CDI). Published in 1977 by Kovacs and Beck, the CDI is similar to the BDI. It is a self-report questionnaire that consists of twenty-seven items. Each item includes a set of three statements from which the test-taker is to choose the one statement that best reflects how he has been feeling over the past two weeks. The main difference between the BDI and the CDI is the content of the questions; for example, the adult version asks about changes in sexual interest and work performance, whereas the child version asks about play and school activities. The CDI has been extensively studied, and is capable of distinguishing depressed children and adolescents from normal youngsters (Cohen, Swerdlik, and Smith, 1992).

Parents often play an important role in the clinical assessment of children, especially very young children. In fact, parents are usually responsible for seeking mental health care for their child. Clinicians rely on parents to provide information about the child's behavior and developmental history. Much of this information comes from a clinical interview. But there are also many standardized questionnaires that are designed for completion by parents. One of these, the Achenbach Child Behavior Checklist (CBCL), is used in clinical and research settings throughout the country. It has over 100 questions that concern specific problem behaviors, from shyness to delinquent acts. Like the MMPI, the CBCL yields scores on multiple aspects of personality and psychopathology. There are norms published for the CBCL, and an individual child's scores can be compared to these norms to gauge the severity of her behavior problems.

PROJECTIVE TESTS

For some psychologists, especially those who are psychodynamically oriented, the focus of assessment is on unconscious conflicts, latent fears, sexual and aggressive impulses, and hidden anxieties. They believe that structured inventories, because they inquire about conscious experience and feelings, do not get at these deeper dynamics. In contrast to the inventories described above, **projective tests** utilize ambiguous stimuli, such as inkblots or pictures. The goal is to minimize reality constraints, encourage imaginative processes, and maximize the opportunity for conflictual or unconscious concerns to emerge (Murray, 1951). The key assumption behind projective tests is that people impose, or "project," their own, unique psychological tendencies and conflicts onto their perceptions of an ambiguous stimulus. Two of the most widely used projective tests are the Rorschach Test and the Thematic Apperception Test.

Before discussing these projective tests, it is important to mention that they are surrounded by a great deal of controversy. The primary reason these tests are subject to criticism is that many psychologists are not convinced that they have adequate reliability. Often, interpretations seem to be influenced by personal biases of the clinician (Garb, Florio, and Grove, 1998). Further, like the self-report measures, projective tests have typically been used in the United States and Europe. There has been very little research on projective tests used with non-European cultural groups. Nonetheless, despite these limitations, projective tests continue to be used in some clinical assessments and research studies. We will describe the tests, then examine the pro and con positions on their value in psychological assessment.

As part of a psychological assessment, a psychologist is administering a Rorschach test to his client. The client is looking at the inkblot and describing what he sees on the card. The psychologist will then score the responses and try to interpret the client's unconscious motivations.

The Rorschach Test   More than any other psychological measure, the Rorschach inkblots have fascinated the general public. People are intrigued by the idea that hidden aspects of one's personality can be revealed by spontaneous reactions to a meaningless inkblot. The **Rorschach test** was invented by Hermann Rorschach, a Swiss psychiatrist. It consists of ten bilaterally symmetrical "inkblots," some in color, some in black, gray, and white, and each on an individual card. The respondent is shown each card separately and asked to tell the examiner everything she sees on the card; that is, everything she thinks the inkblot could resemble. Figure 2–3 shows two inkblots that are similar to such cards.

Here are the responses made by one person to the card on the left (Exner, 1978, p. 170):

Patient:	I think it could be a woman standing in the middle there. . . . Should I try to find something else?
Examiner:	Most people see more than one thing.
Patient:	I suppose the entire thing could be a butterfly. . . . I don't see anything else.

Responses to these inkblots are scored in several ways. First, they are scored for the nature and quality of what has been seen. In this instance, the woman and the butterfly are well-formed percepts, indicative of someone whose view of the world is relatively clear. Second, whether the percept is commonly seen by others, or relatively rare (and if rare, whether

Figure 2—3

THE RORSCHACH TEST

Facsimiles of Rorschach Test cards. These projective instruments are composed of stimuli that seem like inkblots and that allow the respondent to project impressions of what those inkblots might be. (Source: Gleitman, 1981, p. 635)

creative or bizarre) is scored. Seeing a woman and a butterfly on this inkblot is a common occurrence. It suggests that this person is capable of seeing the world as others do. Additional scoring examines whether the entire inkblot or only part of it was used, and whether color is used and integrated into the percept. These scores, as well as what is seen in the inkblot, are integrated to give an overall picture of the respondent's inner life. It is assumed that the responses can tell us something about the respondent's psychological conflicts, the degree to which he can control sexual and aggressive urges, and the like.

Perusal of the inkblot on the left in Figure 2–3 will give some sense of the thinking that goes into Rorschach interpretation. Imagine someone who has only responded to the bits of ink that surround the main part of the inkblot. You might hypothesize (and it is only a hypothesis) that this individual has difficulty confronting "central" realities and, instead, turns her attention to trivia, as if they were central. Using the responses to a single inkblot, of course, would be merely one clue to an individual's personality. There might, for example, be something about the central percept of this particular card that the respondent finds aversive. If so, the response would indicate little about generalized tendencies. If, however, such responses occurred on several cards—if on each of them the respondent "missed" the central percept and puttered about at the edges, an examiner might feel that the hunch was well substantiated. On the other hand, if all the responses are very common ones, the person might be judged to be a behavioral

conformist, especially if other test results are consistent with that view. This is the kind of thinking that is used to examine the use of color, of forms, of the popularity of the responses, and so on.

The Rorschach is sometimes used in clinical settings as part of a battery of tests for diagnostic assessment. Clinicians undergo extensive training in order to interpret the Rorschach. It is a fascinating and complex process, but it has its hazards. Precisely because the process and the logic behind it are so fascinating, there may be a tendency to believe in it without validation, and to disregard contrary evidence. In the past, some clinicians found the assumptions underlying the Rorschach so compelling that they did not question them. But in psychological testing, and in other areas, there are many examples of assumptions that seemed compelling, but turned out to be inaccurate (Chapman and Chapman, 1969).

When researchers have conducted empirical studies on the Rorschach, they have often found that neither the validity nor the reliability of the Rorschach is high (Garb, Florio, and Grove, 1998; Wood, Nezworski, and Stejskal, 1996). The modest level of reliability is especially surprising, given the detailed scoring manuals that are available to assist the clinician (for example, Exner, 1993; Exner and Weiner, 1994). But the ultimate question is whether a particular test can tell us something important about psychological functioning that no other test can tell us. Does the Rorschach yield unique insights about psychological processes? We cannot yet answer this question with confidence (see Box 2–1).

Box 2—1

Science and Practice

The Controversy Surrounding the Rorschach

There have always been some detractors of projective testing, but in recent years the criticism has escalated. The controversy has been most pronounced in the case of the Rorschach Inkblot test. Due to widespread criticism of the test, the Rorschach was not included in the model assessment curriculum recently recommended by the Division of Clinical Psychology of the American Psychological Association. Serious questions have been raised about fundamental methodological issues such as validity, the reliability of scoring, test-retest reliability, cross-cultural bias, clinical utility, and accessibility of research results. Such issues underscore even more basic questions: Does the Rorschach test have any use in diagnosis? What is the clinical utility of this psychological measure?

In a recent article, Wood, Lilienfeld, Garb, and Nezworski (2000) attacked popular claims that the Rorschach test can be used to diagnose a wide variety of psychiatric disorders. They acknowledge that deviant verbalizations and unusual responses to the inkblots are related to schizophrenia, bipolar disorder, schizotypal personality disorder, and perhaps borderline personality disorder. Yet, due to the test's methodological flaws, they suggest that researchers should take a more conservative approach to the test's use in the diagnosis of depression, borderline personality disorder, post-traumatic stress disorder, narcissism, and antisocial personality disorder. Further, for the few disorders where Rorschach scores and psychiatric diagnosis have been shown to be related, the test does not contribute any information beyond what can be obtained through clinical interviews, self-reports, and other tests like the MMPI. In sum, these researchers propose that the Rorschach is best used as an experimental instrument for personality research, rather than as a clinical tool for assessment and diagnosis. Their predominantly negative judgment of the Rorschach draws the same conclusion as that offered by a previous researcher nearly forty years ago. He said that the Rorschach has some empirical validities . . . but the Rorschach is a most imperfect instrument, not qualified to perform the tasks that many psychologists demand of it" (Schaeffer, 1959).

Proponents of the Rorschach counter by claiming that the Rorschach was not intended to be a diagnostic test, especially if "diagnosis" means DSM classification. Irving Weiner (2000) states that the Rorschach "is a personality-assessment instrument designed and intended to measure aspects of personality structure and dynamics. . . . Associations between Rorschach indices and DSM categories accordingly have little bearing on the utility of the Rorschach for achieving its intended purposes." Weiner believes that clinical psychologists are more specifically interested in identifying and treating adjustment problems, and that the Rorschach accurately identifies personality strengths and weaknesses that have implications for treatment. He concludes his counterargument by writing, "There is little to be gained in this process by pondering whether psychological tests can predict how someone will be classified by a psychometrically shaky, inferential nosological scheme involving criteria and definitions that change from one revision to the next."

Sol Garfield, a famous psychologist, has written papers in support of the clinical use of the Rorschach since the 1940s. Like Weiner, Garfield (2000) continues to defend the use of the Rorschach. He claims that the Rorschach is not a psychometric test and that the emphasis that researchers place on scores rather than total test performance marginalizes the projective nature of the test.

So, what is the future of the Rorschach and other projective tests in clinical practice? At this point, the future does not look promising. As we mentioned, the American Psychological Association has excluded the Rorschach from its suggested graduate curriculum in clinical psychology. This event may mark the demise of the Rorschach in clinical practice. On the other hand, as pointed out by Wood and his colleagues (Wood, Lilienfeld, Garb, and Nezworski, 2000), the Rorschach has proven to be very useful as a research tool. If its use in research studies continues, new empirical discoveries about the Rorschach might emerge. Eventually the Rorschach may make a "comeback" in clinical practice.

SOURCES: Garfield, 2000; Schaeffer, 1959; Weiner, 2000, Wood, Lilienfeld, Garb, and Nezworski, 2000.

On the other hand, we do know that responses to the Rorschach cards differ among people and among diagnostic groups. When occurrences of "abnormal thought" in Rorschach responses are scored, researchers have found that the scores are associated with the person's diagnosis. For example, patients diagnosed with schizophrenia, have higher thought disorder scores on the Rorschach than do people without this diagnosis. This provides some support for the validity of the Rorschach. But we also know that some researchers have shown that the MMPI is better than the Rorschach in predicting other psychological indicators (Garb, Florio, and Grove, 1998). Nonetheless, the possibility remains that there are special circumstances in which the Rorschach has advantages over the MMPI (Exner, 1999; Weiner, 1996).

Thematic Apperception Test   Another commonly used projective test is the ***Thematic Apperception Test,*** or the ***TAT*** (see Figure 2–4). It consists of a series of pictures that are not as ambiguous as Rorschach cards, yet not as clear as photographs. Respondents are asked to look at each picture and to make up a story about it. They are told to tell how the story began, what is happening now, and how it will end. As with the Rorschach, it is assumed that because the pictures are ambiguous, the stories will reflect the respondent's proclivity to see situations in a particular way. A respondent who repeatedly uses the same theme to describe several different pictures may be revealing personal psychological conflicts (Bellak and Abrams, 1997).

The TAT has been used extensively as a research instrument to explore a variety of personality characteristics and motives, particularly the need for achievement (Atkinson, 1992; Cramer, 1999; McClelland, Atkinson, Clark, and Lowell, 1953). Its use in that context has been fruitful and provocative. For example, one study revealed that the TAT achievement measure was better than questionnaire measures in predicting career success (Spangler,

1992). The TAT is also used in many clinical settings as part of a larger battery of tests for diagnostic assessment. But its use as a clinical instrument for assessing individual personality is prey to the same problems that beset the Rorschach (Garb, 1998b). Although reliability of scoring is adequate (Harrison, 1965), the interpretations of TAT protocols by different clinicians are quite diverse (Murstein, 1965).

Another limitation of the TAT is that all of the people depicted in the pictures are white. Many psychologists have expressed concern about this. Does the fact that all of the characters are white affect the responses of people who are not white? In order to answer this question, some researchers administered both the standard TAT and a new projective measure called the TEMAS (Tell Me a Story), a test depicting ethnic minority characters, cultural themes, and urban backgrounds (Costantino and Malgady, 1983). Both Hispanics and African Americans gave more responses to the TEMAS than to the TAT cards. This suggests that the cultural content of projective measures does make a difference in the way people respond. This highlights the importance of considering cultural factors when conducting psychological assessments.

Let us return now to the question of whether projective tests are useful. As we mentioned, both the Rorschach and the TAT have been shown to have predictive validity when used in research. In clinical settings, however, the focus is on a single case, and the clinicians often base their conclusions on past experience and clinical hunches. This is where problems may arise. In one recent study, experienced clinicians were given batteries of psychodiagnostic test results, which included the Rorschach, the TAT, and the Draw-a-Person (Ben-Shakhar, Bar-Hillel, Bilu, and Shefler, 1998). They were asked to analyze the results and propose a diagnosis. It was suggested to some of the clinicians that the person might be suffering from borderline personality disorder. Others were told that the client might have a paranoid personality disorder. The suggestions had a significant impact on the way the clinicians interpreted the test results. Even when the test results were identical, those who expected to see signs of paranoia saw them, and those who anticipated borderline signs were more likely to see them. Does this mean that projective tests are useless? Not necessarily. But it does mean that care

Figure 2–4

THE THEMATIC APPERCEPTION TEST

TAT pictures, such as this one, are designed to be sufficiently vague to allow respondents to project their own meaningful story onto it. (Source: Gleitman, 1981, p. 685)

must be taken to minimize bias in interpretation of the test results.

INTELLIGENCE TESTS

Perhaps the most reliable and, for many purposes, the most valid of all psychological tests are those that measure intelligence (McGrew and Flanagan, 1998). All intelligence tests are very structured, and most are administered individually by an examiner. Because consistency is so important in the administration of intelligence tests, they are *standardized;* the wording of the questions and the order of presentation are described in detail in a manual. The first standardized test of intelligence was developed by Alfred Binet and Theodore Simon in France to differentiate "slow" schoolchildren from those who were mentally retarded. Their test measured attention, perception, memory, reasoning, and verbal comprehension, skills needed to do well in school. It included puzzles, defining words, building a tower from blocks, and solving math problems. Over the years, the test underwent many revisions, including translation into English and revisions by Lewis Terman of Stanford University, culminating in the most recent, fourth edition of the Stanford-Binet Intelligence Test for Children (Dacey, Nelson, and Stoeckel, 1999).

David Wechsler standardized individually administered intelligence tests for both adults and children. These tests include the Wechsler Adult Intelligence Scale (WAIS), the Wechsler Intelligence Scale for Children (WISC), and the Wechsler Preschool and Primary Scale of Intelligence (WPPSI). All of the Wechsler intelligence tests have been revised over the years. The WAIS was revised and restandardized as the Wechsler Adult Intelligence Scale–Revised (WAIS-R) in 1981. The latest version of the test, published in 1997, is the WAIS-III. This revision of the test has updated content and standardization data.

Published in its original version in 1949, the Wechsler Intelligence Scale for Children (WISC) is administered to children from ages five years to fifteen years and eleven months. The revised version of the test, the WISC-R, was published in 1974, and the WISC III became available in 1991. The WISC III is administered to children from ages six years to sixteen years and eleven months. In 1967, Wechsler published the WPPSI to extend the coverage of the Wechsler tests to include years below the age range

A second grader is taking a WISC test administered by a psychologist. The WISC is used to assess a child's IQ and to diagnose learning and attention disabilities.

encompassed by the WISC. The revised version, the WPPSI-R, came into use in 1991. The WPPSI-R covers the age range of three to seven years.

As on most standardized tests of intelligence, the Wechsler intelligence tests contain many different types of mental tasks. For example, the WAIS includes subtests such as "Arithmetic," "Vocabulary," "Similarities," "Information," "Picture Arrangement," and "Mazes," to name a few. Each of the subtests is scored separately, so the examiner can see the individual performance "profile." These performance profiles can be helpful in the diagnosis of learning and attention disabilities.

Scores from the subscales are combined to give an overall score. Based on the scores on the test and the child's age, an ***intelligence quotient,*** or ***IQ,*** is calculated. The Wechsler scales provide a total IQ, which is composed of two subscores: Verbal IQ and Performance IQ. The Verbal IQ score is based on the subtests that measure various language capacities, such as vocabulary, ability to comprehend verbal statements and problems, and general information. Performance IQ measures intelligence in ways that are less dependent upon verbal ability, such as the ability to copy designs and to associate symbols with numbers.

All versions of the WISC and WPPSI contain subtests similar to those on the WAIS; however, the tasks are much simpler on the WISC and WPPSI. For example, on the WISC there is a subtest of visual memory that uses geometric symbols. There is a similar subtest on the WAIS, but it uses numerals rather than symbols. On the Maze subtest of the WISC, printed mazes of different length and complexity from those on the WAIS are used. Information, Vocabulary, Arithmetic, Comprehension, and Similarities subtests are all included in the WPPSI. The Sentences subtest replaces the Digit Span subtest in the Verbal Scale subtests as a measure of memory. The Performance Scale of the WPPSI consists of Picture Completion, Mazes, and Block Design, which are all WISC counterparts. Two subtests that are only included in the WPPSI are Animal House and Geometric Design. Animal House requires the child to place the appropriate colored peg beneath the designated animal to which it is assigned in the model at the top of the pegboard. Geometric Design is a simple copying task that utilizes ten basic geometric figures as models.

Although the Wechsler and Stanford-Binet tests are the most widely used intelligence tests, several other tests of intelligence are also available. These include individually administered tests, such as the Kaufman Assessment Battery for Children (K-ABC). The K-ABC is similar to other individualized IQ tests in that it contains subtests that vary in content. But the K-ABC is unique in its emphasis on multiple areas of intelligence, and in its distinction between aptitude and achievement. In addition, there are several paper and pencil measures of intelligence. These are intended to be brief and to provide a general estimate of IQ. One thing that virtually all standardized measures of intelligence have in common is that they are designed to yield scores that have a normal distribution, often referred to as a "bell-shaped" curve. This kind of distribution has only one peak, and most scores are around the middle of the distribution, with fewer at the extreme high and low ends. The average score, usually 100, is at the middle of the peak. During the process of test development, items are selected and rejected until the test gives a normal distribution of scores, with an average of 100.

Intelligence tests can provide useful information in the diagnosis of disorders such as psychoses or depression. Subtle abnormalities in thought, for example, are often detected by the verbal subtests of the WAIS in persons who are later diagnosed with a psychotic disorder, such as schizophrenia. But more than any other measure, intelligence tests play the major role in assessing learning problems, mental retardation, and brain damage. Moreover, intelligence tests are the only psychological tests that are routinely used in schools, and thus they determine, in some measure, the kind of education children will obtain.

It is important, therefore, to understand what intelligence tests actually measure.

Intelligence itself is not directly observable. It can only be inferred from behavior. Intelligence tests sample behaviors on certain standardized tasks, particularly those that predict success in school. Other behaviors, like the ability "to make it on the street" or the ability to comprehend classical music, are simply not measured. For that reason, intelligence has often been defined as "what an intelligence test measures." That is not a very satisfying definition, but it is accurate. On the other hand, intelligence tests do seem to be measuring something that is related to "what" or "how" we do in the real world. IQ scores are correlated with indicators of occupational success. Nonetheless, the correlations are not very high, which means that most of the explanation for occupational success probably lies in personality, drive, and "being in the right place at the right time."

Over the years, as IQ tests have been revised, they have been designed to be more and more difficult. Why? Because successive generations seem to be scoring higher (Flynn, 1998, 1999). For example, when the first version of the WAIS was introduced, the average IQ score was about 100. When subsequent generations took the test, their average IQs gradually went up, so they exceeded 100. The same has held for all the other standardized intelligence tests that have been studied over time. Moreover, this

"WE REALIZE YOU DO BETTER ON YOUR IQ TESTS THAN YOU DO IN ANYTHING ELSE, BUT YOU JUST CANNOT MAJOR IN IQ."

has occurred in many nations in the world. The researcher James Flynn was among the first to document this, so it has come to be known as the "Flynn effect." In fact, based on his mathematical calculations, the average Briton born in 1877 would score in the retarded range on a contemporary IQ test. By the current guidelines for classifying mental retardation, most Britons born at that time would have had great difficulty understanding the basic rules of cricket. Were most British citizens of that time retarded? Needless to say, neither Flynn nor anyone else believes this was the case. What does all of this mean? Are recent generations simply learning more? Or is the IQ gain caused by better nutrition? So far, the origins of the "Flynn effect" have eluded researchers. But even though we do not know why it occurs, the Flynn effect is certainly telling us something about the potential for changing IQ!

NEUROPSYCHOLOGICAL ASSESSMENT

As we emphasize in Chapter 4, the brain is an exceedingly complex organ. Much of it remains to be mapped. But increasingly, researchers are able to identify the links between damage in certain parts of the brain and changes in mood, thought, and behavior. Neuropsychological tests are designed to aid in the diagnosis of brain dysfunction and in assessing the behavioral consequences of brain damage (Goldstein, 1998). Thus, in clinical settings, they are usually administered when a person has experienced a head injury, or when it is suspected that a patient has a disorder that is impairing brain function. Neuropsychological tests are also widely used in research. Many studies, for example, have examined the performance of psychiatric patients on neuropsychological tests.

In neuropsychological assessment, a group, or *battery,* of tests is administered. Each of the tests measures a particular ability, such as memory for words, spatial reasoning, planning, or motor speed. The tests that are selected for the battery measure abilities that have been shown to be associated with particular brain regions. For example, certain memory tasks are known to be sensitive to damage to the hippocampus, whereas other tests measure abilities that depend on the frontal lobes. The neuropsychologist examines the test results to identify areas of average ability as well as special strengths or weaknesses. In this way, the neuropsychologist can answer several important questions. What is the person's average level of mental functioning? Is there a particular area of weakness? If so, is this weakness associated with a specific brain region and/or disorder?

Many neuropsychologists tailor the battery of tests they administer to fit each clinical case. Thus, if a patient is referred because of suspected damage to the frontal lobe, the battery will include several tests of frontal lobe function, as well as other tasks. However, as described below, there are some neuropsychological test batteries that are standardized: the same tests are administered to all patients, and the results are compared to norms for the battery. The advantage to this approach is that the neuropsychologist can compare his client's performance pattern with the norms for the battery. Of course, the disadvantage is that special areas of potential difficulty, such as verbal comprehension, are not targeted.

The Bender Visual-Motor Gestalt Test   This is one of the oldest and most widely used neuropsychological tests, perhaps because it is also the simplest to administer. Consisting of nine cards, each of which shows a design, the client is asked first to copy the design, and then to draw those designs from memory (Figure 2–5). Errors either in direct reproduction or in recall are often, though not always, associated with neurological impairment. The emphasis here is on the *possibility* that test results reflect disorder, because difficulties on the test may arise from many sources, only some of which are neurological. Thus, a tremor that shows itself in an inability to draw a straight line or to copy small circles can arise from brain impairment. But it may also arise from simple "test nervousness." Good examiners are sensitive to the difference.

Trail Making Test   Originally part of a test used by the military, the Trail Making Test has become a widely used instrument in psychological assessment. The test is divided into two parts. Part A presents the client with a worksheet of numbered circles scattered across the page. The person is asked to draw a line connecting the numbered circles in consecutive order. Part B consists of a worksheet with both numbers and letters. The client is asked to connect both series, numbers and letters, consecutively by alternating between the two sequences. The test is scored for accuracy and response speed. The Trail Making Test provides the clinician with clues as to how effectively the client plans ahead, handles multiple stimuli, alternates between activities, and responds to complex

Figure 2—5

THE BENDER VISUAL-MOTOR GESTALT TEST

On the Bender Visual-Motor Gestalt Test, nine cards, each of which has a different design, are presented to clients. The clients must copy the designs and then draw them from memory.

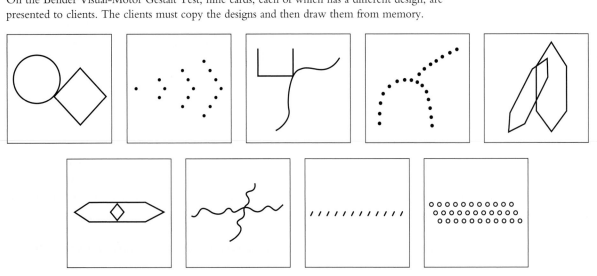

visual presentations. The test is sensitive to the presence of brain damage, especially frontal lobe problems.

Wisconsin Card Sorting Test   The Wisconsin Card Sorting Test (WCST) is an instrument that is able to detect several kinds of cognitive deficits, including impaired concept formation, the tendency to perseverate or "get stuck" on the same response, and the inability to maintain and act upon a set concept. Four stimulus cards are presented to the client: one red triangle, two green stars, three yellow crosses, and four blue circles. The client is given a deck of sixty-four cards on which a different combination of color, symbol, or number is printed. The client's task is to place each card under the stimulus card it matches, according to a specific principle. The task is difficult because the client is forced to deduce the principle based on the examiner's response ("right" or "wrong") to the placement of each card. The test begins with color, symbol, or number as the first principle for sorting. After the client successfully sorts ten cards, the test administrator shifts the sorting principle. Based on a "right" or "wrong" response from the administrator upon placement of the new card, the client must deduce the new sorting principle and begin to place each card accordingly. Perhaps more than any other test, the WCST has gained a reputation for being sensitive to prob-

lems with frontal lobe function. In fact, early studies of the test compared the performance of people with no brain damage to that of patients who had injuries to the frontal lobes. The patients with injury to the frontal lobes had greater difficulty determining the sorting principle and made more perseverative errors.

Wechsler Memory Scales   The Wechsler Memory Scales (WMS), devised by David Wechsler in 1945, consist of seven subtests. The first two subtests, Personal/Current Information and Orientation ask questions such as age, current events, and time and place. The remaining subtests include the Mental Control test, which tests simple concepts, and the Logical Memory test, which assesses immediate recall of verbal material presented to the client in a story format. Digit Span, Visual Reproduction, and Associate Learning tests are also included in the WMS. The WMS has been criticized for its emphasis on testing verbal rather than nonverbal memory. Such weaknesses prompted a revision of the WMS by E. W. Russell in 1975. Russell included the Visual Reproduction and Logical Memory subtests of the original WMS to create a balanced assessment of both visual memory and memory for linguistic or verbal information. After the administration of both subtests in their original format, the battery includes a delayed recall trial that produces a short-term memory score, a delayed recall score, and a percent retained score. Patients with damage to the hippocampus have particular difficulty with the WMS.

The Halstead-Reitan Neuropsychological Battery

The Halstead-Reitan Battery is widely used in research and clinical settings (Horton, 1997; Reitan and Davison, 1974). As originally developed by Ward Halstead in the 1940s, the main goal of the test battery was to discriminate people with brain damage from normal individuals. The battery was later revised in collaboration with Ralph Reitan. They carefully selected additional tests that appeared to be good measures of the various abilities associated with different brain areas. They wanted the clinicians who used the test to be able to draw reasonable conclusions about the likely location of the brain deficit. Among the many things the battery assesses is the individual's ability to:

1. categorize a variety of items as either similar or different;
2. place blocks quickly into slots on a board, while blindfolded;
3. detect whether the rhythm of pairs of sounds is similar or different;
4. tap rapidly on a small lever (finger tapping);
5. squeeze a "dynamometer," which measures strength of grip;
6. remember a string of words;
7. identify spoken "nonsense" words.

For each of the tests that involve a motor component, such as the dynamometer, the person performs the task with both the left and right hands. This helps to determine whether there is damage on only the left or only the right side of the brain, or both. When the scores from all of the tests are combined to create a "performance profile," the clinician offers a diagnosis about the presence and location of the brain impairment.

The Halstead-Reitan, however, is a very time-consuming test, requiring as many as six hours to administer. It consists of six simple subtests, as well as a variety of optional tests, the scores on which are interpreted in light of what is presently known about the relationship between brain structures and behavior. An alternative battery that has become popular with clinicians is the Luria-Nebraska.

The Luria-Nebraska Neuropsychological Battery

Based on the work of the eminent Russian psychologist, Alexander Luria, this 269-item battery provides information about a broad spectrum of psychological functions. Among the data that emerge from such an examination are information about tactile and kinesthetic skills, verbal and spatial skills, fine and complex motor coordination, writing, reading, speech, and arithmetic skills, as well as intellectual and memory processes. The patterns of scores across the entire test are thought to reveal impairments in various parts of the brain (Golden, Hammeke, and Puriosch, 1980). A children's version of the test permits diagnosis of brain disorders among children from ages eight to twelve (Golden, 1981). One virtue of the test is the fact that it takes less time to administer than the Halstead-Reitan. Psychologists believe that the Luria-Nebraska is able to detect effects of brain damage that are not yet discernible on neurological examination. Finally, the Luria-Nebraska permits control for level of education, such that a person who is less educated does not receive a lower score simply because of that fact (Brickman, McManus, Grapentine, and Alessi, 1984).

We have already described modern technologies for obtaining images of the living human brain, including magnetic resonance imaging (MRI), computerized-axial tomography (CAT), functional magnetic resonance imaging (fMRI), and positron emission tomography (PET). It has been suggested by some that neuropsychological assessment will become obsolete now that so many neuroimaging techniques are available for use. There is no doubt that neuroimaging procedures have revolutionized research and the clinical assessment of brain function. But we do *not* believe that they will make neuropsychological testing obsolete. At this point in time, most of the abnormalities in brain function that affect behavior cannot be measured with neuroimaging. For example, we know that certain disorders, such as learning disabilities, schizophrenia, dementia, and autism involve brain dysfunction. When the brain scans from a group of individuals with any of these disorders is compared to a group of normal people of the same age and sex, *average differences* in brain structure are usually found. But, when one person with any of these disorders undergoes neuroimaging, his brain does not necessarily look abnormal in any way. This is probably because these disorders involve subtle abnormalities in brain circuitry that cannot be visualized in one person with current imaging techniques. In contrast, the vast majority of people suffering from learning disabilities, schizophrenia, dementia, or autism show significant performance deficits on neuropsychological testing.

For clinicians, the main concern is the functional consequence of brain abnormality, not the brain abnormality itself. A child's dyslexia and an elderly person's memory loss are matters of concern, whether or not a specific brain lesion is identified. Neuropsychological tests have proven to be very reliable and informative (Dikmen, Heaton, Grant, and Temkin, 1999). Neuropsychological assessment will continue to be a critical part of clinical research; it is needed to document the nature and extent of functional impairment, so that an educational or rehabilitative program can be implemented. It is unlikely that neuropsychological assessment will be replaced by neuroimaging any time in the near future.

Assessment enables psychologists to pinpoint areas of abnormality, whether in the brain, in thoughts, or in behavior. Based on what they learn from the various assessment tools, the clinicians make a diagnosis of what is wrong with the patient, which then gives them guidelines for treatment.

Diagnosis

In Chapter 1, we discussed various approaches to classifying mental illnesses. In the field of mental health, classification involves the identification of similarities and differences among the behavioral abnormalities manifested by people. One approach to classification is the *categorical* approach, in which behavioral symptoms that tend to occur together are assigned to a category. Guidelines for diagnosis are then based on symptom criteria. This is currently the dominant way of classifying mental disorders around the world. Taking this approach, a person either does or does not meet clinical criteria for a specific psychological disorder, such as depression. In order to meet the clinical criteria, the key symptoms must be present, and they must meet a specific threshold for severity. Thus, if the feeling of sadness is not severe enough, it will not meet the clinical criterion for that symptom, and the person may not meet the overall criteria for depression. This person's symptoms would be viewed as *subclinical*, or below the threshold for a diagnosis.

An alternative approach to classification is to measure behavioral or symptom *dimensions*, and rate people on those dimensions. For example, rather than viewing a person as either being depressed or not depressed, she would be rated somewhere along the continuum from extremely happy to extremely depressed. If people are rated on multiple dimensions, the result is a kind of *profile*. For example, we might conclude that a particular person is high on depression, low on impulsivity, and about average on persistence. With the dimensional approach, all levels—low, moderate and high—of the dimension are taken into consideration.

Time is also a factor in classifying mental disorders. Has the symptom lasted for years, or did it just arise last week? If it has persisted over a long period of time, it would be considered a *chronic* problem. If it arose recently in response to a significant life change, it would be viewed as *acute*. Related to the distinction between chronic and acute problems, is the notion of *continuous* versus *episodic* disorder. Do the symptoms remain at the same level of intensity over time? If so, it is a continuous pattern. In contrast, a person may only experience a particular set of symptoms every three to four months. This would be an episodic pattern.

The two most widely used diagnostic classification systems for mental disorders are the *International Classification of Diseases (ICD)*, and the *Diagnostic and Statistical Manual of Mental Disorders (DSM)* (Blashfield and Livesley, 1999). The ICD was introduced in Europe in 1900. It is a classification system for all diseases, including mental disorders. It has undergone several revisions since that time, and it is now undergoing another revision. But the ICD was never widely used in the United States. Until 1950, clinicians in the United States used a variety of different systems for classifying mental illnesses. In order to have a more consistent approach, the American Psychiatric Association introduced the DSM in 1952. The DSM, in turn, influenced the revision of the ICD, so that there is now greater similarity between the two.

Although the ICD and the DSM are used in countries around the world, the cross-cultural validity of the diagnoses has been a long-standing concern. Can the same criteria be used for diagnosing mental disorders across cultures? Although there has not been a great deal of research on this issue, the studies that have been published indicate that cultural bias in the diagnostic categories of the most recent edition of the DSM is not a major problem (Mason, Harrison, Croudace, Glazebrook, and Medley, 1997; Mezzich et al., 1999; Ormel et al., 1994). In other words, the rates of occurrence of various mental disorders, especially the more severe ones, are fairly similar across countries. However, continued efforts are underway to improve the cross-cultural sensitivity of diagnoses.

Reasons for Diagnosis

Diagnosis is a long and complicated procedure, and an accurate diagnostic assessment of a mental disorder takes time, as well as clinical skill. There are five reasons to take the time to make a careful diagnosis: (1) diagnosis is a communication shorthand, (2) it may have implications for understanding etiology, (3) it gives the clinician some hypotheses about treatment, (4) it aids scientific investigation, and (5) it allows clinicians to be paid for their services by insurance companies or "HMOs."

COMMUNICATION SHORTHAND

As we will see in upcoming chapters, troubled people often have a host of symptoms. A young man may have trouble keeping his thoughts straight, believe that people are out to get him, be unable to go to work, feel tense all the time, and have hallucinations of a voice making threatening statements. All of these symptoms may be present simultaneously, in the absence of any drug use. If a clinical psychologist were trying to describe the person's condition to a consulting psychiatrist, she could list each of the symptoms. Or, alternatively, she could simply say, "this young man meets criteria for paranoid schizophrenia." A single diagnosis, in this case, paranoid schizophrenia, implies all of the symptoms listed above. Rather than going down an endless list of troubles, the diagnostician can merely communicate the *syndrome* (that is, the collection of symptoms that occur together) in a single phrase. With respect to communication among clinicians, the advantage of diagnosis is clear.

ETIOLOGY

The origins of adjustment problems and mental disorders are varied, but certain problems are more reliably associated with particular *etiologies,* or causes. For example, autism seems to be a consequence of genetic factors and problems during prenatal development. Childhood phobias, on the other hand, are more likely to be the result of experience and sociocultural factors. When contemporary diagnostic manuals are developed, committees of experts try to distinguish among diagnostic categories based on what is known about the causes of the syndrome. If there is evidence that a certain syndrome is associated with a particular causal factor, that syndrome is listed as a separate disorder. For this reason, knowing the diagnosis may tell something about the underlying cause.

TREATMENT POSSIBILITIES

Many treatments are available for psychological disorders, and most are specific to certain disorders. Diagnosis enables the clinician to concentrate on the specific treatments that might be useful in particular situations. Paranoid symptoms, for example, do not yield readily to verbal psychotherapies, nor are they effectively treated by Prozac. But the symptoms of paranoid schizophrenia often respond well to drugs called antipsychotics. An accurate diagnosis, then, suggests a small number of treatments that might alleviate the symptoms.

AID TO SCIENTIFIC INVESTIGATIONS

One of the most important reasons for psychological diagnosis is not clinical, but rather scientific. Clinical psychology and psychiatry are young sciences that are far from discovering all the causes and cures of human misery. By grouping together people with like syndromes, diagnosis allows investigators to learn what people with that syndrome have in common, both in terms of etiology and effective treatment. Indeed, for a developing science, this may be the single most important function of diagnosis.

ENABLING THIRD-PARTY PAYMENTS

The care and treatment of people with psychological disorders is funded mainly by "third-party payers"— in other words, insurance companies, Medicare, and the like. These institutions will not cover the costs of assessment and care unless the patient has a diagnosis that indicates a need for treatment. Diagnosis, then, is essential for the economics of mental health care.

Evaluating Assessment and Diagnosis

Psychologists recognize that for assessment and diagnosis to be accurate and useful, high standards must be applied to diagnostic tools. As we mentioned earlier, assessment devices and diagnoses must be both reliable and valid to be of use to clinicians. Before we describe the current approach to the diagnosis of mental disorders, the DSM-IV, we will explore the concepts of reliability and validity in greater detail. As you will see, they are the hallmarks of good assessment strategies and diagnostic systems.

RELIABILITY

In order to arrive at a diagnosis, psychologists must use assessment tools and procedures that will give them a true picture of a patient and his or her problems. As mentioned earlier, they use clinical interviews, observation, and psychological tests. If two or more psychologists arrive at the same impression on the basis of a psychological test, diagnostic interview, or observational procedure, this is evidence of *inter-judge* or *inter-rater reliability.* A high level of inter-judge reliability indicates that the results of the assessment are not likely to vary among examiners. But what about change over time? To what extent will a test administered today yield the same results when given a week or month from now? This is referred to as *test-retest reliability* or *test stability.*

In general, it is desirable for a test to yield the same result in repeated trials. But there are some exceptions. If a test is designed to measure a characteristic that is expected to change over time, then we would not expect a high level of test-retest reliability. As an example, consider a questionnaire measure of anxiety that was designed to be sensitive to a person's reaction to a stressful situation, such as public speaking. This would be referred to as a test of *state anxiety*, because it is intended to measure the person's mental state in a particular situation. It is assumed that the individual's score on the test does not reflect a stable, or traitlike characteristic. We would thus expect the person's score to change over time, depending on the circumstances. On the other hand, if we administer a questionnaire that is intended to measure a personality trait, like extroversion, we would want the score to be highly stable over time.

As anyone who has tried to measure a floor knows, even using physical yardsticks, one rarely gets perfect reliability. There are tiny measurement differences. Depending upon the purpose of the measurement, such differences may mean a great deal or nothing at all. A difference of an eighth of an inch means little to the height of an oak, but a lot to the diameter of a diamond. So it is with psychological

measurement. How reliable an instrument needs to be depends upon many things, among them the purposes for which it is being used and the consequences of small and large errors. Generally, a high degree of reliability is required when individuals are being assessed, especially when the findings are to be used for individual diagnosis and treatment rather than, say, research. The human consequences of error in diagnosis and treatment are harsh: nothing less than an individual's well-being is at stake. Therefore, the reliability standards should be more stringent.

Many factors influence inter-judge and test-retest reliability. In the case of clinical interviews, test-retest reliability that is determined from the results of separate interviews is usually lower than inter-judge reliability determined from a joint interview. Decreases in test-retest reliability may arise from several sources. To name just a few, there may be actual changes in the patient's condition between the interviews, there may be differences in the information provided by the patient during the interviews, or the interviewer's behavior or personal characteristics (for example, personality, sex) may differ (Robins, 1985; Williams, Barefoot, and Shekelle, 1985).

VALIDITY

The term *validity* refers to the usefulness of a test or diagnostic procedure; in other words, whether it does what it is supposed to do (Cureton et al., 1996). People who obtain high scores on a good test of extroversion, for example, should perform better than those with low scores in situations requiring them to interact with many people. With regard to diagnostic systems, we want to know whether they serve the main functions of clinical diagnosis. Do they facilitate communication by describing patients, and by differentiating patients in one category from those in another? This is called *construct validity.*

Do diagnostic categories enable one to predict the course and especially the outcome of treatment? This is called *predictive validity* (Blashfield and Draguns, 1976). Of course, low reliability undermines validity. To the extent that clinicians cannot agree about how the diagnostic categories should be applied, the usefulness of the diagnostic system is very limited. When a diagnosis has high predictive validity, the predictions that derive from the diagnosis are borne out by subsequent events. This can be especially crucial, because it may bear directly on the kind of treatment that is selected (Robins and Helzer,

1986). A diagnostic system with good outcome or predictive validity should also tell something about the future course of the disorder. A valid test or diagnostic system will help us answer questions such as: Will the problem respond to a particular kind of treatment? Will the individual be violent or suicidal? Will the nature or the seriousness of the symptoms change as the person matures?

For diagnostic categories, predictive validity is high when a diagnosis can tell the clinician, with a fair degree of certainty, what is likely to be an effective treatment. For example, the predictive validity for "bipolar disorder" is quite high because certain medications are very effective in treating it. Here, the diagnosis performs a predictive function, in that a specific treatment is mandated. Predictive validity is also high for "enuresis" (bed-wetting) in that the disorder responds well to certain behavioral and social learning treatments. In these instances, the diagnosis indicates a treatment that has a high probability of succeeding. For some diagnostic categories, however, there is no established treatment. Moreover, the diagnosis does not say much about the causes of the disorder. When more is learned about the nature and causes of particular forms of abnormality, we will be able to judge with greater certainty whether a particular diagnostic scheme is valid.

The Diagnostic and Statistical Manual of Mental Disorders (DSM)

Let us now turn to a discussion of one of the most widely used diagnostic systems for mental disorders, the *Diagnostic and Statistical Manual of Mental Disorders (DSM)*. In 1952, the DSM was developed in the United States, and approved by the American Psychiatric Association. Since then, the DSM has been revised and expanded several times with the goal of improving its accuracy. One of the most extensive revisions took place in 1968, when the DSM was replaced by DSM-II. The diagnostic categories in DSM-II were heavily influenced by psychoanalytic theory. But the diagnoses that were made using DSM-II were problematic; when asked to diagnose a troubled person using the DSM-II categories, diagnosticians had difficulty agreeing with each other (Beck, Ward, Mendelson, Mock, and Erbaugh, 1962; Rosenhan, 1975; Spitzer, 1975). As a result of these concerns, DSM-III was published in 1980. The diagnostic categories in DSM-III included more objective descriptions of behaviors, rather than inferred traits. Moreover, the number of diagnostic categories was expanded, from fewer than one hundred in DSM-II to well over two hundred in DSM-III. Because of continuing reliability problems, however, DSM-III was replaced by DSM-III-R (for revised) in 1987. It began as an attempt to fine-tune DSM-III, but it ended up as a major revision. Finally, DSM-III-R was replaced by DSM-IV in 1994. While touted as being based on empirical efforts (Blashfield and Livesley, 1991; Widiger, Frances, Pincus, Davis, and First, 1991), well-informed authorities consider that it relies mainly on expert opinion (Spitzer, 1991) and may continue to have the same problems with diagnosis as did its predecessors. The next revision of the DSM, DSM-V, is currently being developed. It will probably be published within the first few years of the new millennium. In the meantime, DSM-IV is likely to remain the "diagnostic bible."

CRITERIA FOR DEFINING DISORDERS

In DSM-IV, a ***mental disorder*** is defined as a behavioral or psychological pattern that has either caused the individual distress or disabled the individual in one or more significant areas of functioning. One must be able to infer that there is a genuine dysfunction, and not merely a disturbance between the individual and society. The latter is social deviance, and social deviance is not a mental disorder.

Beyond defining mental disorder, DSM-IV seeks to provide specific and operational (that is, clearly stated and reproducible) diagnostic criteria for each mental disorder. To a great extent, the shortcomings of previous diagnostic systems, especially DSM-II, arose from the fact that its definitions were vague and imprecise. For example, DSM-II described a depressive episode, but left it to the diagnostician to determine what precisely an "episode" consisted of. The definition left unresolved such practical questions as: Would a one-hour depressive experience qualify? Would depression that continued for a month be considered more than a single episode? The new approach takes some of the guesswork out of diagnosis by offering sharper definitions. With regard to a major depressive episode, for example, DSM-IV states that "At least five of the following symptoms have been present during the same two-week period . . . at least one of the symptoms is either (1) depressed mood, or (2) loss of interest or pleasure . . . ," and it lists nine different symptoms. It was hoped that the use of functional definitions would contribute to the reliability of diagnosis.

DSM-IV describes the essential and associated features of each diagnosis. It then provides the research findings about factors such as age of onset, predisposing conditions, and prevalence of each disorder. Finally, it describes the specific criteria for each diagnostic category: the symptoms and their duration. Using the various assessment measures discussed earlier in the chapter, clinicians then determine which categories of DSM-IV best describe the individual and his condition.

The diagnoses in DSM-IV are organized into classes or clusters. As an example, the "mood disorders" include major depressive disorder and bipolar disorder, among others. The class of disorders referred to as "anxiety disorders" lists fourteen diagnostic categories, including generalized anxiety disorder and obsessive-compulsive disorder. The disorders within the various classes and clusters do share certain symptoms in common. But it has not been established that the disorders within the groupings have the same or similar causes. We must await the results of future research to determine whether DSM has divided the disorders into valid groups.

One advantage of DSM-IV is that cultural factors have been given greater consideration in the diagnostic process (Mezzich et al., 1999). Improvements in the cultural sensitivity of the DSM were spawned by concerns that cultural differences were not addressed in previous editions. DSM-IV contains a discussion of the cultural factors that might influence the way various disorders are manifested. It also provides some guidelines for the clinician to use when evaluating and reporting the impact of the person's culture on their mental disorder. Finally, DSM-IV contains a list of what are called "culture-bound" disorders that are observed in some cultures, but not others.

MULTIAXIAL CLASSIFICATION

DSM-IV uses a multiple axis system, rather than a single classification, to make a diagnosis. All told, there are five dimensions or *axes* that are used, not only to classify a disorder, but also to evaluate the person's physical health, personal experiences, and social setting. Thus, the axes reflect the assumption that mental disorders involve biological, psychological, and social factors. The main reason for the multiaxial system is to assure that the whole person, rather than the disorder alone, is considered in the diagnostic process. The information gleaned from these multiple levels of analysis helps in planning treatment and predicting outcome. DSM-IV provides useful information for functional diagnoses on the following axes:

- *Axis I—Clinical Syndromes.* The traditional clinical labels are included here, among them such familiar diagnostic terms as paranoid schizophrenia, major depression, and the various anxiety disorders. Also included on this axis are conditions that are not mental disorders, but that might nevertheless require treatment. Among the latter are school, marital, and occupational problems that do not arise from a mental disorder.
- *Axis II—Personality Disorders.* The personality disorders are not listed on Axis I but often accompany Axis I disorders. Axis II disorders generally begin in childhood or adolescence and persist in stable form into adulthood. Often, such disorders are overlooked by the diagnostician. Listing them as a separate axis ensures that they will be attended to. Axes I and II, then, comprise all of the psychological diagnoses.
- *Axis III—General Medical Conditions.* All medical problems that may be relevant to the psychological problems are listed here.
- *Axis IV—Psychosocial and Environmental Problems.* Included here are sources of difficulty during the past year, or anticipated events such as retirement, which may be contributing to the individual's present difficulties.
- *Axis V—Global Assessment of Functioning.* The level of adaptive functioning has powerful prognostic significance, since individuals commonly return to their highest level of functioning when their psychological events become less intense. The assessment on Axis V considers three areas: social relations with family and friends, occupational functioning, and use of leisure time, and is noted on a scale that runs from 1 (very low) to 100.

Information gathered along all five axes can yield a broader understanding of a person's difficulty than can a simple descriptive diagnosis based on Axis I (see Box 2–2). The first two axes classify the disorders, with the other axes giving a fuller picture of the per-

Diagnosing with DSM-IV

Although the DSM-IV is a manual of "mental" disorders, the symptom criteria for many diagnostic categories also involve physical signs. This reflects the fact that human disorders do not come in neat packages; disorders that originate with psychological problems can lead to physical problems, and vice versa. In order to conduct a comprehensive assessment of a client, the clinician must explore both physical and mental symptoms. The following case is a very clear illustration of the interplay between biological and psychological dysfunction. It serves as a good vehicle for showing how diagnosis is done with DSM-IV.

When Peggy was sixteen, she undertook a diet to lose six unwanted pounds. The diet was successful. Friends and family pointed out how much better she looked, and she herself felt better, too. Encouraged by the compliments and her own self-perceptions, she proceeded to lose another eight pounds. Over the next two years, she continued to diet and to exercise vigorously until her weight had declined to sixty-four pounds, and she stopped menstruating. She was admitted to a hospital, treated for peptic ulcer disease, and discharged, only to be readmitted some three months later to the psychiatric unit of the same hospital. During that hospitalization, her weight rose to one hundred pounds, and she was able to go off to college.

College brought with it increased academic and social demands. Peggy began to diet again. Her eating habits became quite ritualized, consisting of cutting her food into very small pieces, moving those pieces around her plate, and eating very slowly. She resisted eating food with high fat content or with carbohydrates. She worried about her figure, became much more anxious generally, ultimately left school, and entered the hospital again. There she underwent a behavioral treatment program, where she was expected to gain two pounds each week and was restricted to bed rest if she failed to do so. It was a difficult program for her. She was slowly guided to discuss her feelings and to actually look at herself in the mirror.

A clinician would use DSM-IV to diagnose Peggy along the five axes. In addition to the diagnosis of an eating disorder on Axis I, the clinician would decide whether to give Peggy another Axis I diagnosis, whether there was an Axis II personality disorder, whether there were Axis III medical conditions, any Axis IV psychosocial and environmental problems, and finally what her Axis V global assessment of functioning would be. Here is how Peggy would be diagnosed:

Axis I Clinical Disorder: *Anorexia Nervosa, severe*

After her first bout with extreme weight loss, her physician discovered that Peggy had peptic ulcers. Had she been limiting her food intake because eating caused physical discomfort? If so, the clinician would not look to DSM-IV for a diagnosis. On the other hand, the peptic ulcer may have been a result of an eating disorder. Putting all of the information together, this was the clinician's conclusion. There was strong evidence that psychological problems and a change in eating habits preceded the peptic ulcer.

But some ambiguities remained. Recall that Peggy was given to cutting her food into very small pieces before eating it. This may have indicated an obsessive-compulsive disorder, which might be an additional diagnosis. And, during her treatment, Peggy suffered depression and panic, and so she might also have been given a diagnosis of a mood and/or anxiety disorder.

Axis II Personality Disorder: *None*

While there were some indications that Peggy was dependent for her self-evaluations on her friends and family, there was no evidence that her dependence amounted to a dependent personality disorder.

Axis III General Medical Conditions: *Peptic Ulcer, in remission*

Not all physical disorders qualify to be mentioned on Axis III, but those that might interact with the psychological disorder surely deserve mention. In Peggy's case, her early bouts of dieting had been accompanied by peptic ulcers. It seems that psychological problems precipitated reduced food intake which, in turn, contributed to peptic ulcers.

Axis IV Psychosocial and Environmental Problems: *None*

There is no evidence that Peggy was suffering additionally from a social, vocational, or academic difficulty.

Axis V Global Assessment of Functioning: *50 (perhaps even 20)*

While Peggy is quite responsive to treatment, she is nevertheless in substantial danger. Anorexia nervosa is a serious and often life-threatening disorder.

SOURCE: Adapted from the *DSM-IV Casebook: A Learning Companion to the Diagnostic and Statistical Manual of Mental Disorders.*

son, beyond the actual symptoms. A person's medical problems as well as any psychosocial and environmental stressors will certainly affect his condition. The level of the person's global functioning will be a factor in determining how well the individual can cope with his condition and the stressors in his life.

THE RELIABILITY OF THE DSM

The earliest *Diagnostic and Statistical Manuals* were badly flawed by problems with reliability. Experienced diagnosticians using DSM-II, for example, found they often did not agree with each other. In some instances, inter-judge reliability was so low as to make a diagnostic category useless. Indeed, in a review of all the reliability studies of DSM-II, Spitzer and Fleiss (1974) found that only three broad categories were sufficiently reliable to be clinically useful: mental retardation, alcoholism, and organic brain syndrome. These are fairly broad categories, and when diagnosticians attempted to use finer categories—to distinguish the different kinds of alcoholism or brain damage, for example—diagnostic reliability was even lower.

The committees that worked on DSM-III hoped to change all that. They made the categories more specific and precise. They also established behavioral and *temporal* criteria for including and excluding individuals from each diagnostic category. The temporal criteria specified the length of time the symptoms must be present. In the case of major depressive disorder, for example, a minimum number of symptoms (at least five) must be present for at least two weeks. The majority of the diagnostic categories in DSM-III specified both the number of symptoms and the required time period. All of the changes were intended to increase the reliability of the DSM.

Unfortunately, the reliability studies were quite disappointing, both in the manner in which they were conducted and in their actual outcome. Practicing clinicians were asked to examine patients and to arrive at independent diagnoses. DSM-III encouraged clinicians to use multiple diagnoses, both within Axis I and Axis II. But multiple diagnoses, of course, increase the likelihood of agreement among clinicians. If clinician A makes six diagnoses and clinician B makes five, the likelihood that they will agree on one of those diagnoses is much higher than if each had only made a single diagnosis.

Thus, reliability studies on DSM-III were "stacked" in favor of inflated reliabilities. Despite the need to know the diagnostic reliabilities of specific diagnoses, reliabilities were established for clusters or classes of diagnosis. Thus, if two clinicians arrived at quite different diagnoses—if, for example, one found "agoraphobia with panic attacks" while the other found "obsessive-compulsive disorder"—diagnostic agreement would be considered "perfect" because the diagnoses were in the same class, even though there was no agreement on the specific diagnosis (Kirk and Kutchins, 1992). But the central issue is the reliability of the specific diagnoses. And when reliabilities were ultimately computed for specific diagnoses, they varied from quite reliable (for such diagnoses as panic disorder, agoraphobia, and obsessive-compulsive disorder) to utterly unreliable (for the simple phobias and for generalized anxiety disorder) (Mannuzza et al., 1989).

The development of the current *Diagnostic and Statistical Manual*, DSM-IV, was focused on improving reliability. Was the revision successful? In general, there was an increase in diagnostic reliability, although the extent of the improvement varies, depending on the way reliability is examined and on the diagnostic category (Bertelsen, 1999; Nathan and Lagenbucher, 1999). As a case in point, the diagnosis of dysthymic disorder (a type of depression) shows good reliability (Han, Schmaling, and Dunner, 1995). For the diagnosis of major depression, reliability is quite satisfactory when two judges diagnose in the same clinical setting, but it falls precipitously when they are from different clinical centers (Keller et al., 1995). With regard to the diagnosis of sleep disorders, within-site reliability is at best fair, and it declines to poor and worse for specific sleep difficulties (Buysse et al., 1994). So, too, reliabilities were moderate for people whose problems consisted of mixed anxiety and depression (Zinbarg et al., 1994).

Why are some diagnoses more reliable than others? We cannot be sure, but it is likely that the nature of the diagnostic criteria has something to do with it. For example, the definition of some disorders is based mainly on what patients tell the clinician, whereas other diagnoses rely more on the clinician's observations. There is a great need for more research on strategies for refining the diagnostic process. In the meantime, while acknowledging the limitations of the DSM-IV, many believe that refinements will occur and reliability will improve as research gradually uncovers the causes of mental disorder (Frances and Egger, 1999). This is especially true of the Axis I disorders.

There is less agreement about the Axis II personality disorders. These disorders do not necessarily involve any personal discomfort on the part of the individual. Nonetheless, people who meet criteria for these disorders are often very severely impaired in their daily functioning. For example, as described in Chapter 9, many of those who meet criteria for antisocial personality disorder never seek mental health services, yet they are usually impaired in their relationships with others and their occupational functioning. The Axis II disorders have also been criticized on the grounds that the diagnostic criteria are too extreme, and thus they fail to include people with milder personality problems. A recent study found that the vast majority of patients being seen for psychotherapy did not meet criteria for any DSM-IV Axis I or II disorder (Westen and Shedler, 1999). But when a person does meet criteria for any one Axis II disorder, the chances are very high that he will also meet criteria for another disorder on Axis II. This has been referred to as **comorbidity**, the co-occurrence of two or more diagnoses. Does this mean that having one personality disorder puts people at risk for having another one? Or, does it simply indicate that the categories are incorrect, and that there should be a separate category for co-occurring disorders (for example, instead of assigning one person two separate diagnoses, such as schizotypal personality disorder and antisocial personality disorder, give him one diagnosis for "schizotypal-antisocial" personality disorder).

The DSM-IV criteria for personality disorders have also been criticized for failing to take into consideration the "dimensional nature" of personality characteristics (Westen and Shedler, 1999). In other words, personality traits tend to fall along a continuum; for example, from highly dependent to highly independent, or from extremely optimistic to extremely pessimistic. Most people fall somewhere in the middle, but there is no clear cutoff point for "abnormality." Thus, some have suggested that the categories of personality disorder should be abandoned in favor of ratings along various dimensions of personality. It is likely that the next revision of the DSM will entail some significant changes in the Axis II diagnoses to address this problem. Finally, the test-retest reliability of the DSM-IV Axis II disorders is especially low. Yet, the theoretical basis of the DSM-IV assumes that these disorders reflect stable personality problems that are relatively persistent over time.

Factors That Bias the Diagnosis of Mental Disorders

Why should experienced psychologists and psychiatrists have difficulty in agreeing on a diagnosis or being consistent in their diagnoses across time? As mentioned earlier, one of the main reasons is that we do not know the causes of most psychological disorders. Persons with mental disorders are grouped together based on similarities in behavioral signs. Thus, those with a particular syndrome, or set of behavioral signs, are diagnosed with schizophrenia, and those with another syndrome meet criteria for dysthymic disorder. But we do not know for sure that all of those who are diagnosed with schizophrenia are really suffering from the same illness with the same causes. There is no laboratory test on which to base a decision. Evidence of psychological disorder cannot be found with X-rays or blood tests. Instead, the evidence is behavioral, more subjective and, therefore, subject to a variety of social and psychological factors (Garb, 1998a; Garb, Florio, and Grove, 1998). Three of the most important factors that can influence diagnoses are context, expectation, and source credibility. Indeed, it is often these factors that contribute to the unreliability of diagnoses.

CONTEXT

Throughout the years, psychological research has repeatedly shown that the context in which a behavior is observed can dramatically affect the meaning that is ascribed to it (Asch, 1951; Garb, Florio, and Grove, 1998; Gergen, 1982). In one famous study, a group of people who were free from major psychological symptoms simulated a particularly idiosyncratic symptom to the admitting doctors at general psychiatric hospitals (Rosenhan, 1973). The "patients" alleged that they heard a voice and that the voice said "dull," "empty," and "thud." Now those particular verbalizations were quite idiosyncratic, but nothing else about these people was unusual. Indeed, they had been carefully instructed to behave as they commonly behaved, and to give truthful answers to all questions, except those that dealt with their auditory hallucinations. Had they been outside of the hospital context, their simulation would have been detected, or at least suspected. Surely someone would have indicated that this single symptom with no other accompanying symptoms was strange indeed. But this did not happen in the hospitals in which these patients sought admission. Rather, they were admitted mainly with the diagnosis of schizophrenia, and they were discharged with the diagnosis of schizophrenia in remission. The fact that most patients in hospitals who hallucinate are suffering from schizophrenia created a compelling context for these "pseudopatients" to be considered to have schizophrenia. Although their symptoms were not those of schizophrenia, the context of the symptoms seemed to matter more in the diagnosis than did the symptoms themselves.

Not only hospital settings, but the diagnoses themselves can constitute contexts that admit certain kinds of information and interpretations, bias other kinds, and disallow still others. For example, once the pseudopatients were admitted to the hospital, they of course began to observe their surroundings carefully and to take copious notes on their observations. Patients asked them what they were writing. Soon the patients concluded that the writers were not patients at all, but rather were journalists or college professors doing a study of the hospital. It was not an especially ingenious inference for the patients to make, since the pseudopatients did in fact behave quite differently than many of the real patients did. But the staff, on the other hand, made no such inference. They too noted that the pseudopatients often wrote. "Patient engages in writing behavior," the staff recorded about a particular patient. But they interpreted his writing within the context of the diagnosis itself, viewed the writing as yet another confirming bit of psychopathology, and they closed off any explanation that lay outside of the diagnostic context.

EXPECTATION

Whether a diagnostician is expecting to see a person in distress or a normal person may also influence diagnostic judgment. For example, one hospital administrator, having heard how easily the pseudopatients previously described had been diagnosed as having a schizophrenic disorder and admitted to a hospital, insisted that "it can't happen here." As a result, a simple study was devised (Rosenhan, 1973). The hospital was informed that sometime during the following three months, one or more pseudopatients would appear at the admissions office. During this period, each staff member—attendants, nurses, psychiatrists, and psychologists—was asked to rate each patient who sought admission or who was already on the ward, using a scale that indicated how likely it was that the patient was, in fact, a pseudopatient. More

The power of psychological diagnosis can make it as dangerous as it is indispensable. If this Bosnian boy is considered "irrecoverable" by hospital staff, he could spend the rest of his life in these conditions.

than 20 percent of the patients who were admitted for psychiatric treatment were judged, with high confidence, to be pseudopatients by at least one staff member, and nearly 10 percent were thought to be pseudopatients by two staff members. Set in the direction of finding a pseudopatient, they found many. In fact, not a single pseudopatient ever presented himself for admission—at least not from this study!

SOURCE CREDIBILITY

Psychological diagnosis is particularly vulnerable to suggestions from highly credible sources. This was demonstrated in one study in which groups of diagnosticians heard a taped interview of a man who seemed to be going through an especially happy and vigorous period in his life (Temerlin, 1970). His work was rewarding and going well, his relationships with others were cordial and gratifying, and he was happily married and enjoyed sexual relations. He was also entirely free of the symptoms that commonly generate a psychiatric diagnosis: depression, anxiety, psychosomatic symptoms, suspiciousness, hostility, and thought disturbance. After listening to the interview, one group of diagnosticians heard a respected authority say that the man seemed neurotic but was actually "quite psychotic." Other diagnosticians heard the same authority say that the person was quite healthy. Yet others heard someone on the tape say that it was an interview for a job. The results of this study are quite dramatic. Psychologically trained diagnosticians—psychiatrists, psychologists, and clinical psychology graduate students—were highly influenced in their conclusions by the assertions that this man might be quite disturbed. Indeed, they were somewhat more influenced by that assertion than were untrained diagnosticians, including law students and undergraduates. Correspondingly, when a mixed group of diagnosticians (including both trained and untrained diagnosticians) were told that the individual was "healthy," their evaluations contained no mention of disturbance.

CULTURAL CONTEXTS AND INFLUENCES

We mentioned that DSM-IV pays more attention to cultural factors than its predecessors, and actually includes an appendix on "culture-bound" syndromes (see Box 2–3). Nonetheless, there has been relatively little research on the nature and extent of cultural influences on mental health and disorder. Why is such research important? Consider the case of ataque de nervios, described in Box 2–3. The nature and extent of ataque de nervios was unknown until the 1980s when the disorder was included in an epidemiological study of adult mental health in Puerto Rico (Guarnaccia and Rogler, 1999). Much to the surprise of many researchers, 16 percent of the people interviewed reported having had at least one episode of ataque de nervios. The syndrome was recognized by the vast majority of study participants, and most knew someone who had the disorder. As a result of these findings, some researchers began to routinely question their Puerto Rican patients about their experience with ataque de nervios. They discovered that 75 percent of the patients interviewed in mental health clinics reported that they had experienced

---

Society and Mental Health

Box 2–3

Culturally-Specific Disorders

Below are some of the culturally bound disorders described in DSM-IV. Despite the progress in cultural sensitivity, some people question a basic assumption of DSM-IV: namely, that a universal classification system is possible. Further, some argue that, despite the inclusion of these culturally bound disorders, DSM-IV still does not pay enough attention to the cultural contexts of mental disorder, diagnosis, and treatment.

Ataque de nervios

An idiom of distress principally reported among Latinos from the Caribbean but recognized among many Latin American and Latin Mediterranean groups. Commonly reported symptoms include uncontrollable shouting, attacks of crying, trembling, heat in the chest rising into the head, and verbal or physical aggression. Dissociative experiences, seizurelike or fainting episodes, and suicidal gestures are prominent in some attacks but absent in others. A general feature of ataque de nervios is a sense of being out of control. Ataques de nervios frequently occur as a direct result of a stressful event relating to the family (e.g., news of the death of a close relative, a separation or divorce from a spouse, conflicts with a spouse or children, or witnessing an accident involving a family member). People may experience amnesia for what occurred during the ataque de nervios, but they otherwise return rapidly to their usual level of functioning. Although descriptions of some ataques de nervios most closely fit with the DSM-IV description of panic attacks, the association of most ataques with a precipitating event distinguish them from panic disorder. Ataques span the range from normal expressions of distress not associated with having a mental disorder to symptom presentations associated with the diagnoses of anxiety, mood, dissociative, or somatoform disorders.

Koro

A term, probably of Malaysian origin, that refers to an episode of sudden and intense anxiety that the penis (or, in females, the vulva and nipples) will recede into the body and possibly cause death. The syndrome is reported in south and east Asia, where it is known by a variety of local terms, such as *shuk yang, shook yong,* and *suo yang* (Chinese); *jinjinia bemar* (Assam); or *rok-joo* (Thailand). It is occasionally found in the West. Koro at times occurs in localized epidemic form in east Asian areas. This diagnosis is included in the *Chinese Classification of Mental Disorders*, Second Edition (CCMD-2).

Pibloktoq

An abrupt dissociative episode accompanied by extreme excitement of up to thirty minutes' duration and frequently followed by convulsive seizures and coma lasting up to twelve hours. This is observed primarily in arctic and subarctic Eskimo communities, although regional variations in name exist. The individual may be withdrawn or mildly irritable for a period of hours or days before the attack and will typically report complete amnesia for the attack. During the attack, the individual may tear off his or her clothing, break furniture, shout obscenities, eat feces, flee from protective shelters, or perform other irrational or dangerous acts.

Source: American Psychiatric Association. (1994). *Diagnostic and Statistical Manual of Mental Disorders* (4th ed.). Washington, DC: Author.

ataque de nervios. These findings demonstrate the need to sensitize researchers and clinicians to culture-bound syndromes because they may affect large numbers of people and, therefore, constitute a significant mental health problem. Further, research can help to clarify the nature of the syndrome. For example, although seizures and suicidal gestures had been viewed as key symptoms of ataque de nervios, clinical studies showed that these symptoms were only present in about one-third of the cases. Instead, patients described loss of emotional and physical control (screaming uncontrollably, crying uncontrollably, shaking, and heart palpitations) as the most common symptoms.

When studies of the epidemiology of ataque de nervios were conducted, it was found to occur most often in women over the age of forty-five, especially those who were unemployed, had a limited education, and had experienced a stressor, such as marital separation or divorce. This demographic profile is very similar to that observed for depression in the United States. This raises an important question about culture-bound syndromes. Should they be considered separate mental disorders? Will it be necessary to have culture-specific diagnostic systems? Or, are they simply culturally "flavored" manifestations of one of the basic DSM-IV disorders? Perhaps the individual's culture determines how people show their distress or feelings of sadness. In Puerto Rico, strong displays of emotion may be more acceptable than in the mainland United States. Evidence to support the assumption that culture-bound syndromes are alternative manifestations of DSM-IV disorders is provided by studies of comorbidity; about 63 percent of Puerto Ricans with ataque de nervios meet diagnostic criteria for an Axis I or Axis II disorder (Guarnaccia and Rogler, 1999).

Although there is not a great deal of research on cultural differences in traditional categories of mental disorder, there is some evidence that national rates of certain disorders vary (Ormel et al., 1994). As a case in point, somatization disorder, which involves a preoccupation with bodily symptoms that have no apparent physical basis, seems to be the most common psychological disorder in South American countries (Gureje, Simon, Ustun, and Goldberg, 1997). Researchers found the prevalence to be 8.5 percent in Rio de Janeiro, Brazil, and 17.7 percent in Santiago, Chili. Rates under 1 percent were found in Ibadan, Nigeria; Manchester, England; Nagasaki, Japan; and Verona, Italy. What is the cause of these differences? One possibility, of course, is that there is a true difference in prevalence. But alternative explanations cannot be ruled out. It may be that differences in the translation of symptom questionnaires or interviews produced the disparity. For example, the meaning of the symptom of somatization disorder might differ when they are translated into different languages.

Interpreting the meaning of cross-cultural differences in mental disorder may prove to be the most challenging aspect of this research. But investigators cannot abandon the problem. In particular, as our society becomes more diverse, cultural influences on mental disorders will take on increasing importance in the United States. The proportion of Asians and Hispanics in the United States is increasing at an especially fast pace, so the cultural factors that influence their mental health and response to treatment should be the focus of greater research.

The Need for Categorization and Diagnosis

Currently available tests and diagnostic procedures for assessing mental disorders have limitations. Because the diagnosis of mental disorders relies so heavily on behavioral signs, there is much room for error. But can we do without diagnosis? Absolutely not. There can be no science, and no advance in understanding psychological abnormality, without somehow differentiating one kind of syndrome from another. By differentiating a behavioral syndrome associated with one disorder from other mental disorders, researchers ultimately made the treatment breakthrough possible. Without diagnosis, advances in treatment would not have been possible.

Although it is wise to take a critical approach to the diagnosis of mental disorders, we must not forget that there are limits on diagnostic reliability in virtually all fields of medicine. Over time, as scientific research progresses, we come to understand which diagnoses are useful and which are not. Similar breakthroughs in diagnosis have occurred in the treatment of many physical disorders. As researchers have systematically examined symptoms and syndromes of physical disorders, they have discovered new and important distinctions. This has occurred in research on diabetes, cancer, heart disease, and AIDS. Similarly, some DSM-IV diagnoses, such as dysthymia, a form of mood disorder, have already proven to be reliable and valid, and many other diagnoses are promising. There is no doubt, however, that some DSM-IV diagnostic categories are not based on strong empirical data. Chief among these are some of the personality disorders. Ultimately, only careful research will tell us whether these speculative diagnostic categories should be retained. The accuracy and utility of any diagnosis must be demonstrated.

Research Methods

The twentieth century witnessed amazing advances in science, especially behavioral science. The application of the scientific method to the study of human behavior laid the groundwork for a revolution in our understanding of ourselves and others. In this section, we will discuss the basic assumptions and approaches used by behavioral scientists. Then, in later chapters, we will see how these approaches have shed light on the nature and causes of various mental disorders.

Research on mental disorders began with the simplest of all approaches: the *clinical case history* method. It is the simplest method because it relies on individual case histories as a source of hypotheses. It is extremely useful as the starting point for more complex scientific studies. Clinical case histories were the basis for early theories about the nature of schizophrenia and many other mental disorders. They have also led to research on physical illnesses such as AIDS. In fact, the Centers for Disease Control (CDC), which is responsible for monitoring and reducing illness in the United States, relies heavily on case histories to monitor the onset of epidemics and the spread of disease. The case method approach is very limited, however. How can we know that what holds for a particular client also holds for other people with the same disorder? For example, if we discover that the mother of a particular child with autism suffered from rubella (German measles) during her pregnancy, does that mean the rubella caused the autism? The answer is "no." We cannot assume that a single observation proves a general principle. Nonetheless, case history information can provide us with a *hypothesis,* a theory about the cause, that we can test with further research.

In order to test a hypothesis, we need to get information on a large sample of research participants. When testing the hypothesis that prenatal exposure to rubella increases the risk of autism, we might systematically examine the prenatal records of a large group of children with autism and a comparison group of children without autism. If the hypothesis that rubella can cause autism is correct, then the group with autism should have a higher rate of prenatal exposure to rubella than the comparison group. In other words, we would look for a relation between prenatal rubella and autism. If we find such a relation, we can take this as support for the hypothesis. But have we shown that rubella *causes* autism? Not exactly.

In order to show unequivocally that a particular factor (rubella) causes a particular outcome (autism), we would have to conduct a true experimental study. In experimental studies, the researcher manipulates or "controls" the factor that is assumed to play a causal role. But for ethical and practical reasons, it is usually not possible to do experimental studies to determine causes of psychological disorders. In other words, we cannot intentionally expose a group of pregnant women to rubella, then study their children to see if they are more likely to develop autism. That would violate our basic moral assumptions. Of course, if our goal were to test the hypothesis that prenatal vitamins prevent a certain disorder in children, then there would not necessarily be a problem with using the experimental method. Intentionally exposing human beings to something that we believe will help them is very different from intentionally exposing them to a factor that we believe will harm them.

One powerful use of the experimental method is in the study of treatments for behavioral abnormality. Treatment studies, known as *outcome studies,* compare the effects of one treatment approach, either biological or psychological, to another treatment, or to no treatment. In studies of this type, the researcher is controlling the research participant's exposure to treatment. Of course, if the results indicate that a particular treatment is highly effective in reducing the severity of a certain disorder, then it may eventually become part of clinical practice.

Before we begin our examination of these varied research methods, a key point should be mentioned. No one study is considered sufficient to prove that a particular relationship exists or that a specific treatment is clinically effective. In scientific research, we rely on *replication.* This means the study must be repeated, using the same or similar methods. If the original findings are supported, we are one step closer to accepting the hypothesis. But good researchers are, by nature, skeptics. They consider all the alternative explanations for a particular research finding, not just the explanation favored by a certain hypothesis. Valid research findings stand up to the tests of time and replication.

The Clinical Case History

If we keep in mind that the ultimate goal of any research method is the discovery of evidence about cause, we will see that a variety of approaches can lead toward this goal. The first, the clinical case history, is the record of part of the life of an individual. The clinician who is observing and recording the case history can make informed guesses or hypotheses. And, beyond this, the clinician can sometimes use the information to develop hypotheses and treatment plans. The following case of an anxious adolescent is such an instance:

Rebecca was a 16-year-old black female in the ninth grade who was brought in for psychiatric evaluation by her mother, at the request of school personnel. She was evaluated at an outpatient clinic which specialized in the assessment and treatment of children and adolescents with anxiety disorders.

Rebecca's presenting complaint was a longstanding problem with school attendance that began during sixth grade, when Rebecca showed some mild reluctance to attend school. It is noteworthy that this problem began following the transition from elementary to middle school, and as the literature suggests, such transition times are associated with an increase in school-related fears. No other precipitating events were identified. During seventh grade, Rebecca missed 40 days of school by the end of the first grading period. Although she repeated both seventh and eighth grades due to lack of sufficient attendance, she was promoted to ninth grade on the basis of her age; however, at the time of her evaluation, Rebecca had attended only two days during the first four months of school. Prior to sixth grade, Rebecca attended school regularly and without reluctance, reportedly enjoyed school, and received above-average grades.

Rebecca lived with her mother, Mrs. H, and 15-year-old sister. Her mother was a 35-year-old single parent who worked as a secretary. Family psychiatric history was significant for social phobia of public speaking (mother, sister) as well as major depression (mother).

Rebecca's mother was unsure why Rebecca was so reluctant to attend school. At first, Rebecca pretended to go to school and it was not until three months into seventh grade that Mrs. H became aware of the excessive absenteeism. However, once the absenteeism was discovered, Rebecca began to refuse openly to attend school. She reported feeling sick and worried in the mornings before school and, thus, unable to attend. Although Rebecca was noncompliant about attending school, she did not exhibit acting-out behavior or pervasive problems with noncompliance.

Rebecca acknowledged that school attendance had been a major problem for her over the past four years and that she felt extremely uncomfortable and nervous when in the school setting. She described feeling self-conscious about having to speak in class, eat in the cafeteria, and dress for gym, unable to tolerate the crowded classrooms, and was fearful of doing or saying "something stupid" in front of the other kids. She also reported feeling very embarrassed when in a variety of social situations outside of school, such as crowded places, stores, and waiting in lines. Rebecca described feeling anxious whenever she was around groups of people because she felt as though she was being scrutinized.

Rebecca's presenting symptoms were indicative of anxiety-based school refusal due to social phobia. Although a diagnosis of separation anxiety disorder was a possibility given Rebecca's avoidance of leaving home, her anxiety did not appear to be related to being away from her mother or from her home per se; instead, she was fearful of possible embarrassment in social situations. It appeared as though Rebecca was described best as suffering from pervasive social anxiety and avoidance consistent with a diagnosis of social phobia.

The goal of Rebecca's outpatient treatment was to decrease her anxiety about, and avoidance of, social situations. Although return to school was a high priority, it appeared as though Rebecca first would need to experience success confronting less anxiety-provoking social situations. A program consisting of graduated in vivo exposure to anxiety-provoking situations, and additional anxiety management techniques, such as cognitive coping strategies, was developed. However, as Rebecca responded quickly and well to graduated exposure alone, additional anxiety management techniques were not necessary. Treatment consisted of nine, one-hour sessions over the course of a 3-month period.

The first session was spent gathering additional assessment information and developing a list of anxiety-provoking situations to be used for the hierarchy. Rebecca was instructed to include a variety of situations, ranging from the least to the most anxiety provoking. The pertinent variables were time spent getting ready, degree to which the situation was crowded, and whether the situation was to be faced alone or with someone. Following the delineation of the hierarchy, Rebecca was asked to rate her anxiety regarding each item using a nine-point scale ranging from 0 (do not avoid, no anxiety) to 8 (invariably avoid situation, very severe/continuous anxiety—near panic). The least anxiety-provoking items were "going to a department store with someone," and "standing in line at a fast food place with someone," all of which were given an anxiety rating of 4. In contrast, the most anxiety-provoking items, receiving an anxiety rating of 8, were "taking out the trash without getting ready first" and "going to school and staying all day."

Rebecca's anxiety ratings for items on the hierarchy decreased over the course of treatment. By the end of treatment she was able to approach most social situations with minimal anxiety. In those situations in which her anxiety level remained high (e.g., walking in a crowded park alone), she no longer exhibited avoidance behavior. Rebecca was clearly able to see that exposure to anxiety-provoking situations led to decreased anxiety. In addition, by the end of treatment Rebecca had passed the GED and enrolled in a local community college. Not only was she exposed to large groups of people while attending classes at the community college, but Rebecca also was required to ride the bus for transportation to and from campus. She frequently went out with her boyfriend and family members, and reported feeling very satisfied with the outcome of treatment. (Francis and Ollendick, 1990)

ADVANTAGES OF THE CLINICAL CASE HISTORY

As a method of inquiry, the study of the clinical case history has several advantages. One is that it can document a rare phenomenon or disorder that cannot easily be studied with other standard forms of investigation. But its major advantage is that it can serve as a source of hypotheses about the etiology and treatment of psychological disorders. The case history method can generate hypotheses that can then be tested systematically in the laboratory and the clinic. In Rebecca's case, for example, the clinician might develop several hypotheses after interviewing her and her mother. One obvious candidate would be

that Rebecca's problem with school attendance was due to a specific fear of school. Alternatively, it might be the result of a more generalized social phobia. In addition, the clinician might consider the possibilities that Rebecca's problem was a result of academic difficulties or extreme dependency on her mother. Rebecca's response to the clinical intervention would then provide a test of these hypotheses.

DISADVANTAGES OF THE CLINICAL CASE HISTORY

There are four major disadvantages to clinical case histories: selectivity of memory, lack of repeatability, lack of generality, and insufficient evidence for causality.

The reported "evidence" may be distorted because it deals with incidents in the past, often in the distant past. The patient may have an axe to grind; he may, for example, want to absolve himself of blame or, conversely, emphasize his guilt. To accomplish this, he may select the evidence that serves these purposes, magnifying trivial events or ignoring important ones as he talks to the therapist. Moreover, sometimes it is the therapist, not the patient, who has the axe to grind. A therapist might believe in a particular theory, which may influence what evidence she considers relevant and what evidence she ignores.

Because case histories are real, they are not repeatable. They are often "one of a kind," making it difficult to line up several clinical cases that point to a definite cause. Even a convincing case history, like Rebecca's, is specific to one person and lacks generality. Does all school avoidance begin with a fear of social situations? A single case history can, at best, tell us only that one such case of school avoidance began in this way.

Single clinical case histories should not convince us about etiology, or causality. In cases like Rebecca's, the cause seemed clear, but usually cause is more ambiguous. In most cases, there are several incidents, each of which might be the cause, or there is no obvious incident at all. This is the most serious problem with clinical case histories. It is simply too difficult to isolate which possible incident might cause the disorder.

Scientific Experimentation

The major goal of all scientific experiments is to obtain information about causal effects: Does A cause B? The basic experimental method is fairly simple. First, you make a guess (hypothesis) about the cause of an event. Then, you either (a) remove the suspected cause, and see if the event fails to occur, or (b) you add the suspected cause, and see if the event does occur.

An experiment, then, consists of a procedure in which the hypothesized cause is manipulated, and the occurrence of the effect is measured. The hypothesized cause, which the experimenter controls, is called the ***independent variable.*** The effect, which the experimenter measures, is called the ***dependent variable,*** because its occurrence depends on whether the cause precedes it. Both independent and dependent variables have an ***operational definition.*** An operational definition is the set of clear-cut, measurable criteria. So, for example, obesity can be operationally defined as being 15 percent or more above the specified "ideal" weight for a given height as listed in a table of weights. Depression can be defined as having greater than a given score on a checklist of depressive symptoms. When manipulating an independent variable produces changes in a dependent variable, an ***experimental effect*** has been obtained. Let's consider one particular experiment.

SETTING UP AN EXPERIMENT

To determine whether an experimental effect has occurred, researchers must first set up an experiment. They must identify the dependent and independent variables based on their hypothesis about cause. Researchers who were looking for treatments for depression, for example, set up an experiment that was based on several clinical case histories about sleep deprivation. It appeared that, in some instances, depressed individuals who missed several whole nights of sleep, surprisingly, became less depressed. Putting this together with the fact that antidepressant drugs can reduce the amount of dreaming, investigators hypothesized that dream deprivation itself might relieve depression (Vogel, 1975; Vogel, Buffenstein, Minter, and Hennessey, 1990).

When we dream, our eyes move rapidly back and forth beneath our closed lids. Since we can monitor when an individual is dreaming, we can deprive him of dreams by waking him up every time these signs appear. Such dream deprivation, carried out in a sleep laboratory for several nights running, was the independent variable that was manipulated in a series of experiments (Vogel, 1975). Individuals who had been hospitalized for depression were the subjects, and the dependent variables were changes in ratings of the severity of depression on a variety of symp-

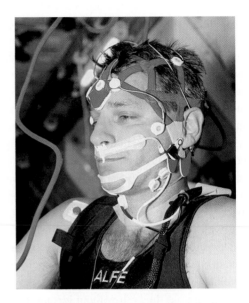

Experiments are set up to determine whether an experimental effect has occurred. Here an astronaut is being monitored to determine how being in space affects sleep patterns and mood. The "sleep cap" and wires are measuring electrical impulses from the brain, muscles, eyes, and heart.

toms. The investigators obtained the expected experimental effect. When the group of depressed people were deprived of dreaming over a period of several weeks, their average level of depression decreased, although not all the depressed people improved.

Can we now conclude that dream deprivation causes relief from depression? Not yet. Let's consider an alternative explanation for the findings. Perhaps it was not the dream deprivation that was effective, but some other aspect of what was done to the depressed patients. For example, the patients had electrodes placed on them, got less total sleep than normal, got lots of individual attention from the researchers, and slept in a novel environment—a laboratory. Any one of these might have been effective, rather than the specific manipulation of preventing them from dreaming.

Factors other than the independent variable that might produce an experimental effect and that occur along with the independent variable are called ***confounds.*** Thus, in the study described above, the independent variable, dream deprivation, was confounded with at least four other factors: electrode placement, shorter sleep time, attention from researchers, and a novel environment. So, which one of these produced the change in the dependent variable, depression severity?

In order to deal with confounds, experimenters use control procedures, the most typical of which is the ***control group.*** In principle, a control group is composed of subjects who are as similar as possible to those in the experimental group. In other words, people in the two groups are as close as possible to each other in such variables as age, economic background, and mental health. The control group experiences only the confounded factors (that is, electrode placement, shorter sleep time, attention from researchers, and a novel environment), but not the hypothesized cause (that is, dream deprivation). In contrast, people in the ***experimental group*** experience both the confounds and the independent variable. In general, whenever there is reason to suspect that some factor confounded with the independent variable might produce the effect, groups that control for that confounding factor must be included (see Figure 2–6).

In the dream deprivation study, the investigators ran an appropriate control group, which controlled for a number of confounds. Other depressed patients were put through exactly the same procedure as above. They spent three weeks sleeping in the laboratory, electrodes were taped on them, and they were awakened the same number of times during each night as were those in the experimental group. But there was one crucial difference: the awakenings occurred, not when the patients were dreaming, but during nondreaming phases of sleep. The patients in the control group did not become less depressed. This leads us closer to the conclusion that dream deprivation alleviates depression in some patients.

There are many examples of therapy outcome studies that are true experiments: one group receives the treatment and the control group does not. These investigations are referred to as ***efficacy studies,*** and they are usually conducted in a controlled laboratory setting. However, some treatment studies are

---

Figure 2—6

THE EXPERIMENTAL EFFECT

When manipulating an independent variable produces changes in a dependent variable, an experimental effect has been obtained. In the experiment above, the independent variable is dream deprivation, the dependent variable is depression, and the experimental effect is less depression as a result of the dream deprivation. To make sure that the experimental effect is not occurring because of the confounds (here, electrodes taped on, sleep in lab, awakened four times during the night), experimenters use control procedures. Control groups experience only the confounds; experimental groups experience both confounds and the hypothesized cause.

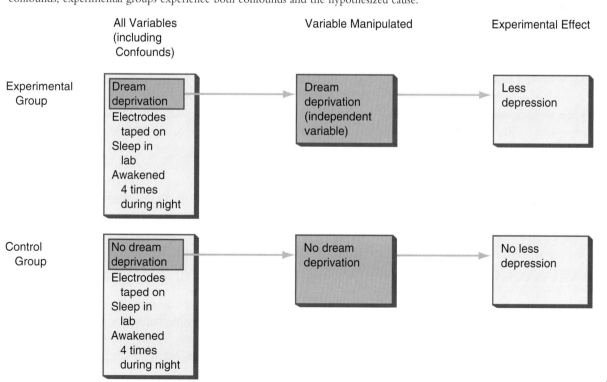

conducted in natural settings. These are referred to as *effectiveness studies,* and they focus on the outcome of treatment as it is delivered in the field. Both kinds of studies are considered outcome studies, and they allow us to determine which therapies work. When the results of efficacy and effectiveness studies converge on the same conclusion, we have the best evidence for the usefulness of a therapy.

LABORATORY ANIMAL MODELS

As mentioned earlier, it is not ethical to conduct research with human beings that has a good chance of putting their physical or mental health at risk. Researchers do not, for example, study the effects of vaccines on humans until they have conducted animal studies that convince them that the benefits of the vaccine probably outweigh the risks. Indeed, animal research has played a major role in the development of treatments for physical illnesses, such as cancer, respiratory disease and AIDS. But what about mental disorders? Can we learn anything about the causes and treatments of mental disorders by studying a nonhuman species? Most agree that the answer is "yes."

A *laboratory animal model* is the production, under controlled conditions, of a behavioral syndrome in animals, that is analogous to naturally occurring human mental disorders. That is, a particular symptom or syndrome is produced in an experimental study to test hypotheses about cause and cure. Confirmed hypotheses can then be further tested in situations outside the laboratory.

As an example of the use of the laboratory model, let us see how scientists have created an animal model of major depression. About twenty-five years ago, investigators noticed that animals who received electric shock that was uncontrollable—that went on and off regardless of what the animal was doing—later became very passive. Later on in a different situation, they failed even to try to escape shock that was actually escapable. They just sat and took the shock (Maier and Seligman, 1976; Seligman and Maier, 1967). Evidence soon began to accumulate that such "learned helplessness" had many of the same symptoms as depression in humans.

Learned helplessness has been systematically evaluated to find if it is a valid model of depression (Weiss, Simson, Ambrose, Webster, and Hoffman, 1985). For a person to meet the DSM-IV criteria for a diagnosis of depression, at least five of these nine

symptoms must be present: (1) loss of interest in usual activities, (2) weight loss and poor appetite, (3) insomnia, (4) psychomotor alterations, (5) fatigue or loss of energy, (6) diminished ability to think or attend, (7) depressed mood, (8) feelings of worthlessness, and (9) suicidal thoughts.

Animals who have experienced uncontrollable events show each of the first six symptoms. They would receive a diagnosis of depression if they were human. The last three symptoms (depressed mood, feelings of worthlessness, and suicidal thoughts) cannot be measured in animals. Is the learned helplessness model applicable to humans? It seems to be. When humans are given uncontrollable noise, they display depressed mood and feelings of worthlessness in addition to the hallmark symptoms above (Abramson, 1978; Breier et al., 1987; Hiroto and Seligman, 1975). In the study by Alan Breier and his colleagues, human research participants were exposed to the stress of loud noise in the laboratory under controllable and uncontrollable conditions. Those who experienced the uncontrollable loud noise showed higher self-ratings of helplessness, lack of control, tension, stress, unhappiness, anxiety, and depression. There were also biological effects of the uncontrollable stress, including elevations in stress hormone release and skin conductance ("electrodermal") activity. Thus, lack of control over a mildly aversive stimulus can produce alterations in mood, as well as neuroendocrine and autonomic nervous system changes. These results mean that eight of the nine symptoms of depression can be produced in the laboratory by uncontrollable events.

Investigators have taken on the challenge of looking for the biochemical basis of learned helplessness and for drug treatments that can cure learned helplessness in animals. Moreover, researchers have also explored the brain chemistry of those suffering from learned helplessness and have found that it looks quite similar to what is known about the brain chemistry of those suffering from depression (Lachman et al., 1993; Weiss, Simson, Ambrose, Webster, and Hoffman, 1985; Wu et al., 1999). In addition, researchers have found that drugs that reduce helplessness in animals also alleviate depression in humans (Sherman and Petty, 1980).

All of this seems to argue that learned helplessness in animals is a convincing laboratory model of depression in humans. This model may help us to understand the brain chemistry of human depression, to understand how drugs can relieve depression, and to find new treatments for depression.

EXPERIMENTAL CONFOUNDS

A well-done experiment can allow us to determine whether A causes B. But experimenters must be on their guard against a variety of subtle confounds. Sometimes confounding factors produce an effect that is misinterpreted as an experimental effect. Some common problems with experimental control are nonrandom assignment, experimenter bias, subject bias, and demand characteristics.

Nonrandom Assignment   In an experiment that includes an experimental group and a control group, it is important that subjects are assigned to groups on a random basis. Such **random assignment** means that each subject should have an equal chance of being assigned to each group. If subjects are not assigned by random selection, mistaken inferences can sometimes be made. For example, in research on a new treatment for depression, the investigator must make sure that there is no bias in the way the depressed patients are assigned to the experimental and control groups. Researchers use a number of strategies to assure random assignment. Sometimes they simply alternate assignment of participants to the experimental and control groups. Other times they use a table of random numbers.

When **nonrandom assignment** occurs, it often, although not always, causes problems. Imagine that a clinical researcher is conducting a study of a new treatment for depression. He decides to assign all the depressed patients who came to his clinic during the day to the control group, and all the patients who came to the clinic in the evening to the experimental group. This would *not* be random assignment. Nonetheless, the researcher decides to do it this way for a pragmatic reason. He has to hire additional therapists with expertise in the new treatment approach to provide the experimental treatment. They are only available in the evening. The therapists who work at the clinic during the day will provide the standard treatment, and their patients will serve as the control group. Do you see any potential problems with this?

What if the patients who come to the clinic for evening appointments differ in some important way from those who come during the day. Chances are

that a higher proportion of the daytime patients will be female homemakers and young students with flexible schedules. Moreover, the daytime patients may be more seriously depressed and unemployed as a result of their depression. If this were the case, then the control group would be composed of people who differ in important ways from the experimental group. The control group members would be more likely to be female, young, unemployed, and seriously depressed. So, we could not necessarily draw any conclusions about differences between the experimental and control groups after the study—because they were different *before* the study.

Experimenter Bias   Another source of mistaken inference from experiments comes from **experimenter bias.** If an experimenter wants or expects a particular result, he can subtly influence the process to produce that result, sometimes without being aware of it. In recent years, there has been increasing concern about the effect of experimenter biases on the findings from studies of psychological therapies. Several reviews of the research literature have found that the treatment favored by the researcher is more likely to be the one that shows the greatest efficacy in an outcome study (Luborsky et al., 1999). This is referred to as the *allegiance effect:* the researcher's allegiance to a particular treatment has an impact on the outcome of the study. How does this happen? There are several ways this can occur without the investigator being aware of it. First, the researcher may select the most committed and competent clinicians to provide his favorite treatment. The "control" treatment might be provided by mediocre clinicians. Another source of the allegiance effect is the enthusiasm generated by the investigator. The treatment providers may sense that the researcher favors a particular therapeutic approach and try harder to make it work. Finally, the research participants themselves may be playing a role. The patients may sense greater enthusiasm for the experimental treatment and convey this in self-reports of decreased symptoms.

Experimenter bias is also a potential problem in observational studies. This has been shown in many areas of research. For example, in one study, observers were asked to rate the behavior of infants, all of whom were normal (Woods, Eyler, Conlon, Behnke, and Wobie, 1998). They were told that certain infants had been exposed to prenatal cocaine and others had not. Their ratings of the babies were highly influenced by this information. When the observer thought the baby had been exposed to prenatal cocaine, she rated the baby more negatively. This raises obvious questions about the problem of *self-fulfilling prophecies:* the tendency for people to conform to others' expectations of them. Will adults inadvertently communicate negative expectations to children who have been exposed to cocaine? Could this contribute to problematic behavior on the part of the child? We have to wait for the results of future research to answer this question.

Subject Bias   An even bigger problem than experimenter bias is *subject bias.* Human subjects routinely form beliefs about what they are expected to do. When someone believes that a drug that is actually useless is going to help him, he may still sometimes get better after taking the drug. For example, following major surgery, pain is frequent and severe. Yet, about 35 percent of patients report marked relief after taking a sugar pill, or *placebo* (Beecher, 1959). Morphine, even in large doses, relieves pain only 75 percent of the time. We can conclude from this that the power of suggestion probably provides some of the pain-killing benefits of morphine. To deal with subject bias, investigators use an experimental group that receives a real drug and a control group that is given a placebo. Both groups are given identical instructions. The mere belief on the part of all subjects that any pill should work has powerful effects. For it to be considered effective, the investigators must then find the real drug to be more potent than the placebo alone.

If neither the experimenter nor the subject knows whether the subject is in the experimental or the placebo control group, the results cannot be affected by either experimenter or subject bias. This elegant design in which both subject and experimenter are "blind" as to which subjects have received a drug or placebo is called a *double-blind experiment.* An experiment in which only the subject (and not the experimenter) does not know whether he is receiving a drug or placebo is called a *single-blind experiment.* The design in which only the experimenter is blind and the subject is not is an *experimenter-blind design.*

Demand Characteristics   The term *demand characteristics* refers to aspects of the research procedures that convey clues to the research participants. Subtle information about the purpose of the study might be conveyed in the announcements to recruit partici-

A subject participates in a sensory deprivation experiment. Will he have stress-induced hallucinations because of the isolation or because he *believes* he should be having hallucinations during such an experience?

pants, the behavior of the experimenter, the instructions, or the setting of the laboratory. Any of these demand characteristics could influence research findings. There are some classic examples in the literature.

In the 1950s, the topic of sensory deprivation was fashionable. In studies of this phenomenon, college students were paid $20 for a twenty-four-hour day of lying on cots in darkened, sound-deadened rooms. They wore translucent goggles that made sight impossible, gloves and cuffs that made feeling impossible, and they listened to masking noise that blocked hearing (Bexton, Heron, and Scott, 1954). The investigators found that the subjects had hallucinations, and that they also felt highly stressed, nauseated, agitated, and fatigued. Researchers concluded that removing vision, touch, and hearing for normal human subjects produced stress-induced hallucinations.

But in reviewing these sensory deprivation experiments, Martin Orne and his associates noticed something fishy about their design. There seemed to be some powerful demand characteristics: subjects were first greeted by a doctor in a white coat, a sign "Sensory Deprivation Laboratory" was on the door, the subjects had to sign awesome release forms absolving the experimenter of responsibility should any complications arise. There was even a panic button that would release the participant from the experiment if "anything undesirable should happen." Could it be that these trappings communicated to the subject that he was expected to be stressed, and perhaps to have hallucinations? This would mean that it was not the sensory deprivation but the demand characteristics that produced the experimental effect.

To test this, subjects were led into a room labeled "Memory Deprivation Laboratory," and they were greeted by a doctor in a white coat with a stethoscope. Awesome release forms were signed. Subjects were told that if the experiment proved to be too much for them, they could use the red panic button conspicuously installed in the wall of the experimental room. No sensory deprivation whatsoever was imposed on the subjects. Rather, they sat in a well-lighted room with two comfortable chairs, they were provided with ice water and sandwiches, and they were also given an optional task of adding numbers. In this situation, the subjects also reported stress-induced hallucinations, indicating that the demand characteristics and not the sensory deprivation may have caused the hallucinations (Orne, 1962).

STATISTICAL INFERENCE

How do we know that an experimental treatment really worked, that there is a meaningful difference between two diagnostic groups, or that a particular causal factor is really associated with a psychological problem? As we have emphasized in this chapter, it is important that our research designs are well controlled. But assuming experimental confounds have been ruled out, how do we interpret the results of scientific research? Imagine a situation in which most subjects in the experimental group show an effect, such as a reduction in symptoms, and only a few subjects in the control group do. How do we decide whether an effect is real rather than just a chance occurrence?

Statisticians have developed a set of procedures and ground rules to help researchers draw conclusions from their studies. **Inferential statistics** are the mathematical procedures used to decide whether the research findings are meaningful or more likely to have occurred by chance alone. Psychologists apply these procedures to data from **samples** of people who are drawn from a larger **population.** For example, a researcher might be interested in studying the nature of depression among college students. Depressed college students are the population of interest. Needless to say, the researcher cannot study the entire population; in this case *all* depressed college students. Instead, she will "sample" a group of students from the population. In doing so, her chief concern should be that the sample is representative of the population. This is another way of saying that the sample should be unbiased. If the researcher went to the weekly campus meeting of Phi Beta Kappa to recruit depressed college students for her study, she would not

get a representative sample of students. Most college students do not belong to Phi Beta Kappa. The sample of depressed students the researcher would recruit at a Phi Beta Kappa meeting would not be representative of the population of depressed students. Ideally, the researcher would like to recruit a **random sample** of depressed college students. When a sample is randomly selected, there is no bias. In this example, every depressed college student, those with stellar records as well as those who are failing, would have an equal chance of being in the sample.

Suppose we try out a new drug therapy on a sample of ten patients with schizophrenia, and at the end of a year, six of them show no symptoms of schizophrenia. We will operationally define the absence of symptoms as a recovery. Did the drug cause the recoveries, or would the patients have improved over time without the drug? To begin with, we need to compare the drug therapy group to a control group of patients with schizophrenia who were given placebos. Let's say we have an excellent control group: there are 100 wards in our hospital, each of which contains ten patients with schizophrenia who have been given placebos and are, therefore, untreated. On the average, across all 100 wards, three out of ten patients have recovered by the end of the year. Does the difference between six out of ten recoveries with the drug and an average of three out of ten recoveries with the placebo really mean anything? Or, could as many as six out of ten of the patients have recovered, untreated, by chance alone? If this were so, the new drug would be of little value. It is vital to decide this, for unless we can, we will not know if it is worthwhile to use the drug for the population of patients with schizophrenia as a whole.

To decide if the difference between six out of ten and three out of ten could have occurred by chance, we need to know the frequency distribution of recoveries from ward to ward. A **frequency distribution** is the number of occurrences in each given class observed; in this case, the number of wards showing no recoveries, one recovery, two recoveries, and so on (see Figure 2–7). This frequency distribution shows how different numbers of recoveries among the wards are distributed. We know that the average (that is, the total number of recoveries divided by the total number of patients) is three out of ten. But for how many of the other wards did six (or more) out of ten patients improve? With a mean of three out of ten, six could be a very infrequent occurrence. For example, if exactly three out of ten recovered in each and

Figure 2—7

FREQUENCY DISTRIBUTION

The frequency distribution graphically represents the spontaneous recovery of patients with schizophrenia. The graph shows the number of patients recovering without drug treatment out of ten patients in a given ward. Each bar represents the number of wards that had the particular number of recovering patients. The bars in gold show the wards in which six or more patients recovered without treatment.

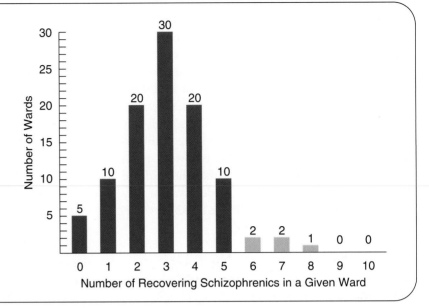

every ward, then six out of ten would be a rare occurrence. We might be tempted to conclude that our new drug treatment had some real advantages.

But don't jump to any conclusions yet. With a different distribution, six out of ten recoveries might be a very common occurrence. If six out of ten patients recovered in fifty of the wards, and zero out of ten recovered in the other fifty wards, the mean rate of recovery would still be three. But the frequency distribution would be *very* different. A recovery rate of six out of ten would be an extremely common event—nothing to get excited about. The effect produced by our new experimental drug would not be viewed as impressive. We would have very little confidence that the drug worked, and we might conclude that six out of ten recoveries was just a chance fluctuation in the recovery rate.

Scientists are taught to be very conservative about making claims. According to the guidelines of inferential statistics, a real "effect" is defined as one that would occur solely by chance *less than 5 percent of the time*. In other words, if our imaginary new drug treatment for schizophrenia had absolutely no effect on the disorder, then there would be a six out of ten recovery rate, by chance alone, less than 5 percent of the time. This can all be stated another way: a *statistically significant* effect can be claimed only when there is at least 95 percent confidence that

chance did not produce the result. When this conventional confidence level is exceeded, an *experimental effect* is inferred. By intention, the criteria used in inferential statistics are very stringent.

Making inferences in this way, however, can result in two kinds of mistakes: *misses* (saying X is false when it is true) and *false alarms* (saying X is true when it is false). Let's say the experimental drug is, in reality, very effective. But we don't know this, so we conduct a study. A miss can occur when, for example, confidence does not exceed the 95 percent level: say we are only confident at the 90 percent level that the number of drug recoveries was not due to chance. Thus, we reject the hypothesis that the drug is effective, and yet the drug really does reduce the symptoms of schizophrenia. We have missed a real cure by our conservative procedure.

On the other hand, imagine that the new experimental drug is actually no more effective than a placebo. But we don't know this, so we conduct a study. In this situation, a false alarm can occur when confidence does exceed the 95 percent level. So we accept the hypothesis that the drug causes recovery, but in reality, this is one of the 5 percent of the wards in which six people would have recovered without treatment. The drug is actually useless. Here, not being conservative enough caused us to draw a false conclusion. It is easy to see why scientists are only convinced by findings when they are replicated, preferably by several researchers.

EXPERIMENTS WITH A SINGLE SUBJECT

Most experiments involve an experimental group and a control group, each with several subjects. Several subjects, as opposed to one, increase our confidence in the causal inference we draw. There are two reasons why we can have greater confidence in group findings: (1) *repeatability*—the experimental manipulation is repeated because it has its effect on several individuals; and (2) *generalizability*—several randomly chosen individuals, not just one, show the effect, and this increases our confidence that any other person, randomly chosen, would also show the effect.

But despite the advantages of studying multiple research participants at one time, useful experiments can be carried out with just one subject. A very well-designed single-subject experiment can accomplish the goal of demonstrating repeatability. Jones and Friman (1999) conducted such an experiment on a young boy who had an insect phobia (entomophobia). They first observed the boy as follows:

> Mike, a 14-year-old boy who was enrolled at the middle school at Boys' Town, was referred by his school principal because the presence of insects in his classroom and taunts about insects seriously disrupted his academic performance. Mike reported that he had difficulty concentrating and working when he thought bugs might be present and that he was often teased by his peers (e.g. "Mike, there is a bug under your chair!"). His response to seeing an insect was ignoring his work, pulling the hood of his jacket over his head, or yelling. Mike identified crickets, spiders, and ladybugs as the insects that he feared most. (Jones and Friman, 1999)

Phobic stimuli can alter behavior in a number of ways. Jones and Friman decided to conduct a single-subject experiment on the effect of the phobia on Mike's academic performance, because that was the primary concern of his school principal.

> The dependent measure was Mike's work completion rate in the presence of crickets purchased from a local pet store. Two or three four-minute math probes were administered each session, during which Mike sat at a desk in a workroom with one of 30 alternate-form third-grade math sheets on the desk. Mike was instructed to complete as many problems as possible and his response rate was the mean number of correct digits per four-minute probe. (Jones and Friman, 1999)

Jones and Friman used two behavioral treatment conditions for their study: (1) graduated exposure, and (2) graduated exposure plus reinforcement. The graduated exposure condition involved a systematic strategy for getting Mike accustomed to the presence of bugs:

> Mike engaged in 15 to 20 minutes of graduated exposure exercises immediately before each math probe. These exercises included a hierarchy of behavioral approach tasks, ranging from holding a jar of crickets to holding a cricket in each hand for one minute. Mike selected the initial exposure level for each session and continued until he refused to proceed with the next step. Mike completed six steps with assistance during the first session, and independently completed nine steps by the final session of the exposure alone phase. Thereafter, time requirements were increased (e.g., holding a cricket for 40 seconds or 60 seconds). (Jones and Friman, 1999)

In the second treatment condition, graduated exposure plus reinforcement, Mike had the opportunity to gain a reward for his academic success:

> This phase was identical to the exposure condition except that Mike earned points for each correct digit. These points were exchanged at the end of each week for items from a reinforcement menu, including Blockbuster gift certificates, videos, candy, and Legos. (Jones and Friman, 1999)

For the baseline period and each experimental condition, the researchers recorded the number of math calculations completed during each four-minute period. The results are presented in Figure 2–8. The data in the first panel of the figure were collected during the baseline period. We can see that there were higher rates of correct digits in the no-bugs condition, relative to the other conditions. Thus, the bug phobia did interfere with Mike's performance. The level of performance was initially low in the

Figure 2—8

SINGLE-SUBJECT EXPERIMENT

A boy with an insect phobia was treated using a multielement design. The mean number of correct calculations per 4-minute probe was assessed in **A** (baseline measure, before treatment, for three conditions: no bugs, talking about bugs, and holding a jar of bugs), **B** (graduated exposure treatment), **BC** (graduated exposure treatment followed by reinforcement, including video gift certificates, videos, candy, and Legos), **A** (baseline measure, no treatment), and **BC** (graduated exposure treatment followed by reinforcement). (Source: Jones and Friman, 1999, p. 97).

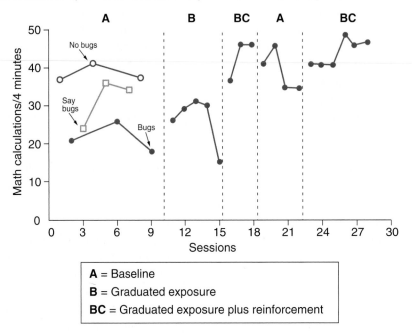

A = Baseline
B = Graduated exposure
BC = Graduated exposure plus reinforcement

"say bugs condition" but increased rapidly. This indicates that Mike became accustomed to verbal statements about bugs fairly quickly. In the "bugs" condition, where Mike actually saw bugs, the rate of calculations was consistently low. In the second panel, the graduated exposure condition, there was no improvement. But significant improvement occurred when graduated exposure was combined with reinforcement. The removal of both the reinforcement and exposure resulted in a modest decline in scores, but there was a rebound when the graduated exposure and reinforcement was started again. These results indicate that rewarding "on task" behavior was very effective. But what about exposure? Was it necessary? The study doesn't give us any clues about that.

It could be that Mike was unique in the way he responded to the intervention. Most other phobic boys might not improve with attention to constructive behavior. Only repeating the procedure with several other children would show generalizability. When there is only one subject available, however, as in a rare disorder or unique therapy, single-subject designs are an ideal way of determining causality.

EVALUATION OF THE EXPERIMENTAL METHOD

Laboratory models have two strengths: (1) as experiments, they can isolate the cause of the disorder, and (2) they are repeatable. Like all other methods, they also have several weaknesses: (1) as laboratory creations, they are not the natural phenomenon, only a model of it. Thus, they are analogous to, but not identical with, the real disorder itself; (2) since observers often use animal subjects in laboratory models, they must infer that humans and the species being investigated are similarly susceptible to the disorder. This may or may not be a correct assumption. In humans, we can manipulate potentially helpful treatments, but we cannot manipulate factors that might cause serious psychopathology. Performing certain experiments may be unethical, or simply impractical. In later chapters, we will see examples of models that have given insight into the cause and cure of such disorders as depression and phobias. Sophisticated laboratory modeling is a new development in the field of abnormality. The verdict is not entirely in on any one model, but the technique promises to add to our understanding of abnormality.

Experiments of Nature

Nature sometimes performs an experimental manipulation that scientists themselves could not do because of ethical or practical considerations. Usually these are striking events that change peoples' lives. Such an occurrence is an **experiment of nature,** in short, a study in which the experimenter observes the effects of an unusual natural event. An alert investigator can use these events to make inferences about what causes psychological problems.

Of course, ethical concerns (if not practical considerations) prevent scientists from intentionally subjecting humans to traumatic stress. But because knowledge about the effects of trauma is so important to the study of abnormality, scientists sometimes visit the scenes of natural disasters to observe the effects of such experiments of nature. One such study looked at the effects of Hurricane Andrew,

Psychologists study natural disasters such as the aftereffects of this tornado in Alabama to observe how people cope with the effects of traumatic stress. This is considered an experiment of nature.

which struck Florida in 1992 (Bahrick, Fraser, Fivush, and Levitt, 1998). The researchers wanted to know whether the severity of the stress the children had experienced during the hurricane was related to their memories for the events. They found that children who had experienced moderate levels of stress had the most detailed memories of their experiences in the hurricane. Those who had experienced very little disruption in their lives, as well as those who had experienced extreme disruption (for example, they had lost their home), recalled less. These findings fit with the assumption that the relationship between memory and stress level is like an inverted "U": moderate levels of stress can enhance memory, but extreme levels will impair memory. Other studies of the victims of natural disasters have also found evidence of cognitive deficits, higher rates of physical illness and suicide, and increased levels of the stress hormone, cortisol (Krug et al., 1998; Rotton et al., 1997).

Experiments of nature can also tell us about the factors that help people cope with stress. One investigation focused on adult men with HIV infection who were exposed to a hurricane. The investigators found that men with higher levels of coping ability showed less emotional distress and post-traumatic stress disorder (PTSD) after the hurricane. In addition, greater coping ability was associated with a less pronounced biological response to the hurricane in the HIV-infected men (Benight et al., 1997).

An experiment of nature is usually *retrospective,* with interviews of the subjects beginning after the precipitating event. But experiments of nature can also be *prospective,* with observation beginning before an expected outcome occurs. When prospective studies are *longitudinal* as well, looking at the same subjects on the same variables at different points over their lifetime, they are particularly powerful methods of investigation (Baltes, Reese, and Lipsitt, 1980). Suzanne King and her colleagues at McGill University, for example, designed a prospective longitudinal experiment of nature to study how maternal exposure to significant stress during pregnancy affects the development of children (King et al., 1999). In 1998, there was a major winter ice storm in Montreal, Canada, that resulted in loss of electrical power, gas, and water for many people. It lasted for almost two weeks. Power lines were down, water pipes broke, trees fell, and many buildings were damaged. Livestock died, and food production suffered. Travel was extremely hazardous, yet many could not stay in their homes because they had no heat and temperatures were sub-zero. Some moved to hotels, or to the homes of friends or relatives who did have heat. Others suffered through the dark, cold nights. Following this natural disaster, Dr. King and her colleagues began to draw up a plan to locate all women who were pregnant during that time period. Using hospital and clinic records, the researchers were able to locate a group of over 200 women who had either been pregnant at the time of the storm or became pregnant within three months afterward. Some of the pregnant women lived in the most severely affected areas and experienced a high level of stress during the ice storm, whereas others lived in areas that were minimally affected. The researchers plan to follow the infant offspring of these mothers through early childhood to determine whether the mothers' experiences during pregnancy are associated with the child's physical, cognitive, and behavioral development. As we will describe in Chapter 4, animal research has shown that pregnant females exposed to stress have offspring who have a variety of developmental problems, including an exaggerated biological response to stress. Will the same hold true for humans? The Montreal study will help us answer this question.

EVALUATION OF EXPERIMENTS OF NATURE

Experiments of nature have three strengths as a method of inquiry: (1) like a case history, they document an actual happening and lack artificiality as opposed to a planned laboratory experiment, (2) no unethical manipulation is performed, and (3) the general event that caused the outcome is identified. In fact, the general cause defines the investigation as an experiment of nature. But the method also has three weaknesses: (1) we cannot isolate the specific elements in the event that are causative from those that have no impact; for example, we cannot know which aspects—the suddenness of a disaster, seeing others die, or the uprooting of a community—produce the psychological reactions; (2) experiments of nature, as they are rare, natural events, are not repeatable; and (3) this method is subject to retrospective bias by both victim and investigator.

Comparative Studies

Despite the power of the experimental method, much of the research conducted on abnormal human behavior is *nonexperimental*. The researcher does not directly manipulate any factors. Therefore, compared with true experimental studies, nonexperimental research does not allow us to draw firm conclusions about causality. Nonetheless, the ultimate goals of experimental and nonexperimental research are the same: to find out whether *A* causes *B*. Nonexperimental research studies can help us in this endeavor. They can tell us a great deal about relationships among factors, and this is often the first step in understanding causality. Comparative and correlational studies are the most common approaches in research on abnormal psychology.

Comparative studies contrast two or more groups. Typically, the objective is to find out how people with a particular symptom or disorder differ from individuals with no disorder or some other psychological disorder. Using this method, researchers have attempted to answer a broad range of questions dealing with the psychological, developmental, and biological aspects of various syndromes.

For example, when adults who suffer from depression and certain kinds of personality disorders are compared to those who do not have the disorders, it has been found that they are more likely to have been exposed to childhood abuse (Weiss, Longhurst, and Mazure, 1999; Zlotnick, 1999). This fits well with some current theories about the origins of adult disorders. And at the biological level of analysis, when autistic children are compared to normal children or children with other disorders, investigators find that those with autism show more brain abnormalities than do the other children (Rapin, 1999).

In comparative studies, the grouping variable is referred to as the independent variable, and the dependent variable is the one that is hypothesized to differ among the groups. In this case, the independent variable would be the particular disorder that was diagnosed (depression or autism), and the dependent variable would be child abuse or brain abnormality. As with experimental studies, the data from comparative studies are analyzed with inferential statistics. The researcher uses specific guidelines to decide whether the results of the study justify the conclusion that there is a real difference between the diagnostic groups. The conclusion that there is a real difference will only be drawn when the probability of finding a particular difference by chance alone is *very* low.

It is easy to see how the findings of comparative studies, such as those described above, can contribute to our understanding of abnormal psychology. Yet, there are limitations. Did the childhood physical abuse cause the adult disorder? Did the brain abnormality cause the autism? We cannot answer either of these questions with any sense of certainty. It is possible that adults with personality disorders had more behavioral problems as children. These problems may have caused their parents to punish them more often and more severely than other children. Using the same line of reasoning, the autistic disorder may have existed before the brain abnormality. Perhaps autistic children are more likely to engage in risky behaviors that result in injuries to the head.

The researcher does not manipulate the independent variable in a comparative study. As a result, conclusions about causality cannot be drawn with any sense of confidence. But we can conclude that there is a relationship between the independent variable (diagnostic group) and the dependent variable (child abuse or brain abnormality). Demonstrating a relationship is no small matter—it can lead to major scientific breakthroughs.

Correlational Studies

Correlational studies are also concerned with the relationship between two or more factors. The researcher looks at relationships as they exist in the real world, without manipulating any independent variable. Let's label the two variables we are studying as *X* and *Y*. There are three possible relationships between *X* and *Y*. First, as *X* increases, so does *Y*. This is called *positive correlation.* If we are studying the relation of height *(X)* and weight *(Y)* in 100 college sophomores, for example, we would find that height *(X)* correlates positively with weight *(Y)*, for the taller a person is, generally the more he weighs. This correlation is shown graphically in Figure 2–9A. The second possibility is that as *X* increases, *Y* decreases. This is called a *negative correlation.* We would not expect height and weight to be negatively correlated. But we would expect study time *(X)* and test errors *(Y)* to be negatively correlated. Studying is, in general, negatively correlated with errors on tests, because the more we study, the fewer mistakes we are likely to make (Figure 2–9B). The third possibility is that there is no relationship between the two variables. As one changes, the other does not change in any systematic way. Two such events are said to be unrelated or *uncorrelated.* As an illustration, we would expect hair length to be uncorrelated with failure on algebra exams, for how long our hair is, in general, makes no difference as to whether or not we fail (Figure 2–9C). The central point here is that in correlational studies, we are observers of the variables; we do not manipulate weight, height, hair length, studying, or failure. Instead, we measure and examine the relationships among the variables.

Let us now see how correlation can be applied to important issues of abnormal psychology by working through an example of a negative correlation. One famous psychologist proposed an elegantly simple theory of human depression: that depression is caused by having too few rewards in daily life (Lewinsohn, 1975). Experimentation on this is limited by ethical considerations: we cannot take nondepressed people and withhold rewards in their daily lives to see if depression results. But we can examine relationships among variables: does depth of depression correlate with the number of pleasant activities

Figure 2—9

CORRELATIONS

Here are three scatterplots illustrating a positive correlation (A), a negative correlation (B), and a lack of correlation (C). The positive correlation indicates that taller individuals tend to weigh more. The negative correlation indicates that individuals who study less tend to fail more. The lack of correlation indicates no relationship between hair length and failure on algebra exams.

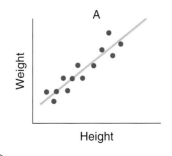

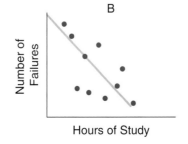

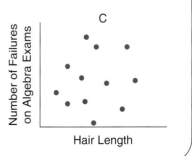

that different individuals engage in? The experimenter predicted a negative correlation: as pleasant activities decrease, the degree of depression increases. Both variables can be operationally defined and measured. Degree of depression can be measured by a self-report test (the Beck Depression Inventory), which totals up the number and severity of mood, thought, motivational, and physical symptoms of depression. Daily life rewards can be measured by the Pleasant Events Scale, which totals up the number of pleasant events, such as going on a date, listening to music, watching TV, dancing, that the individual has recently engaged in. The predicted negative correlation was found: the higher the degree of depression, the fewer pleasant events the person engaged in.

CORRELATION COEFFICIENTS

We have talked about the nature of the relationship between two variables: positive, negative, or unrelated. But what about the strength of the relationship between variables? How is this measured? The strength of the relationship between two variables can be expressed by a ***correlation coefficient,*** the symbol for which is *r* (representing the Pearson Product Moment Correlation Coefficient, which is named after its inventor, Karl Pearson). The range for *r* is as follows: *r* can be as great as +1.00, for a perfect positive correlation; it can vary through 0.00, meaning no relationship at all; and it can go down to −1.00 for a perfect negative correlation. The *r* for depression scores and pleasant activities turns out to be −.87, a strong negative correlation. The level of confidence that the relation did not occur by chance, or its statistical significance, is determined for *r* to see if a real relationship exists. In general, the farther the correlation coefficient is from .00, in either the positive or negative direction, and the more observations or subjects there are, the higher is our confidence that the relationship did not occur by chance. Conventionally, the 95 percent level of confidence is chosen to define statistical significance.

CORRELATION AND CAUSALITY

The main disadvantage of the correlational approach is that finding a strong correlation does not mean that we have discovered a cause. As an illustration, consider the negative correlation between pleasant events and depression. There are really three causal possibilities in this relationship: (1) engaging in only a few pleasant activities might cause depression;

(2) depression itself might cause people to engage in fewer pleasant activities; for example, perhaps depression blunts the desire to be social; and (3) both depression and lower activity could be caused by some third variable that was not measured. As an example, some biochemical imbalance might cause both depression and lack of interest in pleasurable activities. In general, when there is a correlation between *X* and *Y*, it can be either that *X* causes *Y*, that *Y* causes *X*, or that *Z* causes both *X* and *Y*.

But there are some exceptions. One exception occurs when variables are separated in time. For example, positive correlations have been found between the number of major life events, such as divorce and job loss, and illness in the following year; the more life events before, the more illnesses after (Holmes and Rahe, 1967). Here, temporal sequence narrows the possibilities of cause from three to two: a hassled life could produce illness, or some third variable, like unstable personality, could produce both more illness and more life events, but the hypothesis that the illness causes the increases in life events is ruled out. Another situation in which a significant correlation suggests something about causality involves relationships between certain physical characteristics and life experience. Imagine we show, for example, that height is positively correlated with the number of times high school boys are asked if they play on the basketball team. We would, of course, rule out the possibility that being asked the question caused the boys to grow. It is also unlikely that some third unmeasured variable produced the relation. The most plausible and simplest explanation is that height determines whether or not a boy will be asked if he plays basketball.

In most cases, correlational studies can offer sound guidance for an investigator's next step. This next step might be further correlational studies, or it might be an experiment. For example, an experiment has actually been done to test causation for the depression example above. In this experiment, depressed students were induced to increase the number of pleasant events they engaged in each day. Depressed students who increased their activities did not become any less depressed than the control group of depressed students, who did not change their activity level; rather they became more depressed (Hammen and Glass, 1975). So the fact that activity and depression correlate negatively does not seem to reflect a causal relationship. Having few rewards probably does not cause depression, rather depression either causes individuals to engage in fewer rewarding activities, or both are caused by an unobserved third variable. We infer this because the number of pleasant activities has been experimentally manipulated, yet depression has not been alleviated.

EVALUATION OF THE CORRELATIONAL METHOD

Despite the limitations, especially the inability of this method to isolate the cause of a relationship, we should not overlook the advantages to correlational studies of abnormality. The correlational approach allows a quantitative and rigorous observation of relations among variables. Also, because the observations are on natural phenomena, correlational studies do not have the artificiality of laboratory studies. Further, they can easily be reproduced. Correlational studies are the best option when performing an experiment is not a possibility, whether for practical or for ethical reasons.

Epidemiological Studies

Since the advent of operational diagnostic criteria (in DSM-III and DSM-IV), a concerted effort has been made in the United States and Europe to determine just how much mental illness exists. The initial purpose of these studies was practical: by determining the rate of occurrence of the various disorders, training and therapeutic resources could be allocated in a rational way. If there turned out to be a great deal of depression, for example, programs could be mounted to train more therapists to treat depressed patients, better antidepressant drugs could be developed, more money could be spent on research into the etiology of depression and to learn how to prevent depression.

In the best studies, such as the Epidemiologic Catchment Area (ECA) study (Robins et al., 1984) and the National Comorbidity Study (Kessler et al., 1994), trained diagnosticians went door to door to a representative sample of almost ten thousand individuals, and administered detailed structured diagnostic interviews. The disorders studied had clear operational definitions. The most important statistic they gathered was on the *lifetime prevalence* of each major disorder; that is, the proportion of people in a sample who have ever experienced that particular disorder.

Table 2–2 presents the lifetime prevalence for the major disorders based on data from three of the main sites of the ECA study. As you can see, the estimated prevalence rates of mental disorder are alarmingly high—with around one-third of the people in America suffering at least one major disorder in their lifetime. But recent studies have raised some questions

TABLE 2–2

Data

LIFETIME PREVALENCE RATES (PERCENT) OF DISORDERS

Disorders	New Haven (N = 3,058)	Baltimore (N = 3,481)	St. Louis (N = 3,004)
Any disorder	28.8	38.0	31.0
Substance use disorders	15.0	17.0	18.1
Alcohol use/dependence	11.5	13.7	15.7
Drug abuse/dependence	5.8	5.6	5.5
Schizophrenia	1.9	1.6	1.0
Affective disorders	9.5	6.1	8.0
Manic episode	1.1	0.6	1.1
Major depressive episode	6.7	3.7	5.5
Dysthymia	3.2	2.1	3.8
Anxiety/somatoform disorders	10.4	25.1	11.1
Phobia	7.8	23.3	9.4
Panic	1.4	1.4	1.5
Obsessive-compulsive	2.6	3.0	1.9
Somatization	0.1	0.1	0.1
Anorexia	0.0	0.1	0.1
Antisocial personality	2.1	2.6	3.3
Cognitive impairment (severe)	1.3	1.3	1.0

SOURCE: Robins et al., 1984.

TABLE 2-3

Data

DEMOGRAPHIC CORRELATES (ODDS RATIOS) OF LIFETIME DISORDERS

	Any Affective Disorder	Any Anxiety Disorder	Any Substance-Use Disorder
Sex			
Male	1.00	1.00	1.00
Female	1.82	1.85	0.40
Age			
15–24	0.85	1.13	1.36
25–34	0.97	1.13	1.99
35–44	1.06	1.05	1.58
45–54	1.00	1.00	1.00
Race			
White	1.00	1.00	1.00
Black	0.63	0.77	0.35
Hispanic	0.96	0.90	0.80
Income, $			
0–19,000	1.56	2.00	1.27
20,000–34,000	1.19	1.52	1.06
35,000–69,000	1.16	1.48	1.06
≥70,000	1.00	1.00	1.00
Education (years)			
0–11	0.98	1.86	0.99
12	1.00	1.76	1.25
13–15	1.05	1.44	1.20
≥16	1.00	1.00	1.00
Urbanicity			
Major metropolitan	1.26	0.98	1.09
Other urban	1.20	1.00	1.10
Rural	1.00	1.00	1.00

SOURCE: Kessler et al., 1994.

about the reliability of the diagnostic procedures used in the ECA study (Eaton, Neufeld, Chen, and Cai, 2000). About twelve years after the ECA interviews were conducted, researchers went back and interviewed a randomly selected sample of the ECA participants a second time. When they examined the agreement between lifetime diagnoses of depression from the first and second interviews, the results were not encouraging: 33 percent of those who were diagnosed with depression in 1981 were classified as having no history of depression based on the second interview. Part of the problem was that many people failed to recall symptoms they had reported during the first interview. These results highlight the challenges that researchers face when they are trying to come up with accurate estimates of the lifetime prevalence of mental disorders. The findings also indicate that we should view data on prevalence rates as "best estimates," rather than solid facts.

The National Comorbidity Study focused less on estimating overall prevalence rates, and instead it concentrated on differences among groups (see Table 2–3). In this study, the researchers sampled 8,098 Americans and examined the influence of sex, race, income, education, and "urbanicity" on the various disorders. The data on relative risk were presented in "odds ratios" (OR), where 1.00 equaled no increased risk, numbers greater than 1.00 equaled increased risk, and numbers lower than 1.00 equaled decreased risk. Being female markedly increased risk for anxiety and depression, and markedly decreased risk for substance use. Being black lowered risk for anxiety and substance-use disorders, particularly alcoholism. Being poor increased risk for all disorders, and living in a city increased risk for depression and substance abuse.

One of the largest studies of national differences in the rates of mental disorder was conducted by

Myrna Weissman and her colleagues (Weissman et al., 1997). Although some cross-cultural differences were found in the prevalence of certain disorders, the differences were not large. The annual rate of panic disorder, for example, ranges from 2.9 percent in Florence, Italy, to .4 percent in Taiwan. Cross-national diffferences in mental disorders tend to be even smaller for the more serious illnesses, like schizophrenia.

Putting It All Together

A thorough diagnostic assessment of an individual who is experiencing psychological problems requires a multilevel approach. It is important to know about the person's current living situation, physical health, and psychological symptoms. This information can be obtained from interviews, physical examinations, and reviews of past medical records. In some cases, standardized psychological tests will be administered to get an in-depth picture of the person's mental status. By combining information from all of these sources, clinicians hope to be able to make an accurate diagnosis.

Diagnosis plays an important part in the treatment of mental disorders, as well as in research on their causes. The most commonly used diagnostic classification systems for mental disorders, the ICD and DSM, take a categorical approach. In other words, based on the nature and severity of the person's symptoms, he either does or does not meet the criteria for the disorder. Some have criticized the DSM on the grounds that it is of questionable reliability and validity. But critics need not fear that the DSM will remain as it is. We can anticipate another revision, DSM-V, to appear before 2003. We hope that the new revision will move us a step closer to more reliable and valid diagnoses.

Clinical researchers rely on diagnostic schemes to identify samples for their studies. But, at the same time, scientific research yields information that results in changes in existing diagnostic procedures. A wide variety of research approaches are used to study abnormal behavior. Clinical case histories, experimental studies with animals (laboratory models) and humans, experiments of nature, comparative studies, correlational studies, and epidemiological studies can all provide some insight. Each research method has strengths and weaknesses (Table 2–4). Each by itself can, on occasion, provide very convincing evidence.

TABLE 2–4

STRENGTHS AND WEAKNESSES OF VARIOUS METHODS

Method	Strengths	Weaknesses
Single Clinical Case	1. Is not artificial. 2. Documents rare events. 3. Generates causal hypotheses.	1. Is selective and susceptible to retrospective bias. 2. Is not repeatable. 3. Lacks generalizability. 4. Does not isolate causal elements.
Experiments	1. Isolate causal elements. 2. Are general to population sampled (not true of single-subject experiments). 3. Are repeatable.	1. Are artificial; do not capture full reality of the disorder. 2. Inferences are probabilistic or statistical, rather than certain. 3. It is unethical or impractical to manipulate many crucial variables.
Experiments of Nature	1. Are not artificial. 2. There is no unethical manipulation. 3. Isolate gross cause.	1. Do not isolate active elements of the cause. 2. Are not repeatable. 3. Are susceptible to retrospective bias.
Comparative Studies	1. Statistical analysis of relationships. 2. Are not artificial. 3. Are repeatable.	1. Do not isolate causal elements.
Correlations	1. Quantify and observe relationships. 2. Are not artificial. 3. Are repeatable.	1. Do not isolate causal elements.

But most of the time, each taken in isolation resembles blind men groping at an elephant: one has hold of the tail, another the trunk, another a foot. Each captures only one aspect of being an elephant, but none captures the whole thing.

The clinical case history method, when done properly, best conveys the natural development of a disorder, but it usually fails to isolate the cause. The experiment, when conducted properly, isolates the cause, but it remains artificial. Comparative and correlational studies identify crucial relationships, but not necessarily causal ones. But when the findings from several methods converge on the same conclusion, a fabric of understanding is woven. A scientific fabric of converging evidence has already been woven for phobias, for the genetics of schizophrenia, for depression, and for certain kinds of brain damage. For some of the specific disorders that we will discuss in subsequent chapters, the reader will see that much still remains to be discovered before the disorder can be understood. For most others, the reader probably will feel that they are partially understood, but that pieces of the puzzle are still missing.

Summary

1. Psychological assessment techniques may be divided into three processes: interviewing, observing, and testing. Assessment devices must be reliable and valid. *Reliability* refers to the stability of a measure, whether it yields the same findings with repeated use. *Validity* refers to how useful the device is, whether it can be used for the purposes for which it is intended.

2. The *clinical interview* may be structured and have standardized questions, or it may be unstructured and therefore more flexible.

3. *Behavioral assessment* is based mainly on observation. It consists of a record of the patient's behavior and thoughts—their incidence, duration, and intensity. Behavioral observation is often used in conjunction with treatment.

4. Psychological tests fall into four categories: *psychological inventories* such as the MMPI and the MMPI-2; *projective tests,* including the Rorschach and the TAT; *intelligence tests;* and *neuropsychological tests* such as the Luria-Nebraska and the Halstead-Reitan, which assess a variety of cognitive and motor skills that are known to involve

various regions of the brain. All of these tests are used in various clinical settings to assess mental functions.

5. *Neuroimaging* technologies, such as *PET* (positron emission tomography) scans and *MRI* (magnetic resonance imaging), involve visualization of brain abnormalities that may be relevant to behavior. Neuropsychological assessment and neuroimaging are complementary approaches.

6. *Diagnosis* is the categorization of psychological disorders according to behavioral or psychological patterns. Five reasons for making a diagnosis are: it indicates a syndrome, suggests treatments that may alleviate symptoms, suggests causes of the symptoms, is an aid to scientific investigation of symptoms, and enables third-party payments for clinical services.

7. DSM-IV is a multidimensional diagnostic system. It seeks to provide specific and operational diagnostic criteria for each mental disorder. Within DSM-IV, there are five dimensions, or axes, to classify a disorder and to help plan treatment and predict outcome.

8. When two psychologists arrive at the same assessment of a patient, there is said to be *inter-judge* or *inter-rater reliability*. The reliability of the various diagnostic categories in DSM-IV differs, with the Axis II disorder showing the least inter-rater and inter-judge reliability. The reliability of its progenitor, DSM-III, is only fair.

9. For diagnostic categories, *validity* refers to whether a particular set of diagnostic criteria successfully differentiates patients in one category from those in another. *Outcome* or *predictive validity* refers to whether the diagnosis tells something about the future course of the disorder, what gave rise to the disorder, and whether the disorder will respond to treatment.

10. Reliability is reduced by factors that bias diagnoses. The accuracy and usefulness of a diagnosis may be compromised by the *context* in which it occurs and by the *expectations* and *credibility* of the diagnosticians and their informants.

11. Diagnosis and assessment are fundamental to treatment and necessary for scientific advancement. However, that does not mean that every assessment is useful or necessary. Some diagnoses may be useful for scientific purposes, but relatively useless for clinical ones.

12. The *clinical case history* is the record of part of the life of an individual. Information for the case

history is usually obtained when the person appears for treatment. Based on the patient's case history, the clinician will hypothesize about possible causes of the problem. Often case histories set the stage for more extensive, systematic research on a particular disorder.

13. A *scientific experiment* consists of a procedure in which the hypothesized cause (the *independent variable*) is manipulated and the occurrence of the effect (the *dependent variable*) is measured. Both independent and dependent variables are operationally defined. An *operational definition* is a very precise description of an event or condition, one that is clear enough that the event or condition can be reproduced by other researchers. When the manipulation of an independent variable produces changes in a dependent variable, an *experimental effect* has been produced.

14. In a *laboratory model,* investigators produce, under controlled conditions, phenomena that are analogous to naturally occurring mental disorders. This is done to test hypotheses about biological and psychological causes and cures of symptoms.

15. *Confounds* are factors other than the independent variable that might produce an experimental effect. An experimental group experiences both the confounds and the hypothesized cause. The *control group* is similar to the *experimental group,* but the control group only experiences the confounds. Subtle confounds that might produce the experimental effect include non-random assignment, experimenter bias, subject bias, and demand characteristics.

16. *Statistical inferences* are the procedures used to determine whether the *sample* truly represents the *population.* When effects exceed a conventional confidence level, they are called *statistically significant.*

17. A relationship is *statistically significant* if it is unlikely to have occurred by chance. Generally, the farther the correlation is from .00 in either the positive or negative direction, and the more observations that are made, the higher the level of confidence and the greater the likelihood that the relationship did not occur by chance.

18. *Comparative studies* contrast a clinical group with a comparison group, usually comprised of individuals with no mental or physical disorder.

19. *Correlation* is pure observation without manipulation. In a correlation, two classes of events are measured, and the relationship between them is recorded. In a *positive correlation,* as one variable increases, the other does too. In a *negative correlation,* as one variable increases, the other decreases. Events are *uncorrelated* when, as one variable changes, the other does not change in any systematic way.

20. *Epidemiological* data concerning the *lifetime prevalence* of disorders can be used to make inferences about the etiology of the disorder as well.

21. *Experiments of nature* are studies in which the experimenter observes the effects of an unusual natural event. Prospective longitudinal studies are a powerful means of assessing the effects of events on the development of psychopathology.

22. No one assessment method alone will provide complete understanding of psychopathology. But each method may lead us to an understanding of various aspects of abnormality. When all these methods converge in confirmation of a theory, we can say that scientific progress has been made.

Psychological Approaches

Paul Goesch, *Traumphantasie (Dream Fantasy)*.

Learning Objectives

→ Familiarize yourself with the psychodynamic approach, particularly with Freud's concepts of the id, ego, and superego, and be able to describe how conflict between them can give rise to defense mechanisms to cope with underlying anxiety.

→ Learn how the existential and humanistic approaches stress the importance of freedom and choice to psychological health, and how existential therapists help patients to assume responsibility, set goals, and become independent.

→ Be able to describe the basic concepts of Pavlovian conditioning and operant conditioning, and such behavioral treatments as exposure, systematic desensitization, selective positive reinforcement, selective punishment, and extinction.

→ Understand how the cognitive approach emphasizes the importance of thoughts and beliefs, and how cognitive therapists try to change negative expectations, attributions, and beliefs.

→ Be able to explain why the cognitive and behavioral approaches are compatible and the treatment known as cognitive-behavioral therapy.

→ Learn how some theorists are combining cognitive-behavioral therapy with psychodynamics, and how others are combining it with neuroscience.

→ Be able to explain how each kind of therapy can address different aspects of disorders and build different strengths in patients.

A t the present time, there are only two serious levels of analysis of abnormality: the psychological and the biological approaches. In this chapter, we will take up the four main psychological approaches to abnormality. We categorize these four traditions—the psychodynamic, the existential and humanistic, the behavioral, and the cognitive—as psychological approaches because each of them seeks to explain both normal and disordered behavior by underlying mental and behavioral principles. We will consider each of these traditions and examples of the therapies that arise from them. Finally, we will consider how psychologists can integrate these various approaches, using them to treat different aspects of a disorder. To illustrate each approach, we will look at how a therapist from each of the four traditions would treat the very same person:

Angela, twenty-two years old, lived at home with her mother and was a secretary in a large insurance company. She was troubled with crying spells and despondency, of much greater severity than the blues she used to have frequently. She could not concentrate on her job, her future seemed empty to her, she could not get to sleep at night, and food did not interest her. Angela had a clear case of unipolar depression.

Her depression began when she and Jerry broke up. After months of turmoil in which she could not make her mind up about whether to marry Jerry, he demanded an answer. Her mother hated Jerry and urged her to break it off. Caught in the middle, Angela could not decide. After several more fights, Jerry told her that he believed she would string him along forever, and he had made up his mind never to see her again.

Angela said that she was relieved that Jerry had made the decision for her, and she did not attempt to contact him. But over the next month, she became more and more despairing. She stayed home from work several times and just sat around the house and cried. (Adapted from Leon, 1990, Chapter 15).

The Psychodynamic Approach

The *psychodynamic approach* to personality and abnormality is concerned with the psychological forces that—consciously and unconsciously—influence the

Sigmund Freud (1856–1939) in 1909.

mind. These inner desires and motives are forces that often collide. The "dynamic" part of "psychodynamic" means that when a collision of such forces occurs, some change must happen as a result. According to this approach, when these conflicts are well resolved, they produce growth and vigor. But when they are poorly resolved, or remain unresolved, the conflicts generate anxiety and unhappiness, against which people try to defend themselves. Here we examine some of the causes and consequences of conflict and the conditions that lead to its resolution, for better or for worse.

The psychodynamic approach to personality and abnormality began with the work of a single towering genius—a Viennese physician named Sigmund Freud. Born in 1856, Freud produced some twenty-four volumes of theoretical observations and case histories before he died in 1939. His own method of

studying and changing personality, as well as those of his students, is called **psychoanalysis.**

Throughout his life, Freud's consuming intellectual and clinical passion was with **psychic energy.** He assumed that people are endowed with a fixed amount of psychic energy. For this reason, the approach is also called "psychodynamic," to embody the premise that emotion is energy—if suppressed in one realm, it will emerge in another, often unwelcome, realm. Why is it, the theory asks, that sometimes people seem to be vigorous and full of life, while at other times they seem listless? How is it that some people devote their energies to love and work, while others are largely concerned with their aches and pains?

Id, Ego, and Superego

According to Freud, human personality is structured by three kinds of forces: the id, the ego, and the superego (see Table 3–1). These are neither objects nor places in the mind. Rather, they are dynamic and interactive processes, with their own origins and specific roles. The word "id" originates from the German "es," literally meaning "it," and connotes processes that seem to lie outside of an individual's control. "Ego" in German means "ich" or "I," and designates those capacities that enable a person to cope with reality, while "superego" (in German "Uberich" or "over I") describes those processes that transcend the self—conscience, ideals, and morals.

The **id** represents raw and urgent biological drives. The id clamors for immediate gratification. It is guided by the **pleasure principle,** which demands immediate impulse gratification and tension reduction. The id is like a spoiled child. It wants what

TABLE 3–1

THREE PROCESSES OF PERSONALITY

Process	Principle	Reality Concerns?	Characteristics
Id	Pleasure principle	No	Aims to achieve immediate gratification of biological drives
Ego	Reality principle	Yes	Directs impulses toward targets that are appropriate and that can be achieved
Superego	(Idealism)	No	Directs actions toward morality, religion, ideals

it wants when it wants it. The id seeks external gratification, and id drives know nothing of appropriateness, or even danger. If people were wholly dominated by id processes, they would, like spoiled children, eat any food when they were hungry, regardless of whether it was theirs, good for them, or even still alive.

Whereas the id seeks pleasure, the *ego* seeks reality. One function of the ego is to express and gratify the desires of the id, but in accordance with the requirements of reality. While the id operates on the pleasure principle, the ego utilizes the *reality principle.* It tests reality to determine whether the expression of an impulse is safe or dangerous. It delays the impulses of the id until the time is right, and it tries to divert those impulses toward appropriate targets. The ego's success in enabling impulses to be realistically and safely gratified depends on its ability to use thought processes like reasoning, remembering, evaluating, and planning. The ego is the executive of the personality, carrying out the demands of the id in such a way as to minimize negative consequences.

Lastly, the *superego* represents both conscience and idealistic striving. Nonetheless, superego processes are just as irrational as id processes; neither cares or knows much about reality. Conscience can be overly harsh, suppressing not only permissible behaviors, but even the very thought of those behaviors. Whereas the person whose id processes are relatively uncontrolled seems impulse-ridden, the person who is overly dominated by his or her superego seems wooden and moralistic, unable to be comfortable with pleasure and overly sensitive to "Thou shalt not. . . ."

The processes that regulate normal personality and development are identical to those that regulate abnormal personality. What distinguishes normal from abnormal personality is the manner in which psychic energy is distributed between the three components of personality. In normal personality, psychic energy is strongly invested in ego processes, as well as those of the id and superego. In abnormal personality, psychic energy is distributed improperly, with the result that either the id or the superego is too strong, and ego processes are unable to control desire or conscience.

Freud believed that much of the interaction among the id, ego, and superego goes on at an *unconscious level,* which includes both forgotten memories and repressed memories (those actively barred from consciousness). Certain personality processes operate more at the unconscious level than do others. Id impulses are entirely unconscious, as are many superego processes. In contrast, ego processes, because they must mediate between desire, conscience, and reality, are often conscious.

Anxiety and Defense Mechanisms

Conflicts among the id, ego, and superego regularly give rise to a kind of psychic pain that Freud termed *anxiety.* Anxiety can be conscious or unconscious, and its presence is always a signal that conflict is at hand. When the conflict causes the person to feel overwhelmed, helpless, and unable to cope, anxiety arises. The degree of anxiety that a person experiences depends on the anticipated consequences to self.

The experience of anxiety, even the anticipation of anxiety, is an uncomfortable experience that people try to relieve immediately. Humans are particularly well endowed with strategies for alleviating anxiety. Beyond "overcoming fear" as we do when we learn to ride a bicycle, or "fleeing the field" when pursued by strong enemies, humans can, in their own minds, alter the very meaning and significance of troublesome drives and impulses. They perform these alterations by using *coping strategies,* or *defenses.* The more common of these include such defenses as repression, projection, denial, displacement, and sublimation (Vaillant, 2000).

REPRESSION

According to psychoanalytic theory, *repression* is the most fundamental means for altering psychological realities. It is a defense by which the individual unconsciously forces unwanted thoughts or prohibited desires out of mind. Memories that evoke shame, guilt, humiliation, or self-deprecation—in short, affective memories (Davis and Schwartz, 1987)—are often repressed. Repressed events live on, and all the more vigorously, because they are not subject to rational control. They reveal their potent identities in normal fantasies and dreams, in slips of the tongue and "motivated" forgetting, under hypnosis, and in a variety of abnormal psychological conditions. By far, unconscious forces are the dominant ones in personality, as can be seen in the following case:

> Ann was in love with two men, Michael and Jules. Both wanted to marry her, and she could not decide between them. Finally, after more than six months, she decided for Michael. The next night, she had the following dream:

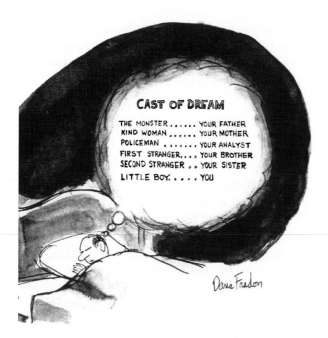

CAST OF DREAM

THE MONSTER . . . . . . YOUR FATHER
KIND WOMAN . . . . . . YOUR MOTHER
POLICEMAN . . . . YOUR ANALYST
FIRST STRANGER. . . . YOUR BROTHER
SECOND STRANGER . . YOUR SISTER
LITTLE BOY. . . . . YOU

Dana Fradon

> I was climbing the fire escape outside my dormitory. It was a dark and rainy night, and I was carrying a big box under my raincoat. I came to the fifth floor, opened the door silently, and tiptoed quickly to my room. Once inside, I double-locked the door, and put this box—it's a treasure chest—on my bed. I opened it and it was full of diamonds and rubies and emeralds.

Now, there is no evidence at all that dreams regularly mean anything (Seligman and Yellin, 1987). Yet, it is hard to escape the possibility that in Ann's dream, "diamonds and rubies and emeralds" = jewels = Jules. Her dream reveals her continuing attachment to her former lover, and quite possibly her desire to maintain the relationship secretly. The mind's extraordinary capacity to play on Jules's name and to transform it into visual symbols is revealed in this dream.

Repression can be nearly complete, or it can be partial. When an idea or memory is partially repressed, some aspects may be consciously available, while others are not. For example, a person who had had a difficult relationship with a parent may recall crying at that parent's funeral but may not recall what he or she cried about or anything else about the event. The available evidence also suggests that it is partially repressed conflicts and memories that play a significant role in abnormal behavior (Perkins and Reyher, 1971; Silverman, 1976). In dissociative identity disorder (also called multiple personality disor-

der; see Chapter 6), for example, an individual has two or more personalities that are alien to each other. When one personality is dominant, the others are repressed.

The capacity of the mind to be "its own place" is not limited merely to its ability to repress, to reject images and memories from consciousness, as important as that ability is. Rather, the mind is an editor, deleting whole chapters of experience and reorganizing others. Ordinarily, even in the absence of conflict, both perception and memory are reconstructive (Anderson and Bower, 1973). This is to say that minds take direct experience, edit, and make something "new" of it, by adding to, or subtracting from, perception, by embellishing memory in ways that range from innocent decoration to filling memorial gaps with new "memories." It is no surprise, then, that these enlivening capacities of the mind should be used in the coping process, when anxiety is experienced or when conflict occurs between self-image and impulse or behavior. Here, sometimes consciously, but more often unconsciously, editing processes are invoked to enable the individual to cope by making perception and memory more pleasant.

The notion that memories and experiences can be partially or wholly repressed has been widely, though far from universally, accepted among psychologists (see, for example, Ganaway, 1989; Holmes, 1990). But recently that acceptance has been questioned as people report the "return" of repressed memories, and on the basis of those newly returned memories, accuse others of sexual molestation, satanic behaviors, and even murder (Loftus, Grant, Franklin, Parr, and Brown, 1996). We examine this matter at greater length in Chapter 15, where we explore the legal implications of "repressed memories."

PROJECTION

Projection consists of attributing to others those feelings and experiences that we personally *deny* having and that we usually repress. Think of the preacher who sees and decries sin everywhere but denies having a sinful impulse himself. Research has shown that people who deny or repress their own sexual impulses often project them onto others and rate others as more lustful than they are (Halpern, 1977).

Projection plays a double role in psychological distress. First, it reduces distress by allowing a person to attribute an anxiety-provoking impulse to another person, rather than to the self. Thus, if anger makes us feel anxious, then attributing that anger to someone else can reduce the anxiety that anger creates. Second, projection allows us to do something about anger. When someone is angry with us, we are permitted to take aggressive or retaliative action in our own defense. Thus, projection can provide the rationale for engaging in the behavior that would have been forbidden in the first place.

DISPLACEMENT

When the strategy of **displacement** is used, the individual edits the target of his or her emotions by replacing the true object with one that is more innocent and less threatening. People who are angry and frustrated at work, but who cannot vent those feelings at work, are unconsciously using displacement strategies when they return home and vent their feelings on innocent spouses and children.

DENIAL

If repression obliterates inner facts, **denial** does away with distressing external ones. Denial commonly occurs when our sense of security and of being loved is threatened. The fact that people generally find it difficult to accurately perceive negative feelings directed toward themselves suggests that the denial process is widespread (Tagiuri, Bruner, and Blake, 1958). Denial is often used when people are threatened by death. The parents of a fatally ill child, much as the fatally ill themselves, often deny that anything is wrong, even though they have the diagnosis and prognosis in hand.

SUBLIMATION

Sublimation is the process of rechanneling psychic energies from socially undesirable goals to constructive and socially desirable ones. Capacities for love, work, altruism, and even humor involve such rechanneling of raw sexual and aggressive impulses. According to Freud, love is an especially powerful form of sublimation because it allows people to achieve sexual gratification in a socially acceptable context. Simultaneously, however, loving leaves one vulnerable to rejection or the death of a loved one. Thus, the gratifications of loving and working are often matched by the anxieties to which they give rise. In Freud's view, sublimation is as fragile as it is constructive. For modern psychoanalysts, however, subli-

mation is seen as a robust, mature defense that is crucial to health and success. People who engage in the mature defenses—sublimation, altruism, anticipation, and humor—are physically healthier, materially more successful, and more resistant to mental illness than people who do not display these defenses (Vaillant, 2000).

Psychodynamic Theorists after Freud

Though they were rejected at first, Freud's ideas later came to attract a number of highly original thinkers, known as **neo-Freudians,** who elaborated on his views and often disagreed with them. Carl Jung (1875–1961), for example, placed greater emphasis on the unconscious. Jung felt that there was a **collective unconscious,** consisting of the memory traces of the experience of past generations and not just memories of early childhood as Freud had thought. In Jung's view, which anticipated modern evolutionary psychology, we are born wiser than we think, already afraid of darkness and fire because our ancestors were, and already knowing of death because past generations have died. Jung called these universal ideas with which we are born **archetypes.** For Jung, these archetypes form the basis of personality, accounting for why people are not merely driven by their past experiences but also strive to grow and become something better. In essence, Jung saw the self as striving for wholeness.

Alfred Adler (1870–1937) placed less emphasis than Freud on the sexual and aggressive needs arising

Left: Carl Jung (1875–1961). *Right:* Alfred Adler (1870–1937).

from the id and mediated by the ego. According to Adler, the self serves a more meaningful purpose. The self aspires to power and control and enables us to fulfill our lifestyle, to become more than the genes with which we are endowed and the environment that presses on us. The self creates something new, something unique, something that is not wholly determined by biological impulse or cultural press (Ansbacher and Ansbacher, 1956).

Neo-Freudians differed considerably with Freud in another area, that of psycho*sexual* versus psycho*social* development. Fundamentally, that difference reduced to whether people are fundamentally biological or social animals. For example, Karen Horney (1885–1952) saw basic anxiety as arising from social rather than biological needs. For her, basic anxiety consisted of "the feeling a child has of being isolated and helpless in a potentially hostile world" (Horney, 1945, p. 41).

Similarly, Harry Stack Sullivan (1892–1949) held that the very notion of personality is itself an illusion that cannot be separated from the social context in which it is seen and operates. According to Sullivan, psychological problems do not merely originate in faulty social development, they consist of faulty social relationships and need to be examined and treated as such. Sullivan's concerns are mirrored in the modern emphasis on the social context in which personality operates (Gergen, 1982; Nisbett and Ross, 1980).

Erik Erikson (1902–1994) provided a broader theory of development, one that stresses the psychosocial nature of people and the interrelations between indi-

Left: Erik Erikson (1902–1994). *Right:* Erich Fromm (1900–1980).

viduals and society. Unlike Freud, who believed that the foundations of personality were essentially completed in childhood, Erikson saw human personality as developing and changing through eight stages, from infancy through adulthood and old age.

Erich Fromm (1900–1980) also saw personality as fundamentally social. At birth and with development, humans find themselves increasingly isolated from others. That isolation—the fundamental human condition—is painful, and however much people cherish their freedom, they also seek to terminate their isolation. They can do this either through love and shared work—a constructive mode—or through conformity and submission to authority, a very destructive mode.

As a group, the neo-Freudians brought refinements to basic Freudian theory. Since then, other theorists and practitioners have proposed further modifications. Today, there really is no single coherent psychodynamic theory of personality. Rather, the work that goes on in many clinics and laboratories sheds light on *aspects* of personality and human development, and it greatly revises Freud's notions and those of his immediate followers. The core of that revision has to do with the nature of the *self*—the processes and crises that shape it, the role of the defenses in shaping consciousness, and those aspects of the self that contribute to growth.

Modern psychodynamic theorists ask what gives personality its unity. What leads individuals to believe that they are the same person across time and place, that they are not fractured and fragmented psychologically? How is it that even though they are doing

Left: Karen Horney (1885–1952). *Right:* Harry Stack Sullivan (1892–1949).

different things at different times with different people, they remain the very same person? For some people, these questions have little meaning: they are the same person physically, and therefore psychologically. For others, however, especially those who have had a "shaky" self, or who see themselves as having undergone great change, such that they can say that "I am not the person that I was five years ago," these questions are significant and worth pursuing.

The self is the vast subjective psychological space that is the storehouse of personal experience within each of us. Central to psychodynamic formulations is the self in all its senses, and especially the ways in which it emerges, is experienced, and often becomes embattled and defended (Kohut, 1971, 1977; Mahler, 1979; Stern, 1985; Vaillant, 2000; Winnicott, 1971). According to Heinz Kohut (1913–1981), for example, there are three aspects of self that arise sequentially and are especially important in modern psychodynamic theory: the core self, the subjective self, and the verbal self.

The *core self* arises sometime between the second and sixth months of an infant's life, when he becomes aware that he and his caregiver are physically separate. This is the "body self," and it is pretty much taken for granted. Usually, people are unaware of their core self. Nevertheless, it serves a very important function. The core self gives each person his sense of separateness, coherence, and identity. Moreover, the core self enables individuals to confer coherence and identity on others. So long as these features of the core self remain strong, personality remains strong. But if one develops the sense that "things are happening to me outside of my control" or that "I can control other people's minds," there is fertile ground for disruption.

At about seven to nine months of age, the *subjective self* emerges. It encourages the development of intersubjectivity—the sense that we can empathize with other people, understand one another's intentions and feelings, as well as share experiences about things and events (Kohut, 1978). Disturbances in the subjective self may result in difficulties in feeling connected to other people and in relating to them or to oneself. The sense of being out of touch with self and others is what may arise when there are disturbances in the subjective self.

At about fifteen to eighteen months of age, children begin to develop the third sense of self: the self as a storehouse of knowledge and experience. That *verbal self* develops by using symbols and language.

Selfobjects are people and things that support and sustain the self throughout life.

The use of language, of course, opens a world of infinite variety and action for the infant. It permits rapid and direct communication. But language has a special down side, for it can distort the same reality that it might otherwise extend and enrich. Imagine a child who is visibly bored or tired, and whose parent says, "My! Aren't we having a wonderful time!"

The various selves are not sturdy, and they are not wholly independent structures. Much as they are formed by interactions between caregivers and infant, so they require support and sustenance from others throughout life. Those centrally important people who provide support for personality cohesiveness are called *selfobjects,* people and things that each of us requires to keep our personality functioning at its optimum level (Kohut, 1977). The notion of selfobjects underscores the importance of attachment for optimal personality functioning. It shows that none of us are islands unto ourselves, free and independent of the contexts in which we are found. As we will see, problems with attachment are associated with anxiety, depression, and eating disorders, as well as being implicated in borderline personality disorder (Fonagy et al. 1996).

Psychodynamic Treatment

Freud's own views and those of his disciples and descendants find expression in the modes of treatment that they have generated. Here, theory and practice come together, for it was from the clinic that Freud's most popular ideas developed. We therefore turn to psychodynamic treatment in order to examine those views in practice. Much as psychoanalytic theory spawned a variety of psychodynamic theories, so did psychoanalysis as a mode of treatment give birth to numerous and varied treatment modes. Among these are a variety of brief psychoanalytically "inspired" treatments that alter classical treatment in a variety of important ways.

Brief psychoanalytically inspired treatments have much in common with classical psychoanalysis. Both seek to alter thought and behavior. Both do so by examining early conflicts in the context of present relationships, and by making conscious that which is repressed. Both examine *free association* (saying whatever comes to mind without censoring), dreams, and **resistance** (momentary blocking in dealing with a particular issue). In so doing, psychic energy is freed for more constructive purposes, and the individual is able to find more constructive resolutions for conflict. Anxiety is reduced because impulses now find "safe" methods of expression. And coping strategies, where they are required, are now more mature. These matters become much clearer when we examine an actual case of psychodynamic psychotherapy.

It had been more than two years since Patty had had a moment's peace. Her problems were in her head, quite literally. There, continually pounding, intense headaches kept her in bed all day, every day, unable to sleep, unable to rise, clawing at the sheets. Patty had sought help for these headaches for well over a year. She had had several medical and neurological work-ups. She finally requested neurosurgery in the hope that the severing of nerve endings would alleviate the pain. Informed that nothing could be done surgically, she became exceedingly depressed. The situation by now seemed entirely hopeless to her. A burden to her husband, useless to her young children, there seemed little to do but end it all. It was then that she was referred for psychodynamic therapy.

The early part of her first meeting was spent describing the problem. With great pain, she described her headaches but quickly ran out of things to say. She didn't think that the problem was psychological, nor that anyone in their right mind would feel as she did under the circumstances. There being nothing more to say, she turned to the therapist and asked, "What should I talk about now?"

"Tell me about your childhood," he said.

She began slowly and then, with growing animation, described her father. (Indeed, during the remainder of that very long interview, Patty alluded to her mother only in passing.) Her father had come originally from a stretch of land that borders Greece and Turkey. He was a man of violent passions and frustrations, a man who had once angrily left his family for four years, only to return as suddenly as he had gone. In her earliest memory of him, he threatened to take a train to a far-off place, never to return.

"Did you ever go to bed with your father?" The question came suddenly, without warning. Patty paled. "How did you know?" she asked. And then, not waiting for the answer, she burst into tears.

"Yes, it was him. And I still hate him. He's an old man now. And I still hate him. On Sunday morning, my mother would clean the house. All of us, except my mother, slept late on Sunday. When she cleaned my room, I went into her bed. I would get under the covers, close my eyes, and go back to sleep. My father was there. He would touch me . . . rub . . . the rat. How could he do that to his own daughter?"

In anger, in sadness, and in shame, she cried as she tore furiously into incidents that had occurred more than a quarter-century ago, when she was eight years old.

Suddenly, she stopped crying, even talking. Then smiling in disbelief, she said, "They're gone. The headaches are gone." She rose slowly and walked around the office, moving her head from side to side. For the first time in more than two years, she felt normal.

Before the session was over, those headaches would return again. But regardless, a connection had been made between her present suffering and her early memories of her father.

During subsequent sessions, Patty was able to retrieve from memory more experiences with her father. Her father, it appeared, had had another family, which he had left behind in Greece when he came to America and married her mother. Patty felt it was her responsibility to keep him in America by making him so happy that he would not want to return. The fear of abandonment ran deep in both Patty and her mother.

She could not recall what her father had done to her in bed, but she knew that it was bad and that even he must have thought so. Once, after an outing with a group of friends, her father spotted her on a subway platform. He pulled her roughly aside from her schoolmates, slapped her hard across the face, and called her "Whore."

Those recaptured events—relived, remembered, re-experienced during therapy—brought relief over longer and longer periods. But certain experiences and even thoughts brought on headaches suddenly and fiercely, as when:

- she was shopping for a brassiere;
- Phil, her husband, was bouncing their young daughters on his lap, and the three of them were laughing;
- friends suggested that they go to a movie;
- she had gone with the family to a Greek wedding celebration, and all the young people were dancing; and
- she was washing the children's laundry.

All of these scenes vaguely connoted sexuality and therefore brought pain. Talking about them was difficult. There was a tension between exploring the psychodynamics of her situation and risking disturbing a trouble-free day. But she pushed on, pursuing her mental and emotional associations to early experiences and memories, not only about father and mother, but also about husband, children, friends, and later even about the therapist.

To a psychodynamic therapist, this search into Patty's past suggested that her headaches resulted from severe sexual conflicts, which paralyzed her, rendering her unable to even initiate caregiving activities for her husband, children, and increasingly, even herself.

The headaches were themselves testimony to the power of the conflicts, as well as the coping strategies. They symbolically suggested a conflict about rape. But since the conflict was going on in Patty's own mind, it also suggested a conflict about her own sexual desires. By some process that is not yet understood, these conflicting desires were repressed and displaced, not outward to other people, but upward to her head.

Patty clearly projected much of this conflict onto her husband and even her children. Their horseplay was seen, not as an innocent rumpus, but as a highly sexualized event. Shopping for underclothes, weddings, Greek dancing, and the weekly laundry were all similarly sexualized. Ego processes that normally differentiate these events and allow people to share social perceptions of them were clearly defective here. The defects, psychodynamic therapists hold, arose because of the intense and poorly contained pressure that was generated from Patty's own sexual conflicts.

It was **catharsis,** the uncovering and reliving of early traumatic conflicts, that enabled Patty to remit her symptoms rapidly. But in psychodynamic theory, symptom remission is only part of the treatment, often the smallest part. Much more significant is the fact that enduring patterns of perceiving and reacting in adults are laid down in childhood and pervade all adult activities. They need to be altered because they are transferred from the people and impulses that originally stimulated the conflict to other significant people in one's life. Psychodynamic therapy seeks, therefore, not merely to relieve symptoms, but to alter personality—the very attitudes, perceptions, and behaviors that were misshaped by early experience.

How does psychodynamic treatment achieve personality changes? In practice, psychodynamic therapists must be nonreactive. They must listen calmly and intensely; they must not appear shocked by the client's revelations, nor should they offer opinions or judgments. They should act as blank screens, onto which clients can project their own expectations, imaginings, and attributions. Over time, therapists themselves become central in the lives of their clients. This centrality is of such therapeutic importance that it is given a technical name in psychodynamic theory: transference. *Transference* describes the process during psychodynamic therapy whereby clients transfer emotions, conflicts, and expectations from the diverse sources from which they were acquired onto their therapists. Therapists become mother, father, son, daughter, spouse, lover, and even employer or stranger to their clients. In this emotional climate, clients are encouraged to speak

Hamlet, played by Kenneth Branagh, speaks with his mother, played by Julie Christie. Hamlet is experiencing a catharsis as he relives the trauma of his father's death and his mother's betrayal.

frankly, to let their minds ramble, and to free-associate to emotionally charged ideas, even if the resulting ideas seem silly, embarrassing, or meaningless. Under these conditions, what was formerly repressed and distorted becomes available to consciousness and therefore more controllable by ego processes, as can be seen from further examination of Patty's case:

> In less than three months, Patty's symptoms had abated. Her attention turned away from her headaches to other matters. Her mother, for example, was a "pain." She had always been melancholy and merely obedient, surely no fun to live with. Patty quickly related the impression that "she was no fun to live with" to her own relationship with her father. He had already abandoned a family in Greece. Had she been trying to keep him in the family? Might he not abandon them? More important, could her own sexual involvement with her father have been little more than an attempt to keep him at home? That possibility cast her memories in a much more positive light, relieving her of the guilt that the memories evoked. Shortly thereafter, she could observe her husband and children playing together, without suffering from headaches and guilt.
>
> Gradually, attention turned from her parents, even from her husband and children, to the therapist himself. His lack of reacting now provoked discomfort: his occasional lateness caused her to feel anxiety; and when her therapist took a weeklong vacation, she experienced dread. In turn, these feelings led to long, blocked silences during the therapy sessions. What thoughts lay behind these silences? It was difficult for her to say, and nearly impossible for her to free-associate. But finally, she was able to allude to the embarrassing sexual fantasies that attended these events, fantasies now about the therapist himself. This was transference, for it shortly became clear that she interpreted his silences, lateness, and absences as abandonment, and she was unconsciously motivated to do what she had wanted to do in the past to retain the affections of significant others. She was, of course, initially unaware of the unconscious connection between abandonment and sexuality, and she was therefore deeply embarrassed by the thoughts that assailed her. Once she understood the reasons for those thoughts, however, she was able to see her relationship to the therapist in more objective terms, to recognize that an occasional lateness or absence is not the same as abandonment, and to find less self-demeaning and guilt-provoking ways to express her affections.

> At about this time, and seemingly for no good reason, Patty began to explore an entirely new matter: what to do with her life. Upon graduating high school, she had considered going to college, but had given up that idea as "simply ridiculous." She had also been attracted to dance, but had not acted on that interest either. Now both ideas returned, as well as the desire to take a job again, and she began to explore those ideas with great enthusiasm. In Freud's view, energies that had once been bound up in repression and other defensive maneuvers were now freed for other activities. A stronger and more mature identity resulted from achieving a greater understanding of herself and greater control over her impulses. Moreover, the more Patty probed, the less clear it became that she had actually had a sexual relationship with her father. Eventually, that "memory" came to be seen as a false one, reflecting her own desire to retain his affections, rather than his actual behavior. In this, Patty repeated the experience of many of Freud's clients, for the mind, Freud observed, is a powerfully inventive place in which even "memories" can arise from desires, conflicts, and defenses.

Evaluating Psychodynamic Theory

STRENGTHS OF PSYCHOANALYSIS

Psychodynamic theory is nothing less than a comprehensive description of human personality. This theory describes personality's development, the way personality functions, and every aspect of human thought, emotion, experience, and judgment—from dreams through slips of the tongue to normal and abnormal behavior.

Because of this, Freud is considered, along with Marx and Darwin, as one of the great geniuses of the nineteenth century. Perhaps the most important of his ideas is the view that the psychological processes that underlie normal and abnormal behaviors are fundamentally the same. Neither conflict, nor anxiety, nor defense, nor unconscious processes are the sole property of abnormal people. Rather, the *outcome* of conflict and the *nature* of defense will determine whether behavior will be normal or abnormal.

In addition, Freud developed a method for investigating psychodynamic processes and treating psychological distress: the talking cure. This was important for several reasons. First, his method of investigation shed light on abnormal processes and thus demystified them. By accounting for why they behaved as they did, Freud "rehumanized" the distressed, making their suffering more comprehensible to the rest of humankind. Second, by providing a method of treatment, Freud encouraged an optimism regarding psychological distress that had been sorely lacking before him. Finally, while Freudian psychoanalysis must be distinguished sharply from modern psychodynamic therapies, the former was the progenitor of the modern efforts, and the modern therapies have been found to be quite effective (Consumer Reports, 1995; Crits-Christoph, 1992; Smith, Glass, and Miller, 1980).

SHORTCOMINGS OF PSYCHODYNAMIC THEORIES

Any theory that aspires to be as comprehensive as psychodynamic theory inevitably has faults, and Freud's theories and those of his successors are no exception. Central to the problems of psychodynamic theory and therapy are: (1) the theory is simply too difficult to prove or disprove, (2) studies indicate that psychodynamic theories often fail to be supported, and (3) in emphasizing the role of the person, these theories overlook the situation.

Some of the difficulty in supporting or disproving psychodynamic theories arises because they take complex views of personality and behavior. Many behaviors are held to be *overdetermined,* that is, determined by more than one force and with more than the required psychic energy. Altering a particular psychological force—for example, by recovering a crucial early memory—may have no visible effect on a particular trait or behavior because the latter are supported and sustained by many interrelated psychological forces.

Moreover, only rarely is it possible to confirm that a particular unconscious motive is really operating. Precisely because the motive is unconscious, it is invisible to the client and only *inferred* by the therapist. Even in Patty's case, where confirmation was apparently obtained because the headaches gradually disappeared, we cannot be sure that these changes were due to her increasing awareness of sexual motives and fears of abandonment. Might not the cure have arisen, with equal plausibility, from the fact that she had finally found someone whom she trusted and in whom she could confide?

Psychodynamic theories have been subjected to a variety of ingenious studies, many of which have failed to confirm the theories. Many aspects of psy-chodynamic theories have yet to accrue sufficient scientific support to merit belief.

Psychodynamic theories overwhelmingly emphasize the impact of traits and dispositions, those stable constellations of attitude and experience that are held to influence behavior. But what of *situations?* Because psychodynamic theories are derived mainly from information conveyed by clients during treatment, and because clients are encouraged to talk about their own reactions rather than the situation in which they find themselves, psychodynamic theory underestimates the role of situation and context. For example, it is much easier to infer that a person's continuing irritation with his employer results from unconscious and unresolved conflicts about authority when the employer's behavior has not been observed directly than when it has been. Similarly, it is easier to construe marital conflicts in terms of the traits of the spouse who has sought consultation precisely because one has no first-hand experience with that spouse's marital situation.

Psychoanalysis and the Medical Model

Freud was a physician, and although he broke with many of the intellectual traditions of medicine, he did not break with the underlying **medical model** of abnormality. In essence, this means that the medical model approaches abnormality as medical researchers approach an illness: It groups diverse, but co-occurring symptoms together into a coherent *syndrome.* It then searches for the *etiology,* or cause, of the syndrome. It recognizes that the symptoms are not the illness itself, but merely reflect the underlying etiology. In the medical tradition, there are four possible causes: (1) germs, (2) genes, (3) the biochemistry of the patient's brain, and (4) the patient's neuroanatomy. To this array of etiologies, Freud added intrapsychic conflict. Once an etiology has been discovered in the medical model, some *treatment* that attacks the root cause will be sought to alleviate the abnormality. For modern physicians, this is usually a drug; for Freud, it was the talking cure involving transference and catharsis. The talking cure "worked through" the underlying etiology of the neuroses. We highlight the psychoanalytic embodiment of the medical model, because as we shall see, this model is rejected by the other three psychological traditions. Now let's look at how a psychoanalyst would treat Angela, whose case we presented at the beginning of the chapter:

> Angela was referred to a psychoanalyst. The central issue they explored was anger—anger at her mother and anger at being abandoned by Jerry. Anger turned upon the self is, from the psychoanalytic point of view, the key dynamic in depression, and therapy often consists of recognizing the anger and learning to express it constructively.
>
> Angela had always been an inward person, even as a child, and when she was angry, she kept it bottled up. Once, as a six-year-old, she got separated from her mother in a shopping mall and was lost for two hours. She was furious at her mother for "abandoning" her, but when they were reunited by an alert mall policeman, Angela said nothing at all. "I was like stone," she told her analyst when they relived this formative event.
>
> In the course of the analysis, Angela realized that she was furious at Jerry for abandoning her, and even more furious at her mother for trying to keep her living at home and dependent. She learned to recognize her anger and not to fear that expressing it would lead to even more abandonment. She became able to express anger to her mother, and as she did, her despondency began to lift. By the end of treatment, she was dating Sal, and she was, for the first time in her life, open about her emotions with another human being.

The Existential and Humanistic Approaches

Some theorists have sought to examine what is especially human in human experience, and particularly those aspects of human experience that contribute to growth or to abnormality. These existential and humanistic theorists discuss the elements of freedom and choice—responsibility and will—and the fundamental anxiety—the fear of dying.

Freedom and Choice

Existential theorists stress the importance of freedom and choice. They believe that individuals must use their freedom to make authentic choices based on their own desires and goals, not those of others. Existential theorists believe that growth will occur when people take responsibility for their actions and work toward their own freely chosen goals. Such authentic

modes of thought and behavior will enable them to make the most of their potential (Schneider, 1998).

RESPONSIBILITY

The assumption of *personal responsibility* is central to existential thinking. It says that we are responsible for the way we perceive the world and for the way we react to those perceptions. To be responsible "is to be aware that one has created one's own self, destiny, life, predicament, feelings and, if such be the case, one's own suffering" (Yalom, 1980).

Existential psychologists generally pay careful attention to language; they are especially sensitive to the use of such words as "can't" and "it." People often say, "I just can't study" or "I can't get up in the morning," implying that the behavior is somehow removed from their control. What they really mean is, "I won't do it." They bury an act over which they have control beneath the appearance of disability. Young children who break something are inclined to say, "it broke," not "I broke it." Similarly, for adults to say that "something happened" or "it happened" is to imply that one is passively influenced by a capricious world. In short, they do not want to be held responsible. Generally, the use of the passive rather than the active voice, the avoidance of first-person pronouns, as well as the attributions of the causes of current events to historical sources (for example, my upbringing, my parents, the things I did as a child), are seen as signs of avoidance of responsibility.

Existentialists believe that we are responsible for the way we perceive the world and for the way we react to those perceptions. This includes taking responsibility for those close to us when they need us.

Goal-directed will can certainly be seen in Lance Armstrong, who survived testicular cancer to win cycling's biggest race, the Tour de France, in both 1999 and 2000.

CAPACITY TO WILL

The capacity to *will* is also a central feature of existential and humanistic views. Yet, despite its centrality, will is difficult to define unambiguously. Will is used psychologically in at least two senses. First, there is will as in willpower: the will of gritted teeth, clenched jaw, and tensed muscle. This is ***exhortative will.*** It can be useful at times, as when we force ourselves to work when we would rather play.

A second and more significant kind of will is associated with future goals. It is called ***goal-directed*** will. Much as memory is the organ of the past, goal-directed will has been called "the organ of the future" (Arendt, 1978). It is quite different from exhortative will, for it develops out of hope, expectation, and competence. Unlike exhortative will, it is not urged upon us but is rather a freely chosen arousal in the service of a future that is willingly embraced. This kind of will cannot be created; it can only be unleashed or disinhibited.

Fear of Dying

Existential psychologists assert that the central human fear, and the one from which most psychopathology develops, is the *fear of dying.* Anxiety about death is most prominent in, and best recalled from childhood. Perhaps because children are vulnerable, and because their worst imaginings are barely informed by reality, their fears are stark, vivid, and memorable. How do people deal with the fear of dying? Broadly speaking, there are two kinds of strategies: by believing themselves special, and by fusion (Yalom, 1990).

SPECIALNESS

One way through which some people protect themselves from death fears is by cultivating in themselves the notion that they are special. It is a peculiar notion in that it holds that the laws of nature apply to all mortals except oneself. The *notion of specialness* manifests itself in many ways. For example, the terminally ill simply cannot believe that it is they who are dying. They understand the laws of nature fully well, but they believe themselves somehow to be exempt from them. Similarly, people who smoke heavily, overeat, or fail to exercise sufficiently may also believe that somehow they are exempt from nature's laws.

The notion of specialness underlies many valued character traits. Physical courage may result from the belief that one is inviolable, as may ambition and striving, and especially striving for power and control. But at the extreme, the unconscious belief in one's specialness may also lead to a spectrum of behavior disorders. The workaholic who compulsively strives to achieve success and power may also harbor the delusion that achieving that one kind of specialness may confer the other, immortal kind. Narcissistic people who devote enormous attention to themselves, and are correspondingly insensitive to the requirements of others, may believe that only that kind of self-indulgence will protect them from death and its associated anxieties.

FUSION

Protection against the fear of death or nonbeing can also be achieved by fusing with others. **Fusion** is an especially useful strategy for those whose death fears take the form of loneliness. By attaching themselves to, and making themselves indistinguishable from others, they hope that their lot is cast with them. They believe that much as these others continue to live, so will they. They also develop a fear of standing apart, as they believe that if they do stand apart, they will no longer be protected from death, as can be seen in the following case:

A well-trained, enormously presentable business executive had held seven positions in as many years, and he was now finding it difficult to gain employment.

People may attempt to protect themselves against non-being by fusing with others. In an extreme case of fusion, these five people had plastic surgery to change their faces to those of rock stars Jim Croce, Linda Ronstadt, Kenny Rogers, Elvis Presley, and Buddy Holly, merging their identities with those of their favorite stars.

Each of his employers had been impressed both by his credentials and his industriousness. He was moved gradually into positions of greater responsibility. Oddly, however, just as he had begun to inspire faith in others, he would "foul up." His errors were as costly as they were inexcusable, and they led quickly to termination from the job. In the course of treatment with an existential therapist, it was found that success had a powerfully unconscious meaning for him. He feared success, for it meant isolation, standing apart from others. For him, success was analogous to death, in that it destroyed fusion. He unconsciously felt that it was better to be indistinguishable from the mass of people than to stand alone, even successfully.

The fear of standing apart has socially valuable features. Why else would we marry and have children if not to create fusions? Why else would we form clubs, communities, and organizations? Such attachments protect against loneliness, against being separated from the flow of life. Yet, fusion may also lead to much unhappiness. A person may engage in inauthentic, or false, modes of behavior. He may say things to others that he hopes will please them, but that he does not really mean. For example, he may conform his opinions to theirs, bend his behaviors to suit them, do the things they do, even though his mind and body would rather believe and do something else. Gradually, he may come to lose sight of what he wants to do, while finding his conformity to others' opinions and behaviors only a pale pleasure. He may pay for a tenuous security against the fear of death by sacrificing his own authenticity.

Existential Treatment

Sometimes people need assistance in handling pain and risk. The existential and humanistic movement has spawned therapies that focus on developing independence, goal-directed will, and personal responsibility. Here, we see a patient who presents with major depression, which comes from not knowing what she wants to do with her life:

Susan was bright enough to do well in college but nevertheless was having a struggle. It was difficult for her to get up in the morning, difficult to crack the books, and difficult to put away the temptations that deflected her from achievement. She had no sense of what she wanted to study in college and, therefore, little motivation to work in her courses. After her mid-year grades were posted, she went to the counseling center to "try to get myself down to work."

Disorders of will are found among people who know what they should do, what they ought to do, and what they must do, but who have no notion of what they want to do. Lacking that knowledge of what they want, their goals seem apparently lusterless, and movement toward them is correspondingly difficult. People may fail to know what they want for three reasons. First, they may simply fear wanting. Wanting makes them vulnerable to failure and hurt, and that is especially difficult for those who wish to appear strong. Second, they may fail to know what they want because they fear rejection. They long ago learned that if their wishes departed from those of their friends or family, their wishes would infuriate and drive others away. Third, they may fail to know what they wish because they want others, magically, to discover their silent wishes and fulfill them.

> During therapy sessions, the existential therapist who was counseling Susan helped her overcome depression by focusing on goal-directed will. During several counseling sessions, Susan came to realize that although she had plenty of intelligence, she lacked confidence in her ability to do well in college and, as a result, found it difficult to commit herself to any career. Susan had had a difficult start in the primary grades, and in the counseling sessions she acknowledged that those bruises had remained with her. During one significant and productive session, Susan realized that grade school was far behind her and that she had achieved a great deal since those experiences. Nearly simultaneously, a long-buried desire surfaced: to be a doctor. As her disorder of will was overcome, her depression lifted. At the next session, Susan reported that "her life had come together during the past week." No longer did she find it difficult to get up in the morning or to resist going to the movies. It was easy to study now, and indeed, she bounded out of bed and headed for the books effortlessly. "Now that I know what I want to do, everything else has fallen into place. I no longer have to force myself."

In another case, a student explored with an existential therapist why she was unable to motivate herself to do what was necessary to complete her graduate studies:

> Most graduate students complete a dissertation before receiving their doctoral degree, and they often view the dissertation as a significant hurdle in their graduate career. For some, however, that final hurdle is insurmountable. Such seemed to be the case for Cathy. She had done well until that point. Her course grades were excellent, and the research that she had completed while in graduate school had been quite interesting. But somehow she found it difficult to get down to the dissertation. In fact, she had begun three separate studies and had dropped each of them for no particular reason other than that she had lost interest. The fact of the matter was that she viewed the dissertation as a major undertaking, much bigger than any-

thing she had undertaken before, and much beyond her abilities.

> Cathy's fear of being criticized by her teachers or, worse, of failing her oral examination prevented her from finding a study that she really wanted to do. But there was more to her concerns than mere fear of criticism, or even fear of failure. Completing her degree meant no longer being a graduate student, and surprisingly, that was troublesome on at least two fronts. First, it meant leaving the cozy, comfortable place that had been hers for four years: the friends, the local haunts, the predictable professors as well as all the other fusions that had served her so well during her graduate career. Second, it meant becoming a full-fledged adult, being responsible for herself and her actions, choosing her life rather than having it chosen for her. Those two issues quickly formed the core of her treatment. As Cathy became comfortable with her own separateness and her freedom to live as she pleased, her fear of being criticized and of failing diminished correspondingly, and she got back to work on her dissertation, which she completed in record time.

Evaluating the Existential Approach

The existential approach to personality and its disorders is very difficult to evaluate, largely because the approach is really a group of philosophical positions rather than a scientific theory. For example, whether people are capable of goal-directed will or fully responsible for their acts are matters of belief rather than facts that can be proven or disproven. Because the approach is made up of a diverse collection of views and is based on beliefs rather than facts, it is difficult to know where to begin in evaluating the views and treatments derived from them.

Among the very attractive features of this approach, however, is the degree to which it accords with everyday notions of personality. People do behave as if they and others are responsible, as if they are free to do what they will, and as if their lives are not predetermined. Thus, the law, for example, holds people responsible for their behavior with fairly rare exceptions. It reflects the common belief that people act freely, for better or for worse, and that they should be held accountable for their actions. Rightly or wrongly, the existential approach reflects a great deal of common sense. Let's look at how an existential therapist would treat Angela:

> Angela was referred to an existential therapist. The central issue they explored was Angela's failure to make decisions and to take responsibility for her own life. From an existential point of view, depression can result from a paralysis of the will, and in such a case, treatment centers on breaking the ice-jam of dependency.
>
> Angela had always been dependent on her mother. Even in the smallest things, like what kind of pizza to order, she deferred to her mother. Furthermore, her mother was happy to take charge and never encouraged Angela's independence. "This is my life, not Mom's," became the theme and central insight of therapy. As Angela recognized that continuing to live with her mother, failing to apply to college, and finally being able to make a decision about Jerry all stemmed from the same weakness, her depression began to lift. She practiced taking responsibility for small things, such as what supermarket to shop in, and soon she took charge of planning a trip to the Catskills with her best friend, Tanya. By the end of therapy, she had decided to attend a community college part-time and to share an apartment with Tanya.

The Behavioral Approach

A single movement—*behaviorism*—dominated academic psychology in the United States and Soviet Russia for almost fifty years, roughly from 1920 until the mid-1960s. Behaviorism is an ambitious effort to discover in the laboratory the general laws of human and animal learning and to apply these laws to the classroom, the workplace, the penitentiary, and to society as a whole. Thus, the behavioral approach is not only a way to study abnormal behavior, it is a worldview. Its first assumption is *environmentalism,* which states that all organisms, including humans, are shaped by the environment (see Box 3–1). We learn about the future through the associations of the past. This is why our behavior is subject to rewards and punishments. If our employers paid us twice as much per hour for working one Saturday, we would be more likely to work on future Saturdays.

The second assumption of behaviorism is *experimentalism,* which states that through an experiment, we can find out what aspect of the environment caused our behavior and how we can change it. If the

crucial element is withheld, the present characteristic will disappear. If the crucial element is reinstated, the characteristic will reappear. For example, what causes us to work on Saturdays? Remove double-time pay, and work on Saturday will stop. Reinstate double-time pay, and work on Saturday will resume. This is the heart of the experimental method (see Chapter 2). From the experimental method, we can determine what causes people, in general, to forget, to be anxious, to fight, and we can then apply these general laws to individual cases.

The third assumption of behaviorism is *optimism,* the belief that people can be changed. If an individual is a product of the environment and if those parts of the environment that have molded him can be known by experimentation, he will be changed when the environment is changed.

These three assumptions apply directly to abnormal behavior. First, abnormal as well as normal behavior is learned from past experiences. Psychopathology consists of acquired habits that are maladaptive. Second, we can find out by experiment what aspects of the environment cause abnormal behavior. Third, if we change those aspects of the environment, the individual will unlearn his old, maladaptive habits and will learn new, adaptive habits.

How do we learn, and what is it we learn? For the behavioral psychologist, two basic learning processes exist, and it is from these two that all behaviors, both normal and abnormal, derive. We can learn *what goes with what* through **Pavlovian,** or *classical conditioning.* And we can learn *what to do* to obtain what we want, and rid ourselves of what we do not want, through **instrumental,** or *operant conditioning.*

Pavlovian Conditioning

Just after the turn of the century, the Russian physiologist Ivan Pavlov (1849–1936) began work on a phenomenon that would change the nature of psychology. Pavlov was studying the digestive system of dogs, specifically the salivary reflex. He received the Nobel Prize in 1904 for his studies of digestive physiology. During his experiments, he would put food powder in the dog's mouth, and he would then measure the drops of saliva by way of a tube surgically inserted into the dog's mouth. But in the course of his work, Pavlov noticed that dogs began to salivate merely when he walked into the room. This salivation could not be a reflex since it did not occur the first few

Can Heritable Disorders Be Treated Psychologically?

In Chapter 4, you will read about the heritability of personality and of psychological disorders. Briefly, studies of identical twins reared separately and of the resemblance of adopted children and biological children to their adoptive and biological parents demonstrate that many personality traits and many disorders are roughly 50 percent heritable. IQ, job satisfaction, alcohol and drug abuse, crime, and even religiosity are at least partly heritable (Bouchard, Lykken, McGue, Segal, and Tellegen, 1990). It is a natural and easy inference that disorders and traits that are genetically inherited can only be changed by biological interventions, like drugs. Should we therefore give up on trying to change heritable traits like sadness and heritable disorders like alcohol abuse by psychological interventions?

Consider the likelihood that personality traits and disorders are only indirectly heritable—that "nature works *via* nurture." Here's an example. Optimism is 50 percent heritable.: Identical twins are much more similar for optimism (and pessimism) than are fraternal twins (Schulman, Keith, and Seligman, 1993). But optimism is produced by lots of success (and pessimism by lots of failure) in life. Success and failure, in turn, are caused by characteristics like looks, strength, and motor coordination, all of which are physical and heritable. Identical twins are more concordant (similar) for these characteristics (for example, tallness or runtiness) than are fraternal twins. So what might be directly heritable are the physical characteristics, with the personality trait actually wholly caused by the environment.

This argument applies to all personality characteristics and all psychological disorders. This mode of heritability is called "gene-environment covariation." The point is that it turns out to be the environment that is primarily causal here, not the genes. The genes get the person selectively into specific environments, and those environments shape the personality trait. So having genes that make you handsome gets you into environments in which people pay more attention to you and in which you are able to succeed more often. All that success makes you more optimistic.

We believe that much of the future of psychological treatments for biologically heritable problems may be dis-covering ways to break the gene-environment covariance. Gene-environment covariance can be broken by psychological interventions, allowing lots of change to occur even in the heritable fraction of personality. An example is the predisposition to committing crimes (Mednick, Gabriella, and Hutchings, 1987). This is partly heritable, and children who go on to commit crimes tend to have alienated their parents and teachers when they were young. Their parents and teachers often gave up on them because they were so irritable. The children, lacking a relationship with an adult, may have turned to gangs for support and ultimately become street-smart criminals. This is gene-environment covariance. Irritability, which is partly heritable, gets you thrown out of warm relationships with responsible adults and by default gets you into relationships with street-smart criminals. But the covariance can be broken if the parents stand by the "irritable" child and don't reject him. By breaking the covariance, the child may be prevented from becoming a criminal.

As you will read throughout this book, many of the disorders—for example, depression, substance abuse, and the anxiety disorders—which are somewhat heritable can be just as effectively treated by a variety of psychological interventions as by medications. We believe that part of the reason that psychological treatment works on these problems is that it breaks up the malignant environments that genetics predispose a person to enter. Depression, for example, is mildly heritable. One gene-environment covariance path is that introversion and shyness, which are partly heritable, lead certain individuals to avoid social gatherings. Their genetic "steersman" steers them away from other people. A life devoid of social contact is usually depressing, and so individuals predisposed to introversion are predisposed to depression. Cognitive-behavior therapy teaches such a person to defy her genetic steersman and to engage in social contact more often, thus breaking the gene-environment covariance (Lykken, 1999). We believe that much of the future benefit of the psychological approaches will come from identifying what the specific gene-environment covariances are for many of the disorders, and discovering the psychological ways to break them.

---

times Pavlov walked in; it only occurred once the dog had learned that Pavlov's appearance signaled food. That is, Pavlov's appearance became associated with a future event: food. He called this a psychic reflex, or a conditional reflex, since it was conditional upon past experience. It has come to be called, through mistranslation, a **conditioned response,** or **CR.** A typical Pavlovian conditioning experiment goes as follows:

We know that food (unconditioned stimulus, US) produces salivation (unconditioned response, UR):

$$\text{US (food)} \rightarrow \text{UR (salivation)}$$

We present a tone just prior to presenting the food. Because the tone itself does not produce salivation, it is a neutral stimulus. But after pairing the tone with the food several times, we discover that salivation will

Ivan Pavlov (1849–1936).

occur upon presentation of the tone. The tone can now be called a *conditioned stimulus,* or *CS,* because it produces salivation, the *conditioned response,* or *CR.* In short:

CS (tone) → US (food) → UR (salivation)

After several pairings of CS and US:

CS (tone) → CR (salivation)

This kind of experiment has been carried out using many species (Siamese fighting fish, rats, dogs, and humans), conditioned stimuli (tones, lights, tastes), and unconditioned responses (salivation, fear, nausea). It also can be used in therapeutic situations to eliminate unsatisfactory behaviors. For example, Pavlovian conditioning might be used to treat a person with a foot fetish, as in the following case:

> Steven has been in trouble with the police for fondling strange women's shoes in public places. He is a person with a foot fetish who has a strong erotic attachment to women's feet and footwear. He agrees to undergo Pavlovian therapy rather than go to jail.
>
> In the therapist's office, Steven fondles women's shoes. He then drinks ipecac, a drug that causes him to become nauseated in a few minutes. He vomits. A week later, the same procedure is repeated. The shoes are the CS, the US is ipecac, and the UR is nausea and vomiting. After several sessions, the pairing of shoes and vomiting produces a major change in Steven's sexual preferences. Women's shoes no longer arouse him, and he throws away his collection of five thousand pictures of shoes.

THE BASIC PAVLOVIAN PHENOMENA

There are two processes in Pavlovian conditioning that occur time and time again, regardless of what species, what kind of CS or US, or what kind of a response is tested: acquisition and extinction.

Acquisition is the learning of a response based on the contingency between a CS and a US. Depending on the response to be learned, acquisition usually takes from three to fifteen pairings. *Extinction* is the loss of the CS's power to produce the formerly acquired response. This is brought about by presenting the CS, and no longer following it with the US. For example, it is possible to condition fear in humans. Fear can be measured by increased heart rate, perspiration, and muscle tension. When mild shocks (US) are given to humans, these measures become evident; that is, pain (UR) is produced. After several pairings of tone (CS) and shock (US), the tone (CS) alone will begin to elicit fear (CR). That is what we call acquisition. But if we now repeatedly present the tone (CS) no longer followed by the shock (US), the individual will no longer show signs of fear. The tone (CS) will no longer signal a shock (US). We call this process extinction.

PAVLOVIAN CONDITIONING, EMOTIONS, AND PSYCHOPATHOLOGY

There are situations in the world that arouse strong emotions in us. Some of these arouse the emotion unconditionally, or from our very first encounter with them: a loud clap of thunder startles us the very first time we hear it. Other objects acquire emotional significance: the face of a person we love produces a sense of well-being; seeing a stranger in a dark alleyway arouses dread. Pavlovian conditioning provides a powerful account of how objects take on emotional significance; it is this account that makes conditioning of great interest to the student of abnormality.

According to the behavioral account, the basic mechanism for all acquired emotional states is the pairing of a neutral object (CS) with an unconditioned emotional state (US). With enough pairings, the neutral object will lose its neutrality, become a CS, and all by itself produce the emotional state (CR). Consider the case of a child who is continually beaten with a tan hairbrush by his father. Before the beatings, the child had no feelings about the brush whatsoever. But, after several beatings (US), the brush becomes a CS, and merely seeing the tan brush produces fear (CR).

If normal emotions are acquired in this way, the same should be true of acquired emotional disorders. Several of the psychopathological disorders explored in the following chapters involve the acquisition of an exaggerated or unusual emotional state in regard to inappropriate objects. For example, phobias are said to be a result of Pavlovian conditioning. (see Figure 3–1). A phobia is a fear greatly out of proportion to how dangerous the phobic object actually is (see Chapter 5). For example, a person with a cat phobia had a history of cats (CS) paired with painful events such as being scratched (US). As a result, cats became terrifying to the individual, despite the fact that cats generally are not dangerous.

Here we can contrast the behavioral view of what causes emotional disorders with the psychodynamic model. The psychodynamic model is a part of the medical model, but the behavioral view is emphatically not. According to the behavioral view, the symptom of the disorder *is* the disorder. In the case above, the phobic individual's fear of cats is the disorder. There is no underlying pathological state that produces the symptoms. For the medical model, an underlying pathology such as a "virus," a disordered biochemistry, or a dysfunctional organ causes the symptoms. For the psychodynamic view, an intrapsychic conflict, usually sexual or aggressive in nature and stemming from childhood fixations, causes the symptoms.

The therapeutic optimism of the behavioral view follows directly from its view of the cause of the disorder. If the disorders are the symptoms and do not reflect an underlying pathology, eliminating the symptoms will cure the disorder. Since the symptoms of emotional disorders are emotional responses acquired by Pavlovian conditioning, it follows that those techniques that have been found experimentally to extinguish conditioned emotional responses will cure emotional disorders. This contrasts with the medical model and the psychodynamic approach, which hold that eliminating symptoms is not enough, that cure consists of removing the underlying cause. A strong test, then, of the behavioral approach, as opposed to the psychodynamic approach to emotional disorders, would be whether the symptoms can be removed by extinction procedures, and whether other symptoms would then occur, reflecting an uncured underlying pathology. For now, we will leave you in suspense about what the data show.

Figure 3—1

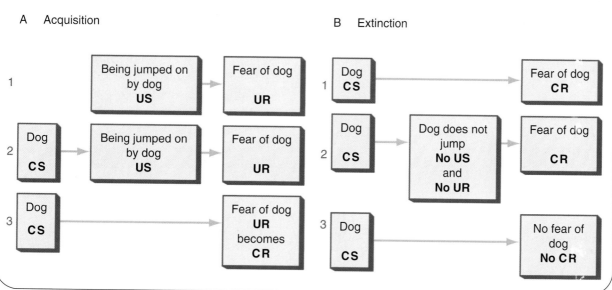

PAVLOVIAN CONDITIONING AND PHOBIAS

A person who has a phobia has an exaggerated emotional reaction to an object. The person is terrified of the phobic object and unable to function in its presence. Pavlovian conditioning explains that the phobia is acquired when a neutral object (CS) is repeatedly paired with an unconditioned emotional state (US) until it loses its neutrality and evokes a conditioned fear response (CR) from the person with the phobia. Therapy consists of extinguishing the phobia by continuous pairing of the phobic object (CS) without the original trauma (US–UR) until the fear of the object (CR) is eliminated.

THE PAVLOVIAN THERAPIES

In the chapters on phobias (Chapter 5) and sexual dysfunction (Chapter 13), we will examine in detail the therapies involving Pavlovian extinction of emotional disorders. But we briefly set forth some of the specific therapies now.

Two Pavlovian therapies involving extinction have been applied to phobias and other anxiety disorders. In **exposure,** the patient is immersed in the phobic situation (either real or imagined) for several consecutive hours. For example, a person with claustrophobia (a terror of being in small enclosed places) would be placed in a closet (CS), the original trauma (US) would not occur, and the fear of being enclosed would diminish (Marks, 1969; Stampfl and Levis, 1967). Or a rape victim with post-traumatic stress disorder would be told to imagine the rape and to narrate the story repeatedly, in detail, and with emotion, to the therapist. The CS's here are sex, men, and the place—all of which produce terror after the rape—but the original trauma (US) no longer occurs. This treatment diminishes anxiety symptoms (Bouchard et al., 1996; Foa, Rothbaum, Riggs, and Murdock, 1991).

In another kind of Pavlovian therapy, **systematic desensitization** (developed by Joseph Wolpe, then a South African psychiatrist), the patient would imagine a set of gradually more frightening scenes involving the phobic object (CS), at the same time as he would make a response incompatible with fear. Pavlovian extinction would occur with this exposure to the CS (thoughts about and, eventually, the actual phobic object) without the US (original trauma) and the UR (terror) (Nelissen, Muris, and Merckelbach, 1995; Turner, Beidel, and Jacob, 1994; Wolpe, 1969).

Pavlovian conditioning, then, provides a theory of how we normally learn to feel a given emotion toward a given object. By applying its basic phenomena to emotional disorders, we can arrive at a theory of how emotional disorders come about, and we can

In this mild form of exposure, a child who had acquired a fear of dogs is gently prodded toward one. Upon learning that the dog no longer presents danger, the child's fear of dogs disappears.

deduce a set of therapies that should undo abnormal emotional responses.

Operant Conditioning

At about the same time that Pavlov discovered an objective way to study how we learn "what goes with what," Edward L. Thorndike (1874–1949) began to study objectively how we learn "what to do to get what we want." Thorndike was studying animal intelligence. In one series of experiments, he put hungry cats in puzzle boxes and observed how they learned to escape confinement and get food. He designed various boxes—some had levers to push, others had strings to pull, and some had shelves to jump on—and he left food—often fish—outside the box. The cat would have to make the correct response to escape from the puzzle box.

Thorndike's first major discovery was that learning what to do was gradual, not insightful. That is, the cat proceeded by trial and error. On the first few trials, the time to escape was very long; but with repeated success, the time gradually shortened to a few seconds. To explain his findings, Thorndike formulated the **law of effect.** Still a major principle, it holds that when, in a given stimulus situation, a response is made and followed by positive consequences, the response will tend to be repeated; when followed by negative consequences, it will tend not to be repeated. Thorndike's work, like Pavlov's, was an objective way of studying the properties of learning.

This tradition was refined, popularized, and applied to a range of real-life settings by B. F. Skinner (1904–1990), who worked largely with rats pressing levers for food and with pigeons pecking lighted

B. F. Skinner (1904–1990) formulated the basic concepts of operant conditioning.

discs for grain. It was Skinner who formulated the basic concepts of operant conditioning.

THE CONCEPTS OF OPERANT CONDITIONING

Through his basic concepts, Skinner defined the elements of the law of effect rigorously. His three basic concepts consist of the reinforcer (both positive and negative), the operant, and the discriminative stimulus.

A **positive reinforcer** is an event whose onset increases the probability that a response preceding it will occur again. In effect, a positive reinforcer rewards behavior. A **negative reinforcer** is an event whose removal increases the probability of recurrence of a response that precedes it. **Punishers,** on the other hand, are events whose onset will decrease the probability of recurrence of a response that precedes it. The same stimulus whose onset acts as a punisher will usually act as a negative reinforcer when removed.

An **operant** is a response whose probability can either be increased by positive reinforcement or by the removal of negative reinforcement. If a mother reinforces her twelve-month-old child with a hug every time he says "Daddy," the probability that he will say it again is increased. In this case, the operant is "saying Daddy." If the mother hugs the child for saying Daddy only when the child's father is in sight, and does not hug him for saying Daddy when the father is not around, she is teaching the child to respond to a discriminative stimulus. In this case, the father in sight is the **discriminative stimulus,** a signal that means that reinforcement is available if the operant is made.

Edward L. Thorndike (1874–1949) studied animal intelligence and formulated the "law of effect."

Figure 3–2

ACQUISITION AND EXTINCTION

This typical curve depicts the growth in the frequency of lever pressing over the course of a number of experimental sessions, followed by its extinction when reinforcement is discontinued. (SOURCE: Adapted from Schwartz, 1984)

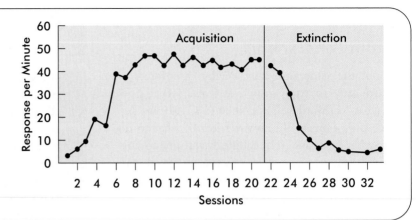

The phenomena of *acquisition* and *extinction* in the operant conditioning of voluntary responses parallel the Pavlovian conditioning of involuntary responses. Consider a typical operant paradigm. A hungry rat is placed inside an operant chamber. The desired operant is the pressing of a lever. Each time the rat presses a lever, food is delivered down a chute. During this acquisition procedure, learning to lever press proceeds gradually, as shown in Figure 3–2. It takes about ten sessions for the rat to learn to press at a high and constant rate. Extinction is then begun (in session 22), and the reinforcer (food) is no longer delivered when the rat presses the lever. As a result, responding gradually diminishes back to zero.

THE OPERANT THERAPIES

The operant therapist uses operant principles in asking three essential questions: (1) What undesirable behavior or maladaptive operants does the patient engage in? (2) What reinforcers maintain these maladaptive responses? (3) What environmental changes—usually reinforcement or discriminative stimulus changes—can be made to change the maladaptive behavior into adaptive behavior (Ullmann and Krasner, 1965)? A variety of operant therapies have been employed for a variety of forms of psychopathology (see Table 3–2). We will look at selective positive reinforcement, selective punishment, and extinction now and discuss other therapies in more detail in the chapters that involve the specific disorders that these therapies treat.

TABLE 3–2

OPERANT THERAPY

Maladaptive Behavior	Reinforcers That Maintain Behavior	Therapy	Response
Not eating by anorexic	Staying thin	Selective positive reinforcement (e.g., anorexic allowed to watch television after she has eaten)	Eating
Self-mutilation by autistic child	Self-stimulation	Selective punishment (e.g., pinches, spanking, cold water)	No self-mutilation
Hitting brother	Attention from parent	Selective punishment (e.g., television turned off)	No hitting brother
Patient disrupting nurses at nurses' station	Attention from nurses	Extinction (nurses ignore patient)	No disruptive visits

Selective Positive Reinforcement In the technique of **selective positive reinforcement,** the therapist selects a target behavior or adaptive behavior that is to be increased in probability. By the systematic delivery of positive reinforcement contingent on the occurrence of the target behavior, this behavior becomes more frequent.

Anorexia nervosa is a life-threatening disorder that, for the most part, afflicts women in their teens and early twenties. They literally starve themselves to death. By engaging in bizarre eating habits, such as eating only three Cheerios a day, a person with anorexia will lose 25 to 30 percent of her body weight within a couple of months. When they are hospitalized, the first objective with these patients (who may weigh as little as seventy-five pounds) is not curing them, but just saving their lives. Such patients usually do not cooperate with regimes that attempt to force them to eat. One highly effective way of saving the life of a woman with anorexia is to selectively reinforce her for eating by using a reinforcer that is more highly desired than is eating. But, if you ask her what would be a reward that would induce her to eat, she will probably not tell you. In order to discover what is positively reinforcing, a therapist will look for a behavior that the patient engages in frequently and will only give her the opportunity to perform it if she first eats (Premack, 1959). If we observe and time what such a patient does during the day, we might find, for example, that she watches television for an hour and a half, spends forty-five minutes talking with fellow patients, and spends an hour pacing the halls. An operant therapist would then set up a regime such that in order to be allowed to do any one of these three activities, the patient would first have to eat a fixed amount. For example, if she first ate a tablespoon of custard, she would then be allowed to watch television for ten minutes; if she ate all of her steak, she would then be allowed to pace the halls for twenty minutes (Stunkard, 1976).

During thirty years of research, selective positive reinforcement has been shown to be an effective technique across a very wide range of behavioral disorders. When a discrete and specifiable instrumental response is missing from the adaptive repertoire of an individual, application of selective positive reinforcement will generally produce and maintain that response.

Selective Punishment In **selective punishment,** the therapist selects a target behavior that is maladaptive. By applying an aversive event when this target behavior occurs, the therapist causes its probability of occurrence to decrease. An example might be eliminating or decreasing chronic nail-biting through applying mild aversion treatments (Allen, 1996).

Although we are not sure why, some children who have autism (a disorder characterized by severe social withdrawal) engage in self-mutilation (see Chapter 8). This maladaptive behavior is persistent, and most attempts at intervention on the part of a therapist will produce no, or only temporary, effects. In some of these cases, operant therapists have applied selective punishment. In one particular case, whenever the child hit himself, a shock was delivered to him. The child soon learned that his behavior brought punishment, and he engaged less often in self-mutilation (Dorsey, Iwata, Ong, and McSween, 1980; Lovaas and Simmons, 1969). This procedure did not cure the child's autism, but it did stop his maladaptive behavior.

Punishment in the form of pinches, spanks, and cold water is now widely used to curtail the self-destructive behavior of children with autism. Punishment in this form strikes some people as cruel, and in 1986, the Office for Children of the State of Massachusetts barred the use of such punishments in a school for children with autism. The children promptly regressed to their self-destructive behavior, and their parents went to court to overturn the ban, claiming that this was the only effective treatment their children had ever received. The court overturned the ban, charging that, out of sentimentalism, the Office of Children had played "Russian Roulette with the lives and safety of the students" by banning selective punishment (*New York Times,* June 5, 1986).

Extinction **Extinction** is another strategy for eliminating maladaptive behaviors: one can eliminate a behavior by merely omitting some highly desired event whenever the target behavior occurs. The most common use of extinction in behavior therapy is when the therapist suspects that some maladaptive target behavior is being performed in order to get some positive reinforcement. The therapist then arranges the contingencies so that this behavior no longer produces the reinforcement. If the behavior decreases in frequency, extinction has been successful. For example, there was a case of a female psychotic patient who would make numerous disruptive visits to the nurses' office on the ward. An operant therapist believed that the attention the patient received from the nurses when she barged into their office was a positive reinforcer that maintained the disruptive behavior. So the therapist instructed the nurses to ignore the patient completely when the patient entered their office, thereby eliminating what was believed to be positive reinforcement. After seven weeks of treatment, the patient's visits dropped from an average of sixteen per day to two per day (Ayllon and Michael, 1959).

Avoidance Learning

As we have seen, learning theorists regard human beings as capable of learning two sorts of relationships: the Pavlovian relationship—what goes with what—and the operant relationship—what to do in order to get what you want (see Table 3–3). There are many situations in which both sorts of learning go on at the same time. Prominent among such situations is learning to avoid aversive events. In an avoidance situation, two relationships have to be learned: (1) what predicts the aversive event, and (2) how to get away from it (Mowrer, 1948; Rescorla and Solomon, 1967). The avoidance situation combines both a Pavlovian relationship and an operant relationship. To investigate avoidance, behavior theorists typically place a rat in a two-compartment chamber called a shuttlebox. After a while, a tone is turned on. Ten seconds after the tone has gone on, an electric shock is delivered through the floor of the apparatus. If the rat runs to the other side of the shuttlebox before the shock comes on, the tone terminates and the shock is pre-

vented from occurring. Rats, dogs, and people usually learn to avoid shock altogether in these circumstances. In order to avoid the shock, the subject must learn two relationships: (1) He must learn that the tone predicts shock, and he must become afraid of the tone. This is a Pavlovian relationship in which the CS is the tone, the US is the shock, and the CR is the fear. (2) Having learned to fear the tone, he must learn what to do about it—that running to the other side of the shuttlebox terminates the fearful tone and prevents the shock from occurring. This is an operant relationship in which the discriminative stimulus is the tone, the operant is running to the other side of the shuttlebox, and the reinforcer is the termination of fear and the prevention of shock.

An understanding of avoidance learning helps in the treatment of certain psychopathologies. The behavioral view of obsessive-compulsive disorders, for example, involves the concept of avoidance learning. According to this view, the obsessive-compulsive checker believes that by engaging in the compulsive behavior of checking the stove several hundred times a day, she can prevent disaster from befalling her family. In this case, the occurrence and persistence of the compulsion may be explained by avoidance learning. Moreover, the relief of obsessive-compulsive checking by flooding can be explained by the Pavlovian extinction of fear and the operant extinction of the ritual (Griest, 1994). Behavior therapists often use both operant and Pavlovian procedures. Recall Steven, the person with a foot fetish who came to

TABLE 3–3

PAVLOVIAN VS. OPERANT THERAPIES

	Example of Problem	Origin	Therapy	Outcome
Pavlovian Therapies	Fear (CR) of closed spaces (CS)	CS (closed space) associated with US (abuse)/UR (terror)	CS (closed space) presented without US (abuse)/UR (terror) through flooding or systematic desensitization	CS (closed space) no longer produces CR (debilitating fear)
Operant Therapies	No social skills	Insufficient rewards for acquiring operant response (social skills)	Desired operant response (social skills) is rewarded through selective positive reinforcement (e.g., gets ice cream after interacting with others)	Operant response (social skills) is learned; patient interacts better with others

hate women's shoes after he received vomit-inducing ipecac. Whenever Steven made the operant response of reaching out to touch shoes, he felt queasy and withdrew his hand. By Pavlovian conditioning, the sight and feel of shoes had become nauseating. By operant conditioning, Steven had learned that withdrawing his hand from the shoes would reduce his queasiness. Let's look at how a behavior therapist would treat Angela:

> Angela was referred to a behavior therapist. This school of thought formulates depression as a lack of positive reinforcement and aims to extinguish maladaptive coping responses and to reinforce positive responses. Getting Angela engaged in active behaviors that would bring about gratification became the theme of therapy.
>
> Angela engaged in a "graded task assignment," in which the patient creates a hierarchy of instrumental behaviors that used to bring her gratification, with the least effortful one the first task, and a major, complex, organized set of actions the final task. Angela chose "ordering a book on Salsa dancing from Amazon.com" as her first assignment, and carried it out, with some reluctance. When the book arrived, she carried out the second assignment, which was to find a dance studio in which Salsa dancing was taught, and to designate an evening in which she would attend. As she worked her way up the hierarchy, through making an appointment and paying a deposit, she found her despair lifting. By the time she had completed the last item—taking six Salsa dancing lessons—she had begun to date Tony, one of her fellow Salsa dancing students. She was now looking forward to the future, and her appetite had returned.

The Cognitive Approach

The cognitive approach is an outgrowth and a reaction to the behavioral approach. Cognitive psychologists believe that what a person thinks, believes, expects, attends to, and how she interprets events— in short, her mental life—influences how she behaves. For the cognitive therapist, as for the behavior therapist (but not for the psychodynamic therapist), the symptoms are the disorder. Specifically, cognitive psychologists contend that these symptoms are disordered cognitions and that by changing these cognitions these disorders can be alleviated and perhaps

even cured. The following case demonstrates the role that thoughts can play in producing anxiety:

> Two individuals have the same speaking skills, but one is very anxious when giving a public speech, and the other speaks with ease in public. On different occasions, each gives a public speech and, as is common during the course of almost any speech, a few members of the audience walk out of the room during each speech. When these two people record what they were thinking when a member of the audience walked out, a very different pattern emerges. The anxious individual thinks, "I must be boring. How much longer do I have to speak? This speech is going to be a failure." In contrast, the low-anxiety person says to herself, "The person walking out must have a class to make. Gee, that's too bad, he will miss the best part of my talk." The same environmental event—people walking out of the room during the speech—produces a very different set of thoughts: the high-anxiety individual has depressing and tension-inducing thoughts, whereas the low-anxiety individual does not. (Meichenbaum, 1977)

How do behavioral and cognitive therapists look at this? On the one hand, the behavior therapist will focus on the particular environmental event—people walking out during a speech—and how this affects behavior. (In this example, the environmental event is the same, but the consequences are different.) The cognitive therapist, on the other hand, will focus on the difference in the thoughts of the two speakers, on how the speakers interpret the very same event. For the cognitive therapist, a person's thoughts are of primary importance.

Cognitive Therapy

Underlying the cognitive approach is the view that mental events—that is, expectations, beliefs, memories, interpretations, and so on—can cause behavior. If these mental events are changed, behavior change will follow. Believing this, the cognitive therapist looks for the cause, or etiology, of psychological disorders in disordered mental events. For example, if someone is depressed, the cognitive therapist will look for the cause of the individual's depression in her beliefs or thoughts. Perhaps she believes that she has no control over her husband, children, and workplace. Thinking that she has no control, she may well become passive, sad, and eventually clinically depressed. Successful therapy for such disorders will consist of changing these thoughts. In the case of the depressed individual, a cognitive therapist will draw out, analyze, and then help change the individual's thoughts that had caused the feeling of hopelessness.

To understand what a cognitive therapist does, let us return to the case study of the two speech-givers. What if the high-anxiety speaker becomes increasingly depressed when he sees members of the audience walking out? He may label the speech, and himself, a failure. Perhaps he gets so depressed that he can no longer give a good speech, or worse, refuses to speak before an audience. Because of this problem, he may enter therapy. What will a cognitive therapist then do?

Because a cognitive therapist is concerned primarily with what a person thinks and believes, the therapist will inquire about the anxious speaker's thoughts. Upon finding out that the speaker thinks that he is boring his audience, the therapist will pursue two hypotheses. First, there is the hypothesis that the speaker in reality is boring. But if in the course of the therapy, the therapist learns that the person's speeches have in the past been received very well, and that some have even been reprinted, the therapist will conclude that the first hypothesis is wrong.

After discarding the hypothesis that the speaker really is boring, the therapist will turn to the hypothesis that the speaker's thoughts are distorting reality. According to this hypothesis, the speaker is selecting negative evidence by focusing too narrowly on one event: He is thinking too much about those members of the audience who walked out. He believes that they think he is boring, that they dislike him, and so on. Here, the therapist gets the client to point out the contrary evidence. First, he has a fine speaking record. Second, only a very small number of people walked out; some probably had important appointments to catch and were glad to have heard at least part of the speech. Perhaps some of them were bored. But third, and most important, he minimized the fact that almost all of the audience remained, and he paid no attention to the fact that the audience applauded enthusiastically. The therapist's job is to draw out all of the distorted negative thoughts, to have her client confront the contrary evidence, and then to get him to change these thoughts.

What kinds of mental events do cognitive therapists deal with? For the purposes of therapy, cognitive processes can be divided into short-term and long-term processes. The short-term processes are

conscious. We are aware of them, or with practice, we can become aware of them. These include expectations, appraisals, and attributions. The long-term cognitive processes are not, generally speaking, available to consciousness. They are dispositions that show themselves in the way they govern the short-term processes. One long-term process involves beliefs. We will discuss the short-term processes first.

CHANGING EFFICACY EXPECTATIONS

Expectations are cognitions that explicitly anticipate future events. The speech-giver who, when he sees a few people walk out, thinks "this is going to be a failure" is reporting an expectation. He anticipates future consequences—in this case, bad ones. There are two kinds of expectancies: an ***outcome expectation*** is a person's estimate that a given behavior will lead to a particular outcome, and an ***efficacy expectation*** is the belief that he can successfully execute the behavior that produces this outcome. Outcome and efficacy expectations are different because a person may be certain that a particular course of action will produce a given outcome, but he may doubt that he can perform this action. For example, he may realize that touching a snake will reduce his snake phobia, but he may still be unable to touch the snake. The cognitive psychologist Albert Bandura believes that the success of systematic desensitization and modeling therapies in curing phobias (see Chapter 5) is attributable to changes in efficacy expectations. In both situations, the patient learns that he can make those responses—relaxation and approach—which will overcome the phobia. A "micro-analysis" of efficacy expectations and behavioral change in snake phobics has confirmed this speculation. Successful therapy created high efficacy expectations for approaching a boa constrictor. The higher the level of efficacy expectations at the end of treatment, the better was the approach behavior to the snake (Bandura, 1977, 1982, 1993; Bandura and Adams, 1977; Biran and Wilson, 1981; Rodgers and Brawley, 1996; Saigh, Mroueh, Zimmerman, and Fairbank, 1996; Staats, 1978).

Bandura (1977) argues that people with high self-efficacy:

1. are more likely to have high aspirations, take long views, set themselves difficult challenges, and commit themselves firmly to meeting those challenges;

2. will persevere longer and bounce back in the face of failures and setbacks;

3. will experience less stress, anxiety, and depression;

4. will attract support from others and so develop the satisfying relations that make hardship easier to bear.

MODIFYING NEGATIVE APPRAISALS

We are constantly evaluating both what happens to us and what we do. These ***appraisals*** are sometimes very obvious to us, but at other times, we are unaware of them. For cognitive therapists, such ***automatic thoughts*** precede and cause emotion (Beck, 1976, 1999). The speech-giver becomes anxious and depressed once he thinks, "This is going to be a failure." He is not only expecting future consequences, but he is also appraising his actions. He judges them to be failures, and this appraisal causes his negative emotions. This appraisal process is automatic. After a lifetime of practice, it occurs habitually and rapidly. The individual in therapy must be trained to slow down his thought process to become aware of such thoughts. Automatic thoughts are not vague and ill formed; rather, they are specific and discrete sentences. In addition, while they may seem implausible to the objective observer, they seem highly reasonable to the person who has them (Alden and Wallace, 1995; Beck, Steer, and Epstein, 1992; Kanfer and Karoly, 1972).

One instrument for discovering the frequency of automatic thoughts is the Automatic Thoughts Questionnaire (Hollon and Kendall, 1980). In answering its questions, clients record the frequency with which they make the following sorts of automatic appraisals of themselves, "I'm no good," "I'm so weak," "My life is a mess," "No one understands me," "It's just not worth it." The results show that when people are depressed, they have many more frequent negative automatic thoughts than when they are not depressed, and further, that these thoughts are specific to people with depression. Those who suffer from schizophrenia, substance abuse, or anxiety disorders do not record having frequent negative thoughts about themselves unless they are also depressed (Hollon, Kendall, and Lumry, 1986).

One of the two founders of cognitive therapy, Aaron T. Beck (1976, 1999), argues that specific emotions are always preceded by discrete thoughts. Sadness is preceded by the thought "something of value has been lost." Anxiety is preceded by the thought "a threat of harm exists," and anger is preceded by the thought "my personal domain is being trespassed against." This is a sweeping and simple formulation of emotional life: the essence of sadness, anxiety, and anger consists of appraisals of loss, threat, and trespass, respectively. Thus, cognitive therapists believe that modifying those thoughts will alter the emotion (Macleod and Cropley, 1995; Sokol, Beck, Greenberg, Wright, and Berchick, 1989).

CHANGING ATTRIBUTIONS

Another kind of short-term mental event that cognitive therapists try to modify is attribution. An ***attribution*** is an individual's explanation of why an event has befallen him. When a student fails an examination, he asks himself, "Why did I fail?" Depending on the causal analysis he makes, different consequences ensue. The student might make an ***external*** or ***internal attribution*** (Rotter, 1966). He might believe that the examination was unfair, an external cause. Alternatively, he might believe that he is stupid, an internal cause. A second dimension along which attributions for failure are made is ***stable*** or ***unstable*** (Weiner, 1974). A stable cause is one that persists in time; an unstable cause is one that is transient. For example, the student might believe that he failed because he did not get a good night's sleep, an unstable cause (which is also internal). Alternatively, the student might believe that he has no mathematical ability, a stable cause (which is also internal). Finally, an attribution for failure can be ***global*** or

Most observers would guess that these athletes' attributional styles are internal: they are taking personal responsibility for the loss of the game.

specific (Abramson, Seligman, and Teasdale, 1978; Seligman, 1991). An attribution to global factors means that failure must occur on many different tasks, and an attribution to specific factors means that failure must occur only on this task. For example, the student who fails might believe that he failed because he is stupid, a global cause (which is also stable and internal). Or he might believe that he failed because the form number of the test was 13, an unlucky number. This latter is a specific attribution (which is also external and stable). Table 3–4 presents these alternative attributions (Heider, 1958; Kelley, 1967; Seligman, 1991; Weiner, 1972).

Cognitive therapists try to change an individual's attributions. For example, women with low self-esteem usually make internal attributions when they fail. They believe that they have failed because they are stupid, incompetent, and unlovable. To deal with this attribution, each week the therapist has them record five different bad events that have occurred during each week, and then he has them write down *external* attributions for the events. For example, one woman might write, "my boyfriend criticized my behavior at a party last night, not because I am socially unskilled, but rather because he was in a bad mood." The goal is to get the woman to shift from internal to external what she believes to be the causes of bad events. After a few weeks, clients begin to see that there are alternative causes for their failures. As a result, low self-esteem and depression brought about

by the internal attributions begin to lift (Beck, Rush, Shaw, and Emery, 1979; Seligman, 1995).

CHANGING LONG-TERM BELIEFS

The short-term mental events that we have examined—expectations, appraisals, and attributions—are available to consciousness. Long-term cognitive processes are different. They are dispositions inferred to govern the mental events now in consciousness. One of these long-term cognitive processes is *belief.*

Albert Ellis, the other founder of cognitive therapy, argues that psychological disorder stems largely from irrational beliefs. He gives an example of a client who, over the course of a lifetime, had had a set of destructive beliefs instilled in him by his parents and by society. Among these were the ideas that: (1) it is a dire necessity for an adult human being to be loved or approved by virtually every significant other person in his community; (2) one should be thoroughly competent, adequate, and achieving in all possible respects in order to be worthwhile; (3) it is awful and catastrophic when things are not the way one would very much like them to be; (4) human unhappiness is externally caused, and we have little or no ability to control our own sorrows; (5) our past history is an all-important determinant of our present behavior; if something once strongly affected our life, it should always have a similar effect; and (6) there is invariably a right, precise, and perfect so-

TABLE 3–4

ATTRIBUTIONS OF STUDENTS WHO DO POORLY ON THE GRADUATE RECORD EXAMINATION

| | Internal | | External | |
	Stable	Unstable	Stable	Unstable
Global	Lack of intelligence (Laziness)	Exhaustion (Having a cold makes me stupid.)	ETS gives unfair tests. (People are usually unlucky on the GRE.)	Today is Friday the 13th. (ETS gave experimental tests this time that were too hard for everyone.)
Specific	Lack of mathematical ability (Math always bores me.)	Fed up with math problems (Having a cold ruins my arithmetic.)	ETS gives unfair math tests. (People are usually unlucky on math tests.)	The math test was form No. 13. (Everyone's copy of the math test was blurred.)

NOTE: ETS = Educational Testing Service, the maker of Graduate Record Examinations (GRE).
SOURCE: Abramson, Seligman, and Teasdale, 1978.

lution to human problems, and it is catastrophic if this perfect solution is not found (Ellis, 1962).

These irrational and illogical beliefs shaped the short-term distorted expectations, appraisals, and attributions that produced psychological disorder. The client was afflicted with a "tyranny of shoulds," and the job of the therapist was to break the hold of these "shoulds." Once the patient abandoned the above beliefs, it was impossible for him to remain disturbed. The job of the therapist was to rid the individual of these beliefs. The therapy was an aggressive one. It made a concerted attack on the client's beliefs in two ways: (1) the therapist was a frank counter-propagandist who contradicted superstitions and self-defeating propaganda embodied in the irrational beliefs of the patient, and (2) the therapist encouraged, persuaded, cajoled, and occasionally insisted that the patient engage in behavior that would itself be forceful counter-propaganda against the irrational beliefs (Ellis, 1962; Kendall, Haaga, Ellis, and Bernard, 1995). This is called *rational-emotive therapy,* and it is among the most active and aggressive of psychotherapeutic procedures. The following case illustrates the force of therapeutic persuasion:

> During his therapy session, a twenty-three-year-old man said that he was very depressed and did not know why. A little questioning showed that this severely neurotic patient, whose main presenting problem was that he had been doing too much drinking during the last two years, had been putting off the inventory keeping he was required to do as part of his job as an apprentice glass-staining artist.
>
> PATIENT: I know that I should do the inventory before it piles up to enormous proportions, but I just keep putting it off. To be honest, I guess it's because I resent doing it so much.
>
> THERAPIST: But why do you resent it so much?
>
> PATIENT: It's boring. I just don't like it.
>
> THERAPIST: So it's boring. That's a good reason for disliking this work, but is it an equally good reason for resenting it?
>
> PATIENT: Aren't the two the same thing?
>
> THERAPIST: By no means. Dislike equals the sentence, "I don't enjoy doing this thing, and therefore I don't want to do it." And that's a perfectly sane sentence in most instances. But resentment is the sentence, "Because I dislike doing this thing, I shouldn't have to do it." And

> that's invariably a very crazy sentence.
>
> PATIENT: Why is it so crazy to resent something that you don't like to do?
>
> THERAPIST: There are several reasons. First of all, from a purely logical standpoint, it just makes no sense at all to say to yourself, "Because I dislike doing this thing, I shouldn't have to do it." The second part of this sentence just doesn't follow in any way from the first part. Your reasoning goes something like this: "Because I dislike doing this thing, other people and the universe should be so considerate of me that they should never make me do what I dislike." But, of course, this doesn't make any sense. Why should other people and the universe be that considerate of you? It might be nice if they were. But why the devil should they be? In order for your reasoning to be true, the entire universe, and all the people in it, would really have to revolve around and be uniquely considerate of you. (Ellis, 1962)

Here the therapist directly attacks the client's belief, arguing that it is irrational. This is an important distinction between cognitive therapists, on the one hand, and behavioral or psychodynamic therapists on the other. Behavioral and psychodynamic therapists point out that a client's actions and beliefs are maladaptive and self-defeating. Cognitive therapists emphasize that, in addition, the beliefs are irrational and illogical. Let's look at how a cognitive therapist would treat Angela:

> Angela was referred to a cognitive therapist. In cognitive theory, depression is seen as resulting from automatic, catastrophic, and irrational thoughts about loss. Therapy consists of learning to recognize these automatic thoughts and learning to dispute them in the same way you would dispute the false accusations of a third person whose mission in life was to make you miserable.
>
> Angela began to keep a diary of what she thought at the times during the day when she suddenly became sadder. She found that whenever she thought about dating again, she felt particularly despondent, and when she was on her way home from work, she often began to cry. The automatic thoughts that accompanied the dating fantasies were "I'm unlovable," "No man would put up with me," "Love always dies."

When going home, the automatic thoughts were "Mom always starts a fight with me" and "the evening will be empty."

She learned to marshal evidence against the thoughts and to actively dispute all these catastrophic thoughts. So, for example, when she thought "I'm unlovable," she disputed it with "I'm quite presentable-looking" (Angela was, in fact, very pretty), "I've got a great sense of humor and tell funny stories all the time," and "I'm a sympathetic listener—there is a lot about me the right guy could love." She found that when she disputed these thoughts successfully, the despair lifted momentarily, and returned with less force and less often.

Cognitive-Behavioral Therapy

Cognitive therapists, then, believe that distorted thinking causes disordered behavior and that correcting the distorted thinking will alleviate and even cure the disordered behavior. Behavior therapists, in contrast, view disordered behavior as learned from past experience, and they attempt to alleviate the disorders by training the patients to use new, more adaptive behaviors. These two positions are increasingly compatible, and many therapists try both to correct distorted cognitions and to train patients to engage in new behaviors. When therapists combine both techniques, it is called *cognitive-behavioral therapy (CBT)* (Beck, Rush, Shaw, and Emery, 1979; Craske, Maidenberg, and Bystritsky, 1995; Ellis, 1962; Mahoney, 1974; Meichenbaum, 1977).

Arnold Lazarus is one of the therapists who integrates cognitive and behavioral techniques in therapy (Lazarus, 1993). He calls this combination of techniques *multimodal therapy.* Lazarus argues that a disorder occurs in the same patient at seven different levels, and that there are levels of therapy appropriate to each level of disorder. The mnemonic device for these seven levels is BASIC ID, where B is behavior, A affect, S sensation, I imagery, C cognition, I interpersonal relations, D drugs. The job of the therapist using such multimodal therapy is to separate the disorder into its different levels and to choose appropriate techniques for each level. Lazarus is willing to use cognitive techniques, behavioral techniques, and even psychodynamic procedures. Table 3–5 shows the variety of treatments used in the course of the

TABLE 3–5

BASIC ID TECHNIQUES

Modality	Problem	Proposed Treatment
Behavior	Inappropriate withdrawal responses	Assertiveness training
	Frequent crying	Nonreinforcement
	Excessive eating	Low-calorie regimen
Affect	Unable to express overt anger	Role playing
	Frequent anxiety	Relaxation training and reassurance
	Absence of enthusiasm and spontaneous joy	Positive imagery procedures
Sensation	Stomach spasms	Abdominal breathing and relaxing
	Out of touch with most sensual pleasures	Sensate focus method
	Tension in jaw and neck	Differential relaxation
Imagery	Distressing scenes of sister's funeral	Desensitization
	Recurring dreams about airplane bombings	Vivid imagery evoking feelings of being safe
Cognition	Irrational self-talk: "I am evil." "I must suffer." "Sex is dirty." "I am inferior."	Deliberate rational questioning and corrective self-talk
	Overgeneralization	Critical analysis of irrational sentences
Interpersonal relationships	Childlike dependence	Specific self-sufficiency assignments
	Easily exploited and submissive	Assertiveness training
	Manipulative tendencies	Training in direct and confrontational behaviors
Drugs	Disordered biochemistry	Antipsychotic drugs

SOURCE: Adapted from Lazarus, 1976.

thirteen-month therapy for Mary Ann, a twenty-four-year-old woman diagnosed as having chronic undifferentiated schizophrenia with a very poor prognosis. She was overweight, apathetic, and withdrawn. She had been heavily medicated, but with little effect. By the end of the thirteen months of these techniques, she was functioning well and engaged to be married.

Combining Cognitive-Behavioral Therapy and Psychodynamics

There has been a movement among psychodynamically oriented therapists to combine cognitively oriented concepts and psychodynamic therapy. Lester Luborsky (1984) argues that what a patient consciously thinks about in three spheres of life reveals an underlying, and often unconscious, core conflictual relationship theme (CCRT). The three spheres are: (1) current in-treatment relationship (the relationship with the therapist), (2) current out-of-treatment relationships, and (3) past relationships. Common cognitions about these spheres, and their recurrent overlap point to the patient's basic conflicted theme about interpersonal relations (Luborsky, Popp, Luborsky, and Mark, 1994).

Ms. N. thinks, "I am trying to do well in my work," a thought about her current out-of-treatment relationships. She tells this to the therapist, and she begins to cry. The therapist then remarks, "You get tearful and cry when I refer to your attractiveness," a result of her thoughts about the in-treatment relationship. Ms. N. then spontaneously thinks about her past, "Father could never stand my being attractive." The content of these three conscious spheres reflects the main unconscious CCRT. By disentangling the cognitions involved in the three spheres, the therapist can discover the client's wish: "I wish I could find a suitable man to provide me with the physical and emotional support I need." The therapist can also discover (and attempt to alter) the negative consequence, or automatic thoughts, that follow from the wish: "But I shouldn't because I am independent, and I can't because I will be rejected, and the man will not be able to provide that kind of support."

By attending to the conscious automatic thoughts that cognitive therapists emphasize, psychodynamically oriented therapists are beginning to bring these two disparate models closer together (Horowitz et al., 1993). Other integrations across models are likely in the future, and as Box 3–2 shows, the integration of neuroscience with cognitive-behavioral therapy is one highly promising arena.

Evaluating Behavioral and Cognitive Therapy

There are several virtues of behavior therapy and cognitive therapy: they are effective in treating a number of disorders; therapy is generally brief and inexpensive; they seem to be based on a science of behavioral and cognitive psychology; and their units of analysis—stimuli, responses, reinforcers, expectations, and attributions—can be measured. Behavioral and cognitive therapies, however, are not without problems. Perhaps the most serious allegation is that they are superficial.

Are humans more than just behavior and cognition? Are psychological disorders more than disordered behavior and disordered thinking? Must therapy, in order to be successful, do more than merely provide more adaptive behaviors and more rational ways of thinking? Because behavior therapists and cognitive therapists restrict themselves to an analysis of the discrete behaviors and cognitions of the human being, they miss the essence: that individuals are wholes, that they are free to choose. A patient with a cat phobia is more than a machine who happens to be afraid of cats. He is an individual whose symptoms are deeply rooted in his personality and psychodynamics, as well as in his genes and his neurochemistry. Alternatively, he is an individual who has made bad choices, but who can still choose health. A child with autism who treats other human beings as if they were pieces of furniture may be taught by behaviorists to hug other people in order to receive food or to escape from shock. But in the end, all we have is a child with autism who hugs people. Merely changing how one behaves fails to change the underlying disorder.

Those who object to the behavioral and cognitive views feel that there are deeper, underlying etiologies that produce symptoms. Because of this, seemingly superficial behavioral change may be short-lived, as in the behavioral treatments of obesity. Most people can lose 10 percent of their body weight in a couple of months by following

Science and Practice

Box 3—2

Combining Neuroscience with Cognitive-Behavioral Therapy

It is not only psychodynamics that has been fruitfully integrated with cognitive-behavioral therapy, but neuroscience as well. Jeffrey Schwartz at UCLA administers a "cognitive-biobehavioral" treatment for obsessive-compulsive disorder (OCD). OCD, which you will read about in Chapter 5, is a disorder in which the individual is haunted by repetitive and alien thoughts and images (the obsessions) and engages in seemingly senseless rituals (the compulsions) to neutralize the anxiety the thoughts generate.

Schwartz tells his patients that OCD is a brain disorder, and that the first step in therapy is learning to *relabel* their intrusive thoughts as a medical condition (Schwartz, 1998). The patients then learn to *reattribute* the bothersome and persistent nature of the thoughts to mere "false brain messages." Then patients learn to *refocus* by working around the stress of the intrusive thought and changing their rituals while conscious of the upsetting thought. Finally, the patients *revalue* the obsessive thoughts, seeing them as mere symptoms of false brain messages, and anxiety fades. To bolster the theory, Schwartz measures brain activity of his patients before, during, and after cognitive-biobehavioral sessions. He uses a PET scan to display brain changes, and finds three basic neural alterations as a result of his four-stage cognitive-behavioral therapy:

1. Individuals who respond to therapy show greater decreases in activity in the caudate nucleus on both sides of the brain than individuals who fail to improve.
2. The stronger the relief of OCD symptoms in treatment, the larger the brain activity change.
3. Before treatment, three brain areas involved in OCD (the caudate nucleus, the cingulate gyrus, and the right thalamus) all fired together. After treatment, this correlation of activity was broken up, which Schwartz calls "freeing the patient from the brain lock."

While much of this thinking is metaphorical or "neuromythological," this kind of research is important and lights a beacon toward the eventual integration of neuroscience and psychotherapy.

---

behavioral treatments for weight loss. In a long-term study of obese dieters, researchers found that after one year many obese individuals who had undergone behavior therapy had kept their weight down. But after five years, the weight returned in the case of more than 85 percent of the dieters (Seligman, 1994). Although behavioral therapy had led to change by removing the symptom of obesity, the underlying problem, probably biological in nature, remained and ultimately sabotaged the treatment.

How might behavioral and cognitive therapists respond to these charges of superficiality? A militant response might be to deny the concept of the "whole person." To radical behaviorists, such a concept is romantic; it makes sense in literature and in poetry, but not for human beings in distress and in need of relief. We would make a less militant reply. Removing symptoms—either behavioral or cognitive—at least helps. Symptom substitution has rarely, if ever, followed successful behavioral or cognitive therapy. Some disorders are highly specific, peripheral to the heart of an individual's being, and amenable to behavior and cognitive therapies. Phobias, stuttering, and some sexual dysfunctions are such disorders. On the other hand, there may be deeper disorders left untouched by behavioral and cognitive therapy: schizophrenia and antisocial personality disorder, for example. For these disorders, successful treatment most likely necessitates changing personality, uncovering dynamics, and administering drugs.

Behavioral and cognitive theorists believe that human misery, including problems of psychological disorder, is sometimes, but not always, produced by an unfortunate set of environmental circumstances or by distorted cognition. To counteract such circumstances by applying behavioral and cognitive therapy does not diminish or devalue human wholeness or freedom, but rather enlarges it. An individual who is so crippled by a phobia of leaving his apartment that he cannot work or see those he loves is not free. By applying behavioral and cognitive therapy to such an individual, one can remove this phobia. Such an individual will then be free to lead a rational life.

Putting It All Together

Psychodynamics is, by design, not about symptoms, but about underlying character. Psychodynamic therapy is very long and very expensive, and what it seems to work on is not alleviating the symptoms of DSM disorders, but creating personality change. Few people can afford the time or money needed, and health insurance schemes are unwilling to reimburse such long-term, difficult-to-measure, and uncertainly-related-to-health treatment. Psychoanalysts have become an endangered species. This is unfortunate, since surely some, and perhaps many, of the disorders we will read about involve deep issues of character, and not mere symptoms. The future viability of psychodynamic theory and therapy, in our view, will depend on delineating those problems, which require character change, welcoming rigorous measurement of such change, and making its blessings more accessible to more people.

The existential and humanistic approaches were an important corrective to the dismal psychodynamic view of human beings as driven by irrational sexual and aggressive conflicts inside themselves. The hearts of these existential and humanistic thinkers were certainly in the right place. Unfortunately, however, they not only revolted against a negative view of humanity but also against rigorous and cumulative science. They advocated, along with their salutary emphasis on will and responsibility, a "science" that was absent rigorous measurement, absent experimentation, and largely absent statistics. In brief, they combined a useful idea with less-than-useful methodology. Existential and humanistic thinking, therefore, has not been cumulative. Nonetheless, we believe that the humane premises of existential therapy wedded to solid empirical science will provide a viable future for this approach.

The behavioral approach advocates getting rid of maladaptive symptoms using behavioral techniques grounded in the animal laboratory. After an initial flowering of interest in the 1960s and 1970s, behavior therapy became quite stagnant. There are several reasons for this, including a waning of interest in animal learning, divorced as it is from human cognition, as well as the recognition that behavioral symptoms at least sometimes flow from underlying processes like cognition and personality. We believe that the future of behavior therapy lies in being able to delineate which disorders are merely their behavioral symptoms, and which are deeper. To understand the full panoply of disorders, the behavioral approach will have to adopt or explain cognitions and personality. To treat the deeper disorders effectively, the behavioral approach will need to wed itself to the cognitive, psychodynamic, and biological approaches.

There was a great burgeoning of cognitive therapy in the 1980s and 1990s as it took up where behavior therapy left off. But increasingly cognitive therapists have found that successful treatment is not nearly as brief as they had originally hoped. Issues of underlying character and conflicts from early in life keep rearing their heads when cognitive therapists treat the mere conscious cognitions about loss, danger, and anger. Further it has not been enough for a patient merely to replace a destructive, negative thought with a healthier, positive cognition. Rather, the patient must *believe* the new cognition as well—and change in belief does not come easily, and is not explained by cognitive theory. Moreover, buoyed by its successes in treating depression and anxiety, cognitive therapy has imperialistically branched out to all the disorders, but with mixed success. We believe the future of cognitive therapy lies in delineating which disorders it works best on and why, and marrying it to deeper processes—both of personality and of biology—when encountering deeper disorders.

It is a common finding that each of the psychological approaches is effective with most of the disorders (Seligman, 1996). This is not a mystery. We believe that this is so because each school of thought addresses one or more of the problems that constitute each disorder, and that each approach identifies and builds a variety of strengths in the patients that buffer them against further troubles, as in Angela's case:

> All four psychological approaches to Angela's depression worked. The psychoanalytic approach worked by putting Angela in better touch with her angry feelings and helping her to express them constructively and appropriately. Existential therapy worked by getting Angela to realize that she was passive and indecisive, and pushing her into taking responsibility for own future. Behavior therapy worked by getting Angela out into the world, interacting with other people, and discovering that she could act to bring about gratification. Cognitive therapy worked when Angela came to recognize and effectively dispute her own irrational thoughts about being unlovable.

The four psychological approaches can themselves be seen as different levels of analysis, parallel to the difference in level between biological and psychological approaches. The levels can be ordered as levels of "depth." At the surface level is the behavioral approach with its doctrine that the disorder *is* the behavioral symptoms and that getting rid of these symptoms *cures* the disorder. This turns out to be occasionally true, as you will read in Chapter 5, such as in the case of many specific phobias. But often, behavioral approaches just do not go deep enough. At the next level down, the cognitive approach holds that symptoms are produced by underlying conscious thoughts, and that changing these thoughts will cure the symptoms. This too sometimes works, as you will read in Chapter 7, as in many cases of depression. But often, it does not go deep enough. Sometimes the issues crucially concern will and responsibility—yet another level deeper—and here the existential therapies do useful work. But beneath that layer are issues of abiding character traits, the issues that psychodynamic approaches have wrestled with for more than one hundred years. And beneath that is our biology and our genetic inheritance. So it is our view that the future of psychological approaches to abnormality lies in understanding and in integrating the different layers of depth that make us what we are.

Summary

1. *Psychodynamic theories* are centrally concerned with conflict, anxiety, and defense. *Conflict* arises when desires cannot find immediate gratification because such gratification is not permitted by reality or conscience. Conflict generates *anxiety,* a form of psychic pain that arises when individuals feel they cannot cope. Anxiety can be either conscious or unconscious and gives rise to *defense mechanisms,* which are the mind's flexible editing mechanisms that allow individuals to alter or entirely obliterate painful stimuli that arise from either desire or reality.

2. Freud divided the personality into three kinds of processes: id, ego, and superego. The *id* is concerned with sexual and aggressive desires and is dominated by the *pleasure principle.* The *ego* is concerned with the individual's safety, allows desire to be expressed only when aversive consequences from other sources are minimal, and is dominated by the *reality principle.* The *superego* consists of the individual's conscience and ideals, and regardless of what reality permits, it either forbids individuals to express desires, or urges them toward the achievement of higher goals.

3. Many of our inner conflicts occur in the *unconscious,* which includes forgotten memories and repressed memories. *Repressed memories* live on because they are not subject to rational control; they are the dominant forces in personality.

4. Our inner conflicts can bring about much anxiety. To relieve anxiety, individuals use such defense mechanisms, or coping strategies, as *repression, projection, displacement, denial,* and *sublimation.*

5. The *neo-Freudians,* Jung, Adler, Horney, Sullivan, Erikson, and Fromm, generally found Freud's formulations too narrowly focused. Some stressed the impact of social relationships on psychological development. More recent theorists like Kohut focus on the central role of *ego processes* in personality. These modern psychodynamic theorists stress the importance of the self as the repository of values and the source of continuity across time and place. There are at least three significant aspects of self: the *core self,* the *subjective self,* and the *verbal self. Selfobjects* are people and things that are especially important for maintaining the self.

6. Psychodynamic therapies seek to make conscious that which is unconscious through encouraging the client to *free-associate* and to examine dreams, resistances, and the *transference* that occurs between the client and therapist. Psychodynamic treatment aims to enable the client to reduce the amount of *psychic energy* that is invested in defensive maneuvers, and to achieve greater control over impulse expression. Psychodynamic practice follows the *medical model* in attempting to remove the underlying conflict to effect a lasting cure of symptoms.

7. Critics of psychoanalysis cite difficulties of proof, indifference to the scientific method, and disregard of the situation and gender.

8. *Existential* and *humanistic theorists* hold that we are the authors of our experience. We determine what we perceive and what we experience; we are responsible for how we behave. *Freedom* and *responsibility,* however, may create anxiety. Responsibility avoidance is occasionally achieved through denying ownership of behavior and thought.

9. Existentialists often posit two kinds of will: *exhortative will* forces us to do what we know we

should do, and *goal-directed will* is unleashed when we have freely chosen our goals and want to pursue and achieve them.

10. Existentialists believe that the fundamental anxiety is *fear of death.* Psychologically, death means nonbeing. Because the fear of death is so threatening, people attempt to endow themselves with immortality by becoming *special* or by *fusion* with others, which may lead to inauthentic, or false, modes of behavior.

11. The *behavioral approach* aims to discover, by laboratory experiment, what aspect of the environment produces maladaptive learning, and it sees successful therapy as learning new and more adaptive ways of behaving.

12. Two kinds of basic learning processes exist: *Pavlovian* and *operant conditioning.* These have each generated a set of behavior therapies.

13. Pavlovian therapies begin with the assumption that emotional habits have been acquired by the contingency between a *conditioned stimulus* and an *unconditioned stimulus.* The formerly neutral conditioned stimulus now produces a *conditioned response,* which is the acquired emotion. Two Pavlovian therapies, *systematic desensitization* and *exposure,* extinguish some maladaptive emotional habits quite successfully.

14. Operant conditioning is based on three concepts: *reinforcer, operant,* and *discriminative stimulus.* Operant therapies are based on the assumption that people acquire voluntary habits by *positive* and *negative reinforcement* and *punishment.* Operant therapies provide new and more adaptive repertoires of voluntary responses and extinguish maladaptive voluntary responses. Among such therapies are *selective positive reinforcement, selective punishment,* and *extinction.* These have been applied with some success to such disorders as anorexia nervosa and autism.

15. The understanding of *avoidance learning* combines operant and Pavlovian theory, and it helps in the treatment of obsessive-compulsive disorders.

16. The *cognitive approach* holds that mental events can cause behavior. More particularly, disordered cognitions can cause disordered behavior, and changing these disordered cognitions can alleviate and sometimes cure psychopathology.

17. Cognitive therapy is carried out by attempting to change different sorts of mental events, which can be divided into short-term mental events and long-term mental events. Short-term mental events consist of *expectations,* including *outcome and efficacy expectations, appraisals* (mental evaluations of our experience), and *attributions* (the explanations of the causes of events that befall us).

18. Many therapists practice both cognitive and behavioral therapy and are called *cognitive-behavioral therapists. Multimodal therapy* is an example of the use of cognitive and behavioral techniques along with techniques from the other models. Contrary to the medical model, both cognitive and behavioral therapists believe that the symptoms—disordered behavior and disordered thought—constitute the entire problem.

19. Critics of cognitive and behavioral therapy argue that human beings are more than their behaviors and cognitions, and that it is superficial to treat only the symptoms rather than the whole person and the underlying etiology. Cognitive and behavioral therapists reply by arguing that it is often helpful to the client merely to remove the symptoms.

20. We believe that the future of the psychological therapies lies in viewing the panoply of disorders as having different *depth,* understanding which kind of psychological treatment applies best to which depth of disorder, and *integrating* these therapies with one another and with biological conceptions.

4

The Biological Approach and Neuroscience

Chapter Outline

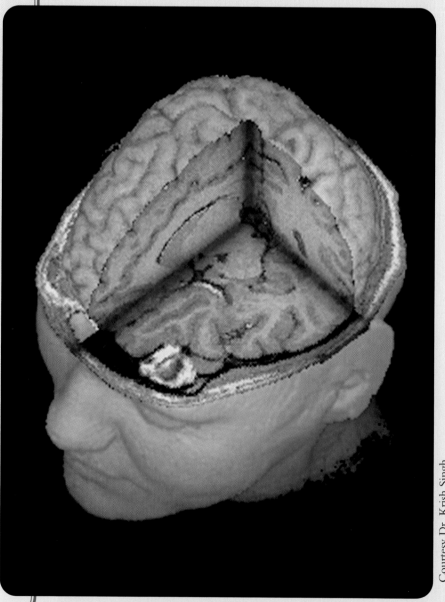

Courtesy Dr. Krish Singh.

Learning Objectives

→ Begin to understand how the interaction between biological and psychological stressors can lead to abnormal behavior.

→ Learn about genes and how researchers study their effects on behavior.

→ Understand why a person's phenotype may differ from his genotype and why heredity does not necessarily lead to psychopathology.

→ Be able to describe the structure of neurons, how they communicate with each other, and how neurotransmission may become disordered.

→ Familiarize yourself with the various regions of the nervous system, the functions they serve, and the brain circuits that are especially relevant to psychopathology.

→ Learn about the changes in the brain that occur during prenatal and postnatal development, and how disruptions in neurodevelopment can lead to abnormality.

→ Become familiar with neuroscience research methods and recent findings that have important implications for abnormal psychology.

A group of scientists and government officials dubbed the 1990s "the decade of the brain" because of the rapid advances in knowledge about the brain derived from new methods of studying the brain and its functions (Hyman, 2000). To begin to understand the explosion of new findings about the brain and how it works, we take this chapter to examine the nervous system, especially the brain, and the way it develops, functions, and affects behavior, particularly abnormal behavior. In the past, it was common to hear such questions as: Is a mental disorder biological or psychological? Is it due to nature or nurture? Is it caused by genes or the environment? Some observers contended that biological explanations were not compatible with psychological explanations. For example, they asked whether depression stemmed from a biological malfunction or psychological factors. But as modern research shows, mental disorders are never a matter of psychological versus biological, but always reflect the *interaction* of both.

This intertwining of biological and psychological factors leads us to pose a more complex kind of question about the causes of any mental disorder: How do our genes, our prenatal environment, our brain development, and our general physical health *combine* with our life experiences to predispose us either toward mental health or mental disorder? We need to be aware of the different ways these factors can interact. Certain genes or combinations of genes may make us more susceptible to certain psychological environments. But these same psychological environments can determine whether certain genes become "expressed" in the first place. Similarly, abnormalities in brain function can predispose us to mental disorder, but our experiences can be the key to whether or not we actually develop the disorder. Given this complexity, how can we even begin to understand the causes of mental disorder? To give us a start, we present the case of Tom, who began to exhibit some worrisome behavior soon after he took his first job. Throughout the chapter, we will periodically revisit the case of Tom and try to make sense of his behavior.

Upon graduation from college with a degree in electrical engineering, Tom Clark got his own apartment and accepted a position as a research assistant at the university. Tom worked along with several faculty members on a research project that was funded by the

Department of Defense. The position required a security clearance because the research involved the development of new electronic control systems for missiles. Tom was pleased and so were his parents. But about three months after beginning the job, he called his mother from a phone booth to tell her that she should avoid calling him at his apartment. He informed her that his phone had been tapped because of the research he was doing. This seemed strange to Tom's parents, although they complied with his request. But as Tom became more and more distant from them and his friends, his parents began to worry. He spent almost every evening and weekend alone in his apartment. He had lost weight recently, and he was less conscientious about his appearance. After this went on for several months, Mr. and Mrs. Clark became convinced that the change in his behavior was due to some physical problem.

Although Tom's parents might first have suspected that he was on drugs or associating with the wrong crowd, they also would have good reasons for suspecting a physical problem. The media have been flooded with reports on new drugs, new therapies, and new procedures for studying and treating the brain. Tom's parents may have read articles or seen TV programs on how researchers have made enormous advances in scanning the brain, in mapping the human genome (that is, identifying the location of the genes that influence various human characteristics), and in finding biological causes and treatments for various physical and mental disorders. With such knowledge, Tom's parents could easily believe that his loss in weight, his suspiciousness, his isolation, and the other changes in his behavior might indicate that something physical and possibly psychological could be wrong with him.

We now turn to our examination of the biological approach and neuroscience to try to find out what may have been wrong with Tom, and to learn about normal and abnormal brain function. This chapter will introduce you to the biological structures and processes that affect behavior. We begin with a discussion of the ways researchers have thought about, and studied, the biological determinants of abnormality. Then, we turn to an overview of the nervous system, starting with the tiniest, microscopic elements and moving through the larger structures of the nervous system. In our exploration of genes, we will examine how hereditary factors can contribute to both physical and behavioral characteristics. As our journey proceeds, we will move from the neuron, the cellular building block of the nervous system, to the brain, then to the entire nervous system.

The Biological Approach

Early theories of the biological roots of psychological problems paved the way for what came to be known as the **biomedical model.** This model applied the same terms to psychological and behavioral abnormalities that were used to describe physical illnesses. For example, the terms "illness" and "disease" were applied to abnormal behavior. Diagnosticians searched for specific sets of criteria to distinguish normal from abnormal behavior. The model also led many to think of biology as the initial and main cause of psychological problems. Proponents of the biological approach, in its original and simplest form, assumed that abnormal behavior indicated biological malfunction, with optimal treatment necessarily involving some kind of biological intervention such as surgery or medication. Researchers began to search for biological causes and cures.

But something was missing from both the early theories and the standard biomedical model that grew out of them. As we indicated earlier, the missing piece of the puzzle was the interplay between the individual and the environment. We now know that biological processes, especially the way the brain functions, are influenced by experience, and that experience is influenced by biological factors. This new perspective is reflected in modern theories about the causes of abnormal behavior. These theories consider both biology and the environment and how they interact (see Figure 4–1). The "interactional" perspective has also influenced clinicians who treat individuals with psychological problems. They now want to know about the person's physical condition, as well as her current living situation and social relationships. Thus, biological explanations of abnormal behavior have undergone change, but they have continued to flourish.

When we use the term "biological," we are referring to physical characteristics, especially a person's brain structure and biochemistry. An individual may have a biological vulnerability to mental illness that involves an imbalance in brain biochemistry, or an abnormality in the way the various parts of the brain are interconnected. Today, many researchers are

Figure 4—1

INTERACTION OF BIOLOGY AND ENVIRONMENT

Biology and environment affect each other before and after birth. The genotype and prenatal environment interact to produce the phenotype of the newborn. Both the phenotype and the individual's physical and social environment influence the course of brain development, which affects behavior. Behavior in turn has an impact on the individual's environment.

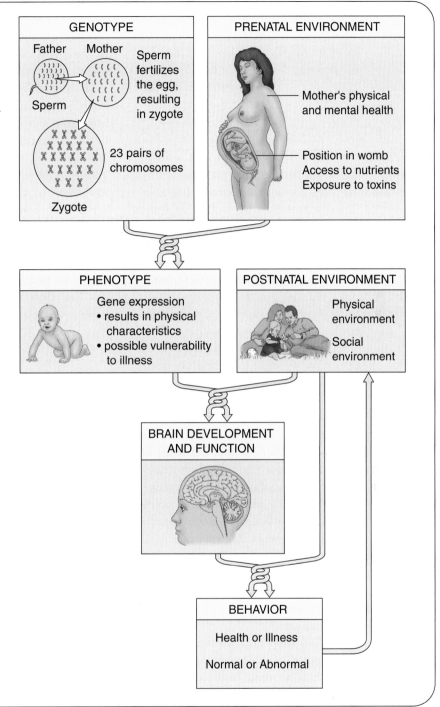

GENOTYPE

Father   Mother

Sperm

Sperm fertilizes the egg, resulting in zygote

23 pairs of chromosomes

Zygote

PRENATAL ENVIRONMENT

Mother's physical and mental health

Position in womb
Access to nutrients
Exposure to toxins

PHENOTYPE

Gene expression
• results in physical characteristics
• possible vulnerability to illness

POSTNATAL ENVIRONMENT

Physical environment

Social environment

BRAIN DEVELOPMENT AND FUNCTION

BEHAVIOR

Health or Illness

Normal or Abnormal

searching for the origins of biological vulnerability. In some cases of mental illness, vulnerability is inherited; it is the consequence of genes passed from one generation to the next. In other cases, the biological vulnerability is acquired; it arises when the individual is exposed to certain environmental factors.

Determining Causes and Treatment

Early biological theorists had relatively little to say about where the biological problem was located. They had even less to say about etiology: the cause of the biological problem. Indeed, prior to the 1950s, progress in understanding the relation between brain function and behavior was very slow. This is because the only available means of studying the brain, or any other internal organ, was on postmortem examination—hardly the way to study the living, functioning brain.

ETIOLOGY (CAUSATION)

In attempting to explain the etiology of abnormal behavior, biological approaches have examined many factors. Because they assume that mental disorders are due to a brain malfunction, researchers typically address two questions: First, what caused the brain malfunction? Second, what is the nature of the brain malfunction? In the search for causes of the malfunction, genetics has been a considerable focus of interest. For example, has the person with depression inherited genes that predispose her to developing a mood disorder? In the search for the nature of the brain malfunction, some researchers have focused on brain biochemistry. For example, could neurochemical deficiencies or excesses lead to obsessive-compulsive disorder? Other researchers have tried to link certain mental disorders to neuroanatomical abnormalities; for example, structural defects in the nervous system. Yet others believe that the roots of some mental disorders lie in neurodevelopment—the growth and maturation of the nervous system. Researchers have hypothesized that problems in the womb may lead to abnormal behaviors like autism. It has been known for many years that environmental factors, such as viral infections in the mother, can damage the developing nervous system of a fetus. Thus, it is not surprising that some researchers have explored the relation between prenatal viral infection and abnormal behavior.

Valuable clues about the causes of mental disorders come from studies of who gets them. Researchers doing such epidemiological studies have found that there are age and sex differences in the rates and course of various psychological disorders. Such differences may hold some clues to the causes of mental disorder. For example, males are more likely to be diagnosed with autism, antisocial personality disorder, and addiction to drugs. Women are more likely to carry diagnoses of depression, phobia, and anxiety. One of the controversies surrounding these findings is whether the differences are due to social learning or biology. For example, researchers have asked whether women are more depressed because of social pressure or because certain biochemicals (for example, female sex hormones) contribute to the risk for depression. The most likely answer to the question is "both."

Before we go on, it is important to keep the following in mind: To say that behavior, normal or abnormal, is a product of genes, brain chemistry, brain function or neurodevelopment is NOT to say that biology holds all the answers to human behavior. While biological factors influence behavior, environmental input is also absolutely essential for our brains to function. Further, the environment has a profound impact on the brain. It does this by changing the activity of genes. So, when you finish reading this chapter, the information you store will have changed your brain cells! There is no doubt that the effects of experience on brain function are among the most provocative findings in behavioral neuroscience.

TREATMENT

Biological approaches to the treatment of mental disorders have also changed over time. In the past, brain surgery was sometimes performed to alleviate symptoms, leading to the term "psychosurgery." Prefrontal lobotomy, the most common form of psychosurgery, involved severing certain connections in the front of the brain. These attempts to change the patient's neuroanatomy were not based on any clear theory of brain function. And as medications for mental disorders improved, the use of these surgical approaches has been seriously restricted, with most modern biological approaches now attempting instead to change the patient's neurochemistry.

So-called "psychotropic medications" typically affect the actions of the biochemical messengers in the brain's communication system. Although less common than medication, another biological treatment currently in use is electroconvulsive therapy (ECT). In ECT, pulses of electric current are applied to the brain through electrodes placed on the scalp. This treatment is used to alleviate depression or mania when medication and psychotherapy have proved ineffective.

Just as research has been influenced by the interactional perspective, so has the treatment of mental disorders. Clinicians often combine psychological treatments with medication. Studies have shown that this approach works best for many types of mental disorders, including certain types of depression.

The Diathesis-Stress Model

In studying biological causes and treatment, contemporary researchers have developed biological theories of abnormal behavior that are much more sophisticated than earlier views. In the past few decades, the *diathesis-stress model* of psychopathology has come to dominate the field. The term "diathesis" is used to refer to a constitutional vulnerability to a particular disorder. The model reflects the interactional point of view, and it assumes that exposure to a stressful environment can trigger behavioral disturbance in the vulnerable individual. The other side of this coin is the notion of "buffering" environments; that is, environments that provide experiences that make the person more resilient to stress. Thus, mental illness is assumed to be the product of the interplay between biology and experience. So, for example, an individual who has no vulnerability to panic attacks will not show them, no matter how unpleasant her life has been. In contrast, someone who has a moderate vulnerability might first begin to have attacks after confronting some severe life challenges (this is illustrated by the case of Celia, described in Chapter 1). And for individuals with a high vulnerability, even normal life experiences may be enough to trigger panic attacks.

The same principles of interactions also apply in everyday life. These interactions between biology and experience may be subtle, but they can precipitate changes in our mood and behavior. We have all had an experience in which a minor stressful event takes on much greater significance because it occurs when we are coming down with a cold or the flu. We might have thoughts like, "I could deal with this at any other time, but not now!" In this situation, a biological state (for example, a viral infection) is making us more vulnerable to an environmental event (for example, lost keys)—one that we might have taken in stride any other day. Of course, each of us has our own unique set of life experiences and memories, and these also influence our interpretation of events. For example, our interpretation of a new experience as being good, neutral, bad, or disastrous depends in part on learned beliefs. Compared to other species, humans are equipped with an un-

paralleled capacity for learning from experience. We owe this capacity to our extraordinary brains.

Genes and Abnormal Behavior

Having set forth some general information on the biological approach, we now turn to one of the possible determinants of abnormal behavior—genetics. We will see that researchers have found genetic vulnerability to various physical and mental disorders. *Genes* are the basic functional units of heredity that contain the code or "program" for our inherited traits. *Neurodevelopment,* the development of the nervous system, is dictated by the actions of genes that are shared by most members of the human species. Abnormalities in the genetic program for brain development may contribute to some mental disorders (for example, schizophrenia). Of course, genetic factors also contribute to individual differences in brain structure and function within the normal range.

Genes and Chromosomes

Genes dictate the design and operation of organisms ranging from the microscopic, one-celled amoeba to the human being. Genes are made up of *DNA (deoxyribonucleic acid),* which consists of strands of phosphate, sugar, and four nucleotide bases. The DNA molecule has two such strands wrapped around each other like a double helix and stores the blueprint, or template, for the production of proteins from amino acids (see Figure 4–2). These proteins, in turn, determine how the cell develops and functions. The genes themselves are specific sequences of DNA located on the *chromosomes* contained in the nucleus of each normal human cell. A single DNA strand may contain thousands of genes. The combination of genes on the chromosomes affects the physical and behavioral characteristics of an individual and is presumed to play a role in the symptoms of many DSM mental disorders. Humans have twenty-three pairs of chromosomes in each cell, with one of each pair coming from the mother, and the other from the father. The *zygote,* which is an egg from the mother fertilized by a sperm from the father, must divide to create two cells, each of which divides, and so on, for all the cells, until an entire

Figure 4—2

GENES AND DNA

Each human cell contains twenty-three pairs of chromosomes, which are made up of DNA containing the individual's genes. The DNA is composed of sugar-phosphate "ropes" and rungs of sequences of nucleotide bases: A (adenine), which binds with T (thymine); G (guanine), which binds with C (cytosine). The genes direct the construction of proteins from amino acids; the proteins both make up parts of the cell and control cell activity.

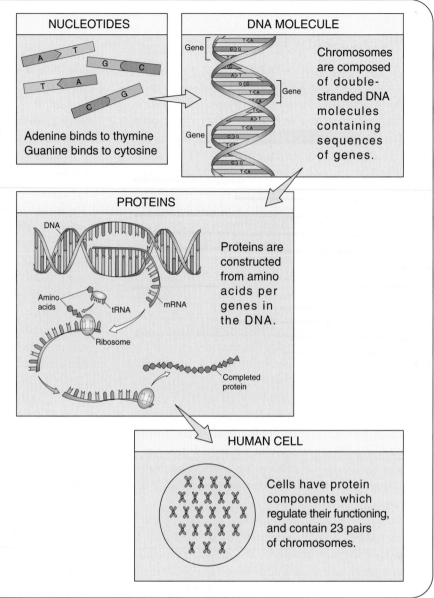

NUCLEOTIDES

Adenine binds to thymine
Guanine binds to cytosine

DNA MOLECULE

Chromosomes are composed of double-stranded DNA molecules containing sequences of genes.

PROTEINS

Proteins are constructed from amino acids per genes in the DNA.

DNA
Amino acids
tRNA
mRNA
Ribosome
Completed protein

HUMAN CELL

Cells have protein components which regulate their functioning, and contain 23 pairs of chromosomes.

organism is created. In order to so divide, however, the chromosomes must duplicate themselves. This is possible through replication of the DNA, whereby the two strands unwind and the nucleotide bases attract other bases, until a new double strand is formed that is identical to the original double strand.

SEX CHROMOSOMES

The twenty-third chromosome pair determines the genetic sex of an individual. The father's sperm con-

tributes either an X or Y chromosome. The ovum, contributed by the mother, always contributes an X chromosome. Different sex hormones are produced, depending on the combination of sex chromosomes. The addition of a Y chromosome by the male parent results in the development of testes and the heightened prenatal production of male sex hormones—most notably testosterone—which stimulate the formation of male sex organs. If the sperm contributes another X chromosome, then ovaries and female sex characteristics develop.

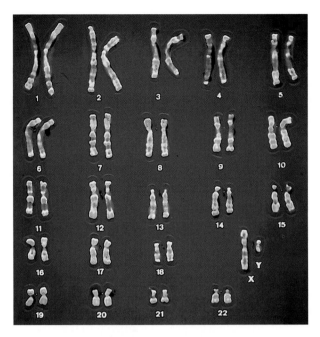

Humans have twenty-three pairs of chromosomes, of which the twenty-third pair determines the sex of the individual. Females have an XX sex chromosome, and males have an XY sex chromosome.

RECESSIVE AND DOMINANT GENES

Genes come in pairs, with one form, or *allele,* on each of the paired chromosomes. Genes are expressed when the DNA leads to the production of specific proteins. Genes can be dominant or recessive. **Dominant genes,** on their own, can produce a specific trait. A **recessive gene** can determine a trait only when paired with another copy of the same recessive gene. For example, in the case of eye color, brown is a dominant gene, and when paired with any other color will result in brown eyes. Blue is a recessive gene, and blue eyes will only result if both gene pairs are blue. There are some human physical characteristics and nervous system disorders that result from the activity of single genes. For example, Huntington's chorea is a degenerative disorder of the nervous system that results in involuntary body movements and cognitive problems, such as memory deficits. A dominant gene on chromosome 4 causes it. Virtually all individuals who inherit this gene will eventually show Huntington's chorea. So if your biological parents live past middle age, and neither of them develops Huntington's chorea, neither will you.

Genotypes and Phenotypes

Resemblance among family members in appearance and behavior is partially due to the genes they share.

In Tom's case, his behavior resembled the behavior of one of his uncles:

> As Tom's mother struggled to understand his behavior, she came to the realization that there were some disturbing similarities between her son and her older brother. Mrs. Clark's brother had joined the army as a young man and been stationed in Korea. She recalled that he had written home about various problems he was having with his commanding officer. He was convinced that he was the target of especially cruel treatment, and he was suspicious that his food was being poisoned. After less than six months, he was relieved of duty and returned home. He refused to share any details about the events with his family. From that time on, he remained aloof and isolated. He never married. Mrs. Clark worried about the similarities between Tom and her older brother. Did this kind of problem run in the family? She wondered if it was due to the genes in her family.

Tom inherited his genes from his parents, but genes aren't always expressed in physical attributes or behaviors. Thus, Tom might inherit genes that would predispose him to certain disturbing behaviors, but such genes would not necessarily lead to such behaviors. The term **genotype** refers to the specific genes inherited by the individual. Each of us has a unique genotype. The term **phenotype** is used to refer to the specific physical or behavioral characteristics associated with a particular genotype. For example, eye color is a physical phenotype. One allele of the gene for eye color contributes to the blue phenotype, whereas another results in brown.

Behavioral phenotypes are not as clear-cut as those for physical characteristics. They vary along a continuum of behavior. In the description above, the behavioral phenotype manifested by Tom involved suspiciousness and social withdrawal. A milder version of this syndrome might have involved skepticism and a tendency toward introversion.

As we discuss the influence of genes, however, keep in mind that the association between particular genotypes and phenotypes is stronger for physical characteristics than for behavior. It appears that most behavioral phenomena, especially human behaviors such as aggression or mental disorders, are influenced by the activity of many genes. Characteristics that are influenced by multiple genes are called **polygenic.** Thus, it is likely that most normal and abnormal human behaviors are polygenic in that they are influenced by a large

Figure 4–3

FORMATION OF IDENTICAL AND FRATERNAL TWINS

Monozygotic (identical) twins develop from one zygote (fertilized egg) and can have one or two placentas and amnionic sacs. Dyzygotic (fraternal) twins develop from two zygotes and always have two separate placentas and two separate amniotic sacs. (Source: Based on Cunningham, 1989, Figure 6.19)

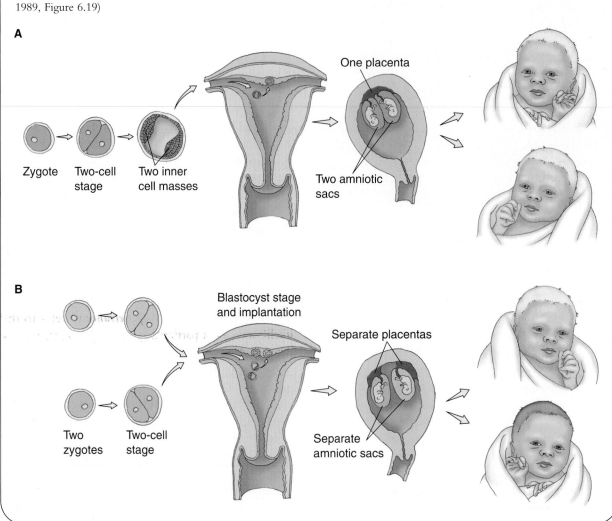

A

Zygote → Two-cell stage → Two inner cell masses

One placenta

Two amniotic sacs

B

Two zygotes → Two-cell stage

Blastocyst stage and implantation

Separate placentas

Separate amniotic sacs

number of genes. In addition, environmental factors play a significant role in determining whether the genes are expressed (that is, whether they show up in behavior or physical characteristics).

Researchers have found that tracing the development of twins from conception throughout their lives provides many insights into the interaction between genes and the environment. There are two kinds of twins: *dizygotic* (DZ, or fraternal) twins, which originate from two fertilized eggs (zygotes); and *monozygotic* (MZ, or identical) twins, which de-

velop from a single fertilized egg (see Figure 4–3). Thus, the two members of a MZ twin pair inherit the same set of genes from their mother and father. This usually results in the two members of the twin pair having the same genotype and, therefore, the same DNA. If one of the twins commits a crime and DNA is used to identify him, his co-twin could be mistaken for the prime suspect.

But there are some interesting exceptions to the general rule that identical twins have the same genotype. Genetic mutations can occur during or after the cellular process of separation that forms two zygotes. When this happens, the two members of the MZ twin pair will have different genotypes. We do not know how often this occurs, but some believe it is quite common (Machlin, 1996). Most of the time, these genotype differences do not result in any dramatic phenotypic differences between the twins, but occasionally they do. For example, if the mutation results in an irregularity that occurs on the sex chromosomes, the two members of the pair can actually differ in genetic sex! They can also differ in genetically determined disorders, such as Down syndrome (Trisomy 21), which involves mild to severe mental retardation and a characteristic facial appearance. Down syndrome is a disorder that is caused by a mutation of chromosome 21. This can occur after the fertilized egg separates into two zygotes, with one twin experiencing the mutation on chromosome 21, while the other does not. Some researchers have suggested that genetic mutations may be responsible for cases where one member of an MZ twin pair has a serious mental illness and the other one does not (Petronis, 1995).

Even when their genotypes are identical, members of monozygotic twin pairs can differ in physical characteristics at birth; in other words, they can have different phenotypes. In fact, significant differences between monozygotic twins in their weight, length, and general health at birth are very common. These differences arise in the womb (in utero), partially as a function of the position of the twins in the uterus. The twin's position can determine its access to the nutrients and oxygen that are required for development. What this means is that environmental influences begin at conception. This fact has implications for our interpretation of differences between MZ twins in their behavior and mental health. It may explain why the two members of an MZ twin pair can differ dramatically in mental health—for example, why one twin may have schizophrenia while the other does not, despite having the same genotype.

You may recall that Tom's mother suspected that the suspicious and withdrawn tendencies she observed in both her son and her brother might run in the family. In the terminology of genetics, this implies that Tom may have inherited a predisposition (or diathesis) to his adjustment problems. If he did, it is not likely that a single dominant gene is responsible, because his mother does not show the same behaviors. But the genetic predisposition Tom has is likely to involve a genotype—a specific combination of genes that his mother does not possess. It may be that Mrs. Clark contributed some of the genes and her husband contributed the others that led to such a predisposition. But if Tom has this predisposition because of his genes, that means he was born with it. Why didn't it show up earlier? We will consider some answers to this question below.

Gene-Environment Interaction

In the past, when psychologists talked about gene-environment interactions, they were referring to the physical and social environment experienced by the person after birth. For example, a person like Celia (described in Chapter 1) might have inherited a genetic vulnerability to panic disorder, but she did not show it until she was in a stressful environment. But today's scientists also study the activity of genes within cells, an even smaller environment. They find that gene-environment interactions also take place at the microscopic level. They have found that the biological environment within the cell has a dramatic impact on whether a gene will be expressed or remain silent (unexpressed).

Scientists use the term **penetrance** to refer to the likelihood that a particular gene or genotype will be expressed. The genetic predispositions for some illnesses, like certain neurological disorders, are virtually always expressed, no matter what kind of environment the person is in. Other genetic predispositions are only expressed under certain unusual circumstances.

Researchers have made some important discoveries about the biological processes that are involved in whether or not genes are expressed. DNA serves as the template for the synthesis of *ribonucleic acid* (RNA). The process of DNA synthesizing RNA is called *transcription* (see Figure 4–4). Scientists say that a gene has been "expressed" when there has been transcription of its coded information from the template DNA into the messenger RNA, which carries the genetic code from the cell nucleus to the cell's cytoplasm (the fluid of the cell), where it attaches to a ribosome. The messenger RNA translates the genetic code by telling the ribosome to add amino acids to the protein it is synthesizing. This final step, the synthesis of proteins (long chains of amino acids that control the activities of the cell and are part of the structure of the cell), is the one that has the potential for influencing behavior.

Figure 4—4

DNA AND RNA

DNA and RNA are responsible for the expression of genes. (1) Genes are located on double-helix DNA strands, which are in the nucleus of the cell. (2) Genes are expressed when part of the DNA strand unravels and serves as a template for transcription of the genetic code from the DNA to messenger RNA. The messenger RNA carries the genetic information from the nucleus of the cell into the cell's cytoplasm (inner fluid). (3) In the cytoplasm, the messenger RNA attaches itself to a ribosome, which moves along the strand, adding amino acids to proteins, until translation of the genetic information is finished and the construction of the protein is completed. (Source: Based on Cunningham, 1989, Figure 10.7)

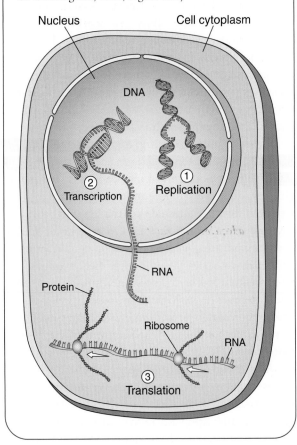

Many genes in the nervous system are regulated in their expression by the biochemical environment surrounding the cell. So, for example, a lack or deficiency in a certain biochemical could result in a failure of gene expression. The gene's DNA would not transcribe the messenger RNA. Thus, the cell's im-

mediate environment plays a major role in determining whether a gene will have the opportunity to use its DNA blueprint. A prime example of this is the effect of certain hormones on prenatal development. Even if the fetus has a male genotype, it will not show the typical male phenotype (male sex organs and body type) unless adequate levels of hormones are present in utero.

Turning to the behavioral level, we mentioned earlier that some identical twins are *discordant* (they differ) for mental illnesses such as schizophrenia and depression. When one MZ twin has an illness and the co-twin does not, researchers assume that environmental factors have produced the difference between them. These environmental differences may occur in the womb or after birth. Thus, despite their virtually identical genotypes, if the two members of the MZ twin pair are exposed to different environments (physical or social), they may manifest very different behaviors. This is an example of the diathesis-stress model. Just because the genes are present for a certain illness does not necessarily mean the illness will occur. In the absence of stressors, the genes may not be expressed, and the person will remain free of the illness.

Some scientists who study the genetic determinants of behavior assume that genes actually affect our experiences. They refer to this as reciprocal gene-environment influences. In other words, genes influence our behavior, which in turn influences the kind of experiences we will have. Risk takers, for example, will be more likely to experience accidental injuries because of the situations they become involved in. Of course, it is also true that our experiences influence our behavior. Thus, the experience of a painful accident might reduce future risk-taking behavior.

When researchers study the relation between experiences and behavior, they often ask the participants to tell them about past events in their lives. But what if genetic factors are influencing their view of the world and what they describe? This runs counter to the average person's assumption that their opinions are caused by personal experience, rather than by their genes. Nonetheless, it appears that genes do have some influence on the way people view their life experiences. This should be kept in mind when we interpret the results of research studies that rely on people's self-reports.

Investigators have studied the effect of genetic factors on self-reported life experiences. Study participants complete questionnaires about various past life events and their perceptions of their childhood family environment. The results of this research indicate that adult MZ twins report more similar past experiences than same-sex DZ twins (Hur and Bouchard, 1995; Plomin et al., 1988). For example, MZ twins report similar childhood stressful events and similar attitudes toward their parents. This effect cannot be entirely accounted for by the similarity of the environments to which the twins are exposed. In both the studies cited here, the twins were reared apart during childhood! Thus, the results indicate a significant contribution of genetic factors to self-reported past experiences. These findings raise some intriguing questions. Are genes influencing the probability that the twins will remember certain past events? Or are genes influencing the likelihood that the twins will actually experience certain events? The answer is probably "yes" to both questions.

Research Methods in Behavioral Genetics

Behavioral geneticists have developed a variety of research designs for exploring the role of genes in animal and human behavior. In animal research, systematic breeding is a very common approach. Of course, experimental manipulation of reproduction or rearing environments cannot be used in human research. Instead, studies of humans rely on our knowledge of genetic relatedness to estimate the influence of genetic and environmental factors.

The *family study method* simply documents the occurrence of characteristics or disorders in individuals who vary in their genetic relatedness. For example, your siblings and parents (first-degree relatives) share more of their genes in common with you than do your grandparents (second-degree relatives). Researchers who use the family study method interview family members about their psychological adjustment. If genes are influencing a particular symptom or disorder, the disorder will tend to run in families. For example, researchers have used the family study method to find out whether genes influence illnesses like schizophrenia and other psychotic disorders (Gottesman, 1991). The results show a clear tendency for these disorders to run in families. However, one problem is that the family study method can't easily disentangle the effects of genes from the

effects of experience. This is because family members share environments as well as genes.

Other approaches in behavioral genetics make it easier to separate environmental and genetic effects. The *twin method* is one example. The twin method is based on the assumption that most MZ twins share 100 percent of their genes in common—that is, they share both the genes that are the same in all members of the human species and those that vary among humans. In contrast, DZ twins share, on average, only 50 percent of the genes that vary among humans. Using statistics, researchers estimate the similarity between MZ and DZ twin pairs on various characteristics. To the extent that genetic factors are influencing a characteristic, MZ twins will be more similar than DZ twins. One widely publicized study of twins was conducted in Minnesota (Bouchard, Lykken, McGue, Segal, and Tellegen, 1990). A subgroup of the MZ twins who participated in this research had been separated at birth. The researchers found some striking similarities between these twins, including similar professions, physical characteristics, and mannerisms, despite the fact that they had not been reared together. The twin method has been used to study a variety of behavioral abnormalities, including criminality, sexual disorders, schizophrenia, and addiction. When we discuss the findings of twin studies in later chapters, you will see what they tell us about the importance of both genetics and the environment.

The *adoption method* is also a useful research strategy. The basic question in this approach is whether the adopted child is more like the biological parents or the adoptive parents. In research on mental disorders, the adopted offspring of parents who have a particular illness are followed to determine if they also develop the illness. If they do, despite the absence of contact with the biological parents, genetic influences are suggested. A group of investigators in Finland has been using this method to determine the role of genes in schizophrenia (Tienari, 1991). They have found that the adopted offspring of mothers with schizophrenia have a heightened risk for schizophrenia themselves, especially if they are reared in unstable adoptive homes. But like all research approaches, the adoption method has some limitations. One of the critical assumptions of the adoption method is that the biological mother has little influence on the child if he is adopted as an infant. Yet, some researchers have argued that environmental influences begin before birth, so that the adoption

Here are twins who were separated at birth and reared apart. When they were reunited, they found out that both were fire chiefs and had the same mustache, sideburns, eyeglasses, drank the same beer, and used the same gestures.

method doesn't completely separate genetic and environmental influences. The question of prenatal influences will be discussed again later in this chapter.

During the past two decades, researchers have been examining the genes of people with mental disorders. One approach, called **genetic linkage analysis,** begins by locating families where several members are suffering from a particular disorder. The investigators then focus on specific human genes, or "genetic markers," that have a known location on a particular chromosome. They look for these markers in all the family members, those with and without the disorder. If the gene or genes that actually contribute to the disorder are close to the marker gene, then there will be a "linkage" between the marker and the presence of the mental disorder in family members. This gives researchers strong clues about the likely location of the genes that cause the disorder. Some famous linkage studies of the genetics of bipolar disorder were conducted in Amish communities, where family records are kept across generations, and showed a genetic predisposition for bipolar disorder (Egeland and Hostetter, 1983). The researchers believed they had found a specific location on chromosome 11 that was linked to bipolar disorder. However, subsequent studies did not replicate these findings (Kelsoe et al., 1989). This has, unfortunately, been the case with many linkage studies of mental illness. Nonetheless, researchers continue to refine this method and apply it in the search for a genetic predisposition to psychological disorders.

As we mentioned earlier, it is believed that most mental disorders are the result of many genes, rather than one or even a few genes. How are researchers able to make the connection between multiple genes and abnormal behavior? They use **quantitative genetic methods** that involve mathematical equations, statistics, and data on large samples of people. With these procedures, the researchers try to estimate just how much a person's genotype, versus the environment, contributes to a particular trait or disorder. This strategy does not involve actually looking at genes. So, quantitative genetics is not able to tell us whether any particular gene or group of genes contributes to a disorder. But it can tell us something about the overall strength of the genetic contribution.

Another research method to study the effects of genes involves altering specific genes (see Box 4–1). By studying the consequences of manipulating individual genes in animals, researchers are coming closer to understanding the precise influence of genes on behavior. These cutting-edge techniques already have implications for research on abnormal human behavior. For example, researchers have conducted studies on animals to identify the specific gene(s) responsible for the activity of certain biochemicals called neurotransmitters. Other investigators have used information from this research to examine similar genes in people with mental disorders and in their family members.

One dramatic technique involves manipulating animals' genes through injecting DNA into the nucleus of embryos when they are still at the stage of

Human Gene Therapy

Research on gene therapy for human disease is now being conducted. Scientific advances have made it possible to identify the genetic defects associated with such diseases as cystic fibrosis, sickle cell anemia, and certain types of hemophilia. The principle behind gene therapy is relatively straightforward: identify people with the genetic defect and insert new genetic information into their tissue. The main technique used to transfer genes is called "somatic cell gene therapy." In this procedure, one or more genes is delivered to target cells in the patient's body via a "delivery system," such as a virus, or through direct injection of DNA.

In France, researchers used such gene therapy to successfully treat three infants with severe combined immune deficiency (SCID). Without this treatment, the infants might have died or had to live their lives in germ-free bubbles. The disease is caused by mutations that destroy the functions of a gene needed to make white blood cells that fight germs. Researchers were able to send functioning genes into the infants' bone marrow. The functioning genes proliferated, and the defective genes died. While gene therapy for this disorder was effective, researchers still have a long way to go in applying the technique to treat other disorders. Moreover, there are ethical and social implications to this gene therapy.

Regardless of the successes in France, the methods that are currently used to deliver genetic material to a patient's host cells continue to be plagued by both known and unknown risks (Eisenberg and Schenker, 1997). One risk is the inability to control the integration of the new DNA into the host cell. The insertion of the new gene in the patient's cells may result in the deactivation of genes that control tumor generation or growth, leading to a new illness. Another risk involves the use of viruses to deliver genes. "Recombination" may occur between the genetic material from the "delivery" virus and other viruses already in the patient. This could result in a life-threatening infection if the patient is unable to mount an appropriate immune response.

Unfortunately, what was once considered a potential risk of gene therapy became reality on September 17, 1999. Eighteen-year-old Jesse Gelsinger died of respiratory distress syndrome after participating in an experimental gene therapy trial at the University of Pennsylvania. The trial used gene therapy to treat a gene defect that causes the overproduction of ammonia in the liver. After the injection of the new gene,

the boy developed a "diffuse activation of his immune system" and died four days later (Barbour, 2000). On January 21, 2000, all gene therapy studies at the University of Pennsylvania were suspended indefinitely. Since then, the NIH (National Institutes of Health) has been bombarded with a total of 691 reports of "serious adverse events" resulting from gene therapy. Although federal law requires that deaths and illnesses attributed to gene therapy must be reported to the NIH and the FDA (Food and Drug Administration), 652 of these events were never reported (Nelson and Weiss, 2000). The FDA and NIH are currently proposing new plans and measures to enhance patient safety, such as quarterly meetings with gene therapy researchers to exchange new information and safety reports. Likewise, safety monitoring plans will now have to be submitted for review before the experiments will be approved by the FDA. The agency is also proposing a guideline that will require them to publicly disclose the details regarding the safety of gene therapy (Collins, 2000).

At the present time, gene therapy is only being used in attempts to treat diseases caused by single genes. But new technology is being developed to prevent disease by changing the genetic structure of eggs and sperm (Eisenberg and Schenker, 1997). "Germline alteration" involves the insertion of a gene into reproductive cells, thus allowing the correction to be passed on to the patient's offspring. So far, researchers have not attempted this with humans, but it may be feasible in the near future. This has raised serious questions in the minds of ethicists. They are concerned that researchers may be tempted to try to use germline alteration to produce human beings with "superior" mental and physical traits. Other concerns are that germline alteration could lead to unforeseen problems by reducing genetic diversity, by creating a situation in which problematic recessive genes are expressed, or by inadvertently altering the germline so that adaptive genes are eliminated. Moreover, if such procedures are not covered by insurance, only the wealthy will have enough money to avail themselves of such techniques, further adding to differences between the "haves" and the "have-nots."

SOURCE: Based on Barbour, 2000; Collins, 2000; Eisenberg and Schenker, 1997; Kolata, 2000; Nelson and Weiss, 2000.

being a single cell. If the procedure is successful, the DNA is incorporated by one of the cell's chromosomes and is therefore present in the replicated genes of all the cells that are produced by division of the original cell. The resultant animal is called *transgenic* because researchers have artificially combined the

genes. The other side of the coin is eliminating specific genes. Researchers eliminate genes in embryos using **knockout procedures.** These scientific methods have great potential for understanding the role of various genes on communication within the brain and from the brain to the different parts of the body.

The findings of molecular genetic studies on animals are helping researchers to identify promising leads for studies of specific genes in humans. Such research has the potential for shedding light on genetic causes of human mental illness. You can expect to hear more about this in the future!

Neurons and Biochemical Etiology

Most of our genes are devoted to the development and ongoing function of the nervous system. This is because the nervous system is the most structurally diverse and, therefore, the most complex of all the systems in our body. Logically, to understand both normal and abnormal behavior, we need to understand how the nervous system works. We begin our discussion of the nervous system at a microscopic level, describing the cells that make up the nervous system and the ways they communicate. In everyday life, we can't directly observe the communication among neurons, but we can see the behavior that results from this communication. The result may be normal behavior, when everything goes right, or abnormal behavior when it does not.

Neural Activity

Neurons, or nerve cells, are the building blocks of the nervous system. There are approximately 10^{11} neurons in the human brain. Most neurons have three distinct parts: the soma (or cell body), the axon, and the dendrites (see Figure 4–5A). The soma contains the nucleus of the neuron, and it is the command center of the cell. DNA is contained in the nucleus and determines what kind of neuron the cell

Figure 4—5

NEURONS AND NEUROTRANS-MISSION

Schematic diagram of the principal parts of the neuron and of neurotransmission across the synaptic gap between neurons. (A) The neuron consists of a cell body containing a nucleus and branch-like dendrites, an axon sheathed in myelin, and axon terminal endings, which contain the synaptic vesicles. (B) Neurotransmission occurs from the presynaptic neuron across the synaptic gap to the postsynaptic neuron. The neurotransmitter is synthesized in the presynaptic neuron and stored in synaptic vesicles. Release of the neurotransmitter is stimulated by nerve impulses in the presynaptic neuron. Some of the neurotransmitter diffuses across the synaptic gap, attaches to receptors on the postsynaptic membrane, and induces electrical charges in the postsynaptic neuron. The neurotransmitter that does not bind to postsynaptic receptors is deactivated either through degrading by enzymes or by reuptake into the presynaptic neuron.

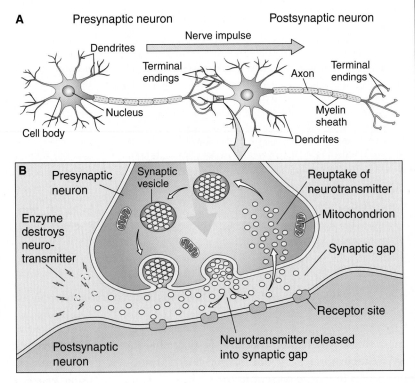

will become, where it will end up living, and in part when it will die. DNA determines the cell's developmental process, and it plays a central role in the cell's functions, especially in the synthesis of biochemicals. The axon projects from the cell body; it is insulated by a myelin sheath that speeds electrical signals through the axon.

There are many different types of nerve cells, and they vary in their structure and their biochemical makeup. Neurons can be distinguished based on which chemicals are inside the cell and which chemicals they produce. Those with similar biochemical properties tend to be located near one another, or in identifiable clusters running through the nervous system. Neurons with biochemical similarities also tend to serve the same function.

COMMUNICATION AMONG NEURONS

All of our mental and physical activities require communication within and among neurons. The nervous system uses some very elegant ways of communicating that rely on electrical and chemical signals. When a neuron is stimulated, action potentials (electrical signals) move along the axon of the presynaptic neuron, until they come to the axon terminals. The signal ends at the presynaptic axon terminals. These hold the neuron's primary chemical messengers, or *neurotransmitters,* which have been synthesized and stored in synaptic vesicles according to the blueprint provided by the cell's DNA. When the action potential arrives at the presynaptic axon terminal, it causes the release of the neurotransmitter into the synaptic gap separating one neuron from another (see Figure 4–5B).

The release of neurotransmitters, a process called *neurotransmission,* is the primary means of communication among neurons. Most neurons receive and send impulses to many other neurons, thus contributing to the massive number of interconnections in the brain's circuitry. Neurotransmitters either increase or decrease the activity of the postsynaptic neuron, which is the neuron receiving the input. Postsynaptic neurons typically receive input through receptors on their dendrites (branchlike structures that are part of the cell body). Receptors are made up of proteins and are specialized to be responsive to different types of neurotransmitters. The process is analogous to a lock and key. When the receptor

(lock) "recognizes" a neurotransmitter (key), the postsynaptic neuron responds. The neurotransmitter binds to the postsynaptic membrane. This triggers an electrical process in the postsynaptic cell. If the receptor is an *excitatory* one, the neurotransmitter will increase activity in the postsynaptic neuron. If the receptor is an *inhibitory* one, it will decrease activity in the postsynaptic neuron.

Finally, excess neurotransmitter must be removed from the synapse. This last step is an important one for controlling the flow of information through the brain. If it does not occur, information flow through the brain is seriously disrupted. There are three main ways that neurotransmitters are removed from the synapse. *Diffusion* of the excess neurotransmitter is one means of clearing the synapse. The process of diffusion is similar to what occurs when a gas mixes with air. When neurotransmitters are diffused, they intermingle with other substances outside the neurons, and their concentrations are reduced. *Degradation* is another mechanism. It involves the elimination of the neurotransmitter through the action of enzymes, which are proteins that are produced by cells and which decompose the neurotransmitters into chemicals that can be reused or excreted. The third and most common means of removing neurotransmitter from the synapse is through *reuptake,* in which the excess neurotransmitter is taken back up by the presynaptic neuron.

Psychoactive drugs affect psychological functions by mimicking the action of naturally occurring substances. They can have an effect on one or more steps in the process of neurotransmission. Drugs that increase activity in particular neurotransmitter systems are called *agonists.* They can act by increasing the synthesis of the neurotransmitter or reducing its uptake. This means more neurotransmitter will be available. *Antagonists,* in contrast, reduce the activity of a neurotransmitter by interfering with synthesis or blocking postsynaptic receptors so that neurotransmitters cannot occupy them.

NEUROTRANSMITTERS

Researchers have identified over forty substances that function as neurotransmitters in the brain. It is expected that more will be found. Some key neurotransmitters that are thought to be involved in psychopathology are the catecholamines (dopamine, epinephrine, and norepinephrine), serotonin, and

Figure 4—6

NEUROTRANSMITTER PATHWAYS

(A) Dopamine pathways go from the substantia nigra to the caudate nucleus and putamen and to the nucleus accumbens. Other dopamine pathways are from the ventral tegmental area to the amygdala and the prefrontal cortex. (B) Norepinephrine pathways lead from the locus coeruleus to the hippocampus, amygdala, hypothalamus and thalamus, to the cortex. (C) Serotonin pathways go from the raphe nuclei to the cerebellum and spinal cord, to the hippocampus, amygdala, hypothalamus, thalamus, striatum, and nucleus accumbens, to the basal ganglia, to the cortex. (Source: Based on Bigler and Clement, 1997, Figures 1.32, 1.33, and 1.34)

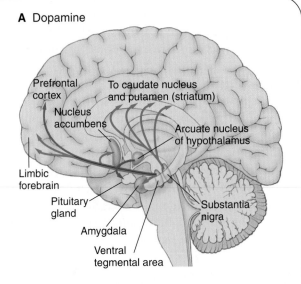

A Dopamine

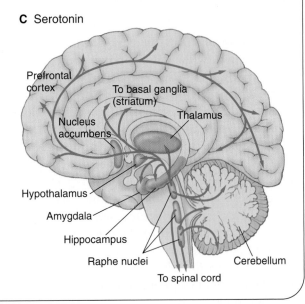

B Norepinephrine

C Serotonin

the amino acids (glutamate, gamma aminobutyric acid—GABA). Another neurotransmitter is acetylcholine, which plays an important role in cognitive functions, and may be involved in disorders such as Alzheimer's disease.

There are several dopamine pathways in the brain (see Figure 4–6A). Dopamine appears to be involved in a number of neurological and mental disorders, including Parkinson's disease and schizophrenia. In some areas of the brain, dopamine release is increased by stress. Moreover, the dopamine system also appears to play a role in the "reward" systems of the brain. Some researchers have proposed that when too little

dopamine is available, animals and humans tend to engage in activities that make more dopamine available. In humans, this can take the form of extreme risk-taking behavior or the abuse of illegal drugs.

Dopamine also influences attention, mood, and motivation, and it plays a central role in muscle movements. Nicotine is a dopamine agonist, and people may smoke cigarettes because the nicotine makes them feel good and better able to focus. When dopamine is lost or depleted, Parkinson's disease may develop. This disease results in tremors and slowed movements. When Parkinson's patients are given L-dopa, a dopamine agonist, their motor symptoms tend to subside. L-dopa has side effects, however, and some patients manifest psychotic symptoms when given the drug. This observation, among others, led researchers to suggest the involvement of dopamine in schizophrenia, a topic we will consider in Chapter 10.

Norepinephrine (sometimes called noradrenaline) is best known for its effects on arousal. The neurons that release norepinephrine originate in an area of the brain stem called the locus coeruleus (see Figure 4–6B). The axons of these neurons extend into the hippocampus, cerebellum, and cortex. Because norepinephrine can increase blood pressure, people who have high blood pressure take drugs to block the action of norepinephrine on certain receptors. Like dopamine, norepinephrine release is increased by stress. In addition, norepinephrine has effects on mood and behavior. Elevation of norepinephrine is associated with depression and anxiety (Ninan, 1999; Ressler and Nemeroff, 1999). Although it is not known whether norepinephrine plays a causal role in these disorders, some drugs used to treat mood disorders do reduce norepinephrine. Psychological treatment also changes norepinephrine levels; one study showed that medical patients who received cognitive behavior therapy to manage stress showed lower post-treatment anxiety, anger, and norepinephrine levels when compared to patients who did not receive therapy (Antoni et al., 2000).

The neurons that use serotonin to communicate mainly originate in the midbrain, but they spread throughout higher brain areas (see Figure 4–6C). Because of this wide distribution, serotonin modulates the activity of many neurons in the brain and affects the way we process information (Spoont, 1992). Public familiarity with serotonin has increased dramatically in recent years because the most widely used antidepressant medications (the selective serotonin reuptake inhibitors—SSRI's) act by increasing serotonin activity. Most notable among these is Prozac (fluoxetine), which has been used by millions of people worldwide. Prozac increases the concentration of serotonin in the brain and reduces depression and anxiety.

Glutamate, an excitatory amino acid, is distributed throughout the brain; an excess of glutamate can be toxic and can kill neurons. "Glutamate excitotoxicity" results from excessive release of glutamate, and it is thought to be responsible for the brain damage resulting from stroke and some degenerative disorders, like ALS (amyotropic lateral sclerosis, or "Lou Gehrig's disease"). At the same time, glutamate is vital to many brain functions, such as learning. Glutamate activity in the hippocampus and cortex is necessary for the consolidation of long-term memories.

Gamma aminobutyric acid (GABA) is an inhibitory amino acid neurotransmitter that is found in many regions of the brain. Receptors for GABA play a role in anxiety. Drugs that are GABA agonists (for example, Xanax) have a calming effect and are often used to treat anxiety disorders.

HORMONES

Neurotransmitters are not the only biochemicals that influence brain function. The body's **hormones** also affect neural activity (McEwen, 1994a). Hormones affecting neural activity are often referred to as neurohormones. Like neurotransmitters, hormones act as chemical messengers in the nervous system. Rather than being released by neurons, however, they are secreted by the endocrine glands (see Figure 4–7): the

Figure 4–7

MAJOR GLANDS OF THE ENDOCRINE SYSTEM

Each of the glands produces and releases hormones into the bloodstream. The arrow shows the hypothalamic-pituitary-adrenal (HPA) axis, which controls the release of the stress hormone cortisol.

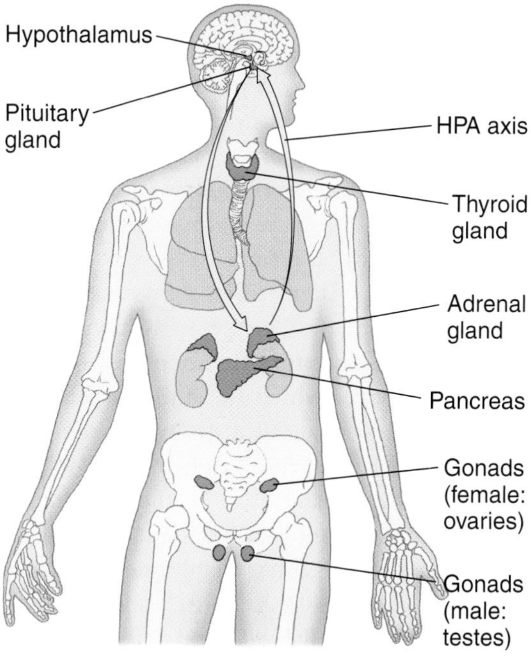

Hypothalamus
Pituitary gland
HPA axis
Thyroid gland
Adrenal gland
Pancreas
Gonads (female: ovaries)
Gonads (male: testes)

thyroid, the adrenal, the pituitary, and the gonads (ovaries in females, and testes in males). Neurons contain intracellular receptors for hormones, and recent research suggests that there are also surface hormone receptors. Some of the actions of hormones are temporary, and others are permanent.

The sex hormones (androgens such as testosterone, and female sex hormones such as estrogen) not only stimulate the development of sex organs, they also influence the development of brain structure and the function of neurons (Breedlove, 1994). Both male and female fetuses are exposed to circulating levels of sex hormones from the mother. When researchers manipulate prenatal sex hormones in animals, the results are changes in nervous system development and behavior. For example, increases in prenatal testosterone change the shape of the hypothalamus in female offspring and cause them to show more masculine sexual behavior in adulthood (Berenbaum, 1998).

Neurohormones can influence neuronal development and activity through receptors that are located in the cell's nucleus. This is the mechanism through which sex hormones are able to trigger or suppress the expression of genes, and thereby influence the structural characteristics of neurons as well as brain regions (McEwen, 1994a). In mammals, the adrenal glands secrete hormones called glucocorticoids (among them, the hormone cortisol), which are sometimes known as the "stress hormones." In some regions of the brain, the neurons contain a large number of glucocorticoid receptors. Researchers have conducted numerous studies of the effects of experience on levels of glucocorticoids in primates and rodents. Levels of these glucocorticoids can be measured in blood, urine, or saliva. In humans, exposure to acute stressful experiences, such as final exams, inoculations, or public speaking, results in increased glucocorticoid release, followed by a return to preexisting levels (Sapolsky, 1992). Other studies show that there is a greater glucocorticoid release in response to demanding mental tasks that are uncontrollable, compared to those over which the individual has some control (Peters et al., 1998). Along the same lines, rodents exposed to acute stressors (for example, noise, temporary separation from the mother, social isolation, or placement in a small enclosure that restricts movement) manifest heightened glucocorticoid responses (Sapolsky, 1992), especially when the stress is uncontrollable (Henry, 1992).

High levels of circulating stress hormones are not good for the body or mind. When glucocorticoid levels are high, performance on mental tasks declines. In addition, stress hormones slow down the healing process in humans and animals (Kiecolt-Glaser, Page, Marucha, MacCallum, and Glaser, 1998). This helps to explain why presurgical interventions aimed at reducing stress enhance postsurgical recovery (Wells, Howard, Nolin, and Vargas, 1986).

Disordered Neural Activity

Neural transmission can go awry in many ways. Changes in brain function can arise due to abnormalities in: (1) the interconnections among neurons, (2) the synthesis, release, or reuptake of neurotransmitters, (3) the distribution or function of neurotransmitter receptors, and (4) the actions of hormones. Further, neurotransmitter and neurohormone systems do not act in isolation from one another. A disturbance in one system can affect activity in the other. For example, an increase in stress hormones can lead to an increase in dopamine in certain regions of the brain and a decrease in serotonin in other regions.

Thus, abnormal behavior can result when there is too much or too little neurotransmitter or abnormal hormonal levels. An excess or deficiency in a chemical messenger could occur for several reasons. There may be a problem in synthesizing the neurotransmitter or in reabsorbing the neurotransmitter after it is released. Or the problem may lie with the receptors on the postsynaptic neuron. If the postsynaptic receptors do not respond to the chemical messenger, there will be no neural intercommunication. As you might expect, all of the drugs that are currently used to treat mental disorders change the activity of neurotransmitters. This includes the increasingly popular "herbal" remedies, such as St. John's Wort, that are available over the counter.

Efficient communication among neurons can also be hampered by damage to surrounding elements. Neurons are sheathed in glial cells, and there are ten to fifty times more glial cells than neurons in the brain. Glial cells do not process information themselves, but they do serve to enhance the organization and flow of neural information. One way they do this is by producing a myelin sheath, which insulates axons and speeds action potentials. A breakdown in the myelin sheath can lead to multiple sclerosis, a progressive neurological disorder that often results in blindness, numbness, and paralysis. Communication among cells may be disrupted if glial cells are damaged. Such damage may result from exposure to toxic chemicals and might be considered in a case like that of Tom:

> After working as a research assistant for about a year and a half, Tom showed up late one night at his parents' home. He was irritable and very annoyed. He explained that some of his co-workers were failing to clean their work areas after handling small microprocessors that contained toxic metals. As a result, he believed he had inhaled some hazardous materials that were affecting his concentration. He said, "The toxins are interfering with my mind. They must be destroying my brain cells." He told his parents a story he had heard about a research assistant in another lab who had developed a neurological condition because the protective covering on his brain cells was destroyed by chemicals. Upon calling his supervisor, his parents were assured that Tom was not working with any hazardous materials, and the supervisor told them that it was very unlikely that the work environment was contributing to his symptoms.

Although the supervisor doubted that Tom's problems were due to toxins in his workplace, he was aware that some substances can be **neurotoxic** (destructive to nerves or nervous tissue). Precautions must be taken with certain chemicals and metals used in research laboratories because they can interfere with the communication among nerve cells by altering the balance of neurotransmitters or by causing cell death. Some substances can actually destroy glial cells and seriously interfere with brain function. On the other hand, it is also true that the effects of some chemicals on the nervous system can be beneficial. This is the basis of modern advances in psychopharmacology. For example, medications that enhance communication among nerve cells have been developed to treat disorders such as Alzheimer's disease and Parkinson's disease. To assess whether Tom's symptoms were physical, his parents scheduled a physical examination to see if his physician could determine if there was a medical problem:

> Tom's physical exam included chest X-rays, an electroencephalogram (EEG), a sensory examination, and blood tests for a range of toxins and infectious agents. The results came back a week later. Nothing was out of the ordinary. His blood chemistry was perfectly normal. This made Tom more irritable and frustrated than ever. He insisted that there was indeed something wrong with his "nerves," and that the doctors had simply failed to find it. Tom accused the physician of conspiring with the Department of Defense. He didn't contact his parents or respond to their messages for a month after that.

The tests administered by Tom's physician can detect the kind of nervous system dysfunction produced by toxins. An EEG can detect significant abnormalities in the electrical currents in a person's brain. A sensory exam can reveal deficits in his vision or hearing. Blood tests can provide information on blood cell counts and the presence of toxic substances. Although these tests cannot tell us anything about the structure of a person's brain or how well it processes information, they are useful because they help the physician to rule out alternative causes of symptoms.

Molecular Techniques and the Study of Neurons

In order to study neurons, cellular functions, and genetic mechanisms in the nervous system, a variety of sophisticated techniques have been used in research on animals. We mention these techniques here because they have helped generate some promising theories about the causes of abnormal behavior. These techniques are also widely used in research on drug development. Before a medication can be marketed for human consumption, its effects on cellular function must be studied in animals (see Box 4-2).

Recording of activity from neurons is often done with living animals. Studies using this procedure have answered such questions as: How does a particular kind of neuron respond to different neurotransmitters? Are some neurons uniquely sensitive to a specific kind of visual or tactile input? What effect do drugs have on the activity of neurons in a particular brain region?

Similar procedures are used to stimulate groups of neurons experimentally. Tiny electrodes are inserted in the brain, and current is passed through that

Science and Practice

Box 4–2

The Validity of Animal Models

Findings from research with animals have played a central role in our understanding of the causes of human illnesses and effective treatments for them. For example, virtually all vaccines used to prevent human disease are the product of extensive experimentation with animals. The reason this is possible is because there is a great deal of similarity between the biological processes that govern organic systems in humans and other mammals. Similarly, researchers have gained a better understanding of human depression by studying the behavior of animals when they are confronted with uncontrollable negative events (see Chapter 7).

Yet, how far can we extend the analogy? We know that in many ways the human brain is more complex than that of any other species. Perhaps some of the psychological disorders that occur in humans are due to this complexity. Along these lines, the British psychologist Timothy Crow, has proposed that schizophrenia is a uniquely human disorder that

has evolved in conjunction with human language (Crow, 1997). Certainly, no other species appears to possess a system of symbolic communication commensurate with human language. If Crow's proposal is correct, then there may indeed be limits on what we can learn about human mental disorders from animal research.

Similar concerns apply to animal models of depression. Rodents certainly do not experience the worries that so commonly plague depressed persons, such as concerns about financial security, health, and the future. On the other hand, there is no doubt that research with animals has revealed many kinds of behavior that resemble aspects of human depression, such as lack of motivation and irritability. On the biological level, animal research has also illuminated brain processes that have parallels in human brain function. This is aptly illustrated by the research on stress described in this chapter.

region. Animals will work to receive stimulation of some brain regions and will actively avoid stimulation of others. This has given researchers a critical tool in the search for brain regions that are involved in reward and punishment, and that may play a role in drug abuse (for example, of cocaine).

Histochemical techniques are used to identify specific groups of neurons. Such techniques can include visual staining of neurons for microscopic inspection, or tagging neurons chemically or radioactively for later detection. Such histochemical techniques (for example, tagging of neurons) can be used within the living brain, or applied to tissue samples extracted from the brain (for example, visual staining). These techniques have allowed researchers to discover some of the ways in which learning and experience change neuronal structure and function.

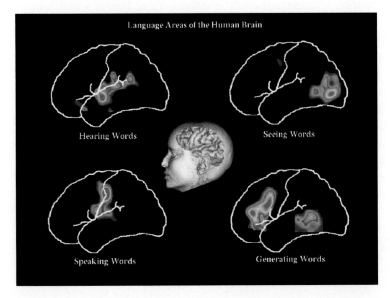

Histochemical techniques are used to identify the different areas of the brain that are activated when a person hears words, speaks words, sees words, and generates words.

Brain Structures and Abnormal Behavior

Up to this point, we have discussed parts of the nervous system that are not visible to the human eye. We have explored the microscopic building blocks that make up the nervous system—neurons and glial cells. We have also described the biochemicals that energize the nervous system—the neurotransmitters and hormones. Now we will take a look at the larger structures that make up the nervous system, especially the brain, which is the most complex of all our organs.

The brain affects both normal and abnormal behavior. It affects what we perceive and what we remember, what we feel and what we think, which in turn affect how we behave. Not only do we need to understand what the structures and the functions are, we also must learn about how these structures relate to each other and affect behavior. Thus, understanding brain-behavior relationships also requires some knowledge of the complex interconnections (called brain circuits) within and among brain regions that make it possible for our species to engage in sophisticated behaviors, such as the symbolic communication of emotions and abstract ideas.

The structures of our brain are determinants of our behavior and our experiences, and at the same time, experiences mold the structures of our brain. Thus, experiences with the physical and social world influence how our brain functions and how it develops. Exposure to environments that are enriched, deprived, or stressful can alter brain function and may actually change brain structure. Experiences become part of our memory by physically altering brain cells and making a biological "impression" that can have a lasting impact on thoughts and behavior. Discovering how the brain determines, and changes with, experience is critical for understanding psychopathology. To better understand the interplay between the brain and experience, we need to first present the basic structures of the nervous system, and then discuss how they function and how they can malfunction.

The Central Nervous System

The human nervous system is made up of the **central nervous system (CNS)** and the **peripheral nervous system (PNS)** (see Figure 4–8A). The CNS has three major divisions: the spinal cord, the brain stem, and the forebrain (or cerebral hemispheres) (Kandel, Schwartz, and Jessel, 1991). Neurons

---

Figure 4–8

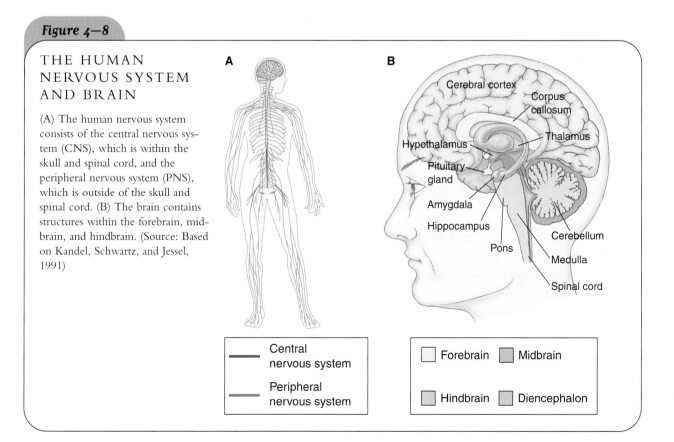

THE HUMAN NERVOUS SYSTEM AND BRAIN

(A) The human nervous system consists of the central nervous system (CNS), which is within the skull and spinal cord, and the peripheral nervous system (PNS), which is outside of the skull and spinal cord. (B) The brain contains structures within the forebrain, midbrain, and hindbrain. (Source: Based on Kandel, Schwartz, and Jessel, 1991)

A

B

Cerebral cortex

Corpus callosum

Thalamus

Hypothalamus

Pituitary gland

Amygdala

Hippocampus

Pons

Cerebellum

Medulla

Spinal cord

— Central nervous system

— Peripheral nervous system

☐ Forebrain ☐ Midbrain

☐ Hindbrain ☐ Diencephalon

composing these divisions perform particular functions based, in part, on where they are located.

SPINAL CORD AND BRAIN STEM

The spinal cord processes sensations and controls movements in the trunk and limbs. Spinal cord injuries can result in partial or complete paralysis of the limbs. The brain stem is divided into the hindbrain (medulla, pons, cerebellum), the midbrain (reticular activating system), and the diencephalon (thalamus and hypothalamus). From the standpoint of evolution, the brain stem is the oldest part of the mammalian brain. The brain stem controls automatic functions—actions done without conscious thought. When damage occurs, the simplest actions, such as turning the head, or moving the arm, or walking a few steps, or even breathing, coughing, or swallowing, may become impossible. The regions of the hindbrain play a role in processing sensory input, particularly to the head, neck, and face. The cerebellum is important for maintaining control of posture, balance, and movements. The medulla helps to regulate and maintain breathing, heart rate, and blood pressure. The midbrain processes auditory, visual, and olfactory input. Damage to this region is a common cause of deafness and blindness.

The diencephalon is located between the cerebral hemispheres. Extensive neural pathways connect its two main regions, the thalamus and hypothalamus. These brain regions have connections with the cerebral cortex. The thalamus plays a major role in processing sensory and motor information that is directed toward the cortex. The hypothalamus has a unique function in controlling hormone secretion from the pituitary gland and in modulating activation of the autonomic nervous system. It also influences physical growth by regulating appetite and controlling the pituitary gland's release of hormones that cause maturation. Finally, the hypothalamus secretes gonadotropin-releasing hormone, which triggers the pituitary gland's release of hormones that influence the reproductive organs and regulate sexual interest. Damage to the hypothalamus can lead to changes in sexual interest, mood, and weight. Some theorists have also suggested that abnormalities in the hypothalamus may be responsible for eating disorders.

FOREBRAIN

The forebrain is highly developed in human beings, and its increased size contributes to our uniqueness

Figure 4–9

THE RIGHT AND LEFT HEMISPHERES

Schematic diagram of the human brain, as seen from above, to illustrate the corpus callosum, the specialized functions of each hemisphere, and the contralateral organization of the sensory pathways, such that information from the left visual field projects to the right hemisphere, while information from the right visual field projects to the left hemisphere. (Source: Based on Levy, 1972, p. 163)

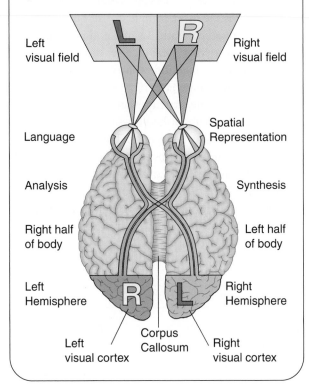

as a species. It is important for conscious thought, reasoning, and memory. Damage to various areas in this region can impair self-control, emotional engagement, and memory. Major structures are the cerebral cortex, basal ganglia, amygdala, and hippocampus (see Figure 4–8B).

Nerve cell bodies are concentrated in the exterior layers of the cortex, referred to as the gray matter. Axons are concentrated in the underlying white matter, which gets its name from the white myelin sheath surrounding the axon. A concentrated tract of myelinated nerve fibers, the corpus callosum, connects the right and left cerebral hemispheres, permitting communication between the two hemispheres (see Figure 4–9).

The left hemisphere is generally specialized for linguistic/analytic functions and the right hemisphere for spatial/holistic functions. The differences between the two hemispheres have many clinical implications. Language disorders are much more common with left hemisphere damage (for right-handers and most left-handers), while disorders in getting around in space or recognizing complex configurations occur much more frequently with right hemisphere damage. People with greater right hemisphere activation (or damaged left hemisphere) may be more prone to depression (see Chapter 7). But the division of labor between the hemispheres is not absolute; both participate, to some extent in all of cognition and behavior, with the corpus callosum integrating activities and information from the two hemispheres (Davidson, 1998, 1999).

The Cortex and Higher-Order Functions In primates, the cortex has a wrinkled surface, with clefts and ridges that are referred to as convolutions. Humans have a highly convoluted cortex. It is believed that this evolved as the volume of the cortex increased more rapidly than the volume of the cranium (skull). The chief regions of the cortex are the frontal, parietal, temporal, and occipital lobes (see Figure 4–10). The ***limbic system*** is made up of the middle areas of the frontal, temporal, and parietal lobes. This system sends signals from the brain stem, which senses bodily changes, to the frontal cortex. The limbic system is thought to play a major role in disorders of mood and anxiety.

There is a system of cavities in the brain containing cerebral spinal fluid. These cavities, called ***ventricles,*** vary in size and shape among individuals. Reductions in the volume of regions of the brain surrounding the ventricles (periventricular areas) can result in an apparent enlargement of the ventricles. Enlargement of the ventricles is associated with many brain disorders, including schizophrenia.

Cognitive, sensory, and motor functions tend to be localized (concentrated in certain areas of the brain). But we emphasize that the use of the term "localized" does not mean that a specific function, such as the ability to differentiate threatening from nonthreatening events, is due solely to a particular brain region. Instead, areas of the brain are specialized for certain functions that they perform in cooperation with other brain regions, via neuronal interconnections. Thus, groups of nerve fibers connect

Figure 4–10

THE LOBES OF THE CEREBRAL HEMISPHERES

The frontal, parietal, temporal, and occipital lobes, and their primary functions.

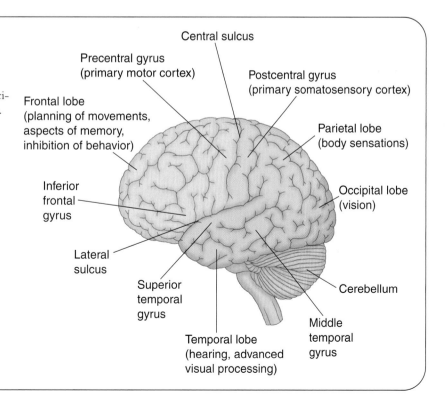

Central sulcus

Precentral gyrus (primary motor cortex)

Postcentral gyrus (primary somatosensory cortex)

Frontal lobe (planning of movements, aspects of memory, inhibition of behavior)

Parietal lobe (body sensations)

Inferior frontal gyrus

Occipital lobe (vision)

Lateral sulcus

Superior temporal gyrus

Cerebellum

Middle temporal gyrus

Temporal lobe (hearing, advanced visual processing)

Electrical-Chemical Storms in the Brain

In practice, most clinical psychologists are confronted with a broad range of problems. It is not uncommon for people with very specific neurological disorders to begin their search for treatment in the psychologist's office. This is because so many neurological illnesses first become apparent when there is a deterioration in the person's emotional well-being. Epilepsy is a prime example. It is a common disorder that affects over 1 million Americans. The early signs might be described by the patient as feelings of confusion, intense anger, or even panic. Epilepsy is caused by damage to neural tissue. This can be produced by any of a number of different agents or diseases. The result is a region of brain tissue that is irritable and produces increased synchronized neural activity, either because of damage to inhibitory systems or because the residue of the damage (for example, scar tissue) excites neighboring neurons. The excessive activity that is produced, known as seizures, can lead to an exaggerated expression of the function of the area.

Seizures occur intermittently, with sudden discharge of neurons. These discharges may be localized, or they may be much more widespread, leading to muscle contraction throughout the body and loss of consciousness. For many patients, seizures are precipitated by stress. The part of the brain or type of mental event that appears first in the seizure is an indicator of the location of the brain damage.

Depending on the location of the irritable tissue (the seizure foci), the primary symptoms may be sensory (for example, an hallucination), motor (for example, twitches or larger muscle contractions), or emotional (for example, fear or laughter). Also, the nature of the symptoms may vary, depending on whether the seizure originates in the right or left hemisphere. For example, seizures are more often associated with hallucinations and delusions if they occur in the left hemisphere. Patients sometimes experience unusual ideas, emotional impulses, or sensory experiences before the onset of the seizure. With time, some patients and their family members can actually predict an impending seizure from these behavior changes.

A psychologist who is conducting an assessment of a new client may detect subtle signs of seizure activity, such as sensory or motor abnormalities. This signals the need for more in-depth assessment and referral to a neurologist. It is fortunate that certain medications can be very effective in reducing or even eliminating seizures. After their seizures are brought under medical control, epilepsy patients often seek psychological treatment to help them cope with their illness. For some, this entails dealing with the distress of having a chronic illness. For those whose seizures are worsened by stress, the psychological treatment might be directed at helping the patient reduce his reactions to stress.

---

regions of the brain so that they can share tasks and information, but this may also mean that damage may spread through the brain, as may happen with epileptic seizures (see Box 4–3).

The specialization of a brain region can change over time. Brain injury, especially when it occurs early in life, can result in functions being relocated to brain regions that would not typically serve them (Broman and Michel, 1995; Stein, 2000). Plasticity of the brain allows for such relocation of function and is a key factor in the ability of people to recover from brain injuries. Nonetheless, there are limitations to the brain's plasticity, and so recovery does not always occur when there are brain injuries.

Many high-level cognitive functions are performed by the **association areas,** which serve to integrate information from diverse sources. They have extensive neural interconnections with other brain regions. The limbic association area is concerned with integrating past memories, emotional/motivational impulses, and motor plans. The prefrontal asso-

ciation area of the cortex plays a major role in formulating and executing plans for cognitive and motor activity. In fact, the term "executive functions" is sometimes used to refer to the unique functions served by the prefrontal cortex. Research on patients with damage to the frontal lobes has contributed greatly to our knowledge of this brain region. Dramatic changes in personality can occur when the frontal lobes are damaged. One famous case is that of Phineas Gage:

Phineas Gage was the twenty-five-year-old foreman of a group of men working on railroad track in Vermont in 1848. An explosion caused an iron bar, over an inch in diameter, to pass through the front of his skull, damaging a large part of the frontal area of his brain. Miraculously, Gage survived, with no more than a few moments of loss of consciousness. After recovery, he reapplied for his job as foreman. His contractors, who had regarded him as the most efficient and capable foreman in their employ previous to his injury, considered the change in his mind so marked that they could not give him his place again. The equilibrium or balance, so to speak, between his intellectual faculties and animal propensities, seemed to have been destroyed. He was fitful, irreverent, indulging at times in the grossest profanity (which was not previously his custom), manifesting but little deference for his fellows, impatient of restraint or advice when it conflicted with his desires, at times perniciously obstinate, yet capricious and vacillating, devising many plans of future operations, which are no sooner arranged than they are abandoned in turn for others. . . . his mind was radically changed, so decidedly that his friends and acquaintances said he was "no longer Gage." (Harlow, 1868, pp. 339–40)

This case shows the effect of frontal damage on an entire personality (Harlow, 1868; see also Damasio, Grabowski, Frank, Galaburda, and Damasio, 1994). Like other patients with frontal lobe damage, Gage was impulsive, easily distracted, and unable to follow through on plans or to evaluate their consequences. The emotional and personality changes that he underwent may have had similar causes. He could no more control, modulate, inhibit, or evaluate his emotional responses than he could his actions. Other studies have also shown that individuals who have a history of violent behavior often have abnormalities in the structure of the frontal lobes, such that the frontal lobes are unable to inhibit impulsive behav-

iors like those shown by Phineas Gage (Raine and Buchsbaum, 1996). Thus, brain damage may contribute to criminal behavior in some individuals. These findings raise challenging questions about personality and responsibility for criminal behavior (see Chapter 9).

A particular higher-order function controlled by the frontal lobes is going from one action to another. After damage to the frontal lobe, particular parts of individual actions are intact, but there is a problem putting them together. A striking clinical sign of this deficit is **perseveration,** a difficulty in making transitions between one action and the next, or in simply stopping a behavior or response (see Figure 4–11). It often shows up as excessive repetition. Patients with frontal damage may repeat an action over and over and have great difficulty in alternating two actions. They are particularly poor at abandoning a strategy they have learned, even after it ceases to work.

Higher levels of the nervous system often inhibit lower levels. When the higher levels are damaged, the lower-level response can be released. A particularly clear example of release is the **Babinski reflex,** which is normally shown only by infants. When the sole of the foot is stroked, the big toe turns upward and the other toes fan out. This reflex disappears early in life. The circuits of neurons that are responsible for it remain intact, but they are inhibited by higher centers. When there is damage to higher motor centers (that is, to the motor cortex), however, this reflex is

Figure 4–11

PERSEVERATION

Drawings made by two patients with damage to the frontal lobes, in response to the instruction printed above each drawing. Each row represents the sequence of requests made to one patient. The tendency to repeat the previous response is called perseveration. (Source: Luria, 1970, p. 71)

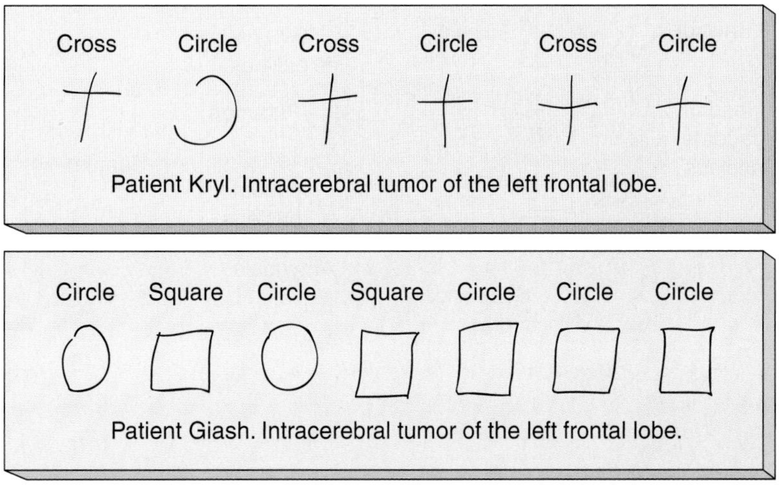

Patient Kryl. Intracerebral tumor of the left frontal lobe.

Patient Giash. Intracerebral tumor of the left frontal lobe.

released; this is one of the cardinal signs of damage to the motor cortex. Some researchers suggest that frontal lobe damage has a similar effect on behavior. In other words, if the frontal lobes are not able to inhibit lower brain regions, the person may show impulsive behavior, as did Phineas Gage.

Subcortical Areas and Abnormal Behavior   There are three subcortical regions of the cerebral hemispheres that appear to be especially relevant to psychopathology, especially to the experience of emotion and stress. These are the basal ganglia, the hippocampus, and the amygdala. Each of these regions is part of one or more brain systems that have figured prominently in theories of psychopathology. The basal ganglia, made up of the caudate, putamen, and globus pallidus, are located within the white matter of the cortex surrounding the ventricles of the brain (see Figure 4–12A). The basal ganglia are part of several circuits that connect subcortical and cortical brain regions. For example, the basal ganglia are essential to motor behavior and are part of a motor circuit that passes through the thalamus and into the motor cortex. The basal ganglia, as well as the hippocampus and amygdala, are also connected with

the limbic system (see Figure 4–12B), which influences emotion and cognition.

Jeffrey Gray, a neuropsychologist, has identified one of the circuits connecting subcortical and cortical regions: the **behavioral inhibition system (BIS),** which Gray believes plays an important role in the experience of anxiety (Gray, 1987). It connects the brain area next to the olfactory bulb, called the septal region, with the hippocampus (Gray, 1985). Serotonin and norepinephrine are the chief neurotransmitters in this pathway. Both the amygdala and the cortex are connected to the "septal-hippocampal" system. The BIS is turned on when the organism encounters an unexpected, disturbing or threatening event. This leads to feelings of arousal and anxiety. Gray has also proposed another circuit that connects subcortical and cortical regions: the **behavioral activation system (BAS),** which is sensitive to signs of pleasure and reward. The BAS inhibits the activity of the BIS. Gray further suggests that both of these systems can be over-ridden by the **fight/flight system (FFS),** which is associated with intense arousal and with attempts to flee or resist threat. Other researchers have suggested that an excess of BAS over

Figure 4–12

THE BASAL GANGLIA AND THE LIMBIC SYSTEM

Frontal views of the brain showing (A) the basal ganglia, which include the caudate nucleus, putamen, and the globus pallidus, and (B) the limbic system, which includes the amygdala, the hippocampus, the cingulate cortex, the fornix, the septum, and the mammillary body. Structures of the limbic system are involved in memory and emotion.

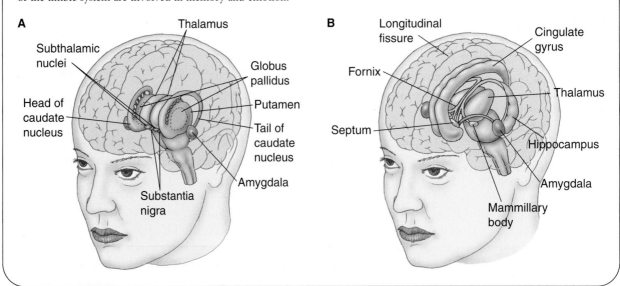

Figure 4–13

THE HPA AXIS

Various brain circuits connecting brain structures (especially those in the limbic system, which is shown in blue) are implicated in the experience of both stress and anxiety. The HPA axis is involved in the stress response and includes the hypothalamus, the pituitary gland, the adrenal gland, and their chemical messengers. Activation of the hypothalamus causes the release of CRH (corticotropin-releasing hormone), a hormone that travels to and stimulates the pituitary gland, which secretes other hormones, including ACTH (adrenocorticotropic hormone), which activates the adrenal gland, which secretes the stress hormone cortisol. At the same time, neurons in the locus coeruleus release norepinephrine, which affects various brain structures.

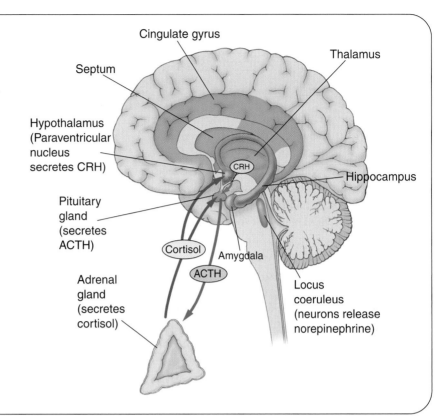

BIS system activation may underlie antisocial behavior (Newman, 1997).

The amygdala is a key component of the system of emotion and reward. It has direct and indirect connections with other brain regions, including the cortex and the other subcortical areas such as the hippocampus, thalamus, hypothalamus, nucleus accumbens, and basal ganglia. These connections enable it not only to receive information about sensory experience but also to influence our thoughts, motor behavior, the autonomic nervous system, and the stress response (Rolls, 1995). Animal studies have shown that lesions of the amygdala reduce emotion and the ability to learn from reward and punishment (LeDoux, 1992). In contrast, electrical stimulation of the amygdala is rewarding to animals, and they will learn new tasks in order to obtain such stimulation. Thus, some view the amygdala as a key brain region for triggering emotional responses. Further, addiction to some illegal drugs, such as the stimulants (for example, amphetamine and cocaine), may be due to their effects on the amygdala. The emotional turmoil that results from drug withdrawal might be a conse-

quence of disruptions in neural communication through amygdala circuits.

The inputs from the amygdala to the hypothalamus also stimulate activity in the **hypothalamic-pituitary-adrenal (HPA) axis.** The HPA axis is one of the primary systems mediating the biological response to stress (see Figure 4–13). When the organism is exposed to a stressful event, a cascade of biological events is triggered in the HPA system, leading to the secretion of glucocorticoids, including the stress hormone cortisol. There are receptors for glucocorticoids throughout the brain, and particularly in the hippocampus. When these receptors are activated by glucocorticoid release, they contribute to a process of negative feedback that dampens or inhibits the activation of the HPA axis, thereby affecting the body's response to stress.

If stress persists, and the HPA axis is activated for an extended period of time, there can be negative effects on the body and mind. For example, rodents who experience periods of isolation from their social groups are more susceptible to disease (Popovic, Popovic, Eric-Jovicic, and Jovanova-Nesic, 2000).

Heightened release of cortisol may also trigger or worsen the symptoms of mental disorders, probably due to the effect cortisol has on neurotransmitter activity (for example, it can increase the activity of dopamine) (Walker and Diforio, 1997). Such an effect can be seen in Tom:

> In December, almost a year after first experiencing problems concentrating, Tom called his mother and told her his car had been stolen. He was convinced that his car had been taken by spies from the Department of Defense who were monitoring his activities. Tom's father picked him up and brought him home. Mr. and Mrs. Clark knew that Tom's suspicious ideas and emotional upset got worse when he was stressed, so they did all they could to calm him down. Mr. Clark called the police and reported the vehicle as stolen. The next day, the police called to say that the car was found in the possession of someone who claimed to be a friend of Tom's. When his parents shared this information with Tom, he became furious and lunged at his father. Mrs. Clark began to scream, and Tom backed off. But he continued a barrage of verbal threats that frightened his parents. Mrs. Clark went into her bedroom and called the police. Two officers were there within ten minutes, and drove Tom to the State Psychiatric Hospital.

The Peripheral Nervous System

The peripheral nervous system (PNS) is made up of the neural pathways located outside the central nervous system (outside the brain and spinal cord). It sends messages to glands, organs, and muscles. It is responsible for the effects our thoughts have on our physical well-being. For example, the gastrointestinal discomfort produced by the anticipation of a frightening or challenging event results from actions of the peripheral nervous system. Moreover, it is also responsible for our ability to execute movements. Feedback is carried by afferent nerves that send information to the brain from muscles and internal organs. They make it possible for us to coordinate movements and to be aware of internal changes.

The somatic system is one of two main divisions of the peripheral nervous system. It controls the muscles and includes the sensory neurons that carry the input from the skin and muscles. The other major division, the autonomic division of the peripheral nervous system, is responsible for maintaining balance, or homeostasis, in the nervous system. It keeps arousal at an appropriate level. The autonomic nervous system is further subdivided into the sympathetic and parasympathetic systems (see Figure 4–14). The sympathetic system innervates blood vessels, hair follicles, smooth muscle, visceral organs, the reproductive organs, heart, lungs, and glands (for example, sweat, adrenal and salivary glands). For example, it accelerates heart action, opens respiratory passages, and inhibits digestion, salivation, and erection. Because it is activated by exposure to threat and stress, the sympathetic system has been viewed as mediating the "flight or fight" reaction, whereby the individual's body readies itself to stand and fight or to run away from a threatening situation. This system has also been implicated in panic attacks, where the body readies itself to fight or flee in situations where there is no actual danger.

The parasympathetic system innervates most of the same organs, but its influence is restorative, in that it conserves energy and works to restore normal conditions in organ systems. For example, it inhibits heart action, constricts respiratory passages, and restores salivation, digestion, and the capacity for erection. Thus, when confronted with a stressful situation, the sympathetic nervous system is called upon to prepare the individual to react mentally and physically. It calls the body to a general state of preparation. But if such a state persisted too long, the individual would become too exhausted to cope. So within a short period of time, the parasympathetic system's restorative effect is triggered. When the sympathetic system remains activated over a prolonged period of time, perhaps because of stress or anxiety, it can have long-term effects on how an individual is able to cope and on his health, as in the case of Tom:

> When he was admitted to the psychiatric hospital in December, Tom's physical condition was very poor. He had lost over twenty pounds in the past year. He complained about stomach pains and nausea. Tom told the physician on the ward that he had trouble sleeping because he often woke up with heart palpitations. However, a thorough physical exam revealed no gastrointestinal or cardiovascular disease. The doctor told Tom that his physical symptoms were due to stress.

Given what we know about the autonomic nervous system, it is not surprising that Tom had physical

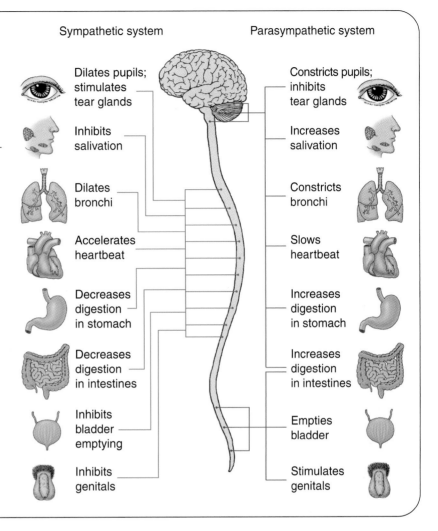

Figure 4–14

THE AUTONOMIC NERVOUS SYSTEM

The autonomic nervous system includes the sympathetic and parasympathetic sections. This diagram of one side of the body shows the parasympathetic nerve connections and functions (in red) and the sympathetic nerve connections and functions (in green).

Sympathetic system

Dilates pupils; stimulates tear glands

Inhibits salivation

Dilates bronchi

Accelerates heartbeat

Decreases digestion in stomach

Decreases digestion in intestines

Inhibits bladder emptying

Inhibits genitals

Parasympathetic system

Constricts pupils; inhibits tear glands

Increases salivation

Constricts bronchi

Slows heartbeat

Increases digestion in stomach

Increases digestion in intestines

Empties bladder

Stimulates genitals

symptoms. Whether or not he was really in danger, Tom was genuinely worried about threats to his well-being. He perceived himself as being in danger. The resulting activation of the sympathetic nervous system affected critical organ systems and produced physical symptoms.

Neurodevelopment and Abnormal Behavior

The human nervous system undergoes change, both in its structure and its biochemistry, across the life span. **Neurodevelopment,** the development of the nervous system, extends from the embryonic stages through old age. As we mentioned, our genes dictate some of the developmental change. In addition, environmental factors also influence the growth of the nervous system. Scientists have discovered that the brain is not a static entity. Rather, normal processes of brain maturation occur throughout life, beginning in the prenatal period and extending through old age. We also know now that as various aspects of brain structure mature cognitive and behavioral capacities also change. Some of the most dramatic changes are those that occur before birth, when the nervous system is forming. This is the main reason why there is such an emphasis on good prenatal care for pregnant women. Without normal prenatal brain development, there can be serious negative consequences for the child. Some mental illnesses seem to be due to such prenatal brain abnormalities.

The Prenatal Period

With a few exceptions, all the cells of the human body contain the same set of genes. Yet, we know cells differ greatly in their form and function. What determines whether a cell becomes a neuron versus a glial cell or a kidney cell or any other type of cell? The answer lies in the *expression* of genes in the cell. You will recall from our earlier discussion that genes only affect the person's phenotype if they are expressed. During the development of the embryo, chemicals inside and outside the cells serve to turn on or turn off the expression of certain genes. This is how the cell's ultimate identity is determined. Thus, all human cells start out as general-purpose cells, but they specialize as they develop.

In addition to neuron formation, the prenatal period is also associated with loss of neurons, or cell death (Sastry and Rao, 2000). Many find it surprising that programmed neuronal death is a normal developmental process in the mammalian nervous system. But research clearly shows that a high proportion of the neurons that develop in the embryo die before they migrate and form connections with other cells. Researchers believe that this process increases the likelihood that neurons that develop abnormal interconnections will not survive. Although it is known that neuron death occurs in normal human brain development, its extent has not been established.

Among humans, the first two trimesters are critical periods for the development of nervous system structures (see Figure 4–15). By the fourth week of gestation, divisions among the areas that will become the forebrain, midbrain, and hindbrain are clearly visible. Cellular layers of the cortex have begun to form by the seventh week. The thalamus and hypothalamus are visible by the tenth week, and the basal ganglia by the twelfth week. Also by the twelfth week, the cerebral hemispheres have differentiated and are convoluted. *Myelination,* the formation of the myelin sheath around the neuron, begins in the spinal cord in the first trimester and on the neurons of the brain in the second trimester. As described below, myelination and some other neurodevelopmental processes continue far into the postnatal period (in fact, the brain's myelination isn't finished until about twenty years of age). Nonetheless, when the fetus enters the third trimester (at the seventh month), it has a nervous system capable of processing information and engaging in motor behavior, such as sucking amniotic fluid, sucking the thumb, turning in the womb, and blinking.

The prenatal development of the human nervous system thus proceeds rapidly during the first and second trimesters of the pregnancy. It is influenced by genetic factors, some of which are unique to the individual. Prenatal development is also affected by environmental factors, some of which may be other cells or chemicals and some of which may be the mother's psychosocial environment. During the first two trimesters, the nervous system is especially vulnerable. Maternal nutritional deprivation during pregnancy, as well as exposure to alcohol, certain drugs, neurotoxins, and oxygen deprivation, can disrupt neurodevelopment in offspring (Walker and Diforio, 1997). Moreover, the mother's stress level during pregnancy can permanently alter fetal nervous system development. Studies of rodents, as well as nonhuman primates, have shown that offspring of mothers who experienced repeated stress while pregnant show an increase in glucocorticoid release, as well as abnormalities in the hippocampus (Smythe, McCormick, Rochford, and Meaney, 1994; Weinstock, 1996). These abnormalities can persist into adulthood, and the animal will manifest behavioral abnormalities, such as hypersensitivity to stress and deficits in social behavior (Clarke et al., 1994; Schneider, 1992). Further, there is evidence that some of the consequences of prenatal stress are only apparent after the onset of puberty (Henry et al., 1995). This suggests that vulnerabilities can be latent during some stages of development, then can be expressed after certain maturational processes occur, as in the case of Tom:

> Two days before Christmas, the unit physician asked Tom's parents to come to the hospital for a meeting. The clinical team had completed an evaluation that lasted five days. The physician wanted to share the results with Mr. and Mrs. Clark. It was at that time that they were first told their son was suffering from paranoid schizophrenia. They were devastated. They didn't know much about the illness, but it was clear from the physician's somber demeanor that the news was not good. Mr. and Mrs. Clark spent the morning of December 23 in an interview with the unit social worker. She asked them to provide an account of Tom's developmental history, including the prenatal period. Mrs. Clark was surprised at the details she was able to recall. In part, this was due to the fact that her pregnancy with Tom had been difficult, much more difficult than her previous two pregnancies. Because of complications, her physician had directed her to remain in bed during the last two months. Nonetheless, Tom was born prematurely and had to be kept in an incubator for several

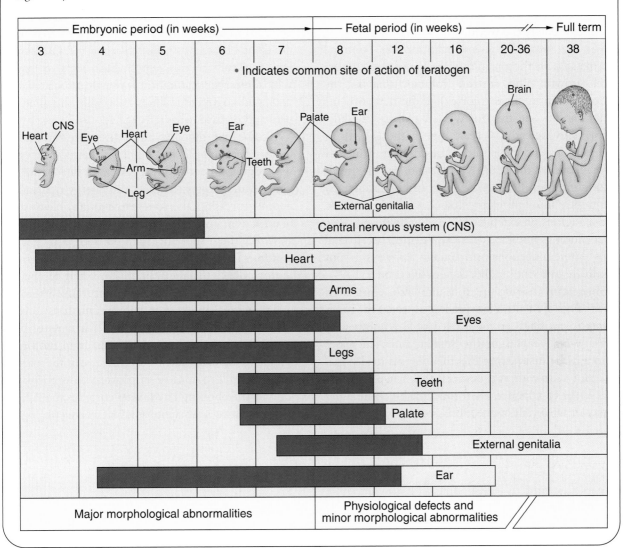

CRITICAL PERIODS OF PRENATAL DEVELOPMENT

The figure shows the development from embryo to fetus to full-term infant. Neurodevelopment can go awry at any time during prenatal development. The dark purple bars indicate periods during which various structures are most sensitive to damage by teratogens (harmful environmental agents), although physiological defects and abnormalities can occur later in the fetus's development, as indicated by the light purple bars. (Source: Based on Cunningham, 1989, Figure 6.9)

days. As Mrs. Clark recounted these details, she wondered how they could be related to Tom's current problems. After all, he didn't seem to have any psychological problems until recently—at the age of twenty-three.

It was unclear to Tom's mother why the social worker would inquire about her pregnancy. Wouldn't a problem that was due to pregnancy complications

show up as soon as the child was born? It is certainly true that some prenatal complications are so severe that they produce nervous system abnormalities that are obvious at birth. For example, brain abnormalities resulting from prenatal oxygen deprivation can result in motor abnormalities at birth, ranging from relatively subtle deficits in muscle tone to paralysis of a limb. If the abnormality is in a brain region that is mainly involved in symbolic communication or abstract reasoning, however, the abnormality may not be detected until the child is older.

Postnatal CNS Development

Prenatal complications can have effects that are not detected until later in life. This may be perplexing at first, but it makes sense when we examine the brain changes that occur after birth. As you will see, brain development is by no means complete at the time the infant enters the world.

Several neurodevelopmental processes continue postnatally, even into adulthood. One of these is cortical growth. The cortical volume (that is, the amount of tissue in the cortex) of the newborn infant is about one-third of what it will be in adulthood. The increase is largely due to the growth of the neurons and their interconnections and further myelination of the brain. Myelination (which speeds communication between neurons and brain circuits) continues through early childhood, and in some brain regions, it extends into early adulthood. Recent findings indicate that myelination of frontal lobe interconnections and limbic pathways is not complete until the third decade of life (Benes, 1994). Connections among neurons are also eliminated with development. This process is referred to as **synaptic pruning** (see Figure 4–16). The number, or density, of synapses in the human brain increases through the first year of life, then begins to decline. As with cell death, it is assumed that synaptic pruning serves to enhance brain function by eliminating faulty or irrelevant connections.

Neuroimaging studies have revealed a pattern of human brain growth through adolescence that includes an increase in nerve fibers connecting various areas within each hemisphere, an increase in the volume of the corpus callosum, the group of nerve fibers that connect the two hemispheres (Thompson et al., 2000), and a decrease in the volume of the gray matter in the cortex, especially the frontal cortex (Sowell et al., 1999). Keeping in mind that the gray matter contains cell bodies and the white matter contains myelinated fibers, the pattern of changes in the frontal lobes is assumed to reflect a refinement of neural circuits in this region. This helps to explain why adolescent maturation is usually associated with increased cognitive abilities, especially the ability to plan and control behavior.

Studies of glucose metabolism in the human brain reveal significant changes in neural processing with development (Chugani, 1994). The brain uses glucose and oxygen to meet the energy demands of neural processing, and so researchers are able to study brain activity in living subjects by measuring the rate at which these substances are consumed by various regions. They have found that in newborns, the motor cortex, thalamus, brain stem, and cerebellum show the greatest metabolic activity. Given that the brain regions involved in motor functions develop early, it is not surprising that the first signs of brain damage detected in infants are usually in motor behaviors. Gradually, during the first year, the parietal and temporal regions of the cortex show increasing glucose metabolism. The frontal cortex is the last area to show a rise in metabolism. Electroencephalogram

Figure 4–16

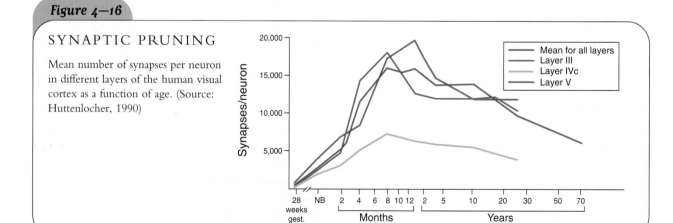

SYNAPTIC PRUNING

Mean number of synapses per neuron in different layers of the human visual cortex as a function of age. (Source: Huttenlocher, 1990)

(EEG) research measures electrical fields on the surface of the head and has revealed similar developmental changes (Thatcher, 1994). Patterns of brain electrical activity show especially marked changes around six years of age and again in adolescence.

Developmental changes in brain metabolism show parallels with the changes that have been found in brain structure. For example, during early childhood, when cortical growth and synaptic production are increasing rapidly, so is cortical metabolism. Similarly, during the developmental periods characterized by synaptic pruning, metabolism is declining. Cognitive psychologists assume that developmental changes in the human brain are, in part, responsible for the remarkable growth in cognitive ability observed during childhood and adolescence. Thus, for example, there are significant increases in cognitive capacity around seven years of age and again following puberty—around the same time that the greatest changes are observed in EEG and metabolic activity. At about age seven, children advance markedly in their abilities to solve social problems and to think about mathematics. Adolescents demonstrate notable improvements in abstract reasoning.

Adult development is also associated with changes in brain structure and function. Beginning in middle age, the brain gradually loses volume, and brain metabolism shows a more dramatic decline. These changes are most noticeable in the cortical regions. Several studies have documented significant age-related declines in the volume of the hippocampus (Sapolsky, 1992). Neurotransmitter concentrations and receptors also change with age (Walker, 1994). For example, research with human subjects has shown age-related decreases in the number of receptors for serotonin, dopamine, and acetylcholine. Finally, there appears to be an increase in activity of the HPA system with age, so that older adults show higher cortisol levels than younger persons (Nicolson, Storms, Ponds, and Sulon, 1997). Many of the brain changes that occur with advanced age appear to be associated with risk for various psychological symptoms. As a case in point, age-related declines in memory with age may be related to changes in the hippocampus. Reduced dopamine activity may be responsible for the lowered risk of schizophrenia beyond the age of forty.

The extended period of normal brain maturation that takes place in humans is part of our genetic blueprint. Our large and complex brains have developed significantly over the course of human evolution. It takes about two decades for our brains to fully mature; perhaps it is because they are such sophisticated biological machines.

But what if there is something wrong with an individual's neurodevelopmental blueprint? Could brain development proceed normally for a while, then go awry? The answer is a qualified yes. Scientists have not identified any specific abnormalities in the human genes that control brain development. But such genes have been identified in animals, and there is every reason to believe that they also occur in humans. This could explain how a genetic predisposition to a mental illness might be present at birth, but not be apparent in behavior until the individual matures. The case of Tom shows his developmental history and that clinical symptoms of schizophrenia did not appear until he was an adult:

When the social worker asked Tom's mother to describe his childhood, she began to make a mental comparison between Tom and his siblings. There was no doubt that Tom walked later than his brother and sister. He didn't take his first step on his own until he was fourteen months, whereas both Tom's siblings walked before the age of eleven months. Tom was also less coordinated than his older brother, and less interested in sports. Another thing that stood out in Mrs. Clark's mind was Tom's childhood fears. Tom had more nightmares and was more likely to be frightened by unusual noises, animals, or storms. But aside from these problems, Tom was a good boy. His grades were always average or above. He never got into serious trouble in school and didn't hang out with a bad crowd. In fact, during high school he only had a couple of friends. He never dated, although he had a crush on a girl. It was during the high school years that Tom first developed an interest in science fiction. On several occasions, he shared some ideas with his parents that seemed rather far-fetched. When he was a senior in high school, he developed an "astrological theory" to explain why he was teased by some of his peers. He seemed to fit in somewhat better in college and went out with a few girls, but generally he was still a loner. As Mrs. Clark shared this information with the social worker, she became conscious of the fact that she had always had nagging worries about Tom. Had she been denying it all this time? Were there signs she should have seen?

Tom's developmental history is fairly common among patients diagnosed with serious mental illnesses. Many begin to show adjustment problems during adolescence, then, in their early twenties, diagnosable signs and symptoms arise. Some researchers believe that the brain changes that occur during adolescence and early adulthood play a role in this developmental course. For example, it has been suggested that schizophrenia involves an abnormality in the frontal cortex that is present at birth (Weinberger, 1988). But the abnormality is not detected until this brain region approaches maturity. When the abnormal region is fully mature, the individual begins to show clinical symptoms. Although there is currently no direct evidence to support this particular theory, the general notion that brain development influences the expression of behavioral abnormalities is very plausible.

Critical Periods for Psychological Development

A question that has been of great interest to researchers who study abnormal behavior is whether the environment is more important during some periods of development than in others. The existence of developmental critical periods was demonstrated by biologist Konrad Lorenz in the 1950s when he showed that ducklings could only form attachments during a relatively brief time period after hatching. Further research has shown that critical periods also exist in mammals.

Researchers have found that critical periods are a consequence of the organism's neurodevelopmental stage. For example, in rodents, undernutrition is more likely to impair brain growth if it occurs on the tenth day of life than if it occurs before or after that time (Yoshioka, Yoshida, Okana, and Yamazoe, 1995). In an "adoption" study of rodents, those placed with the adoptive mothers on the day of birth were compared to those placed on the fifth or twelfth day after birth (Barbazanges et al., 1996). Only the rat pups who were placed after the first day showed significant deficits in maze performance as adults. It appears that rat pups form a bond with the caregiver within the first day, and severing this bond once it has formed has negative consequences. Along these same lines, studies of humans have found that children who are adopted as infants show better cognitive ability and fewer behavior problems than those adopted later in childhood (Castle et al., 1999; Sharma, McGue and Benson, 1996).

Many psychologists have assumed that the first few years of life are especially important in human development. In part, this is because attachment bonds between the child and his caregiver are formed during these years. Researchers have conducted some very creative studies with animals that have shed light on the biochemical underpinnings of attachment bonds (Insel, 1997). They have shown that certain hormones play a significant role in the attachments animals form with their offspring and their mates. We must await future research to find out whether human bonding also depends on hormones.

Environmental Input and Abnormal Behavior

Learning and experience affect both normal and abnormal behavior. We know, for example, that learning plays a role in phobias and anxiety. Within the past decade, researchers have made tremendous advances in clarifying the biological events that take place when learning occurs. These findings help us to better understand why some kinds of maladaptive behavior persist, and how psychotherapies can change such behavior.

Effects of Learning and Memory

Learning depends upon both perception and memory. Psychologists who study learning have long assumed that changes in the brain occurred when new memories were acquired. But only in the past decade has research shown where and what these changes are. We have learned a great deal about the brain regions involved with various kinds of sensory input, and the nature of the changes that occur at the microscopic level when memories are formed.

By recording the activity of neurons in living animals, researchers have discovered that the processing of sensory information involves the simultaneous activity of "ensembles," or groups of neurons (Deadwyler and Hampson, 1997). Different types of input activate groups of neurons in different brain regions. Memories are represented in the nervous system by relatively permanent changes in the firing patterns of the ensemble, which in turn are controlled by the expression of genes in the neurons involved. This cellular process is referred to as ***long-term potentiation (LTP),*** and it is believed to play a pivotal function in memory formation (Malenka and Nicoli, 1997).

Which brain regions are involved in memory depends on the type of memory being formed (Rugg et al., 1998). The term ***explicit memory*** refers to stored knowledge about objects, people, and events. Acquiring these memories often involves conscious attention, and recalling them requires conscious effort. Forming and recalling ***implicit memories,*** in contrast, does not depend on conscious awareness. Implicit memory includes stored knowledge about perceptual and motor skills and various procedures and principles. For example, rules of grammar are, for the most part, stored and utilized without conscious awareness of the process. Implicit memories have also been implicated in recognition of emotional stimuli and events. There have been many stories in the news about adults who have "recovered memories" of childhood sexual abuse. These situations may involve implicit memories that become explicit. Implicit memories might also play a role in post-traumatic stress disorder, a disorder in which traumatic memories continue to disturb the individual long after the actual events have occurred. Even though the patient may not consciously recall the traumatic memories, they nonetheless can affect his actions and reactions to new events in his life.

Damage to different brain structures can affect different types of memories. The hippocampus seems to play a role in many forms of memory, but especially explicit memory (Uecker et al., 1997). Damage to the amygdala may lead to more pronounced problems with implicit memory, such that patients show deficits in classifying facial expressions of emotion (Adolphs, Russell, and Tranel, 1999; Adolphs, Tranel, Damasio, and Damasio, 1994), and in making socially relevant judgments (as to approachability or trustworthiness, for example) based on facial appearances (Adolphs, Tranel, and Damasio, 1998). In a unique study of patients undergoing surgery for epilepsy, researchers monitored neural activity and discovered that neurons in the amygdala responded differentially when the patient was shown faces of strangers versus friends or family members (Seeck et al., 1993).

In Chapter 8, we discuss autism, an early-onset disorder that involves a failure to form social attachments. It is possible that the brain abnormality involved in autism involves the brain regions that are responsible for the processing and storage of social information, particularly the facial expressions and gestures that comprise human nonverbal communication.

Effects of Experience

Let us now consider how our experiences affect our capacity to acquire information and, in doing so, might contribute to or reduce risk of mental disorder. Early in this chapter, we described the diathesis-stress model, which assumes that abnormal behavior is the result of an interaction between constitutional vulnerability and experience. As you will see, recent findings are leading us to reconsider what the "interaction" may be. This is because "diathesis" and "stress" cannot be easily separated. Our brain determines the kinds of environments we seek, and thus the stressors we will encounter. But we now know that our brain structure is malleable and is altered by our experience. In other words, the causal arrow points both ways. How does environment affect brain development? This is the focus of much ongoing research, as we discuss next.

ENRICHED AND IMPOVERISHED ENVIRONMENTS

The sensory nervous system requires stimulation in order to develop normally. For example, the visual system shows abnormal neuron shapes and interconnections if visual input is reduced or distorted (Hubel, 1995). Similarly, research has also shown that environmental enrichment can change the structure of the brain (Blakemore, 1998). Rodents who are exposed to enriched or novel environments show enlargement of the volume of certain brain regions (Fuchs, Montemayor, and Greenough, 1990; Katz, Davies, and Dobbing, 1980). Mice reared in an environment rich in stimulus complexity show faster nerve conduction velocity than those reared in less stimulating environments (Reed, 1993). Thus, experience influences the brain in ways that change its capacity to learn new information.

The effects of environmental enrichment also extend to animals and humans who have experienced brain damage. In one study, rats with lesions in the hippocampus were either placed in an impoverished environment or an enriched environment (Galani, Jarrard, Will, and Kelche, 1997). Those who had a recovery period in an enriched environment

Researchers have shown that rats exposed to such a stimulating environment as this one show increased volume in certain brain regions and faster nerve conduction. Enriched environments may also affect human brains and increase the ability to learn.

Hou, and Cook, 1996). Differences among animals have also been found in the effects of drugs on behavior and on neurotransmitters (Gendreau, Petitto, Gariepy, and Lewis, 1997). Finally, the effects of brain damage on learning are more pronounced for some strains of rats than others (Rossi-Arnaud, Fagiolo, and Ammassari-Teule, 1991). These findings illustrate the kind of gene-environment interactions that are assumed to play a role in the development of psychological disorders.

STRESSFUL ENVIRONMENTS

Many studies have documented a relationship between exposure to stressful experiences and psychological problems. Researchers who study stress typically define a stressor as any event that threatens the individual's homeostasis or "balance." Usually the event is a negative one, although very unusual events can also be stressful.

Most contemporary theories of the etiology of mental disorders, such as depression and schizophrenia, have included stress as a factor that triggers illness onset or worsens symptoms (Post, Weiss, Smith, and Leverich, 1996; Walker and Diforio, 1997). Of course, mental disorders are not distinct from general medical illnesses in this regard. It is well established that stress can exacerbate many physical illnesses, including cardiovascular disorders, respiratory conditions, diabetes, and cancer. Stress, and the way we cope with it, also influences the speed of our physical recovery from injuries (Kiecolt-Glaser, Page, Marucha, MacCallum, and Glaser, 1998).

showed better performance on certain measures of learning. Can the environment affect human recovery from brain damage in a similar manner? The tentative answer is "yes." A longitudinal study of children with traumatic brain injury showed that the quality of the child's family environment was associated with outcome twelve months later (Yeates et al., 1997). Brain-injured children who were in supportive and emotionally stable families showed greater improvement in cognitive functions and behavior.

There is now direct evidence that the favorable effect of environmental enrichment on brain growth and function is a consequence of gene activity. One study found that male rats housed in a stimulus-rich environment (lots of rat toys!) for thirty days had significantly higher levels of nerve growth factor in the visual cortex and hippocampus than rats who did not experience stimulus enrichment (Torasdotter, Metsis, Henriksson, Winblad, and Mohammed, 1998). Nerve growth factor is a substance that is present in the brain throughout development. It promotes neuronal growth and survival. Thus, the results of this study show that postnatal experiences can turn genes on and improve brain function.

As described at the beginning of this chapter, diathesis-stress models of psychopathology assume that individuals differ in their response to the same environment. Researchers have discovered many examples of this. Studies of rodents have shown differences among genetic strains in the effects of environmental factors on brain neurotransmitters (Jones,

In January, Tom was released from the hospital. He was on a medication that made him less irritable and reduced his preoccupation with the Department of Defense. He had lost his job at the university. Tom was somewhat disappointed about this, but at the same time, he was relieved. The daily demands of working with the lab group had been too stressful. Also, the medication he was taking made him groggy in the morning, so he couldn't concentrate on work. Tom moved back in with his parents and began weekly therapy sessions with a psychologist at the local community mental health center. Most of the time his irritability and paranoid ideas were controlled by the medication. He had also become more sociable. Like many patients, however, Tom experienced drug side effects, especially involuntary movements. When these became too annoying, he stopped taking his medication. Tom's parents always knew when he had failed to take his medication, because within a few days, Tom was pacing, irritable, and confused. Over the next ten years, he was rehospitalized seven times. Five of the seven times the hospitalizations followed a period when he had failed to take his medication. The other two hospitalizations occurred after stressful events: the death of his grandfather and the retirement of his therapist.

Genetic factors influence the biological response to stress. Animal studies have shown that the magnitude of the biological response to stress differs as a function of genotype, so that strains of rats vary in their hormonal response to the same stressor (Driscoll et al., 1998). In humans, twin studies reveal that genetic factors partially determine the release of stress hormones; monozygotic twins are more similar in their cortisol levels than are dizygotic twins (Kirschbaum, Wust, Faig, and Hellhammer, 1992; Linkowski, Van Onderbergen, Kerkhofs, Bosson, Mendlewicz, and Van Cauter, 1993). Scientists have recently begun to manipulate stress sensitivity in laboratory mice by altering the genes that control their sensitivity to stress hormones (Stroehle, Poettig, Barden, Holsboer, and Montkowski, 1998). The transgenic mice who receive genes that impair function of the HPA system show more behavioral signs of anxiety.

When stress is chronic or severe, there may be lasting effects on brain function. Repeated exposure to a stressful experience can result in an abnormality of the HPA axis that is reflected in a chronic increase in glucocorticoid release, as well as greater biological and behavioral responses to later stressors (Chrousos, McCarty, Pacak, Cizza, Sternberg, Gold, and Kvetnansky, 1995; Prasad, Sorg, Ulibarri, and Kalivas, 1995). The apparent increase in stress sensitivity produced by repeated exposure is called *sensitization.* Early stressful experiences can also alter sensitivity to drugs. For example, rodents who experience a period of maternal deprivation show a greater behavioral reaction to amphetamines than do controls who are not separated from their mother (Zimmerberg and Shartrand, 1992).

In addition to changes in stress hormones, rodents exposed to repeated stress show changes in brain structure. Researchers have found that stress reduces the density of glucocorticoid receptors in the hippocampus and the size of the hippocampus (Sapolsky, 1992), especially when the stress is uncontrollable (Wellman, Cullen, and Pelleymounter,

1998). Like other mammals, humans subjected to chronic stress show brain abnormalities. For example, several neuroimaging studies indicate that stress contributes to abnormalities of the hippocampus in humans. When compared to women with no history of abuse, women who were abused in childhood show a shrinkage of the hippocampus (Bremner et al., 1997b; Stein et al., 1997). Similarly, men suffering from post-traumatic stress disorder who were exposed to intense combat during war show shrinkage in the hippocampus (Gurvits, Shenton, Hokama and Ohta, 1996). Of course, the investigations of humans exposed to severe trauma are not controlled experimental studies. As a result, we can't rule out the possibility that the brain abnormalities were present before the individuals had the stressful experiences. But it is certainly plausible that, like other mammals, humans can sustain nervous system damage from exposure to traumatic events.

As you may recall from Celia's case (a panic disorder case described in Chapter 1), Celia's panic attacks began after she experienced a series of stressful events. How can we explain this correlation? Could these events have caused her panic attacks? Or did the occurrence of panic attacks lead her to interpret the events as especially stressful? Or did some less obvious factor lead both to Celia's panic attacks and to her experience that she was under stress? Some of the research findings we have reviewed here suggest that Celia may have been biologically predisposed to panic attacks. Then what are we to make of the fact that cognitive therapy eliminated the attacks? Cognitive therapy is aimed at changing the individual's attitudes and beliefs about the world. Perhaps the therapy provided Celia with an effective means of coping with the stressors that precipitated the attacks. This may have put her at a lower level of overall biological stress, and placed her further from the threshold for having a panic attack. We will explore the plausibility of this notion in Chapter 5.

Putting It All Together

So, has the "decade of the brain" lived up to its promise? As we enter the next decade, many now believe the enthusiasm surrounding new research and information on the brain was warranted. Certainly, our knowledge of the nervous system has increased exponentially. This new knowledge compels us to reevaluate some of our long-standing and simplistic assumptions.

Older theories about the causes of some psychological disorders often assumed that mental illness arose when a constitutional, and typically innate, vulnerability combined with a stressful environment. We now know that constitutional vulnerabilities can be acquired, as well as inherited. For example, hippocampal abnormalities can result from genetic defects, but they may also be a consequence of prenatal factors. Further, constitutional vulnerabilities can be acquired after birth, whether the agent is an abrupt blow to the head, exposure to a neurotoxin, abnormal hormone levels, or persistent psychological stress.

Originally, the biomedical conception of mental illness led to the belief that psychologists could clearly distinguish mental illness from mental health, just as internists could clearly distinguish a cancerous lung from a healthy one. But we now know that, in reality, there is little evidence for such clear-cut distinctions between mental illness and mental health. Moreover, mental health falls on a continuum, from high levels of resilience and invulnerability to extreme psychological vulnerability. The same holds for biological factors. Brain function falls on a continuum, so there is no clear-cut dividing line between brain normality and abnormality.

The biomedical model once meant that biology is the initial and main cause of abnormal behavior. The research findings we have discussed in this chapter have shown us that this is an incorrect assumption. The causal chain has proven much more complex, with experience often coming at the beginning, and brain malfunction as an intermediate step on the road toward psychopathology.

As we mentioned earlier in this chapter, it was once common to hear questions such as: Is it biological or psychological? Is it nature or nurture? Do genes cause this disorder, or is it the environment? It now appears that these are the wrong questions. The following are just a few of the questions that we should now ask: How do our genes affect our central nervous systems and therefore our behavior? How does our environment influence our gene expression and brain structure? What particular kinds of brain-environment interactions predispose us to become mentally ill or stay mentally healthy?

Clearly, researchers have moved far beyond simple ideas about the etiology of mental disorders. When our theories were simpler and our knowledge more limited, textbooks in abnormal psychology were less challenging. But the reality is that human behavior, normal and abnormal, is the product of many causal factors. There is no doubt that this makes the task of explaining abnormal behavior more interesting.

Summary

1. Biological theories of abnormal behavior have been with us for a long time, but in recent years scientists have gained a better understanding of the interplay between experience and biology. This has changed the way we think about the causes and treatments of mental disorders.

2. The *diathesis-stress model* assumes that mental disorders arise from the interaction between constitutional vulnerabilities and the environmental factors that act on the individual throughout life. In addition, certain positive characteristics of the person and his or her environment may act as a buffer against psychological problems.

3. Genetic predispositions are one source of vulnerability. At conception, the human *zygote* possesses *genes* inherited from both mother and father. Genes come in pairs, and one member of each pair comes from each parent. *Dominant genes* are genes whose effect is almost always shown, whereas a *recessive gene* does not have an effect unless it is paired with another copy of the recessive gene.

4. The particular combination of genes inherited by a person is called the *genotype*. This genotype is a blueprint that includes detailed instructions on how to build a human being. The *phenotype* is the combination of physical and behavioral characteristics associated with the genotype. Only some of the genes in the person's genotype are expressed in a way that affects behavior. *Gene expression* involves a process called *transcription,* in which the gene's DNA provides the template for messenger RNA, thereby activating the "code" for the synthesis of proteins.

5. From the moment of conception, the zygote is surrounded by an intrauterine environment that begins to influence its development through the expression of genes. The mother's physical health and personal experiences determine the nature of the intrauterine environment, which in turn, influences the expression of genes that guide the development of the fetal nervous system. When the infant is born, it enters the world with a ner-

vous system that reflects the interaction between its inherited genotype and its intrauterine environment. Thus, the infant's congenital (present at birth) "biological constitution" already reflects both nature and nurture.

6. Researchers who study behavioral genetics use a variety of methods, each with its own advantages and disadvantages. The *family study method* examines the occurrence of characteristics in people who are genetically related. The *twin study method* relies on the differences between monozygotic and dizygotic twins in their genetic similarity. *Adoption studies* trace the development of children who are offspring of biological parents with a disorder, but who are reared by adoptive parents without the disorder. Some newer techniques in behavioral genetics are *genetic linkage studies* and *quantitative genetic methods*.

7. *Neurons* are the cells of the nervous system. They communicate with each other through the release of neurotransmitters. Dopamine, serotonin, norepinephrine, glutamate, and GABA are *neurotransmitters* that are believed to play a role in some forms of psychopathology. Sex hormones and stress hormones also influence the way neurons function. Exposure to chronic or severe stress can change neuronal function and produce behavioral abnormalities.

8. Communication among neurons is disrupted when there is too little or too much of any neurotransmitter or changes in the neurotransmitter receptors. Damage to the glial cells that surround neurons and hormonal imbalances can also interfere with *neurotransmission*. Using sophisticated techniques, researchers can examine the activity of individual neurons in animal studies. These techniques have furthered our understanding of how neurotransmitters and drugs work to affect brain function.

9. The *central nervous system (CNS)* is comprised of the spinal cord, the brain stem, and the forebrain. The forebrain is highly developed in humans. The cortex is the largest region of the brain, and it is important for complicated mental abilities. Areas under the cortex, especially the basal ganglia, hippocampus, and amygdala, play an important role in emotion and behavior, as well as in mental abilities. The *hypothalamic-pituitary-adrenal (HPA) axis* mediates the response to stressful events.

10. The *peripheral nervous system (PNS)* is made up of the neurons outside the central nervous system. Its two divisions are the *somatic* and *autonomic nervous systems*. The autonomic nervous system is further divided into the *sympathetic* and *parasympathetic nervous systems*. The sympathetic nervous system comes into play during activation, whereas the parasympathetic nervous system dampens arousal.

11. The genotype contains plans for prenatal and postnatal nervous system development. All of the components of the nervous system are formed during prenatal life, and their development is affected by the mother's health. Fetal exposure to toxins, insufficient oxygen, or maternal stress can interfere with *neurodevelopment*.

12. As the child matures, the nervous system undergoes further changes that are dictated by the genetic blueprint. These maturational processes include the refinement of interneuronal communication and the gradual activation of brain regions that are responsible for higher-level cognitive abilities. But environmental factors come into play as well. The nature of the environment in which these processes occur can influence the pace and quality of the child's nervous system development.

13. Some neurodevelopmental processes extend into adulthood. Our chances of developing various psychological problems and disorders change significantly with age. A few disorders (for example, autism and pervasive developmental disorder) have an onset in early childhood, but most do not have their clinical onset until late adolescence or young adulthood. This suggests that post-pubertal brain maturation is playing some role in triggering mental illness among vulnerable individuals.

14. Biological processes mediate the effects of the environment and play a role in learning and memory. The amygdala and the hippocampus are areas of the brain that are involved in the formation and storage of memories. When memories are formed, there are changes in the way neurons respond to input and send information.

15. Stimulating and supportive environments can have beneficial effects on the nervous system. This occurs through changes in gene expression. Stressful environments can have detrimental effects, largely due to the influence of stress hormones on gene expression. Consistent with the diathesis-stress model, people vary in their vulnerability to environmental stress. These differences contribute to individual differences in risk for abnormal behavior.

5

Anxiety Disorders

Chapter Outline

Marc Chagall, *Nu.*

➙ Be able to describe the elements of fear and anxiety, and to distinguish fear from anxiety.

➙ Learn about the different kinds of phobias, and be able to discuss how biological and behavioral explanations and therapies both help to account for the selectivity and persistence of phobias.

➙ Understand how some people may be more vulnerable to post-traumatic stress disorder than others, and how such therapies as exposure, disclosure, and EMDR may help to relieve the suffering of those with PTSD.

➙ Describe how both the biological and cognitive approaches can help us to understand panic disorder, and why the cognitive explanation can be said to "subsume" the biological explanation.

➙ Understand why agoraphobia is now considered a subtype of panic disorder, rather than a kind of phobia.

➙ Learn about the biological explanations for generalized anxiety disorder, as well as the role of uncontrollability and unpredictability in GAD.

➙ Be able to describe how a person with obsessive-compulsive disorder uses compulsions as a way to ward off the anxiety created by obsessive thoughts, and how depression is often comorbid with OCD.

We have all felt fear and anxiety. Both are part of the human experience. All of us would feel fear if we saw an out-of-control car hurtling toward us. Most of us would feel anxious if suddenly called upon to perform a difficult task for which we were unprepared, such as speaking before a large group about Estonian economic recovery. When fear and anxiety prevent normal functioning, however, they are called *anxiety disorders.*

Terry's problems began in his first year of residency. His schedule as an internal medicine resident had him on call for thirty-six straight hours at a time. The constant emergencies and the daily 6 A.M. rounds were grueling and exhausting. He began to notice that his fellow residents were making small errors in the care of their patients. Terry found himself ruminating about their oversights and, worse, he began to hesitate when making medical decisions himself, lest he make a serious mistake. He found himself avoiding difficult cases and began calling in sick. By the end of the year, he resigned rather than be dismissed for incompetence.

His father, also a physician, helped him get into a less demanding residency. But again, he felt overwhelmed with dread of making a catastrophic mistake, and he quit after six months. He then took a more relaxed job as a researcher in the Food and Drug Administration. But even in this job, he couldn't handle all the decisions. His contract expired after six months and was not renewed.

Besides crippling his career, Terry's anxieties ruin his closest relationships. He is afraid to go home because he fears that his father has a low opinion of him. He avoids talking about any touchy subject with his girlfriend, because he is afraid he will say something wrong and it will "blow the relationship."

Terry is always very tense, complains of throbbing headaches and a constant feeling of fatigue. He describes himself as "worthless" and "lazy," but he knows his fears are much exaggerated. After persuasion he will admit to being an intelligent and capable person, but he feels utterly unable to control his anxiety. (Adapted from Vitkus, 1996, Case 1)

In this chapter, we discuss six disorders in which anxiety is felt. We group phobia and post-traumatic stress disorder together because they are both provoked by fear of specific danger. *Fear* is distinguished from *anxiety* in that it is characterized by distress about specific, dangerous objects; whereas **anxiety** is a general feeling of unease about some unspecified danger. In phobic disorders, the individual is afraid of an object (such as cats), and the fear is out of proportion to the reality of the danger the object presents. In post-traumatic stress disorders, the individual experiences fear, numbness, and repeated reliving of the trauma after experiencing a specific event that involves actual or threatened death or injury. For example, an undergraduate who was raped in her dormitory may subsequently relive the trauma repeatedly in memory and in her dreams, becoming numb to the world around her, avoiding men, and experiencing intense fear whenever she is alone with a man.

In panic disorder, agoraphobia, and generalized anxiety disorder, no specific object threatens the individual, yet she feels very anxious. Thus, in panic disorder, an individual is suddenly and repeatedly overwhelmed with brief attacks of intense anxiety and terror. In agoraphobia in which there is no history of panic disorder, the individual fears going out to public places because he fears that he will experience a panic attack and that no one will come to his aid. In generalized anxiety disorder, such as Terry experiences, the individual experiences pervasive anxiety and worry that can be more or less continually present for months on end.

In obsessive-compulsive disorder (OCD), the individual is plagued with uncontrollable, repulsive thoughts, and he engages in seemingly senseless rituals in order to ward off feelings of anxiety. A person with OCD might think that he left the gas stove on and get out of bed to check it twenty times during the night.

Another person might have continual thoughts of killing her children and go to great lengths to keep all knives and sharp objects out of reach. People with obsessive-compulsive disorder often feel anxiety, but they develop ways to deflect it quickly.

In this chapter and the next, we discuss the disorders that used to be grouped together as the "neuroses." Freudian theory claimed that all the neuroses were accompanied by underlying anxiety, whether or not anxiety was felt. DSM-III and DSM-IV abandoned the term "neuroses" because it was too inclusive and presumed prematurely that anxiety was the root cause. We believe the distinction between anxiety felt and anxiety inferred is still valuable and can often provide insights into the causes of not only the anxiety disorders but also the somatoform and dissociative disorders. In this chapter, we consider the disorders in which anxiety is actually felt. In Chapter 6, we will deal with the somatoform and dissociative disorders, in which anxiety usually is not felt, although its existence is often inferred from the other symptoms.

All the anxiety disorders share in common a grossly exaggerated version of normal and adaptive distress that each of us has felt on many occasions. We begin our discussion of these disorders by examining this kind of distress: normal fear and normal anxiety.

Fear and Anxiety

Fear is commonplace, and it is simply a reaction to danger. How much danger we face depends in large part on our job, where we live, and so on. Being a member of a team responsible for constructing an oil

Fear is a quickly recognizable state, as shown by Drew Barrymore's face in *Scream*.

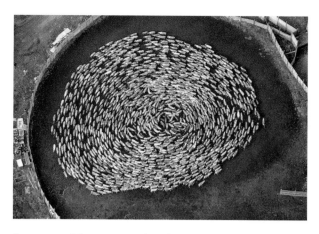 

Symptoms of fear are normal or abnormal according to context. In these frightened reindeer *(left)* or these civilians and U.N. soldier in Bosnia taking cover from sniper fire *(right)*, we would expect to find the somatic, emotional, cognitive, and behavioral elements of fear.

rig in the wintry North Sea presents more danger than being an accountant. But an accountant living in New York City may experience more danger than one working in Maui. When the oilman experiences fear, it is directly related to the danger of his situation; his reactions will be appropriate and normal. Similarly, the accountant's heart has every reason to beat rapidly upon hearing a noise at the window at 3 A.M. Unlike the disorders we will discuss in this chapter, normal fear and anxiety are in keeping with the reality of the danger.

Elements of Fear

The definition of fear is multidimensional and doesn't depend upon any one particular element being present although there must be some combination of the various elements (see Chapter 1). Thus, fear can take different forms in different individuals. Nonetheless, the more intense any element and the more elements present, the more confident we are in labeling the state as "fear."

When we sense danger, we experience the fear response, which is made up of these four aspects: (1) cognitive elements—discernment of an immediate threat to life or limb; (2) somatic elements—the body's emergency reaction to danger; (3) emotional elements—feelings of dread and terror and panic; and (4) behavioral elements—fleeing, freezing, or fighting (Lang, 1967; Rachman, 1978).

- **Cognitive elements.** These are appraisals of immediate, near-certain harm from a specific, identifiable threat. A large Doberman growls menacingly

at you. You think, "He's going to bite me," and you feel a surge of fear and cringe. On a dark and lonely street, you sense a sudden movement behind you. You think, "It's a mugger," and you run. Notice that appraisals evoke the bodily reactions of fear (Lang, 1979; Thorpe and Salkovskis, 1995).

- **Somatic elements.** These include two classes of bodily reactions: external and internal changes. Our external reactions can be observed by anyone who sees us: our skin becomes pale, goose bumps may form, beads of sweat appear on our forehead, the palms of our hands become clammy, our pupils dilate, our lips tremble, our muscles tense, and our face shows fear. Our internal reactions cannot be observed by others. Internally, our body's resources are mobilized in the **emergency reaction** (often called the **fight or flight response**), wherein the sympathetic branch of the autonomic nervous system is activated, causing our heart rate to increase, our spleen to contract and release scores of red blood cells to carry more oxygen, our respiration to accelerate and deepen, our air passages to widen to take in more oxygen, adrenaline to be secreted from the adrenal medulla into the bloodstream, the liver to release glucose and fatty acids for use by the muscles, stomach acid to be inhibited, the immune system to shut down, and—with intense, sudden stress—the loss of bladder and sphincter control.

- **Emotional elements.** These may include a sense of dread, terror, panic, queasiness, the chills, creeping sensations, and a funny feeling in the pit of the stomach. These elements are familiar to us because we talk about them when describing fear. We are generally more conscious of the emotional elements of fear than of our cognitions and the inner physiological workings that have been set off by fear.

- **Behavioral elements.** These include two kinds of behavior. First are involuntary reactions to being afraid, which are in many cases the result of classical conditioning. Second are instrumental responses, which are voluntary attempts to do something about the object we fear.

Bullies sometimes pick on a hapless child on his way home from school, perhaps in what was once a safe alley. After this occurs a few times, the child will become afraid when approaching the alley. He will display a number of involuntary fear reactions, like sweating and a faster heartbeat. This is an example of the classical conditioning of fear. From Chapter 3, we know that classical fear conditioning takes place when a previously neutral signal is paired with a traumatic event. As a result of this pairing, the signal itself will cause fear reactions. In this case, the alley is the conditioned stimulus (CS), the encounter with the bullies is the unconditioned stimulus (US), and fear is the conditioned response (CR). Once conditioning has occurred, the signal alone causes the physiological emergency reaction to occur, profoundly changing other voluntary behavior. In our example, as the hapless child approaches the alley, he will stop munching on potato chips and will cease reading his comic book.

Fleeing, freezing, and fighting are the main instrumental behaviors in response to fear. There are two types of flight responses: escape and avoidance. In *escape responding,* the harmful event actually occurs, and the subject leaves the scene. For example, the child who is being beaten up by his schoolmates will run out of the alley if given the chance. Similarly, a rat will jump across a hurdle to escape from and terminate an electric shock. In contrast, in *avoidance responding,* the subject will leave before the harmful event occurs. A signal will herald the bad event; the alley is a signal that some bullies might await the child, just as a tone might signal shock to a rat. The child will run out of the alley and take another route home, even if no bullies are beating him up. Responding to the tone, a rat will avoid the shock before it comes on, thereby preventing the shock from occurring at all. The signal, because of its previous pairing with shock (in early trials, in which

the subject failed to make the avoidance response, shock occurred), produces fear, and the subject responds during the signal to remove itself from fear.

Degree of Fear

The degree of fear varies in different people and in different situations. Some people actually like to step inside a cage with a chair and whip to teach lions tricks. Lion tamers probably experience some fear, whereas most of us would be terrified. Hence, we do not go into cages. Instead, we go to the circus or the zoo. This is considered normal behavior.

There is a range of dangerous situations, as well as a range of fear responses. We accept our fear response when it reflects the degree of danger in the situation. But when the fear response is out of proportion to the amount of danger, we label it abnormal; in short, a phobia (Rosen and Schulkin, 1998). While fear is normal and a phobia is abnormal, they are both on the same continuum; they differ in degree, not in kind (see Figure 5–1).

Anxiety Distinguished from Fear

Anxiety has the same four components as fear, but with a crucial difference in the cognitive element. The cognitive component of fear is the thought that there is a clear and specific danger, whereas the cog-

The degree of danger we encounter often has to do with our jobs. Although most people would experience fear if they were close to tigers, this animal trainer does not look as if he is afraid of the tigers behind him.

Figure 5—1

PHOBIA VERSUS NORMAL FEAR

This figure gives us a schematic way of distinguishing normal fear from a phobia. It plots the degree of the reality of the danger (as measured by societal consensus) against the degree of accompanying fear (as measured by the strength of the emergency reaction). The 45-degree line indicates normal fear. The area in purple shows the phobic range. *A* plots an accountant at work, *B* plots an oil rig construction worker in the wintry North Sea. He probably feels more fear, but the level of fear is in proportion to what he should feel compared to an accountant. *C*, however, plots a phobic, whose reaction to the feared object is far out of proportion to the real danger. *D* plots decorated bomb disposers, who, when placed in laboratory fear tasks, show a lack of reaction. Although these courageous individuals are in dangerous situations that would cause a high level of fear in most individuals, the bomb disposers display only a minimal emergency reaction (Source: Based on Cox, Hallam, O'Connor, and Rachman, 1983)

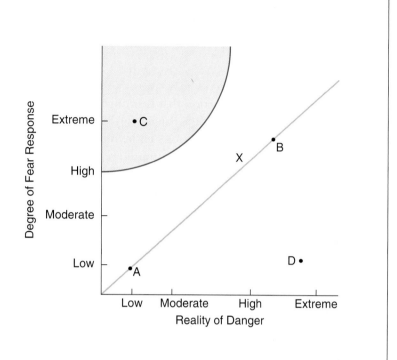

nitive component of anxiety is the expectation of a more diffuse and uncertain danger. With fear one might identify a specific threat to life or limb and think, "Help, a dog is chasing me and is about to bite me!" With anxiety the thought might be, "I feel something terrible might happen, but I don't know what it will be." The somatic component of anxiety is the same as that of fear: the elements of the emergency reaction. Many of the emotional elements of anxiety also occur in fear: the funny feeling in the pit of the stomach, the dread, for example. But whereas with fear one feels impelled to act (freeze or flee), with anxiety one feels uncertain how to act. Finally, the behavioral components of anxiety and fear are similar and may include flight or fight. Nonetheless, with fear we target the threatening stimulus and react to it; with anxiety we're frantic to discover what the stimulus is but have difficulty reacting. Whereas with fear we react quickly, with anxiety we

scan vigilantly for cues that will help identify the threat while keeping ourselves prepared in case we must eventually fight or flee. Thus, fear is based in reality, or on an exaggeration of a real danger, whereas anxiety is based on a more formless danger.

We now turn to the specific disorders themselves. Psychologists diagnose anxiety disorders based on the presence of symptoms that are typical of specific disorders. But before such a diagnosis is warranted, they must rule out certain rather common physical conditions that may cause abnormal amounts of anxiety. These include ruling out hyperthyroidism, overconsumption of caffeine or nicotine, use of simulant medications such as asthma inhalers, and even adrenal gland tumors.

In keeping with our distinction between fear and anxiety, we will first examine the disorders in which the individual experiences fear: phobia and post-traumatic stress disorder. Then, we will discuss the disorders in which the individual experiences anxiety: panic disorder, agoraphobia, and generalized anxiety disorder. We conclude with obsessive-compulsive disorder (OCD), in which the patient goes to great lengths to deflect any feelings and thoughts of anxiety.

Phobia

A *phobia* is a persistent fear reaction that is strongly out of proportion to the reality of the danger. Such a fear reaction may interfere with a person's entire life. A person with a cat phobia, for example, cannot even be in the same room with a house cat because of her extreme fear of cats. Although we can repeatedly tell the person that house cats rarely attack humans, the fear will persist untouched. Consider the following case in which fear is so great that the woman is even afraid to leave her home:

> Anna was housebound. Six months ago, the house next door had become vacant and the grass had begun to grow long. Soon, the garden had become a rendezvous for the local cats. Now Anna was terrified that if she left her house, a cat would spring on her and attack her. Her fear of cats was of thirty years' status, having begun at age four when she remembered watching in horror as her father drowned a kitten. In spite of saying that she believed it was unlikely that her father actually did such a thing, she was haunted by fear. At the sight of a cat, she would panic and sometimes be completely overwhelmed with terror. She could think of nothing else but her fear of cats. She interpreted any unexpected movement, shadow, or noise as a cat.

Anna is housebound because she is afraid that a cat might attack her if she goes outside. Her fear is greatly out of proportion to the reality of the danger of actually being injured by a cat. The real danger is near zero, but her fear is extreme and irrational. Her problem is more than normal fear; it is a phobia.

There is little trouble diagnosing a phobia when it is present, since its symptoms are unambiguous: (1) persistent fear of a specific situation out of proportion to the reality of the danger, (2) great anxiety and panic produced by actual exposure to the situation, (3) recognition that the fear is excessive or unreasonable, (4) avoidance of the phobic situation, and (5) symptoms that are not due to another disorder (APA, 1994; Marks, 1969).

There is no question that phobias are abnormal. Many of the elements of abnormality discussed in Chapter 1 are present. They cause the individual to suffer. They are maladaptive, since the individual's activities are greatly restricted. They are irrational, since the sense of danger is out of proportion to the reality of the danger. People with phobias make others uncomfortable, and their behavior is considered socially unacceptable. Phobias are out of the individual's control, and those who suffer from them want to be rid of their fear.

While phobic symptoms are the same in all who suffer from phobia, the objects of phobias vary greatly. Although there are reports of such unusual phobias as fear of flowers (anthophobia), the number 13 (triskaedekophobia), and snow (blanchophobia), these are very rare. The most common phobias in our society are social phobias and specific phobias (see Table 5–1).

Specific Phobia

There are five classes of *specific phobias*: (1) phobias of particular animals, usually cats, dogs, birds (most commonly pigeons), rats, snakes, and insects; (2) natural environment phobias, including dirt, heights, darkness, wind, water, and storms; (3) situational phobias, usually bridges, elevators, flying in airplanes, tunnels, closed places, public transportation; (4) blood, injections, and injury phobias; and (5) other phobias, including illness or death. Together, these make up about half of all phobias (Boyd, Rae, Thompson, and Burns, 1990). The most recent estimate of the lifetime prevalence of specific phobias in the United States is 11.3 percent,

A specific childhood incident may set off a phobia. This child may grow up to be a person with a dog phobia.

TABLE 5–1

THE SPECIFIC PHOBIAS

Phobia		Sex Difference	Age of Onset
Animal Phobias		vast majority are women	childhood
Cats (ailurophobia)	Birds (avisophobia)		
Dogs (cynophobia)	Horses (equinophobia)		
Insects (insectophobia)	Snakes (ophidiophobia)		
Spiders (arachnophobia)	Rodents (rodentophobia)		
Natural Environment Phobias		more women	any age
Dirt (mysophobia)	Darkness (nyctophobia)		
Storms (brontophobia)	Thunderstorms and		
Heights (acrophobia)	lightning (astraphobia)		
	Water (hydrophobia)		
Situational Phobias		more women	childhood and mid-twenties
Closed places (claustrophobia)			
Bridges			
Elevators			
Airplanes			
Tunnels			
Blood-Injection-Injury Phobias		probably more women	late childhood
Other phobias		none	middle age
Death phobia (thanatophobia)			
Cancer (cancerophobia)			
Venereal disease (venerophobia)			

but only about 1 percent of adults have phobias so severe as to keep them housebound (Magee, Eaton, Wittchen, McGonagle, and Kessler, 1996; Regier, Narrow, and Rae, 1990).

- **Animal phobias.** Like Anna's cat phobia, these almost always begin in early childhood, and most are outgrown by adulthood. A dog phobia might develop after a child was bitten by a dog; a bird phobia might begin if a bird landed on a child's shoulder. Animal phobias are highly focused: Anna may be terrified of cats, but she is rather fond of dogs and birds. The vast majority of animal phobias are reported by women (Bourdon, Boyd, Rae, and Burns, 1988; Fredrikson, Annas, Fischer, and Wik, 1996; Marks, 1969).

- **Natural environment phobias.** Irrational fear of heights, storms, dirt, darkness, running water, and wind make up the majority of these phobias. As in animal phobias, the symptoms are focused on one object, and the individuals are otherwise psychologically normal. These phobias are somewhat more common than animal phobias, they usually begin in childhood, and they occur about equally in women and men (Fredrikson, Annas, Fischer, and Wik, 1996).

- **Situational phobias.** Flying in airplanes, bridges, public transportation, tunnels, enclosed spaces, and elevators trigger these phobias. More women

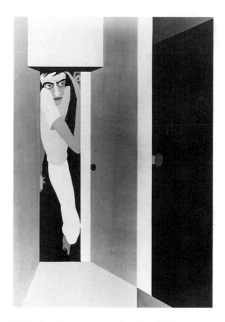

This drawing conveys the fear felt by someone who has claustrophobia, the fear of enclosed spaces.

DSM-IV Criteria

Specific Phobia

A. Marked and persistent fear that is excessive or unreasonable, cued by the presence or anticipation of a specific object or situation (e.g., flying, heights, animals, receiving an injection, seeing blood).

B. Exposure to the phobic stimulus almost invariably provokes an immediate anxiety response, which may take the form of a situationally bound or situationally predisposed panic attack. (*Note:* In children, the anxiety may be expressed by crying, tantrums, freezing, or clinging.)

C. The person recognizes that the fear is excessive or unreasonable. (*Note:* In children, this feature may be absent.)

D. The phobic situation(s) is avoided or else is endured with intense anxiety or distress.

E. The avoidance, anxious anticipation, or distress in the feared situation(s) interferes significantly with the person's normal routine, occupational (or academic) functioning, or social activities or relationships, or there is marked distress about having the phobia.

F. In individuals under age 18 years, the duration is at least 6 months.

G. The anxiety, panic attacks, or phobic avoidance associated with the specific object or situation are not better accounted for by another mental disorder, such as Obsessive-Compulsive Disorder (e.g., fear of dirt in someone with an obsession about contamination), Post-Traumatic Stress Disorder (e.g., avoidance of stimuli associated with a severe stressor), Separation Anxiety Disorder (e.g., avoidance of school), Social Phobia (e.g., avoidance of social situations because of fear of embarrassment), Panic Disorder with Agoraphobia, or Agoraphobia without History of Panic Disorder.

SOURCE: APA, DSM-IV, 1994.

---

than men have these phobias. Onset can occur in childhood or early adulthood, and the phobia is sometimes embedded in a traumatic incident. For example, a nineteen-year-old develops an airplane phobia after a plane he has just gotten off crashes at its next stop.

- *Blood-injection-injury phobias.* People with such phobias become highly anxious in situations involving the sight of blood, injections, and injuries. They often avoid medical procedures because of their phobia. They cannot bear to watch gory films or think about mutilation. About 4 percent of the normal population show this phobia at least to a moderate extent (Agras, Sylvester, and Oliveau, 1969; Costello, 1982). It is probably somewhat more common in women than in men, and its onset is usually in late childhood (Kleinknecht, 1994; Kleinknecht and Lenz, 1989; Öst, 1987).

- *Other types of phobias.* These include phobias about choking (McNally, 1994) or vomiting or contracting an illness (nosophobia). A person with nosophobia fears having one specific illness, although the kind of illness feared has changed throughout the centuries. In the nineteenth century, a person with a nosophobia feared he had tuberculosis or perhaps syphilis and other vene-

real diseases. More recently, cancer, heart disease, stroke, and AIDS have been the terrors. Such a person is usually perfectly healthy, but he worries endlessly that he may have or will soon contract a particular disease. He searches his body for the slightest sign of the disease, and since fear itself produces symptoms like tightness in the chest and stomach pain, he interprets these symptoms as further evidence that the disease is upon him. And so it spirals to more stomach or chest pain and to more certainty that he has the dreaded disease. There are no sex differences in overall reports of nosophobia, although cancer phobias tend to occur more in females, and phobias of venereal disease almost always occur in males (Fredrikson, Annas, Fischer, and Wik, 1996). Other psychological problems accompany the disorder frequently, and it usually arises in middle age. People with nosophobia often know someone who has the feared disease.

Social Phobia

People with a *social phobia* fear being observed. They are afraid that they will act in a way that will be humiliating or embarrassing and that they will end up having a panic attack. They recognize that the fear is excessive or unreasonable, but they still avoid social situations that they think will provoke anxiety. Thus, for example, a person with a social phobia may be unable to eat in a restaurant for fear of vomiting and being humiliated. A student may stop writing during an exam when he is being watched by a teacher for fear of shaking violently. A factory worker may stop going to work because he fears that he will not be able to do his job if he is being observed. The fears are often unrealistic; people who fear they might shake do not shake, nor do those who fear vomiting in public actually vomit in public. The phobia may be *general,* with wholesale avoidance of conversation, parties, and dating; or it may be *specific* to one kind of social situation, such as speaking to an authority figure.

Culture probably has a major influence on the content and vulnerability to social phobia. Japanese culture is considerably more interdependent than ours, and in Japan, taijin kyofusho (TKS), appears to be a social phobia. TKS is a fear of offending or embarrassing others by blushing, breaking wind, staring, making inappropriate facial expressions, or having a deformity. This fear produces the avoidance of social situations, lest a person bring shame upon his family or social group. So, for example, a person who fears blushing will not go to social gatherings if possible, but if forced to attend, he will wear layers of facial creams to mask his complexion. The typical age of onset of TKS, as for Western social phobias, is adolescence; more Japanese males appear to have TKS than females (Kleinknecht et al., 1997).

Social phobias usually begin in adolescence, occasionally in childhood, and only rarely after age twenty-five (Schneier et al., 1992). They may have antecedents in early childhood, however. Schwartz, Snidman, and Kagan (1999) followed seventy-nine thirteen-year-olds from age one. Those toddlers who were subdued and avoided novelty grew into socially anxious teenagers, and this was more pronounced among girls. Researchers have found that women in general have more social phobias than men, and that social phobias are markedly more frequent among poor people. Why this is so is not known, but it seems likely that the economic costs of avoiding other people may be high and that individuals who are socially phobic may drift down toward poverty.

DSM-IV Criteria

Social Phobia

A. A marked and persistent fear of one or more social or performance situations in which the person is exposed to unfamiliar people or to possible scrutiny by others. The individual fears that he or she will act in a way (or show anxiety symptoms) that will be humiliating or embarrassing. (*Note*: In children, there must be evidence of the capacity for age-appropriate social relationships with familiar people and the anxiety must occur in peer settings, not just in interactions with adults.)

B. Exposure to the feared social situation almost invariably provokes anxiety, which may take the form of a situationally bound or situationally predisposed panic attack. (*Note*: In children, the anxiety may be expressed by crying, tantrums, freezing, or shrinking from social situations with unfamiliar people.)

C. The person recognizes that the fear is excessive or unreasonable. (*Note*: In children, this feature may be absent.)

D. The feared social or performance situations are avoided or else are endured with intense anxiety or distress.

E. The avoidance, anxious anticipation, or distress in the feared social or performance situation(s) interferes signif-icantly with the person's normal routine, occupational (academic) functioning, or social activities or relationships, or there is marked distress about having the phobia.

F. In individuals under age 18 years, the duration is at least 6 months.

G. The fear or avoidance is not due to the direct physiological effects of a substance (e.g., a drug of abuse, a medication) or a general medical condition and is not better accounted for by another mental disorder (e.g., Panic Disorder with or without Agoraphobia, Separation Anxiety Disorder, Body Dysmorphic Disorder, a Pervasive Developmental Disorder, or Schizoid Personality Disorder).

H. If a general medical condition or another mental disorder is present, the fear in Criterion A is unrelated to it, e.g., the fear is not of Stuttering, trembling in Parkinson's disease, or exhibiting abnormal eating behavior in Anorexia Nervosa or Bulimia Nervosa.

SOURCE: APA, DSM-IV, 1994.

The adolescent girl at the right may have a social phobia. She may crave companionship but avoid it out of a fear of humiliating or embarrassing herself.

Both specific and social phobias are highly "comorbid" (two or more disorders occur in the same person, but not necessarily at the same time) with other disorders, most commonly with depression or another anxiety disorder. In the National Comorbidity Study of 8,098 representative Americans, the lifetime prevalence for social phobia in the United States was found to be 13.3 percent for social phobia (Beekman et al., 2000; Magee, Eaton, Wittchen, McGonagle, and Kessler, 1996). This study also looked at the patterning of disorders. Reseachers found that 83.4 percent of people with a specific phobia had another disorder, as did 81 percent of those with a social phobia. One possible explanation for the high comorbidity of anxiety and depression is that neither alone is a fundamental emotion and that both are part of a more basic general level of distress termed **negative affect** (Joiner, Catanzaro, and Laurent, 1996).

Etiology of Phobias

Both biological and behavioral explanations have been proposed to explain phobia. We will begin with some of the biological theories, and then we will discuss the behavioral theories. We will also discuss how biological and psychological theories may interact in explaining how evolution prepares us to be conditioned to fear certain objects and for these fears to be difficult to extinguish.

BIOLOGICAL EXPLANATIONS

Two of the biological explanations of phobias are genetic and neurophysiological accounts. For example,

researchers have found that monozygotic twin pairs are more likely to both have phobias than are dyzygotic twin pairs (Kendler, Neale, Kessler, Heath, and Eaves, 1992). This suggests that one's genotype may contribute to the development of phobias. Other studies have found that about 31 percent of the first-degree (mother, father, sibling) relatives of patients with specific phobias also have a phobia themselves (Fyer et al., 1990). This indicates a role for genetic vulnerability, but also leaves much room for an environmental contribution as well.

Neurophysiological factors have also been proposed as possible contributors to phobia. People who have phobias have been shown to have abnormalities in serotonin and dopamine pathways in their limbic system that seem particularly involved in anxiety (Stein, 1998). They have also been found to have low levels of gamma aminobutyric acid (GABA), which typically helps inhibit physiological arousal. For many investigators, these abnormalities may result in a tendency to be especially reactive in anxiety-provoking situations, thus increasing the chances of developing a phobia. Recent research also suggests that the formation of phobias heavily involves the actions of the amygdala, an area of the limbic system associated with the development of emotional associations (LeDoux, 1998; Merckelbach, deJong, Muris, and van den Hout, 1996; Ninan, 1999).

BEHAVIORAL EXPLANATIONS

Although these genetic and neurobiological factors are suggestive, the most useful way of understanding phobias has been through behavioral explanations. Many researchers and clinicians believe that phobias develop in people much the same way that conditioned responses develop in laboratory animals during classical conditioning (Eysenck, 1979; Seligman, 1970, 1972). This behavioral analysis of phobias begins by assuming that normal fear and phobias are learned in the same way. Both fear and phobias arise when a neutral signal happens to occur at the same time as a bad event. If the bad event is mild, the neutral signal becomes mildly fear provoking. If the bad event is particularly traumatic, however, the signal becomes terrifying, and a phobia develops. Phobic conditioning is simply an instance of classical fear being conditioned by a particularly traumatic unconditioned stimulus.

Recall that classical conditioning consists of a procedure in which a conditioned stimulus (CS)—or

Figure 5—2

THE BEHAVIORAL ACCOUNT OF PHOBIA

When the signal (CS) is paired in time with the traumatic event (US), this elicits a reaction (UR). Later when the CS again occurs, it produces a phobia (CR).

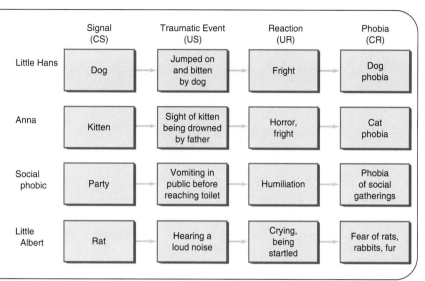

	Signal (CS)	Traumatic Event (US)	Reaction (UR)	Phobia (CR)
Little Hans	Dog	Jumped on and bitten by dog	Fright	Dog phobia
Anna	Kitten	Sight of kitten being drowned by father	Horror, fright	Cat phobia
Social phobic	Party	Vomiting in public before reaching toilet	Humiliation	Phobia of social gatherings
Little Albert	Rat	Hearing a loud noise	Crying, being startled	Fear of rats, rabbits, fur

signal—happens to occur at the same time as an unconditioned stimulus (US)—or traumatic event in the case of fear conditioning—which evokes a strong unconditioned response (UR). Thereafter, the previously neutral CS produces a conditioned response (CR) that resembles the UR. The CR is the phobic response and the CS is the phobic object. This thinking originated with a pioneering, but in modern eyes, ethically suspect experiment conducted in 1920 by John B. Watson and Rosalie Rayner:

> Little Albert B. was a normal, healthy eleven-month-old who, from birth, had been reared in the hospital in which his mother worked as a wet nurse. On the whole, he was big, stolid, and unemotional. One day, Albert was presented with a white rat, and he eagerly began to reach for it. Just as his hand touched the rat, the experimenters struck a metal bar suspended above Albert's head with a hammer. This produced such a loud and startling sound that Albert jerked violently, buried his head in the mattress, and whimpered. This pairing of the rat and the sound was repeated several times. When Albert was shown the rat later, he began to cry. He fell over on his side, and began to crawl away as rapidly as he could. Watson and Rayner had conditioned a phobia in Little Albert.

Today, clinicians see numerous cases of phobias that arise as conditioned responses in fearful situations. For example, a child might by mistake startle a dog while it is eating. The startled dog (CS) jumps on the child and bites him (US). The child becomes terrified (UR) and develops a fear of all dogs, that is, a dog phobia (CR). Every time he sees a dog (CS), the child is now terrified and phobic (CR) (see Figure 5–2). But the story must be more complicated than simple classical conditioning. Specific instances of classical conditioning with trauma only lead to phobias some of the time, and a direct frightening experience is not the only way that a phobia can be acquired (Fredrikson, Annas, and Wik, 1997).

SELECTIVITY OF PHOBIAS

Phobias occur almost entirely to a highly restricted set of objects, but ordinary classical conditioning of fear occurs to any object that happens to be around at the same time as trauma. Why are phobias of the dark so common but phobias of pillows nonexistent, although both are paired with nighttime trauma? Why are phobias of knives so rare even though knives are often paired with injury? Why have we never heard of a phobia of electric outlets? Why are there rat, dog, and spider phobias, but not lamb phobias?

Watson and Rayner found it simple to condition Little Albert to fear rats, but E. L. Thorndike (1874–1949), the early American learning theorist, had difficulty trying to train his children to stay away from sharp objects and to stay out of the street, even though such trespasses were paired with spankings. Apparently, phobic conditioning, both in and out of the laboratory, is highly selective.

Classically conditioned fear of dogs would begin with the pairing of an unconditioned stimulus—dogs—with an unconditioned response—terror. According to an evolutionary account, a child who encountered dogs like these would be "prepared" to develop a phobia (conditioned response) to all dogs (conditioned stimulus).

The biological level of analysis makes sense of selectivity. It seems that the great majority of common phobias are of objects that were once actually dangerous to pre-technological man (De Silva, Rachman, and Seligman, 1977; Zafiropoulou and McPherson, 1986). Natural selection probably favored those of our ancestors who, once they had minimal exposure to trauma paired with such signals, were highly prepared to learn that strangers, crowds, heights, insects, large animals, and dirt were dangerous. Such primates would have had a clear reproductive and survival edge over others who learned only gradually about such real dangers.

Thus, evolution may have selected a certain set of objects, all once dangerous to man, that are readily conditionable to trauma. Evolution may have left out other objects that are much more difficult to condition to fear (such as lambs, electric outlets, knives), either because they were never dangerous or because their origin was too recent to have been subject to natural selection. According to such evolutionary accounts, it is utterly futile to try to convince a person with a cat phobia by arguing that cats aren't dangerous, while it is quite easy to convince the very same person that the building he works in has been effectively fireproofed.

Arne Öhman, Kenneth Hugdahl, and their collaborators at the University of Uppsala in Sweden created a laboratory model of evolutionarily prepared phobias (Öhman, Fredrikson, Hugdahl, and Rimmo, 1976). Fear was conditioned in student vol-unteers using pictures of a variety of prepared fear CS's (for example, snakes and spiders) or unprepared fear CS's (for example, pictures of houses, faces, or flowers). In a typical experiment, the "prepared" group was presented with pictures of snakes that signaled the occurrence of a brief, painful electric shock ten seconds later. In the "unprepared" group, pictures of houses signaled shock. Fear conditioning, as measured by galvanic skin response (akin to sweating), occurred much more rapidly to prepared signals than to unprepared ones when each was paired with shock. In fact, conditioning took place in one pairing with snakes or spiders, but it took four or five pairings with houses or flowers. Moreover, at the end of the conditioning, when the electrodes were removed and the subjects were told that shock would not be delivered anymore, fear extinguished immediately to houses and faces, but remained full-blown to snakes and spiders (Hugdahl and Öhman, 1977).

This study demonstrates that humans seem more prepared to learn to be afraid of certain objects than of others. Consider guns, therefore, as a potentially phobic object. Guns are too recent to have been prepared for fear conditioning by evolution, but guns have had voluminous cultural preparation: stories, TV shows, parental warnings. Does the fear of guns have the same properties as the fear of snakes and spiders, or the fear of houses and flowers? Guns turn out to resemble houses and flowers, not spiders and snakes, in their conditioning properties. This indicates that the preparedness to fear spiders and snakes is biological, not cultural. Along these lines, one researcher tells the story of a four-year-old girl who saw a snake while walking through a park in England. She found the snake interesting, but she was not greatly frightened by it. A short time later, she returned to the family car, and her hand was smashed in the car door. She developed a lifelong phobia, not of cars or doors, but of snakes (Marks, 1977).

Susan Mineka and her colleagues have pointed to an evolutionary edge for prepared phobias in experiments with rhesus monkeys. These studies have also shown that phobias can develop through observation and that young monkeys raised by parents who have a fear of snakes do not need a direct experience with a snake to acquire this fear. In one of the studies, the young monkeys saw their parents behaving fearfully in the presence of real or toy snakes. Five of these six adolescent rhesus monkeys then suddenly showed an intense and persistent fear of snakes (Mineka, Davidson, Cook, and Keir, 1984). Human children can also develop phobias through "vicarious" conditioning— that is, by seeing parents or friends display a phobia. Moreover, human children may develop a phobia after hearing frightening stories about the to-be-feared object (Annas, 1997; King, Eleonora, and Ollendick, 1998; Mineka, Davidson, Cook, and Keir, 1984; Rachman, 1990). Such ease of conditioning points to preparedness. The selectivity and irrationality of phobias suggest that phobias are not instances of ordinary classical conditioning; rather, they are instances of **prepared classical conditioning.** Certain evolutionarily dangerous objects are prepared to become phobic objects when paired with trauma, but others are not and require more extensive and traumatic conditioning to become phobic objects (McNally, 1987; Menzies and Clark, 1995; Regan and Howard, 1995).

Some phobias may even erupt with no pairings at all. One long-term study followed over one thousand children from Dunedin, New Zealand, from early childhood to age twenty-six. Researchers tracked whether the children developed any major mental illnesses as well as whether they experienced any traumatic events. For example, they assessed fear of heights, fear of water, separation fears, and dental fears, as well as the occurrence of relevant trauma. One important and surprising result occurred for heights, water, and separation phobia—all evolutionarily prepared fears. Those participants who became phobic had *fewer, not more,* bad encounters with these objects. In contrast, those with dental fears (an unprepared fear) had *more* bad dental experiences. This suggests that early experience with potentially phobic objects allows habituation to these objects and prevents phobia, whereas lack of experience with the object allows the object to remain potentially phobic. Thus, even though the person has *not* experienced a history of pairing of phobic object and trauma, when he experiences an irrelevant stressful event (one that is unrelated to the phobic object), the prepared fear can now erupt anyway (Poulton and Menzies, 2000).

PERSISTENCE OF PHOBIAS

A phobia is, by definition, resistant to change. Can the behavioral analysis also offer an account of persistence, a defining feature of phobias? After fear is classically conditioned in the laboratory by pairing a tone with shock a few times, extinction will occur rapidly when the tone is presented without the shock. Within ten or twenty presentations of the tone without shock, fear will always disappear (Annau and Kamin, 1961). Phobias, on the other hand, are very robust. They seem to resist extinction; some persist for a lifetime. How can a model based on an ephemeral phenomenon, classical fear conditioning, capture phobias that last and last? An extinction trial in fear conditioning occurs when the fear-evoking signal is presented to the subject, but the traumatic event no longer follows. For example, a rat is put into the box in which it has received shocks. A fear-evoking tone that has been paired with shock comes on, but no shock is presented. The rat can do nothing to escape the tone and is exposed to the fact that the tone no longer predicts shock. Because the rat cannot escape, it reality tests and finds out that the trauma no longer follows the signal. Under these conditions, fear extinguishes rapidly.

In contrast, people who have phobias rarely test the reality of their fears. When the phobic object is around, they rarely wait to be passively exposed to an extinction trial. Rather, they run away as quickly as possible. For example, Anna would avoid cats as best she could, but if she did happen across a cat, she would flee as fast as she could. She would not reality test by staying in the presence of the cat and finding out what would happen. We see a parallel situation in the animal laboratory. If given a chance to escape, a rat will do so upon hearing the tone (CS) that signals

This film still of Charles Dickens' *Great Expectations* shows Jean Simmons playing Miss Havisham, who continued to dress in her veil and wedding clothes decades after her groom failed to show up for her wedding. After suffering the embarrassment of being left at the altar, Miss Haversham thereafter remained secluded in her home, only seeing those whom she chose to see. Her social phobia may have persisted because she never again attempted to appear in public.

shock (US). This means that the rat will never stay long enough to discover that the shock is no longer being presented at all on subsequent trials (Baum, 1969; Rescorla and Solomon, 1967; Seligman and Johnston, 1973).

Consider the individual with a social phobia who no longer goes to parties because he was humiliated when he once vomited at a party. He avoids parties altogether, and if he must attend one, he escapes as quickly as he can. He is afraid that if he finds himself at a party (CS—the signal), he will again vomit (US—the trauma) and be publicly humiliated (UR—the reaction). His fear does not extinguish because he does not allow himself to be exposed to extinction trials—being at a party and finding out that he does not vomit and is not humiliated. He does not test the reality of the fact that parties (CS) no longer lead to vomiting (US) and humiliation (UR). The ability to avoid and escape the phobic object protects fear of the phobic object from being extinguished, just as allowing a rat to escape the signal and avoid the trauma protects fear from extinguishing.

In line with this is the possibility that prepared conditioning may resist extinction. Joseph LeDoux (1996) has investigated the neural circuitry involved in the conditioning of fear. When an animal is frightened, it exhibits the emergency reaction with freezing, raised blood pressure, increased heart rate, and the release of stress hormones into the bloodstream. When the fear response is classically conditioned, LeDoux argues that the amygdala, an area of the temporal lobe, is the active memory processor. This is a different system from the system that remembers nonfearful information, such as places and times. The conditioning of this system is fast, but more important, LeDoux contends that once these brain circuits are established, they are difficult or impossible to delete. Furthermore, there may be a genetic predisposition to phobias. In seven of eight pairs of identical twins, both of the twins had phobic features, but in only five of thirteen fraternal twins did both have phobic features (Carey and Gottesman, 1981; Marks, 1986; Neale et al., 1994). The selectivity of phobias, vicarious conditioning, and genetic differences in vulnerability all add up to a picture of phobias as evolutionarily prepared classical conditioning.

Therapy for Phobias

The behavioral analysis can make direct predictions about therapy: those procedures that extinguish fear conditioning in the laboratory should also cure phobias. There are three behavioral therapies that have proven highly effective against phobias: systematic desensitization, exposure, and modeling. In addition, applied tension, a new therapy developed for blood phobia, has also been proven to be highly effective. All were developed within the framework of the behavioral analysis.

SYSTEMATIC DESENSITIZATION

Developed in the 1950s by Joseph Wolpe, a South African psychiatrist, *systematic desensitization* involves three phases: training in relaxation, hierarchy construction, and counterconditioning. First, the therapist trains the phobic patient in deep muscle relaxation, a technique in which the subject sits or lies with eyes closed, with all his muscles completely relaxed. This state of relaxation will be used in the third phase to neutralize fear, since individuals cannot be deeply relaxed and afraid at the same time (that is, fear and relaxation are incompatible responses). Second, with the aid of the therapist, the patient constructs a hierarchy of frightening situations, in which the most dreaded possible scene (for example, meeting someone with a physical deformity) is on the highest rung for a person with an injury phobia, and a scene evoking some min-

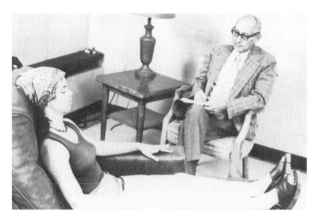

Psychiatrist Joseph Wolpe conducts systematic desensitization with a patient. The patient imagines a fear-evoking scene while engaging in deep muscle relaxation. She will signal by lifting her forefinger if the fear becomes unbearable.

imal fear (for example, seeing an ambulance) is on the lowest rung (Wolpe, 1969).

The third phase removes the fear of the phobic object by gradual counterconditioning; that is, causing a response that is incompatible with fear to occur at the same time as the feared CS. The patient goes into deep relaxation, and simultaneously imagines the first, least-arousing scene in the hierarchy. This serves two purposes. First, it pairs the CS, ambulances, with the absence of the original traumatic US. (You will recall that presenting the CS without the original US is an extinction procedure that will weaken the fear response to the CS.) Second, a new response, relaxation, which neutralizes the old response of fear, occurs in the presence of the CS. This is repeated until the patient can imagine scene 1 of the hierarchy without any fear at all. Then scene 2, which provokes a slightly greater fear than scene 1, is paired with relaxation. And so the patient progresses up the hierarchy by the graded extinction procedure until she reaches the most terrifying scene. Therapy is considered successful when the patient can tolerate being in the actual presence of the most terrifying item on the hierarchy. Eighty to 90 percent of specific phobias improve greatly with such treatment. These gains are usually maintained over follow-ups of a year or two without new symptoms being substituted for those that have been eliminated (Kazdin and Wilcoxon, 1976; Paul, 1967).

EXPOSURE

While systematic desensitization was the first effective therapy for phobias historically, it has now been largely replaced by exposure therapy. Recall that behaviorists believe that phobias persist because patients with phobias will avoid the phobic object if at all possible, and if forced into its presence, they will escape rapidly. This failure to find out that the phobic object no longer predicts the original traumatic event will protect the phobia from extinction.

What happens when a person with a phobia forces herself to be in the presence of a phobic object? What happens when a rat that avoids shock by escaping a tone is exposed to the tone and finds out that shock no longer occurs? Such an **exposure treatment** is also called **flooding** or **reality testing,** and in rats it reliably brings a reduced amount of fear and eliminates future avoidance (Baum, 1969; Tryon, 1976). The success of eliminating fear in animals by exposure led behavior therapists to try this treatment with human patients (Stampfl and Levis, 1967).

In an exposure procedure, the patient with a phobia agrees, usually with great apprehension, to imagine the phobic situation or to stay in its presence for a long period without attempting to escape. A person with claustrophobia might be put in a closet for four hours, or an individual with a fear of flying (aviaphobia) will take a course including a real, aborted jet takeoff and a real flight (McCarthy and Craig, 1995; Serling, 1986). Exposure also seems to be the treatment of choice for social phobia (Scholing and Emmelkamp, 1996; Taylor, 1996).

In general, exposure has proven to be equal, and sometimes even superior, to systematic desensitization in its therapeutic effects. It is also a briefer treatment that can be largely accomplished in just a single

Through exposure treatment, this woman is gradually losing her fear of water.

Virtual reality has been used as an exposure treatment for those with a fear of flying or heights. The computer simulates flight, which the woman who wears the virtual-reality helmet experiences as if she were actually flying in a plane.

three-hour session (Öst, 1996). By forcing a patient to reality test and stay in the phobic situation and thereby to find out that catastrophe does not ensue, extinction of the phobia can usually be accomplished. This directly confirms the hypothesis that phobias are so persistent because the object is avoided in real life and therefore not extinguished by the discovery that it is harmless.

Exposure therapy, in its most hi-tech incarnation, uses virtual reality. Computers can simulate some of the objects of the specific phobias, so there is no need to climb mountains to carry out exposure therapy with a person who has a height phobia or take transatlantic flights with a person who has a phobia of flying. In one pioneering study, Barbara Rothbaum and her colleagues simulated footbridges as high as 80

meters above water, twentieth-floor balconies, and forty-nine-story elevators. Twelve students with height phobia had seven sessions learning to cope with these virtual heights, and they were markedly more improved when compared to eight wait-list controls (Rothbaum, Hodges, Alarcon et al., 1999; Rothbaum, Hodges, Kooper et al., 1995; Rothbaum, Hodges, Watson, Kessler, and Opdyke, 1996).

MODELING

The third effective therapy for phobias is **modeling.** In a typical modeling procedure, the patient with a phobia watches someone who does not have the phobia perform the behavior that the phobic patient is unable to do himself. For example, a person with a snake phobia will repeatedly watch a nonfearful model approach, pick up, and fondle a real snake (Bandura, Adams, and Beyer, 1977; Bandura, 1986). Seeing that the other person is not harmed, the phobic patient may become less fearful of the situation. The therapist will then gradually involve the patient in the exercises. First, the patient may be asked to describe aloud what he sees, then to approach the snake, and finally to touch it. The procedure will be repeated until the phobia diminishes.

Overall, modeling seems to work about as well as both desensitization and exposure in curing both mild and severe clinical phobias (Moore, Geffken, and Royal, 1995; Rachman, 1976). This therapy brings about cognitive change, as well as behavioral change. Once a patient has observed a model, the single best predictor of therapeutic progress is the extent to which he now expects that he will be able

In modeling therapy for snake phobia, a patient learns to handle snakes by first watching a person who is not afraid of snakes handle one, and eventually handling the snake herself.

to perform the actions he formerly was unable to do (Bandura, Adams, and Beyer, 1977).

APPLIED TENSION

Another therapy for phobias is **applied tension,** and it is the therapy of choice for blood phobias. It derives from the same logic that Wolpe used when he created systematic desensitization. Wolpe reasoned that relaxation would countercondition fear because it mobilized the opposite biological system: relaxation was incompatible with the muscular tension and sympathetic arousal components of fear. So, the patient could not be fearful at the same time that he was relaxing. Lars-Goren Öst, a Swedish psychologist, noted that when confronted with the phobic stimulus of blood, people with a blood phobia have the opposite bodily reaction to that of people with other phobias when confronted with their phobic stimulus: people with blood phobia have a drop in blood pressure and heart rate, and they often faint. Öst reasoned that making these patients tense their muscles would raise their blood pressure and heart rate, so that they could not have the phobic reaction of fainting at the sight of blood.

In the applied tension technique, the patient tenses the muscles of his arms, legs, and chest until he feels warmth suffusing his face. Then he lets the tension go. He practices this repeatedly so that he can use it when he encounters blood. In an outcome study involving thirty patients with blood phobia, Öst compared the applied tension technique to the relaxation technique and found that both helped considerably, but applied tension produced clinically meaningful improvement in 90 percent while relaxation produced meaningful improvement in only 60 percent (Öst, Sterner, and Fellenius, 1989; Öst, Fellenius, and Sterner, 1991). Just one two-hour session of applied tension produces meaningful improvement in people with blood phobias (Hellstrom, Fellenius, and Öst, 1996).

A single underlying process—extinction—seems to be the operative element in all the effective therapies for phobias. In all four treatments, the patient is exposed, repeatedly and enduringly, to the phobic object in the absence of the original traumatic event. Each technique keeps the phobic patient in the presence of the phobic object by a different tactic so that extinction can take place: systematic desensitization by having the patient relax and imagine the object, exposure by forcibly keeping the patient in the pho-

bic situation, modeling by encouraging the patient to approach the phobic object as the model has done, and applied tension by preventing fainting in the presence of blood. The fact that each of these therapies works and employs classical fear extinction supports the view that the phobia was originally acquired by classical fear conditioning.

DRUGS

The minor tranquilizers, such as the benzodiazepines (for example, Valium) and alprazolam (Xanax), are not useful for long-term treatment of specific phobias. These anti-anxiety drugs (or anxiolytics) produce calm and relaxation when the patient takes them in high doses during the phobic situation itself. The calm is accompanied by drowsiness and lethargy. So for a person with a phobia of flying who must suddenly take a plane, a minor tranquilizer will often help, but only temporarily. Once the drug wears off, however, the phobia is still there undiminished (Noyes, Chaudry, and Domingo, 1986; Roy-Byrne and Cowley, 1998).

More success for medications is reported with social phobia than with specific phobia. MAO (monoamineoxidase) inhibitors (a strong antidepressant) have been used with some success in treating patients with social phobia. From 60 to 80 percent of patients improve while on the drug. In one recent well-controlled study, phenelzine (an MAO inhibitor) and cognitive-behavior therapy both did equally well, with the drug superior on some measures (Heimberg et al., 1998). But the relapse rate was high once the drug was discontinued. Moreover, MAO inhibitors have dangerous, even deadly, side effects, such as hypertension and stroke when they are combined with certain foods.

Somewhat lower improvement (around 50 percent) in social phobia occurs with the stronger anti-anxiety agents, like alprazolam (Xanax). But again, the relapse rate is very high, and the drugs have marked side effects, such as drowsiness and memory loss. A high relapse rate upon drug discontinuation suggests only a temporary effect on phobic anxiety (Roy-Byrne and Cowley, 1998; Versiani et al., 1988).

The selective serotonin reuptake inhibitors (SSRI's), popular antidepressant drugs, are now also becoming widely prescribed for social phobia. Results are still preliminary, however. In the most recent, well-controlled study, 55 percent of those people with social phobias who were treated with

Treatment

TABLE 5-2

PHOBIA

Specific (Simple) Phobia	Extinction Therapy[*]	Drugs
Improvement	60–80% markedly improved	probably better than placebo
Relapse[†]	10% or fewer relapse	high relapse
Side Effects	none	moderate
Cost	inexpensive	inexpensive
Time Scale	weeks	days/weeks
Overall	**excellent**	**marginal**

Social Phobia	Extinction Therapy	Drugs[‡]
Improvement	60–80% markedly improved	50–80% markedly improved
Relapse[†]	10–20% relapse	high relapse
Side Effects	none	moderate
Cost	inexpensive	inexpensive
Time Scale	weeks/months	days/weeks
Overall	**very good**	**useful**

[*]Extinction therapy includes exposure, systematic desensitization, modeling, and applied tension.
[†]Relapse after discontinuation of treatment.
[‡]Drugs include SSRI's, MAO inhibitors, and benzodiazepines.
SOURCE: Based on Seligman, 1994, pp. 78–79; revised with Barlow, Esler, and Vitali, 1998, pp. 288–318; and Roy-Byrne and Cowley, 1998.

paroxetine (an SSRI) were much improved after twelve weeks compared to 24 percent of controls. As usual, in such drug studies, patients were not followed after discontinuation of medication, but virtually complete relapse is likely (Roy-Byrne and Cowley, 1998; Stein et al., 1998).

Table 5–2 compares the use of the extinction therapies and drugs to treat specific phobia and social phobia.

Post-Traumatic Stress Disorder

Trauma used to be a part of everyone's life—the incorrigible human condition. Until this century, most people experienced life as a vale of tears. Bad things still happen all too frequently: we get disappointing grades; our stocks go down; we don't get the job we had hoped for; people we love reject us; we age and die. We are usually prepared for many of these losses, or at least we know ways to soften the blow. Once in a while, however, the ancient human condition intrudes, and something irredeemably awful, something beyond routine setback, occurs. But modern technology, medicine, and a growing sense of social

justice have created a world in which the experience of trauma is not inevitable and its consequences are no longer accepted passively as fate. Psychology has discovered in the last decade ways of relieving—but not extinguishing—the pain and suffering that irredeemably awful events cause.

So devastating and long-lasting are the effects of certain types of extraordinary loss, they have been given a name and a diagnostic category of their own: ***post-traumatic stress disorder (PTSD).*** The following case shows a Vietnam veteran who is suffering from post-traumatic stress disorder:

Vince first came to the clinic after he became upset during the funeral of a Vietnam buddy who had killed himself. When a helicopter flew overhead during the service, he panicked and thought he was back in Vietnam. This set off a series of horrific combat memories, including one in which he had stuck his gun in the face of a Viet Cong officer. "My God!" he remembered, "My bullet hit her above the right eye. It took her face away. The guys were laughing. They cut off her hair and ripped off her clothes. They took her head to get her earrings." The night of the funeral, he almost killed his wife, sticking a gun in her face.

Before being drafted, Vince had had no serious psychological difficulties. He was twenty-five, married, a father, and he worked as a machine operator. He returned to this job after discharge. But Vietnam changed him forever. At least two helicopter incidents haunted him and triggered his panic at the funeral.

In one, he was pushed out of a helicopter hovering above the ground. For a second, he was furious at his crew for shoving him out. The next second, he watched as the helicopter exploded, blowing everyone remaining on board to pieces. In another, on July 4, 1969, he and his company had planned to shoot off firecrackers and have a steak barbecue. Instead, they walked into an ambush that left many members of his outfit dead. Vince drew the duty of stuffing the mutilated remains of his dead friends into bags and loading them onto a helicopter. (Adapted from Lindy, Green, Grace, MacLeod, and Spitz, 1988).

Characterizing Post-Traumatic Stress Disorder

The objects that set off a phobia are commonplace; for example, crowds, embarrassment, cats, and illness. But the precipitant of a post-traumatic stress disorder, in contrast, is unusual (see Table 5–3). There is debate about what kind of precipitating events should qualify for a diagnosis of PTSD. At the most extreme, some claim that the events must be catastrophic, beyond the usual range of human suffering: living through an earthquake, watching one's chil-

Vietnam veterans may experience post-traumatic shock disorder as a result of the trauma of their experiences in Vietnam. Here a Vietnam veteran is overcome by his memories of Vietnam and the friend who died there when he visits a traveling replica of the Washington Vietnam Veteran's Memorial Wall, which contains the names of members of the U.S. armed forces who were killed or missing in action during the Vietnam War.

dren being tortured, being in a concentration camp, being kidnapped, experiencing hand-to-hand combat. This was the criterion used in DSM-III to diagnose many psychologically crippled veterans of the Vietnam War. But it is important to note that some

TABLE 5–3

PHOBIA AND PTSD COMPARED

	Origin	Symptoms	Course	Therapy
Simple Phobia	Classical conditioning in which prepared (or occasionally unprepared) stimulus becomes a CS for fear reaction	Usually confined to phobic reaction to one object or situation; patient often functions well in other areas	Dissipates in most children, but unremitting if found in adults without therapy	Drugs ineffective; patient often responds well to brief behavioral/cognitive therapy
PTSD	Confrontation with threat of death or injury responded to with horror or helplessness	Wide range of emotional, behavioral, and somatic symptoms; reliving of trauma, pervasive numbness, and anxiety are common	Symptoms may persist and interfere with many areas of functioning for decades	Drugs largely ineffective; early intervention with both stress inoculation and exposure therapy may work well

Diagnosis

DSM-IV Criteria

Post-Traumatic Stress Disorder

A. The person has been exposed to a traumatic event in which both of the following were present: (1) the person experienced, witnessed, or was confronted with an event or events that involved actual or threatened death or serious injury, or a threat to the physical integrity of self or others; (2) the person's response involved intense fear, helplessness, or horror. (*Note*: In children, this may be expressed instead by disorganized or agitated behavior.)

B. The traumatic event is persistently reexperienced in one (or more) of the following ways: (1) recurrent and intrusive distressing recollections of the event, including images, thoughts, or perceptions (*Note*: In young children, repetitive play may occur in which themes or aspects of the trauma are expressed.); (2) recurrent distressing dreams of the event (*Note*: In children, there may be frightening dreams without recognizable content.); (3) acting or feeling as if the traumatic event were recurring (includes a sense of reliving the experience, illusions, hallucinations, and dissociative flashback episodes, including those that occur on awakening or when intoxicated) (*Note*: In young children, trauma-specific reenactment may occur.); (4) intense psychological distress at exposure to internal or external cues that symbolize or resemble an aspect of the traumatic event; (5) physiological reactivity on exposure to internal or external cues that symbolize or resemble an aspect of the traumatic event.

C. Persistent avoidance of stimuli associated with the trauma and numbing of general responsiveness (not present before the trauma), as indicated by three (or more) of the following: (1) efforts to avoid thoughts, feelings, or conversations associated with the trauma; (2) efforts to avoid activities, places, or people that arouse recollections of the trauma; (3) inability to recall an important aspect of the trauma; (4) markedly diminished interest or participation in significant activities; (5) feeling of detachment or estrangement from others; (6) restricted range of affect (e.g., unable to have loving feelings); (7) sense of a foreshortened future (e.g., does not expect to have a career, marriage, children, or a normal life span).

D. Persistent symptoms of increased arousal (not present before the trauma), as indicated by two (or more) of the following: (1) difficulty falling or staying asleep; (2) irritability or outbursts of anger; (3) difficulty concentrating; (4) hypervigilance; (5) exaggerated startle response.

E. Duration of the disturbance (symptoms in Criteria B, C, and D) is more than 1 month.

F. The disturbance causes clinically significant distress or impairment in social, occupational, or other important areas of functioning.

SOURCE: APA, DSM-IV, 1994.

---

people endured the Holocaust with no trace of PTSD, and that other people in contrast show full-blown PTSD when their spouse dies or after a purse-snatching or even when sued in court. A wider, but specific, criterion has therefore been given in DSM-IV: having experienced, witnessed, or been confronted by an event or events that involved the threat of death, injury, or threat to the physical integrity of self or others. This would include rape, mugging, watching a bloody accident, shooting a female Viet Cong officer, or committing an atrocity. What is crucial is the person's reaction to this "exceptional" stressor: intense fear, horror, helplessness, and a sense of ruination.

The criteria for the disorder are: (1) the person relives the trauma repeatedly, in dreams, in flashbacks, and in reverie; (2) the person becomes numb to the world, and avoids stimuli (for example, thoughts, feelings, places, people) that remind him of the trauma;

(3) the person experiences symptoms of anxiety and arousal that were not present before the trauma, including trouble sleeping, over-alertness, trouble concentrating, exaggerated startle, and outbursts of anger; (4) the person is unable to remember an important part of the traumatic event; (5) the person has less interest or participation in activities and feels detached (or dissociated) from others, which significantly impairs his or her functioning; and (6) the symptoms last for more than a month. Under this definition, even in our relatively insulated and comfortable culture, the lifetime prevalence of PTSD is a shocking 7.8 percent, with women having twice as much PTSD as men (Kessler et al., 1995). During the first month after a trauma, the problem cannot by definition be PTSD. So during that time, the syndrome is called *acute stress disorder.*

It was once thought that victims of disaster recovered briskly. An early psychiatric study of the aftermath of disaster was of the relatives of the victims of a catastrophic nightclub fire during the 1940s. Interviews with the survivors and the families of the dead led to the belief that an "uncomplicated grief reaction" would be gone in four to six weeks (Lindemann, 1944). Dr. Camille Wortman, a psychologist at the State University of New York at Stony Brook, found evidence that contradicted this assumption. She went through the microfilm records of every auto fatality in Michigan between 1976 and 1979. She randomly chose thirty-nine people who had lost a spouse and forty-one couples who had lost a child. She then interviewed them at length and compared them to matched controls.

Her interviews occurred four to seven years after the tragedy, and she found that the parents and spouses were still in decidedly poor shape. They were much more depressed than the controls. They were less optimistic about the future, and they did not feel good about their lives. They were more "worn out," "tense," and "unhappy." More of those who had lost a spouse or child had died than had the controls. While they did not differ on income before their child died, the bereaved parents now earned 25 percent less than did the controls. Twenty percent were now divorced (versus 2.5 percent of the controls). People were just as bad off seven years later as four years later, so there does not seem to be a noticeable natural healing process going on. Almost everyone asked "Why me?" Sixty percent could find no answer to this wrenching question (Lehman, Wortman, and Williams, 1987).

NATURAL DISASTERS

The Turkish Earthquake of 1999, the recurrent floods in the U. S. Midwest, Hurricane Mitch in Central America in 1998, and Hurricane Floyd in 1999 produced a large number of people with PTSD. Much of what we know about the suffering of these victims and the course of their problems begins with a study of a flood at Buffalo Creek, West Virginia, in 1972. This flood produced devastation and death in a small Appalachian community, setting off many cases of PTSD among its survivors (Erikson, 1976; Green, Gleser, Lindy, Grace, and Leonard, 1996). In the early morning of February 26, 1972, the dam on Buffalo Creek in the coal region of West Virginia collapsed, and within a few seconds, 132 million gallons of the sludge-filled black water roared upon the residents of the mountain hollows below. Wilbur, his wife Deborah, and their four children managed to survive. Here is how they describe what happened to them (Erikson, 1976, pp. 338–44):

> For some reason, I opened the inside door and looked up the road—and there it came. Just a big black cloud. It looked like 12 or 15 foot of water . . .
>
> Well, my neighbor's house was coming right up to where we live, coming down the creek. . . . It was coming slow, but my wife was still asleep with the baby—she was about seven years old at the time—and the other kids were still asleep upstairs. I screamed for my wife in a bad tone of voice so I could get her attention real quick. . . . I don't know how she got the girls

While a specific object triggers the fear response in phobia, an unusually traumatic event—often a natural or manmade disaster—precipitates post-traumatic stress disorder. On the left, flood waters break a window during Hurricane Andrew in 1992; on the right, an exhausted firefighter covers his mouth from smoke as he takes a break from battling yet another wildfire in Montana during the summer of 2000.

downstairs so fast, but she run up there in her sliptail and she got the children out of bed and downstairs . . .

We headed up the road. . . . My wife and some of the children went up between the gons [railway gondolas]; me and my baby went under them because we didn't have much time. . . . I looked around and our house was done gone. It didn't wash plumb away. It washed down about four or five house lots from where it was setting, tore all to pieces.

Two years after the disaster, Wilbur and Deborah describe their psychological scars, the defining symptoms of a post-traumatic stress disorder. First, Wilbur relives the trauma repeatedly in his dreams:

What I went through on Buffalo Creek is the cause of my problem. The whole thing happens over to me even in my dreams, when I retire for the night. In my dreams, I run from water all the time, all the time. The whole thing just happens over and over again in my dreams . . .

Second, Wilbur and Deborah have become numb psychologically. Affect is blunted, and they are emotionally anesthetized to the sorrows and joys of the world around them. Wilbur says:

I didn't even go to the cemetery when my father died [about a year after the flood]. It didn't dawn on me that he was gone forever. And those people that dies around me now, it don't bother me like it did before the disaster. . . . It just didn't bother me that my dad was dead and never would be back. I don't have the feeling I used to have about something like death. It just don't affect me like it used to.

And Deborah says:

I'm neglecting my children. I've just completely quit cooking. I don't do no housework. I just won't do nothing. Can't sleep. Can't eat. I just want to take me a lot of pills and just go to bed and go to sleep and not wake up. I enjoyed my home and my family, but outside of them, to me, everything else in life that I had any interest in is destroyed. I loved to cook. I loved to sew. I loved to keep house. I was all the time working and making improvements on my home. But now I've just got to the point where it don't mean a thing in the world to me. I haven't cooked a hot meal and put it on the table for my children in almost three weeks.

Third, Wilbur experiences symptoms of anxiety, including hyper-alertness and phobic reactions to events that remind him of the flood, such as rain and impending bad weather:

. . . I listen to the news, and if there is a storm warning out, why I don't go to bed that night. I sit up. I tell my wife, "Don't undress our little girls; just let them lay down like they are and go to bed and go to sleep and then if I see anything going to happen, I'll wake you in plenty of time to get you out of the house." I don't go to bed. I stay up.

My nerves is a problem. Every time it rains, every time it storms, I just can't take it. I walk the floor. I get so nervous I break out in a rash. I am taking shots for it now . . .

Wilbur also suffers from survival guilt:

At that time, why, I heard somebody holler at me, and I looked around and saw Mrs. Constable. . . . She had a little baby in her arms and she was hollering, "Hey, Wilbur, come and help me; if you can't help me, come get my baby." . . . But I didn't give it a thought to go back and help her. I blame myself a whole lot for that yet. She had her baby in her arms and looked as though she were going to throw it to me. Well, I never thought to go help that lady. I was thinking about my own family. They all six got drowned in that house. She was standing in water up to her waist, and they all got drowned.

These symptoms persisted. Fourteen years after the Buffalo Creek Flood, 193 survivors were examined. Sixty percent had PTSD initially, and 25 percent still had it fourteen years later. Thirty-five percent had major depression initially, and 19 percent had it fourteen years after the flood (Green, Lindy, Grace, and Leonard, 1992).

MANMADE CATASTROPHES

The catastrophe that brings out a post-traumatic stress reaction need not be a naturally occurring one like the Buffalo Creek Flood. It can be manmade like the one that Vince suffered in Vietnam. Human beings have made a hell of the lives of other human beings since time immemorial: concentration camps, war, and torture ruin lives long after the victims have ceased to experience the original trauma. Unfortunately, the disorders following these catastrophes may

Manmade catastrophes can lead to post-traumatic shock disorder. Survivors of concentration camps or refugees forced from their homes by armed soldiers or former friends and neighbors may experience survivor guilt, depression, and nightmares. *(Left)* These Jews in the Warsaw Ghetto were rounded up by German soldiers and then sent to concentration camps, where they experienced unspeakable horrors. *(Right)* These ethnic Albanians were forced to leave their homes in Kosovo.

be even more severe and long-lasting than those following natural disasters; it may be easier for us to deal with the "acts of God" than with the acts of men.

The survivors of the Nazi concentration camps illustrate how long-lasting and severe the post-traumatic stress reaction can be. In a study of 149 camp survivors, 142 (or 97 percent) were still troubled with anxiety twenty years after they were freed from the camps (Krystal, 1968). Anxiety symptoms were marked: 31 percent were troubled with fears that something terrible would happen to their mates or their children whenever they were out of sight. Many of them were phobic about certain people whose appearance or behavior reminded them of their jailors; for example, the sight of a uniformed policeman or the inquisitive behavior of a doctor might be enough to set off panic. Seven percent had such severe panic attacks that the individual became confused and disoriented, entering a dreamlike state in which he believed himself to be back in the concentration camp.

The survivors relived the trauma in dreams for twenty years: 71 percent of these patients had anxiety dreams and nightmares, with 41 percent having severe ones. These nightmares were usually of their persecution. Particularly terrifying were dreams in which only one detail was changed from the reality; for example, dreaming that their children who had not yet been born at the time of the camps had been imprisoned with them in the camps.

Eighty percent of the patients suffered survivor guilt, depression, and crying spells. Survival guilt was especially strong when the patient's children had been killed; those who were the most severely depressed had lost an only child or had lost all of their children, with no children being born since. Ninety-two percent expressed self-reproach for failing to save their relatives, and 14 percent wished they had been killed instead of their relatives (Krystal, 1968). One hundred and twenty-four Holocaust survivors were examined more than forty years after the war, and the findings were grim. Almost half were suffering PTSD, with sleep disturbance the most pervasive symptom. Survivors of Auschwitz were three times as likely to still have PTSD as survivors who had not been in concentration camps (Kuch and Cox, 1992).

Fifty-five relatives of persons killed in the Lockerbie air bombing of 1988 were examined, and the majority had PTSD, with victims over sixty-five, unlike younger victims, also having major depression (Brooks and McKinlay, 1992; Livingston, Livingston, Brooks, and McKinlay, 1992). Among evacuees of the SCUD missile attacks in Israel during the Gulf War of 1991, almost 80 percent met the criteria for PTSD. The more danger they encountered, the worse were their symptoms (Solomon, Laor, Weiler, and Muller, 1993). Pol Pot's murderous regime left a wake of PTSD among Cambodian children. A group of forty-six refugees to North America who were children at the time of the massacres have been followed and subsequently examined. PTSD was found to persist in many through their adolescence and into their adulthood, but depression markedly decreased

Survivors of war often suffer from PTSD, even if they were not in the armed forces. *(Left)* These Rwandan refugees, mainly Hutus, are returning to Rwanda from refugee camps in Zaire. *(Right)* These refugees from the conflict in East Timor over independence from Indonesia return to their homes.

from adolescence to adulthood (Sack, Clarke, Him, and Dickason, 1993).

Inhumanity to other humans has not abated in recent years, and among its more awful consequences has been lasting PTSD. The genocides in Rwanda (850,000 Tutsi murdered by neighbors in three months), Bosnia, East Timor, and Kosovo should be sufficient to tell us that mass political murder is still with us. It is not just the dead who should have our compassion, but even more the living relatives. Seven hundred and ninety-one children who survived the siege of Sarajevo by the Serbs in 1994 were closely examined for PTSD. Massive depression and PTSD symptoms were seen, with girls worse off than boys, and those who had lost a family member, been deprived of water, or had come under direct sniper fire were in worse shape (Husain et al., 1998).

RAPE

Sarah was sixteen when she was raped:

> He came closer to me, and I could feel his breath. He was taller than me, but then everyone was tall to me. All I saw was black until I looked around and saw, for the first time, a long knife in his left hand. It sparkled in the light, and, again, I could only make out a manly figure. I never saw his face because he was wearing a ski mask, but I could feel his eyes, and that was enough for me. I am so glad I didn't see his face, or my nightmares would probably be worse and more

vivid than they are now. He pulled me out of the light and pushed me back toward some bushes. He told me I could either run and he would kill me, or I could stay and we could have a lot of fun. I still remember his voice. I can't describe it, but it is permanently in my mind. I didn't answer. He held the knife up to my throat and looked at me. Then he pushed me down to the ground on my back and ripped off my shorts and underpants. It took him a little time to get ready himself. Then he forced himself down on me. He was very heavy and strong. I felt that, so I didn't struggle, and I think that was smart. He did have a knife and who knows what else. Then I felt the pain from the lower end of my body, and then that's when I knew what this horrible man was doing to me. He was raping me. Not only raping up my insides, but my trust, my honesty, my cleanliness, my pride, my sleep, my friends, my family, my happiness—and, most of all, my life. I just lay there not doing anything, but thinking, "What am I going to tell my family?" I don't recall how long this went on, but I do recall the pain and the powerlessness. Then a wet feeling. Then he got up and said, "Thanks." That's all he said, and he left and went on his way to rape another woman, or home to his wife and kids, or back to a house out on the street. I don't know and don't care at all. (Foa and Rothbaum, 1998)

About 100,000 rapes are reported every year, and possibly seven times as many go unreported. A woman's reaction to rape is a kind of post-traumatic stress disorder that was originally called the "rape trauma syndrome" (Burgess and Holmstrom, 1979).

When a woman is raped, her first reaction is called the phase of "disorganization." In one study, researchers found that immediately following rape, a roughly equal number of women exhibited one of two emotional styles: expressive—showing fear, anger, anxiety, crying, sobbing, and tenseness—or controlled—showing a calm exterior. The symptoms of post-traumatic stress disorder were usually present as well. Within two weeks as many as 95 percent of the victims may show the symptoms of what would later be diagnosed as post-traumatic stress disorder (Rothbaum, Foa, Riggs, Murdock, and Walsh, 1992). The victim relives the rape time and again, in waking life and in dreams. Sleep disturbance sets in, and she has trouble with both getting to sleep and sudden awakening. Rape victims startle easily. Women who were suddenly awakened by the rapist ("blitz" rape) find that they awake each night at about the same time, screaming from rape nightmares. Normal sexual activity is difficult to resume, and a complete avoidance of sex sometimes develops.

Most victims get over the phase of "disorganization" in time and enter the "reorganization" phase. In the long-term process of reorganization, most women take action to ensure safety. Many change their telephone numbers, and half of the women make special trips home to seek support from family members. Half of the victims move. One victim who couldn't afford to move first stayed with relatives and then rearranged her home. As the rape had occurred in her bedroom, she did what she could to change that

room: "Wouldn't sleep in my own bed. Stayed with friends for a while. Changed my bedroom around, and got a new bedroom set." Many of the victims begin to read about rape and to write about their experience. Some become active in rape crisis centers and assist other victims, and of these, 70 percent recover in a few months (Burgess and Holmstrom, 1979; Meyer and Taylor, 1986).

Four to six years after the rape, about 75 percent of rape victims said they had recovered. More than half of these recovered in the first three months, and the rest within two years. Victims with the least fear and the fewest flashbacks in the week following the rape recovered more quickly. The very distressed or numbed victims had a poor outcome. The violence of the assault and how life threatening it was perceived as being also predicted worse long-term outcome. Distressingly, 25 percent of rape victims said they had not recovered, even after four to six years. Seventeen years later, 16 percent still had post-traumatic stress disorder (Foa and Meadows, 1997; Rothbaum, Foa, Riggs, Murdock, and Walsh, 1992).

Course of Post-Traumatic Stress Disorder

The course of post-traumatic stress disorder varies, but it can be agonizingly long. Sometimes the symptoms disappear within a few months, resembling recovery from a depressive disorder (see Chapter 7). DSM-IV labels PTSD as "acute" if the symptoms last for less than three months, as "chronic" if they last for more than three months, and as "delayed" if symptoms first occur six or more months after the trauma.

Overall, the prognosis for those who suffer from PTSD is probably bleak, particularly for the victims of very severe trauma. As we have seen, a high percentage of concentration camp victims were still troubled with anxiety and guilt twenty years later, and people who had lost a child or spouse in a motor accident were still more depressed and anxious four to seven years later (Lehman, Wortman, and Williams, 1987). Even with the milder stress of injury in a traffic accident, 32 percent still had PTSD one year later, and in a prospective study of people injured and admitted to emergency wards, 17.5 percent still had PTSD four months later (Koren, Arnon, and Klein, 1999; Shalev et al., 1998).

A very long course also seems to be true for some veterans of combat. Sixty-two veterans of

Many women experience the symptoms of PTSD after they are raped. Rape counseling in which they can talk candidly to a therapist may relieve the feelings of distress caused by the trauma.

World War II who suffered chronic "combat fatigue," with symptoms of exaggerated jumpiness, recurrent nightmares, and irritability, were examined twenty years later. Irritability, depression, restlessness, difficulties in concentration and memory, blackouts, wakefulness, fatigability, and jumpiness persisted for twenty years. These symptoms were more prominent in the veterans suffering from combat fatigue than in noncombat patients or in healthy combat veterans (see Figure 5–3; Archibald and Tuddenham, 1965).

An entire lifetime of PTSD is not uncommon after particularly brutal combat experience. Two hundred and sixty-two World War II and Korean War veterans, who had suffered the multiple traumas of combat and imprisonment, were assessed for problems when they were senior citizens. Fifty-three percent had suffered PTSD, and 29 percent were still suffering from it. The POW's held by the Japanese, who were the most brutal captors, had an 84 percent lifetime rate of PTSD, with 59 percent still suffering from PTSD later in their lives (Engdahl, Dikel, Eberly, and Blank, 1997).

Years after the end of the Vietnam War, veterans still experienced post-traumatic stress disorder, particularly those who had seen buddies killed in action. Those who had seen, and particularly those who had participated in, atrocities, have been shown to be at severe risk for post-traumatic stress disorder (Breslau and Davis, 1987). One group of Vietnam War veterans interviewed six to fifteen years after participating in violent combat had lives full of problems. They had more arrests and convictions, more drinking, more drug addiction, and more stress than veterans who had not seen combat (Yager, Laufer, and Gallops, 1984). Moreover, twenty years after the end of the war, Vietnam War veterans were found to be more likely to suffer from PTSD, generalized anxiety disorder, and depression than non–Vietnam War veterans (Boscarino, 1995).

In the aftermath of the Gulf War, the rate of PTSD jumped markedly from 3 percent immediately after the war to 8 percent two years later (Wolfe, Erickson, Sharkansky, King, and King, 1999). While those who had PTSD at time 1 were twenty times as likely to still

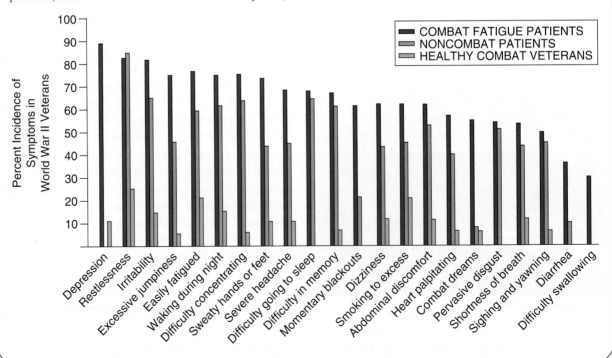

Figure 5–3

POST-TRAUMATIC STRESS DISORDER IN VETERANS

The bars indicate the percentage of incidence of symptoms twenty years after World War II in veterans who suffered combat fatigue in comparison to healthy combat veterans and noncombat patients. (Source: Archibald and Tuddenham, 1965, p. 478.)

Men who have been through combat, such as these American soldiers in Vietnam, may later suffer from post-traumatic stress disorder.

have it at time 2, many new cases appeared. There are several possibilities as to why: Perhaps there is delayed PTSD, a notion that was formerly fashionable, but for which minimal evidence appeared. Perhaps some combat trauma "kindles" a hypersensitivity to later peacetime stress. Or perhaps, all the publicity about Gulf War syndrome and PTSD itself exaggerates the symptoms.

Vulnerability to Post-Traumatic Stress Disorder

Who among us is particularly at risk? Psychologists comb over disasters looking for the people who thrive without any signs of PTSD and for those who collapse. Overall, the factor that most predicts who will suffer is the degree of threat to one's life—those individuals who were surest they would die were the most vulnerable to PTSD. Over and above the brutality of the event itself, what psychological factors protect or predispose some people to PTSD? Here is what psychologists have found:

- A prior life history free of mental problems predicted who did best after a catastrophic factory explosion in Norway (Malt and Weisaeth, 1989; Weisaeth, 1989).
- Among 469 firefighters caught in a disastrous Australian brushfire, those most at risk for getting chronic PTSD scored high on neuroticism and had a family history of mental disorders. These were better predictors than even how much phys-

ical trauma each one had experienced (McFarlane, 1989).

- After fighting in Lebanon, Israeli combat casualty veterans who were the children of Holocaust survivors (called "second-generation casualties") had higher rates of PTSD than control casualties (Solomon, Kotler, and Mikulincer, 1988).
- Among Israeli combat veterans of two wars, those who experienced PTSD after the second war had had more combat stress reactions during the first war (Solomon, Oppenheimer, Elizur, and Waysman, 1990).
- After Hurricane Andrew struck Florida in 1992, prior high anxiety and low academic achievement predicted those children who would show the worst problems (LaGreca, Silverman, and Wasserstein, 1998).
- Among eighty-nine torture survivors from Turkish prisons, those who resisted PTSD best had prior experience with trauma, training in mental and physical stoicism, the expectation that they would be tortured if caught, and a belief system that construed their torture as repression by the ruling class (Basoglu et al., 1997)

These findings indicate that people who are psychologically healthiest and most prepared before the trauma are at least risk for PTSD, while those who show psychological disturbances before the traumatic event are at greater risk. But if the bad event is awful enough, previously good psychological health is not protective.

People who are poor and have lower educational backgrounds are more likely to develop PTSD than those at higher educational and socioeconomic levels (Blazer, Hughes, George, Swartz, and Boyer, 1991). There are many reasons for this. One factor may be the greater risk of traumatic events in the bad neighborhoods in which they reside. An additional factor may be the lack of social support. Not having someone to talk to and commiserate with may also cause previously healthy individuals to crumble under the strains of trauma and loss. During natural disasters, friends and relatives may be dispersed and absorbed by their own troubles, depriving victims of solace and affection (Kaniasty and Norris, 1995).

Genetic predisposition also affects vulnerability to PTSD. The sheer scale of the American participation in the Vietnam War has allowed the first major study of the heritability of PTSD. After the war, over 4,000 twin pairs who were Vietnam veterans were examined for PTSD symptoms. Overall, PTSD symptoms occurred in roughly half the veterans who saw intense combat, but the identical twins showed more similar levels of PTSD symptoms than did the fraternal twins, suggesting that PTSD has a heritable component (True et al., 1993).

Given that PTSD is always triggered by an external event like combat, what exactly is heritable in PTSD? One possibility concerns differences in the neural circuitry associated with PTSD (Yehuda, 2000). Biological studies of children and adults who suffer trauma sufficient to produce PTSD suggest an array of neural and hormonal changes (Lipschitz, Rasmusson, and Southwick, 1998). Researchers have found that the extreme stress experienced during a traumatic event may lead to a long-term and even lifelong increase in activity in the HPA (hypothalamic-pituitary-adrenal) axis, which governs responses to prolonged stress (see Chapter 4). The resulting chronic release of such stress hormones as cortisol permanently damages the hippocampus, an area involved in long-term memory (Gurvits, Shenton, Hokama, and Ohta, 1996).

Other physical changes occur in traumatic stress. Physical abuse is associated with a smaller corpus callosum, the major neural tract that conducts messages between the two hemispheres of the brain. Researchers have shown that traumatized children have signs of chronic autonomic overarousal, including a faster resting heart rate, disrupted regulation of catecholamines such as epinephrine (adrenaline) and norepinephrine, increased startle response, and overreactivity of the hypothalamic-pituitary-adrenal (HPA) axis (Bremner et al., 1997b). These physiological changes help to explain the persistence of PTSD and its resistance to treatment.

In one PET scan study, seven combat veterans with PTSD and seven without the disorder viewed pictures of combat and generated their own mental images (Shin et al., 1997). Compared to the veterans without the disorder, those with PTSD showed more heightened blood flow in the cingulate gyrus and the amygdala (which are part of the limbic system) when generating images, and reduced blood flow in Broca's area when viewing pictures. Heritable differences in the reactions of these structures could be responsible for the heritability of PTSD.

These biological differences may be accompanied by cognitive vulnerabilities. Some individuals may be genetically predisposed to recurring thoughts about the trauma (rumination) and to reexperiencing bad events in flashbacks. Similarly, some individuals may be genetically predisposed to catastrophic interpreta-

tions of bad events. Further research on the heritability of rumination and catastrophizing will shed light on their relation to PTSD.

Who recovers from PTSD and who does not? Ninety-two assault victims completed questionnaires about their cognitions concerning the assault (Dunmore, Clark, and Ehlers, 1999; Ehlers and Clark, 2000). Those who recovered from PTSD responded in ways that differed markedly from those who still had the disorder. Those still affected had the following pattern of thoughts:

1. Mental defeat: "If something like that happened to me again, I'd go to pieces."
2. Mental confusion: "I couldn't believe this was happening to me."
3. Negative appraisal of emotions: "If I can react like that, I must be very unstable."
4. Negative appraisal of initial symptoms: "My reactions must mean I'm losing my mind."
5. Negative appraisal of others' reactions: "Other people are ashamed of me now."
6. Permanent change: "My life has been destroyed by the assault."

This pattern amounts to a belief in personal ruination, coupled with the shattering of a person's global assumptions that the world is just and her future is controllable and predictable.

Treatment of PTSD

In spite of the fact that so many of our fellow human beings are victims of trauma, it is only recently that we have learned anything substantial about how to alleviate post-traumatic stress reactions. Relatives, friends, and therapists are inclined to tell the victims of catastrophe to try to "forget it," but it should be apparent that such painful memories are not easily blotted out. The last ten years, however, have witnessed considerable progress in the treatment of PTSD. A decade ago, PTSD was basically untreatable. Now the most recent meta-analysis of seventeen controlled studies of PTSD involving 690 patients shows a "success" rate of 62 percent against only 38 percent in control groups (Sherman, 1998).

Therapists have tried both drug therapy and psychotherapy with victims of trauma (see Table 5–4). The psychotherapies seem more promising than medications, however. Two types of psychotherapy have been widely used to treat the disorder: exposure and disclosure (opening up).

TABLE 5–4

Treatment

POST-TRAUMATIC STRESS DISORDER

	Exposure Therapy*	Antidepressant and Anti-anxiety Drugs†
Improvement	about 60% moderately improved	probably better than placebo
Relapse‡	infrequent relapse	moderate relapse
Side Effects	mild	moderate
Cost	inexpensive	inexpensive
Time Scale	weeks/months	weeks
Overall	**good**	**marginal**

*Most data come from the exposure therapy of rape victims. Results with other traumas are uncharted. See also the promising findings for EMDR (Box 5–1).

†Medication data are based mainly on outcome studies of MAO inhibitors, SSRI's, tricyclics, and minor tranquilizers.

‡Relapse after discontinuation of treatment.

SOURCE: Based on Seligman, 1994, p. 143; revised with Foa and Meadows, 1997; Foa et al., 1999; Keane, 1998; Yehuda, Marshall, and Giller, 1998.

DRUG THERAPY

In the best-controlled drug study, forty-six Vietnam veterans with post-traumatic stress disorder were given either antidepressants or a placebo. After the patients were given antidepressants, the number of nightmares and flashbacks decreased but did not drop into the normal range. Numbing, a sense of distance from loved ones, and general anxiety were not relieved. Overall, antidepressants and anti-anxiety drugs produce some symptom relief for some patients, but drug treatment alone is never sufficient to relieve the patient's suffering in post-traumatic stress disorder (Demartino, Mollica, and Wilk, 1995; Marshall, Stein, Liebowitz, and Yehuda, 1996; Rothbaum, Ninan, and Thomas, 1996; Yehuda, Marshall, and Giller, 1998).

EXPOSURE

Exposure therapy is an extinction or habituation procedure in which individuals are repeatedly exposed to the feared stimulus. It has been used to treat post-traumatic stress disorder and is perhaps the best documented of the successful treatments. In the exposure treatment of PTSD, victims relive the trauma in their imagination while overcoming the tendency to dissociate from the experience. They describe it aloud to the therapist, with emotion and in the present tense. This is repeated session after session. The reliving is tape-recorded, and the patient plays it back at home frequently as a homework assignment.

When the efficacy of exposure therapy is tested, it is usually compared to a wait-list control and to stress inoculation training (SIT). SIT teaches a variety of anxiety management skills, including deep muscle relaxation, thought-stopping (the patient yells "Stop!" to herself when she finds herself ruminating, which is dwelling on the traumatic thoughts), and cognitive restructuring ("My love life wasn't actually *ruined* by the rape, since my husband and children still love me.").

In the best-controlled study of exposure treatment to date, Edna Foa and her colleagues treated ninety-six women who were victims of assault, usually rape (Foa et al., 1999). Women were assigned randomly to eighteen sessions of prolonged exposure treatment (PE); to stress inoculation training (SIT), which included deep muscle relaxation, thought-stopping ruminations, and cognitive restructuring; to PE plus SIT; or to a wait-list control group. At the end of the study, women in the three active treatment groups all had less PTSD and less depression than did women in the wait-list control group, and these gains continued through a one-year follow-up. The good outcomes for the treatment groups did not differ from one another. At completion of treatment, none of the women in the wait-list group had lost their PTSD diagnosis, whereas 60 percent of the women in the three treated groups had. There was a trend for the PE group to be superior to the other two treated groups at the end of one-year follow-up: 51 percent of the PE group were "functioning well" after one year, compared to 31 percent (SIT group) and 27 percent (PE plus SIT group) (see also Foa, Rothbaum, Riggs, and Murdock, 1991; Foa and Riggs, 1995; Frueh, Turner, and Beidel, 1995; Keane, 1998).

In a briefer version of this treatment for women who had recently been raped, Foa, Hearst-Ikeda, and Perry (1995) added elements of education, relaxed breathing, and cognitive restructuring (see also Marks, Lovell, Noshirvani, Livanou, and Thrasher, 1998). In follow-up, only 10 percent of those in the treated group still had PTSD, while 70 percent of those in the matched control group still had PTSD. These new findings are the best outcome yet for treatment of rape victims, who are usually reluctant to go for treatment because they want to avoid thinking about the rape.

Although more controversial, a therapy that incorporates some of exposure therapy called Eye Movement Desensitization and Reprocessing (EMDR) is also widely used. We discuss both the techniques and the controversy surrounding EMDR in Box 5–1.

Science and Practice   Box 5–1

EMDR

Francine Shapiro came across EMDR (Eye Movement Desensitization and Reprocessing) therapy quite serendipitously. She was walking in a park in 1987, ruminating about a distressing event, when she noticed that the disturbing thoughts were markedly losing their hold. Paying close attention to what she had been doing, she noticed that her eyes had been moving spontaneously and rapidly back and forth in an upward diagonal (saccadic eye movements). Eager to try this out as a therapeutic technique, she began asking colleagues and friends to concentrate on disturbing beliefs and simultaneously to move their eyes back and forth while holding on to the images. When people varied their eye movements—faster, slower, different trajectories—the disturbance caused by the image seemed to wane markedly (Shapiro, 1995).

From these simple observations, Shapiro developed one of the most widely used, and one of the most controversial, psychotherapies of the 1990s. She created the EMDR Institute, and she and her colleagues have trained many thousands of therapists in the technique.

The core technique is exposure accompanied by saccadic eye movements. The patient and therapist select a target visual memory that causes distress, and the patient generates a negative verbal thought about the memory (for example, "I am unlovable"). The patient also generates a positive thought designed to replace the negative one (for example, "I am kind"). The therapist rapidly moves her finger back and forth in front of the patient's eyes, and the patient follows the moving finger with his eyes while concentrating on the disturbing image or memory. After a set of ten to twenty eye movements, the patient rates his distress and how strongly he believes in the positive thought. This is repeated until the image becomes less disturbing, and the belief in the positive cognition is much stronger.

Many therapists have found strong and sudden improvement in patients with anxiety problems, and encouragingly so with patients suffering from post-traumatic stress disorder. EMDR therapists were dispatched to Bosnia and to Oklahoma City in the wake of those traumas. Based on the preliminary evidence and clinical enthusiasm, researchers have carried out several controlled outcome studies. In one such study, eighty participants who were "experiencing traumatic memories" received three ninety-minute sessions of EMDR, with half receiving treatment immediately and half acting as a control group with EMDR received later. The disturbing memories included physical and mental abuse, death of a loved one, health crises, sexual abuse, and the like. Forty-six percent of the participants were diagnosed as suffering from full-blown PTSD. Substantial and rapid improvement occurred for the treated group relative to the group yet-to-be-treated, and their improvement was maintained over a ninety-day follow-up. There was less subjective distress about the memory, as well as fewer symptoms of depression and anxiety (Wilson, Becker, and Tinker, 1996). In another study, twenty-one rape victims were randomly assigned to either a wait-list control or EMDR. PTSD symptoms were markedly alleviated and at the end of treatment only one of the ten women in the EMDR group had PTSD, while 88 percent of the wait-list controls did (Rothbaum, 1997). At any rate, these preliminary findings on EMDR are strong enough that thorough scientific exploration of the technique is in order.

In spite of apparently promising results, EMDR has been the subject of scathing criticism particularly among clinical outcome scientists (Lohr, Kleinknecht, Tolin, and Barrett, 1995). In fact, the tone of the criticism is as hostile as any we have seen in the entire psychological literature. McNally (1999) compares the EMDR movement to mesmerism, a precursor of hypnotism in the eighteenth century, which was widely regarded as charlatanism. There are several grounds for the hostility: First, why this treatment works remains a mystery, as do its active ingredients. It seems that the eye movements are not necessary to successful outcomes. Second, the treatment did not arise out of either the psychological or psychiatric "establishment," but rather from the fringes of science. Third, the therapy has been an enormous financial success and some clinicians have criticized Shapiro both for training so many people in the technique before controlled outcome studies were done and for the cultish secrecy surrounding the technique (McNally, 1996). Successful commerce and scientific respectability are not easy bedfellows.

OPENING UP (DISCLOSURE)

"Opening up" is derived from James Pennebaker's important work on silence. Pennebaker has found that Holocaust victims and rape victims who do not talk about the trauma later suffer worse physical health than do those who confide in somebody. Pennebaker got sixty Holocaust survivors to open up and disclose what happened to them. They finally related to others scenes that they had relived in their heads thousands of times over the last fifty years.

Ironically, the interviewers themselves had nightmares from hearing these long-buried stories, but the health of the disclosers improved. Similarly, Pennebaker had students write down their secret traumas: sexual abuse by a grandfather, death of a dog, a suicide attempt. The immediate consequence was increased depression. But in the long term, the number of physical illnesses of the students dropped—by 50 percent—and their immune systems became stronger (Pennebaker, 1990). In a confirming, but preliminary study of Bosnian refugees in America, those who gave testimony about their experiences showed relief from PTSD symptoms (Goenjian et al., 1997; Weine, Kulenovic, Pavkovic, and Gibbons, 1998).

Psychological treatment thus produces good relief, but as yet, no cures for PTSD, and future research in this domain is essential. Evidence indicates that exposure, EMDR, and disclosure are all useful in treating PTSD patients. More controlled outcome studies are needed to verify and extend these results.

Panic Disorder

How many of us have at some time been suddenly overwhelmed by intense apprehension? Physically, we feel jumpy and tense. Cognitively, we expect that something bad—we don't know what—is going to happen. Such an attack comes out of nowhere; no specific object or event sets it off, and the attack gradually subsides. But some people have more severe attacks, and they have them frequently. These people suffer from *panic disorder.* Panic disorder consists of recurrent panic attacks. In the United States, 1.7 percent of the adult population suffers from panic disorder. Germany and Italy have the highest rates (2.6 and 2.9 percent), and Taiwan, which has a very low prevalence of psychopathology across the board, has the lowest rate at 0.4 percent. Women have panic disorder two to three times as often as men, and the average age of onset is in the late twenties (Weissman et al., 1997).

DSM-IV classifies panic disorder with and without agoraphobia. People with *agoraphobia* fear going out to places of assembly, open spaces, and crowds, or being in any situation in which they might get sick, not be able to escape, and not get help. Agoraphobia often begins with a panic attack, and the individual fears that another panic attack will occur if she goes out into a public place.

Symptoms of a Panic Attack

A panic attack consists of the four elements of fear, with the emotional and physical elements most salient.

Emotionally, the individual is overwhelmed with intense apprehension, terror, or depersonalization.

> It was just like I was petrified with fear. If I were to meet a lion face to face, I couldn't be more scared. Everything got black, and I felt I would faint; but I didn't. I thought "I won't be able to hold on . . ." (Laughlin, 1967, p. 92)

Physically, a panic attack consists of an acute emergency reaction (including shortness of breath, dizziness, racing heart, trembling, chills, or chest pains).

> My heart was beating so hard and fast I thought it would jump out and hit my hand. I felt like I couldn't stand up—that my legs wouldn't support me. My hands got icy and my feet stung. There were horrible shooting pains in my forehead. My head felt tight, like someone had pulled the skin down too tight and I wanted to pull it away. . . .
> I couldn't breathe; I was short of breath. I literally got out of breath and panted like I had run up and down the stairs. I felt like I had run an eight-mile race. I couldn't do anything. I felt all done in; weak, no strength. I couldn't even dial a telephone. . . . (Laughlin, 1967, p. 92)

Cognitively, the individual thinks he might have a heart attack and die, or go crazy, or lose control.

> Even then I can't be still when I am like this. I am restless and I pace up and down. I feel like I am just not responsible. I don't know what I'll do. These things are terrible. I can go along real calmly for a while. Then, without any warning, this happens. I just blow my top. (Laughlin, 1967, p. 92)

Such an attack begins abruptly, usually peaks within ten minutes, and subsides gradually. Panic

DSM-IV Criteria

Panic Disorder without Agoraphobia

A. Both (1) and (2): (1) recurrent unexpected panic attacks; (2) at least one of the attacks has been followed by 1 month (or more) of one (or more) of the following: (a) persistent concern about having additional attacks; (b) worry about the implications of the attack or its consequences (e.g., losing control, having a heart attack, "going crazy"); (c) a significant change in behavior related to the attacks.

B. Absence of Agoraphobia

C. The panic attacks are not due to the direct physiological effects of a substance (e.g., a drug of abuse, a medication) or a general medical condition (e.g., hyperthyroidism).

D. The panic attacks are not better accounted for by another mental disorder, such as Social Phobia (e.g., occurring on exposure to feared social situations), Specific Phobia (e.g., on exposure to a specific phobic situation), Obsessive-Compulsive Disorder (e.g., on exposure to dirt in someone with an obsession about contamination), Post-Traumatic Stress Disorder (e.g., in response to stimuli associated with a severe stressor), or Separation Anxiety Disorder (e.g., in response to being away from home or close relatives).

SOURCE: APA, DSM-IV, 1994.

attacks are the defining symptom of panic disorder, and they come in two forms: *unexpected* ("uncued" or "spontaneous") and less commonly, *situationally triggered* ("cued"). Cued panic attacks may be set off by social situations or specific objects (for example, cats). After a few attacks, the individual worries persistently about having another one and about the consequences (for example, going crazy or dying). An occasional panic attack is quite common, with as many as 20 percent of students and about 5 percent of senior citizens reporting one episode of panic in the preceding week (Barlow, 1988). When panic attacks are frequent, however—

Lost and disoriented, while hearing terrifying noises from afar, this college student in search of the Blair Witch is certainly experiencing the emotional and physical symptoms of a situationally triggered panic in the 1999 film *The Blair Witch Project*.

three in three weeks or four in a month—and when the individual has extreme fear of losing control, the condition is severe enough to warrant a diagnosis of panic disorder.

Etiology of Panic Disorder

When researchers have looked for the causes of panic disorder, they have encountered a prime example of a head-on collision between the biological level and the psychological level of analysis. Many investigators—strangely, both biological and psychological—have regarded this issue as either/or. While the first theme of this book is the integration of biological and psychological levels of analysis of disorders, this is not always possible. Both levels of analysis can illuminate the causes and treatments and complement each other for such disorders as phobia and PTSD. But there are two other kinds of cases. In one, when all evidence is considered, the disorder turns out to be basically biological, with psychological considerations useful only at the margin. In the other, the disorder is basically psychological, and the biological aspects are wholly explained by the psychological analysis. Thus, sometimes one level of analysis *subsumes,* or totally explains, all the evidence from the other level of analysis. Panic disoder falls into the category of a disorder in which both biological and psychological explanations contribute to our understanding, but in which one explanation is subsumed by the other.

BIOLOGICAL APPROACH

Up until about 1990, panic disorder was almost universally seen as a biological disorder. Exponents of the biological viewpoint looked at four questions that each bears on whether a psychological problem is primarily biological:

- Can it be induced biologically?
- Is it heritable?
- Can medication control it?
- Are specific brain areas or functions involved?

Biological researchers found evidence that the answer to each question was "yes." First, panic attacks can be induced chemically in the laboratory in patients who experience them frequently. Such patients are hooked up to an intravenous line that slowly infuses into their bloodstream sodium lactate, a chemical that normally produces rapid, shallow breathing and heart palpitations. Similar effects are produced by the botanical extract yohimbine. Within a few minutes after either drug is administered, between 60 and 90 percent of patients with panic disorder have panic attacks, while normal controls have them only rarely (Klein, 1996a; Liebowitz, Fyer, Gorman, et al., 1985; Liebowitz, Gorman, Fyer, et al., 1985).

A second line of evidence supporting a biological view of panic disorder involves genetics. If one of two identical twins has panic disorder, then there is a 25 to 30 percent chance that the other twin also has the disorder. Such is not the case with fraternal twins; if one has panic disorder, the odds are only about 10 to 15 percent that the other twin will have it. Nonetheless, panic runs in families, and more than half of patients with panic disorder have close relatives who have some anxiety disorder or suffer from alcoholism (Crowe, 1990; Torgersen, 1983; see also Crowe et al., 1990)

Third, medication can be quite effective in controlling panic attacks. Two main classes of medications are currently favored: antidepressants (tricyclics, MAO inhibitors, atypical antidepressants, or preferably, the SSRI's), and the benzodiazepines (for example, Xanax or Klonopin). Both classes work better than placebos, with panic attacks dampened or even eliminated. General anxiety and depression also decrease (Michelson et al., 1998; Pecknold, Swinson, Kuch, and Lewis, 1988; Roy-Byrne and Cowley, 1998; Svebak, Cameron, and Levander, 1990; Tesar, 1990). Because the benzodiazepines can be addictive, they are largely reserved for short-term use, and the SSRI's are currently the favored treatment for panic disorder.

Fourth, there is some evidence that patients with panic disorder may have a neurochemical abnormality in particular areas of the brain. PET scans have shown that patients who have panic attacks after sodium lactate infusion have abnormally high blood flow and oxygen use in anxiety-related areas of their brain. One such area has been repeatedly implicated: the locus coeruleus, a part of the brain's arousal system (Reiman et al., 1986). The locus coeruleus is a major site of action of yohimbine (mentioned above). Moreover, when animals are stimulated in the locus coeruleus, they exhibit panic-like behavior (Gorman, Liebowitz, Fyer, and Stein, 1989).

But the locus coeruleus cannot account for the whole phenomenon, because it is composed largely of norepinephrine-containing neurons, while the SSRI's act exclusively on serotonin systems. Researchers now consider the locus coeruleus to be just one part of a neural "fight/flight system" (Gray, 1982, 1985) that starts in the brain stem, travels through the limbic system (which includes the amygdala, the hippocampus, and the hypothalamus—with the actions of the latter affecting the entire HPA axis), and ends up in the prefrontal cortex (see Figure 5-4). According to this model, patients with panic disorder may have a poorly regulated fight/flight system (Gray and McNaughton, 1996; Roy-Byrne and Cowley, 1998).

What causes such poor regulation? It now appears that the norepinephrine-containing neurons of the fight/flight system may normally be held in check by serotonin neurons. This normal inhibition is reduced by deficiencies in serotonin, as is the efficiency of the circuits in the brain that dampen the emergency reaction once it has begun (Charney and Heninger, 1986; Gorman, Kent, Sullivan, and Coplan, 2000; Nesse, Cameron, Curtis, McCann, and Huber-Smith, 1984). The result of this unbridled action of the fight/flight system is the runaway phenomenon of the panic attack (Gray and McNaughton, 1996; see also Goddard, Woods, and Charney, 1996).

With all this evidence amassed, biological psychiatrists made a strong case for viewing panic disorder primarily as a biological problem. Panic attacks could be induced chemically. Panic disorder was heritable, treatable by medication, and traceable to specific brain areas. Yet, even this case was not airtight, because panic disorder was found to respond to distinctly *psychological* treatment.

Figure 5—4

THE FIGHT/FLIGHT SYSTEM

Panic attacks may be set off by stimulation of a brain circuit known as the fight/flight system. As shown in the figure, this circuit includes the raphe nuclei and locus coeruleus of the brain stem, limbic structures such as the amygdala and the hypothalamus, and the frontal cortex. Stimulation of this system in animals leads to an alarm and escape response that resembles panic in humans.

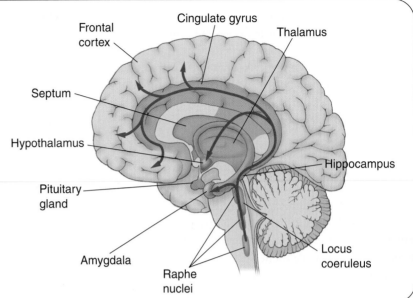

COGNITIVE APPROACH

In the 1990s, cognitive therapists offered an alternative view of panic disorder in which the basic cause is held to be catastrophic misinterpretations of bodily sensations (see Table 5–5). The patient misinterprets normal anxiety responses, such as racing heart, breathlessness, suffocation, and dizziness, as indicating impending disaster. The patient, who is often hyperaware of his heartbeats, interprets palpitations as meaning a heart attack is about to occur, and interprets dizziness as meaning insanity and loss of control (Beck and Emery, 1985; Bouwer and Stein, 1997; Clark, 1988, 1989, 1999; Ehlers and Breuer, 1992; Salkovskis, Clark, and Gelder, 1996; Van der Does, Antony, Ehlers, and Barsky, 2000).

TABLE 5–5

THE BIOLOGICAL AND COGNITIVE EXPLANATIONS OF PANIC

Fact	*Biological Explanation*	*Cognitive Explanation*
Panic attacks can be induced by sodium lactate infusions and yohimbine.	Lactate causes panic attacks in people with the disorder because these agents produce panic directly in biochemically vulnerable people.	People with panic disorder panic to these agents because they misinterpret the drug-produced increases in heart rate and breathing; their cognitions produce acute anxiety, compounding those effects.
Concordance for panic disorder is higher in identical twins than in fraternal twins.	The biochemical vulnerability that produces panic is a heritable defect of the neural alarm system.	Vulnerability to panic disorder is heritable either because the hyperawareness of certain physical symptoms is heritable or because higher heart rate is heritable.
Patients with panic disorder enter the panic state and show less inhibition of the alarm reaction.	Poor regulation of the alarm reaction is caused by a heritable brain abnormality and is not under the patient's control.	Poor regulation of the alarm reaction is a symptom of panic, caused ultimately by the patient's cognitions.
Antidepressants and anti-anxiety drugs alleviate panic.	Drugs block the biochemical process that produces panic.	Drugs block the symptoms that are misinterpreted in ways that induce panic.

The cognitive view reinterprets each line of evidence of the biological view by saying that panic attacks result from misinterpreting the meaning of bodily sensations. It goes over all the evidence as follows:

- Lactate and yohimbine induce panic because they make the heart race. These chemicals create the bodily sensations that are misinterpreted as catastrophe.
- Panic attacks are partially heritable because having a particularly noticeable bodily sensation, such as heart palpitations, or being hyperaware of bodily sensations, or even the tendency to misinterpret bodily sensations is heritable, not because

panic itself or a malfunctioning neural alarm circuit is directly heritable.

- The poorly regulated activity of the neural alarm pathways that prevent the dampening of anxiety is a result or a mere correlate of the panic attack, not the cause of it.
- Drugs relieve panic because they quiet the bodily sensations that get misinterpreted as catastrophe. When these drugs are no longer taken, panic attacks recur in full force because the misinterpretations remain uncorrected.

Which view is correct? Or are they compatible? In Box 5–2, we examine a possible rapprochement between the biological and psychological explanations.

Levels of Analysis

Box 5—2

The Etiology of Panic Disorder: A Rapprochement

How can we resolve the either/or dispute between the psychological and biological levels of analysis? In Chapter 4, we discussed the complex reciprocal causality involved in current explanations of mental disorder. The interaction of biology and psychology, and their reciprocal causality, is especially evident in cases of panic disorder.

According to the biological approach, panic attacks are caused by a heritable defect in the brain's alarm system, with the sufferer's misinterpretation caused by this defect. According to the psychological approach (specifically, the cognitive approach), panic attacks are caused by catastrophic misinterpretations of bodily systems. The panic-prone individual is hypersensitive to bodily symptoms and prone to misinterpret them (and these symptoms and misinterpretations are heritable). The activity of the neural alarm circuits is then a mere consequence of the misinterpretation.

As we see it, both the biological and the cognitive approach have made major contributions to the mounting evidence about the cause of panic disorder. Both bottom-up and a top-down causes of panic attacks have been shown: lactate and yohimbine produce panic attacks, and reading panic-loaded words produces panic attacks. At the moment, we see the evidence as showing both a psychological route and a biological route. Neither approach has shown that its route *alone* (without the other route activated) can cause panic. Evidence showing that panic attacks occur when the neural alarm circuit is activated even when there are no catastrophic misinterpretations would support a primarily biological causation of panic. Evidence showing that panic

attacks occur when there are catastrophic misinterpretations of bodily sensations but no activation of the neural alarm system would support a primarily cognitive causation of panic. Such experiments have not yet been done.

Both approaches have also produced therapies that relieve panic. The biological approach uses medications and claims that these work by regulating the neural alarm system. The cognitive approach changes people's misinterpretations of bodily sensations. The cognitive treatments have the edge as treatments of choice because they prevent recurrence of panic attacks in the long term, whereas once the medications are stopped, panic attacks return full-blown. But neither approach has the edge theoretically, for it is possible that correcting misinterpretations works by regulating the neural alarm system, or, conversely, that the medications work by correcting the misinterpretations. Decisive evidence would show that correcting misinterpretations works even when the alarm system continues to be poorly regulated, or, conversely, that regulating the alarm system ends panic attacks even though the misinterpretations continue. These decisive experiments have not been done.

So the evidence points to two routes to panic—one biological and one psychological—and to two treatments for panic—one using medications and one correcting misinterpretations of bodily sensations. These two routes are not independent, but the evidence does not yet tell us what the relationship actually is between the biological and the psychological routes to cause and treatment.

Treatment of Panic Disorder

As we've already discussed, tricyclic antidepressant drugs, anti-anxiety drugs, and SSRI's can relieve panic during an attack. Psychological treatments have also been found to treat panic and to prevent recurrence of attacks. In the 1990s, cognitive therapists carried out a novel series of experiments and created a new therapy. David Clark and Paul Salkovskis compared patients with panic disorder to patients who had other anxiety disorders and to normal people. Everyone was asked to read the following sentences aloud, but the last word presented was blurred. For example:

> If I had palpitations I could be   *dying.*
> *excited.*
> If I were breathless I could be   *choking.*
> *unfit.*

When the sentences were about bodily sensations, the patients with panic disorder, but no one else, saw the catastrophic endings fastest. This indicates that patients with panic disorder possess the habit of thinking catastrophically.

Next Clark and Salkovskis asked if words alone would activate this habit of catastrophic thinking, thereby inducing panic. Everyone read a series of word pairs aloud. When patients with panic disorder got to "breathlessness-suffocation" and "palpitations-dying," 75 percent had a full-blown panic attack—right there in the laboratory. No one without panic disorder had panic attacks, no patients who had recovered from panic disorder had panic attacks, and only 17 percent of other anxious patients had panic attacks.

Clark and Salkovskis reasoned that if catastrophic misinterpretations of bodily sensations are the cause of panic disorder, then changing the misinterpreta-

tion should cure the disorder. The therapy they developed to do this is straightforward and brief. Patients are told that panic results when they mistake normal symptoms of mounting anxiety for symptoms of heart attack, going crazy, or dying. Anxiety itself, they are informed, produces shortness of breath, chest pain, and sweating. Once you misinterpret these normal bodily sensations as an imminent heart attack, this makes the symptoms even more pronounced because it changes your anxiety into terror. A vicious circle has set in, culminating in a full-blown panic attack.

Patients are taught to reinterpret their symptoms more realistically—as mere anxiety symptoms. Then they are given practice in dealing with the anxiety symptoms. First, the symptoms of anxiety are brought on right in the office. Patients are told to breathe rapidly into a paper bag. This will cause a buildup of carbon dioxide and shortness of breath, mimicking the bodily sensations that provoke a panic attack. The therapist will then point out that the symptoms the patient is now experiencing—shortness of breath and heart racing—are harmless. They are simply the result of overbreathing, not a sign of a heart attack. The patient will then learn to interpret the sensations correctly. The following case illustrates how a cognitive therapist would proceed:

> One patient upon feeling somewhat faint would have a panic attack. He became afraid that he would actually faint and collapse. He interpreted his anxiety as a further symptom of fainting. This escalated to panic in a few seconds.

> THERAPIST: Why are you afraid of fainting? Have you ever actually fainted?
> PATIENT: I always managed to avoid collapsing just in time by holding on to something.
> THERAPIST: That's one possibility. An alternative explanation is that the feeling of faintness that you get in a panic attack will never lead you to collapse, even if you don't control it. In order to decide which possibility is correct, we need to know what has to happen to your body for you to actually faint. Do you know?
> PATIENT: No.
> THERAPIST: Your blood pressure needs to drop. Do you know what happens to your blood pressure during a panic attack?
> PATIENT: Well, my pulse is racing. I guess my blood pressure must be up.

David Clark (1954–) proposes that panic results from catastrophically misinterpreting bodily sensations of anxiety, such as a racing heart, as symptoms of a heart attack. He teaches people to correct these misinterpretations and to recognize that the symptoms signify anxiety, not physical catastrophe.

TABLE 5–6

Treatment

PANIC DISORDER

	Cognitive Therapy	*Medication**[*]
Improvement	more than 75% markedly improved	60–80% markedly improved
Relapse[†]	very frequent	moderate to high
Side Effects	none	moderate
Cost	inexpensive	moderate
Time/Scale	weeks	inexpensive
Overall	**excellent**	days/weeks
		good

[*]Based mainly on outcome studies of tricyclic antidepressants fluoxetine (Prozac), and alprazolam (Xanax).
[†]Relapse after discontinuation of treatment.
SOURCE: Based on Seligman, 1994, p. 67; revised with Barlow, Esler, and Vitali, 1998; Roy-Byrne and Cowley, 1998.

THERAPIST: That's right. In anxiety, heart rate and blood pressure tend to go together. So you are actually less likely to faint when you are anxious than when you are not.

PATIENT: But why do I feel so faint?

THERAPIST: Your feeling of faintness is a sign that your body is reacting in a normal way to the perception of danger. When you perceive danger, more blood is sent to your muscles and less to your brain. This means that there is a small drop in oxygen to the brain and that is why you feel faint. However, this feeling is misleading because you will not actually faint since your blood pressure is up, not down.

PATIENT: That's very clear. So next time I feel faint, I can check out whether I am going to faint by taking my pulse. If it's normal or quicker than normal, I know I won't faint. (Clark, 1989)

How well does this simple therapy work? Seventy-five to 90 percent of the patients treated with this therapy became panic free by the end of therapy and remained panic free twenty-four months later (Brown, Barlow, and Liebowitz, 1994; Margraf, Barlow, Clark, and Telch, 1993; Westling and Öst, 1995).

Two sets of "official" treatment guidelines for panic disorder have been promulgated recently. The guidelines from the American Psychiatric Association recommend both the medications and cognitive therapy as effective and approximately equally so (Gorman and Shear, 1998). The guidelines from the Practice Guidelines Coalition, a multiorganization body, has three major recommendations (Practice Guidelines Coalition, 1999):

1. The clear majority of patients show a positive response to either drugs or cognitive-behavioral therapy (see Table 5-6).
2. Both are equally effective in the short term.
3. Cognitive-behavior therapy has greater durability than drug therapy.

Agoraphobia

Agoraphobia usually occurs in the context of panic. As the name agoraphobia, literally "fear of the marketplace," implies, this disorder used to be classed as a phobia. But two important facts gradually emerged from careful study of many patients with agoraphobia: (1) most cases begin with a panic attack (Klein, Ross, and Cohen, 1987), and (2) the individual is not afraid of the marketplace or of places of assembly in themselves, but of having a panic attack there, being helpless, and of no one coming to her aid. These facts tell us that agoraphobia is not a true phobia, in the sense of fear of a specific situation, but rather it is a more global anxiety disorder. DSM-IV sensibly categorized agoraphobia as a subtype of panic disorder. Nonetheless agoraphobia can also occur without full panic attacks. In these cases, which DSM-IV calls "agoraphobia without history of panic disorder," the individual is afraid to leave home and go out in public lest she have "panic-like" symptoms, such as fainting, dizziness, loss of bladder control, or diarrhea.

DSM-IV Criteria

Agoraphobia

A. Anxiety about being in places or situations from which escape might be difficult (or embarrassing) or in which help may not be available in the event of having an unexpected or situationally predisposed panic attack or panic-like symptoms. Agoraphobic fears typically involve characteristic clusters of situations that include being outside the home alone; being in a crowd or standing in a line; being on a bridge; and traveling in a bus, train, or automobile. (*Note*: Consider the diagnosis of Specific Phobia if the avoidance is limited to one or only a few specific situations, or Social Phobia if the avoidance is limited to social situations.)

B. The situations are avoided (e.g., travel is restricted) or else are endured with marked distress or with anxiety about having a panic attack or panic-like symptoms, or require the presence of a companion.

C. The anxiety or phobic avoidance is not better accounted for by another mental disorder, such as Social Phobia (e.g., avoidance limited to social situations because of fear of embarrassment), Specific Phobia (e.g., avoidance limited to a single situation like elevators), Obsessive-Compulsive Disorder (e.g., avoidance of dirt in someone with an obsession about contamination), Post-Traumatic Stress Disorder (e.g., avoidance of stimuli associated with a severe stressor), or Separation Anxiety Disorder (e.g., avoidance of leaving home or relatives).

SOURCE: APA, DSM-IV, 1994.

SYMPTOMS OF AGORAPHOBIA

People with agoraphobia are beset not only with a terror of being caught with panic in the marketplace, but they also fear open spaces, crowds, bridges, and streets, or being in any situation in which escape might be difficult or embarrassing, or in which help might not be available in the event of suddenly getting sick. They typically believe that some disaster,

The woman looking out the window may suffer from agoraphobia, literally "fear of the marketplace." People who have agoraphobia fear leaving the safety of their homes because they worry that they will experience a panic attack while they are in the street, in a crowd, or in an open space.

usually a panic attack, will befall them when they are traveling away from the security of their homes, and that no one will help them. They then go to great lengths to avoid such places. Agoraphobia is crippling because many people with agoraphobia are unable to leave their homes, as in Celia's case from Chapter 1:

> Celia, nineteen, suddenly came home from work at McDonald's and screamed that she was going to die. While standing at her counter, she had experienced the worst sensations in her life. Her heart began to pound like a jackhammer, she could not catch her breath, she was gripped by panic and dread, she felt the ground underneath her was about to give way, and she was convinced she was having a stroke or a heart attack. She spent the next two weeks in bed and, thereafter, she refused to walk beyond the front gate.

People with agoraphobia dread a variety of objects connected with open space: smooth bodies of water, bleak landscapes, the street, train travel on clear days. These objects are much less terrifying when the space is more comfortably circumscribed, as by a snowstorm or trees, or when an enclosed space is easily within reach.

Agoraphobia is not uncommon, having a lifetime prevalence of about 3 percent (Boyd, Rae, Thompson, and Burns, 1990; Kessler et al., 1994; Regier, Narrow, and Rae, 1990). Twice as many women as men are diagnosed with agoraphobia, and the first panic attack usually begins in late adolescence, followed shortly by avoidance of going out of the home. People with agoraphobia are prone to panic attacks even when they are not in the agoraphobic situation. Moreover, they have more psychological problems—other than their disorder itself—than do those with true phobias. People with agoraphobia are often globally anxious and generally depressed (Magee, Eaton, Wittchen, McGonagle, and Kessler, 1996). Seventy percent of fifty-five patients with agoraphobia and panic also suffered depression (Breier, Charney, and Heninger, 1986). Substance abuse is also a frequent complication of agoraphobia. Obsessive-compulsive disorders occasionally accompany agoraphobia as well, and the relatives of these patients are at greater risk for the entire range of anxiety disorders (Harris, Noyes, Crowe, and Chaudry, 1983). Untreated, agoraphobia will sometimes remit spontaneously, and then return mysteriously, or it may be unabating (Marks, 1969; Zitrin, Klein, Woerner, and Ross, 1983).

CAUSE

The role of panic is crucial to understanding the cause of agoraphobia. Agoraphobia, you will recall, occurs either with or without panic. But both cases are marked by the terror of becoming ill while outside and not getting help. In the case of agoraphobia with panic, the feared illness is full-blown panic, while in the case of agoraphobia without panic, only some panic-like symptoms, including dizziness, fainting, and vomiting are the object of fear. Both can be explained by a classical conditioning analysis.

This model suggests the following analysis of the acquisition of agoraphobia with panic: The CS is the "agora" (a stimulus complex in which panic might occur and help not come), the US is the first panic attack that sets off agoraphobia, the UR is the panic response, and the CR is fear and avoidance of the agora. The same analysis holds for agoraphobia without panic, save that the US-UR is the panic-like symptoms. Based on this analysis, agoraphobia would be cured by removing the possibility of panic attacks with drugs and then showing the patient in exposure therapy that panic no longer occurs.

TREATMENT

It appears that the antidepressant, imipramine, reduces and removes panic. Groups that receive both imipramine and exposure therapy show improvement in that they experience less panic and tend to avoid the agora less. In contrast, groups that receive only exposure therapy show no less panic and only partial improvement in avoidance of the agora (Klein, Ross, and Cohen, 1987). This suggests that imipramine works by quelling the patient's spontaneous panic attacks. Once the panic attack is controlled, the patient no longer fears going out because the panic attack had been the traumatic event (the US) that he had feared and that he now knows will not happen (Ballenger, 1986; De Beurs et al., 1995; Mattick, Andrews, Hadzi-Pavlovic, and Christensen, 1990; Mavissakalian and Michelson, 1986; Telch et al., 1985).

Each of these two treatments employed separately has been quite effective for agoraphobia (see Table 5–7). In an exposure procedure, the patient agrees, usually with great apprehension, to enter a crowded public setting and to stay there without attempting to escape for a long period. This can be done first in imagination and then in reality. When it is done in imagination, the patient with agoraphobia will listen to a long and vivid tape recording that describes a scenario in which she goes to a shopping

TABLE 5–7

Treatment

AGORAPHOBIA

	Extinction Therapy	*Drugs**	*Combination*
Improvement	50–85% moderately improved	at least 50% moderately improved	60–80% markedly improved
Relapse[†]	10–30% relapse	very high relapse	10–20% relapse
Side Effects	none	moderate	moderate
Cost	inexpensive	inexpensive	inexpensive
Time Scale	weeks/months	weeks	weeks/months
Overall	**very good**	**good**	**very good**

*Medication data is based on tricyclics, MAO inhibitors, and SSRI's.
[†]Relapse after discontinuation of treatment.
SOURCE: Based on Seligman 1994, pp. 78–79; revised with Barlow, Esler, and Vitali, 1998.

center, falls down, is trampled by crowds, and hears them laugh as they observe her vomiting all over herself. Usually she is terrified for the first hour or two of exposure, and then gradually the terror will subside as she realizes that nothing is really going to happen to her. When she is actually taken to a shopping center subsequently, she will usually be greatly improved, and the anxiety may be gone. Between 60 and 85 percent of patients markedly improve. Treatment gains are maintained: five years after exposure, 77 percent of a group of ninety patients with agoraphobia remained in remission (Barlow, Esler, and Vitali, 1998; Fava, Zielezny, Savron, and Grandi, 1995; Marks, Boulougouris, and Marset, 1971). The combination of *in vivo* (in real life, as opposed to imagination) exposure and cognitive therapy may be the psychological treatment of choice. At one-year follow-up, 65 percent of the exposure-only patients were functioning well as compared to 87 percent of those treated with the combination of exposure and cognitive therapy (Michelson, Marchione, Greenwald, Testa, and Marchione, 1996).

Antidepressant and anti-anxiety drugs—the tricyclics, MAO inhibitors and SSRI's—may also be helpful in alleviating agoraphobia, either alone or when given in concert with the psychological therapies. But there is an important distinction between who will benefit from medication and who will not. The distinction is between patients who do and who do not have full-blown panic attacks. The patients with agoraphobia who do not have panic attacks do not seem to benefit from medication. This is probably because the way the medications work is to end the full-blown attacks, but not the "panic-like" symptoms of dizziness and the like (Ballenger, 1986; Klein, Ross, and Cohen, 1987; Mavissakalian and Perel, 1995; Pollard, Bronson, and Kenney, 1989). When these drugs work, it is important to stay on them, for the rate of relapse when the drug is discontinued is very high (Mavissakalian and Perel, 1999).

Generalized Anxiety Disorder

In contrast to a panic attack, which is sudden and acute, generalized anxiety is chronic, and may last for months on end, with the elements of anxiety more or less continually present. DSM-IV requires a period of six months during which most days are filled with worry and excessive anxiety for a diagnosis of *generalized anxiety disorder (GAD)*.

Symptoms and Prevalence of GAD

An individual with generalized anxiety disorder has trouble controlling the worry and anxiety. His symptoms cause him considerable distress and problems at work and in relationships.

Emotionally the individual feels restless, jittery and tense, vigilant, and constantly on edge.

> I feel tense and fearful much of the time. I don't know what it is. I can't put my finger on it. . . . I just get all nervous inside. . . . I act like I'm scared to death of something. I guess maybe I am. (Laughlin, 1967, p. 107)

Cognitively the individual expects something awful but doesn't know what.

> I am frightened, but don't know what I fear. I keep expecting something bad to happen. . . . I have thought I could tie it to definite things, but this isn't true. It varies, and is unpredictable. I can't tell when it will come on. If I could just put my finger on what it is. . . . (Laughlin, 1967, p. 107)

Physically the individual experiences chronic muscle tension. There are increases in EEG beta activity in the frontal lobes, especially in the left hemisphere, indicating intense worry. The person with GAD tires easily, has difficulty concentrating, is irritable, tense, and has trouble sleeping.

Behaviorally he flails around, looking for what to do to relieve his worries.

> For the past week or so I don't want to get away from the house. I fear I might go all to pieces, maybe become hysterical. . . . Sometimes I get fearful and tense when I am talking to people and I just want to run away. (Laughlin, 1967, p. 107)

Considerably less is known about GAD than about any other anxiety disorder. Indeed, there has been controversy about whether it is a disorder at all, because it can be difficult to distinguish GAD from panic and obsessive-compulsive disorder on the one hand and from normal worrying and fretting on the other. Here are a few of the better-documented findings: with a lifetime prevalence of 5.1 percent, GAD is somewhat more prevalent than panic disorder; it is more frequent in females; and it is mildly heritable.

DSM-IV Criteria

Generalized Anxiety Disorder

A. Excessive anxiety and worry (apprehensive expectation), occurring more days than not for at least 6 months, about a number of events or activities (such as work or school performance).

B. The person finds it difficult to control the worry.

C. The anxiety and worry are associated with three (or more) of the following six symptoms (with at least some symptoms present for more days than not for the past 6 months) (*Note*: Only one item is required in children): (1) restlessness or feeling keyed up or on edge; (2) being easily fatigued; (3) difficulty concentrating or mind going blank; (4) irritability; (5) muscle tension; (6) sleep disturbance (difficulty falling or staying asleep, or restless unsatisfying sleep).

D. The focus of the anxiety and worry is not confined to features of an Axis I disorder, e.g., the anxiety or worry is not about having a panic attack (as in Panic Disorder), being embarrassed in public (as in Social Phobia), being contaminated (as in Obsessive-Compulsive Disorder), being away from home or close relatives (as in Separation Anxiety Disorder), gaining weight (as in Anorexia Nervosa), having multiple physical complaints (as in Somatization Disorder), or having a serious illness (as in Hypochondriasis), and the anxiety and worry do not occur exclusively during Post-Traumatic Stress Disorder.

E. The anxiety, worry, or physical symptoms cause clinically significant distress or impairment in social, occupational, or other important areas of functioning.

F. The disturbance is not due to the direct physiological effects of a substance (e.g., a drug of abuse, a medication) or a general medical condition (e.g., hyperthyroidism) and does not occur exclusively during a Mood Disorder, a Psychotic Disorder, or a Pervasive Developmental Disorder.

SOURCE: APA, DSM-IV, 1994.

GAD is more common among poorer people and those in lower educational groups, and the highest incidence is among young black Americans (Blazer, Hughes, George, Swartz, and Boyer, 1991). Those who live in poverty may live in unsafe neighborhoods and have chronic anxiety about violence or jobs or health care. Moreover, GAD has also been found to be more common in urbanized countries in which people must cope with the stresses of social change or in countries in which there is war or political oppression than in less urbanized countries and in countries at peace (Compton et al., 1991).

GAD patients are worriers, with daily life dominated by worrisome thoughts. Their muscles are unusually tense, and they have reduced flexibility in their cardiac system (Borkovec and Inz, 1990; Thayer, Friedman, and Borkovec, 1996). Family studies suggest that GAD is separable from panic disorder since relatives of patients with GAD have more GAD than panic disorder, and relatives of patients with panic disorder have more panic disorder than GAD (Kendler, Neale, Kessler, Heath, and Eaves, 1992; Kendler, Walters, Neale, Kessler, et al., 1995; Rapee, 1991; Weissman, 1990).

In this painting called *The North Beach Cafes,* the people look as if they may suffer from generalized anxiety disorder.

Etiology of GAD

Researchers have proposed both biological and psychological explanations for GAD. One biological explanation proposes that the same brain circuitry involved in fear and panic—involving the locus coeruleus, parts of the limbic system (particularly the amygdala), and the prefrontal cortex—is also involved in the experience of anxiety. Jeffrey Gray calls this circuit the behavioral inhibition system (Gray, 1982, 1985; see Chapter 4). This circuitry normally inhibits behavior during threat—stopping the person dead in his tracks, triggering fear and the appraisal of the next course of action. Unlike fear and panic, however, in GAD the activation of this circuit is chronic.

What might cause this chronic activation? Some investigators look to the neurophysiological phenomenon known as "kindling," in which groups of neurons that are activated repeatedly develop lower thresholds for subsequent activation—in effect, "breaking in" well-used pathways (Gorman, Kent, Sullivan, and Coplan, 2000). Such kindling phenomena are well-known in the amygdala, and they are used to explain the spread of epilepsy in the brain (Bear and Fedio, 1977). Conceivably, then, frequent experiences of fear make fear easier to experience—so much so that nearly any stimulus might become sufficient to trigger it. The result is a continual fear that would become generalized anxiety. And as in fear and panic, GABA is the main neurotransmitter implicated in GAD, with GABA deficiencies associated with the disorder (Redmond, 1985). We discuss the implications for medication below.

In contrast to these biological explanations, cognitive researchers have focused on the role of uncontrollability and unpredictability in GAD. People who have GAD may feel that they have no control over the important events of their lives and that bad things can happen to them at any time (Mineka and Zinbarg, 1996). Other researchers have examined the role of maladaptive thoughts. One such automatic thought in people with GAD might be "Any strange situation should be regarded as dangerous" (Beck and Emery, 1985). Recurrence of such thoughts may lead to worry and anxiety (Wells and Butler, 1997).

Treatment of GAD

Two kinds of treatment have been tested in controlled outcome studies of GAD: anti-anxiety drugs and cognitive-behavioral techniques (see Table 5–8). The drug evidence is consistent: anti-anxiety drugs, such as the benzodiazepines, produce clear reduction in anxiety symptoms for as long as the drug is taken.

The effectiveness of the benzodiazepines in reducing anxiety has led to a neural theory of GAD. The benzodiazepines enhance the release of GABA in the brain. As mentioned above, GABA is a widespread inhibitory neurotransmitter that, among other effects, inhibits anxiety. If GAD patients have too few GABA receptors, or otherwise process GABA inadequately, the anxiety-relieving effect of the benzodiazepines in GAD follows. Unfortunately, benzodiazepines can be addictive. They also have additive effects with alcohol, which means that the anxious patient who drinks while on benzodiazepines runs the risk of a fatal overdose on the combination. Moreover, long-term use of the benzodiazepines can cause memory loss and depression. For all these reasons, the benzodiazepines

TABLE 5–8

GENERALIZED ANXIETY DISORDER

Treatment

	Cognitive-Behavioral Therapy	Antidepressant and Anti-anxiety Drugs
Improvement	about 50% moderately improved	better than placebo
Relapse*	moderate relapse	high relapse rate
Side Effects	mild	moderate
Cost	inexpensive	inexpensive
Time Scale	weeks/months	days/weeks
Overall	**useful**	**marginal**

*Relapse after discontinuation of treatment.

SOURCE: Based on Barlow, Esler, and Vitali, 1998; Roy-Byrne and Cowley, 1998.

tend to be used mainly for acute anxiety, and they are restricted to patients with no alcohol problems.

How do physicians treat chronic anxiety? Several classes of medications have proven nearly as effective as the benzodiazepines, but without their liabilities. Now under investigation is the drug abecarnil, which also increases the availability of GABA but may have fewer harmful side effects (Ballenger et al., 1991; Lydiard, Ballenger, and Rickels, 1997; Rickels, DeMartinis, and Aufdembrinke, 2000). Other anti-anxiety drugs are already in wide use. The actions of these drugs do not directly involve GABA, and so they call into question the comprehensiveness of the GABA-based theory of anxiety. The most widely used non-benzodiazepine anti-anxiety drug is buspirone (Buspar), which is non-addictive, has no effect on GABA, and seems to operate on dopamine, norepinephrine, and serotonin systems (Gobert, Rivet, Cistarelli, Melon, and Millan, 1999). Additionally, antidepressant medications such as imipramine (Tofranil), and especially the SSRI's (such as Prozac), exibit strong anxiety-reducing effects in the laboratory (Zhang et al., 2000) and can be quite effective in patients who have chronic anxiety (Enkelmann, 1991; Michelson et al., 1999; Roy-Byrne and Cowley, 1998; Thompson, 1996).

Cognitive and behavioral techniques have also been tried on those with GAD, and there are three well-done outcome studies on their effectiveness. In one, fifty-seven patients with GAD were randomly assigned to either cognitive-behavioral therapy (CBT), behavioral therapy alone, or wait-list control. Treatment lasted from four to twelve sessions, and follow-up was continued for eighteen months. Cognitive-behavioral treatment fared best (Butler, Fennell, Robson, and Gelder, 1991). The second study compared cognitive-behavioral treatment to an anti-anxiety drug (diazepam) in 101 GAD patients. A six-month follow-up showed clear superiority for CBT, with the drug no more effective than a placebo (Power, Simpson, Swanson, and Wallace, 1990). The third study found both CBT and relaxation superior to nondirective therapy, and emphasized imagery as an active ingredient (Borkovec and Costello, 1993; see also Durham et al., 1994; Peasley-Miklus and Vrana, 2000; Silverman et al., 1999). Overall, anti-anxiety and antidepressant drugs produce temporary relief from GAD until the drug is discontinued, while cognitive and behavioral techniques produce more lasting gains.

Perhaps the most important development about anxiety concerns prevention rather than treatment. A group of Australian psychologists devised an early intervention program for anxious children aged seven to fourteen. One hundred and twenty-eight children were randomly assigned to a treatment or a no treatment control group. The treatment consisted of cognitive-behavioral skills and practicing graduated exposure to fear-provoking situations. Six months later, the treated group showed sustained gains (Dadds, Spence, Holland, Barrett, and Laurens, 1997; Dadds et al., 1999). This is cause to hope that school-based prevention programs may markedly reduce future cases of severe anxiety disorders.

Obsessive-Compulsive Disorder

All of us at least occasionally have distasteful and unacceptable thoughts. Many people at one time or another have had the following thoughts: "Might I become violent to someone I love?" "Am I absolutely sure that I've locked all the doors and windows?" "Have I left the gas in the stove on?" "Is my essay absolutely perfect?" Most of us pay little attention to these thoughts when they occur; if we do, we soon dismiss them. Such is not the case in individuals with *obsessive-compulsive disorder (OCD).*

My favorite description of OCD is sane people doing insane stuff. With me, it was erasing. That's right. Erasing. It started when I started college. You know, college is supposed to be, like, the greatest time of your life? For me, it was the worst. My usual perfectionism just got totally out of control when it came to writing papers and essays. Good was not good enough for me. I'd erase sentences over and over until I'd erase a hole in the paper, and have to start all over again. The act of erasing became a compulsion I had no control over. I'd no sooner start to write something than I'd start erasing it. I'd try so hard to stop. But I couldn't.

My friends thought this was hilarious at first. But then they got worried. So did my girlfriend. She knew about OCD because someone in her family has it. She wanted me to go to a doctor for help. I told her any doctor would think I was crazy if I showed up with a story about not being able to stop erasing. She said I was wrong, that they heard this kind of stuff all the time, that now, doctors treat behavior like mine all the time. "Oh, right," I said, "like there are millions of people out there who can't stop erasing!" She looked at me, and you know what she said? She said, "Get a new attitude or get a new girlfriend." (Hyman and Pedrick, 1999)

Obsessive-compulsive disorder consists of the two components from which we derive its name: obsessions and compulsions. **Obsessions** are repetitive thoughts, images, or impulses that invade consciousness, are often abhorrent, and are very difficult to dismiss or control. These thoughts are not mere excessive worries about real-life problems. The person with an obsession recognizes that the thoughts are products of his mind rather than imposed from outside. He is also aware that his obsessions are excessive and unreasonable and inappropriate, and he attempts to suppress or neutralize them with another thought or action as in the case above.

Compulsions are the responses to obsessive thoughts. They consist of rigid rituals (such as hand washing or checking or erasing) or mental acts (such as counting or praying or silently repeating words) that the person feels driven to perform in response to the obsession or according to rigid rules. The compulsions are aimed at preventing or reducing distress or averting some dreaded event or situation; these actions, however, are not connected in a realistic way with what they are designed to prevent, and they are clearly excessive. The student above, for example, reacts to his thoughts of failure and imperfection by compulsively erasing his work.

What distinguishes obsessions of clinical proportions from more harmless recurring thoughts? There are three hallmarks: (1) obsessions are distressing and unwelcome and intrude on consciousness; a person with a clinical obsession complains, "The thought that I might strangle my child keeps returning and prevents me from concentrating on my work," whereas mere recurring thoughts do not interfere with work; (2) obsessions arise from within, not from an external situation; and (3) obsessions are very difficult to

DSM-IV Criteria

Obsessive-Compulsive Disorder

A. Either obsessions or compulsions:

Obsessions as defined by (1), (2), (3), and (4): (1) recurrent and persistent thoughts, impulses, or images that are experienced, at some time during the disturbance, as intrusive and inappropriate and that cause marked anxiety or distress; (2) the thoughts, impulses, or images are not simply excessive worries about real-life problems; (3) the person attempts to ignore or suppress such thoughts, impulses, or images, or to neutralize them with some other thought or action; (4) the person recognizes that the obsessional thoughts, impulses, or images are a product of his or her own mind (not imposed from without as in thought insertion).

Compulsions as defined by (1) and (2): (1) repetitive behaviors (e.g., hand washing, ordering, checking) or mental acts (e.g., praying, counting, repeating words silently) that the person feels driven to perform in response to an obsession, or according to rules that must be applied rigidly; (2) the behaviors or mental acts are aimed at preventing or reducing distress or preventing some dreaded event or situation; however, these behaviors or mental acts either are not connected in a realistic way with what they are designed to neutralize or prevent or are clearly excessive.

B. At some point during the course of the disorder, the person has recognized that the obsessions or compulsions are excessive or unreasonable. (*Note:* This does not apply to children.)

C. The obsessions or compulsions cause marked distress, are time consuming (take more than 1 hour a day), or significantly interfere with the person's normal routine, occupational (or academic) functioning, or usual social activities or relationships.

D. If another Axis I disorder is present, the content of the obsessions or compulsions is not restricted to it (e.g., preoccupation with food in the presence of an Eating Disorder; hair pulling in the presence of Trichotillomania; concern with appearance in the presence of Body Dysmorphic Disorder; preoccupation with drugs in the presence of a Substance Use Disorder; preoccupation with having a serious illness in the presence of Hypochondriasis; preoccupation with sexual urges or fantasies in the presence of a Paraphilia; or guilty ruminations [repeated thoughts] in the presence of Major Depressive Disorder).

E. The disturbance is not due to the direct physiological effects of a substance (e.g., a drug of abuse, a medication) or a general medical condition.

SOURCE: APA, DSM-IV, 1994.

Drawing by W. Miller, © 1982
The New Yorker Magazine, Inc.

control. Someone with merely recurring thoughts can readily distract himself and think of something else; someone with a clinical obsession, in contrast, complains, "I can't help myself—I keep saying the numbers over and over again."

Obsession, Anxiety, and Depression

What motivates a person with obsessive-compulsive disorder to perform such strange actions as flushing a toilet in multiples of three? How does he feel when he has obsessive thoughts and performs his compulsive rituals? The thoughts (the obsessive component) are very disturbing. Typically, the individual suffers considerable internal distress. A mild emergency reaction is often present; he feels foreboding and dread. If the ritual is performed frequently and fast enough in response to the thoughts, he can reduce or even ward off the ensuing anxiety. The patient finds ways of dealing with the anxiety—by acting out his compulsions. But if his compulsive ritual is prevented, he will first feel tension similar to what we would feel if someone prevented us from answering a ringing telephone. If the barrier persists, intense distress will sweep over the patient. Here, of course, the anxiety will be felt. At this point, the individual can only relieve his distress by carrying out the compulsion, thereby neutralizing the anxiety evoked by the obsessive thoughts and images. The case below illustrates this:

A middle-aged woman complained of an obsession concerning colors and heat. "The main problem is colors. I cannot look at any of the colors that are in the fire, red, orange or pink."

She believed the colors blue, green, brown, white, and gray were neutral, and she used these colors to "neutralize" the fiery colors. "If I happen to see a fire color, I've got to immediately look at some other color to cancel it out. I've got to look at a tree or flowers out on the grounds, something brown or white, to neutralize it." She used to walk around with a small piece of green carpet in order to neutralize the effects of any orange colors she might happen upon and see or imagine.

She described the traumatic feelings that images of colored stimuli (or hot stimuli) evoked:

It starts in my mind, and when I look at the color, I start to tremble and I go hot all over, just as though I'm on fire. I cannot stand up; I've got to sit down or else I'll fall. I feel sick, and all I can say is that it is a traumatic feeling, that's the only word I can think of to describe it. If it is the last color I look at before I get into bed, I just won't sleep all night. . . .

I try to fight it, and get into bed and tell myself it is ridiculous. I know it can't hurt me physically, although it does harm me mentally. I lie there and this hot feeling comes over me, and I start to tremble. If that happens, I have to get up, put all my clothes on again and start once more, as though I am getting into bed. Sometimes I have to do this four or five times before finally getting to sleep. (Rachman and Hodgson, 1980)

Anxiety is not the only negative affect associated with obsessions. Depression bears an intimate relationship as well. Obsessions and clinical depression appear frequently in the same person; as such, they are comorbid. In fact, as many as 66 to 67 percent of those with OCD may experience major depression at some time in their life (Edelmann, 1992, Gibbs, 1996), and at any time, from 6 to 35 percent of depressed patients may have obsessions as well (Beech and Vaughan, 1979; Fava et al., 2000; Ricciardi, 1995). The symptoms wax and wane unpredictably over time, but stress exacerbates them. During periods of depression, the incidence of obsessions triples over the rate before and after the depression (Videbech, 1975). Not only do depressed patients tend to develop obsessions, but patients with OCD are prone to develop depression as well (Teasdale and Rezin, 1978; Wilner, Reich, Robins, Fishman, and

Van Doren, 1976). In fact, between 35 and 50 percent of patients with OCD meet criteria for concurrent depression (Kruger, Cooke, Hasey, Jorna, and Persad, 1995; Perugi et al., 1997).

Vulnerability to Obsessive-Compulsive Disorder

Obsessive-compulsive disorders are not uncommon. Between 2 and 3 percent of adults are diagnosed as having obsessive-compulsive disorder. Overall, women are probably twice as vulnerable as men, but males have more compulsive urges than females, while females have more obsessions (Karno, Golding, Sorenson, and Burnam, 1988; Mancini, Gragnani, Orazi, and Pietrangeli, 1999). The problem may be partially heritable, since identical twins show double the concordance of fraternal twins for OCD. Furthermore, relatives of patients with OCD often do not have obsessive-compulsive disorders themselves, but they do suffer from other anxiety disorders as well as subclinical (not full-blown) obsessions and compulsions (Billett, Richter, and Kennedy, 1998; Black, Noyes, Goldstein, and Blum, 1992). Occasionally the disorder may arise following a traumatic experience, such as rape, leading to a filth and cleaning obsession (Da Silva and Marks, 1999). The disorder usually comes on gradually, beginning in childhood and early adolescence in boys, but in early adulthood in women. Males are more likely to be "checkers," and females to be "cleaners." Our patient with the color obsession describes the typically vague and gradual onset of her disorder:

> It is hard to say exactly when the obsession started. It was gradual. My obsession about colors must have been coming on for a couple of years very, very gradually. I only noticed it fully during the past twelve years when it got worse and worse. I can't look at certain colors, can't bathe, can't do any cooking, have to repeat many activities over and over again. . . .
>
> I think it all began some years ago when I had a sort of nervous breakdown. At the onset, I went very hot; it seemed to happen overnight somehow. I was in bed, and woke up feeling very hot. It was connected with an obsession that I had about my ailing mother at the time. I feared for her safety, and when I got a horrible thought that she might have an accident or a serious illness, this horrible hot feeling came over me. (Rachman and Hodgson, 1980)

Is there a specific type of personality that is vulnerable to an obsessive-compulsive disorder? Here we should make an important distinction between OCD and obsessive-compulsive personality. The popular notion is that a person with an obsessive-compulsive personality is methodical and leads a very well-ordered life. He is always on time. He is meticulous in how he dresses and what he says. He pays exasperatingly close attention to detail, and he strongly dislikes dirt. He may have a distinct cognitive style, showing intellectual rigidity and focusing on details. He is deliberate in thought and action, and often highly moralistic. He is preoccupied with rules, lists, order, organization, or schedules, to the point where he cannot see the forest through the trees. His perfectionism interferes with completing a task. He works so devotedly that he has no leisure and few friends. He is not a warm individual. In addition, he is reluctant to delegate tasks or to work with others (Rheaume et al., 2000; Sandler and Hazari, 1960; Shapiro, 1965).

The crucial difference between having an obsessive-compulsive personality and having an obsessive-compulsive disorder has to do with how much the person likes having the symptoms. A person with an obsessive-compulsive personality views his meticulousness and love of detail with pride and self-esteem. For an individual with an obsessive-compulsive disorder, however, these characteristics are abhorrent, unwanted, and tormenting. They are "ego-alien."

Melvin Udall, the character played by Jack Nicholson, shows his disgust with his neighbor's dog in the 1997 film *As Good As It Gets*. The character suffers from obsessive-compulsive disorder, as shown by the fact that he takes his own utensils to restaurants, goes to great lengths not to step on cracks in the sidewalk, and wears gloves when he goes outside.

Testing for OCD

Among the tools that are useful to clinicians are questionnaires, or inventories, that reliably aid in diagnosis. S. J. Rachman and Ray Hodgson of the Maudsley Hospital in London developed a questionnaire that helps determine who might have OCD. The questionnaire isolates three major components of obsessive-compulsive disorders: cleaning, checking, and doubting. The answers are those typically given by OCD patients.

SAMPLE QUESTIONS FROM THE MAUDSLEY OBSESSIVE-COMPULSIVE INVENTORY

Components of Obsessive-Compulsive Disorder	*Disorder Answer*
Cleaning	
1. I am not excessively concerned about cleanliness.	False
2. I avoid using public telephones because of possible contamination.	True
3. I can use well-kept toilets without any hesitation.	False
4. I take a rather long time to complete my washing in the morning.	True
Checking	
1. I frequently have to check things (gas or water taps, doors) more than once.	True
2. I do not check letters over and over again before mailing them.	False
3. I frequently get nasty thoughts and have difficulty getting rid of them.	True
Doubting-Conscience	
1. I have a very strict conscience.	True
2. I usually have serious doubts about the simple everyday things I do.	True
3. Neither of my parents was very strict during my childhood.	False

SOURCE: Rachman and Hodgson, 1980.

When one actually looks at the personality of individuals with obsessive-compulsive disorders, little evidence emerges showing that they also have an obsessive-compulsive personality. A majority of patients with OCD have no history of an obsessive-compulsive personality, and few people with an obsessive-compulsive personality develop OCD. What they do have are excessive concerns about cleanliness, checking, and conscience (see Box 5–3). They may also have an exaggerated sense of responsibility, believing that they are pivotal in bringing about or preventing disasters (Salkovskis, 1985).

Theories of Obsessive-Compulsive Disorder

What causes an obsessive-compulsive disorder? There are three major theoretical views: psychodynamic, cognitive-behavioral, and neuroscience (see Table 5–9). Their strengths complement each other well and yield an integrated picture of how OCD is caused. The psychodynamic view wrestles with the question of the genesis of the obsession—who gets it and why it takes a particular form—but it is not illuminating about why it persists for years once it has started. The cognitive-behavioral view explains its persistence, but leaves us in the dark as to who gets it and what its content will be. The neuroscience view points to the brain structures underlying OCD.

PSYCHODYNAMIC THEORY

The questions "Who will get an obsessive-compulsive disorder?" and "What form will it take?" lie at the heart of the psychodynamic view of obsessive thoughts. According to this view, an obsessive thought is seen as a defense against the anxiety produced by an even more unwelcome and unconscious thought (Lang, 1997; Meares, 1994). This defensive process involves displacement and substitution (see Chapter 3). What happens is that an unconscious, dangerous thought, such as "my mother might die of a fever" in the previously mentioned case of the woman with color and heat obsession, threatens to break into the

TABLE 5–9

VIEWS OF OBSESSIVE-COMPULSIVE DISORDER

Theoretical View	Who Develops OCD?	What Happens?	How Is It Sustained?	How Is It Cured?
Psychodynamic view	People with specific unconscious conflicts (e.g., thoughts of injuring or murdering one's child or mother.	Obsessive thought begins as a defense against a more unacceptable thought.	Obsession and accompanying compulsion are maintained because they successfully defend against anxiety.	Unconscious conflict is recognized and worked through.
Cognitive-behavioral view	People who cannot distract themselves easily from troubling thoughts, often combined with depression	Obsessive thoughts (present in normals also) become frequent and persistent, while depression simultaneously weakens ability to distract oneself.	Patient discovers a ritual that temporarily relieves anxiety, which is then reinforced through repetition.	Response blocking of compulsion extinguishes obsession.
Neuroscience view	People with overactive cortical-striatal-thalamic circuit	Repetitive behavior may be poorly inhibited; anxiety may be inadequately dampened; filtering of irrelevant information may be inadequate.	Obsessive thoughts and compulsive behaviors are directed toward objects and situations evolution has prepared us to see as threatening.	Drugs (e.g., clomipramine) down-regulate overactive cortical-striatal-thalamic circuit

individual's consciousness. This arouses anxiety. To defend against this anxiety, the individual unconsciously displaces this anxiety from the original terrifying thought onto a less unwelcome substitute, like hot and fiery colors. The defense has a powerful internal logic, and the thoughts that are substituting for the underlying thought are not arbitrary. Fiery and hot colors symbolize the fever that her ailing mother might die of.

Psychodynamic theory explains who will develop an obsession in response to underlying conflict-arousing anxiety, and what content the obsession will take on to symbolize the underlying conflict. The following case of obsession about infanticide illustrates why the particular individual would be susceptible to the particular form of obsession she developed:

A thirty-two-year-old mother of two had obsessional thoughts of injuring and murdering her children and more infrequently, her husband. These thoughts were almost as threatening and as guilt-provoking as the very act itself. Therapy uncovered even more threatening impulses from her childhood, which had been displaced onto her children. She had been the eldest of three siblings and while very young had been given undue responsibility for their care. She felt deprived

of affection from her parents and was greatly resentful of her younger sister and brother. She entertained murderous fantasies about them, which were accompanied by tremendous guilt and anxiety. As a result, these fantasies had been completely driven from consciousness. When she became an adult, her children symbolically stood for her siblings, whose destruction would make her the sole object of parental love and relieve her of her childhood burden. Her own mother's occasional visits triggered the obsessions. She was particularly susceptible because she had unresolved and anxiety-provoking resentment against her own parents and siblings. Her obsession had the content of death as it symbolized the death of her siblings, which would have solved her childhood problem. (Adapted from Laughlin, 1967, pp. 324–26)

Thus, the psychodynamic view of obsessions claims that powerful, abhorrent wishes and conflicts that have been repressed and threaten to break into consciousness put an individual at risk for obsessions, and that adopting the defense of displacement and substitution provides the immediate mechanism for relief (Wegner and Zanakos, 1994). In addition, the particular content of the obsessions these individuals acquire will be a symbol for the underlying conflict.

COGNITIVE-BEHAVIORAL THEORY

S. J. Rachman and Ray Hodgson have formulated the most comprehensive cognitive-behavioral theory of obsessions (Rachman and Hodgson, 1980; Rachman and Shafran, 1998). The theory begins with the assumption that we all experience obsessional thoughts occasionally. The thought "Step on a crack and you'll break your mother's back" followed by an avoidance of sidewalk cracks is a common obsessive-compulsive ritual in children. For others, memories of radio jingles often intrude, unbidden, into consciousness. But most of us outgrow the sidewalk ritual, and we easily are able to distract ourselves from or habituate to the radio jingles. We can also dismiss the more awful thoughts that occasionally run through our heads. Individuals with obsessive-compulsive disorders, however, differ from the rest of us in that they are unable to habituate, dismiss, and distract themselves from such intrusive thoughts.

The more anxiety provoking and depressing the content of the obsession, the more difficult it is for anyone—someone with or without OCD—to dismiss the thought or distract himself from it. When normal individuals are shown a brief but stressful film, most of them have intrusive and repetitive thoughts. For example, a stressful film depicting a gruesome woodshop accident brought about anxiety and repetitive thoughts about the accident. The more emotionally upset an individual was made by the film, the more intrusive and repetitive were the thoughts (Horowitz, 1975). Furthermore, anxious

individuals find threatening words more intrusive than do normal controls (MacLeod and McLaughlin, 1995; Matthews and MacLeod, 1986; Matthews, Mogg, Kentish, and Eysenck, 1995). This supports two of the assumptions of the cognitive-behavioral view of obsession: (1) we all have unwanted and repetitive thoughts; and (2) the more stressed we are, the more frequent and intense are these thoughts.

Recall now the link between depression and obsession. To the extent that an individual is depressed beforehand, obsessive thoughts will be more disturbing and therefore more difficult to dismiss. In addition, as we will see in Chapter 7, depressed individuals display more helplessness (Seligman, 1975). This means that they are less able to initiate voluntary responses to relieve their own distress. The act of distracting oneself is a voluntary cognitive response, and like other such responses, it will be weakened by depression. A background of depression is therefore fertile soil for an obsessive-compulsive disorder.

Here, then, is the chain of events that distinguishes a person with obsessive-compulsive disorder from someone who does not have OCD, according to the cognitive-behavioral view. For someone without OCD, some initiating event, either internal or external, leads to a disturbing image or thought. He may find this thought unacceptable but will not be made anxious by it. If he is not in a state of depression, he will easily dismiss the thought or distract himself from it. In contrast, the person with obsessive-compulsive disorder, often believing that he is responsible for preventing a disaster, will be made anxious by the thought, and the anxiety and depression will reduce his ability to dismiss it. The thought will persist, and the person's inability to turn the thought off will lead to further anxiety, helplessness, and depression, which will increase his susceptibility to the intrusive thought (Salkovskis, Forrester, and Richards, 1998; Salkovskis, 1999).

The cognitive-behavioral view also attempts to explain compulsive rituals. The temporary relief from anxiety that they bring reinforces these rituals. Since the person with obsessive-compulsive disorder cannot remove the thoughts by the distraction and dismissal techniques that the rest of us readily use, he resorts to other tactics. He attempts to neutralize the bad thought, often by substituting a "good" action. The person with the fiery color obsession neutralized the color orange by looking at a swatch of green carpet. Individuals who are obsessively afraid that

S. J. Rachman has formulated a comprehensive cognitive-behavioral theory of obsessions.

their doors are not locked check them dozens of times a night. These compulsive rituals produce temporary relief, but they also produce a stronger tendency to check, wash, or seek reassurance, since they are followed by anxiety reduction and are therefore strengthened or reinforced. But the rituals can only be cosmetic; that is, the relief they provide is only temporary. The obsessions are left intact, and they return with increased frequency and intensity. Each time a thought recurs, the ritual must be performed in order to produce any relief.

The strength of the cognitive-behavioral view is that it provides an account of why obsessions and compulsions, once started, might be maintained. The strength of the psychoanalytic view is that it tries to explain both the content of the obsessions and who is vulnerable. The next view we turn to, the neuroscience view, can claim to be the most basic of the three: it looks for the brain structures underlying OCD.

THE NEUROSCIENCE VIEW

Neuroscience researchers view OCD as a brain disease. There are four lines of evidence for this view: (1) neurological signs, (2) brain scan abnormalities, (3) the primitive content of obsessions and compulsions, and (4) an effective drug (which we will discuss in more detail in the treatment section).

Neurological Signs　OCD has been known to develop right after a brain trauma. On neurological examination, many OCD patients show a number of abnormalities: poor fine motor coordination, more involuntary jerks, and poor visual-motor performance. The more pronounced such "soft signs" are, the more severe the obsessions (Hollander et al., 1990; Tien et al., 1992). This is consistent with the presence of an underlying, but subtle, neurological disorder.

> Jacob, eight years old, was playing football in the backyard. He collapsed and went into a coma with a brain hemorrhage. When he came out of brain surgery, which went very well, he was now plagued by numbers. He had to touch everything in 7's. He swallowed in 7's and asked 7 times for everything. (Rapoport, 1990)

OCD is also comorbid with neurological disorders such as epilepsy. After the great sleeping sickness

epidemic (a viral brain infection in Europe from 1916 to 1918), there was an apparent rise in the number of OCD patients (Rapoport, 1990). Tourette's syndrome is a compulsive-like disorder of motor tics and uncontrollable verbal outbursts, apparently of neurological origin. There is a high concordance between OCD and Tourette's syndrome in identical twins, and many patients who have Tourette's syndrome also have OCD (Allen, Leonard, and Swedo, 1995; George et al., 1993; Leonard et al., 1992; Robertson, Trimble, and Lees, 1988; Swedo and Kiessling, 1994).

Brain Scan Abnormalities　The second line of neuroscience evidence comes from brain scan studies of patients with OCD. Several areas of the brain show high activity in patients with OCD: the caudate nucleus in the basal ganglia, the orbital region of the frontal cortex, and the thalamus. Together, they constitute a "cortical-striatal-thalamic" circuit (Cottraux and Gerard, 1998; Gehring, Himle, and Nisenson, 2000; Rosenberg and Keshavan, 1998; Saxena, Brody, Schwartz, and Baxter, 1998; see Figure 5–5). These areas are related to filtering out of irrelevant information and perseveration (or repetition) of behavior. In fact, inability to turn off distracting thoughts and perseveration of behavior seem like central problems in obsessions and compulsions. When these patients are treated successfully with drugs, these brain areas decrease their activity.

Unfortunately, different brain scan studies conflict on exactly which brain areas increase and decrease in

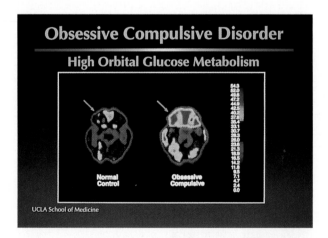

These PET scans of *(left)* a normal control and *(right)* a person with obsessive-compulsive disorder show how brain function changes in people with OCD. Yellow and red indicate greater metabolic activity. In the person with OCD, we can see greater activity in the basal ganglia, the frontal cortex, and the thalamus than in the normal control.

Figure 5—5

THE CORTICAL-STRIATAL-THALAMIC CIRCUIT AND OCD

Several areas of the brain are implicated in patients with obsessive-compulsive disorder. The caudate nucleus, the frontal cortex, and the cingulate cortex (part of the striatum) together constitutes the "cortical-striatal-thalamic circuit" (shown in red). These areas are related to filtering out irrelevant information and disengaging attention. Malfunction of the circuit may lead to the symptoms of OCD whereby the patient is unable to filter out irrelevant information and unable to disengage attention.

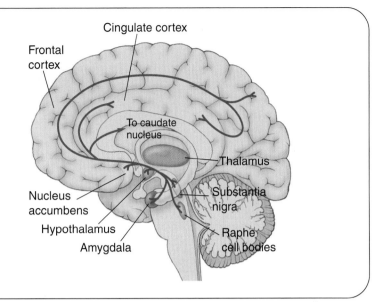

activity (Baxter et al., 1992; Berthier, Kulisevsky, Gironell, and Heras, 1996; Insel, 1992; Robinson et al., 1995; Rubin et al., 1992; Swedo et al., 1992). The next decade promises exciting research in this field, with the possibility of tracking down how the hyperactive cortical-striatal-thalamic circuit actually works and how drugs and behavior therapy affect this circuit. Consistent with this hypothesis is the finding from a study in which surgical interruption of this circuit produced substantial reduction in OCD symptoms in about one-third of thirty-three patients (Jenike et al., 1991).

Primitive Content The third line of evidence for a biological view concerns the specific content of OCD. The content of obsessions and compulsions is not arbitrary. Like the content of phobias, consisting mostly of objects that were once dangerous to the human species, the content of obsessions and of compulsive rituals is also narrow and selective. The vast majority of patients with OCD are obsessed with germs or with violence, and they wash or they check in response. Why such a specific focus? Why not obsessions about particular shapes, like triangles, or about socializing only with people of the same height? Why no compulsions about push-ups, or about hand clapping, or about crossword puzzles? Why germs and violence? Why washing and checking?

Across evolution, washing and checking have been very important. The grooming and physical security of oneself and one's children are central pri-

mate concerns. Perhaps the brain areas that kept our ancestors grooming and checking are the very areas gone awry in OCD. These same areas may be those involved with the mediation of excretion, sexuality, and violence. Perhaps the recurrent thoughts and the rituals in OCD are deep vestiges of primate habits run amok (Marks and Tobena, 1990; Rapoport, 1990; Swedo et al., 1992).

Drug Therapy Useful drug therapy to alleviate serotonin dysfunction is the final line of evidence for the biological theory. The drug Anafranil (clomipramine), a serotonin reuptake inhibitor (SRI), and the SSRI's (selective serotonin reuptake inhibitors)—Prozac (fluoxetine) and Luvox (fluvoxamine)—have been found to alleviate the symptoms of obsessions and compulsions in many patients with OCD. These drugs affect the serotonergic systems, which seem to be dysfunctional in those with OCD (Dolberg, Iancu, Sasson, and Zohar, 1996; Murphy et al., 1996). While the exact mechanism is still unknown, researchers have proposed that these drugs are causing a down-regulation of serotonin receptors, which decreases serotonin activity, and partially explains symptom remission (Gross, Sasson, Chopra, and Zohar, 1998).

Treatment of OCD

Until the 1990s, the prognosis for those with obsessive-compulsive disorders, either treated or untreated, was not particularly promising. But at present, both behavior therapy and drug therapy are being used to produce considerable relief for those with OCD.

BEHAVIOR THERAPY

Behavior therapies for obsessive-compulsive disorder result in considerable relief, but not in complete cures. A combination of three basic techniques of behavior therapy—response prevention, exposure, and modeling—is used in treating obsessive-compulsive disorder (Franklin and Foa, 1998; Griest, 1994; Marks and Rachman, 1978). These three procedures all encourage and persuade but do not force the patient to endure disturbing situations. For example, these techniques were used to treat a patient who had obsessive thoughts that he might be contaminated with germs and who, as a result, spent four hours a day washing himself. In therapy, he first watched the therapist contaminate himself with dirt (modeling). The therapist urged him to rub dirt and dust all over himself (exposure) and endure it without washing it off (response prevention). After a dozen sessions of covering himself with dirt and just sitting there without washing it off, the patient's thoughts of contamination diminished and the washing rituals no longer occurred in his daily life.

In this case, exposing the patient to filth and preventing him from washing cured the compulsion. In addition to such case histories, there have been at least sixteen controlled studies of exposure, response prevention, and modeling in patients with OCD (Abramowitz, 1998; Franklin and Foa, 1998; Marks and Rachman, 1978; Rachman, Hodgson, and Marks, 1971; Salzman and Thaler, 1981). These studies indicated marked improvement in about two-thirds of the patients. Follow-up for as long as six years indicates that improvement is maintained in all but about 10 percent of respondents (Emmelkamp, Hoekstra, and Visser, 1985; Foa and Kôzak, 1993; O'Sullivan et al., 1991). Moreover, in a summary of sixteen studies involving more than 300 patients with OCD who were given behavior therapy, an average of 83 percent were judged "improved" by the end of therapy, and 76 percent were still improved over an average of two and one half years of follow-up. The behavior therapies are specific in their effects: obsessive thoughts, compulsive rituals, and anxiety all decrease, but depression, sexual adjustment, and family harmony are not clearly helped.

The American behavior therapist Edna Foa has pioneered the use of exposure therapy for post-traumatic stress disorder following rape and contributed to the evaluation of behavior therapy for obsessive-compulsive disorder.

These are not cures, however, since very few patients lose all their symptoms completely or are functioning well in all areas of life at follow-up. In addition, roughly 20 to 30 percent fail to improve at all (Beech and Vaughan, 1979; Dominguez and Mestre, 1994; Hackmann and McLean, 1975; Meyer, 1966; Rabavilos, Boulougouris, and Stefanis, 1976; Rachman et al., 1979).

Why do exposure, response prevention, and modeling usually work, and what are their critical elements? Reconsider the man who washed himself for four hours a day. He had the obsession that some terrible illness would strike him if he did not wash. When he was persuaded to endure being dirty without washing, his obsessive thoughts of illness waned, and his compulsive rituals of washing vanished. What had he learned during exposure and response prevention? By covering himself with dirt and then not washing, his fear that dirt would lead to illness extinguished. The conditioned stimulus (CS) was the dirt, and the anticipated unconditioned stimulus (US) was illness. He received stark exposure to being dirty without getting sick, and Pavlovian extinction occurred. In addition, he learned that illness did not happen even though he did not wash. This was an instrumental extinction procedure for the compulsive ritual of washing. So, exposure and response prevention may work for two reasons: (1) by showing the patient that the dreaded event does not occur in the feared situation (Pavlovian extinction), and (2) by showing the patient that no dreaded event occurs even though the compulsive ritual is not performed (instrumental extinction of the compulsion).

TABLE 5–10

Treatment

OBSESSIVE-COMPULSIVE DISORDER

	Behavior Therapy	*Drugs*[*]
Improvement	50–60% moderate-marked improvement	40–60% moderate-marked improvement
Relapse[†]	10–20% relapse	marked relapse
Side Effects	none	moderate
Cost	inexpensive	inexpensive
Time Scale	weeks/months	weeks
Overall	**good**	**useful**

[*]Drug treatment includes the SRI clomipramine (Anafranil) and the SSRI's—fluoxetine (Prozac), fluvoxamine (Luvox), and sertraline (Zoloft).

[†]Relapse after discontinuation of treatment.

SOURCE: Based on Seligman 1994, p. 93; revised with Franklin and Foa, 1998; Pato, 1999; Rauch and Jenike, 1998.

DRUG THERAPY

There is a medication that works markedly better on OCD than do placebos. Clomipramine (trade name: Anafranil) has been used with thousands of people who suffer from OCD in more than a dozen controlled studies. Clomipramine is a potent antidepressant drug, a serotonin reuptake inhibitor (SRI). When OCD sufferers take clomipramine, obsessions wane and compulsions can be more easily resisted (Rauch and Jenike, 1998, for a review; see also Clomipramine Collaborative Study Group, 1991; Griest et al., 1995; Jefferson and Griest, 1996; Leonard et al., 1991, 1993). An average of 50 to 60 percent of patients with OCD improve when treated with clomipramine (Foa and Kozak, 1993). The SSRI's, including fluoxetine (Prozac), fluvoxamine (Luvox), sertraline (Zoloft), and paroxetine (Paxil), all work better than placebo on OCD as well.

Clomipramine, however, is not a perfect drug. A large number of patients (almost half) do not get better, or they will not take it because of its side effects, which include drowsiness, constipation, and loss of sexual interest. Those who benefit are rarely cured; their symptoms are dampened, but traces of the obsessive thoughts usually remain, and the temptation to ritualize is still present. When those who do benefit stop taking the drug, many—perhaps most—of them relapse completely. But clomipramine is decidedly better than nothing (Leonard, 1997; Pato, Zohar-Kadouch, Zohar, and Murphy, 1988; Rauch and Jenike, 1998). The combination of behavior therapy and medication has not been clearly demonstrated to be superior to either alone, but many experts still advocate doing both at the same time (Franklin and Foa, 1998; Pato, 1999). See Table 5–10 for a comparison of behavior therapy and medications in the treatment of OCD.

Overall then the behavioral, psychoanalytic, and the neuroscience views of OCD complement one another nicely. The psychoanalytic view helps us to understand who gets OCD and who does not and why it takes the particular form it does with that individual. The behavioral view tells us why such maladaptive behavior is maintained and has generated three therapies that produce substantial relief for OCD sufferers. The neuroscience view gives us a schema of the brain circuits that are disrupted in OCD and is compatible with the drugs that produce symptom relief.

Everyday Anxiety

Let's say you do not fit the diagnostic criteria for phobia or PTSD or panic or agoraphobia or GAD or OCD. Does this mean that all is well in your emotional life? Hardly. Your everyday anxiety may be unacceptably high and debilitating. Box 5–4 allows you to assess its intensity. Everyday anxiety level is not a category to which psychologists have devoted a lot of attention. The vast bulk of work on emotion is about "disorders." One hope, however, comes from two recent prevention studies (Dadds, Spence, Holland, Barrett, and Laurens, 1997; Seligman, Schulman, DeRubeis and Hollon, 1999). In both of these

Assessment

Box 5—4

Assessing Anxiety

Is your life dominated by anxiety? Dr. Charles Spielberger, past president of the American Psychological Association, is also one of the world's foremost testers of emotion. He has developed well-validated scales for calibrating how severe anxiety and anger are. He divides these emotions into their "state" form ("How are you feeling right now?") and their "trait" form ("How do you generally feel?"). You can use the trait questions in his Self-Analysis Questionnaire below to evaluate whether your everyday anxiety is too high.

SELF-ANALYSIS QUESTIONNAIRE

Read each statement and then mark the appropriate number to indicate how you generally feel. There are no right or wrong answers. Do not spend too much time on any one statement but give the answer which seems to describe how you generally feel.

1. I am a steady person.

Almost Never	Sometimes	Often	Almost Always
4	3	2	(1)

2. I am satisfied with myself.

Almost Never	Sometimes	Often	Almost Always
4	3	(2)	1

3. I feel nervous and restless.

Almost Never	Sometimes	Often	Almost Always
1	(2)	3	4

4. I wish I could be as happy as others seem to be.

Almost Never	Sometimes	Often	Almost Always
1	(2)	3	4

5. I feel like a failure.

Almost Never	Sometimes	Often	Almost Always
1	(2)	3	4

6. I get in a state of tension and turmoil as I think over my recent concerns and interests.

Almost Never	Sometimes	Often	Almost Always
1	(2)	3	4

7. I feel secure.

Almost Never	Sometimes	Often	Almost Always
4	3	(2)	1

8. I have self-confidence.

Almost Never	Sometimes	Often	Almost Always
4	(3)	2	1

9. I feel inadequate.

Almost Never	Sometimes	Often	Almost Always
1	(2)	3	4

10. I worry too much over something that does not matter.

Almost Never	Sometimes	Often	Almost Always
1	2	3	4

Scoring. Simply add your numbers over the ten questions. Be careful to notice that some of the rows of numbers go up and some go down. The higher your total, the more the trait of anxiety dominates your life. Adult men and women have slightly different scores on average, with women being somewhat more anxious generally.

If you scored **10–11,** your anxiety level is in the lowest 10th percentile.

If you scored **13–14,** your anxiety level is in the lowest 25th percentile.

If you scored **16–17,** your anxiety level is about average.

If you scored **19–20,** your anxiety level is around the 75th percentile.

If you scored **22–24 and you are male,** your anxiety level is around the 90th percentile.

If you scored **24–26 and you are female,** your anxiety level is around the 90th percentile.

If you scored **25 and you are male,** your anxiety level is at the 95th percentile.

If you scored **27 and you are female,** your anxiety level is at the 95th percentile.

SOURCE: "Self-Analysis Questionnaire": developed by Charles Spielberger in collaboration with G. Jacobs, R. Crane, S. Russell, L. Westberry, L. Barker, E. Johnson, J. Knight, and E. Marks. We have selected the trait anxiety questions from the questionnaire, inverting some of the scoring of the negatively worded items for easy self-scoring.

studies, young people at risk for anxiety or depression were taught cognitive-behavioral anti-anxiety techniques before any disorder had developed. Participants learned to recognize and then dispute the catastrophic thoughts that automatically came to mind when they faced threatening situations. So, for example, an anxiety-prone individual might think, "No one at this party is going to pay any attention to me." She might then counter this thought with, "Wait. The last time I went to a party I met two people, both of whom later called and asked me out." Both anxiety symptoms and anxiety disorder were thereby prevented. These techniques and the results are discussed in Chapter 16.

TABLE 5–11

Treatment

EVERYDAY ANXIETY

	Meditation	*Relaxation*	*Tranquilizers*
Improvement	60–80% markedly improved	at least 50% moderately improved	60–80% markedly improved
Relapse*	10-20% relapse	moderate relapse	high relapse
Side Effects	none	none	moderate
Cost	inexpensive	inexpensive	inexpensive
Time Scale	weeks/months	weeks	minutes
Overall	**very good**	**useful**	**marginal**

*Relapse after discontinuation of treatment.
SOURCE: Based on Seligman, 1994, p. 58.

There is enough research, however, for us to recommend two techniques that quite reliably lower everyday anxiety levels (see Table 5–11). Both techniques are cumulative, rather than quick fixes. They require devoting twenty to forty minutes a day of your time for them to work.

The first is **progressive relaxation,** done once or twice a day (better) for at least ten minutes. In this technique, you tighten and then turn off each of the major muscle groups of your body until your muscles are wholly flaccid. Relaxation engages a response system that competes with anxious arousal (Öst, 1987).

The second technique is regular **meditation.** "Transcendental Meditation" (TM) is one useful, widely available version of this. Twice a day for twenty minutes, in a quiet setting, you close your eyes and repeat a "mantra" (a syllable whose "sonic properties are known") to yourself. Meditation works by blocking thoughts that produce anxiety. It complements relaxation, which blocks the motor components of anxiety but leaves the anxious thoughts untouched. Done regularly, most meditators enter a peaceful state of mind. Anxiety at other times of the day goes down, and hyperarousal to bad events is dampened. Done regularly, TM probably works better than relaxation alone (Butler, Fennell, Robson, and Gelder, 1991; Eppley, Abrams, and Shear, 1989; Kabat-Zinn et al., 1992).

We urge you to weigh your everyday anxiety. If it is mild and not irrational or paralyzing, live with it. Listen to its dictates, and change your outer life accordingly. If it is intense or irrational or paralyzing, act now to reduce it. Intense everyday anxiety is sometimes quite changeable. Meditation and pro-gressive relaxation practiced regularly may change it—and lastingly so.

Putting It All Together

Nowhere is progress in understanding psychopathology more apparent than in the anxiety disorders. The changes are striking. As late as the 1970s, the maladies we now call the "anxiety disorders" were all grouped with depression, the dissociative disorders, and sexual dysfunctions within an ill-defined category called "the neuroses," whose causes were believed to lie in the murky world of unconscious conflicts, defense mechanisms, and processes of symptom formation (American Psychiatric Association, 1980). Anxious people were seen as having a basic character defect that could only be remedied with long-term psychodynamic therapy, or merely suppressed with the tranquilizers of the day. Today, researchers have come to realize that anxiety as a symptom is a manifestation of a distinctive process whose aspects are not only psychological but also genetic, hormonal, and neurophysiological. Clinicians have now reached some consensus on what specific disorders should be called "anxiety disorders," defined the boundaries of each, and developed a system for diagnosing them reliably.

This new precision in classification and identification has had many implications. One lies in understanding the relationship between anxiety and depression. Since we now diagnose anxiety and depression separately, we are able to study systematically cases in which the two disorders co-occur and cases in which they do not. We can also examine through well-constructed studies whether members of families with high rates of depression have high rates of anxiety disorders as well, and whether anxiety tends to precede depression and vice versa (Fava et al., 2000).

The precision of the current diagnostic system has also clarified how the anxiety disorders relate to each other. For example, we now know that many but not all cases of agoraphobia begin as panic disorder (Langs et al., 2000), that 75 percent of people with OCD have another anxiety disorder simultaneously (Steketee, Eisen, Dyck, Warshaw, amd Rasmussen, 1999), and that most people with generalized anxiety disorder will go on to have another type of anxiety disorder in their lifetime (Hunt and Andrews, 1995).

Considerable progress has also been made in understanding the physiological bases of the various anxiety disorders. We now know that panic disorder involves norepinephrine and serotonin systems in the brain stem, the amygdala, and the frontal cortex. Generalized anxiety disorder is intimately related to GABA systems. OCD involves some kind of malfunction in the basal ganglia. Prolonged cortisol hypersecretion is integral to PTSD. These localization findings are increasing our knowledge of the brain and our potential for engineering better treatments.

Treatments for the anxiety disorders have already improved markedly. Whereas the treatments for the "anxiety neuroses" were formerly ill-defined, researchers have now verified that specific anxiety disorders require specific treatments. For example, obsessive-compulsive disorder responds especially well to the SSRI's and to exposure, specific phobias are very effectively treated using exposure and systematic desensitization, generalized anxiety disorder is best treated by anxiety-reducing medications or relaxation training, and PTSD often improves with exposure and group therapy. This specificity of treatments has also improved the odds of successful treatment. For example, before 1970, if you had a specific phobia, you were doomed to have it for the rest of your life. Today, your chances of getting marked relief are well above 70 percent. Obsessive-compulsive disorder was an agonizing, unremitting, and untreatable affliction, while today more than 65 percent of sufferers can function well with appropriate treatment.

Much remains to be learned. What is the nature of the genetic diathesis that connects depression, anxiety, and alcoholism? Do prenatal and infantile trauma predispose to anxiety disorders in adulthood, particularly PTSD (Ladd et al., 2000)? Why is panic disorder found so often in patients with inner ear disease (Simon, Pollack, Tuby, and Stern, 1998)? Does early infection by streptococcal bacteria lead to later OCD (Swedo et al., 1998)? For which disorders and which kinds of patients is psychotherapy superior to medication, and vice versa? These questions are at the frontier of anxiety research, which holds the promise of even more progress in understanding and treating anxiety and its disorders.

Summary

1. Phobias and post-traumatic stress disorder are both disorders in which fear is felt and in which specific objects or events set them off. Panic disorder, agoraphobia, and generalized anxiety disorder are disorders in which the individual feels very anxious, although the danger anticipated is less specific. Obsessive-compulsive disorder is characterized by thoughts and rituals to ward off unbearable feelings of anxiety.

2. The state of fear consists of four elements: *cognitively*, the individual expects danger; *somatically*, the individual experiences the emergency reaction; *emotionally*, the individual feels apprehension, terror, or dread; and *behaviorally*, the individual tries to flee the feared situation. The elements of anxiety are identical to those of fear except for the cognitive element; the anxious individual does not expect a specific danger but simply that something bad will happen.

3. A *phobia* is a persistent fear of a specific object in which the fear is greatly out of proportion to the amount of danger actually present. There are *social phobias* and four *specific phobias:* phobias of particular animals and insects; phobias of the natural environment; phobias of situations; phobias of blood, injection, and injury.

4. The behavioral school holds that phobias are merely instances of the normal classical conditioning of fear to an innocent object that happened to be around when a traumatic event occurred. The behavioral model is consistent with case histories and laboratory evidence, and it has generated four effective therapies based on classical fear extinction: *systematic desensitization*,

exposure, modeling, and *applied tension* for blood phobia. This latter appears to be a virtual cure for blood phobia.

5. *Post-traumatic stress disorder* is a fear disorder that is set off by a specific event. In some cases, the specific event is a catastrophic happening such as natural disasters, combat, and imprisonment in a concentration camp. More commonplace adversities—death of a relative, divorce, and mugging—may also set off the symptoms of PTSD in some individuals. Following the event, symptoms of anxiety and avoidance, reliving the event in dreams and waking, and numbness toward the external world may develop. Also, the individual may experience survivor guilt. The symptoms may last a lifetime. *Exposure therapy* and *disclosure* show considerable promise, particularly after rape, but medications do not.

6. *Panic attacks* come out of the blue, with no specific event or object setting them off. They last for only a few minutes and consist of the four elements of the anxiety reaction. *Panic disorder* consists of recurrent panic attacks. Panic disorders can be relieved by drugs and markedly relieved by learning to reinterpret frightening bodily sensations as resulting from stress and not impending doom. Both the biological and cognitive approaches have recently contributed to an understanding of panic, and the cognitive model may have developed a cure.

7. *Agoraphobia* is a subtype of panic disorder and not a true phobia. It consists of anxiety about venturing into public places lest a panic attack occur there, and it usually begins with a panic attack in a public place. The combination of antidepressant drugs and exposure therapy seems to be the treatment of choice. Each alone works reasonably well.

8. *Generalized anxiety disorder (GAD)* is similar to panic disorder in that there is no specific event that sets it off. In generalized anxiety disorder, however, the anxiety is milder and is chronic, with the elements of anxiety strongly present almost daily for months on end. Cognitive-behavioral therapy provides some relief as do antidepressant drugs, but to a lesser extent.

9. *Obsessive-compulsive disorders (OCD)* consist of *obsessions,* which are repetitive thoughts, images, or impulses that invade consciousness, are often ab-

horrent, and are very difficult to dismiss or control. In addition, most obsessions are associated with *compulsions,* which are repetitive, stereotyped, and unwanted thoughts or actions to counter the obsession. Compulsions can be resisted only with difficulty.

10. An obsessive-compulsive individual displays anxiety when his or her rituals are blocked. In addition, depression is associated with this disorder. When such an individual is depressed, obsessions occur much more frequently. Such individuals are more prone to depression than are people who do not have OCD.

11. There is no personality type that seems predisposed to obsessive-compulsive disorder. Individuals who are obsessive-compulsive in their daily life and concerned with order are not more vulnerable to obsessive-compulsive disorder. What distinguishes these individuals from individuals with the disorder is that individuals with the obsessive-compulsive personality are proud of their meticulousness and love of detail, whereas individuals who have obsessive-compulsive disorder are tormented by their symptoms.

12. Psychoanalytic theory explains who is vulnerable to the disorder and why it has the particular content it does. Cognitive-behavioral theory explains why the disorder and its rituals are maintained. The theory claims that individuals with the disorder are unable to habituate, dismiss, or distract themselves from disturbing thoughts.

13. Behavior therapies for obsessive-compulsive disorder include *exposure,* forcing the patient to endure the aversive situation; *response prevention,* blocking the individual from engaging in the ritual; and *modeling,* watching another person refrain from the ritual. These therapies bring about marked improvement in about two-thirds of the patients with obsessive-compulsive disorder.

14. Neurological signs, brain scan findings, the evolutionarily primitive content of obsessions and compulsions, and the success of clomipramine, an SRI drug, all provide evidence for the biological underpinnings of OCD. Clomipramine produces improvement in 40 to 60 percent of patients with OCD, but relapse is almost universal when the drug is stopped.

15. Mild, *everyday anxiety* can be relieved by regular relaxation or meditation.

6

Somatoform and Dissociative Disorders

Adolf Wölfli, *Ville Géante aux Oiseaux Соисои.*

Learning Objectives

→ Be able to identify the five general symptoms of somatoform disorders.

→ Describe how clinicians can identify motor and sensory deficits that have resulted from conversion disorders as opposed to physical disorders, and how culture contributes to the form the conversion will take.

→ Familiarize yourself with the evidence for a genetic etiology of somatization disorder.

→ Be able to describe the psychoanalytic, communicative, and percept blocking views of the somatoform disorders, and the various therapies for treating these disorders.

→ Describe the dissociative states of amnesia, depersonalization, derealization, identity confusion, identity alteration, and how they can enable the individual to escape from feeling intolerable anxiety.

→ Understand who is especially vulnerable to dissociative identity disorder, the role of amnesia, the steps that lead to the formation of new identities (personalities or alters), and the most effective therapy for these disorders.

→ Be aware of the controversy surrounding the dissociative identity disorder diagnosis, and why many people remain skeptical about some of the stories recounted by patients with DID, and even the very existence of DID.

In the disorders we discussed in the previous chapter, the victims felt anxiety: a person with agoraphobia is terrified when she walks around a shopping center, an individual with generalized anxiety disorder is filled with dread, and a patient with obsessive-compulsive disorder panics when he is blocked from performing his rituals. In contrast to these disorders, anxiety is not usually felt by an individual who suffers from a somatoform or dissociative disorder. In fact, he may be surprisingly indifferent to his symptoms, as in the following case:

Bear was a burly twenty-five-year-old construction worker who was paralyzed from the waist down—totally without movement or feeling—and had been so for three weeks. What's more, he was not particularly upset by his paralysis; that is, he was a bit concerned that he could not walk, but he was not emotional or excessively anxious.

After three days of tests that failed to show anything, the neurologist examining Bear had decided that there was nothing wrong with him physically and had sent him to Psychiatry.

In Psychiatry, there was the same frustration as that experienced by the neurologist. Bear's recent life seemed uneventful to him, and he recalled no precipitating incident. He had used drugs occasionally, and he drank a bit, but he had no previous psychiatric history. Mystified, groping for any lead, one of the residents asked him if he knew anybody else who was paralyzed. At first, Bear couldn't think of anyone, but after a minute or so, he mumbled, without any show of emotion:

"Yeah, come to think of it, Tom, a good friend of mine, is paralyzed from the waist down. Broke his neck."

"How did that happen?"

"It was really sad, and, you know, I guess it was pretty much my fault. Tom's a virgin, like in every way possible. Doesn't even drink or smoke. Well, we were together at a party about a month ago, and I was riding him. I thought he should live a little, try some LSD. I guess he couldn't take it, so he gave in.

"Well, we downed a couple of tabs, and within a few minutes he was flying. Seeing all sorts of weird things. He ran out of the apartment, and I followed, a little afraid for him. God, it was awful! He was running away from something in his head. Next thing I knew, he jumped off the bridge. You know, the one over the tracks at 30th Street Station. He was still alive when the rescue squad got him down from the high-tension lines. They say he'll never walk, or any-thing, again."

"Bear, tell me again when your problem started."

"Out of nowhere. About three weeks ago. I was at work, driving my forklift down at the station. As I crossed over the tracks under the high-tension lines, suddenly I was all dead down there. I shouted for help, and my buddies took me off to. . . . Oh, my God! Don't you see what I've done!"

And within a few days, Bear walked home. (Stinnett, 1978)

Bear believes he caused the paralysis of his friend. He has assumed the symptoms of paralysis and is not much bothered by the fact that he can no longer walk. Similarly, a teenager who is plagued with unre-solvable troubles at home and in school may forget who he is, wander to a new city, and blithely assume a new identity. Historically these disorders used to be classified as "anxiety disorders," because the conflicts that preceded these disorders led psychoanalytic clin-icians and researchers to infer that the symptoms were an attempt to control underlying anxiety that otherwise threatened to overwhelm the individual. Today, however, because anxiety is not manifest, only inferred, DSM-IV classifies somatoform and dissocia-tive disorders separately from the anxiety disorders.

We will discuss two categories of disorders. The first are the somatoform disorders, and they include conversion, somatization, pain disorder, hypochondri-asis, and body dysmorphic disorder. These disorders are characterized by a loss of physical functioning not due to any physical disorder but apparently resulting from psychological conflict. Bear, who was diagnosed with conversion disorder, suddenly became paralyzed for no biological reason but as a result of psychologi-cal stress. The second category consists of the disso-ciative disorders, in which the individual's very identity is fragmented. Among these are dissociative amnesia, in which an individual loses the memory of who he is, depersonalization disorder, and dissociative identity disorder (multiple personality disorder), in which more than one identity exists in the same indi-vidual, and each identity has a relatively rich and sta-ble life of its own.

Somatoform Disorders

A woman is brought into a psychologist's clinic. She cannot see, but curiously, she expresses little concern about being blind. Following an initial interview with the patient, the clinician calls in a neurologist and then an opthamologist. After several tests, the patient goes back to the clinician with two sealed reports indicating "no neurological problem." Having seen this before, the clinician must now try to discover the psychologi-cal problem underlying the woman's blindness.

Such a disorder is called a **somatoform** (taking bodily form) **disorder,** and this disorder has fascinated clinicians and researchers from Jean Charcot and Sig-mund Freud to our contemporaries. There are five factors to consider when diagnosing a patient sus-pected of having a somatoform disorder: First, the patient has lost or altered physical functioning. She may present with symptoms of blindness, deafness, or paralysis. Second, the symptom cannot be explained by a known physical or neurological condition. There is no evidence of neurological damage to pro-duce the blindness, deafness, or the paralysis. Third, there is positive evidence that psychological factors are related to the symptom. Fourth, the patient is often, but not always, indifferent to the physical loss. Specifically, she does not feel anxiety about the symptoms. Finally, the symptoms are not under vol-untary control.

Types of Somatoform Disorders

Conversion, somatization disorder, pain disorder, hypochondriasis, and body dysmorphic disorder are all categorized as somatoform disorders in DSM-IV, and we will consider each in turn.

CONVERSION

Conversion, once known as hysterical conversion, is a disorder in which psychological stress is converted into physical symptoms. Consider Bear's case: Bear's paralysis has the five symptoms of somatoform dis-order. First, he has lost physical functioning: he is paralyzed. Second, physical damage cannot explain the paralysis, since he is neurologically sound. Third, the paralysis is not under voluntary control. Fourth, Bear seems remarkably indifferent to his paralysis; he feels no anxiety about his paralysis. And fifth, there is good evidence that psychological factors are cer-tainly related to, and probably caused, the symptoms: (1) Bear has a friend with paralysis caused partly by Bear's actions; (2) Bear's paralysis began at the same site where his friend's paralysis occurred; (3) Bear did not easily remember the incident when his friend was paralyzed, nor did he relate it to his own

DSM-IV Criteria

Conversion Disorder

A. One or more symptoms or deficits affecting voluntary motor or sensory function that suggest a neurological or other general medical condition.

B. Psychological factors are judged to be associated with the symptom or deficit because the initiation or exacerbation of the symptom or deficit is preceded by conflicts or other stressors.

C. The symptom or deficit is not intentionally produced or feigned (as in Factitious Disorder or Malingering).

D. The symptom or deficit cannot, after appropriate investigation, be fully explained by a general medical condi-

tion, or by the direct effects of a substance, or as a culturally sanctioned behavior or experience.

E. The symptom or deficit causes clinically significant distress or impairment in social, occupational, or other important areas of functioning or warrants medical evaluation.

F. The symptom or deficit is not limited to pain or sexual dysfunction, does not occur exclusively during the course of Somatization Disorder, and is not better accounted for by another mental disorder.

SOURCE: APA, DSM-IV, 1994.

---

paralysis; and (4) Bear could not control his paralysis, but when he gained insight into this, his paralysis remitted.

SOMATIZATION DISORDER (BRIQUET'S SYNDROME)

In **somatization disorder,** also called Briquet's syndrome, the person has had many physical complaints that began before age thirty, resulting in a complicated history of medical treatment. These complaints involve many different organs and cannot be fully explained from known physical causes, nor are they under voluntary control. The symptoms include a history of pain related to at least four different areas, such as the head, stomach, back, joints, arms and legs, rectum, chest, or pain on sexual intercourse, menstruation, or urination.

DSM-IV Criteria

Somatization Disorder

A. A history of many physical complaints beginning before age 30 years, that occur over a period of several years and result in treatment being sought or significant impairment in social, occupational, or other important areas of functioning.

B. Each of the following criteria must have been met, with individual symptoms occurring at any time during the course of the disturbance: (1) four pain symptoms: a history of pain related to at least four different sites or functions (e.g., head, abdomen, back, joints, extremities, chest, rectum, during menstruation, during sexual intercourse, or during urination); (2) two gastrointestinal symptoms: a history of at least two gastrointestinal symptoms other than pain (e.g., nausea, bloating, vomiting other than during pregnancy, diarrhea, or intolerance of several different foods); (3) one sexual symptom: a history of at least one sexual or reproductive symptom other than pain (e.g., sexual indifference, erectile or ejaculatory dysfunction, irregular menses, excessive menstrual bleeding, vomiting throughout pregnancy); (4) one pseudoneurological symptom: a history of at least

one symptom or deficit suggesting a neurological condition not limited to pain (conversion symptoms such as impaired coordination or balance, paralysis or localized weakness, difficulty swallowing or lump in throat, aphonia [loss of voice], urinary retention, hallucinations, loss of touch or pain sensation, double vision, blindness, deafness, seizures; dissociative symptoms such as amnesia; or loss of consciousness other than fainting).

C. Either (1) or (2): (1) after appropriate investigation, each of the symptoms in Criterion B cannot be fully explained by a known general medical condition or the direct effects of a substance (e.g., a drug of abuse, a medication); (2) when there is a related general medical condition, the physical complaints or resulting social or occupational impairment are in excess of what would be expected from the history, physical examination, or laboratory findings.

D. The symptoms are not intentionally feigned or produced (as in Factitious Disorder or Malingering).

SOURCE: APA, DSM-IV, 1994.

The fifteen most common symptoms that contribute to the diagnosis of somatoform disorder are: fatigue; fainting; palpitations; menstrual problems; nausea, gas, and indigestion; back pain; joint or limb pain; dizziness; chest pain; stomach pain; headache; sexual problems; sleep complaints; diarrhea or constipation; breathing difficulties (Kroenke, Spitzer, De-Gruy, and Swindle, 1998).

The patient may also have a history of at least one "pseudoneurological" or conversion symptom that is not limited to pain, such as impaired coordination, paralysis, blindness, deafness, or loss of the sensation of touch. Unnecessary surgery, addiction to prescription medicines, depression, and attempted suicide are common complications of this syndrome. The fundamental difference between somatization and conversion is that the patient with somatization disorder will suffer from many physical problems, while the patient with conversion disorder generally has only one complaint.

Intriguingly, the presenting symptoms usually occur more often on the right side of the body than the left side, suggesting left-hemisphere involvement (Min and Lee, 1997). The left hemisphere is the site of our verbal life, so this suggests that verbal interventions, such as we will see below, may be on the right track.

PAIN DISORDER (PSYCHALGIA)

The third main somatoform disorder is *pain disorder (psychalgia)*. In pain disorder, pain in one or more parts of the body causing marked distress or impairment is the central symptom. Psychological factors account for its onset, its severity, its undue persistence, or for the worsening of the pain. The symptom is not under voluntary control. Statistically, it may be the most frequent of the somatoform disorders (Drossman, 1982; Verhaak, Kerssens, Dekker, Sorbi, and Bensing, 1998; Watson and Buranen, 1979). The following case illustrates psychalgia:

> Harry, a forty-one-year-old man, suffered a sudden onset of severe abdominal pain. Emergency surgery was about to be performed, but there was no elevated white cell count, and other physical symptoms were normal. In addition, Harry seemed emotionally indifferent to the pain and the fact of impending surgery. He was obviously in pain, but not anxious about it.
>
> Upon consultation, it was decided to abandon urgent preparations for surgery, and to explore for a possible psychological basis. It emerged that Harry had had a childhood that predisposed him to psychalgia. His parents had been materially wealthy, but they had given him very little love and affection. The one break in this emotional barrenness of his childhood had been his appendectomy. The love he had received during this period was meaningful, real, and what he had "always longed for."
>
> The present abdominal pain was set off by an incident of domestic deceit. His wife had become infatuated with another man and had threatened to go off with him. At this very point, the abdominal pain had begun. (Adapted from Laughlin, 1967, pp. 667–68)

The hypothesis in Harry's case is that whenever he is in serious distress, he will suffer pain in his abdomen. This pain becomes a somatic excuse for not suffering the anxiety brought on by the stressful events.

DSM-IV Criteria

Pain Disorder

A. Pain in one or more anatomical sites is the predominant focus of the clinical presentation and is of sufficient severity to warrant clinical attention.

B. The pain causes clinically significant distress or impairment in social, occupational, or other important areas of functioning.

C. Psychological factors are judged to have an important role in the onset, severity, exacerbation, or maintenance of the pain.

D. The symptom or deficit is not intentionally produced or feigned (as in Factitious Disorder or Malingering).

E. The pain is not better accounted for by a Mood, Anxiety, or Psychotic Disorder and does not meet criteria for Dyspareunia.

SOURCE: APA, DSM-IV, 1994.

Hypochondriasis

A. Preoccupation with fears of having, or the idea that one has, a serious disease based on the person's misinterpretation of bodily symptoms.

B. The preoccupation persists despite appropriate medical evaluation and reassurance.

C. The belief in Criterion A is not of delusional intensity (as in Delusional Disorder, Somatic Type) and is not restricted to a circumscribed concern about appearance (as in Body Dysmorphic Disorder).

D. The preoccupation is not better accounted for by Generalized Anxiety Disorder, Obsessive-Compulsive Disorder, Panic Disorder, a Major Depressive Episode, Separation Anxiety, or another Somatoform Disorder.

Specify if With Poor Insight: if, for most of the time during the current episode, the person does not recognize that the concern about having a serious illness is excessive or unreasonable.

SOURCE: APA, DSM-IV, 1994.

HYPOCHONDRIASIS

Hypochondriasis is defined by the conviction that one has a serious medical disease, or the preoccupation with fears about contracting one, in spite of extensive evidence and reassurance to the contrary. Patients dwell on their bodily functions, such as sweating or rapid heartbeat. They worry endlessly about minor physical symptoms, such as a cough or a little sore. They "doctor shop" and change physicians frequently, believing they are getting inadequate care. Both the patient and the physician, usually a family practitioner, feel anger and frustration. Family and social life is also strained, with the patient's complaints about his poor health the central irritant. The patient usually refuses to believe that he is suffering a mental disorder and not a physical one.

Men and women seem equally predisposed to hypochondriasis, and around 4 percent of medical patients may display it. It can be found at any stage of life, but particularly in adolescence, in middle age, and after age sixty (Barsky, Wyshak, Klerman, and Latham, 1990; Kellner, 1986). Culture greatly influences what particular physical problems will preoccupy a person who has hypochondriasis. Among Chinese males, panic about the possibility that one's penis will retract into the abdomen *(Koro)* occurs; in India, some men report *Dhat,* which is a preoccupation about losing semen, and is associated with dizziness and fatigue.

Making a diagnosis of hypochondriasis involves a process of elimination. First, a medical condition must be ruled out. Then, a series of related mental disorders, such as generalized anxiety disorder, obsessive-compulsive disorder, illness phobia, panic disorder, and somatization disorder should be eliminated. Further, the patient must not be experiencing the bodily delusions that can occur in psychosis. What is left over is hypochondriasis. Unfortunately, little is know about the course, vulnerability, and effective treatment of this understudied problem.

BODY DYSMORPHIC DISORDER

Have you ever thought you were ugly? Much too freckled? Too fat? Too thin-lipped? All elbows and knees? Taken to extremes and become a preoccupation, this is the essence of *body dysmorphic disorder* *(BDD).* A person with BDD exaggerates a slight bodily defect into the perception of wholesale ugliness, and this concern comes to dominate his or her life. Baldness, acne, scars, pale or red complexion, hairiness, fatness or thinness, and scars are common preoccupations of those with BDD. A person with this disorder might obsess over the size and shape of her nose, ears, eyes, mouth, legs, hips, breasts, genitals, buttocks, or feet. When the preoccupation becomes tormenting, when she avoids others, when she cannot resist falling into rumination, the line has been crossed from worry about appearance to a clinical problem.

A person with BDD checks herself endlessly in the mirror, using special lighting and magnification

DSM-IV Criteria

Body Dysmorphic Disorder

A. Preoccupation with an imagined defect in appearance. If a slight physical anomaly is present, the person's concern is markedly excessive.

B. The preoccupation causes clinically significant distress or impairment in social, occupational, or other important areas of functioning.

C. The preoccupation is not better accounted for by another mental disorder (e.g., dissatisfaction with body shape and size in Anorexia Nervosa).

SOURCE: APA, DSM-IV, 1994.

---

to scrutinize the defect. A woman may comb her hair for hours, pick at her skin, or engage in prolonged makeup rituals. A man may try to camouflage the defect by wearing a beard to cover a small or scarred chin, a wig to disguise hair loss, or a sock in his bathing trunks to enhance his "small" penis. At the extreme, he or she may avoid any social contact, becoming housebound, or dropping out of school or work. Depression, suicide, and repeated plastic surgery are all common outcomes.

BDD usually begins in adolescence and may last a lifetime (Wilhelm et al., 1999). It is uncommon in severe form (Hollander and Aronowitz, 1999). Women have the disorder slightly more frequently than men. Usually a family member goads the reluc-

tant patient into treatment. What counts as ugly is subject to wide cultural variation: too wide a face in Peru or Greenland, too short a neck in Burma, too large feet in China. Therefore, the preoccupations of those with BDD differ, based on their cultural background. Moreover, differential diagnosis is called for: the diagnostician must rule out anorexia and bulimia, depression, obsessive-compulsive disorder, and social phobia (Phillips, Gunderson, Mallya, McElroy, and Carter, 1998; Zimmerman and Mattia, 1998). Even then, little is known about cause, and less is known about effective treatment. There have been only two uncontrolled studies to date. In one, thirteen eighteen- to forty-eight-year-old females diagnosed with BDD were treated in small groups that met for twelve weekly ninety-minute sessions. Patients improved significantly over the course of treatment, with reductions in both BDD and symptoms of depression (Wilhelm, Otto, Lohr, and Deckersbach, 1999). In the other study, a serotonin reuptake inhibitor (SRI) was effective in ten of eighteen individuals (Albertini and Phillips, 1999).

Diagnosing Somatoform Disorders

A somatoform disorder is one of the most difficult disorders to diagnose correctly. In the case study discussed earlier, how can we tell if Bear was faking paralysis or if he had some obscure physical illness that was as yet undiagnosed?

In an attempt to make diagnosis clearer, let us distinguish somatoform disorders from four other disorders with which it can be confused, sometimes tragically. These conditions are malingering, psychosomatic disorders, factitious disorder, and undiagnosed physical illness.

Body dysmorphic disorder may lead a person to undergo repeated plastic surgery to correct a body defect that he or she perceives as wholesale ugliness. Michael Jackson had surgery to change his appearance, as can be seen when comparing these photos of Jackson as a child and as an adult.

Malingering—faking symptoms—is a frequent problem in diagnosing somatoform disorders in the American and European welfare and disability systems (Hiller, Rief, and Fichter, 1997).

In principle, there are two differences between malingering and an authentic somatoform disorder—neither of which is easy to pin down in practice. First, the symptoms of a malingerer are under his voluntary control, whereas they are not under the voluntary control of an individual with a somatoform disorder. A malingerer can turn the paralysis on and off, although it may be difficult to induce him to display this voluntary control for you. The individual suffering conversion cannot. For example, even if we had offered Bear an irresistibly large amount of money to get up out of his wheelchair and walk away, he would not have been able to do so. One trick diagnosticians have used to distinguish a malingerer feigning deafness is to drop a silver dollar on the concrete floor behind the subject. The malingerer would react, the deaf person would not.

Second, the malingerer acquires an obvious environmental goal as a result of his symptom (for example, getting out of the army by feigning paralysis; winning large disability payments by feigning pain), whereas an individual with a conversion disorder does not necessarily achieve anything obvious by his symptom.

Malingering itself should be distinguished from *secondary gain.* Secondary gain consists of deriving benefits from one's environment as a consequence of having abnormal symptoms. Individuals with somatoform disorders frequently get secondary gains. So, for example, a person with pain disorder may get more love and attention from his family when he is in pain. The use of secondary gain seems to be part of the universal human trait of making the best of a bad situation. A person with a somatoform disorder who derives secondary gain, however, differs from a malingerer. The malingerer is faking the initial symptoms and then may, in addition, use them to benefit. The individual with the somatoform disorder, in contrast, is not faking the symptoms but may well derive benefit from having them. The pattern of symptoms sometimes distinguishes malingering from somatoform disorders. Hysterically blind patients do not crash into objects, but malingerers may.

Psychosomatic disorders, which are taken up in Chapter 12, also resemble somatoform disorders. What distinguishes psychosomatic disorders from somatoform disorders is the existence of a physical basis that can explain the psychosomatic symptom, but not

the somatoform symptom. Although some people who have peptic ulcers or high blood pressure may have these conditions exaggerated or even initiated by psychological factors, the ulcers and hypertension are actually being caused by specific known physical mechanisms. In contrast, glove anesthesia, a conversion symptom in which nothing can be felt in the hand and fingers, but in which sensation is intact from the wrist up, cannot be induced by any known pattern of damage to the nerves controlling the hand.

The third disorder from which somatoform disorder must be distinguished is *factitious disorder,* also called ***Münchhausen syndrome.*** This disorder is characterized by multiple hospitalizations and operations in which the individual voluntarily produces the signs of illness, not through underlying anxiety, but by physiological tampering (Folks, 1995; Pope, Jonas, and Jones, 1982). There was one documented case of a thirty-four-year-old man who, over a decade, had made 200 visits to physicians under dozens of aliases at more than sixty-eight hospitals and who had cost Britain's health service $2 million. In contrast to malingering, a factitious disorder has no obvious goal other than gaining medical attention. It is crucially different from somatoform disorders because the symptoms are voluntarily produced by the person who has them, and they are physically based.

Finally, a somatoform disorder may be misdiagnosed and actually result from an undiagnosed physical illness. The diagnosis of a somatoform disorder is for many people degrading, as the patient and his family are told that the disease is in his mind, not in his body. Current medical diagnosis is far from perfect, and occasionally an individual who has been diagnosed as having a somatoform disorder will eventually develop a full-blown physical disease, such as multiple sclerosis, which in fact had caused the earlier symptoms. This is one reason the diagnosis must be made with caution (Binzer and Kullgren, 1998).

Table 6–1 summarizes the distinctions among conversion, malingering, psychosomatic disorders, factitious disorders, and undiagnosed physical illness.

Vulnerability to Somatoform Disorders

Conversion disorders are not common. Estimates vary widely, but probably not more than 5 percent of all nonpsychotic patients (or much less than 1 percent of the entire American population) have conversion disorders (Laughlin, 1967; Rogers et al., 1996; Woodruff, Clayton, and Guze, 1971). Conversion symptoms usually are displayed from late adolescence to middle adulthood; they occur in children and old people, but rarely (Fritz, Fritsch, and Hagino, 1997; Kotsopoulos and Snow, 1986; Lehmkuhl, Blanz, Lehmkuhl, and Braun-Scharm, 1989). Although the large majority of patients with conversion disorder are women, between 20 and 40 percent of conversion disorders occur in men (Chodoff, 1974; Tomasson, Kent, and Coryell, 1991). Culture is an important determinant of the form that conversion takes. The feeling of ants crawling over the skin or of burning feet are common in Africa and South Asia. In a study of Hmong refugees in the United States who were originally from Southeast Asia, considerable somatoform disorders were observed (see Box 6-1). Somatoform disorders in these refugees were also strongly associated with depression. Those who were most acculturated to America (had American friends, used the mass media, owned a car) were less likely to somaticize (Westermeyer, Bouafuely, Neider, and Callies, 1989). This suggests that those refugees least able to communicate mental distress in their new world expressed it through bodily distress.

Somatization disorder, in which the patient has a complicated medical history before the age of thirty-five, with a large number of symptoms ranging across many organ systems, and with no known medical explanations, is more common. As many as 2 to 10 percent of all adult women may display this disorder, and it is rarely diagnosed in men (Cloninger et al.,

1984; Woodruff, Clayton, and Guze, 1971). Except for stomach pain, which is often seen in children and adolescents, psychalgia is largely an adult problem (Fritz, Fritsch, and Hagino, 1997).

In contrast to only marginal evidence that somatoform disorders as a whole run in families (Torgersen, 1986), one of them—somatization disorder—clearly does. The sisters, mothers, and daughters of women with this disorder are ten times more likely to develop it than women in the general population (Woodruff, Clayton, and Guze, 1971). Beyond this familial association, family members (particularly the parents) of individuals with somatization disorder tend to have unexpectedly high rates of three other disorders: depression, alcoholism, and antisocial personality disorder (Golding, Rost, Kashner, and Smith, 1992; Sigvardsson von Knorring, Bohman, and Cloninger, 1984; Weller et al., 1994). Much of the evidence for these associations comes from studies of children adopted in early childhood by nonrelatives. Overall, the results show that if one or both biological parents were alcoholic, then the sons were much likelier than other adoptees to be alcoholic and/or have antisocial personality disorder. The daughters, on the other hand, showed unexpectedly high rates of somatization disorder. One emerging view is that somatization disorder and psychopathy and/or alcoholism, may represent alternative outcomes of the same genetic diathesis (Bohman, Cloninger, von Knorring, and Sigvardsson, 1984; Bohman, Cloninger, Sigvardsson, and von Knorring 1987; Cloninger, Martin, Guze, and Clayton, 1986; Cloninger, von Knorring, Sigvardsson, and

TABLE 6–1

Diagnosis

CRITERIA FOR DIFFERENTIAL DIAGNOSIS OF SYMPTOMS SUGGESTING PHYSICAL ILLNESS

Disorder	Can a known physical mechanism explain the symptom?	Are the symptoms linked to psychological causes?	Is the symptom under voluntary control?	Is there an obvious goal?
Conversion	Never	Always	Never	Sometimes
Malingering	Sometimes	Sometimes	Always	Always
Psychosomatic Disorders	Always	Always	Never	Sometimes
Factitious Disorder	Sometimes	Always	Always	Never (other than medical attention)
Undiagnosed Physical Illness	Sometimes	Sometimes	Never	Never

SOURCE: Based on Hyler and Spitzer, 1978.

Sight Loss as Conversion Disorder?

Under the regime of Cambodian leader Pol Pot, it is estimated that between one and two million people (out of a total population of only eight million) were killed. Many were exiled from their homes in the city to the countryside, and there abused and even tortured. Survivors of the atrocities perpetuated by Pol Pot's political party, the Khmer Rouge, were forcibly marched 160 miles across the Cambodian-Thai border. Many watched countless others die on the march, weakened by starvation and exhaustion. It became common for relatives to see the murder and torture of family members.

Clinicians have treated and studied the survivors of these atrocities. One woman, they report, watched as her three-

These civilian survivors of the atrocities perpetrated by Pol Pot's political party, the Khmer Rouge, were forcibly marched 160 miles across the Cambodian-Thai border. Many watched countless others die on the march, weakened by starvation and exhaustion.

month-old nephew was clubbed to death against a tree by Khmer Rouge soldiers. Soon after, she saw three other nephews and nieces beaten to death, and then her brother and his wife were murdered in front of her. She eventually immigrated to the United States and reacted to her Cambodian experiences by becoming blind.

Two researchers have studied 150 cases of this sort just in the Long Beach, California, area. After finding no evidence of neurophysiological damage to the visual system, Gretchen Van Boehmel, an electrophysiologist, and Patrick Rozee, a psychologist, interviewed thirty of these women, aged fifty-one to seventy. They became convinced that the visual problems were conversion symptoms. Using a skill building and group therapy intervention with ten of the women, Van Boehmel and Rozee reported improved vision in four of them.

Unlike malingerers, these women had little to gain from blindness. Malingerers "play up" their symptoms by walking with exaggerated tripping motions and pretending they are not able to touch their nose with their fingers. But these women did not. Further, the longer the women spent under the Khmer Rouge and in Thai refugee camps, the worse their visual problems became.

These could possibly be cases of conversion on a massive scale in which the women no longer "wanted" to see. This is biologically plausible as well as psychologically plausible. When some parts of the brain that control vision are destroyed, individuals report that they can see nothing at all in specific regions of their visual field. But in spite of consistent reports of blindness, such patients perform above chance on visual discrimination problems. When confronted with this fact, the patients, like the hysterically blind, insist they saw nothing at all and were merely guessing (Weiskrantz, Warrington, Sanders, and Marshall, 1974).

Alternatively, however, undiagnosed physical illness must be considered. Undetected neurological damage resulting from years of malnutrition and abuse also might be the cause.

SOURCE: Based on DeAngelis, 1990.

Bohman, 1986; Guze, 1993; Lilienfeld, Van Valkenburg, Larntz, and Akiskal, 1986).

The Etiology of Somatoform Disorders

What causes the loss of the function of a bodily organ in the absence of any underlying physiological basis? This remains one of the great questions of psychopathology (see Table 6–2).

THE PSYCHOANALYTIC VIEW

While psychoanalytic thinking has gone out of fashion for explaining many disorders, usually for want of empirical evidence, somatoform disorders are a domain in which its explanations remain quite viable. The psychoanalytic view was put forth by Sigmund Freud in 1894 and remains a pillar of psychoanalytic thinking today. Freud believed that the physical symptom resulted from a defense that absorbed and neutralized the anxiety generated by an unacceptable

TABLE 6–2

VIEWS OF SOMATOFORM DISORDERS

Theory	Who Is Vulnerable	Cause of Symptom	Therapy
Psychoanalytic view	People with specific unresolved conflicts	Unconscious conflict causes anxiety; conversion into a physical symptom defends against anxiety while at the same time symbolizing the conflict	Recognize and work through unconscious conflict
Communicative view	People who have trouble expressing distress verbally	Physical symptom communicates distress to others in an acceptable and easily understood way	Recognize communicative function of symptom and find more acceptable means of expressing distress
Percept blocking view	People with unbearable anxiety or distress	Unbearable anxiety, or need to communicate distress, or reinforcement of anxiety reduction	Work through conflict and/or find more acceptable ways to express distress

unconscious conflict (Freud, 1894/1976, p. 63). Today, the psychodynamic explanation of conversion still revolves around this notion and postulates three distinct processes: First, the individual is made anxious by some unacceptable idea, and the conversion is a defense against this anxiety. Second, psychic energy is transmuted into a somatic loss. The anxiety is detached from the unacceptable idea, rendering it neutral. Because anxiety is psychic energy, it must go someplace—this is what "psychodynamic" means—and in this case, it is used to debilitate a physical organ. Third, the particular somatic loss symbolizes the underlying conflict. For Bear, the three processes seem to play a role: Bear is unconsciously anxious and guilty about causing Tom's paralysis, and he walls off these feelings from consciousness by transmuting the guilt and anxiety into his own paralysis. The particular symptom—paralysis—obviously symbolizes the real paralysis suffered by his friend.

This theory is just about the only idea that can explain one of the strangest symptoms of conversion: "la belle indifference." Unlike patients with actual physical loss due to injury, conversion patients are often strangely indifferent to their physical symptoms. For example, a patient with conversion paralysis may show much more concern over a minor skin irritation on his legs than the fact that he cannot move them (Laughlin, 1967, pp. 673–74). In the psychoanalytic view, a conversion symptom may absorb anxiety so well by transmuting it into a physical loss that the patient can actually be calm about being crippled, blind, deaf, or insensate.

While no complete behavioral view of somatoform disorders has been put forward, the psychoanalytic view gives a hint of what the behavioral view might look like. If conversion symptoms do, in fact, absorb anxiety, anxiety reduction reinforces the patient for having a symptom.

THE COMMUNICATIVE VIEW

There are negative emotions other than anxiety: sadness, anger, guilt, awe, bewilderment, and shame are all elements of the human experience. People with phobias or obsessive-compulsive disorders experience these emotions as well as anxiety, particularly sadness and anger. Moreover, patients with conversions—if they are defending at all—might not be defending against anxiety but against depression, guilt, or anger. This possibility has spawned another theory of conversion, which emphasizes the communicative, rather than the defensive, function of the symptom. The communicative model claims that the patient uses the disorder to deal with a variety of distressing emotions—not only anxiety—and to negotiate difficult interpersonal transactions. He expresses his underlying distress to himself in terms of physical illness, thereby distracting himself from his distress. He then communicates the fact that he is distressed to others with his physical loss. He unconsciously chooses his symptoms according to his own conception of a physical illness—which will derive in part from the illnesses that important people in his life have had—and according to what does and doesn't count as an illness in his culture. His particular symptoms will then simulate physical illness either expertly or crudely, depending on how much medical knowledge he has (Ziegler and Imboden, 1962).

The communicative model views the case study of Bear in the following way: Bear is depressed, anxious, and guilty over his role in paralyzing his friend. In addition, he cannot talk about his distress because he is not verbal about his troubles. By paralyzing himself, he is able to distract himself from these emotions, so he shows his distress to others by his paralysis. Bear's particular symptom derives directly from identification with his friend's paralysis. Bear is *alexithymic*. The term "alexithymia" (literally, no words for feelings) has been coined to categorize people who cannot easily express their feelings (Sifneos, 1973). When asked about how they feel about highly charged events, such as the death of a spouse, they describe their physical symptoms or simply fail to understand the question. For example, they may say, "My headaches got worse . . . it was like a band around my head . . . that's all I felt" (Bach and Bach, 1995; Lesser, 1985). Alexithymic people are particularly susceptible to somatoform disorders and the psychosomatic problems discussed in Chapter 12.

Experiencing a trauma but not talking about it may precede physical health problems. In a survey of 2,020 respondents, 367 reported having at one time experienced a sexual trauma. These people had higher rates of virtually all physical diseases inquired about than did those who had not experienced a trauma (Pennebaker, 1985; Rubenstein, 1982). In another study, 115 students were classified into a group that had not experienced a trauma, a group that had experienced a trauma but had confided in others, and a group that had experienced a trauma but had not told anybody. Those in the trauma/no confide group had more diseases, symptoms, and took more medication. Among nineteen people whose spouses had died by accident or suicide, the illness rate was substantially greater in those who did not talk to their friends about the death (Pennebaker, 1985). While these studies are not definitive, the possibility that silence hurts is intriguing and important. The mechanism by which silence hurts may be rumination (thinking constantly about a problem); the

less people talk to others about tragedy or distress, the more they talk to themselves, and there may be some as yet unknown way in which rumination undermines physical health (Rachman and Hodgson, 1980).

The communicative model holds that conversion reactions "talk." They are a cry for help, particularly among individuals who are reluctant or unable to talk about their emotional distress. Such people may be forced to rely on physical symptoms to tell the people they love and their physicians that all is not well in their emotional lives (Karon, 1999).

THE PERCEPT BLOCKING VIEW

There is a third view of somatoform disorders that is compatible with either the psychoanalytic or communicative views. It focuses on how a perception can be blocked from conscious experience. This view is best illustrated by hysterical blindness, a conversion disorder in which blindness is the physical loss. Surprisingly, in spite of the claim that he is aware of no visual input at all, the behavior of a hysterically blind person is often controlled by visual input. Such individuals usually avoid walking in front of cars and tripping over furniture, even though they report no awareness of actually seeing anything. In the laboratory, they also give evidence that some visual material is getting through. When given discrimination tasks that can only be solved by visual cues, such as "pick the side—left or right—that has the square, as opposed to the circle, on it," they perform significantly below chance. They do worse than if they were guessing at random, and they systematically pick the side that has the circle. In order to be so wrong, the patient must be right—the square of which he is not aware must register at some level of his mind, and then be reacted to by choosing the circle (Theodor and Mandelcorn, 1978; see also Brady and Lind, 1961; Bryant and McConkey, 1989; Gross and Zimmerman, 1965).

What are we to make of this? If we assume that the hysterically blind individual is not lying when he says he is not aware of anything visual, then we are led to the following model: visual input can register in the sensory system and directly affect behavior (hence the avoidance of furniture and below-chance performance), while being blocked from conscious awareness (hence the report "I see nothing"). The conversion process consists in blocking the percept from awareness (Hilgard, 1977; Sackeim, Nordlie, and Gur, 1979). This is compatible with both the psychoanalytic and communicative models since it makes no claims about what motivations can cause blocking—a need to defend against anxiety or a desire to distract oneself from inner distress. So we conclude that the mechanism of hysterical blindness may be the blocking of a visual percept from awareness. The blocking could be motivated either by anxiety (as Freud held), by a need to communicate distress, or it might be reinforced by anxiety reduction (as a behaviorist would hold).

Treatment of Somatoform Disorders

There is an ancient Persian legend about a physician named Rhazes who was called into the palace for the purpose of diagnosing and treating a young prince. Apparently, the prince could not walk. After the usual examination of the day, Rhazes determined that there was nothing wrong with the prince's legs, at least not physically. With little more than a hunch, Rhazes set out to treat what may be the first recorded case of conversion. In doing so, he took a risk: Rhazes unexpectedly walked into the prince's bathroom brandishing a dagger and threatened to kill him. Upon seeing him, "the startled prince abruptly fled, leaving his clothes, his dignity, his symptom, and undoubtedly part of his self-esteem behind" (Laughlin, 1967, p. 678).

CONFRONTATION

Modern clinicians tend to approach their "princes" brandishing a less drastic treatment. They will sometimes confront a conversion patient and try to force him out of his symptom. For example, therapists may tell hysterically blind patients that they are performing significantly below or above chance on visual tasks in spite of seeing nothing, which may cause visual awareness gradually to return in the patient (Brady and Lind, 1961; but see also Gross and Zimmerman, 1965). But these recoveries are usually temporary, and they may produce conflict and loss of self-esteem in the patient. They also may make the patient feel that the therapist is unsympathetic, and so they may ultimately undermine therapy.

SUGGESTION

Simple suggestion, merely telling a patient in a convincing manner that the symptoms will go away, may fare somewhat better than confrontation does. Conversion patients are particularly suggestible, and cer-

tain therapists have found improvement by directly telling the patient, in an authoritative-sounding way, that the symptom will go away. In an account of 100 cases of patients with conversion symptoms, one investigator found that following strong suggestion 75 percent of the patients were either symptom-free or much improved four to six years later (Carter, 1949). But since there was no comparison group that might have controlled for the spontaneous disappearance of conversion without suggestion, we cannot be sure that suggestion had any real effect (Bird, 1979).

INSIGHT

Insight, or coming to recognize the underlying conflict producing the physical loss, is psychoanalysts' therapy of choice for conversion disorders, or for any disorder for that matter. According to these therapists, when the patient comes to see, and emotionally appreciate, that there is an underlying conflict that is producing a conversion disorder, the symptom should disappear. A number of dramatic case histories confirm this. For example, when Bear realized that his paralysis expressed his guilt over his friend's paralysis, the symptom remitted. Unfortunately, there does not exist a well-controlled study that tests whether psychoanalytic insight has any effect over and above suggestion, confrontation, spontaneous remission, or the mere formation of a helping alliance with a therapist.

OTHER THERAPIES

There are suggestions of promising effects from a variety of other approaches. Amitriptyline, an antidepressant with pain-killing effects, seems to have some beneficial effects on a minority of pain disorder patients, although its biochemical mechanism is unknown (Van Kempen, Zitman, Linssen, and Edelbroek, 1992). A meta-analysis of eleven studies treating somatoform pain disorder with antidepressants shows quite substantial pain relief overall (Fishbain, Cutler, Rosomoff, and Rosomoff, 1998). Sensible advice also helps pain disorder: telling the patient that the treatment goal is not to cure the pain, but to help him achieve a sense of control over pain and improve his functioning in life (Lipowski, 1990). Family therapy also may help. In a study of eighty-nine youngsters with conversion disorders, family therapy approaches produced recovery within two weeks for half the patients (Turgay, 1990). Because suggestion is such a strong factor in conversion, however, skepticism is in order. Placebo-controlled studies of therapy for somatoform disorders are still very much needed—more than 100 years after the first cures were claimed by the very people who founded abnormal psychology as we know it.

Dissociative Disorders

Each of us has, at one time or another, awakened in the middle of the night and, being somewhat befuddled, wondered, "Where am I?" Sometimes the disorientation is more profound. "Who is the person sleeping next to me?" "Who am I, anyway?" When such an event happens—most commonly following fatigue, travel, or drinking—it usually wears off in a few seconds or minutes, and knowledge of who we are—our identity—returns. But for some people, it is different. People who have suffered a strong psychological trauma sometimes experience a profound and lasting disturbance of memory, and this is at the heart of the **dissociative disorders.** They are called "dissociative" because two or more mental processes co-exist or alternate without becoming connected or influencing each other (Gregory, 1987). Some area of memory is split off or dissociated from conscious awareness.

The dissociative disorders have much in common with our last topic, the somatoform disorders, particularly conversion. In conversion, anxiety is not experienced by the victim; in fact, complete indifference is common. Rather, the symptom can be seen as a way to prevent underlying anxiety from surfacing. So it seems with dissociative disorders. For example, when an individual suddenly loses his memory following an unbearable trauma, he is not necessarily overtly anxious. Rather, theorists infer that the loss of memory allows him to escape from intolerable anxiety brought on by the trauma (Spiegel and Cardena, 1991).

The experience of dissociation consists of either: (1) **amnesia,** in which a substantial block of time in one's life is forgotten—after the catastrophic collapse of the Hyatt Hotel skywalks in Nevada, 28 percent of the survivors had memory deficits (Wilkinson, 1983); (2) **depersonalization,** in which one feels detachment from oneself—as if one is just going through the motions or looking at oneself from the outside; 57 percent of survivors of a series of deadly tornadoes reported such detachment (Madakasira and O'Brien, 1987); (3) **derealization,** in which the world, not the self, seems unreal; 72 percent of sur-

vivors of life-threatening dangers reported feeling as if space and time had altered (Noyes and Kletti, 1977); (4) **identity confusion,** in which one is confused or uncertain about who one is; (5) **identity alteration,** in which one displays a surprising skill—for example, speaking Flemish or tightrope walking—that one did not know one had (Steinberg, Rounsaville, and Cicchetti, 1990). Dissociative states are not rare; for example, 3 percent of the Dutch and Flemish population, mostly male, report serious dissociative experiences (Vanderlinden, Van Dyck, Vandereycken, and Vertommen, 1991).

We will discuss three dissociative disorders: **dissociative amnesia,** a loss of personal memory caused by severe trauma such as the death of a child or the dashing of a career; **depersonalization disorder,** the persistent experience of feeling detached from one's mind or body, and **dissociative identity disorder** (also called **multiple personality disorder**), in which two or more distinct identities exist within the same individual, and each leads a rather full life.

Dissociative Amnesia

Timmy was fifteen years old and attending high school in upstate New York. He was teased mercilessly by his fellow students and was doing poorly in his schoolwork. In addition, he fought constantly with his parents. He was very upset about his problems, and it seemed to him that they had become absolutely unsolvable. One spring afternoon, he went home from school extremely distressed and threw his books down on the porch in disgust.

At that moment, Timmy became a victim of amnesia. This was his last memory for a year, and we will never know exactly what happened next. The next thing we know with certainty is that a year later, a young soldier was admitted to an army hospital after a year of military service. He had severe stomach cramps and convulsions of no apparent physical origin. The following morning, he was better, calm and mentally clear. Astonishingly, he was at a total loss to explain where he was or how he got there. He asked how he came to be in the hospital, what town he was in, and who the people around him were. He was Timmy, all right, awake and in a military hospital with his last memory that of throwing his books down on the porch in disgust. Timmy's father was phoned, and he corroborated the story. At his father's request, Timmy was discharged from the service as underage. (Adapted from Laughlin, 1967, pp. 862–63)

After witnessing the brutal murder of her husband, Betty, played by Renee Zellweger in the 2000 film *Nurse Betty,* loses her memory and flees to Los Angeles, where she takes on the new identity of a nurse.

Timmy was the victim of amnesia (the loss of memory of one's identity). As in many cases of amnesia, Timmy wandered and took up a new life by joining the army. Such unexpected travel away from home during amnesia is called a ***fugue state,*** from the Latin *fuga,* meaning flight. Timmy's loss of memory and fugue are understandable as a flight from intolerable anxiety caused by his problems at home and at school. Timmy adopted the most extreme defense against a painful situation: he became amnesic, not only for the situation, but for his very identity, and he took up a new identity. By becoming amnesic, he was able to escape from his anxiety. During his army

life, he remembered nothing about his previous painful life and, following recovery of his earlier memories, he was totally amnesic for his year in the army.

KINDS OF DISSOCIATIVE AMNESIA

What happened to Timmy is called a ***global*** or ***generalized amnesia:*** all the details of his personal life had vanished when he joined the army. Dissociative amnesia, like Timmy's, tends to be recurrent, with up to 40 percent of patients reporting a second episode (Coons, 1998). Amnesia can be less global than this. ***Retrograde amnesia*** is a more localized amnesia, in which all events immediately before some trauma are forgotten. For example, an uninjured survivor of an automobile accident may be unable to recall anything that happened during the twenty-four hours up to and including the accident that killed the rest of her family. ***Post-traumatic amnesia*** is the memory loss for events after the episode. The rarest amnesia is ***anterograde amnesia,*** in which there is difficulty remembering new material. This form of amnesia almost always has an organic cause, like a stroke. Finally, there exists ***selective*** or ***categorical amnesia,*** in which only the memories of events related to a particular theme vanish (Hirst, 1982; Roediger, Weldon, and Challis, 1989).

DISSOCIATIVE VERSUS ORGANIC AMNESIA

Amnesia can also be caused by physical trauma, such as a blow to the head or a gunshot wound to the brain, alcoholism, Alzheimer's disease, and stroke. Such

---

DSM-IV Criteria

Dissociative Amnesia

A. The predominant disturbance is one or more episodes of inability to recall important personal information, usually of a traumatic or stressful nature, that is too extensive to be explained by ordinary forgetfulness.

B. The disturbance does not occur exclusively during the course of Dissociative Identity Disorder, Dissociative Fugue, Post-Traumatic Stress Disorder, Acute Stress Disorder, or Somatization Disorder and is not due to the direct physiological effects of a substance (e.g., a drug of abuse, a medication) or a neurological or other general medical condition (e.g., Amnestic Disorder Due to Head Trauma).

C. The symptoms cause clinically significant distress or impairment in social, occupational, or other important areas of functioning.

SOURCE: APA, DSM-IV, 1994.

organically caused amnesia is different from dissociative amnesia. Aside from its physical basis, organic amnesia differs from dissociative amnesia in several ways. First, a person with dissociative amnesia is usually sorely troubled by marital, financial, or career stress before the amnesia, whereas an individual who suffers organic amnesia need not be (Coons, Bowman, Pellow, and Schneider, 1989). Second, dissociative amnesia does not result from any known neural damage.

A person with dissociative amnesia shows a four-fold pattern of memory loss that no one with organic amnesia has ever shown. First, the person with dissociative amnesia loses his past, both recent and remote—he cannot remember how many brothers and sisters he has; he cannot remember a well-learned fact from the distant past, nor can he remember what he had for breakfast right before the amnesia started. Those with organic amnesia, on the other hand, remember the distant past well—after a blow to the head, they can tell you perfectly well who taught them Sunday school when they were six years old, or the starting lineup of the 1964 Phillies—but they remember the recent past poorly. Second, an individual with dissociative amnesia loses his personal identity—name, address, occupation, and the like—but his store of general knowledge remains intact. He still remembers who the president is, what the date is, and what the capital of Saskatchewan is (Regina). People with organic amnesia, in contrast, tend to lose both personal and general knowledge.

Third, those with psychogenic amnesia have no anterograde loss; they remember well events that happened after the moment the amnesia started. In contrast, patients with organic amnesia have severe anterograde amnesia, and this is their primary symptom; they remember very little about episodes that happened after the organic damage (like the name of the doctor treating them for the blow to the head). Finally, dissociative amnesia often reverses abruptly. Dissociative amnesia often ends within a few hours or days, and within twenty-four hours of the return of his memory the individual may even recall the traumatic episode that set off the memory loss. In organic amnesia, memory only gradually returns for retrograde memories and hardly ever returns for anterograde memories following organic treatment, and memory of the trauma is never revived (Suarez and Pittluck, 1976).

Finally, it should be emphasized that the very existence of dissociative amnesia is not universally accepted. The belief in the category is based entirely on isolated, intriguing case histories. Skeptics have reviewed the literature in which a documented severe trauma happened and the victims were later asked if they remembered the trauma. In the dozens of such studies, there were quite a number of instances in which the victims did not report the trauma when they were asked about it. Are any of these cases dissociative amnesia? Once organic trauma and ordinary forgetfulness are ruled out, the possibility of nondisclosure is examined. It is commonplace that people will often not disclose humiliating, shameful, and otherwise untoward events. The reviewers conclude that there are no substantiated cases in which nondisclosure has been satisfactorily ruled out, and they suggest that the existence of dissociative amnesia has yet to be proven in prospective studies of trauma victims (Pope, Hudson, Bodkin, and Oliva, 1998). On the other hand, the exponents of dissociative disorder argue that not only is it real, it is underdiagnosed for two reasons: First, dissociative amnesia is comorbid with so many other disorders (for example, conversion, PTSD, self-mutilation, and sexual dysfunction) that it is easily overshadowed or overlooked. Second, few clinicians know how to do a probing chronological interview that reviews the recent and distant past in enough detail to expose huge gaps of memory (Coons, 1998). Be that as it may, it is obvious that the dissociative disorders—as they were 100 years ago—are still a battleground on which the different basic beliefs about the nature of human beings continue to play themselves out.

VULNERABILITY AND CAUSE OF DISSOCIATIVE AMNESIA

Only a few other facts about dissociative amnesia are known, and they tell us a bit more about vulnerability to this disorder. Dissociative amnesia and fugue states (assuming a new identity) are rare disorders in peacetime, but in times of war and natural disaster they are much more common. They apparently occur in men more than in women and in younger people more than in old people.

The cause of dissociative amnesia is a mystery, more shrouded even than the causes of the somatoform disorders, which it resembles. We can speculate on how it might be caused, however. If we take the symptoms of conversion at face value, we can assume that the mind sometimes deals with emotionally distressing conflicts by producing physical losses. This is the lasting insight of psychodynamic thinking. So, Bear, anxious and guilty about causing his friend's paralysis, converted his distress into his own paralysis. We do not know the mechanism of this conversion, but whatever it is, it might also be working in the person with amnesia. What happens when a vulnerable individual faces an even more traumatic conflict, such as occurs during war? What happens when one's physical existence is suddenly threatened, or when one's entire life plans are shattered? Enormous anxiety is generated. Perhaps we have one ultimate psychological escape hatch—to forget whom we are and thereby neutralize our anxiety about our possible death, our shattered future, or our insoluble problems. Both the psychoanalytic model and the behavioral model are compatible with this explanation. For the psychoanalyst, the painful memory of who we are is repressed, and this defends successfully against anxiety. For the behaviorist, anxiety reduction reinforces the symptom of taking on a new identity. In short, amnesia may be the most global of defenses against anxiety produced by very traumatic and unacceptable circumstances.

Depersonalization Disorder

> Cardiopulmonary resuscitation was begun. . . . I did indeed observe my body as the physicians were working with me. At this point, I "left" the room, traveled through the tunnel at rapid speed, although time was totally irrelevant, and had multiple subsequent experiences. There was a travel through a misty area, hearing voices and sounds, not seeing anyone at this time, but being acutely aware of both positive and negative

> forces. . . . I experienced a panoramic view of my entire life, had glimpses into the "future" regarding not only myself but of other possible events, saw in the distance beautiful palaces and areas which I presumed represented "knowledge."
>
> Throughout this experience, there was no fear whatsoever. I felt totally warm and comforted, enveloped by compassion and love. There was a specific verbalization that I indeed heard . . . "it was not my time," and the next thing that I remember was awakening in the Intensive Care Unit where I had apparently been for two days." (Greyson, 1997).

This near-death experience reported by a physician is a typical report of a profound depersonalization experience. In depersonalization, one feels detached and separate from one's body or mind. When there are recurrent episodes, DSM-IV classifies this as *depersonalization disorder.* In this state, one can feel like an automaton or like one is in a dream or movie. Emotion is flat and dreamy, and one feels a lack of control. This is not a delusional state, since reality testing is present and one remains aware that this is not real. While depersonalized states are common, with up to 50 percent of people reporting a brief episode, the disorder itself is rare.

Individuals with the disorder are highly hypnotizable and often experience distortions in the shapes and sizes of objects. The disorder is comorbid with depression, hypochondriasis, and substance abuse, and differential diagnosis requires ruling these out, as well as panic, phobia, and PTSD, since these all entail the kind of massive threat that brings on depersonalization (Simeon et al., 1997)

DSM-IV Criteria

Depersonalization Disorder

A. Persistent or recurrent experiences of feeling detached from, and as if one is an outside observer of, one's mental processes or body (e.g., feeling like one is in a dream).

B. During the depersonalization experience, reality testing remains intact.

C. The depersonalization causes clinically significant distress or impairment in social, occupational, or other important areas of functioning.

D. The depersonalization experience does not occur exclusively during the course of another mental disorder, such as Schizophrenia, Panic Disorder, Acute Stress Disorder, or another Dissociative Disorder, and is not due to the direct physiological effect of a substance (e.g., a drug of abuse, a medication) or a general medical condition (e.g., temporal lobe epilepsy).

SOURCE: APA, DSM-IV, 1994.

DSM-IV Criteria

Dissociative Identity Disorder
(formerly Multiple Personality Disorder)

A. The presence of two or more distinct identities or personality states (each with its own relatively enduring pattern of perceiving, relating to, and thinking about the environment and self).

B. At least two of these identities or personality states recurrently take control of the person's behavior.

C. Inability to recall important personal information that is too extensive to be explained by ordinary forgetfulness.

D. The disturbance is not due to the direct physiological effects of a substance (e.g., blackouts or chaotic behavior during Alcohol Intoxication) or a general medical condition (e.g., complex partial seizures). (*Note:* In children, the symptoms are not attributable to imaginary playmates or other fantasy play.)

SOURCE: APA, DSM-IV, 1994.

Dissociative Identity Disorder (Multiple Personality Disorder)

Dissociative identity disorder (DID), also called ***multiple personality disorder (MPD),*** is defined as the occurrence of two or more distinct identities (historically referred to as "personalities" and often called "alters") in the same individual, each of which is sufficiently integrated to have a relatively stable life of its own and recurrently to take full control of the person's behavior (DSM-IV). This is another disorder in which amnesia plays a major role. Here it is quite clear that the multiple identities and their attendant amnesia for each other function to minimize unbearable anxiety. This is as astonishing a form of psychopathology as exists. Multiple personality disorder was formerly thought of as a very rare disorder—only 200 cases had been reported—but now that clinicians are looking for it, much more of it seems to be around. Very few cases were reported before 1970. But one researcher, Eugene Bliss, started the cascade when he saw 14 cases of it in the late 1970s, just in Utah (Bliss, 1980; Bliss and Jeppsen, 1985). Another 100 cases were reviewed by other researchers in the 1980s (Putnam et al., 1986). At present, the rate of diagnosed dissociative identity disorder may run as high as 5 percent of inpatient psychiatric admissions in some clinics (Ross, 1991; Ross, Anderson, Fleisher, and Norton, 1991; Coons, 1998).

The upsurge in the number of cases may be more than just a diagnostic fad. There seem to be three basic reasons for why dissociative identity disorder is seen so often: First, the diagnostic probe for amnesia is crucial ("Are there large parts of the week that you can't remember?"). If the answer to the question turns out to be "yes" many times, there is a possibility that other distinct identities may exist. Thus, amnesia is now part of the diagnosis, with "inability to recall important personal information that is too extensive to be explained by ordinary forgetfulness" a hallmark.

Second, dissociative identity disorder fits the psychoanalytic model to a T, and so psychodynamic therapists are highly prepared, even eager, to diagnose it. As we shall see, the disorder begins with a childhood trauma that is repressed, and other identities are generated as a defense against the trauma (Loewenstein and Ross, 1992). Treatment consists of cathartic reintegration of the identities. It is not an exaggeration to say that dissociative identity disorder has breathed new life into the psychodynamic movement.

Third, diagnosis of dissociative identity disorder has surged with the new and highly visible awareness of child abuse. As we will see, child abuse—often sexual abuse—is generally claimed to be the trigger for the disorder. The immensely popular "Recovery Movement" sees such adult problems as depression, anxiety, eating disorders, and sexual dysfunction as resulting from child abuse (Bradshaw, 1990). Adherents of this movement believe that only by coming to grips with this early, and often unrecognized, abuse, can an adult regain mental health. Dissociative identity disorder is perhaps the best-documented example of the claims that child abuse has effects that last into adulthood (Lewis, Yeager, Swica, Pincus, and Lewis, 1997). All these claims, however, are speculative and controversial.

DISSOCIATIVE IDENTITY DISORDER DESCRIBED

Eugene Bliss, who is the pioneer of modern work on multiple personality disorder, had his first introduction to the disorder in 1978 when he received a call from a distressed supervisor of nurses at a Salt Lake City hospital. The supervisor suspected that one of her nurses had been secretly injecting herself with Demerol. The supervisor and Bliss called the nurse into the office and accused her of improper conduct. They asked the nurse to roll up her sleeves because they wanted to examine her arms for needle marks. The nurse complied, and the telltale marks were there. But in the process of complying, the nurse underwent a remarkable transformation. Her facial expression, her manner, and her voice all changed, claiming that she was not Lois, the demure nurse, but Lucy, the brazen drug addict. Almost everyone has heard of other famous multiple personalities, as in *The Three Faces of Eve* (Thigpen and Cleckley, 1954), Sybil (Schreiber, 1974), or Dr. Jekyll and Mr. Hyde. Among these cases is that of Julie-Jenny-Jerrie:

Julie came to therapy through her son, Adam, age nine, who had been referred for counseling because of very poor school performance, poor relations with peers, and aggressive behavior at home. Eventually it was decided to see his thirty-six-year-old mother, Julie, in hope that she could help in the therapeutic process.

Julie was highly cooperative, sophisticated, and concerned about Adam. She seemed to have a good understanding of herself, and her general style of solving interpersonal problems was discussion and compromise. She felt that she had trouble setting limits for her son, and she worried that she sometimes behaved too rigidly toward him.

During a session in the sixth week of discussions with Julie, she suddenly announced that she wanted to introduce someone to the therapist. The therapist assumed there was someone out in the waiting room, but to his astonishment he witnessed the following: Julie closed her eyes for a few seconds, frowned, and then raised her eyelids slowly. Putting out her cigarette, she said, "I wish Julie would stop smoking. I hate the taste of tobacco." She introduced herself as Jerrie, and later in the hour and in the same way, she introduced Jenny, yet a third personality.

Jenny revealed that she was the original personality and said that she created Jerrie at age three and subsequently created Julie at age eight. Both times Jenny created the new personalities to cope with her disturbed family life. Jerrie emerged as the outer personality when Jenny was recovering from a severe case of measles, and Jerrie became a buffer who allowed Jenny to keep her distance from seven rejecting siblings and two frightening parents. Jenny said that observing Jerrie was like observing a character in a play.

Between the ages of three and eight, Jenny remembers that her physical welfare was neglected, that she was sexually molested by a neighbor, and was given away for permanent adoption at age eight, with her parents telling her she was "incorrigible." At this

Chris Sizemore, on whose life the film *The Three Faces of Eve* is based, was diagnosed with multiple personality disorder (now called dissociative identity disorder). Here the real Chris Sizemore is shown next to her own painting, which shows the coexistence of three of her identities.

time, Jenny created Julie, a gentle personality who was better able to cope with rejection and not as vulnerable to cruelty as either Jerrie or Jenny. Remarkably, while Julie was allowed to know about Jenny, the original personality, Julie was kept unaware of the existence of Jerrie. Julie did not find out about Jerrie until age thirty-four, two years before therapy began.

At age eighteen, Julie-Jenny-Jerrie left home for good. Jerrie and Julie by this time were always the alternating outer personalities, and Jenny was always inside. In fact, Jenny had been "out" only twice since age seven. At age twenty-six, Jerrie married, and the couple adopted Adam, who was the husband's son by a woman with whom he was having an affair while he and Jerrie were married. Jerrie soon divorced him, but she kept Adam.

The three personalities were strikingly different. Jenny—the original—was a frightened person, very shy and vulnerable. She was the most insecure and childlike of the three and felt "exposed" whenever she was out. Jenny felt she had created two Frankensteins who were now out of her control. She liked Julie better, but she was put off by Julie's stubbornness and strong individuality. She felt Jerrie was tougher than Julie and better able to cope with the world, but she didn't like her as well. Jenny's main hope in therapy was that Julie and Jerrie would come to get along better with each other and therefore be better mothers to Adam.

Julie seemed to be the most integrated of the three personalities. Julie was heterosexual, and emotionally invested in being a good mother—this in spite of the fact that it was Jerrie who had adopted Adam.

Jerrie was the opposite of Julie. Jerrie was homosexual, dressed in masculine fashion, sophisticated, and sure of herself. She was accomplished and proficient in the business world, and she enjoyed it. Jerrie didn't smoke, whereas Julie was a heavy smoker, and Jerrie's blood pressure was a consistent twenty points higher than Julie's.

Jerrie had known about Julie since Julie was "born" at age eight, but she had been in touch with her only in the past two years. She wanted to have nothing to do with Julie because she was afraid Julie would have a mental breakdown. Julie and Jerrie did not get along. When one of them was out and having a good time, she would resist relinquishing her position. But when a crisis was at hand, the personality who was out would duck in, leaving the inner personality to face the problem. For example, Julie took

LSD and then let Jerrie out so that Jerrie would be the victim of the hallucinations.

Ultimately Jerrie was able to tell Adam that there were two personalities who had been contributing to his misery, and Adam's immediate response was amusement and curiosity. He was able to accept the explanation that "Mother is two people who keep going in and out, but both of them love me." Adam appeared relieved rather than disturbed. Soon thereafter, Jerrie terminated therapy. Julie, in a suicidal depression, had gotten herself admitted to a state hospital against Jerrie's will, but Jerrie had gained control and talked her way out of the hospital. Julie wrote the therapist that she wanted to come to therapy, but Jerrie would not allow it and refused to come anymore. And this was the last that was seen of Julie-Jenny-Jerrie. (Adapted from Davis and Osherson, 1977)

This fascinating case exemplifies much of what is known about dissociative identity disorder. Amnesia of some kind almost always exists. Generally, one of the identities is aware of the experience of the others (Jenny knew of both Julie and Jerrie, and Jerrie knew of Julie), and one is amnesic about the others (Julie did not know of Jerrie). The presence of unexplained amnesia—hours or days each week that are missing—is a crucial clue to the undetected presence of dissociative identity disorder.

In the history of a person with dissociative identity disorder, the distinct identities within an individual—like Julie-Jenny-Jerrie—differ along many dimensions. Not only do they differ in their memories, but also in their wishes, attitudes, interests, learning ability, knowledge, morals, sexual orientation, age, rate of speech, personality test scores, and physiological indices such as heart rate, blood pressure, and EEG (Lester, 1977). In a systematic study of the autonomic patterns of nine patients with dissociative identity disorder compared to five hypnotized controls at the National Institute of Mental Health, the distinct identities in the patients with dissociative identity disorder showed highly distinct patterns of breathing, sweating, heart rate, and habituation (Putnam, Zahn, and Post, 1990). Remarkably, some women with dissociative identity disorder report that they menstruate much of the month because each identity has her own cycle (Jens and Evans, 1983). Moreover, each distinct identity can have different handwriting (see Figure 6–1). Most patients with dissociative identity disorder are women. Nor is the disorder restricted to the wealthiest Western cultures, since the parallel symptoms have been well documented in Turkey (Yargic, Sar, Tutkun, and Alyanak, 1998).

Figure 6—1

HANDWRITING SAMPLES OF FOUR PEOPLE DIAGNOSED WITH DISSOCIATIVE IDENTITY DISORDER

Handwriting has been shown to differ in the different identities of people with dissociative identity disorder. Researchers studied twelve murderers who were diagnosed with dissociative identity disorder. Writing samples from ten of the subjects revealed markedly different handwriting in each of their identities. We see here handwriting samples and signatures from one subject (A and B), as well as handwriting samples from another subject (C), and signatures from a different subject (D). The handwriting is obviously very different, depending on which identity (personality or alter) of the subject is doing the writing. (Source: Lewis, Yeager, Swica, Pincus, and Lewis, 1997, p. 1706)

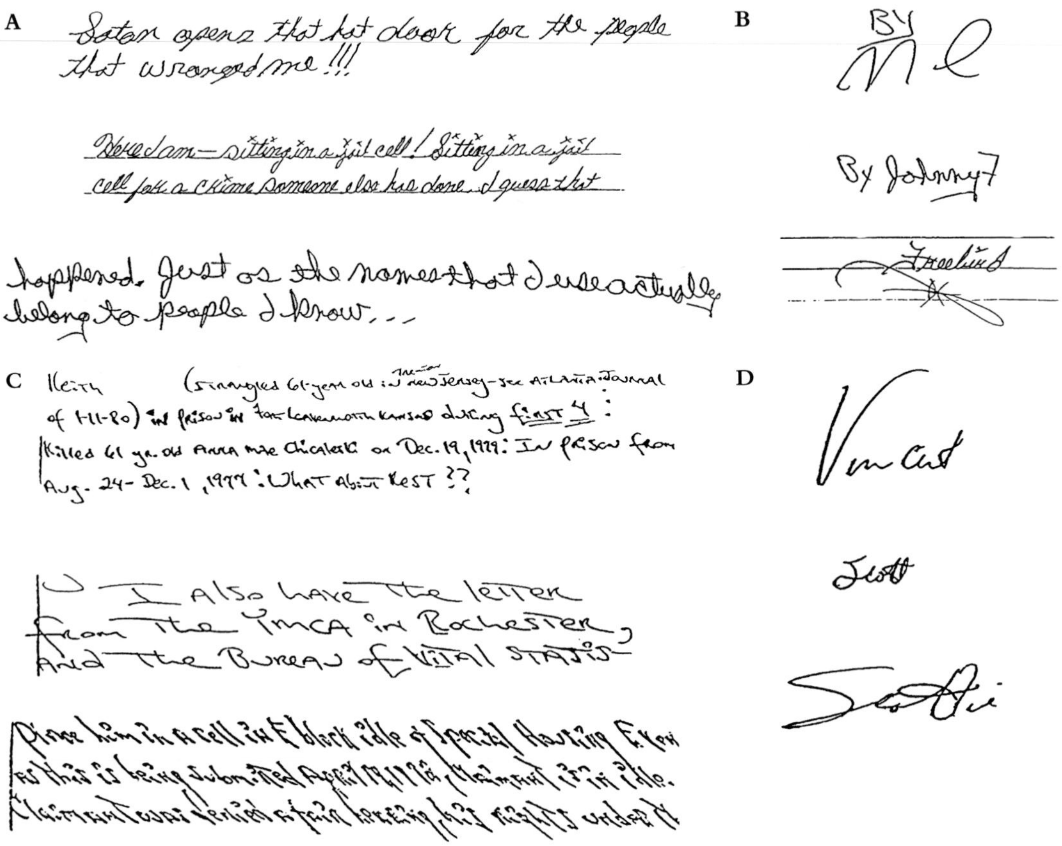

The identities also differ in psychological health. Often, the dominant identity is the healthier personality. One patient, a proper Southern lady, was accused of wanton sexuality, including intercourse with strangers. She made a clumsy attempt at a self-induced abortion, but she could not remember it. Her submerged identity said, "I did it because I suspected a pregnancy. I took a sharp stick and shoved it inside, then I started to bleed badly" (Bliss, 1980). The dominant identity, however, is not always the healthiest, and a submerged identity may actually sympathize with an unhealthy dominant identity and try to help. In one case, the submerged identity wrote to the dominant identity giving her helpful information to try to make her healthier (Taylor and Martin, 1944).

ETIOLOGY OF DISSOCIATIVE IDENTITY DISORDER

Where does dissociative identity disorder come from? The fourteen cases of multiple personality disorder that were seen by Bliss shared some important common features, and provide us with some clues as to how the disorder begins and how it develops. Bliss's hypothesis about how multiple personality disorder proceeds has three steps: First, an individual between

The distinct identities in a person with dissociative identity disorder may be created by self-hypnosis. The identities may be unconsciously created to cope with unbearable stress and trauma. The sense of dissociation and multiple selves trapped together in the patient's mind is depicted by Jacqueline Morreau in this painting titled *Divided Self I*.

ages four and six experiences a traumatic emotional problem. Indeed, dissociative identity disorder has much in common with post-traumatic stress disorder (Spiegel, 1984), and the rate of claims of child abuse experienced by those who develop dissociative identity disorder may be as high as 97 percent (Coons, 1994; Keaney and Farley, 1996; Putnam et al., 1986; Ross et al., 1990). She copes with the trauma by creating another distinct identity to take the brunt of the problem. Second, the individual is particularly vulnerable because she is highly susceptible to self-hypnosis, a process by which one is able to put oneself at will into trance states that have the properties of formal hypnotic inductions. Third, the individual finds out that creating another distinct identity by self-hypnosis relieves her of her emotional burden, so that in the future, when she confronts other emotional problems, she creates new distinct identities to take the brunt (see Figure 6–2; see also Kluft, 1984, 1991).

There is some evidence for each of these three steps: First, all fourteen of the patients that Bliss saw did, in fact, create their first alternative identity between the ages of four and six, and each seemed to be created in order to cope with very difficult emotional circumstances. Roberta, for example, created the first of her eighteen distinct identities when her mother held her under water and tried to drown her. This identity had the purpose of controlling and feeling

Figure 6–2

MODEL OF DISSOCIATIVE IDENTITY DISORDER

One theory about the origin of dissociative identity disorder holds that an early trauma triggers the creation of a new personality, an elaborate defense that is repeated as the patient grows up.

Childhood trauma between ages 4 and 6

People less easily hypnotized use other coping strategies and DID does not develop

People skilled at self-hypnosis use it to develop a second personality, which bears the brunt of the trauma

When a new and different trauma is experienced, a third personality is created, because the strategy of creating another personality successfully relieved the earlier trauma

Roberta's anger and of handling Roberta's homicidal rage without Roberta's having to do so. Another patient was molested at age four by an adult man. She created her first alternative identity in order to handle the molestation and thereafter used this identity to handle all sexual encounters.

Second, there is evidence that these patients are extraordinarily good at self-hypnosis (Ganaway, 1989). All fourteen of Bliss's patients were excellent hypnotic subjects. When Bliss hypnotized them, they went rapidly into a trance on the first induction. During the hypnosis, when he instructed them to have amnesia for what happened during hypnosis, they did this as well. In addition, when these patients reported the way in which they created the identities, they described a process that sounds like hypnotic induction. One of the identities of a patient said, "She creates personalities by blocking everything from her head, mentally relaxes, concentrates very hard and wishes." Another said, "She lies down, but can do it sitting up, concentrates very hard, clears her mind, blocks everything out and then wishes for the person, but she isn't aware of what she is doing." Once these patients were introduced to formal hypnosis in therapy, most reported that this experience was identical to experiences they had had dating back to their childhood, and that an inordinate amount of their lives had been spent in this altered state of consciousness. One patient described what she was experiencing as follows: "I spent an awful lot of time in hypnosis when I was young. . . . I've always lived in a dream world. Now that I know what hypnosis is, I can say that I was in a trance often. There was a little place where I could sit, close my eyes and imagine, until I felt very relaxed, just like hypnosis—and it could be very deep."

Third, patients used new identities to defend against distress later in life. Jenny, you will recall, created Julie, a gentle identity, to cope with her parents' putting her up for adoption at age eight. Most of the patients reported instances in which they created new identities to cope with new stresses even when they were adults (see Table 6–3).

Overall, dissociative identity disorder, like somatoform disorders and dissociative amnesia, can be seen as an attempt to defend against severe emotional distress. A child of four to six who is unusually capable of self-hypnosis creates a new identity—an imaginary companion and ally—to help her deal with the anxiety generated by a possible traumatic experience. This innocent, childhood ploy inadvertently becomes an adult disaster as the patient repeatedly uses this technique to cope with the stresses she encounters as she grows up. The identities multiply, and new problems arise as a result of the fractured self.

PSYCHOTHERAPY FOR DISSOCIATIVE IDENTITY DISORDER

As in the case of Julie-Jenny-Jerrie, the treatment of patients with dissociative identity disorder is difficult and frustrating. Therapy for the disorder has been conceptualized both in psychodynamic terms and as "tactical integration," a cognitive therapy approach (Fine, 1991). In the cognitive approach, the therapist identifies the automatic thoughts of the patient, teaches skills of disputing and challenging irrational thoughts, and tries to find the basis for why these irrational thoughts were credible to the patient. Hypnosis is used in both the cognitive treatment and in the more widely used psychodynamic treatment.

In psychodynamic treatment, the first step is to make the patient aware of the problem. Although she may have lived in this strange state for many years, had amnesia, and been told by others about her bizarre behavior, she may not yet have confronted the fact of other identities. Under hypnosis, the therapist calls up the alter egos and allows them to speak freely. In addition, the patient herself is asked to listen and then is introduced to some of these identities. She is told to remember the experience when she emerges from hypnosis. Enormous distress and turmoil often follow this discovery, but it is important for her to keep hold of the facts of many identities. At this point, she may display one of the most troublesome problems for therapy—dodging back into a self-hypnotic state and so avoiding the unpleasant reality. The therapist may then try to enlist the aid of various identities (Kluft, 1987).

After the patient is made fully aware of her many distinct identities, the therapist explains to her that they are products of self-hypnosis induced at an early age and without any conscious or malicious intent. The patient is told that now she is an adult, strong and capable, and that if she has the courage, she can flush these specters out and defeat them. The other identities may object, or want to continue their own life, but she is the only real person here. There is only one body and one head, and the other identities are her creations. She will have the privilege of deciding what aspects of the identities she will retain. In one study of thirty-four patients treated by an experienced therapist, 94 percent apparently showed strong improvement, with a two-year follow-up (Kluft, 1987).

TABLE 6–3

SIGNS AND SYMPTOMS OF DISSOCIATION
IN FIVE MURDERERS WITH DID

Subject	Sex	Age (years)	Symptoms and Signs in Childhood	Symptoms and Signs in Adulthood	Corroboration of Symptoms
1	M	40	Considered "possessed"; vivid imaginary companions; auditory hallucinations; dramatic demeanor changes	Trances; vivid imaginary companions; voice changes/switches to foreign-sounding language; different names/handwritings; command hallucinations; amnesias; two male personality states identified	Mother, sister, aunt; police record; legal assistant's notes; handwritten documents and letters
2	M	32	Trances ("phasing out") since age 15 months; called "possessed"; vivid imaginary companions; auditory hallucinations; episodic shaking with eyes open; considered epileptic	Trances; voice, accent, demeanor changes; different names/signatures; wrote different ages on forms; auditory hallucinations; amnesias; three male personality states identified	Mother, brother, wife, teacher, housemates; handwritten documents and letters
3	M	41	Trances; fugue states; called "possessed"; vivid imaginary companion; auditory hallucinations; amnesias	Trances/"conscious blackouts"; voice and demeanor changes; regression to small child; legally changed name to that of most powerful alternate personality; different signatures/handwritings; auditory hallucinations; amnesias; three male personality states identified	Wife, brother, sister, friends, neighbors, co-workers; court records of legal name change to that of alternate personality; handwritten documents and letters
4	M	33	Trances ("glassy eyed"); fugues (age 8, found across town; age 14, found in distant state); vivid imaginary companions; auditory, visual, and tactile hallucinations; amnesias; falling and shaking episodes; considered epileptic	Trances/time loss; vivid imaginary companions; voice and demeanor changes/dresses and sounds female; different clothing (sizes, sexes); different signatures/handwritings; auditory hallucinations; amnesias; two female and four male personality states identified	Mother, father, brother, friends, cell mates; prosecution psychiatrist interviewed alternate personalities; trial transcripts; police audiotapes; handwritten documents and letters
5	M	30	Fugues; vivid imaginary companion; auditory hallucinations; amnesias; wore girls' panties and sanitary napkins	Trances (i.e., "astral projection"); fugues/time loss; voice and demeanor changes/dresses as a female; different names/signatures/handwritings; different visual acuities; auditory hallucinations; amnesias; two female and four male personality states identified	Mother, brother, aunt, uncle, stepmother, stepfather, childhood friends; adult and child psychiatric/psychological records; school records; handwritten documents and letters

SOURCE: Lewis, Yeager, Swica, Pincus, and Lewis, 1997; p. 1704.

In a survey of 305 clinicians who treat dissociative identity disorder, Putnam and Loewenstein (1993) found that the average patient is in treatment for almost four years. Individual therapy (both psychodynamic and cognitive) and hypnosis were most widely used. Antidepressant and anti-anxiety drugs were also prescribed by two-thirds of the clinicians, with "moderate" relief reported. In a two-year follow-up of 135 DID patients, about half of those who could be located (only 54), showed marked improvement on dissociative symptoms, mood, and need for medication. Those patients who had achieved "integration" in therapy showed the most long-term improvement (Ellason and Ross, 1997).

DOUBTS ABOUT DISSOCIATIVE IDENTITY DISORDER

And yet, many doubts remain about the reality of dissociative identity disorder. It is not surprising that DID should be a battleground since several different interest groups and ideologies clash about this disorder. First, DID has led to a rejuvenation of psychoanalysis, long embattled by lack of empirical evidence for its tenets.

At its very heart, DID invokes repression of the memory of childhood abuse as its cause. In opposition, cognitive and behavioral thinkers are unwilling to accept the existence of unconscious motivated processes like repression and hence—lacking a theory to explain DID—are prone to doubt whether DID really exists at all. Second, lawyers and the courts are very much a part of the battle. DID is used as a plea to excuse serious crime, so both sides in many court cases have had a stake in its validity or invalidity. Third, DID, with its reliance on memories of abuse during childhood, is inextricably linked to the heated false memory controversy (see Chapter 15). Finally, DID can be faked by an individual knowledgeable about its symptoms, and so the question of malingering is always present.

The most salient grounds for doubt concern the memories of childhood sexual abuse in many DID patients. With the exception of the study of the twelve murderers by Dorothy Lewis (Box 6–2), almost all reports of DID are based on the adult patient's uncorroborated memory that abuse occurred when she was a small child. Some psychologists have been concerned about the veracity of the adult patients' memories of child abuse (Ganaway, 1989; Putnam, 1989). Society has recently become much more willing to listen to buried family secrets and to "believe the children." As a result, in the early 1990s, following the explosion in the diagnosis of DID, "memory retrieval" therapy became quite fashionable. In such a treatment, the therapist strongly encourages the patient to explore and find long-buried memories of abuse, usually sexual, that might be at the root of the patient's adult problems. There has been a trend toward facile acceptance of extensive, incredible, and contradictory accounts of abuse. This has placed the hard-won scientific credibility of the field of dissociative identity disorder into jeopardy. Memory retrieval therapy is now highly controversial, and some evidence suggests that it may sometimes be based on false memories and may sometimes make patients worse, whether the memories are true or false.

In discussing dissociation and DID, David Spiegel (1990) points to the existence of the "grade 5" hypnotizable person. Only 5 percent of the population fall into this category. Grade 5's are extremely hypnotizable, very suggestible, show pathological compliance with their therapists, and give up critical judgment. They report vivid, rich, detailed "memories" from trance states—which are without factual foundation. Virtually all patients with dissociative identity disorder are grade 5's (Ganaway, 1989).

The reports of patients with DID must be considered at high risk for contamination by such pseudo-memories. George Ganaway's many patients have told him in vivid detail of encounters with demons, angels, lobsters, chickens, tigers, God, and a unicorn. In one case, Sarah, a fifty-year-old woman diagnosed with dissociative identity disorder, was shocked when Carrie, a five-year-old "alter," relived in vivid detail the brutal rape and murder of twelve girls from her Sunday school class. The cult leader spared Carrie because she was unlucky number 13. On further exploration, Sherry, another alter, revealed that she had created Carrie to absorb the terror she had felt when her grandmother read grisly murder stories to her (Ganaway, 1989).

While the Lewis study of the twelve murderers may put to rest some of the doubts about the origin of DID in childhood sexual abuse, other doubts remain. There are particular concerns about the potentially destructive possibilities of memory retrieval in therapy. In 1990, Washington State let people receive treatment under the Crime Victims Act if they claimed repressed memory of childhood sexual abuse. So in 1996, the Washington Department of Labor and Industries gathered preliminary statistics on the outcome of treatment for thirty randomly selected patients (Loftus, Grant, Franklin, Parr, and Brown, 1996). Before the repressed memories were retrieved in therapy, 10 percent had suicidal ideation, 7 percent had been hospitalized, and 3 percent had self-mutilated. After the memories were recovered, 67 percent had suicidal ideation, 37 percent had been hospitalized, and 27 percent had self-mutilated. Ninety-seven percent claimed that they had been abused by parents or family members in satanic rituals, with the abuse beginning at seven months of age on average. The patients, it was noted, saw master's level therapists (87 percent). They were well educated, and 83 percent had had jobs before therapy. Three years later, only 10 percent were employed, 50 percent had been separated or divorced from their spouses, and all of them were estranged from their extended families. It cannot be known if the memories were true, but recovering them made many of their lives dramatically worse.

At this point, we should remain skeptical about the validity of some of the patients' tales of abuse, particularly the more outlandish ones, and about whether memory retrieval therapy actually benefits all patients (Lilienfeld et al., 1999). Some of the memories may be true, and some may be false; some of the therapy may help patients, and some may actually make them worse. The truth or falsity of the memories, however,

Murderers with Dissociative Identity Disorder

Scientists have expressed considerable doubt about whether dissociative identity disorder (DID) exists at all, to say nothing of the three-stage process postulated by psychodynamic thinkers to account for it. One particularly important criticism is the absence of outside verification of the childhood trauma alleged to have set off DID. Dramatic documentation of this process, however, comes from the history of twelve murderers diagnosed with DID (Lewis, Yeager, Swica, Pincus, and Lewis, 1997). In felons, the DID claim is doubly suspect, since an insanity defense based on DID invites malingering. The first author, Dorothy Lewis, did case eval-

uations of about 150 murderers over the last twenty years. Of these, twelve—eleven men and one woman—met the criteria for DID. All of these individuals had amnesia for both violent and nonviolent behavior, all had auditory hallucinations of voices of their alternate personalities, and in all cases, Lewis was able to speak with at least one of the alters. Researchers documented that 10 of the 12 went into trances as adults. Eleven of the 12 had experienced sexual and physical abuse—better described as torture—during their childhood, and the abuse was confirmed by external evidence. The table below presents the evidence of childhood abuse for 5 of these murderers.

Subject	Physical Abuse	Sexual Abuse	Documentation	Informants	Scars
1	Severe beatings by mother, father; tied up and beaten by mother; neglect	Sexual abuse by mother; incest with sisters	Trial testimony regarding father's incarceration for violence to his family; neglect petitions; mother declared unfit; children removed from home	Mother, sister, aunt	Head, back
2	Thrown into wall by father (ages 14 months and 3 years), causing indentation of skull; leg fractured by father (age 5); tied up naked and beaten by mother; set afire by siblings	Sexual abuse by father, including "circumcision" (age 3)	Childhood hospital records document numerous injuries, losses of consciousness, "seizures"; father's military records indicate court martial and dishonorable discharge for beating subject's 7-month-old sibling; father's medical records document fist traumas coincident with subject's unexplained injuries	Mother, brother	Head, back, chest
3	Severe beatings by mother, father; neglect	Sexual abuse by mother; incest with sisters, brother	Neglect petitions; petition for termination of parental rights; brother's social work, welfare records reveal subject's incest with mother; school records report father's violence	Brother, childhood friend, neighbor, wife	Head, face, back, chest
4	Severe beatings by father; scalded by mother; set afire by parents	Sexual abuse, including sodomy with bizarre objects, by father; sexual abuse by older brother	Hospital records document several admissions starting at age 2 for "convulsions" and loss of consciousness; police reports call father "highly emotional and erratic"	Mother, father, brother	Head, back, chest, arms, thighs, buttocks, penis
5	Severe beatings by mother, father, stepmother; burned and thumbs pulled out of sockets by stepmother; locked in closets and basement by stepmother; abandoned by mother	Sexual abuse by stepmother, including sodomy with bizarre objects; being tied down and given blood enemas; dressed as a girl by stepmother	Child medical, psychiatric, and foster care records document abuse by father, mother, stepmother; mother declared unfit, children removed from home; police records document stepmother's violence	Mother, aunt, uncle, childhood friend	Head, back, chest

SOURCE: Lewis, Yeager, Swica, Pincus and Lewis, 1997, p. 1708.

does not matter nearly as much as the fact of their telling, the needs that such telling reveal about the patient, and the usefulness of such material for healing. Therapists of patients with DID must take care in encouraging patients to talk about such memories and in helping them to work through their problems as adults so that their emotional lives can become richer rather than more impoverished.

Putting It All Together

In this chapter and the previous one, we examined disorders that appear, on the surface, to be quite varied: phobia, post-traumatic stress disorder, panic disorder, generalized anxiety disorder, obsessive-compulsive disorder, somatoform disorders, dissociative amnesia, depersonalization, and dissociative identity disorder. In the past, these disorders looked more like a coherent whole than they do today. Historically, they were all viewed as "neuroses," and all were thought to involve anxiety as the central process. In the case of phobia and post-traumatic stress disorder, fear is on the surface; in panic disorder and generalized anxiety disorder, anxiety (fear without a specific object) is also on the surface. The individual with one of these problems feels anxiety, apprehension, fear, terror, and dread in his daily life. In obsessive-compulsive disorders, on the other hand, anxiety is present, but it is not consciously felt if the compulsion is frequent and effective. In contrast, in the somatoform disorders and the dissociative disorders, anxiety is not usually observed. But in order to explain the bizarre symptoms of these disorders, theorists have had to infer that, with his symptoms, the individual is defending against underlying anxiety. To the extent that the defense is successful, the symptoms will appear, and anxiety will not be felt.

The last forty years have witnessed a sea change in the field of psychopathology: our categories have become more descriptive and less theoretical. DSM-IV disavows a common process—defending against anxiety—as the mechanical cause of these disorders. The dissociative disorders and somatoform disorders are of central historical importance in this change. They were the cornerstone disorders on the basis of which Freud postulated that transmuted anxiety caused all neuroses, even those in which no anxiety was felt. In a decisive move, DSM-IV no longer classifies these as "anxiety disorders." Rather, DSM-IV includes as anxiety disorders only those disorders from the previous chapter in which anxiety is manifest: phobia, panic disorder, generalized anxiety disorder, post-traumatic stress disorder, and obsessive-compulsive disorder. Descriptively, it makes good sense to segregate those disorders in which anxiety is observed from those in which anxiety is only inferred by a theory. But at a theoretical level, the dissociative and somatoform disorders cry out for a common explanation.

Where will such a theory come from? One possibility is from the growing discourse between neuroscience and psychology. Even though the somatoform and dissociative disorders involve such apparently "biological" states as amnesia, blindness, deafness, and paralysis, it is noteworthy that no biological theory has emerged. But there are a variety of clues that a neuroscience of these disorders might be illuminating. Hysterical blindness, for example, shares some of the features of "blind-sight" (Rafel, Smith, Krantz, Cohen, and Brennan, 1990). Patients with occipital cortex brain damage, who act and feel as if they are blind, do much better than chance at locating visual stimuli. Similarly, an hysterically blind person usually avoids walking in front of cars and tripping over furniture, even though he feels blind. Another clue is that such neurologically and hormonally controlled processes as handwriting, handedness, and even menstrual periods differ among the different personalities in dissociative identity disorder. Yet another clue is that conversion symptoms usually occur more often on the right side of the body than the left side. This suggests left-hemisphere involvement (Min and Lee, 1997).

Another possibility is that such a theory may reemerge from modern psychodynamic thinking. Psychodynamic thinking has always been most concerned with the underlying deep processes that produce symptoms. Many of those processes have failed to be of much use in explaining disorders in which anxiety is manifest. Rather, for phobia and post-traumatic stress disorder, theories that come out of behavioral and cognitive models seem appropriate. In both of these disorders, we can postulate a trauma that imbued parts of the environment with terror, and the symptoms, the course, and the therapies roughly follow known behavioral and cognitive laws. But we saw that obsessive-compulsive disorder is not as easy to handle in this way. How obsessions stay around once they have been acquired fits reasonably well within behavioral views, as do therapies that alleviate obsessions. But this is only part of the story. Cognitive and behavioral investigators do not answer the questions of who is vulnerable to obsessions and what content obsessions will take, nor is there even a useful theory from these traditions. Finally, we have somatoform disorders, dissociative amnesia, and dissociative identity disorder. Here, theories of surface anxiety are useless, and in the absence of an adequate behavioral or cognitive theory, these theorists are more inclined to doubt the reality of these disorders than to account for their existence. These disorders, in which underlying emotional distress is creating troubling symptoms, may be best viewed within a psychodynamic tradition, where anxiety or some other unpleasant emotion that lies beneath the surface and is being defended against, seems to make some sense of the symptoms of these disorders. Nonetheless, the details of their etiology and which therapy is best for them remain questions to be resolved in the future.

Overall, then, we find that when fear and anxiety are on the surface, behavioral and cognitive models serve us well. As fear and anxiety tend to disappear from the surface, however, we find ourselves in need of deeper models to attempt to explain what we do observe. It seems likely that for the present we still need for disorders like conversion disorder, dissociative amnesia, and dissociative identity disorder, either theories from cognitive neuroscience or a theory derived from the psychodynamic approach. Such an approach postulates deep, unobserved emotional conflict and psychological defenses that are so rich as to inspire awe in those who study these disorders closely.

Summary

1. This chapter discussed two classes of disorders: the *somatoform disorders* and the *dissociative disorders.*

2. The somatoform disorders have five symptoms: (1) lost or altered physical functioning, (2) the absence of a known physical cause, (3) positive evidence that psychological factors are associated with the symptom, (4) indifference to the physical loss, and (5) the absence of voluntary control over the symptom.

3. Five kinds of somatoform disorders are: (1) *conversion,* in which one physical function is lost or altered; (2) *somatization disorder,* in which there is a dramatic and complicated medical history for multiple and recurrent bodily complaints in many organs, without any physical cause; (3) *pain disorder,* in which the onset, severity, or persistence of pain is not attributed to physical cause; (4) *hypochondriasis,* in which the individual is convinced he has, or will soon contract, a serious medical disease, in spite of ample reassurance to

the contrary; and (5) *body dysmorphic disorder,* in which the individual is preoccupied with an imagined or greatly exaggerated defect in his or her physical appearance.

4. Psychoanalytic theory holds that somatoform disorders are a defense against anxiety, that psychic energy is transmuted into somatic loss, and that the particular somatic loss symbolizes the underlying conflict. The communication view of somatoform disorder holds that the disorder is the alexithymic's way of saying she is distressed psychologically. The percept blocking view focuses on how a perception can be blocked from conscious experience and makes no claims about the motivation causing this blocking. Malingering is always a possibility in the somatoform disorders.

5. *Dissociative amnesia* is a loss of memory for important personal information caused by unbearable trauma. It can either be general or highly specific. *Retrograde amnesia* is a specific amnesia in which events immediately before some trauma are forgotten. *Anterograde amnesia* is difficulty remembering anything that occurs after a trauma. Dissociative amnesia sometimes involves *fugue,* which is the leaving of one place and taking up an identity in a new place.

6. *Depersonalization disorder* consists of recurrent episodes of feeling detached from one's body or mind. The individual who is having such an episode feels like an outside observer of real, and usually highly threatening, events that are actually happening.

7. *Dissociative identity disorder (DID),* formerly called *multiple personality disorder,* is the existence of two or more distinct identities in the same individual. Each identity is sufficiently integrated to have a relatively stable life of its own and to be able to recurrently take full control over the person's behavior. This disorder is more frequent than previously believed and seems to involve individuals who are highly susceptible to self-hypnosis, who claim to have experienced a serious trauma between ages four and six, and who use the creation of alternative identities to bear this trauma, which they are unable to cope with in any other way.

8. While case study evidence continues to accumulate for the existence of the dissociative disorders, particularly those created around childhood sexual abuse, critics doubt the very existence of these disorders and the veracity of the memories of childhood abuse. Some critics worry that memory retrieval in therapy can be destructive.

7 Mood Disorders

Chapter Outline

Else Blankenhorn, Untitled.

Learning Objectives

→ Be able to describe signs and symptoms of depressive disorders.

→ Learn who is most vulnerable to clinical depression, and why young people and women are particularly at risk.

→ Learn about the biological and psychological approaches to depression.

→ Be able to describe drug therapies for depression and why they are effective as long as they continue to be taken, as well as cognitive therapies and why they are more likely to prevent relapse.

→ Understand bipolar disorder and how it differs from unipolar depression, and be able to describe the course, probable cause, and effective treatments for bipolar disorder.

→ Familiarize yourself with seasonal affective disorder and the most effective treatment for SAD.

→ Learn who is at risk for suicide, how it is motivated, and how it might be prevented.

There is growing evidence that we now live in an Age of Melancholy and that prosperous young Americans are particularly afflicted. This is a very revealing paradox. People usually think that depression is intimately related to bad life circumstances, but things have never been better *objectively* for young Americans. The hands on the nuclear clock are farther away from midnight than ever before. There are fewer soldiers dying on the battlefield than at any time in the last hundred years. Fewer children are now dying of starvation than at any time in human history. We now have unprecedented purchasing power and access to music, education, books, and worldwide instant communication. But as all the statistics of "objective well-being" are improving, all the statistics on the depression and demoralization of the young are getting worse. These facts tell us that depression is not only about life circumstances, but also about how we *think* about life circumstances.

Depression is a disorder of guilt, sadness, hopelessness, and passivity. The incidence of mood disorders has increased greatly in America over the last thirty years. This is the largest increase in the incidence of any psychological disorder on record. Depression has become so common that it is considered the common cold of mental illness in America. Depression used to be a disorder that took years to treat successfully. Today, new medications like Prozac seem to alleviate some of the worst symptoms, at least for a time, and if the drugs continue to be taken. The general public has come to believe that depression is a biochemical illness that can be beaten by these new wonder drugs. Yet, is this media hype or truth or in-between? Is depression at bottom a biochemical illness? Can it be cured by antidepressant medication? What is the role of psychotherapy? In this chapter, we will discuss how depression and other mood disorders are understood and diagnosed. We will speculate on why depression has become so rampant today, and describe the treatments that work. We start by describing a common, but nonetheless very painful, depressive reaction to a loss:

> Within a two-day period, Nancy received a double blow: she got a C on her Abnormal Psychology midterm, and she also found out that her high school boyfriend had become engaged to someone else. The week that followed was awful. For the first few days, she had trouble getting out of bed to go to class. She burst into tears over dinner one evening and had to

leave the table. Missing dinner didn't much matter anyway. She wasn't hungry. Her future looked bleak since she now believed that she would never be accepted by any clinical psychology graduate school, and that she would never again find anyone she would love as much. She blamed herself for these failures in the two most important arenas of her life. After a week or two, the world started to look better. The instructor said that because everyone's grades were so low on the midterm, everyone had the option of writing a paper to cancel out their midterm grade, and Nancy found herself looking forward to a blind date that her roommate had arranged for the weekend. Her usual bounce and enthusiasm for life began to return, and with it, her appetite. She thought, "It will be an uphill battle, but I'm basically OK and I think I may find love and success."

How does such "normal depression" relate to "depressive "disorders"? In many ways, normal depression differs only in degree, not in kind, from the clinical disorder (Flett, Vredenburg, and Krames, 1997). Both are characterized by the same kinds of symptoms, and both show similar emotional difficulties and problems at work and at home (Judd, Paulus, Wells, and Rapaport, 1996). For the person with a depressive disorder, however, the symptoms are more severe, more frequent, and last far longer.

Mood disorders are quite varied in their signs and symptoms. We will first discuss these variations. Then we will discuss unipolar depressive disorder, how it looks and feels. We will do the same for the flip side of depression: mania. We will then show how in some mood disorders—bipolar disorder—depression and mania can intermingle. We will conclude the chapter by examining what is perhaps the most catastrophic outcome of the mood disorders: suicide.

Classifying the Mood Disorders

DSM-IV divides the **mood disorders** (also known as the **affective disorders**) into the depressive disorders, mania, and the bipolar disorders. In **major depression** (or **unipolar depression**), the individual suffers only depressive symptoms (for example, sadness, hopelessness, passivity, sleep and eating disturbances) without ever experiencing mania. In **mania,** the individual experiences symptoms of excessive elation, expansiveness, irritability, talkativeness, inflated self-esteem, and flight of ideas. In **bipolar disorder** (or **manic-depression**), the individual experiences both depression and mania.

By DSM-IV's definition, a major depressive episode generally lasts at least two weeks. The patient experiences five or more emotional, cognitive, motivational, and somatic symptoms, and one of the symptoms must be depressed mood or loss of interest or pleasure. Such **episodic depression** lasts for less than two years and has a clear beginning, which distinguishes it from previous nondepressed functioning. In contrast, **dysthymic disorder** is chronic depression in which the individual has been depressed for at least two years without more than a two-month return to normal functioning. **Chronic depression** is much less common than episodic depression. Some unfortunate people have both a chronic depression and an episodic depression on top of it. This is called **double depression.** Those suffering from double depression have more severe symptoms and a low rate of recovery (Keller and Shapiro, 1982; Wells, Burnam, Rogers, and Hays, 1992).

DSM-IV also distinguishes between depression "with melancholia" and depression "without melancholia." The distinction was originally an attempt to

Tsing-Fang Chen's *Bombardment* conveys the despair that is present in the mood disorders.

separate biologically based (endogenous—coming from within the body) depressive episodes from psychologically based (reactive or exogenous—coming from outside the body) depressive episodes. "Melancholic features" include a loss of pleasure in all activities and numbing or general lack of reaction to pleasurable events, which is worse in the morning; early morning awakening; lethargy; weight loss; and guilt. The attempt to distinguish depressive episodes as a biological illness from depressive episodes as a psychological problem is still highly controversial.

Two different symptom clusters have been found for the two kinds of episodes: depression with melancholia and depression without melancholia. People who have depression with melancholia have slow speech and movement, more severe symptoms, a lack of reaction to environmental changes during the episode, loss of interest in life, and somatic symptoms. They also smoke more, have had more anxiety, and have an abundance of melancholia in their families (Kendler, 1997). In addition, early morning awakening, guilt, and suicidal behavior may be more strongly associated with a melancholic depressive episode (Haslam and Beck, 1994; Mendels and Cochran, 1968).

The distinction between depression with melancholia and depression without melancholia has treatment implications: melancholic depressive episodes may respond better to antidepressant drugs and electroconvulsive shock, while nonmelancholic depressions may fare better with psychotherapy alone. The results of differential treatment studies have not been uniform, however, and the distinction must be viewed with caution (Fowles and Gersh, 1979; Sackeim and Rush, 1995; Thase et al., 1996).

Bipolar disorders are clearly different from normal depressive reactions to loss and from major unipolar depression. Bipolar depression has great swings between episodes of mania and episodes of depression, and as we will see, it probably has a large genetic component. DSM-IV distinguishes between two kinds of bipolar disorders, depending on whether the depression has full manic episodes or just "hypomanic" episodes (manic episodes that are not as severe as full manic episodes). Bipolar disorders develop at a younger age than depressive disorders, and are often more crippling to the individual. Fortunately, a specific drug, lithium carbonate, provides very considerable relief to those with bipolar disorders.

Depression and Depressive Disorders

Two astonishing things have happened to depression over the last two generations. First, depression has become the most widespread psychological disorder. If you were born after 1975, you are at least ten times more likely to become depressed than were your grandparents. Second, depression has become widespread among teenagers. In 1960, the average age for the first onset of depression was thirty; now the average age is less than fifteen. One out of six teenagers now suffers a serious episode of depression before graduating from high school. If you are a young adult today, your risk for becoming depressed has never been higher.

Almost everyone has suffered from depression, at least in its mild forms. Loss and pain are inevitable parts of growing up and growing older. Sometimes people we care for reject us, we write bad papers, our stocks go down, we fail to get the job we want, we don't get the grades we expect, people we love reject us or die. When these losses occur we go into mourning, and then emerge, our lives poorer, but with hope for the future. Almost everyone reacts to loss with some of the signs and symptoms of depression. We become sad and discouraged, apathetic and passive, the future looks bleak, some of the zest goes out of living. Such a reaction is normal—and we have repeatedly found in our surveys of college courses that at any given moment 25 to 30 percent of undergraduates have at least mild symptoms of depression.

Signs and Symptoms of Depression

Depression is called a disorder of "mood" by DSM-IV, but this is a misleading oversimplification, as can be seen in the words of this patient who was diagnosed with major depressive disorder:

> When you are in it there is no more empathy, no intellect, no imagination, no compassion, no humanity, no hope. It isn't possible to roll over in bed because the capacity to plan and execute the required steps is too difficult to master, and the physical skills needed are too hard to complete. For me, the loss of academic skills—reading, writing coherently, basic math—was particularly hard to deal with since I had excelled

in all those areas throughout my life and I took pride in my intellectual capacity.

Depression steals away whoever you were, prevents you from seeing who you might someday be, and replaces your life with a black hole. Like a sweater eaten by moths, nothing is left of the original, only fragments that hinted at greater capacities, greater abilities, greater potentials now gone. Nothing human beings value matters any more—music, laughter, love, sex, children, toasted bagels and the Sunday *New York Times*—because nothing and no one can reach the person trapped in the void. You have no idea of what will happen next, when it might be over, or even where you are now. Suicide sounds terrific, but much too difficult to plan and complete. (Karp, 1996, p. 24)

There are actually four sets of symptoms in depression. In addition to mood symptoms, there are thought or cognitive symptoms, motivational symptoms, and physical symptoms. An individual does not have to have all these symptoms to be correctly diag-

nosed as "depressed," but the more symptoms he or she has and the more intense each set, the more confident we can be that the individual is suffering from depression (see Box 7–1).

MOOD SYMPTOMS

When a depressed patient is asked how she feels, the most common adjectives she uses are: "sad, blue, miserable, helpless, hopeless, lonely, unhappy, downhearted, worthless, humiliated, ashamed, worried, useless, guilty." Sadness and guilt are the most obvious emotional symptoms in depressed people, and indeed some depressed people are unable to carry on a social conversation without excessive crying. Yet, this mood varies with time of day. Most commonly, depressed people feel worse in the morning, but their mood seems to lighten a bit as the day goes on. Along with feelings of sadness and guilt, feelings of anxiety are very often present in depression, so frequently in fact that depressive disorders are often "comorbid" with anxiety disorders (Fowles and

DSM-IV Criteria

Major Depressive Episode

A. Five (or more) of the following symptoms have been present during the same 2-week period and represent a change from previous functioning; at least one of the symptoms is either (1) depressed mood or (2) loss of interest or pleasure. (*Note:* Do not include symptoms that are clearly due to a general medical condition, or mood-incongruent delusions or hallucinations.) (1) depressed mood most of the day, nearly every day, as indicated by either subjective report (e.g., feels sad or empty) or observation made by others (e.g., appears tearful) (*Note:* In children and adolescents, can be irritable mood.); (2) markedly diminished interest or pleasure in all, or almost all, activities most of the day, nearly every day (as indicated by either subjective account or observation made by others); (3) significant weight loss when not dieting or weight gain (e.g., a change of more than 5% of body weight in a month), or decrease or increase in appetite nearly every day (*Note:* In children, consider failure to make expected weight gains.); (4) insomnia or hypersomnia (excessive sleeping) nearly every day; (5) psychomotor agitation or retardation nearly every day (observable by others, not merely subjective feelings of restlessness or being slowed down); (6) fatigue or loss of energy nearly every day; (7) feelings of worthlessness

or excessive or inappropriate guilt (which may be delusional) nearly every day (not merely self-reproach or guilt about being sick); (8) diminished ability to think or concentrate, or indecisiveness, nearly every day (either by subjective account or as observed by others); (9) recurrent thoughts of death (not just fear of dying), recurrent suicidal ideation without a specific plan, or a suicide attempt or a specific plan for committing suicide.

B. The symptoms do not meet the criteria for a Mixed Episode.

C. The symptoms cause clinically significant distress or impairment in social, occupational, or other important areas of functioning.

D. The symptoms are not due to the direct physiological effects of a substance (e.g., a drug of abuse, a medication) or a general medical condition (e.g., hypothyroidism).

E. The symptoms are not better accounted for by bereavement, i.e., after the loss of a loved one, the symptoms persist for longer than 2 months or are characterized by marked functional impairment, morbid preoccupation with worthlessness, suicidal ideation, psychotic symptoms, or psychomotor retardation.

SOURCE: APA, DSM-IV, 1994.

Measuring Depression

Lenore Radloff at the Center for Epidemiological Studies of the National Institutes of Mental Health has developed a widely used inventory of depressive symptoms. Each of the questions describes one of the symptoms of depression, and each question provides a severity score of 0 through 3 for that symptom. The person circles the answer that best describes how he or she feels right now. The symptoms divide into mood, thought, motivational, and physical sets. The statements below show responses to eight of the twenty questions of the CES–D (Center for Epidemiological Studies–Depression).

This test is designed, not as a way of diagnosing depression, but as a way of knowing how many symptoms are present and how severe they are once depression is clinically diagnosed. A high score alone is not diagnostic of clinical depression or mental illness. Generally speaking, research has shown that the average score (for the total of the numbers from the eight questions) in a North American college population is about 3 or 4, and students who score below this can be considered nondepressed. Mildly depressed students typically have scores from about 5 to 9, and scores of 10 or higher suggest moderate to severe depression. If an individual scores 10 or more for a period of one or two weeks, it would probably be in his best interest to seek help. If he has serious or persistent thoughts of suicide, regardless of his score, it is imperative that he seek aid.

CENTER FOR EPIDEMIOLOGICAL STUDIES–DEPRESSION INVENTORY

Mood A (Sadness)
I felt sad.
0   Rarely or none of the time (less than 1 day)
1   Some or a little of the time (1–2 days)
2   Occasionally or a moderate amount of time (3–4 days)
3   Most or all of the time (5–7 days)

Mood B (Enjoyment of life)
I did not enjoy life.
0   Rarely or none of the time (less than 1 day)
1   Some or a little of the time (1–2 days)
2   Occasionally or a moderate amount of time (3–4 days)
3   Most or all of the time (5–7 days)

Thought C (Pessimism)
I felt hopeless about the future.
0   Rarely or none of the time (less than 1 day)
1   Some or a little of the time (1–2 days)
2   Occasionally or a moderate amount of time (3–4 days)
3   Most or all of the time (5–7 days)

Thought D (Failure)
I thought my life had been a failure.
0   Rarely or none of the time (less than 1 day)
1   Some or a little of the time (1–2 days)
2   Occasionally or a moderate amount of time (3–4 days)
3   Most or all of the time (5–7 days)

Motivation E (Work initiation)
I felt that everything I did was an effort.
0   Rarely or none of the time (less than 1 day)
1   Some or a little of the time (1–2 days)
2   Occasionally or a moderate amount of time (3–4 days)
3   Most or all of the time (5–7 days)

Motivation F (Sociability)
I talked less than usual.
0   Rarely or none of the time (less than 1 day)
1   Some or a little of the time (1–2 days)
2   Occasionally or a moderate amount of time (3–4 days)
3   Most or all of the time (5–7 days)

Physical G (Appetite)
I did not feel like eating; my appetite was poor.
0   Rarely or none of the time (less than 1 day)
1   Some or a little of the time (1–2 days)
2   Occasionally or a moderate amount of time (3–4 days)
3   Most or all of the time (5–7 days)

Physical H (Sleep loss)
My sleep was restless.
0   Rarely or none of the time (less than 1 day)
1   Some or a little of the time (1–2 days)
2   Occasionally or a moderate amount of time (3–4 days)
3   Most or all of the time (5–7 days)

SOURCE: Seligman, 1994.

Gersh, 1979; Kessler et al., 1994). Almost everyone who is depressed is also anxious, but anxiety can occur in the absence of depression (Barlow, 2000; Keller et al., 2000).

Just as pervasive as sadness and guilt in depression is loss of gratification, the numbing of the joy of living. Activities that used to bring satisfaction feel flat. Loss of interest usually starts in only a few activities, such as work or child rearing. But as depression increases in severity, it spreads through practically everything the individual does. The pleasure derived from hobbies, recreation, and family diminishes. Gregarious individuals who used to enjoy parties now avoid social gatherings altogether. Finally, even pleasurable biological functions, such as eating and sex, lose their appeal. Ninety-two percent of depressed patients no longer derive gratification from some major interests in their life, and 64 percent of depressed patients lose their enjoyment of other people (Clark, Beck, and Beck, 1994).

This woman clearly shows the sadness and numbness that characterize a major depression. People who are diagnosed with major depression have lost interest in their family, friends, jobs, and hobbies.

COGNITIVE SYMPTOMS

A depressed person thinks of himself in a very negative light. These negative thoughts color his view of himself and of the future. He believes he has failed and that he is the cause of his own failures. He believes he is inferior, inadequate, and incompetent. But these views of failure and incompetence are often distortions. One patient managed to wallpaper a kitchen although very depressed. Here is how he distorted this achievement into a failure:

THERAPIST: Why didn't you rate wallpapering the kitchen as a mastery experience?

PATIENT: Because the flowers didn't line up.

THERAPIST: You did in fact complete the job?

PATIENT: Yes.

THERAPIST: Your kitchen?

PATIENT: No. I helped a neighbor do his kitchen.

THERAPIST: Did he do most of the work?

PATIENT: No, I really did almost all of it. He hadn't wallpapered before.

THERAPIST: Did anything else go wrong? Did you spill the paste all over? Ruin a lot of wallpaper? Leave a big mess?

PATIENT: No, no, the only problem was that the flowers did not line up.

THERAPIST: So, since it was not perfect, you get no credit at all.

PATIENT: Well . . . yes.

THERAPIST: Just how far off was the alignment of the flowers?

PATIENT: (holds out fingers about ⅛ of an inch apart) About that much.

THERAPIST: On each strip of paper?

PATIENT: No . . . on two or three pieces.

THERAPIST: Out of how many?

PATIENT: About 20–30.

THERAPIST: Did anyone else notice it?

PATIENT: No. In fact, my neighbor thought it was great.

THERAPIST: Did your wife see it?

PATIENT: Yeah, she admired the job.

THERAPIST: Could you see the defect when you stood back and looked at the whole wall?

PATIENT: Well . . . not really.

THERAPIST: So you've selectively attended to a real but very small flaw in your effort to wallpaper. Is it logical that such a small defect should entirely cancel the credit you deserve?

PATIENT: Well, it wasn't as good as it should have been.

THERAPIST: If your neighbor had done the same quality job in your kitchen, what would you say?

PATIENT: . . . pretty good job!

(Beck, Rush, Shaw, and Emory, 1979)

Depressed people not only have low self-esteem, but they blame themselves and feel guilty for the troubles that afflict them. When failure occurs, depressed individuals tend to take the responsibility on themselves.

In addition to negative beliefs about the self, the depressed individual almost always views the future with great pessimism and hopelessness, believing that his actions, even if he could undertake them, are doomed. For example, when a middle-aged, depressed woman was told by her therapist that it would be a good idea for her to get a job, she replied, "I just couldn't possibly do it. How would I find the number of an employment agency? Even if I found the phone number, no one would want to hire me because I'm unqualified." Upon being reminded that she held a Ph.D. she replied, "Well, they might hire me, but they will eventually fire me because I'm incompetent; and even if they kept me on it wouldn't be because of competence, but only because I'm so pathetic." The depressed individual has a whole host of reasons for future failure, and no reasons at all to expect success.

These negative beliefs can translate into disastrous interpersonal relations. In a study of 150 husbands and their spouses (some of whom were depressed and some of whom were not depressed), positive communications from the husband led to increased negativity from their wives. This may have been because the positive communications of the depressed husbands were less positive and compelling than those of nondepressed husbands, or because the wives of depressed husbands were, in general, emotionally exhausted by their husbands' depression and could not respond positively even to positive communications. With either interpretation, the negative beliefs continued to have an effect on the mood state of the partner and to be a central influence on the long-term success of the marriage (Johnson and Jacob, 2000).

MOTIVATIONAL SYMPTOMS

Depressed individuals have great trouble getting up in the morning, going to work, beginning projects, and even entertaining themselves. An advertising executive loses his initiative in planning a major sales campaign; a college professor cannot bring herself to prepare her lectures; a student loses the desire to study.

One depressed man who was hospitalized after a suicide attempt merely sat motionless day after day in the ward lounge. His therapist decided to prepare a schedule of activities to get the patient engaged:

THERAPIST: I understand that you spend most of your day in the lounge. Is that true?

PATIENT: Yes, being quiet gives me the peace of mind I need.

THERAPIST: When you sit here, how's your mood?

PATIENT: I feel awful all the time. I just wish I could fall in a hole somewhere and die.

THERAPIST: Do you feel better after sitting for two or three hours?

PATIENT: No, the same.

THERAPIST: So you're sitting in the hope that you'll find peace of mind, but it doesn't sound like your depression improves.

PATIENT: I get so bored.

THERAPIST: Would you consider being more active? There are a number of reasons why I think increasing your activity level might help.

PATIENT: There's nothing to do around here.

THERAPIST: Would you consider trying some activities if I could come up with a list?

PATIENT: If you think it will help, but I think you're wasting your time. I don't have any interests.

(Beck, Rush, Shaw, and Emory, 1979)

Ambivalence also seems to be a common symptom of depression (Hammen and Padesky, 1977). For a depressed individual, making a decision may be overwhelming and frightening. Every decision seems momentous, of make-or-break significance, and fear of making the wrong decision can be paralyzing. In its extreme form, this lack of initiative is called "paralysis of the will." Such a patient cannot bring himself to do even those things that are necessary to life. He has to be pushed and prodded out of bed, clothed, and fed. In severe depression, there may be psychomotor retardation in which movements slow down and the patient walks and talks excruciatingly slowly.

PHYSICAL SYMPTOMS

Perhaps the most insidious symptoms in depression are the physical changes. As depression worsens, every joy that makes life worth living dwindles, and poor physical health often follows.

Loss of appetite is common. A gourmet finds that food has lost its taste. Weight loss occurs in moderate and severe depression, although in mild depression weight gain sometimes occurs. Sleep disturbance occurs as well, with depressed individuals sometimes having trouble getting to sleep at night or more typically beset by early morning awakenings that leave them fatigued for the rest of the day. A depressed individual also may lose interest in sex and experience erectile difficulties or lack of arousal.

A very high percentage of individuals diagnosed with depression also have somatic symptoms. In a major international study of 1,146 depressed individuals, almost 70 percent on average also had somatic symptoms, ranging from around 90 percent in Turkey, Greece, Nigeria and India, to around 50 percent in Italy and France, with the U.S.A. in between (Simon, VonKorff, Piccinelli, Fullerton, and Ormel, 1999). A depressed individual is often self-absorbed and focused on the present. His body absorbs his attention, and increased worry about aches and pains occurs. In addition to more worrying about health, depressed individuals may, in fact, be more susceptible to physical illness, and this is especially so for depression with melancholia (Kendler, 1997). Depression is often an early sign of infectious illness, cancer, and heart disease (Carney, Freedland, and Jaffee, 1991; Imboden, Cantor, and Cluff, 1961; Seligman, 1991).

Vulnerability and Prevalence of Depression

Who is at risk for clinical depression? At this very moment about one out of twenty Americans is severely depressed, and your chances are about one in seven of having a depressive episode of diagnosable proportions at least once in your lifetime (Angst, 1992; Myers et al., 1984; Robins et al., 1984).

As it turns out, *everyone* is vulnerable to depression. No group—not blacks or whites, not women or men, not young or old, not rich or poor—is spared. While depression is found universally, some groups seem especially susceptible. For example, if you were born after 1970 or you live in a prosperous nation like the United States or you are female, you are at particularly high risk for depression.

Four lines of evidence point to a huge increase in depression over the last fifty years. The first is the Epidemiologic Catchment Area (ECA) study, which sampled a large and representative group of Americans and showed that people born earlier in this century have experienced much less depression in their lifetime than people born later (Robins et al., 1984). Table 7–1 shows the lifetime prevalence of different age groups in three cities. These data are remarkable. They suggest that those born around 1910 had only a 1.3 percent chance of having a major depressive episode over the course of the seventy-five years they had lived. In contrast, those born after 1960 already

had a 5.3 percent chance, even though they had lived only twenty-five years. These are huge differences, suggesting a roughly tenfold increase in risk for depression across two generations (Murphy, Laird, and Monson, 2000).

The second line of evidence for a similar rise in depression was provided by a massive, parallel international study (Cross-National Collaborative Group, 1992). In this study, a sample of almost 40,000 adults from the United States, Canada, Puerto Rico, Germany, France, Italy, Lebanon, New Zealand, and Taiwan had diagnostic interviews. All nations, with the exception of Hispanic samples, showed dramatic increases in risk for depression across this century. The rise in North America, however, is steepest of all (see Figure 7–1). This huge increase in depression has prompted the World Health Organization (WHO) to predict that depression will be the second leading cause of disability in the world by 2020 (Holden, 2000).

The third line of evidence is provided by studies of relatives of people with severe depression. These studies show that younger relatives are much more susceptible to depression than older relatives (Klerman et al., 1985). Specifically, 2,289 relatives of 523 people with affective disorders were given a structured diagnostic interview probing for their lifetime prevalence of major depressive disorder. Consider, for example, women born in 1950 versus women born before 1910. By age thirty, about 65 percent of the women born in 1950 had had one depressive episode, whereas fewer than 5 percent of women in the 1910 cohort had had such an episode by the time they were thirty. For almost all age groups, a more recent year of birth confers greater and earlier risk for major depressive disorder. Overall, we again estimate a risk increase of at least tenfold across two generations.

TABLE 7–1

Data

LIFETIME PREVALENCE OF MAJOR DEPRESSIVE EPISODES BY AGE

	18–24 years born c. 1960 n = 1397	25–44 years c. 1945 n = 3722	45–64 years c. 1925 n = 2351	over 65 c. 1910 n = 1654
New Haven	7.5	10.4	4.2	1.8
Baltimore	4.1	7.5	4.2	1.4
St. Louis	4.5	8.0	5.2	0.8

SOURCE: Adapted from Robins et al., 1984.

Figure 7–1

LIFETIME RATES OF DEPRESSION ACROSS COUNTRIES

The figure shows cumulative lifetime rates of major depression by birth cohort and age of onset in the United States (based on the Epidemiologic Catchment Area results), Puerto Rico, Munich, and Taiwan. (Source: Cross-National Collaborative Group, 1992, pp. 3100–02)

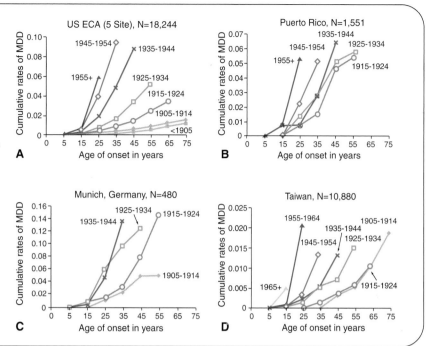

The fourth line of evidence comes from the study of the Old Order Amish living in Lancaster County, Pennsylvania. This study used a parallel diagnostic interview and showed very low rates of unipolar depression. The Amish are an ultraconservative Protestant sect descended entirely from thirty eighteenth-century progenitors. No electricity is permitted in their homes, horses and buggies are used for transportation, alcoholism and crime are unknown, and pacifism is absolute. For the five-year period from 1976–1980, forty-one active cases of major depressive disorder were found; this is a five-year prevalence of about 0.5 percent (there are 8,186 adult Amish). If we compare this rate to the parallel figures from the ECA studies, we can roughly estimate that the Amish have about one-fifth to one-tenth the risk for unipolar depression as neighboring Americans from modern cultures. Importantly, the rate of bipolar depression is the same as for modern Americans (Egeland and Hostetter, 1983).

AGE DIFFERENCES

Young people are now particularly at risk for depressive disorder (see Box 7–2). Forty years ago, the average age for the first episode of depression was 29.5 (Beck, 1967), and depression was unusual among teenagers. Now teenagers are affected fairly often. Figure 7–1 not only shows that the total amount of depression is much higher among younger people, but that the age of onset is now much younger than it used to be. Peter Lewinsohn and his colleagues gave diagnostic interviews to 1,710 randomly selected western Oregon adolescents. By age fourteen, 7.2 percent of the youngest adolescents, born in 1972–1974, had had a severe depression; in contrast, 4.5 percent of the older adolescents, born in 1968–1971, had had a severe depression (Lewinsohn, Rohde, Seeley, and Fischer, 1993). In a study of over 3,000 twelve- to fourteen-year-olds in the southeastern United States, 9 percent had experienced major depressive disorder (Garrison, Addy, Jackson, McKeown, and Waller, 1992). This high a percentage of youth suffering severe depression and at such a young age is surprising and dismaying. Because depression tends to recur, a first onset as a teenager adds up to several more episodes in a lifetime than does a first onset in middle age.

The earliest psychological state that may be related to depression was described by the American psychiatrist René Spitz in 1946 and was called ***anaclitic depression.*** Spitz observed that when infants between the ages of six and eighteen months were separated from their mothers for prolonged periods

Society and Mental Health

Box 7—2

Why Young Americans Are Suffering an Epidemic of Depression—A Speculation

Depression is a disorder of individual helplessness and individual failure. When a person finds himself helpless to achieve his goals, he suffers depression. Why then is there an epidemic of depression, particularly among young people in America today?

First, in contemporary America, the balance between the "I" and the "we" has become overly weighted toward the "I." Individualism has become rampant and the self all-important, while at the same time the "we"—the attachment to larger things that buffer against depression, such as God, nation, community, family—has weakened. Second, for the last forty years, America has seen a movement in parenting and education that has stressed instilling self-esteem in children. Paradoxically, the doctrine of raising our children to feel good and enjoy high self-esteem at all times, may have contributed to the epidemic of feeling bad (Bushman and Baumeister, 1998). This may be because the more that a child believes that he is all that matters and that his goals, his successes, and his pleasures are of paramount importance, the more hurtful the blows when life brings its inevitable failures. In attempting to cushion bad feeling, the self-esteem movement has effectively minimized the three good uses of feeling bad.

The first good use of strong negative emotions, such as anxiety, sadness, and anger, is to galvanize us into action to change ourselves or the world, and by doing so to terminate the negative emotion. We become anxious amid danger, sad with loss, and angry when we feel violated. All these reactions are by themselves painful, but we can use them as cues to actions we may need to take.

But using our feelings as guides to action is not problem-free. Some of our emotional reactions are false alarms—the kid who elbowed you is not a bully but just clumsy, and the bad grade does not mean your teacher thinks you're stupid. When bad feelings become chronic and paralyzing, and when they set off too many false alarms, we call this state "emotional illness," and we try to dampen it with drugs or correct it with psychotherapy.

We can also use our bad feelings to overcome boredom and to achieve "flow." Flow is a state in which time seems to stop, when we feel truly at home and want to be nowhere else—perhaps when we are playing a sport, listening to a CD, writing a poem, painting a fence or picture, gardening, making love, or engaging in good conversation. Researchers who have been studying it—who experiences it, when it occurs, what impedes it—find that it often occurs when our skills are used to their utmost—matched against a challenge just barely within our grasp. Too little challenge can produce boredom. Too much challenge or too little skill can produce

helplessness and depression. Success after success—unbroken by failure, regrouping, and trying again—will not produce flow. Rather, overcoming frustration, working through anxiety, and confronting the highest challenges are needed to achieve flow (Csikszentmihalyi, 1990).

The third good use of bad feeling is to overcome helplessness. Any complicated task we undertake requires many steps, and we can succeed or fail at each. Only by persevering can we surmount failure at any one step and proceed on to complete the entire task. Nonetheless, persevering isn't always painless, because any temporary setback is an emotional setback as well. But momentary failure and bad feeling can be building blocks for ultimate success and feeling good.

We may be teaching our children not to persevere when we insist that bad feelings are to be avoided altogether. Children need to fail sometimes. When we always protect our children from failure, as the "feel good" society suggests, we deprive them of learning perseverance. When they encounter obstacles, and we leap in to bolster their self-esteem and to soften the blows, we make it harder for them to achieve mastery. And if we deprive them of mastery, we weaken their self-esteem just as certainly as if we had abused, belittled, humiliated, and physically thwarted them at every turn.

Finally, American ideology has drifted from individual responsibility to "victimology." It has become routine for us to blame our troubles on other people, circumstances, the system, anything but our own actions, our own character, or our own decisions. While shifting the blame away from ourselves may protect our self-esteem, it is, unfortunately, a recipe for learned helplessness and passivity. As we shall see later in this chapter, whatever increases learned helplessness probably increases depression.

So it is possible that the self-esteem movement in particular and the "feel good" ethic in general have had the untoward consequence of producing low self-esteem on a massive scale. By cushioning feeling bad, it has made it harder for our children to feel good and to experience flow. By circumventing feelings of failure, it has made it more difficult for our children to feel mastery. By blunting warranted sadness and anxiety, it has created children at high risk for unwarranted depression. By encouraging cheap success, it may have produced a generation at risk for depression.

Source: Adapted from Seligman, Reivich, Jaycox, and Gillham, 1995.

Young people are particularly at risk for depression, as can be seen in this child, who seems to be overwhelmed with sadness.

of time, a state of unresponsive apathy, listlessness, weight loss, increased susceptibility to serious childhood illness, and even death occurred. The mothers' return, or the substitution of a different, permanent mother, reversed these effects (Spitz, 1946).

Sensitive psychological tests have revealed as high a rate of depressive symptoms in children as among adults, along with the expected intellectual deficits (Blumberg and Izard, 1985; Kaslow, Tannenbaum, Abramson, Peterson, and Seligman, 1983; Kovacs and Beck, 1977). While the rate of major depressive disorder among children is less than 3 percent, at puberty the prevalence rises to at least 6.4 percent (DuBois, Felner, Bartels, and Silverman, 1995).

One common loss for a child occurs with divorce and separation, as well as its precursor, parental turmoil. In a longitudinal study of 400 children who were followed as they went from third grade through sixth grade, 20 percent developed moderate to severe depressive symptoms (Nolen-Hoeksema, Girgus, and Seligman, 1986, 1992). Among the salient precipitants of depression was parental turmoil—the report that parents had been fighting more lately. Parents' fighting probably undermines the child's sense of security and often leads to a string of bad life events, such as separation and economic problems, and so

increases a child's risk for depression. Finally, when divorce occurs, and the child "loses" a parent, he may start to exhibit depressive symptoms:

> Peter, age nine, had not seen his father, who lived nearby, more than once every two to three months. We expected that he would be troubled, but we were entirely unprepared for the extent of this child's misery. The interviewer observed: "I asked Peter when he had last seen his dad. The child looked at me blankly and his thinking became confused, his speech halting. Just then, a police car went by with its siren screaming. The child stared into space and seemed lost in reverie. As this continued for a few minutes, I gently suggested that the police car had reminded him of his father, a police officer. Peter began to cry and sobbed without stopping for 35 minutes. (Wallerstein and Kelly, 1980)

Depressed adolescents share all the symptoms seen in adults (Lewinsohn, Gotlib, and Seeley, 1995). In addition to the core symptoms, depressed adolescents, particularly boys, are commonly negativistic and even antisocial. Restlessness, grouchiness, aggression, and strong desire to leave home are also common symptoms, and sulkiness, uncooperativeness in family activities, school difficulties, alcohol and drug abuse can also be symptoms.

Depression among adults does not increase in frequency and in severity with age as was once supposed (Myers et al., 1984; Robins et al., 1984). Complicating depression in the elderly is the helplessness that results from decreasing physical strength and, sometimes, mental abilities. Nonetheless, the frequency of depression among old people is at present much lower than among younger people.

SEX DIFFERENCES

The evidence is strong that women are diagnosed with depression twice as much as men (Nolen-Hoeksema, 1988; Silberg et al., 1999). Methodologically sound studies of depression (those that use standardized assessment, large sample sizes, and diagnosis that separates out unipolar and bipolar depression) can be divided into treated cases—people undergoing therapy—and door-to-door community studies. In seven of the eight studies of treated cases in the United States, females outnumbered males, with a mean ratio of 2:1. In the ten studies of treated

When faced with loss, women are more likely to cry and remain passive, while men are more likely to express anger or indifference.

cases outside the United States, nine showed more females than males with depression, with a mean ratio of 2.3:1. Treated cases may not reveal underlying sex differences in depression, however, because women might be more likely to seek out treatment than men. To get around this problem, a large number of community studies have been conducted; most of these studies show a preponderance of depression in females over males, with a mean ratio slightly under 2:1.

Why this is so is not clear. Several hypotheses have been advanced. First, women may be more willing to say they are depressed than men are in Western society. When they confront loss, women are more reinforced for passivity and crying, while men are more reinforced for anger or indifference (Nolen-Hoeksema and Girgus, 1994; Weissman and Paykel, 1974). Second, biological hypotheses suggest that vulnerability to depression in women may be related to hormonal changes or genetic proneness. Thus, some pin the vulnerability on monthly bouts of premenstrual depression, tentatively called "premenstrual dysphoric disorder" by DSM-IV and characterized by such symptoms as feeling suddenly sad or tearful, angry, tense, depressed, apathetic, fatigued, overwhelmed, and experiencing difficulty concentrating, appetite changes, sensitivity to rejection, and sleep changes. There is also the possibility that female carriers of a depressive gene become depressed, whereas male carriers of the same gene become alcoholic (Robinson, Davis, Nies, Ravaris, and Sylvester, 1971; Winokur, 1972). A third hypothesis

grows out of the learned helplessness theory of depression (see pp. 270–74). If depression is related to helplessness, then to the extent that women learn to be more helpless than men, depression will appear more frequently in women than in men. A society that rewards women for brooding and becoming passive in the face of loss while rewarding men for active coping attempts may pay a heavy price in later female depression (Radloff, 1975). Fourth, women ruminate about bad life events (foremost among them, depression itself), whereas men are inclined to more action and less thought (Nolen-Hoeksema, 1987, 1991). Rumination about depression will amplify depression (Zullow and Seligman, 1985), whereas an action orientation may dampen or distract from a depressive mood.

The last hypothesis has to do with the pursuit of thinness through dieting. As we will see, one root cause of depression is failure and helplessness. Dieting sets up a cycle of failure and helplessness: pitting the goal of slimming to an almost unattainable "ideal" weight against untiring biological defenses. At first, dieters lose weight, and with it, the depression about being overweight lifts. Ultimately, however, dieters become dismayed as the pounds come back, as they do in 90 percent of dieters. Repeated failure and all the daily re-

If people who are dieting fail to lose weight or start to gain weight again, depression may set in.

minders of being overweight again bring depression in their wake (Seligman, 1994; Wadden, Stunkard, and Smoller, 1986). On the other hand, about 10 percent of dieters keep the weight from coming back, but they have to stay indefinitely on an extremely low-calorie diet to do so. A side effect of prolonged malnutrition is depression. Either way, the pursuit of thinness makes people vulnerable to depression (Garner and Wooley, 1991). Moreover, researchers have found that the eating disorders—anorexia nervosa and bulimia—arise in cultures that have a thin ideal for women. These cultures also have roughly twice as much depression in women as in men (Jeffrey, Adlis, and Forster, 1991). Women in cultures like Egypt, Iran, India, and Uganda, which do not have the thin ideal, do not have eating disorders. Most importantly, in those cultures the rate of depression in women and men is roughly the same (McCarthy, 1990; Stice, 1994).

RACIAL AND SOCIAL CLASS DIFFERENCES

The National Comorbidity Study of 8,098 Americans shows that the rate of mood disorder among blacks is only about two-thirds that of whites and Hispanics (Kessler et al., 1994). Suicide rates in Africa are much lower than in the rest of the world (Lester and Wilson, 1988). These data should remind us that depression is a psychological process more directly than it is an economic one, since on all measures of economics and bad life events, African Americans have bleaker statistics than whites and Hispanics, and Africans have bleaker economic statistics than most of the rest of the world. Some caution should be kept

in mind, however, in interpreting any study of cross-ethnic or cross-cultural psychological disorders. Hispanic samples, both in Los Angeles and in Puerto Rico, show a major difference from North American, European, and Asian samples: older and younger Hispanic samples do not differ, with both showing a similar fairly high rate of depression and a fairly young onset (Cross-National Collaborative Group, 1992). But since diagnosis is, for the most part, made by middle-class psychiatrists and psychologists, insensitivity to symptoms of depression in another class, race, or culture, or elicitation of greater hostility among the patients may contaminate the results (Tonks, Paykel, and Klerman, 1970).

No strong differences occur in depression among social classes or with poverty. Unlike schizophrenia, which is less frequent in middle and upper classes, depression is democratic and affects people from all classes about equally. In the National Comorbidity Study (Kessler et al., 1994), poor people were found to have somewhat higher rates of depression, but not dramatically so. Again, however, it is possible that depression may have different manifestations according to the patient's social class. Lower-class patients may show more feelings of powerlessness and hopelessness, middle-class patients stronger feelings of loneliness and rejection, and upper-class patients greater pessimism and social withdrawal (Schwab, Bialow, Holzer, Brown, and Stevenson, 1967). But overall, while some differences can be seen, the similarities in the occurrence of depression among black people, Hispanic people, and white people, and between rich people and poor people far outweigh the differences.

EFFECTS OF LIFE EVENTS

It is commonly believed that depression is routinely triggered by bad life events. Most depressions are preceded by a recent loss, or at least by the perception, if not the reality, that one has lost something of value. The thwarting of cherished goals, breakup of a romance, failure at work, marital separation, failure at school, loss of a job, rejection by a loved one, death of a child, illness of a family member, and physical illness are common precipitants of depression (Monroe, Rohde, Seeley, and Lewinsohn, 1999). Individuals who become depressed show a greater number of such losses preceding their depression than matched controls (Breslau and Davis, 1986; Paykel, 1973). Indeed, there used to be a category called "reactive" depression (as contrasted to "endogenous" depression),

Children show as high a rate of depressive symptoms as do adults, although African Americans are less likely than whites to become depressed.

The loss of a job may lead to depression, especially if the person has been depressed in the past and is predisposed to becoming depressed.

in which some bad external event was the major cause. Because the characteristics of a depression following a bad event and a depression that just came out of the blue do not seem to differ much, this distinction has been abandoned. But the question remains: "Are the lives of depressed people, before the onset of their depression, different from the lives of people who do not become depressed?"

The answer is a qualified "yes" (Kessler, 1997). The role of bad life events is surprisingly small once other predisposing factors are taken into account. Having had prior depression is by far the life event that most predisposes an individual to further depression and this greatly overshadows all other life events (Coryell et al., 1993; Klinkman, Schwenk, and Coyne, 1997). Furthermore, genetic predisposition, as measured in twin studies, also overshadows life events (Kendler, Kessler, Walters, et al., 1995). Nonetheless some life events may, in addition, predispose to depression—for example, interpersonal loss, physical illness, sexual abuse.

Depressed individuals have experienced more bad early childhood events, including sexual abuse (Levitan et al., 1998), than nondepressed individuals and more frequent stressful losses within a year or two before the onset of depression. Yet, many individuals suffer both early childhood loss and recent loss without becoming depressed, and a substantial number of depressed individuals do not suffer early childhood loss or recent loss.

The death of a child's mother before the child is eleven years old may predispose the person to depression in adulthood. One study found that the rate of depression was almost three times higher among women who, before age eleven, had lost their mother and had also experienced a severe recent loss, than among women who, before age eleven, had not lost their mother but had experienced a similar recent loss. Death of the mother after the child reached age eleven had no effect on risk for depression (Brown and Harris, 1978). Death of the father while the child is young is also probably associated with later depression (Barnes and Prosin, 1985). But only half the women who, before age eleven, had lost their mother and also had suffered a recent loss became depressed. What about the other half? Brown and Harris proposed that there are four invulnerability factors that can help prevent depression from occurring, even in the presence of the predisposing factors and recent loss. The invulnerable women had either (1) an intimate relationship with a spouse or a lover, or (2) a part-time or full-time job away from home, or (3) fewer than three children still at home, or (4) a serious religious commitment. So intimacy, employment, a life not overburdened by childcare, and strong religious belief may protect against depression. Perhaps what these four invulnerability factors have in common is that they contribute confidence and a sense of mastery, while undercutting the formation of an outlook pervaded by hope-

If a woman has more than three young children at home, she may be more vulnerable to depression after a stressful loss.

lessness. This articulates well with the findings that a good relationship with parents protects adolescents from depression and good social support prevents depression among cardiac patients (Holahan, Holahan, Moos, and Brennan, 1997; Holahan, Valentiner, and Moos, 1995).

The main lesson to be drawn from the evidence about bad life events and depression is not that bad life events, in part, cause depression. Rather, it is the relatively small, but real, effect bad events have. Only about 10 percent of those persons who experience losses equivalent in severity to those of an average depressed person become depressed themselves. This evidence should be taken together with the evidence that the privileged youth of all prosperous nations now have very high rates of depression and that African Americans have less depression than white Americans. This evidence tells us that depression is an eminently psychological problem, not a problem of objective bad events. As the song goes, the mind can make a heaven of hell, and in the case of depression, a hell of heaven. We will turn later to the question of why the other 90 percent of people who experience very bad life events do not become depressed.

The Course of Depression

When a vulnerable individual becomes depressed, what is likely to happen if the individual fails to seek out treatment? If anything good about depression can be said, it is that it usually dissipates in time. After the initial attack, which comes on suddenly about three-quarters of the time, moderately severe depression seems to last an average of about three months. Very severe episodes last about six months on the average. At first, the depression gets progressively worse, eventually reaching the bottom, but then the depressed individual begins to recover gradually to the state that existed before the onset (Beck, 1967; Robins and Guze, 1972). What our grandmothers told us about our own personal tragedies—time heals all wounds—is certainly true for depression. The mind, or the body, seems incapable of sustaining a dark mood forever, and in time the disorder inexorably lifts. The mechanism is unknown; it could be the restoration of a neurochemical state, it could be habituation to the painful loss, or it could be some more benign re-framing of the loss (Hunt, 1998).

The time that a depressive episode lasts, however, is painfully long, and to an individual suffering from it, it seems like forever. For this reason, a therapist should provide hope by emphasizing that the depressive episode will go away in time. Without minimizing the suffering the patient is feeling now, the therapist should tell the patient that complete recovery from the episode occurs in 70 to 95 percent of the cases. For some, this ray of hope may speed the time when the depression will lift.

Once a depressive episode has occurred, one of three patterns develops. The first is recovery without recurrence. "Recurrence" is defined as the return of symptoms following at least six months without significant symptoms of depression. If the patient goes for six months free of symptoms, however, it is generally believed that the episode has run its course. "Relapse" into the same episode, which may occur when drug therapy or psychotherapy relieves symptoms for only a short while, is defined as a return of symptoms in less than six months. Only 15 percent of 380 patients who recovered from a major depressive episode did not have another one over the next fifteen years. Of those who remained well for five years after the first episode, 42 percent did not have a recurrence in the next ten years (Mueller et al., 1999). Generally, the more stable a person is before the episode, the less likely depression will recur. On the other hand, most depressed individuals will show the second pattern: recovery with recurrence.

Who is most likely to suffer a relapse or recurrence of depression? Fifty depressed patients were followed after their recovery from a depressive episode, and two-thirds of them relapsed within two years. The presence of a personality disorder (see Chapter 9) comorbid with the initial depression greatly increased the risk for relapse: seventeen of the twenty-two patients with a personality disorder relapsed in the first six months, but only four out of twenty-eight without a personality disorder relapsed over that period (Ilardi, Craighead, and Evans, 1997). The presence of pessimism is an additional factor predicting who relapses. The belief that good events are transient, in particular, made recovered patients more likely to relapse (Evans et al., 1992). Being a woman, never marrying, having suffered more depressive episodes—especially within a short period—all make it more likely that the individual would suffer another recurrence (Mueller et al., 1999; Solomon et al., 2000).

Depression tends to recur in people and may itself lead to further bad life events. This homeless man may have become depressed because he lost his job, but his depression may have also caused him to lose his home and his family and may prevent him from taking steps to set his life back on course.

The second depressive episode, if it occurs, will tend to be of about the same duration as the first attack. On the average, however, most individuals who have recurrent episodes of depression can expect a symptom-free interval of more than two years before the next episode. But the interval between episodes in recurrent depression tends to become shorter over the years. The period of greatest risk for recurrence is the first six months after recovery (NIMH, 1984). It must be noted, however, that depression itself brings further bad life events such as romantic indifference and breakup in its wake, and that such a cascade of bad events increases vulnerability to recurrence (Harkness, Monroe, Simons, and Thase, 1999).

For some individuals, the third pattern will develop: chronic depression, or dysthymic disorder. Roughly 10 percent of those individuals who have a major depressive episode will not recover and will remain chronically depressed (Angst and Wicki, 1991; Keller, Lavori, Mueller, and Endicott, 1992; Schuyler, 1974). Recovery from chronic depression does occur, however: 38 percent of patients who had been depressed for five years recovered during the next five years, with an average remission rate of 9 percent a year (Mueller et al., 1996).

Therapy for depression tries to make the current episode shorter or to postpone the time at which the next episode might strike. The therapies for depres-

sion derive from two different approaches, and it is to these theories that we now turn.

Theories of Depressive Disorders

What causes depression? Although several theories with substantial evidence attempt to explain the origins of depression, we still cannot say with certainty that one theory totally explains what depression is or how it can best be treated. Different factors—both biological and psychological—interact to lead to depression. The biological approach and the cognitive approach provide the two main theories for depression. These theories overlap, and there is also a good deal of overlap in the therapies each recommends, but each focuses on only one aspect of depression. Taken together, rather than in opposition, however, the two approaches are a step on the road toward an integrated picture of the disorder.

The Biological Approach to Depression

Many researchers believe that depression is best understood by treating it just like any other medical illness, and that discovering the physiological basis for depression will lead to both its cause and cure. If the biological model has yet to provide any final answers, it has certainly revealed many biological aspects of depression. These include a genetic predisposition, alterations in neurotransmitter and hormone systems, and localized changes in specific areas of the brain. This section surveys what is known about each.

GENETICS AND UNIPOLAR DEPRESSION

Undoubtedly, genes play a role in determining one's vulnerability to depression. First-degree relatives of patients with depressive disorders are between two and five times more at risk for depression than are those in the general population (Keller et al., 1986; Weissman, Kidd, and Prusoff, 1982). So having a depressed family member confers risk for depression, but is this risk genetic or does it come from the common family environment? Twin studies and adoptive studies implicate genetics. Studies of twins show that genetic factors play a small, but probably real, role in unipolar depression. Kenneth Kendler and his colleagues studied the entire set of twins registered in the state of Virginia, over 1,000 pairs. Identical twins show a concordance rate for unipolar depression of 48 percent, somewhat higher than the 42 percent concordance shown by fraternal twins (Kendler, Neale, Kessler, Heath, and Eaves, 1992). Further evidence comes from studies of adoptive versus biological relatives of depressed patients. Biological relatives had an eightfold increased risk for unipolar depression relative to adoptive relatives (Wender et al., 1986).

While unipolar depression has a weak to moderate genetic component, bipolar depression has a strong genetic component (Kendler, 1997; Torgersen, 1986a). At least 60 percent of identical twins are discordant for unipolar depression, but only 28 percent of identical twins are discordant for bipolar disorder (Allen, 1976; McGuffin, Katz, Watkins, and Rutherford, 1996). Nonetheless, there may be a common genetic substrate that underlies both unipolar depression and bipolar depression, as having bipolar depression increases the risk that relatives will have both bipolar and unipolar depression. Moreover, common genetic factors have been implicated in both anxiety and depression (Kendler, Neale, Kessler, Heath, and Eaves, 1992a; Kendler, Walters, Neale, et al., 1995). Why a genetically predisposed individual ends up with one disorder as opposed to another is an excellent question that future research will illuminate.

NEUROTRANSMITTERS AND DEPRESSION

From the start, researchers on depression believed that, whatever ultimately caused depression, changes in brain and body chemistry certainly accompany depression (see Figure 7–2). Four lines of evidence led them to this conclusion: First, depression occurs with some frequency following periods of natural physiological change in women—after giving birth to a child, at menopause, and just before menstruation. Second, there is considerable similarity of symptoms across cultures, sexes, ages, and races, indicating an underlying biological process. Third, drug

Figure 7—2

THE NEUROCHEMICAL BASIS OF DEPRESSION

The biogenic amines are neurochemicals that facilitate neural transmission. Depression may result from decreased availability of norepinephrine or serotonin. Researchers have mapped norepinephrine and serotonin neurons in the brain. There is a high concentration of such neurons in the limbic system, which regulates emotional behavior, and hence may be implicated in depression. The figure shows a schematic representation of norepinephrine and serotonin pathways. Although these pathways are not limited to being located on the left and right sides of the brain, the figure attempts to simplify the depiction of these pathways by representing norepinephrine pathways on the left side of the drawing and representing serotonin pathways on the right side of the drawing. (Source: Based on Snyder, 1986, p. 108)

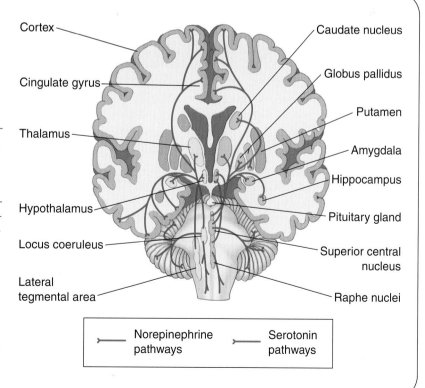

Cortex — Caudate nucleus — Globus pallidus — Putamen — Amygdala — Hippocampus — Pituitary gland — Superior central nucleus — Raphe nuclei

Cingulate gyrus — Thalamus — Hypothalamus — Locus coeruleus — Lateral tegmental area

Norepinephrine pathways Serotonin pathways

Figure 7–3

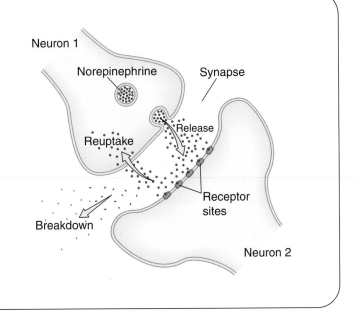

NOREPINEPHRINE IN NEURAL TRANSMISSION

When a nerve impulse occurs in neuron 1, norepinephrine is discharged into the synapse (the gap between neuron 1 and neuron 2). This stimulates neuron 2 to fire when the NE makes contact with the receptors on the membrane of neuron 2. Norepinephrine is now sitting in the synapse and on the membrane of neuron 2. Neuron 2 will continue to fire until the NE is inactivated. There are several ways that decreased availability might occur. One way is by reuptake, in which neuron 1 reabsorbs norepinephrine, thereby inactivating NE and decreasing the amount of norepinephrine at the receptors. A second way is by breakdown, in which norepinephrine is broken down chemically and rendered inactive. In addition, there might be decreased synthesis of NE from its precursors.

therapies, in particular tricyclic antidepressants, selective serotonin reuptake inhibitors (SSRI's), and monoamine oxidase inhibitors (MAO inhibitors), are all effective treatments for depression. Fourth, depression is occasionally induced in normal individuals as a side effect of drugs such as reserpine, formerly used to treat hypertension (Schuyler, 1974).

These initial lines of evidence led to the formulation of the influential hypothesis that depression is a disorder of motivation caused by chemical abnormalities in brain systems containing a class of transmitters known as monoamines (or *biogenic amines*). The specific monoamines implicated in this biogenic amine theory of depression are norepinephrine (NE), dopamine (DA), and serotonin (5-HT, for serotonin's chemical name, 5-hydroxy-tryptamine).

What are these abnormalities? Early on, researchers speculated that depression resulted from a decreased availability of norepinephrine and dopamine in certain systems of synapses in the brain (Schildkraut, 1965; see Figure 7–3). By the 1970s and 1980s, evidence pointed to a reduced availability of serotonin as well (Maas, 1975; McNeal and Cimbolic, 1986; Potter and Manji, 1994).

If these neurotransmitters were actually involved, then people with mood disorders, compared to those without mood disorders, should show lower levels of these neurotransmitters. Directly assessing these neu-

rotransmitters would require neurosurgery, so investigators resorted to a simpler tactic: they measured the metabolic breakdown products of these transmitters normally found in the blood or urine. Many experiments were designed to discern whether mood disorders altered the levels of these breakdown products, but the results have been inconsistent.

Another finding also complicated the picture: antidepressant medications typically take two to three weeks to produce any relief from depression, but these medications were found to increase neurotransmitter availability immediately. In fact, the long-term effect of these drugs is to decrease, not increase, availability. They do this by reducing the receptors for norepinephrine and serotonin in the postsynaptic neurons. For all these reasons, the simple norepinephrine and serotonin hypotheses have been abandoned (Thase and Howland, 1995).

How can these findings be reconciled? Several theories have arisen, but none has been well confirmed. Among them is a "downregulation" theory, which suggests, not that monoamine levels are low, but that the number of postsynaptic monamine receptors is inadequate. Thus, although antidepressant medications might immediately increase neurotransmitter levels, their real antidepressant effects might have to wait for another set of changes, either the growth of new receptors or the heightening of the sensitivity of existing receptors (Thase and Howland, 1995). A second theory invokes "kindling," a process by which certain neurons, by firing repeatedly, make themselves more sensitive to subsequent stimulation. Robert Post (1992) has noted that each episode of depression makes subsequent ones increasingly likely, a fact that he suggests is because the relevant neurotransmitter systems become more easily "dysregulated." Thus, while the first bout of depression may require a strong external stressor to trigger it, the relevant neurochemical systems are now sensitized, and lesser triggers will set off another episode in the future.

Even though none of these neurotransmitter theories has proven adequate to explain depression, they have been of enormous value in leading to new medications to treat depression. Indeed, all the neurochemical theories of depression receive their strongest support, not from studies of blood or urine chemistry, but from a more direct finding—some patients' clear relief from depression after taking certain drugs known to produce neurochemical changes. Finally, two important lessons have been gleaned from the mass of studies done to test neurochemical theories of depression. First, the neurochemical deficits are observed only when the individual is depressed, but are not seen before or after the episode. Second, the drugs that relieve depression produce a panoply of other changes. This suggests that although monoamine levels correlate with depression and relief from depression, they do not cause either one. Causal theories, like one we will propose later, focus on both psychological and biological factors as working together to cause or cure depression.

HORMONES AND DEPRESSION

Changes in some of the brain's neurotransmitter systems are but a part of depression. Many of our hormone systems show alterations as well. For example, individuals whose thyroid glands are underactive (hypothyroidism) show many of the features of unipolar depression, but their depression remits quickly once they receive the thyroxin they need. In fact, some researchers believe that as many as 10 to 15 percent of people who suffer from depression may have undiagnosed hypothyroidism. Thyroxin (made synthetically and known as Synthroid) is also effective for some depressed people with normal thyroid levels, and it is occasionally prescribed in order to augment the benefits of standard antidepressants (Jackson, 1998; Lasser and Baldessarini, 1997).

The same principle holds for men whose testes are manufacturing inadequate levels of testosterone. Injections or skin patches of testosterone reverse their depression, and the affected men typically experience more energy, enhanced libido, and buoyant mood (Seidman and Walsh, 1999).

As we mentioned earlier, women suffer bouts of depression before menstruation, after childbirth, and at menopause. Each of these changes is associated with a falloff in levels of estrogen, which—like testosterone for men—seems necessary for maintenance of normal mood. Just as in men, restoration of normal hormone levels in women reverses their depression. This may be through the natural increase in estrogen post-menstrually, or via estrogen patches worn by new mothers and post-menopausal women (Epperson, Wisner, and Yamamoto, 1999; Gregoire, Kumar, Everitt, Henderson, and Studd, 1996). These hormones may be linked to depression through playing a role in regulating the availability of serotonin in the brain (Fink, Sumner, Rosie, Wilson, and McQueen, 1999; Osterlund, Overstreet, and Hurd, 1999).

In addition to studying these notable hormonal effects, researchers on depression are also focusing increasingly on changes in the hormone systems involved in our responses to stress. These changes are controlled in great part by the hypothalamus in the brain, the pituitary gland at the base of the skull, and the adrenal glands atop the kidneys—the coordinated hierarchical system known as the hypothalamic-pituitary-adrenal (HPA) axis (see Chapter 4).

Researchers have found that depressed people show hormonal changes at each level of the HPA axis. Some of the first findings are that depressed individuals, especially severely depressed patients, show greatly increased levels of cortisol in their blood and cerebrospinal fluid. Cortisol is secreted whenever a person encounters stress for an extended period of time (for more than ten to twenty minutes). Cortisol has numerous actions in the body. While it ramps up the delivery of glucose to the bloodstream to enable defensive action against a stressor, it also shuts down many of the body's necessary housekeeping activities, such as wound healing and the deactivation of germs by the immune system (see Chapter 12). Because depression can last months or years, the effects of heightened cortisol can be quite harmful, leaving the depressed individual prone to injury and infection. Long-term secretion of cortisol is also toxic to brain cells, especially to those in the hippocampus, the part of the limbic system involved in long-term memory (Sapolsky, Romero, and Munck, 2000).

These "neurotoxic" effects were shown dramatically in a study of twenty-four women who had averaged about five bouts of depression each (although one participant suffered eighteen depressive episodes). Compared to control participants with no history of depression, MRI scans of the brains of the patients showed that each had a smaller hippocampus (about 10 percent smaller, by volume) than nondepressed women. The amount of the shrinkage of the hippocampus was proportional to the number of depressions suffered. This shrinkage had visible consequences; for example, upon neuropsychological testing, those patients with a history of depression showed poorer verbal memory (Sheline, Sanghavi, Mintun, and Gado, 1999).

Apart from the cortisol elevations, depressed patients have also been shown to have abnormally high levels of the pituitary hormone that releases cortisol, adrenocorticosteroid hormone (ACTH). Moreover, the depressed patients also showed high levels of corticotropin releasing hormone (CRH), a chemical released by the hypothalamus and causing the release of ACTH (Nemeroff, 1996). Some investigators suggest that CRH itself is pivotal in determining whether depression occurs. Researchers have shown that infusion of CRH directly into the brains of animals produces many of the signs of depression, including anorexia, insomnia, and reduced mating behavior. In humans, elevated CRH levels can be returned to normal by some of the same procedures—antidepressant medications or electroconvulsive therapy (ECT)—effective in successfully treating depression itself (Arborelius, Owens, Plotsky, and Nemeroff, 1999; Heim, Owens, Plotsky, and Nemeroff, 1997; Mitchell, 1998).

One particular set of CRH findings may have important, if unfortunate, implications concerning vulnerability to depression. In this research, newborn rats were intermittently separated from their mothers for the first twenty-one days of their life, and then moved to a normal rat colony. Compared to young rats reared normally, the maternally deprived rats showed CRH elevations and greater numbers of CRH receptors in several areas of their brains consistent with the pattern that occurs in depression. These changes were permanent, and they suggest a mechanism whereby lifelong vulnerability to depression might be conferred (Liu et al., 1997).

BRAIN REGIONS AND DEPRESSION

Besides the hippocampus, there are other areas of the brain that are implicated in depression. Some theories emphasize regions of the cortex, for example. One theory claims that overactivity of the right frontal lobe produces depression. This is based on three lines of evidence: First, normal subjects express more negativity about pictures of faces presented to the right hemisphere (left visual field) than about pictures presented to the left hemisphere (right visual field). This is particularly strong in depressed people (Davidson, Schaffer, and Saron, 1985). Second, brain damage to the left hemisphere due to stroke (neuron death due to vascular leaks or clots)—resulting in a dominance of right brain activity—more often results in depression than does damage to the right hemisphere (Sackeim et al., 1982). Third, one brain-imaging study showed that the blood flow to the left frontal lobe decreased in patients with major depression. The blood supply to the same region increased when these patients recovered from their depression following drug therapy (Bench, Friston, Brown, Frackowiak, and Dolan, 1993; Bench, Frackowiak, and Dolan, 1995).

Other studies have linked depression to the underactivity of specific parts of the left frontal lobe, as opposed to overactivity of the right. In unipolar depressed patients, these spots appear "cooler," or less active, on brain scans, when compared to the same areas in nondepressed controls. Researchers believe that this underactivity leads to the apathy of depres-

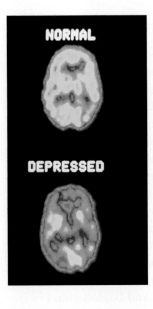

PET scans comparing a normal brain *(top)* and the brain of a person diagnosed with depression *(bottom)*. Note that there is less metabolic activity in general (as shown by more of the blue color and less of the yellow color), and especially less activity in the frontal lobes (the top of the brain) of the person who is depressed than of the person who is not depressed.

sion. Indeed, patients who have permanent damage in these locations often show blunted emotions, low arousal, decreased motivation, and lack of interest (Biver et al., 1994). Recent research on autopsied brains suggests that clinically depressed patients may also have structural defects in their brain. Compared to the brains of nondepressed controls, the brains of people who had been depressed and committed suicide had marked reductions in the size of their prefrontal cortex, an area of the brain involved in memory and planning.

Direct neurological stimulation promises to clarify which brain areas are involved in depression. In one study, a patient was undergoing high-frequency deep-brain electrical stimulation to treat her Parkinson's disease (Bejjani et al., 1999). One of the stimulating electrodes was placed in a subcortical area called the substantia nigra, a region that is traditionally implicated in smooth muscular movements and shows degeneration in Parkinson's disease. Upon stimulation, the patient showed unequivocal signs and symptoms of depression, even though she had suffered no previous depressive episodes. The investigators speculate that there may be a close and under-appreciated relationship between depression and Parkinson's disease. First, 40 percent of Parkinson's patients are depressed. Second, several signs and symptoms are common to both disorders, including sleep problems; reduced appetite, motivation, and energy; and slowed movements. This study may indicate some common neurological basis as well.

A technique using powerful magnetic fields to disable specific areas of the brain for brief periods of time has provided additional evidence regarding an anatomical basis for depression. The procedure, known as transcranial magnetic stimulation (TMS), can produce temporary mood changes in normal people. In one study, repeated magnetic pulses to the brain area above the left eyebrow caused subjects to feel sad and apathetic, while applying the pulses to the area above the right eyebrow caused subjects to feel happier and more energetic. Moreover, magnetic pulses can increase the activity of specific regions, and when used to stimulate the left frontal lobe, severely depressed patients feel better. TMS may one day replace electroconvulsive therapy, in which electric shock is administered to the brain. Currently, however, not everyone responds to the treatment, and the effects tend to wear off (George et al., 1995).

The Psychological Approach to Depression

The psychological approach encompasses both psychodynamic and cognitive theories about depression, but the cognitive approach has been more valuable in that cognitive researchers have been able to test their theories and have derived treatments that are quite effective. The psychodynamic approach is largely based on unconscious motivations and conflicts and is much more difficult to confirm and test. It hypothesizes that anger against the self, dependence on others for self-esteem, and helplessness at achieving one's goals cause depression. There are two main cognitive models of depression, and both view particular thoughts as the crucial cause of depressive symptoms. The first, developed by Aaron T. Beck, derives mainly from extensive therapy with depressed patients, and it views depression as caused by negative thoughts about the self, about ongoing experience, and about the future. The second, developed by Martin E. P. Seligman, derives mainly from experiments with dogs, rats, and mildly depressed people. It views depression as caused by the expectation of future helplessness, which is seen as permanent and pervasive. A depressed person expects bad events to occur, believes that there is nothing she can do to prevent them from occurring, and she believes that this will last for a long time and undermine everything she undertakes.

BECK'S COGNITIVE THEORY OF DEPRESSION

Aaron T. Beck (along with Albert Ellis) founded a type of therapy called cognitive therapy. According to Beck, two mechanisms, the cognitive triad and errors in logic, produce depression.

The Cognitive Triad   The *cognitive triad* consists of negative thoughts about the self, about ongoing experience, and about the future. The negative thoughts about the self consist of the depressed person's belief that he is defective, worthless, and inadequate. His low self-esteem derives from his belief that he is defective. When he has unpleasant experiences, he attributes them to personal unworthiness. Since he believes he is defective, he believes that he will never attain happiness.

The depressed person's negative thoughts about ongoing experience consist of his interpretation that

Aaron T. Beck has developed cognitive theories and treatments for depression.

what happens to him is bad. He misinterprets small obstacles as impassable barriers. Even when there are more plausible positive views of his experience, he is drawn to the most negative possible interpretation of what has happened to him. Finally, the depressed person's negative view of the future is one of helplessness. When he thinks of the future, he believes the negative things that are happening to him now will continue unabated because of his personal defects.

Errors in Logic   Beck believes that systematic *errors in logic* are the second mechanism of depression. According to Beck, the depressed person makes five different logical errors in thinking, and each of these darkens his experiences: arbitrary inference, selective abstraction, overgeneralization, magnification and minimization, and personalization.

Arbitrary inference refers to drawing a conclusion when there is little or no evidence to support it. For example, an intern became discouraged when she received an announcement that said that in the future all patients worked on by interns would be reexamined by residents. She thought, incorrectly, "The chief doesn't have any faith in my work." *Selective abstraction* consists of focusing on one insignificant detail while ignoring the more important features of a situation. In one case, an employer praised an employee at length about his secretarial work. Midway through the conversation, the boss suggested that he need not make extra carbon copies of her letters anymore. The employee's selective abstraction was, "The boss is dissatisfied with my work." In spite of all the good things said, she only remembered this.

Overgeneralization refers to drawing global conclusions about worth, ability, or performance on the basis of a single fact. Consider a person who fails to fix a leaky faucet in his house. Most people would call a plumber and then forget it. But a depressed patient will overgeneralize and may go so far as to believe that he is a bad person. *Magnification* and *minimization* are gross errors of evaluation, in which small bad events are magnified and large good events are minimized. The inability to find the right color shirt is considered a disaster, but a large raise and praise for good work are considered trivial. And lastly, *personalization* refers to incorrectly taking responsibility for bad events in the world. A neighbor slips and falls on her own icy walk, but the depressed next-door neighbor blames himself unremittingly for not having alerted her to her icy walk and for not insisting that she shovel it.

LEARNED HELPLESSNESS, HOPELESSNESS, AND DEPRESSION

The second cognitive model of depression is the *learned helplessness model,* along with its cousin, the *hopelessness model.* The learned helplessness model is cognitive because it holds that the basic cause of depression is an expectation: the individual expects that bad events will happen to him and that there is nothing he can do to prevent their occurrence. We will discuss the phenomenon and theory of learned helplessness, and then we will discuss the relationship between learned helplessness and depression.

Learned helplessness theory argues that the basic cause of deficits observed in helpless animals and humans after uncontrollable events is the expectation of future noncontingency (unrelatedness) between responding and outcomes. The theory says that dogs, rats, and people given inescapable events will become profoundly passive later on when they are given escapable events. They will be unable to learn later that responding could enable them to escape (Hiroto, 1974; Miller and Seligman, 1976; Overmier and Seligman, 1967). This expectation that future responding will be futile causes the two helplessness deficits: (1) it produces deficits in responding by undermining the motivation to respond, and (2) it produces later difficulty in seeing that outcomes are contingent upon responding. The experience of shock, noise, or problems in themselves does not produce the motivational and cognitive deficits; only uncontrollable shock, noise, and problems produce these deficits (see Figure 7–4).

When a human being experiences inescapable noise or unsolvable problems and perceives that his responding is ineffective, he goes on to ask an important question: What caused my present helplessness?

Figure 7–4

LACK OF CONTROL AND LEARNED HELPLESSNESS

The figure shows the effects of matched escapable and inescapable shocks on later escape learning. It shows the escape latencies in the shuttlebox for three groups of dogs: (a) those given escape training in the shuttlebox as naive subjects, (b) those given prior escape training in a different situation, and (c) those given prior inescapable shocks, but matched in duration and temporal distribution to the shocks for the esape-training groups. (Source: Maier, Seligman, and Solomon, 1969)

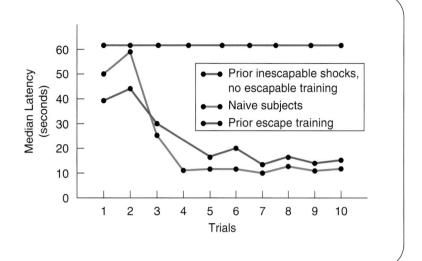

The causal attribution (explanation) that a person makes is a crucial determinant of when and where he will expect future failure. There are three attributional dimensions that govern when and where future helplessness deficits will be displayed (Abramson, Seligman, and Teasdale, 1978).

The first dimension is *internal-external*. Consider an individual who has received unsolvable problems in an experiment. When he discovers that responding is ineffective, he can either decide that he is stupid (internal) and the problem is solvable, or that the problems are rigged to be unsolvable (external) and he is not stupid. In addition to deciding whether or not the cause of failure is internal or external, an individual who has failed also considers the second dimension, the *stable-unstable* dimension: "Is the cause of my failure something permanent or temporary?" An individual who has failed may decide that the cause of the failure is stable and unchangeable and so it will persist into the future. Examples of such stable factors are stupidity (which is internal as well as stable), or the difficulty of the task (which is stable but external). In contrast, an individual may decide that the cause of his failure is unstable. An individual who has failed an exam may believe that the cause was his bad night's sleep, an unstable cause that is internal. Alternatively, he may decide that he failed because it was an unlucky day, an unstable cause that is external. When the person attributes the cause of failure to a stable factor, his helplessness deficits will persist in time, and he will probably fail in the future. Con-

versely, if the individual believes that the cause of his failure is unstable, he will not experience helplessness and will not necessarily fail again when he encounters the task months later. According to the attributional model of learned helplessness, stable explanations lead to permanent deficits, and unstable explanations to transient deficits.

The third and final dimension is *global-specific* (see Figure 7–5). When an individual finds that he has failed, he must ask himself whether or not the cause of his failure is global—a factor that will produce failure in a wide variety of circumstances—or specific—a factor that will produce failure only in similar circumstances. For example, an individual who has failed to solve a laboratory problem may decide that he is unskilled at solving laboratory problems and probably unskilled at other tasks as well. In this instance, he perceives being unskilled as global and will expect failure in a wide variety of other situations. It is also a stable and internal factor. Alternatively, he might decide that these particular laboratory problems are too hard. Here he will perceive the difficulty of laboratory problems as a specific factor, since it will only produce the expectation that future responding will be ineffective in other laboratory problems and not in real life. This factor, aside from being specific, is stable and external. The attributional model of helplessness holds that when individuals make global explanations for their failure, helplessness deficits will occur in a wide variety of situations. When individuals believe that specific factors cause

Figure 7–5

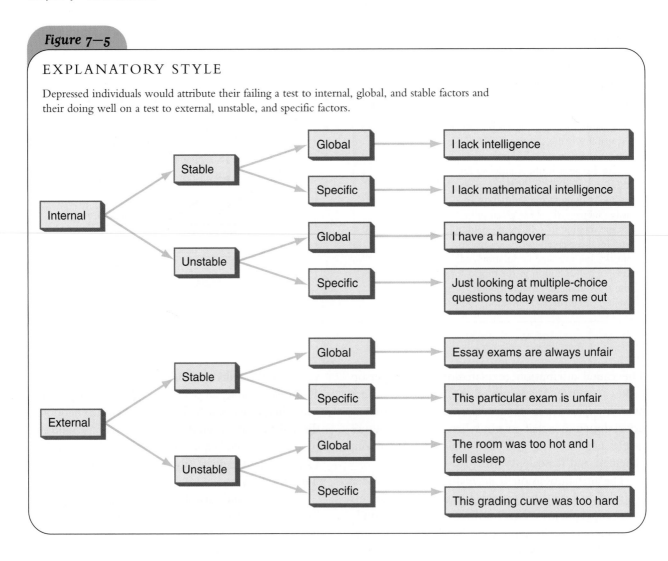

EXPLANATORY STYLE

Depressed individuals would attribute their failing a test to internal, global, and stable factors and their doing well on a test to external, unstable, and specific factors.

their failures, the expectation of response ineffectiveness will be narrow, and only a narrow band of situations will produce helplessness.

There are notable similarities in symptoms, cause, cure, prevention, and predisposition between learned helplessness in the laboratory and major depression as it occurs in real life (see Table 7–2; Seligman, 1975; Weiss, Simson, Ambrose, Webster, and Hoffman, 1985). And in fact, the helplessness model suggests that a pessimistic explanatory style or attributional style (attributing failure to internal, global, and stable factors; attributing success to external, unstable, and specific factors) predisposes an individual to depression. The latest version of the theory is the hopelessness theory of depression (Abramson, Metalsky, and Alloy, 1989; Alloy, Lipman, and Abramson, 1992). The theory emphasizes the stable and global dimensions for negative events as determinants of hopelessness, and proposes a subtype of depression, hopelessness depression. It says

that when the individual feels that nothing he does now or in the future will make a difference, he feels hopeless and experiences the symptoms of depression. Thus, the theory hypothesizes that the expectation of no control and the certainty that something bad will happen or that something good will not happen is what leads to depression. Some researchers have suggested that the expectation of helplessness creates anxiety, but that this anxiety turns into depression when helplessness becomes hopelessness (Alloy, Kelly, Mineka, and Clements, 1990). Hopelessness theory is being tested in various research studies, including one of college students at risk for major depression (Alloy and Abramson, 1997). It remains to be seen if hopelessness is merely a symptom or a cause of depression.

The failure to escape noise and to solve problems after experience with uncontrollable events is the basic *passivity deficit* of learned helplessness. This passivity seems similar to the *motivational deficits* of de-

(Left) Someone with an external, unstable, and specific explanatory style may blame Hurricane Andrew for the damage to his life but may be able to pull his life together more quickly than *(right)* a person with an internal, stable, and global explanatory style, who may feel helpless and hopeless in the face of a natural disaster.

pression (Miller and Seligman, 1975, 1976; Price, Tryon, and Raps, 1978). Nondepressed individuals given inescapable noise or unsolvable problems show the cognitive deficit of learned helplessness: they have difficulty learning that responding is successful, even when it is. Depressed individuals show exactly the same deficit. Nondepressed human beings made helpless fail to see patterns in anagrams and fail to change expectancy for future success when they succeed and fail in skill tasks. Depressed students and patients show these same deficits in the laboratory

(Abramson, Garber, Edwards, and Seligman, 1978; Miller and Seligman, 1975, 1976).

When individuals are made helpless by inescapable noise and attribute their failure to their own shortcomings as opposed to external causes, not only are the motivational and cognitive deficits of helplessness and depression observed, but self-esteem drops as well. This parallels the low self-esteem that occurs in depressed individuals, particularly among those who blame themselves for their troubles (Abramson, 1978).

TABLE 7–2

SIMILARITY OF LEARNED HELPLESSNESS AND DEPRESSION

	Learned Helplessness	*Depression*
Symptoms	Passivity	Passivity
	Cognitive deficits	Negative cognitive triad
	Self-esteem deficits	Low self-esteem
	Sadness, hostility, anxiety	Sadness, hostility, anxiety
	Loss of appetite	Loss of appetite
	Loss of aggression	Loss of aggression
	Sleep loss	Sleep loss
	Norepinephrine and serotonin depletion	Norepinephrine and serotonin depletion
Cause	Learned belief that responding is independent of important outcomes (plus attributions to internal, global, and stable factors)	Generalized belief that responding will be ineffective
Therapy	Change belief in response futility to belief in response effectiveness	Cognitive and behavioral therapy
	ECT, MAO-I, tricyclics, fluoxetine	ECT, MAO-I, tricyclics, fluoxetine
	REM deprivation	REM deprivation
	Time	Time
Prevention	Immunization	Optimism training
Predisposition	Pessimistic explanatory style	Pessimistic explanatory style

Parallel mood changes occur both in learned helplessness and depression. When nondepressed subjects are made helpless by inescapable noise or unsolvable problems, they become sadder, more hostile, and more anxious. These reports parallel the emotional changes in depression: more sadness, anxiety, and perhaps more hostility.

In the laboratory, rats that receive inescapable shock eat less food, lose more weight, aggress less against other rats, and lose out in competition for food with rats that had received either escapable shock or no shock. This loss of appetite and loss of aggression produced by helplessness in the laboratory parallel the somatic symptoms of depressed individuals: they lose weight, eat less, lose sleep, their social desires and status drop, and they become less aggressive. Finally, learned helplessness in the rat is accompanied by norepinephrine and serotonin depletion (Peterson, Maier, and Seligman, 1993; Weiss, Glazer, and Pohoresky, 1976).

The learned helplessness hypothesis says that depressive deficits, which parallel the learned helplessness deficits, are produced when an individual expects that bad events may occur and that they will be independent of his responding. When this is attributed to internal factors, self-esteem will drop; to stable factors, the depression will be long-lived; and to global factors, the depression will be general. The experimental evidence confirms this. This pessimistic attributional style has been found in depressed students, children, and patients, and it predicts the outcome of therapy (Jacobson et al., 1996). Depressed patients believe that the important goals in their life are less under their control than do other patients (Seligman, Abramson, Semmel, and Von Baeyer, 1979; see also Raps, Reinhard, and Seligman, 1980). Most important, individuals who have this explanatory style, but are not depressed, become depressed at a much higher rate when they later encounter bad events (Peterson and Seligman, 1984; see also Hilsman and Garber, 1995).

Treatment of Depressive Disorders

Between 80 and 90 percent of severe depressions can now be markedly relieved with a brief course of treatment—either biological or psychological. But recurrence remains substantial with all forms of treatment.

Biological Therapy for Depression

The biological model approaches the treatment of unipolar depression, particularly when it is severe, in two ways. The first is to treat the patient with drugs (see Figure 7–6). Relief is moderate, but the relapse rate is very high when the drugs are stopped. The second approach is to administer electroconvulsive shock (ECT). There is immediate, marked improvement, but the relapse rate is also very high, and public dislike of the procedure relegates it all too often to being a treatment of last resort.

DRUG TREATMENT

Three classes of moderately effective drugs are used to treat depression: tricyclic antidepressants (TCA's), monoamine oxidase inhibitors (MAO inhibitors), and selective serotonin reuptake inhibitors (SSRI's). Moreover, there are now atypical antidepressants such as Wellbutin, which are also used to treat depression. Tricyclic antidepressants block the reuptake of norepinephrine (NE). As a result, more NE is available. On average, between 60 and 75 percent of depressed patients given tricyclics show significant clinical improvement. Further, maintaining a patient with recurrent depression on tricyclics between attacks also reduces recurrence (Gelenberg and Klerman, 1978; Gorman, Nemeroff, and Charney, 1999; Kocsis et al., 1996). Increasing availability of NE in the brain is no longer seen as strong confirmation of the NE unavailability hypothesis, however, because these drugs also have many other effects. For example, research with laboratory animals has shown that administering tricyclic antidepressants over long periods reduces the number of "5-HT receptors," which participate in the reuptake of serotonin. The reduction of these receptors may be responsible for the effectiveness of tricyclic antidepressants in clinical trials (Taylor et al., 1995).

The MAO inhibitors prevent the breakdown of norepinephrine by inhibiting the enzyme MAO. With more NE available, the patient is thought to become less depressed. But MAO inhibitors are prescribed less often than tricyclics or SSRI's, largely because the MAO inhibitors can have lethal side effects. When combined with aged cheese, red wine, beer, shellfish, narcotics, or high-blood-pressure-reducing drugs, MAO inhibitors can be fatal. Most studies show MAO inhibitors to be superior to placebos in alleviating depression, however, and if SSRI's and the tricyclics fail, the MAO inhibitors should be tried.

DRUG TREATMENTS FOR DEPRESSION

Norepinephrine is discharged into the synapse when a nerve impulse from neuron 1 to neuron 2 fires. In a normal person, the norepinephrine is inactivated by either reuptake, whereby neuron 1 reabsorbs the norepinephrine, or breakdown of the norepinephrine by the enzyme MAO. In a depressed person, breakdown or reuptake or both of either norepinephrine (indicated by the blue part of the arrow) or serotonin (indicated by the red part of the arrow) removes the norepinephrine or serotonin, leaving the person depressed. MAO inhibitors work by preventing the breakdown of norepinephrine; tricyclic antidepressants work by preventing the reuptake of norepinephrine; fluoxetine works by preventing the reuptake of serotonin.

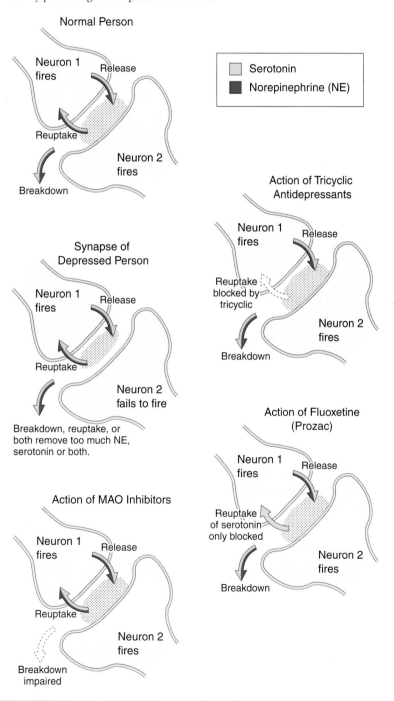

SSRI's like fluoxetine (Prozac) and its cousins sertaline (Zoloft) and paroxetine (Paxil) are very widely prescribed, particularly for less severe depressions. Some patients are rhapsodic about its transformative effects:

> Those first few mornings were fairy tales, tall tales, replete with all the bent beauty of a new world. I saw a raven, an egg full of gold. I blinked, and blinked again . . . . I spent hours imagining myself inside the plethora of houses the world suddenly made available to me. I started going to open houses. I saw chandeliers sprouting down through intricate ceiling medallions, old gas lamps and blue vases on cream-colored windowsills . . . . In the month that followed, I began to range farther and wider, getting reckless, hungry from all the time I'd lost to illness. I started going out late at night, prowling around by myself until two or three in the morning, standing by the edge of the dirty river and admiring the waxy sheen of light on the water or exploring the alleys of Boston, where broken things glittered. I felt invulnerable. (Slater, 1998).

Prozac and the other SSRI's (for example, Zoloft and Paxil) selectively inhibit the reuptake of serotonin (Wong et al., 1974). They produce relief in 60 to 70 percent of those who have major depressions, with low risk of overdose (Hirschfeld, 1999). Having a patient with recurrent depression continue to take fluoxetine reduces the occurrence of relapses (Lonnqvist et al., 1995). In severe depression, Prozac produces less drowsiness, dry mouth, sweating, and risk of overdose than the tricyclic antidepressants, but it produces more nausea, nervousness, and insomnia (Boulos, Kutcher, Gardner, and Young, 1992; Hirschfeld, 1999; Wernicke, 1985). Because their side-effect profile is somewhat less noxious and because they have had very good press, Prozac, Zoloft, and Paxil are now much more popularly prescribed than the norepinephrine-raising drugs. Nonetheless, careful study of outcomes among large numbers of patients reveals about the same efficacy as the tricyclics and the MAO inhibitors (Mulrow et al., 1998). Moreover, despite all these good results, there is still some concern about whether Prozac may lead to suicidal ideation and behavior in some patients (see Box 7–3).

The SSRI's are not the only new antidepressants in wide use. Physicians are increasingly using a heterogeneous class of medications known as atypical depressants (Trazadone, Serzone, Effexor, and Wellbutin), which affect the availability of both serotonin and norepinephrine. Wellbutrin (buproprion), the most widely used of these drugs, also affects the availability of dopamine. Wellbutrin has stimulating as well as antidepressant effects, making it useful not only for depression but also for attention deficit hyperactivity disorder (see Chapter 8). Although Wellbutrin has its own side effects (among them, an increased risk of seizures in vulnerable individuals), it is conspicuously free of the sexual side effects that plague other kinds of antidepressants.

What should not be forgotten in the administration of any antidepressant drugs is their powerful placebo effect. It is a commonplace belief that depression is a biochemical illness that can be relieved by drugs. Whether or not this is actually a true belief, it provides an important opening wedge for hope, and inspiring hope is crucial to relieving depression. Not surprisingly, a large part of the effect of the antidepressant drugs—around 30 to 40 percent—has been estimated to be a placebo effect (Kirsch and Sapirstein, 1998). In a very large trial of the effects of seven antidepressant medications, researchers compared the medications and placebos to see their effects on suicidal patients. Among 19,639 patients, the suicide rate for the drug-treated group was 0.8 percent and 0.4 percent for the placebo controls. The attempted suicide rate was 3.4 percent for those treated with the medications, and 2.7 percent for those treated with a placebo. Symptom reduction was 40.7 percent for those given medication versus 31 percent for those given a placebo (Khan, Warner, and Brown, 2000). Not surprisingly, this major study engendered a torrent of methodological criticism from drug researchers (Quitkin and Klein, 2000; Quitkin, Rabkin, Gerald, Davis, and Klein, 2000), but it adds to the concern that much of the effect of antidepressant medication is a placebo effect.

Not only do all drug therapies have a sizable placebo effect and moderate to good alleviation of symptoms in common, they all also have high relapse and recurrence rates once the drug is stopped. The recurrence rate for unipolar depression may be as high as 85 percent over fifteen years (Levitan et al., 1998), and there is no evidence that drug treatment, unless continued, prevents recurrence. Although some have suggested that drug treatments work better than psychotherapy for depression, particularly when depression is severe (Schulberg and Rush, 1994), comparisons of psychotherapy and drugs actually reveal an equal effect for severe depression (Munoz, Hollon, McGrath, Rehm, and VandenBas, 1994). Nonetheless, in profound psychotic depres-

Does Prozac Cause Suicide?

Although the published empirical evidence for a relationship between Prozac and suicidal behavior is limited to a handful of case studies (Teicher, Glod, and Cole, 1990) controversy still surrounds this issue (Healy, 1994; Healy, Langmaak, and Savage, 1999). Recently, a lawsuit was filed against the manufacturer of Prozac, Eli Lilly, claiming that Prozac was responsible for the suicide of a retired businessman named Bill Forsythe.

Bill Forsythe was a successful former businessman who was having a difficult time adjusting to the slower-paced living of retirement. Bill's marriage began to suffer after he and his wife moved from California to Hawaii to be closer to their son. The constant togetherness was too much for the both of them. After a few trial separations, Bill and his wife sought counseling and were able to repair their relationship. Six months later, however, Bill started having panic attacks. His doctor prescribed several ineffective medications before settling on Prozac. The day after Bill took his first pill, he experienced the "Prozac miracle" — he felt markedly better than the day before. And yet, the very next day Bill committed himself to a psychiatric ward, complaining that he didn't feel like himself. During his week-long stay at the hospital, he continued to receive Prozac. The day after Bill's return home, his son came upon a gruesome scene: Bill had stabbed his wife fifteen times and impaled himself on a knife tied to a stool.

David Healy, an expert on antidepressant medication, served as an expert witness for the plaintiffs. Bill Forsythe's death, says Healy, was caused by an abnormal reaction to Prozac called "akathisia." Patients with akathisia become extremely restless and panicked and sometimes have intense thoughts of harming self and/or others. Further supporting Healy's claim is the fact that Bill had no history of suicidal ideation or behavior and his actions were seen as completely out of character by those closest to him. Though the jury decided in favor of Eli Lilly, this case provided another controversial ending to the ongoing debate about Prozac.

The task of proving that Prozac induces suicidal behavior requires the disentangling of the drug's effects from the effects of the person's disorder. Eli Lilly points to studies where the rate of suicidal behavior and ideation for people with depression who are on Prozac is not any worse than what one would expect to find in a sample of people with depression who are not taking Prozac (Beasley et al., 1991; Leon et al., 1999; Tollefson et al., 1993; Warshaw and Keller, 1996). Healy claims that such studies are flawed for various reasons, one of which is that the studies use the rate of suicidality in people who have been hospitalized for depression, when most people on Prozac are not inpatients in a psychiatric ward. Thus, the rate of suicidal tendencies should be markedly lower for those on Prozac, but this is not the case. When all is said and done, both parties are far from being able to conclude when Prozac causes suicide and when depression causes it. Healy realizes this, and he does not want to see Prozac banned, but he wants a warning given so that doctors know to closely monitor first-time recipients of the drug. Healy claims that Eli Lilly refuses to include such a warning because of the detriment such a move would have on their sales.

Source: Adapted from S. Boseley, They said it was safe, *The Guardian,* October 30, 1999.

---

sion, psychotherapy is useless, and only drugs or ECT will work.

In general, you should keep in mind that there are two kinds of medications: curative and palliative. Antibiotics, for example, are curative. If you have a bacterial infection and take the right antibiotic, it kills the bacteria and cures the infection. Once you stop taking the antibiotic, the infection does not re-occur. On the other hand, quinine is palliative. If you have malaria and take quinine, the symptoms are suppressed for as long as you take the drug. Once you stop taking the drug, however, the symptoms return, since quinine merely suppresses the symptoms.

We must not forget that every single drug in the arsenal against mental illness is palliative rather than curative. All the antidepressant drugs are palliative but not curative. They suppress the symptoms of de-

pression (moderately well), but the symptoms have the same risk of returning once the patient stops taking the drug, as if he had never taken the drug in the first place. Patients who respond well to antidepressant drugs, however, may decide to take the drug indefinitely to prevent recurrence (Antonuccio, Danton, DeNelsky, Greenberg, and Gordon, 1999; Kocsis et al., 1996; Kupfer et al., 1992).

ELECTROCONVULSIVE SHOCK TREATMENT (ECT)

Electroconvulsive shock treatment (ECT) is, to the layman, the scariest of the antidepressant treatments. In the two decades following ECT's discovery as a psychotherapeutic treatment in 1938, enthusiasm was high, and it was prescribed for a very broad range of

Treatment

TABLE 7–3

DEPRESSION

	Cognitive Therapy	Interpersonal Therapy	Drugs*	Electroconvulsive Shock Therapy
Improvement	60–75% markedly improved	60–75% markedly improved	60–75% markedly improved	80% markedly improved
Relapse[†]	moderate relapse	moderate relapse	high relapse	high relapse
Side Effects	none	none	moderate	rather severe
Cost	inexpensive	inexpensive	inexpensive	inexpensive
Time Scale	one month	months	weeks	days
Overall	**very good**	**very good**	**very good**	**very good**

*Drugs include tricyclics, MAO inhibitors, and selective serotonin reuptake inhibitors.
[†]Relapse after discontinuation of treatment.
SOURCE: Based on Seligman, 1994, p. 114.

disorders. The treatment, particularly in its less refined forms, can have very serious side effects, however, and it has come to be regarded by the general public as "barbaric" and "punitive." Unfortunately, it is still widely used for nonspecific purposes (Hermann, Dorwart, Hoover, and Brody, 1995), but strong evidence exists that ECT, when given to patients with severe unipolar depression, is a highly effective antidepressant therapy (see Table 7–3). Modern techniques have greatly reduced the common and severe side effects of yesteryear, and about 80 percent of patients with major depression respond to ECT (Devanand, Sackeim, and Prudic, 1991; Fink, 1979; Malitz et al., 1984).

Typically, a medical team consisting of a psychiatrist, an anesthesiologist, and a nurse administers ECT. Metal electrodes are taped to either side of the patient's forehead, and the patient is anesthetized. The patient is given a short-acting anesthetic, along with drugs to induce muscular relaxation in order to prevent the breaking of bones during the convulsion. A high current is then passed through the brain (often through only one side of the brain) for approximately a half-second. This is followed by convulsions that last for almost one minute. As the medications wear off, the patient will awaken and not remember the period of treatment. Within twenty minutes, the patient will

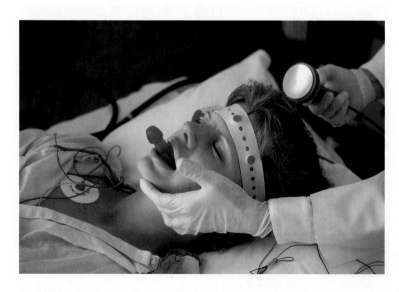

A patient is prepared for electroconvulsive shock treatment. The object in her mouth is to prevent her from swallowing her tongue when the electric current passes through her body.

be functioning reasonably well and will have little, if any, physical discomfort. A course of electroconvulsive shock therapy usually consists of a half-dozen treatments, one every other day (Schuyler, 1974).

Electroconvulsive shock is often administered unilaterally; that is, to only half of the brain. Producing the convulsion on the side of the brain that does not contain the speech centers (in the non-dominant hemisphere) greatly reduces the possibility of the side effect of impaired speech following ECT. Although unilateral ECT is an effective anti-depressant, in the past is was not as effective as bilateral ECT (Abrams et al., 1983; Scovern and Killman, 1980). The rate of response for bilateral ECT was about 50 percent greater than for unilateral ECT, but the intensity of the patient's disorientation and amnesia in the following week was also much greater. Recently, high dosage ECT given unilaterally to the right hemisphere has been shown to be as effective as bilateral ECT and to have fewer cognitive side effects (Sackeim et al., 2000). Nonetheless, recurrence of depression after ECT is substantial, with almost 60 percent of those treated with ECT becoming depressed again the next year (Sackeim et al., 1993).

Exactly how ECT works is unknown. Isolating the effective ingredient in ECT is quite difficult, as it is such a gross technique—shocking half, sometimes the entire, brain—and it has so many other effects, including memory loss and motivational changes (Devanand, Fitzsimons, Prudic, and Sackeim, 1995; Philibert, Richards, Lynch, and Winokur, 1995; Squire, 1986).

Psychological Therapy

Psychological therapies include both cognitive and psychodynamic therapies. Cognitive therapy works to alleviate depressive symptoms directly and over the short term. In contrast, most classical psychodynamic treatments emphasize long-term change rather than short-term alleviation of symptoms of depression. Psychodynamic therapy consists of making the patient conscious of misdirected anger and the early conflicts that produced it, and in resolving these conflicts. Interpersonal therapy is a form of psychodynamic therapy, but it focuses on present rather than past social relationships. Like cognitive therapy, it is a brief form of treatment. We begin with a discussion of cognitive therapy.

COGNITIVE THERAPY

In cognitive therapy, the patient is taught to conquer problems and master situations that he previously believed were insuperable. Cognitive therapy differs from most other forms of psychotherapy. In contrast to the psychoanalyst, the cognitive therapist actively guides the patient into reorganizing his thinking and his actions, not about the past, but primarily about the present. The cognitive therapist talks a lot and is directive. She argues with the patient. She persuades; she cajoles; she leads.

Beck's Cognitive Therapy Cognitive therapy attempts to counter negative thoughts and errors in logic (Beck, 1967; Beck, Rush, Shaw, and Emery, 1979). There are four specific cognitive therapy techniques that are used: detecting automatic thoughts, reality testing automatic thoughts, reattribution training, and changing depressogenic (depression-causing) assumptions.

Beck argues that there are discrete, negative sentences that depressed patients say to themselves quickly and habitually. These "catastrophic," automatic thoughts maintain depression. Cognitive therapy helps patients to identify such automatic thoughts. Once the patient has learned to identify such thoughts, the cognitive therapist engages in a dialogue with the patient in which evidence for and against the thoughts is scrutinized. This is not an attempt to induce spurious optimism, but rather to encourage the patient to use the reasonable standards of self-evaluation that nondepressed people use. A young student despondent over the belief that she would not get into a particular college would be taught to criticize her automatic negative thoughts, as in the following case:

THERAPIST:	Why do you think you won't be able to get into the university of your choice?
PATIENT:	Because my grades were really not so hot.
THERAPIST:	Well, what was your grade average?
PATIENT:	Well, pretty good up until the last semester in high school.
THERAPIST:	What was your grade average in general?
PATIENT:	A's and B's.
THERAPIST:	Well, how many of each?
PATIENT:	Well, I guess almost all of my grades were A's, but I got terrible grades in my last semester.
THERAPIST:	What were your grades then?

PATIENT: I got two A's and two B's.

THERAPIST: So your grade average would seem to me to come to almost all A's. Why don't you think you'll be able to get into the university?

PATIENT: Because of competition being so tough.

THERAPIST: Have you found out what the average grades are for admission to the college?

PATIENT: Well, somebody told me that a B+ average should suffice.

THERAPIST: Isn't your average better than that?

PATIENT: I guess so.

(Beck, Rush, Shaw, and Emory, 1979)

By learning to recognize, scrutinize, and dispute her catastrophic thoughts and marshaling evidence against them, the patient would undermine her negative automatic thoughts, and they would wane.

Depressed patients tend to blame themselves for bad events for which they are not, in fact, responsible. To counteract such irrational blame, the therapist and the patient review the events, applying the standards of nondepressed individuals in order to come up with an assignment of blame. This is not to absolve the patient of blame, but to let him see that there may be other factors besides his own incompetence that contribute to a bad event.

The final technique is the explicit change of assumptions as created by Albert Ellis in his "Rational-Emotive" therapy, a forerunner of cognitive therapy (Ellis, 1962). Beck outlines six assumptions that depressed individuals base their lives upon, thereby predisposing themselves to sadness, despair, and disappointment: (1) in order to be happy, I have to be successful in whatever I undertake; (2) to be happy, I must be accepted by all people at all times; (3) if I make a mistake, it means I am inept; (4) I can't live without love; (5) if somebody disagrees with me, it means he doesn't like me; and (6) my value as a person depends on what others think of me. When the patient and therapist identify one of these assumptions, it is vigorously attacked. The validity of the assumption is examined, counterarguments are marshaled, plausible alternative assumptions are presented, and the disastrous consequences of holding the assumption are exposed.

In one study of cognitive therapy for depression, many patients experienced enormous symptom improvement in a single period between two sessions. These sudden gains accounted for half of these patients' total improvement. Moreover, these patients were less depressed than the other patients after treatment, and they remained so eighteen months later. Substantial cognitive improvement—such as arriving at a new belief—occurred in the therapy sessions preceding sudden relief from depression. This strongly suggests that cognitive change in the pregain session triggered the sudden relief (Tang and DeRubeis, 1999). Further, there is reason to believe that behavioral activation may also be a central aspect of gain in cognitive therapy (Jacobson and Gortner, 2000).

Therapy for Learned Helplessness   Since the cause of learned helplessness and depression is hypothesized to be the expectation that responding will be ineffective in controlling future events, the therapist attempts to change this belief to one in which the patient feels effective and can avoid anticipated bad events. So, for example, learned helplessness theory suggests that therapies such as teaching social skills and assertiveness training should be antidepressive because they teach the individual that he can control the affection and the esteem of other people by his own actions. Further, techniques such as criticizing automatic thoughts (it's not that I'm an unfit mother; rather, I'm grouchy at 7 A.M.) help alleviate depression because they change attributions for failure from internal, stable, and global (unfit mother) to external, unstable, and specific (7 A.M.). These strategies are the techniques of cognitive therapy that we have just reviewed. Interestingly, studies that ask about the active ingredients of cognitive therapy find that it is the change from pessimistic to optimistic attributions that plays an important role in the therapy and prevention of depression (DeRubeis, Evans, Hollon, and Garvey, 1990; Seligman, Schulman, DeRubeis, and Hollon, 1999).

Flexible Optimism   The shift from pessimism to optimism seems to occur when people learn the skill of making unstable, specific, and external explanations for the bad events that occur to them. People who make these attributions do better in several realms of life. These optimists fight off depression better, achieve more in school, sports, and the workplace, and enjoy better physical health than do pessimists, people who see bad events as stable, global, and internal.

Optimism is no panacea, however. For one thing, it may sometimes keep people from seeing things as they really are. For another, it may help them to evade responsibility for failure by blaming it on others. But these limits are just that, limits. They do not nullify the benefits of optimism; rather, they put it in perspective (Seligman, 1991).

Cognitive therapy teaches people to curtail depression by disputing their catastrophic thoughts. But sometimes it is better not to dispute such thoughts. For example, if a student fails his midterms because he did not study enough for them, it might be more valuable for him to look at himself with merciless clarity, rather than trying to ward off his depression. The cost of being wrong here may affect his academic future and outweighs the importance of fighting off demoralization. He can use this as a time to take stock and appreciate more clearly his need to study hard.

People can choose to use optimism when it will lead to less depression, more achievement, or better health. But they can also choose not to use it, when they judge that clear sight or taking responsibility are called for. Learning optimism need not erode a person's sense of values or his judgment. Rather, it can free him to use cognitive techniques as a tool to achieve the goals he sets.

The fundamental guideline for whether or not to deploy the skills of optimism and cognitive therapy is to ask what the cost of failure is in the particular situation. If the cost is high, optimism is the wrong strategy. In the cases of a pilot in the cockpit deciding whether to have the plane deiced one more time, or a partygoer deciding whether to drive home after drinking, or a student deciding to go skiing for the weekend rather than studying for her final exams, the costs of failure are, respectively, death, an auto accident, and academic failure. Using techniques that minimize those costs are a disservice. On the other hand, if the cost of failure is low, cognitive techniques that promote optimism are invaluable. The sales agent deciding whether to make one more call only loses her time if she fails. The shy person deciding whether to attempt to open a conversation only risks a single episode of rejection. The teenager contemplating learning a new sport only risks temporary frustration. The disgruntled executive, passed over for promotion, only risks some refusals if he quietly puts out feelers for a new position.

INTERPERSONAL THERAPY

Another psychological treatment for depression is ***interpersonal therapy (IPT),*** which originated in the

psychoanalytic treatments of Harry Stack Sullivan and Frieda Fromm-Reichman. Such traditional forms of psychoanalytic therapy have not been documented to help relieve depression, but IPT has. Unlike classical psychoanalysis, IPT is brief, has procedures outlined in a manual, and does not deal with childhood or defense mechanisms. Rather, IPT focuses on social relations in the present, and specifically deals with current interpersonal problems. Ongoing disputes, frustrations, anxieties, and disappointments are the main material of therapy.

Interpersonal therapy looks at four problem areas: grief, fights, role transitions, and social deficits. When dealing with grief, IPT looks at abnormal grief reactions. The therapist brings out the delayed mourning process and helps the patient find new social relationships that can substitute for the lost one. When dealing with fights, the IPT therapist helps determine where the disrupted relationship is going: Does it need renegotiation? Is it at an impasse? Is it irretrievably lost? Communication, negotiation, and assertiveness skills are taught. When dealing with role transitions, including retirement, divorce, and leaving home, the IPT therapist gets the patient to reevaluate the lost role, to express emotions about the loss, to develop social skills suitable for the new role, and to establish new social supports. When dealing with social deficits, the IPT therapist looks for recurrent patterns in past relationships. Emotional expression is encouraged. Role playing and enhanced communication skills are used to overcome recurrent weaknesses in social relationships.

IPT is probably useful at preventing relapse and recurrence of depression (Frank and Spanier, 1995). In a randomized three-year maintenance trial, 128 patients with recurrent depression who had responded to combined treatment with imipramine hydrochloride and interpersonal psychotherapy were given additional IPT and/or drugs. Imipramine was an effective means of preventing recurrence, as was monthly IPT, which lengthened the time between episodes in patients not receiving active medication (Frank et al., 1990). IPT has also proven useful in treating depression in teenagers. Adolescent patients who received IPT had a greater decrease in depressive symptoms and greater improvement in overall social functioning, functioning with friends, and specific problem-solving skills than controls. Because the patients were mostly low-income Latino teenagers, and treatment was brief—twelve weeks—this is a very promising approach for treating depression in urban

Levels of Analysis

Drugs or Psychotherapy: Is There a "Treatment of Choice"?

The advent of safer and more effective medication has resulted in much greater use of antidepressants than ever before. Is this change warranted, or does psychotherapy offer equivalent benefits? This issue is often stated dichotomously, as one of determining whether drugs are "better" than "psychotherapy," or vice versa. This issue of "treatment of choice" for unipolar depression is a hotly disputed empirical question, with psychiatrists, psychologists, managed care companies, and drug companies taking sides. Literally billions of dollars in health-care costs hang on the ultimate answer.

Over the last two decades, hundreds of well-controlled studies have been conducted supporting the effectiveness of both medication and psychotherapy for depression. It turns out that for most patients and most depressions, medication, cognitive-behavioral therapy, and interpersonal therapy seem roughly equivalent. Over the many studies on symptom relief, the range for all the treatments is between 60 to 75 percent of patients with moderate or better symptom relief (DeRubeis, Evans, Hollon, and Garvey, 1990; Fava, Grandi, Zielezny, and Rafanelli, 1996; Lewinsohn and Clarke, 1999; Reinecke, Ryan, and DuBois, 1998; Spangler, Simons, Monroe, and Thase, 1997). Antidepressant medications work faster initially, but after three to four months of treatment, the psychotherapies catch up (Elkin, Shea, Imber et al, 1986; Elkin, Shea, Watkins, et al., 1989; Imber, Pilkonis, Sotsky, and Elkin, 1990; Shea, Elkin, Imber, and Sotsky, 1992). Thus, statistically, patients are improved by both drugs and psychotherapy. But are particular patients more likely to respond to drugs, and other patients more likely to respond to psychotherapy? Would the same patients improve if given therapy rather than drugs, or drugs rather than therapy? Some patients don't want to or are unable to talk about their problems, and for them medication may be a better treatment. Some patients may be unable to take drugs because of their medical condition, unwilling because of unpleasant side effects, or they may just need a sympathetic ear to listen to them.

The National Institutes of Mental Health (NIMH) sponsored a landmark collaborative study comparing the efficacy of cognitive-behavioral therapy, interpersonal therapy (IPT), and tricyclic antidepressants (Elkin, Shea, Imber, et al., 1986). Two hundred and fifty unipolar patients were randomly assigned to one of four groups (cognitive-behavioral therapy, interpersonal therapy, tricyclic antidepressant drugs, and placebo), and the design was carried out at three different treatment centers. More than 50 percent of the patients recovered in the two psychotherapy groups and in the drug group. Only 29 percent recovered in the placebo group.

Drugs worked better than psychotherapy with severely depressed patients, but statistically there was no difference between drugs and psychotherapy for less severe depression. As a result of these findings, practice guidelines issued by the American Psychiatric Association (1993, 2000) and the Agency for Health Care Policy and Research (1993) suggest that clinicians should use medication instead of psychotherapy to treat severe depression. Nonetheless, more research is needed to establish whether drugs are best for treating severe depression, as the evidence supporting these guidelines is thin (Antonuccio, 1995; Munoz, Hollon, McGrath, and Rehm, 1994), the severity difference did not prove to be strong at every treatment site in the NIMH study (Jacobson and Hollon, 1996), and a recent major meta-analysis (an analysis that combines all the subjects from several studies) shows no difference between cognitive-behavioral therapy and antidepressant medication, even in severe depression (DeRubeis, Gelfand, Tang, and Simons, 1999).

We believe that the issue of whether to use medication or psychotherapy to treat severe depression boils down to how severe the depression is, and how a particular case of depression is manifested. For example, profound depression can leave the patient passive, mute, and incontinent. Moreover, many depressed patients show pronounced deficits in concentration and attention. In neither case is the patient a good psychotherapy candidate, and antidepressant medication is the logical alternative. This may mean that it is best to treat severely depressed patients with drugs or even with ECT, at least initially, in order to get them past a crisis. If a fast fix is needed—perhaps to pull a patient out of depression so that he can return to work or take care of his children, or so that he doesn't commit suicide—antidepressant medication may be better than psychotherapy because drugs work faster initially.

---

teenagers—a problem that now goes largely untreated (Mufson, Weissman, Moreau, and Garfinkel, 1999).

The main virtues of this approach are that it is brief (it takes a few months), sensible, and inexpensive. A manual for it exists (Klerman, Weissman, Rounsaville, and Chevron, 1984). It has no known side effects, and it has been shown to be quite effective against depression, bringing relief in around 70 percent of cases Its main problem is that it has not been widely practiced or disseminated, so not enough research has been done to discover how it works. For a discussion of the relative merits of both drugs and psychotherapy, see Box 7–4.

If the patient is still able to function and is not in danger of suicide, psychotherapy may be a better treatment since psychotherapy does not have the side effects that may accompany medication. Moreover, psychotherapy may be more effective for preventing relapse and recurrence of symptoms. Both cognitive-behavioral therapy and interpersonal therapy teach skills that can be used the next time depression strikes (Fava, Rafanelli, Grandi, Canestrari, and Morphy, 1998; Frank and Spanier, 1995; Jarrett et al., 1998; Paykel et al., 1999; Seligman, Schulman, DeRubeis, and Hollon, 1999; Teasdale et al., 2000).

Treatment by antidepressant medication teaches no new skills, and so once the patient stops taking antidepressants, the risk for relapse and recurrence returns to the norm for unmedicated patients. Nonetheless, so long as the antidepressant medication is continued, recurrence is considerably reduced or prevented (Kupfer et al., 1992). The issue comes down to whether patients should remain on antidepressant medication indefinitely, even for life. To many patients, this presents an undesirable dependency, and they seek to go off the drugs as soon as possible—even at the risk that their depression will return. But what if patients decide to remain on antidepressants? No one can be sure, but research thus far has detected no "time bombs" in antidepressant medications—no long-term health risks with indefinite use.

In the present era of managed care, the net cost of treatment will often override other considerations like treatment effectiveness. It is commonly thought that drug treatment is cheaper than psychotherapy; after all, Prozac—one of the more expensive antidepressants —currently costs about $1.75 per day, or about $12 per week. This is considerably less than the $65 to $150 per week cost of individual psychotherapy. This cost computation, however, is complicated by the fact that treatment by medication must include monitoring of the drug by a physician, side effect cost, differential clinical success, and differential cost of relapse. In the calculations of most insurers, medication is still cheaper than psychotherapy, but the verdict is very far from in.

Should patients receive both medication and psychotherapy? There is ample rationale for dual treatment, because even if the patient's medication handles the depression, psychotherapy should still be invaluable to discuss issues such as the fact of having depression, and the consequences for one's personal, social, and work life. Further research is needed to elucidate when and for whom combination therapy is superior. In the meantime, however, evidence on this key question is mixed, depending on what kind of depression is being treated. Several studies have concluded that there is no additive effect using both drugs and psychotherapy to treat acute unipolar depression (Craighead, Craighead, and Ilardi, 1998; Nemeroff and Schatzberg, 1998).

The story is different for chronic depression, however, and happily so. In one study, 519 chronically depressed patients received twelve weeks of treatment: medication, an "atypical" antidepressant, Serzone, alone; cognitive-behavioral "analysis" (a blend of cognitive therapy and interpersonal therapy) alone; or the two in combination. Fifty-five percent of the Serzone group improved, 52 percent of the cognitive-behavioral group improved, and a surprising 85 percent of the combination group improved (Keller et al., 2000). Thus, in contrast to the typical findings of no additive effect of medication and psychotherapy, these two treatments are additive with chronic depression.

So, which is better, psychotherapy or medication? Forty years ago, the mental health professions were preoccupied with the question of whether psychotherapy worked at all. One observer, Gordon Paul, reminded researchers that the question was wrong from the start. As he pointed out, the issue wasn't whether psychotherapy worked, but rather which therapy worked for which patients and for which disorders? (Paul, 1969).

We now know that the same issue applies to the question at hand. Not all depressions respond to psychotherapy or medication. Not all patients are good psychotherapy candidates, and some patients have medical conditions that preclude medication. So the question isn't drugs or therapy. Rather, it is, "For which patients, and for which kinds of depressions, is one kind of therapy better than another, or one kind of medication better than another, and for which is either of the two preferable"?

Bipolar Disorder

Thus far, we have discussed the disorder of major (unipolar) depression, which accounts for 80 to 95 percent of all depressions. Another kind of depression, which is more severe in many respects, is seen in many people who also have suffered episodes of mania. These bipolar depressions, along with manic episodes, constitute the fluctuating, unstable condition known as **bipolar disorder** (formerly called **manic–depression**).

Whether a person is diagnosed with bipolar disorder depends on his history of manic and/or depressed

DSM-IV Criteria

Manic Episode

A. A distinct period of abnormally and persistently elevated, expansive, or irritable mood, lasting at least 1 week (or any duration if hospitalization is necessary).

B. During the period of mood disturbance, three (or more) of the following symptoms have persisted (four if the mood is only irritable) and have been present to a significant degree: (1) inflated self-esteem or grandiosity; (2) decreased need for sleep (e.g., feels rested after only 3 hours of sleep); (3) more talkative than usual or pressure to keep talking; (4) flight of ideas or subjective experience that thoughts are racing; (5) distractibility (i.e., attention too easily drawn to unimportant or irrelevant external stimuli); (6) increase in goal-directed activity (either socially, at work or school, or sexually) or psychomotor agitation; (7) excessive involvement in pleasurable activities that have a high potential for painful consequences (e.g., engaging in unrestrained buying sprees, sexual indiscretions, or foolish business investments).

C. The symptoms do not meet the criteria for a Mixed Episode.

D. The mood disturbance is sufficiently severe to cause marked impairment in occupational functioning or in usual social activities or relationships with others, or to necessitate hospitalization to prevent harm to self or others, or there are psychotic features.

E. The symptoms are not due to the direct physiological effects of a substance (e.g., a drug of abuse, a medication, or other treatment) or a general medical condition (e.g., hyperthyroidism). (*Note:* Manic-like episodes that are clearly caused by somatic antidepressant treatment (e.g., medication, electroconvulsive therapy, light therapy) should not count toward a diagnosis of Bipolar I Disorder.)

SOURCE: APA, DSM-IV, 1994.

---

episodes. A person in a manic state who has never had a depressive episode is diagnosed as having only a **manic episode.** Likewise, a person is diagnosed with only a major depression if she has had no manic episodes. An individual, however, is diagnosed with bipolar disorder if he is currently either depressed with a history of mania, or manic with a history of depression. Individuals with bipolar disorder differ greatly in whether they suffer only from manic or depressed episodes, or, over time, from both. It is rare, however, to have manic episodes with no history of depression.

The depressive component of bipolar disorder is superficially similar to major depression, but there are differences. For one thing, bipolar depressions tend to be more severe (Angst et al., 1973; Depue and Monroe, 1978; Fogarty, Russell, Newman, and Bland, 1994; Loranger and Levine, 1978). They also tend to be accompanied, not by insomnia and reduced appetite, but by overeating (especially of carbohydrates) and hypersomnia (always feeling sleepy, despite getting too much sleep already). Unipolar and bipolar depression may also differ in their neurochemistry: patients with bipolar depression, when treated with antidepressant medications like Prozac that are so effective in unipolar depressions, some-

times flip instead into a manic episode (Boerlin, Gitlin, Zoellner, and Hammen, 1998).

The onset of a manic episode usually occurs fairly suddenly. Here is what it feels like to be in the manic state of a manic-depressive disorder:

> When I start going into a high, I no longer feel like an ordinary housewife. Instead, I feel organized and accomplished, and I begin to feel I am my most creative self. I can write poetry easily, I can compose melodies without effort. I can paint. My mind feels facile and absorbs everything. I have countless ideas about improving the conditions of mentally retarded children, how a hospital for these children should be run, what they should have around them to keep them happy and calm and unafraid. I see myself as being able to accomplish a great deal for the good of people. I have countless ideas about how the environmental problem could inspire a crusade for the health and betterment of everyone. I feel able to accomplish a great deal for the good of my family and others. I feel pleasure, a sense of euphoria or elation. I want it to last forever. I don't seem to need much sleep. I've lost weight and feel healthy, and I like myself. I've just bought six new dresses, in fact, and they look quite good on me. I feel sexy and men stare at me. Maybe I'll have an af-

fair, or perhaps several. I feel capable of speaking and doing good in politics. I would like to help people with problems similar to mine so they won't feel hopeless. (Fieve, 1975, p. 17)

Symptoms of Mania

The euphoric or irritable thoughts, frenetic acts, and resulting insomnia of mania stand in marked contrast to the person's usual functioning. Mania presents four sets of symptoms: mood, cognitive, motivational, and somatic.

MOOD SYMPTOMS

The mood of an individual in a manic state is expansive and either euphoric or quite irritable. A highly successful manic artist describes his mood:

I feel no sense of restriction or censorship whatsoever. I'm afraid of nothing and no one. During this elated state, when no inhibition is present, I feel I can race a car with my foot on the floorboard, fly a plane when I have never flown a plane before, and speak languages I hardly know. Above all, as an artist, I feel I can write poems and paint paintings that I could never dream of when just my normal self. I don't want others to restrict me during this period of complete and utter freedom. (Fieve, 1975)

As we have described, euphoria is not universal in mania. Often the dominant mood is irritability, and this is particularly so when a manic individual is thwarted in his ambitions. People with mania, even

In the 1988 film *Good Morning, Vietnam,* Robin Williams plays a manic disc jockey on Armed Forces Radio during the Vietnam War. Williams himself is diagnosed with bipolar disorder.

when high, are peculiarly close to tears, and when frustrated may burst out crying. This is one reason to believe that mania is not wholly the opposite state of depression, but that a strong depressive element co-exists with it.

COGNITIVE SYMPTOMS

The manic thoughts are appropriate to the mood. They are grandiose. The patient does not believe in limits to his ability, and worse, he does not recognize the painful consequences that will ensue when he carries out his plans. A patient who spends $100,000 buying three automobiles in a week may not recognize that he will have a great deal of trouble making payments on them; a manic patient who calls the president in the middle of the night to tell him about her latest health-care proposal does not recognize that this call may bring the police down on her; the manic patient who enters one sexual affair after another does not realize the threats to his health and reputation.

A person in a manic state may have thoughts or ideas racing through his mind faster than he can write them down or say them. This flight of ideas easily becomes derailed because the manic patient is highly distractible. In some extreme cases, the manic patient has delusional ideas about himself. He may believe that he is a special messenger of God, or an intimate friend of famous politicians and movie stars. The patient's thinking about other people is black and white: the individuals he knows are either all good or all bad; they are his best friends or his sworn enemies. The following is a case showing a manic flight of ideas:

I went mad at the winter Olympics in Innsbruck. My brain got cloudy, as if a fog from the Alps had enveloped it. In that condition I came face to face with one gentleman—the Devil. He looked the part! He had hooves, fur, horns, and rotten teeth that looked hundreds of years old. With this figure in mind I climbed the hills above Innsbruck and torched a farm building. I was convinced that only a brilliant bonfire could burn off that fog. As I was leading the cows and horses from the barn, the Austrian police arrived. They handcuffed me and took me down into the valley. . . Back over the border I was delivered to the doctors in Prague . . .

Then the bad times began. The doctors, with their pills, got me into a state in which I realized I was mad. That is sadness, when you know that you are no Christ but a wretch whose brain, which makes a man a man, is sick . . .

. . . I know I suffered terribly. There are no words to describe it. And if there were such words, people would not believe them because they do not want to hear about madness. It frightens them. "When I felt better, I tried to remember what had been beautiful in my life. I did not think about love or how I had wandered all over the world. . . . I remembered most the river I had loved most in my life. Before I could fish in it again I would take its water in the shell of my hands and kiss it as I would kiss a woman. . . . Sometimes, when I sat at the barred window and fished in memory, the pain was almost unbearable. I had to block it out, the beauty, and I had to remind myself that dirt, foulness, and muddy waters also ran the world. When I succeeded in this, I did not long so much for my freedom . . .

I wanted to kill myself a hundred times when I felt I couldn't go on, but I never did. Maybe my desire to kiss the river and catch the silver fish again kept me going. Fishing taught me patience and my memories helped me go on. (Pavel, 1990)

MOTIVATIONAL SYMPTOMS

Manic behavior is hyperactive. The patient who is in a manic state engages in frenetic activity, be it in his occupation, in political or religious circles, in sexual relationships, or elsewhere. Describing the mania of a woman, one author wrote:

Her friends noticed that she was going out every night, dating many new men, attending church meetings, language classes, and dances, and showing a rather frenetic emotional state. Her seductiveness at the office resulted in her going to bed with two of the available married men, who didn't realize she was ill. She burst into tears on several occasions without provocation and told risqué jokes that were quite out of character. She became more talkative and restless, stopped eating and didn't seem to need any sleep. She began to talk with religious feeling about being in contact with God and insisted that several things were now necessary to carry out God's wishes. This included giving herself sexually to all who needed her. When she was admitted to the hospital, she asked the resident psychiatrist on call to kiss her. Because he refused to do so, she became suddenly silent. Later, she talked incessantly, accusing the doctor of trying to se-

duce her and began to talk about how God knew every sexual thought that she or the doctor might have. (Fieve, 1975, pp. 22–23)

The manic activity of the patient has an intrusive, demanding, and domineering quality to it. People in a manic state often make us uncomfortable because of this. It is difficult to spend much time with an individual who delivers a rapid succession of thoughts and who behaves in a frenetic way almost in disregard of those around him. Other behaviors that commonly occur during mania are compulsive gambling, reckless driving, poor financial investments, and flamboyant dress and makeup.

PHYSICAL SYMPTOMS

With all this flurry of activity comes a greatly lessened need for sleep. Such hyposomnia virtually always occurs during mania. After a couple of days of this, exhaustion inevitably sets in, and the mania slows down. In fact, an experimental treatment is to "sleep off" a mania using sleeping medication. It is the opposite of the finding that sleep deprivation reduces depression.

Course of Bipolar Disorder

Between .6 and 1.1 percent of the population of the United States will have bipolar disorder in their lifetime (Keller and Baker, 1991; Robins et al., 1984). Unlike unipolar depression, which affects more women than men, bipolar disorder affects both sexes equally. The onset of bipolar disorder is sudden; usually a matter of hours or days, and typically no precipitating event is obvious. The first episode is usually manic, not depressive, and it generally appears between the ages of twenty and thirty. Ninety percent of people with bipolar disorder will have had their first attack before they are fifty years old.

Bipolar disorder tends to recur, and each episode lasts from several days to several months. Over the first ten years of the disorder, the frequency and intensity of the episodes tend to worsen. Surprisingly, it seems to burn out, and not many episodes occur twenty years after the initial onset. Both manic and depressive episodes occur in the disorder, but regular cycling (for example, three months manic, followed by three months depressive, and so on) is rare.

Bipolar disorder is not a benign, remitting disorder. For some, extreme manic episodes may bring about much hardship. Their hyperactivity and bizarre behavior may lead to problems at work and at home. Employers often become annoyed at their behavior, and some people with bipolar disorder then find themselves without a job. For others, entire careers may be lost. In addition, their social relationships tend to break down. The person with bipolar disorder is hard to deal with. A much higher percentage of married manic-depressive patients divorce than do married unipolar depressive patients. Alcohol abuse, either in attempted self-medication or due to poor judgment and impulsiveness, is very high in those with bipolar disorder. The more severe the mania, the more frequent the alcoholism (Maier, Lichtermann, Minges, Delmo, and Heun, 1995). In all, between 20 and 50 percent of people with bipolar disorder suffer chronic social and occupational impairment. In most extreme cases, hospitalization is required. And for a few, suicide is a constant threat. The rate of attempted and successful suicides is also higher in bipolar than in unipolar depressions. As many as 15 percent of those with bipolar disorder may end their life by suicide (Brodie and Leff, 1971; Carlson, Kotin, Davenport, and Adland, 1974; Dunner, Gershom, and Goodwin, 1976; Reich, Davies, and Himmelhoch, 1974; Sharma and Markar, 1994).

When the mania is more moderate and the depressions are not too debilitating, however, the ambition, hyperactivity, talkativeness, and grandiosity of the person with bipolar disorder may lead to great achievements. This behavior is conducive to success in our society. It is no surprise that many creative people, leaders of industry, entertainment, politics,

There is evidence that Theodore Roosevelt had bipolar disorder, and that the manic phase of his disorder contributed to his political success.

and religion may have been able to use and control their less severe levels of bipolar disorder. Abraham Lincoln, Winston Churchill, and Theodore Roosevelt probably all suffered from bipolar disorder.

Cause of Bipolar Disorder

The cause of bipolar disorder is unknown. On the surface, the expansiveness and hyperactivity of mania are in stark contrast to the withdrawal and inertness of depression, an observation that has led to theories proposing that mania is the physiological opposite of depression. Some theorists, for example, believe that bipolar disorder results from self-correcting biological processes that have become ungoverned. Generally, when an individual becomes depressed, the depression is allegedly ended by switching in an opposite, euphoric state that cancels it out. Conversely, when an individual becomes euphoric, this state is kept from spiraling out of bounds by switching in a depressive state that neutralizes the euphoria. Investigations of the biochemistry of this switching process seem to indicate that bipolar disorder may result from a disturbance in the balance of mania and depression, specifically from an overshooting of the reaction to either (see Figure 7–7).

Another theory about the underlying biological basis for bipolar disorder identifies three separate systems in the brain that may become unbalanced and cause different groups of symptoms. First, the switching from the lack of interest and lack of enjoyment of the depressed phase to the excessive pleasure-seeking activity of the manic phase may involve disturbances in the brain's reward system, with an excess or a lack of pleasure "inhibition" determining whether the individual is overly enthusiastic or apathetic. Second, high sensitivity to pain and negative events in depression and low sensitivity to them in mania may result from a separate disinhibition-inhibition process. Third, the shift from the hyperactivity of the manic state to the retarded motor activity of the depressive state may stem from an unregulated movement processing system. Different neurotransmitters are thought to control the switching processes within each of these three systems (Carroll, 1994).

Each of these theories, however, considers depression and mania to be separate and reciprocal phases of bipolar disorder. They have a difficult time explaining how mania and depression could co-occur in the same person at the same time. But this is

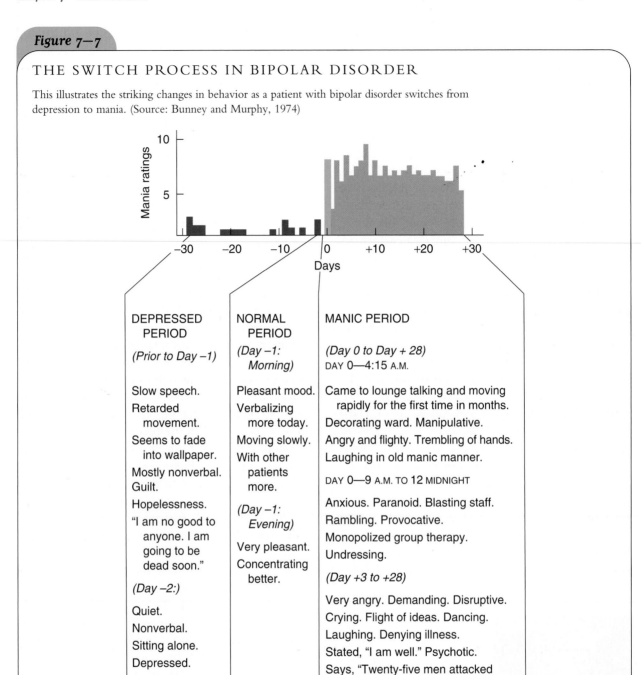

Figure 7-7

THE SWITCH PROCESS IN BIPOLAR DISORDER

This illustrates the striking changes in behavior as a patient with bipolar disorder switches from depression to mania. (Source: Bunney and Murphy, 1974)

DEPRESSED PERIOD

(Prior to Day −1)

Slow speech.
Retarded movement.
Seems to fade into wallpaper.
Mostly nonverbal.
Guilt.
Hopelessness.
"I am no good to anyone. I am going to be dead soon."

(Day −2:)

Quiet.
Nonverbal.
Sitting alone.
Depressed.

NORMAL PERIOD

(Day −1: Morning)

Pleasant mood.
Verbalizing more today.
Moving slowly.
With other patients more.

(Day −1: Evening)

Very pleasant.
Concentrating better.

MANIC PERIOD

(Day 0 to Day + 28)
DAY 0—4:15 A.M.

Came to lounge talking and moving rapidly for the first time in months.
Decorating ward. Manipulative.
Angry and flighty. Trembling of hands.
Laughing in old manic manner.

DAY 0—9 A.M. TO 12 MIDNIGHT

Anxious. Paranoid. Blasting staff.
Rambling. Provocative.
Monopolized group therapy.
Undressing.

(Day +3 to +28)

Very angry. Demanding. Disruptive.
Crying. Flight of ideas. Dancing.
Laughing. Denying illness.
Stated, "I am well." Psychotic.
Says, "Twenty-five men attacked me today."

---

exactly what seems to happen in *mixed episodes,* in which individuals meet criteria to be diagnosed with *both* mania and depression. Such patients typically look depressed but show agitation, irritability, and psychotic thinking. As we have seen, feelings of depression are often close at hand during the mania. The bipolar individual, when manic, is close to tears; he voices more hopelessness and has more suicidal thoughts than is normal. This has led some theorists to believe that mania is a brittle defense against an underlying depression. Clearly they are not reciprocal disorders that are somehow related and can co-occur.

Individuals are genetically vulnerable to bipolar disorder. Individuals with manic-depression are more often found in families in which successive generations have experienced depression or mania. Relatives of bipolar patients have five times the normal 1 percent risk for developing the disorder (Rice et al., 1987). Identical twins have five times the concordance for bipolar disorder than do fraternal twins. Thus, the familial risk is probably genetic, at least in part for bipolar disorder, but less so for major depression. Meanwhile, the search for gene loci is underway but as yet inconclusive (Allen, 1976; Berrettini et al., 1997; Carroll, 1994; McGuffin and Katz, 1989).

Treatment of Bipolar Disorder

The classic first-line treatment for bipolar disorder is lithium carbonate (see Table 7–4). Lithium was originally used as a table salt substitute. In 1949, John Cade, an Australian physician, having found that lithium salts made guinea pigs lethargic, thought that it might make people with mania lethargic. So he tried it to dampen mania in humans and found that administering lithium ended severe manic attacks. Since that time, lithium carbonate has been shown to be an effective treatment both for mania and for the depressive aspects of bipolar disorder. Approximately 80 percent of patients with bipolar disorder will show a full or partial alleviation of symptoms during lithium administration (Schou, 1997). It is also clear, however, that the other 20 percent of patients do not respond to the lithium (Depue, 1979; Manji, Potter,

and Lenox, 1995; Solomon, Keitner, Miller, Shea, and Keller, 1995).

Although lithium can be viewed as a miracle drug for bipolar disorder, its side effects, particularly on the heart and kidneys, can be physically damaging and even lethal. Because lithium is quite toxic on overdose, it is a precarious drug to prescribe to patients with bipolar disorder who are far from conscientious about taking their medications. This explains why, after fifty years of effective use of lithium for bipolar depression, lithium treatment is being supplanted. The new treatments use anticonvulsant drugs such as carbamazepine (Tegretol), valproate (Depakote), lamotrigine (Lamictal), and gabapentin (Neurontin). Many case studies have been reported, but to date only one well-controlled study. In this double-blind randomized controlled trial, researchers showed that lamotrigine was effective against depression in bipolar patients (Calabrese et al., 1999). The next few years will see wider experimental testing of the anticonvulsants (Post et al., 1998), but due to their more manageable side effects, treatment with anticonvulsants has already become standard practice.

You will recall the hot dispute about whether to view unipolar depression in the biological framework or in the cognitive framework. There is no such dispute about bipolar depression: Both the evidence on the robust effectiveness of lithium and on strong genetic vulnerability suggest that bipolar disorder is best understood within the biological model.

TABLE 7–4

Treatment

BIPOLAR DISORDER

	Psychosocial Treatment*	Medications[†]
Improvement	marginal	80% marked relief from mania; 60–80% moderate relief from depression
Relapse[‡]	unknown	high relapse rate
Side Effects	none	moderate to severe
Cost	inexpensive	moderately expensive
Time Scale	months/weeks	weeks/months
Overall	**marginal**	**very good**

*Psychosocial treatment is given as an adjunct of medication only. Both family interventions and cognitive-behavioral therapy have been used coupled with medication in several controlled trials.

[†]Medications include lithium for bipolar disorder, as well as valproate and carbamazepine for acute mania.

[‡]Relapse after discontinuation of treatment.

SOURCE: Based on Craighead, Miklowitz, and Vajk, 1998; Keck and McElroy, 1998.

Seasonal Affective Disorder (SAD)

The most recent addition to the mood disorder classification is called *seasonal affective disorder (SAD),* and in its latest incarnation is dubbed a "seasonal pattern specifier" in DSM-IV. In principle, it can be a specifier for any of the mood disorders, but most commonly it is seen in conjunction with bipolar disorder. For millennia, human activity in the temperate zones has been strongly influenced by the seasons, with highly active behavior occurring during spring and summer, and withdrawal from the frenzy of life tending to occur during fall and winter. This may be the evolutionary basis for SAD (Whybrow, 1997).

When John moved to Washington, D.C., from Florida at age twenty-one, he experienced his first depression. He went there to attend medical school, and for each of the next four winters the depression recurred. He was hospitalized and became hopeless about his goal of becoming a physician because of his depression problem. He plodded on through his internship in Maryland, with the depressions continuing yearly.

He noticed that each year his depression remitted in the spring. The depression started around the first of December, when the days were getting short, and it lifted by the first of April. In some years, the depressions came on gradually, but in other years a bad event, like a patient dying, precipitated the depression. His mood was worse in the morning; he had trouble sleeping; he craved carbohydrates and gained weight. He was apathetic, irritable, and felt pessimistic.

After reading about SAD, he entered light therapy treatment at the National Institutes of Mental Health. He found that brilliant grow lights, on for two hours before dawn, markedly relieved his depression. Finally, he treated himself. He moved, and opened a practice in San Diego. He has not experienced a winter depression since. (Adapted from Spitzer, Gibbon, Skodol, Williams, and First, 1989, pp. 19–21)

SAD is characterized by depressions that begin each year in October or November and fully remit, sometimes switching toward mania, as the days lengthen (March and April). Patients complain of fatigue, oversleeping, and carbohydrate craving as well as of the more typical symptoms of depression. Women are diagnosed more than men, and young children show the problem as well. In a nationwide Japanese survey, only 1 percent of the over 5,000 depressed outpatients were identified as having SAD (Sakamoto, Kamo, Nakadaira, and Tamura, 1993). In contrast, among a random sample of 283 Alaskans, who have less sunlight, twenty-six (9.2 percent) had SAD (Booker and Hellekson, 1992; but see Magnusson, Axelsson, Karlsson, and Oskarsson, 2000, for lack of SAD in Iceland). In one of the first major studies, twenty-nine patients with SAD reported their clinical history of depression by month. Depressive episodes were yoked to the sunlight and temperature of each month, with greatest depression in the winter months and least in the summer (see Figure 7–8).

DSM-IV Criteria

Seasonal Pattern Specifier

DSM-IV suggests criteria for describing recurrent episodes of mood disorders with Seasonal Pattern (can be applied to the pattern of Major Depressive Episodes in Bipolar I Disorder, Bipolar II Disorder, or Major Depressive Disorder, Recurrent):

A. There has been a regular temporal relationship (occurring at the same time) between the onset of Major Depressive Episodes in Bipolar I or Bipolar II Disorder or Major Depressive Disorder, Recurrent, and a particular time of the year (e.g., regular appearance of the major Depressive Episode in the fall or winter). (*Note:* Do not include cases in which there is an obvious effect of seasonal-related psychosocial stressors; e.g., regularly being unemployed every winter.)

B. Full remission (or a change from depression to mania or hypomania) also occur at a characteristic time of the year (e.g., depression disappears in the spring).

C. In the last 2 years, two Major Depressive Episodes have occurred that demonstrate the temporal seasonal relationships defined in Criteria A and B, and no nonseasonal major Depressive Episodes have occurred during that same period.

D. Seasonal Major Depressive Episodes substantially outnumber the nonseasonal Major Depressive Episodes that may have occurred over the individual's lifetime.

SOURCE: APA, DSM-IV, 1994.

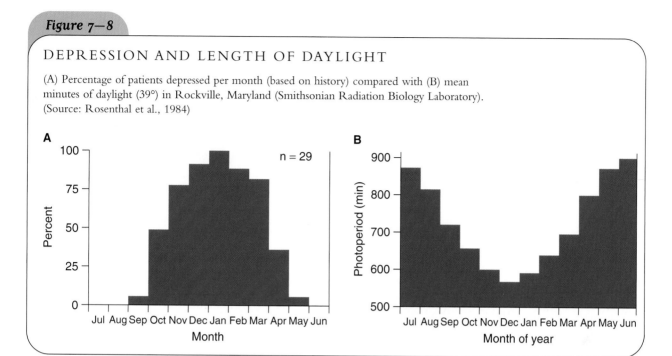

Figure 7—8

DEPRESSION AND LENGTH OF DAYLIGHT

(A) Percentage of patients depressed per month (based on history) compared with (B) mean minutes of daylight (39°) in Rockville, Maryland (Smithsonian Radiation Biology Laboratory). (Source: Rosenthal et al., 1984)

Not only is depression governed by the amount of sunlight where these patients live, but when they travel their depression changes. When they travel south in the winter, depression remits in a few days, and when they travel north in the winter it tends to worsen (Molin, Mellerup, Bolwik, Scheike, and Dam, 1996; Rosenthal et al., 1984).

These findings led to the use of artificial light as therapy. Bright "Gro-Lights" (natural-sunlight phosphor fluorescent lamps) are strategically located in the homes of the patients and come on very early in the morning and after sunset to lengthen daylight hours artificially. Prompt relief of depressive symptoms, particularly with the morning lights, has been reported, and relapse occurs when light is withdrawn (Hellekson, Kline, and Rosenthal, 1986; Lewy, Sack, Miller, and Hoban, 1987; Rosenthal, Moul, Hellekson, and Oren, 1993). Exposure to natural light in the morning also seems to reduce depressive symptoms (Lewy et al., 1998; Wirz-Justice et al., 1996).

In a form of light therapy for Seasonal Affective Disorder, this woman sits in front of a fluorescent light screen for several hours each day. This light therapy relieves the depressive symptoms she experiences during the winter months, when there is less sunlight.

Suicide

Suicide is the most disastrous consequence of depression, whether bipolar or unipolar. Depression is the precursor of a vast majority of suicides. Death only rarely results directly from other psychological disorders: the patient with anorexia who refuses food; the hallucinating patient with schizophrenia who, believing he is Christ, attempts to walk on water; the heroin addict who administers an overdose. But it is depression that most frequently results in irreversible harm: death, by suicide.

Suicide is the third most frequent cause of death among high school and college students. This age group, which once accounted for only 5 percent of suicides, now accounts for more than 15 percent (Harvard Mental Health Letter, 1996; Monthly Vital

Statistics Report, 1996). The death of a young person, because of all his or her unfulfilled promise, is a keenly felt tragedy. As a young man, Beethoven almost took his own life before composing his second symphony. What held him back was the thought that he had not yet produced his best work.

Suicide is an act that most societies forbid. Many religions regard it as a sin; and it is, ironically, a crime in several states. No act leaves such a bitter and lasting legacy among friends and relatives. It leaves in its wake bewilderment, guilt, shame, and stigma that relatives may carry to their own graves.

The individual who is deciding whether or not to take his own life is usually strongly ambivalent about the decision. One vote can tip the balance, as in a declaration of war (see Table 7–5). For example, when his physician had to cancel an upcoming appointment, one patient saw this as the last straw in a series of disappointments, and it tipped the balance toward his suicidal death.

The ethical quandaries of suicide are immensely difficult. Does an individual have a right to take his own life without interference by others, just as he has a right to dispose of his own property at will (Szasz, 1974)? There is a movement within the United States today, symbolized by Dr. Jack Kevorkian, which holds that individuals have such a

Dr. Jack Kevorkian believes that an individual should have the right to take his own life without interference from others. Here he talks to reporters during a break at his 1996 trial for assisted suicide.

right. On the other side, however, are those who contend that most suicides have a depressive disorder behind them. The lifetime suicide rate among people with mood disorders is over twenty-five times the rate in the general population (Caldwell and Gottesman, 1990, 1992). Once the depression has lifted, either with the passage of time or with treatment, the suicidal desires also lift. It is problematic to regard a

TABLE 7–5

FABLES AND FACTS ABOUT SUICIDE

Fable	Fact
Individuals who talk about killing themselves do not kill themselves.	Of every ten persons who have killed themselves, eight gave definite warnings of their intentions.
Suicidal individuals have made a clear decision to die.	Most are undecided about living or dying. They often gamble with death, leaving it to others to save them.
Once an individual is suicidal, he is forever suicidal.	Usually individuals who wish to kill themselves are suicidal only for a limited period. Suicidal wishes are often linked to depression, and depression usually dissipates in time.
The suicidal risk is over when improvement occurs following a suicidal crisis.	Most suicides occur while the individual is still depressed, but within about three months after the beginning of "improvement." It is at that time that the individual has better access to weapons and more energy to put his suicidal plans into effect than when he is in the hospital or at the lowest point in his depression.
Suicide occurs more often among the rich.	Suicide is equally frequent at all levels of society.
The suicidal act is the act of a sick person.	While the suicidal person is almost always extremely unhappy, he is not necessarily "mentally ill." Suicide can be a rational act.

SOURCE: Adapted from Shneidman, 1976.

decision that waxes and wanes with depression as a rational decision (McHugh, 1997).

Who Is at Risk for Suicide?

At the very least, 25,000 people end their lives by suicide every year in the United States. There were at least 30,000 completed suicides and more than three times as many hospitalizations for attempted suicide in 1996 (Monthly Vital Statistics Report, 1996), the most recent year for which there are reliable data. There are also estimated to be at least ten times as many suicide attempts as successful suicides, and it has been estimated that in the United States today, 5 million people are alive who have attempted suicide. An attempted suicide is the biggest risk factor for a completed suicide, carrying a risk 100 times greater than average in the next year. About 10 percent of people who make an attempt will succeed in the next ten years (Harvard Mental Health Letter, 1996).

Suicide may run in families, and to the extent that depressive disorders are heritable, suicide itself may be heritable (Arango and Underwood, 1997). In a study of the Amish, a highly insular group of people who tend to marry within the group and to live in Lancaster County, Pennsylvania, all twenty-six suicides over the last hundred years were analyzed. Twenty-four of these individuals had had major affective disorders; 16 percent of the families accounted for 73 percent of the suicides (Egeland and Sussex, 1985).

The risk for suicide may even have a biochemical component. Among depressed patients, suicide attempts were most frequent in those having low sero-

tonin levels, and when low-serotonin patients attempted suicide, they used more violent means (Asberg, Traskman, and Thoren, 1976). The brains of suicide victims have lower serotonin in their brain stem and cerebrospinal fluid, but not in their frontal cortex (Bourgeois, 1991; Mann, Arango, and Underwood, 1990; Traskman-Bendz et al., 1993).

DEPRESSION AND SUICIDE

Although suicide can occur in the absence of depression and even though the large majority of depressed people do not commit suicide, depressed individuals are the single group most at risk for suicide. An estimated 80 percent of suicidal patients are significantly depressed. Depressed patients ultimately commit suicide at a rate that is at least twenty-five times as high as control populations (Flood and Seager, 1968; Pokorny, 1964; Robins and Guze, 1972).

But depression is not the only disorder with high suicide rates: about 20 percent of suicides are alcohol abusers (almost all of whom are also depressed), and 5 to 10 percent of people with schizophrenia attempt suicide. Homicidal people also commit suicide at a great rate: the suicide rate among white murderers is 700 times the national average (Harvard Mental Health Letter, 1996).

SEX DIFFERENCES AND SUICIDE

Women make roughly three times as many suicide attempts as men, but men actually succeed in killing themselves four times more often than women (Canetto and Lester, 1995). The combination of an individual who is impulsive and aggressive and has low serotonin—a more common combination in men than women—may explain the male preponderance of completed suicides. The greater rate of suicide attempts in women is probably related to the fact that more depression occurs in women, whereas the greater completed suicide rate in men probably has to do with choice of methods: women tend to choose less lethal means, such as cutting their wrists and overdosing on sleeping pills; whereas men tend to shoot themselves and jump off buildings. More than half the completed suicides in the United States use a gun. The suicide rate for both men and women is higher among individuals who have been divorced and widowed; loneliness, as well as a sense of failure in interpersonal affairs, surely contributes to this statistic. Men who kill themselves tend to be motivated by failure at work, and women who kill themselves tend

Kurt Kobain committed suicide at the height of his popularity. Unlike Beethoven, who considered suicide after writing his first symphony but did not kill himself, we will never know what other music Kobain might have writen had he not taken his life.

Men are more likely than women to actually kill themselves when attempting to commit suicide, as women tend to cut their wrists or overdose on sleeping pills, while men are more likely to shoot themselves or to jump off bridges or buildings. Here a young man decides whether or not to jump to his death, as the police department tries to coach him to go back inside or to catch him below if he actually jumps.

to be motivated by failure at love (Linden and Breed, 1976; Mendels, 1970; Shneidman, 1976). As one female patient who tried to commit suicide after being rejected by her lover said, "There's no sense in living. There's nothing here for me. I need love and I don't have it anymore. I can't be happy without love—only miserable. It will just be the same misery, day in and day out. It's senseless to go on" (Beck, 1976).

CULTURAL DIFFERENCES AND SUICIDE

Race, religion, and nationality contribute somewhat to vulnerability to suicide. The suicide rate of young black and white men is approximately the same (Hendin, 1969; Linden and Breed, 1976; McIntosh, 1989), but black women and older black men, probably kill themselves less often than whites (Swanson and Breed, 1976; McIntosh, 1989). Alarmingly, among young black men the rate of suicide tripled from 1960 to 1987 (Summerville, Kaslow, and Doepke, 1996). There is some evidence that American Indians may have a higher suicide rate than the rest of the population (Frederick, 1978). In the United States, one's religious beliefs appear to offer little protection against suicide, as the rate of suicide in the United States is roughly the same whether the individual is nonreligious, Catholic, Protestant, or Jewish.

Suicide rates tend to increase in places of forced social changes, as in Russia after the fall of the Soviet Union. Here Russians who have lost their jobs during the financial crisis of 1998 wait in line to attend a job fair, their despair and hopelessness evident in their faces.

Suicide occurs in all cultures, but it seems to be more common in industrialized countries (see Table 7–6). Studies have shown that Hungary, Sri Lanka, and Russia have the highest suicide rates in the world; roughly triple the rate in the United States (WHO, 1995). The suicide rate in the former Soviet Union almost doubled over the period from 1965 to 1984. Then, during the period of democratization from 1984 to 1988, the suicide rate halved again. In regions of strong political antagonism (Baltic States) and of forced social changes (Russia) the rate was high, but in regions where families and religious faith were strong, the rate was low (Varnik and Wasserman, 1992). Mexico and Egypt have very low suicide rates, perhaps because suicide is considered a mortal sin in these cultures. The suicide rate in Ireland has increased fivefold in fifty years as the Catholic Church has taken a more benign view. On the world scale, the United States has an average suicide rate. Sweden has a middling high rate of suicide. Some have blamed this on the lack of incentive provided by its social welfare system, but its suicide rate has remained the same since about 1910, before the introduction of social welfare (Shneidman, 1976; see also Department of International Economic and Social Affairs, 1985).

AGE AND SUICIDE

Among children, suicide is rare, with probably fewer than 200 suicides committed in a year in the United States by children who are under the age of fourteen. Suicide is difficult to predict under any circumstances, but is known that preschoolers who are suicidal tend to be more impulsive and hyperactive, show less pain and crying when hurt, and have parents who abuse and neglect them (Rosenthal and Rosenthal, 1984).

Discussing her wish to die, Michelle (M), age nine, talks with the late Joaquim Puig-Antich (JPA), a leading expert on childhood depression:

JPA: Do you feel you should be punished?

M: Yes.

TABLE 7–6

Data

WORLD SUICIDE RATES

Country	Available Data	Total	Male	Female	Ratio
Hungary	1991	38.6	58.0	20.7	2.8
Sri Lanka	1986	33.2	46.9	18.9	2.5
U.S.S.R.	1990	21.1	34.4	9.1	3.8
China	1989	17.1	14.7	19.6	0.8
Japan	1991	16.1	20.6	11.8	1.7
Germany, Fed. Rep.,	1990	15.8	22.4	9.6	2.3
Australia	1988	13.3	21.0	5.6	3.8
Singapore	1990	13.1	14.7	11.5	1.3
Canada	1990	12.7	20.4	5.2	3.9
United States	1989	12.2	19.9	4.8	4.1
Hong Kong	1989	10.5	11.8	9.1	1.3
Puerto Rico	1990	10.5	19.4	2.1	9.2
Uruguay	1990	10.3	16.6	4.2	4.0
Ireland	1990	9.5	14.4	4.7	3.1
India	1988	8.1	9.1	6.9	1.3
Korea, Rep. of	1987	7.9	11.5	4.4	2.6
United Kingdom	1991	7.9	12.4	3.6	3.4
Israel	1989	7.8	11.0	4.6	2.4
Argentina	1989	7.1	10.5	3.8	2.8
Costa Rica	1989	5.8	9.3	2.1	4.4
Thailand	1985	5.8	7.1	4.5	1.6
Chile	1989	5.6	9.8	1.5	6.5
Venezuela	1989	4.8	7.8	1.8	4.3
Mexico	1990	2.3	3.9	0.7	5.6

SOURCE: WHO Division of Mental Health, unpublished statistics, except India and China. Source for India: National Crime Records Bureau, Government of India, 1992.

JPA: Why?

M: I don't know.

JPA: Have you ever had the thought that you might want to hurt yourself?

M: Yes.

JPA: How would you hurt yourself?

M: By drinking a lot of alcohol, or jumping off the balcony.

JPA: Have you ever tried to jump?

M: I once stood on the edge of the terrace and put one leg over the railing, but my mother caught me.

JPA: Did you really want to jump?

M: Yes.

JPA: What would have happened if you had jumped?

M: I would have killed myself.

JPA: Did you want to get killed?

M: Uh-huh.

JPA: Why?

M: Because I don't like the life I live.

JPA: What kind of life do you live?

M: A sad and miserable life.

(Jerome, 1979)

Suicide among young people in the United States is on the rise. In the past thirty-five years, the suicide rate among college-age groups has tripled. Males between the ages of twenty and twenty-four are hardest hit, with a rate of about 28 per 100,000 compared to a rate of 12 per 100,000 in the general population. Studies of the psychological "autopsies" of young suicides have strongly implicated substance abuse and untreated depression as precursors (Holden, 1986).

The suicide rate rises dramatically, particularly among men, through middle age and into old age. Men over eighty-five have the highest suicide rate of all age groups (Statistical Abstract of the United States, 1993). Increasing depression, loneliness, moving to a strange setting, loss of a meaningful role in family and society, and loss of people they love all surely contribute to the high rate of suicide among old people. In cultures and communities in which the aged are revered and remain important in the life of the family, suicide is infrequent.

The Motivation for Suicide

In the first major modern study of suicide, the French sociologist Emile Durkheim (1858–1917) distinguished three motivations for suicide, all of them intimately related to the way an individual sees his place in society. He called these motives anomic, egoistic, and altruistic. *Anomic suicide* is precipitated by a shattering break in an individual's relationship to his society: the loss of a job, economic depression, and even sudden wealth. *Egoistic suicide* occurs when the individual has too few ties to his fellow humans. Societal demands, principal among them the demand to live, are not registered by the egoistic individual. Finally, *altruistic suicide* is for the sake of the society. The individual takes his own life in order to benefit his community. Hara-kiri is an altruistic suicide. The Buddhist monks who burned themselves to death to protest the injustices of the Vietnam War are other reminders of individuals who committed altruistic suicide.

Modern thinkers see two more fundamental motivations for suicide: *surcease* and *manipulation.* Those who wish surcease have simply given up. One man wrote in a suicide note, "I wanted to be too many things, and greatness besides—it was a hopeless task. I never managed to love another person—only to make the sounds of it. I never could believe what my society taught me to believe, yet I could never manage to quite find the truth" (Shneidman, 1976). Their emotional distress is intolerable, and they see no alternative solution. In death, they see an end to their problems. Fifty-six percent of the suicide attempts observed in a systematic study were classified as individuals trying to achieve surcease. These suicide attempts involved more depression, more hopelessness, and tended to be more lethal than the remaining suicide attempts (Beck, 1976).

The other motivation for suicide is the wish to manipulate other people by a suicide attempt. Some wish to manipulate the world that remains by dying: to have the final word in an argument, to have revenge on a rejecting lover, to ruin the life of another person. More commonly in manipulative suicide, the individual intends to remain alive, but by showing the seriousness of his dilemma, he is crying out for help from those who are important to him. Trying to prevent a lover from leaving, getting into the hospital and having a temporary respite from problems, and being taken seriously are all manipulative motives for suicide with intent to live.

In one study, 13 percent of suicide attempts were found to be manipulative; these involved less depression, less hopelessness, and less lethal means than did the surcease attempts (Beck, 1976). Those suicides that are manipulative are clearly cries for help, but it should be apparent that these do not account for all

Altruistic suicide is killing yourself for what you perceive to be the good of your community. *(Left)* A Buddhist monk set himself on fire in 1963 in a ritual suicide to protest and thereby try to change the policies of the South Vietnamese government. *(Right)* A Tamil rebel killed herself and eight other people in 1998, when she blew up the van she was driving, thereby hoping to draw attention to the rebels' fight for a homeland for the minority Tamil people of Sri Lanka.

suicides. The individual who wishes to escape because life is not worth living is not crying out for help, but for an end to his troubles. The individual is usually constricted, his field of consciousness has narrowed, and he is in despair. This is not a state conducive to creativity, as shown by the following words in this suicide note: "Dearest darling I want you to know that you are the only one in my life I love you so much I could not do without you please forgive me I drove myself sick honey please believe me I love you again and the baby honey don't be mean with me please I've lived 50 years since I met you, I love you—I love you" (Shneidman, 1976). The remaining 31 percent of suicide attempts combine surcease and manipulative motivation. Here the individual is not at all sure whether he wishes to live or die, whether he wishes surcease or a change in the world. In this undecided group, the more hopeless and the more depressed the individual, the stronger is the underlying desire for surcease (Beck, Rush, Shaw, and Emery, 1979).

Prevention and Treatment of Suicide

In the initial therapeutic interview with a depressed individual, suicide should be the diagnostician's overriding concern. If clear suicidal ideation or intent are evident, crisis intervention, close observation, and hospitalization may be indicated. If they are not,

treatment will be oriented toward the longer term; antidepressant medication and/or psychotherapy will be started, with the latter directed toward careful understanding of the factors leading to the depression.

In the late 1960s, a network of more than 300 suicide prevention centers was established in the United States to deal with suicidal crises. In addition, hospitals and outpatient units set up hotlines to deal with the crises of acutely suicidal individuals. It was believed that if someone was available for the suicidal individual to talk to, the suicide could be prevented.

In terms of prevention of suicide, once the suicidal person makes contact with a telephone hotline volunteer, a psychologist, a psychiatrist, a family physician, a pastor, or emergency room doctor, evaluation of the suicidal risk takes first priority. Does the individual have a clear plan? Does he have access to a weapon? Does he have a past history of suicidal acts? Does he live alone? Once suicidal risk in a crisis is assessed, a treatment decision must be hastily made: home visit, hospitalization, medication, the police, or outpatient psychotherapy. In some cases, merely holding the person on the phone may be the appropriate action. Long-term follow-up and after-care must then occur.

Are the suicide prevention centers effective? To ascertain this, the total number of prevention centers in each state was tabulated, and the number of suicides in that state over the next decade was compared to the rates that existed before the prevention centers were started. The more suicide centers that had been established, the larger the drop in suicide rate. The effect, however, was not large, and whether the centers caused the drop, or some other demographic variable did, was unclear (Diekstra, 1992; Hazell and Lewin, 1993; Lester, 1993). In one five-year study, however, the suicide rate was found to decrease among white women who were under twenty-five years old, the most frequent users of the hotline; an estimated 600 lives were saved (Harvard Mental Health Letter, 1996). Overall, then, suicide prevention centers seem to be moderately effective.

Psychosocial interventions have also been used to try to prevent suicide. Marsha Linehan (1997) reviewed twenty treatments aiming to reduce suicide among vulnerable individuals. Four psychosocial intervention studies and one pharmacotherapy study have reported efficacious results when compared to treatments-as-usual or placebo controls. Psychosocial interventions include problem-oriented counseling, home visits, and crisis intervention; they appear to be most effective with higher-risk individuals.

In addition to suicide prevention, psychological intervention in the lives of the surviving friends and relatives is also important (Hazell and Lewin, 1993). As we have seen, these survivors are themselves more vulnerable to later depression and suicide. They are faced with shame, guilt, bewilderment, and even social ostracism. This is a neglected group that can benefit greatly from systematic care.

Putting It All Together

Through the years, unipolar depression has been regarded as either a psychological disorder or a biological disorder. Until the final decades of the twentieth century, depression was considered by most of Western society to be "all in your head," an entirely mental disorder whose treatment had to be mental as well. But the popularity of Prozac and other antidepressant medications led public opinion to swing to the opposite extreme. Today, most people endorse the view that unipolar depression is a biochemical disorder.

Nonetheless, should depression really be considered a brain disorder? In some sense, this question is the wrong one because, like the drugs versus medicine debate we discussed earlier, the dichotomy is false. Moreover, the biology versus psychology question may have different answers, depending upon whether one is considering (1) the cause of the disor-

der, (2) the manifestations of the disorder, or (3) the treatments for the disorder.

To illustrate how hard it is to separate biology and psychology, let's take a tension headache suffered by an at-home mother. What caused it? The causes might include her son's defiant behavior (a psychological cause) as well as the fact that she got a poor night's sleep or has a pre-existing problem with her neck (biological causes). How is the headache manifest? Symptoms of tension headache include crankiness (a psychological manifestation) and heightened muscle tension (a biological one). And how will she get rid of her headache? She may sit down and practice meditation (a psychological treatment) or take aspirin (a biological treatment).

To make things even more complex, at each step the psychological and biological aspects interact. Both the mother's lack of sleep and her neck problem may very well make the son's behavior especially annoying, and indeed her son's behavior the day before may have contributed to her current insomnia and neck pain. Regarding the manifestations of her headache, they also interact. Her crankiness may help make her muscles more tense, which makes her even crankier. Finally, the treatments even interact. Her meditating may help the aspirin work faster, while the aspirin will take the edge off the headache pain so she can relax more.

Understanding depression in a general way is no less complex. What causes it? Researchers have pinpointed both psychological risk factors, such as life events and a pessimistic explanatory style, and biological ones, such as "bad" genes and neurotransmitter deficiencies. How is it manifest? Depression shows both psychological manifestations, such as hopelessness, guilt, and loss of pleasure, and biological ones, such as sleep problems, appetite disturbances, and hypersecretion of cortisol. And how is depression treated? Treatments include both psychological ones, such as psychotherapy, and biological ones, such as ECT and antidepressant medication.

Is depression, then, biological or psychological? Or is it more psychological or biological? This question, too, is impossible to answer, because here, as in tension headache, the psychological and biological aspects interact. Thus, helplessness and hopelessness can reduce serotonin levels, and lowered serotonin levels can increase helplessness and hopelessness. Depression's manifestations interact as well: insomnia can contribute to hopelessness and guilt, and either can keep one awake at night. Finally, the treatments interact. The positive changes in behavior associated with psychotherapy can induce changes in neurotransmitter levels, just as changes in neurotransmitter levels induced by medication can effect positive changes in behavior.

How can we make sense of this quandary? The answer, as we discussed in Chapter 4, is that mental disorders, like physical disorders, are the products of a complex interaction of biology and psychology—an interaction that must be factored not only into the causes of mental disorders, but into the manifestations and treatments as well.

Such causal complexities lead us to look for neither the smoking gun that causes depression, nor the magic bullet that will cure it. The task instead is more daunting: it is to understand how all the aspects of affective disorder interact. What combinations of genotype, intrauterine environment, life experiences, and ongoing attitudes and beliefs, are likely to predispose us to affective disorder or to inoculate us against it? What combinations of interventions at each point—interventions that one day may range from gene therapy to psychotherapy—are most effective in controlling or even eliminating affective disorder? These are tougher questions, to be sure, but they are likelier to provide bigger payoffs.

Summary

1. The *mood disorders* consist of *major depressive disorder (unipolar depression)* and *bipolar disorder (manic-depression).* Unipolar depression (major depressive episode) consists of depressive symptoms only and involves no symptoms of mania. It is by far the most common of the depressive disorders, and has become much more frequent since World War II. *Dysthymic disorder* consists of chronic (lasting more than two years) depressive symptoms. Bipolar disorder occurs in individuals who have both periods of depression and periods of mania as well.

2. There are four basic symptoms of unipolar depression: mood symptoms, largely sadness; motivational symptoms, largely trouble making decisions or taking action; cognitive symptoms, largely hopelessness and pessimism; and physical symptoms, including loss of weight and loss of appetite. Untreated, these symptoms will usually dissipate in about three months.

3. Women are more at risk than men for unipolar depression.

4. Two theories—biological and cognitive—have shed light on the causes of unipolar depression and have generated effective treatments.

5. The biological approach holds that depression may have a genetic component; it may be due to depletions in certain central nervous system neurotransmitters—serotonin, norepinephrine, or dopamine; it may result from hormonal deficiencies; it may result from underactivity in certain areas of the brain.

6. The cognitive approach concentrates on particular ways of thinking and how these cause and sustain depression. There are two prominent cognitive models: the view of Aaron Beck, which holds that depression stems from a *negative cognitive triad,* and Seligman's *learned helplessness* explanatory style model of depression, which holds that a pessimistic explanatory style predicts risk for depression and that changing this attribution style to an optimistic style may relieve and prevent depression.

7. Unipolar depression can now be effectively treated: nine out of ten people who suffer a severe unipolar depressive episode can be markedly helped either by drugs (including tricyclic antidepressants, MAO inhibitors, and selective serotonin reuptake inhibitors), ECT, cognitive therapy, or interpersonal therapy.

8. *Bipolar disorder (manic-depression)* is the most crippling of the affective disorders. It results in ruined marriages, irreparable damage to reputation, and not uncommonly, suicide. *Mania* consists of four sets of symptoms: euphoric mood, grandiose thoughts, frenetic activity, and lack of sleep.

9. Eighty percent of bipolar depressions can now be greatly helped by lithium and anticonvulsant drugs. This disorder is best viewed within the biological model.

10. *Seasonal affective disorder (SAD)* is characterized by depression that begins each year in October or November and ends in the early spring. Light therapy has been shown to be effective.

11. *Suicide* is the most disastrous consequence of depression. Its frequency is rising among young people, and it is the second most frequent cause of death among college students. Women make more suicide attempts than men, but men actually succeed in killing themselves more often than women. There are two fundamental motivations for suicide: *surcease,* or desire to end it all, and *manipulation,* or desire to change the world or other individuals by a suicide attempt.

12. Unipolar depression is best viewed as multiply caused and treated. Biological, cognitive, and social factors can each cause depression, as well as relieve depression. These factors interact in their effects.

8

Early-Onset Disorders

Irene Phillips, Untitled work.

Learning Objectives

→ Learn about the difficulties in identifying and diagnosing childhood disorders, and how the risk for various disorders changes as children grow older.

→ Be able to describe the major symptoms of childhood emotional disorders, and how the ratio of males to females having these disorders changes with age.

→ Describe the essential features, course, and some biological and psychological causes and treatments of autism, and be able to distinguish autism from Rhett's disorder, childhood disintegrative disorder, and Asperger's disorder.

→ Learn about mental retardation, including some of the measures psychologists use to assess it, the known biological and environmental causes, and different philosophies of treating children suffering from retardation.

→ Distinguish anorexia nervosa and bulimia, and be able to describe some psychosocial theories of the eating disorders, as well as some cognitive-behavioral therapies that have been especially helpful in treating them.

→ Describe how biological and psychological factors can interact to produce conduct disorder, and why it is important to involve the family in treatment of a child with this disorder.

→ Learn about Attention-Deficit Hyperactivity Disorder (ADHD), including symptoms and treatment of ADHD, and be able to discuss the controversy over whether this disorder is overdiagnosed.

The onset of a mental disorder is tragic at any age, but it is especially so when it occurs in childhood. Childhood is viewed as a period of growth—one that should be filled with joy and learning. When the course of development is interrupted by psychological problems, the child is often deprived of experiences that are important for psychological growth. He may, for example, miss out on close peer relationships that set the stage for establishing independence. Moreover, parents must cope with the unexpected challenges of rearing a child who has special needs. This can place major demands on their financial and emotional resources. In this chapter, we will explore the psychological disorders and adjustment problems that typically have their onset in childhood. Symptoms, etiology, and current treatments will be examined, as will the intricate interaction between the child's biological constitution and the caregiving environment. We begin by introducing a child who was experiencing difficulties at school and at home and whose parents took her to a clinical psychologist for an evaluation:

> Robert and Carol Jenkins scheduled an appointment with me because they were having some problems with their four-year-old daughter, Jennifer. Her preschool teacher said that Jennifer was not playing with the other children and that she didn't participate in the organized activities. There were also some problems at home. Sometimes Jennifer was destructive and hostile. At times she seemed indifferent toward her parents and at other times she was affectionate. Mr. and Mrs. Jenkins wanted a psychological evaluation of their daughter.
>
> When I see a child like Jennifer in my clinical practice, I do a comprehensive evaluation. I get information from all of the adults who interact with her on a regular basis. I observe the child and administer psychological tests. It's like putting the pieces of a puzzle together. My job is to get the clearest possible picture of the child's developmental history and psychological needs.
>
> The Jenkins family arrived for their appointment fifteen minutes early. As I walked into the waiting room to greet them, Jennifer was paging through some of the magazines lying on a table. I introduced myself to Jennifer's parents, then I greeted Jennifer. She looked up at my face, but she didn't make eye contact or respond verbally. I met with Mr. and Mrs. Jenkins first in order to get some background information about Jennifer.

They described Jennifer's first two years of life as "normal." All the milestones—potty-training, walking, and speaking—occurred at the normal times. She was playful and active, and her parents did not notice any "out of the ordinary" behavior problems. Jennifer was talking in simple sentences by the time she was two, although she did have a tendency to repeat words. But when her parents took her to events where there were other children, Jennifer was aloof. She didn't join in the activities. Her parents decided Jennifer needed more opportunities for interaction with other children, so when she turned four they enrolled her in a local preschool. Jennifer was very distressed about being left at the school; sometimes she would cling to her mother and cry. Only a few weeks after she started preschool, the teacher began to express concerns about her social adjustment. Her parents were disappointed, but not surprised.

Jennifer exhibited symptoms that indicated a possible psychological disorder, as we will see when we return to her case throughout the chapter. How common are psychological disorders in children? Several large-scale epidemiological studies conducted in the United States, Europe, and Australia have sought to answer this question by interviewing parents and children from the general population (Bird, 1996; Brandenburg, Friedman, and Silver, 1990). On the basis of information from these interviews, researchers estimate that, at any point in time, between 14 and 20 percent of children suffer from moderate to severe psychological problems. According to a report from the surgeon general of the United States, one in five children experience signs and symptoms of DSM-IV disorders during the course of a year (Department of Health and Human Services, 1999). Usually the early signs are recognized by parents, primary-care physicians, and/or the child's teacher. Preventing and treating these disorders should be high priorities for our society.

Identifying Childhood Disorders

Our discussion of childhood disorders will emphasize the importance of maturational change and experience. One of the major questions faced by clinicians and researchers who work with children is,

In *Hide and Seek,* a painting by Pavel Tchelitchew, frightened children crowd in on a charred tree. Children's minds and behaviors are molded by their social and physical experiences, and anxiety can change the brain itself.

"Which psychological problems will disappear as the child matures, and which ones will persist, or even lead to more serious difficulties?" The normal course of human development involves constant change, and the child's behavioral capacities and propensities are always evolving. Memory, concentration, and impulse control improve dramatically throughout childhood, and during the teenage years abstract reasoning abilities begin to approach adult levels. This is partially due to the fact that the human brain undergoes a prolonged period of maturation after birth. In addition, the child's behavioral capacities are molded by social and physical experiences, and these experiences can vary dramatically.

Experimental research with rodents and nonhuman primates has shown that deprived environments can thwart brain development and alter behavior, and that enriched environments can promote brain growth and behavioral adaptation. While it is not ethical to conduct experimental research in which the rearing environment of human beings is intentionally deprived so that we can examine changes in their brains, there is every reason to believe that the formative period of human life is just as sensitive as the formative period of animals is to environmental input. In fact, the human brain may be more sensitive than the rodent or monkey brain because it is so well equipped to process environmental input.

Vulnerabilities to Disorders

As you will see, abnormal child development, like normal child development, is a result of many factors. Vulnerability to some disorders is present at birth and may be the consequence of genetic factors or prenatal complications. One example of a disorder that is influenced by genetic factors is schizophrenia, a mental illness that involves abnormalities in clarity of thought and communication. Prenatal complications are also associated with risk for schizophrenia, as well as a variety of learning disorders. In Chapter 4, we described the growth of the fetal nervous system and how the normal pattern of prenatal brain growth can go awry. But the ultimate developmental outcome also depends upon the quality of the postnatal environment. Children are highly dependent on adults. The nature of the environment experienced by children, especially when they are infants, is mainly determined by the adults who care for them.

Clinical psychologists who conduct assessments of children want to know about the child's environment and cultural background. What was the quality of the home environment when the child was born? How stable is the home? What is the family's daily schedule? What, if any, stressors are impinging on the family? How do the parents deal with the child? The psychologist who evaluated Jennifer wanted answers to these questions.

> During my first meeting with the Jenkins family, I asked about their family life. Jennifer's parents, Carol and Robert, told me they had been married for five years before Jennifer was born. Robert worked as a computer specialist with an international bank, and Carol was employed as a nutritionist in a university hospital. The couple had waited to have a child until they had saved enough money to purchase a home. Robert's parents were very pleased that their youngest son was going to be a father. Carol's parents were eager to have their first grandchild, so they were delighted when they found out Carol was pregnant. The hospital had granted Carol a six-month leave of absence, beginning two weeks before the due date. Her co-workers gave her a baby shower, and her in-laws purchased new furniture for the baby's room. The two prospective grandmothers were planning on taking turns in helping with childcare when the baby was born.
>
> Carol and Robert reported that they had no trouble adjusting to the demands of parenthood. They were devoted to their daughter and thoroughly enjoyed her, despite some sleepless nights during the first six months. Carol took Jennifer to baby swim lessons and a play group. The family spent their weekends together, often taking long walks through their neighborhood. When Carol's leave of absence ended and she returned to work, Jennifer stayed with one of her grandmothers during the day. Jennifer and her grandmother were very attached to each other.
>
> As I examined my notes from this interview, I could see no indication that Jennifer had experienced any undue stress during the four years of her life. Her parents were very conscientious and loving, and they provided Jennifer with a stable home. I concluded that we needed to look elsewhere for the origins of Jennifer's problems.

The birth of some infants, like Jennifer, is greeted by a network of devoted parents and family members. The infant's welfare is paramount, and the parents seek out a diversity of growth-enhancing experiences for the child. But sadly, at the other extreme, some infants enter a world that offers no easy solutions. Their parents may even be addicted to drugs and prone to violent outbursts against them. For these children, life is like a minefield, and basic survival is the best they can hope for.

The childhood disorders we will examine vary in their etiology. Some are mainly due to the child's experiences after he enters the world. Anxiety disorder following exposure to trauma is one example. Other disorders, such as autism, appear to be caused solely by inborn abnormalities in the way the brain functions. But most childhood disorders involve both constitutional vulnerabilities and environmental influences. Whether the vulnerable child succumbs to a disorder will depend on the quality of the environment, as well as the strengths, or resilience factors, possessed by the child. Thus, the diathesis-stress model, which we described in earlier chapters, fits well with much of what we know about the etiology of early-onset psychological disorders.

As we discuss the prevalence rates for the various disorders covered in this chapter, you will see that there are substantial differences between males and females in their rate of occurrence. Although no one knows for sure, it is likely that these differences are a consequence of sex differences in brain development and socialization experiences. The general pattern is one in which males tend to outnumber females in having disorders that involve disruptive behavior, such as conduct disorder and attention deficit hyperactivity disorder. In contrast, females tend to show higher rates of eating disorders, depression, and anxiety.

Unique Aspects of Childhood Disorders

Several aspects of childhood disorders distinguish them from disorders that first occur in adulthood. First, normal psychological development proceeds at different rates for different children. As a result, it can be difficult to distinguish a genuine psychological problem, one that requires professional attention, from a problem that simply reflects the child's current developmental stage. For example, most children are toilet-trained by the time they are three years old. Of those who are not, some are merely on the extreme end of the normal distribution, while for others, continued bed-wetting may reflect deeper emotional insecurities. When diagnosing children, psychologists must differentiate normal variability in rates of development from psychological problems that indicate a need for treatment.

A second unique aspect of childhood psychological problems is the fact that they are less predictable than adult disorders. Children often change dramatically over a relatively short period of time, so that it is difficult to predict which children are vulnerable to persistent problems (Bennett, Lipman, Racine, and Offord, 1998; Lipman, Bennett, Racine, Mazumdar, and Offord, 1998). Some young children who are very aggressive, for example, become teenagers who are very subdued. Conversely, shy, withdrawn toddlers can develop aggressive tendencies later in life. It is also common for children to manifest regression. This is illustrated in some developmental disorders where the child shows normal language development during the first few years of life, then loses language skills.

Third, children cannot communicate their problems as easily as adults. Instead, a child's distress may be manifested indirectly through disruptive behaviors. When this happens, it is up to parents and teachers to identify behaviors that are indicative of "real" problems. This is not always a simple task. Sometimes adults mislabel a child's behavior as a "psychological problem" when it is merely a normal developmental phase. At other times, adults will ignore children's problem behaviors, believing the child will grow out

It is often difficult to diagnose a child's problem because children cannot communicate their problems as easily as adults. This girl may be merely lost in thought, or she may have fears that are preventing her from playing with the other children on the playground.

of them, when in fact the child really does need professional help. Large-scale studies of children in the general population find that only a minority of those qualifying for a diagnosis of a DSM-type psychological disorder had ever been taken by their parents to a mental health professional (Burns et al., 1995; Cohen and Hesselbart, 1993; Zahner, Pawelkiewicz, DeFrancesco, and Adnopoz, 1992).

There are also differences among adults in how they perceive children's behavior. John Weisz and his colleagues found this in their studies of American and Thai children (Weisz et al., 1995). When teachers from Thailand and the United States were asked to rate the behavior of the children in their classes, the Thai children were rated as having more behavior problems. But when observers recorded the children's behaviors, they found that the Thai children actually showed fewer problem behaviors than the U.S. children. In part, behavior problems are in the eye of the beholder. Evidently, Thai teachers have a lower threshold for labeling a behavior as problematic. Because clinicians are so dependent on adults' interpretations of children's problems, we often know less about the children than we do about the adults who care for them.

Finally, children's problems are often quite specific to particular situations or contexts. For example, a child might be physically aggressive at home, but not at school. Similarly, overactivity—a common complaint of teachers—depends on the circumstances. One study of clinic-referred children found that 75 percent of children who were viewed as overactive in school were not viewed as overactive at home or in the clinic (Klein and Gittelman-Klein, 1975). This highlights the importance of taking the child's physical and social context into consideration when conducting an evaluation.

Types of Childhood Disorders

All of the childhood disorders listed in DSM-IV involve behaviors in which a child deviates from what is expected of her at a particular age and cultural setting. In addition, these behaviors are persistent and severe, and they interfere with the child's development and day-to-day functioning. Thus, in order for a behavioral or psychological problem to be considered a "disorder" the child must either be suffering (for example, she might be paralyzed with fear resulting from an animal phobia) or the child's behavior must be making others suffer (for example, she may be hurting her schoolmates or pets).

What distinguishes a childhood disorder from normal variation in development is often only a matter of degree. In other words, there is a quantitative rather than a qualitative difference between abnormal and normal behaviors. In fact, with few exceptions, the childhood-onset disorders listed in DSM-IV involve behaviors that are not qualitatively different from what many normal children manifest. Minor versions of these problem behaviors can be found in well-adjusted children (Rutter, 1985). For example, the occasional temper tantrums that occur in many preschoolers would hardly be labeled a psychological disorder. But frequent tantrums, or tantrums that occur in peculiar circumstances, or for a very long time, might be considered abnormal. The child's developmental stage is also important. Most preschoolers show anxiety about separating from their parents, especially when they have just started to attend school. This anxiety is seldom persistent or predictive of future problems. But separation anxiety occurring when the child is twelve years old is more likely to reflect an adjustment problem. This is why psychologists take maturational stage into consideration when they conduct an assessment of a child.

Table 8–1 lists four groups of childhood disorders contained in DSM-IV. For each group, the major diagnostic categories are listed. The *emotional disorders*

involve negative affective states, particularly insecurity, fear, anxiety, and sadness. In reactive attachment disorder, which has the earliest onset of all the DSM disorders, the infant fails to bond to caregivers because of early deprivation. *Developmental disorders* are characterized by marked deficiencies in the child's acquisition of intellectual, communicative, and social skills. This category includes autism and other pervasive developmental disorders, which are characterized by severe deficits in communication skills and social responsiveness. It also includes mental retardation, as well as less severe learning disorders (such as developmental reading disorder). *Eating and habit disorders* include a rather wide variety of syndromes that involve repetitive maladaptive or nonfunctional behaviors. Examples of eating disorders include anorexia and bulimia; examples of habit disorders include bed-wetting, stuttering, and motor tics. *Disruptive behavior disorders* are characterized by deficits in self-control and involve behavior tendencies like hyperactivity, inattention, aggressiveness, destructiveness, and defiance of authority.

Estimating the prevalence of mental disorders is always difficult, but this is especially true of disorders in children. We cannot assume that all children who are suffering from a particular disorder are brought into a clinic for treatment (Department of Health and Human Services, 1999). Children do not come to the attention of mental health professionals unless their parents, or some other adult, decides they are in need of psychological help. Given this reality, we must be cautious in interpreting estimates of the rates of childhood disorders, especially those based on clinic samples.

Note that some of the most severe mental disorders, such as bipolar disorder, major depressive disorder, and schizophrenia, do not appear in Table 8–1. It is uncommon for children to show signs of these disorders, but when they do, the adult diagnostic criteria are used. The childhood manifestations of these severe mental illnesses are discussed in Chapters 7 and 10. Similarly, the developmental precursors of substance abuse, anxiety disorders, and personality disorders are described in the chapters devoted to these categories of abnormal behavior. In the present chapter, our focus will be on syndromes of abnormal behavior that are first diagnosed in childhood.

Many children meet criteria for more than one of the diagnoses listed in Table 8–1. This is referred to as comorbidity, meaning multiple diagnoses. For example, among children and adolescents, about 40 percent of

TABLE 8-1

Data

MAJOR CLUSTERS OF CHILDHOOD DISORDERS

Diagnostic Class	Disorder	Typical age of onset	Prevalence
Emotional disorders	Reactive attachment disorder	Birth–5 years old	No data available
	Separation anxiety disorder	Preschool–18 years old	4%
	Phobias	Varies according to type	10–11.3%
	Childhood depression	Birth–17 years old★	1.9–4.0%★
Developmental disorders	Autistic disorder	Birth–3 years old	.02–.05%
	Rett's disorder	Birth–4 years old	.001–.01%†
	Childhood disintegrative disorder	3–4 years old	Very rare
	Asperger's disorder	Preschool period	.10–.26%★
	Mental retardation	Birth–18 years old	1%
	Learning disorders	Varies among subtypes	2–10%
Eating and habit disorders	Bulimia nervosa	Late adolescence	1–3%
	Anorexia nervosa	17 years old	0.5–1.0%
	Elimination disorders (e.g., Enuresis)	5 years old	Males 7% Females 3%
	Speech disorders (e.g., Stuttering)	2–7 years old	0.8–1.0%
	Tourette's disorder	2–18 years old	.04–.05%
Disruptive behavior disorders	Conduct disorder	5–16 years old	Males 6–16% Females 2–9%
	Oppositional defiant disorder	Birth–8 years old	2–16%
	Attention deficit hyperactivity disorder (ADHD)	Elementary school age	3–5%

★Data from Volkmar, 1996.
†Data from Weiner, 1997; Lomborso, 2000.
SOURCE: Based on data from DSM-IV (unless otherwise specified).

those who meet criteria for one disorder also meet criteria for another disorder (Loeber, Farrington, Stouthamer-Loeber, and Van Kammen, 1998; Simonoff et al., 1997). It is especially common for depression to co-occur with other disorders in children, particularly with conduct disorder and anxiety disorder. Researchers do not know why syndromes tend to occur together. One possible explanation is that there is a causal relationship; in other words, having a disorder like depression may cause the child to seek attention by violating rules. Another possibility is that a single causal factor can produce more than one type of disorder.

Emotional Disorders

The phrase ***emotional disorders*** loosely describes the diagnostic categories that involve subjective distress for the child, without a disruption in his perception of reality. These include anxiety states, mood disorders, obsessive-compulsive disorder, and phobias. The symptoms of these childhood disorders are similar to those seen in adult emotional disorders: for example, feelings of inferiority, self-consciousness, social withdrawal, shyness, fear, sadness, and the like.

But there are some differences between childhood emotional disorders and adult emotional disorders. Among adults, all of the emotional disorders, especially depression, are more common in women. In contrast, the ratio of males to females is more balanced for childhood depression. Depression only begins to be more prevalent in girls at the onset of adolescence (Hankin et al., 1998). It is also worth noting that the onset of some emotional disorders is stage-specific; that is, the disorders begin at particular ages. Animal phobias, for example, almost always begin in early childhood, while agoraphobia is rarely experienced before late adolescence or early adulthood.

Social withdrawal of a child from other children may indicate shyness or more serious disturbances, including social phobia or even reactive attachment disorder.

Because several of the emotional disorders of childhood bear a strong resemblance to those of adulthood, we do not discuss them in detail here. Rather, we describe their unique "childhood" features here, and refer you to the other chapters for more information. We begin by describing an emotional disorder that is assumed to originate in infancy: reactive attachment disorder.

Reactive Attachment Disorder

The chief symptom of **reactive attachment disorder** is a marked disturbance in the child's ability to relate to other people (Richters and Volkmar, 1994). By definition, the disturbance begins before the age of five years. Children who receive this diagnosis fail to show social attachments that are appropriate for their age. There are two subtypes. The *inhibited subtype* entails a persistent failure to initiate or respond to interpersonal situations. The child tends to be highly inhibited, constantly observes the behavior of others, and resists physical contact or comforting. The *disinhibited subtype* shows an opposite pattern of behavior: these children are indiscriminate in their social responses. They respond to strangers and familiar people in the same way—with lots of physical contact and expressed need for comforting.

The diagnostic criteria for reactive attachment disorder include the child's early experiences, as well as symptoms. In order to receive this diagnosis, the child must have been exposed to serious neglect or outright abuse during some period before the symptoms began. It is assumed that inadequate care causes the syndrome. Thus, unlike most DSM-IV categories, there are specific assumptions about the etiology of reactive attachment disorder.

Because reactive attachment disorder is a new diagnostic category in DSM-IV, there has been relatively

DSM-IV Criteria

Reactive Attachment Disorder

A. Markedly disturbed and developmentally inappropriate social relatedness in most contexts, beginning before age 5 years, as evidenced by either (1) or (2): (1) persistent failure to initiate or respond in a developmentally appropriate fashion to most social interactions, as manifest by excessively inhibited, hypervigilant, or highly ambivalent and contradictory responses (e.g., the child may respond to caregivers with a mixture of approach, avoidance, and resistance to comforting, or may exhibit frozen watchfulness); (2) diffuse attachments as manifest by indiscriminate sociability with marked inability to exhibit appropriate selective attachments (e.g., excessive familiarity with relative strangers or lack of selectivity in choice of attachment figures).

B. The disturbance in Criterion A is not accounted for solely by developmental delay (as in Mental Retardation) and does not meet criteria for a Pervasive Developmental Disorder.

C. Pathogenic care as evidenced by at least one of the following: (1) persistent disregard of the child's basic emotional needs for comfort, stimulation, and affection; (2) persistent disregard of the child's basic physical needs; (3) repeated changes of primary caregiver that prevent formation of stable attachments (e.g., frequent changes in foster care).

D. There is a presumption that the care in Criterion C is responsible for the disturbed behavior in Criterion A (e.g., the disturbances in Criterion A began following the pathogenic care in Criterion C).

SOURCE: APA, DSM-IV, 1994.

little research on its prevalence, specific causes, or treatments. Its inclusion in DSM-IV stemmed, in large part, from the findings of research on children who were cared for in institutional settings. For example, John Bowlby conducted landmark studies of infants reared in orphanages where they received only basic care and very little stimulation (Bowlby, 1989). He found that these children were apathetic, nonresponsive, and seemed to have no attachments to their caregivers. More recently, psychologists have studied the development of Romanian orphans who are adopted by families from the United States and Canada. Most of these children have experienced institutional care before their adoptions. When compared to other children who are their age, they show a higher rate of adjustment problems and signs of being less securely attached to their adoptive parents (Markovitch, Goldberg, Gold, and Washington, 1997).

To date, there has been little research on the treatment of reactive attachment disorder. But despite the absence of sound information, some practitioners have advocated certain forms of therapy that they believe are effective (Magid, McKelvey, and Schroeder, 1989). In "holding" or "rage reduction" therapy, the child is held down by an adult and then provoked to anger. The adult is then instructed to express feelings of love and concern for the child. Some believe this procedure reawakens the child's traumatic experiences and forces the child to confront his or her need for attachment to others. Other clinicians have expressed grave doubts about the appropriateness of these treatments and believe they only serve to make matters worse by reawakening unpleasant memories and making the child feel intimidated by adults (James, 1997).

A recent case illustrates the ambiguity surrounding the diagnosis and treatment of reactive attachment disorder:

Renee and David Polreis adopted their second child, a one-year-old boy from Russia, in 1996. They named him David, Jr., and took him to their middle-class home in Colorado. David, Jr., had been reared in an institution prior to his adoption. According to reports, the parents began to encounter problems with David, Jr., shortly after he arrived from Russia. Mrs. Polreis took David, Jr., to a psychotherapist, Bryon Norton, for treatment. She told Mr. Norton that David, Jr., threw terrible tantrums, bit people, spat on them, threw his food, refused to use the toilet, and hit his head repeatedly on the floor. Mr. Norton diag-

nosed David, Jr., as having reactive attachment disorder. Several months later, on Friday, February 9, Mr. Polreis went on a business trip, leaving David, Jr., in the care of Mrs. Polreis. The following Saturday morning, at 4:00 A.M., Mrs. Polreis called her mother, who lived nearby, and told her that David, Jr., had been sleeping with her when he suddenly began choking. Mrs. Polreis's mother came over immediately. By the time she arrived, Mrs. Polreis was giving David, Jr., mouth-to-mouth resuscitation. When the paramedics arrived they found David, Jr., lying on the bathroom floor. He was rushed to the hospital where he was found to be bruised over 90 percent of his body. He had finger imprints on his arms, blistered buttocks, cuts on his abdomen, and massive internal injuries. His father, David, Sr., rushed home and went to the hospital, only to find that his son had died. Mrs. Polreis did not come to be with David, Jr., because she reported being phobic of hospitals. When police searched the Polreis's home the next day, they found two broken wooden spoons and bloody diapers in the trash. They also found DNA from David, Jr., on the spoons.

Mrs. Polreis was charged with the murder of her son. She maintained that all of the child's injuries were self-inflicted, due to his reactive attachment disorder. Similarly, her defense attorney argued that David, Jr., was suffering from a form of reactive attachment disorder that caused him to act out against others and injure himself. When interviewed for the trial, the teachers at David, Jr.'s preschool described him as a loving child who was eager to see his parents when they came to pick him up. The prosecution maintained that Mrs. Polreis had murdered David, Jr. In 1997 Mrs. Polreis was convicted of murder and was sentenced to twenty-two years in prison.

We do not know for sure whether David, Jr., was suffering from reactive attachment disorder. Nonetheless, there is every reason to expect that a child reared in an institution for the first year of his life might have some adjustment problems. It is possible that these adjustment problems, combined with Mrs. Polreis's low level of tolerance, created a volatile situation. When alone with David, Jr., Mrs. Polreis may have been unable to control her rage. There is no evidence that Mrs. Polreis had any trouble with parenting her older adopted son, Isaac. This may have been because her older son was adopted at birth and, according to reports, was a very compliant child. Mrs. Polreis may have assumed that David, Jr., would be the same.

Many experts in the field of adoption have cautioned prospective parents to be prepared for the possibility of reactive attachment disorder in children who are coming from institutions. It is likely that the reported incidence of this disorder in the United States will increase in the coming years as more institutionalized children from abroad are adopted. The attachment problems manifested by these children are especially distressing for parents who have waited many years to have children.

Separation Anxiety Disorder

In several respects, children with separation anxiety disorder are a striking contrast to those with reactive attachment disorder. Rather than rebuffing contact with their caregiver, children with separation anxiety disorder have an excessive need for it. In the normal course of development, children go through a period, usually from about six months to four years, when they protest separation from parents. Most of us can remember an incident sometime in our childhood in which we suddenly realized we had been separated from our parents. At first, we may have searched calmly, but after a few minutes without finding them, our fear became more intense. Eventually we felt terror about being alone; we wondered if our parents would ever return. We were finally reunited with our parents, with great relief. For a short period following the incident, we were somewhat more anxious about being separated from our parents, and tried to stay close to them in stores or other public places. But for the most part, the separation was an isolated incident that we forgot within a relatively short period of time.

In contrast, there are some children who live every minute of the day with terror that they might be separated from their families. They worry that terrible things will happen to their parents, siblings, or other loved ones. They resist being separated from them, and they become panicked if they must be apart. These children often cling to loved ones and follow them around the house. They have nightmares with themes of separation. Some show continual physical symptoms of anxiety, such as headaches, stomach aches and nausea, particularly on days that they must be separated from parents (such as school days). Children who show such symptoms for at least two continuous weeks may be suffering from *separation anxiety disorder.*

Separation anxiety appears to be one of the most common of childhood emotional disorders, with a

Children with separation anxiety disorder live with the constant fear that they may be separated from their families. This boy is leaving his father in the besieged city of Sarajevo during the Bosnian War of 1992. The child may later suffer from a fear of being separated from his family as a result of his wartime experiences.

prevalence of 4 percent among preadolescents (Bell-Dolan and Brazeal, 1993; Fischer, Himle, and Thyer, 1999). It is nearly twice as common in girls as in boys. In its severe form, separation anxiety can be incapacitating for children, preventing them from attending school or extracurricular activities. Physical complaints are often used as a ploy to stay home with the parents. As a result, these children often undergo repeated physical examinations to find the cause of their aches and pains. Episodes of separation anxiety often occur repeatedly throughout childhood and adolescence for children with this diagnosis. As they get older, they are at increased risk for panic attacks (Bernstein and Borchardt, 1991).

A first episode of separation anxiety often occurs after some traumatic event in the child's life, such as the death of a relative or pet, being hospitalized, or moving to a new town. Children whose parents suffer from depression or anxiety disorder, particularly agoraphobia, are at an increased risk for separation anxiety (Leonard and Rapoport, 1991). In addition, children with this disorder tend to come from very close-knit families. In part, the relation between familial characteristics and separation anxiety in the child is due to shared genetic influences (Hewitt et al., 1997). In addition, modeling of parental fears also seems to contribute (Fischer, Himle, and Thyer, 1999).

Cognitive-behavioral procedures have been used with success to treat separation anxiety disorders

DSM-IV Criteria

Separation Anxiety Disorder

A. Developmentally inappropriate and excessive anxiety concerning separation from home or from those to whom the individual is attached, as evidenced by three (or more) of the following: (1) recurrent excessive distress when separation from home or major attachment figures occurs or is anticipated; (2) persistent and excessive worry about losing, or about possible harm befalling, major attachment figures; (3) persistent and excessive worry that an untoward event will lead to separation from a major attachment figure (e.g., getting lost or being kidnapped); (4) persistent reluctance or refusal to go to school or elsewhere because of fear of separation; (5) persistently and excessively fearful or reluctant to be alone or without major attachment figures at home or without significant adults in other settings; (6) persistent reluctance or refusal to go to sleep without being near a major attachment figure or to sleep away from home; (7) repeated nightmares involving the theme of separation; (8) repeated complaints of physical symptoms (such as headaches, stomach aches, nausea, or vomiting) when separation from major attachment figures occurs or is anticipated.

B. The duration of the disturbance is at least 4 weeks.

C. The onset is before age 18 years.

D. The disturbance causes clinically significant distress or impairment in social, academic (occupational), or other important areas of functioning.

E. The disturbance does not occur exclusively during the course of a Pervasive Developmental Disorder, Schizophrenia, or other Psychotic Disorder and, in adolescents and adults, is not better accounted for by Panic Disorder with Agoraphobia.

SOURCE: APA, DSM-IV, 1994.

(Eisen, Engler, and Geyer, 1998). The parents play a major role in this treatment, and they are provided with new techniques for reinforcing independence and confidence in their child. At the same time, the therapist works to desensitize the child to separation from the parents. For children whose symptoms persist despite therapy, antidepressant medication may be helpful.

Although it is not uncommon for preschool-aged children with adjustment problems to protest separation from their parents, in many of these cases, separation anxiety is not the central problem. Clinicians must draw on their skills in differential diagnosis to arrive at a valid assessment. The case of Jennifer illustrates this:

I questioned Carol and Robert Jenkins about Jennifer's problems with adjustment to preschool. They said she did all right the first two days, when Carol and Robert stayed for an hour before leaving her there alone. She didn't cry or cling to either parent. But she didn't pay any attention to the other children or the teachers either. By the end of the first week, Jennifer began to protest going to the school. Her mother had to pick her up and carry her in. During the second week, she began to protest in the car on the way to school. On Monday of the third week, Jennifer ran away from her mother in front of the school. Carol had to chase her to prevent her from running into a busy street. A similar scenario occurred on Tuesday and Wednesday.

Around the same time, the teacher mentioned to Carol that Jennifer had a tendency to get very upset whenever any of the other children made a loud noise. She reported that Jennifer would startle, then begin to cry. It was often difficult to console her. One day Jennifer became upset at school, then consoled herself by sitting in the corner with a teddy bear. After a few minutes she got up and went out the back door of the classroom. The teacher immediately went out to get her, but Jennifer protested and had to be carried back into the school.

As I made notes from Carol and Robert's descriptions of their daughter, it seemed implausible that her problems at school were solely due to anxiety about separation. Jennifer didn't show the consistent clinging behavior that characterizes most children with separation anxiety disorder. She never protested being left with her grandmother or a baby-sitter. Also, the fact that she ran away from her mother, rather than enter the school, suggested more of a fear of the school than a concern about separation.

Phobias

At some point, virtually every child experiences an unjustified fear so extreme that he or she is immobilized. You may recall a childhood fear of being in the dark, or a fear that something was under the bed just waiting to reach up and snatch you. Because children have less knowledge of the world and are more physically vulnerable and dependent, their fears tend to be more intense than those of adults. Childhood fears are a universal phenomenon, although there are cultural differences in their content and intensity. For example, Nigerian children report a higher level of fear than American, Australian, and Chinese youth (Ollendick et al., 1996). Fear of burglars intruding in their homes and getting lost in unfamiliar places are highly prevalent among Australian and American children. In contrast, Chinese and Nigerian children express a higher rate of fear of electricity and potentially dangerous animals.

The nature of fears varies with age (Last, 1992; Ollendick and King, 1994). The most common fears reported at various developmental stages are listed in Table 8–2. Infants and toddlers show a strong fear reaction to loud noises and loss of physical support. Strangers are also frightening to most youngsters in this developmental stage. As children enter preschool, their imaginations expand. During this period, their fears involve more fantasized objects and anticipated events. For example, a preschooler does not need to hear thunder to express fear of it; just

Childhood fears can immobilize a child. In the 1999 film *The Sixth Sense,* Haley Joel Osment freezes in fear.

hearing about an impending storm can be enough to trigger the fear response. Imaginary creatures and ghosts, typically from books and movies, can also preoccupy children at this age. Of course, fears of certain tangible objects, such as animals and insects, are present in many young children and can persist into adulthood. Fears of tangible objects rarely begin after age five. In contrast, school-connected fears usually begin after age five, when children are first enrolled in school, and they increase markedly between the ages of nine and twelve. From about age

TABLE 8–2

COMMON CHILDHOOD FEARS

Age Group	*Common Fears*
Infants and Toddlers (0–2 years old)	loss of support, loud noises or large objects, changes in house, strangers, separation, dark, animals
Preschool Children (3–6 years old)	separation, masks, dark, animals, insects, night noises, "bad people," bodily harm, thunder and lightning, supernatural beings, being alone
School-Aged Children (7–12 years old)	supernatural beings, dark, being alone, bodily harm or injury, tests, school performance, physical appearance, thunder and lightning, death, snakes, burglar breaking into the house, not being able to breathe
Adolescents (13 years old or older)	problems at home and with family, political concerns, preparation for the future, personal appearance, social relations, school, snakes

SOURCE: Based on data from Last, 1992; Ollendick, 1983; Ollendick and King, 1994.

twelve through adolescence, children's fears begin to resemble those of adults, including fears about social relationships and anxieties about identity. Once we become adults, it can be difficult for us to remember how truly terrifying childhood fears were.

Across all ages, it is consistently found that women express more fears than men (Muris, Merckelbach, Meesters, and Van Lier, 1997). Does this reflect the fact that women are more physically vulnerable than men? Or are females simply more willing to express their fears? The latter explanation has some indirect support. Among children and adolescents, girls tend to rate their classmates as less fearful than themselves, whereas boys rate their classmates as more fearful than themselves (Ollendick et al., 1995). It appears that being perceived as fearful relative to one's peers is not as problematic for girls as for boys. This may be a consequence of the gender role expectations that children acquire from adults and peers.

Fears become phobias when they are out of proportion to the reality of the danger that an object presents. The prevalence of simple phobias in preadolescents is about 2 to 8 percent (Rutter, 1989; Silverman and Rabian, 1993). As with normal childhood fears, phobias are more common in females, with twice as many girls as boys showing the disorder. Sometimes children's phobias develop in complex and unpredictable ways. The following case demonstrates the transition from fear to phobia:

> Sara was referred for treatment of her phobias when she was thirteen. The referring physician indicated that the girl was afraid of airplanes and bees, but Sara, like so many such children, found it hard to put in words just what she was scared of. She acknowledged that, beyond airplanes and bees, she was also afraid of elevators, but nothing more. Yet, after she came to know and trust her therapist, it emerged that there was a fear that underlay and linked all the others: that was a fear of anesthesia. The link between airplanes, elevators, bees, and anesthesia was not immediately obvious, and it took some care to piece the following history together.
>
> A number of years earlier, Sara had to have a tooth extracted. The dentist used a general anesthetic. As she "went under," everything went black, but Sara could still hear voices and rushing noises. (In fact, this is an almost universal experience since, physiologically, the nerves controlling vision are affected seconds before the nerves controlling hearing.) Sara was not prepared for these sensations, and they terrified her. Ever since, she has studiously avoided putting herself in a situation where she might be injured and therefore might be rushed to a hospital, where she might be given an anesthetic. Airplanes crash. So do elevators. Bees sting. Any one of these might land her in the hospital.
>
> Like everyone else, Sara's parents did not understand the connection between her phobias and what gave rise to them, Rather, they tended to see her simply as a fearful child. Sara's shifting fears were complicated, but not unusual. The therapist explained that what Sara had originally experienced, though unexpected and unpleasant, was understandable and very treatable. He then trained Sara in relaxation techniques that could be used in situations of high anxiety. By focusing on her fears of elevators, the therapist demonstrated to Sara that she could conquer one fear in therapy, then go on and conquer the others by herself. Within three months, Sara had reported no more difficulties.

In Sara's case, a plausible traumatic event was easily identified. But in most cases, triggering events are more difficult to trace. In many children, phobias are associated with general anxiety or emotional disturbance, and with having parents who are phobic or anxious themselves (Barlow, Chorpita, and Turovsky, 1996; Rutter and Garmezy, 1983).

School phobia is one of the most common and problematic childhood phobias. It creates great distress in both children and their parents. About 5 percent of all clinic-referred children and 1 percent of children in the general population experience school phobia (Burke and Silverman, 1987). Adolescents who refuse to go to school tend to be more severely impaired and less responsive to treatment than younger children. When they grow up, children who have had school phobia are at risk for several problems, including agoraphobia, job difficulties, and personality disorders (Blagg and Yule, 1994).

Many children with school phobia do well in school and express a desire to attend, but they experience intense anxiety when they get ready to go to school. For example, they may go to the toilet frequently, feel sick, or sweat profusely when the topic of school is brought up. Unlike the truants whose parents are often unaware that their child was not at school, these children stay at home during their prolonged absences, and their parents know exactly where they are. Consider the following case:

Richard was a twelve-year-old who had been out of school almost continuously for five months. The previous summer he had won a scholarship to a well-known private school. He did exceedingly well in his first term. Then, just after the beginning of the second term, he contracted severe influenza which left him feeling very weak. He was worried that he would lose ground academically, and his anxious parents shared that concern. He tried to go back to school, but once in the classroom, he had a panic attack and ran home. Thereafter, he worried about what to say to the other boys and how to explain his flight and long absence. He was brought to a therapist for help in overcoming his fear (Yule, Hersov, and Treseder, 1980).

In his therapy, Richard was given some training in relaxation and was accompanied to his school in graded stages during the summer vacation. He and his therapist rehearsed what he would say to his friends when he returned in the fall. The therapist accompanied him to school for the first three mornings, but thereafter, he was on his own. Follow-up during the two years revealed no further difficulty.

School phobia presents a serious challenge because it is so puzzling to teachers, to parents, and to the child who suffers from it. The situation is made more tragic when the child was previously a good student who enjoyed school, then suddenly and for no apparent reason, stopped going to school. Careful investigation often reveals many causes of school refusal. In Richard's case and in many others, threats to self-esteem and an unrealistically high level of aspiration play significant roles in refusal. To a child who regularly receives straight A's, the threat of even a "B" can be highly aversive and anxiety-producing.

As discussed below, there are some very specific and effective behavioral treatments for phobias (Blagg and Yule, 1994). One is desensitization, which involves gradual exposure to the feared object. The therapist who worked with Richard used this technique. At the same time, therapy for childhood phobias typically involves some work with the parents. It is especially important that parents be involved in the process, so that they can monitor the child's behavior. The therapist also helps the parents identify any behaviors on their part that might be subtly encouraging and maintaining the child's phobia.

The clinical psychologist who conducted the evaluation of Jennifer also considered the possibility that she was suffering from school phobia. But her clinical profile didn't quite fit:

Although it was clear that something about school was aversive to Jennifer, the behavioral pattern didn't conform to a simple school phobia. Jennifer's parents told me that she had also resisted attending a play group with Carol when she was three years old. She never formed any relationships with the other children, and eventually seemed to find them annoying.

Jennifer's parents gave me permission to talk to her preschool teacher. The teacher told me that, at first, Jennifer showed no interest in the other children in her class. But by the second week, she became irritable with them. She resisted the teacher's attempts to involve her in group activities. She hoarded toys in the corner to keep the other children from playing with them. According to the teacher, Jennifer's happiest moments in the classroom were when the other children were outside playing.

As the picture of Jennifer's daily life became clearer, I ruled out several possibilities. First, Jennifer was not anxious about separating from her mother; her clinging behavior at school was more a function of her desire to leave the school than it was a need to maintain physical proximity to her mother. Second, Jennifer did not have a phobia of any kind. There was no object or situation that consistently elicited an unrealistic fear response in Jennifer. Instead, the chief problem—the one that made her resist attending school—was an aversion to other children. She manifested the same reaction earlier in her life when her mother took her to a play group on a regular basis. I recalled Carol telling me that Jennifer rarely made a fuss when she was in a public place where there were large numbers of people, or when she was at a social gathering that included many people she didn't know. So the mere presence of people was not the source of discomfort. Instead, it appeared that Jennifer was uncomfortable in situations where she knew there would be expectations for her to interact with other children; namely, the play group and school. The next step would be to conduct a psychological evaluation of Jennifer. Her parents scheduled the next appointment for the end of the week.

In order to arrive at an accurate assessment of Jennifer's problems, the psychologist gathers as much information as he can about her history and current behavior. It is fortunate that he is able to get information from several sources, so that his conclusions will not be biased by the perspective of one individual. Based on the reports he has received from the parents and teachers, the psychologist is inclined to rule out separation anxiety and school phobia as the central problem.

Childhood Depression

We turn now to the emotional disorder that has the highest lifetime prevalence—depression. Prior to the 1970s, many clinicians assumed that preadolescent children were unlikely to develop depression. This belief was based on the assumption that children did not have the sense of self or the concern about the future that would lead to the low self-esteem, guilt, or hopelessness associated with depression (Rie, 1966). Research over the last two decades has shown, however, that preadolescent children can and do develop the symptoms that make up the syndrome of depression (Kovacs, Gatsonis, Paulauskas, and Richards, 1989).

Among adults, the lifetime prevalence of major depression is 21.3 percent for women compared to 12.7 percent in men (Kornstein, 1997). By comparison, the prevalence of major depression in children is lower; most studies find a prevalence ranging from .4 to 3 percent in children and .4 to 8 percent in adolescents (Birmaher et al., 1996a). Thus, children are much less likely than adults to suffer from severe depression. But milder forms of depression appear to be just as common in childhood as in adulthood (Nolen-Hoeksema, 1988). Moreover, the rate of depression shows a marked increase in adolescence. The increase during adolescence is especially pronounced for girls, and by late adolescence the rate of depres-

A nine-year-old child painted this picture to describe a recurring nightmare she had of being trapped in a hole. The milder forms of depression are as common in children as they are in adults, although major depression appears less often in children.

sion for girls is approaching the lifetime prevalence rate for women. In Chapter 7, we described these developmental trends in greater detail. We also discussed some theories about the causes of sex differences in depression.

One of the most alarming scientific findings in recent years is that the rate of depression seems to be going up and the age at onset of depression is going down (Birmaher et al., 1996a, 1996b). In other words, people born in the latter part of the twentieth century are more likely to suffer from depression than those born earlier in the century, and they tend to suffer from it at an earlier age. The reasons for this are not known, but many have suggested that it is a result of social changes that have destabilized communities. These and other ideas were discussed at length in Chapter 7.

The risk factors for depression in children are similar to those for adults: family history of depression, stressful life events, low self-esteem, and pessimistic attitudes (Angold, 1994; Fleming and Offord, 1990; Kovacs, Gatsonis, Paulauskas, and Richards, 1989; Silberg et al., 1999). Family dysfunction, such as parental conflict, may be a source of depression for children, because they are physically and emotionally dependent on the adults who care for them (Silberg et al., 1999). Many clinicians believe that they cannot treat depression in children without treating the family as a whole.

Although most children who become depressed recover quickly when positive changes in their environment are made, a substantial minority of them remain depressed for months, sometimes even years (Nolen-Hoeksema, Girgus, and Seligman, 1992). An episode of depression in childhood may affect a child's functioning during critical periods in the development of skills and self-concept such that it has long-lasting effects on his or her beliefs about the self and the world. Like depressed adults, children with depression are at high risk for suicide. Among youth hospitalized for depression, one study found that the proportion who attempted suicide was 59 percent (Ivarsson, Larrson, and Gillberg, 1998).

Treatment of Emotional Disorders

Increasingly, psychiatrists are using psychotropic drugs, usually antidepressants, to treat emotional disorders in children (Birmaher and Brent, 1998). These drugs in-

Children who become depressed generally recover quickly if positive changes in their environment are made and if the child is treated in the context of the family.

clude selective serotonin reuptake inhibitors (SSRI's), such as Prozac, Luvox, and Zoloft. There have been relatively few outcome studies on the effectiveness of these drugs for children, however. Some researchers suggest that antidepressants, especially the SSRI's, can be helpful for separation anxiety and depression. Nonetheless, the side effects of antidepressants, such as changes in appetite, have caused concern for many clinicians (Wilens, Spencer, Frazier, and Biederman, 1998). Moreover, some clinicians are worried that adults may be taking the "easy way out" by prescribing antidepressants to children at increasing rates. Thus, with the exception of extreme cases of anxiety or depression, experts advocate psychological therapy as the first approach to treating emotional disorders in youth (Birmaher and Brent, 1998).

Phobias in children, like those in adults, respond very well to behavioral treatments, especially modeling (Blagg and Yule, 1994; Rosenthal and Bandura, 1979). In these treatments, children are exposed to models who are both attractive and relatively fearless. They are encouraged to imitate the model's behavior. The use of such models enables children to overcome their fears quickly. Specific fears, such as fear of animals or a fear of heights, respond best to such treatment.

As mentioned earlier, treatment of school refusal also follows a behavioral approach. Sometimes this disorder is treated like a simple phobia, using system-

atic desensitization and modeling techniques. In other cases, school refusal is seen as the result of secondary reinforcements from parents. In these situations, the therapist's intervention focuses on reducing the reinforcements parents give children for avoiding school. The therapist also works on improving parents' skills at rewarding positive behaviors in their children.

Cognitive therapies, like those designed by Aaron Beck (see Chapter 7), are now being used to treat emotional disorders in older children and adolescents (Graham et al., 1998). Obviously, cognitive therapy must be adapted to the developmental level of the child being treated. Outcome studies of cognitive therapies for depressed and anxious children and adolescents have indicated that these therapies can be effective (Barrett, 1998; Lewinsohn, Clarke, Hops, and Andrews, 1990; Stark, 1990). Again, however, many clinicians believe that children with emotional disorders such as depression need to be treated in the context of their entire family, since family stress or dysfunction is so frequently related to the child's disorder.

Developmental Disorders

According to DSM-IV, the essential feature of developmental disorders is that the predominant disturbance is in the acquisition of cognitive, language, motor, or social skills. The course of developmental disorders tends to be chronic, with some signs of the disorder persisting into adult life. But, in many mild cases, adaptation or full recovery may occur. DSM-IV contains a general category called ***pervasive developmental disorders,*** which includes autism, Rett's disorder, childhood disintegrative disorder, and Asperger's disorder. These disorders involve noticeable abnormalities in the child's social adjustment. In contrast, the other developmental disorders, such as mental retardation and learning and communication disorders, impair the child's cognitive functioning, but these disorders do not necessarily affect social adjustment.

Autism

Of all the childhood disorders listed in DSM-IV, the pervasive developmental disorders are the most devastating and the most perplexing. These disorders involve problems in many domains of functioning: language, attention, social responsiveness, perception, and motor development. The term "pervasive" is used because early developmental processes are often so seriously impaired that the child usually requires a special educational setting. We begin with a discussion of **autism,** a pervasive developmental disorder whose symptoms are first observed very early in life—usually in infancy.

The essential feature of autism is that the child's ability to respond to others does not develop normally within the first three years of life. Even at this young age, the child's social deficits are quite noticeable, as are the bizarre responses these children make to their environment. They lack interest in people and do not respond to them. They fail to develop normal attachments to the adults who care for them. In infancy, these tendencies are reflected in their failure to cuddle, lack of eye contact, or even aversion to physical affection. These children may fail entirely to develop language, and if language is acquired, it is usually abnormal. For example, it might be characterized by echolalia—the tendency to repeat or echo precisely what one has just heard—and echopraxia—to repeat the actions of others. Another common

characteristic is pronominal reversal—the tendency to use "I" where "you" is meant, and vice versa. Such children also respond very negatively to change in their routines or in their environments. These symptoms will be taken up at greater length momentarily. But first, some of the difficulties created by autism can be seen in the following case:

> Looking at family photographs of John, one sees a good-looking, well-built, sandy-haired ten-year-old. He looks like thousands of other ten-year-olds—but he's not. If one saw a movie of John it would be immediately obvious that his behavior is far from normal. His social relationships seem peculiar. He seems distant, aloof. He seldom makes eye contact. He rarely plays with other children, and when he does, he plays like a three-year-old, not like someone who is ten.
>
> Some things fascinate him, and his most recent fascination has been with shiny leather belts. He carries one around with him nearly always and at times whirls it furiously, becoming more and more excited in the process. At the height of his excitement, he lets out high-pitched, bird-like noises, jumps up and down on the spot, and flaps his hands at eye level. At other times, John appears to be living in a world of his

DSM-IV Criteria

Autistic Disorder

A. A total of six (or more) items from (1), (2), and (3), with at least two from (1), and one each from (2) and (3): (1) qualitative impairment in social interaction, as manifested by at least two of the following: (a) marked impairment in the use of multiple nonverbal behaviors such as eye-to-eye gaze, facial expression, body postures, and gestures to regulate social interaction; (b) failure to develop peer relationships appropriate to developmental level; (c) a lack of spontaneous seeking to share enjoyment, interests, or achievements with other people (e.g., by a lack of showing, bringing, or pointing out objects of interest); (d) lack of social or emotional reciprocity; (2) qualitative impairments in communication as manifested by at least one of the following: (a) delay in, or total lack of, the development of spoken language (not accompanied by an attempt to compensate through alternative modes of communication such as gesture or mime); (b) in individuals with adequate speech, marked impairment in the ability to initiate or sustain a conversation with others; (c) stereotyped and repetitive use of language or idiosyncratic language; (d) lack of varied,

spontaneous make-believe play or social imitative play appropriate to developmental level; (3) restricted repetitive and stereotyped patterns of behavior, interests, and activities, as manifested by at least one of the following: (a) encompassing preoccupation with one or more stereotyped and restricted patterns of interest that is abnormal either in intensity or focus; (b) apparently inflexible adherence to specific, nonfunctional routines or rituals; (c) stereotyped and repetitive motor mannerisms (e.g., hand or finger flapping or twisting, or complex whole-body movements); (d) persistent preoccupation with parts of objects.

B. Delays or abnormal functioning in at least one of the following areas, with onset prior to age 3 years: (1) social interaction, (2) language as used in social communication, or (3) symbolic or imaginative play.

C. The disturbance is not better accounted for by Rett's Disorder or Childhood Disintegrative Disorder.

SOURCE: APA, DSM-IV, 1994.

own, entirely impervious to what is happening around him. A car can backfire near him, but he does not flinch. He stares into space, gazing at nothing in particular, occasionally flicking his fingers at something in the periphery of his vision.

In addition to the peculiar squeaks, John's speech is most unusual. He can follow a few simple instructions, but only if he is in familiar surroundings. He will say, "Do you want a drink?," and his parents will know that he means *he* wants a drink. Often, he will repeat complex phrases that he has heard a few days before; television commercials particularly feature in this sort of meaningless speech. At other times, he will echo back large chunks of his parents' speech, but they have realized that this is a signal that he has failed to understand them. He can ask for some things, but even simple requests come out muddled. When he fails to get meaning across—and this can be several times a day—he will fly into temper tantrums that can become quite wild.

John's parents are both intelligent, articulate, professional people who, right from the early months after John was born, were convinced that something was wrong with him. But since John was their first child, they shrugged off their worries and attributed them to inexperience. So, too, did their family physician. But gradually, no amount of bland reassurance that John would soon "grow out of it" gave any comfort. John was still too good, too quiet, yet too little interested in them as people, and entirely unwilling to be cuddled.

Worried still, they brought John to child specialists. Again the opinions were reassuring. But as John approached age two and was not yet speaking, the experts' views began to change. Words like "slow," "backward," and "retarded" began to be used more frequently. Finally, John was formally tested by a psychologist, and a surprising fact emerged. Although he was grossly retarded in language development, he was advanced for his age on nonverbal puzzles. Difficulties with hearing were ruled out, and it was during these investigations that autism was first suggested.

Oddly, merely knowing that what was wrong with John had a name provided his parents with some relief. But it was only momentary, for as they read popular accounts of autism, they found that many experts blamed the parents for the child's bizarre problems. Damning accounts of obsessional, emotionally remote parents—dramatized as "refrigerator mothers"—soon had them questioning whether they were fit parents. Their relationship to each other, as well as to John, was undermined.

John's parents managed to get him into a small class in a school for children with learning handicaps. The teacher took a special interest in John and, encouraged by his parents, she adopted a firm, structured approach to teaching him. To everyone's surprise, he took to some aspects of schoolwork readily. He loved counting things and could add, subtract, multiply, and divide by the time he was seven. Moreover, he learned to read fluently—except that he could not understand a single word of what he read. This was brought home to his parents when he picked up a foreign language journal of his father's and read a whole page in phonic French—without, of course, understanding a word! At about this time, he began talking. He referred to himself as "John," got his personal pronouns in a dreadful muddle, and learned to say "no." He used telegraphic sentences of a sort more appropriate to a boy many years younger than he, but at least he was beginning to make himself understood.

John seemed to cherish all kinds of monotonous routines. His diet consisted of a very restricted selection of foods, and he could not be induced to try new foods. He went to school by a prescribed and invariable route, watched television from the same armchair, and strenuously resisted change. Taking him outside was a nightmare, for there was no anticipating when he might throw an embarrassing tantrum. Try as she might, his mother could not help but be hurt by the glares and comments from passersby as she struggled to get John out of the supermarket or into their car. "If only he looked abnormal," she often said, "people would be more understanding."

Some of the behaviors shown by children with autism are also observed in children who have reactive attachment disorders. For example, children with either of these disorders may be indifferent to social contact, prone to temper tantrums, or delayed in learning. But in the case of autism, there is no clear-cut evidence of early neglect or abuse. Further, as described in detail below, autistic children tend to show characteristic abnormalities in their language and motor behavior.

It is fortunate that the severe disorders of childhood are rare. Autism occurs in approximately 4 cases per 10,000—about as frequently as deafness occurs among children, and twice as often as blindness (Fombonne, 1998; Ritvo et al., 1989). With regard to sex differences, boys outnumber girls by about three to one. The disorder does not appear to be related to

A child with autism may become more attached to objects than to people.

socioeconomic status or race. The prevalence of autism is similar across different countries, income levels, and ethnic groups.

SYMPTOMS OF AUTISM

The central feature of autism, according to Leo Kanner, a child psychiatrist who was the first to recognize this disorder as a distinct syndrome, is the "inability to relate . . . in the ordinary way to people and situations . . . an extreme autistic aloneness that, whenever possible, disregards, ignores, shuts out anything that comes to the child from outside" (Kanner, 1943). This striking aloneness takes a variety of forms in the areas of language, behavior, cognitive development, and social relationships.

Language Development One of the striking features of children with autism is their poor use and understanding of spoken language. The severity of the language delay manifested by these children is the most powerful predictor of their clinical outcome (Eisenmajer et al., 1998). Most parents of children with autism report that the child's language development was unusual right from the beginning. The stage of enthusiastic babbling observed in normal infants does not occur in many children with autism. When they do begin to vocalize, they fail to show the typical pattern of language development. By the age of one, most normal children use some simple, one-syllable words. But about half of children with autism do not.

When children with autism do begin to use language, their very peculiar use of sounds and words becomes noticeable. In the early stages, the child often uses a high-pitched, bird-like squeaking voice, as John did. Again, like John, both immediate and delayed echolalia occur for long periods after speech develops. The child latches on to a phrase or word that has been spoken to him and repeats it for no apparent reason. Some children with autism show perseveration, which involves the repetition of a sound, word, or phrase over an extended period of time. When comprehensible sentences do emerge, children with autism show many of the same sorts of grammatical errors that normal children do. But in children with autism, these errors are more long-lasting and peculiar. We will look at two of these errors; pronoun reversal and the misuse of the rule for adding -*ing*.

Children with autism tend to reverse the pronouns *I* and *you*. For example, when the child wants candy, he may say "*You* want a candy?" instead of "*I* want a candy." They also tend to refer to themselves using their own proper name (Lee, Hobson, and Chiat, 1994). For example, a ten-year-old boy named David who suffers from autism was asked the question "Are you going to the party?" He replied, "David going to party. David going with me, with me, with me. Me come." In this case, David was referring to himself by name. He referred to the therapist as "me." As David uttered "with me" he began to tug at the arm of the therapist who had asked him the question. When the therapist failed to respond, David tugged harder and urged him to come along.

The causes of pronominal reversal are not yet known. Nonetheless, since personal pronouns occur more frequently at the beginning of sentences, and since children with autism have difficulty processing long sentences, they tend to echo the last few words only. When they are given artificial sentences with "I" and "me" placed at the end (for example, "give candy to me"), they are less likely to reverse pronouns (Bartak and Rutter, 1974). Thus, pronominal reversal can be understood as an integral part of a more general language disorder.

While normal children sometimes misuse the -*ing* rule, children with autism continue to make this error long after the age when normal children have learned the rule. One nine-year-old girl with autism described a man smoking a pipe as "Daddy piping," while a boy blowing bubbles was "boy bubbling" (Wing, 1976). Children with autism also often identify objects by their use, such as "make-a-cup-of-tea" for kettle, and "sweep-the-floor" for broom.

For some children with autism, language development does not proceed very far, and communication skills remain noticeably deficient. These children do learn to talk, but they continue to use language in a peculiar manner. For children with autism who acquire age-appropriate verbal skills in adulthood, language is often too perfect and too grammatical, rather like a person using a foreign language he learned in a classroom. There is a lack of colloquialism. Conversation is stilted. These individuals can maintain a concrete question-and-answer interchange, but the subtleties of emotional tone are lost on them. They seem to know the formal rules of language, but they do not comprehend the idea of communication. This defect extends to the nonverbal aspects of communication as well.

Most children with autism fail to imitate gestures or to initiate imaginative play, both of which are crucial for early language development (Smith and Bryson, 1998). For example, they are slower to acquire simple social gestures such as waving "bye-bye." Unlike deaf children, who understand the ideas of communication and who develop nonverbal communication skills, children with autism fail to use nonverbal strategies to make their needs known. They may point to objects they need, but if an object is not immediately present, their ability to communicate about it is very limited. Similarly, their use of toys as symbols in imaginative play is limited if, indeed, it ever develops. Some believe the key to understanding communication deficits in children with autism lies in their lack of understanding of social interactions.

Social Development Usually the first symptoms observed in children with autism involve some aspect of their social behavior. One striking characteristic is aloofness, a physical and emotional distance from others that is especially troublesome to parents. John was clearly aloof, and his mother was very troubled by it. This aloofness reflects a fundamental failure to develop social attachments. This is shown by the fact that when children with autism can choose where to spend their time, they will spend more time near a nonreacting adult than near an empty chair (Hermelin and O'Connor, 1970). Thus, active avoidance (which would have been shown by choosing to be near the empty chair) is not the case for children with autism. Many children with the disorder gradually improve in their social relationships. But even for those with the best outcomes, some problems persist. They continue to show lack of cooperative group activities with others, fail to make personal friendships, and have difficulty in responding appropriately to others' feelings. Recent evidence suggests that children with autism have fundamental problems in understanding expressions of emotions in others and in using their own faces, voices, and gestures to communicate their own emotions (Charman et al., 1998).

Several theorists have suggested that a critical problem for children with autism is that they do not understand that other people exist as separate individuals and have their own ideas and feelings (Baron-Cohen, 1995). In other words, children with autism suffer from a sort of "mindblindness" that causes an impairment in their ability to imagine what others

Children with autism often hold themselves aloof from others. *(Left)* Although they may not interact with other children, they nonetheless often prefer to be near other people than to be alone. *(Right)* They often become more attached to objects than to people, and they may make up elaborate games and patterns with these objects.

are experiencing. They cannot make sense of the actions of other people, and have trouble decoding nonverbal cues of the human face and eyes.

Insistence on Sameness   Many normal children react badly to changes in their environment, particularly if those changes are sudden. But for reasons that are not at all clear, children with autism show this trait in greatly exaggerated form (Durand and Mapstone, 1999). For example, some children with autism will have severe temper tantrums if the furniture in the house is moved around. Others insist on being driven to school over the same route every day. Parents find that what began as a harmless routine becomes so rigid that it seriously interferes with everyday life.

Insistence on sameness is seen in other ways. Children with autism frequently use toys and other objects to make long lines or complex patterns. They seem more interested in the pattern than in the functional or imaginative play qualities of the objects. Frequently, these children become intensely attached to one or more objects. John, you recall, carried around a long belt and gyrated it. Other children may refuse to part with a dirty blanket or pacifier. These intense attachments interfere with normal development and everyday living in a number of ways. If the object is lost, life is made unbearable for the child and the rest of the family. If it is a large object, it prevents hand-eye coordination since the child's hands are not free to play with other objects.

Some children with autism show stereotypies; the repetition of a motor behavior or activity. For example, the child might repeatedly move his fingers in a

Children with autism often have severe temper tantrums, particularly when their environment suddenly changes.

particular sequence, or rock back and forth in his chair. In some extreme cases, children with autism engage in repeated self-injurious behavior. For example, they might bang their head against a wall until it is bruised, or bite their own hands until they bleed. These behaviors often require physical restraints, such as helmets or bandages, to prevent the child from seriously injuring himself.

Intellectual Development   The measured IQ of the child with autism is one of the best predictors of later progress: those with higher scores do better in a variety of educational and remedial settings (Gittleman and Birch, 1967; Lockyer and Rutter, 1969; Szatmari et al., 1989). Only about 25 to 40 percent of children with autism score above 70 on IQ tests (Ritvo et al., 1989). Thus, a significant proportion of children with autism have IQs in the range of mental retardation. Although some studies have found that the siblings of children with autism also have low IQ scores, others find no evidence that low IQ scores occur in other family members (Freeman et al., 1989).

One of the most mystifying things about autism is that it is often accompanied by "savant" capacities. The term "savant" is used to refer to an unusually high area of ability in an individual with low or moderate abilities in other areas. For example, some children with autism show the amazing ability to identify with great speed and accuracy the day of the week associated with a particular date (Heavey, Pring, and Hermelin, 1999). Others show exceptional ability to memorize things (Mottron, Belleville, Stip, and Morasse, 1998). Some display great spatial abilities, or talent in music or drawing. The fact that these talents are present in persons who score in the retarded range on measures of basic reasoning is perplexing. It suggests that humans have many separable mental abilities.

The diagnosis of autism is often challenging because the diagnostic criteria require that the symptoms be present before the child turns three. If the parents delay having their child evaluated, despite concerns about the child's development, it can be very difficult for the clinician to reconstruct a picture of the early years. This happened in the case of Jennifer. Her parents were concerned about her development, but as long as she remained in the care of her grandmother during the day, they did not feel compelled to seek treatment. Jennifer's deficits became more glaring when she began preschool and

In the 1988 film *Rain Man,* Dustin Hoffman played an "autistic savant," someone who had difficulty interacting with and touching or being touched by other people but who could memorize the phone book and make lightning-quick calculations of the square roots of large numbers.

was contrasted with her peers. The psychologist who evaluated Jennifer had to rely on current observations and retrospective accounts in order get a developmental view of her behavior:

Jennifer and her parents arrived promptly for their second appointment. I greeted them in the waiting room, then Jennifer accompanied me to my office. She looked somewhat apprehensive, but she kissed and hugged her mother, then followed me. She walked on tiptoe to my office. On that day, I planned to administer a battery of tests designed for preschoolers. I began with a test called the Peabody Picture Vocabulary test (PPVT). In this test the child is shown an array of four pictures, and is asked to point to the one that represents a particular concept. For example, at the simplest level, the pictures might be of a ball, bat, glove, and apple. The child is asked to point to the ball. The items get more difficult as the test progresses. On the first nine trials, Jennifer was able to point to the correct picture. But when I pointed to a picture and asked her to name it, she said nothing. When I repeated the question, she said "no." Jennifer then began to ask me questions about the pictures. Her questions were restatements of mine. When I said, "Show me the scissors," Jennifer said, "Point me to the scissors."

It was not possible to complete any of the standardized tests. After the first few items, Jennifer would stop attending to the test materials, or would start repeating my queries in her own words. Nonetheless,

I learned a great deal from the assessment. Jennifer's visual-motor coordination was excellent. She drew and colored a detailed picture of a cat. The drawing was typical of what a six- or seven-year-old would produce. Similarly, her gross motor coordination was excellent. She caught a ball with ease from across the room. But I also observed several atypical behaviors. She rocked back and forth in her chair and twisted her hair in her fingers. On several occasions, she opened and closed a small red purse that was on a string around her neck. She did not make eye contact with me at any time.

After spending over an hour with Jennifer, I asked her parents to meet with me again. Jennifer stayed with the receptionist in the waiting room, watching the tropical fish swimming in the aquarium. I shared some of my observations about Jennifer's behavior with Carol and Robert. They confirmed them. I then asked Jennifer's parents some specific questions about the onset of each of the abnormalities I noticed. They said Jennifer's speech seemed perfectly normal, maybe even above average, until she was three, then she started repeating things and stopped using some words. They said she was very affectionate up to the age of about three, although she always had a tendency to stare off in space sometimes, as if she was daydreaming. When she turned three, Jennifer became more irritable and hostile; she vacillated between affection and aggression. Her play was less organized and more repetitive. After questioning Jennifer's parents for about an hour, I asked them if they would sign forms giving me permission to talk to her grandmother and to observe her at school. They readily agreed.

Later that afternoon, I reviewed my notes from the interview with Jennifer's parents. After observing Jennifer's behavior during the testing, I had considered the possibility that she was autistic. But the developmental history provided by her parents led me to doubt that diagnosis. They had described a period of relatively normal development up to age three. They also described Jennifer as socially responsive. I hoped to interview the grandmother to see whether she shared this impression of Jennifer's development. If she did, I would have to rule out autism.

CAUSES OF AUTISM

The sorts of behavior associated with autism are so far removed from people's expectations of normal development that most now believe that there must be some biological abnormality underlying the syndrome. The professional community has not always taken this position, however. Those who first studied the disorder tended to focus on the parents and their traits (Kanner, 1943). By examining parental traits, they hoped to come up with possible psychological causes of autism. Since the evidence on parental traits is now fairly clear, let us examine this first.

Psychogenic Theories   From the perspective of some early psychodynamic and behavioral theorists, the parents of children with autism seemed to be introverted, distant, intellectual, and meticulous (Bettelheim, 1967; Ferster, 1961). They were described as creating an environment of "emotional refrigeration," and many clinicians referred to the "refrigerator mothers" of these children. It was assumed that the parents' behavioral tendencies were reflected in their offspring: parental distance was seen in the child's aloofness, while parental meticulousness was mirrored in the child's repetitive behaviors. Even if one accepted this evidence, however, it does not necessarily mean that the parents' behavior caused the child's disorder. It is equally plausible that, faced with such a challenging child, parental attitudes and behaviors changed. This alternative hypothesis was overlooked in the rush to demonstrate parental culpability.

There is little evidence to suggest that the parents of children with autism behave differently when compared to the parents of children with serious physical illnesses. No confirmation of extremely damaging parental behavior exists. Few children with autism actually come from broken homes, and most have not experienced early family stresses. There is no evidence that their parents are overly introverted or obsessional, nor do they show any excess of thought disorder. Most children with autism experience the normal range of parental attitudes and child-rearing practices (Cantwell, Baker, and Rutter, 1978).

Biological Theories   Because psychogenic theories of autism have not been substantiated, increasing attention has been directed to the biological origins of the disorder (Rapin and Katzman, 1998). Behavior genetic studies have been conducted to determine whether vulnerability to autism can be inherited. Because autism is a relatively rare condition, however, it is difficult to gather extensive data on the genetics of this disorder. But one study found that about 10 percent of families with one child with autistic disorder have at least one other child with the disorder (Ritvo et al., 1989). Twin studies show a high rate of concordance for autism in MZ twins (60 percent) when compared to DZ twins (0 percent) (Bailey, Le Couteur, Gottesman, and Bolton, 1995). Also in twin pairs that are discordant for autism, it is not uncommon for the healthy twin to show mild cognitive and social abnormalities (Quay, Routh, and Shapiro, 1987). Thus, the genetic vulnerability to autism may result in a cognitive problem that can appear in subtle or more extreme ways.

The fact that the behavioral abnormalities associated with autism are so severe led researchers to expect brain abnormalities. So far, neuroimaging studies have shown only a few consistent differences between children with and without autism (Deb and Thompson, 1998). To the surprise of many, the results of several of these studies indicate that children with autism tend to have larger than normal brain volumes. Another finding is that children with autism have an abnormality in the structure of the cerebellum, with certain areas of the cerebellum showing a reduction in size (Courchesne, Townsend, and Saitoh, 1994). However, some research findings indicate that these

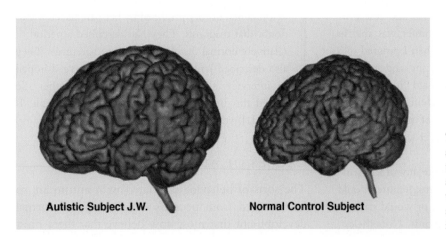

Autistic Subject J.W.   **Normal Control Subject**

These MRI scans compare the brain of a three-year-old boy with autism with the brain of a boy who does not have autism. The brain volume of the child with autism was 6 standard deviations above the normal average brain volume for a child his age.

cerebellum abnormalities are also present in other pervasive developmental disorders, including Rett's disorder, which is described below (Schaefer, Thompson, Bodensteiner and McConnell, 1996).

It has been suggested that there may be a certain brain region that plays a special role in our abilities to "read" members of our own species. In Chapter 4, we described research that showed that certain "limbic" regions of the brain, particularly the amygdala, may be responsible for our ability to recognize familiar faces, especially members of our own species (Seeck et al., 1993). Damage to these regions may interfere with the ability to recognize what other people are feeling. In a creative study, Michael Tomasello and Luigia Camnioni compared the nonverbal communication abilities of normal children, children with autism, and a group of chimpanzees raised by humans (Tomasello and Camnioni, 1997). The normal children showed clear advantages over the other two groups in their ability to use gestures and other symbolic means to communicate their needs to an adult human. The researchers concluded that children with autism do indeed behave as if they are not aware that other people have thoughts and intentions.

Additional evidence for a biological basis to autism is the fact that children with the disorder tend to have seizures. During adolescence, about 30 percent of children with autism develop epileptic seizures, even though they had shown no clear evidence of neurological disorder when they were younger (Rapin, 1997). Furthermore, electroencephalographic (EEG) studies—that is, studies that examine the electrical activity of the brain—reveal that children with autism have a higher rate of abnormal brain waves than do normal children. These findings support the notion that the causes of autism may be biological. Further, the fact that only some children with autistic disorder show seizures or EEG abnormalities suggests there may be several subtypes of autism, each with different causes (Prior, 1987).

Another possible biological cause of autism is faulty neurotransmission. When neurotransmitter activity is abnormal, the brain is unable to pass messages efficiently from one neuron to another. This could produce the behavioral and cognitive abnormalities observed in children with autism. Researchers have found differences between children with and without autism in levels of the catecholamine neurotransmitters, dopamine and serotonin (Gilberg and Svennerholm, 1987; Hameury et al., 1995; Winsberg, Sverd, Castells, Hurwic, and

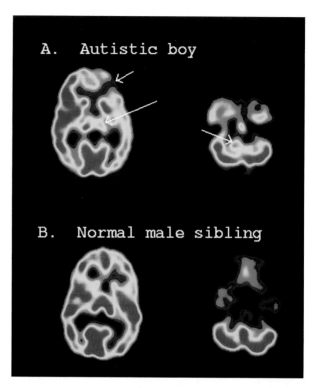

PET scans of a six-year-old boy who is diagnosed with autism and his nine-year-old brother show a difference in serotonin activity in the brains of the two boys. The boy with autism has decreased serotonin activity in the left frontal cortex (shown with the top arrow; more blue indicates less activity; the left side of the brain appears on the right side of the brain image) and in the left thalamus (shown with the longer arrow; yellow indicates less activity than red). The set of scans on the right indicate increased serotonin activity in the dentate nucleus (a part of the cerebellum involved in motor planning) in the boy with autism (more yellow than blue) than in his brother.

Perel, 1980). To date, the most consistent evidence is for an increase in serotonin activity in children with autism (McBride et al., 1998). But other findings suggest that it may be an imbalance in serotonin between the left and right hemispheres of the brain. A study using PET scans revealed such an imbalance in serotonin, with the brains of children with autistic disorder showing lower levels in the left cortex and thalamus when compared to the right side of the brain (Chugani et al., 1997). The authors point out that the abnormalities are located in brain regions that are important for language production and integrating visual and auditory input.

A significant percentage of autistic children also experience other severe biological disorders. These include Fragile X syndrome, phenylketonuria, rubella (German measles), and encephalitis (Barak,

Kimhi, Stein, Gutman, and Weizman, 1999; Prior, 1987). Finally, autism is associated with a higher rate of obstetric and neonatal complications (Ciaranello and Ciaranello, 1995; Goodman, 1990). One of these complications, maternal rubella infection, not only increases the risk for autism, but also for a range of developmental disorders, including mental retardation. The very clear-cut evidence that "German measles" can cause serious problems with fetal development has resulted in more widespread efforts to protect pregnant women from the disease.

TREATING AUTISM

A variety of medications are used in the treatment of autism. However, they are prescribed for limited periods of time to treat specific symptoms, rather than the entire syndrome (Cohen and Volkmar, 1997; Rapin, 1997). For example, methylphenidate (Ritalin) is used for improving attentional capacity, whereas SSRI's (for example, Prozac) and other antidepressants are used to control stereotypies, perseveration, and mood swings. But the main treatment for autism is intensive behavioral therapy and educational interventions.

Considerable effort, for example, has focused on language development and social responsiveness (American Academy of Pediatrics, 1998; Lovaas and Buch, 1997; Risley and Wolf, 1967). Treating problems with language ability is considered crucial, because the inability to communicate properly is so central to this disorder (see Box 8–1 for a discussion of a controversial treatment of language deficits). At the same time, it is very important that the child learn to attend to others so that efforts to reinforce communication are effective. Ivar Lovaas has been in the forefront of developing intensive treatment programs for children with autism. The behavioral techniques developed by his research group are now widely used. In these treatments, children's vocalizations are reinforced by the therapist to increase their frequency. Next, the children are rewarded for imitating the sounds produced by the therapist. When imitation is established, children are taught to label everyday objects. And finally, the same techniques are used to teach them to ask questions. Early studies of the effectiveness of these methods engendered considerable optimism that these behavioral techniques might enable children to completely overcome the deficits associated with autism. But this optimism was tempered somewhat by the studies showing that gains made during treatment often disappeared when the children were returned to institutional care (Lovaas, 1973).

Nonetheless, follow-up studies of children with autism who undergo intensive treatment show that there are significant improvements in their functioning (Freeman, 1997). In general, the research findings indicate that if children with autism are given behavioral treatment for an extended period of time (for example, forty hours per week for at least two years) at an early age, long-term prognosis can be good. In one study, 47 percent of the children receiving such intensive treatment achieved intellectual and educational functioning within the normal range by age six to seven. In contrast, this occurred in only 2 percent of the children who had received minimal or institutional care (Lovaas, 1987). Furthermore, when parents participate in treatment programs, both their behaviors and those of the children undergo change. And the more the parents are involved in the treatment program, the more likely the language gains will be maintained (Hemsley et al., 1978).

In conjunction with behavioral therapies, structured educational approaches have also proven beneficial to children with autism (Hung, Rotman, Consentino, and MacMillan, 1983; Jordan and Powell, 1995). These approaches zero in on the specific cognitive, motor, and perceptual handicaps of the child. A carefully designed educational program minimizes the kinds of distractions that accompany ordinary teaching. For example, when normal children are taught to read, some texts and teaching materials print vowels in one color and consonants in another.

Behavioral techniques may successfully treat specific deficits caused by autism. These children receive positive reinforcement for hugging each other.

Science and Practice

Box 8—1

Facilitated Communication: Fact or Fiction?

Researchers who have devoted their careers to finding effective treatments for children with autism are well aware that progress can be slow and painstaking. For parents of a child with this disorder, the process can be grueling; they are eager to see their child live a normal life. Often the eagerness to find a miraculous cure leads parents and professionals to fall prey to faddish treatments. An example is facilitated communication (FC) (Holster, 1996). This treatment is intended to stimulate the development of language in nonspeaking children with autism and other communication disorders. FC was developed in Australia and then introduced in the United States around 1990. In FC, the therapist is referred to as the facilitator. The facilitator provides physical assistance to the child to help him communicate with mechanical devices, usually a computer keyboard. The facilitator guides the child's hand, wrist, elbow, or shoulder to letters on the keyboard, and encourages him to type words and sentences. Early reports alleged that children who had never spoken suddenly began expressing their inner thoughts and feelings through FC. Proponents of FC state that the facilitator's belief in both the child's potential to communicate and in the FC procedures is necessary for success. However, problems began to arise as facilitators reported that some patients were revealing incidences of sexual and physical abuse by family members or treatment providers. These claims led to more controlled studies of the efficacy of FC.

Wheeler, Jacobson, Paglieri, and Schwartz (1993) studied twelve autistic children in a residential program where the staff used FC. The aim was to determine whether FC was actually facilitating communications from the children, or whether the facilitator herself was the source of the messages. The researchers made a set of thirty photographs of familiar objects in the child's environment. These objects had been used in vocabulary training with the children. The facilitator/child pair sat at one end of a long table with a lengthwise divider. Each could see the photograph presented at the other end of the table on their own side, but not on the other side. The task required the child to label the photograph. The two were shown each stimulus photograph under three conditions: (1) assisted typing with the facilitator unaware of the content of the photograph presented to the subject, (2) unassisted typing, and (3) assisted typing/facilitation, where both the child and the facilitator were presented with photographs, but where some photograph pairs were identical and some pairs were different. None of the children were able to label the photograph correctly without facilitator assistance. On trials where facilitators and children had different photographs, the only correct responses were for photographs shown to the facilitator. The researcher concluded that all the correct responses originated with the facilitators. At the same time, there was no evidence that the facilitator was intentionally influencing the child.

Despite the fact that this and other experimental studies have failed to show the effectiveness of facilitated communication, some practitioners have continued to use it in the treatment of children with autism (Duchan, 1999). These therapists have defended this practice on the grounds that they have observed improvements in some children who receive it. Is this justified? Or should it be required that all treatments for behavioral disorders meet certain scientific standards? If so, what should those standards be? These questions have been the topic of debate among leading psychologists, and most have concluded that psychological treatments should be empirically validated (Kazdin, 1998a). This means that only those treatments that have been shown to be effective in controlled studies should be offered to the public.

While this helps normal children differentiate between vowels and consonants, it confuses children with pervasive developmental difficulties (Schreibman, 1975). Generally, structured education aimed at overcoming the specific handicaps of children with the disorder seems to be the best method presently available for helping these children. Again, including parents in these treatments and teaching them how to overcome their child's specific deficits increases the effectiveness of the treatments.

It appears that intensive treatment programs also make a difference for the intellectual functioning of the child with autism (Smith, 1999). On average, research has shown increases of 7 to 28 IQ points after

treatment with behavioral programs. Of course, children vary in their responses to treatment: most improve, but others remain stable or decline. Language ability may be a critical factor in determining who benefits from treatment.

Long-term follow-up studies of children with autism indicate that the prognosis varies a great deal. In one study, children diagnosed with autism were followed up into adolescence or young adulthood (Ballaban-Gil, Rapin, Tuchman, and Shinnar, 1996). These children had received treatment, but not the intensive approaches that are now routinely used. The researchers found that behavior problems persisted in 69 percent of the children. Thirty-five percent of the

The IQ's of children with autism can increase when they are treated in behavioral programs. Here the child is practicing his eye/hand coordination at a water table.

adolescents and 49 percent of the adults engaged in self-injurious behavior, and slightly more than 50 percent of the total sample exhibited some stereotypies. More than 90 percent continued to have social deficits. Language improved with age, although only 35 percent showed fluency in the normal range. At the time of the follow-up, 53 percent of the adults were living in residential placement, and 27 percent of the adults were employed in menial jobs or in sheltered workshops. Clearly, in the absence of intensive treatment, the long-term prognosis for independent living is not good. Nonetheless, many children with autism are able to live satisfying lives as adults, and the proportion of those who are able to do so will probably increase in the future, mainly because of better treatment (Wing, 1997).

The level of functioning achieved in adulthood is strongly related to the child's level of functioning. As mentioned earlier, the IQ score of the child with autism turns out to be one of the most sensitive early indices of later outcome. The higher the child's IQ, the better his prognosis. Another good prognostic indicator is the presence of some useful spoken language before the age of five. Finally, children who do not develop seizures have a better outcome than those who do (Gilberg, 1991).

Rett's Disorder

Although autism is the most well-known pervasive developmental disorder, there are several other syndromes that involve dramatic delays in development. They are distinguished from autism because they show a different developmental course and pattern of symptoms.

Rett's disorder typically has its onset between five and forty-eight months of age, although the age of onset may range from birth to four years of age as described by DSM-IV (Ghuman, Ghuman, and Ford, 1998). It is known to be a rare disorder, with a prevalence estimate of 1 in 10,000 (Lomborso, 2000). Unlike the other pervasive developmental disorders, Rett's disorder only occurs in females. It is believed that this is because it is a genetically determined disorder that involves the X chromosome and is lethal in

DSM-IV Criteria

Rett's Disorder

A. All of the following: (1) apparently normal prenatal and perinatal development; (2) apparently normal psychomotor development through the first 5 months after birth; (3) normal head circumference at birth.

B. Onset of all of the following after the period of normal development: (1) deceleration of head growth between ages 5 and 48 months; (2) loss of previously acquired purposeful hand skills between ages 5 and 30 months with the subsequent development of stereotyped hand movements (e.g., hand-wringing or hand washing); (3) loss of social engagement early in the course (although often social interaction develops later); (4) appearance of poorly coordinated gait or trunk movements; (5) severely impaired expressive and receptive language development with severe psychomotor retardation.

SOURCE: APA, DSM-IV, 1994.

DSM-IV Criteria

Childhood Disintegrative Disorder

A. Apparently normal development for at least the first 2 years after birth as manifested by the presence of age-appropriate verbal and nonverbal communication, social relationships, play, and adaptive behavior.

B. Clinically significant loss of previously acquired skills (before age 10 years) in at least two of the following areas: (1) expressive or receptive language; (2) social skills or adaptive behavior; (3) bowel or bladder control; (4) play; (5) motor skills.

C. Abnormalities of functioning in at least two of the following areas: (1) qualitative impairment in social interaction (e.g., impairment in nonverbal behaviors, failure to develop peer relationships, lack of social or emotion-al reciprocity); (2) qualitative impairments in communication (e.g., delay or lack of spoken language, inability to initiate or sustain a conversation, stereotyped and repetitive use of language, lack of varied make-believe play); (3) restricted, repetitive, and stereotyped patterns of behavior, interests, and activities, including motor stereotypies and mannerisms.

D. The disturbance is not better accounted for by another specific Pervasive Developmental Disorder or by Schizophrenia.

SOURCE: APA, DSM-IV, 1994.

---

the male fetus (Anvret and Clarke, 1997). Thus, only females with the genetic susceptibility survive to have the disorder. However, because individuals with Rett's disorder tend not to have offspring themselves, the vulnerability is probably due to a gene mutation, rather than being inherited from parents.

The developmental course of Rett's disorder is unique. At first the child's physical and emotional development is normal. Studies of the home movies of infants who later develop Rett's disorder reveal no observable abnormalities until the child approaches one year of age (Carmagnat-Dubois et al., 1997). When the disorder does begin to manifest itself, however, the child shows a slowing down in head growth and a decline in motor and communication skills. She then begins to withdraw from social interactions, rigidly adheres to nonfunctional routines or rituals, and begins to manifest stereotypic and repetitive hand or finger movements or whole-body movements. Most children with Rett's disorder suffer from mental retardation. It is unfortunate that Rett's disorder is usually persistent and progressive.

Due to advances in genetics, scientist recently succeeded in identifying a gene that is responsible for about a third of the cases of Rett's disorder (Amir et al., 1999). Using linkage analysis (described in Chapter 4), they discovered that Rett's syndrome is caused by mutations in a specific gene on the X chromosome. This gene codes for a protein (MeCP2) that is very important for brain function. It appears that the

MeCP2 protein is responsible for silencing the transcription of some other genes that affect nerve cells. When the MeCP2 protein is not working appropriately, the activity of these other genes is out of control. We must await the results of future research to find out how this results in the marked developmental regression that characterizes Rett's disorder. Researchers are also trying to find out why the mutation occurs in the first place; a prenatal event is a likely source.

Childhood Disintegrative Disorder

In *childhood disintegrative disorder,* development is within the normal range at least until the child reaches two years of age (Durand and Mapstone, 1999). According to DSM-IV, the typical age of onset of the disorder is between three and four years. At that time, the child begins to show a loss of skills in at least two of three areas: language, social, and motor. The symptoms are very similar to those shown by autistic children, including abnormalities in communication, motor stereotypies, and an aversion to social interaction. Childhood disintegrative disorder is much less common than autism, and occurs more often in males than in females. The cause of this mysterious disorder is unknown, however researchers believe it probably involves some abnormality in the early development of the nervous system. The treatments are the same as those for autism: intensive behavioral therapy and educational programs, and in some cases, medication.

Asperger's Disorder

Of all the pervasive developmental disorders, **Asperger's disorder** has the latest onset; usually it is not detected until the preschool period or later (Schopler, Mesibov, and Kunce, 1998). The estimated prevalence for Asperger's disorder is relatively low; .1 to .26 percent of the population (Volkmar, 1996). Further, it is associated with less severe deficits. The primary symptom is impairment in social interaction, usually accompanied by repetitive patterns of behavior and limited interests. When interacting with others, most individuals with Asperger's disorder fail to make eye contact, and their facial expressions rarely change. Their body posture and gestures seem almost mechanical. They have few friends and express little interest in recreational activities or humor. There is some controversy about the distinction between autism and Asperger's. Some believe that Asperger's is a milder form of autism. Like autism, it is more common in males than females. The following description of a young man diagnosed with Asperger's disorder illustrates the awkward social interaction that is the hallmark of this syndrome:

Samuel was diagnosed as having Asperger's syndrome when he was ten years old. Prior to that, although an average student, he was viewed as "very unusual" by adults and his peers. Sam went on to complete high school with the help of a tutor. He then got a job packing groceries at a local supermarket. He has now worked there for over ten years. He is the most reliable employee at the store. Nonetheless, Sam has very obvious signs of Asperger's disorder. He virtually never makes eye contact, and he greets everyone with the same phrase in the same high-pitched tone of voice. As patrons enter the store he says "Welcome today and I hope you are doing fine." He turns his head toward the person, but averts his gaze to the right and shows no facial expression of emotion. He packs the groceries in a very precise manner, and occasionally initiates a brief conversation while doing so. As the customer leaves the store, Sam says "Good-bye and I hope you come back real soon." Sometimes he repeats this several times, usually in the same high pitch and with the same pattern of intonation.

One intriguing aspect of Asperger's is that some children who suffer from this disorder are unusually gifted in certain areas. Dr. Fred Volkmar and his colleagues describe an eleven-year-old boy named Robert who showed exceptional math and com-

DSM-IV Criteria

Asperger's Disorder

A. Qualitative impairment in social interaction, as manifested by at least two of the following: (1) marked impairment in the use of multiple nonverbal behaviors such as eye-to-eye gaze, facial expression, body postures, and gestures to regulate social interaction; (2) failure to develop peer relationships appropriate to developmental level; (3) a lack of spontaneous seeking to share enjoyment, interests, or achievements with other people (e.g., by a lack of showing, bringing, or pointing out objects of interest to other people); (4) lack of social or emotional reciprocity.

B. Restricted repetitive and stereotyped patterns of behavior, interests, and activities, as manifested by at least one of the following: (1) encompassing preoccupation with one or more stereotyped and restricted patterns of interest that is abnormal either in intensity or focus; (2) apparently inflexible adherence to specific, nonfunctional routines or rituals; (3) stereotyped and repetitive

motor mannerisms (e.g., hand or finger flapping or twisting, or complex whole-body movements; (4) persistent preoccupation with parts of objects.

C. The disturbance causes clinically significant impairment in social, occupational, or other important areas of functioning.

D. There is no clinically significant general delay in language (e.g., single words used by age 2 years, communicative phrases used by age 3 years).

E. There is no clinically significant delay in cognitive development or in the development of age-appropriate self-help skills, adaptive behavior (other than in social interaction), and curiosity about the environment in childhood.

F. Criteria are not met for another specific Pervasive Developmental Disorder or Schizophrenia.

SOURCE: APA, DSM-IV, 1994.

puter abilities (Volkmar, Klin, Schultz, Rubin, and Bronen, 2000). Robert clearly met the diagnostic criteria for Asperger's disorder; he was not responsive to other people's facial expressions or gestures, tended to ignore social stimuli, actively avoided eye contact, and "seemed to look through people." On a test of social knowledge, he scored at age level two years, seven months. But on the WISC-III, his verbal IQ was 145, his performance IQ was 119, and his full-scale IQ was 135. His score on a test of math achievement was in the superior range, 159, and he was enrolled in a math program for gifted children. Nonetheless, Robert had few friends and felt rejected by his peers.

PDD-NOS

One other diagnostic category listed with the developmental disorders in DSM is pervasive developmental disorder NOS (not otherwise specified), or "PDD-NOS" as it is often called. This diagnostic label is applied when the child shows "autistic-like" behavioral abnormalities and developmental delays, but does not meet criteria for autism or any of the other disorders. In clinical practice, the PDD-NOS diagnosis is about as common as autism. What this indicates is that it is often very difficult to distinguish among these diagnostic categories. In fact, many consider them to be tentative. For example, some have suggested that autism, PDD-NOS, childhood disintegrative disorder, and Asperger's disorder may be variants of the same disorder. We will only be able to resolve this issue when we have identified the etiological processes. In the meantime, clinicians like Jennifer's psychologist must try to apply the current diagnostic labels as accurately as possible.

I spoke to Jennifer's grandmother on the phone for about thirty minutes. She was very concerned about her grandchild and had prepared some notes to share with me. Her observations were similar to those of Jennifer's parents. She described Jennifer as developing more or less normally up to age three, then deteriorating in her language and social development. But even now, according to the grandmother, Jennifer often shows spontaneous affection.

Jennifer's teacher arranged for me to observe Jennifer in her classroom from an adjacent office. During the forty-five minutes I was there, Jennifer had no interaction with the other children. She followed the teacher's directions, and sat appropriately at the table for

a snack, but she manifested no interest in interacting with the other children. When the other children were playing, Jennifer retreated to a corner of the room where art supplies were stored and drew pictures of cats.

My conversation with Jennifer's grandmother led me to conclude that I must rule out autism as a diagnosis. Yet, it was clear that Jennifer showed several "autistic-like" features, and that she was likely suffering from a pervasive developmental disorder. Because her development was normal, at least up to two years, and she deteriorated in both language and social skills after three years of age, I concluded that Jennifer met the criteria for childhood disintegrative disorder. My next responsibility was to share my conclusions and recommendations with Jennifer's parents.

Mental Retardation

The definition of mental retardation most used in the United States is the one provided by the American Association on Mental Retardation (AAMR): "Mental retardation refers to substantial limitations in present functioning. It is characterized by significantly subaverage intellectual functioning, existing concurrently with related limitations in two or more of the following applicable adaptive skill areas: communication, self-care, home living, social skills, community use, self-direction, health and safety, functional academics, leisure, and work. Mental retardation manifests before age eighteen" (Luckasson et al., 1992). This definition has been incorporated into DSM-IV as criteria for diagnosing mental retardation. DSM-IV lists mental retardation as an Axis II disorder. Thus, it can be diagnosed along with other DSM disorders, and it is often present in children with autism and schizophrenia.

According to the DSM-IV, mental retardation has a 1 percent prevalence rate. But prevalence estimates vary a great deal from one study to the next, depending on the definition of retardation. What has been clearly established, however, is that there are more males than females suffering from the disorder. Severe mental retardation, which requires extensive special support services, has a prevalence of about 4 per 1,000 (Simonoff, Bolton, Rutter, 1996; Roeleveld, Zielhuis, and Gabreels, 1997). Thus, compared to other disorders in DSM-IV, mental retardation is a highly prevalent disorder. Despite its prevalence, however, it is a controversial disorder, and it is often difficult to diagnose. In part, the difficulty arises from the stereotypes that people have about mental retardation. But in larger measure, the difficulty occurs

DSM-IV Criteria

Mental Retardation

A. Significantly subaverage intellectual functioning: an IQ of approximately 70 or below on an individually administered IQ test (for infants, a clinical judgment of significantly subaverage intellectual functioning).

B. Concurrent deficits or impairments in present adaptive functioning (i.e., the person's effectiveness in meeting the standards expected for his or her age by his or her cultural group) in at least two of the following areas:

communication, self-care, home living, social/interpersonal skills, use of community resources, self-direction, functional academic skills, work, leisure, health, and safety.

C. The onset is before age 18 years.

SOURCE: APA, DSM-IV, 1994.

because the notion of intelligence is at the heart of mental retardation, and intelligence is very difficult to define (Gould, 1981; Kamin, 1974).

MEASURES OF MENTAL RETARDATION

For the purposes of diagnosis and intervention planning, several measures have been developed to assess the abilities of individuals with mental retardation. Factors that have contributed to the development of these tests include the AAMR definition of retardation and the passage and updating of the Education for All Handicapped Children Act (PL94-142). The diagnosis of mental retardation can only be made when low IQ is accompanied by deficits in ability to cope with the demands of daily life. Similarly, the requirements of PL94-142 state that the classification of students must be based on a comprehensive evaluation, that people with mental retardation have the right to be educated in the least restrictive environment possible, and that their assignment to special education classes cannot be made on the basis of IQ tests alone.

An IQ score of less than 70 remains the criterion of mental retardation. The WISC-R and other intelligence tests continue to be regarded as acceptable measures to provide a meaningful criterion of mental retardation. One problem with the use of IQ tests, however, is that there are not enough easy items for children with severe impairments. One possible solution to this problem would be to use infant scales, such as the Bayley Scales of Infant Development, with children who are beyond that test's age range but who have mental ages that are within the age range (Sullivan and Burley, 1990).

Intelligence tests developed for use with infants and preschool children typically are performance tests that measure a variety of motor, social, and cognitive skills. Tests for infants are designed to assess sensorimotor development, communication skills, and social responsivity. Tests for preschoolers assess a wider range of abilities, including perceptual and motor skills, immediate memory, ability to follow directions, simple discrimination, recognition of inconsistencies, and identification of body parts and common objects and their functions. These tests typically use a developmental approach, in that the test items distinguish among children at various developmental levels.

Adaptive behavior scales assess the degree to which an individual meets the standards of personal independence and social responsibility expected for a child's age or cultural group (Grossman, 1983a). For example, the Vineland Adaptive Behavior Scale measures skills in four domains: communication (receptive, expressive, written); daily living skills (personal, domestic, community); socialization (interpersonal relationships, play and leisure time, coping skills); and motor skills (gross, fine; primarily for young children). One difficulty with this type of assessment, however, is that standards of behavior and achievement are determined by an individual's society. The System of Multicultural Pluralistic Assessment (SOMPA) was developed by Jane Mercer (1979), based on Mercer's belief that all cultural groups have the same average potential, and in response to concern about the misclassification of minority group children as mentally retarded based solely on their IQ test scores. The SOMPA is unique in its integration of three assessment components: a medical component that assesses the physical health conditions that affect a child's learning ability, a social system component that measures a child's social-adaptive behaviors, and a pluralistic component that evaluates a child's sociocultural background.

Correlations between intelligence tests and adaptive behavior scales where parents serve as the informants are moderate to low (Kamphaus, 1993). This finding implies that psychologists should not expect much agreement between test scores and parent-reported adaptive behavior scores. It further implies that adaptive behavior scales are adding information to the diagnostic process that is different from intelligence tests. It is likely that adaptive behavior will continue to become more important in the diagnosis and intervention planning of mental retardation.

Some researchers believe that, in the future, we will rely less on performance measures to identify mental retardation. Instead, they suggest that there will be an increasing reliance on genetic tests and neuroimaging (Crow and Tolmie, 1998). On the other hand, some would argue that the ultimate concern is the behavioral capacity, not the biological index. As described below, Down syndrome is a genetic disorder associated with mental retardation. It is known, however, that a subgroup of children with Down syndrome score within the normal range on measures of intelligence. So a prediction of future intelligence that is based solely on the person's genotype would be far from perfectly accurate.

LEVELS OF RETARDATION

The various levels of mental retardation and their associated IQ scores on a standard test of intelligence are shown in Table 8–3. What do these levels of retardation mean?

Mild Mental Retardation   The largest group of children with mental retardation, about 85 percent of them, fall into this category. These children develop social and communication skills just like all others and at the same times. In fact, their retardation is often not noticed until they are in the third or fourth grade, when they begin to have academic difficulties. Without help, they can acquire academic skills through the sixth grade; with help, they can go beyond that level. In all other respects, their needs and abilities are indistinguishable from those of other children. Special education programs often enable these children to acquire the vocational skills that are necessary for minimal self-support. When under social or economic stress, they may need guidance and supervision, but otherwise they are able to function quite adequately in unskilled and semiskilled jobs.

Moderate Mental Retardation   Children in this category make up 10 percent of those with mental retardation. Like other children, they are able to learn to talk and communicate during the preschool period. But unlike other children, those with moderate mental retardation have difficulty learning social conventions. During the school-age period, they can profit from training in social and occupational skills, but they are unlikely to go beyond the second-grade level in academic subjects. Physically, they may be clumsy, and occasionally they may suffer from poor motor coordination. They may learn to travel alone in familiar places and can often contribute to their own support by working at semiskilled or unskilled tasks in protected settings.

Severe Mental Retardation   Before they are five, those with severe mental retardation show poor motor development, and they develop little or no communicative speech. At special schools, they may

TABLE 8–3

Data

SEVERITY LEVELS OF MENTAL RETARDATION		
Level	*Percent of Retarded People*	*IQ Levels*
Mild	85	50–55 to approximately 70
Moderate	10	35–40 to 50–55
Severe	4	20–25 to 35–40
Profound	>1	below 20 or 25

learn to talk and can be trained in elementary hygiene. Generally, they are unable to profit from vocational training, though as adults they may be able to perform simple, unskilled job tasks under supervision.

Profound Mental Retardation   Children in this category are severely handicapped in adaptive behavior, and they are unable to master any but the simplest motor tasks during the preschool years. During the school years, some development in motor skills may occur, and the child may respond in a limited way to training in self-care. Severe physical deformity, central nervous system difficulties, and retarded growth are not uncommon. Health and resistance to disease are poor, and life expectancy is shorter than normal. These children require custodial care.

CAUSES OF MENTAL RETARDATION

Our knowledge of the causes of mental retardation is ever expanding. Mental retardation is a symptom, not a specific disease, and there are a multitude of causes. The more severely impaired an individual, the more likely a specific cause can be found. Mental retardation may result from chromosomal disorders, prenatal exposure to certain drugs, infections, complications during labor and delivery, postnatal physical trauma to the brain, metabolism or nutrition problems, brain disease, and psychosocial disadvantages, including deprivation, abuse, and neglect. Table 8–4 presents some common causes of mental retardation.

Genetic Influences   A major cause of mental retardation is a chromosomal disorder known as ***Down syndrome,*** named for Langdon Down, a physician who first recognized it in 1886. While the most

This three-year-old girl has Down syndrome. A child with Down syndrome has an extra chromosome (number 21) and a distinctive appearance (rounded face and wide-set and upwardly slanting eyes) and may be born with physical anomalies such as heart defects.

common form of Down syndrome is not inherited, it occurs at conception and immediately affects the development of the fetus. It arises because there are forty-seven chromosomes, rather than the usual forty-six, in the cells of the children born with the disorder. There is an "extra" chromosome 21, so Down syndrome is sometimes referred to as Trisomy 21. The reason for this chromosomal abnormality is not presently known. Interestingly, while the risk for the disorder is about 1 in 1,500 for children born to mothers in their twenties, it increases to 1 in 40 when the mother is over forty. This may be due to the cumulative effects of exposure of the older

TABLE 8–4

PHYSICAL CAUSES OF MENTAL RETARDATION

Genetic Abnormalities	Infectious Diseases	Other Conditions
Down Syndrome	Rubella	Rh Factor
Phenylketonuria (PKU)	Syphilis	Malnutrition
Tay-Sachs Disease	Toxoplasmosis	Lead Poisoning
Klinefelter's Syndrome	Encephalitis	Irradiation
Fragile X Syndrome	Meningitis	Anoxia
	Herpes Simplex	Head Injuries
		Drug Reactions

mother's eggs to toxins and radiation, which produce genetic mutations.

Down syndrome children have a characteristic facial appearance that usually includes wideset, slanted eyes. Many babies born with Down syndrome suffer from physical anomalies, especially heart malformations, as well as cognitive delay (Nadel, 1999). Fortunately, with the advent of infant heart surgery, advanced surgical skills, and the development of better antibiotics, most of these defects are readily correctable or treatable. With advanced age, however, another challenge faces people with Down syndrome: they are at increased risk for Alzheimer's disease (Visser, Aldenkamp, van Huffelen and Kuilman, 1997). The reason for this is not yet known.

Other chromosomal abnormalities associated with mental retardation include Fragile X syndrome, Trisomy 13, and Trisomy 18. Fragile X syndrome is caused when a tip of the X chromosome breaks off.

The syndrome is characterized by severe to profound mental retardation, autistic behaviors, and speech defects (see Box 8–2). In addition, males with Fragile X syndrome have large ears, long faces, and enlarged testes. Trisomy 13 and Trisomy 18 are caused when chromosomes 13 and 18 are present in triplicate rather than in pairs. Both disorders cause more severe retardation than Down syndrome, and a shorter life expectancy.

It is possible to detect chromosomal problems through amniocentesis, a test that is administered to the mother after the thirteenth week of pregnancy. In this procedure, a small amount of amniotic fluid (the fluid that surrounds the fetus) is drawn off and examined for the presence of abnormal chromosomes. When they are found, mothers have the option of continuing the pregnancy or undergoing an abortion. Another test, known as chorionic villus sampling (CVS), can be done earlier in a pregnancy, between the eighth and twelfth weeks, to test for

Levels of Analysis

Box 8–2

Fragile X

Researchers considered it a major breakthrough when they discovered that a certain type of mutation on the long arm of the X chromosome can produce mental retardation as well as many of the symptoms associated with pervasive developmental disorders (Meyer, Blum, Hitchcock, and Fortina, 1998). It is now routine for children with mental retardation, pervasive developmental disorder, or physical anomalies to be screened for mutations on their X chromosome. At the molecular level, there is an abnormal expansion or "repeat" of the genetic code when Fragile X occurs. This mutation is the most common genetic cause of mental retardation and autism in boys, with an incidence of 1 in 4,000. It appears to occur much less often in females. Fragile X syndrome is sometimes associated with physical abnormalities, such as prominent ears, a long narrow face and, in males, enlargement of the testicles.

Although Fragile X is caused by a genetic abnormality, the prenatal environment plays a significant role in the physical and behavioral aspects of the disorder. The most clear-cut evidence for the interaction between the prenatal environment and the Fragile X "diathesis" comes from studies of identical twins. For example, one study found that a pair of monozygotic twins with Fragile X syndrome differed in their genotype, such that one had more expansions than the other (Helderman-van den Enden et al., 1999). Further, it

appears to be the extent of the expansion that determines the severity of the psychological symptoms. In this twin pair, the boy with the greater mutations showed the most extreme phenotype. In other words, a larger number of repeats was related to more severe mental retardation and behavioral abnormalities. The findings of this study also illustrated something very interesting about the nature of how genes work to influence our behavior. The more severely disturbed twin showed the Fragile X mutation in all of his cells. In contrast, his brother only showed the mutation in some of his cells. So the twin who was less impaired had some cells with the mutation and other cells with a "premutation." Premutations on the X chromosome do not seem to be expressed, so they do not affect behavior. Geneticists use the term "mosaicism" to refer to the presence of cells with different genotypes in the same individual.

As we mentioned in Chapter 4, scientists do not yet know how or when differences between MZ twins in genetic mutations come about. They only know that such differences have their origins somewhere in the course of prenatal events. Their occurrence raises some interesting questions for scientists. Is it possible to reduce or prevent genetic mutations in the fertilized egg? If scientists were able to do so, could mutations like Fragile X be prevented? We may have at least tentative answers to these questions within your lifetime.

Down syndrome and other chromosomal abnormalities. A sampling of cells is taken via the mother's vagina and cervix, or through her abdominal wall. The advantage of CVS is that earlier detection of birth defects is possible, allowing for an earlier and perhaps less complicated abortion, if the mother chooses one. The disadvantage of CVS is that it is somewhat less accurate than amniocentesis.

There are a number of metabolic diseases that are associated with mental retardation. The most well known among these is ***phenylketonuria (PKU),*** a metabolic disease that occurs in roughly 1 out of 20,000 births. PKU results from the action of a recessive gene that is inherited from each parent. The infant cannot metabolize phenylalanine, an amino acid that is an essential component of proteins. As a result, phenylalanine and its derivative, phenyl pyruvic acid, build up in the body and rapidly poison the central nervous system, causing irreversible brain damage. About a third of such children cannot walk; nearly two-thirds never learn to talk; and more than half have IQ's that are below 20.

Carriers of PKU can be identified through genetic testing and can receive genetic counseling (American Academy of Pediatrics, 1996). In addition, it is possible to identify affected babies by a simple test of their urine shortly after birth. Provided they are kept on a diet that controls the level of phenylalanine in their system until age six, when the brain is more fully developed, their chances of surviving with good health and intelligence are fairly high.

We have described some specific genetic causes of mental retardation, but for many mentally retarded persons, there is no clear chromosomal abnormality (Hatton, 1998). Rather, there seem to be nonspecific factors in their genetic backgrounds that have contributed to their condition. Cognitive ability (as measured by IQ tests) appears, to some extent, to be passed through the genes. The IQ's of identical (MZ) twins reared together are more similar than the IQ's of DZ twins reared together (Bouchard, 1997). Some findings indicate that even MZ twins reared apart have more similar IQ's than DZ twins reared together (Scarr, 1975). The IQ's of adopted children correlate more powerfully with the IQ's of their biological parents than with the IQ's of their adoptive parents (Munzinger, 1975). These findings suggest that intelligence is partly inherited. But there may not be a specific genetic predisposition to mental retardation. Rather, it may be intellectual ability in general that is partially influenced by genetics.

Environmental Influences   Environment appears to play an important role in the development of intelligence. The prenatal environment to which the fetus is exposed can have a profound effect on intellectual development. Some chronic medical conditions in the mother, such as high blood pressure or diabetes, if untreated, can interfere with fetal brain development. Infectious disease, such as German measles (Rubella), can also cause neurodevelopmental abnormalities. In addition, drugs that the mother takes while pregnant can affect fetal development. ***Fetal alcohol syndrome (FAS)*** is a condition involving a variety of physical defects and deformities and mental retardation in fetuses exposed to alcohol through the mother's drinking during pregnancy. Children whose mothers severely abused alcohol during pregnancy have an average IQ in the 70s (Mattson, Riley, Gramling, Delis, and Lyons-Jones, 1997). It is unclear whether there is a safe amount of alcohol mothers can ingest during pregnancy.

Lower-income mothers are more likely to give birth to premature infants with low birth weights, and low birth weight is a risk factor for retardation (Kiely, Paneth, and Susser, 1981). Sometimes there are problems during the delivery process that interfere with the oxygen supply to the infant's brain. Children from impoverished backgrounds also face a number of postnatal environmental challenges to intellectual growth. Some of these children ingest toxic levels of lead by eating fragments of lead-based paint that peel off the walls of the old buildings in which they live. Such exposure to lead is associated with retarded intellectual growth. In addition, children from lower-class families are more likely than upper-class children to be malnourished, to receive poor health care, and to suffer from a variety of illnesses across childhood. Such factors impede the full expression of the child's intellectual abilities.

Physical abuse of children and accidental falls or blows to the head can also cause brain damage and mental retardation. Brain trauma can occur if an infant is simply shaken hard. Because the infant's head is large and heavy, the neck muscles are too weak to control the infant's head movements. The infant's soft brain literally bangs against the inside of the skull, causing bruising.

The term ***cultural-familial mental retardation*** has been used to refer to cases of retardation where there is no identified biological basis (Weisz, 1990). Many in the field assume that this form of retardation is caused by insufficient intellectual stimulation from the child's environment. This is because most of these children come from low-income homes where the parents have limited educational backgrounds and few resources. As we described in Chapter 4, being reared in a stimulating environment improves brain development and cognitive functions in animals. So it is very plausible that some forms of retardation in humans are due to environmental deprivation. But other researchers believe that genetic factors account for retardation in children from deprived backgrounds. In attempting to resolve this debate, researchers have examined the effects of improving the environments of disadvantaged youngsters.

Early intervention studies have focused on preventing retardation by enriching the experiences and environment of lower-class children who are at risk. Among the leading researchers in this field are Craig and Sharon Ramey (Ramey and Ramey, 1998). They have studied the effects of various intervention programs on the intellectual development of children from very low-income homes, some of whom were also premature or had low birth weight. Follow-up evaluations of the children who experienced one of their intensive early interventions showed significant advantages in academic performance seven to ten years after the intervention ended. At twelve years of age, the children who received early intervention in the form of an enriched preschool program scored above the control group on IQ and achievement tests by about 5 to 10 points. Greater parental involvement in the program was associated with higher gains.

TREATMENT

In the past, many children with mental retardation, especially those with physical disabilities, were placed in institutional settings. This is clearly not the best environment for any child; intellectual deficits are often exacerbated in institutional settings, and the children fail to gain the skills necessary for living effectively outside the institution (Birenbaum and Rei, 1979; Chinn, Drew, and Logan, 1979; Ohwaki and Stayton, 1978). Today, the rate of institutionalization of those with mental retardation has declined throughout the Western world (Bouras and Szymanski, 1997). Youngsters with severe retardation are now educated in regional facilities that offer a broad range of educational programs to prepare them for independent living. These programs try to help the children learn the basic skills they need to care for

themselves. Children with mental retardation also benefit from help with acquiring social skills that enable them to interact more easily with people in school and community settings (Elliott and Gresham, 1993). As adults, most people with mental retardation live in the community, either with family members or in structured group homes or halfway houses.

Today, most school districts in the United States have special educational opportunities for children with mental retardation. Special educational programs usually begin in preschool and extend through the high school years (Wacker, Berg, and Harding, 1999). Children with mental retardation often have defects in language skills that manifest themselves even before the child enters school. Training in language necessitates that the required sounds be demonstrated, and that the child be rewarded for closer and closer approximations to normal speech. Such training, whether conducted by professionals or by parents who have been trained to do such teaching, can be very useful in helping the child to communicate more effectively. Behavioral training methods have also been used successfully to teach self-care skills, wherein the children are rewarded for performing closer and closer approximations of simple skills as well as more complex behaviors (Watson and Uzzell, 1981).

As we indicated earlier, many children, particularly those who are mildly handicapped, are not identified as requiring assistance until they enter school. There is considerable continuing controversy about the kind of remedial help they need once they are in school. One view holds that they should be "mainstreamed," that is educated with other schoolchildren, in the same classes and with the same teachers, since the vast majority of them will ultimately live with their "normal" peers (Snell, 1998). Another view holds that the needs of those with intellectual disabilities are so different from those of their normal peers that they need to be educated separately, with separate teaching methods and different schedules and curricula. According to this view, the education of children with mental retardation proceeds best when they are segregated in different institutions, or at least in separate classes. The fact is that a combination of both regular classroom experiences and special education approaches may be optimal (Mills, Cole, Jenkins, and Dale, 1998). And regardless of their views on mainstreaming, all would agree that there is no substitute for a good teacher. This is particularly true when it comes to children with mental retardation. It is important that the teachers who work with these children have both a commitment to special education and expectations that their students can learn.

Learning Disorders

Much more common than mental retardation are the *learning disorders,* difficulties that reflect developmental delays, mainly in the areas of language and mathematical skills (Lyon et al., 1994; Lyon, 1996). Children with learning disorders are considered to be learning disabled. Like youngsters with mental retardation, they are entitled to special education services under the law.

DSM-IV lists three main types of learning disorders: reading disorder, mathematics disorder, and disorders of written expression. In contrast to people with mental retardation, individuals with learning disorders are delayed in *specific* cognitive skills, not in all areas of mental functioning. Moreover, children with learning disorders do not have the severe social problems that characterize those with pervasive developmental disorders. However, learning disorders occur frequently in combination with other difficulties, and in fact, may spawn them.

To function well in industrial societies, people must be able to learn a language, to learn to read and to do simple arithmetic. Because of this, modern industrial societies make education compulsory for about ten years of a child's life. As in most developmental matters, children progress in their education at different speeds. A certain amount of lagging behind is to be expected of many children some of the time. But when a child is significantly below the expected level, as indexed by the child's schooling, age, and IQ, then the matter is viewed as a psychological problem. For children between the ages of eight and thirteen—the critical ages for the acquisition and implementation of academic skills—a significant problem may exist if a child is more than two years behind his or her age level.

Usually learning disorders are not identified until the child enters elementary school. Often within the first few years of grade school, the teacher and parents notice that there is a discrepancy between the child's actual academic performance and the level of performance one might expect based on the child's intellectual capacity. Psychological testing is usually the next step. If the child's scores on a standardized measure of intelligence are in the normal range or above, but the achievement scores are significantly lower, there is reason to suspect a learning disorder.

READING DIFFICULTIES

Of all the learning disorders, reading difficulties have been studied most (Morgan and Hynd, 1998). Reading disorder, or *dyslexia,* as it is sometimes called, is the most common of all the learning disorders, affecting about 2 percent of school-aged children. As a group, poor readers are late in acquiring language, are poor spellers, and are more likely to have a history of reading difficulty in their families. Many children who have reading difficulties also have trouble with other domains of learning. More than three times as many boys as girls suffer serious reading difficulties. Children with severe reading difficulties at age ten are at increased risk of other psychological disorders, particularly behavior disorders.

Theories of the causes of reading disorder focus on various aspects of brain development (Pennington, 1999). One dominant view is that dyslexia is caused by a delay in the development of the brain. This implies that the individual will eventually "catch up." Another perspective is that there is actually an abnormality in the structure of the brain. One prevalent theory is that there is some abnormality in the "wiring" of the left hemisphere (Morgan and Hynd, 1998). Researchers have just begun to do neuroimaging studies of the brains of people with dyslexia. It is likely that this research will shed more light on the causes of the disorder.

A combination of training in reading skills and behavior therapy designed to maintain a child's interest in learning has proven effective for many children with reading disabilities. This training must start early in a child's school career and be maintained throughout the school years for the child to sustain the gains that have been made and to continue to improve. It is crucial, therefore, that reading problems be identified early in the elementary school years. Most current programs for training children with dyslexia to read emphasize helping the child develop strategies for breaking words down into smaller parts ("phonemes") and distinguishing the sounds they make (Wise, Olson, Ring, and Johnson, 1998). Other programs give the child intense experience in scanning moving text to improve their reading speed (Krischer, Coenen, Heckner, and Hoeppner, 1994). Computer programs have also proven to be very useful in providing systematic training in reading skills. Many programs for enhancing reading skills are available for use on home computers.

The social implications of serious reading problems are disturbing. Poor readers who are of average intelligence rarely read books or newspapers. Some aspire to little that involves reading and, therefore, they often fail to graduate from high school. Children with reading disabilities sometimes emerge from the school system handicapped educationally, socially, and economically, and their employment opportunities may be limited. Their self-esteem often suffers because they view themselves as lacking a basic skill. But on the other side of the coin, a surprising proportion of children with learning disabilities grow up to be highly successful adults (Reiff, Gerber, and Ginsberg, 1997). These may be people with highly creative minds, strong motivation, and/ or exceptional interpersonal skills. We should probably expect to see an even larger proportion of people with learning disabilities achieve high levels of success now that computer technology can be used to help them overcome some of their difficulties.

AN EDUCATIONAL OR PSYCHOLOGICAL DISORDER?

The learning disorders are often correlated with, or give rise to, a host of distinctly psychological symptoms. It is not uncommon for youngsters with learning disabilities to express frustration and sadness, to withdraw, or to act out aggressively. It is mainly for this reason that these developmental disorders are considered psychological, rather than educational. But fundamentally, these are skills disabilities; they are in the domain of education rather than psychology and psychiatry. And many believe that they should continue to be viewed that way (Garmezy, 1977).

The argument is not without merit. There is no evidence, for example, that psychological treatment or drugs have any positive effect on say, the developmental reading disorder. Calling the difficulty a *psychological* disorder in fact may lead teachers to believe that a reading disability is outside of their sphere, leaving the child helped neither by the teacher nor by the psychologist. Moreover, terming reading delay a psychological disorder may stigmatize the child without contributing a solution to the problem. Indeed, it may simply compound the difficulties. Consider the case of Nelson Rockefeller, former governor of New York and vice president of the United States. Rockefeller had a severe reading dis-

ability that handicapped him from childhood through adulthood. Even when he was an undergraduate, friends and others had to read his textbooks to him. Throughout his career, he much preferred oral communications to written ones. His problems were difficult enough to deal with. Would his life have been made easier if those difficulties had been described as a severe psychological disorder of childhood? Indeed, could he have been elected to high office if he had been so diagnosed?

Eating and Habit Disorders

In this section we discuss disorders whose primary symptoms involve a disruption in the individual's patterns of eating, elimination, movement, or communication. The *eating disorders* can occur at either extreme: excessive consumption of food or dramatic reductions in food intake. Both can have life-threatening consequences. The *habit disorders* include disorders of elimination, movement, and communication. These are very basic domains in human development; acquiring socially appropriate habits with respect to these behaviors is of critical importance for healthy development. Problems with elimination, referred to as enuresis and encopresis, can have significant psychosocial causes and consequences. Similarly, the abilities to communicate clearly and maintain conscious control over movements are central to the child's functioning in society. In these domains, we will discuss stuttering and tic disorders.

Eating Disorders: Anorexia and Bulimia

There are two major categories of eating disorders: anorexia nervosa and bulimia. Although these two disorders have distinct features, they share some common symptoms, and, possibly, common etiologies (see Table 8–5). They also show a similar developmental course. They tend to begin in adolescence and usually don't extend past early adulthood.

The main symptoms of *anorexia nervosa* are an intense fear of gaining weight despite being much underweight, the refusal to maintain body weight at or above a minimal expected weight for one's age and height, and a distorted body image. Even when they are emaciated, people with anorexia often feel fat.

TABLE 8–5

MODELS OF EATING DISORDERS

Model	Proposed Cause	Effect or Process
Sociocultural model of anorexia and bulimia	Cultural emphasis on thinness as ideal, combined with increase in women's average weight in recent years, leads to poor body image in many	Some women respond by dieting excessively; people who are overweight and those who enter puberty early may be especially vulnerable
Stress reduction model of bulimia	Stress and anxiety	Those who develop bulimia seek short-term relief of stress in eating, then relief through purging of the distress caused by eating
Autonomy/control model of anorexia	Overcontrolling family leads to fierce need for autonomy and difficulty communicating emotions	Eating becomes the one area of her life the person with anorexia can control; her control over it defines her self-esteem

There appear to be two subtypes of those with anorexia: restricters and purgers. **Restricters** are thin primarily because they refuse to eat. **Purgers** also refuse to eat much of the time, but when they do eat, use vomiting and laxatives to purge what they have eaten. Often, the disorder is accompanied by a variety of other physical changes. The consequences of anorexia can be severe: blood pressure and body temperature may be lowered, life-threatening cardiac arrhythmias may occur, bone growth can be retarded, and anemia is common. Most importantly, the low level of serum potassium caused by starvation can lead to irregularities in the heart rate that may cause death. Amenorrhea, the absence of menstrual periods, is common among girls or women with anorexia.

About 95 percent of those with anorexia are female. The prevalence of this disorder appears to be rising, such that about 1 in 100 females suffer from it (Amara and Cerrato, 1996; Fairburn, Welch, and Hay, 1993). The reason anorexia is considered a disorder of childhood is that its onset is usually in early to late adolescence, although it can begin at any age. The following case illustrates some of the common features of anorexia:

Frieda had always been a shy, sensitive girl who gave little cause for concern at home or in school. She was bright and did well academically, although she had few friends. In early adolescence, she had been somewhat overweight and had been teased by her family that she would never get a boyfriend unless she lost some weight. She reacted to this teasing by withdrawing and becoming very touchy. Her parents had to be careful about what they said. If offended, Frieda would throw a tantrum and march off to her room—hardly the behavior they expected from their bright and sensitive fifteen-year-old.

The woman on the left suffers from anorexia nervosa and is starving to death as surely as the person on the right, who suffers from famine.

DSM-IV Criteria

Anorexia Nervosa

A. Refusal to maintain body weight at or above a minimally normal weight for age and height (e.g., weight loss leading to maintenance of body weight less than 85% of that expected; or failure to make expected weight gain during period of growth, leading to body weight less than 85% of that expected).

B. Intense fear of gaining weight or becoming fat, even though underweight.

C. Disturbance in the way in which one's body weight or shape is experienced, undue influence of body weight or shape on self-evaluation, or denial of the seriousness of the current low body weight.

D. In postmenarcheal females, amenorrhea, i.e., the absence of at least three consecutive menstrual cycles. (A woman is considered to have amenorrhea if her periods occur only following hormone, e.g., estrogen, administration.)

SOURCE: APA, DSM-IV, 1994.

Frieda began dieting. Initially, her family was pleased, but gradually her parents sensed that all was not well. Mealtimes became battle times. Frieda hardly ate at all. Under pressure, she would take her meals to her room and later, having said that she had eaten everything, her mother would find food hidden away untouched. When her mother caught her deliberately inducing vomiting after a meal, she insisted they go to the family physician. He found that Frieda had stopped menstruating a few months earlier. Not fooled by the loose, floppy clothes that Frieda was wearing, he insisted on carrying out a full physical examination. Her emaciated body told him as much as he needed to know, and he arranged for Frieda's immediate hospitalization.

People with anorexia nervosa are preoccupied with body image, as illustrated in this painting made by a patient during the severest stage of her illness.

Bingeing on food is not uncommon; about 24 percent of white women report that they have done so at some point in their life (Sullivan, Bulik, and Kendler, 1998). Among college students, as many as 30 percent say they binge at least twice a month, and 16 to 20 percent say they binge once per week (Schotte and Stunkard, 1987). People with *bulimia,* however, are excessively self-critical about their binges, and more generally about their physical appearance. As a result, they attempt to purge after a binge, by self-induced vomiting, by misusing laxatives, diuretics, or other medications, by fasting, or by excessive exercising. Often the binge/purge episodes take hours out of each day, and become habitual. People with bulimia often wish they could restrict their food intake better. Nonetheless, people with bulimia find themselves bingeing, often on large quantities of food, with a sense that they completely lack control over their eating. The sense of shame, distress, and helplessness that follows these episodes is often overwhelming. It is not surprising that many of those who suffer from bulimia also suffer from severe depression.

As with anorexia, most people who suffer from bulimia are women. Although poor eating patterns may be rampant among adolescents and young adults, only about 1 percent of persons in this age range will qualify for a diagnosis of bulimia (Fairburn and Wilson, 1993; Kendler et al., 1995; Lucas, Beard, O'Fallon, and Kurlan, 1991). Some people with bulimia are excessively thin, but many are of normal weight. Bulimia is still a very dangerous disorder physically, however. Stomach acid vomited up can lead to severe tooth decay (Muscari, 1998). Many women with bulimia also experience menstrual problems. Frequent vomiting and other types of

DSM-IV Criteria

Bulimia Nervosa

A. Recurrent episodes of binge eating. An episode of binge eating is characterized by both of the following: (1) eating, in a discrete period of time (e.g., within any 2-hour period), an amount of food that is definitely larger than most people would eat during a similar period of time and under similar circumstances; (2) a sense of lack of control over eating during the episode (e.g., a feeling that one cannot stop eating or control what or how much one is eating).

B. Recurrent inappropriate compensatory behavior in order to prevent weight gain, such as self-induced vom-

iting; misuse of laxatives, diuretics, enemas, or other medications; fasting; or excessive exercise.

C. The binge eating and inappropriate compensatory behaviors both occur, on average, at least twice a week for 3 months.

D. Self-evaluation is unduly influenced by body shape and weight.

E. The disturbance does not occur exclusively during episodes of Anorexia Nervosa.

SOURCE: APA, DSM-IV, 1994.

---

purging can lead to severe loss of body fluids and an imbalance in electrolytes, which regulate the heart. Such an imbalance can result in heart failure.

THE CAUSES OF ANOREXIA AND BULIMIA

Some researchers believe that both anorexia and bulimia are variants of a mood disorder (Agras and Kirkley, 1986; Lilienfield et al., 1998). Dysphoria and depression are common among both those with anorexia and those with bulimia, and the families of people with eating disorders often have histories of depression and anxiety disorders (Hudson, Pope, Jonas, and Yurgelun-Todd, 1987). But it is unclear whether depression is a cause or consequence of eating disorders. Similarly, although the metabolic changes that occur in anorexia have led some researchers to suggest that a malfunction of the hypothalamus is the cause (Licinio, Wong, and Gold, 1996), it is not known whether changes in hypothalamic functioning precede or follow self-starvation by those with anorexia.

There are a number of psychosocial theories of the eating disorders (Becker, Grinspoon, Klibanski, and Herzog, 1999). Both anorexia and bulimia have increased in prevalence in recent decades, and are more common in developed countries than in underdeveloped countries (Garfinkel and Garner, 1982; McCarthy, 1990). There are also ethnic group differences in the prevalence of eating disorders in the

United States. Fewer black women than white women have eating disorders (Edwards-Hewitt and Gray, 1993). These findings have led many researchers to argue that cultural norms play a role in the etiology of these disorders. In the case of ethnic differences in the United States, for example, thinness is viewed as more desirable by the white major-

Women may be vulnerable to a poor body image and hence to eating disorders because of Western society's "thin ideal," as shown by pervasive images of very thin models throughout the culture.

ity culture than by the African-American culture. There is no doubt that thinness is considered a virtue in American society, especially for females. The "ideal" shape for women, as indicated by television stars, fashion models, and winners of beauty pageants has become thinner over the last forty years. Over the same time period, there has been an increase in the average weight of women due to improvements in nutrition. Thus, women are being told to become thin when it is increasingly hard to do.

Some women succumb to this pressure by going on extremely restrictive diets. These women may be especially sensitive to society's messages about thinness because they are naturally slightly heavier than their peers. In addition, girls who enter puberty earlier than their peers also appear more vulnerable to a poor body image (Brooks-Gunn, 1988). Restrained eating can lead to both perceived and real physical deprivation, however, which in turn leads to a breakdown of restraint and overeating (Herman and Mack, 1975). Many women who develop bulimia have a history of going on extremely restrictive diets, which are chronically stressful and frustrating. These women, when they break their dietary rules, tend to lose their sense of control over their eating and end up bingeing. Then the guilt and fear of fatness that follow the bingeing can lead them to purge (Cooper, Todd, and Wells, 1998; Garner, 1993). Stress reduction models of bulimia suggest that bingers eat when faced with stressful circumstances to escape anxiety and distress (Heatherton and Baumeister, 1991). They focus on the short-term gratification of food in lieu of their long-term goals for weight control, and end up eating large amounts of food even though they are not hungry. Purging is then a way of reducing the distress that the binge has caused.

Some of the psychosocial theories of anorexia suggest that it arises from a deep need for autonomy, which comes from being in an overcontrolling family (Bruch, 1982; Hart and Kenny, 1997). These theories hold that the parents of girls with anorexia are overinvolved in their daughters' lives, not allowing them adequate independence or a sense of self apart from their role in the family. The parents also tend to restrict shows of emotion or conflict and tend to demand perfection from their children, so that the adolescent girl is not allowed to express her needs or her anger at her parents. Eventually, she may discover that she can control at least one aspect of her life— her eating. Gaining complete control over her food

intake becomes all important, the way the girl defines her self-esteem. Moreover, some females who develop eating disorders have a history of sexual abuse, usually by a family member (Kanter, Williams, and Cummings, 1992). In such a case, the eating disorder may develop as a result of a distorted body image or low self-esteem caused by the abuse, or out of a need to control some aspect of her life. In the meantime, her weight loss may lead to expressions of concern from her parents—attention that the girl may not be getting in any other way.

Others are convinced that the social influences on eating disorders come from popular culture. Joan Brumberg of Cornell University has documented the way our modern industrial society has caused so many young women to view their body as the most important feature of their identity (Brumberg, 1998). She traces the links between this "body fetish" and the development of eating disorders in Western cultures. Brumberg and others believe that the media have been the primary vehicle for conveying the values that promote an obsession with thinness. But it is only recently that researchers have obtained convincing evidence that the media does indeed have a direct impact on the rate of eating disorders in any culture. In one study, Anne Becker, a psychiatrist at Harvard University, interviewed young girls on the island of Fiji in the South Pacific (*New York Times International,* May 20, 1999). Fiji is a relatively small island, and the inhabitants had virtually no access to television prior to 1995. Becker began collecting data in 1995, just one month after the introduction of television to the island. In response to a questionnaire administered in 1995, only 3 percent of the girls said they had ever induced vomiting to control their weight. But in 1998, 15 percent of the girls said they had induced vomiting. Between 1995 and 1998, there was also a significant rise in the Fijian girls' average score on a measure of risk for eating disorders. In 1995, only 13 percent scored at the high end of the eating disorders scale; in 1998, the proportion rose to 29 percent. During the same three-year period, there was a 50 percent rise in the number of girls who described themselves as "too big or fat." What shows were these girls watching? Becker and her colleagues found that the most popular shows included *Xena, Warrior Princess; Beverly Hills 90210;* and *Melrose Place,* all of which had thin female leads.

These results support Brumberg's contention that eating disorders are, at least in part, a consequence of cultural influences that make young women aspire to meet a standard of "beauty" that is unrealistic for many of them. How do we change this? Assuming that the media promote images that sell products, ranging from shampoo to TV sitcoms, consumers may hold the power to change the media's promotion of thinness.

TREATMENT FOR EATING DISORDERS

Early approaches to therapy with the families of patients with eating disorders had a psychoanalytic orientation and focused on the ways family members control each other and express conflict (Minuchin, Rosman, and Baker, 1980). More recent approaches rely heavily on behavioral and cognitive therapy techniques to help the family reduce the patient's symptoms (Garner and Garfinkel, 1997). Cognitive-behavioral therapies have proven especially effective for treating bulimia (Agras, 1993; see Table 8–6). Therapists teach patients to identify environmental triggers for bingeing, to introduce feared foods into their diets while controlling the amount they eat, and to identify and change distorted cognitions about food intake, weight, and body shape. Agras and his colleagues found that 56 percent of patients with bulimia cease bingeing and purging by the end of treatment with cognitive-behavioral ther-

apy (Agras, Schneider, Arnow, Raeburn, and Telch, 1989a, 1989b). Although the success rate of cognitive-behavioral therapy for anorexia is not as high, it is effective in some cases (Fairburn, Shafran and Cooper, 1999).

Antidepressant drugs, in particular the SSRI's (for example, Prozac), are helpful for some people with eating disorders, but many patients with anorexia do not show a significant response to these drugs (Mayer and Walsh, 1998; see Table 8–7). Whether these drugs relieve an underlying biological dysfunction that is the cause of the eating disorder, or simply make it easier for the women to participate in psychotherapy and to change their eating habits is unclear. Most clinicians agree, however, that psychotherapy is also necessary for eating disorders, even for people who are taking antidepressant drugs (Barker and O'Neil, 1999).

Patients with anorexia often do not enter therapy until the anorexia reaches a crisis point, at which time the patient is dangerously ill. It may be necessary to hospitalize the patient to stabilize her health. Even then, some people with anorexia will protest that they have no problem, and as many as 30 percent will refuse treatment (Crisp, 1980). Obviously, force-feeding a patient in the hospital can tap into the very autonomy issues that are supporting her anorexia. The family may also deny that there is

TABLE 8–6

BULIMIA NERVOSA

Treatment

	Interpersonal Therapy	Cognitive-Behavioral Therapy (CBT)	Antidepressant Drugs Alone	Cognitive-Behavioral Therapy and Antidepressant Drugs
Improvement	about 75% at least moderately improved	about 85% at least moderately improved	about 60% at least moderately improved	similar to CBT alone
Relapse*	moderate	low to moderate	high	low to moderate
Side Effects	unclear	unclear	moderate	moderate
Cost	moderately expensive	moderately expensive	inexpensive	moderately expensive
Time Scale†	months	weeks/months	weeks/months	weeks/months
Overall	**good**	**good**	**useful**	**good**

*Relapse after discontinuation of treatment.
†Time to achieve maximal effect.
SOURCE: Based on Mitchell, Raymond, and Specker, 1993, pp. 229–47; Seligman, 1994, Chapter 12; Wilson and Fairburn, 1998; drug data updated with Goldstein, Wilson, Ashcroft, and Al-Banna, 1999.

TABLE 8–7

Treatment

ANOREXIA NERVOSA

	Outpatient Family Therapy	*Outpatient Behavior Therapy*	*Outpatient Cognitive Therapy*	*Outpatient Dietary Advice*
Improvement	about 70% moderately improved	about 65% at least moderately improved	about 65% at least moderately improved	about 40% with moderate improvement; effective for restoring body weight with improved sexual and social function
Relapse★	moderate	moderate	moderate	moderate
Side Effects	unclear	unclear	unclear	unclear
Cost	moderately expensive	moderately inexpensive	inexpensive	inexpensive
Time Scale†	months	months	months	weeks/months
Overall	**good**	**good**	**good**	**marginal**

★Relapse after discontinuation of treatment.
†Time to achieve maximal effect.
SOURCE: Based on Wilson and Fairburn, 1998; Yates, 1990; revised with Geist, Heinman, Stephens, Davis, and Katzman, 2000; Hsu, 1980.

anything wrong within the family, identifying the patient as their only "problem." Thus, anorexia can be a difficult disorder to treat. Clinicians and researchers are continuing to explore combinations of drug and psychological therapies that will be most effective.

Elimination Disorders

For most children in Western society, the first major confrontation with social expectations for impulse control occurs in the context of potty training. By the age of three and one-half years, the majority of children gain bladder control. But sometimes things don't go as planned. ***Enuresis (bed-wetting)*** is arbitrarily defined as involuntary urination at least twice a month for children between five and six, and once a month for those who are older. It is estimated that between 3 million and 7 million school-aged children in the United States suffer from sleep-related enuresis (Sheldon, 1996). After elementary school, the proportion of children who have difficulty controlling urination, either during the day or while in bed, drops markedly. At age twelve, only 8 percent of boys and 4 percent of girls have enuresis (Friman and Warzak, 1990). Thus, there is a marked decrease in enuresis with age, and most who continue to have the problem into late childhood are males.

The problems of the child with enuresis are compounded by the social consequences of the disorder (Goin, 1998). Parents object to soiled clothes and bedding, and they commonly stigmatize the child as immature. Schoolmates and friends are likely to tease the child who has an "accident," especially when those accidents are regular occurrences. Children with enuresis find it awkward to accept overnight invitations from friends or to go to camp. These social consequences may create a fertile ground for other more serious psychological problems.

Encopresis, the failure to control bowel movements, is much less common than enuresis. Children are not diagnosed with encopresis unless they are four years old or older. The disorder is often associated with physical health problems (Geffken and Monaco, 1996). But when there are no specific physical causes, encopresis is frequently associated with conduct disorder or oppositional defiant disorder. To date, there has been relatively little research on the causes and treatments for encopresis.

CAUSES OF ENURESIS

A distinction is made between primary enuresis, where the child never attains bladder control, and secondary enuresis, which occurs after the child has achieved control. Some assume that primary enuresis

DSM-IV Criteria

Enuresis

A. Repeated voiding of urine into bed or clothes (whether involuntary or intentional).

B. The behavior is clinically significant as manifested by either a frequency of twice a week for at least 3 consecutive months or the presence of clinically significant distress or impairment in social, academic (occupational), or other important areas of functioning.

C. Chronological age is at least 5 years (or equivalent developmental level).

D. The behavior is not due exclusively to the direct physi-

ological effect of a substance (e.g., a diuretic) or a general medical condition (e.g., diabetes, spina bifida, a seizure disorder).

Specify type:
Nocturnal Only
Diurnal Only
Nocturnal and Diurnal

SOURCE: APA, DSM-IV, 1994.

---

is caused by a biological abnormality, whereas psychosocial factors, such as stress, contribute to secondary enuresis.

There is evidence that biological factors do, indeed, contribute to enuresis. Behavior genetic studies indicate that the predisposition to enuresis can be inherited. Approximately 75 percent of children with enuresis have first-degree relatives who have or have had enuresis, and the concordance for enuresis is higher in identical (MZ) twins than in fraternal (DZ) twins (Abe, Oda, Ikenaga, and Yamada, 1993). So, the more similar a person's genetic blueprint is to a person with enuresis, the more likely the individual will also have enuresis. Recent linkage studies have shown an association between nocturnal enuresis and certain regions on chromosomes 8, 12, and 13 (von Gontard and Lehmkuhl, 1997), but additional research is needed to confirm this.

Physical illnesses can also contribute to enuresis (Goin, 1998). It is not uncommon for children to develop enuresis after experiencing an illness that disrupts their daily schedule and sleep patterns. The link between physical illness and the onset of enuresis may be a direct consequence of a decrease in the physical control of bladder function. But it could also be a result of stress. A clear-cut example of the role of stress is provided by Dollinger (1985), who studied the effects of a tragedy in which a child was struck by lightning and killed. He collected information about fifth- and sixth-graders who were aware of the incident. While most of these children reported feelings of anxiety, especially during storms, the most disturbed children experienced nocturnal enuresis.

These findings and others suggest that stress can trigger the onset of enuresis.

Some researchers have suggested that children with enuresis may have less sensitivity to the cues that signal bladder extensions, especially during sleep (Arajaervi, Kivalo, and Nyberg, 1977). In other words, their bodies may not "hear" the biological alarm clock that signals that it is time to get up and go to the bathroom. The failure to wake up may result from a tendency for the child to remain in deep stages of sleep for a longer period of time than the average child (Sheldon, 1996). As described below, the effectiveness of behavioral approaches in treating enuresis lend support to this idea.

TREATMENT

Some drugs, namely the antidiuretics or antidepressants such as imipramine and the SSRI's, can suppress bed-wetting, at least temporarily (Wilens, Spencer, Frazier, and Biederman, 1998). But often children begin to wet the bed again once the drug is stopped (see Table 8–8). Nonetheless, even a few dry nights can be an enormous morale-booster to a child with enuresis, particularly if it allows the child to visit friends overnight or to go to camp without fear of embarrassment. Recall, however, that antidepressant drugs can have side effects, such as weight loss and cardiovascular problems. For some children, the side effects outweigh the usefulness of the medication.

Behavioral treatments have been quite successful with enuresis, and the effects may be more lasting than drug treatment (Goin, 1998). Most common is

TABLE 8–8

Treatment

ENURESIS

	Behavior Therapy	*Desmopressin*★
Improvement	about 70–98% significantly improved or cured	about 25% significantly improved or cured
Relapse[†]	low	high
Side Effects	low	mild
Cost	moderate	inexpensive
Time Scale[‡]	months	months
Overall	**excellent**	**useful**

★An antidiuretic drug used to treat enuresis.
[†]Relapse after discontinuation of treatment.
[‡]Time to achieve maximal effect.
SOURCE: Based on Thompson and Rey, 1995, pp. 266–71; revised with Moffitt, 1997b.

a procedure that was first described over fifty years ago (Mowrer and Mowrer, 1938). The child sleeps in his or her own bed. Beneath the sheets is a special pad which, when moistened by urine, completes a harmless electric circuit that sounds a bell and awakens the child, who then goes to the toilet. A number of studies have shown that approximately 75 percent of children treated by the "bell and pad" method gain bladder control during the two-week treatment period. There is a relapse rate of up to 35 percent, but that can be reduced to 15 to 25 percent by giving a longer treatment period or by offering an additional "booster" dose of treatment (Doleys, 1979; Houts, 1991). Behavioral treatments are most effective with children who are under the age of twelve (Bath, Morton, Uing, and Williams, 1996).

Stuttering

Stuttering or stammering is a marked disorder in speech rhythm. While most children go through transient periods of hesitating over particular words, the dysrhythmia is both more pronounced and more prolonged in those who are regarded as stutterers. Often, it is the initial consonants in certain words that cause real problems. "I d-d-d . . . don't know what to d-d-d-do!" is a typically problematic sentence that is often accompanied by a flushed or pained face.

About 1 percent of all children are diagnosed with stuttering, and another 4 to 5 percent experience transient stuttering for a period of up to six

months. Usually the signs are first apparent by the time the child is three years old. For unknown reasons, boys outnumber girls by four to one. The causes of stuttering are still unclear, but abnormalities in the left hemisphere motor regions are suspected (Ludlow, 1999). Genetic factors also play a role in stuttering. Children who stutter are more likely to have a biological relative who also has the problem (Ambrose, Yairi and Cox, 1993). As in many other physical disorders, there are psychological consequences. Children who stutter tax the patience of other children and teachers. They are often taunted and ostracized by peers. Teachers may avoid calling on them in class, with the result that their academic interest and performance may flag. It is not surprising that most children who stutter persistently also suffer from anxiety, and many become depressed (Watson and Miller, 1994).

TREATMENT

By the time a child who stutters seeks help, he or she is likely experiencing considerable tension that both results from the speech problem and magnifies it. Consequently, most treatments of stuttering combine psychotherapeutic counseling with specific reeducational techniques. The latter serve to distract the stutterer from his own speech while training him to speak fluently.

Three techniques seem particularly promising. The first is called **delayed auditory feedback** and involves hearing one's own speech played back over

DSM-IV Criteria

Stuttering

A. Disturbance in the normal fluency and time patterning of speech (inappropriate for the individual's age), characterized by frequent occurrences of one or more of the following: (1) sound and syllable repetitions, (2) sound prolongations, (3) interjections, (4) broken words (e.g., pauses within a word), (5) audible or silent blocking (filled or unfilled pauses in speech), (6) circumlocutions (word substitutions to avoid problematic words), (7) words produced with an excess of physical tension, (8) monosyllabic whole-word repetitions (e.g., "I-I-I-I see him").

B. The disturbance in fluency interferes with academic or occupational achievement or social communication.

C. If a speech-motor or sensory deficit is present, the speech difficulties are in excess of those usually associated with these problems.

SOURCE: APA, DSM-IV, 1994.

---

earphones at about a .1 second delay. When fluent speakers hear their own speech delayed in this manner, they stutter enormously. But when speakers who stutter receive delayed auditory feedback, they become nearly fluent. These paradoxical findings suggest that feedback from one's own speech contributes to stuttering, and that any interference in that feedback will reduce it. The problem, of course, is affecting feedback outside of the treatment situation. Delayed auditory feedback works quite well in the clinic but transfers hardly at all outside of the clinic.

Shadowing is a variant of the delayed auditory feedback technique. Here, the therapist reads from a book, and the stutterer repeats the therapist's words shortly after the latter has spoken them (and without reading the words). This requires the stutterer to concentrate carefully on what the therapist is saying, and in the process, to ignore his own stuttering. Several studies indicate that shadowing may be useful in alleviating stuttering (Cherry and Sayers, 1956; Kondas, 1997).

A third method, called *syllable-timed speech,* requires stutterers to speak in time to a metronome or beeper that sounds in an earpiece. This procedure, too, may have the effect of distracting the stutterer from his own stuttering. Combined with a system of rewards for maintaining nonstuttering, this procedure has been found relatively effective in reducing stuttering (Ingham, Andrews, and Winkler, 1972; Meyer and Mair, 1963).

Whether it is begun in childhood or adulthood, treatment for stuttering results in significant improvement, on average, for about 70 percent of all cases (Conture, 1996). Considering the tremendous com-munication problems that stuttering can produce, the available treatments are certainly worth pursuing.

Tic Disorders

A *tic* is a repetitive, involuntary movement or vocalization that has a very sudden onset. Examples of motor tics are intense eye blinking, neck jerking, and grimacing. Commonly occurring vocal tics are grunting, sniffing, and barking. Although individuals with tics do not manifest them all of the time, the occurrence of tics is not under voluntary control. They tend to worsen with stress and rarely occur during sleep. Occasional tics are relatively common in children, with 12 to 24 percent showing mild tics in certain situations (Ollendick and Ollendick, 1990). Tics occur at a high rate in several psychological disorders, but the most widely recognized disorder that involves tics is Tourette's disorder.

TOURETTE'S DISORDER

The chief symptoms of Tourette's disorder are multiple motor tics and at least one or more vocal tics. The tics occur many times a day. In order to meet the DSM-IV criteria for Tourette's disorder, the individual must manifest the symptoms for at least a year and the symptoms must cause distress or some impairment of functioning. Also, the diagnostic criteria specify that the disorder has an onset before eighteen years of age. Typically, the child's age at initial onset is about seven years old. According to DSM-IV, Tourette's disorder has a prevalence rate of .04 to .05

percent, however more recent estimates of the prevalence of Tourette's range from .5 to 1 percent (Zohar et al., 1999). Many youngsters with Tourette's also suffer from obsessive-compulsive behaviors. It is much more common in boys than girls. A typical case is that of Eddie:

> Eddie first showed a motor tic when he was six years old. He would blink his eyes very hard ten to twenty times, then let out a few soft grunts. After observing this several times, Eddie's parents started asking him what he was doing and encouraged him to stop. Although Eddie would say "O.K.," as if he had intentional control, there was no reduction in the frequency of his tics. Instead, the tics became lengthier and more frequent. Several weeks later, Eddie's eye blinking tic was accompanied by repeated vocalizations of a single word. Usually, while the eye tic was occurring, Eddie would repeatedly say "O.K.," as if he was anticipating his parents' response to the tic. It quickly became apparent to Eddie's parents that the tics were not under his control. Further, the tics would increase when Eddie was stressed. Eddie's parents scheduled an appointment with the pediatrician. By the time they took him to the doctor one week later, he had acquired several more vocal tics. The most disturbing one was the repetition of four-letter words during his eye blinking.
>
> Eddie's pediatrician suspected Tourette's disorder and referred Eddie to a specialist for further evaluation. The diagnosis was confirmed, and Eddie was treated with an antipsychotic drug. The tics continued through early adolescence, although they were less intense when Eddie was on the medication. He had to attend special classes for children with learning problems. This was not because Eddie had any academic deficits, but rather because his behavior disrupted the other students. This was especially true of his vocal tics, which involved curse words.
>
> As Eddie approached fourteen years of age, the tics gradually decreased in frequency and severity. By the time he was fifteen, Eddie's tics were so rare his dose of antipsychotic medication was reduced, then withdrawn altogether. He returned to a regular classroom setting in the tenth grade.

The most dramatic and troublesome of the symptoms associated with Tourette's disorder is *coprolalia,* the repetition of socially unacceptable words. Although coprolalia only occurs in a minority of patients with Tourette's, it is so disruptive in social settings that it has received a great deal of attention in the media. In Eddie's case, the coprolalia resulted in his attending special classes. Fortunately, like Eddie, most children with Tourette's show diminished symptoms over time. No one knows why this is the case, although it has been suggested that it may be due to the maturation of certain brain circuits that connect subcortical and cortical regions.

Causes Current theories about the origins of Tourette's disorder focus on the subcortical areas of the brain, especially the basal ganglia, which have a high concentration of dopamine receptors (Peterson

DSM-IV Criteria

Tourette's Disorder

A. Both multiple motor and one or more vocal tics have been present at some time during the illness, although not necessarily concurrently. (A *tic* is a sudden, rapid, recurrent, nonrhythmic, stereotyped motor movement or vocalization.)

B. The tics occur many times a day (usually in bouts) nearly every day or intermittently throughout a period of more than 1 year, and during this period there was never a tic-free period of more than 3 consecutive months.

C. The disturbance causes marked distress or significant impairment in social, occupational, or other important areas of functioning.

D. The onset is before age 18 years.

E. The disturbance is not due to the direct physiological effects of a substance (e.g., stimulants) or a general medical condition (e.g., Huntington's disease or postviral encephalitis).

SOURCE: APA, DSM-IV, 1994.

(Left) As can be seen in this photo of a man experiencing a tic while riding on a bus, those who suffer from Tourette's disorder feel an irresistible urge to perform tics—twitches, jerks, grimaces, blinks, grunts, throat clearing—as someone feels the urge to sneeze or to scratch an itch. The urge to perform these tics increases when the person is tense or stressed. *(Right)* It decreases when the person feels relaxed or is concentrating on an absorbing task, such as playing the piano, as pictured in this film still from *The Tic Code,* which is the story of a boy with Tourette's disorder.

et al., 1999). The thalamus has also been implicated. These particular regions play a significant role in controlling movements of the limbs and face. It is thus plausible that an abnormality in these areas might result in a failure of motor control that could be expressed in involuntary vocalizations and facial or limb movements. Investigators have recently begun to use functional neuroimaging procedures to study brain activity while Tourette's patients are experiencing tics (Heinz et al., 1998). Increased activity in the midbrain, particularly the thalamus, has been detected during vocal tics. The use of functional neuroimaging in research on tics holds great promise for identifying the causes of Tourette's disorder.

Genetic factors are often involved in the etiology of Tourette's disorder (Pauls, Alsobrook, Gelernter, and Leckman, 1999). Genes and environment interact in determining the phenotypic expression of the genotype. Twin studies of Tourette's disorder have shown concordance rates of around 50 percent for MZ twins, whereas DZ twins show less than 10 percent concordance (Hyde, Aaronson, Randolph, Rickler, and Weinberger, 1992). When all tic disorders are considered, the concordance rate rises to nearly 80 percent in MZ twins and about 25 percent in DZ twins. While these

results suggest a primary genetic contribution to Tourette's disorder, they also indicate that nongenetic factors must also play an important role, since only about half of the MZ twins are concordant for full-blown Tourette's disorder, and the twins exhibited considerable differences in the frequency, intensity, and character of tics, despite their identical genetic endowment. Moreover, in many cases of the disorder, there is no evidence of a family history of Tourette's, indicating the role of environmental factors, such as brain damage, in the etiology of the disorder.

Treatment   Drugs that block dopamine receptors of the D2 subtype continue to be the most effective treatment for Tourette's disorder (Tourette Syndrome Study Group, 1999). The most common of these drugs are the antipsychotics. The fact that these drugs are so effective in treating Tourette's disorder has led some researchers to suspect that the syndrome may share some common features with psychotic disorders. Behavioral management and stress reduction procedures have also proven useful in treating tic disorders (King, Scahill, Findley, and Cohen, 1999). These procedures are usually used as an adjunct to drug treatment.

Disruptive Behavior Disorders

The symptoms of ***disruptive behavior disorders*** tend to emerge in the preschool and elementary school years. Unlike the emotional disorders, all of the diagnoses classified as disruptive disorders are more common in boys than in girls. There are three types of disruptive behavior disorders. ***Conduct disorders*** are characterized by persistent behaviors that seriously violate the rights of others and basic societal norms. Children with conduct disorders often get in trouble with the law, and some become career criminals. ***Oppositional defiant disorder*** also involves noncompliant behavior, but not serious violations of others' rights. Children with this disorder show a pattern of negativistic, hostile, and defiant behavior. A third disorder in the disruptive category is ***attention deficit hyperactivity disorder (ADHD).*** It is characterized by impulsiveness, inattention, and hyperactivity. Among preadolescent children, it is the most common of the three diagnoses.

Conduct Disorder

When discussing conduct disorder it is important to keep in mind that most children, at one time or another, transgress important rules of conduct. A survey of 1,425 British boys aged thirteen to sixteen years, from all socioeconomic groups, found that 98 percent of them admitted to keeping something that did not belong to them (Belson, 1975). In only 40 percent of the instances were the goods worth more than $2.00, but even so the rate of dishonesty in children is quite high. Similar results are reported from other countries. For example, about 89 percent of nine- to fourteen-year-olds in Norway and Sweden confessed to petty illegal offenses (Elmhorn, 1965). For better or worse, it seems that stealing is a part of most children's development. But these offenses are usually isolated incidents. Children who meet diagnostic criteria for conduct disorder *repeatedly* violate very basic norms for interpersonal behavior. They are often physically aggressive and cruel to others. They may habitually lie and cheat.

There is a significant sex difference in the rate of conduct disorder. It is at least three times more common in boys than in girls, with 6 to 16 percent of boys and 2 to 9 percent of girls qualifying for a diagnosis of conduct disorder (APA, 1994; Robins, 1991; Smith, 1998). Thus, sex is one of the most powerful predictors of conduct disorder. Also, the behavioral patterns differ for males and females. Girls are less likely to show physical aggression and more likely to lie and be truant. Some of the factors that might contribute to these sex differences are discussed below.

The pattern of behaviors associated with conduct disorder changes with age (Johnston and Ohan, 1999). In early and middle childhood, conduct disorder often takes the form of lying, fighting, and aggression against animals. During adolescence, the rate of conduct disorder increases dramatically, and the behavior problems become more serious. Some of these children engage in muggings, armed robberies, and even rapes. Further, children with conduct disorder are at increased risk for showing antisocial per-

Conduct disorder in early and middle childhood may take the form of lying, fighting, and aggression against animals. If these boys who are fighting on the playground constantly pick fights with other children, they may suffer from conduct disorder.

DSM-IV Criteria

Conduct Disorder

A. A repetitive and persistent pattern of behavior in which the basic rights of others or major age-appropriate societal norms or rules are violated, as manifested by the presence of three (or more) of the following criteria in the past 12 months, with at least one criterion present in the past 6 months: *Aggression to people and animals*—(1) often bullies, threatens, or intimidates others; (2) often initiates physical fights; (3) has used a weapon that can cause serious physical harm to others (e.g., a bat, brick, broken bottle, knife, gun); (4) has been physically cruel to people; (5) has been physically cruel to animals; (6) has stolen while confronting a victim (e.g., mugging, purse snatching, extortion, armed robbery); (7) has forced someone into sexual activity. *Destruction of property*—(8) has deliberately engaged in fire setting with the intention of causing serious damage; (9) has deliberately destroyed others' property (other than by fire setting). *Deceitfulness or theft*—(10) has broken into someone else's house, building, or car; (11) often lies to obtain goods or favors or to avoid obligations (i.e., "cons" others); (12) has stolen items of nontrivial value without confronting a victim (e.g., shoplifting, but without breaking and entering; forgery). *Serious violations of rules*—(13) often stays out at night despite parental prohibitions, beginning before age 13 years; (14) has run away from home overnight at least twice while living in parental or parental surrogate home (or once without returning for a lengthy period); (15) is often truant from school, beginning before age 13 years.

B. The disturbance in behavior causes clinically significant impairment in social, academic, or occupational functioning.

C. If the individual is age 18 years or older, criteria are not met for Antisocial Personality Disorder.

SOURCE: APA, DSM-IV, 1994.

---

sonality disorder in adulthood (Langbehn, Cadoret, Yates, Troughton, and Stewart, 1998). In fact, the presence of childhood conduct disorder before age fifteen is one of the diagnostic criteria for antisocial personality disorder (see Chapter 9). The following case is representative of a child with one type of conduct disorder:

Derrick was always small for his age, but according to his mother, he was never short on energy. From the time he began walking, he was constantly getting into things. He was fearless. Nothing seemed to worry him, including physical punishment. In preschool, his teachers reported that he was physically aggressive and took things from other children. The redeeming quality that kept Derrick from being rejected by the other boys was his quick wit. He was the class clown.

Derrick's mother and father were divorced when he was a baby. He lived with his mother and two older brothers and a sister. It was a struggle for Derrick's mother to feed and clothe the children. She worked part-time, and occasionally her former husband gave her some money for the children. Even though Derrick was a behavior problem, he and his mother had a close relationship.

By the time Derrick was in the third grade, he had a reputation at his elementary school for being a difficult child. He was suspended from school for a week for vandalizing the classroom. His behavior improved somewhat the rest of the year. But in the fourth grade he was again suspended for leaving the school grounds during the day. It was not until the sixth grade that he had an encounter with the police. A local merchant reported him for shoplifting. Derrick's father attended the hearing at juvenile court, and convinced the judge that he would spend more time with his son and monitor his behavior more closely. For a period of about one year, Derrick's father did visit him more often. Around the time Derrick entered the eighth grade, his father lost his job and moved to another state with his new girlfriend.

The teacher reports of noncompliant and aggressive behavior increased during junior high, and the principal recommended that he be sent to a special high school for children with behavior problems. Derrick's mother believes that his exposure to the children at the high school made matters worse. Derrick started smoking cigarettes and marijuana. He violated curfew and began hanging out with a group of older boys who were always getting into trouble. Shortly after Derrick turned fifteen, his mother received a threatening phone call from the father of a girl in the neighborhood. He said he would shoot Derrick if he didn't stay away from his daughter.

When he was sixteen, Derrick became involved with a girl who was twenty. Although Derrick's mother didn't approve of the relationship, Derrick did seem to settle down for a while. But that was only the calm that preceded the storm. Before he turned seventeen, Derrick dropped out of school and was arrested for burglary the following week. Again, however, Derrick's charm served him well, and he managed to convince the judge that he should be on probation, rather than being placed in a detention facility. During his first interview with Derrick, the probation officer was impressed by his personable manner and intelligence. Derrick seemed to have potential for getting back on the right track.

SUBTYPES OF CONDUCT DISORDER

When researchers conduct longitudinal studies of children with conduct disorder, several subtypes are found. One subtype involves children with persistent antisocial and aggressive tendencies from childhood into early adulthood (Huesmann, Eron, Lefkowitz, and Walder, 1984; Moffitt, 1997a). About half of the children who meet diagnostic criteria for conduct disorder are eventually classified as juvenile delinquents in adolescence, and 30 to 40 percent of children with conduct disorder develop antisocial personality disorder as adults (Myers, Stewart, and Brown, 1998). Another subtype involves people who were not classified as juvenile delinquents but who still showed conduct problems as children and continue to experience chronic problems in social functioning in adulthood, such as unstable work histories, stormy personal relationships, physical aggression, and spouse abuse (Zoccolillo, Pickles, Quinton, and Rutter, 1992). As described above, Derrick's criminal behavior is typical of children with conduct disorder who have problems that continue into adulthood.

Some of the strongest predictors of which children with persistent conduct disorder will go on to engage in serious criminal behavior are: (1) high frequency of deviant acts as a child, (2) greater variety of conduct problems, (3) problem behaviors across multiple settings, (4) early onset of deviant acts, and (5) the co-occurrence of conduct disorder with impulsivity and cognitive deficits (Lipsey and Derzon, 1998; Loeber, 1990; Lynam, 1998; Rogers, Johansen, Chang, and Salekin, 1997). Given Derrick's developmental course up to age fourteen, he is certainly at risk for showing persistent behavior problems.

A third subtype of conduct disorder has a more favorable outcome; it involves a noneventful child-

hood course followed by the onset of behavior problems in adolescence. If the behavior problems do not emerge until adolescence, there is a much greater likelihood that they will be short-lived (Moffitt, 1997a). It is likely that these transient problems represent a way for some youth to assert their independence (Seiffge-Krenke, 1993). Whatever the case, it is encouraging that the majority of youth who first manifest conduct problems during adolescence do not go on to more serious antisocial behavior.

Although the majority of youngsters with conduct disorders do not commit serious crimes, there is a small subgroup of children who commit lethal acts of aggression before they enter adulthood. In recent years, newspaper headlines have featured stories about youth who show serious aggressive behavior that has deadly consequences. These headlines are startling because they undermine many of our assumptions about the nature of childhood. Consider the following cases:

"Kip" Kinkel The youngest of two children, fifteen-year-old Kipland Kinkel (nicknamed "Kip" by his peers) lived a middle-class lifestyle in rural Springfield, Oregon. Kip's parents, both teachers, were well-respected and involved in a number of community activities. His older sister was a pretty and popular college student. Kip, however, was known to be

On May 22, 1998, Kip Kinkel was led away to his arraignment for the shooting deaths of his parents and two students at his high school. Kinkel had exhibited many symptoms of conduct disorder, particularly his behavioral problems at school and his aggression toward people and animals.

aggressive with others and to curse at adults. Despite being awkward and small for his age, it was rumored that Kip was voted "Most Likely to Start World War III" at school. At one point, Kip was prescribed Ritalin to improve his school behavior, and his parents took him to counseling for anger management.

High school peers reported that Kip had been preoccupied with violence and was fascinated with bombs. He had downloaded information on the creation of explosives from his home computer. Kip told his friends he enjoyed torturing and hurting animals. He reportedly killed cats by beheading them, then displayed their heads on posts. When Kip began to express a strong interest in weapons, his father finally relented and purchased a gun as a gift for his son. Mr. Kinkel hoped that doing so would allow Kip to learn the safety procedures for gun use.

In May 1998, Kip was expelled for bringing a gun to school. On May 19, his parents took away his gun as a form of punishment. The following night, on May 20, Kip fatally shot both of his parents in the family home. He talked on the phone to a friend and watched television after the murders. The next day, he took his gun to school, walked into the cafeteria, and opened fire, killing two students and injuring twenty-two others. (Based on *Time Magazine,* July 6, 1998)

Luke Woodham Luke Woodham lived with his divorced mother in the small town of Pearl, Mississippi. Often teased and disliked by other children, sixteen-year-old Luke was overweight and wore glasses. He was described as a withdrawn and quiet student. He had few opportunities for social interaction, so when a girl at his school showed an interest in becoming friends, Luke asked her out. Luke's mother would often insist on accompanying the couple on dates. Luke considered his mother overprotective, and at one point said he "hated her." After a few months, the girl ended the relationship.

Luke was a member of a self-styled "demonic cult" comprised of other boys who were viewed as unpopular by their peers. The boys were preoccupied with violence. They had even planned brutal acts toward a list of "enemies" they kept. Luke himself had a propensity for aggression toward animals. He killed his own dog, Sparkle, by beating it, setting it on fire, and throwing it in a pond to drown. Luke bragged about this incident.

On October 1, 1997, Luke awoke and stabbed his mother to death while she was sleeping in bed. He then hid his hunting rifle under his coat and went to his school. Luke went directly to the commons area and began shooting. He eventually killed two students, including the only girl he had ever dated. Seven others were injured. (Based on *Washington Post,* October 22, 1997)

Michael Carneal Fourteen-year-old Michael Carneal lived with his parents and an older sister in West Paducah, Kentucky. Michael and his sister attended the same school. However, the two were strikingly different. Michael's sister Kelly was popular, whereas Michael had few friends and struggled with his schoolwork. Michael was often taunted and threatened by peers. Although he had a reputation as a jokester, he was small for his age and worried that other kids were talking about him. Organized group activities did not hold his interest. Michael was often depressed, preferred to remain alone, and passed time playing violent video games at home. He often expressed violent thoughts and had talked about throwing a cat into a fire for fun.

Michael began to learn how to handle and use guns at a very early age at summer camps. A neighbor had taken him on shooting and hunting trips, as well. At the age of fourteen, Michael was well-experienced in the use of firearms. He once pulled a gun on a few kids at school when they threatened to beat him up. Fortunately, this incident did not end in violence. But on the morning of December 1, 1997, Michael brought a stolen gun to school. He walked into a morning prayer group. There he shot and killed three students and wounded five others. (Based on *Time Magazine,* July 6, 1998)

Dylan Klebold and Eric Harris Littleton, Colorado, a small, affluent town outside of Denver, was the home of seventeen-year-old Dylan Klebold and eighteen-year-old Eric Harris. Both boys lived with their parents in comfortable middle-class homes and attended Columbine High School. But despite the fact that their families "fit in" with the community, Dylan and Eric felt like outsiders. They were members of a self-styled group of teens called the "Trench Coat Mafia." This group was comprised of students who had strong negative feelings about minorities and popular, athletic students.

Web sites, diaries and e-mail messages left behind by Dylan and Eric revealed an obsession with death and violence, as well as a preoccupation with Adolf Hitler and the Nazi movement. In 1998, both

Dylan and Eric were arrested for breaking into a car, and they were sentenced to community service for the offense. Eric was also accused of physically and verbally threatening another student. Although the parents of this student informed the police about the threats on several occasions, no charges were pressed.

On April 21, 1999, Dylan Klebold and Eric Harris entered Columbine High School and began a rampage of violence that shocked the nation. With smiles on their faces and sarcastic comments to their victims, Dylan and Eric went through the school with guns and killed twelve students, one teacher, and finally themselves. The shooting spree lasted about an hour. (Based on *New York Times,* April 22, 1999)

These cases were just the most sensational of those occurring in the late 1990s. Others have occurred both before and after those we have described. In fact, among fifteen- to nineteen-year-olds, there was a startling increase in firearm homicides between 1985 and 1993 (Fingerhut, 1993; National Center for Health Statistics, 1985–1993). The rate was 5.8 per 100,000 population in that age group in 1985 compared to 18.10 per 100,000 in 1993. According to the most recent data from 1997, however, there has been a decrease in the rate of homicides by youth, down to 16.5 per 100,000. Nonetheless, such a rate is still extremely high for a society that is not at war (Zimring, 1998).

Most of these homicides involve individual victims and take place in low-income, urban areas. The perpetrators are usually boys from single-parent homes in which the mother is struggling to make ends meet, and the child is exposed to negative environmental influences. But one of the most disturbing aspects of the homicides described above is the fact that they occurred in stable, rural, and small-town communities. The boys did not grow up in crime-infested urban areas where gang activity flourishes. They were not members of ethnic minorities who experienced isolation and discrimination. There is no evidence that these youngsters had experienced poverty or physical abuse. So what is the explanation?

There are some striking similarities among these youngsters. One similarity is their preoccupation with violence and aggression. They also all had difficulty with peer relations, and they showed little interest in organized group sports. Another notable commonality is the fact that at least two of them were cruel and aggressive toward animals. This is consistent with research findings; longitudinal studies have shown that cruelty toward animals is one of the most powerful predictors of future antisocial behavior (Felthous, and Kellert, 1986). A lack of empathy for the suffering of animals is an ominous sign, which may indicate a generalized lack of sensitivity to the feelings of others.

It is likely that all five of these boys would meet criteria for conduct disorder. In addition, they might also meet DSM criteria for one or more other disorders. Several studies have shown that many children with conduct disturbances have problems in maintaining attention (Anderson, Williams, McGee, and Silva, 1987; Quay, 1986). Thus, they often do poorly in school, and they do not experience the self-esteem and feelings of competence that academic success engenders. But what caused their behavior? We turn to this question next.

POSSIBLE ORIGINS OF CONDUCT DISORDER

What causes a child to violate social norms and show aggressive and delinquent behavior? First, we shall discuss the possible social origins of conduct disorder. Then we will explore biological influences on the development of conduct disturbances.

Social Sources of Conduct Disorder   Let us begin by considering the social factors that might play a role in the most serious cases of conduct disorder; those involving homicidal behavior in youth. Many critics have blamed these violent crimes on the increased availability of guns. Franklin Zimring, an expert on youth crime, attributes the fluctuations in youth homicide to the availability of guns. He claims there is no evidence of a "violent new breed" of disturbed youth. Rather, he believes that the increase in youth homicides between 1985 and 1993 was due to the increased availability of guns, and that the decrease in 1997 was due to a police crackdown on gun possession that began after 1993 (Zimring, 1998).

It has been shown that children are much more likely to seriously injure themselves or others if there is a gun kept in the house (Brent and Perper, 1995). Kip Kinkel's father hoped that by educating his son about the use of weapons, problems would be avoided. But education in gun safety may not be the solution, at least not for younger children. In a recent study, a group of four- to six-year-old children were shown real and toy guns, then provided with information about them and specific instructions not to play with them (Hardy, Armstrong, Martin, and Strawn, 1996). This intervention had no effect on the children's behavior when the adult left the room; those who received the intervention were just as likely to play with the guns as those who had received no instructions. Guns may simply hold too much appeal for children. Such findings have led some to conclude that keeping guns out of homes with children is the only solution (Berkowitz, 1994).

We might also question the influence of the media. In April 1999, the families of the three children killed by Michael Carneal sued several entertainment companies, charging that violent computer games, Internet pornography, and the movie industry contributed to Michael's propensity to violence. In particular, the families targeted a movie entitled *The Basketball Diaries,* which depicted a drug-addicted young man who gunned down a teacher and some classmates at his school. Michael Carneal had been fascinated by this film.

It is certainly plausible that exposure to media violence contributed to the aggressive behavior shown by Michael, as well as by Kip, Luke, Dylan, and Eric. It is well established that exposure to aggressive behavior increases the likelihood of aggression in children (Berkowitz, 1994; Smith and Donnerstein, 1998). Yet, there is also ample evidence that all of these boys were psychologically vulnerable, perhaps

Pictured above is a scene from the 1995 film *The Basketball Diaries,* which tells the story of three boys' descent into drug abuse and crime. The parents of murdered students in West Padukah, Kentucky, have filed a $130 million damage suit against several Hollywood entertainment companies, including Polygram Filmed Entertainment, which owned the rights to the film. Michael Carneal repeatedly watched the dream sequence in the film in which one of the boys gunned down a teacher and students at school.

deeply disturbed. In the case of Michael Carneal, the judge accepted his attorney's plea of guilty but mentally ill. Michael was sentenced to life in prison. The attorneys for Kip and Luke argued that their clients were suffering from a psychological disorder. They argued that, when combined with exposure to media violence and access to a deadly weapon, their disorder led to murder. It is fortunate that this outcome is rare; most children with conduct disorder do not commit crimes that endanger the lives of others.

What about the family environment? Does it contribute to conduct problems? Numerous studies have shown that children with conduct problems are more likely to come from disorganized social environments than from warm, stable families. The home environment is often characterized by a lack of affection, high levels of discord, and harsh and inconsistent discipline (Farrington, 1978; Hetherington and Martin, 1979; Loeber and Dishion, 1983; Loeber, 1990; Toupin, Dery, Pauze, Fortin, and Mercier, 1997). In many cases, the children's activities are poorly supervised and monitored. As might be expected, parental divorce and separation are quite common. Some of the most interesting findings on this issue come from adoption studies (Cadoret and Stewart, 1991). Adopted children who show aggressive and antisocial behaviors as young adults are more likely to come from adoptive homes characterized by low socioeconomic status and poor parental adjustment. This relation cannot be attributed to genetic factors, because the parents and children have no genetic relation. Nonetheless, adoptees whose biological parents show aggressive or antisocial behavior seem to be at greater risk for showing the same behavior if they are reared in unstable environments.

In the families of children with conduct disorder, patterns of interaction between family members are often characterized by coercive behaviors and a lack of reinforcement for prosocial behaviors (Frick, 1994; Patterson, Reid, and Dishion, 1998). One family member's anger or aggressive behavior elicits similar behavior from another family member, and this, in turn, produces a further aggressive response from the first person. As the cycle continues, the negative emotion escalates. Sometimes parents unintentionally reinforce these cycles of coercive behavior. The parent often backs down, deciding it is not worth the struggle, and the child ends up doing whatever he originally wanted to do. The child has essentially won the battle by engaging in coercive anger and aggression. As a result, the frequency of this behavior increases.

Members of the Diamond Street Gang in Los Angeles make diamond signs as they sit in front of a wall containing their gang's graffiti. Gangs supply the motivation and opportunity to engage in deviant acts.

Many children with conduct disorders also have difficulty forming peer relationships. They are often rejected by other children (Coie, Terry, Lenox, and Lochman, 1995; Dodge, 1983). Others become members of deviant peer groups (gangs) that supply the child with the motivation and rationalizations to support delinquent acts, as well as opportunities for engaging in such behaviors (Elliott, Hulzinga, and Ageton, 1985; Patterson, DeBaryshe, and Ramsey, 1989).

Family difficulties are augmented by poverty. Conduct disorder is particularly prevalent among inner-city youth. And even there, different schools, different housing areas, or different parts of town are associated with enormous variation in rates of conviction. Areas of high delinquency are characterized by high unemployment, poor housing, and poor schooling. Moreover, delinquency is highly related to indices of social pathology, such as illegitimate births, drug dependence, and venereal disease (Loeber, 1990).

In Chapter 4, we talked about some of the ways that experience can change the brain. Could this be a factor in conduct disorder? Serotonin has been linked with conduct disorder and aggression in humans. Studies of rhesus monkeys have shown that some of the same factors that are believed to contribute to aggression in children can produce serotonin abnormalities in rhesus monkeys (Higley, Suomi, and Linnoila, 1990). For example, young monkeys who do not have free access to their moth-

ers show lower levels of serotonin when compared to animals who have consistent contact with their mothers. The animals deprived of maternal contact also show higher levels of aggression. So it is possible that the seeds of constitutional vulnerability to conduct disorder are planted by negative social experiences that occur early in the child's life.

Throughout this book, we have highlighted the diathesis-stress model and the interaction between biology and the environment. Does this also hold for conduct disorder? Research findings indicate that it does. For example, several studies have shown that children who score high on measures of minor physical anomalies or were exposed to obstetrical complications are much more likely to develop conduct disorder if they are reared in unstable environments (Raine, 1993; Raine, Brennan, and Mednick, 1997). Similarly, the rate of antisocial behavior in adopted children who have a biological parent with a criminal history is significantly higher if they are reared in unstable adoptive homes (Cadoret, 1986; Cloninger and Gottesman, 1987; Rutter, Quinton, and Hill, 1990; Rutter, Macdonald, et al., 1990). All of these findings are consistent with the diathesis-stress model. They also suggest, however, that even children who are genetically predisposed to conduct problems are less likely to show them if they are reared in stable, supportive families.

Biological Influences on the Development of Conduct Disorder　We now know that some children have a constitutional vulnerability to conduct disorder and that this can arise from several sources. Heredity is one source. Genetic factors play a role in determining which children have conduct problems and which do not. For example, twin studies show a higher concordance rate for conduct disorder in MZ twins than in DZ twins (Eaves et al., 1997). Wendy Slutske and her colleagues reported a concordance rate of .53 for conduct disorder in male MZ twin pairs and .30 in male DZ twin pairs (Slutske et al., 1997). Similarly, twin studies show that there is a genetic component to antisocial personality disorder in adults (McGuffin and Thapar, 1998). Finally, when the criminal records (rather than the clinical diagnoses) of adopted children are compared with those of their natural and adoptive fathers, it is found that the criminal records of adopted children most closely resemble those of their biological fathers, with whom they never lived (Cloninger and Gottesman, 1987; Mednick, Gabriella, and Hutchings, 1987).

The twin study by Slutske, described above, was one of the few to test the "equal environments" assumption; in other words, the assumption that the experiences of MZ twins are no more similar than those of DZ twins. It was not supported; rather, MZ twins reported sharing more childhood experiences and friends in common than did DZ twins. The MZ twin pairs were also more likely than the DZ twin pairs to keep in touch as adults. How might this have influenced the results of the study? It was found that MZ twin pairs were more likely to be similar on conduct disorder signs if they spent more time together, communicated with each other more often, and shared more close friends. These results alert us to the potential role played by environmental factors.

In previous chapters, we discussed the effect of prenatal complications on the development of the nervous system. Do prenatal events play any role in conduct disorder? Recent studies have revealed some surprising links. For example, several longitudinal studies have found that the children of mothers who smoke cigarettes during pregnancy are at increased risk for developing conduct problems (Brennan, Grekin, and Mednick, 1999). Similarly, the occurrence of pregnancy complications puts children at greater risk for delinquent behavior (Brennan, Mednick, and Kandel, 1991). Given these findings, it is not surprising that children with conduct disorder show more signs of abnormal prenatal development; they have more minor physical anomalies of the head and limbs (Raine, 1993).

The evidence strongly suggests that biological factors play a part in determining who develops conduct problems. But how might that come about? Surely one is not born with a blueprint for deviant behavior, because most human behaviors are learned. What exactly is the vulnerability?

At the biological level, the vulnerability might involve an abnormality in neurotransmitters or a structural irregularity in the brain. Both animal studies and research with humans suggest that the neurotransmitter serotonin plays some role. Researchers have studied "knockout" mice who lack the gene for serotonin receptors (Brunner and Hen, 1997). These mice show a high rate of aggressive and impulsive behavior. They also show a greater interest in alcohol and cocaine. Similarly, among rhesus monkeys, those who show high rates of aggression tend to show lower levels of serotonin (Higley et al., 1992; Higley et al., 1996). Some studies of boys with conduct disorder also indicate a relation between aggression and serotonin activity (Moffitt et al., 1998; Pine et al., 1997; Unis et al., 1997).

At this point, we do not know why low levels of serotonin would be associated with antisocial and aggressive behavior. But it is interesting that a reduction in serotonin activity has also been linked with depression. (The role of serotonin in depression is discussed in detail in Chapter 7.) Perhaps low levels of serotonin contribute to a generalized negative mood state that leads to sadness and depression in some, and anger and aggression in others. It is likely that future research will shed light on this issue.

It has been proposed that abnormalities in the frontal lobes of the brain might contribute to conduct disorder, as well as disruptive behavior in general (Miller and Cummings, 1999; Pennington and Bennetto, 1993). You may recall that damage to the frontal lobes can result in dramatic changes in personality and behavior (see Chapter 4). The most common behavioral response is a decrease in inhibition; individuals with damage to the frontal lobes often engage in impulsive behaviors that would have been out of character for them before the injury. The behavior of patients with frontal lobe damage is similar to that observed in children with conduct disorder (Scarpa and Raine, 1997). These children fail to inhibit their impulses, especially their aggressive impulses. In addition, like frontal lobe patients, they perform below average on measures of "executive" functions, such as the ability to plan ahead and refrain from impulsive responses.

Another theory holds that the biological basis of vulnerability to conduct disorder is reduced physiological arousal (see Figure 8–1). Evidence for this comes from studies that have revealed much lower resting heart rates in aggressive and delinquent boys (Raine, 1993). Reduced arousal is also suggested by the results of conditioning studies. Certain unpleasant stimuli, such as loud noises and mild electric shocks, cause a skin conductance response in humans. This skin conductance response is assumed to reflect the person's increased arousal. When a neutral stimulus, such as a low tone, is repeatedly paired with the unpleasant stimulus, it eventually causes a skin conductance response on its own. In other words, after a certain number of pairings, the neutral stimulus has the same effect as the unpleasant stimulus. For children with conduct disorders, more pairings of the two stimuli are required in order for the neutral stimulus to cause a response (Raine, 1993). In other words, they show less conditioning. It has been hy-

Figure 8—1

LOW AROUSAL AS A POSSIBLE CAUSE OF DISRUPTIVE BEHAVIOR DISORDERS

A summary of low arousal theories for both conduct disorder and attention deficit hyperactivity disorder.

	Cause	Deficits	Behaviors	Treatment
Conduct Disorder	Low emotional arousal	Deficits in avoidance learning (from negative reinforcement) and in socialization (from positive reinforcement)	Children do not become socialized; impulsive, aggressive, and manipulative behaviors develop	Most promising treatment: behavioral resocialization programs that compensate for learning deficits
Attention Deficit Hyperactivity Disorder	Chronic underarousal (to all stimuli)	Difficulty maintaining attention	Impulsive and frenetic behavior; school difficulties may develop	Stimulants may raise arousal level and improve symptoms; behavior management may teach adaptive behaviors; both therapies combined seem most promising

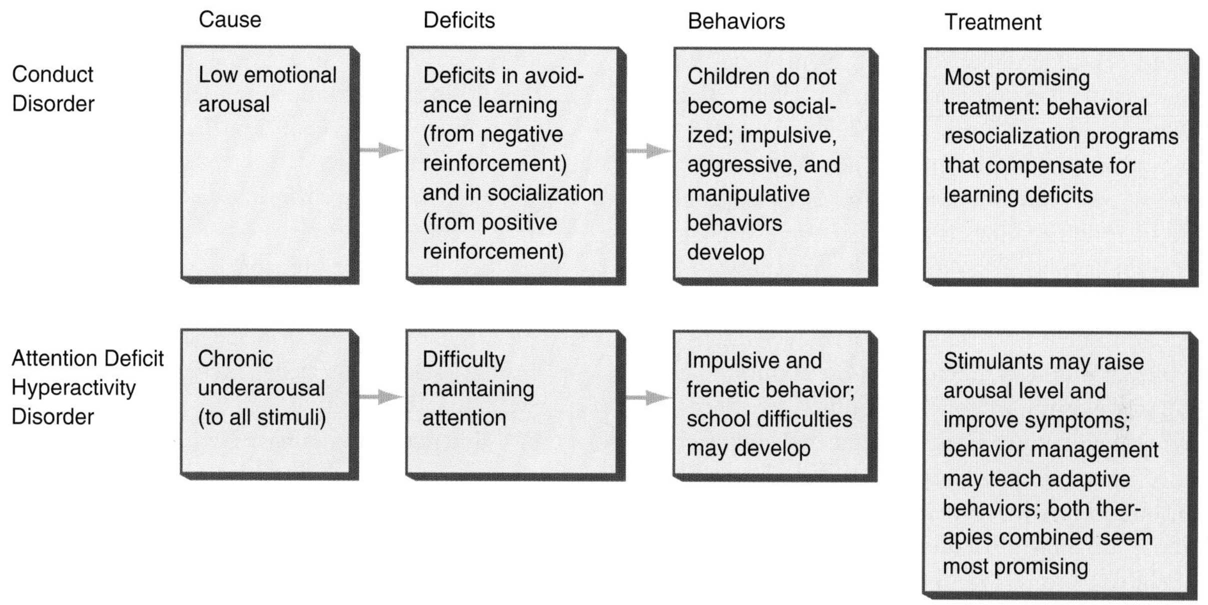

pothesized that the reason children with conduct disorder seek out "risky" or "stimulating" experiences is because they want to increase their level of physiological arousal (Zuckerman, 1994).

Some researchers have interpreted the findings of reduced heart rate and lower "conditionability" to mean that children with conduct disorder are less capable of social learning. In other words, they are less emotionally aroused and therefore less responsive to praise and punishment (Robins, 1991). As a result, they experience less discomfort when they violate social norms. Researchers have also shown that children with conduct disorder have less empathy than other children. For example, youth with conduct disorder have difficulty identifying the emotion experienced by people in videotaped interactions (Cohen and Strayer, 1996). These children also report that they do not personally experience the emotions shown by other people. The combination of low empathy and low emotional arousal might explain the cruel behavior shown by some of the children we have described in this chapter. Similar explanations have been offered for antisocial behavior in adults.

As we consider the evidence for the role of biology in conduct disorder, there is an important point we must keep in mind. All of the biological indicators we have mentioned here, such as minor physical anomalies and reduced heart rate and conditionability, also occur in individuals who do not engage in antisocial behavior. In fact, some individuals who engage in altruistic behavior, in which they risk their lives for others, may have a low resting heart rate (Raine, 1993). Although the reason for this is unknown, it is possible that the same biological tendencies that lead some people to take illegal risks can lead others to take risks that benefit society. In the case of altruistic behavior, those with a below average physiological reaction to dangerous situations may be more likely to take the initiative to come to the aid of others.

TREATING CONDUCT DISORDER

Amazingly, only about 23 percent of children showing conduct disorders such as Derrick's, or the less severe oppositional defiant disorder, are referred for counseling (Anderson, Williams, McGee, and Silva, 1987). Apparently, even when children are being extraordinarily disruptive, parents are reluctant to seek out mental health professionals. This is very unfortunate, because effective treatments are now available (see Table 8–9; Brestan and Eyberg, 1998; Ollendick, 1996).

Historically, treatment of conduct disorder has focused on interventions derived from social learning theory (Brestan and Eyberg, 1998; Kazdin, 1998b; Lochman, White, and Wayland, 1991) and family therapy (Chamberlain and Rosicky, 1995). Goals of such interventions include: (1) helping the child identify situations that trigger aggressive or antisocial behavior, (2) teaching the child how to take the perspective of others and care about this perspective, (3) reducing the aggressive child's tendency to attribute hostility to others, and (4) training the child in adaptive ways of solving conflicts with others, such as negotiation. Each of these goals is accomplished by reinforcing positive behaviors in the child, punishing negative behaviors, modeling, and observational learning procedures (see Chapter 3). Often the child's family will be involved in treatment, since the family's interaction patterns may be supporting the child's conduct disorder. Interventions such as these have proven promising in outcome research, although it may be crucial for these interventions to take place soon after the child begins to exhibit antisocial behavior and to include the child's parents or family for the interventions to have long-term positive effects (Lochman, White, and Wayland, 1991). It is not surprising that interventions that use multiple strategies seem to be most effective (Frick, 1998).

As an example of the application of these interventions, consider John, whose conduct problems were mild in severity and stemmed from communication problems with his parents:

John was fourteen when he was referred to a treatment center because he had been stealing from his mother. He frequently stole large sums of money, often in excess of $20. His mother, however, knew precisely how much money she had, and there was no way in which John could pretend that his stealing would go unnoticed.

Interestingly, during early discussions with the therapist, it became clear that John respected his parents, and that they loved him. The problem was that they could no longer discuss things together. John's stealing had driven a wedge of distrust between them, such that his parents could think of nothing else, yet John resented not being trusted.

In fact, stealing was simply the most irritating of a group of problems that typically arise during adoles-

TABLE 8–9

Treatment

CONDUCT DISORDER

	Cognitive Problem-Solving Skills Training	Parent Management Training	Family Therapy	Multisystemic Therapy
Improvement	about 45% at least moderately improved	about 50% moderately improved	unclear	about 60–70% improved
Relapse*	moderate	low to moderate	moderate	low to moderate
Side Effects	unclear	unclear	unclear	unclear
Cost	moderately expensive	moderately expensive	moderately expensive	highly expensive
Time Scale†	months	months	months/years	months/years
Overall	**good**	**good**	**good**	**good to excellent**

*Relapse after discontinuation of treatments.
†Time to achieve maximal effect.
SOURCE: Based on Campbell and Cueva, 1995, p.10; Kaplan and Hussain, 1995, pp. 291–98; Kazdin, 1998c; Offord and Bennet, 1994, p 8; revised with Borduin et al., 1995; Dishion and Andrews, 1995; Gordon, Arbuthnot, Gustafson, and McGreen, 1988; Howard, Kopta, Krause, and Orlinsky, 1986; Kazdin, 1993.

Interventions for conduct disorder include helping the child to identify situations that lead to violence and teaching adaptive ways of resolving conflicts. Pictured here are several hundred gang members who are being given legal, health, and educational advice in a program targeted at ending drive-by shootings.

cence and that neither John nor his parents knew how to discuss and resolve. Among these problems were conflicts over curfew, neatness, personal cleanliness, and table manners.

Recognizing that these conflicts were by no means trivial irritants, the therapist arranged a series of meetings with John and his parents. During these sessions, the rewards and penalties for violating or conforming to explicit agreements were made clear to both sides. In these contracts, John acknowledged that his lateness might be a source of great concern to his parents, while they recognized that his room was his own "space" which, subject only to fundamental rules of sanitation, was his to do with as he pleased. At the same time, the therapist encouraged John and his father to role-play how they might settle differences of opinion at home. After the first meeting, stealing was never discussed nor was it targeted as an area for contract or discussion. Nevertheless, it stopped altogether and long before the eight-week treatment was completed.

While a variety of methods are used in the treatment of childhood conduct disorders, certain behavior management treatments are recognized to be most effective. Alan Kazdin, a psychologist at Yale University, has devoted much of his career to developing and evaluating treatment approaches for conduct disorder. Kazdin has been a pioneer in the field and has made significant advances in two techniques for reducing conduct problems: cognitive problem-solving skills training and parent management training (Kazdin, 1997).

Cognitive problem skills training, or PSST, helps the child develop the necessary skills for interper-

sonal problem solving. Research has shown that children with conduct disorder tend to misperceive social cues and make inaccurate attributions about people's motives (Dodge and Schwartz, 1997). For example, they tend to think other people have malicious motives even when they don't. PSST tries to change these faulty cognitive processes.

Kazdin describes several important aspects of PSST. The first is a step-by-step approach to the child's thought processes in interpersonal situations. The therapist works with the child to understand his or her "cognitions" about social interactions. For example, the therapist might ask the child to describe his interpretations of a particular experience, such as not being invited to join a playground game. Often children with conduct disorder will automatically conclude that there must have been some malevolent intent; in other words, that another child intentionally excluded him from the game. Taking this one

Alan Kazdin has developed and evaluated many treatment approaches and programs for reducing conduct disorder.

step further, the child might decide to retaliate in some way. The therapist's task is to change these perceptions and assumptions. This requires great skill and sensitivity on the part of the therapist, because many children find it difficult to verbalize their thoughts and are very resistant to change.

A second aspect of PSST involves identifying the behaviors that are appropriate in the child's daily life. Such behaviors are encouraged through modeling and direct reward. Third, specific activities are used to train the child in behaviors that will eventually be applied in real-life situations. These activities can include structured games, stories, and academic tasks. Fourth, the therapist tends to play an active part in modeling appropriate interpersonal behaviors. The combination of these strategies makes PSST an effective behavioral approach to the treatment of conduct disorders.

Parent management training (PMT) is used to help parents learn new approaches to managing their child's behavior in the home environment. In PMT, the parents are first trained to identify, define, and observe problem behavior in new ways. They are given an overview of social learning principles, such as positive reinforcement, mild punishment, and negotiation. Parents observe the therapist model techniques for working with the child, then they role-play the techniques to be used at home. Of course, the therapist must form a good relationship with the parents in order for PMT to work. In addition, the treatment is more effective if the therapist also works with the child's teacher.

Kazdin advocates the combined use of PSST and PMT in working with children and their families. Thus, one therapist might work with the child using PSST at the same time another therapist is implementing a PMT program with the parents.

Sometimes a child's behavior is so disruptive, or his family environment is so dysfunctional, that he will be sent to a treatment home, such as Achievement Place (Kirigin and Wolf, 1998). At Achievement Place, which began at the University of Kansas and is now in several locations around the country, professionally trained "teaching parents" live together in a family-style arrangement with six to eight delinquent adolescent children. Often the children's homes are in the same community, and they can continue to attend their regular school and visit in their own homes.

The aim of Achievement Place is to teach prosocial behaviors. The teaching parents develop a mutually reinforcing relationship with their charges; the parents model, role-play, and reinforce the kinds of social skills they want the children to acquire. They emphasize skills such as responding appropriately to criticism, as well as the academic skills that are necessary to make school interesting and to obtain employment afterward. Moreover, Achievement Place emphasizes self-government, whereby the children take increasing responsibility for their own behavior and for helping their housemates.

How successful has the Achievement Place approach been? One measure of success is to look at what happens to adolescents during and after Achievement Place, compared to a similar group that spent time in a traditional facility. One such study found that the Achievement Place children showed greater improvement in conduct (Kirigin, Braukmann, Atwater, and Wolf, 1982). During the year of treatment, 56 percent of the boys and 47 percent of the girls assigned to Achievement Place were involved in a criminal offense, compared to 86 percent of the boys and 80 percent of the girls in more traditional institutions. One year following treatment, the Achievement Place children continued to be less likely to be in trouble with the law; 57 percent of the boys and 27 percent of the girls from Achievement Place had an offense, compared to 73 percent and 47 percent of the boys and girls, respectively, who received traditional treatment. The Achievement Place program had a positive effect, but many of the children continued to have conduct problems. One reason so many of the children in both types of treatment got into trouble when they were released was that many had to return to difficult home environments that may have undermined the effects of the treatment. This has led researchers to explore treatment approaches that also change the family.

One of the most successful of the new approaches to the treatment of conduct disorder is **multisystemic therapy (MST)** (Borduin, 1999). MST is typically used with the most severely disturbed and aggressive children. It is a family-based approach that intervenes in all aspects of the child's daily life: home, school, and peer groups. In MST, the therapist works intensively with the child and his environment. Parents are trained in new techniques for managing their child's behavior. Behavioral management and specialized academic programs are also developed with the child's teacher. The therapist meets directly with the child's peers to help them develop new strategies for dealing with the child. In working directly with the child, the therapist focuses on the development of social skills and better impulse control. The success of MST is believed to be due to the fact that it uses basic principles of cognitive-behavioral therapy and applies them to all aspects of the child's natural environment. Needless to say, MST is costly. But that may simply be the high price we have to pay for successful treatment. In the long run, intensive interventions like MST may not only improve the life of the child, but may also save the lives of others who could eventually be victims of the child's conduct-disordered behavior.

Oppositional Defiant Disorder

Children who meet diagnostic criteria for *oppositional defiant disorder (ODD)* are negativistic, hostile, temperamental, and defiant toward authority figures over at least six months. They lose their temper, argue with adults, actively defy or refuse to comply with requests or rules, deliberately do things to annoy other people, are angry and resentful, spiteful, or vindictive. Although the noncompliant behaviors of children with ODD are usually manifested toward adults, these children are also prone to be negativistic toward peers. They often blame others for the consequences of their behavior, especially the social rejection they experience from other children. The prevalence of ODD is estimated to be about 2 percent during the course of childhood. Like conduct disorder, ODD is more common in boys than in girls, especially prior to adolescence.

The distinction between ODD and conduct disorder is based on the presence of violations of the law or basic social mores. Children with ODD do not engage in repeated physical aggression, property destruction, theft, or deceit. Yet, the two disorders do tend to occur in sequence; many children who manifest ODD during childhood gradually develop conduct disorder in adolescence. Both disorders are associated with problems in understanding and solving interpersonal problems (Matthys, Cuperus, and van Engeland, 1999). Further, both ODD and conduct disorder are associated with an increased risk for antisocial behavior in adulthood (Langbehn, Cadoret, Yates, Troughton, and Stewart, 1998).

Research findings suggest that the causes of ODD are similar to the causes of conduct disorder. For example, children with ODD tend to come from unstable homes where the parents use harsh, inconsistent punishment, and are less involved in the child's activities (Frick, Christian, and Wooton, 1999). Children with ODD also show a reduction in indicators of serotonin activity (van Goozen, Matthys, Cohen-Kettenis, Westenberg, van Engeland, 1999). Given these similarities, it is not surprising that the treatments administered to children with ODD are similar to those used with conduct disorder. They rely on behavioral principles, as well as cognitive theories about the misinterpretation of events (Barkley, Edwards, and Robin, 1999; Christophersen and Finney, 1999).

Some have questioned whether the distinction between ODD and conduct disorder is a valid one—

DSM-IV Criteria

Oppositional Defiant Disorder

A. A pattern of negativistic, hostile, and defiant behavior lasting at least 6 months, during which four (or more) of the following are present: (1) often loses temper, (2) often argues with adults, (3) often actively defies or refuses to comply with adults' requests or rules, (4) often deliberately annoys people, (5) often blames others for his or her mistakes or misbehavior, (6) is often touchy or easily annoyed by others, (7) is often angry and resentful, (8) is often spiteful or vindictive. (*Note:* Consider a criterion met only if the behavior occurs more frequently than is typically observed in individuals of comparable age and developmental level.)

B. The disturbance in behavior causes clinically significant impairment in social, academic, or occupational functioning.

C. The behaviors do not occur exclusively during the course of a Psychotic or Mood Disorder.

D. Criteria are not met for Conduct Disorder, and, if the individual is age 18 years or older, criteria are not met for Antisocial Personality Disorder.

SOURCE: APA, DSM-IV, 1994.

perhaps the two syndromes are simply alternative forms of the same basic disorder. There are no firm answers to this yet. Nonetheless, one study of adopted children and their families revealed a pattern of correlations that suggests that vulnerability to ODD and conduct disorder do tend to run "separately" in families (Langbehn, Cadoret, Yates, Troughton, and Stewart, 1998). In other words, if one child has ODD, his siblings are somewhat more likely to show ODD than conduct disorder. Further, many children who meet diagnostic criteria for ODD never get involved in any delinquent or aggressive behavior. This is often the case during adolescence, where some youth show extreme negativism and verbal hostility toward their parents, but never violate the law.

Attention Deficit Hyperactivity Disorder (ADHD)

We now turn to the most frequently diagnosed disruptive disorder of childhood—**attention deficit hyperactivity disorder (ADHD)**. DSM-IV distinguishes three subtypes of this disorder: attention deficit hyperactivity disorder—combined type; attention deficit hyperactivity disorder—predominantly inattentive type; and attention deficit hyperactivity disorder—predominantly hyperactive-impulsive type. These distinctions are made because children may show only one aspect of the syndrome: attention problems or excessive activ-

A child with attention deficit hyperactivity disorder has trouble controlling his impulses and often engages in behaviors that are disruptive in the classroom.

ity level. In the majority of cases, however, they show problems with both attention and activity level, so the combined type is the most common.

The frequency with which ADHD is diagnosed is the main reason it is so controversial. Some people think it is overdiagnosed. They believe ADHD has become a convenient label that absolves adults of the responsibility for disciplining children. Even some experts think ADHD is overdiagnosed in the United States. However, cross-cultural studies do find that children from non-Western societies, such as China, also meet diagnostic criteria for ADHD, although the prevalence is somewhat lower than in the United States (Leung et al., 1996).

It is certainly not uncommon for parents and teachers to complain that children are overactive and restless, that they won't sit still, and that they cannot concentrate for long. What they usually mean is that the youngster won't concentrate for as long as adults would like. Most of these children are well within the normal range for their age. In contrast, there are children who show extreme attentional problems and overactivity, both at home and at school, and they can truly be regarded as having ADHD.

In order to be diagnosed with ADHD, a child must show developmentally inappropriate attentional problems, impulsiveness, and motor hyperactivity. In the classroom, the attentional difficulties are often manifested in an inability to stick with a specific task. Children with ADHD have difficulty organizing and completing work. They often give the impression that they are not listening or that they have not heard what they have been told. Just sitting still seems to be a major challenge for them. These children do not appear to have specific problems with processing information (such as a learning disorder); instead their problems lie in self-regulation (Henker and Whalen, 1989).

When they interact with peers, children with ADHD are sometimes awkward and disorganized. It is not surprising that they are often rejected by others as annoying and intrusive (Hinshaw and Melnick, 1995). Similarly, at home they are described as failing to follow through on parental requests and failing to sustain activities, including play, for periods of time that are appropriate for their age. A good example of a child with attention deficit hyperactivity disorder is provided in the following case:

James was four years old when he was first admitted to a children's psychiatric ward as a day patient. Ever since infancy he had made life difficult for his parents.

DSM-IV Criteria

Attention Deficit Hyperactivity Disorder

A. Either (1) or (2): (1) *inattention:* six (or more) of the following symptoms of inattention have persisted for at least 6 months to a degree that is maladaptive and inconsistent with developmental level: (a) often fails to give close attention to details or makes careless mistakes in schoolwork, work, or other activities; (b) often has difficulty sustaining attention in tasks or play activities; (c) often does not seem to listen when spoken to directly; (d) often does not follow through on instructions and fails to finish schoolwork, chores, or duties in the workplace (not due to oppositional behavior or failure to understand instructions); (e) often has difficulty organizing tasks and activities; (f) often avoids, dislikes, or is reluctant to engage in tasks that require sustained mental effort (such as schoolwork or homework); (g) often loses things necessary for tasks or activities (e.g., toys, school assignments, pencils, books, or tools); (h) is often easily distracted by extraneous stimuli; (i) is often forgetful in daily activities. (2) *hyperactivity-impulsivity:* six (or more) of the following symptoms of hyperactivity-impulsivity have persisted for at least 6 months to a degree that is maladaptive and inconsistent with developmental level: *Hyperactivity*—(a) often fidgets with hands or feet or squirms in seat; (b) often leaves seat in classroom or in other situations in which remaining seated is expected;

(c) often runs about or climbs excessively in situations in which it is inappropriate (in adolescents or adults, may be limited to subjective feelings of restlessness); (d) often has difficulty playing or engaging in leisure activities quietly; (e) is often "on the go" or often acts as if "driven by a motor"; (f) often talks excessively. *Impulsivity*—(g) often blurts out answers before questions have been completed; (h) often has difficulty awaiting turn; (i) often interrupts or intrudes on others (e.g., butts into conversations or games).

B. Some hyperactive-impulsive or inattentive symptoms that caused impairment were present before age 7 years.

C. Some impairment from the symptoms is present in two or more settings (e.g., at school [or work] and at home).

D. There must be clear evidence of clinically significant impairment in social, academic, or occupational functioning.

E. The symptoms do not occur exclusively during the course of a Pervasive Developmental Disorder, Schizophrenia, or other Psychotic Disorder and are not better accounted for by another mental disorder (e.g., Mood Disorder, Anxiety Disorder, Dissociative Disorder, or a Personality Disorder).

SOURCE: APA, DSM-IV, 1994.

As soon as he could crawl, he got into everything. He had no sense of danger. He slept very little at night and was difficult to pacify when upset. It was only because he was their only child and they could devote all of their time to him that his parents managed to maintain him at home.

His problems were noticed by others just as soon as James began preschool at age three. He made no friends among the other children. Every interaction ended in trouble. He rushed around all day, and could not even sit still at story time. His flitting from one activity to another completely exhausted his teachers. After some eighteen months of trying, his teachers suggested that he be referred to the hospital for assessment and treatment.

On examination, no gross physical damage could be found in his central nervous system. Psychological examinations revealed that James had a nearly average intelligence. In the hospital, he was just as hyperactive as he had been in school and at home. He climbed dangerously to the top of the outdoor swings.

He ran from one plaything to another and showed no consideration for other children who were using them. Left to his own devices, he was constantly on the move, tearing up paper, messing with paints—all in a nonconstructive manner.

James was placed in a highly structured classroom, with two teachers and five other children. There his behavior was gradually brought under control. He was given small tasks that were well within his ability, and he was carefully shown how to perform them. His successes were met with lavish praise. Moreover, patience and reward gradually increased the length of time he would spend seated at the table.

James had an especially severe form of ADHD. He was hyperactive, always on the go, with apparently boundless energy. He was impulsive, doing whatever came to mind, often without regard to physical danger. And he had problems focusing his attention on any one task without a great deal of support from teachers. Eventually, James was placed in a small, structured, residential school. By age sixteen, he had settled down a great deal. He was no longer physically overactive, but his conversation still flitted from one subject to another. He had no friends among his peers, although he could relate reasonably well to adults. James showed little initiative in matters concerning his own life, and his prospects for gaining employment were not good.

Conservative estimates of the prevalence of attention deficit disorders in preadolescents ranges from 2 to 5 percent, with male to female ratios ranging from 4:1 to 9:1 (Cantwell, 1998; Elia, Ambrosini, and Rapoport, 1999). DSM-IV cites prevalence rates ranging from 3 to 5 percent. As noted earlier, ADHD is a controversial disorder, in part because many people believe it is overdiagnosed. The proportion of children who meet the diagnostic criteria for ADHD varies as a function of (1) how information about the child's behavior is obtained (from parents, teachers, or clinical observers), (2) the nature of the setting (classroom, playground, or home), and (3) the child's family background. Of course, children with ADHD encounter the greatest problems in the classroom, where they are expected to sit in one place and pay attention for an extended period of time. So, teachers are often the first to recognize ADHD in a child. This is especially true of children from lower-income families.

As we mentioned, the behavior of children can change dramatically as they mature. This is certainly true of children with ADHD. Many children "grow out" of the symptoms as they get older, but follow-up studies of clinical samples indicate that 40 to 80 percent of children still meet the criteria for ADHD in adolescence, and some continue to show symptoms in adulthood (Fischer, Barkley, Fletcher, and Smallish, 1993; Zametkin and Ernst, 1999). Children with ADHD are also prone to conduct disturbances. About 45 to 60 percent of children with ADHD develop conduct disorder, delinquency, or drug abuse, compared to about 16 percent of youngsters without ADHD (Barkley, Fischer, Edelbrock, and Smallish, 1990; Hinshaw and Melnick, 1995; Moffitt and Silva, 1988). Not surprisingly, children with ADHD also tend to do poorly in school, and over 20 percent have a learning disorder. As adults, they are at greater risk for interpersonal problems, frequent job changes, traffic accidents, marital disruptions, and legal infractions (Fischer, Barkley, Fletcher, and Smallish, 1993; Henker and Whalen, 1989).

POSSIBLE CAUSES OF ATTENTION DEFICIT HYPERACTIVITY DISORDER

Genetic factors are involved in at least some cases of ADHD. Evidence for this comes from twin and family studies of children with ADHD (Rhee, Waldman, Hay and Levy, 1999). In a recent twin study, the authors found that concordance for ADHD was .67 in MZ twins and .00 in DZ twins (Shermaan, McGue, and Iacono, 1997). This suggests a substantial genetic contribution to ADHD. But these concordance rates are based on behavioral ratings provided by the mothers. When the concordance rates for the same twins were based on teachers' ratings, they were .53 for MZ twins and .37 for DZ twins. These figures yield a much lower estimate for the heritability of ADHD. While both sets of statistics indicate a role for genetic factors in ADHD, they also sound a note of caution about how we interpret research findings.

More recently, through the use of molecular genetic techniques, scientists have been able to look at specific candidate genes for ADHD. Some have found evidence that the genes that code for the D2 and D4 subtypes of the dopamine receptor may play a role, but more research is needed to confirm this (Faraone and Biederman, 1998). These findings fit with the theory that some abnormality in the dopamine receptor may produce a decrease in dopamine activity in children with ADHD (Sagvolden and Sargeant, 1998). The idea that dopamine is involved in ADHD also receives support from research on treatment.

As with conduct disorder, vulnerability to ADHD is also increased by environmental factors that interfere with brain function. Children exposed to prenatal complications are more likely to develop ADHD (Faraone and Biederman, 1998). Environmental toxins may also be involved. Children with high blood levels of lead show higher rates of hyperactivity, distractibility, impulsiveness, and problems following simple instructions (Fergusson, Horwood, and Lynskey, 1993). Elevations in blood lead levels are usually the result of youngsters ingesting chips of lead-based paints.

Theories about brain function in ADHD have focused on the regions that control arousal and behavioral inhibition (Barkley, 1997). In the past, many researchers believed that hyperactive children suffered from overarousal. This seems intuitively plausible, but the fact that children with ADHD are actually made more calm by stimulant drugs is inconsistent with this viewpoint. In contrast, recent theories assume that hyperactive children suffer from underarousal (see Figure 8–1; p. 357), which makes it more difficult for them to maintain attention. The limbic region is one brain area that could be involved in ADHD underarousal. The problems that children with ADHD have with inhibiting their motor behavior have led some to suspect that the frontal lobes are also involved. This is another parallel between conduct disorder and ADHD. When brain electrical activity is monitored in children with ADHD, there is a slowdown in the activation of the frontal lobes (Silberstein et al., 1998). This is most noticeable when children with ADHD are expected to be paying attention to specific visual stimuli.

The child's social environment may also be a factor in the symptoms of ADHD. Children with ADHD have often been exposed to more disruptions in their families, such as frequent changes in residence or parental divorce (Frick, 1994). Also, the fathers of children with ADHD are more prone to irresponsible and antisocial behavior (Barkley, Fischer, Edelbrock, and Smallish, 1990). But these findings leave some unanswered questions: Are family disruptions causes or merely correlates of ADHD? Do fathers influence their children's risk for ADHD through genetic or environmental routes? Although we do not know for sure, it is likely that the familial influences are both genetic and environmental.

TREATMENT

Children with ADHD can be very difficult to deal with. They can quickly exhaust their teachers and parents. But the real tragedy of ADHD is the fact that it can interfere with the child's academic success and peer relationships. Every clinician who has worked with these children has had the experience of hearing a tearful child describe his most recent rejection by a peer. The sadness and loss of self-esteem can be profound. These children are certainly deserving of the best treatment mental health professionals have to offer. The two main treatment approaches to ADHD are medication and behavior therapy (see Table 8–10). We will describe both of these, as well as the controversy that surrounds them.

Drug Therapy Paradoxically, many children with ADHD are made worse by tranquilizers. In contrast, most show decreases in attention problems and overactivity when given stimulant drugs (Cantwell, 1998). The most common stimulant is an amphetamine called methylphenidate, whose trade name is Ritalin. Methylphenidate is a dopamine agonist; it increases the level of activity in the brain systems that use dopamine as their neurotransmitter. Another drug used to treat ADHD is premoline (trade name "Cylert"). Like Ritalin, Cylert is a stimulant that acts

TABLE 8–10

Treatment

ATTENTION DEFICIT HYPERACTIVITY DISORDER (ADHD)

	Stimulants	*Antidepressants*	*Behavior Therapy*	*Combined Stimulant and Behavior Therapy*
Improvement	about 80% at least moderately improved	about 50% moderately improved	about 40% moderately improved	slightly better than stimulants alone
Relapse★	high	high	low to moderate	moderate
Side Effects	mild to moderate	mild to moderate	unclear	mild to moderate
Cost	inexpensive	inexpensive	expensive	expensive
Time Scale†	weeks/months	months	weeks/months	months
Overall	**good**	**useful**	**marginal**	**good**

★Relapse after discontinuation of treatment.
†Time to achieve maximal effect.
SOURCE: Campbell and Cueva, 1995, p. 10; Greenhill, 1998; Hinshaw, Klein, and Abikoff, 1998; revised with MTA Cooperative Group, 1999a, 1999b.

Society and Mental Health

Box 8—3

Treating Children or Drugging Children?

While there are a number of methods used in the treatment of ADHD, the prescription of stimulant medication (primarily methylphenidate, or Ritalin) remains the most common but most controversial treatment. Psychologist Richard DeGrandpre is among those who believe that Ritalin is being overprescribed for a disorder that does not necessarily exist (DeGrandpre, 1999). In his book, *Ritalin Nation,* DeGrandpre argues that Ritalin has become a chemical tool for controlling childhood behaviors that are a consequence of an overstimulating culture. He believes that increasing numbers of children are being prescribed the drug unnecessarily. DeGrandpre also points out that Ritalin is a relatively new drug and its long-term side effects have not been clearly identified. Moreover, the well-established short-term side effects include the aggravation of psychosis, depression, motor tics, anxiety, and insomnia. These should not be taken lightly.

Peter Breggin, of the International Center for the Study of Psychiatry and Psychology, is also concerned about the recent, sharp increase in the diagnosis of ADHD and the use of medication for treatment (Breggin, 1998). Breggin notes that the U. S. Drug Enforcement Administration indicated a "sixfold increase" in the production of Ritalin over a five-year span, and that approximately 4 to 5 million more children are on Ritalin per year. Breggin believes we are "pathologizing" normal childhood behavior by diagnosing so many children as having ADHD and as needing medical treatment.

On the other side of this argument is Jerry Wiener, a psychiatrist at George Washington University Medical Center. Wiener argues that ADHD is a disorder that does, in fact, exist, and that Ritalin is the most effective means of treatment (Wiener, 1996). He points to data indicating that 75 to 85 percent of children benefit from its ability to reduce major symptoms, such as inattention, impulsivity, and hyperactivity. But Wiener believes that medication alone should not be the only method used in treating ADHD. Along these same lines, Russell Barkley, a psychologist at the University of Massachusetts Medical Center, maintains that Ritalin is not being overprescribed. He notes that the prescription of

Ritalin is not equivalent to the production of Ritalin, so that reports of a significant increase in production do not necessarily reflect actual usage of the drug (Barkley, 1998a). Barkley also points to recent studies that indicate that the number of children on Ritalin is actually less than half of what Breggin states. Both Wiener and Barkley allege that Ritalin use is well below the estimated percentage of children diagnosed with ADHD; Ritalin may even be underprescribed in school-aged children.

It is unlikely that the controversy surrounding ADHD will be resolved in the near future. It brings into clearer focus the problems clinical researchers face when they are trying to define a disorder. It seems most likely that what we call ADHD is the extreme end of the "normal" distribution of attentional capacities and activity levels observed in children, just as "high blood pressure" is the extreme end of the normal distribution of blood pressures. But does ADHD qualify as a disorder? What about the fact that methylphenidate helps 75 to 85 percent of children with ADHD? Should this be taken as evidence that ADHD is a biologically based disorder? The answer is "no." You may recall that the research shows that methylphenidate also improves attention in normal children, as well as in adults. Nonetheless, ADHD does qualify as a disorder if one uses the criterion that a disorder must cause some discomfort for the individual. ADHD would qualify because it is usually accompanied by academic problems or peer rejection.

Ultimately, the question of whether it is wise to give children methylphenidate will only be resolved when we have more data on long-term outcome. If we discover that there are negative long-term effects, then we will have to weigh them against the short-term positive effects produced by the drug. If the negative effects of methylphenidate are too great, clinicians and parents will probably opt for behavioral therapy, a treatment that is more time-consuming, but that has no known negative side effects.

SOURCE: Based on Barkley, 1998a; Breggin, 1998; Bromfield, 1996; DeGrandpre, 1999; Wiener, 1996.

---

on the dopamine system. Children taking these drugs show increases in interpersonal responsiveness and goal-directed efforts, plus decreases in activity level and disruptive behavior. But these beneficial effects also occur in normal children. So there is really nothing unique about the impact that stimulant medication has on children with ADHD (see Box 8–3 for a further discussion).

There can be side effects of stimulant drugs, and these have been well documented for meth-

ylphenidate. It can cause insomnia, headaches, and nausea. Further, there is no evidence that the gains children make when taking stimulants are lasting; children with ADHD who receive these medications do not have a better long-term prognosis than children who do not (Henker and Whalen, 1989). Moreover, there are large differences between children in their responses to these drugs. Some children respond rapidly to small doses of Ritalin, whereas others respond only to large doses.

A computerized biofeedback system has been developed to treat children with ADHD. The patient's brain-wave activity is monitored while playing computer games. The computer then modifies the game so that the patient is increasingly challenged, which then causes increases in the range of brain-wave activity, thereby strengthening the brain.

Behavioral Therapy Behavioral therapies are the chief alternative to medication in the treatment of ADHD. Operant conditioning programs have been found to be effective in treating overactivity and attentional deficits, particularly in the short run (Barkley, 1998b; Pelham, 1989). Several investigators have used these techniques to reduce the child's problem behaviors—for example, distracting others—while simultaneously extending the amount of time the child attends. In one case, for example, after carefully establishing how overactive a nine-year-old boy was—that is, his base rate of overactive behavior—the boy was rewarded for sitting still. For every ten seconds that he sat quietly, he earned a penny. The first experimental session lasted only five minutes. But by the eighth session, the boy's overactivity had virtually ceased and, at follow-up four months later, his teacher reported that not only was he much quieter but he was also progressing in reading and making friends. Thus, the straightforward use of attention and tangible reinforcers can produce significant and rapid changes when they are systematically applied.

The critical question is whether behavioral therapy is as effective as medication in treating ADHD (see Table 8–10). Findings from studies that compare the two indicate that medication is more effective than behavioral therapy in treating the symptoms of ADHD (Klein and Abikoff, 1997; MTA Cooperative Group, 1999a, 1999b). But the results also suggest that a combination of drug therapy and behavioral therapy is the most effective treatment for reducing some of the conduct problems often associated with ADHD (DuPaul and Barkley, 1993; Hinshaw, Klein, and Abikoff, 1998; MTA Cooperative Group, 1999a, 1999b). Medications may make it easier for children to learn from behavioral interventions. It is clear, however, that children's responses to both stimulant medications and behavioral therapy are highly idiosyncratic (DuPaul and Barkley, 1993). An effective dose of either stimulant medications or behavioral therapy for one child may be an ineffective dose for another. Thus, clinicians must carefully monitor children's responses to these interventions, and vary dosage levels and techniques to meet an individual child's needs.

Putting It All Together

In this chapter, we have discussed a broad range of childhood disorders. Some, like autism, involve behavioral abnormalities that are so pronounced few would fail to notice the child's disability. Others, like enuresis, may only be known to a small number of people who have regular contact with the child. But to varying degrees, all the disorders we have discussed have the potential to interfere with the child's happiness and opportunities for healthy growth and development.

It appears that virtually all of the disorders of childhood are the consequence of multiple causal factors. This is even true of Fragile X syndrome, the only disorder whose genotype is known. In the case of Fragile X, events that occur during the early development of the fertilized egg influence the genetic mutations that take place in the cells. These are "micro" environmental events that can result in noticeable differences between identical twins in their physical appearance and behavior. During postnatal life, environmental events continue to influence the course of development. The impact will vary, of course, depending on the person's constitutional strengths and vulnerabilities. Thus, it seems that the diathesis-stress model provides a valid framework for viewing childhood disorders.

Through careful study, researchers have made significant progress in understanding the etiology of virtually all the childhood disorders. But we still have much to learn. Throughout this chapter, we have pointed out gaps in our knowledge. There are at least four broad questions about childhood psychopathology that need to be addressed over the next few years. First, does the current DSM-IV classification system for childhood disorders accurately represent the breakdown of childhood syndromes? For example, are autism and Asperger's disorder really separate disorders with different causes? Or is Asperger's disorder a much milder subtype of autism with the same basic causes? It is often difficult to translate children's adjustment problems into specific syndromes with clear-cut criteria for diagnosis. This is because the symptom configuration of any disorder may change with the child's development. Also, some symptoms, such as aggressive behavior, are associated with many different disorders. The classification of children's disorders is expected to undergo much revision in the future.

The second question is related to the first: How can we better identify children who have serious psychological problems? There are several challenges here. First, we must rely on the adults in a troubled child's life to bring the child to the attention of clinicians. In addition, children's underdeveloped language skills make it difficult to obtain information from them about their condition. We need to know how to ask better questions of parents, teachers, and children that will provide the information clinicians need to access children's psychological health.

The third question concerns the long-term effects of various treatments for children. What treatments, biological or psychological, are the most effective at helping a child to recover from a given problem and at preventing the recurrence of that problem in later years? Longitudinal studies of the treatment outcomes will be expensive, but the need for them is obvious (Klykylo, Kay, and Rube, 1998). When objective data on the effectiveness of various treatments are not available, clinicians are forced to rely on their best hunches. Sometimes this works, because the clinician has a great deal of knowledge from professional experience. But sometimes the outcome is not so good, and the clinician is left to wonder whether another treatment would have yielded a better outcome. The ideal situation is one in which the practitioner can use the findings from studies that compare various treatments to give the parents and child some options. In the case of Jennifer, discussed at the beginning of the chapter, the psychologist concluded that she was suffering from a pervasive developmental disorder and would benefit from an intensive psycho-educational approach:

> When I met with Carol and Robert Jenkins for the third time, they were eagerly awaiting my conclusions. My usual procedure is to first share my observa-

tions with the parents. I described the behaviors Jennifer showed during my assessment and the school observation. I described the limited test results I was able to obtain. I then explained the process I went through as I excluded certain alternative diagnoses. When I told them Jennifer met the criteria for a diagnosis of childhood disintegrative disorder, Carol and Robert looked worried and confused. Carol had tears in her eyes. The next step was to explain to them, to the best of our current knowledge, what causes this disorder. Of course, they had many questions, which I tried my best to answer.

The final, and most important, step was to explore the treatment alternatives for childhood disintegrative disorder. In our community, as in many others in the United States, the public school system provides some very good programs for children with special needs. They are mandated to do so because of federal guidelines. There are also several private schools that offer programs for children with pervasive developmental disorders. I described the typical content of these programs to Jennifer's parents, as well as the differences among them. It is not surprising that Carol and Robert were eager to know what to expect of the treatment outcome. How much improvement should they expect to see in Jennifer? Would she regain the skills she lost? It is fortunate that there are several well-conducted outcome studies on the treatment of pervasive developmental disorders. I told them about some of the findings. I also told them that it would be very important to focus on Jennifer's language development and social skills, because these two areas are linked with the long-term prognosis.

As a clinical psychologist, I have a professional obligation to tell parents about the limits of our understanding of childhood disorders. For example, I told Jennifer's parents that there are no studies that specifically compare the outcomes of various treatments for all the subtypes of pervasive developmental disorder. We have to draw some inferences from the general research findings.

Toward the end of our ninety-minute session, we addressed a topic that most parents bring up at this point; namely, what if anything could have been done to prevent the child's disorder? This is probably the most difficult issue for a psychologist to address. The truth is, prevention of childhood disorders has received relatively little attention from researchers.

This bring us to the fourth broad issue for research on childhood disorders—prevention. Early-onset disorders can be especially tragic because they have the potential to rob the individual of the joys of childhood. We know some of the environmental factors and biological indicators that are associated with risk for childhood disorders. Can we identify those at risk and develop new programs for preventing the onset of adjustment problems? By bolstering the child's emotional and cognitive strengths, it may be possible to increase resilience. This can have ripple effects that reverberate throughout society. Preventing childhood disorders would not only benefit the child, but would have positive consequences for society in general. Perhaps, if such programs had been available, the tragedy in Littleton, Colorado, would not have occurred.

Summary

1. Children's psychological disorders are often difficult to diagnose because they occur in a developmental context; physical and mental abilities and behavior undergo rapid change during childhood and adolescence. Also, because children cannot always communicate their problem directly through language, clinicians and researchers must often rely on observation or on adult informants.

2. The early-onset disorders result from both biological and social causes. Some, like autism, are more strongly determined by constitutional vulnerabilities that are present at birth. Other disorders, such as those involving conduct problems and anxiety, appear to be heavily influenced by the child's experiences. The diathesis-stress model, which assumes an interaction between constitutional factors and experience, fits well with what is known about many of the early-onset disorders. On the whole, children's problems can be divided into four areas: *emotional disorders, developmental disorders, eating and habit disorders,* and *disruptive behavior disorders.*

3. The emotional disorders include reactive attachment disorder, separation anxiety disorder, phobias, and depression. *Reactive attachment disorder* involves severe problems with the child's capacity to form attachments with caregivers. The most common emotional disorder in children is *separation anxiety disorder.* Children with this disorder have a marked fear of separation from loved ones. *Phobias,* such as school phobia, are also common among children. Although early theories posited that children could not suffer from *depression,* we now know that it can occur in children and that its prevalence is actually increasing.

4. The developmental disorders involve pervasive difficulties in the acquisition of interpersonal and/or communication skills. *Autism* involves severe disturbances in the way the child interacts and communicates with others. The signs are often apparent soon after birth, and always present by the time the child reaches three years of age. *Rett's disorder* and *childhood disintegrative disorder* are preceded by a period of normal development, then the child gradually loses abilities. The key feature of *Asperger's disorder* is an impairment in the capacity to relate to others, without significant language problems. Most children with a pervasive developmental disorder have at least some residual signs in adulthood, even if they have undergone intensive treatment.

5. The eating disorders include *anorexia* and *bulimia.* Both usually have their onset in adolescence, and they are more common in females. The eating disorders appear to be heavily influenced by social factors. Habit disorders include the elimination disorders, especially *enuresis (bed-wetting)* and *encopresis,* which tend to occur in early childhood, as well *stuttering* and *Tourette's disorder,* whose main symptoms are motor and verbal tics.

6. The disruptive behavior disorders include *conduct disorder, oppositional defiant disorder,* and *attention-deficit hyperactivity disorder.* Children with these disorders have difficulty controlling their behavior, and sometimes show adjustment problems that continue into adulthood.

7. There is still much to be learned about childhood disorders, and especially about their treatment. Drug therapies have been used for some disorders, but there are reasons for concern about the use of drugs in the treatment of children. Behavioral treatments are effective for many childhood disorders, including attention deficit hyperactivity disorder, separation anxiety disorder, phobias, bed-wetting, stuttering, and some symptoms of autism. Many therapists also advocate involving a child's parents in therapy in order to facilitate the child's recovery.

9

Personality Disorders

Chapter Outline

Kenny McKay, Untitled work.

→ Describe some of the problems of diagnosing the personality disorders, and the differences between the categorical and dimensional approaches to personality disorders.

→ Understand how both genes and experience contribute to the development of personality disorders, and what some cross-cultural differences are in their diagnosis.

→ Learn how schizotypal personality disorder is genetically related to schizophrenia, as well as what physical and behavioral abnormalities these disorders share in common.

→ Be able to characterize antisocial personality disorder and to identify causes and treatments for the disorder, as well as possibilities for prevention.

→ Describe the central features of the "dramatic-erratic" disorders, and be able to explain why people with these disorders have unstable relationships with others.

→ Be able to describe the symptoms, causes, and possible treatments for borderline personality disorder, and why this diagnosis is so often accompanied by self-destructive behavior.

→ Learn about the central features of the "anxious-fearful" disorders and why some people question whether these should be viewed as personality disorders.

The term "personality" is used to refer to the relatively stable psychological and behavioral characteristics of an individual, the way the person views the world and relates to it. Personality remains, more or less, the same across various situations. Thus, when someone says that a particular behavior is "out of character" for a person, they are implying that it is not consistent with his personality. An individual's typical style might be flexible, upbeat, and outgoing, and he might often take a leadership role. Researchers who study personality would use words such as cooperative, optimistic, extroverted, and dominant to describe such a person. These various aspects of personality are referred to as personality traits. Another person might share the same traits of cooperativeness, optimism, and extroversion, but tend to be a follower, being more submissive than dominant. The two individuals would differ on the trait of dominance. Nonetheless, people are judged, in part, by their personalities; both of these individuals would probably be described as having a "good personality." People who are cooperative, optimistic, and extroverted tend to be perceived as well-adjusted.

But what about those who are so negativistic, withdrawn, manipulative, and/or rigid that it interferes with their life? Such persistent patterns of dysfunctional behavior are referred to as *personality disorders.* People with personality disorders have enduring, inflexible, and maladaptive patterns or traits that can affect their thinking, emotional responses, interpersonal relations, and impulse control. These dysfunctional behaviors differ significantly from the expectations of the individual's culture and can lead to significant distress for the individual or others and can impair social or occupational functioning.

In the previous chapter, we described a boy named Derrick who showed persistent conduct problems from the preschool years through adolescence and who was diagnosed with conduct disorder. As a young adult, he was less aggressive and succeeded in getting a high school degree, but problems persisted:

> Derrick was proud of the fact that he had completed a high school equivalency degree program. He bragged to his friends that he hadn't even studied, and actually had someone else take the final exam for him. The degree opened some doors for Derrick, and he got a job as a sales trainee at a local car dealership when he was nineteen. His mother was very pleased that Derrick seemed to be more mature.

Again, Derrick's skills with people served him well, and he breezed through the training period. He didn't always show up on time for work, but when he was there he did extremely well. His supervisor was impressed at the way Derrick managed to get customers to agree to take a test drive. But problems started to crop up. A woman who claimed that Derrick was her baby's father showed up at the dealership and made a scene. One evening Derrick drove a demonstration car home without asking, and it was reported stolen by the morning supervisor. Some money was missing from the register in the parts department, and several other employees suspected Derrick. They were right. But by that time Derrick was dating one of the cashiers, and he was able to convince her to implicate another employee in the theft. The other employee was fired. Somehow Derrick was able to put out all of the little "fires" that seemed to surround him at the dealership. He had a feeling of satisfaction that he managed to keep the job for seven months. But he abruptly quit at that point, and informed his co-workers that he was going into business for himself. Derrick told his mother there was no future at the dealership, and that he was planning to buy a fast-food franchise with a loan he received from a friend.

The personality disorders are fundamentally disorders of traits; they are enduring, maladaptive ways of perceiving, relating to, and thinking about the world and oneself. Two of Derrick's maladaptive traits are manipulativeness and dishonesty. These tendencies cause others to be suspicious of him; they interfere with his functioning at work; and they ultimately can lead to serious legal problems. Further, these tendencies are pervasive, as they are manifested in a variety of situations. As people get to know Derrick, they begin to view honesty as "out of character" for him.

Diagnosing Personality Disorders

In contrast to most of the behavioral syndromes we have discussed up to this point, the personality disorders are considered Axis II disorders in DSM-IV. The Axis I disorders, such as major depression and schizophrenia, are typically associated with such severe symptoms that other people can readily notice that the person suffering from the disorder is not mentally healthy. In contrast, the suffering is often muted in individuals with a personality disorder. But even when people with personality disorders do not view themselves as having a problem, their behaviors usually strike friends and family members as odd, deviant, or abnormal. Their characteristic ways of thinking about themselves and their environment are inflexible, and a source of social and occupational problems. Derrick's case illustrates the difficulties that a specific type of personality disorder, antisocial personality disorder, can create in the work environment.

DSM-IV Criteria

Personality Disorder

A. An enduring pattern of inner experience and behavior that deviates markedly from the expectations of the individual's culture. This pattern is manifested in two (or more) of the following areas: (1) cognition (i.e., ways of perceiving and interpreting self, other people, and events); (2) affectivity (i.e., the range, intensity, lability, and appropriateness of emotional response); (3) interpersonal functioning; (4) impulse control.

B. The enduring pattern is inflexible and pervasive across a broad range of personal and social situations.

C. The enduring pattern leads to clinically significant distress or impairment in social, occupational, or other important areas of functioning.

D. The pattern is stable and of long duration and its onset can be traced back at least to adolescence or early adulthood.

E. The enduring pattern is not better accounted for as a manifestation or consequence of another mental disorder.

F. The enduring pattern is not due to the direct physiological effects of a substance (e.g., a drug of abuse, a medication) or a general medical condition (e.g., head trauma).

SOURCE: APA, DSM-IV, 1994.

Although it is difficult to estimate the rate of personality disorders in the general population, the best estimates indicate that 10 to 13 percent of people would meet diagnostic criteria for a personality disorder (Cloninger, 1999; Weissman, 1993). Further, there is a tendency for people to meet criteria for more than one personality disorder, either at the same time or through the course of development (Kasen, Cohen, Skodol, Johnson, and Brook, 1999). This is referred to as the **comorbidity** of personality disorders, and it has been estimated that about 50 percent of people who meet criteria for one personality disorder will also meet criteria for another personality disorder. There is especially comorbidity with substance abuse; one study showed that 60 percent of patients with substance-use disorders also have a personality disorder (Skodol, Oldham, and Gallaher, 1999).

There has been some controversy about the best interpretation of comorbidity (Lilienfeld, Waldman and Israel, 1994; Pfohl, 1999). Some believe it reflects the actual existence of two or more separate disorders, noting that the use of the term "comorbidity" for psychological syndromes implies that there are true boundaries to the disorders and that DSM-IV has correctly defined them. Others disagree and have argued that comorbidity simply shows that we have not correctly identified the boundaries of mental disorders.

Categories or Dimensions of Personality?

In DSM-IV, each personality disorder is listed as a separate diagnostic category, just as paranoid schizophrenia and Alzheimer's disease are listed separately. The person either meets the behavioral criteria, and falls in the category (that is, he or she has the mental illness), or fails to meet the criteria and is deemed to not have that particular disorder. This is a **categorical approach.** In contrast, some view the behaviors and traits that define the personality disorders as falling on a continuum; and they take a **dimensional approach.** They believe that personality disorders represent extreme versions of normal personality traits or "dimensions." For example, they believe there is a continuum of emotional dependence, and that everyone falls somewhere along the continuum. Even healthy and competent adults are emotionally dependent on others sometimes, but at the extreme are adults who are unable to function autonomously

because they can't make decisions about even the most mundane, everyday issues.

In general, when researchers have compared categorical to dimensional approaches, the results suggest that the dimensional approach may be more reliable (Clark, Livesley, and Morey, 1997). For example, in one study, five clinicians judged each of ten client case histories and provided both dimensional ratings and categorical diagnoses (Heumann and Morey, 1990). Reliability was higher for the dimensional judgments than for the categorical diagnoses. But these findings do not address the question of validity. Nor do they help us understand what the true nature of human personality is, or what the critical dimensions of personality are.

One of the main questions researchers have tried to answer is how many personality dimensions are there? Controversy still surrounds this question, but the most well-known theory is the five-factor model, which proposes a set of five personality dimensions, sometimes called the "Big Five" (Clark, 1999; Clark, Livesley, and Morey, 1997; Costa and Widiger, 1994; McCrae and Costa, 1999; Widiger, Verheul, and van den Brink, 1999). The five personality dimensions in this model are: extraversion (ranging from assertive to passive), conscientiousness (ranging from organized and thorough to negligent and unreliable), agreeableness (ranging from warm and kind to selfish and hostile), emotional stability (ranging from calm and even tempered to nervous and moody), and openness to experience (ranging from creative and curious to shallow and inflexible). Everyone falls somewhere on each of these personality dimensions. Although the five dimensions were originally identified in research on normal individuals, they also apply to people who meet DSM diagnoses (Costa and Widiger, 1994). But could the five-factor model, or any other dimensional approach to personality, take the place of categories of personality disorder? Researchers are continuing to explore this possibility.

It appears that the five-factor model can be generalized to people from many different cultural settings. When people from countries as different as Japan, Germany, Portugal, Israel, Korea, Italy, Croatia, and China complete self-report measures of personality, researchers find the same five dimensions of personality (McCrae and Costa, 1997; McCrae et al., 1999; Trull and Geary, 1997). The age changes in personality are also similar across cultures; as people age, there are decreases in extraversion and openness, and

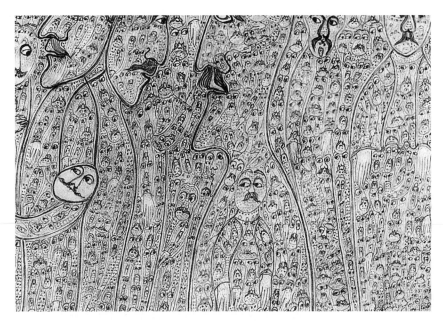

The dimensional approach says that personality disorders are extreme versions of personality traits that fall along a continuum, while the categorical approach says that personality disorders are discrete categories based on specific criteria. This pencil drawing of wide-eyed faces by Edmund Monsiel seems to illustrate the dimensional approach where stronger faces emerge from the continuum of faces.

increases in agreeableness and conscientiousness. These findings indicate that the personality dimensions defined by the five-factor model are not just a product of American culture, but rather shared human tendencies that transcend culture.

Some, like Robert Cloninger, have proposed a biological basis for personality dimensions. Cloninger and his colleagues believe that personality dimensions involve different neurotransmitter systems (Cloninger, 1998; Svrakic, Svrakic, and Cloninger, 1996). They originally proposed a model that assumed the existence of three brain systems (behavioral activation, inhibition, and maintenance), each of which is based on one of three neurotransmitters: dopamine, serotonin, and norepinephrine. They believe that each of these brain systems are linked with three personality dimensions: novelty seeking, harm avoidance, and reward dependence. Cloninger theorizes that a person's behavior is determined by where he or she stands on each of these dimensions. For example, people who are low on novelty seeking and high on harm avoidance will avoid risks and prefer to lead a very predictable life. Those high on novelty seeking and average on harm avoidance will take more risks and enjoy spontaneity. Those who are too high on novelty seeking and low on harm avoidance will engage in foolhardy behavior. More recently, Cloninger and his colleagues have added a fourth personality dimension, persistence, and three "character dimensions," self-directedness, cooperativeness, and self-transcendence.

Cloninger believes that people who are low on these character dimensions, especially self-directedness and cooperativeness, are more likely to have personality disorders. Using Cloninger's model, someone with antisocial personality disorder would be characterized by high novelty seeking, low harm avoidance, low reward dependence, and low persistence, combined with low self-directedness, low cooperativeness, and low self-transcendence. It is obvious how these traits would interfere with occupational functioning.

Development of Disorders

One long-held assumption about personality is that it is not entirely formed until the person reaches adulthood. The developers of DSM-IV shared this assumption. Consequently, another key feature of personality disorders is that they are usually not diagnosed until adulthood (generally to have such a diagnosis, the patient must be eighteen years of age or older). Although children can be given a personality disorder diagnosis if they meet all of the criteria for one of them, they must also meet the criterion that the behavioral signs are present for at least one year. The only exception is antisocial personality disorder; children under eighteen who show this syndrome receive a diagnosis of conduct disorder (see Chapter 8). The reason for this is that so many youngsters who show signs of antisocial behavior in adolescence go on to be well-adjusted young adults. Nonetheless, it has been shown that personality disorders can be reliably diagnosed in adolescents (Kasen, Cohen, Skodol, Johnson, and Brook, 1999). Furthermore, adolescents who meet criteria for a DSM-IV personality disorder are more likely to meet criteria for an Axis I or II diagnosis when they are young adults. Thus, the presence of a personality disorder during adolescence may be an indicator of risk for a chronic course of psychological problems.

There are also some sex differences in the occurrence of certain personality disorders. Among the most well-established sex differences are that antisocial and paranoid personality disorders tend to be more common in men, whereas histrionic and dependent personality disorders occur more often in women (Livesley, 1995). Although it has been suggested that this may be due to sex bias in the diagnosis of disorders by clinicians, recent evidence suggests that this is not the case (Funtowicz and Widiger, 1999). In general, the personality disorders that tend to predominate in females involve less social and occupational dysfunction, and more personal distress, than those that occur more often in males.

It is also well established that personality, and personality disorders, are influenced by both genetic factors and experiences. Research findings support this; it appears that only a moderate proportion of the variance in the ratings of personality disorder symptoms and syndromes is due to heredity (Nigg and Goldsmith, 1994). Thus, experiences, especially childhood experiences, play a significant part in molding the development of personality traits.

Knowing that childhood experiences influence personality development, we would expect to find cross-cultural differences in personality disorders. A number of such differences have been observed (Cohen, Slomkowski, and Robins, 1999). For example, there are national differences in the rate of antisocial personality disorder (Zoccolillo, Price, Ji, Hyuns and Hwu, 1999) and the symptoms of narcissistic personality disorder (Warren and Capponi, 1996). With respect to antisocial personality disorder, the United States has a somewhat higher rate than several other countries. Also, in the United States, people with narcissistic personality disorder are more "exhibitionistic" than their counterparts in Japan. These and other personality differences are, in part, a product of cultural differences in the emphasis on certain personality characteristics, such as assertiveness and self-orientation. Thus, just as the cross-cultural

differences in the physical environment impact on rates of medical diseases, so cross-cultural differences in the social environment influence the occurrence of behavioral disorders.

Compared to the Axis I disorders listed in DSM-IV, the treatment of personality disorders has received less attention from researchers. There are at least two reasons for this. One is that the personality disorders have been conceptualized as "trait-like," and clinicians have been somewhat pessimistic about the prognosis. Also, with a few exceptions, most people with personality disorders are not so dysfunctional that their behavior results in involuntary treatment, as is often the case for those with psychotic disorders. In recent years, researchers have focused more attention on developing new treatments for personality disorders, and some of these will be discussed in this chapter (Costa and Widiger, 1994).

Clusters of Disorders

DSM-IV lists three general categories of personality disorders. Cluster A disorders all involve some type of odd, eccentric ideas or behaviors. There are three Cluster A disorders in DSM-IV: schizotypal, schizoid, and paranoid personality disorders. Cluster B disorders are characterized by dramatic, emotional, or erratic behaviors. These include antisocial, histrionic, narcissistic, and borderline personality disorders. The disorders listed in Cluster C share the common thread of anxious or fearful behavioral propensities. There are three: avoidant, dependent, and obsessive-compulsive personality disorders. Our discussion of the DSM-IV personality disorders will be organized around these three clusters. We begin with the Cluster A disorders.

Odd-Eccentric Disorders

Although the clusters of personality disorders described in DSM-IV have not been validated by research, those disorders in Cluster A share several features. All of the personality disorders that are considered to be odd-eccentric disorders involve some form of discomfort with or suspicion about other people. Individuals with these disorders have a hard time establishing relationships with others and fitting into a social network.

Schizotypal Personality Disorder

Of all the personality disorders, the volume of laboratory research on **schizotypal personality disorder** ranks second to that on antisocial personality disorder. Schizotypal personality disorder affects about 3 percent of the general population, with males being more likely to meet the diagnostic criteria (Carter, Joyce, Mulder, Sullivan, and Luty, 1999). The disorder involves long-standing oddities in thinking, perceiving, communicating, and behaving—oddities that are severe enough to be noticed, but not serious enough to warrant the diagnosis of schizophrenia. Indeed, many of the disturbances that characterize schizotypal personality disorder are similar to those seen among chronic schizophrenics, although in milder forms. It would be an error, however, to identify this disorder wholly with schizophrenia, because differences of degree are very important as far as psychological distress and prognosis are concerned (McGlashan, 1986b). McCreery and Claridge (1996) conducted a study of people who report having "out of body" experiences. It is not surprising that these people also tended to score above average on questionnaires that measure "schizotypal" tendencies (see Box 9–1). The authors describe these individuals as "happy schizotypes," people who are relatively well-adjusted and functional despite, and in some cases even because of, their anomalous perceptual experiences. Also, it should be kept in mind that people

Odd thinking and communication characterize schizotypal personality disorder. Many people with this disorder experience constricted or inappropriate emotions, as might be inferred from this painting by Josef Wittlich.

with schizotypal personality disorder do not lose contact with reality; they are aware of who they are and where they are.

Odd thinking, one of the key features of schizotypal personality disorder, can be manifested in ex-

DSM-IV Criteria

Schizotypal Personality Disorder

A. A pervasive pattern of social and interpersonal deficits marked by acute discomfort with, and reduced capacity for, close relationships as well as by cognitive or perceptual distortions and eccentricities of behavior, beginning by early adulthood and present in a variety of contexts, as indicated by five (or more) of the following: (1) ideas of reference (excluding delusions of reference); (2) odd beliefs or magical thinking that influences behavior and is inconsistent with subcultural norms (e.g., superstitiousness, belief in clairvoyance, telepathy, or "sixth sense"; in children and adolescents, bizarre fantasies or preoccupations); (3) unusual perceptual experiences, including bodily illusions; (4) odd thinking and speech (e.g., vague circumstantial, metaphorical, overelaborate, or stereo-

typed); (5) suspiciousness or paranoid ideation; (6) inappropriate or constricted affect; (7) behavior or appearance that is odd, eccentric, or peculiar; (8) lack of close friends or confidants other than first-degree relatives; (9) excessive social anxiety that does not diminish with familiarity and tends to be associated with paranoid fears rather than negative judgments about self.

B. Does not occur exclusively during the course of Schizophrenia, a Mood Disorder with Psychotic Features, another Psychotic Disorder, or a Pervasive Developmental Disorder.

SOURCE: APA, DSM-IV, 1994.

Characterizing the Schizotypal Personality: Selected Items from The Schizotypal Personality Questionnaire

Ideas of Reference

1. Do you sometimes feel that things you see on the TV or read in the newspaper have a special meaning for you?
28. Have you ever noticed a common event or object that seemed to be a special sign for you?

Excessive Social Anxiety

2. I sometimes avoid going to places where there will be many people because I will get anxious.
11. I get nervous when I have to make polite conversation.

Odd Beliefs or Magical Thinking

39. Can other people feel your feelings when they are not there?
47. Have you had experiences with astrology, seeing the future, UFOs, ESP, or a sixth sense?

Unusual Perceptual Experiences

31. I often hear a voice speaking my thoughts aloud.
40. Have you ever seen things invisible to other people?

Odd or Eccentric Behavior

14. People sometimes comment on my unusual mannerisms and habits.

No Close Friends

6. I have little interest in getting to know other people.
41. Do you feel that there is no one you are really close to outside of your immediate family, or people you can confide in or talk to about personal problems?

Odd Speech

16. I sometimes jump quickly from one topic to another when speaking.
58. Do you tend to wander off the topic when having conversation?

Constricted Affect

17. I am not good at expressing my true feelings by the way I talk and look.
43. I tend to avoid eye contact when conversing with others.

Suspiciousness

59. I often feel that others have it in for me.
9. I am sure I am being talked about behind my back.

SOURCE: Raine, 1991.

---

treme superstitiousness or paranoid ideas—the feeling that one is the object of special attention from others. The latter sense, which is technically called an *idea of reference,* can also be a fertile breeding ground for further suspiciousness and paranoia. Communication may be odd, but not incomprehensible. It may be tangential, digressive, vague, or overly elaborate, but it is not loose or incoherent. In general, it is the odd thinking and communication that play the greatest role in diagnosing schizotypal personality disorder (Siever, Bernstein, and Silverman, 1995). But there are also marked signs of interpersonal problems. Depersonalization—a sense of estrangement from oneself and from one's environment—may be present. Many suffering from this disorder experience constricted or inappropriate emotions, with the result that they find it difficult to maintain rapport in face-to-face interactions. Finally, social anxiety is often pronounced in schizotypal disorder, to the extent that the person avoids most social situations. The following case illustrates the syndrome of schizotypal personality disorder:

At twenty-one, Mark complains that he feels "spaced out" and "creepy" much of the time. Unemployed, he lives with his parents and spends much of his time watching television or staring into space. He says that he often feels as if he is outside himself, watching himself through a TV screen, or running through a script that someone else has written. Mark has had several jobs, but none has lasted more than a month. He was fired from his last position as a toy salesman after several customers had complained that he had talked to them in vague terms about irrelevant things.

Mark is convinced that people do not like him, but he does not understand why. He is certain that people change their seats on buses to avoid sitting next to him. He is unhappy about his loneliness and isolation, but he has made no attempt to reestablish old relationships.

Several months ago, Mark learned that one of his parents' friends planned to open a chain of athletic shoe discount stores. Although he has no experience or training in business, Mark is "waiting" for an offer to manage one of these stores.

CAUSES

It is well established that schizotypal personality disorder can be influenced by genetic factors (Nigg and Goldsmith, 1994). It is also known that schizotypal personality disorder is genetically related to schizophrenia (Raine, Lencz, and Mednick, 1995; Roitman et al., 1997; Siever, Bernstein, and Silverman, 1991). It occurs at a higher rate in the biological relatives of patients with schizophrenia than in the relatives of individuals with other mental disorders. Is schizotypal personality disorder one of the possible phenotypes that results from the genotype for schizophrenia? Many believe it is. Researchers have focused on schizotypal personality disorder with the hope of finding clues about the etiology of schizophrenia.

People who meet the diagnostic criteria for schizotypal personality disorder show many of the physical and behavioral abnormalities observed in patients with schizophrenia. For example, they show more minor physical anomalies of the limbs and head, and more irregularities in their fingerprints than either normal individuals or those with other personality disorders (Weinstein, Diforio, Schiffman, Walker, and Bonsall, 1999). The course of childhood adjustment problems is strikingly similar for patients with schizophrenia and for those with schizotypal personality disorder (Walker, Baum, and Diforio, 1998). There are also parallels in cognitive functions (Bergman et al., 1998) and brain structure, with people diagnosed with schizotypal personality disorder showing reductions in temporal lobe volume similar to the reduced volume seen in patients with schizophrenia (Dickey et al., 1999).

TREATMENT

Cognitive-behavioral therapy has been used to treat schizotypal personality disorder (Beck and Freeman, 1990). The first step is the identification of the client's distorted cognitions. The primary goal is to teach clients to evaluate their environment objectively, rather than relying on their subjective responses. They are taught to disregard inappropriate thoughts and to consider the consequences that will ensue if they continue to function under such unrealistic belief systems. Increasing social appropriateness is another goal of treatment. Social skills training is accomplished through modeling of appropriate behavior and speech, and teaching the client to identify his own inappropriate responses. At the same time, the therapist helps the client to establish a safe and supportive social network to improve his social interactions.

In recent years, there has been increasing interest in the idea of preventing the onset of schizophrenia by treating people with schizotypal symptoms. When people with schizotypal personality disorder are given antipsychotic drugs, they often show improvement (Coccaro, 1998). Nonetheless, the issue is still controversial (see Box 9–2). Only some of those taking drugs would have gone on to develop schizophrenia, even if they weren't treated. Most clinicians are skeptical about administering medication when the person is not yet experiencing actual psychotic symptoms. They worry about the side effects of the antipsychotic medications. Even though the newer antipsychotic drugs, such as clozapine and olanzapine, may have fewer short-term side effects than the earlier drugs, we do not yet know the long-term consequences of regular use. On the other side of the controversy, it has been shown that the longer the untreated episodes of psychosis go, the worse the long-term prognosis. Thus, failing to prevent the onset of the first psychotic episode in someone who is vulnerable to psychosis may have dire consequences. To date, systematic attempts at the prevention of schizophrenia have mainly focused on people who have had a psychotic episode, rather than on those with schizotypal personality disorder (McGorry and Jackson, 1999). Many in the field of schizophrenia research are eagerly awaiting longitudinal studies on the prevention of psychotic episodes, both with medication and psychological treatments.

Schizoid Personality Disorder

Schizoid personality disorder is a syndrome that shares some features with schizotypal disorder. The key sign of schizoid personality disorder is a defect in the capacity to form social relationships, as reflected in the absence of desire for social involvement, indifference to both praise and criticism, insensitivity to the feelings of others, and/or lack of social skills. People with this disorder have few, if any, close friends. They are withdrawn, reserved, and seclusive. Other people view them as being "in a fog." In short, they are extreme introverts. Their feelings tend to be bland and constricted; they seem to lack warm feelings or the capacity for emotional display, and they are therefore perceived as cold, aloof, or distant. Sometimes, and especially in jobs that require a good deal of social isolation, these characteristics can be assets. But more often, the lack of social skills restricts occupational and social success. Unlike schizotypal disorder, the diagnostic criteria for schizoid person-

Box 9—2

Levels of Analysis

Psychopharmacologic Treatment of Personality Disorders

Until the late 1960s, personality disorders either went untreated or were treated with psychotherapy. But as psychopharmacology proved to be effective for schizophrenia and mood disorders, the utility of drug therapy for personality disorders became a topic of discussion among clinical researchers (Marin, De Meo, Frances, Kocsis, and Mann, 1989). Clinicians observed the similarities between some of the symptoms experienced by patients with personality disorders and those with Axis I disorders. For example, many who are diagnosed with borderline personality disorder show the mood swings and exaggerated emotion characteristic of bipolar disorder. In addition, research has shown that there are genetic links and biological similarities between certain personality disorders and Axis I disorders. Schizotypal personality disorder and schizophrenia are a prime example of this.

Given these and other findings, biological psychiatrists have proposed that effective drug treatments exist for patients with personality disorders (Klar and Siever, 1984; Silk, 1996). For example, Soloff published a study showing that haloperidol, an antipsychotic, significantly reduced symptoms of obsessive-compulsiveness, depression, anxiety, hostility, paranoid ideation, and impulsiveness in patients with borderline personality disorder and schizotypal personality disorder (Soloff, 1986). In subsequent years, there have been numerous reports documenting the effect of selective serotonin reuptake inhibitors (such as Prozac) and serotonin transport inhibitors on personality (Ekselius and von Knorring, 1999; Marchevsky, 1999). The SSRI's are now widely accepted treatments for a variety of personality disorders, including obsessive-compulsive personality disorder, and have been greeted with enthusiasm in some quarters (Kramer, 1994; Silk, 1996; Swinson, Antony, Rachman, and Richter, 1998).

But how effective are drug treatments compared to psychotherapy? Donald Black and his colleagues compared the personality changes that occurred in outpatients treated with cognitive therapy, medication (an SSRI), and placebo treatments (Black, Monahan, Wesner, Gabel, and Bowers, 1996). On a self-report measure of personality, 82 percent of those who received cognitive therapy showed a decline in traits of personality disorder, whereas only 47 percent of those on medication changed. Placebo treatment had little effect on personality scores. In fact, 41 percent of subjects given placebos showed an increase in signs of personality disorder. Thus, cognitive therapy was associated with the greatest reduction in what are considered abnormal traits, particularly in the schizotypal, narcissistic, borderline, and compulsive categories.

Besides concerns about the efficacy of drug treatments as compared to psychotherapy, other concerns about the use of drugs to treat personality disorders have also been raised (DeGrandpre, 1999). Researchers have asked such questions as: Are we "manufacturing" personality? In the future, will people select medications to alter their personalities based on current fads? Will psychopharmacology change personality tendencies that particular ethnic groups encourage through socialization (Jacobsen, 1995)? Will this result in a "homogenization" of human cultural diversity? Is psychopharmacology capable of eliminating our individuality? Yet, perhaps the first question that we must all ask ourselves is: Are we comfortable with the idea of changing personality in general, whether through psychotherapy or medication?

SOURCE: Based on Black, Monahan, Wesner, and Bowers, 1996; DeGrandpre, 1999; Ekselius and von Knorring, 1999; Jacobsen, 1995; Klar and Siever, 1985; Kramer, 1994; Marin, De Meo, Frances, Kocsis, and Mann, 1989; Marchevsky, 1999; Silk, 1996; Soloff, 1986, Swinson, Antony, Rachman, and Richter, 1998.

ality disorder do not involve abnormal ideas or perceptions. It is likely that many people who meet diagnostic criteria for schizoid personality disorder are simply at the extreme end of the continuum of introversion.

PREVALENCE AND CAUSES

It is estimated that the incidence of schizoid personality disorder is between 0.4 and 0.9 percent of the population and that it is more common in men than in women (Fabrega, Ulrich, Pilkonis, and Mezzich, 1991; Weissman, 1993). Like the other Cluster A personality disorders, there is some evidence that ge-

netic factors contribute to schizoid personality tendencies (Nigg and Goldsmith, 1994). But the genetic association between schizoid personality disorder and schizophrenia is not clear. The results of some studies indicate that the disorder tends to occur more often in the families of patients with schizophrenia, but other studies do not find this association (Battaglia et al., 1995).

TREATMENT

A chief goal in the cognitive-behavioral treatment of schizoid disorder is to reduce the client's social isolation and to facilitate the development of intimate

DSM-IV Criteria

Schizoid Personality Disorder

A. A pervasive pattern of detachment from social relationships and a restricted range of expression of emotions in interpersonal settings, beginning by early adulthood and present in a variety of contexts, as indicated by four (or more) of the following: (1) neither desires nor enjoys close relationships, including being part of a family; (2) almost always chooses solitary activities; (3) has little, if any, interest in having sexual experiences with another person; (4) takes pleasure in few, if any, activities; (5) lacks close friends or confidants other than first-degree relatives; (6) appears indifferent to the praise or criticism of others; (7) shows emotional coldness, detachment, or flattened affectivity.

B. Does not occur exclusively during the course of Schizophrenia, a Mood Disorder with Psychotic Features, another Psychotic Disorder, or a Pervasive Developmental Disorder and is not due to the direct physiological effects of a general medical condition.

SOURCE: APA, DSM-IV, 1994.

relationships with others (Beck and Freeman, 1990). Group therapy can provide a successful forum for establishing a social network for schizoid individuals. It also provides a setting for self-disclosure and social feedback. Thus, the client can be taught how to handle positive, negative, and neutral reactions from others. Teaching social skills can also be accomplished through role-playing and homework assignments. Because people with schizoid tendencies are often inattentive to the emotional state of others, another goal of therapy is to identify emotions and the emotional responses of others, thus increasing the client's ability to empathize.

Paranoid Personality Disorder

The prominent characteristics of **paranoid personality disorder** are a pervasive and long-standing distrust and suspiciousness of others (Bernstein, Useda, and Siever, 1995). Persons with this disorder are hypersensitive, and they have a tendency to scan the environment for cues that they are being singled out for mistreatment. Those who suffer from the paranoid personality disorder are often argumentative, tense, and humorless. They seem ready to attack. They tend to exaggerate, to make mountains out of molehills, and to find hidden motives and special meanings in the innocent behavior of others. They tend to blame others for whatever difficulties they experience, and they cannot themselves accept any blame or responsibility for failure.

PREVALENCE AND CAUSES

Like schizoid personality disorder, there is some evidence that paranoid personality disorder is influenced by genetics and occurs at a higher rate in families of patients with schizophrenia (Kendler and Gruenberg, 1982; Nigg and Goldsmith, 1994). Because people with this disorder tend to externalize blame and guilt, they are not inclined to seek out treatment in clinics or psychiatric hospitals. The best estimate of the incidence is somewhere between 0.4 to 1.8 percent of the population (Weissman, 1993). More men than women suffer from paranoid per-

In this detail of a painting by Scottie Wilson, we can see the withdrawn, reserved, seclusive look that characterizes a person with schizoid personality disorder.

371 - 75
382 - 97
648 - 07

sonality disorder (Kass, Spitzer, and Williams, 1983), and the rate of comorbidity with Axis I disorders, especially depression, anxiety, and substance abuse is high (Bernstein, Useda and Siever, 1993). Often, the signs of the disorder have their onset with advanced age, especially after significant life changes, as in the following case:

> After his wife died, Seymour moved to a retirement community in Florida. Healthy and attractive, he joined a folk dancing group, a current events discussion group, and a ceramics class. Within six weeks, however, he had dropped out of all the programs, complaining to his children that other residents were talking about him behind his back, that he was unable to find a dancing partner, ignored in the current events group, and given improper instruction in ceramics.
>
> Before his retirement, Seymour had been a physicist. He had always been closedmouthed about his work. His home study had always been locked. He had not permitted anyone to clean it, and he had become angry if anyone entered it without his permission. His son reported that his parents had been close and affectionate, but that his father had had few other friends. He had been wary of new faces and concerned about the motives of strangers. A hard worker throughout his life, he was now gripped by fear. He spent much of his time overseeing his investments, fearful that his broker would give him poor advice, or neglect to tell him when to buy and when to sell.

In the 1997 film *Conspiracy Theory,* the character played by Mel Gibson distrusts others and finds hidden meaning and conspiracies all around him, characteristics that typify those who suffer from paranoid personality disorder.

TREATMENT

Seymour would be viewed as a good candidate for cognitive-behavioral therapy aimed at reducing paranoid tendencies. Cognitive-behavioral therapy for paranoid personality disorder emphasizes self-disclosure and trust (Beck and Freeman, 1990). The primary goals are to increase the client's sense of self-efficacy regarding his or her ability to handle problem situations, and to establish a more realistic perspective of the intentions and actions of others. This allows the client to discard the defensive guard

DSM-IV Criteria

Paranoid Personality Disorder

A. A pervasive distrust and suspiciousness of others such that their motives are interpreted as malevolent, beginning by early adulthood and present in a variety of contexts, as indicated by four (or more) of the following: (1) suspects, without sufficient basis, that others are exploiting, harming, or deceiving him or her; (2) is preoccupied with unjustified doubts about the loyalty or trustworthiness of friends or associates; (3) is reluctant to confide in others because of unwarranted fear that the information will be used maliciously against him or her; (4) reads hidden demeaning or threatening meanings into benign remarks or events; (5) persistently bears grudges, i.e., is unforgiv-

ing of insults, injuries, or slights; (6) perceives attacks on his or her character or reputation that are not apparent to others and is quick to react angrily or to counterattack; (7) has recurrent suspicions, without justification, regarding fidelity of spouse or sexual partner.

B. Does not occur exclusively during the course of Schizophrenia, a Mood Disorder with Psychotic Features, or another Psychotic Disorder and is not due to the direct physiological effects of a general medical condition.

SOURCE: APA, DSM-IV, 1994.

that he might typically use to defend against his perceived sense of danger. Establishing a collaborative relationship between a therapist and client is always important, but it is especially important when working with paranoid clients who are suspicious and tend to think that others are malevolent and deceptive. An effective method for increasing a client's comfort in therapy is to give him more freedom and control over the content and frequency of the sessions.

Dramatic-Erratic Disorders

A central feature of the Cluster B disorders is overt behavior that is inappropriate and/or extreme. People with dramatic-erratic disorders fail to conform to certain social norms, and they may seem quite self-centered to others.

Antisocial Personality Disorder

Perhaps the most fascinating of the Axis II disorders is **antisocial personality disorder.** This disorder has been given many different names over the decades, but the core symptoms remain remarkably the same. In the past, the terms "sociopathy" or "psychopathy," were sometimes used interchangeably to refer to antisocial personality disorder. Today, the term "sociopathy" is not commonly used, and most researchers now differentiate between antisocial personality disorder and psychopathy. In part, the distinction is based on the approach to assessment. The diagnostic label "antisocial personality disorder" is based on behavioral diagnostic criteria, whereas psychopathy is based on personality traits that are assessed with a checklist or questionnaire.

Harvey Cleckley wrote extensively about the "psychopathic personality." In his famous book, *The Mask of Sanity,* he was largely responsible for bringing the problem of psychopathy to the attention of clinicians (Cleckley, 1964). Cleckley listed many features of the psychopath's personality, including the following: superficial charm, insincerity and dishonesty, lack of remorse or shame, egocentricity, poor judgment, lack of emotional responsivity, lack of insight, absence of nervousness or anxiety, and absence of delusional thinking. Robert Hare and his colleagues expanded on Cleckley's work and developed a measure, the Revised Psychopathy Check-

list (PCL-R), to rate people on the personality traits that are associated with psychopathy (Hare, 1996).

Although criminals as well as people who meet DSM criteria for antisocial personality disorder will tend to get high scores on the PCL-R, this is not always the case. Further, some people who score very high on the PCL-R do not meet criteria for antisocial personality disorder and never commit illegal acts. For example, using DSM criteria, a person who scores very high on the traits of manipulativeness, dishonesty, shamelessness, and unreliability would not be diagnosed with antisocial personality disorder if she did not show clear signs of conduct disorder before the age of fifteen. Moreover, we know that some people with these traits never get into trouble with the law, so they are not criminals.

But we should not let these distinctions overshadow the fact that there is a great deal of overlap among the three populations: those who meet criteria for antisocial personality disorder, those who score high on psychopathy, and those who are convicted criminals. Even though high scores on self-report measures indicating psychopathy are not synonymous with antisocial personality disorder, there is considerable overlap between the signs of antisocial personality disorder and the items that are used to measure psychopathy. Also, while criminality is not synonymous with antisocial personality disorder, many persons who meet criteria for this disorder do commit crimes. And, among individuals who are incarcerated for crimes, those who show more signs of antisocial personality disorder are much more likely to be repeat offenders (Hemphill, Hare, and Wong, 1998).

In the following discussion, we will explore the results of research on individuals with DSM antisocial personality disorder. Some relevant findings from studies of persons who score high on measures of psychopathy, including some who are incarcerated, will also be covered.

CHARACTERIZING THE ANTISOCIAL PERSONALITY DISORDER

Throughout most of history, antisocial behavior was not thought about in psychological terms. But in the nineteenth century especially, the idea developed that certain kinds of criminal behavior might arise from conditions over which the individual had no control— that is, from social, psychological, or biological sources. Their crimes then were not acts of will, but rather the result of circumstances beyond their control.

In the nineteenth century, the notion that some people have a disorder that prevents them from conforming to social expectations became more widespread. From this perspective, people who showed persistent antisocial tendencies were said to be afflicted with "moral insanity," which was viewed as a disorder of the will. Although the term "moral insanity" has been displaced by "antisocial personality disorder," it continues to be viewed as a disorder of will. Whether for biological, social, or psychological reasons, these people are found "to be incapable . . . of conducting [themselves] with decency and propriety in the business of life." When people are capable of exercising will and of conducting themselves properly, but simply choose not to do so, they continue to be called criminals.

In recent years, antisocial personality disorder has been studied extensively, and is among the best understood of all the personality disorders. In part, interest in the disorder stems from the fact that it has direct negative consequences for society; its hallmark is a chronic insensitivity and indifference to the rights of other people that is manifested in lying, stealing, cheating, and worse. Whereas those who suffer other psychological difficulties may be unpleasant, contact with people who have antisocial personality disorder may be dangerous. Because their numbers are not small, they constitute a major social and legal problem, as well as a psychological one.

In Chapter 8, we discussed the developmental roots of antisocial personality disorder. The disorder originates in childhood conduct disorder, where it is characterized by behaviors such as truancy, persistent lying, theft, and vandalism. Similar behaviors persist into adulthood, taking the forms of assaults against persons and property, defaulting on major debts and financial responsibilities, and involvement in the underworld. This developmental pathway has been observed in a subgroup of individuals from cultures all over the world (Robins, 1999). There are also similarities across cultures in the epidemiology of antisocial personality disorder: it is much more common in males than in females, and in persons who grow up in homes characterized by poverty and instability.

The severity of antisocial behavior decreases significantly with age, beginning around age thirty (Robins, 1966; Robins and Price, 1991). Particularly between the ages of thirty and forty, there is a marked behavioral improvement. Although no one knows for sure, it is assumed that this developmental improvement is due to several factors. Social learning is one factor; as the individual gains more experience with the negative consequences of his antisocial behavior, there is a decline in the frequency of these behaviors. Biological factors may also be involved. As we described in previous chapters, there are changes in brain characteristics, hormones, and physical abilities across the life span. For example, maturation of the frontal lobes of the brain probably plays a role in the developmental increase in the ability to plan ahead and to inhibit inappropriate behavior.

From the perspective of the average adult, antisocial personality disorder can be perplexing. How can a mature person fail to develop emotional connections to others and fail to understand the importance of ethics? Robert Kegan (1986) suggests that people who have antisocial personality disorders most resemble ten-year-old children in their psychological makeup. Neither can handle responsibility, both have difficulty understanding others, and both are awfully concrete-minded. Some of the latter is represented in the following interchange between a reporter and the famous bank robber, Willy Sutton:

> Why do you rob all these banks, Willy?
> Because that's where they keep the money.
>
> (Kegan, 1986)

The presence of antisocial behavior alone is not sufficient for the diagnosis of antisocial personality disorder. Such behavior would merely qualify as "adult antisocial behavior," which in DSM-IV is ruled out as a mental disorder. In order to qualify as a personality disorder, the antisocial behavior must meet two primary criteria. First, the behavior has to be long-standing. Although the diagnosis cannot be applied to a person who is under eighteen, current diagnostic criteria require substantial evidence of a conduct disorder before the age of fifteen. Such evidence can include habitual lying, early and aggressive sexual behavior, destructiveness, theft, vandalism, and chronic rule violation at home and at school. Second, the present antisocial behavior must be manifested in at least three classes of behavior, among which are: repeated aggressiveness; recklessness that endangers others; deceitfulness, lack of remorse, and consistent irresponsibility as seen by such behaviors; a failure to honor financial obligations. The antisocial personality disorder then is defined by sustained antisocial behaviors that, having begun by adolescence, continue in a variety of areas during adulthood.

These criteria make clear who should be diagnosed as having an antisocial personality disorder and who should not. Nonetheless, that does not mean it

DSM-IV Criteria

Antisocial Personality Disorder

A. There is a pervasive pattern of disregard for and violation of the rights of others occurring since age 15 years, as indicated by three (or more) of the following: (1) failure to conform to social norms with respect to lawful behaviors as indicated by repeatedly performing acts that are grounds for arrest; (2) deceitfulness, as indicated by repeated lying, use of aliases, or conning others for personal profit or pleasure; (3) impulsivity or failure to plan ahead; (4) irritability and aggressiveness, as indicated by repeated physical fights or assaults; (5) reckless disregard for safety of self or others; (6) consistent irresponsibility, as indicated by repeated failure to sustain consistent work behavior or honor financial obligations; (7) lack of remorse, as indicated by being indifferent to or rationalizing having hurt, mistreated, or stolen from another.

B. The individual is at least age 18 years.

C. There is evidence of Conduct Disorder with onset before age 15 years.

D. The occurrence of antisocial behavior is not exclusively during the course of Schizophrenia or a manic episode.

SOURCE: APA, DSM-IV, 1994.

---

is easy to diagnose the disorder. As you can imagine, there are differences between how people describe themselves and the way others describe them (Lilienfeld, Purcell, and Jones-Alexander, 1997). A person with antisocial personality disorder may view himself as clever and strategic, while people who know him describe him as manipulative and conniving. So what source of information should the diagnostician use? As is the case with all disorders, the best approach in the diagnosis of antisocial personality disorder is to use multiple sources of information.

What personality characteristics are reflected in antisocial personality disorder? Let us consider the facets of psychopathy suggested by Cleckley (1964). The characteristics listed by Cleckley can be reduced to three broad categories: inadequately motivated antisocial behavior, the absence of a conscience and sense of responsibility to others, and emotional poverty. These tendencies are certainly represented among individuals who meet the criteria for antisocial personality disorder (see Table 9–1).

Inadequately Motivated Antisocial Behavior Most criminals are motivated by the desire to get rich—quick—and, in the process, to gain status among their peers. These are motivations we can understand, however much we disapprove of the behaviors. But the crimes of those with antisocial personality disorder often seem aimless, random, and impulsive. As a case in point, Derrick whom we described previously in this chapter, took a demonstration car from the dealership he worked for without asking. There was no reason for him to do this. The dealership had a policy of letting sales representatives take "demo" cars home several times a month. Derrick had never taken one home, so he was entitled to do so. His behavior did not seem to be motivated by any rational purpose, but rather seemed perversely impulsive, as is typical of in-

TABLE 9–1

Diagnosis

THE ANTISOCIAL PERSONALITY DISORDER

Definition	Childhood Antecedents	Adult Behaviors	Influencing Factors
Long-standing antisocial behavior manifested across a spectrum of activities, among which are aggressiveness, irresponsibility, recklessly endangering others, failure to honor financial obligations	Habitual lying	Deceitfulness	Deficiencies in social learning abilities, especially in avoidance learning
	Theft	Irritability	
	Aggressive sexuality	Repeated aggressiveness	Emotional underarousal
	Vandalism	Criminal behavior	
	Truancy	Failure to plan ahead	Genetic predisposition to criminality
	Impulsivity	Lack of remorse	
			Brain abnormalities

dividuals with antisocial personality disorder. Neither Derrick nor we understand why he did what he did. A more extreme case is Gary Gilmore, a convicted murderer who would likely meet the DSM-IV criteria for antisocial personality disorder (see Box 9–3). His life personified the trait of inadequately motivated antisocial behavior:

On October 7, 1976, Gary Gilmore was sentenced to death by a Utah court after a seemingly purposeless crime spree, and on January 7, 1977, he became the first person to be executed in the United States since 1966. During a psychological evaluation to determine whether Gilmore was competent to stand trial, it was determined that he suffered an antisocial personality

---

Society and Mental Health

Box 9–3

Criminal or Mentally Ill?

Psychologists are often called upon to evaluate the mental health of people who have committed serious crimes. Often these individuals meet diagnostic criteria for antisocial personality disorder. However, a diagnosis of personality disorder, including antisocial personality disorder, is not considered to be a mental disorder that qualifies a defendant for the insanity defense. This is because personality disorders are not viewed as illnesses that impair the person's ability to control his emotions or differentiate right from wrong. In contrast, episodes of serious mood disorders, such as bipolar disorder, are viewed by the court as illnesses that are capable of interfering with a person's emotional control and judgment.

In the following case of a man who committed multiple murders, two mental health professionals disagreed about the defendant's mental status. The psychiatrist testifying on behalf of the defendant stated that the man suffered from bipolar disorder and was in a manic state when he committed the crime. If this were true, the insanity defense would be an option. In other words, the man's attorney would argue that the defendant was not responsible for his criminal acts. He would try to convince the jury that the defendant had a mental illness that caused uncontrollable emotional reactions and impaired his ability to differentiate right from wrong. In contrast, a forensic psychologist believed the defendant showed a pattern of behavior throughout his life history that suggested antisocial personality disorder. If this were correct, we would not expect the defendant to be highly emotionally aroused during the commission of the crime. Thus, the success of the insanity defense in this case hinged on evidence that the defendant was "acting" when he was in a state of extreme emotional arousal.

The thirty-five-year-old man had a lengthy history of aggressive behavior, and he had physically and sexually assaulted his wife on several occasions. A series of events in the perpetuator's life occurred the week prior to the crime. His wife, the victim of repeated domestic violence during their fifteen years of marriage, told him that she intended to leave him and move in with a friend. Three days later, she took custody of their son and had a restraining order issued against her husband. The following week the perpetrator shaved his head and moustache and pur-

chased a .50 caliber rifle. He arrived at the local grocery store where his wife was employed, and shot his wife, wounding her. He then straddled his spouse and fired five more rounds into her chest and abdomen. The killing spree culminated in the murder of the store manager and the county sheriff. There were three wounded victims who were treated and later released. The perpetrator had a long history of antisocial behavior; there was more than sufficient evidence to diagnose him with antisocial personality disorder. Further, based on the evidence that was gathered from the scene and testimony from observers, the perpetrator's psychological state just prior to the event was characterized by minimal emotional arousal. Witnesses to the crime reported that the offender appeared calm and self-confident, and there were no signs of frustration, irritability, or temper. In fact, the perpetrator appeared emotionally aloof. More than thirty-four people who interacted with the defendant in the week before the crime reported that he was not overly emotional. It was reported that his remarks concerning his wife the day before the murders took place were devoid of emotion. Witnesses at the scene of the crime commented on the defendant's tone of voice, "It was a monotone voice just as if he were talking about working on cars." Similarly, immediately after the crime was committed, witnesses reported that the offender walked away from the scene with a look of confidence and calm. A videotape made at the crime site confirmed these observations.

Contrary to the testimony of the psychiatrist who served as a defense expert witness, there was no evidence that the perpetrator was suffering a manic episode. Instead, the offender seemed emotionless and indifferent, characteristics more consistent with antisocial personality disorder. The argument that the defendant suffered from bipolar disorder was further undermined by the fact that he was not diagnosed and treated for bipolar disorder until five months after the offense.

The man was convicted and sentenced to life in prison on three counts of murder and three counts of attempted murder.

SOURCE: Meloy, 1997, 326–29.

disorder. Gilmore's activities provide an interesting example of crime without understandable motives.

Gilmore had been released from prison only six months earlier, after serving time for armed robbery. He promptly violated parole by leaving the state. His probation officer gave him another chance. But shortly thereafter, following a heated argument with his girlfriend, Gilmore stole a stereo. Once again, he persuaded the police not to bring charges. Gilmore himself described the next events: "I pulled up near a gas station. I told the service station guy to give me all his money. I then took him to the bathroom and told him to kneel down and then I shot him in the head twice. The guy didn't give me any trouble but I just felt like I had to do it."

The very next morning, Gilmore left his car at another service station for minor repairs and walked to a motel. "I went in and told the guy to give me the money. I told him to lay on the floor and then I shot him. I then walked out and was carrying the cash drawer with me. I took the money and threw the cash drawer in a bush and I tried to push the gun in the bush too. But as I was pushing it in the bush, it went off and that's how come I was shot in the arm. It seems like things have always gone bad for me. It seems like I've always done dumb things that just caused trouble for me."

Convicted killer Gary Gilmore (second from right) was examined by psychologists in 1976, as shown here. He would have been given the diagnosis of antisocial personality disorder under DSM-IV.

Absence of a Conscience and a Sense of Responsibility to Others

The absence of shame or remorse for past misdeeds, or of any sense of humiliation, is one of the most common characteristics of antisocial personality disorder. Those with antisocial personality disorder lack conscience, and with it, any deep capacity to care about other people (Millon, 1996; Williamson, Hare, and Wong, 1987). Their relationships, therefore, tend to be quite shallow and exploitative. They lack a capacity for love and sustained attachment and are unresponsive to trust, kindness, or affection. They lie shamelessly and can mercilessly abuse those who have trusted them.

Gary Gilmore did not have a romantic relationship until several weeks before he committed the two murders. He was then thirty-six years old. Describing the affair, he said that it was "probably the first close relationship that I ever had with anyone. I just didn't know how to respond to her for any length of time. I was very insensitive to her. . . . I was thoughtless in the way I treated her. . . . [H]er two children bugged me and sometimes I would get angry at them and slap them because they were so noisy."

Emotional Poverty

One of the major differences between the person with antisocial personality disorder and the person who is a criminal but does not have antisocial personality disorder lies in the depth of experienced emotion. Ordinary criminals presumably experience the same emotions as other people. But people with antisocial personality disorder experience very shallow emotions. They seem to lack the capacity for sustained love, anger, grief, joy, or despair. During a psychiatric interview, Gilmore observed that "I don't remember any real emotional event in all my life. When you're in the joint, you stay pretty even all the time. I'm not really excitable you know. I don't get emotional." Indeed, their incapacity to experience emotion may be significantly related to their lack of conscience and to the ease with which they violate the expectations of others (Hare, 1998; Patrick, Bradley, and Cuthbert, 1990; Patrick, Cuthbert, and Lang, 1990; Stoff, Breiling, and Maser, 1997).

PREVALENCE AND SEX DIFFERENCES

The prevalence of antisocial behavior is roughly 2 to 3 percent, with men accorded the diagnosis as much as four times more often than women (Weissman, 1993; American Psychiatric Association, 1994). But does this difference reflect a sex bias in the eyes of diagnosticians, or a true base-rate sex difference in the prevalence of this disorder? There is indeed evidence of a sex bias in the diagnosis of certain personality disorders. In a study conducted in 1978, mental health professionals were asked to offer a diagnosis on a hypothetical case history (Warner, 1978). They were offered eight possible diagnoses, among them histrionic personality disorder (a disorder in which the person is charming, attention seeking, and self-absorbed) and antisocial personality disorder. When the client was described as female, therapists were inclined to diagnose her as hysterical or histrionic. But when the same hypothetical client was described as male, diagnostic perceptions shifted in the direction of the antisocial personality. It might be argued that these findings would not hold today because sex-role stereotypes are less pronounced. But in fact, more recent studies yield the same pattern of findings (Ford and Widiger, 1989; Widiger, 1998). Thus, there may be a sex bias in these diagnoses that is generated by the sex-role expectations of the diagnostician.

But diagnostic bias does not account for all of the difference between the sexes in the incidence of antisocial personality disorder. When the occurrence of antisocial personality disorder is examined across cultures, the same-sex differences are apparent, even when sex-role stereotypes are vastly different (Wrangham and Peterson, 1996). Some psychologists who study the evolutionary origins of human behavior believe that the greater propensity of males to engage in antisocial and aggressive behavior is biologically determined. In their controversial book entitled *Demonic Males: Apes and the Origins of Human Violence*, Richard Wrangham and Dale Peterson present evidence to support the hypothesis that evolution has "selected" for certain traits in males that can be problematic in modern society. They propose that the tendencies to be aggressive, to take risks, and to engage in indiscriminate sexual behavior are more pronounced in males because they are based on biological differences between the sexes.

THE CAUSES OF ANTISOCIAL PERSONALITY DISORDER

This brings us to the origins of antisocial personality disorder. What are its causes? We are not yet certain, but research findings point to several factors, including: (1) inherited vulnerabilities, (2) early damage to the developing nervous system, (3) abnormalities in physiological reactions and in brain activity, (4) the family and social context, and (5) defects in learning.

Genetics   The notion that antisocial personality disorder has a genetic basis has a long history. In popular culture, antisocial behavior has been associated with the "bad seed," and particularly the bad seed that came from a family of "bad seeds." But the problems of sorting environmental from genetic influences are as difficult here as elsewhere. And the task is further compounded by the fact that it is criminals with antisocial personality disorder—those who have been apprehended and convicted of a crime—who are most likely to come to our attention, not those who have eluded apprehension. Of course, not all criminals have antisocial personality disorder, but a substantial proportion do.

The research findings on the causes of antisocial personality disorder parallel the findings on the causes of childhood conduct disorder; it appears that both heredity and environment play a role. We begin by considering twin and adoption studies. But before doing so, one point should be mentioned. Some of the studies we describe are concerned with the genetic determinants of criminality. Criminality, as we indicated earlier, is not synonymous with antisocial personality disorder.

Recall again that monozygotic (MZ) or identical twins share essentially the same genetic heritage, whereas dizygotic (DZ) or fraternal twins share about 50 percent of their genes (see Chapter 4). If concordance for criminality or antisocial personality disorder is higher for MZ than for DZ twins, we can infer that genetic factors play a role.

Studies that have examined the rates of criminality among MZ and DZ twins indicate that MZ twins do show a higher rate of concordance for criminality than DZ twins. This suggests a genetic influence on criminal behavior. Karl Christiansen

Hannibal Lecter (played by Anthony Hopkins) in the 1991 film *Silence of the Lambs* showed no remorse for his crimes and seemed to lack a conscience and to be incapable of deep emotional feeling. This serial killer would probably have been diagnosed as having an antisocial personality disorder.

TABLE 9–2

PREVALENCE AND TWIN CORRELATIONS FOR SYMPTOMS OF ANTISOCIAL PERSONALITY DISORDER [*]

JUVENILE CRITERIA (before the age of 15)

DSM CRITERIA	PREVALENCE (%)	CORRELATION for MZ twins	CORRELATION for DZ twins
Often truant	13.6	.26	.19
Initiates fights	5.0	.37	.18
Uses weapons	1.3	.39	.22
Ran away	1.9	.47	.78
Forced sex	0	…	…
Cruel to animals	8.6	.21	.11
Cruel to people	6.1	.10	.28
Damaged property	5.1	.26	.37
Starts fires	5.7	.38	.47
Lies often	9.9	.38	.27
Steals, without confrontation	29.4	.46	.36
Steals, with confrontation	0.3	…	…

ADULT CRITERIA (since the age of 15)

DSM CRITERIA	PREVALENCE (%)	CORRELATION for MZ twins	CORRELATION for DZ twins
Inconsistent work	16.1	.34	.15
Fails to conform to social norms	20.5	.49	.32
Aggressive	38.5	.50	.27
Fails to honor financial obligations	5.1	.39	.20
Impulsive	7.0	.41	.23
No regard for truth	2.7	.15	.28
Reckless	47.8	.47	.31
Irresponsible parent	1.2	.22	…
Never monogamous	4.2	.30	.19
Lacks remorse	4.0	.22	.14

[*]Criteria and correlations for 6,452 MZ and DZ twins.

SOURCE: Lyons et al., 1995, pp. 906–15.

studied over 300 MZ male twin pairs and 611 same-sex DZ pairs who were listed in the Danish Twin Register (Christiansen, 1977). He found that 35 percent of the MZ twins, and 13 percent of the DZ pairs were concordant for criminality. Although the results do indicate a genetic effect, the concordance rates are moderate for both types of twins.

Twin studies of antisocial personality disorder also reveal an influence of genetic factors. In one investigation, researchers examined data on a large sample of over 3,000 military veterans, all of whom were members of an MZ or DZ twin pair. The men were interviewed and DSM-III-R was used to rate the occurrence of antisocial personality disorder symptoms (Lyons et al., 1995). The results for the childhood (behavior occurring before age fifteen)

and adult (occurring after age fifteen) criteria are listed in Table 9–2. In general, the investigators found that the correlations for the MZ twins tended to be somewhat higher than those for the DZ twins, but mainly for the traits measured in adulthood. The MZ twins were more similar than the DZ twins on several of the signs of antisocial personality disorder, including impulsiveness and inconsistent work history. Nonetheless, many of the correlations for the DZ twin pairs were also positive and high, indicating that the members of the DZ twin pairs were similar to each other on some of the traits. For some DSM criteria, the DZ twins were actually more similar than the MZ twins. In twin studies, the heritability of a trait is measured by comparing the MZ and DZ correlations. When genetic factors have a significant influence on the trait, the MZ correlation is much higher than the DZ correlation. The pattern of results shown in Table 9–2 generated heritability estimates that were not very high. On average, the heritability for the adult antisocial traits was .43, suggesting a moderate genetic effect. But the researchers were surprised to find that the average heritability estimate was only .07 for the criteria based on behavior before the age of fifteen. Such a low heritability indicates that environmental influences were largely responsible for the antisocial traits measured in childhood.

When children are raised by their natural parents, it is impossible to separate the effects of genetics from those of environment on their development. But studies of children who have been adopted at an early age allow these influences to be separated. These studies also provide evidence for the influence of heredity in both criminality and antisocial personality disorder. One study examined the criminal records of adopted persons in Denmark (Mednick, Gabriella, and Hutchings, 1984). Their names were drawn from the Danish Population Register, which records the names of both the adoptive and the biological parents of these adoptees. The incidence of crime among these offspring was lowest when neither the biological nor the adoptive fathers had been convicted of a criminal offense (see Table 9–3). Nearly indistinguishable from that low rate was the rate among adoptees whose adoptive fathers had been convicted, but whose biological fathers had not. The incidence of criminal conviction among adoptees jumped, however, when the natural father had a criminal record, providing clear support for the view that genetic factors are involved in the tendency to engage in criminal acts. But highest of all was the incidence of criminality among adoptees when both their natural and adoptive fathers had criminal records, underscoring again the combined influence of heredity and environment on criminality.

Although criminality is not identical with antisocial personality disorder, when antisocial personality disorder or behaviors are examined in adoption studies, the results are similar (Cadoret, Yates, Troughton, Woodworth, and Stewart, 1995; Langbehn, Cadoret, Yates, Troughton, and Stewart, 1998; Schulsinger, 1972). Adopted children whose biological parents have antisocial tendencies are more likely to manifest antisocial behavior. However, the interaction between genes and experience is powerful (Rutter, 1997). If the adopted child has a biological parent with antisocial tendencies and the adoptive home is unstable, there is a much higher rate of antisocial personality disorder later in life.

There is strong evidence for both genetic and environmental influences on antisocial behavior. But oddly, although women are much less likely than men to become criminals, the biological children of women who are convicted of a crime are at greater risk for criminal conviction than are the biological children of men who are convicted of a crime. Convicted females seem to have a larger genetic predisposition than convicted males (Cloninger, Reich, and Guze, 1975). Why should that be? One reasonable explanation rests on the observation that antisocial behavior is less common among women. In order for

TABLE 9–3

CRIMINALITY OF ADOPTED SONS ACCORDING TO THE CRIMINALITY OF THEIR ADOPTIVE AND BIOLOGICAL FATHERS

Father		Percentage of Sons Who Are Criminal Offenders	Number
Biological	*Adoptive*		
No registered offense	No registered offense	10.5	333
No registered offense	Criminal offense	11.5	52
Criminal offense	No registered offense	22.0	219
Criminal offense	Criminal offense	36.2	58
Total			662

SOURCE: Modified from Hutchings and Mednick, 1977, p. 132.

women to engage in criminal behavior, they may require a stronger genetic predisposition, as well as more adverse environmental circumstances, than do males (Baker, Mack, Moffitt, and Mednick, 1989).

Prenatal and Birth Complications   Like conduct disorder, antisocial personality disorder is linked with exposure to prenatal and birth complications. As mentioned in Chapter 4, maternal smoking during pregnancy is associated with an increased risk of criminal behavior in the offspring (Brennan, Grekin, and Mednick, 1999). Exposure of the fetus to alcohol also increases the likelihood of later antisocial behavior (Streissguth and Kanter, 1997). Moreover, infants with low birth weight and other complications of birth are more likely than infants of normal birth weight to engage in antisocial behavior, especially if they are reared in nonoptimal environments (Mednick, Brennan, and Kandel, 1988; Piquero and Tibbetts, 1999; Shanok and Lewis, 1981). Adrian Raine, an expert on antisocial personality disorder, and his colleagues studied a group of over 4,000 Danish men and found that exposure to birth complications, when combined with early maternal rejection, predisposed the men to aggressive behavior at age thirty-four years (Raine, Brennan, and Mednick, 1997).

Most researchers believe that all of these obstetrical factors are correlated with antisocial behavior because they can have a profound effect on brain development. If this assumption is correct, it means that some individuals who show antisocial personality disorder are the "victims" of brain damage that was sustained when they were fetuses. Should these persons be held responsible for criminal acts? This is a controversial issue—one that will probably become increasingly salient as researchers identify more of the biological factors involved in antisocial behavior.

Physiological Dysfunctions   To the extent that genetics and perinatal problems are related to antisocial personality disorder, the relationship is probably not a direct one. As described above, research has shown that environmental factors interact in some way with the biological vulnerabilities that are produced by perinatal complications or the person's genotype. Nonetheless, if the nature of the biological vulnerability can be identified, we will be in a better position to help children at risk.

People with antisocial personality disorder manifest abnormalities in their physiological reactions to emotional and fear-producing stimuli. In one study, male prison inmates who scored high on a measure of psychopathic tendencies performed a task in which they responded to a series of letter strings, only some of which were real words (Williamson, Harpur, and Hare, 1991). They had to respond as quickly as possible, indicating whether or not the letter string was a real word. Some of the real words were emotionally charged (for example, grief), and others were neutral. Their reaction times and EEG (electroencephalogram) responses were recorded. The inmates who did not have psychopathic tendencies showed faster reaction times and larger amplitude EEG responses to the emotional words than to the neutral words. In contrast, those with psychopathic tendencies were significantly slower in responding to the emotional words, and their EEG responses were smaller for emotional words than for neutral words. These results indicate that the inmates with psychopathic tendencies were less physiologically reactive to emotional meaning.

Cleckley's observation that people who engage in antisocial behavior are emotionally nonresponsive was confirmed in this experiment. The emotions that ordinarily inhibit antisocial behavior are not sufficiently aroused. At the same time, the emotions that propel people into crimes of passion are usually also absent. People with antisocial personality disorder are mainly responsible for "cool" crimes such as burglary, forgery, and con games. When they are involved in violence, as Gilmore was, it tends to be impulsive, irrational, and perverse because it lacks passion or feeling.

In fact, generalized reductions in psychophysiological responses seem to characterize people with antisocial tendencies. These include low resting heart rate and reduced electrodermal (skin conductance) responses (Fowles and Furuseth, 1994; Raine, 1996). Perhaps the most serious consequence of this reduced arousal is that it might limit the individual's reactions to the suffering of others. When compared with controls, individuals who have psychopathic tendencies show reduced skin conductance responses to stimuli depicting distress in others (Blair, Jones, Clark, and Smith, 1997). This may underlay the lack of remorse and the increased capacity for cruel violence associated with antisocial personality disorder.

Looking at the other side of the coin, Patricia Brennan and her colleagues tested the hypothesis that high nervous system reactivity is a "protective" factor against antisocial behavior (Brennan et al., 1997). They compared the skin conductance and heart rate responses of four groups: criminals who had criminal fathers, noncriminals with criminal fathers, criminals with noncriminal fathers, and noncriminals with noncriminal fathers. Consistent with their predictions, skin conductance and heart rate responses to stimuli were largest for the men who were not criminals but had a father with a history of crime. In other words, among those who were presumably at high risk for crime because they had a criminal father, heightened nervous system responsiveness was associated with a lower likelihood of criminal outcome.

Some investigations have revealed abnormalities in the activity of the brain in people with antisocial personality disorder. Chief among these is an apparent decrease in the activity of the frontal lobes (Raine, 1997). This has been shown in studies using EEG (Deckel, Hesselbrock, and Bauer, 1996) and SPECT (single photon emission tomography) (Intrator et al., 1997; Kuruoglu et al., 1996). In their study of young men in their twenties, Deckel and colleagues found that reduced frontal EEG activity was linked with ratings of past childhood conduct disorder, as well as current signs of antisocial personality disorder. Adrian Raine has proposed that frontal dysfunction can contribute to antisocial behavior because it results in a failure of behavioral inhibition. It may thus contribute to the risk taking, impulsivity, and disregard of social norms that characterize antisocial personality disorder.

In considering the findings on biological factors in antisocial personality disorder, it is important to keep two things in mind. First, personality disorders probably represent the extremes along a continuum of variations in personality. Second, there are undoubtedly some contexts in which the extremes can be advantageous. The same propensity that leads a youngster from a deprived environment to engage in antisocial behavior may lead a young man from a privileged environment to be a success on Wall Street. We would be misguided in our efforts if we concluded that there are specific biological "risk" factors for antisocial behavior that are dysfunctional under all circumstances.

The Family and Social Context

Because people with antisocial personality disorder seem not to have internalized the moral standards of the larger society, it is natural to examine the agents of socialization, par-

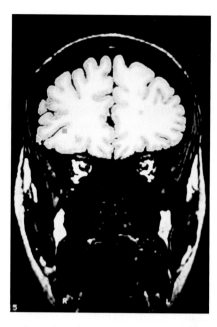

MRI scans of people with an antisocial personality disorder indicate an 11 percent reduction in the gray matter of the frontal lobe compared with subjects who do not have the disorder. The resulting frontal dysfunction in people with this disorder may lead to a failure of behavioral inhibition and consequently to antisocial behavior.

ticularly the family and social context, for clues about antisocial personality disorder. There is a great deal of evidence, for example, that people who grow up in low-income families have more difficult childhoods and are more likely to develop antisocial personality disorder (Miech, Caspi, Moffitt, Wright, and Silva, 1999). In one of the most well-known longitudinal studies of antisocial behavior, Lee Robins and her colleagues at Washington University followed a large group of people who had been seen at a child guidance clinic between 1924 and 1929 (Robins, 1966; Robins and Price, 1991). Fortunately, the clinic had maintained careful records on the presenting problems and family circumstances of its clients. When these children grew up, they were interviewed, along with a control group that had never been seen at the clinic. About 22 percent of the clinic referrals showed adult antisocial behavior, while only 2 percent of the control group did. What early experiences were correlated with the diagnosis of antisocial personality disorder in adulthood? The children treated at the clinic who later developed antisocial personality disorder tended to come from impoverished homes that were broken by divorce or separation. Their fathers themselves were often people with antisocial tendencies who may well have served as negative role models for their children, while simultaneously creating the marital discord that may have spawned problems in their children.

A number of studies indicate that losing a parent through desertion, divorce, or separation (rather than through death or chronic hospitalization) is highly correlated with the later development of antisocial behavior (Greer, 1964; Oltman and Friedman, 1967). Some believe, however, that it is not the parental loss per se that promotes antisocial behavior—otherwise the findings would include deprivation through death and hospitalization. Instead, it is the emotional climate that precedes the divorce—the arguments, the parental instability, the neglectful father—which contributes to antisocial personality disorder in offspring (Smith, 1978). Consistent with this idea, research has shown that separation and divorce are not linked with an increase in the rate of antisocial behavior if the level of discord between the parents is minimal, the mother is affectionate and self-confident, the child is supervised, and the father is nondeviant (McCord, 1979). Indeed, parental monitoring of the child and association with healthy peer groups are linked with lower levels of antisocial behavior in children (Ary, Duncan, Duncan, and Hops, 1999).

Again taking Gary Gilmore's life as an example, we find that although Gilmore's parents were never formally separated, his father spent so much of his time away from home that Gilmore considered himself to have been raised by "a single parent." During some of that time, his father was in prison, serving eighteen months on a bad check charge. His mother was simultaneously overindulgent and neglectful: Gilmore was often left to fend for himself. Reflecting on his family, he described it as "typical" and noted that "there wasn't much closeness in it."

It is not surprising that there is also a significant relationship between antisocial behavior and early experiences of witnessing violence and being abused or neglected (Widom, 1997, 1998). But it may not be necessary for the experience to fall in the category of "abuse" in order to see a rise in antisocial behavior. A study of corporal punishment, defined as slapping or spanking the child, revealed that the more corporal punishment experienced by a child, the greater the tendency for the child to engage in antisocial behavior and to act impulsively (Straus and Mouradian, 1998). This relationship was observed across social classes, for children of all ages, and for both males and females. The strongest relation was for impulsive corporal punishment in which the parent acted without advance planning in response to anger at the child. Based on these findings, and the results of several previous studies of spanking, the authors concluded that physical punishment is an important risk indicator for the development of impulsive and antisocial behavior.

From the standpoint of cause and effect, however, these findings are not that easily interpreted. They certainly do not provide support for the belief that physical punishment improves children's behavior. But is it the parental punishment that causes an increase in antisocial behavior in offspring? Or, is the association between parental behavior and antisocial characteristics in offspring the result of heredity? Most of the research on the relation between the rearing environment and children's behavioral outcomes was conducted on children reared by their biological parents. Studying adoptive families helps get around this problem. As we described in the section on genetic factors, studies of adopted children have found that growing up in an environment characterized by discord and maladaptive parental behavior does increase the rate of antisocial behavior in children, especially if the biological parents had a history of antisocial behavior (Cadoret, Yates, Troughton, Woodworth, and Stewart, 1995; Ge, Conger, Cadoret, and Neiderhiser, 1996). This pattern of findings highlights the interaction between genetic and environmental factors in the etiology of antisocial disorders (see Figure 9–1).

Defects in Learning   Many clinicians have been struck by the seeming inability of people with antisocial tendencies to learn from experience. Prichard (1837) called them "moral imbeciles." Cleckley (1964) observed that they failed especially to learn from punishing experiences, and as a result, had poor judgment. But some are "savvy" and intelligent. If they suffer a defect in learning, it must be a fairly subtle one. Consider the following description of Derrick's lifestyle and its consequences:

> Derrick went from one job, or "get-rich-quick" scheme, to the next throughout his twenties. He was always in debt and moved frequently to avoid bill collectors. Yet, his good looks and charming personality made it possible for him to date a lot of women. At the age of twenty-eight, he was living in the apartment of a woman named Lauren whom he had been

Figure 9—1

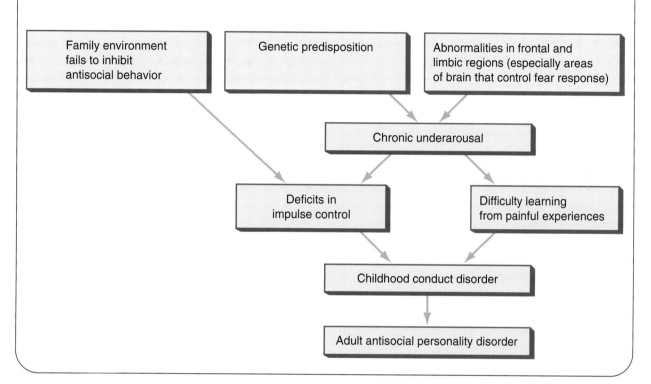

SOURCES OF THE ANTISOCIAL PERSONALITY DISORDER

Both genes and environment play a role in whether someone will develop antisocial personality disorder. Family and social context may lead to deficits in impulse control in an individual. This in combination with a genetic predisposition to chronic underarousal, which may be caused by a dysfunction in the frontal and limbic regions of the brain, may lead to difficulties in learning, as well as problems with impulse control, resulting in childhood conduct disorder and ultimately antisocial personality disorder.

dating for four months. Derrick was seeing two other women at the same time. None of the three women knew about the others. One night he came back to the apartment and found the door locked and his clothes in bags on the porch. Lauren was inside, but refused to let him in. Derrick became enraged that Lauren would not let him in to get his CD player, so he kicked the door in. Lauren called the police, and Derrick was taken to jail. He was booked on several charges, including attempted assault. Because he could not post bond, he was held pending a hearing.

Why did Derrick keep making the same mistakes? Cleckley's observations, in particular, suggested that people with antisocial tendencies were especially deficient in avoidance learning. Ordinary people rapidly learn to anticipate and avoid punitive situations. But those with antisocial personality dis-

order, perhaps because they are underaroused or underanxious, fail to do so. In one of the earliest and most famous experiments addressing this issue, Lykken (1957) examined the effects of punishment on learning in a group of individuals with psychopathic tendencies (they were referred to as "sociopaths" by Lykken). The laboratory task involved learning to press a "correct" lever, but the investigators' real interest was to find out which group learned to avoid punishment.

Participants sat in front of a panel that had four levers. Immediately above each lever was a red light and a green light (see Figure 9–2). The subjects' task was to find and press the lever that turned on the green light on each of a series of twenty trials. Because the correct lever changed on each trial, the subjects had to remember their sequence of responses from the first trial to the one they were now

Figure 9—2

AVOIDANCE LEARNING

This is the apparatus for Lykken's famous (1957) study of avoidance learning in sociopaths. On any given trial, only one of the four levers is correct, and the correct lever changes from trial to trial. Subjects must learn a pattern of twenty correct lever-presses. A correct lever-press turns on a green light. Of the remaining three levers (each of which is wrong), two turn on red lights, while the third delivers electric shock.

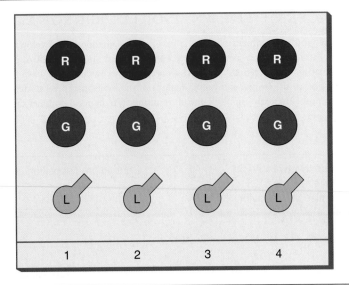

working on. A certain pattern had to be learned, and it was quite a complicated task, a veritable mental maze. On each trial, the subject had four choices, only one of which turned on the green light. Two of the levers turned on a red light—clearly a wrong response—while the third delivered electric shock. Having two kinds of wrong responses, one that simply says "wrong" and the other that delivers physical punishment, enabled the investigator to answer a telling question. Is it the case that people who score high on psychopathy cannot learn from negative experience, or are there particular negative experiences, namely avoidance experiences, from which they cannot learn?

As expected, there were no differences in the total number of mistakes made by those who score high on psychopathy and those who do not. But, whereas normals quickly learned to avoid the electrified levers, those who score high on psychopathy made the most errors that led to shock, suggesting that their particular learning defect was an inability to learn from painful experiences (Lykken, 1957). In effect, punishment or threat of punishment did not seem to influence their behavior; they appeared to be deficient in "passive avoidance learning."

Although not all of the "psychopaths" in this study would meet contemporary criteria for antisocial personality disorder, they certainly fall on the continuum of antisocial tendencies. So what inferences can we draw? Why should people who score high on psychopathy be deficient in avoidance learning? One possibility is that they do not avoid shock because they do not find shock as noxious as do normal people, and they do not find shock as noxious because they are chronically underaroused. Put differently, those who score high on psychopathy may actually seek stimulation in order to elevate arousal to an optimal level. Indeed, it has often seemed to clinical observers that that is the case (Cleckley, 1964). Gary Gilmore may well have experienced underarousal and the need for stimulation as a child. Gilmore said, "I remember when I was a boy I would feel like I had to do things like sit on a railroad track until just before the train came and then I would dash off. Or I would put my finger over the end of a BB gun and pull the trigger to see if a BB was really in it. Sometimes I would stick my finger in water and then put my finger in a light socket to see if it would really shock me."

But what about other kinds of punishment? Do individuals with psychopathic or antisocial tendencies have any problem learning when the punishment does not involve physical discomfort? There are several kinds of punishment (see Table 9—4). There is physical punishment to which people who score high on psychopathy do not respond. But there is also tangible punishment such as the loss of money, and social punishment such as disapproval. Are people who score high on psychopathy as unresponsive to the latter kinds of punishment as they are to physical punishment? The same "mental maze" was used to examine this question. But this time, if one of the wrong levers was pressed, the subject lost a quarter. If another was pressed, the subject received social disapproval, and the third wrong lever brought electric shock. Once again, those who score high on psychopathy learned the task as quickly as normals. But, again, they were considerably less responsive to physical punishment than were normals. They were also less responsive to social disapproval. But they did not have a problem learning to avoid the lever that would cost them a quarter. These findings led the investigator to the conclusion that those who scored high on psychopathy can learn to avoid punishment, provided that the punishment is noxious to them; in other words, if it means the loss of a reward (Schmauk, 1970).

Subsequent studies of people who score high on psychopathy have confirmed and extended these findings. In a series of studies, Joseph Newman and his colleagues have shown that individuals with antisocial tendencies have difficulty with passive avoidance learning, even when loss of money is the punishment (Newman and Schmitt, 1998). But the monetary loss to participants in Newman's research was only ten cents, whereas in the study by Schmauk (conducted in 1970—almost thirty years earlier) the participants lost a quarter. Thus, it may be that individuals who score high on psychopathy can only overcome their deficit in passive avoidance learning when the value of the lost reward exceeds a certain level.

In their effort to make sense of the research findings on passive avoidance, Patterson and Newman (1993) proposed a theory referred to as the "response modulation theory." They based this theory on the observations that individuals who score high on psychopathy have less difficulty avoiding punishment if (1) avoidance is their only goal, (2) the avoidance goal is made clear from the beginning, or (3) there is an extended period of time between trials so that the consequences of their responses can be processed. These findings suggest that there may be a deficiency in the processing of contextual information that is unexpected or outside of the current focus of attention. Patterson and Newman labeled it as a deficit in response modulation: the ability to make rapid and relatively automatic shifts in attention so that the focus of attention can be evaluated and redirected, if appropriate for the context (Newman, Schmitt, and Voss, 1997).

Newman and his colleagues tested the merits of the response modulation theory with samples of prison inmates who were either high or low on psychopathy (Newman and Schmitt, 1998). The researchers asked the participants to perform a task in which they classified pairs of stimuli, pictures or words, as related or unrelated. For each trial of the test, the two stimuli in each pair were presented quickly, in succession, on a computer screen. The participants were told before each trial to either focus on the target picture or the target word. The first stimulus in each pair always contained an irrelevant (nontarget distractor) word or picture that they were instructed to ignore. The irrelevant word or picture was potentially distracting, because it was sometimes related to the second stimulus. The reaction times to label the stimulus pairs as related or unrelated were

TABLE 9–4

AVOIDANCE LEARNING IN NORMALS AND PSYCHOPATHS

Stimulus	Normals	Psychopaths
Electric shock	Learn quickly to avoid; anxious while anticipating	Have trouble learning to avoid; less anxious while anticipating
Social disapproval (red light)	Learn to avoid	Have trouble learning to avoid
Loss of a quarter	Learn to avoid	Learn more quickly than normals to avoid

recorded. Most people found the task to be more difficult when the irrelevant word or picture was related to the second stimulus; their reaction times were slower because the irrelevant word or picture interfered with their focus of attention. But the central finding of this study was that this did not hold for the inmates who were high on psychopathy. They did not show the same interference effect. What does this mean? The authors conclude that the inmates who are high on psychopathy are showing a response modulation deficit—they fail to process peripheral cues when they are involved in goal-directed behavior. In the real world, this may translate into a failure to respond to subtle environmental cues that ordinarily influence behavior and, therefore, a failure to change behavior to make it conform to social expectations. For example, the person who is high on psychopathy may fail to notice looks of disapproval from others when he is focused on a particular goal.

One recurrent finding in this research is that people who are high on both anxiety and psychopathic tendencies are much less likely to show abnormalities in learning or task performance (Newman, Schmitt, and Voss, 1997; Newman and Schmitt, 1998). It is as if a high level of anxiety increases their ability to attend to stimuli and learn. Another interesting and potentially important aspect of the findings on avoidance learning is the presence of ethnic group differences. Specifically, when the subjects are incarcerated whites and African Americans, the African Americans show less or no deficiency in avoidance learning (Newman, Schmitt, and Voss, 1997; Newman and Schmitt, 1998). Considering this in light of the fact that African-American men are more likely than white men to be stopped by the police, investigated, arrested, and imprisoned, the end result may be a higher proportion of "nonpsychopathic" African-American men in jail.

TREATMENT AND PREVENTION

Among both clinicians and researchers, there has been a great deal of pessimism about the potential for treating people who have personality disorders. This is because the symptoms have been viewed as characterological in nature and thus indicative of long-standing problems. Clients with personality disorders are less likely to follow through with treatment plans, and their rate of attendance at therapy

sessions is poor (Hilsenroth, Holdwick, Castlebury, and Blais, 1998). The pessimism has been especially great about the treatment of antisocial personality disorder. Most approaches to psychotherapy emphasize the importance of the therapeutic relationship, a relationship that is based on commitment and trust. If the client has a limited capacity for trust and commitment, as is the case for people with antisocial personality disorder, the therapeutic relationship is not formed. We described the case of Derrick, whose childhood conduct disorder emerged as antisocial personality disorder in adulthood. Derrick's experience illustrates the obstacles that can be encountered in the psychotherapeutic treatment of personality disorder:

> In order to get out of jail, Derrick staged a suicide attempt and feigned symptoms of depression. He was placed in a secure unit in a local psychiatric hospital. He was assigned a psychiatric nurse who saw him every other day to monitor his depression. Derrick convinced the nurse and several other staff members that he had become clinically depressed when he discovered his girlfriend was unfaithful. He claimed that her infidelity caused him to lose control. The nurse referred him for psychotherapy with the unit psychologist. Again, Derrick's charm helped him win over the psychologist. He told the psychologist that he was the oldest of five children and that he had supported his ill mother for years while he went to school at night. In Derrick's chart the psychologist described him as "a deeply wounded young man who has great potential for growth and the capacity to benefit from self-exploration in therapy." For almost a week, Derrick was the recipient of sympathy and attention from almost everyone on the staff. But the façade began to crack when he made a pass at a nurse, he "borrowed" money from a vending machine, and staff members found inconsistencies in the stories he told them. When he was confronted about these issues by his therapist, Derrick became defensive and belligerent. Within two weeks of beginning therapy with Derrick, the psychologist recorded in his chart, "this client repeatedly engages in manipulation of staff, and becomes very hostile when he is thwarted in his attempts to control others. He appears to be using therapy as a means of avoiding responsibility for his behavior."

The manipulative behavior shown by Derrick would not surprise an experienced clinician. Despite the pessimistic views of some, however, there is evidence that the signs of antisocial personality disorder can be reduced with certain psychological treatments. In developing effective treatment approaches for people with antisocial personality disorder, it is important to keep in mind the nature of the cognitive abnormalities they are likely to show. For example, clinicians who specialize in the treatment of people with antisocial personality disorder tailor their approach to the propensities of the person. In most cases, the therapist attempts to improve the client's ability to empathize and identify with others (Lowenstein, 1996). Another specific strategy is "positive practice," a behavioral technique in which the individual's negative patterns of behavior are corrected and appropriate behavior repeatedly presented. Further, assuming that these individuals suffer from deficits in response modulation, cognitive therapy techniques can be modified to improve the client's ability to process subtle cues that ongoing behavior should be inhibited (Wallace, Vitale, and Newman, 1999). Experienced clinicians also emphasize the importance of starting treatment early, before antisocial behavior becomes habitual and therefore more difficult to treat.

At the present time, there are no specific drug treatments for antisocial personality disorder. Many people with this diagnosis do receive medication, but it is usually for the treatment of other conditions, such as co-occurring psychotic symptoms, anxiety, or depression.

In the long run, society might be best served if efforts were put into the prevention of antisocial behaviors and syndromes, rather than their treatment (McCord, Tremblay, Vitaro, and Desmarais-Gervais, 1994). Based on her findings from extensive research on the childhood precursors of antisocial disorders, psychologist Cathy Spatz Widom has offered some specific recommendations for prevention programs, including: (1) early intervention, (2) paying special attention to neglected children, (3) prevention programs that are tailored to the unique needs of various groups of children, since "one size does not fit all," and (4) accessible resources for at-risk youth and their families (Widom, 1998). Instead of waiting to respond when cases of child abuse or neglect come to our attention in court proceedings, primary prevention efforts should target childhood victims to reduce their risk of becoming offenders in the future.

Because unstable environments can lead to antisocial behavior, a possibility for prevention is to change the environments of at-risk youth. Indeed, researchers have shown that early intervention studies that involve "experimental" manipulations of the environment can change the outcomes for children from impoverished backgrounds (Olds et al., 1998). David Olds and his colleagues at Cornell University provided young pregnant women with one of four intervention programs: Groups 1 and 2 (comparison groups) were provided prenatal and well-child care. Group 3 was provided prenatal and well-child care and a nurse who visited the women at home during their pregnancy. Group 4 was provided the same services as Group 3, except the nurse continued to visit through the child's second birthday. Fifteen years later, the researchers gathered information on the children's criminal behavior, school suspensions, behavior problems, and substance use. Adolescents born to women in Group 4 had fewer episodes of running away, fewer arrests and convictions, less promiscuity, and lower rates of cigarette smoking and alcohol consumption than did their counterparts in the comparison groups.

Preventive intervention programs, like the one implemented by David Olds and his colleagues, are feasible and compatible with our cultural assumptions about personal rights. The success of David Olds's home visitation program lends support to the idea that intensive early intervention with at-risk children can reduce the rate of antisocial behavior later in life. This program only involved home visitations by a childcare worker up to the child's second birthday—perhaps an intervention that extended to adolescence would have an even greater impact.

At this point, we can only speculate on the possibilities for the prevention of antisocial personality disorder. Future research will help us understand what the possibilities for prevention are. In the meantime, clinicians focus their attention on the treatment of individuals who already have a history of antisocial behavior. As described above, the symptoms of this disorder present unique challenges for clinicians. In addition, the difficulty is compounded by the fact that there is a high rate of comorbidity among the personality disorders (Livesley, 1995). For example, a large proportion of those who meet diagnostic criteria for antisocial personality disorder also meet criteria for another DSM personality disorder, including schizotypal personality disorder.

Histrionic Personality Disorder

People who meet diagnostic criteria for **histrionic personality disorder** have long histories of drawing attention to themselves and of reacting to insignificant events with dramatic emotional displays. They are often superficially charming, warm, and gregarious, but they are usually viewed by others as insincere and shallow (Bornstein, 1999). Individuals with histrionic personality disorder seem to be seeking admiration by playing continually to unknown audiences. Once they form relationships, they become demanding, inconsiderate, egocentric, and self-absorbed. They can be enormously flirtatious and seductive, and their sexual adjustment is often poor. The incidence of histrionic personality disorder is about 1.3 to 3 percent of the population (Weissman, 1993). The diagnosis is more common among women than men (Kass, Spitzer, and Williams, 1983). The case of Shelly is an example:

Shelly had problems relating to her peers throughout childhood. Even though she was very attractive, and a talented singer and gymnast, she had few long-term friendships. Her mother and other family members attributed Shelly's problems to the fact that she "wanted to be the focus of attention," and when she was not she became "irritable." As an adolescent, her concern with her physical appearance became excessive, and she wore very provocative clothing. She was also very flirtatious with boys and encouraged their interest in her. Shelly spent a great deal of time talking to boys on the telephone and going on dates. She usually had several boyfriends at one time. But none of her relationships with other girls lasted longer than a few months. Other girls sometimes initiated relationships with Shelly, and these "friendships" often became very intense, very quickly. Shelly would call her newfound friend constantly, seeking advice and reassurance. But just as quickly, the friendships dissolved, usually over an emotional conflict.

Shelly considered it a challenge to get the attention of a boy who she knew was involved with someone else. As a result, she gained a negative reputation with the other girls in her high school. Through a variety of manipulations, Shelly managed to get a very popular boy on the football team to invite her, rather than his long-time girlfriend, to the prom. This created a great deal of animosity. The situation was made worse by the fact that Shelly appeared at the prom in an evening gown that was brightly colored and semi-transparent. She followed her date around constantly at the prom and clung to him as if she feared he would leave her.

After graduating from high school, Shelly completed a year of college, then quit because she felt she needed a break to make some money. Her first job was as a receptionist in the executive offices of a department store. Within a few months, Shelly began to have an affair with the vice president of the company, a married man. Shelly was very flagrant and dramatic in her conversations with other employees, openly displaying gifts that the man had purchased for her. The vice president was reprimanded and counseled by the CEO to terminate the affair immediately. When he attempted to do so, Shelly protested dramatically, and began to tell other employees that she believed she was pregnant and that the father was one of the company executives. She persisted in calling the home of her former lover until he had to have his

DSM-IV Criteria

Histrionic Personality Disorder

A pervasive pattern of excessive emotionality and attention seeking, beginning by early adulthood and present in a variety of contexts, as indicated by five (or more) of the following: (1) is uncomfortable in situations in which he or she is not the center of attention; (2) interaction with others is often characterized by inappropriate sexually seductive or provocative behavior; (3) displays rapidly shifting and shallow expression of emotions; (4) consistently uses physical appearance to draw attention to self; (5) has a style of speech that is excessively impressionistic and lacking in detail; (6) shows self-dramatization, theatricality, and exaggerated expression of emotion; (7) is suggestible, i.e., easily influenced by others or circumstances; (8) considers relationships to be more intimate than they actually are.

SOURCE: APA, DSM-IV, 1994.

number changed. Eleven months after being hired, Shelly was asked to leave. In the following two years, Shelly had four different jobs. She was terminated from three of the four because of inappropriate relationships or behavior with male supervisors.

When she finally went to seek psychotherapy, Shelly lamented that most of her problems stemmed from the fact that she was the victim of "her own good looks and personality." According to Shelly, "I am just too much of a threat to other women."

If, upon perusing Shelly's history, you have the sense that her diagnosis is not entirely clear, that it seems to overlap with other personality disorders, perhaps especially with the borderline personality (see below), or even the antisocial personality disorder—you may well be right. There seems to be considerable overlap between the histrionic personality disorder and other disorders (Grueneich, 1992; Pfohl, 1991). It has been proposed that histrionic personality disorder and antisocial personality disorder share some of the same underlying causes, in particular a lack of concern for others and a preoccupation with one's own desires (Hamburger, Lilienfeld, and Hogben, 1996). But in general, when these propensities occur in females, they are channeled into a histrionic personality type, whereas in males they are expressed as antisocial traits.

Most theories about the causes of histrionic personality disorder have drawn on psychodynamic concepts (Bornstein, 1999). The earliest theories emphasized the "hypersexuality" of histrionic people, and proposed that it is due to penis envy in women and castration anxiety in men. Later psychodynamic theories held that the key feature of histrionic personality disorder is an extreme dependency need, and that this stems from a fixation in the oral stage of development. In other words, as a child, the person failed to have his or her needs for emotional sustenance met. In adulthood, this can lead to an intense preoccupation with seeking and receiving attention from others. More recently, theorists have focused on early learning, suggesting that histrionic tendencies stem from inconsistent patterns of reinforcement provided by parents (Millon and Davis, 1996). Again, in adulthood, the result is a personality style that involves seeking others' attention. To date, there is not sufficient evidence from research to favor one theory over the other. Moreover, there has been very little empirical research on the cognitive or biological correlates of the disorder.

People with a histrionic personality disorder like to dramatize everything they do in order to draw the attention and admiration of others. The person in this drawing by Martha Grunenwalt seems to exhibit such characteristics.

There is also very little known about the treatment for histrionic personality disorder. It has been recommended that the therapist should focus on the highly defensive style and interpersonal dependency needs of the client (Horowitz, 1997). Lorna Benjamin suggests an interpersonal therapy approach along with a "structural analysis of social behavior" (Benjamin, 1996).

Narcissistic Personality Disorder

Narcissistic personality disorder is characterized by an inflated sense of self-importance and a lack of empathy. There is "grandiosity" and self-absorption in fantasies of unlimited success, power, and/or beauty, and a need for constant admiration. People with narcissistic personality disorder use a less stringent standard for evaluating themselves than for judging others (Ronningstam, 1998; Tangney, Wagner, and Gramzow, 1992). Criticism, the indifference of others, and threats to self-esteem are met with responses of rage, shame, or humiliation. Of course, the near-total preoccupation with self disturbs interpersonal relationships in a variety of ways. Such people seem to lack the ability to recognize how others feel. They may have an exaggerated sense of "entitlement," expecting that the world owes them a living without assuming reciprocal responsibilities. They may simply be exploitative, taking advantage of others to indulge their own desires. When they are able to establish a relationship, they may vacillate between the extremes of over-idealization and enormous devaluation of the

DSM-IV Criteria

Narcissistic Personality Disorder

A pervasive pattern of grandiosity (in fantasy or behavior), need for admiration, and lack of empathy, beginning by early adulthood and present in a variety of contexts, as indicated by five (or more) of the following: (1) has a grandiose sense of self-importance (e.g., exaggerates achievements and talents, expects to be recognized as superior without commensurate achievements); (2) is preoccupied with fantasies of unlimited success, power, brilliance, beauty, or ideal love; (3) believes that he or she is "special" and unique and can only be understood by, or should associate with, other special or high status people (or institutions); (4) requires excessive admiration; (5) has a sense of entitlement, i.e., unreasonable expectations of especially favorable treatment or automatic compliance with his or her expectations; (6) is interpersonally exploitative, i.e., takes advantage of others to achieve his or her own ends; (7) lacks empathy: is unwilling to recognize or identify with the feelings and needs of others; (8) is often envious of others or believes that others are envious of him or her; (9) shows arrogant, haughty behaviors or attitudes.

SOURCE: APA, DSM-IV, 1994.

---

other person. But the hidden roots of narcissism may also involve fragile self-esteem and deep-seated fear of failure. Below is a case of a man with narcissistic personality disorder:

Bill is a handsome twenty-four-year-old man from a small town in the Midwest. An only child, he continues to be close to his parents and receives some financial support from them. A seemingly self-assured young man, Bill has excellent communication skills, dresses very neatly, and prides himself on being organized and efficient. After graduating with a master's degree in business, Bill was hired as a sales manager in an advertising firm. He had made a favorable impression when applying for the job, in part because of the many personal accomplishments he described to the interviewer. During the interview, Bill was very gregarious and enthusiastic. He stated that he had been instrumental in the dramatic success of a small start-up company where he had worked part time as a student.

By the beginning of his second week with the company, Bill began to have trouble with some of his co-workers. They avoided having lunch with him, and confided their dislike of him to each other. They found Bill annoying because he bragged endlessly about his successes, and criticized his former co-workers for their incompetence. He maintained that it was a bad policy to have lunch with co-workers, because it is unwise to get too close to people who are your competitors. Bill seemed to have no clues about the impact his behavior had on others. One day, Bill threw out the entire contents of the refrigerator in the employee lounge. When other employees arrived and asked what happened to the things they had stored in the refrigerator, Bill laughed in amusement and expressed surprise that they wanted to keep "that garbage." He also speculated openly to the other male employees that several of the female employees in his department had crushes on him. He dated, in succession, four women in his department. But all of these dating relationships ended, with Bill claiming that the women "weren't very interesting." In fact, in two cases the women chose not to continue dating Bill because they found his self-centered attitudes intolerable.

It was clear to the branch manager that Bill was not very popular with the other employees. However, he attributed this to jealousy over Bill's accomplishments. Bill did have a sales record that was slightly above average. He assumed that the other employees were concerned that Bill would outshine them. But the branch manager's perception changed when Bill began to complain to him about the poor treatment he was receiving. After working at the company for two months, Bill requested that the furniture in his office be replaced. He was told that the furniture in all of the sales managers' offices was only three years old, and that there were no plans to replace it. Bill complained to the division manager, stating that his performance exceeded that of all his co-workers, and that his achievements should be rewarded. He openly accused the branch manager of being a "wimp" because he was unwilling to "reward excellence" due to fear of reprisals from "mediocre" employees. Bill accused his co-workers of being threatened by his competence.

At the end of his first year of employment, Bill was estranged from both his co-workers and supervisors. He repeatedly complained that he was being victimized by them because he was so much more successful. He perceived even their most innocent oversights as personal insults. The perception shared by his co-workers was that Bill was an "egotist" who needed constant praise and attention to bolster his self-esteem.

We can see some similarities between the case of Bill and that of Shelly, described earlier in the discussion of histrionic personality disorder. Both seem to have a grandiose sense of themselves and are constantly seeking admiration from others. Yet, there are obvious differences. Shelly manifests strong dependency needs and seems to strive for the approval of others. In contrast, Bill views dependency as dangerous, and he primarily relies on himself for evaluation.

In a study of the daily life experiences of people who score high on measures of narcissism, several distinguishing characteristics were found (Rhodewalt, Madrian, and Cheney, 1998). When compared to the control group, they displayed greater mood variability, mood intensity, and fluctuations in self-esteem. They also reacted differently to daily events. Normals showed relatively little change in self-esteem as a function of their daily experiences. In contrast, for those high on narcissism, negative inter-personal events increased self-esteem instability, whereas positive interpersonal events seemed to stabilize their self-esteem.

The incidence of narcissistic personality disorder is less than 0.5 percent of the population (Allnut and Links, 1996). It has been proposed that childhood experiences contribute to it. Some theorists suggest that these expectations arise because empathic relationships with caregivers failed to develop (Kohut, 1978), resulting in a fragmented sense of self that is especially vulnerable to feelings of emptiness and low self-esteem, and the compensatory behaviors that these generate. Perhaps the parents failed to respond to the child unless it furthered their own needs, rather than the child's. Those who have narcissistic personality disorder simply expect too much from others (Benjamin, 1987).

Borderline Personality Disorder

The essential feature of the **borderline personality disorder** is instability in many aspects of daily functioning, including interpersonal relationships, behavior, mood, and self-image. People with borderline personality disorder tend to fluctuate between depression, anxiety, and anger with the slightest provocation. They are prone to suicide, substance abuse, unsafe sex, self-mutilation, and intense, but unstable, relationships (see Box 9–4). These areas of dysfunction are themselves so broad that people with quite different problems can meet the criteria for this diagnosis.

Somewhere between 1 to 3 percent of the population meet the DSM criteria for borderline personality disorder (Swartz, Blazer, George, and Winfield, 1990; Widiger and Weissman, 1991). Although many have viewed borderline personality disorder as being more common in women, recent studies indicate that it occurs as often or more often in men (Carter, Joyce, Mulder, Sullivan, and Luty, 1999). Most who suffer from this disorder feel distressed, and many seek treatment. Consequently, the borderline personality diagnosis is by far the most prevalent of the personality disorder diagnoses in both inpatient and outpatient settings (Grueneich, 1992). Yet, clearly any diagnosis that is so broad and potentially inclusive runs the risk of becoming a "kitchen sink" diagnosis. In order to increase the validity of the borderline diagnosis, as well as to limit its use to a restricted range of people, DSM-IV requires that evidence for at least five of the following problems be present before the diagnosis can be made:

The character played by Annette Bening in the 1999 film *American Beauty* lacked empathy and was so self-absorbed that she failed to see the pain of those around her, characteristics of the narcissistic personality disorder. Her narcissism may have emerged from low self-esteem and a fear of failure.

Science and Practice

Box 9—4

Self-Mutilation in Borderline Personality Disorder

Perhaps more than any other abnormal behavior, self-mutilation has been a puzzle to researchers and clinicians. Self-mutilation is defined as deliberate, self-inflicted injury to one's body (Winchel and Stanley, 1991). Forms of self-injurious behavior reported in the clinical literature include cuts on the wrists and body, cigarette burns, carving letters in the skin, arm and head banging, sandpapering the face, overdosing on drugs, intentionally breaking the bones of the body, and washing body parts with acid. Clearly, self-injurious behaviors can manifest in a wide array of destructive, bizarre, and reckless forms. Ironically, however, death is usually not the stated intent (Gardner and Cowdry, 1985). Most who engage in self-mutilation do not express the desire to end their life.

Self-injurious behavior frequently occurs as a symptom of borderline personality disorder (Winchel and Stanley, 1991). Patients with borderline personality disorder experience dysphoria, a mixture of negative emotions such as depression, anxiety, anger, emptiness, depersonalization. It is during these periods of dysphoria that individuals with borderline personality disorder are most likely to commit acts of self-mutilation. While engaging in self-mutilation, many report a sort of numbness and a sense of being disconnected from their body parts. Those who report experiencing physical pain during the self-injurious act are, at the same time, overwhelmed by a sense of relief from their previous state of dysphoria (Gardner and Cowdry, 1985). Many report experiencing a state of calm and greater clarity of thought.

Treatment strategies for self-mutilation consist of both behavioral and biological techniques. Behaviorists have focused their attention on the factors that are responsible for the maintenance of self-injurious behavior (Mace, Vollmer, Progar, and Mace, 1998). Self-injury may constitute an escape behavior that is controlled by negative reinforcement processes, or an attention-seeking behavior that is controlled by positive reinforcement processes. Thus, in some cases, self-mutilation serves the function of helping the person escape from or avoid negative reinforcement, such as aversive social interactions. In other cases, the individual engages in the behavior because of the positive reinforcement that results from the expression of concern or attention from others.

The therapist begins by conducting a thorough evaluation of the person's daily activities and the environmental context. Then a treatment plan is formulated, based on the therapist's hypotheses about the antecedents and consequences of the self-mutilation. Behavioral techniques that have been used in the treatment of self-mutilation include extinction, alternative-sensory activities, time-outs, various changes in the environmental contexts, and punishment (Winchel and Stanley, 1991). Punishment is only used as a last resort, however, when other approaches fail. Systematic desensitization has also been used to reduce the emotional stress that often precedes and triggers self-injurious behaviors. Behavior modification is generally preferred over aversion techniques (Van Moffaert, 1990).

Pharmacological agents are now widely used in the treatment of self-injurious behaviors. Commonly used drugs include antipsychotics and antidepressants (Chengappa, Ebeling, Kang, Levine, and Parepally, 1999; Winchel and Stanley, 1991). Clozapine, an antipsychotic drug, has been especially noted for its effectiveness in diminishing hostility and aggressiveness. Patients with borderline personality disorder who display self-mutilating behaviors have been shown to benefit a great deal from clozapine treatment. Research has shown that serotonin deficits are linked with impulsivity, aggression, and suicide. Thus, it is not surprising that selective serotonin reuptake inhibitors have also proven to be effective in reducing self-mutilation.

SOURCE: Based on Chengappa, Ebeling, Kang, Levine, and Parepally, 1999; Gardner and Cowdry, 1985; Mace, Vollmer, Progar, and Mace, 1998; Van Moffaert, 1990; Winchel and Stanley, 1991.

- seemingly frantic efforts to avoid being abandoned;
- a pattern of intense, yet unstable, interpersonal relationships;
- a markedly disturbed, distorted, or unstable sense of self;
- self-damaging, impulsive sexual behavior, substance abuse, spending, reckless driving, or binge eating;
- recurring suicidal behavior, threats of such behavior, or self-mutilating gestures;
- chronic feelings of emptiness;

- emotional instability that lasts for a few hours to a few days;
- lack of control over anger;
- stress-related paranoid thoughts or severe dissociative symptoms.

The following case illustrates some of the difficulties of the person with borderline personality disorder:

Thomas Wolfe was a writer whose first work was published in 1929 and who died less than ten years later, before he was forty. In that brief decade, he was a literary sensation, hailed by the greatest novelists of his time. He was enormously productive and driven. And he was painfully unhappy. Wolfe was described as nervous, surly, suspicious, given to brooding, to drinking, to violent outbursts, and sometimes even to fears that he was going mad. He was rude and dislikable. He said of himself that he was afraid of people and that he sometimes concealed his fear by being arrogant and by sneering magnificently.

It was hard for him to begin writing on any particular day, but once he began it was harder still for him to stop. The words would simply pour out of him. He would sleep late, gulp down cup after cup of black coffee, smoke innumerable cigarettes, pace up and down— and write endlessly. He would scrawl down the words on sheet after sheet of yellow paper, so hastily and hugely that the pages often contained only twenty words apiece, and those in abbreviated scrawl. At night, he would prowl the streets, drinking heavily, or spending hours in a phone booth, calling friends, and accusing them of having betrayed him. The next day, overcome with remorse, he would call again and apologize.

For all his writing, he had difficulty putting together a second book after *Look Homeward, Angel*. Although he had written a million words, ten times that of an average novel, it still was not a book. He was fortunate to have as his editor Maxwell Perkins, who had discovered his talent and who cared to nurture it. Wolfe wrote: "I was sustained by one piece of inestimable good fortune. I had for a friend a man of immense wisdom and a gentle but unyielding fortitude. I

Thomas Wolfe (1900–1938) may have suffered from borderline personality disorder.

think that if I was not destroyed at this time by the sense of hopelessness . . . it was largely because of . . . Perkins . . . I did not give in because he would not let me give in." Perkins recognized that Wolfe was a driven man, and feared that he would suffer either a psychological or physical breakdown, or both. He proposed to Wolfe that, having written a million words, his work was finished: it only remained for both of them to sit down and make a book out of his effort.

That collaboration was difficult. A million words do not automatically make a book. Wolfe was reluctant to cut. Most of the editing, therefore, fell to Perkins. And as Perkins slowly made a book out of Wolfe's words, Wolfe's resentment of Perkins increased. The work was not perfect, Wolfe felt. And it upset him to bring forth a book that did not meet his standards.

DSM-IV Criteria

Borderline Personality Disorder

A pervasive pattern of instability of interpersonal relationships, self-image, and affects, and marked impulsivity beginning by early adulthood and present in a variety of contexts, as indicated by five (or more) of the following: (1) frantic efforts to avoid real or imagined abandonment. (*Note:* Do not include suicidal or self-mutilating behavior covered in Criterion 5.); (2) a pattern of unstable and intense interpersonal relationships characterized by alternating between extremes of idealization and devaluation; (3) identity disturbance: markedly and persistently unstable self-image or sense of self; (4) impulsivity in at least two areas that are potentially self-damaging (e.g., spending, sex, substance abuse, reckless driving, binge eating). (*Note:* Do not include suicidal or self-mutilating behavior covered in Criterion 5); (5) recurrent suicidal behavior, gestures, or threats, or self-mutilating behavior; (6) affective instability due to a marked reactivity of mood (e.g. intense episodic dysphoria, irritability, or anxiety usually lasting a few hours and only rarely more than a few days); (7) chronic feelings of emptiness; (8) inappropriate, intense anger or difficulty controlling anger (e.g., frequent displays of temper, constant anger, recurrent physical fights); (9) transient, stress-related paranoid ideation or severe dissociative symptoms.

SOURCE: APA, DSM-IV, 1994.

Until the book was published, Wolfe believed it would be a colossal failure. The reviews were magnificent, however. But although Wolfe was at first heartened by the reviews, he gradually began to feel again that the book was less than perfect, a matter for which he held Perkins responsible. His relationship with Perkins deteriorated. He became suspicious, even paranoid. Yet, apart from Perkins, he had no close friends. He became increasingly unpredictable, yielding easily to incensed anger, unable to control it. Ultimately, he broke with Perkins. Rosenthal (1979) has suggested that Wolfe's emotional lability, his inability to control his anger, the difficulties he had in being alone, his many self-damaging acts, as well as his identity problems point to the diagnosis of a borderline personality disorder. At the same time, Wolfe also had personality features that were consistent with the schizotypal personality disorder, especially his ideas of reference that made him so suspicious.

The rate of suicide and suicide attempts is high among people with borderline personality disorder. It is estimated that about 8 percent die by suicide (Maltsberger and Lovett, 1992; Paris, 1990). However, the disorder becomes less severe as the individual ages. Erratic behavior decreases, and interpersonal relationships improve.

What about those who show some signs of borderline personality, but would not necessarily meet DSM-IV criteria for the disorder? When researchers assessed personality traits in a sample of randomly selected young adults, they found that those who showed more of the features of borderline personality had more life problems in the subsequent years (Trull, Useda, Conforti and Doan, 1997). Those who scored high on borderline traits were more likely to have academic difficulties, to have interpersonal problems, and to meet criteria for a mood disorder over the next two years. Thus, even within a "normal" population, borderline traits are associated with poorer outcome.

CAUSES

What causes the instability and unpredictability that is so characteristic of the borderline personality disorder? A great deal of controversy has surrounded this question. Psychodynamic explanations dominated in the past (Kohut, 1977). In recent years, the psychodynamic approach has been refined and extended. Otto Kernberg and his colleagues have been at the forefront of this work, and they have called attention to the tendency for persons with borderline personality disorder to "split" or dichotomize the world into extremes of good and bad (Clarkin, Yeomans, and Kernberg, 1999). They believe this tendency is a central feature of borderline personality disorder, because it causes the person to behave in extreme and erratic ways.

As research findings accumulated, it became clear that individuals with borderline personality disorder reported a high rate of early childhood abuse and trauma (Arntz, Dietzel, and Dreessen, 1999; Zanarini et al., 1997). But is the link a causal one? Some have argued that it may not be. Bailey and Shriver (1999) interviewed psychologists about their perceptions of clients with borderline personality disorder. The practicing psychologists described the patients as being especially likely to misinterpret or misremember social interactions, to be manipulative, and to have voluntarily entered destructive sexual relationships. So the link between childhood experiences and adult borderline personality disorder may not be causal.

Some recent findings suggest there may be biological correlates of borderline personality disorder. The biological relatives of people with borderline personality disorder tend to have a higher rate of var-

People who are diagnosed with borderline personality disorder may have suffered from childhood abuse and tend to have unstable and destructive interpersonal relationships. Their chronic feelings of emptiness, unstable self-image, and manipulative behavior may be seen in this woman painted by Jennie Maruki.

ious psychiatric disorders, especially mood disorders (Nigg and Goldsmith, 1994). Reduced serotonin activity seems to be associated with borderline personality disorder, and drugs that increase serotonin activity lead to improvement in some patients (Coccaro, Silverman, Klar, Horvath, and Siever, 1994). Brain trauma may also play a role. When researchers examined the medical histories of veterans suffering from borderline personality disorder, they found that they were more likely than a control group to have experienced traumatic brain injury (Streeter et al., 1995). In fact, 42 percent of the group with borderline personality disorder had a previous history of trauma to the head, compared to 4 percent of the controls. Consistent with this, a recent neuroimaging study revealed evidence of structural brain abnormality in persons with borderline personality disorder (Lyoo, Han, and Cho, 1998). Specifically, when compared to a normal group of the same age and sex, those with borderline personality disorder had significantly smaller frontal lobes, but there were no differences in the volumes of the temporal lobes, the lateral ventricles, or the cerebral hemispheres. Of course, we do not know whether the brain abnormalities caused the disorder, were produced by the disorder, or were a consequence of some other factor, like early trauma, that caused both the brain abnormality and the personality disorder.

Marsha Linehan has proposed one of the most comprehensive theories of the causes of borderline personality disorder (Wagner and Linehan, 1997). Her "biosocial" model postulates that the disorder involves both heritable traits and psychosocial experiences. She and her colleagues assume that children who develop borderline personality disorder later in life have a biological vulnerability that makes them more emotionally sensitive to negative events; they react more strongly and take a longer time to recover. When these children encounter an "invalidating environment," one in which there is more stress and less support, they begin to manifest the signs of borderline personality disorder. Linehan's theory fits well with the research findings.

Some writers have noted that persons being treated for borderline personality disorder often manifest certain positive qualities, such as unusual perceptiveness and insight into the feelings of other people (Park, Imboden, Park, Hulse, and Unger, 1992). In part, these observations may reflect the fact that patients with borderline personality disorder who are in treatment tend to have a higher than av-

erage educational level and to come from the upper social classes (Taub, 1996).

TREATMENT

Although many clinicians view borderline personality disorder as being very difficult to treat, recent research indicates that it can be treated effectively with a form of therapy called "dialectical behavior therapy" developed by Marsha Linehan (Dimeff, McDavid, and Linehan, 1999). Dialectical behavior therapy is a very systematic treatment that includes weekly individual psychotherapy and group skills training. The therapy is based on a motivational-skills deficit model that presumes that people with borderline personality disorder lack important interpersonal, self-regulation (including emotional regulation), and distress tolerance skills. Dialectical behavior therapy targets the reduction of suicidal behavior, as well as behaviors that interfere with treatment, and behaviors that interfere with quality of life. Weekly individual therapy focuses primarily on motivational issues and skill training. Behavioral techniques aimed at change are balanced with supportive strategies aimed at providing acceptance. Weekly group sessions also usually focus on behavioral skill acquisition and follow a psychoeducational format, in which the therapist offers systematic information about strategies for achieving greater behavioral control. A recent review of the published research on dialectical behavior therapy concluded that it does help those with borderline personality disorder in the short run, but that the longevity of the improvement is not known (Scheel, 2000). This is an important point, because personality disorders are, by definition, chronic disorders.

The psychodynamic approach also continues to be used in the treatment of borderline personality disorder (Clarkin, Yeomans, and Kernberg, 1999). A new psychodynamic technique called "transference focused psychotherapy" (TFP) focuses on the patient's unconscious reactions, especially reactions to the therapist (the "transference"). TPF's main goal is to bring the patient's unconscious reactions and conflicts to the surface, so that they can be discussed and worked through within a structured therapeutic setting. The developers of TFP believe it is important to help the individual with borderline personality disorder control the destructive impulses that can undermine the therapeutic process.

Some have raised the question of whether the psychotherapeutic treatment of borderline personality disorder is cost-effective, particularly in the

TABLE 9-5

Treatment

BORDERLINE PERSONALITY DISORDER

	Individual Psychodynamic Therapy	Dialectical Behavior Therapy	Serotonergic Agents	Noradrenergic Agents	Antipsychotic Drugs
Improvement	about 30% moderately improved	about 65% moderately improved	decrease impulsivity, aggressiveness, and depressive symptoms	about 40% improved; improved mood, but not irritability; may worsen impulsivity	about 70–75% of borderline patients with psychotic symptoms improved; also reduce anger and hostility
Relapse*	unclear	unclear	moderate to high	unclear	unclear
Side Effects	unclear	unclear	mild to moderate	moderate	moderate to severe
Cost	expensive	moderately expensive	inexpensive	inexpensive	moderately expensive‡
Time Scale†	years	months	weeks/months	weeks/months	weeks/months
Overall	**marginal**	**useful**	**useful**	**marginal**	**useful§**

*Relapse after discontinuation of treatment.
†Time to achieve maximal effect.
‡Atypical antipsychotics are moderately expensive.
§Useful for those with psychotic symptoms.
SOURCE: Based on Crits-Cristoph, 1998; Woo-Ming and Siever, 1998; revised with Bendetti, Sforzini, Colombo, Marrei, and Smeraldi, 1998; Koerner and Dimeff, 2000; Schulz, Camlin, Berry, and Jesberger, 1999; Soloff, 2000; Verhoeven et al., 1999.

current climate of managed care. Recently Gabbard and Lazar (1999) addressed this question in a "cost-benefit" study and concluded that the benefits appear to offset the costs, such that treating borderline conditions results in a reduction in: (1) outpatient visits and hospital stays for physical conditions; (2) psychiatric inpatient days, and (3) indirect expenses associated with lost work productivity.

Although medication is not routinely prescribed for borderline personality disorder, there is evidence that it can be beneficial for some persons with this disorder (see Table 9–5). Antipsychotic medications can be used effectively with severe cases, and the results have been favorable (Gitlin, 1993). Antidepressant drugs, including the SSRI's, are most helpful for patients with borderline personality disorder who show a high level of negative emotionality (Hirschfeld, 1997).

Anxious-Fearful Disorders

The disorders in Cluster C are characterized by high levels of worry and anxiety, and a tendency to hold feelings in. These are the anxious-fearful disor-

ders. Unlike those with Cluster B disorders, who tend to show dramatic expressions of emotion, those with Cluster C disorders tend to be more subdued. Cluster B and C disorders are also distinguishable on the basis of attitudes toward others. Cluster B disorders are associated with a lack of concern about social mores, whereas Cluster C disorders usually entail excessive concern about ethical guidelines.

Avoidant Personality Disorder

At the core of the **avoidant personality disorder** is a turning away: from people, from new experiences, and even from old experiences. The incidence ranges from 0.4 to 1.3 percent of the population (Millon and Martinez, 1995; Weissman, 1993). The syndrome involves a fear of appearing foolish, with an equally strong desire for acceptance and affection. Individuals who experience this disorder want very much to enter into social relationships or new activities, but they may find themselves unwilling to take even small risks, unless they are given strong guarantees of uncritical acceptance. They are shy. The slightest hint of

DSM-IV Criteria

Avoidant Personality Disorder

A pervasive pattern of social inhibition, feelings of inadequacy, and hypersensitivity to negative evaluation, beginning by early adulthood and present in a variety of contexts, as indicated by four (or more) of the following: (1) avoids occupational activities that involve significant interpersonal contact, because of fears of criticism, disapproval, or rejection; (2) is unwilling to get involved with people unless certain of being liked; (3) shows restraint within intimate relationships because of the fear of being shamed or ridiculed; (4) is pre-occupied with being criticized or rejected in social situations; (5) is inhibited in new interpersonal situations because of feelings of inadequacy; (6) views self as socially inept, personally unappealing, or inferior to others; (7) is unusually reluctant to take personal risks or to engage in any new activities because they may prove embarrassing.

SOURCE: APA, DSM-IV, 1994.

disapproval by others and the slightest whiff of potential failure lead them to withdraw. They may interpret apparently innocuous events as ridicule. People suffering from this disorder are likely to be distressed by their relative inability to relate comfortably to others, which adds to their low self-esteem, which in turn makes them even more sensitive to criticism and humiliation—an especially vicious cycle.

But is the avoidant personality disorder truly a separate disorder, or is it indistinguishable from generalized social phobia, which we examined in Chapter 5? The available evidence suggests that the diagnosis of avoidant personality disorder overlaps with the Axis I diagnosis of social phobia (Turner, Beidel, and Townsley, 1992; Widiger, 1992). Nonetheless, avoidant personality disorder is a valid syndrome, in that the symptoms tend to co-occur (Baillie and Lampe, 1998).

It has been suggested that biologically based differences in temperament are involved in avoidant personality disorder (Millon and Davis, 1995). Specifically, it has been proposed that children who are highly sensitive to sensory stimuli, especially social cues related to negative emotion, are at greatest risk for developing this disorder. When combined with an environment that affords little in the way of parental support, the individual develops low self-esteem and an avoidant strategy in dealing with the stress of social interactions. Longitudinal research on young children who are shy and withdrawn has shown that these youngsters are more likely than outgoing children to show avoidance of social interactions in adolescence (Schwartz, Snidman, and Kagan, 1999).

The treatment of avoidant personality disorder, like social phobia, typically involves behavioral strategies. Both graduated exposure to social settings and training in social skills have been found to be effective (Alden and Capreol, 1993). But the treatment should be tailored to the individual in order to optimize the outcome. For example, some people with social avoidance and nonassertiveness also have interpersonal problems related to distrustful and angry behavior. These individuals can benefit from graduated exposure, but they may not make progress in social skills training. Another subgroup of people with avoidant personality disorder may experience interpersonal problems that are mainly a result of being coerced and controlled by others. Social skills training that emphasizes the development of intimate relationships is especially helpful for these clients.

Deference and fearfulness characterize the person with dependent personality disorder.

Dependent Personality Disorder

People with *dependent personality disorder* allow others to make the major decisions, to initiate the important actions, and to take responsibility for significant areas of their own life. They often defer to spouse, parent, or friend regarding where they should live, the kind of job they should have, and who their friends should be. They subordinate their own needs to the needs of the people upon whom they are dependent, feeling that any assertion of their own needs may jeopardize the relationship. Such people will often tolerate enormous physical and/or psychological abuse for fear that they will be abandoned. Correspondingly, when they are alone even for brief periods of time, they may experience intense discomfort and helplessness. Thus, they often seek companionship at great cost. They lack self-esteem, and they often refer to themselves as stupid or helpless.

> The mother of two small children, Joyce was brought to the emergency room with multiple facial abrasions and a fractured jaw. She was no stranger to the hospital staff. Eight months earlier, she had been treated for two broken ribs and assorted bruises. Joyce was reluctant to give the details of her injuries. But the neighbor who brought her to the hospital reported that Joyce had been physically assaulted by her husband. According to the neighbor, Joyce's husband frequently abused her verbally and "slapped her around" on a number of occasions. Although Joyce feared for her own safety and that of her children, she was unresponsive to suggestions that she move out and separate from her husband.

> The middle child of three, Joyce was given neither great responsibility nor great attention during her childhood. Her father was a man of strong opinions and made all the decisions in the family. He believed adamantly that women belonged at home, and joked often and coarsely about "buns in the oven and bums in bed." He controlled the family finances, and delegated no responsibility in that area.

> Apart from a course in typing, Joyce learned no vocational skills in high school, and dropped out to get married. Indeed, other than baby-sitting and summer jobs as a mother's helper, Joyce had no work experience at all. During the five years of her marriage, Joyce left all decisions to her husband. Her husband was intensely jealous of her friendships, and she therefore abandoned all of them. Indeed, except for visits to her mother who lived in the neighborhood, she went nowhere without her husband.

Dependent personality disorder appears to be more common than the other personality disorders, with an incidence of up to 7 percent of the population (Allnut and Links, 1996). The disorder may have its origin in parental behavior that is both overprotective and authoritarian. Such behavior may well be synergistic. Overprotective parents encourage dependency in children, and such dependent behavior brings forth comforting protectiveness from parents (Bornstein, 1992; Hunt, Browning, and Nave, 1982).

The dependent personality disorder occurs more frequently among women than among men (Bornstein, 1996). Pregnant women who suffer this disorder are much more anxious at the time of birth if their husbands are not in the delivery

DSM-IV Criteria

Dependent Personality Disorder

A pervasive and excessive need to be taken care of that leads to submissive and clinging behavior and fears of separation, beginning by early adulthood and present in a variety of contexts, as indicated by five (or more) of the following: (1) has difficulty making everyday decisions without an excessive amount of advice and reassurance from others; (2) needs others to assume responsibility for most major areas of his or her life; (3) has difficulty expressing disagreement with others because of fear of loss of support or approval (*Note:* do not include realistic fears of retribution.); (4) has difficulty initiating projects or doing things on his or her own (because of a lack of self-confidence in judgment or abilities rather than

a lack of motivation or energy); (5) goes to excessive lengths to obtain nurturance and support from others, to the point of volunteering to do things that are unpleasant; (6) feels uncomfortable or helpless when alone because of exaggerated fears of being unable to care for himself or herself; (7) urgently seeks another relationship as a source of care and support when a close relationship ends; (8) is unrealistically preoccupied with fears of being left to take care of himself or herself.

SOURCE: APA, DSM-IV, 1994.

HE SAID HE'D NEVER HIT YOU AGAIN . . .

BUT THAT'S WHAT HE SAID LAST TIME.

Hedda Nussbaum, who was brutalized by her lover Joel Steinberg, testified at his trial for murdering the child she thought they had adopted. Nussbaum, like the woman in the poster, may have suffered from a dependent personality disorder, which prevented her from taking the child and leaving Steinberg, despite years of abuse.

room, whereas women who do not suffer the disorder seem unaffected by their husbands' absence during delivery (Bornstein, 1992; Keinan and Hobfoll, 1989). Moreover, the disorder impairs occupational functioning if the nature of the job requires independent decision making. Social relations may be restricted to the few people upon whom the person is dependent. There is a high rate of comorbidity, such that dependent personality disorder often co-occurs with Axis I mood disorders (Loranger, 1996).

Obsessive-Compulsive Personality Disorder

Obsessive-compulsive personality disorder is characterized by a pervasive pattern of striving for perfection. Excessively high standards cause people with this disorder to demand perfection in themselves as well as others. They are rarely pleased with their own accomplishments, however excellent the outcome. And because they anticipate being unable to meet their own unattainable standards, they often procrastinate in important matters, allocating their time poorly and leaving the things that mean most to them to the very last. While they prize work and productivity over pleasure and interpersonal relationships, they get overly involved in details, in lists and rules and schedules. They

have great trouble making decisions in most domains of their life, and they are especially prone to avoid making decisions about pleasurable activities. People who suffer this disorder tend to have difficulty expressing emotion, and they are often seen by others as formal, stiff, overly conscientious, and moralistic.

Laura and Steve began to see a marriage counselor because Steve insisted on it. He had become extremely distressed by Laura's unavailability and perfectionism. At thirty-seven, Laura was a partner in one of the nation's largest accounting firms. She worked long hours at the office, brought work home, was unwilling to go out more than once a week, and resisted taking vacations. At home, she snapped out orders to the children about housework and schoolwork. She could not tolerate an unwashed dish or a jacket on the sofa and was critical and demanding of household help.

Laura did not believe she had a "marriage problem," though she freely acknowledged feeling harassed at work and at home. She attributed her long hours at work to the demands of her profession. Snapping at the children and nit-picking about domestic order were, she insisted, the result of being the person who had to clean up after everyone else. Laura did not consider herself sexually unresponsive, but she did think she was often tense and fatigued. The only child of upwardly

DSM-IV Criteria

Obsessive-Compulsive Personality Disorder

A pervasive pattern of preoccupation with orderliness, perfectionism, and mental and interpersonal control, at the expense of flexibility, openness, and efficiency, beginning by early adulthood and present in a variety of contexts, as indicated by four (or more) of the following: (1) is preoccupied with details, rules, lists, order, organization, or schedules to the extent that the major point of the activity is lost; (2) shows perfectionism that interferes with task completion (e.g., is unable to complete a project because his or her own overly strict standards are not met); (3) is excessively devoted to work and productivity to the exclusion of leisure activities and friendships (not accounted for by obvious economic necessity); (4) is overconscientious, scrupulous, and inflexible about matters of morality, ethics, or values (not accounted for by cultural or religious identification); (5) is unable to discard worn-out or worthless objects even when they have no sentimental value; (6) is reluctant to delegate tasks or to work with others unless they submit to exactly his or her way of doing things; (7) adopts a miserly spending style toward both self and others; money is viewed as something to be hoarded for future catastrophes; (8) shows rigidity and stubbornness.

SOURCE: APA, DSM-IV, 1994.

striving immigrant parents, Laura had been encouraged to excel. She was valedictorian of her high school class and among the top ten of her college graduating class. The social milieu in which she grew up put great stress on the value of close family relationships. Laura never doubted that she would be a wife and mother, and she married soon after graduating from college.

It is estimated that the prevalence of obsessive-compulsive personality disorder is about 1 percent of the general population. People with obsessive-compulsive tendencies are more inclined to seek treatment than are individuals with other personality disorders. As a result, the rates of the disorder are much higher in clinical samples (Weissman, 1993). The disorder occurs in both sexes, but somewhat more frequently among men (Carter, Joyce, Mulder, Sullivan, and Luty, 1999).

It has been theorized that obsessive-compulsive personality disorder has its roots in punitive parental responses to everyday childhood mishaps (Millon, Davis, Millon, Escovar, and Meagher, 2000). The parents are hypothesized to be emotionally distant, yet rigid and demanding. In response to repeated parental punishment, the person becomes preoccupied with following rules and maintaining order in the environment. When patients with various personality disorders are asked to describe their childhood experiences, those with obsessive-compulsive personality disorder report lower levels of paternal concern, but higher levels of paternal overprotection (Nordahl and Stiles, 1997).

Cognitive approaches have proven useful in the treatment of obsessive-compulsive personality disorder (Kyrios, 1998). The therapist focuses on the person's dysfunctional cognitions, restricted behavioral repertoires, negative affect, and issues relating to interpersonal relationships and identity. Supportive psychotherapy is also effective in treating obsessive-compulsive personality disorder (Barber, Morse, Krakauer, Chittams, and Crits-Cristoph, 1997). Barber and his research colleagues found that clients with obsessive-compulsive personality disorder remained in therapy longer than those with avoidant personality disorder, and that they showed greater and more rapid improvement. This may be a consequence of the fact that individuals with obsessive-compulsive personality disorder are more motivated

"SEE — IT'S NOT IMPOSSIBLE FOR AN OBSESSIVE-COMPULSIVE TO GET A RESPONSIBLE JOB."

to follow rules and conform to social expectations, including those of the therapist. In contrast, those with avoidant personality disorder are inclined to avoid interpersonal interaction.

Putting It All Together

By definition, the personality disorders are manifestations of traits that interfere with everyday functioning. Because they are assumed to originate in childhood or adolescence, they are long-standing features of the person's style of dealing with life. Further, people with personality disorders do not necessarily experience subjective emotional pain, so they may not seek treatment, or even open themselves to feedback from friends or family members.

Over the years there has been a great deal of controversy about the personality disorder diagnoses (Arntz, 1999; Glaser, 1993). The major controversy that has surrounded the personality disorders concerns their classification as "disorders" that can be separated from normal functioning. Some believe the reliability of the current diagnostic categories for personality disorders is too low to justify their inclusion as separate categories, and that further research is needed. Others believe that personality disorders are not really "mental illnesses." Rather, they believe that they are characterological traits that happen to cause people problems in living. Related to this is the question of how to conceptualize the personality disorders (Cloninger, Bayon, and Przybeck, 1997). Are they discrete categories that describe people who are qualitatively different from the rest of us? Or is it best to think of them as in dimensional terms, as extreme ends of a normal continuum of personality traits?

Many psychologists believe that they are extreme manifestations of the personality dimensions along which we all vary. Others are more inclined to view them as discrete entities that involve specific kinds of biological or psychological vulnerabilities. In fact, it is likely that both of these viewpoints are accurate, but for different personality disorders. For example, there is a well-established relationship between schizophrenia and schizotypal personality disorder. It is likely that some individuals who meet the diagnostic criteria for schizotypal personality disorder do, in fact, have a unique, biologically based vulnerability for schizophrenia. In contrast, it is plausible that individuals with dependent personality disorder are manifesting an extreme level of the same tendency to rely on others that many adults show.

To the extent that a personality disorder is simply an extreme manifestation of a normal human tendency, should it be viewed as a "disorder" per se? Our answer to this question has important implications, especially in the legal arena (Winick, 1995). If, for example, antisocial personality disorder is viewed as a disorder, especially one with a biological basis, then it seems reasonable that a diagnosis of antisocial personality disorder should be grounds for the insanity defense. In Chapter 15, we will discuss the reasons why the legal system does not hold people responsible for criminal acts that are a result of impaired mental capacity or mental illness. But in most states, personality disorders do not qualify as mental illnesses. Should an individual who has one or more personality disorders be held responsible for illegal behavior that appears to be a consequence of the disorder? There is no easy answer to this question; we can expect to see it debated for some time to come.

The way we conceptualize personality disorders also has implications for the special protections we afford to people who suffer from these disorders. For example, people who suffer from Axis I mood disorders or schizophrenia are eligible to receive disability payments if they are unable to support themselves because of their illnesses. Should those who suffer from personality disorders also be eligible for disability if their disorder makes it hard for them to hold down a job? At the present time, they are not legally entitled to disability. Some clinical researchers believe that the treatment of personality disorders should be approached from a medical and biological perspective, as if they were Axis I disorders (Joseph, 1997). They advocate that each of the symptoms of personality disorders should be individually targeted for treatment using specific drugs. Others are concerned that this will result in such a broad expansion of the concept of mental illness that it will become meaningless. Again, we can expect to see further debate about this issue, especially if more biological correlates of the personality disorders are identified by researchers.

Clinical psychologists and psychiatrists are also well aware of the difficulties involved in diagnosing personality disorders. Because the signs of personality disorder must be long-standing in order to meet diagnostic criteria, the clinician must often rely on personal recollections of past behaviors and experiences. As a result, distortions of memory or failure to obtain and properly assess information are potential sources of error for these diagnoses. Consider the case of Seymour, described above, who was diagnosed as suffering from a paranoid personality disorder. The behavioral facts relating to his difficulties were quite accurate. But subsequently, a careful investigation of the sources of his difficulties yielded a quite different picture. It turned out that Seymour had been experiencing a marked hearing loss. He had not mentioned it during his early interviews both because he underestimated its extent and because he dreaded wearing a hearing aid. He had difficulty getting dancing partners because, while he heard the music, he often missed the instructor's calls and was commonly out-of-step. In the discussion group, he often repeated comments that had already been made by others or, worse, misheard others' comments, such that his own were inappropriate and disruptive. Similar difficulties pervaded his experience in the ceramics class. Moreover, his seeming distrust of others, which had been manifested in the locking of his study and in not talking about his work, takes on a somewhat different meaning when one learns that as a physicist, he had spent his entire career working on classified military problems. In addition, like many professionals of the 1950s and 1960s, Seymour had moved a great deal. Making new friends in each new location required a heavy expenditure of time and energy. Precisely because he had a close relationship with his wife and because he was deeply involved in his work, Seymour was simply unwilling to invest himself in new, but transient, relationships.

Thus, the possibility of misinterpreting lifelong behaviors is potentially dangerous because the contexts in which those behaviors developed may not be readily retrievable now. But even when considerable information is available, therapists of different theoretical persuasions or in different cultural contexts may arrive at different diagnostic conclusions. Consider Laura, who appeared to have all of the characteristics of an obsessive-compulsive personality disorder. Would a feminist therapist, who is sensitive to the conflicts that arise from the competing demands of gender and work roles, see the case differently? Laura, who was traditional in her attitudes toward family and home, was simultaneously ambitious in her professional life. In attempting to fulfill both roles with excellence, she unwittingly aspired to the impossible: to be a "superwoman." She wanted her house neat, her children at the top of their class, and herself at the top of her male-dominated profession. Her insistence that the house be spotless re-

flected this competition between roles, for if the house was not spotless, to whom would it fall to clean it up? Similarly, in her refusal to take holidays and her long working hours, she was behaving like the ambitious men in her profession.

The field of personality disorders is challenging. Yet, it is an area where we are likely to see major advances in the coming years. Researchers are making progress in their efforts to identify the experiences and biological processes that are associated with both adaptive and maladaptive behavioral propensities. Future diagnostic systems for the personality disorders will undoubtedly reflect these advances. We can also expect to see progress in treatment, as researchers continue to explore the best strategies for tailoring therapies to clients (Benjamin, 1996; Gabbard and Lazar, 1999).

Summary

1. The *personality disorders* are fundamentally disorders of traits, that is, disorders that are reflected in the individual's tendency to perceive and respond to the environment in maladaptive ways. The notion of a personality disorder assumes that people have a tendency to respond consistently across different kinds of situations.

2. The personality disorders are considered Axis II disorders in DSM-IV, and people tend to meet the criteria for more than one personality disorder, giving rise to the question of whether the disorders should be considered as discrete *categories* or as *dimensions* on a continuum.

3. The *five-factor model* proposes a set of five personality dimensions, sometimes called the "Big Five": extraversion, conscientiousness, agreeableness, emotional stability, and openness to experience.

4. The *"odd-eccentric" disorders* are disorders involving some form of discomfort with or suspicion about other people. These include schizotypal personality disorder, schizoid personality disorder, and paranoid personality disorder.

5. The hallmarks of *schizotypal personality disorder* are social deficits and abnormal ideas and perceptual experiences. Odd thinking can be manifested in extreme suspiciousness and paranoid ideas. This disorder has been of particular interest to clinical researchers because it is genetically related to schizophrenia. Also, individuals who suffer from schizotypal personality disorder show cognitive deficits and physical signs of central

nervous system abnormality similar to those observed in patients with schizophrenia.

6. *Schizoid personality disorder* is characterized by a defect in the ability to form social relationships and a lack of social skills. When this disorder is treated with psychotherapy, the goal is to reduce the patient's social isolation and to teach him social skills.

7. People with *paranoid personality disorder* have a long-standing distrust and suspiciousness of others and tend to externalize blame and guilt. Cognitive-behavioral therapy for this disorder emphasizes self-disclosure and trust.

8. The *"dramatic-erratic" disorders* are disorders involving a failure to conform to social norms. These include antisocial personality disorder, histrionic personality disorder, narcissistic personality disorder, and borderline personality disorder.

9. Of all the personality disorders, *the antisocial personality disorder* is the most widely studied in the research laboratory. In the past, it was called "sociopathy" and "psychopathy." It is characterized by chronic insensitivity and indifference to the rights of other people and includes repeated aggressive behavior, chronic lying, stealing, cheating, destructiveness, and rule violation. It is a disorder that is characterized clinically by inadequately motivated antisocial behavior, emotional poverty, and the apparent lack of conscience or shame.

10. Antisocial personality disorder originates in conduct disorder in childhood or early adolescence, where it takes the form of truancy, petty thievery, and other rule-violating behavior. Research points to several factors that may contribute to antisocial behavior: inherited vulnerabilities, prenatal damage to the developing nervous system, abnormalities in physiological reactions (emotional underarousal) and brain function, emotionally deprived backgrounds, marginal economic circumstances, and defects in learning (being less able to learn from punishment or to control their impulses).

11. There are no specific drug treatments for antisocial personality disorder, but cognitive therapy has been used to attempt to improve the patient's ability to empathize and identify with others and to improve the patient's ability to process social cues. A behavioral technique called "positive practice" has also been used to correct the patient's negative patterns of behavior and substitute appropriate behavior.

12. Many researchers believe preventive intervention is the most promising approach to reducing the rate of antisocial personality disorder. But there is no consensus on the optimal approach to prevention; some psychologists have called for very invasive interventions that remove the child from his environment, whereas others advocate interventions that bolster parental competence.

13. People with *histrionic personality disorder* react to insignificant events with dramatic and inappropriate emotional displays; they constantly seek others' attention and admiration.

14. Those with *narcissistic personality disorder* have an inflated sense of self-importance and a lack of empathy; they have difficulty maintaining interpersonal relationships because of their near-total self-preoccupation and their resentment of any criticism or lack of attention from others.

15. People with *borderline personality disorder* are characterized by instability in daily functioning, relationships, behavior, mood, and self-image. They are prone to misinterpret social interactions, to be manipulative, and to engage in suicide attempts, substance abuse, unsafe sex, self-mutilation, and intense but short-lived, destructive sexual relationships. People with this disorder often report having experienced early childhood abuse and trauma. Dialectical behavior therapy has led to short-term improvement in those with borderline personality disorder.

16. The *"anxious-fearful" disorders* are characterized by high levels of worry and anxiety and a tendency to hold feelings in. One such disorder is *avoidant personality disorder,* in which the patient wants to enter into social relationships or activities, but turns away from people and experiences out of a fear of looking foolish or feeling disapproval. Another disorder is *dependent personality disorder,* in which the patient allows others to make all major decisions and to take all responsibility out of a fear of being abandoned. A third such disorder is *obsessive-compulsive personality disorder,* which is characterized by excessively high standards and a pervasive striving for perfection.

17. There is genuine disagreement about whether the personality disorders should be classified as "disorders" that can be separated from normal functioning. Related to this are controversies about whether persons with personality disorder should have the legal protections that are afforded to individuals with Axis I mental illnesses.

10

The Schizophrenias

Chapter Outline

Adolf Wölfli, Der Skt. Adolf Ball-Saal 1916.

Learning Objectives

→ Learn about the major misconceptions concerning the origins of schizophrenia and the historical views of the disorder.

→ Familiarize yourself with the substantive criteria and the symptoms of schizophrenia.

→ Describe the different subtypes of schizophrenia, including the DSM-IV subtypes, and acute versus chronic schizophrenia.

→ Learn about the two sources of constitutional vulnerability to schizophrenia: genetics and obstetrical complications, and be able to describe childhood precursors to schizophrenia.

→ Be able to describe the biology of schizophrenia, including neurochemical abnormalities, abnormalities in brain structure, and functional abnormalities in the frontal lobes and in the connections among various brain regions.

→ Learn about the social influences on schizophrenia, particularly about faulty interpersonal communication within the family, how those with schizophrenia often drift into the lower social classes and poverty, and how people from developing nations who have schizophrenia fare better than those from developed nations.

→ Be able to describe treatments for schizophrenia, including typical and antipsychotic drugs and their side effects, as well as cognitive rehabilitation and social skills training.

Schizophrenia is a puzzling and profound psychological disorder. It affects thought, perception, and mood. The thought problems often include difficulties with concentration, abstract thinking, and basic logic. The perceptual signs may involve hearing or seeing things that are not physically present. Some patients with schizophrenia show very little emotion, and they report that they experience no emotion, good or bad. Others are agitated or inappropriately giddy. During serious episodes of the illness, most patients find it very difficult to understand the "reality" we all take for granted. This is what makes the disorder so baffling. It challenges our basic assumptions about human perceptions of the real world, as shown in the case of this patient:

> When I was a kid, my parents always seemed to be worried about me. I'm not sure what their reasons were. I wasn't the most popular kid in the world, but I did pretty well in school, and I never got into any serious trouble. They still acted as if I needed extra attention. They were always asking, "How are you doing, Glenn?" Maybe this is what made me notice I was different. Every once in a while, when I was a kid, I felt like I was watching a movie of life. It didn't seem real. By the time I went to high school, I truly felt like I was an actor in a play. But I didn't always know my lines. I wasn't sure what role I was playing. Sometimes I thought I was being tricked. Maybe everyone was going along with me to make me feel like I was part of the play, but I really wasn't. I drifted in and out of believing I was real. By the time I turned eighteen, I was just hanging on by a thread. I wondered if anyone else could tell.

In the chapter title, we refer to "the schizophrenias" because most experts in the field believe that schizophrenia is not really a single disorder. In other words, they believe that the syndrome we diagnose as "schizophrenia" actually has several different causes. One of the reasons they believe this is because the symptoms vary a great deal among patients. Similarly, as we describe below, the nature and the extent of the cognitive, emotional, and motor abnormalities vary. But perhaps the most convincing evidence that schizophrenia is more than one disorder is the fact that patients differ in their response to the same medication. Nonetheless, we will use the singular (schizophrenia) rather than the plural (schizophrenias) for convenience in our discussion, even though we agree that schizophrenia is probably not a single disorder.

Although patients with schizophrenia can have different symptoms, they all share in common the presence of one or more *psychotic* symptoms. These are the disturbances in thought and perception that make it difficult for the patient to keep in touch with reality. In the case above, we can see from Glenn's description that he had a tenuous grip on reality during adolescence, although he did not show psychotic symptoms until early adulthood.

We will begin our exploration of schizophrenia by sketching out a general picture of the history, prevalence, and nature of schizophrenia. Next, we will describe the symptoms of schizophrenia. We will then turn to the question that has challenged researchers for many decades, "What causes schizophrenia?" Finally, we will examine the various treatments that are available for the disorder.

Society's perception of the person with schizophrenia as being dangerous, unpredictable, and out of control is reflected in Charles Bell's 1806 illustration titled "Madness." Such views reflect society's fears rather than the true nature of the disorder.

What Is Schizophrenia?

Patients with schizophrenia have been called lunatics, madmen, raving maniacs, unhinged, deranged, and demented. These words suggest that patients with this illness are dangerous, unpredictable, impossible to understand, and completely out of control. These ideas, however, say more about a healthy person's fears and ignorance than they do about the nature of schizophrenia itself. Rather than being raving maniacs on the rampage, patients with schizophrenia are more often shy, withdrawn, and preoccupied with their own problems.

Another common misconception about schizophrenia is that it involves a split personality of the Dr. Jekyll and Mr. Hyde sort, with its attendant unpredictability and potential for violence. This error arises from the origins of the words "schizophrenia" (schizo = split, phreno = mind). When Swiss psychiatrist Eugen Bleuler (1857–1939) coined the term, he intended to suggest that certain psychological functions were divided in patients with schizophrenia, not that there were two or more alternating personalities residing in the person. Bleuler believed that thought and emotion are split in patients with schizophrenia. For example, he said that while most people have an immediate emotional reaction following a horrifying incident, such a reaction does not occur in the person with schizophrenia. Although Bleuler's view is no longer as widely accepted as it once was, the misconception that arose

from his view continues to exist, fostered by Hollywood and television, in such productions as *The Three Faces of Eve* (see Chapter 6 on dissociative disorders).

A third misconception about schizophrenia is that once a person is found to have the disorder, he or she will always have it. But in fact, the disorder is not lifelong for all patients. Often a single episode will occur and then disappear, never to recur. Sometimes, after a long period in which the individual has been symptom-free, another episode may occur. Much as one may suffer several colds during a lifetime and yet not always have a runny nose, so too a person can suffer several episodes of schizophrenia during a lifetime, and be quite cogent in between. Many people who have suffered from schizophrenia engage in athletics, read newspapers and novels, watch television, obtain college degrees, and relate to their friends and families in much the same way that others do. Long stretches of time can pass without evidence of their distress. We do not know why an episode occurs any more than we understand why we come down with a cold. As when the symptoms of a cold are absent and the individual is considered healthy, so when the symptoms of schizophrenia are absent the individual is considered mentally healthy.

Historical Views

Until about 1880, little progress was made in differentiating one form of mental disorder from another. There was a sense that there were different kinds of "insanity," but there was no shared view of what those differences might be. Indeed, it was not until 1809 that the syndrome that is presently called schizophrenia was identified clinically (Gottesman, 1991). The first widely accepted classification system for severe psychological disorders was advanced by the German psychiatrist, Emil Kraepelin (1856–1926). One of the disorders he described in 1896 was *dementia praecox,* which literally meant early or premature deterioration.

For Kraepelin, the diagnosis of dementia praecox was indicated when individuals displayed certain symptoms and showed a deteriorating course thereafter. Included among the behavioral signs were inappropriate emotional responses, such as laughter at a funeral or crying at a joke; stereotyped motor behavior, such as bowing repeatedly before entering a room, or clapping before putting head to pillow; attentional difficulties, such as inability to read because of shifting shadows; sensory experiences in the absence of appropriate stimuli, such as seeing people when none are present, or smelling sulfur in a jasmine garden; and beliefs sustained in spite of overwhelming contrary evidence, such as insisting that one is an historical personage like Napoleon, or that one is held together by wire. Emil Kraepelin's views were a strong influence on subsequent generations of psychologists and psychiatrists. He made an important historical contribution by distinguishing and classifying the various forms of mental disorder (Carpenter, 1992).

Eugen Bleuler believed that schizophrenia was part of one's biological makeup. He was convinced that brain disease caused schizophrenia, and he continually resorted to hypothetical brain pathology to account for the symptoms. Bleuler believed that schizophrenia could first occur at any time during a person's life, and that it was likely to recur. While he recognized that schizophrenia was undoubtedly serious, and in many cases chronic, he asserted that recovery was possible. Kraepelin was convinced that the causes of schizophrenia were biological and that the ultimate cure would be biomedical. He hypothesized that a chemical imbalance was produced by malfunctioning glands, which somehow interfered with the nervous system. These two pioneering scientists began the search for a biological basis for schizophrenia.

A completely different approach to understanding the origins and cure of schizophrenia was propounded by a contemporary of Kraepelin and Bleuler, Adolf Meyer (1866–1950). Meyer, a brain pathologist, later became recognized as the dean of American psychiatry. He maintained that there were no fundamental biological differences between patients who have schizophrenia and those who do not have the disorder, and that there were no fundamental differences in their respective psychological processes. Rather, he believed that the cognitive and behavioral disorganization associated with schizophrenia arose from inadequate early learning and reflected "adjustive insufficiency" and habit deterioration. He proposed that individual maladjustment, rather than biological malfunction, lay at the root of the disorder. While Bleuler and Kraepelin strengthened the biological tradition of research in schizophrenia, Meyer gave impetus to a tradition that focused on learning and interpersonal processes. Both of these perspectives have influenced modern views of schizophrenia. We now know, however, that biological vulnerability lays the groundwork for schizophrenia.

Symptoms of Schizophrenia

The definition of schizophrenia has generated heated debate ever since 1896, when Kraepelin described the symptoms of dementia praecox in his *Psychiatrie.* In part, the diagnosis of schizophrenia is controversial because each of its symptoms is quite similar to the symptoms that may arise from physical illnesses, some prescription medications, street drugs, and brain injury. The most recent definition was offered in 1994 in DSM-IV. In order to be diagnosed with schizophrenia now, the symptoms must last for at least six months, and there must be a marked deterioration from the individual's previous level of functioning at work, in social relations, and in self-care. Those are the temporal criteria.

There are also two substantive criteria for the diagnosis: (1) There must be a gross impairment of reality testing, that is, the individual must evaluate the accuracy of his or her thoughts incorrectly and, as a consequence, must make incorrect inferences about reality. As we mentioned, major impairment in the understanding of reality is called **psychosis.** Minor distortions of reality, such as a tendency to undervalue

DSM-IV Criteria

Schizophrenia

A. *Characteristic symptoms:* Two (or more) of the following, each present for a significant portion of time during a 1-month period (or less if successfully treated): (1) delusions; (2) hallucinations; (3) disorganized speech (e.g., frequent derailment or incoherence); (4) grossly disorganized or catatonic behavior; (5) negative symptoms, i.e., affective flattening [dulled feeling], alogia [inability to speak], or avolition [inability to make decisions]. (*Note:* Only one Criterion A symptom is required if delusions are bizarre or hallucinations consist of a voice keeping up a running commentary on the person's behavior or thoughts, or two or more voices conversing with each other.)

B. *Social/occupational dysfunction:* For a significant portion of the time since the onset of the disturbance, one or more major areas of functioning such as work, interpersonal relations, or self-care are markedly below the level achieved prior to the onset (or when the onset is in childhood or adolescence, failure to achieve expected level of interpersonal, academic, or occupational achievement).

C. *Duration:* Continuous signs of the disturbance persist for at least 6 months. This 6-month period must include at least 1 month of symptoms (or less if successfully treated) that meet Criterion A (i.e., active-phase symptoms) and may include periods of prodromal [precursory] or resid-

ual symptoms. During these prodromal or residual periods, the signs of the disturbance may be manifested by only negative symptoms or two or more symptoms listed in Criterion A present in an attenuated form (e.g., odd beliefs, unusual perceptual experiences).

D. *Schizoaffective and Mood Disorder exclusion:* Schizoaffective Disorder and Mood Disorder with Psychotic Features have been ruled out because either (1) no Major Depressive, Manic, or Mixed Episodes have occurred concurrently with the active-phase symptoms; or (2) if mood episodes have occurred during active-phase symptoms, their total duration has been brief relative to the duration of the active and residual periods.

E. *Substance/general medical condition exclusion:* The disturbance is not due to the direct physiological effects of a substance (e.g., a drug of abuse, a medication) or a general medical condition.

F. *Relationship to a Pervasive Developmental Disorder:* If there is a history of Autistic Disorder or another Pervasive Developmental Disorder, the additional diagnosis of Schizophrenia is made only if prominent delusions or hallucinations are also present for at least a month (or less if successfully treated).

SOURCE: APA, DSM-IV, 1994.

---

one's abilities or attractiveness, do not qualify. (2) The disturbance must affect more than one psychological process: thought, perception, emotion, communication, or psychomotor behavior.

The five symptom criteria for schizophrenia are delusions, hallucination, disorganized speech, disorganized or catatonic behavior, and negative symptoms.

DELUSIONS

Delusions are false beliefs that resist all argument and are sustained in the face of evidence that normally would be sufficient to destroy them. An individual who believes that he has drunk of the Fountain of Youth and is therefore immortal suffers a delusion. And the individual who believes that he not only has knowledge of these legendary waters, but also that others are conspiring to pry his secret knowledge from him, is probably suffering from several delusions.

Delusions are among the most striking symptoms of schizophrenia. To the observer, the content of a

delusion seems so bizarre that it automatically suggests that the person is out of touch with reality. How else does one explain the belief that one is being intensely persecuted, or that one is infinitely superior to ordinary mortals, all in the absence of confirming evidence? Indeed, it is the flowering of a delusion in the absence of confirmation, and its resistance to ordinary persuasion, that leads us to conclude that the reasoning processes implicated in delusional activity are different from our own.

Delusions are common in a variety of psychoses. What usually differentiates delusions in schizophrenia from those, say, in psychotic depression, is their mood incongruence. Patients diagnosed with depression have delusions that bear a strong relationship to their moods. In contrast, patients with schizophrenia have delusions that seem incongruent with their present feelings (Junginger, Barker, and Coe, 1992). For example, a person with psychotic depression might be extremely distraught over the false belief that he is guilty of a serious crime. A person with schizophrenia might hold the same false belief, but show no emotion.

There are five kinds of delusions: delusions of grandeur, delusions of control, delusions of persecution, delusions of reference, and somatic delusions. *Delusions of grandeur* consist of convictions that one is especially important. The belief that one is Jesus Christ or fourth in line to the throne of Denmark would indicate a delusion of grandeur.

Delusions of control are characterized by beliefs that one's thoughts or behaviors are being controlled from without. The patient attributes the source of angry, sexual, or otherwise sinful thoughts to external agents. For example, someone who believes that beings from another universe are giving him instructions is suffering from a delusion of control.

Delusions of persecution consist of fears that individuals, groups, or the government has malevolent

intentions and is "out to get me." The focus of the delusion may be quite specific: a neighbor, one's boss, the FBI, or a rather vague "they." When a patient also erroneously believes she is "seeing" or "hearing" evidence of a plot, she may feel continual panic. Confirmation for these imaginings can often be found in misinterpretations of everyday experience, as illustrated by Glenn's experience:

> I began to worry more and more that there was something going on behind my back. The feeling is hard to describe now. The time I hated most in college was lunchtime. I actually started to believe that when I walked through the lunch line in the cafeteria, the other students were speaking in some sort of code to the people serving the food. It was like a secret code, where each word actually symbolized something else. So let's say the person ahead of me in line said, "I want some macaroni and cheese." I would start thinking that he was actually telling the server that he thought I was disgusting. When people waiting in the lunch line talked to the person next to them, I would think they were talking about me. I thought I would hear them say things like, "Let's try to get Glenn to order a cheeseburger," or "Watch Glenn copy my order." I wondered why they were doing this. Then I started to think that it was because they were trying to poison me.

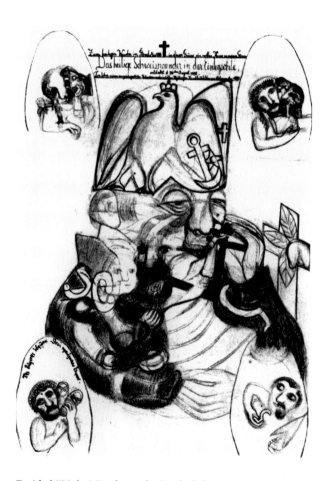

Entitled "Holy Miracle on the Insole," this drawing was done by a patient suffering from a systematic delusion. According to the patient, the Holy Ghost arose from a "miracle in the insole of the victim ruthlessly sacrificed, disinherited, and declared dead, by the secret violent poisoning and brain crushing of assassins possessed by Satan and mentally disturbed . . ."

Ideas of reference involve beliefs that certain events or people have special significance for the person. Some patients with schizophrenia, for example, are convinced that television newscasters are speaking to them, or that strangers in the street are looking at them. When such beliefs become organized into a larger and coherent framework, they are called delusions of reference. As described above, Glenn's psychotic symptoms included delusions of persecution and delusions of reference.

Finally, *somatic delusions* are characterized by the unverified belief that something is drastically wrong with one's body. A patient with schizophrenia who suffers somatic delusions might believe, for example, that something is rotting inside her body. Often these delusions begin with fairly commonplace physical complaints, such as headaches, heart palpitations, or stomach pains. Then gradually the person creates a delusional belief system to explain them.

It is important to emphasize that fleeting false beliefs do not qualify as delusions. Points of view about reality can differ among people with no mental disorder. All theories about how the world operates, including scientific ones, are overthrown only when a more satisfactory theory can be found to replace it. In the case of schizophrenia, it is the patient's persistence in maintaining his false belief, despite contrary evidence, that results in it being labeled a delusion. Because the "theories" held by psychotic patients often rest on intangible evidence, what seems ridiculous to the observer can, nonetheless, provide the patient with a cohesive and satisfactory account of his situation. On those occasions when it is contradicted by particular kinds of data, the theory (that is, the delusion) becomes more elaborate and comprehensive to account for the seeming contradiction, much as scientific theories do when they must account for exceptions. For example, if a patient with schizophrenia believes that he is being poisoned and he encounters a nurse who seems particularly kind, he may expand his delusion to include people who seem kind, but who are really plotting to poison him.

HALLUCINATIONS

Hallucinations are the perceptual signs of psychosis. They involve false sensory perceptions that have a compelling sense of reality, even in the absence of external stimuli that ordinarily provoke such perceptions. In schizophrenia, hallucinations are usually auditory, consisting either of a voice that maintains a running commentary on the individual's behavior, or two or more voices conversing with each other about the patient. But they can also be visual or involve other sense organs, such as taste and smell. An individual who is convinced that she has seen, shook hands with, and had dinner with a minotaur has had an hallucination.

Auditory hallucinations are the most common hallucinations in schizophrenia (Heilbrun, 1993). One finds their origins in ordinary thought; for example, when a person conducts a private dialogue by imagining herself talking to others and others talking back. And at times people actually talk to themselves, or to deities whose presence is only assumed. Of course, the healthy person has considerably greater control over the internal dialogue than does the patient with schizophrenia. The latter, when experiencing an auditory hallucination, does not believe that the voices originate within the self, or that she has the ability to begin or end the talk. The inability to distinguish between external and internal, real and

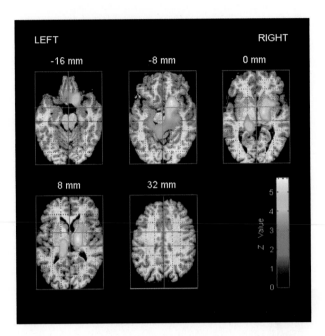

These functional PET scans show brain activity during auditory verbal hallucinations (of voices talking to or about the individual) as experienced by a person diagnosed with schizophrenia. Areas that show greater activity (as indicated by the orange and yellow colors) are at the center of the scans (the bilateral thalamus, the hippocampus and parahippocampal gyrus, the right ventral striatum, and right anterior cingulate) and at the top (the left orbitofrontal cortex). These areas are highly interconnected with limbic regions (affecting emotion) and with the visual and auditory cortices (affecting the perception of reality).

imagined, controllable and imposed, is central to the experience of schizophrenia.

Hallucinations are often gripping, and they are sometimes terrifying. Everyone has a general idea of what a visual hallucination might be like because everyone dreams. But for most people, dreams occur only during a certain portion of sleep, called "rapid eye movement," or REM sleep. They do not occur when we are awake, presumably because there is a neurotransmitter-mediated mechanism that inhibits them. Some researchers believe that this mechanism has failed in persons who hallucinate (Assad and Shapiro, 1986). Is there an actual physical basis to hallucinations? There appears to be. PET scans show that the visual or auditory cortex is activated when patients with schizophrenia are experiencing visual or auditory hallucinations (Silbersweig et al., 1995).

The descriptions of delusions and hallucinations that were just given are based on our clinical and research experience, not our personal experience. Most of us will never know what it is like to experience a delusion or hallucination. When patients who have actually had these symptoms describe their experiences to us, we begin to get a better idea of the extent to which they induce emotional distress, fear and, sometimes outright terror. Consider the case of Carl:

"I am an unreal person. I am made of stone. . . ." *The Song of the Violet,* a painting by Magritte.

Carl was twenty-seven years old when he was first admitted to a psychiatric facility. Gangling and intensely shy, he was so incommunicative at the outset that his family had to supply initial information about him. They, it seemed, had been unhappy and uncomfortable with him for quite some time. His father dated the trouble from "sometime in high school." He reported, "Carl turned inward, spent a lot of time alone, had no friends and did no schoolwork." His mother was especially troubled about his untidiness. "He was really an embarrassment to us then, and things haven't improved since. You could never take him anywhere without an argument about washing up. And once he was there, he wouldn't say anything to anyone." His twin sisters, six years younger than Carl, said very little during the family interview, but rather passively agreed with their parents.

One would hardly have guessed from their report that Carl graduated high school in the upper quarter of his class and had gone on to college where he studied engineering for three years. Though he had always been shy, he had had one close friend, John Winters, throughout high school and college. John had been killed in a car accident a year earlier. (Asked about Winters, his father said, "Oh, him. We don't consider him much of anything at all. He didn't go to church either. And he didn't do any schoolwork.")

Carl and John were unusually close. They went through high school together, served in the army at the same time and, when discharged, began college together and roomed in the same house. Both left college before graduating, much to the chagrin of Carl's parents, took jobs as machinists in the same firm, and moved into a nearby apartment.

They lived together for three years until John was killed. Two months later the company for which they worked went out of business. John's death left Carl enormously distraught. When the company closed, he found himself without the energy and motivation to look for a job. He moved back home. Disagreements between Carl and his family became more frequent and intense. He became more reclusive, as well as sloppy and bizarre; they, more irritable and isolating. Finally they could bear his behavior no longer and took him to the hospital. He went without any resistance.

After ten days in the hospital, Carl told the psychologist who was working with him: "I am an unreal person. I am made of stone, or else I am made of glass. I am wired precisely wrong, precisely. But you will not find my key. I have tried to lose the key to me. You can look at me closely if you wish, but you see more from far away."

Shortly thereafter, the psychologist noted that Carl "smiles when he is uncomfortable, and smiles more when in pain. He cries during television comedies. He seems angry when justice is done, frightened when someone compliments him, and roars with laughter on reading that a young child was burned in a tragic fire. He grimaces often. He eats very little but always carries food away."

After two weeks, the psychologist said to him: "You hide a lot. As you say, you are wired precisely wrong. But why won't you let me see the diagram?"

Carl answered: "Never, ever will you find the lever, the eternalever that will sever me forever with my real, seal, deal, heel. It is not on my shoe, not even on the sole. It walks away."

DISORGANIZED SPEECH

Most people who live in urban areas have had the occasion to see someone on a city street speaking incoherently to themselves. More than any of the other symptoms, it is the disorganized speech of patients with schizophrenia that is most apparent to others.

Clinicians have devised terms to describe the various kinds of disorganized speech. The term *derailment* is used to refer to speech that shifts from one topic to another with no apparent connection. Responses to questions from others may be *tangential,* in that they bear little or no relationship to the question. For example, in response to the query, "How are you doing today?," one patient with schizophrenia answered, "Today, today the bus is late again today and the driver must be sick." In extreme cases, speech is so disorganized that it is *incoherent* and makes no sense to the listener. Some clinicians refer to this as "word salad." An example is the rambling verbalizations of a young male patient, "I usually have to go out when the others come in no doubt to get out of the boat. If they sink with it the dinner is lost and then, maybe, you choose, the other shoe will drop."

Clinicians often use the term *loose association* to refer to more subtle irregularities in the connections made in a patient's statements. For example, when asked, "Will you be at the theatre this evening?," one patient replied, "Yes, I'll go to the theatre, but not the theatre of the absurd, it's too silly. I guess I'm silly too." Some early research on schizophrenia shed light on the semantic nature of loose associations (Chapman and Chapman, 1973; Rattan and Chapman, 1973). Given that many words have a variety of meanings and connotations, investigators presented patients and normals with target words and asked them to select an associated word. Patients with schizophrenia were especially sensitive to the dominant associations to words, and less influenced by the contexts in which they are typically used. Consider the following test item:

> *Pool* means the same as
> 1. puddle
> 2. notebook
> 3. swim
> 4. none of the above.

The correct answer is "puddle." But many patients, as well as a few normals, will offer "swim" as the correct answer.

Of course, all of us have associations that prove to be irrelevant. While listening to a friend speaking about a personal experience, we may find ourselves thinking about our own similar experience, rather than our friend's concerns. Or we may try to concentrate on reading, but instead have recurrent thoughts about an event that will take place tomorrow. The difference lies in the number of associative intrusions, the context in which they arise, and in how they are integrated conceptually. Imagine yourself writing a New Year's greeting to a friend. You wish her a happy and healthy year and then refer to the pleasures and sadness of the previous year. Compare your greeting to that written by one of Eugen Bleuler's patients:

> I wish you then a good, happy, joyful, healthy, blessed and fruitful year, and many good wine-years to come, as well as a healthy and good apple-year, and sauerkraut and cabbage and squash and seed year. (Bleuler, 1950, cited in Martin, 1977)

Here, there are many more associations than are found in normal greetings. These associations, moreover, arise in chains that appear to be generated by specific words that seem to distract the patient from his ultimate goal and impair the overall meaning of the greeting. The word "fruitful" seems to evoke associations to wine, apple, sauerkraut, cabbage, squash, and the like. Moreover, in this context, wine and sauerkraut are not normally the dominant associations of the word "fruitful"; abundance is. But the patient seems to have centered on "fruit" and to have generated associations that are appropriate for that word but not for "fruitfulness."

At times, the speech of patients seems to be moved more by the sound of words than by their meaning. *Clang associations,* that is, associations produced by the rhyme of words such as "my real, seal, deal, heel," abound. Some patients also come up with *neologisms,* new words like "eternalever" that have only a private meaning. In addition, their use of vague, overly abstract or overly concrete, repetitive, or stereotyped words can "impoverish" the content of their speech, such that little information is communicated. These communication disturbances seem not to arise from lack of education or low intelligence but apparently from the disorder itself.

A person with schizophrenia may exhibit catatonic behavior, in which she appears entirely immobile, often maintaining an uncomfortable position for hours.

DISORGANIZED OR CATATONIC BEHAVIOR

The disorganized behavior shown by people who have schizophrenia can vary from bizarre giddiness and excitement to extreme irritability and agitation. In psychiatric hospitals, for example, it is not uncommon to see a patient with schizophrenia sitting alone laughing out loud, while another patient is pacing the halls and wringing his hands in apparent distress. Especially during episodes of illness, many patients are disheveled or show poor hygiene. Patients with schizophrenia are often seen wearing inappropriate clothing or excess clothing, such as multiple coats and pairs of gloves on a hot day.

Catatonic behavior is certainly the most bizarre of all the behavioral features of schizophrenia. It involves a marked decrease in movement, sometimes to the point that the individual appears to be frozen in space! The patient might assume a rigid and strange body posture, and refuse all efforts to be moved. Usually the person is mute at the same time, and thus does not acknowledge communication from others. Yet, the rate of occurrence of catatonia has decreased dramatically in the past few decades;

this may be due to the more effective medications that are being used to treat schizophrenia.

NEGATIVE SYMPTOMS

The term **negative symptoms** is used to refer to symptoms that entail a reduction in normal behavior. (This is in contrast to **positive symptoms,** such as hallucinations and delusions, that involve an excess of sensory perceptions and ideas.) The negative symptoms of schizophrenia usually appear before the positive symptoms.

One of the most common negative symptoms is "blunted" or "flattened" affect (that is, emotion). The patient's face may appear immobile, with no discernible signs of emotion. Her voice may be monotonous, and she may seem entirely unresponsive emotionally. The apparent inability of some people with schizophrenia to display affect should not, however, be mistaken for absence of any emotional experience. In one respect, the experience of a patient with schizophrenia is like our own when we visit unfamiliar places. For example, American guests at a Thai wedding, not knowing what all of the symbols mean, would hardly know how to act or what to feel. Shared symbolic meanings allow feelings to arise, be expressed, and be understood by others. Because schizophrenia interferes with the person's socially shared domain of symbols and meanings, her affective responses to those stimuli are likely to be blunted.

Affective flattening is often accompanied by another negative symptom, *alogia,* or a significant decrease in speech. The patient may give one-word answers to questions, or pause for long periods of time between words. *Avolition,* also a negative symptom, is an apparent lack of energy or interest in activities. The patient may sit and watch television for extended periods of time without showing any emotion or interest. Glenn recalls the onset of negative symptoms in his late teens:

Being around too many people started to be hard for me. I felt like I had to watch them all the time, and it made me nervous. I spent a lot of time alone at home. There were times when I didn't even want to have dinner with my family. I just wanted to sit and be alone. My parents kept trying to humor me, because they said I never laughed anymore. They were right, but I didn't cry either. I was kind of numb. One day I looked at myself as I passed by the mirror in my

Representations of irrationality. *(Left)* Plate from *Urizen* by William Blake. *(Right) Agony-Raving Madness* by Richard Dadd, a nineteenth-century English artist who was hospitalized and diagnosed as having a schizophrenic disorder after he killed his father.

bedroom—I was shocked. I had, like, no facial expression. My face looked kind of lifeless.

IMPAIRED INSIGHT AND DEPRESSION

Clinicians have always considered impaired insight to be a hallmark of schizophrenia (Schwartz, 1998), although it is not part of the diagnostic criteria. Some patients emphatically deny that they have any symptoms or abnormal behaviors (Neumann, Walker, Weinstein, and Cutshaw, 1997; Walker and Rossiter, 1989). Even when they are patients in state psychiatric facilities, about 20 percent deny that they have a mental illness, and another 25 percent say that they are not sure they are mentally ill. Instead these patients attribute their "problems" to the personal vendettas of others or just plain "bad luck." This is not surprising when considered in light of other illnesses that involve brain dysfunction. For example, patients with Alzheimer's disease, especially in the advanced stages, often deny the presence of symptoms (Ceniceros, 1998; Seltzer, Vasterling, and Buswell, 1995). Unawareness of symptoms, referred to as *anosognosia* by neuropsychologists, is also observed in patients with serious strokes and head injuries. Thus, deficits in insight are a common consequence of serious brain disorders.

Some investigators have tried to improve the insight of patients with schizophrenia by providing them with psychological interventions. In a recent

and novel study, a group of researchers filmed patients during the course of an interview (Davidoff, Forester, Ghaemi, and Bodkin, 1998). They wanted to find out whether the patients would show increases in insight if they had the opportunity to view themselves during the interview. Half of the patients viewed the film of themselves, and the others viewed a "placebo" film. The placebo film had neutral content. Indeed, when interviewed several days later, those who viewed themselves showed improvements in insight and had fewer delusions, although other symptoms did not change.

Most people would assume that having "insight" is desirable, so this intervention was a success. Many clinicians would certainly assume so. But recent findings suggest that there may be a trade-off. Improvements in insight may come at the expense of mood. In particular, being too aware of our limitations may make us depressed.

Depression is very common in patients with schizophrenia, especially women (Johnson, 1981). It is so common that many of those with schizophrenia take antidepressants, in addition to antipsychotic drugs. In fact, suicide is the most frequent cause of death among people with schizophrenia, far surpassing any other cause (Gottesman, 1991). More than 10 percent end their lives through suicide. Several explanations have been suggested for this. One is that depression is simply a feature of the illness, caused by the same biological factors that cause the schizophrenic symptoms. Another possibility is that the two have become genetically linked through "assortative mating"; people with psychiatric symptoms may be more likely to marry each other and pass their vulnerabilities on to their offspring. Finally, it has been suggested that awareness that one is suffering from schizophrenia can cause the patient to feel depressed. This last suggestion is supported by recent research.

Although it may seem counterintuitive, several investigations have shown that depression and insight are positively correlated. In other words, among patients with schizophrenia (Carroll et al., 1999), as well as patients with other brain disorders (Ceniceros, 1998; Seltzer, Vasterling, and Buswell, 1995), those with greater insight are more depressed. Further, when Andrew Carroll and his colleagues followed patients over time, they found that those who showed an increase in insight became more depressed (Carroll et al., 1999). What this suggests is that the knowledge that one has a debilitating disorder can contribute to depression. This should come as no surprise. But it highlights the need to provide people who have schizophrenia with supportive psychological intervention.

DSM-IV Subtypes of Schizophrenia

DSM-IV distinguishes among subtypes of schizophrenia based on the pattern of symptoms. There are five subtypes: paranoid, disorganized, catatonic, undifferentiated, and residual (see Table 10–1). Each has a characteristic symptom profile. Past editions of the DSM did not include the same subtypes; the diagnostic categories have changed over time. Have these changes improved the accuracy of our diagnoses? We can't be sure, because we don't know how many kinds of schizophrenia there really are. But we do know that the most recent diagnostic criteria of DSM-IV result in more agreement among diagnosticians when they classify patients' syndromes.

PARANOID SCHIZOPHRENIA

Paranoid schizophrenia is the longest-standing of all the subtypes. It is marked by the presence of delusions or pronounced auditory hallucinations. The patient with paranoid schizophrenia suffers delusions of persecution or grandeur that are remarkably systematized and complex, often like the plots of dark mysteries. For the patient, this complexity may serve the purpose of providing an explanation for confusing thoughts and perceptions. At the same time, the delusions are bewildering to the outside observer.

Beyond experiencing delusions of persecution and/or grandeur, patients with paranoid schizophrenia may also experience delusional jealousy, the deep belief that their sexual partner is unfaithful. But despite the intensity of their feelings, people with paranoid schizophrenia do not display severely disorganized behavior, incoherence, or loose associations. Nor do they experience blunted or inappropriate emotion. Rather, their demeanor tends to be extremely formal or quite intense.

TABLE 10–1

Diagnosis

THOUGHT AND EMOTION IN THE SCHIZOPHRENIAS

Type	Thought	Emotion
Paranoid	Delusions of persecution are complex and coherent	Either intensely emotional or very formal
Disorganized	Less coherent delusions, often centered on own body	Inappropriate and voluble
Catatonic	Delusions often centered on death and destruction	Very inappropriate, either very excited or "frozen" behavior
Residual	No delusions	May be flattened; may show impairment of hygiene or peculiar behavior

Patients who suffer from paranoid schizophrenia have systematic and complex delusions of persecution or grandeur. Edmund Monsiel drew staring faces that may have represented the paranoid delusions he was experiencing.

Patients with paranoid schizophrenia (as well as others who suffer from delusional disorders) are often attracted to prominent places, such as the White House, 10 Downing Street, or the Vatican. Each year, the Secret Service arrests about 100 people after they approach the White House for money, relief from persecution, or to advise the government on how to run the country, and remands them to St. Elizabeth's Hospital for further evaluation (Gottesman, 1991).

DISORGANIZED SCHIZOPHRENIA

The most striking behavioral characteristic of *disorganized schizophrenia* (formerly called *hebephrenic schizophrenia*) is silliness and incoherence. The patient may burst into laughter, grimace, or giggle without an appropriate stimulus. His behavior is often jovial, but quite bizarre and absurd, suggesting extreme sensitivity to internal cues and extreme insensitivity to the external environment. Sometimes the patient is voluble, bursting into meaningless conversation for long periods of time.

Disorganized schizophrenia may also involve delusions and hallucinations, but these tend to be more disorganized and diffuse than those seen in paranoid schizophrenia. The delusions often center on the patient's own body. For example, a patient with disorganized schizophrenia may complain that his intestines are congealed or that his brain has been removed. In some cases, however, the delusions may be quite pleasant and contribute to his giddiness.

Disorganized schizophrenia is often associated with poor hygiene and grooming. Staff members on inpatient units find they have to spend a great deal of time encouraging some patients to bathe, brush their teeth, and comb their hair. In extreme cases, the patient may become incontinent.

CATATONIC SCHIZOPHRENIA

The salient feature of *catatonic schizophrenia* is motor behavior that is either enormously excited or strikingly frozen, and that may, occasionally, alternate between the two states. The onset of the disorder is sudden. When behavior is excited, the individual may seem quite agitated, even wild, vigorously resisting all attempts at control, and dangerous to self and others. Affect is quite inappropriate, while agitation is highly energetic and surprisingly prolonged, commonly yielding only to strong medication.

Stuporous or frozen behavior is also quite striking in this subtype of schizophrenia. Individuals may be entirely immobile, often adopting quite uncomfortable postures and maintaining them for long periods. If someone moves them, they will freeze in a new position. A kind of statuesque "waxy flexibility" is characteristic. After emerging from such a stuporous episode, patients sometimes report that they had been experiencing hallucinations or delusions. These sometimes center on death and destruction, conveying the sense that any movement will provoke an enormous catastrophe.

Negativism—the apparently motiveless resistance to all instructions or attempts to be moved—is a common characteristic of catatonic schizophrenia, so much so that some theorists take negativism to define the category (Maher, 1966). Forbidden to sit, the catatonic will sit. Told to sit, the catatonic will insist on standing. As mentioned earlier, the catatonic subtype is rare, possibly because the defining symptoms are being controlled with antipsychotic drugs (Jablensky et al., 1992).

UNDIFFERENTIATED SCHIZOPHRENIA

A diagnosis of **undifferentiated schizophrenia** is given when the individual does not meet the criteria for the other types of schizophrenia but nonetheless shows psychotic symptoms and poor interpersonal adjustment.

In the case history of Carl, presented above, we see many of the characteristics associated with schizophrenia: lack of interest in life, withdrawal from social activity, seemingly bizarre behavior, incomprehensible communications, and increasing preoccupation with private matters. We would need more information about Carl to classify him with a subtype of schizophrenia. Disorganized or undifferentiated schizophrenia might be appropriate.

RESIDUAL SCHIZOPHRENIA

Residual schizophrenia is characterized by the absence of prominent symptoms, such as delusions, hallucinations, incoherence, or grossly disorganized behavior. Rather, continuing evidence of the disorder is indicated by the presence of two or more symptoms which, though they are relatively minor, are nevertheless very distressing. These symptoms include: (a) marked social isolation or withdrawal; (b) marked impairment in role functioning; (c) very peculiar behavior; (d) serious impairment of personal hygiene and grooming; (e) blunt, flat, or inappropriate emotional expression; (f) odd, magical, or bizarre thinking; (g) unusual perceptual experiences; or (h) apathy or lack of initiative (APA, 1994).

It is common for patients to meet the diagnostic criteria for residual schizophrenia for some period of time after one or more episodes of paranoid or undifferentiated schizophrenia. When the prognosis is good, the patient will eventually show no residual signs of illness.

Other Approaches to Subtyping Schizophrenia

In DSM-IV, symptom profiles are emphasized in the categorization of schizophrenia. For example, the presence of delusions of persecution is a hallmark of paranoid schizophrenia. But clinical researchers have long been aware that schizophrenia can be preceded by a very uneventful life course or by a prolonged downward spiral. Thus, they have also subtyped the disorder based on the way the symptoms develop. One such distinction is between *acute* and *chronic* schizophrenia. This distinction is based on how quickly the symptoms developed and how long they have been present. **Acute schizophrenia** is characterized by the sudden onset of very florid symptoms. Quite frequently, one can point to a specific precipitating incident, usually a crisis that involved a severe social or emotional upset. For some patients, that crisis may involve leaving home, leaving school for a job, breaking up with a lover, or the loss of a family member. Prior to that upset, their history may have been within normal bounds. In contrast, **chronic schizophrenia** involves a more prolonged and gradual period of decline. No specific crisis or stressor can be identified. Rather, the person's childhood history gives evidence of interpersonal problems, poor school adjustment, and social withdrawal.

The distinction between acute and chronic schizophrenia roughly corresponds to the distinction between "good premorbid" and "poor premorbid" patients. Those designated as good premorbid have an average or above level of functioning before they show any clinical signs in early adulthood. The poor premorbid patients are those who have noticeable adjustment problems long before the first psychotic symptoms are recognized. From Glenn's self-description of his childhood, we can see that he experienced interpersonal adjustment problems before the onset of any clinical symptoms. He traced the beginning of social withdrawal and other "negative" signs to his late teens. Yet, he was not diagnosed with schizophrenia until he was twenty-five years old.

Timothy Crow, a British psychiatrist, was among the first to propose a subtyping scheme based on the difference between "negative" and "positive" symptoms of schizophrenia. As mentioned earlier, negative symptoms include flat affect, poverty of speech, social withdrawal, and loss of volition; these symptoms reflect the absence or diminution of normal functions.

Positive symptoms include delusions, hallucinations, and certain forms of thought disorder. They are called "positive symptoms" because they reflect marked departures from ordinary cognition. Crow (1985) referred to cases with a predominance of positive symptoms as **Type I schizophrenia,** and those with mostly negative symptoms as **Type II schizophrenia.** He proposed that the two subtypes might have different etiologies. Type I, or positive-symptom schizophrenia, was thought to be more responsive to medication because it arose from a disturbance in brain chemistry, possibly an abnormality in dopamine neurotransmission. Other researchers proposed that Type I schizophrenia was characterized by a sudden onset of disorder in a person who seemed to be functioning well before the episode (Fenton and Mc-Glashan, 1991). Researchers assumed that the Type II, or negative-symptom schizophrenia, was associated with poorer long-term outcome (McGlashan and Fenton, 1992). Its etiology was thought to be unrelated to dopamine transmission, but rather associated with structural changes in the brain, as well as intellectual impairment.

The distinction between positive and negative symptoms continues to be of interest to researchers. But the idea that Type I and Type II schizophrenia are caused by relatively independent processes has not received much support from research. It does appear that the two types of symptoms follow different time courses. Negative symptoms, especially social withdrawal, begin earlier than positive symptoms. But most patients with schizophrenia have both positive and negative symptoms. It seems most likely that positive and negative symptoms reflect psychopathological processes that are only partially independent and that they tend to coexist in the same individual (Carpenter, 1992; Crow, 1985; Fenton and McGlashan, 1991).

The Epidemiology of Schizophrenia

Schizophrenia is estimated to occur in about 1 percent of the population (Gottesman, 1991; Jablensky, 1997). Although estimates of the prevalence vary among countries, the differences are not dramatic. In fact, the risk rates across countries are surprisingly similar. There may be slight differences among ethnic groups. For example, in Britain, people of Afro-Caribbean origin have somewhat higher rates of schizophrenia than whites (Bhugra et al., 1997; Lloyd, 1998). These differences have been of interest to researchers, and some have raised the possibility that they may reflect differences in etiological factors that contribute to the disorder. For example, researchers have suggested that the ethnic differences in Britain may be due to a lack of immunities to certain infections in recently immigrated Caribbeans. Alternatively, the simple stress of being a member of an ethnic minority may contribute. At this point, no conclusive explanations have been offered.

The first episode of schizophrenia usually occurs in late adolescence or early adulthood (Gottesman, 1991). If the episode goes untreated, it may last for as little as a few weeks or as long as several years. After treatment, some people with schizophrenia return to a level of functioning that allows them to become self-sufficient (Harding and Keller, 1998). But many recover only to the bare level tolerated by society or, at worst, recover only enough to leave the hospital while continuing in a chronic condition of disability.

Occasionally, children are diagnosed with schizophrenia, but this is very rare. For children under the age of twelve, the prevalence is about 2 cases per 100,000 children. In contrast, for children between the ages of twelve and sixteen, the prevalence rises dramatically. Then in late adolescence and early adulthood there is a marked increase, so that the prevalence approaches the lifetime rate of 1 in 100. There is a marked decline in new cases past the age of thirty-five. Clearly the risk for the onset of schizophrenia is strongly linked with developmental changes. Glenn has vivid memories of his first illness episode at the age of twenty-five.

I hit rock bottom when I lost my job with my uncle's printing company. After I dropped out of college, I had a lot of different jobs. Finally my uncle told me I could work for him in his printing company. I started there when I was twenty-five, and I thought it was going to be the beginning of a career for me. Instead, it was the beginning of the end. After less than a year, my uncle told me he was going to lay me off. I knew it was something about me personally, because I was the only one in the company getting laid off. It was pretty devastating. During the next week or so I would just go out all day, so my parents would think I was still working. One day I was hanging out at the mall and kept having this feeling that someone was following me. I didn't want to leave the mall because there was a serious rainstorm and I didn't know where else to go. So I just kept walking and thinking about my uncle and imagining that he had hired people to follow me. I was walking the entire length of the mall for the fifteenth time when I felt a tap on my shoulder and turned around. It was a policeman. It doesn't make any sense now, but something told me to run. So I took off running as fast as I could. The policeman yelled at me to stop, but I just kept going. I really felt like I was running for my life. Two security guards caught me as I turned a corner. They pinned me down, and I started yelling for help. I don't remember all the things I said. They put me in handcuffs, took me to a police car and drove me to a mental hospital. That's where I spent the next month and first got diagnosed with schizophrenia.

There are sex differences in the time of first occurrence: men tend to have their first episode of schizophrenia when they are younger, mainly before age twenty-five, with peak incidence occurring at age twenty-four (Faraone, Chen, Goldstein, and Tsuang, 1994; Goldstein, 1997; Lewine, 1981). Women, on average, have an onset around age twenty-five. Moreover, these sex differences persist. Women with schizophrenia are hospitalized less often than men, and for shorter periods (Goldstein, 1997). The long-term prognosis for women is better than it is for men, perhaps because women with schizophrenia retain better social skills (Mueser, Bellack, Morrison, and Wade, 1990). Men and women differ in their brain structures and their cognitive styles. This is partly due to the effects of sex hormones on the brain. One plausible explanation for the sex differences in schizophrenia is that the female sex hormone, estrogen, acts to reduce the severity of the illness in women. Like stress hormones, sex hormones affect neurotransmitters. So it is possible that estrogen is affecting a neurotransmitter system that is involved in schizophrenia.

As the diagnostic criteria for schizophrenia have become more stringent, there appears to be a higher proportion of males than females who receive the diagnosis (Castle, Wessely, and Murray, 1993). But it is not clear that this actually reflects a sex difference in the likelihood of the illness. As we mentioned in Chapter 7, women are more likely than men to be diagnosed with depression. It is possible that changes in the diagnostic criteria for schizophrenia result in more females receiving diagnoses of mood disorder, such as psychotic depression, instead. Thus, changing diagnostic criteria may simply be shifting more women into the mood disorder categories.

Other demographic factors are also related to schizophrenia. First, the prevalence of schizophrenia among the poor is somewhat higher than among the wealthy (Dohrenwend et al., 1992; Dohrenwend, Levav, et al., 1998). This is especially true of the urban poor. Researchers have asked whether this is so because the stress of poverty causes schizophrenia, or because those with schizophrenia have difficulties keeping up with their schooling and their jobs. We will return to this question later in the chapter. The prevalence is also higher among the unmarried. Compared to the general population, people with schizophrenia are much less likely to marry and establish a household. (Nimgaonkar, 1998). As you might expect, they are also less likely to have children. This is especially true of male patients. In fact, men with schizophrenia do not "replace themselves" in the population. In other words, they have, on average, less than one child (Bassett, Bury, Hodgkins, and Honer, 1996). See Box 10–1 for a discussion about how we might reconcile this lowered reproduction rate with genetic theories of the etiology of schizophrenia.

Deficits in Functioning

The symptoms of schizophrenia can interfere with virtually every aspect of a person's life. This includes how he is able to function in relationships with others and whether he is able to work or study. When one considers the nature of the symptoms of schizophrenia, it is not surprising that they would present problems in so many aspects of daily living.

Cognitive Deficits

The defining clinical symptoms of schizophrenia involve problems with thinking and with communicating thoughts. Researchers have struggled with the question of whether the most basic problem is with patients' thoughts or with the way they are communicating their thoughts. It appears that both are involved. Many patients with paranoid schizophrenia are crystal clear in their communication of very bizarre delusions. The communication of their thoughts is intact, but the content of their thoughts is very abnormal. It is for this reason that cognitive processes have been of great interest to researchers who are striving to understand this disorder. Beginning before the turn of the century, researchers began to conduct systematic studies to try to pinpoint the nature of the cognitive problem that might

Why Does Schizophrenia Stay with Us?

Geneticists have been puzzled by the fact that there does not appear to be a significant decrease in the rate of schizophrenia across generations. Why would they expect a decrease? As we have noted, patients with schizophrenia, especially men, are much less likely to have children than healthy men (Ritsner, Sherina, and Ginath, 1992). In other words, they are not "replacing" themselves in the population. This has been found in studies throughout the world. Thus, they will not pass on whatever genetic vulnerability to schizophrenia they happen to possess. This should result in a decrease in the number of people who are vulnerable and, therefore, a very noticeable decline in the number of people who suffer from schizophrenia. No such decline has been observed.

One possible explanation for this is that individuals who have an unexpressed genetic vulnerability to schizophrenia are *more* likely to reproduce than members of the general population (Battaglia and Bellodi, 1996). Of course, this hypothesis cannot be directly tested because we do not know who is genetically vulnerable. The available evidence from studies of relatives of patients is inconsistent. Some find no evidence that biological relatives of patients have more than the average number of children (Buck, Simpson, and Wanklin, 1977). Another study, however, found that among the female relatives of patients, those with schizotypal personality disorder had more than the average number of children (Bassett, Bury, Hodgkinson, and Honer, 1996).

In order for the persons with the unexpressed genetic liability to reproduce at a higher than average rate, we would expect them to have some sort of trait that confers a reproductive "advantage." What would that be? Some have suggested that the genetic vulnerability that underlies schizophrenia might also be associated with high "creativity." Reporting on a follow-up study of children born to mothers with schizophrenia and placed in adoptive or foster homes shortly after birth, Leonard Heston and Duane Denney note that the children who did not develop schizophrenia were more "spontaneous," "had more colorful life histories," "held more creative jobs," and "followed the more imaginative hobbies . . ." than normals (Heston and Denney, 1968, p. 371). A familial study of schizophrenia in Iceland by Karlsson (1991) led him to conclude that the "genetic carriers" of schizophrenia often exhibit "unusual ability" and display "a superior capacity for associative thinking" (Karlsson, 1972, p. 61). Fascinated by this finding, Karlsson proposes that society may even depend upon "persons with a schizophrenic constitution" for its social and scientific progress. He remarks that a disproportionate number of the most creative people in philosophy, physics, music, literature, mathematics, and the fine arts often developed psychiatric disorders.

In her review of the literature, Andreasen (1978) raises serious questions about the evidence for a link between creativity and schizophrenia. Instead, she points out that depression is more often associated with creative artistic tendencies. It seems that the riddle of why schizophrenia persists will remain for future researchers to solve.

cause the symptoms of schizophrenia. No specific deficit has been found; instead, it appears that patients with schizophrenia have problems in many areas of cognition. These include general intelligence, reasoning, memory, and attention.

In the past, it was quite common for persons who entered psychiatric hospitals to receive tests of general intelligence, such as the Stanford-Binet or the Weschler Intelligence Scales. Numerous studies found that, on average, patients with schizophrenia scored below healthy people who were of the same age and educational background (Aylward, Walker, and Bettes, 1984). We should emphasize that most patients have intelligence scores in the normal range, and some actually score in the superior range. But, in general, schizophrenia tends to be associated with lower-than-expected scores on tests of intelligence. Of course, intelligence tests measure a variety of dif-

ferent cognitive abilities. Is there a specific problem that interferes with the performance of those suffering from schizophrenia?

Several different terms have been used to describe the "essence" of the problems with thinking that characterize schizophrenia. For example, the term "overinclusiveness" refers to the tendency to form concepts from both relevant and irrelevant information. This is believed to arise from an impaired capacity to resist distracting information. The thinking of patients with schizophrenia indeed tends to be overinclusive (Cameron, 1938, 1947; Chapman and Taylor, 1957; Marengo, Harrow and Edell, 1993; Payne, 1966; Yates, 1966). This strongly suggests a defect in cognitive filtering, wherein the person has difficulty ignoring ideas and perceptions that have no relevance to the situation or task at hand.

Overinclusiveness is one of the problems with thinking that characterizes schizophrenia. August Klotz, who was hospitalized and diagnosed as having schizophrenia, drew a person whose hair was a combination of worms, fingers with nails, and caterpillar heads, and described it as follows: "Worm holes (bath faces), worm paths (pianomusickstickteeth), worm strings (spitbathlife of the archlyre-gallery-tin-timeler-reflections: ad mothersugarmoon in the seven-saltnose water . . ."

One cognitive function that seems to be especially impaired by schizophrenia is memory (Kazes et al., 1999; Stevens, Goldman-Rakic, Gore, Fulbright, and Wexler, 1998; Wexler, Stevens, Bowers, Sernyak, and Goldman-Rakic, 1998). Psychologists distinguish between short-term memory and long-term memory. Short-term memory refers to memory for information just presented, such as a phone number or an address you just heard. Long-term memory, as the name implies, is memory for things that happened in the past. Although there is some evidence that patients with schizophrenia have problems with long-term memory, short-term memory deficits are the most pronounced (Stirling, Hellewell, and Hewitt, 1997). For example, they frequently have trouble with memory tests that require the repetition of strings of letters or numbers. The short-term/long-term memory distinction has some overlap with the distinction between explicit versus implicit memory.

Explicit memory involves conscious effort, whereas implicit memory is more automatic (see Chapter 4). For patients with schizophrenia, implicit memory is relatively intact, but explicit memory is impaired (Kazes et al., 1999).

Another area of difficulty is in abstract reasoning (Mitrushina, Abara, and Blumenfeld, 1996). Some of the earliest studies of schizophrenia examined the ability of patients to explain the meaning of proverbs (de Bonis, Epelbaum, and Feline, 1992). Their responses were often very "concrete." For example, when asked to interpret the proverb, "A bird in the hand is worth two in the bush," one patient responded, "If you are able to catch a bird you might be able to sell him for money." Difficulties with abstract reasoning are also apparent in the reactions of patients to humor (Corcoran, Cahill, and Frith, 1997). They often fail to see the humor in cartoons or movies that are viewed as hilarious by healthy people.

In previous chapters, we have discussed the frontal lobes of the brain and the fact that they are especially important for what are called "executive functions," which include the ability to plan ahead and to inhibit impulsive responses. We mentioned that the Wisconsin Card Sorting Test (WCST) is often used to measure these functions. In this test, the person must sort cards containing shapes that vary in color and number. The test is difficult because the person is not told when the criteria for sorting the cards changes during the course of the task; he is only told whether his response is right or wrong. Patients with schizophrenia tend to perform very poorly on this task (Koren et al., 1998). They make a lot of "perseverative" errors—that is, they make the same mistake over and over (see Chapter 4).

Of all the cognitive problems associated with schizophrenia, it is attentional difficulties that seem to be most disturbing to patients. Of course, we have all had trouble paying attention at one time or another, in spite of trying hard to do so. Tired or upset, we sometimes find our attention roaming, and we cannot direct it. What we have experienced briefly and in microcosm, people with schizophrenia often experience profoundly. One patient explains his problem with attention in this way:

> I can't concentrate. It's diversion of attention that troubles me. The sounds are coming through to me, but I feel my mind cannot cope with everything. It's difficult to concentrate on any one sound. It's like trying to do two or three different things at one time. (McGhie and Chapman, 1961, p. 104)

In this drawing by Johann Knüpfer, the merging of the people and the writing demonstrates how in schizophrenia there is a breakdown of the cognitive filter that normally keeps out irrelevant stimuli.

Consider for a moment what normal attention involves. We are continuously bombarded by an enormous number of stimuli, much more than our limited channel capacity can absorb. So we need some means of sorting out stimuli to determine which ones will be admitted and which ones barred. This has been referred to metaphorically as an **attentional filter** (Broadbent, 1958). Recent theories of cognition emphasize the importance of the inhibitory processes that reduce attention to irrelevant stimuli (Houghton and Tipper, 1998). In your daily activities you rely on these processes. Sometimes you must attend to several different stimuli simultaneously, and at other times you need to focus on a specific stimulus. When you drive a car on a clear road, for example, you usually can conduct a conversation with a passenger, often while listening to background music. But when the road is treacherous and winds along a drop-off, attention narrows. It becomes impossible to conduct a conversation, and what was formerly soothing music is now quite an irritant. All of the mind's energy, as it were, is directed to one thing and one thing only: driving safely. Everything else is filtered out. But among patients with schizophrenia, the attentional filter seems to be defective. A former patient puts it well:

Each of us is capable of coping with a large number of stimuli, invading our being through any one of the senses. We could hear every sound within earshot and see every object, line and color within the field of vision, and so on. It's obvious that we would be incapable of carrying on any of our daily activities if even one-hundredth of all these available stimuli invade us at once. So the mind must have a filter which functions without our conscious thought, sorting stimuli and allowing only those which are relevant to the situation in hand to disturb consciousness. And this filter must be working at maximum efficiency at all times, particularly when a high degree of concentration is required. What happened to me was a breakdown in the filter, and a hodgepodge of unrelated stimuli were distracting me from things which should have had my undivided attention. (MacDonald, 1960, p. 218)

Over the years, numerous controlled studies have confirmed the personal statements of patients (Chapman and Chapman, 1973; Cornblatt, Obuchowski, Schnur, and O'Brien, 1997; Garmezy, 1977b; Nuechterlein et al., 1998). For example, on the continuous performance test (CPT) the person is required to identify a target stimulus, such as the letter "t," in a random series of rapidly presented letters of the alphabet. Patients with schizophrenia make more errors of omission and commission on this task; they more often fail to respond to the target, and they more often respond to nontarget stimuli. Their performance is even more impaired when an irrelevant distracter stimulus, such as a noise, is presented when they are performing the CPT. Again, they seem unable to filter out the distracter. It appears that people with schizophrenia are processing and reacting to the irrelevant stimulus even when they would benefit from ignoring it. Is this because they are not motivated to pay attention to the target stimulus? Or, are they simply unable, no matter how hard they try, to ignore the distracter?

Some researchers have suggested that people with schizophrenia find it difficult to inhibit their responses to sensory input. Several lines of investigation support the idea that this is a very basic problem. A good example is "prepulse inhibition" (Swerdlow, Bakshi, Waikar, Taaid, and Geyer, 1998). In this procedure, a "startle stimulus," such as a loud noise, is presented either with or without a "prepulse" such as a weak tone. The person's eyeblink response to the startle stimulus is measured. Most people show a reduction in their response to the startle stimulus when it is preceded by a prepulse. It is as if the prepulse serves as a warning, so that the startle stimulus is not as startling. This is assumed to reflect inhibitory mechanisms in the brain. But for some reason, the prepulse is less effective in reducing the startle response in patients with schizophrenia. These abnormalities on the prepulse inhibition test may be reflected in real-world experiences. If a person is experiencing heightened physiological responses to sensory input, even input he is trying to ignore, this may contribute to hyper-vigilance and to feelings of paranoia.

The prepulse inhibition procedure can be used with animals by recording their motor response to the startle stimulus. Like humans, animals typically show a reduction in the response to the startle stimulus when the prepulse is paired with it. There is a great deal of optimism about the insights that we might gain using the "animal model" of prepulse inhibition. For example, one important question concerns the causes of decreased prepulse inhibition. Recent studies have shown that animals who are exposed to early maternal deprivation show reduced prepulse inhibition, and that this can persist into adulthood (Ellenbroek, van den Kroonenberg, and Cools, 1998). So, early environmental factors may set the stage for individual differences in the inhibition of the startle response. This is probably due to the effect of early experiences on nervous system development. What about genetics? In Chapter 4, we discussed a new genetic approach that involves "knocking out" certain genes in the fertilized egg of mice. These "knockout" mice then develop without the influence of that particular gene. In one recent study, the gene for a certain subtype of serotonin receptor was eliminated (Dulawa, Hen, Scearce-Levie, and Geyer, 1997). When compared to a control group, these knockout mice showed an increase in prepulse inhibition and a general decrease in the startle response. This indicates that the serotonin receptor gene is involved in prepulse inhibition. Later in this chapter, we will discuss the possible role of serotonin in the neurochemistry of schizophrenia.

Our discussion of the research on cognitive functions in schizophrenia has only scratched the surface. Yet, even with this brief overview, it is clear that people with schizophrenia tend to have cognitive deficits that extend across a variety of functions. The next question that we must confront is how these deficits are related to the symptoms of schizophrenia. At this point, we cannot conclude that any of the cognitive deficits that have been found in patients with schizophrenia are causing their symptoms. The main reason for this is that all of the performance deficits we see in people with schizophrenia have also been observed in people with other disorders. For example, children with attention deficit disorder also show significant distractibility and fail to inhibit responses to irrelevant stimuli. In fact, like patients with schizophrenia, children with attention deficit disorder perform poorly on the CPT (Overtoom et al., 1998). Memory impairments are often pronounced in depression and severe in Alzheimer's disease. Prepulse inhibition is abnormal in people who suffer from Huntington's disease, enuresis, obsessive-compulsive disorder, or Tourette's disorder. Yet, none of these disorders is quite like schizophrenia. It may be that future research will shed light on one or more specific cognitive problems that can produce psychotic symptoms. Whatever the case, up to this point the accumulated findings from studies of schizophrenia indicate cognitive problems that extend across many domains of functioning. Glenn's description of his first episode of schizophrenia illustrates this:

> In thinking back on it now, I'm not sure what was going on with me that day in the mall. My mind was racing from one thing to another. As I stopped to look in the store windows, I couldn't concentrate on what I was seeing. I remember going into a department store to buy something, but I couldn't remember what I wanted to buy. A salesclerk asked me if I needed any help, and I said I forgot what I was looking for. I was embarrassed after I said that, so then I told her I remembered that I needed a watch. She asked me what kind of watch I was interested in, and I was speechless. I had a watch on at the time and it was working fine. There was a long period of silence, then the salesclerk asked me if I was O.K. This took me off guard and I just walked away. I don't think I had any mental control that day.

The sense that the world's hodgepodge has invaded the mind, that one cannot control one's attention or one's thoughts or speech, that it is difficult to focus the mind or sustain that focus once it is achieved—these experiences are shared by many patients with schizophrenia. Like Glenn, they may be able to look back and reflect on these episodes. Their personal accounts can be very informative. But, just like the researchers who have studied the illness for decades, they have no definitive answers about the causes of schizophrenia.

Perceptual Deficits

The perception of a sensory input is the earliest stage in any cognitive process. In order to respond to a stimulus, we must first detect it with one of our

Patients with schizophrenia may experience visual and auditory perceptual deficits. Their impaired sensory systems may cause them to hear or see things that aren't there, giving them the feeling that they are being sent secret messages, as depicted in this drawing.

sensory systems. This is a very basic stage in our ability to relate to the world around us. It appears that some patients with schizophrenia have an impairment at this basic level.

When asked to describe their symptoms, patients often report perceptual abnormalities, such as difficulties in understanding others' speech or overly sensitive auditory perception. In the visual modality, there may be spatial distortions. For example, a room may seem much smaller and more constricting than it really is, or objects may seem farther away. Researchers have suggested that these perceptual problems may provide a fertile soil for hallucinations.

One of the clearest illustrations of the sensory processing deficit is the performance of patients with schizophrenia on "backward masking" tasks (Green, Nuechterlein, and Breitmeyer, 1997). In the visual backward masking procedure, the person views a very brief "target" visual stimulus, such as a word or picture presented on a screen. This is followed, within milliseconds, by another visual stimulus referred to as the "mask." This is usually just a bright light or random lines. If the time period between the two is brief, say less than fifty milliseconds, it can be difficult or impossible to report the identity of the target stimulus. It is as if the target stimulus was never presented! Patients with schizophrenia require a longer time period between the presentation of the target and the mask in order to identify the target. This is not due to any basic problem with visual acuity; even patients with 20–20 vision have this problem. This indicates that there is some abnormality in the very early stages of sensory processing. We do not yet know the cause, but it is likely that it has something to do with the way neurons in the sensory system are functioning (Green, Nuechterlein, and Mintz, 1994a, 1994b).

Given that patients with schizophrenia have early-stage deficits in visual processing, it is not surprising that they also show problems with other aspects of visual perception. For example, studies have revealed problems on visual tasks that involve the estimation of sizes (Strauss, Foureman, and Parwatikar, 1974), or the tracking of a moving visual stimulus (Kinney, Levy, Yurgelun-Todd, Tramer, and Holzman, 1998). Similarly, in the auditory modality, patients with schizophrenia have problems in the discrimination of tones (Holcomb et al., 1995; Schall et al., 1996). When reflecting on his first episode of schizophrenia, Glenn recalls some unusual sensory experiences:

> I know I had problems with concentration at that time, but there was something else happening, too. At times it seemed that the things I heard and saw were coming and going very fast. When I was in the mall that day, it looked like people were moving at an abnormal speed. They would speed up, and I would see them like a blur in my peripheral vision. Then they would slow down like a movie in slow motion. The rustling sounds of their paper shopping bags seemed so loud to me that it was annoying. I was tempted to yell out to them and tell them to stop making so much noise. But I didn't because I was afraid they would come after me.

Motor Deficits

The earliest writings on the nature of schizophrenia included comments about abnormalities in movement. The early descriptions mentioned unusual posturing of the head and limbs and involuntary movements of the face and limbs. Keep in mind that there were no drug treatments for schizophrenia until about 1950. The postural abnormalities shown by patients prior to 1950 cannot be attributed to medication. Since that time researchers have conducted controlled studies and, indeed, they have found evidence of postural and movement abnormalities in schizophrenia (Walker, Savoie, and Davis, 1994). It has been estimated that about 30 percent of patients with schizophrenia show some kind of movement abnormality. These are often referred to as "spontaneous" movement abnormalities because they are present in patients who have not received any treatment and have no history of a specific neurological disorder.

When laboratory tests of motor functions are administered to people with schizophrenia, they perform below normals. For example, they tend to score below average on tests of motor proficiency and coordination (Carnahan, Aguilar, Malla, and Norman, 1997). They also have much slower reaction times (Heinrichs and Zakzanis, 1998). Many patients have difficulty maintaining a steady pressure on a device that tests manual force (Rosen, Lockhart, Gants, and Westergaard, 1991; Vrtunski et al., 1998).

Of course, motor abnormalities are viewed by neurologists as a sign of problems in the nervous system. So, the presence of motor abnormalities in patients with schizophrenia is consistent with the idea that there is a biological basis to the disorder. When do these abnormalities arise? This is an important question. If motor abnormalities are present, say, in childhood, long before the onset of the symptoms of schizophrenia, then this would suggest that the vulnerability can be present, but unexpressed. We will return to this issue in the sections below as we explore the developmental precursors of schizophrenia.

Emotional Deficits

We have described a broad range of cognitive and perceptual problems that often accompany schizophrenia. But the one that has the greatest potential for interfering with everyday life is the problem many patients have in recognizing nonverbal cues relevant to human emotion and social interaction. When patients with schizophrenia are shown photographs depicting facial expressions of emotion, they are less likely than normals to correctly identify them (Feinberg, Rifkin, Schaffer, and Walker, 1986; Hellewell, Connell, and Deakin, 1994). For example, they might label surprise as happiness, or fear as anger.

The problem with understanding human emotions is also apparent when people with schizophrenia are asked to explain or resolve an interpersonal problem. In one study, patients viewed videotapes of people interacting while experiencing various levels of conflict (Addington, McCleary, and Munroe-Blum, 1998). The patients were then asked to explain what had occurred in the interaction, and to offer some potential solutions to the problem. This and similar tasks prove to be difficult for some patients. Their inferences about social motives are often inaccurate and, perhaps as a consequence, they offer impractical solutions to the interpersonal problems.

But are these problems specific to human emotions? In other words, is there a special deficit in the ability of patients with schizophrenia to understand emotion? Or do they encounter difficulty in recognizing facial expressions of emotion simply because they have trouble with visual perception? In an attempt to answer this question, several research groups have studied the ability of patients with schizophrenia to recognize facial identities and features, independent of emotion. The results suggest that the problem patients have with recognizing facial emotion may indeed be part of a larger problem with visual perception (Kerr and Neale, 1993). But whatever the source of the problem, the fact that some patients have difficulty understanding the meaning of facial emotion has obvious implications for their interpersonal experiences. Misjudging nonverbal cues of another person's emotional state could make interpersonal interactions unpleasant, and might result in social rejection. Clinicians who treat patients with schizophrenia know all too well how easy it is for patients to misinterpret nonverbal cues. Thus, it is very important for clinicians to speak as clearly and unambiguously as possible to their patients.

Sources of Vulnerability

Although schizophrenia has been the subject of study for more than a century, progress in understanding the origins of the disorder has been painfully slow. Nonetheless, we know much more about the nature of schizophrenia now than we did at the turn of the century. The advances are very obvious to families who have had to deal with the illness in a loved one. The following comments from the father of a son with schizophrenia illustrate the marked changes:

When we first took our son in for treatment in 1964, the doctor questioned us for over four hours. They asked my wife if she had wanted my son when he was born. They tried to suggest that she hadn't really wanted another baby and had somehow rejected him. They asked her about her own childhood and wanted to know if her mother had been affectionate toward her. They even asked her if she had fantasies of abandoning my son when he was a baby. Finally, one of the doctors told us that schizophrenia could be caused by emotional rejection by the mother. By the end of the meeting my wife was in tears. She went home and hid my son's baby pictures so she wouldn't have to look at them. She carried a burden of guilt for many years. It wasn't until the late 1970s that the doctors started talking about the possibility that my son had a brain disorder. We started reading up on the research and our whole outlook changed. My wife doesn't hide the baby pictures anymore. We are saddened by our son's illness, but we love him and we always will.

In the following sections, we will describe some of what is currently known about the causes and treatment of schizophrenia. Research on schizophrenia, like that on other psychological disorders, is multifaceted, involving biological, psychological, and sociological approaches. Taken together, the findings have shown us that schizophrenia results from the complex interplay between genetic and environmental factors (Zubin and Spring, 1977).

Genetics of Schizophrenia

Scientists have conducted a great deal of research to determine whether there is an inherited vulnerability to schizophrenia. Twin studies, family studies, and adoption studies have provided strong evidence for the role of genes in schizophrenia (Gottesman, 1993). At the same time, twin and adoption studies have also provided us with strong support for the role of environmental factors. We do not yet know what these environmental factors are, but, as you will see, there are some promising leads.

CONCORDANCE FOR SCHIZOPHRENIA IN TWINS

The twin study method is a useful strategy for exploring the effects of genes on human behavior. As we discussed in Chapter 4, twins are of two kinds: identical (monozygotic) and fraternal (dizygotic). Monozygotic (MZ) twins develop from a single egg fertilized by a single sperm. The fertilized egg divides and produces two individuals. Dizygotic (DZ) twins develop from two different eggs and two different sperm. Except for the fact that they share the same prenatal environment and are born at the same time, DZ twins are like ordinary siblings. They share approximately 50 percent of their genes in common, and about 50 percent of the time they are of different genders.

The logic of a genetic study is really quite simple. If all other things are equal, the more similar people

The Genain quadruplets (who shared identical genes) were all diagnosed with schizophrenia, suggesting a strong genetic component to the disorder. But other factors, including prenatal factors and a stressful family environment, also played a role, since the women had differing degrees of schizophrenia and adjustment (one sister was hospitalized for most of her life; one sister married, had a child, and held a job).

are in their genetic makeup, the more traits they will have in common if those traits are genetically influenced. MZ twins should resemble each other more than DZ twins or ordinary siblings. And DZ twins and siblings should have more in common than unrelated individuals. If both members of a twin pair have a trait in common, we say that that twin set is **concordant** for that particular trait. If one twin has the trait and one does not, we call the twin pair **discordant** for the trait. If a trait is entirely determined by genetic makeup, there should be 100 percent concordance for MZ twins, meaning that if one twin has the trait, the other should have it too. Anything less than 100 percent concordance (but more than the percentage found in DZ twins) will suggest that heredity influences, but does not solely determine, the presence of the trait.

Irving Gottesman and James Shields (1972) conducted one of the landmark twin studies of schizophrenia. From 1948 through 1964, every patient admitted for treatment to the psychiatric unit at the Maudsley and Bethlehem Royal Hospital in London was routinely asked if he or she was a twin. Over these sixteen years, the investigators located 55 patients (out of more than 45,000 admitted) who were twins and whose co-twin could be located and would cooperate in the study. For analytic purposes, the twin who was first seen at the psychiatric clinic was called the **index case,** or **proband.** The other twin, who was examined for the presence or absence of schizophrenia, was called the **co-twin.**

Of these fifty-five sets of twins, the researchers determined that twenty-two were MZ twins and thirty-three were DZ twins. The twins ranged in age from nineteen to sixty-four, with a median age of thirty-seven initially. Concordance for schizophrenia, where it was already present in the co-twin at the time the proband was admitted to the hospital, could of course be determined immediately. Discordant pairs were followed for at least thirteen and as long as twenty-six years to determine if schizophrenia subsequently developed in the co-twin (Gottesman, McGuffin, and Farmer, 1987).

Such a lengthy study examines more than just the person's diagnosis. In analyzing an enormous variety of psychological, medical, and social data for each twin pair, Gottesman and Shields observed two findings of special relevance to our understanding of the genetic causes of schizophrenia. First, they found that "strict" concordance for schizophrenia was 50 percent for MZ twins and 9 percent for DZ twins, a ratio of roughly 4:1. In other words, for 50 percent of the MZ pairs, both the proband and the co-twin had been hospitalized and diagnosed with schizophrenia. Despite the small sample, this is a very significant finding, one consistent with other genetic studies.

Second, using length of hospitalization to indicate severity of schizophrenia, Gottesman and Shields found substantial concordance differences between MZ twins whose probands had been hospitalized for more than two years and those whose probands had been hospitalized for less than two years. Hospitalization for more than two years is critical to a diagnosis of chronic schizophrenia. It is therefore of enormous interest that concordance rates rose to 77 percent in this sample. For those who were hospitalized for less than two years (very likely the patients with a better prognosis), the concordance rate was only 27 percent (Gottesman and Shields, 1972). What this finding means practically is that severity of schizophrenia in a proband also increases the chances that the co-twin will develop schizophrenia (Torrey, 1992).

The evidence from the many studies summarized in Table 10–2 is strong: concordance rates for MZ twins are higher than they are for DZ twins; concordance rates for DZ twins are higher than the rate for unrelated persons in the general population (about 1 percent). Concordance, however, is never 100 percent, and this means that genes are only part of the story. Genes make one vulnerable to schizophrenia; they do not guarantee that the disorder will occur. Indeed, 89 percent of those diagnosed with schizophrenia have no known relative who has schizophrenia (Cromwell, 1993).

There is something else to consider. The concordance rates in Table 10–2 vary a great deal. Across the studies, concordance for schizophrenia in MZ twins varies from 18 to 58 percent. Why are the rates so different? Some researchers tried to answer this question by looking at the findings from all published twin studies of schizophrenia (Walker, Downey, and Caspi, 1991). They found that the type of sample used in the study determined the size of the concordance rates. Basically, the twin samples came from one of two places: either psychiatric hospitals or government health registries that listed all twins, both healthy and ill, in the population. When the research participants were twins who were identified through

TABLE 10–2

Data

CONCORDANCE RATES FOR SCHIZOPHRENIA IN THE MOST RECENT TWIN STUDIES

Country/Year	MZ Pairs			DZ pairs		
	Total Pairs	Pairwise Rate (%)*	Probandwise Rate (%)†	Total Pairs	Pairwise Rate (%)*	Probandwise Rate (%)†
Finland, 1963/1971	17	0–36	35	20	5–14	13
Norway, 1967	55	25–38	45	90	4–10	15
Denmark, 1973	21	24–48	56	41	10–19	27
United Kingdom, 1966/1987	22	40–50	58	33	9–12	15
United States, 1969/1983	164	18	31	277	3	6
United Kingdom, 1999	106	not given	40.8	118	not given	5.3
Average			44.3			12.55

SOURCE: Cardno et al., 1999; Gottesman, 1991.

*The pairwise rate is the number of concordant pairs divided by the total number of twin pairs.

†The probandwise rate is the number of ill twins who are members of concordant pairs divided by the number of index cases.

psychiatric hospitals, the concordance estimates were much higher. As we described above, Gottesman and Shields found that more severely ill MZ twins were more likely to have a co-twin with schizophrenia. Thus, there is a relation between illness severity and concordance. It is likely that sampling from a psychiatric hospital yields patients who are more severely disturbed, and this may explain why concordance rates are higher when the twin pairs are identified through hospital records.

Although researchers agree that heredity is an important factor in the etiology of schizophrenia, debate continues regarding the magnitude of the genetic contribution. Based on a review of the findings from twin studies of schizophrenia, Fuller Torrey concluded that the genetic contribution to schizophrenia has been overestimated (Torrey, 1992). He reviewed concordance rates for eight twin studies of schizophrenia that used representative samples of twins (that is, health registries) and determined whether they were MZ or DZ twins with reasonable certainty by using techniques such as DNA and red cell typing. The eight studies showed a concordance rate for schizophrenia that is 28 percent for MZ twins and 6 percent for DZ twins. These rates support a lower genetic contribution to schizophrenia. But others set those estimates much higher (Gottesman, 1991; McGue, 1992).

We should also keep in mind the issue of the twins' experiences. The logic of twin studies rests on the assumption that MZ twins do *not* share more experiences in common than DZ twins. What if this assumption is incorrect? What if MZ twins have more similar environmental experiences than DZ twins? This might result in greater similarity between MZ pairs than DZ pairs, but not for reasons of genetics. Some researchers have tried to resolve this issue by asking twins to describe their experiences, or by studying MZ twins who are reared apart (Bouchard, 1994). So far, the results do not indicate that MZ twins share more experiences. But we know from Chapter 4 that the environment begins to have an influence before birth. We also know that during prenatal development, MZ twins often share the same placenta, whereas DZ twins never do. Some researchers believe this may cause MZ twins to be more similar in their development than DZ twins (Phelps, Davis, and Schartz, 1997; Sokol et al., 1995).

Perhaps the most intriguing question raised by the results of twin studies is why MZ twins are not always concordant for schizophrenia. It turns out that the twin method is also very useful for studying environmental effects. In fact, one of the most important research projects in the past twenty years is the National Institute of Mental Health (NIMH) study of MZ twins who are discordant for schizophrenia—twin pairs in which one has schizophrenia and the other one does not (Torrey, Bowler, and Taylor, 1994). The individuals who participated in this study were very generous with their time. They spent several days at the NIMH taking tests, having brain scans, and giving blood samples. The findings of this study proved to be very important. The twins with schizophrenia differed from their healthy co-twins in performance on neuropsychological tests as well as in the structure of their brains. In the sections below, we will discuss some of these findings in greater detail.

SCHIZOPHRENIA IN FAMILIES

Family studies begin from the same premise as twin studies: individuals who have a similar heredity should be more likely to possess a particular trait than those who are unrelated. Further, those who are closely related to the patient (parents and siblings)

should be at greater risk than those who have a more distant relation (aunts, uncles, and cousins). The data from more than a dozen studies support this conclusion (Gottesman, 1991). As can be seen in Figure 10–1, the likelihood that siblings of a patient with schizophrenia will also suffer from schizophrenia is about 9 percent—much higher than the 1 percent one finds among the general population, but much lower than the 48 percent estimated for identical twins. Similarly, it is estimated that when both parents have schizophrenia, each of their children has about a 46 percent chance of developing the illness. The evidence is clearly consistent with the idea that a genetic vulnerability can be shared by relatives.

At the same time, it is important to notice that the overwhelming majority of patients with schizophrenia have no immediate family members (parents or siblings) with the illness. For most families, therefore, the illness would not be predicted. Furthermore, biological relatives typically share more than genes; they also tend to share the same environment.

Figure 10–1

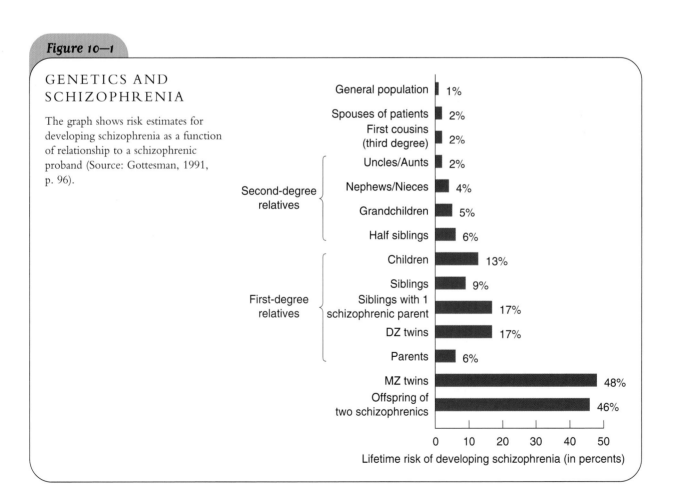

GENETICS AND SCHIZOPHRENIA

The graph shows risk estimates for developing schizophrenia as a function of relationship to a schizophrenic proband (Source: Gottesman, 1991, p. 96).

Family studies cannot disentangle genetic and environmental influences. The only way these two influences can be separated is if biological relatives do not share the same environment. This is most likely to happen when children are adopted.

ADOPTION STUDIES

In one of the first adoption studies of schizophrenia, Leonard Heston (1966) examined children who were born to mothers with schizophrenia, but who were reared in adoptive homes. Most of the "high-risk" children were placed within several weeks after birth. Heston compared these children to adoptees whose biological mothers had no mental illness. When they were adults, the adoptees were interviewed by a psychiatrist. Then two other psychiatrists, not previously involved in the research, were asked to evaluate the participants' medical histories and, if necessary, to diagnose them. Neither psychiatrist knew about the adoptees' origins. Even so, the two psychiatrists diagnosed five of the adoptees as suffering from schizophrenia. All five had a biological mother with the illness. In contrast, none of those from the control group were so diagnosed. Moreover, among the adoptees whose biological mothers suffered from schizophrenia, thirty-seven of the forty-seven were given some kind of psychiatric diagnosis. Only nine of the fifty adoptees from the control group received a diagnosis. These results are striking; they are telling us that the child does not have to be reared by a parent with schizophrenia in order to develop the illness. It is important, however, to state this case precisely, and not to overstate it. Genes contribute to vulnerability to schizophrenia, but what about the experiences of the children after adoption? Does the environment matter at all?

In recent adoption studies, investigators have taken a closer look at the nature of the children's experiences after adoption. Tienari and his colleagues followed the development of a group of 341 adopted children in Finland (Tienari et al., 1994). Almost half, 155, had a biological mother with schizophrenia. As in previous studies, the researchers found that the biological offspring of mothers with schizophrenia were more likely to develop the illness. In this study, the investigators also rated the quality of children's rearing environments. They found that there was a significant increase in the likelihood of schizophrenia in the adoptees reared in "disordered" envi-

ronments; namely, families that were chaotic and unstable. These results give strong support to the diathesis-stress model. Recall from our discussion of gene expression in Chapter 4 that genes can be turned on or off by the environment. The findings from the Finnish adoption study indicate that some of the biological offspring of mothers with schizophrenia inherit a vulnerability that is more likely to be expressed if the children are exposed to environmental stress.

As with twin studies, however, adoption studies have not examined the prenatal environment. Keep in mind that both animal and human research have shown that prenatal factors, including maternal stress, can affect the developing brain. Could it be that the prenatal experiences of the adopted children were also influencing their chances of succumbing to schizophrenia? We will explore this possibility below in our discussion of the role of obstetrical complications and schizophrenia.

LINKAGE ANALYSIS

Some genetic disorders, such as muscular dystrophy or cystic fibrosis, arise from defects in single genes. Schizophrenia, however, does not appear to be due to a single gene (Levinson et al., 1998). Instead, it is a *polygenic* disorder in that it is influenced by multiple genes (see Chapter 4). Schizophrenia may be like cancer in the following way: A single process, analogous to uncontrolled cell division in cancer, is probably at the core of some forms of schizophrenia. But this process may be brought about by various and distinct genetic influences.

When a disorder is due to the action of more than one gene, it is very difficult to identify the genetic causes. A research technique known as **linkage analysis** has been used in studies of disorders like schizophrenia, where it is believed many genes contribute to vulnerability. This technique seeks to evaluate the occurrence of a familial disorder alongside a known genetic marker (a gene that is known to control a particular trait). A decade ago, there were just a few known genetic markers, but with the advent of the Human Genome Project, markers that span the entire genome have been developed. Up to this point, findings from linkage analysis are inconsistent; some studies have reported a relation between specific chromosomal regions and the occurrence of schizophrenia, but none of these has been consistently replicated (DeLisi, 1997; Faraone et al, 1998). One exception is linkage to a region on chromosome 22, as reported by more than one group of researchers (Brzustowicz, Hodgkinson, Chow, Honer, and Bassett, 2000). Nonetheless, the abnormality on chromosome 22 seems to be associated with a very small percentage of cases. Some researchers are optimistic that, with sufficient time and resources, linkage analysis will tell us more about which genes lead to schizophrenia (Kendler and Diehl, 1993). Others have less confidence in its potential to provide definitive answers (Faraone et al., 1998). In the future, it is likely that linkage analysis will be combined with other approaches to refine the search for genetic factors in schizophrenia.

Complications of Pregnancy and Birth

As early as 1960, some researchers believed that prenatal complications might play a role in the etiology of schizophrenia (Jackson, 1960). Since that time, more supportive evidence has accumulated. When the early medical records of patients with schizophrenia and normals are compared, those of the people with schizophrenia are more likely to contain evidence of complications during gestation. For example, the mothers of patients with schizophrenia showed more problems with circulation and swelling of their legs and arms during their pregnancies. Recent studies have also found that viral infections were more common during their pregnancies (Stoeber, Franzek, and Beckmann, 1997). To confirm these findings, researchers have used government health records to compare yearly rates of influenza infection with yearly changes in the birthrate of those who develop schizophrenia. They find that the risk rate for schizophrenia is elevated for persons born shortly after a flu epidemic (Barr, Mednick, and Munk-Jorgensen, 1990; Murray et al., 1992).

We know that the chance that a person will come down with a viral infection varies with the seasons; viral infections are more common in the winter than in the summer. If maternal viral infections do contribute to schizophrenia, then we would expect to find that the births of patients with schizophrenia are clustered in certain months of the year. Numerous studies have found support for this (Bradbury and Miller, 1985; Torrey, Miller, Rawlings, and Yolken, 1997). If the middle part of the pregnancy

overlaps with the winter season, the mother has a greater chance of giving birth to a child who will develop schizophrenia. It appears that period between the fourth through the sixth month of pregnancy is especially sensitive.

In Chapter 4, we described how maternal stress during pregnancy can interfere with fetal brain development. At least two studies have demonstrated that the rate of psychiatric disorder, including that for schizophrenia, is increased in the offspring of pregnant women exposed to stress. One of these studies focused on the children of women whose spouses had died during their pregnancy (Huttunen, 1989), another on women who had been affected by a major military battle while pregnant (van Os and Selten, 1998). It is likely that the maternal exposure to stress triggers an increase in the release of stress hormones and that this negatively influences fetal brain development.

Problems that occur during the delivery process are also linked with increased risk for schizophrenia (Cannon, 1997; Jones, Rantakallio, Hartikainen, Isohanni, and Sipila, 1998). It appears that complications that affect the oxygen supply to the newborn are especially important. These include extended labor, breech position, and the cord around the infant's neck. Many experimental studies of animals have shown that insufficient oxygen, or *hypoxia,* can damage the newborn brain. Recent neuroimaging studies indicate that human infants can also sustain brain damage from hypoxia (Greco, 1995).

The findings on obstetrical complications help us to understand how identical twins can be discordant for schizophrenia. We know that MZ twins can have very different prenatal experiences. At birth, they often differ in weight and physical health. Researchers have found that MZ twins who are discordant for schizophrenia experienced a higher than average rate of obstetrical complications, especially delivery problems (McNeil et al., 1994). Also, in discordant pairs, the ill twin is more likely to show physical signs of exposure to prenatal complications, such as a smaller head circumference (Bracha et al., 1995).

In an innovative study, Bracha and his colleagues examined the fingerprints of twins who were discordant for schizophrenia (Bracha et al., 1992). Fingerprint patterns are determined by two things: genetics and prenatal events. They do not change after birth. Most MZ twin pairs have highly similar fingerprints. But Bracha found that the fingerprints of twin pairs who were discordant for schizophrenia were not as similar as the fingerprints of healthy twin pairs. The differences are readily apparent. Again these results suggest that prenatal events may have affected the twins in different ways. But why would differences in fingerprints be associated with differences between twins in mental health? The answer lies in the way the nervous system develops. The brain develops from the same set of embryonic cells that eventually forms the skin. So abnormalities in fingerprints are like fossilized evidence of abnormalities in nervous system development.

We have seen that a broad range of complications during pregnancy and delivery are associated with schizophrenia. Looking at the individual studies, it is apparent that none of the complications alone accounts for a large proportion of the cases. But, if we add them all up, it appears that obstetrical factors in general do play an important role in the etiology of schizophrenia. What remains unknown at this point is whether obstetrical complications alone can create the vulnerability for schizophrenia, or whether a genetic predisposition is also required. Some believe that obstetrical complications *interact* with a genetic risk in producing schizophrenia (Mednick et al., 1998). From this perspective, genetic risk for schizophrenia involves a heightened sensitivity to the negative effects of prenatal complications. If the fetus has a specific genotype *and* is also exposed to obstetrical complications, the genotype will be expressed in the form of vulnerability to schizophrenia. But we cannot yet rule out the possibility that prenatal factors alone can cause schizophrenia.

Childhood Indicators of Schizophrenia

If vulnerability to schizophrenia can arise from hereditary predispositions or obstetrical complications, then it must be present at birth. Yet, in most cases, the clinical symptoms of the illness are not apparent until the person reaches early adulthood. These facts have puzzled researchers. They suggest that the vulnerability must be "silent," or unexpressed, during the person's formative years. Or perhaps the early signs of vulnerability are very subtle. With the passage of time, as development proceeds and experiences accumulate, the silent vulnerability might gradually show itself.

The search for early indicators of vulnerability to schizophrenia has been a major focus of research.

There are two reasons why this is considered so important. First, by identifying early indicators we may gain a better understanding of the underlying factors that are involved in the illness. Second, in the long run, clinicians would like to be able to prevent the onset of schizophrenia. Doing so will require some means of identifying persons who are at risk. Having information about the person's family history is not enough; as we mentioned above, most patients with schizophrenia do not have a parent or sibling with the illness.

Three strategies have been used in research on the developmental precursors of schizophrenia: The *high-risk method* focuses on children who have a parent with schizophrenia. The *retrospective method* relies on parents' recollections of the patient's early childhood years. In *follow-back studies,* researchers identify adults with the illness, then look back at their childhood records to search for early signs.

HIGH-RISK RESEARCH

Once behavior genetic studies had provided strong evidence that hereditary factors were playing a role in schizophrenia, researchers became interested in the development of children whose parents suffered from the disorder. Knowing that only some of the children who have a parent with schizophrenia will eventually show the illness, researchers wanted to find out whether they could predict whether a child would develop schizophrenia. Are there childhood indicators? In order to find out, several research groups launched large-scale studies of "high-risk" children. These studies have contributed a great deal to our knowledge of schizophrenia.

Most high-risk research projects have focused on individuals who have at least one biological parent with schizophrenia. To study these individuals, researchers use *prospective studies,* which begin when the participants are children, then follow them over an extended period of time. Periodic evaluations of the participants are conducted until they pass through early adulthood, which is the age period of major risk for schizophrenia.

One of the first, and most extensive high-risk projects was spearheaded by Sarnoff Mednick and Fini Schulsinger in Denmark (Mednick, Cudeck, Griffith, Talovic, and Schulsinger, 1984; Olin and Mednick, 1996; Parnas et al., 1993; Walker, Cudeck, Mednick, and Schulsinger, 1981). In 1962, these investigators identified 207 "high-risk" people (they had a parent with schizophrenia) and 104 "low-risk" people (they did not have a parent with schizophrenia) who were matched on such variables as age, gender, years of education, father's occupation, and place of residence. When the study began, the average age of the subjects was about fifteen years, and none of them had schizophrenia. Ten years later, 17 of the high-risk (and only 1 of the low-risk) people were diagnosed with schizophrenia. By 1993, 31 of the high-risk sample were diagnosed with schizophrenia (Parnas et al., 1993). Those who developed schizophrenia were distinguished from the rest of the high-risk sample on a variety of characteristics, including greater adjustment problems in childhood, delays in motor development, and poorer academic performance. Also, the mothers of those who developed schizophrenia had a higher rate of pregnancy complications.

Prospective studies of high-risk children were also conducted in New York City (Erlenmeyer-Kimling et al., 1995; Fish, 1977); Rochester, New York (Sameroff, Seifer, and Barocas, 1983); and Israel (Marcus, Hans, Auerbach, and Auerbach, 1993). All found evidence of abnormalities in social adjustment and in motor and/or cognitive development. Deficits in attention are among the most commonly reported cognitive problems observed in high-risk children (Cornblatt, Obuchowski, Schnur, and O'Brien, 1997; MacCrimmon, Cleghorn, Asarnow, and Steffy, 1980). Fish was the first to study infant offspring of women with schizophrenia, and her landmark study revealed delays in motor and perceptual development. The findings seemed to be consistent; on average, children whose parents suffered from schizophrenia showed more delays in motor development, more academic problems, and more adjustment problems (Cornblatt and Obuchowski, 1997; Fish, 1987; Fish, Marcus, Hans, Auerbach, and Perdue, 1992). Further, these difficulties are most pronounced in the subgroup of high-risk children who manifest schizophrenia in adulthood.

Like all research methods, high-risk studies have some limitations. First, with a few exceptions (Fish, 1977; Sameroff, Seifer, and Barocas, 1983), most of the studies were begun after the subjects had passed through early childhood. There are pragmatic reasons for this: the younger the participants are when the study begins, the longer the researchers have to wait to find out who will succumb to schizophrenia. As a result, we do not have much information on the infancy period in preschizophrenic children. Second,

the subjects of high-risk research are unique, in that they have a biological parent with schizophrenia. Keep in mind that research shows that most patients with schizophrenia do not have a family member with the illness. This raises the question of whether the developmental precursors observed in studies of high-risk children would be apparent in other children who eventually develop schizophrenia. In other words, do preschizophrenic children from families with no mental illness show the same developmental abnormalities we see in the offspring of parents with schizophrenia? Findings based on other research strategies indicate that the answer is "yes."

RETROSPECTIVE AND FOLLOW-BACK STUDIES

Alternatives to the prospective research method are the retrospective and follow-back approaches. In *retrospective studies,* the parents of adult patients are asked to provide information about the patient's childhood development. Numerous studies of this type have been conducted, and the results are consistent. Many parents state that, long before the onset of clinical symptoms, they noticed some unusual behavioral characteristics in their preschizophrenic child: motor delays, emotional instability, and academic problems. Some parents report that they noticed subtle temperamental abnormalities in infancy. These research findings are mirrored in the words of Anne Deveson, the mother of a patient with schizophrenia (Deveson, 1992). In a poignant book documenting her son's personal struggle with mental illness, Deveson describes his life, beginning at birth, to his diagnosis at age nineteen, to his death by suicide at age twenty-five. Her joy at bringing her newborn son home from the hospital was replaced by dismay as she tried to cope with his difficult temperament. Like many other parents, Deveson recalled subtle signs of abnormality in her son, as early as infancy:

> But when we get home, Jonathan cries. He cries during the day, he cries during the night. The only time he isn't crying is when he is feeding. When he is about six months old, Jonathan smiles. The event seems so miraculous, so bathed in light, that I rush out to call the neighbors. At about the same time the pediatrician detects that Jonathan has some physical disability. The muscles on one side of Jonathan's body are weak. He has a weak left leg, a weak left arm,

Photos of Jonathan Deveson at ages sixteen months, five years, and thirteen years. Jonathan was diagnosed with schizophrenia at age nineteen, although very subtle signs of abnormality may have been present even before the full-blown symptoms of the schizophrenia destroyed his life.

and weak muscles in the left side of his neck, so his head flops to one side. I give him daily exercise; after several months his muscles have grown strong and he has put on weight. When he is two, the pediatrician gives him the all-clear (Deveson, 1992, pp. 7–8).

Retrospective reports from parents reveal a gradual increase in adjustment problems as the preschizophrenic child gets older (Neumann and Walker, 1995). The rise becomes especially pronounced in adolescence. As the individual passes through puberty, there is often a marked increase in subtle thought abnormalities and difficulties in social relationships. For this reason, adolescence is considered to be a critical period in the development of schizophrenia. In Deveson's book, she vividly describes her son's decline during young adulthood.

The severity of childhood deficits is strongly associated with the later severity of schizophrenic symptoms. For example, Haas and Sweeney (1992) collected retrospective data and found that patients who had more behavior problems before their first hospital admission had an earlier onset of clinical symptoms and a more chronic illness course. Male patients were more likely than females to have adjustment problems before the onset of clinical symptoms.

But like all research approaches, the retrospective method has limits. The chief question that has been raised about retrospective studies is whether we can be confident that "after-the-fact" reports from parents are accurate. Parents of children who develop serious mental illnesses usually spend a great deal of time trying to figure out "what went wrong." They revisit past events in their minds over and over. Could it be that they are looking so hard for early signs that they imagine them? Perhaps their knowledge that their child has developed a mental illness is biasing their view of the past.

Investigators have used the *follow-back method* to get around this problem. Instead of asking parents, or other informants, to report on the patient's childhood behavior, the investigators go back to medical or school records. Norman Watt and his collaborators did some landmark studies using this approach (Watt, 1978; Watt and Lubensky, 1976). They went back to the elementary and high-school records of people who were diagnosed with schizophrenia as adults. For each patient, the researchers selected a child of the same age and from the same school, but with no history of mental illness, to serve as a comparison subject. The records of children who later suffered from schizophrenia contained more teacher comments about adjustment problems, including social withdrawal and disruptiveness. The preschizophrenic children also had poorer grades. The researchers found that these differences between the preschizophrenic and control children became greater as they entered adolescence. Similar results have been reported from more recent studies of childhood records (Cannon et al., 1997; Jones, 1995). Overall, the findings from follow-back research are highly consistent with the retrospective reports from parents.

But what about the reports from some parents that their preschizophrenic child was noticeably different in infancy? In order to get more direct information about the early development of children who later suffer from schizophrenia, Elaine Walker and her colleagues at Emory University conducted a different kind of follow-back study (Walker and Lewine, 1990). They obtained childhood home movies of individuals who developed schizophrenia, major mood disorder, or no mental illness in adulthood. These included films ranging from the individual's infancy to adolescence. First, examiners rated the children's facial expressions of emotion in each frame of film. (The examiners were not aware of the individual's adult diagnosis.) Comparison of the diagnostic groups revealed that the children who later developed schizophrenia showed less positive and more negative facial expressions of emotion (Walker, Grimes, Davis, and Smith, 1993). This difference was apparent as early as infancy.

Second, specialists in early motor development viewed the films and rated the child's motor functions. Again, the preschizophrenic children differed from their healthy siblings. They showed more delays and abnormalities in motor development during the first two years of life (Walker, Savoie, and Davis, 1994). Among the abnormalities observed were weakness and unusual positioning of the left arm and leg. Note the hyperextension (excessive spreading) of the fingers and unusual posturing of the hands shown in Figure 10–2. Keep in mind that the examiners who rated the films did not know which of the children eventually suffered from a mental illness. The findings cannot be the result of biases on the part of the examiners. Thus, Anne Deveson's description of her son's early motor abnormalities were probably not due to biased recollections. Instead, it appears that abnormalities in early motor development are associated with risk for schizophrenia.

In discussing the precursors of schizophrenia it is important to mention that not all patients follow the same developmental course. The trends we have described above are based on group averages. Some persons who develop schizophrenia in adulthood had no apparent signs of abnormality during childhood. In fact, some were above average in academics and social adjustment. Conversely, some children who showed significant behavior and motor problems grew up to be perfectly healthy adults.

In the future, our knowledge of the precursors of schizophrenia may permit us to identify with a high degreee of accuracy individuals at risk for the disorder. We are not there yet, but this should not be taken as cause for despair. As a case in point, cancer researchers have identified both genetic and environmental factors that are linked with risk for that illness; however, they are far from predicting the onset of cancer (Chakraborty, Little, and Sankaranarayanan, 1998). As in the case with cancer, there are probably multiple subtypes of schizophrenia with multiple causes.

What can we say with confidence about the precursors of schizophrenia? First, it appears that the

Figure 10–2

POSTURAL ABNORMALITIES

Still frames illustrating postural abnormalities in preschizophrenic children show unusual positioning of the hands, as well as hyperextension of the fingers.

early signs of risk fall into several domains of behavior: motor, interpersonal, and cognitive. Second, many preschizophrenic children show the most pronounced adjustment problems when they enter adolescence. Third, the more severe the childhood problems, the earlier the onset and the more severe the illness.

BEHAVIORAL RISK FOR SCHIZOPHRENIA: SCHIZOTYPAL PERSONALITY DISORDER

Research has brought the developmental course of schizophrenia into clearer focus. We now know that many persons who manifest schizophrenia in adulthood showed earlier behavioral signs (Walker, Lewine, and Neumann, 1996). Investigators have begun to use this knowledge to identify individuals for prospective study.

The behavioral signs that often predate the onset of schizophrenia include social withdrawal, unusual ideas, and subtle thought abnormalities (Neumann and Walker, 1995). This combination of behaviors is very similar to the diagnostic criteria for schizotypal personality disorder (SPD). As described in Chapter 9, SPD is a DSM-IV, Axis II, personality disorder that is more common in the biological relatives of people with schizophrenia (Kendler et al., 1995; Raine, Lencz, and Mednick, 1995). So the genetic link between SPD and schizophrenia has been established. Also, research on attentional functions and thought disorder indicates that both adolescent and adult subjects with SPD show deficits similar to those manifested by people with schizophrenia (Asarnow, Goldstein, and Ben-Meir, 1988a, 1988b; Raine, Lencz, and Mednick, 1995).

A substantial proportion of people who eventually develop schizophrenia manifested a syndrome that is equivalent to SPD when they were younger (Tyrka et al., 1995; Walker, Lewine, and Neumann, 1996). Further, SPD can be reliably diagnosed in preadolescents and adolescents (Rawlings and Mac-Farlane, 1994; Weinstein, Diforio, Schiffman, Walker, and Bonsall, 1999). At this date, the risk rate for schizophrenia among youth with SPD is still not known, and this constitutes a gap in our knowledge. Nonetheless, previous research on short-term outcome with young adult SPD participants has shown that the prognosis is poor; although some do show improvement, others manifest persistent signs of personality disorder and a subgroup (25 to 30 percent) develop Axis I disorders, usually in the schizophrenia spectrum (Bernstein et al., 1993; McGlashan, 1986b).

In a recent prospective study, researchers discovered that adolescents with SPD showed some of the physical characteristics of risk that have been observed in patients with schizophrenia (Weinstein, Diforio, Schiffman, Walker, and Bonsall, 1999; Walker, Lewis, Loewy, and Paylo, 1999). The adolescents with SPD were compared to a control group of adolescents who were healthy and a control group of adolescents who had other kinds of personality disorders. First, videotapes of the participants during a clinical interview were scored for the number of movements they made. When compared to both control groups, the youngsters with SPD showed significantly more involuntary movements of the upper limbs, face, and trunk. The researchers also found more abnormalities in the SPD adolescents' fingerprints: specifically, greater differences between their hands in the number of ridges on the fingertips. Earlier in our discussion, we mentioned that fingerprints are formed during prenatal development. The same factors that disrupt the development of fingerprints can also interfere with the development of the nervous system. Along these same lines, the SPD group had more minor physical anomalies—again, a sign of problems during prenatal development. But perhaps most interesting, the adolescents with SPD secreted more of the stress hormone cortisol during the early part of the assessment. These findings suggest two conclusions. One is that SPD, like schizophrenia, may be related to some abnormality in prenatal development. Second, the youngsters with SPD may be more biologically sensitive to stress.

We must await the findings of future research to understand the developmental course for children with SPD. However, we already know that the adolescent period is characterized by significant behavioral changes, and it is the time when the behavioral precursors of schizophrenia are most likely to show up. For these reasons, it is an important period for researchers to study. Certain maturational changes that occur in the brain during adolescence may play some role in triggering the expression of biological vulnerabilities that were, more or less, silent up to that point.

The Biology of Schizophrenia

We have described evidence that both genetic and obstetrical factors are involved in the etiology of schizophrenia. Researchers assume that these factors are doing something to the brain that causes it to malfunction. We do not yet know precisely what is involved in the brain malfunction, but researchers have uncovered some interesting possibilities. Over the past decade, enormous progress has been made in understanding the biology of schizophrenia. Two lines of research have been particularly illuminating. The first has looked at irregularities in neurochemistry, the second at differences in brain structure and function. Both lines of investigation have important consequences for understanding schizophrenia.

THE NEUROCHEMISTRY OF SCHIZOPHRENIA

The idea that there may be a biochemical abnormality in patients with schizophrenia has been around for a long time. Beginning in the 1950s, researchers tried to find a biochemical difference between patients with schizophrenia and normals by testing their blood and urine. But this approach met with little luck. Some early reports of biochemical differences between normals and hospitalized patients with schizophrenia turned out to be erroneous. In hindsight, researchers discovered that the findings were due to differences in the diets of hospitalized and nonhospitalized people, or bad lab technique, or the absence of control groups, or experimenter bias.

In recent years, the strategies have become more sophisticated. Scientists are now searching for abnormalities in specific neurotransmitters and their receptors in the brain. Modern neuroimaging techniques make it possible to examine the activity of neurotransmitters in living patients. For example, with PET scans researchers can identify the locations of specific neurotransmitter receptors and estimate their density (that is, how many there are in a particular area). They can also observe the changes in activation that occur when the individual is injected with a substance that either blocks or turns on certain types of receptors. These and other procedures are being used to test hypotheses about the biochemical basis of schizophrenia.

The longest-standing biochemical hypothesis of schizophrenia is the "dopamine" hypothesis. As illustrated in Figure 10–3, there are four major dopamine

---

Figure 10–3

DOPAMINE PATHWAYS

A coronal section of the brain showing the sites of origin and the targets of the four major dopamine pathways in the brain: (1) the nigrostriatal, from the substantia nigra to the putamen and caudate; (2) the tuberoinfundibular, from the arcuate nucleus of the hypothalamus to the pituitary gland; (3) the mesolimbic, from the ventral tegmental area to many parts of the limbic system; and (4) the mesocortical, from the ventral tegmental area to the prefrontal areas of the neocortex. (Source: Adapted from Kandel, Schwartz, and Jessell, 1991, p. 864.)

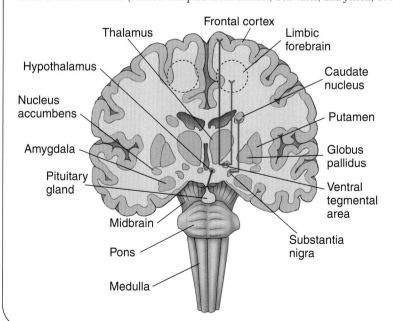

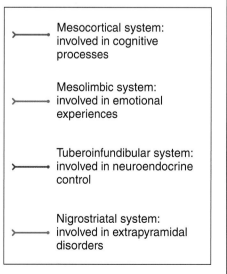

pathways in the brain: the mesolimbic, mesocortical, nigrostriatal, and tuberoinfundibular. The fact that these pathways are so widespread makes it easy to imagine how an abnormality in dopamine could impact many aspects of human behavior.

Several pieces of evidence led researchers to suspect that dopamine was involved in schizophrenia. First, they discovered that all of the drugs used to treat schizophrenia were blocking the activity of dopamine. Researchers found that the effectiveness of the various "antipsychotic" drugs in reducing symptoms was highly related to their effectiveness in blocking dopamine. In other words, the antipsychotic drugs were shown to be dopamine antagonists.

A second line of evidence supporting the dopamine hypothesis concerns the behavioral effects of drugs that increase dopamine activity. Numerous drugs, including amphetamine, L-dopa, and cocaine, are dopamine "agonists." Large doses of any of these drugs can create a psychosis, with symptoms similar to those of acute paranoid schizophrenia. Further, low doses of these drugs can exacerbate the symptoms of schizophrenia: paranoid patients, for example, become increasingly paranoid. It is not surprising that antipsychotic drugs are the best antidotes for amphetamine psychosis (Snyder, 1974a).

L-dopa is also a drug that increases the activity of dopamine in the brain. It has been used for many years to treat the symptoms of Parkinson's disease, which is characterized by stiffness in the arms and legs, and tremors, especially in the hands. In Parkinson's disease, there is a decrease in the release of dopamine by neurons in the nigrostriatal dopamine system—a system that helps coordinate motor activity. When victims of Parkinson's disease are treated with L-dopa, their symptoms are relieved. But some Parkinson's patients develop psychotic symptoms in response to L-dopa. Fortunately, these symptoms usually disappear quickly.

A third source of support for the dopamine hypothesis of schizophrenia is the presence of movement abnormalities in untreated persons with schizophrenia. Many patients with schizophrenia show mild involuntary movements of the face and limbs (Walker, Savoie, and Davis, 1994). As we mentioned, these can be observed as early as infancy in some cases. The type of movement abnormality shown by untreated patients is similar to that associated with excessive dopamine activity. On the other hand, when patients with schizophrenia are treated with certain antipsychotics for a prolonged period of

time, they display motor symptoms very much like those seen in Parkinson's disease: they have stiffness and tremors in their extremities (see Figure 10–4). These motor "side effects" are assumed to be a result of blocking dopamine activity in the brain, particularly in the nigrostriatal system. In the section on treatment, we describe recent advances in antipsychotic medications that have reduced the problem of motor side effects.

The most direct evidence in support of the dopamine hypothesis has come from postmortem and neuroimaging studies. Postmortem examination of the brains of people who had schizophrenia revealed a marked increase in the number of dopamine receptor sites, particularly the "D2" subtype of dopamine receptors. While the precise cause of this increase is not yet known, it does not seem to be the result of drug treatment. Patients who had been drug-free for at least a year before death also showed a greater number of dopamine receptors (Crow, 1980, 1982; Mackay, 1980). Several studies using PET scans of living patients also indicate that there is an increased density of dopamine receptors in the brains of patients with schizophrenia. Nonetheless, several other investigations have not found an excess of dopamine receptors, so further research is needed to clear up this discrepancy (Farde, 1997). If it is established that patients with schizophrenia have excess receptors that are sensitive to dopamine, this would help explain both the symptoms of the illness and their response to drugs that are dopamine antagonists.

As PET scans for measuring neurotransmitter activity have improved, researchers are finding

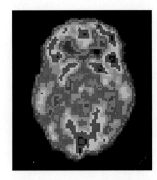 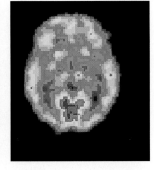

PET scans showing the brain of a nonschizophrenic person *(left)* and the brain of a person with schizophrenia *(right)*. Red indicates greatest metabolic activity. In the patient with schizophrenia, there is less activity in the frontal lobes (near the top of the scan) and greater activity in the basal ganglia and striatum (shown by the red dot near the center of the scan).

Figure 10–4

EVIDENCE FOR THE DOPAMINE HYPOTHESIS

This analysis of the effects of increasing or decreasing the availability of dopamine offers some support for the dopamine hypothesis.

Disorder	Symptom	Drug Treatment	Action	Effect
Amphetamine psychosis	Hallucinations, paranoia	Antipsychotic	Decreases dopamine	Calms
Parkinson's disease	Stiffness and tremors	L-dopa	Increases dopamine	Reduces stiffness and tremors
Schizophrenia	Disordered thought and behavior	Antipsychotic	Decreases dopamine	1. Calms disordered thought and behavior 2. Causes stiffness and tremors

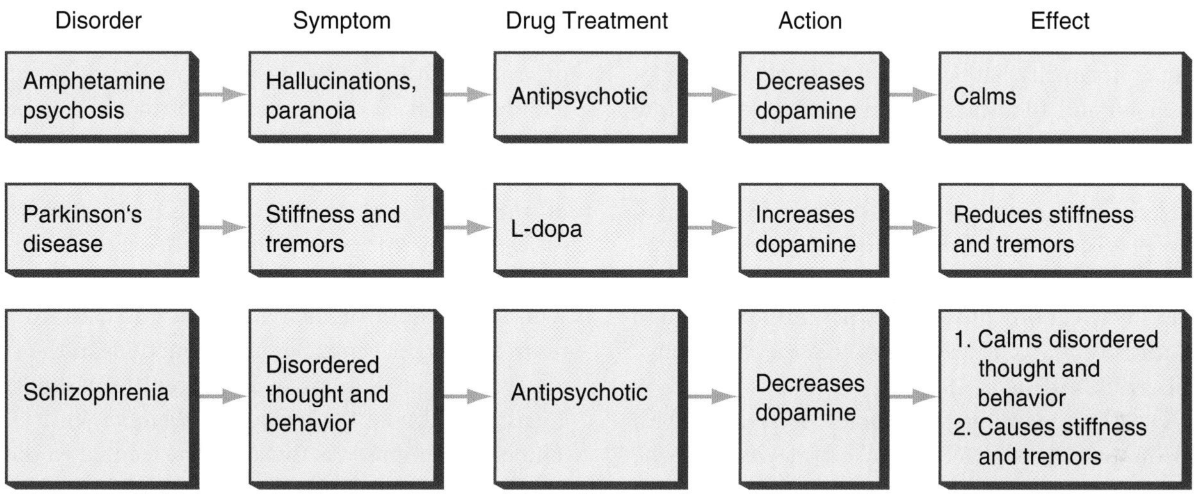

more evidence that dopamine activity is abnormal in schizophrenia. It appears that there is a greater release of dopamine by neurons in the striatum, a subcortical region of the brain, in patients with schizophrenia (Abi-Dargham et al., 1998; Farde, 1997). This was discovered by administering amphetamine to patients, then measuring dopamine activity in the brain with PET scans. Amphetamine is a dopamine agonist, which means it triggers the release of dopamine in the brain. When patients with schizophrenia and normals were given amphetamine, the patients showed more dopamine release. Again, the dopamine hypothesis receives some support!

Although various versions of the dopamine hypothesis have held center stage in biochemical theories of schizophrenia, other neurotransmitters are also plausible candidates. For example, some investigators have found a role for GABA, an inhibitory neurotransmitter. Autopsy studies of the brains of those who had schizophrenia suggested that there might be a decrease in GABA activity (Benes, 1998). A theory implicating glutamate, an excitatory neurotransmitter, originated from observations that phencyclidine (PCP)—(a street drug referred to as "angel dust")—could produce psychotic symptoms in some

people (Tamminga, Holcomb, Gao, and Lahti, 1995; Vollenweider, 1998). PCP acts by blocking certain receptors for glutamate. There is evidence that these same receptors may be abnormal in patients with schizophrenia.

Serotonin has also come under suspicion as a contributor to schizophrenia. While serotonin has been theorized to be involved in depression, there are also theories linking serotonin to psychotic symptoms. Researchers have proposed that there is too much serotonin activity in those diagnosed with schizophrenia (Abi-Dargham, Laruelle, Aghajanian, Charney, and Krystal, 1997; Lewis et al., 1999). Although there has not been consistent evidence that serotonin is involved in schizophrenia (Lewis et al., 1999), studies of newly developed medications for schizophrenia indicated that decreasing serotonin levels may be beneficial (see p. 458).

Our description of the neurochemical theories of schizophrenia has covered only a few of all the possibilities researchers have considered. So which one is true? Keep in mind that we began this chapter with a discussion of the "schizophrenias." There may, in fact, be several causes of the illness. Each of the theories may be correct for a particular subgroup of patients.

BRAIN STRUCTURE IN SCHIZOPHRENIA

In the previous section, we described how neurotransmitters might be involved in schizophrenia. We now turn to the structural aspects of the brain. Are there signs of abnormal brain structure?

The idea that schizophrenia was a result of a brain abnormality has been with us since the time of Kraepelin and Bleuler. Yet, many years passed before there was any solid evidence to support this notion. In the last thirty years, over 300 neuroimaging studies of the brains of patients with schizophrenia have been published. The findings indicate that there are abnormalities in many regions of the brain, and that these involve both the large structural features and the microscopic cellular aspects (Lawrie and Abukmeil, 1998; Videbech, 1997).

The first neuroimaging studies of patients with schizophrenia used CAT scans and showed that the size of the brain ventricles was larger in those with schizophrenia than in normals. Later studies with MRI confirmed these results. As described in Chapter 4, ventricles are cavities in the brain that are filled with cerebrospinal fluid. In people with schizophrenia, the ventricles on the left side of the brain are especially large compared to those on the right side. Enlargement of the ventricles suggests a reduction in brain tissue in the surrounding regions (Bogerts, 1993; Brown et al., 1986). But it is important to mention that enlarged ventricles have also been observed in other disorders, including Alzheimer's disease and Huntington's disease. So, such an enlargement is not unique to schizophrenia, and certainly it is not the cause of the illness. Nonetheless, the presence of enlarged ventricles is a fairly convincing sign of some sort of brain abnormality.

As the results of neuroimaging studies of schizophrenia have accumulated, we have seen that there are reductions in the size of many brain regions (Lawrie et al., 1999). These include the frontal lobes, temporal lobes, amygdala, and hippocampus (Hirayasu et al., 1998; Nelson, Saykin, Flashman, and Riordan, 1998). Of course, some have raised the question of whether these brain abnormalities are present before the onset of the illness, or whether they arise after the clinical symptoms begin. While some have suggested that the brain abnormalities are a consequence of drug treatment, recent findings have indicated that these abnormalities are present before patients with schizophrenia receive any treatment (Hirayasu et al., 1998), although they may get worse over time (Jacobsen et al., 1998). Further, adult patients who show greater abnormalities of the brain on MRI scans also had more behavioral abnormalities prior to the onset of their illness, including problems in early childhood (Alaghband-Rad et al., 1997; Neumann and Walker, 1995). Thus, even though the brain abnormalities were not directly measured until the patients were adults, the abnormalities may have been present at birth and may have subtly influenced their behavior at an early age.

But what is causing the brain abnormalities? Part of the answer to this question comes from the NIMH study of discordant twins. The researchers found that when they compared the brain scans of ill twins with those of their identical co-twins, the ill twins had larger ventricles and reductions in the size of several brain regions (see Figure 10-5; Suddath, Christison, Torrey, Casanova, and Weinberger, 1990). The hippocampus was the area that seemed to differ most in size between the healthy and ill twins. What this suggests is that the ill twins sustained brain damage. The most plausible explanation is that the damage occurred before birth. There are two reasons for this conclusion. First, the ill twins did not have a history of serious head injury after birth. Second, the kinds of abnormalities seen in their brains are often produced by prenatal complications. You may recall from our discussion in Chapter 4 that the hippocampus is a brain structure that is highly sensitive to prenatal damage.

On the other hand, we cannot attribute the brain abnormalities in schizophrenia solely to prenatal factors. When brain scans of the biological relatives of patients with schizophrenia are compared to those of people with no family history of schizophrenia, the relatives are more likely to show abnormalities, including reduced size of the hippocampus, amygdala, and thalamus (Lawrie et al., 1999). The abnormalities in healthy relatives are not as pronounced as those in the patients, but they indicate that genetic factors are probably contributing to the structural abnormalities seen in the brains of the patients. Again, it is plausible that there is an inherited predisposition that makes some fetuses more sensitive to brain abnormalities from obstetrical complications.

The kinds of brain abnormalities that are observed with neuroimaging are usually visible to the human eye. But abnormalities in the structure of neurons (which are too small to see without some level of magnification) also can produce significant

Figure 10—5

BRAIN ABNORMALITIES AND SCHIZOPHRENIA

MRIs of the brains of nonschizophrenic and schizophrenic twins have revealed that the ventricles (cavities filled with fluid) of patients with schizophrenia (indicated in the right MRI) are larger than those of individuals who do not have schizophrenia (indicated in the left MRI).

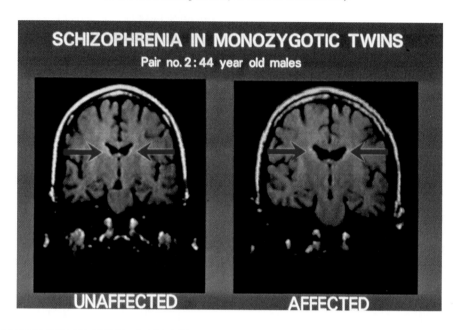

problems with thought and behavior. In fact, molecular studies have revealed that the interconnections among neurons in the brains of patients with schizophrenia are abnormal, especially in the cortex and hippocampus of these patients (Arnold, Ruscheinsky, and Han, 1997; Benes, 1998; Benes, Kwok, Vincent, and Todtenkopf, 1998).

BRAIN FUNCTION IN SCHIZOPHRENIA

Up to this point we have discussed the structure of the brains of patients with schizophrenia. We will now turn briefly to the question of function. In order to examine functional brain differences, researchers have used EEG's (electroencephalograms), PET scans, fMRI (functional magnetic resonance imaging) and, more recently, SPECT (single photon emission computerized tomography) scans. All of these procedures rely on electrical and/or magnetic signals from the brain to estimate the activity (energy utilization) of various brain regions. One finding that has shown up fairly consistently in these studies is

that patients with schizophrenia show less activation in the frontal lobes when they are performing cognitive tasks (Carter and Neufeld, 1998; Fletcher et al., 1998; Kindermann, Karimi, Symonds, Brown, and Jeste, 1997; Morrison-Stewart, Williamson, Corning, Kutcher, and Merskey, 1991; Volz et al., 1997; Weinberger, Berman, and Zec, 1986). When asked to identify odors, patients show reduced activity in the temporal and frontal regions (Malaspina et al., 1998).

Let us now return to the same question we asked about the structural abnormalities: When do the functional abnormalities first arise and what causes them? Given that a reduction in brain activation is present in patients who have not received any treatment, we can at least rule out medication as the cause. But we cannot yet rule out the possibility that the experience of having schizophrenia causes abnormalities in brain activity.

Is any one of the many abnormalities that have been found in the brains of patients the key factor that produces schizophrenia? This does not seem likely, since all of the abnormalities that have been observed in the brains of patients with schizophrenia are also present in certain other disorders. This has led many investigators to conclude that the key factor must be some abnormality in the *connections* among various regions of the brain. In other words, it may be that the brain abnormalities that are found with neuroimaging are general indicators of brain dysfunction. But the critical feature that causes schizophrenia may be the disruption that is produced in a specific brain circuit. For example, one possibility is a disruption in the limbic circuit. In Chapter 4, we described the important role this circuit plays in the integration of emotion and cognition. If neuronal intercommunication is impaired in one or more segments of this circuit, psychotic symptoms might arise. Perhaps this impairment in intercommunication occurs when a structural brain abnormality is combined with a neurochemical abnormality. This is purely speculative at this point. We are still a long way from identifying a unique problem in the brains of patients with schizophrenia. Nonetheless, psychologists and researchers from other disciplines are continuing to make rapid progress in research on brain function. There is reason to be optimistic about our potential for solving the mystery of brain dysfunction in schizophrenia.

Social Influences

By now you have probably been persuaded by the evidence that schizophrenia has a biological basis. Does this mean that interpersonal experiences have no relevance? The answer is that they certainly do have an influence. As is the case with most illnesses, the course of schizophrenia is influenced by the individual's psychosocial environment. Psychosocial influences extend from the level of the patient's immediate family to the larger social context in which the patient lives. Thus, as implied by the diathesis-stress model, environmental factors can serve to buffer the person from developing schizophrenia, or they can trigger the expression of symptoms. At the same time, the patient also has an effect on his or her social context, so the relation is reciprocal.

SCHIZOPHRENIA AND THE FAMILY

There are certain characteristics of interpersonal communication that seem to bear a relationship to the course of schizophrenia. These characteristics are referred to as ***expressed emotion,*** and they include measures of cynical, hostile comments toward the

The 1996 film *Shine* tells the story of David Helfgott (played by Geoffrey Rush), who may have suffered from schizophrenia brought on through an inherited vulnerability to mental disorder and the stress of a critical, domineering father who pressured him to succeed as a concert pianist.

patient and marked emotional overinvolvement by a relative or other care provider. When criticism and hostility are directed at a child who has a diathesis to develop schizophrenia, the person is more likely to develop the spectrum of symptoms associated with schizophrenia (Rodnick, Goldstein, Lewis, and Doane, 1984). When patients with schizophrenia return home after hospitalization for a schizophrenic episode and are then exposed to environments that are high in expressed emotion, they are more likely to have a relapse and to require rehospitalization (Butzlaff and Hooley, 1998; Goldstein, Strachan, and Wynne, 1994; Hooley, 1998; Miklowitz, 1994; Snyder et al., 1995). This holds for both family environments and residental care homes. Correspondingly, living in an environment where expressed emotion is low may buffer patients and contribute to their remission (Falloon, 1988). It is important, however, to note that schizophrenia is not the only mental disorder that is affected by expressed emotion; mood disorders and eating disorders are also worsened in such environments (Butzlaff and Hooley, 1998).

Of course, the link between family members' communications and the patient's illness is not a one-way street. Expressed emotion in family members is also influenced *by* the patient's illness (Scazufca and Kuipers, 1998). When family members are experiencing a high level of caregiver burden, they show higher levels of expressed emotion. Similarly, when the patient's level of functioning declines, the rate of expressed emotion increases. There is no doubt that having a family member who is suffering from a serious and debilitating illness is a stressor (Mueser, Valentiner, and Agresta, 1998). It is not surprising that fluctuations in the patient's symptoms can change the mood and behavior of family members.

The fact that the communication style of family members can affect the symptoms of schizophrenia has significant implications. The findings on expressed emotion point to the importance of providing patients with stable, supportive environments for rehabilitation. For example, the situation for both families and patients would be improved if there were safe and readily accessible daytime programs that offered high-quality treatment and, at the same time, reduced the caregivers' burden.

SCHIZOPHRENIA AND SOCIAL CLASS

As mentioned above, one of the most amazing things about schizophrenia is the fact that it occurs in every human culture and in all socioeconomic classes. It is not unique to any particular subgroup. But, there is a relation between social class and schizophrenia, and this is due to reciprocal influences between the larger social context and the patient with schizophrenia.

Particularly in large urban areas, rates of mental disturbance, and especially of schizophrenia, are inversely associated with social class: the lower the social class, the higher the rate of schizophrenia (see Figure 10–6). In particular, in the United States and the European countries, the highest rates of schizophrenia occur in urban areas and among those with the lowest socioeconomic status (Cohen, 1993; Freeman, 1994; Hollingshead and Redlich, 1958; Saugstad, 1989; Srole, Langner, Michael, Opler, and Rennie, 1962).

Teasing out the relationship between social class and schizophrenia is no simple matter. Do the poverty and stress associated with lower social class cause schizophrenia? Or do people who are predisposed to schizophrenia drift into the lower social classes, or at least fail to rise from them? The notion that adversity and stress cause schizophrenia is termed the *social causation hypothesis,* while the view that constitutionally predisposed persons develop schizophrenia and then drift down into lower social classes is called the *social drift hypothesis.* Which is true?

One logical way to resolve the question would be to examine the occupational status of the fathers of patients with schizophrenia. If patients' fathers

Figure 10–6

THE PREVALENCE OF SCHIZOPHRENIA IN A CITY

In this map of Chicago in 1934, the center zone is the business and amusement section, which is uninhabited, except for transients and vagabonds. Surrounding the center, there is a slum area, largely made up of unskilled workers of low socioeconomic status, and having the highest rate of schizophrenia. The next circle is occupied by skilled workers and has a lower rate of schizophrenia than the slum. The next zone is inhabited by middle-class and upper-middle-class people. The last circle is populated by upper-middle-class commuters and shows the lowest rate of schizophrenia. (Source: Gleitman, 1991, p. 762, based on data from Faris and Dunham, 1939)

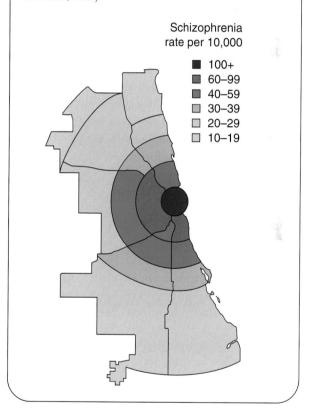

Schizophrenia rate per 10,000

- ■ 100+
- ■ 60–99
- ■ 40–59
- ▨ 30–39
- □ 20–29
- □ 10–19

were at the lowest occupational rung, it would be likely that the patient was born into the lower social class, and that class therefore preceded psychosis. Such a finding would strengthen the view that the stress associated with low social class contributes to schizophrenia. If, on the other hand, patients' fathers had higher occupational status, it would be likely that the patients were not born into the lower social class, and that the clinical symptoms therefore preceded falling into the lower social social class. This would support the view that patients with schizophrenia drift into the lower class. When studies of this kind are conducted, the results generally provide greater support for the social drift hypotheses. On average, patients achieve lower socioeconomic status than their parents (Jones et al., 1993). The downward drift starts to become apparent before the onset of clinical symptoms. On a personal level, this can be a very disheartening experience for patients and their families. Some patients with schizophrenia, like Glenn, express concerns about their capacity for success:

> No one in my family ever said they thought I was a failure. Nobody told me they were worried that I would always be dependent on them. But I knew they thought about this, . . . and so did I. I couldn't help comparing myself to other people in my family. Everyone in my family is a college graduate except me. My brother and sister graduated from college, and they got good jobs. My sister is married to a guy who makes a lot of money, and they have a kid. I didn't go to college, and none of my jobs has lasted more than three months, except the one with my uncle—that lasted seven months.

In one large-scale study, Bruce Dohrenwend and his colleagues examined both the social drift and social causation effects on schizophrenia (Dohrenwend et al., 1992). They conducted a study of schizophrenia in Israel, a country into which people have immigrated for reasons other than social class and which keeps good birth, death, and psychiatric records. Those who immigrated to Israel shortly after it was founded in 1948 were mainly from Europe, had gone to Israel to flee persecution, and were more heavily represented in the higher social classes. Those who immigrated from North African and Middle Eastern countries after 1948 were more likely to be in the lower classes and were more likely to have drifted into them for purely economic reasons rather than for psychiatric reasons. At the same time, lower-class Israelis were subject to a good deal of prejudice from upper-class Israelis, most of whom had arrived from European countries. The social causation hypothesis would predict vast differences between the social classes in the rate of schizophrenia, promoted wholly by the stresses that are created by prejudice. The social selection view, however, would predict fewer differences, because the differences in social class would be produced by economic and educational differences rather than by prejudice.

The researchers found no increase in schizophrenia among people from low-income, ethnic minority families. The rate of schizophrenia was actually higher among Israelis who had a European background, that is, among those in the less-deprived social class. This is more consistent with the social drift theory than the social causation theory. By contrast, the rates for major depression were much higher in the lower classes, especially among women, supporting the view that social causation plays a greater role in depression.

Although the research findings are most consistent with the social drift hypothesis, this does not mean that poverty has no implications for schizophrenia. Although it may not produce an increase in the rate of schizophrenia, there is every reason to believe that it influences the course of the disorder. Access to medication, for example, is influenced by finances. The most recently developed and most effective drugs for schizophrenia are also the most expensive. In some states in the United States, Medicare and Medicaid have refused to reimburse for the more costly medications. This has resulted in lawsuits by patients and their families. In the meantime, unless patients have very good health insurance or financial support from their families, they may be deprived of the best treatment for their illness. But lack of money is not the only issue. Poverty also brings about a host of stressors in daily living that are

People may drift into the lower classes, and sometimes may end up homeless and on the streets, as a result of their schizophrenia, which negatively affects their ability to earn a living.

likely to worsen the illness. We will discuss the general effects of stress on schizophrenia below.

SCHIZOPHRENIA AND CULTURE

The fact that the prevalence of schizophrenia worldwide is about the same, around 1 percent, does not mean that cultural factors have no bearing on schizophrenia. It appears that culture can influence both the clinical expression and the course of the illness.

Over more than two decades, the World Health Organization has been conducting cross-cultural epidemiological studies of a variety of disorders, including schizophrenia. Its most recent collaborative study examined the determinants of severe mental disorders in ten countries. Well over thirteen hundred patients were examined, the majority of whom came from urban areas and from socioeconomic circumstances that are best described as average. And while the study confirmed the ubiquitous nature of schizophrenia and its consistency across cultures, it provided quite a surprise with regard to outcome. Patients from developing nations fared far better than did those from developed countries. For example, the symptoms of 63 percent of the participants in developing countries remitted over the course of the two-year follow-up, while those of only 37 percent remitted in developed nations. Thirty-eight percent of those in developing nations were wholly symptom-free during much of the course of the follow-up, while only 22 percent of those in developed countries were symptom-free. Finally, 38 percent of those from developed countries fall into the category termed "worst possible outcome," while only 22 percent of those from developing nations were in that category (Jablensky et al., 1992; Sartorius et al., 1986).

It is not clear why there are cross-cultural differences in the clinical course of schizophrenia. The explanation for the better outcome of patients in developing countries may lay in the way families respond to the illness. A recent comparison of patients with schizophrenia in the United States and Italy revealed that those in Italy expressed much greater satisfaction with their quality of life (Warner, de-Girolamo, Bologna, Fioritti, and Rosini, 1998). The Italian patients were also more likely to be employed and to be living with their family of origin or a spouse. These cultural differences in the patients' daily life seem to make a big difference in their outlook. Of course, these findings may not be unique to schizophrenia; it is possible that persons suffering from other kinds of illnesses also fare better in Italy.

Cultural factors also have an impact on the expression of psychotic symptoms (Carter and Neufeld, 1998; Kirmayer and Corin, 1998). For example, the content of patients' delusions and hallucinations has a cultural flavor. In predominantly Christian societies, religious delusions often involve concerns about the devil or the belief that one is Christ or the Virgin Mary. Delusions in Islamic cultures are more likely to reflect Islamic religious figures and symbols. Similarly, technological aspects of the culture have an impact on the content of delusions. Consider these two descriptions of somatic delusions:

A young man from New York hospitalized for schizophrenia: The location of my first apartment had something to do with the problems I'm having now. It was right next to a factory where they were assembling computers. They worked all night there. All of us who lived in that building were convenient guinea pigs for their experiments. They wanted to know whether the microchips could control a human body. They put them in our brain stems. We kept our identities but no longer had control of our actions. That is why my hands and feet often feel numb, and they move in strange ways. My migraine headaches are caused by scars from the brain surgery.

A young man from a rural village outside Calcutta, India: Our family was known for making bread and we shared it with others in the village. It gave us a power over the others. I became the scapegoat for their jealousy. A spell was cast on my food, and it caused my internal organs to be diseased. Since that time, I have always felt the burning in my stomach and my head. It is their way of making sure I will not forget them, even though I left my parents' house.

THE STRESSES OF LIVING

In the past, some theorists believed that schizophrenia could be caused by a stressful environment. We now know that stressful experiences alone cannot account for schizophrenia. There is no consistent evidence that patients with schizophrenia have experienced more stressful life events than persons who do not suffer from the illness (Norman and Malla, 1993a, 1993b). Nonetheless, numerous studies have shown that patients with schizophrenia are more likely to relapse following exposure to stressful events (Das, Kulhara, and Verma, 1997; Dohrenwend et al., 1998; Doering et al., 1998; Hultman, Wieselgren, and Oehman, 1997; Norman and Malla, 1993b; Ventura, Nuechterlein, Lukoff, and Hardesty, 1989). Yet, patients are not experiencing a level of stress that is above that experienced by healthy persons. It is simply that the stressors of life have a greater impact on persons with schizophrenia. When researchers study the effects of stress, they try to focus on events that are outside the control of the individual, such as the death of a loved one or unavoidable accidents. This is important, because mental illness alone is stressful *and* because mental illness can result in stressors such as loss of income or relationship problems. If researchers want to understand the effects of stress on illness, as opposed to the effects of the illness on stress, they must focus on independent stressful events.

The results of research on the effects of stress on schizophrenia fit very well with the diathesis-stress model of psychopathology. An individual who does not have a constitutional vulnerability to schizophrenia is unlikely to succumb to it no matter how much adversity he encounters in life. But someone who enters the world with a constitutional vulnerability may respond to the everyday hassles of life with a psychotic episode. Some patients with schizophrenia, like Glenn, are convinced that stress is linked with their symptoms.

> Looking back at it now, I think I see what happened to me. Losing the job with my uncle's company was just much more than I could take. It made me see how my life could just fall apart in a matter of days. I couldn't stop thinking about it. But the more I thought about it the worse I felt, and the more my whole psyche fell apart. Stress gets to me. Maybe if my uncle didn't fire me I would never have had a mental breakdown. My mother told me this isn't true. She doesn't want me to blame my uncle. She could be right.

But demonstrating that relapses are often preceded by stress still leaves us with unanswered questions. What, if anything, is stress doing at the biological level to worsen the patient's symptoms? In Chapter 4, we described some of the biological consequences of stress exposure. An increase in cortisol secretion is one of the chief consequences in primates. Longitudinal studies of patients with schizophrenia have shown that increases in cortisol release precede increases in symptom severity (Franzen, 1971; Sachar, Kanter, Buie, Engle, and Mehlman, 1970). Other research has revealed that cortisol secretion can raise dopamine activity. This may be the biological basis of the link between stress and psychotic symptoms (Walker and Diforio, 1997). The heightened cortisol that follows stress may worsen symptoms by augmenting dopamine activity.

Treatment of Schizophrenia

In our discussion up to this point, we have mentioned several factors that can predict the course of schizophrenia. We now turn to a discussion of various treatments for schizophrenia. The treatment of this devastating illness typically involves medication, and some form of therapy and/or rehabilitation. It is fortunate that all approaches used to treat schizophrenia today are more effective than ever before. The new drugs have fewer side effects, and the psychological interventions target specific impairments.

Occasionally, people suffering from schizophrenia come for treatment on their own. But this is not common, because the illness is associated with impairments in judgment and insight (Smith, Hull, and Santos, 1998). As we mentioned above, many patients deny their symptoms and insist they are not mentally ill. As a result, most receive their first treatment at the urging of friends or family members who are worried about the person's well-being. And too often they are brought to emergency rooms by the police because their symptoms are disturbing to others. This was the case for Glenn. From his vivid description of his arrest at the mall, it is easy to imagine what a terrifying experience it must have been.

Drug Therapy

Until the mid-1950s, treatment of schizophrenia was primarily custodial. Patients were hospitalized for long periods of time in institutions that were sometimes boring and hopeless. Often their disorder and the hospital environment interacted to bring about behavior that required physical restraint. In 1952, however, a lucky accident changed this bleak situation, and led to a drug treatment that revolutionized the treatment of schizophrenia.

While synthesizing new drugs called antihistamines that benefit asthmatics and those with allergies, researchers noticed the strong calming effects of these drugs. In fact, one of the drugs, promethazine, was so tranquilizing that the French surgeon Henri Laborit gave it to his patients as a prelude to anesthesia. Using a close relative of promethazine with even

Until chlorpromazine was used to treat patients with schizophrenia, they generally spent their lives in back wards of psychiatric hospitals, as shown here.

stronger sedative effects, French psychiatrists Jean Delay and Pierre Deniker treated mentally disordered patients with varying results. Those who improved had a common diagnosis: schizophrenia. The drug they took was chlorpromazine, which revolutionized the treatment of schizophrenia. Chlorpromazine and the other antipsychotic drugs that followed it made a tremendous difference in the lives of the mentally ill. These drugs have been so successful that the average hospital stay for patients with schizophrenia has declined to fewer than thirteen days, when formerly it was months, years, even a lifetime.

Since the introduction of antipsychotic drugs, the number of psychiatric inpatients has decreased dramatically. In 1955, there were about 560,000 patients in American psychiatric hospitals. One out of every two hospital beds was devoted to psychiatric care. It was then estimated that by 1971, 750,000 beds would be required to care for the growing psychiatric population. In fact, there were only 308,000 patients in psychiatric hospitals in 1971, less than half the projected estimate, and about 40 percent fewer than were hospitalized in 1955. By 1986, that number had declined further to 161,000 patients, of whom fewer than half were diagnosed with schizophrenia. Of course, by 1986 there had been a major shift in the administration of psychiatric service. More than 1.4 million clients (more than 300,000 of whom were diagnosed with

schizophrenia) were being seen as outpatients, and an additional 133,000 (roughly half of whom had schizophrenia) were being treated in the community (Rosenstein, Milazzo-Sayre, and Manderscheid, 1990). The emphasis on community-based treatment has continued into the 1990s. In Chapter 15, we will examine the pros and cons of the trend away from hospital care. But regardless of your opinion on this, there is no doubt that the advent of antipsychotic medication has made community living possible for many individuals with severe mental illnesses.

THE EARLY ANTIPSYCHOTICS

Chlorpromazine and haloperidol, both of which are neuroleptics, were among the first available and the most commonly used antipsychotics. Their most striking effect is the degree to which they "tranquilize," make peaceful, even sedate. Could it be that these antipsychotics are no different from barbiturates, whose sedative action produces no greater improvements for schizophrenia than placebos? Some evidence suggests that this is not the case. Beyond their sedative effects and even beyond their impact on anxiety, the antipsychotic drugs seem to have specific ameliorating effects on thought disorders and hallucinations. Subjective emotional experiences, such as guilt and depression, however, sometimes continue unabated, despite a course of drug treatment.

The chief mode of action of these drugs is in binding to dopamine receptors, thereby preventing dopamine itself from binding to those receptors. It is estimated that an average dose of any of the "standard" neuroleptics will block about 70 percent of the D2 subtype of dopamine receptors in the patient's brain. Once the dopamine is blocked, the positive symptoms of schizophrenia usually subside, resulting in marked cognitive and behavioral improvement. But chlorpromazine and haloperidol are not as effective in treating the negative symptoms of schizophrenia.

Besides their beneficial effects, the early antipsychotic drugs also have a variety of unpleasant side effects that often lead patients to discontinue using them. Side effects of chlorpromazine (Thorazine), for example, include dryness of mouth and throat, drowsiness, visual disturbances, weight gain or loss, menstrual disturbances, constipation, and depression. For most patients, these are relatively minor problems, but they are sometimes annoying enough to make the patients discontinue medication against the advice of their doctor.

There are two kinds of side effects that are more than just annoying, however. Chlorpromazine produces extrapyramidal or Parkinson-like effects, which appear to arise because, as we have seen, antipsychotic medications affect the dopamine receptors, which are in turn implicated in Parkinson's disease. (These drugs do not cause Parkinson's disease, but they do induce analogous symptoms.) The motor symptoms include stiffness of muscles and difficulty in moving; reduced flexibility of facial muscles, which results in a glum look, as well as an inability to smile; tremors in the extremities as well as spasms of limbs and body; and *akathisia*—a peculiar "itchiness" in the muscles that results in an inability to sit still and an urge to pace the halls continuously and energetically (Snyder, 1974b). Other drugs are often prescribed to help control these side effects.

An even more serious side effect of chlorpromazine is a movement disorder called **tardive dyskinesia**. Its symptoms consist of sucking, lip-smacking, and tongue movements that seem like fly-catching. Tardive dyskinesia is not always reversible. Conservatively, it affects 24 percent of patients with schizophrenia after seven years of cumulative neuroleptic exposure (Jeste and Caligiuri, 1993; Wegner, Catalano, Gibralter, and Kane, 1985). The prevalence and severity of tardive dyskinesia increases with age. And there may well be a relationship between the severity of a person's negative symptoms of schizophrenia and the risk of developing tardive dyskinesia (Barnes and Braude, 1985).

THE NEW "ATYPICAL" ANTIPSYCHOTICS

Research on medications for the treatment of psychotic disorders did not stop in the 1950s. Over the past two decades, progress in the development of new antipsychotic drugs has been especially rapid. In 1990, clozapine, the first "atypical" antipsychotic, was introduced. It is more effective than the previous antipsychotics in successfully treating both the positive and the negative symptoms of schizophrenia (Breslin, 1992). Clozapine was reported to reduce symptoms where other neuroleptics had failed. And, compared to the "standard neuroleptics," it is much less likely to produce either extrapyramidal side effects or tardive dyskinesia. Indeed, clozapine would have become the treatment of choice for schizophrenia were it not for the fact that it sometimes produces a condition called agranulocytosis, a deficiency in white blood cells, which can lead to infections, severe fever, and even death. Because such a condition can ultimately be toxic, clozapine use must be monitored very carefully, which contributes greatly to its cost (Kane and Marder, 1993).

The introduction of clozapine was followed rapidly by several other new drugs. Risperidone was approved by the FDA in 1994. Olanzapine became available for clinical use in 1996, followed by sertindole and quetiapine. All of these drugs promised to offer a significant reduction in antipsychotic symptoms, without the motor side effects of conventional antipsychotics (see Table 10–3).

Why do the newer antipsychotics have fewer motor side effects? No one knows for sure. But it has been shown that the newer drugs have different neurochemical effects. First of all, compared to first-generation antipsychotics, standard doses of the "atypicals" block fewer dopamine D2 receptors, about 40 to 50 percent. They also tend to block certain subtypes of serotonin receptors at rates as high as 70 to 80 percent—an effect not observed with the older drugs. This pattern of neurotransmitter effects is assumed to be the explanation for the reduction in tardive dyskinesia and other side effects.

Clinical psychologists and psychiatrists are often amazed at the changes they observe in patients who were treated with standard antipsychotic drugs for many years, then switched to a newer atypical drug. Some patients appear to come out of a fog, as if all of a sudden they can see things clearly that had been confusing to them. The unfortunate aspect of this is that some patients become depressed. This is usually because their heightened insight makes it possible for them to see how the illness has devastated their life. But most chronic patients with schizophrenia who receive an atypical antipsychotic for the first time benefit greatly. A *New York Times* article describes the experiences of Mr. Ken Steele. He had suffered from schizophrenia since the age of fourteen, and had been treated with chlorpromazine and other typical drugs until he was fifty years of age.

> He remembers the hospital he was in when Apollo 11 landed on the moon, when the Watergate hearings began, when Diana Spencer married Prince Charles, when the space shuttle exploded.
>
> Mr. Steele is now trying to make up for the years that disappeared. His recovery speaks to his per-

TABLE 10–3

PHARMACOLOGICAL TREATMENTS OF SCHIZOPHRENIA

	Conventional Typical Antipsychotics[*]	Atypical Antipsychotics[†]	Antipsychotics and Lithium or Anticonvulsants[‡]	Antipsychotics and Antidepressants
Improvement	50–60% at least moderately improved	about 50–60% of patients who do not respond to conventional antipsychotics are at least moderately improved	moderate improvement for subpopulation of aggressive, agitated patients	significant improvement for patients with both psychotic and depressive symptoms
Relapse[§]	high	high	high	high
Side Effects	severe	moderate	moderate to severe	moderate to severe
Cost	moderately expensive	expensive	expensive	expensive
Time Scale[‖]	months	months	months	months
Overall	**good**	**good**	**useful**	**good**

[*] Typical antipsychotics are chlorpromazine and haloperidol.

[†] Atypical antipsychotics are clozapine, olanzapine, risperidone, sertindole, and quetiapine.

[‡] Anticonvulsants are carbamazepine and valproic acid

[§] Relapse after discontinuation of treatment.

[‖] Time to achieve maximal effect.

SOURCE: Based on Buchanan, 1995; Dixon, Lehman, and Levine, 1995; revised with Buckley, 1997; Carpenter and Buchanan, 1994; Lam, Peters, Sladen-Dew, and Altman, 1998; Pickar, 1995; Sheitman, Kinon, Ridgway, and Liberman, 1998; Stip, 2000; Tollefson, Sanger, Lu, and Thieme, 1998; Wahlbeck, Cheine, Essali, and Adams, 1999.

sonal strength and determination to get well, but it also reflects the benefits of a new generation of antipsychotic drugs, which for many patients control psychotic symptoms without the disabling side effects of older medications, allowing a growing number of people to resume normal lives.

In 1995, Mr. Steele, with the support of Dr. Rita Seiden, a psychotherapist and executive director of the Park Slope Center for Mental Health in Brooklyn, began taking Risperdal [risperidone], which came on the market in 1994. Seven months after Mr. Steele started the medication, the voices, which had tormented him ceaselessly, stopped.

And when, for the first time in three decades, he found himself able to concentrate and to focus his energies, he realized that though he did not have even a high school diploma, his experience put him in an unusual position to educate people about his illness. And he decided to devote his efforts to helping others who suffer similarly.

Mr. Steele is now vice chairman of the Mental Health Association in New York State and chairman of the organization's governmental affairs committee. He was consulted recently by the State Attorney Gen-

eral's office which, in the wake of Mr. Goldstein's arrest [Goldstein is a man with schizophrenia who pushed a young woman onto subway tracks and to her death], has proposed legislation that would allow closer monitoring of some mentally ill people.

Mr. Steele is the publisher of New York City Voices, a newspaper about mental health issues. He frequently gives lectures to psychiatric residents about schizophrenia. And because he believes that isolation is one of the worst consequences of mental illness, he founded Awakenings, a support group where those with schizophrenia, depression, or manic-depression can come weekly to share their experiences and help one another survive.

Perhaps most significantly, Mr. Steele, who lives on a monthly Social Security disability check of $587, has been able to shape for himself an independent life, with a state-subsidized apartment that doubles as meeting hall and drop-in center, a coffee table covered with knickknacks and his cat, Diva, who rubs against his legs when he comes home.

He lives with the physical legacy of the medicines he has taken and the years he spent in hospitals and halfway houses. He is overweight, a frequent side

Treatment with Risperdal, a new generation of antipsychotic drug, has enabled Ken Steele to work and live on his own.

effect of antipsychotic drugs, and suffers from diabetes and emphysema. But after years of coexisting with roommates, he is for the first time living alone—and enjoying it.

"I have a home today," Mr. Steele said. "I never had a home in my life. I feel like a teen-ager just growing up. I have this incredible appetite to do as much as I can and to grow as much as I can." (*New York Times,* January 30, 1999)

Despite their differences, there are also some similarities in the effects of standard and atypical antipsychotics. In controlled studies of animals, all of the antipsychotics have the same general effects on behavior. For example, they tend to reduce locomotion and block the activating effects of amphetamine. The usefulness of medication in the treatment of schizophrenia also extends beyond the short-term reduction of symptoms. Patients treated with antipsychotics are much less likely to relapse (Wyatt and Henter, 1998). While stress, poor premorbid functioning, and being male are among the indicators that tend to be associated with relapse, more than any of these, the patient's adherence to a medication schedule determines the clinical course of schizophrenia. After the first episode of schizophrenia, those who follow through with taking their medication have a much better chance of avoiding another episode. In addition, the sooner they begin to take medication, the better their long-term prog-

nosis. This finding has puzzled researchers. It appears that the longer the duration of untreated psychotic symptoms, the more severe the illness becomes. This may indicate that the medication halts some biological process in the brain that can lead to further problems. Whatever the case, the long-term benefits of antipsychotic drugs are becoming more apparent.

THE REVOLVING DOOR PHENOMENON

The widespread use of psychotropic drugs promised a virtual revolution in the treatment of schizophrenia. Even if the disorder could not be cured, it seemed certain that it could be contained. No longer would thousands spend their lives in back wards. No longer would families and society be deprived of their contribution. And no longer would massive economic resources be wasted on custodial care. But the pharmaceutical revolution has had limitations. While the hospital population of patients with schizophrenia has declined radically since 1955, the readmission rates for those with schizophrenia have soared. In 1972, for example, 72 percent of the people with schizophrenia admitted to hospitals had been there before (Taube, 1976). Subsequent studies have also found that over 70 percent of patients relapse within two to five years of discharge (Brett, Kirkby, Hay, Mowry, and Jones, 1998; Hogarty et al., 1986).

One factor that probably contributes to rehospitalization in the United States is that about 70 to 90 percent of adults with schizophrenia are unemployed (Anthony, Cohen, and Danley; 1988; Priebe, Warner, Hubschmid, and Eckle, 1998; Warner, deGirolamo, Bologna, Fioritti, and Rosini, 1998). This is higher than the rate in other countries, such as Germany and Italy. Priebe and his colleagues found that unemployed patients had more severe symptoms and reported much less satisfaction with life. Another problem is that patients are often returned to communities with inadequate follow-up services. Because so many lack work experience and social skills, it is difficult for them to make the transition back into the community. Indeed, when patients are given social skills training, the relapse rate declines markedly—though it does not disappear by any means (Benton and Schroeder, 1990). Finally, the most common reason why patients are rehospitalized is because they stop taking their medication. This is usually due to their concerns about the drug side effects.

One can interpret this "revolving-door" aspect of psychiatric hospitals both negatively and positively. On the negative side, the readmission rates are discouraging; they suggest that the attempt to treat people with schizophrenia is futile. But on the positive side, is it not better for a patient to be readmitted than never to have been discharged at all?

Even if one opts for the more positive response to the high readmission rate, the task of understanding its cause and of eventually reducing it remains. One thing is clear: antipsychotic drugs help reduce the symptoms of schizophrenia, but they do not cure the illness like an antibiotic cures an infection. Indeed, the fact that these drugs only alter symptoms raises questions about what is meant by treatment, recovery, and cure.

Psychological Treatments

Early psychological approaches to the treatment of schizophrenia used psychodynamic techniques with the patient and family members. There was little evidence that this was beneficial to patients. Contemporary psychological treatments for schizophrenia focus on the cognitive problems and the social adjustment problems associated with the illness. A variety of new approaches have been tried over the past five decades. The results have been mixed, although generally encouraging (see Table 10–4).

COGNITIVE REHABILITATION

The evidence of cognitive deficits in schizophrenia is certainly extensive. Further, the idea that these deficits play some causal role in the symptoms and interpersonal deficits associated with schizophrenia is quite plausible (Green, 1996). Based on this assumption, some researchers have attempted to use various rehabilitative strategies to improve the cognitive functions of patients (Kern and Green, 1998). The ultimate objectives are to reduce symptoms and enhance the patient's adaptive functioning in the real world. It is also assumed that an improvement in cognitive functioning will allow patients to receive

TABLE 10–4

PSYCHOSOCIAL TREATMENTS OF SCHIZOPHRENIA

	Family Therapy	Social Skills Training (SST)	Cognitive-Behavioral Therapy	Cognitive Rehabilitation	Individual Personal Therapy	Integrated Psychological Therapy
Improvement	about 50% moderately improved when used in conjunction with antipsychotics	for stabilized patients, highly effective in conjunction with antipsychotics	about 50–60% moderately improved when used in conjunction with antipsychotics	about 40–70% show improved cognitive functioning when used in conjunction with antipsychotics	about 65% moderately improved when used in conjunction with antipsychotics	rate of improvement not yet established
Relapse*	moderate	moderate	moderate	moderate	moderate	moderate
Side Effects†	unclear	unclear	unclear	unclear	unclear	unclear
Cost	moderately expensive	moderately expensive	moderately expensive	moderately expensive	moderately expensive	expensive
Time Scale‡	months/years	months	months/years	weeks/months	years	months/years
Overall	**good**	**good**	**good**	**good**	**good**	**promising**

★ Relapse after discontinuation of psychosocial treatment but maintenance on antipsychotics.
† Side effects of the psychosocial treatment.
‡ Time to achieve maximal effect.
SOURCE: Based on Kopelowicz and Liberman, 1998; revised with Brenner, Hirsbrunner, and Heimberg, 1996; Dickerson, 2000; Hogarty, Greenwald, et al., 1997; Hogarty, Kornblith, et al., 1997; Lauriello, Bustillo, and Keith, 1999; Sensky et al., 2000; Wexler et al., 1997; Wykes, Reeder, Corner, Williams, and Everitt, 1999.

greater benefits from the psychological treatments that are intended to enhance interpersonal skills. So what are the research findings telling us at this point? Can we treat schizophrenia by boosting patients' cognitive skills?

The idea of *cognitive rehabilitation* grew out of neuropsychological research with brain-damaged patients. Much of this work was concerned with improving the cognitive capacity of individuals who developed memory problems after sustaining brain injuries. The rehabilitation programs designed for patients with schizophrenia have focused on attention, memory, and executive functions. In one study, a group of patients with schizophrenia received training in strategies for improving memory and attention, whereas another group only received training in strategies for improving attention (Corrigan, Hirschbeck, and Wolfe, 1995). The results showed that patients who received training in both attention and memory were able to identify social cues better than patients in the other group. This advantage was still present two days after the training program. These findings are very encouraging, because memory dysfunction is associated with a broad range of problems encountered by patients with schizophrenia, including adjustment to the workplace (Bryson, Bell, Kaplan, and Greig, 1998).

Deficits on measures of frontal lobe function, or "executive" functions as they are often called, have been found in numerous studies of schizophrenia. You may recall the Wisconsin Card Sorting Task (WCST) is one of the main tests used to measure these abilities (see Chapter 2). It requires high-level reasoning skills and strategic planning. Several research groups have attempted to improve patients' performance on this measure by providing very basic training in the required strategy. To date, this approach has not yielded promising findings. Although there are some improvements in performance, they are short-lived (Hellman, Kern, Nielsen, and Green, 1998). This even holds when patients are given money as a "reinforcer" for successful trials! Further, patients who show substantial improvement in WCST scores after training fail to show gains on other measures of problem solving (Bellack, Blanchard, Murphy, and Podell, 1996). In other words, there is no generalization from one task to another. These findings suggest that higher-level reasoning skills are not easily acquired through time-limited training sessions.

Many believe that cognitive rehabilitation has great potential (see Box 10–2 for further discussion).

John Nash, a genius in higher mathematics, wrote a Ph.D. thesis at Princeton that revolutionized the field of game theory. Nash became a professor at M.I.T., but shortly after receiving tenure, he had his first episode of paranoid schizophrenia. He resigned his position there, and for many years, he wandered around Europe. His communications to his family and former colleagues were bizarre, paranoid, rambling letters. Then, more than two decades later, Nash experienced a rapid recovery. While Nash was ill, game theory had flourished. In 1994, almost fifty years after he wrote his thesis at Princeton, Nash received the Nobel Prize in economics for his work.

But some experts in the field argue that cognitive deficits can't be the cause of schizophrenic symptoms because the cognitive problems usually persist even when the symptoms disappear (Laws and McKenna, 1997). Moreover, earlier in this chapter, we described research that shows that some cognitive deficits are present long before the onset of the symptoms. Finally, we should not forget that some people who suffer from schizophrenia have cognitive abilities that are far superior to those of the average person. The Nobel laureate, Dr. John Nash, who suffered from schizophrenia for many years, is a prime example.

Nonetheless, even if cognitive deficits are not the cause of the symptoms, it still makes sense to try to remediate them. At this point, it appears that it may be possible to boost attention and memory in patients with schizophrenia. Given the role these skills play in the workplace, this could have important implications for the daily life of many patients. Clearly this is a very important area for further research.

INTERPERSONAL TRAINING

Social skills training is used in many treatment programs for schizophrenia. Training in social skills usually includes discussions about patients' social experiences, structured role playing of social interactions,

Cognitive Rehabilitation

Cognitive rehabilitation incorporates the disciplines of clinical neuropsychology, rehabilitation, and behavioral psychology in its aim to restore cognitive functioning. The basis of cognitive rehabilitation rests in the assumption that certain brain abnormalities associated with schizophrenia cause cognitive deficits that may be remediated with psychological intervention. The most pronounced of these cognitive impairments are attentional and memory problems. Why focus on remediating these cognitive deficits? First, it is assumed that when cognitive functions are impaired the person is more susceptible to stressful events because coping skills are reduced. Second, many advocates of cognitive rehabilitation believe that patients are handicapped in learning new social skills if they are struggling with deficits in basic cognitive abilities.

Can the cognitive performance of patients with schizophrenia be improved? There is little doubt that it can. Bruce Wexler and his colleagues conducted a study in which patients with schizophrenia (average age about forty-two years) practiced perceptual, memory, and motor tasks five times a week for ten weeks (Wexler et al., 1997). The basic goal was to determine the extent to which patients could improve their performance and sustain their gains. The patients received monetary payment for their participation, as well as supplements for good performance. After ten weeks of practice, sixteen of the twenty-two patients performed *as well or better* than the best normal comparison subject on the perceptual and memory tasks, and eleven patients performed *within the range* of normals on the motor task. When they were retested six months after training, half of the patients maintained their improvement, and the others showed performance declines. The fact that about half showed sustained improvements is very encouraging.

Is it possible that the cognitive training produced some lasting change in the patients' brains? In fact, a recent study of two patients with schizophrenia showed that a training program for remediating cognitive deficits changed their pattern of brain activity: in one case, there was increased temporal lobe activity, and in the other case, there was decreased activation in the motor area of the cortex (Wykes, 1998). This is reminiscent of the finding that cognitive therapy can change patterns of brain activity in patients with OCD (see Chapter 5). Yet, many questions remain: Do the findings mean that the biological basis of the "disease" can be changed with psychological interventions? Will the changes have a generalized impact on cognitive functioning? Or did the intervention merely teach the patients how to be better "takers" of specific tests? What, if anything, do the findings tell us about the potential for cognitive rehabilitation to improve the prognosis for schizophrenia?

Some families of patients who suffer from schizophrenia have expressed great optimism about cognitive rehabilitation. Nonetheless, cognitive rehabilitation for patients with schizophrenia has received a mixed reception. Although the literature suggests that basic cognitive competencies are correlated with real-life skills, the question still arises: Does posttreatment *improvement* in performance on basic cognitive tests predict meaningful improvements in daily functioning? To date, there is no strong evidence to indicate that it does. Furthermore, as we have discussed in this chapter, some patients with schizophrenia have above-average cognitive abilities, yet they still suffer from severe psychotic episodes. For these reasons, some believe that changing cognitions may not necessarily improve symptoms or general functioning (Penn and Mueser, 1996). Thus, patients and their families should not be encouraged to have undue optimism about the efficacy of this or any other experimental treatment.

Spring and Ravdin counter this position by pointing out that an extensive body of research has shown that there are positive correlations between scores from neuropsychological tests and measures of the level of patients' self-care, academic, and vocational functioning (Spring and Ravdin, 1992). They also suggest that psychological interventions, in general, were previously neglected because of advances in psychopharmacology. The belief was that antipsychotic medications suppressed the florid positive symptoms of psychosis and thus, offered sufficient treatment. However, residual deficits such as impaired attention, learning, memory, and motivation remain long after medication has had its maximal effect. Patients whose psychotic symptoms have remitted continue to feel the impact of their cognitive dysfunction on their social and vocational functioning, and on the general quality of their life. Thus, while effective treatment for psychotic symptoms may rest in psychopharmacology, cognitive remediation may also provide a reasonable method for teaching compensatory strategies that will help contain or reduce the impact of the illness on functioning (Green, 1993). In fact, Liberman and Green suggest that psychopharmacology should supplement cognitive and social skills rehabilitation, and that the two may have a synergistic effect on each other; pharmacotherapy may reduce symptoms and make the patient more responsive to the cognitive treatment (Liberman and Green, 1992).

The efficacy of cognitive rehabilitation, in terms of improving patient functioning in the real world, has yet to be clearly demonstrated. But the approach holds a lot of appeal. The idea that we might enhance the lives of people who are suffering from such a debilitating illness through a relatively straightforward, noninvasive "educational" intervention is very appealing to patients and their families. We expect that in the near future clinical research will shed significant light on the potential, and limits, of this approach.

SOURCE: Green, 1993; Liberman and Green, 1992; Penn and Mueser, 1996; Spring and Ravdin, 1992; Wexler et al., 1997; Wykes, 1998.

and various didactic procedures intended to improve social problem solving. Most studies have shown this type of intervention to be beneficial (Penn and Mueser, 1996).

Family therapy that educates relatives about schizophrenia and improves their skills in communicating with the patient has proven to be effective in reducing relapse (Doane, Falloon, Goldstein, and Mintz, 1985; Vaughn, Snyder, Jones, Freeman, and Falloon, 1984). This is especially true if the intervention is combined with a regular medication schedule. Another therapy, developed by a group of researchers at the Western Psychiatric Research Institute in Pittsburgh, has also produced good results. This therapy is an individual "personal therapy" model based on education, stress management, and skills training (Hogarty et al., 1997). Patients who have undergone this treatment have shown significant improvement in social adjustment. The treatment is lengthy, however, lasting about three years. Yet, it is clearly superior to short-term interventions.

In recent years, a structured treatment called Integrated Psychological Therapy has shown great promise (Brenner et al., 1994). This is a set of structured intervention programs that are derived from both cognitive rehabilitation and principles of social skills training. Integrated Psychological Therapy attempts to remedy the cognitive and behavioral dysfunctions that are characteristic of schizophrenia. Evaluative studies of this therapy suggest that as a result of the program patients with schizophrenia show improvement in social behavior, as well as in cognitive processes such as attention, abstraction, and concept formation (Brenner, Hodel, Roder, and Corrigan, 1992; Liberman and Green, 1992; Spaulding et al., 1998). Moreover, there is reason to believe that this and other treatments that focus on social skills work especially well in conjunction with drug therapy (Bellack, 1992).

The ideal treatment for schizophrenia involves carefully monitored psychopharmacological intervention, combined with psychological intervention that is implemented within the framework of a community program. On the community level, researchers have examined the effects of a variety of such structured programs for outpatients. One of the most widely utilized is the Program of Assertive Community Treatment (PACT). PACT is an amalgamation of several strategies that have proven effective (Test et al., 1997). It is a comprehensive,

integrated biopsychosocial treatment that is implemented in the community. It has been shown to improve all aspects of patient functioning, including independent living skills, employment, and interpersonal behavior (Becker, Meisler, Stormer, and Brondino, 1999; Mowbray et al., 1997). Further, although the PACT program clearly costs money, it is cost effective in the long run because it reduces the need for inpatient treatment (Hu and Jerrell, 1998).

In a recent study conducted by Nancy Wolff and her colleagues, two versions of Assertive Community Treatment (ACT), a program similar to PACT, were compared to "brokered case management" (Wolff et al., 1997). The brokered case management condition was essentially what is offered through HMO's in the United States: a case manager evaluated the client, then arranged for the purchase of mental health and psychosocial rehabilitation services from providers in the community. She also monitored the progress of each of her eighty-five clients, but saw them infrequently and rarely made home visits or engaged in outreach. One version of the ACT program included outreach, twenty-four-hour emergency services, assistance in obtaining entitlements and other resources, transportation, skill training, and assistance in activities of daily living, symptom management, supportive counseling, and traditional mental health services. The services were frequently offered in the client's natural environment rather than in an office setting. The main difference between this condition and the original PACT was that the treatment team in this study did not have an assigned psychiatrist and nurse. The other ACT condition included all of these services as well as a community worker who involved the client in "normalizing" activities, such as participation in individual and community leisure activities.

The results clearly favored the two ACT conditions. When compared to patients in brokered case management, those in the ACT programs experienced greater reductions in symptoms and were more satisfied with their treatment. There was no significant difference between treatment conditions in terms of the total costs of treating the patients. These findings are important because they suggest that the kind of mental health service routinely provided for patients with schizophrenia in the United States, namely managed care, may not yield the best outcome that can be achieved for the cost (see Box 10–3).

At the present time, most patients with schizophrenia in the United States who receive rehabili-

Science and Practice

Box 10—3

Managed Care and Psychotherapy for Schizophrenia

Clinicians and managed care representatives often disagree about whether the clinical benefits of psychotherapy for psychotic patients, as an adjunct to psychopharmacological treatment, justify the economic costs. Some treatment studies indicate that psychotherapy may reduce a variety of costs for patients with severe mental disorders, which generally involves substantial hospital stays and an impaired ability to function in daily activities. These studies suggest that psychotherapy should be viewed as an investment in reducing total cost for treatment and to society because it may prove to be beneficial to work performance and in reducing the duration and frequency of hospitalization (Gabbard, Lazar, Hornberger, and Spiegel, 1997).

Hogarty and his colleagues conducted three-year trials of personal psychotherapy for patients with schizophrenia (Hogarty et al., 1997). Their model was applied in the early months after discharge and aimed to create clinical stabilization, therapeutic alliance, and psycho-education. The intermediate phase promoted self-awareness by training individuals to recognize internal affective cues associated with stressors. By focusing on the relationship between the patient's life events and his/her internal state, the goal was to provide opportunities for introspection. Advanced social skills training focused on interpersonal relations and conflict management. These researchers found that only 8 percent of patients who received personal therapy relapsed, whereas 23 percent of those in other treatment groups relapsed. Both of these figures are far below the relapse rate of about 66 percent usually found in treatment studies of schizophrenia. Furthermore, the social adjustment of the patients who received personal therapy continued to improve over the next three years and did not appear to plateau (Fenton and McGlashan, 1997).

It has been argued that managed care systems traditionally focus on cost containment, and fail to grasp a longitudinal perspective. Critics argue that in seeking to limit the cost of treating each discrete episode, managed care systems begin to overemphasize cost and ignore effectiveness (Gabbard, Lazar, Hornberger, and Spiegel, 1997). Thus, the threat lies in whether quality of care is being sacrificed to yield short-term savings. Moreover, although the costs of psychotherapy treatment are obvious and easy to add up, many of the costs of failing to treat severe mental disorders with psychotherapy are "hidden." Among the hidden costs are those associated with work impairment and lost wages, not only for the patient, but also for family members. There are also hidden costs in other sectors of society. Patients with schizophrenia who receive inadequate treatment may be incarcerated. Jails are as expensive as some hospitals, yet the cost of detaining, arresting, and incarcerating psychiatric patients is rarely taken into consideration.

There is little doubt that the controversy surrounding psychotherapy for patients with serious mental disorders will not be resolved soon. But it is important that discussions of this issue factor all of the costs into the analysis, including those incurred by the patient, family, and the larger society.

SOURCE: Fenton and McGlashan, 1997; Gabbard, Lazar, Hornberger, and Spiegel, 1997; Hogarty et al., 1997.

---

tative treatment are in a day-treatment program or in a group residential setting. In these settings, patients with schizophrenia are given pharmacological interventions and various kinds of psychosocial interventions. There are now thousands of group homes and apartments across the United States. These homes are usually located in residential neighborhoods, although communities occasionally fight to keep them out. The recent experience with such homes has been quite positive, however, with community fears and prejudices fading. Most group homes accommodate a small number of people. At the same time, the homes enable individuals to make significant progress toward living fully independent and productive lives (Winerip, 1994).

Putting It All Together

In this chapter, we have discussed an illness that is considered to be the most serious mental disorder experienced by human beings. It afflicts people all over the world, from rural villages in India, to European cities, to American suburbs. Its costs to society and the individual are astronomical. Solving the mystery of its origins will certainly be an accomplishment deserving of a Nobel Prize.

Until about 1970, psychodynamic theories played a significant role in discussions about its cause. But ideas about the causes of schizophrenia have changed dramatically in the past three decades. There is no longer any doubt that it is a disorder of the brain that involves some abnormality in structure and/or function. In other words, some brain region(s) and/or neurotransmitter system(s) are abnormal in schizophrenia.

Further, it is likely that the vulnerability to schizophrenia is present at birth for most patients. There are three pieces of evidence that support this assumption: First, we know that the vulnerability can be inherited, so this implies that it exists when the individual enters the world. Second, prenatal complications appear to contribute to vulnerability. Third, developmental studies indicate that many patients show abnormalities as early as infancy.

Presuming the constitutional vulnerability to schizophrenia is typically present at birth, why does it usually take two decades before the symptoms emerge? This is certainly one of the most challenging aspects of the disorder. The fact that schizophrenia typically has its onset in early adulthood suggests to us that some maturational process is playing a role in triggering it expression. Perhaps the hormone changes that accompany puberty are gradually activating the brain system that is responsible for schizophrenia.

A full account of schizophrenia, especially the long-term course of the illness, also requires attention to the individual's psychosocial environment. Like most of the other psychological disorders described in this book, schizophrenia is influenced by the quality of the social support the patient receives. This extends from the patient's immediate family to the larger society. It is clear from the research findings that the most effective treatment programs for schizophrenia include psychological counseling, support services, and vocational training.

The effects of the environment on schizophrenia fit well with the diathesis-stress models that have dominated the thinking of researchers for many years. As our understanding of the biological effects of psychological stress has broadened, our ideas about the impact of stress on schizophrenia have become more sophisticated. It appears that stress hormones change brain function through their influence on the expression of genes. So stress hormones might affect schizophrenia by triggering the expression of genes that control dopamine neurotransmission. This is one of several possible neural mechanisms.

There is no doubt that the advent of antipsychotic drugs has revolutionized the treatment of schizophrenia. These medications, especially the newer ones, reduce or eliminate the florid symptoms of schizophrenia. They have made it possible for persons with schizophrenia to live independently and to get much greater satisfaction from life. The drugs are not, however, a cure. Residual symptoms usually remain. Further, antipsychotic drugs do not erase the psychological pain caused by schizophrenia.

The tragedy of schizophrenia is amplified by the fact that it strikes at a time when most people are just beginning to embark on an independent life. It derails educational and occupational plans, and it dashes the hopes and dreams of family members. It is not surprising that patients who are more aware of their illness also tend to be more depressed. They are confronted by the losses in time, achievement, and life satisfaction caused by schizophrenia. Patients and their families need and deserve psychological treatments to help them cope with their losses. Glenn, the patient whose personal narrative began this chapter, offers a poignant account:

> There is nothing I can do now to change what happened in the past. I am forty-three years old, and when I look back over my life I see a desolate road. I really haven't accomplished anything that most people would think is worthwhile. The new medication I'm on lifted a veil from my face and made me see things more clearly. At first it was very painful, but my therapist helped me work through this. He helped me put things in perspective. I have lost time, but I still have a future ahead of me, and that is what I need to set my sights on. My new job is full-time and I have had it for five months. I have better relationships with my family since my symptoms are under control. One of the best things is that my parents don't worry so much about me anymore. My Dad just turned seventy-one. At his birthday party, everyone toasted me for my success at work. My Mom was so happy she cried.

Summary

1. Schizophrenia involves abnormalities in thought, perception, emotion, and behavior. *Delusions* and *hallucinations* are among key symptoms of schizophrenia. They are referred to as "psychotic" symptoms because they involve a loss of connection with reality. Abnormalities in emotional expression and overt behavior are also among the defining symptoms.

2. At the subjective level, the patient's experience is often one of being overwhelmed by the world. Many patients with schizophrenia have problems with concentration and find it difficult to focus their thoughts and communication. Thinking may therefore be disorganized, and speech is often dotted with irrelevant associations and repetitions.

3. There are five clinical subtypes of schizophrenia: *paranoid, disorganized, catatonic, undifferentiated,* and *residual.* Schizophrenia can also be differentiated according to whether the condition is *acute* or *chronic,* or whether the symptoms are predominantly *positive* or *negative.*

4. A range of cognitive deficits is associated with schizophrenia. Patients manifest problems with reasoning, memory, and attention. Attending to relevant stimuli is especially difficult for patients, so they are easily distracted. People with schizophrenia also experience perceptual abnormalities or deficits that lead them to experience the world differently from others. But it does not appear that schizophrenia involves a unique cognitive problem. Virtually all of the deficits shown by patients with schizophrenia are also present in those who have other disorders of brain function.

5. There are at least two sources of constitutional vulnerability for schizophrenia. One is genetic; there is extensive evidence that the vulnerability to the disorder can be inherited. This has been shown in twin, adoption, and family studies. The other well-documented source of vulnerability is obstetrical complications. Events that occur during pregnancy and delivery can increase the child's risk for schizophrenia later in life. Included among the prenatal risk factors are maternal viral infection and various kinds of physical and social stressors.

6. Research indicates that the schizophrenia is a biological disorder. Schizophrenia is associated with a variety of structural brain abnormalities, including smaller frontal lobes and enlarged ventricles. But it is not assumed that these irregularities in brain structure cause schizophrenia. Rather, the dominant theory is that schizophrenia involves an abnormality in neurotransmission through certain brain circuits. Although several neurotransmitter systems have been the subject of research, dopamine has been the main neurotransmitter implicated in schizophrenia.

7. Psychological factors, especially exposure to stress, can worsen the symptoms of schizophrenia and contribute to relapse. Critical and hostile communications within the family (specifically, high *expressed emotion*) has been shown to increase the likelihood of relapse in patients. Findings from adoption studies of the biological offspring of women with schizophrenia suggest that these "high-risk" children are more likely to succumb to schizophrenia if they are exposed to stressful environments.

8. Schizophrenia is a disorder that affects the poor more than the rich, in part because patients drift down into lower socioeconomic status because their illness interferes with their academic and work performance. The course of schizophrenia, and especially its outcome, may depend on the culture in which it occurs. Schizophrenia in developed countries appears to have a worse prognosis than the same disorder in developing nations. Cultural differences in social support may be one of the factors producing these differences.

9. Treatment of schizophrenia was revolutionized by the introduction of antipsychotic drugs that reduce symptoms. Hospitalizations have become briefer, and there is a greater probability that the person will return to society. The early or "typical" antipsychotic medications that were introduced in the 1950s had several negative side effects that can be very disturbing. Chief among these is *tardive dyskinesia,* a movement disorder.

10. More recently developed antipsychotic drugs, the "atypicals," have fewer side effects. They also seem to be more effective for some patients. Both the typical and atypical antipsychotics are dopamine antagonists. They achieve their effects by blocking dopamine receptors, especially the D2 subtype. Although not a cure, the antipsychotic drugs have greatly improved the prognosis for schizophrenia.

11. *Cognitive rehabilitation,* which was originally developed for the treatment of brain damage, is now being explored for use in the treatment of schizophrenia. Training programs aimed at improving memory and attention have been successful, but the high-level reasoning deficits shown by some patients do not show stable improvement.

12. Psychotherapy can also be helpful in the treatment of patients with schizophrenia. Recent studies have shown that patients who receive certain forms of supportive psychotherapy are more likely to take their medication and have lower rates of relapse.

11

Late-Onset Disorders

Chapter Outline

Painting by Jean-Marie Heyligen.

Learning Objectives

→ Be able to describe the three sources of bias in estimating the rate of mental illness in the elderly.

→ Learn about how biological vulnerability to certain mental disorders increases with age and how psychological factors affect physical and mental health as people age.

→ Understand the symptoms of dementia, especially the cognitive deficits, and the high comorbidity of dementia with other disorders, and be able to distinguish dementia from delirium.

→ Learn about the hypothesized causes and experimental treatments of Alzheimer's disease, including the differences in causes of early-onset and late-onset Alzheimer's disease.

→ Be able to differentiate Alzheimer's disease from vascular dementia.

→ Understand why depression is less prevalent in the elderly than in the young, but how depression, anxiety, and the risk of suicide are liable to increase with physical illness and disability in the elderly.

→ Learn about the difference between delusional disorder and late-onset schizophrenia, and be able to explain why late-onset schizophrenia is more common in women than in men.

Advances in medicine have extended the average human life span far beyond what it was at the turn of the century. Especially in the developed nations, people are living longer and in good physical health; the rate of physical disability has decreased dramatically in the past two decades (Butler, 1997). In 1999, the population of the United States was about 270 million, with more than 34 million over age sixty-five, and about 4 million over age eighty-five (United States Census Bureau, 1999). Future projections to 2020 estimate that the population over age sixty-five will increase by at least 60 percent. We can expect this trend to continue. Demographers predict that there will also be a significant increase in the proportion of people over the age of eighty during the same time span (Hobbs and Damon, 1996). We are certainly going to witness the "graying of America" in the new millennium.

Of course, the quality of life is determined by more than just physical health; mental health is also a critical element in judging the value of longevity. Thus, as our population ages, the mental health of the elderly has taken on greater importance. During the "golden years," many people have the opportunity to experience the special joys of maturity: seeing their children marry and establish their own families, having grandchildren, retiring and spending more time in leisure activities. The pressures of child rearing and the daily grind of the work world subside. But during this same developmental stage, individuals must often contend with physical illnesses, as well as the loss of longtime friends through death. How people handle these challenges will depend upon their personality and the life skills they have acquired during previous developmental stages. The case of Alicia Cole, a seventy-year-old woman in excellent physical health, highlights both the assets and unique challenges of aging:

> Alicia Cole had been married to her husband Harvey for forty years. Both of them were sixty-seven years old, and it had been two years since they had retired from their positions at a state university. Harvey had been dean of students and Alicia had been a professor in the Department of Biology. As a couple, Harvey and Alicia were socially and physically active, and they were involved in several community organizations.
>
> They were in Florida to meet the youngest of their two children for spring break when Harvey had

his first heart attack. He was treated at a local hospital and released three days later with instructions to refrain from strenuous exercise. Harvey was advised to consider bypass surgery. He did so, but one month later, before the surgery could be scheduled, Harvey suffered another heart attack from which he died.

Harvey's death was a great emotional loss to Alicia, and she relied on her children for support through the grieving process. Alicia was sixty-eight at the time and in excellent health. Her children encouraged her to maintain her involvement in the community. She took this advice, and she began to devote more time to a local program aimed at promoting science education in elementary schools. She worked several days a week in the classroom and attended board meetings. On the weekends, she played tennis, worked in the garden and visited with friends. There was no doubt that she missed Harvey a great deal; on the morning of the first anniversary of his death, she woke up crying. But Alicia was determined to move on with her life, for her own benefit and that of her children.

At the age of seventy, Alicia began spending time with a man in her neighborhood who had also lost his spouse. His name was Cal, and he proved to be a wonderful companion. Alicia and Cal went to the movies, ate dinner together, visited with friends, attended social events, and enjoyed gardening. Alicia's children were very pleased to see their mother remain active and happy with her life. Nonetheless, it was somewhat awkward for Alicia to introduce Cal to her children as her "new friend."

We see in Alicia a continuity in functioning over time. As a young woman, she was an active person, with both a career and a family that kept her very busy. When the children grew up and left home, she and her husband directed their energy into work and community activities and preparation for retirement. Although the loss of her husband was difficult for Alicia, she made an effort to continue her activities and to broaden her social world after his death. Optimism, resilience, and industriousness characterized Alicia throughout adulthood. In general, this is the typical pattern: personality traits and adjustment level remain fairly stable throughout the adult life course (Agronin, 1994). People who are mentally healthy and optimistic in early adulthood are likely to be healthy, optimistic senior citizens.

Yet, there are some adult developmental trends that often result in changing personality styles with age (Molinari, Kunik, Snow-Turek, Deleon, and

After their retirement, older adults can continue to live useful lives, including tutoring young children.

Williams, 1999). Many of these are part of our cultural stereotypes about aging. For example, when compared to young adults, older adults have a greater preference for routines, and they are less impulsive, less aggressive, more suspicious, and more introverted. In part, this is a normal consequence of life experiences. In addition, the hormonal and other physical changes that accompany aging contribute to these developmental trends (Gatz, Kasl-Godley, and Karel, 1996). Among the physical changes are declines in levels of certain hormones, and decreases in muscle and bone density.

Of course, most physical and personality changes that come with aging are not pathological, and the majority of senior citizens are able to adjust to their changing lifestyles without major psychological difficulties. Only a minority of those over age sixty-five encounter serious psychological problems that require treatment. When this does occur, they benefit most from mental health care professionals who are sensitive to the unique experiences and needs of older adults.

In Chapter 8, we described how certain developmental processes associated with childhood can go awry and lead to psychological disorders. In this chapter, we will emphasize the psychological disorders that have their onset with advanced age. One major category is the dementias: impairments in cognitive functioning that are more prevalent among the elderly. We will also discuss the unique features of other mental disorders, including depression and psychosis, when they occur later in life. As shown in Table 11–1, the results of community screening studies indicate that about 13 percent of those over age

Data

TABLE 11–1

PREVALENCE OF PSYCHIATRIC DISORDERS AMONG YOUNGER VS OLDER ADULTS*

Disorder	Younger Adults[†]		Older Adults[‡]		Older Adults
	1-year Prevalence	Lifetime Prevalence	1-year Prevalence	Lifetime Prevalence	Prevalence of Clinically Significant Symptoms
Affective disorders					
Any	2.7 Men	6.6 Men	0.6 Men	1.6 Men	15–25
	7.9 Women	15.3 Women	1.5 Women	3.3 Women	
Major depression	3.9	7.5	0.9	1.4	
Dysthymia		3.8		1.7	
Bipolar I	1.2	1.4	0.1	0.1	
Bipolar II	0.3	0.6	0.1	0.1	
Anxiety disorders					17–21
Panic disorder	0.7 Men	1.8 Men	0.04 Men	0.1 Men	
	1.9 Women	3.1 Women	0.4 Women	0.7 Women	
Phobic disorder	6.1 Men	10.5 Men	4.9 Men	7.8 Men	
	16.1 Women	22.6 Women	8.8 Women	13.7 Women	
Generalized anxiety disorder	3.6	4.9–6.8	2.2	2.6–4.3	
Obsessive-compulsive disorder	2.1	3.3	0.9	1.2	
Alcohol abuse/dependence	14.1 Men	27.9 Men	3.1 Men	13.5 Men	7–8 (community-dwelling elderly persons who consume 12 to 21 drinks per week)
	2.1 Women	5.5 Women	0.5 Women	1.5 Women	10–15 (older primary care patients who have alcohol-related problems)
Other drug abuse/dependence		6.7		0.1	
Schizophrenia	1.5	2.3	0.2	0.3	
Antisocial personality disorder	1.5	3.7	0.0	0.3	
Cognitive impairment					
Severe	0.3 (Aged 35–54)		1.0 (Aged 55–74)		
			5.0 (Aged ≥75)		
	3.1 (Aged 35–54)		7.5 (Aged 55–74)		
Mild			19.1 (Aged ≥75)		
Any psychiatric disorder (excluding cognitive impairment)	23	39	13	21	

*Data are presented as percentages, based on Epidemiologic Catchment Area (ECA) study, which used DSM-III criteria. Where there are no numbers, data was not available.
[†]Younger adults are those aged 30 to 44 years.
[‡]Older adults are those aged 65 years and older.
SOURCE: Jeste et al., 1999.

sixty-five will have suffered from a mental illness other than a cognitive disorder during the previous year (Jeste et al., 1999). Some in the field of mental health research believe this figure is an underestimation. Three sources of bias in estimates of the rate of mental illness in the elderly have been suggested: (1) misattribution of psychiatric symptoms to cognitive problems, physical disorders, or "normal aging"; (2) lack of age-appropriate diagnostic criteria for certain disorders, such as substance abuse and schizophrenia; and (3) underreporting of psychological symptoms due to forgetfulness and/or social stigma (Jeste et al., 1999). It is unfortunate that there is no easy way of determining whether current estimates of the prevalence of mental illness in the elderly are actually too low. But there is no doubt that we can expect a big increase in the number of elderly people with mental illness in the coming decades.

As you will see, when compared to research on early-onset disorders, the literature on abnormal geriatric psychology is limited. But as the proportion of elderly people in the population increases, we can expect that the mental disorders that are associated with aging will be the focus of greater attention from researchers and clinicians. There will also be more psychological research on the factors that enhance cognitive and emotional functioning during this period of the life span.

Vulnerability to Disorders of Aging

Like the psychological disorders that tend to occur in childhood and early adulthood, the disorders that have their onset later in life are a result of multiple etiological factors. The diathesis-stress model provides a useful framework for understanding the causal process. For older adults, as for youth, psychological well-being is determined by the interaction between constitutional factors and the individual's experiences.

Physical Vulnerability

Margaret Gatz and her colleagues point out that biological vulnerability, or the diathesis for certain mental disorders, can be expected to increase with age

(Gatz, Kasl-Godley, and Karel, 1996). This is because of the physical changes, especially changes in the brain, that are associated with aging.

Physical limitations affect the daily living habits of many elderly people (Lamberts, van den Beld, and van der Lely, 1997). About 15 percent of people ages sixty-five to seventy-five require some assistance with daily living, and this number increases to 45 percent for those over eighty-five years of age. The physical limitations confronted by the elderly arise from the biological changes that occur when organs age. There is a decrease in the ability of cells to synthesize proteins, a decline in immune function, muscle mass, and bone density, and an increase in the proportion of body fat. Taken together, these changes result in reduced physical mobility and strength and a higher rate of physical illness. Although lifestyle factors, such as physical exercise, can slow down these aging processes, such factors cannot completely prevent them.

Sensory acuity also decreases with age. There is a visual decline, especially a deterioration of near vision, as well as declines in hearing, sensitivity to odors and tastes, and decreased sensation in the limbs. When the impulses in sensory neurons are measured, a reduction in the amplitudes of action potentials is observed.

The normal aging process is linked with changes in the structure and function of the human brain (Drachman, 1997). Based on neuroimaging studies, researchers have estimated that there is a 10 percent reduction in the weight and volume of the brain by the age of eighty. This reduction is due in part to the

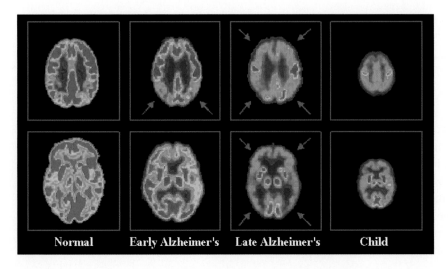

Normal   Early Alzheimer's   Late Alzheimer's   Child

PET scans showing the metabolic activity in the brains of a child, an adult, a person in the early stages of Alzheimer's disease, and a person in the late stages of Alzheimer's disease. The reds and yellows indicate higher metabolic activity, and the blues and greens indicate lower activity. There is greater metabolic activity in the normal brain than in the late Alzheimer's brain, indicating a loss of neurons and a dramatic loss of function. The lower metabolic activity in some portions of the child's brain indicates brain areas that are not fully developed.

loss of neurons, most markedly in the substantia nigra and the temporal region. Loss of neurons in the substantia nigra can interfere with motor functions, whereas temporal lobe neuron decreases may contribute to memory deficits. Neurons in the brain stem, which play a major role in reflexes such as respiration, are less likely to decline with age. In addition to a decrease in number, there is also a decrease in the size of neurons. Similarly, the number of synapses among neurons declines. The behavioral consequences of these changes are not known. Finally, certain abnormalities in the structure and interconnections among neurons increase with age; neural malformations are apparent in about half the people over the age of sixty-five who have no cognitive impairment. However, these abnormalities are most common in people who suffer from Alzheimer's disease, a cognitive disorder described later in the chapter.

Of course, the functioning of the nervous system is dependent on other organ systems, such as the respiratory and cardiovascular systems. The reduced capacity of these systems with advanced age has implications for the functioning of the brain. In addition, age-related declines in the immune system can increase the risk for infections that impair nervous system functioning.

Changes in hormone levels appear to play a major role in the loss of abilities that occur with advanced age (Lamberts, van den Beld, and van der Lely, 1997). Normal human aging is characterized by a significant decline in the activity of several hormone systems (see Figure 11–1). There are gradual decreases in the release of thyroid stimulating hormone and growth hormone. The sex hormones begin to decline in middle adulthood; there are decreases in gonadotropin luteinizing hormone (LH), follicle-stimulating hormone (FSH),

Figure 11—1

DECLINE IN HORMONE SYSTEMS WITH AGE

The graphs show changes in the hormone levels in normal women and normal men as they age. (A) Age-related changes in estrogen in healthy women over their lifetime, (B) age-related changes in testosterone in healthy men over their lifetime, (C) age-related decreases in secretion of dehydroepiandrosterone (DHEA) in 114 healthy women, and (D) age-related decreases in secretion of dehydroepiandrosterone (DHEA) in 163 healthy males. (Source: Lamberts, van den Beld, and van der Lely, 1997)

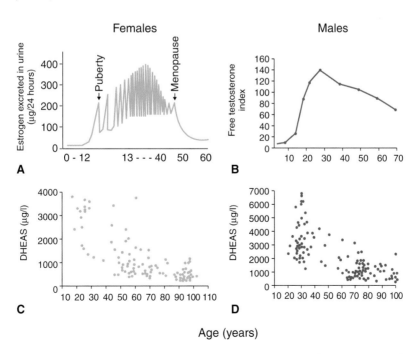

estrogen from the ovaries, and testosterone from the testes. These reductions result in various physical changes, including menopause in women. Another hormonal system that undergoes age-related decline is the secretion of dehydroepiandrosterone (DHEA) from the adrenal gland. Because the administration of DHEA has been linked with the maintenance of youthful characteristics (for example, higher muscle mass) in laboratory animals, it has become a popular dietary supplement in health food stores. However, it has not yet been established that DHEA, or any other drug, retards or reverses the aging process in humans. Age-related changes in estrogen, testosterone and DHEA are illustrated in Figure 11–1.

Psychological Vulnerability

Given the structural changes that occur in the brain with aging, it is not surprising that there are significant cognitive changes (Maki, Zonderman, and Weingartner, 1999; West and Craik, 1999). As noted in Chapter 2, IQ tests are normed to yield an average score of 100. This is done separately for each age level. As a result, people who score 100 at age seventy-five will have gotten many fewer items correct compared to people who score 100 at age twenty-one. The two most pronounced changes in cognitive ability that account for the lower IQ scores are declines in the ability to store new information and in the speed of the individual's reactions to visual and auditory stimuli. As the ability to store new information decreases, everyday failures to remember become more apparent. Misplacing keys and forgetting telephone numbers and names are common occurrences. This is certainly bothersome when it is mild, and can be a source of great discomfort when it starts to interfere with daily life.

But certain aspects of intellectual ability remain intact in elderly people. Vocabulary, for example, changes little with age. Moreover, it is important to keep in mind that there are differences among elderly people in their mental abilities. Some continue to function at an exceptional cognitive level well into their nineties. This is especially true of individuals who were highly educated, indicating that there is continuity across the life span in intellectual functioning.

It appears that there is also continuity in emotional health. In a longitudinal study of a large group of men, researchers found that psychological factors, such as emotional stability, during the college years could be significant predictors of depression at the age of sixty-five (Cui and Vaillant, 1996). In addition, the researchers found that negative life events (for example, loss of a loved one or serious accidents) affected the men's psychological health more than their physical health. Negative life events prior to the age of sixty-five were strongly associated with depressive symptoms at age sixty-five. Another significant predictor was a history of depression in the man's family of origin. Longitudinal research with elderly women has also demonstrated the effect of negative life events on mental health (Penninx et al., 1998). Taken together, these results indicate that vulnerability among the elderly is determined by both hereditary factors and life experiences.

One of the most common psychological challenges faced in old age is the loss of social support. Elderly people tend to have smaller social networks than younger people (Mendes de Leon et al., 1999). This results from the deaths of friends and loved ones, as well as the decrease in everyday contact with people in the neighborhood and workplace. Further, decreased social contacts are a risk factor for psychological disorders in the elderly (Penninx et al., 1998).

In considering the mental health of elderly people, we should not overlook the benefits of the experience and knowledge they have gained in life. The elderly have had the opportunity to acquire life skills that can help them cope with stress. They have observed and personally experienced the benefits of avoiding certain situations and certain kinds of people. By the age of sixty-five, most have gained interpersonal skills and the ability to delay immediate gratification for the sake of long-term goals. They may also be better at avoiding stress. There is evidence that stressful life events decrease throughout adulthood and are much less common in older adults. In part, this is due to the fact that most people over sixty-five no longer have to confront the everyday challenges of the workplace or child rearing. But the lower level of stressors experienced by elderly people is also a function of the choices they make. They are less likely to take risks and more likely to have a regular schedule in their daily habits. All of these factors contribute to a decrease in psychological vulnerability with age.

Figure 11–2 illustrates three kinds of contributions to depression in adults: biological vulnerability, psychological diathesis, and stressful life events. Summing across the three, we see that early and late

Figure 11—2

INFLUENCES ON DEPRESSION ACCORDING TO AGE

The graph shows the relationship between age and depression in three dimensions in adults between 20 and 90 years old: biological vulnerability, psychological diathesis, and stressful life events. Each curve shows the developmental trends in the magnitude of the influence of these different dimensions on symptoms of depression, waxing and waning according to the relationship between age and depressive symptoms. (Source: Gatz, Kasl-Godley, and Karel, 1996, p. 370)

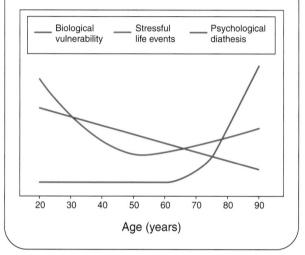

While vocabulary and factual knowledge tend to remain stable or increase with age, psychomotor skills and short-term memory often decrease. But these declines are normal developmental processes, and they do not always pose problems in everyday life. The real concern is when there is a dramatic loss in cognitive functioning that can interfere with independent living.

The disorders that are classified as dementias in DSM-IV involve a variety of cognitive deficits and, it appears, many causal factors. In order for a person to be diagnosed with dementia according to DSM-IV, he or she must display a noticeable decline from a previous level of functioning, including amnesia, an impairment in memory function. The memory impairment is manifested in difficulty with learning new information or recalling previously learned information. For example, the individual may have difficulty remembering new street addresses or telephone numbers. He may forget the titles of books he has read or movies he has seen.

In addition to amnesia, to meet DSM-IV diagnostic criteria for dementia the person must show at least one of the following cognitive disturbances: aphasia, apraxia, agnosia, or a loss of executive abilities. *Aphasia* refers to a deterioration in the ability to communicate with language. The person's speech may become unclear, slow, and repetitive. Patients who have *apraxia* manifest a decline in motor skills. Tying shoes, getting dressed, or doing household chores becomes more difficult and requires more

adulthood are viewed as periods of heightened risk for psychological problems. But the nature of the vulnerability differs at the two ends of the life span. Among youth, the vulnerability is greatest for externalized disorders, such as attention deficit disorder and conduct disorder. For the elderly, the primary risk is for disorders of cognition.

Dementia

When it comes to mental health in old age, there is no doubt that the dementias are the major problem. *Dementia* is the general, progressive deterioration of cognitive functioning that is often accompanied by changes in psychological and emotional states such as depression, agitation, aggression, and apathy. We have mentioned that there is a well-established decline in certain mental functions with aging (Maki, Zonderman, and Weingartner, 1999; West and Craik, 1999).

Society and Mental Health

Box 11–1

Dementia and International Politics

The vast majority of heads of state are older men, often men who are in their sixties and seventies. Their age may bring wisdom! But what are the implications of dementia in a political leader? Several authors have speculated on whether dementia in a world leader might affect the course of international policies. For example, Francois Boller and his colleagues suggest that Paul Deschanel, who became president of France in 1920, was afflicted with Alzheimer's dementia (Boller, Ganansia-Ganem, Lebert, and Pasquier, 1999). Deschanel manifested eccentricities and erratic behavior throughout the election and afterward. Nonetheless, the researchers found no evidence that Deschanel's neurological illness had a lasting political impact.

James Toole (1999) presents evidence that Franklin D. Roosevelt suffered from vascular dementia, and that this impaired his ability to negotiate with Stalin in Yalta after World War II. In particular, Toole suggests that Roosevelt's dementia resulted in the division of Poland, Germany, Vietnam, and Korea into halves, and that this sowed the seeds for the cold war.

Although our former president, Ronald Reagan, showed no evidence of failing health while in the White House, he was diagnosed with Azheimer's disease in 1994, a few years after leaving office. More recently, a Russian psychiatrist, Mikhil Vinogradov, called into question the mental health of then Russian president Boris Yeltsin (The Daily Telegraph, London, October 9, 1998). Vinogradov noted that Yeltsin showed a facial expression of confusion, rambled when he attempted to answer a question, and often appeared not to understand questions asked by reporters. Based on his observations, he concluded that Yeltsin was suffering from dementia.

In the United States, concerns such as these have led some physicians to propose that a "mental health unit" be assigned to the White House to monitor the president's mental health (Annas, 1995). This proposal is based on the assumption that when a world leader is deemed incompetent due to mental impairment, the medical community has a responsibility to express its concern and make appropriate recommendations to Congress. But important questions remain: How much does the public have a right to know about the mental health of the president? Does the president forego rights to privacy about his medical history? There are no easy answers to these questions.

(Left) Paul Deschanel; *(center)* Ronald Reagan; *(right)* Boris Yeltsin.

concentration to complete. **Agnosia** is the failure to identify familiar objects or people. Elderly patients with dementia usually begin showing agnosia when they are attempting to refer quickly to an object in the environment. As the agnosia gets more severe, the patient may fail to recognize family members. Finally, some patients show impairment in the "executive" functions that are controlled by the frontal lobes. The abilities to plan ahead and to inhibit inappropriate behavior may decline. For example, a very conscientious woman who was always careful to avoid offending others might show little concern about making critical comments in public settings.

In order to meet diagnostic criteria for any of the dementias in DSM-IV, the cognitive deficits must not be due to temporary physical conditions, such as infection or intoxication with alcohol or drugs. Thus, they do not have an abrupt onset. Instead, the dementias usually have a gradual onset, beginning with minor lapses in memory, then leading to more significant failures in memory that have a greater impact on functioning and decision making (see Box 11–1).

At first, the memory lapses may only be apparent to the individual, but with time they become obvious to others. In the advanced stages, the person is unable to care for herself, and may even be unaware that she is suffering from cognitive impairment.

Dementia has a high comorbidity with other disorders; in particular, a large proportion of patients who have dementia also show psychotic or depressive symptoms. In fact, there is considerable evidence that depression contributes to the cognitive deficits observed in elderly patients (Benedict, Dobraski, and Goldstein, 1999; Rosenstein, 1998).

Ten subtypes of dementia, each with a different etiology, are listed in DSM-IV. All of the subtypes are characterized by the criteria described above, as well as by other specific symptoms. Four of the subtypes tend to occur in persons over the age of sixty: Alzheimer's disease, vascular dementia, dementia due to Pick's disease, and dementia due to Parkinson's disease. By far, the most common two subtypes of dementia are Alzheimer's disease and vascular dementia.

Alzheimer's Disease

Alzheimer's disease was originally described by Alois Alzheimer at the turn of the century. At that time, it was considered to be a relatively uncommon disorder. But we now know that it is the most common cause of dementia in the elderly. Our knowledge of the biological aspects and course of the disease has improved greatly in recent years. Whether or not Alzheimer's disease should be viewed as accelerated or pathological aging, it is certainly a disease of major proportions.

At least half of all elderly people diagnosed with dementia probably have Alzheimer's disease. An estimated 2 to 4 million people in the United States suffer from the disorder (Menzin, Lang, and Friedman, 1999). About 8 percent of American adults over sixty-five years of age are diagnosed with Alzheimer's disease, and about one-third of these people are severely handicapped. For every five-year increase in age up to age sixty-four, the incidence rates of Alzheimer's and other dementias triple, then the rates double between ages sixty-five and seventy-five (Gao, Hendrie, Hall, and Hui, 1998). For unknown reasons, the rate of increase drops down to 1.5 around age eighty-five. This slowing down of the age-related increase in the rates of dementia and Alzheimer's disease lends support to the hypothesis that these disorders are not inevitable consequences of aging. It appears that the peak risk period occurs before the age of eighty; beyond that age, the likelihood of succumbing is dramatically reduced.

There are also sex differences in the risk of Alzheimer's, with women being at a significantly higher risk for developing the disorder (Gao, Hendrie,

---

DSM-IV Criteria

Dementia of the Alzheimer's Type

A. The development of multiple cognitive deficits manifested by both: (1) memory impairment (impaired ability to learn new information or to recall previously learned information), and (2) one (or more) of the following cognitive disturbances: (a) aphasia (language disturbance); (b) apraxia (impaired ability to carry out motor activities despite intact motor function); (c) agnosia (failure to recognize or identify objects despite intact sensory function); (d) disturbance in executive functioning (i.e., planning, organizing, sequencing, abstracting).

B. The cognitive deficits in Critera A1 and A2 each cause significant impairment in social or occupational functioning and represent a significant decline from a previous level of functioning.

C. The course is characterized by gradual onset and continuing cognitive decline.

D. The cognitive deficits in Criteria A1 and A2 are not due to any of the following: (1) other central nervous system conditions that cause progressive deficits in memory and cognition (e.g., cerebrovascular disease, Parkinson's disease, Huntington's disease, subdural hematoma, normal-pressure hydrocephalus, brain tumor); (2) systemic conditions that are known to cause dementia (e.g., hypothyroidism, vitamin B_{12} or folic acid deficiency, niacin deficiency, hypercalcemia, neurosyphilis, HIV infection); (3) substance-induced conditions.

E. The deficits do not occur exclusively during the course of a delirium.

F. The disturbance is not better accounted for by another Axis I disorder (e.g., Major Depressive Disorder, Schizophrenia).

SOURCE: APA, DSM-IV, 1994.

Hall, and Hui, 1998). The reasons for the apparent higher risk for women are still uncertain.

Alzheimer's disease can have an early onset, with the first signs seen prior to the age of sixty. In general, the onset is considered early if it occurs prior to age sixty-five. But typically it begins gradually after the age of sixty-five. The symptoms usually develop slowly, followed by a continuous decline in cognitive functioning. Its initial symptoms include loss of initiative, forgetfulness, naming disability, and apraxia (impaired ability to perform certain motor tasks, such as cooking, dressing and writing). Some patients show spatial disorientation; they become confused about directions and locations of familiar places. Different symptoms predominate in different patients. In many patients, an amnesic syndrome is the prominent symptom; in other patients, naming or spatial disorders are the primary symptoms (Martin, 1987; Schwartz, Baron, and Moscovitch, 1990). With time, the nervous system in Alzheimer's patients deteriorates further.

The case of Mary provides an example of the gradual onset and pervasive effects of Alzheimer's disease:

For two or three years, Mary's memory was slipping, but she compensated by writing things down. At first, she found herself groping for a word she had always known, and she also noticed that she often lost the thread of a conversation. Though she worried that her mind might be slipping away, she didn't want to think about getting old and, most important, she didn't want to be treated as if she were senile. She was still enjoying life and able to manage.

Then Mary got pneumonia and had to be taken to the hospital. In those strange surroundings, she could no longer compensate for her forgetfulness. People told her where she was, but she forgot. She complained that her daughter-in-law never visited her, though she had been there in the morning.

Although the fever and infection passed, the illness had focused attention on the seriousness of her condition. Her family realized she could no longer live alone. She was taken to live with her son's family where she was given a room. Because only some of her things were there, she thought that perhaps the rest were stolen while she was sick even though she had been told many times where her things were. She got lost in the neighborhood and often could not find her way around the house. . . .

Mary continued to deteriorate. Dressing became an insurmountable ordeal. Because of her apraxia, she no longer knew how to button buttons, to unzip zippers. Mary gradually lost the ability to interpret what she saw and heard. Words and objects began to lose their meaning. Sometimes she would react with terror and panic, or with anger. Her things were gone, her life seemed gone. She could not understand the explanations that were offered or, if she understood, she could not remember them. . . . However, Mary's social skills remained, so that when she finally relaxed she was personable and engaging. She also loved music and sang old familiar songs. Music seemed to be embedded in a part of her mind that she retained long after much else was lost.

The time finally came when the physical and emotional burden of caring for Mary became too much for her family, and she went to live in a nursing home. After the initial days of confusion and panic passed, the reliability of the routine comforted her and gave her a measure of security.

Mary was glad when her family came to visit. Sometimes she remembered their names; more often she did not. (Source: Adapted from Mace and Robins, 1981)

In many patients, sleep is severely disturbed, wandering occurs, and maintaining basic hygiene and cleanliness become problematic. People with Alzheimer's disease may be incontinent of urine and feces; other unmanageable behaviors, such as screaming, aggression, and refusal to eat or drink, may appear. There may be problems in walking and balance that lead to falls and injuries. As the disease

As Alzheimer's disease progresses, intellectual and basic maintenance functions continue to deteriorate. Patients may forget to eat, to brush their teeth, and to use the toilet. Here a woman in a nursing home is being fed.

progresses, more and more severe deficits appear, in more and more systems. Thus, over a period ranging from a few to ten years, it leads to severe deterioration of intellectual and basic maintenance functions. In the final stages, the person may be confined to bed, incontinent, and inert. The immediate cause of death is often a complicating condition such as pneumonia, malnutrition, dehydration, or infection.

The treatment of Alzheimer's disease can be complicated by the presence of psychotic symptoms and disturbances in mood (Richards and Hendrie, 1999). Psychosis is very common and may include delusions and hallucinations. Usually the delusions are paranoid in nature, and they often involve concerns about personal health and safety. For example, patients may complain that their friends or relatives are trying to poison them or steal from them. More than half of all Alzheimer's patients also suffer from feelings of sadness and symptoms of depression, with 10 to 20 percent meeting DSM criteria for a depressive disorder.

In part, the depression observed in patients with dementia seems to be a consequence of the awareness of their symptoms (Seltzer, Vasterling, and Buswell, 1995). When patients are asked about their cognitive and physical limitations, those who are most accurate in describing them are also found to have more symptoms of depression. As the dementia worsens, patients are less accurate in describing their limitations, and the depression often subsides.

In previous chapters, we have discussed the early precursors of many adult-onset disorders, including schizophrenia and the personality disorders. Are there early signs of risk for Alzheimer's dementia? In order to answer this question, David Snowdon and his colleagues enlisted the cooperation of a group of ninety-three nuns (Snowdon et al., 1996). It has been shown that nuns tend to live longer than the average woman, so they are excellent prospects for participation in studies of aging (Butler and Snowdon, 1996). The nuns had written autobiographies about themselves when they were in their early twenties. Given that virtually all of the nuns had at least a college education, they were presumably of at least average intelligence when they wrote their autobiographies. Two measures, idea density (the number of ideas conveyed per sentence) and grammatical complexity, were derived from the autobiographies. Approximately fifty-eight years later, when their ages ranged from seventy-five to ninety-five years, the women

who wrote these autobiographies participated in a cognitive assessment. Brain studies were conducted on the fourteen nuns who had died between seventy-nine to ninety-six years of age. The findings were striking: high idea density and grammatical complexity in autobiographies written in early life were associated with high cognitive test scores in late life. Among the fourteen nuns who died, Alzheimer's disease was confirmed in all of those with low idea density in early life but in none of those with high idea density in early life. These results indicate that the vulnerability to Alzheimer's disease exists in young adulthood for some individuals. The prospect for preventive intervention may, therefore, exist long before the first signs of the illness are detected.

THE ORIGINS OF ALZHEIMER'S DISEASE

The causes of Alzheimer's disease are not known. As mentioned earlier, normal aging is associated with changes in brain structure, including a loss of neurons and an increase in neural malformations. However, it appears that these age-related changes are much more pronounced in Alzheimer's patients. Two types of neural abnormalities are especially common in Alzheimer's patients: groupings of protein inside the neurons (neurofibrillary tangles), accumulation of protein between neurons (senile plaques), and loss of cells in a number of areas of the nervous system. The neurofibrillary tangles inside the neurons are distorted remnants of microscopic tubes that transport nutrients and other materials from the body of the cell to the dendrites and axons. The main component of the senile plaques is beta amyloid, a starch-like protein substance that accumulates gradually. Together, the neurofibrillary tangles and plaques constitute the neuropathological features that confirm a diagnosis of Alzheimer's disease at biopsy or autopsy. Neural malformations in Alzheimer's patients are particularly common in the hippocampus, but they are also observed in the cerebral cortex (Bobinski et al., 1998). In addition, brain imaging reveals shrinkage in the frontal and temporal lobes and enlargement of the ventricles due to cell death in the cortex (Martin, 1999).

Research has shown that beta amyloid can be detected in the cerebral spinal fluid of most patients with Alzheimer's disease (Hulstaert et al., 1999). One hypothesis is that the beta amyloid leads to the formation of the tangles, and then to cell death (Hardy

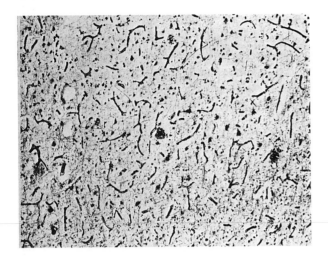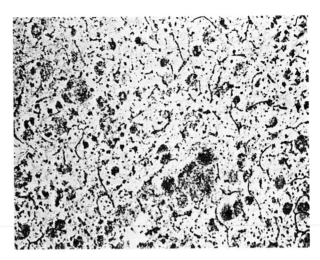

Photomicrographs of brain tissue from the cortex of *(left)* a patient who does not have Alzheimer's disease and *(right)* a patient who does have Alzheimer's disease. Notice the small number of senile plaques (the darker areas) in the normal patient and the larger number of plaques in the patient with Alzheimer's disease.

and Higgins, 1992). It suggests that Alzheimer's disease can be treated by substances that retard or interfere with the accumulation of beta amyloid. Thus, it is not unrealistic to think that Alzheimer's disease may one day be preventable.

A biochemical consequence of the brain impairment in Alzheimer's disease is an abnormally low level of acetylcholine, a brain neurotransmitter that is known to be important in memory (Muir, 1997). It is possible that a decrease in acetylcholine is the main cause of the memory loss associated with aging. Many researchers are studying the effects of various drugs that activate this neurotransmitter, with the goal of finding a medication for dementia.

One controversial hypothesis about Alzheimer's disease is that it is caused by an increase in aluminum in the body (Mjoberg, Hellquist, Mallmin, and Lindh, 1997). Researchers have suggested that the aluminum concentrates in parts of the brain and causes the neural malformations that are associated with Alzheimer's disease. Although early studies of patients with Alzheimer's disease did show that they had a higher rate of exposure to aluminum through their workplaces or from drinking water, more recent studies do not support this (Gun et al., 1997). Nonetheless, there is fairly convincing evidence that excessive levels of aluminum in the brain are associated with neurofibrillary tangles and behavioral abnormalities in animals (Shin, 1997). We must await the results of

future research to clarify the role of aluminum in degenerative brain disorders in humans.

There is accumulating evidence that Alzheimer's disease is inherited in some people. Research on twins has shown that the concordance rate for Alzheimer's disease is 83 percent among MZ twins and 46 percent among DZ twins (Bergem, Engedal, and Kringlen, 1997). This striking difference suggests a significant genetic component for the illness. Family studies have shown that the risk for Alzheimer's disease in first-degree relatives (parents, children, siblings) of patients with the illness is about 50 percent by age ninety, compared to a risk of about 25 percent in the population at large in this age range (Mohs, Breitner, Silverman, and Davis, 1987).

The kind of Alzheimer's disease that runs in families typically has an early onset. St. George-Hyslop and his colleagues (1987) found a defective gene in patients with familial Alzheimer's disease on the same region of chromosome 21 that carries the defective gene for Down syndrome. (And in fact, all people with Down syndrome who live past forty-five years of age develop Alzheimer's disease.) Further investigations have isolated the defect to a mutation of a gene that is involved in forming amyloid; this mutation leads to the formation of beta amyloid, one of the pathogenic substances in Alzheimer's disease. Another rare mutation of the same gene in those with early-onset Alzheimer's disease has been found on chromosome 14, but its defective product has not been

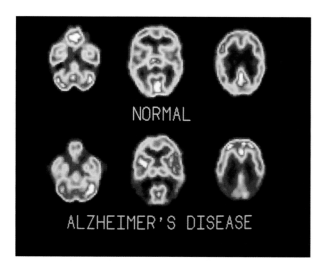

PET scans comparing a normally functioning brain and the brain of a person with Alzheimer's disease show a lower level of metabolism (red and yellow show higher metabolism, while blue and green show lower metabolism) in the brain affected by Alzheimer's disease, especially in the frontal lobes (responsible for planning; located at the top of the scans) and temporal lobes (responsible for memory; located around the center of the scans). The only areas of normal metabolic activity are in the primary motor and sensory areas (at the botton of the scans).

isolated (St. George-Hyslop et al., 1992). A small proportion of early-onset cases of Alzheimer's may also be due to gene mutations on chromosome 1 (Plassman and Breitner, 1996).

Encouraged by the finding of an association between early-onset Alzheimer's disease and chromosomal abnormalities, investigators have searched for a possible chromosomal defect in late-onset, or "nonfamilial" forms of the disease. Such late-onset Alzheimer's disease has now been linked with a defect on a gene on chromosome 19, specifically the allele "APOE-4." This particular gene is thought to play a role in the transport of cholesterol through the blood. Eighty-four percent of those with familial and 64 percent of those with nonfamilial, late-onset Alzheimer's disease have at least one APOE-4 allele. As the number of APOE-4 alleles increases from 0 to 2, so does the risk for Alzheimer's disease, and the age of onset decreases from eighty-four to sixty-eight years. Having both APOE-4 alleles dramatically increases the likelihood of developing Alzheimer's disease by age eighty (Corder et al., 1993; Saunders et al., 1993).

Although the genetic findings are promising, it is important to emphasize that none of these chromo-

somal abnormalities assures the development of Alzheimer's; they only increase the odds. Alzheimer's disease runs in families to some extent, and there is evidence that there is a genetic basis for this, but most patients with Alzheimer's disease do not have another family member with the illness. So other factors must also be operating to cause the disorder.

TREATMENT OF ALZHEIMER'S DISEASE

There has been a tremendous increase in research on medical treatments for Alzheimer's disease (see Box 11–2). Among the most promising are drugs that increase the activity of the neurotransmitter acetylcholine (Mayeux and Sano, 1999; Tune and Sunderland, 1998). These drugs increase the activity of acetylcholine in the synapse. Two such drugs are tacrine and donepezil. These medications can improve performance on measures of cognitive functioning, as well as everyday living skills. However, the severity of the side effects, especially liver problems, caused by tacrine has limited its use. For most patients who show a favorable response to these drugs, the changes are modest. However, some patients show dramatic improvements in functioning that are readily apparent to their family members. There can also be improvements in the patient's mood. Despite the clear benefits, however, these medications do not cure Alzheimer's or slow its progress. Even patients on medication show a gradual decline in functioning. A point eventually comes when the medications are no longer effective. In addition, the uncomfortable physical side effects, such as nausea and insomnia, prevent some Alzheimer's patients from taking the drugs.

One of the most interesting new developments in research on the treatment of patients with Alzheimer's and other dementias is the evidence that nicotine can have beneficial effects (Whitehouse and Kalaria, 1995). Nicotine is a "cholinergic agonist," meaning that it enhances the activity of acetylcholine in the brain. Some epidemiological research findings have suggested that smoking reduces the risk of Alzheimer's and Parkinson's disease. Researchers have also shown that drugs that simulate the effects of nicotine on neurotransmitter receptors in the brain improve learning and memory in animals. This has suggested to researchers that nicotinic compounds might slow the progression of these diseases in humans. One study

Cutting-Edge Research on Alzheimer's Disease

At the very cutting edge of neuroscience research are studies that may ultimately lead to highly effective treatments for dementia. For example, some investigators are doing research that may result in "genetic therapy" for dementia (Tang et al., 1999). Joseph Tsien and his research group have examined the effects of specific genes on memory using the "knockout" procedure described in Chapter 4. They eliminated a gene called "NR1" in laboratory mice. This gene is of interest because it is involved in the development of a receptor for glutamate, the NMDA receptor. NMDA receptors in the hippocampus are known to play a central role in the formation of memories. In their absence, memories are not formed or maintained. Further, the NMDA receptors change in structure with age, and this might contribute to cognitive declines in the elderly. As expected, when Tsien and his colleagues selectively knocked out the NR1 gene in the hippocampus, the laboratory mice did not learn as well. Taking this work one step further, they then took the approach of inserting a gene, "NR2," into fertilized mouse eggs. The NR2 gene was known to improve the function of NMDA receptors by making the receptor channel stay open longer. As predicted, these mice showed superior performance on a maze task that is heavily dependent on memory!

In another line of investigation, scientists are pursuing the possibility of a vaccine for dementia (Josefsen, 1999). A vaccine was developed that is highly effective in reducing amyloid plaques in the brains of mice. As we have discussed, amyloid plaques are made of amyloid proteins and are known to contribute to neuronal cell death in humans with Alzheimer's disease. Researchers immunized mice with a fragment of the amyloid protein to see if it would affect the growth of amyloid plaques in their brains. In young mice, who had not yet developed amyloid deposits, the vaccine was successful in preventing the occurrence of plaques. In older mice, who were well into the developmental period when amyloid plaques would be expected to grow, the vaccine not only prevented the growth of more plaques, but seemed to decrease existing plaques.

These findings certainly raise amazing prospects for the prevention of human memory loss. But at this juncture, we don't know whether these laboratory findings will ever be translated into useful treatments for humans. It would certainly be desirable if we could eliminate dementia by genetic engineering or through the administration of a vaccine. The gap between laboratory animal models and treatments for human disease is very wide, however, and there is no assurance that effects observed with animals will be replicated with humans. In the year 2000, researchers began clinical trials of the "amyloid plaque" vaccine in humans. The initial findings should be available by the end of 2001.

Of course, if scientists do discover that either genetic or vaccine treatments are effective in eliminating age-related brain changes and memory loss, we will be confronted with a new set of dilemmas. Can these interventions be used to improve mental abilities in healthy people? Should we strive to eliminate the cognitive changes that occur naturally with age? We can expect biomedical ethicists to struggle with this, and related questions, during this new millennium.

SOURCE: Based on Josefson, 1999; Tang et al., 1999.

---

found that patients with dementia show improvement in cognitive functioning when they wear nicotine patches (Wilson, Langley, and Monley, 1995). Further investigations are underway to determine the long-term effects of this treatment.

There are currently a number of other compounds under study that may prove to be effective preventative treatments for dementia (Richards and Hendrie, 1999). These include estrogen, nonsteroidal anti-inflammatory drugs (for example, ibuprofen and naproxen), and nerve growth factors. Within the next decade, we can expect to see the results of large-scale follow-up studies of women who received hormone replacement therapy for menopausal discomfort. The findings will tell us whether estrogen can actually prevent the onset of Alzheimer's disease. Another promising lead is antioxidant vitamins; scientists have discovered that certain antioxidants, like vitamin E, may play a major role in the development of Alzheimer's disease. Studies are currently underway to determine whether antioxidant therapy can prevent the onset of Alzheimer's disease, or at least slow its progression (Ravaglia et al., 1998).

In addition to physical treatments, psychological therapies are also important in the treatment of patients with dementia (Zarit and Knight, 1996). The loss of cognitive and physical abilities can be devastating, so counseling and behavioral therapy are provided to help Alzheimer's patients deal with their symptoms, as well as with their emotional reactions

"And here I am at two years of age. Remember? Mom? Pop? No? Or how about this one. My first day of school. Anyone?"

to their illness. The therapist helps the patient develop strategies to reduce the impact of the illness on her daily life. Cognitive therapy can be used to treat the negative cognitions that contribute to the depression associated with dementia (Zeiss and Steffen, 1996).

Disease not only affects the patient but also the patient's family members. Seeing a loved one suffer from the illness and providing care for her can be a heavy burden on family members. The importance of offering supportive counseling and psychotherapy for family members is becoming more apparent to clinicians. Studies have shown that placement of the patient in a hospital or nursing care facility can be

delayed if families receive psychological services (Mittelman, Ferris, Shulman, Steinberg, and Levin, 1996). Providing family members with information about the nature and course of Alzheimer's disease is important. At the same time, the family members who care for the patient on a daily basis can benefit a great deal from supportive counseling that emphasizes the caregiver's personal needs for social activities and recreation that can reduce the emotional burden.

Vascular Dementia

Vascular dementia is often caused by a "stroke," which is a severe interruption of blood flow, typically with a sudden onset. The term "vascular" refers to the capillaries and arteries that supply blood and oxygen to the brain. When there is blockage in the vascular system in the brain, neuronal functions are impaired. If the interruption in the flow of oxygen and nutrients lasts longer than about ten minutes, cells can die. Vascular dementia can result in a pronounced infarct—an area of dead or dying brain tissue. In addition, the patient usually loses some motor and/or speech ability, at least temporarily. If small blood vessels, the capillaries, are partially blocked, the effects are less pervasive, and often referred to as a "silent stroke." The result is a milder form of vascular dementia. In patients who have suffered such silent strokes, brain scans often reveal multiple small infarcts, usually in the cortex or underlying white

DSM-IV Criteria

Vascular Dementia

A. The development of multiple cognitive deficits manifested by both (1) memory impairment (impaired ability to learn new information or to recall previously learned information); and (2) one (or more) of the following cognitive disturbances: (a) aphasia (language disturbance), (b) apraxia (impaired ability to carry out motor activities despite intact motor function), (c) agnosia (failure to recognize or identify objects despite intact sensory function), (d) disturbance in executive functioning (i.e., planning, organizing, sequencing, abstracting).

B. The cognitive deficits in Criteria A1 and A2 each cause significant impairment in social or occupational func-

tioning and represent a significant decline from a previous level of functioning.

C. Focal neurological signs and symptoms (e.g., exaggeration of deep tendon reflexes, extensor plantar response, pseudobulbar palsy, gait abnormalities, weakness of an extremity) or laboratory evidence indicative of cerebrovascular disease (e.g., multiple infarctions involving cortex and underlying white matter) that are judged to be etiologically related to the disturbance.

D. The deficits do not occur exclusively during the course of a delirium.

SOURCE: APA, DSM-IV, 1994.

matter. Researchers have recently found that these silent strokes also put elderly people at risk for depression (Steffens, Helms, Krishnan, and Burke, 1999).

The cognitive signs of vascular dementia parallel those of Alzheimer's disease. In fact, the cognitive signs listed in DSM-IV for the two disorders are identical. The clinical differences lay in the presence of neurological signs and brain abnormalities. In vascular dementia, the patient shows unusual reflexes and movement abnormalities. For example, the tendon reflexes can be exaggerated, and the person may show weakness in a limb or unsteady gait. In addition, there are distinctive abnormalities in the brain.

Vascular dementia is considered to be a leading cause of irreversible dementia, second only to Alzheimer's disease (Nyenhuis and Gorelick, 1998). Stroke is certainly a major risk factor for vascular dementia, but other causes include genetic factors, cardiovascular disease risk factors, and lesions in the white matter surrounding the ventricles (Gorelick, Roman, and Mangone, 1994). Risk for vascular dementia also varies, depending on sex, age, and race. Vascular dementia tends to occur more often in males than in females (Leys and Pasquier, 1998; Neri, De Vreese, Finelli, and Iacono, 1998). While men have a higher tendency to develop vascular dementia, women are at greater risk of developing Alzheimer's disease (Nyenhuis and Gorelick, 1998). There are also ethnic differences; although the reasons are unknown, older African Americans seem to be at higher risk of vascular dementia and stroke than their white counterparts (Gorelick et al., 1994).

Vascular dementia seems to have a more devastating effect on mental health than does Alzheimer's disease. One study showed that the prevalence of major depression was 3.2 percent in patients with Alzheimer's disease and 21.2 percent for patients with vascular dementia (Newman, 1999). Returning to the woman we introduced at the beginning of the chapter, we note what happened to her after she suffered a stroke at age seventy-three. Alicia's clinical course following her stroke involved symptoms of mood disorder, but there was no evidence of dementia:

> Alicia felt dizzy while leaning over in the garden and decided the summer heat was getting to her. She stood up to go inside, took a few steps, then fell to the ground. Her friend Cal happened to see her from the

window, and he immediately ran outside to help. At that point, Alicia couldn't speak and seemed to be partially unconscious. Cal called an ambulance, and Alicia was rushed to the hospital. She was diagnosed as having had a stroke. Alicia's symptoms included a loss of movement in her left arm and leg, as well as some agitation and confusion. Within a few days these symptoms began to clear up. An MRI revealed evidence of a stroke in the right hemisphere, as well as some very mild signs of vascular infarcts in other brain regions.

> Alicia's initial reaction to the stroke was fear and worry. Would she recover her ability to move her limbs? After it became clear that she was going to regain full function, Alicia was relieved. After five days in the hospital, she went home to recuperate, but she began to show signs of depression. She told Cal and her children that she was concerned about becoming a burden to them. She cried often and showed little interest in eating or recreational activities. After two weeks, Alicia's physician prescribed an antidepressant for her. Alicia's daughter scheduled an appointment with a psychologist.

> The psychologist first conducted an assessment to determine whether the stroke had caused any significant cognitive deficits. He administered a brief battery and found that Alicia was functioning at an above-average level, with excellent short-term and long-term memory. Consistent with her high level of education, Alicia's vocabulary and fund of general information was in the superior range. But it was also clear that Alicia was clinically depressed; her score on the Beck Depression Inventory (BDI) was in the "clinical depression range." The psychologist began a course of cognitive-behavior therapy. Within two weeks, Alicia was showing signs of improvement. Her spirits had improved. She looked forward to her therapy sessions, and she believed she was gaining a new and better perspective on life.

> Alicia's family was also pleased by her progress. After three months of therapy, she seemed to be her normal self again, with no traces of depression.

Alicia's case is typical, in that she experienced a deep depression following her stroke. As in many such cases, her response to antidepressant medication and therapy was very favorable. One of the factors that probably contributed to Alicia's success in therapy was her alertness and insight. She showed no signs of dementia, despite her age and history of stroke. This is consistent with the evidence that people with higher levels of education are at lower risk for dementia (Ott et al., 1999; Palsson, Aevarsson, and Skoog, 1999). This may be due to the effects of mental stimulation on brain function, or it may simply reflect the greater "cognitive reserve" available to people with higher educational levels.

Frontal Lobe Dementia

When progressive neuronal degeneration principally affects the frontal lobes, it produces dementia with characteristic frontal signs. Unlike patients with Alzheimer's dementia, which in its initial stages primarily affects the temporal and parietal lobes, patients with *frontal lobe dementia* (sometimes called *Pick's disease*) show variable, often mild memory deficits and little or no visuo-spatial impairment. Indeed, many patients present with symptoms similar to those of Phineas Gage (discussed in Chapter 4): marked changes in personality, disinhibition, unconcern, language problems, and socially inappropriate behavior. As the illness progresses, more cognitive symptoms arise, including memory problems and apraxia. The following case illustrates this condition:

A fifty-year-old shop manager suffered a gradually progressive change in his personality. He became outspoken, rude, and callous, lacking in initiative, self-care, and responsibility toward his family. His mood would fluctuate between facetiousness and jocularity and negativism and irritability, with verbal and physical aggression thought to be totally out of character.

On examination, he was free of neurological signs. He was generally courteous, although mildly disinhibited, talking excessively loudly, and giving frequent and inappropriate guffaws of laughter. His speech was normal. There was no evidence of impaired comprehension. He was left/right oriented, and no word finding difficulty was evident. Repetition tasks elicited perseverations [repetitions] of previous responses. He could read and write, although his spelling was poor. He showed substantial difficulty in calculating. He had no difficulty in perceptual identification of objects, line drawings, and faces of celebrities. He was fully oriented and displayed preserved memory for day-to-day events.

Over a four-year follow-up period his behavior became increasingly rigid and inflexible, and violent outbursts were more common. He was inert and lacked initiative. Stereotyped mannerisms were increasingly evident. His cognitive performance remained qualitatively similar, although increasing impulsivity, carelessness and lack of attention to the task resulted in reduced performance accuracy. (Source: Neary, Snowden, Northern, and Goulding, 1988)

Dementia due to Pick's disease usually has its onset between fifty and sixty years of age. Although it is distinguished from other dementias on the basis of the pattern of clinical symptoms, the diagnosis is confirmed by postmortem examination of the brain, which reveals marked changes in the neurons of the frontal lobe.

Signs of frontal dysfunction are not unique to this form of dementia. The frontal lobes have widespread connections with most other brain regions, and many of these interconnections rely on dopamine as the chemical messenger (Swartz, 1999). Thus, when there are abnormalities in subcortical brain regions, there may eventually be symptoms of frontal lobe dysfunction. Especially in the advanced stages, frontal dysfunction accompanies Alzheimer's disease, vascular dementia, and Parkinson's disease, as described below.

Dementia Due to Parkinson's Disease

Parkinson's disease is a disorder that is the result of a degeneration of dopamine neurons in subcortical

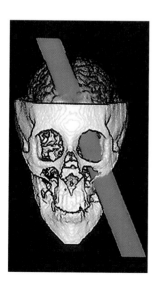

Skull of Phineas Gage showing the hole in the frontal bone made by the iron bar blown through his head.

DSM-IV Criteria

Dementia Due to Parkinson's Disease

A. The development of multiple cognitive deficits manifested by both: (1) memory impairment (impaired ability to learn new information or to recall previously learned information), and (2) one (or more) of the following cognitive disturbances: (a) aphasia (language disturbance); (b) apraxia (impaired ability to carry out motor activities despite intact motor function); (c) agnosia (failure to recognize or identify objects despite intact sensory function); (d) disturbance in executive functioning (i.e., planning, organizing, sequencing, abstracting).

B. The cognitive deficits in Criteria A1 and A2 each cause significant impairment in social or occupational functioning and represent a significant decline from a previous level of functioning.

C. There is evidence from the history, physical examination, or laboratory findings that the disturbance is the direct physiological consequence of Parkinson's disease.

D. The deficits do not occur exclusively during the course of a delirium.

SOURCE: APA, DSM-IV, 1994.

regions of the brain. It affects about 1 out of 100,000 people, and it usually has its onset after sixty years of age. The prominent signs of Parkinson's disease are movement abnormalities, tremors in the limbs and head, muscle rigidity, and a generalized inability to initiate movement. In addition to these motor signs, somewhere between 20 to 60 percent of patients with this disorder also show dementia (Ellgring, 1999; Phahwa, Paolo, Troester, and Koller, 1998). The cognitive symptoms include memory loss, specifically retrieving long-term memories, storing new information, and procedural skills; and deficits in executive functions, such as planning and organization.

Patients with Parkinson's disease who develop dementia come from families with a higher rate of other forms of dementia, including Alzheimer's disease (Marder et al., 1999). One study found that siblings of patients who had Parkinson's disease with dementia were three times as likely as siblings of healthy seniors to develop Alzheimer's disease. Among siblings who were sixty-five years or older, there was a fivefold increase in Alzheimer's disease.

A substantial proportion of patients with Parkinson's disease also show psychotic symptoms and mood disorders (Ellgring, 1999; Gelb, Oliver, and Gilman, 1999). In some cases, the psychotic symptoms are a result of the dopamine agonists, such as L-dopa, that are administered to treat the motoric dysfunction (Wolters, 1999). Chronic psychosis induced by L-dopa afflicts about one-fifth of patients with Parkinson's disease. But the most common disorder among patients with Parkinson's disease is depression; the prevalence rate for depression in these patients is about 50 percent, and approximately 26 percent of them are on antidepressants (Richard and Kurlan, 1997). The mood disorder associated with Parkinson's disease, usually depression, may be a direct consequence of the dopamine deficiency that causes the disorder. In

(Left) Actor Michael J. Fox suffers from Parkinson's disease and quit his award-winning show *Spin City* as his disease worsened. *(Right)* A woman after being treated with L-dopa in the 1990 film *Awakenings*. This film was based on the true story of patients who had contracted encephalitis lethargica ("sleeping sickness") during the flu epidemic of 1918 and had remained frozen and unable to move or speak for over fifty years, exhibiting the signs of extreme Parkinson's disease. While the drug enabled the patients to awake from their catatonic state, it ultimately led to irritability and violence in many of the patients and was discontinued.

DSM-IV Criteria

Delirium Due to a General Medical Condition

A. Disturbance of consciousness (i.e., reduced clarity of awareness of the environment) with reduced ability to focus, sustain, or shift attention.

B. A change in cognition (such as memory deficit, disorientation, language disturbance) or the development of a perceptual disturbance that is not better accounted for by a preexisting, established, or evolving dementia.

C. The disturbance develops over a short period of time (usually hours to days) and tends to fluctuate during the course of the day.

D. There is evidence from the history, physical examination, or laboratory findings that the disturbance is caused by the direct physiological consequences of a general medical condition.

SOURCE: APA, DSM-IV, 1994.

---

part, the depression may also reflect the individual's response to the physical limitations imposed by the illness.

Delirium

Up to this point, we have discussed disturbances in cognitive functions that result from age-related changes in the structure of the brain. But cognitive impairment can also result from transient changes in the biochemistry of the brain. **Delirium** is a cognitive disturbance that has a rapid onset, fluctuates over time, and usually responds rapidly to treatment. As in dementia, there may be memory deficit, sensory deficit, disorientation, and communication problems, but the onset is rapid rather than gradual.

Moreover, delirium is a disorder that can occur at any age, although it is somewhat more common in the elderly.

DSM-IV differentiates between two general types of delirium: delirium due to a general medical condition and substance intoxication delirium. A broad range of medical conditions can produce delirium, including hormonal imbalances, oxygen deprivation, head trauma, and metabolic disorders such as hypoglycemia. Because these conditions are more common among the elderly, so too is delirium.

In young people, substance-induced delirium is often caused by the ingestion of excessive amounts of alcohol or recreational drugs. But elderly people most often experience delirium as a result of prescription drugs that are either taken in excessive doses, or taken in the wrong combination. Many elderly people receive prescriptions from several

DSM-IV Criteria

Substance Intoxication Delirium

A. Disturbance of consciousness (i.e., reduced clarity of awareness of the environment) with reduced ability to focus, sustain, or shift attention.

B. A change in cognition (such as memory deficit, disorientation, language disturbance) or the development of a perceptual disturbance that is not better accounted for by a preexisting, established, or evolving dementia.

C. The disturbance develops over a short period of time (usually hours to days) and tends to fluctuate during the course of the day.

D. There is evidence from the history, physical examination, or laboratory findings of either (1) or (2): (1) the symptoms in Criteria A and B developed during Substance Intoxication; or (2) medication use is etiologically related to the disturbance.

SOURCE: APA, DSM-IV, 1994.

different physicians. If the patient fails to inform each of the physicians about her daily medication regimen, she can end up taking drug combinations that produce excessive sedation or confusion. Thus, when geriatric patients show signs of mental impairment, one of the first questions asked by a good clinician is, "What medications are you currently taking?" Once a substance-induced delirium is identified, the discontinuation of nonessential medications typically eliminates the delirium. The following case of an elderly women with delirium is a clear example:

A 65-year-old Caucasian female was admitted to a general medicine ward of a university hospital due to paranoid behavior and visual hallucinations. The patient had recently been discharged from the same hospital after successful heart surgery. Shortly after arriving home, however, the patient appeared suspicious of family members and then ducked when she perceived bats to be flying out of her refrigerator. She was readmitted to the hospital and a consult was requested from a neuropsychologist. During the evaluation, the patient was well oriented and denied visual hallucinations. She expressed dismay and anger that her husband had been telling the physicians about her behavior and accused him of making the doctors think she was "crazy" so that he could divorce her and marry a younger woman. She was

noted to begin plucking at her bedclothes, and, when asked who had been to visit her that day, she reported visits from improbable individuals. Some time later, the patient took a cup of water, pantomimed opening a sugar packet and stirring the cup, and informed the psychologist that she had fixed the coffee just the way she preferred. The psychologist diagnosed the patient with delirium likely secondary to medication. Investigation revealed that the patient had been discharged from the hospital on 11 medications that she took in conjunction with other medications prescribed by her primary care physician back home. The physician tapered nonessential medications. Three days later the patient evidenced no unusual behavior, reported no concerns or suspicions about her husband's behavior, and was described by her sister as "like her old self." (Source: Lichtenburg, 1999)

Late-Life Depression

In contrast to the dementias, which increase with age, self-reported symptoms of negative mood, particularly depression and anxiety, decrease with age (Henderson, Jorm, et al., 1998). Figures 11–3A and B show the results of a survey of over 2,700 individ-

Figure 11—3

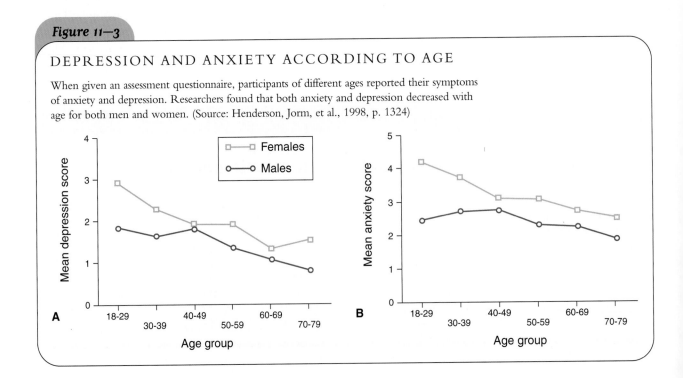

DEPRESSION AND ANXIETY ACCORDING TO AGE

When given an assessment questionnaire, participants of different ages reported their symptoms of anxiety and depression. Researchers found that both anxiety and depression decreased with age for both men and women. (Source: Henderson, Jorm, et al., 1998, p. 1324)

uals ranging in age from eighteen to seventy-nine years. As you can see, scores on self-report measures of depression and anxiety go down sharply with age for both men and women. But does this mean that there is an actual decrease in feelings of anxiety and depression with age? Or could it be what researchers call a "cohort" effect? A cohort is a group of individuals born during a particular time period. People born at different times may also differ in their tendency to report negative feelings. Imagine, for example, that the cohort of people born between 1900 and 1910 always reported less depression and anxiety than those born in the following decades. In other words, if we had asked the 1900 to 1910 birth cohort to rate their depression and anxiety when they were thirty years old, they would have reported the same low level—and there would be no change with age.

One way to address this issue is to ask people the same questions repeatedly, as they age. This requires a longitudinal research design. Joseph Gallo and his colleagues at Johns Hopkins University conducted such a study (Gallo, Rabins, and Anthony, 1999). In 1981, they asked a group of 1,651 adults from the community to report on their feelings of sadness. The researchers asked these same people the same question thirteen years later, when they ranged in age from thirty to over sixty-five years of age. The results showed a clear age effect: there was a decrease in self-reported sadness and other signs of depression as these individuals aged. It was not a cohort effect.

Prevalence and Symptoms of Clinical Depression

Researchers have found an age-related decrease for the clinical diagnosis of depression: when compared to those in younger age groups, persons over the age of sixty-five have the lowest rate of clinical depression (Jeste et al., 1999; Regier et al., 1988). Estimates of depression in those over age sixty-five average between 1 and 3 percent, whereas in middle adulthood (ages thirty to forty-five) the rates are around 6 to 8 percent, and young adult rates exceed 10 percent. Nonetheless, there does appear to be a sharp rise in the rate of depression in those who are past the age of eighty, suggesting that we can expect to see more depression in the elderly as the life span increases (Gatz, Kasl-Godley, and Karel, 1996). The reasons for

this are unknown. It is likely that both psychological factors (such as reactions to physical limitations) and brain changes contribute to depression in those over the age of eighty.

A decrease in depression past the age of sixty-five is the opposite of what many people might expect. Especially in the United States, a great premium is placed on youth and vitality. Many people assume that being old is unpleasant because it is associated with a decline in strength and physical health. So how can it be that those who are approaching the end of their life are actually less likely to be depressed? There is no conclusive answer to this question, but it has been suggested that it is due to the less demanding lives of the elderly (Henderson, Jorm, et al., 1998). Most do not have to contend with work or child-rearing demands, and their relationships are relatively stable.

Even though rates of depression are lower among adults over the age of sixty-five than among younger people, we should not conclude that depression is not a problem for the elderly (Henderson and Hasegawa, 1992; National Insititue of Mental Health, 1989b). In fact, depression is the most common psychological disorder among older adults: the vast majority of elderly people admitted to psychiatric hospitals are diagnosed with depression (Verhey and Honig, 1997). When older adults experience feelings of depression, it is likely to be due to an increase in somatic symptoms linked to physical changes or concerns about the narrowing of long-term opportunities (Christensen et al., 1999). Moreover, research has shown that the risk of depression among older people is linked with the level of physical illness and disability they experience (Roberts, Kaplan, Shema, and Strawbridge, 1997). This is because these physical factors can impose limitations on their ability to care for themselves, to interact with others, and generally to enjoy life.

Depression in the elderly is often accompanied by cognitive deficits (Feinstein, 1999; Rosenstein, 1998). In a longitudinal study of more than 5,000 older women (age sixty-five and above), those who reported more depressive symptoms showed the most dramatic decline in cognitive functioning when they were followed up four years later (Yaffe et al., 1999). Does a decline in mental functioning cause depression among older adults, or does depression contribute to a decline in mental functioning? We do not yet know the answer to this question. But, as described in Chapter 4, we do know that

In older adults, depression may be caused by physical illness, cognitive impairments, or the loss of loved ones and friends.

prolonged exposure to stress can result in brain abnormalities. Thus, the stress associated with depression may contribute to brain changes that impair cognitive functions in elderly people.

Depression in the elderly may also have lethal consequences. It is associated with an increase in death rates from illness (Pulska, Pahkala, Laippala, and Kivela, 1999). And, like younger people with depression, the depressed elderly are much more likely to take their own lives. In virtually all countries where information on suicide rates is available, the rate is highest among the elderly (Shimizu, 1992). The most common precipitating factor is suffering due to serious illness. This is in contrast to younger adults who are more likely to commit suicide in response to financial losses or romantic disappointments. So, why would the suicide rate be higher among older adults when their rate of depression is lower? It is likely that part of the answer lays in the perspective elderly people have on the future and their worries about dependency on others.

As is the case with suicide in early adulthood, there is a sex difference in the rate of suicide among the elderly; men show a much higher rate than women (Shimizu, 1992). One of the explanations for this sex difference is the means employed. Women are more likely to use drug overdoses and to be resuscitated. Men are much more likely to use guns, hanging, or jumping from heights—all very lethal means. In contrast, there is a sex difference in the rate of depression in the elderly that is the opposite of the sex difference in suicide (Henderson, Jorm, et al., 1998). As illustrated in Figures 11–3A and B, women are more likely than men to report symptoms of depression and anxiety at all ages. The findings from some studies have shown that women also have a greater tendency toward late-life clinical depression (Kessler et al., 1993).

The main factors that contribute to late-life depression differ from those that cause depression in young adulthood. Of course, certain personal vulnerability factors, such as a personality disorder or history of depression, are linked with depression in people of all ages. Nonetheless, in older adults, the major risk factors for depression are health problems (including physical illness, cognitive impairment, or disability), and social factors linked with the death or illness of a loved one (bereavement, playing a caregiver role) (Jorm, 1995). As mentioned earlier, there is evidence that vascular disorders of the brain, even those that go undetected, can contribute directly to depression (Conway and Steffens, 1999). In fact, depressive symptoms are very common in persons recovering from stroke. In the social domain, caring for a chronically ill spouse is one of the major causes of depression in elderly people. The case history of "Mr. B" illustrates how the stress and isolation of being a caregiver for an ill spouse can contribute to clinical depression:

Mr. B was a seventy-four-year-old male who had been married for fifty years. He was the primary caregiver to his wife, who had been diagnosed with emphysema seven years earlier. Mr. B was a retired architect with a Master's degree in architectural design. He and his wife had two sons, who were both married and lived out of state. Mr. B was referred to therapy by his physician, who believed that he was experiencing some significant anxiety and depression as a result of being responsible for the care of both his wife and their household. During the intake, he reported with great sadness that he was quite committed to caring for his wife. He also described becoming anxious when she is demanding and hostile to him. Mr. B described an event where she refused to eat breakfast, and was critical of him when he said that he had run out of her favorite bread for her toast. Mr. B reported that these difficulties have been ongoing for the past year, since his wife's health began to decline. Mr. B reported no prior episodes of depression or any prior experience with psychotherapy.

At intake, Mr. B exhibited a significant depression, scoring 20 on the Beck Depression Inventory and 18 on the Hamilton Rating Scale for Depression (Hamilton, 1967). Mr. B expressed a desire to contract for the standard course of twenty sessions of cognitive-behavioral therapy offered at the Older Adult Center at the Department of Veterans Affairs Medical Center, Palo Alto, but he was quite concerned about his wife's reaction to his involvement in therapy. (Source: Dick, Gallagher-Thompson, and Thompson, 1996)

Treatment

Depression in the elderly is treated in the same way as depression in younger people. Cognitive-behavioral therapy is often used to reduce the negative thought patterns that contribute to depression. Recent studies that have compared antidepressant medication and cognitive-behavioral therapy indicate that the two are comparable in effectiveness for treating late-life depression (Dick, Gallagher-Thompson and Thompson, 1996). About 65 percent of elderly patients are improved after one year of either treatment. Another recent "double-blind" study followed elderly patients with major depression over three years (Reynolds et al., 1999). The researchers found that depression recurred in about 43 percent of depressed elderly patients who were treated only with antidepressant medication. But when the medication was combined with interpersonal psychotherapy, the recurrence rate was cut in half, to only 20 percent. The treatment of Mr. B. shows how cognitive-behavioral therapy can be used to alleviate depression in an elderly man:

Early Phase. Initially, it was very uncomfortable for Mr. B to attend the therapy sessions. At first, he told his wife that he was going to see his physician, but later "confessed" to her that he was seeing a psychologist. Consequently, Mr. B would often come in quite anxious because his wife became increasingly demanding moments before he had to leave for his appointment. In order to keep Mr. B focused on the agenda, a brief relaxation exercise was introduced at

the beginning of each session. Mr. B was immediately satisfied with this exercise, as he noticed his physical tension eased, his labored breathing subsided, and his racing thoughts decreased. The therapist provided Mr. B with an audiotaped version of the relaxation exercises, suggesting that he practice them whenever he felt the physical symptoms of anxiety emerging, but he doubted that he could get a moment away from his wife to try it.

Mr. B was able to articulate and define clear goals for therapy: to reduce his depression by understanding and challenging the stressful beliefs that accompany his caregiving duties; to increase his pleasant, social activities; and to reduce his anxiety during situations with his wife where he needed to be assertive.

Mr. B completed an Older Person's Pleasant Events Schedule, which revealed that he still maintained strong interests in social activities and some leisure activities, but he did so infrequently or almost not at all. This measure also demonstrated that Mr. B enjoyed recognition from others, but experienced so few times when someone (particularly his wife) complimented him or thanked him for a job well done.

Mr. B explained that he rarely socialized with friends, because he believed he could not leave his wife alone with any other paid caregiver, as it would "upset her." He also believed he was the only person who could competently take care of her. These beliefs were further complicated by the fact that he reported many situations where his wife would be critical of his care, as well as asking him not to leave the house even to run household errands. Thus Mr. B started to believe that his desire to find time for himself made him a "bad caregiver."

Final Phase. By the final phase of therapy, Mr. B was able to spend one hour in his study each morning, thirty minutes in his study after lunch, and one hour each evening. He was also able to plan outings with old friends, as well as schedule a weekly golf game. Mr. B introduced each of these activities by stating helpful cognitions, such as "In order for me to be a good caregiver, I must take care of myself" and "I deserve to enjoy my retirement and keep up with things and people that I enjoy." Mr. B also demonstrated a significant decrease in his anxiety around asserting his needs to his wife. He also hired a paid caregiver to come to the house for four hours each day to give him a break from the household chores.

Mr. B was also quite collaborative in the creation of a "maintenance guide," which was his summary of all the changes he made, skills he learned, and how he would handle future difficult situations. Mr. B completed therapy with a BDI of 3, and a score of 4 on the Hamilton Anxiety Scale. The therapist asked Mr. B if he would be interested in a "booster session" which could serve as a check to see how he was handling these new skills independently. Mr. B agreed and a booster session was scheduled for one month later. (Source: Dick, Gallagher-Thompson, and Thompson, 1996)

Anxiety in older people may be caused by financial worries, worries about becoming ill or dependent, or by catastrophic events like war and the loss of friends and homes.

One of the most surprising recent findings on depression is that sleep deprivation seems to be useful in treatment. Several studies of older adults have shown that sleep deprivation can result in a rapid, although short-lived, antidepressant effect. Smith and colleagues studied a group of elderly depressed patients to determine whether total sleep deprivation had the same effects on functional brain activity as long-term treatment with antidepressant medication (Smith et al., 1999). PET scans were used to measure brain activity at baseline and after total sleep deprivation. The researchers found that sleep deprivation produced a change in brain activation similar to that observed in patients who receive antidepressant drugs. More specifically, there was a reduction in activity in the anterior cingulate cortex, a brain region that is part of the limbic system. These findings suggest that in elderly depressed patients, sleep deprivation may accelerate the treatment response. At this point, we do not know why sleep deprivation reduces the symptoms of depression.

Finally, psychologists must keep in mind some special considerations when working with older patients. First, it is important that the treatment provider be sensitive to his or her own biases about aging. If the therapist has negative stereotypes about the aging process, it may be difficult to establish rapport and encourage positive change. Second, the treatment provider may have to contend with biased perceptions on the part of the elderly patient. Some elderly depressed patients may view a younger professional with suspicion, and wonder whether someone with less life experience can really understand them. Special care must be taken to build the patient's confidence in the treatment process.

Anxiety in the Elderly

Like depression, the rate of anxiety seems to decline with age (Jeste et al., 1999). As shown in Table 11–1, the best estimate is that about 2 percent of people over the age of sixty-five would meet diagnostic criteria for generalized anxiety disorder. Of course, it is likely that many elderly people who do not meet all of the DSM-IV criteria for generalized anxiety disorder still experience symptoms of anxiety. A recent survey of people over the age of sixty revealed that about 10 percent experienced episodes of severe anxiety that did not meet criteria for anxiety disorder (Papassotiropoulos and Heun, 1999).

It is reasonable to assume that many of the causes of anxiety in the elderly are the same as those that contribute to anxiety in younger adults. These can include financial worries and concerns about the welfare of loved ones. But anxiety in elderly people may also have some causes that are relatively uncommon in younger adults (Fortner and Neimeyer, 1999). For example, with advanced age, anxiety about death increases. In addition to concerns about their own mortality, many elderly people express anxiety about the prospect of becoming very ill and dependent. In fact, like the rates of depression, rates of anxiety among people over the age of sixty-five are higher for those who are ill (De Beurs et al., 1999). Moreover, the risk for anxiety is markedly increased in people who have suffered a stroke.

Some innovative behavioral treatments have been used to treat anxiety in older people. Cognitive-behavioral therapy with the elderly typically focuses on the relief of anxiety through the reduction of thoughts about death and disability, as well as the re-organization of daily routines (Stanley and Averill, 1999). In one case report on a stroke patient, a biofeedback program was very effective in reducing both physiological indices and self-report measures of anxiety (Melton, Van Sickle, Hersen and Van Hasselt, 1999).

Although the physical health benefits of exercise for the elderly are well accepted, the mental health benefits have only recently been recognized (Katula, Blissmer, and McAuley, 1999; King, Taylor, and Haskell, 1993). Over a twelve-month period, Abbey King and her colleagues examined the effects of exercise on anxiety in healthy, older adults. The participants were randomly assigned to take part in light or high-intensity physical exercise, or they were part of a control group. For some, the exercise took place in a group setting, while others exercised alone. Psychological symptoms were measured at the beginning and end of the year. At the end of the year, there was a significant reduction in anxiety for those who were in the exercise group, and the setting and intensity of the exercise did not matter. These and related findings have highlighted the importance of physical activity for maintaining mental health in the elderly.

Drug treatments for anxiety in the elderly are similar to those used in younger patients (Bell, 1999). However, one additional factor to take into consideration with the elderly is the problem of negative side effects and interactions among medications (Ayd, 1994; Berg and Dellasega, 1996). It seems that the benzodiazepines, which are among the main drugs used for anxiety, have great potential for interfering with cognitive functions, especially in older people (Curran, 1994). Extra caution must be used in prescribing these drugs to people over the age of sixty-five. The benefit of reducing anxiety must be weighed against the risk of impairing cognitive abilities.

Substance Abuse in the Elderly

There is a general decline in the use of alcohol and illegal drugs among people who are beyond the age of sixty-five (Adams, Garry, Rhyne, Hunt, and Goodwin, 1990). This trend is consistent with the more conservative lifestyles that people tend to adopt as they get older. When substance abuse does occur, however, it may have more immediate life-threatening consequences for older people than it does for the young.

The most common form of substance abuse in the elderly is alcohol abuse, with about 9 percent of men and 2 percent of women over sixty years of age reporting that they drink more than twenty-one drinks per week (Adams, Barry, and Fleming, 1996). Similarly, 9 percent of the men and 3 percent of the women met criteria for substance abuse within the past three months. When excessive alcohol consumption is combined with the physical changes that accompany aging, the results are especially problematic. For example, aging is associated with a normal decline in reaction time and coordination that can make driving more difficult. The additional effects of alcohol on perceptual-motor skills can seriously compromise an elderly person's ability to drive safely.

Another common substance abuse problem in the elderly is the abuse of prescription medications (Gomberg and Zucker, 1998; Norton, 1998). Many elderly people receive prescriptions for psychotropic drugs (tranquilizers and anxiolytics) in order to help them with anxiety or, more often, with sleeping difficulties (see Box 11–3). As mentioned above, these drugs can interfere with cognitive functions. They also have tremendous potential for addiction and abuse. Although the proportion of elderly people who abuse prescription drugs is not known, it is a familiar problem encountered by primary care physicians who treat geriatric patients. The following case illustrates this problem:

Howard, aged seventy, had retired from his insurance business two years earlier. He expressed great satisfaction with his new lifestyle during the first year, but by the second year he began to express feelings of anxiety and aimlessness. Sleeping was especially difficult. Howard awakened several times on most nights, for no apparent reason, and had trouble getting back to sleep. Most nights he only slept about two hours. Howard's physician prescribed a common drug used to treat anxiety, a benzodiazepine.

The drug seemed to be a lifesaver. Howard slept through the night easily. But after two weeks, when

Box 11—3

Levels of Analysis

Sleeping Pill Abuse in the Elderly

The elderly comprise only 10 percent of the U.S. population, but they consume 25 to 40 percent of the nation's prescription drugs. Among those over age sixty-five, especially those with physical illnesses, the use of sleeping pills is widespread. In fact, over 90 percent of institutionalized elderly persons are prescribed sedative-hypnotic drugs. This is because sleep disturbances are so prevalent among the elderly. Insomnia in later life is commonly associated with increased rates of sleep-disordered breathing, nocturnal muscle spasms, problems with circulation, and physical pain. Physicians are concerned about treating sleep disturbances in the elderly because insufficient restful sleep can diminish the quality of life. Chronic insomnia can lead to excessive fatigue and depression.

Prescribing sleep medication to older patients can be risky, however. Elderly people with memory problems sometimes forget that they have already taken their medica-tion, and they end up "double-dosing." The result can be lethargy, excessive sleep, and an increased frequency of accidents. Other aversive effects of sleeping pills include daytime hangover, exacerbation of sleep-disordered breathing, impaired alertness, drug interaction, drug tolerance, and rebound insomnia. Moreover, the prescription of sleeping pills to treat insomnia in the elderly can also lead to addiction, abuse, and delirium. Because insomnia is often chronic and recurring, there is a need for long-term management strategies for insomnia. In order to counter the dangerous overprescription of sleeping pills to the elderly, alternative nonpharmacological measures to manage sleep disturbances are needed.

SOURCE: Based on Reynolds, Buysse, and Kupfer, 1999; Reynolds, Kupfer, Hoch, and Sewitch, 1985.

---

the doctor advised him that it was time to discontinue the medication, Howard's sleep problems returned. The doctor denied Howard's request for another prescription. But Howard was so convinced he needed the medication, he went to another physician to get "treatment" for his sleep problems. The scenario was repeated with five different physicians. In this way, Howard was able to keep a steady supply of medication. His use of the drug was initially limited to bedtime, but after several months, Howard began to take it during the day to reduce his anxiety level.

By the time he reached his seventieth birthday, Howard was sleeping fifteen or more hours a day. His friends noticed that he seemed to be confused sometimes. One evening, at a reception for a former co-worker, Howard drank a cocktail and became so drowsy that he fell asleep on a sofa and could not be awakened. His hosts were alarmed and called an ambulance to take him to the emergency room. It was discovered that Howard had taken a dose of his antianxiety medication immediately before the party. He was referred for treatment for his addiction after release from the hospital.

Although substance abuse and addiction is not currently a major problem for older people, some experts have predicted that it will be in the near fu-ture (Montoya, Chenier, and Richard, 1996; Patterson and Jeste, 1999). The "baby-boom" generation ushered in the era of recreational drug use among youth. The idea that one could use chemicals to add to the enjoyment of socializing with others, watching a movie, or listening to a concert was popularized in the 1960s. In subsequent years, from the 1960s through the 1990s, our society witnessed a stunning increase in the proportion of people taking drugs to change their mood. The use of alcohol also increased during these decades. As a result, compared to previous generations, the level of substance abuse problems is higher among the baby-boom generation and the generations that have followed it.

What will happen when the baby-boomers and their successors become senior citizens? Will those who have substance abuse problems take these problems into old age? If they do, substance abuse among the elderly will be a significant public health problem. Or will the tendency for older people to adopt a more conservative lifestyle result in a decline in substance abuse? The next few decades will reveal the answer. In the meantime, those in the field of substance abuse are beginning to publicly discuss the treatment implications (Dupree and Schonfeld, 1999). Most existing treatment programs for alcohol and drug abuse are designed for young adult populations. New approaches will be needed for addicts who are also senior citizens.

Delusional Disorder

DSM-IV defines *delusional disorder* as a type of psychotic disorder in which the person experiences nonbizarre delusions for at least one month in duration. What are nonbizarre delusions? They are beliefs that are plausible and potentially believable, yet false. They involve situations that can occur in real life, such as having a disease, being followed, poisoned, infected, having a secret admirer, or being deceived by a spouse or lover. The delusions must not interfere with normal functioning or behavior, aside from the impact of the delusions or its consequences. For example, if the individual with a nonbizarre delusion becomes a complete recluse due to fear of poisoning, refuses to speak to others unless they use a secret language code, and claims to hear messages about poisoning over the radio, he would not receive the diagnosis of delusional disorder. Instead, he is likely to meet diagnostic criteria for schizophrenia. If there are also extended episodes of depression or mania at the same time as the delusions, mood disorder may be the more appropriate diagnosis. Finally, the delusions cannot be a result of the physical effects of a substance or a general medical condition.

Delusional disorder is usually first diagnosed when the person is in middle or late adulthood. Among persons aged sixty-five and older, the prevalence is about .04 percent, with an annual incidence of 15.6 per 100,000 people (Copeland et al., 1998). Other estimates of the prevalence of delusional disorder in older populations range from 0.1 percent (Lindstroem, Widerloev, and von Knorring, 1997) to 1.78 percent in hospital populations (Penin et al., 1993).

A person diagnosed with delusional disorder may be further diagnosed by type, depending upon the predominant delusional theme. The subtypes may include: erotomanic type (another person is in love with the individual), grandiose type (inflated worth, power, knowledge, identity, or special relationship to a deity or famous person), jealous type (an individual's sexual partner is unfaithful), persecutory type (a person is being malevolently treated in some way), somatic type (the existence of some physical defect or general medical condition), mixed type (combination of more than one of the previously described types, with no one type predominating), and unspecified type. The most common type of delusional disorder is the persecutory type (National Institute of Mental Health, 1989a). For example, the person might believe that his family members are plotting among themselves to keep him physically inactive so that he will decline in health and have to be put in a nursing home.

The causes of delusional disorder have not been identified. Some have proposed that it may stem from the same genetic causes as schizophrenia. But the biological relatives of patients with delusional disorder do not show an elevated rate of schizophrenia (Kendler and Hays, 1981). Nonetheless, there is evidence that persons who suffer from delusional disorder are more likely to be socially isolated,

---

DSM-IV Criteria

Delusional Disorder

A. Nonbizarre delusions (i.e., involving situations that occur in real life, such as being followed, poisoned, infected, loved at a distance, or deceived by spouse or lover, or having a disease) of at least 1 month's duration.

B. Criterion A for Schizophrenia has never been met. *Note:* Tactile and olfactory hallucinations may be present in Delusional Disorder if they are related to the delusional theme.

C. Apart from the impact of the delusion(s) or its ramifica-

tions, functioning is not markedly impaired and behavior is not obviously odd or bizarre.

D. If mood episodes have occurred concurrently with delusions, their total duration has been brief relative to the duration of the delusional periods.

E. The disturbance is not due to the direct physiological effects of a substance (e.g., a drug of abuse, a medication) or a general medical condition.

SOURCE: APA, DSM-IV, 1994.

suggesting that insufficient social contact may contribute to delusions (Munro, 1992). There is also a higher rate of sensory deficits in people with delusional disorder (Maher, 1992), and this has led to the notion that the delusional beliefs may represent an attempt to make "sense" of confusing sensory inputs. Schlager (1995) has proposed that delusions can be "manifestations of an adaptive hypersensitivity to important environmental threats or opportunities." This can be shown in Alicia, whom we've discussed earlier in the chapter:

> When Alicia was seventy-eight years old and Cal was seventy-nine, they decided to get married. Their children and grandchildren were delighted. After the wedding, they had a honeymoon in Hawaii. During the subsequent four years, Alicia and Cal traveled together and enjoyed spending time with their families.
>
> At the age of eighty-two, Alicia began having trouble with her vision. She was diagnosed with glaucoma, and by the time she was eighty-four Alicia was almost blind. A year later, Cal died suddenly of a heart attack. Alicia was devastated. In the months following, she became depressed and confused. Her doctor prescribed an antidepressant, but it did not seem to help. Instead, Alicia began to be highly suspicious of her neighbors. She didn't want to be left alone, and called her children on the phone at all hours of the night, yet she refused to come stay with them or enter a nursing home. Alicia insisted that her neighbors were trying to break into her house at night, and that she couldn't sleep. When her children spent the night with her, they heard nothing. When they tried to convince Alicia that she was safe, she argued with them. Alicia's doctor referred her to a psychiatrist, who diagnosed her with delusional disorder. A prescription of an antipsychotic drug reduced Alicia's expressions of fear, but it also made her somewhat lethargic.
>
> When Alicia turned eighty-six, she moved in with her oldest daughter and her husband. The house was large, and Alicia had her own room. During the day, Alicia's daughter worked in her home office and was almost always accessible. In the evening and on weekends, the house was filled with the activity of Alicia's three teenage grandchildren. During this time, the antipsychotic medication was tapered off, then discontinued altogether. There was no reoccurrence of suspiciousness or delusional ideas.

Delusional disorder is often treated with antipsychotic drugs. These drugs can reduce the severity of delusions, as well as the anxiety and agitation that often accompany the disorder (Long, 1990; Munro, 1995). Patients suffering from delusional disorder with jealous and persecutory subtypes have shown some response to the newer antipsychotic medications, such as clozapine (Buckley, Sajatovic, and Meltzer, 1994; Songer and Roman, 1996). Although the use of antipsychotics may help to treat the symptoms of delusional disorder in older adults, side effects may include a loss of emotion or "sparkle," and decreased motivation (Macdonald, 1997). Individual psychotherapy may be beneficial in many cases.

Late-Onset Schizophrenia

In Chapter 10, we talked about developmental changes in the risk for psychotic disorders, the main one being schizophrenia. As we pointed out, psychotic disorders are very rare before adolescence, and once a person passes forty his risk for a first psychotic episode goes down dramatically. This probably reflects developmental changes in the brain, as well as changes in life circumstances. **Late-onset schizophrenia,** sometimes referred to as **paraphrenia,** is more common in women, with 18 percent of female patients having a first episode after the age of sixty-five. Figure 11–4 shows the number of male and female patients with schizophrenia and their various onset ages in a large sample of first-episode patients in England (Howard, Castle, Wessely, and Murray, 1993). The shift in the sex ratio is clearly apparent. In the eighteen- to twenty-five-year age range, most of the new patients are men; past the age of thirty-six years, most are women. Nonetheless, it has been estimated that 4 percent of males with schizophrenia first receive their diagnosis when they are over sixty-five years of age (Castle and Murray, 1993).

In Chapter 10, we discussed the sex difference in the age at which the clinical symptoms of schizophrenia first arise: men tend to develop schizophrenia, on average, about two years earlier than women. This difference may be due to estrogen (Lindamer, Lohr, Harris, and Jeste, 1997). It appears that estrogen can reduce the activity of dopamine, the neurotrans-

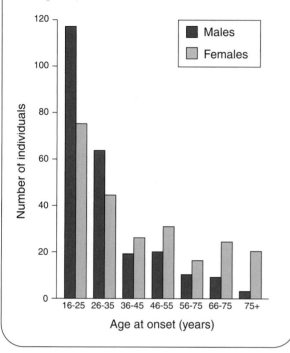

Figure 11—4

FIRST ONSET OF
SCHIZOPHRENIA IN
MEN AND WOMEN

When first-episode patients with schizophrenia were
assessed, researchers found that more of the early-
onset patients were men than women, while more of
the late-onset patients were women than men. But
for both sexes, there is a decline in the risk for onset
of schizophrenia between 25 and 45 years of age.
(Source: Howard, Castle, Wessely, and Murray,
1993, p. 354)

hereditary factors do play a smaller role in late-onset schizophrenia (Henderson and Kay, 1997). In contrast, it appears that sensory deficits, especially hearing problems, are much more common in elderly patients with schizophrenia. The symptom profile in late-onset schizophrenia is also somewhat different: patients who are first diagnosed with schizophrenia after the age of forty-five tend to have more hallucinations and paranoid delusions. Cognitive deterioration and cognitive brain disorders are also more common in first psychotic episodes in those past sixty-five years of age.

Elderly people with schizophrenia tend to be socially isolated and lonely (Almeida, Howard, Levy, and David, 1995). It is not clear, however, whether these social problems are contributing to their risk for psychosis, or are a consequence of the disorder. To some extent, the causal influence is probably in both directions. Thus, the loss in social support that some elderly people experience may cause them to be more vulnerable to mental illness. At the same time, the psychotic symptoms may contribute further to their withdrawal from social interaction.

The drug treatments for late-onset schizophrenia are the same as those used for younger patients, and include the new antipsychotics, olanzapine and clozapine. Special caution must be taken, however, to avoid excessive dosages that sedate the patient and interfere with mobility. Also, the psychiatrist must monitor interactions between the antipsychotic drug and other medications the patient might be taking.

Putting It All Together

The proportion of the U.S. population aged sixty-five or older is larger than ever before, and it is expected to increase. Our chances of living to an advanced age in good health are better than ever. Astronaut John Glenn was launched on a major space voyage in 1998, at the age of seventy-seven. Worldwide, more and more adults are pursuing a physically active and intellectually stimulating life after the age of sixty-five. In fact, according to the data, we may be happier in old age than ever before. On the other side of the coin, these benefits do come with increased risks for certain kinds of mental disorders. As

mitter that is believed to play a key role in schizophrenia. If this is true, then we might expect to see an increase in the rate of schizophrenia among women later in adulthood, when estrogen levels decline. The findings presented in Figure 11—4 seem to support this prediction.

One issue that has puzzled researchers is whether the late-onset psychotic disorders have the same causes as the early-onset psychoses. Because it is unusual for a person to have a first episode of schizophrenia after age forty, some have assumed that it must have a different cause when it arises late in life. Although researchers have not yet identified the cause of any form of schizophrenia, it appears that

a result, the mental health of senior citizens has become a more salient issue.

As birthrates stabilize, or even decline, in some regions of the world, and the life span increases, a growing proportion of the population will suffer from Alzheimer's, Parkinson's, and other forms of dementia. The treatment and prevention of these disorders will consume a larger proportion of the national budget for health care and research. It is therefore not surprising that the development of drugs to prevent the onset of the brain changes that cause dementia is a major focus of the pharmaceutical industry. Along these same lines, depression and other mental disorders in the elderly are receiving greater attention. Psychological treatments and medications are being developed to address the unique needs of older people.

But there is no pharmaceutical "fountain of youth" on the horizon. Advanced age will continue to be associated with a decline in physical abilities and, for many, a decrement in mental abilities. The challenge is to enjoy the benefits of aging, while minimizing the influence of the physical, mental, and interpersonal losses associated with advanced age. We expect that psychologists who specialize in geriatrics will play a major part in the research and clinical work directed at improving the quality of life for those in the "golden years."

It is likely that graduate education in clinical psychology and psychiatry will place an increasing emphasis on geriatric issues. In the clinical area, practitioners will receive more training in the treatment of elderly persons who are coping with the loss of physical and/or mental abilities. Maximizing their sense of autonomy and supporting their independent living skills will be especially important. The emotional losses that tend to come with advanced age, such as the death of friends and family members, will also be a key focus of clinical psychology. Individuals confronted with the death of a spouse are particularly vulnerable to both physical and mental disorders, and many will certainly benefit from preventive psychological intervention.

Summary

1. There is continuity across the life span in personality style and adjustment level. Individuals who lived healthy and productive lives in early and middle adulthood will usually maintain their positive approach to life in old age. However, on average, there is a gradual change toward lower levels of aggression and risk taking and greater cautiousness with advanced age.

2. The most common disorder associated with aging is *dementia*. The two major types of dementia are *Alzheimer's disease* and *vascular dementia*. Alzheimer's disease occurs at a higher rate in women than in men, whereas vascular dementia is more prevalent among males. Dementia due to *Parkinson's disease* and *Pick's disease* is less pervasive.

3. All dementias involve some loss of memory. In addition, each of the subtypes is associated with other cognitive deficits, such as perceptual-motor problems or a decline in frontal or "executive" capacities. Current treatments include various kinds of medications and cognitive therapy aimed at helping the patient accommodate to memory loss and reduce the depression that often accompanies the early stages of the illness.

4. *Delirium* is a cognitive disturbance that has a rapid onset, fluctuates over time, and usually responds quite quickly to treatment. The elderly are at risk for delirium because many of them suffer from general medical conditions that can lead to delirium, including hormonal imbalances, oxygen deprivation, head trauma, metabolic disorders, or excessive doses or wrong combinations of prescription drugs.

5. It appears that the rate of depressive symptoms and clinical depression is lower for those over sixty-five years of age. When depression does occur among the elderly, it is often related to a decline in physical health. Depression in senior citizens is treated with the same psychological therapies and medications that are used with younger persons. However, experienced clinicians tailor the treatment to meet the special needs of older clients.

6. The rate of anxiety also appears to decline with age. The rate of anxiety is lower for those over age sixty-five than for those who are younger. But the rate is higher in elderly people who are physically ill.

7. There is a general decline in the use of alcohol and illegal drugs among those who are over age sixty-five. But a common substance-abuse prob-

lem in the elderly is the abuse of prescription medications.

8. Although *delusional disorder* is not common for any age group, it is most likely to have its onset in middle or late adulthood. Delusional disorder involves extreme suspiciousness and delusions, without the presence of other psychotic symptoms, such as thought disorder or hallucinations. Many persons diagnosed with delusional disorder also have visual or auditory impairments.

9. In a small proportion of cases, the onset of schizophrenia occurs after the age of forty-five. Most of the late-onset cases are women. It has been hypothesized that *late-onset schizophrenia* and other psychoses in women reflect the decline in estrogen that occurs with advanced age. Patients with late-onset schizophrenia are treated with antipsychotic medications, although there are special concerns about overmedicating the elderly patient.

12

Psychological Factors and Physical Disorders

Heinrich Anton Mueller, *L'Homme aux Mouches et le Serpent.*

Learning Objectives

→ Describe how the DSM-IV criteria for a Psychological Factor Affecting a General Medical Condition can be said to define the diathesis-stress model.

→ Explain the general adaptation theory, how recent advances in neuroscience have modified this theory, and how the modern theory of stress revolves around the difference between "homeostasis" and "allostasis."

→ Begin to understand how the immune system works, and learn about the field of psychoneuroimmunology, which studies how psychological factors can change neural activity and the immune system.

→ Be able to describe some psychological moderating factors that affect a person's health.

→ Learn why the Type A personality is particularly at risk for coronary heart disease, and be able to describe the roles of hostility, helplessness, hopelessness, and stress as they contribute to a vulnerability to heart disease.

→ Describe the physiological development of an ulcer and the psychological factors that can affect gastric secretion and may lead to peptic ulcers.

→ Learn about various immune system disorders, including AIDS, cancer, and asthma, whose outcomes are especially affected by the patient's emotional state.

What we think and how we feel can change our physical health. We learned from our discussion of emotion in Chapter 5 that our thoughts and our emotions influence how our body reacts. One of our bodily reactions is, of course, disease, but we do not immediately think of physical disease—heart disease, cancer, or AIDS—as reactions that can be influenced by thoughts and feelings. There is, however, a good deal of evidence that the course, and sometimes the very occurrence, of such physical disorders can be influenced by the psychological state of the sufferer. There are few physical processes more fundamental than growth, and even this fundamental physical process can be influenced by psychological factors, as shown in the following case:

> Shortly after World War II, many German children were raised in orphanages. The government ran the orphanages, and so the orphans in each orphanage received similar nutrition, visits by doctors, and the like. Two such orphanages, however, differed in one important respect, the personality of the two women who ran them. A kind and motherly woman, who often played with the children, ran the first. She was warm and comforting. Singing and laughter were the sounds of the day. A tyrant ran the other orphanage. She avoided the children as much as possible. When she interacted with the children, it was to berate and criticize them, often in front of all the other children. The growth of the children was recorded as a matter of course, and the two homes diverged dramatically. The children of the kindly administrator gained more weight and height than those of the tyrant. When the tyrant was transferred to the first orphanage, however, just the reverse happened despite an increase in the food rations in this orphanage. (Widdowson, 1951)

Conversely, the condition of our body can influence and even trigger a disorder of the mind. The evidence is strong when we consider damage to the brain from without, as in a blow to the head or an attack of a virus, or damage from within as in Alzheimer's disease, dementia, stroke, or tumor, as shown in the following case:

> Doctors removed an enormous tumor that had permanently damaged several areas of Greg's brain, causing blindness, movement difficulties, and memory deficits.

Greg seemed unaware that he had any problems and did not know why he was in the hospital. He experienced retrograde amnesia (loss of memory of the recent past). He did not remember spending six years at a Hare Krishna temple in New Orleans before his hospitalization. He could recall events from the mid- to late sixties, but he had almost no memory of events that took place after 1970. When asked to name the current president and prompted, "Jimmy . . ." [Jimmy Carter was then president], he replied, "Jimi Hendrix," demonstrating his disorientation and confusion. He only became excited when he spoke about rock bands and songs from the sixties. (Adapted from Sacks, 1995)

Such a case is an example of an organic disorder, in which a bodily disorder influences a mental disorder. We discussed such disorders (for example, Alzheimer's disorder, vascular dementia, and delirium) in Chapter 11. In this chapter, we will discuss cases in which the mind influences bodily disorders. Such disorders were formerly called *psychosomatic* or *psychophysiological disorders,* as it was believed that only certain mental disorders had both psychological and physiological components. Because there is mounting evidence that very many physical disorders, not just a limited set, are influenced by the mind, DSM-IV now refers to the process rather than

Society and Mental Health

Placebos: Not "All In Your Head"

"Take these and call me in the morning," says the physician as she hands out medication to her ailing patient. Does it matter what "these" really are? This assumption underlies modern medicine: medical treatments work because they have an active ingredient that produces direct physical changes in the patient. Why does aspirin relieve tension headaches? Because the chemicals in aspirin block certain pain pathways. Why does bypass surgery relieve the symptoms of coronary heart disease? Because it opens the pipelines that improve the heart's blood supply. And—more to our point—why do antidepressants and anti-anxiety drugs work? Because their chemical ingredients change the patient's mood-related neurotransmitters. At least that's the assumption.

A wealth of research suggests, however, that even pretend treatments—whether sugar pills, laying on of hands, or phony surgeries—can have remarkable effects on physical health, a phenomenon called the placebo effect, after the Latin verb "placere" (to please). The importance of placebo effects was brought to medicine's attention in a provocative paper by the anesthesiologist Henry K. Beecher (1995). Beecher concluded that fully one-third of medical patients who improved did so because of placebo effects. This one-third figure became known as the placebo response rate, but we know now that one-third may, in many cases, be far too conservative. Recent studies have shown that up to 70 percent of patients with diagnosed physical illnesses, ranging from asthma and heart disease to Parkinson's disease and pain, show real improvements after taking placebos (Benson and Friedman, 1996; Harrington, 1999; Price et al., 1999; Shetty, Friedman, Kieburtz, Marshall, and Oakes, 1999).

The acknowledgment of the power of placebo treatments rallied medical science to base any claims of treatment efficacy strictly on double-blind experimental procedures, in which neither the patient nor the doctor knows who is get-

ting the active substance and who is getting the placebo. This is supposed to isolate the chemical effects of the drug from all other "mental" effects. The actual procedure's effectiveness, then, is determined only after the effect of the placebo control is subtracted. Of course, some placebos are better than others. For example, placebos that are administered frequently work better. This was shown in a study of patients who received placebo pills for duodenal ulcers. After one month's treatment, ulcers had healed in 44 percent of patients who received their placebos four times per day; the healing rate for those who took placebos once per day was only 32 percent (de Craen et al., 1999).

Apart from frequency, placebos are more powerful if they're believable. For this reason, researchers often distinguish between inactive placebos, such as powder-filled pills which have no measurable side effects, and active ones, which have measurable effects but none that could help the patient's illness. A commonplace example of an active placebo is antibiotic therapy: Physicians often prescribe antibiotics to patients suffering from viral infections. Although antibiotics kill bacteria and have side effects such as gastrointestinal distress, they have no effect on viruses. But patients leave the office feeling they have gotten something helpful—and would feel untreated if they left the office without a prescription.

Placebos are also more effective if they are extensive or painful. For example, placebos that are injected are more powerful than those taken orally (de Craen et al., 2000). Particularly powerful are placebo effects associated with surgery. Forty years ago, Leonard Cobb tested the effects of a surgical procedure to reduce angina (chest pain associated with heart disease). Patients with angina were given either actual surgeries, in which small incisions were made in the chest and then knots were tied in two arteries to increase blood flow to the brain, or sham surgeries (the placebo condition), in which

the disorder, dubbing it "Psychological Factors Affecting a General Medical Condition."

Interaction of Mind and Body

Philosophers and psychologists once believed that the mind and the body were totally separate and unrelated; in other words, that there was a mind-body dualism. Psychologists now recognize that the mind and body are linked, and that they interact to promote health or cause illness. Such a link may also account for the *placebo effect,* whereby a sugar pill or some other inactive treatment leads to improvement (see Box 12–1). Today, many people believe that some heart attacks, ulcers, and other physical problems are partly caused by an adverse psychological state. But how does a clinician know when this is so? Moreover, when there is evidence, how does the clinician classify it?

DSM-IV's criteria for a "Psychological Factor Affecting a General Medical Condition" are: (1) there is a disorder of known physical pathology present, and (2) psychologically meaningful events preceded,

Box 12–1

the patients were anesthetized but only the incisions to the chest were made. After recovering from the procedures, 80 percent of the placebo patients had improved, but only 40 percent of the actual surgery patients (Cobb, Thomas, Dillard, Merendino, and Bruce, 1959). Needless to say, the particular surgical procedure was quickly discontinued.

Thus far, we have restricted our discussion to physical illness. But what about mental disorders? There is evidence that placebo effects in mental disorders may be even more powerful than in physical illness, and placebo response rates of 40 to 50 percent are not unusual. Yet, even these high rates may be conservative. One recent and controversial critique reviewed nineteen studies of antidepressant drugs—mostly SSRI's—and concluded that 70 percent of the effect of antidepressant medications are placebo effects (Kirsch and Saperstein, 1998)!

Such placebo effects in mental disorders apply not only to medication, but also to psychotherapy, and some investigators contend that placebo effects are underestimated in psychotherapy studies as well. These observers reveal the partisan "allegiance effects" inherent in evaluations of medication by pro-psychotherapy investigators or evaluations of therapy by pro-medication investigators. Impartial observers claim that both estimates of placebo effects and treatment effectiveness warrant suspicion (Quitkin, Rabkin, Gerald, Davis, and Klein, 2000).

What accounts for placebo effects? Some investigators believe that the "placebo effect" is a kind of mystical formulation that can be explained more prosaically. For example, most illnesses fluctuate in severity, and people seek out doctors when they are at their worst. They then get better (regression to the mean) and attribute their improvement to whatever treatment they received, whether actual or pretend. As another factor, self-report is the most frequent way of assessing improvement, and politeness dictates that people tell the doctor they feel better (Kienle and Kiene, 1997).

Most theorists, however, contend that placebo effects are real, and several theories have been proposed to explain them. One theory holds that any treatment will diminish a patient's anxiety and lower her physiological stress levels, thereby promoting recovery. Another contends that placebos engender optimism and hope, and these emotions directly affect depression (Seligman, 1991). Another theory applies to pain relief by placebos, and hypothesizes that placebos unleash the brain's endorphins and create analgesia. The evidence suggests that endorphins are certainly involved, but non-opioid pain systems are involved as well (Amanzio and Benedetti, 1999; ter Reit, de Craen, de Boer, and Kessels, 1998).

A psychologically more complex theory involves classical conditioning, and is based on the real relief that patients often receive from seeing their doctor, taking their medicine, or getting the surgery. Placebo effects are thus conditioned responses that occur to a doctor visit, medicine, or surgery, even when the treatment is a placebo. Thus, antibiotics do cure strep throat, and the patient associates pill-taking with relief from throat pain. The next time the patient has a sore throat and takes a pill for it, he will feel relief, even if the sore throat is viral and the antibiotic is functionally a placebo.

On the face of it, placebo effects seem to be a phenomenon worth exploiting. Should practitioners administer placebos to patients? Some practitioners believe that administering placebos always requires some degree of patient deception, and thus even if beneficial, deliberate placebos should not be administered. Other practitioners believe placebo effects should be maximized whenever possible, especially since the "healer mystique" has been decimated in a world where one's doctors are assigned by an HMO. This question is ethically complex, and is a matter of lively debate.

DSM-IV Criteria

[Specified Psychological Factor] Affecting . . . [Indicate the General Medical Condition]

A. A general medical condition (coded on Axis III), for example, heart attack, is present.

B. Psychological factors, for example, a stressful divorce, adversely affect the general medical condition in one of the following ways: (1) the factors have influenced the course of the general medical condition as shown by a close temporal association between the psychological factors and the development or exacerbation of, or delayed recovery from, the general medical condition; (2) the factors interfere with the treatment of the general medical condition; (3) the factors constitute additional health risks for the individual; (4) stress-related physiological responses precipitate or exacerbate symptoms of the general medical condition.

SOURCE: APA, DSM-IV, 1994.

and are judged to have contributed to, the onset or worsening of the disorder. When psychological factors influence physical illness, the individual commonly denies that he is ill, refuses to take medication, and may ignore the presence of risk factors that will likely worsen his physical condition (DSM-IV).

Diathesis and Stress

The two criteria for psychological factors affecting medical conditions define a useful model: the **diathesis-stress model,** which we discussed in Chapter 4. "Diathesis" refers to the constitutional weakness that underlies the physical pathology, and "stress" to the psychological disturbance of meaningful events (see Figure 12–1). According to this model, an individual develops a disorder when he both has some physical vulnerability (diathesis) and experiences psychological disturbances (stress). If an individual is extremely weak constitutionally, very little stress will be needed to trigger the illness; if, on the other hand, extreme stress occurs, even individuals who are constitutionally strong may fall ill. In effect, the model suggests that individuals who develop coronary heart disease are both constitutionally vulnerable to cardiovascular problems and experience sufficient stress to trigger the pathology.

Psychological factors can affect physical conditions in a large number of organ systems: the skin, the skeletal-musculature, the respiratory, the cardiovascular, the blood and lymphatic, the gastrointestinal, the genitourinary, the endocrine systems, or the sense organs (Looney, Lipp, and Spitzer, 1978). There is no evidence, however, that the process causing psychological effects is different for each different organ, although any given individual may be especially vulnerable to psychological influence in only one organ system. Some of us are more likely to react to stress with the stomach, others by sweating, some by muscle tension, and still others with a racing heart. For this reason, DSM-IV does not have separate categories for each physical problem affected by a psychological factor. Rather, it has only one, "Psychological Factors Affecting a General Medical Condition." The diagnostician fills in which psychological factors (for example, a nasty divorce) affect which medical condition (for example, a heart attack).

Biological Mechanisms

Our discussion of the ways in which psychological factors can exacerbate physical disorders begins by outlining the two physical systems that are likely mechanisms: the HPA axis and the immune system. We will then discuss in detail two physical disorders, coronary heart disease and peptic ulcers, in which the HPA axis is strongly implicated. Following this we will discuss other physical diseases—cancer, AIDS, and asthma—in which psychological influences on the immune system play a large role.

STRESS AND THE STRESS RESPONSE

A "stressful" meeting, a "stressful" relationship, and being "stressed out" have all found their way from the scientific literature into common parlance. It has become routine to blame our mental and our physical problems on stress. Even though much abused by the layman, the concept of stress is an organizing principle for discussing psychological influences on

Figure 12–1

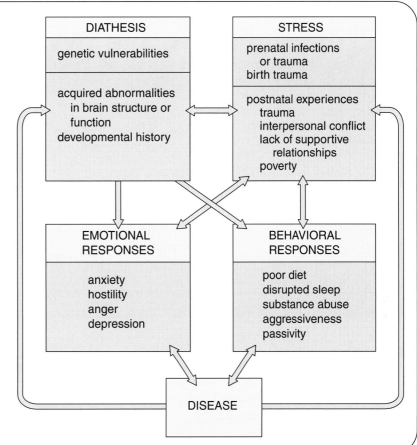

THE DIATHESIS-STRESS MODEL

Diathesis, the constitutional weakness or vulnerability underlying a physical pathology, and stress, the experiences (prenatal, birth, and postnatal) that a person undergoes, interact to affect emotional and behavioral responses that can result in physical disease. While this diagram does not show all the interactions that might occur in real life, it does illustrate the interplay between biological and psychological stress. Moreover, it also shows that disease can ultimately feed back on acquired abnormalities, developmental history, and postnatal experiences and responses, but not on genetic vulnerabilities or prenatal infections or trauma.

physical disorders. But we must begin by asking "what, exactly, is stress?"

Researchers who study stress typically define a stressor as an event that threatens the individual's balance or "homeostasis." Usually the event is a negative one, although very unusual positive events, like winning the lottery, are also said to be stressful. Hans Selye (1907–1983) used the emergency reaction of the sympathetic nervous system as the defining mechanism for his classic theory of stress. Selye held that when an organism is confronted by a stressor, a sequence of three stages called the ***general adaptation syndrome*** ensues (see Figure 12–2). The first stage is the *alarm reaction,* wherein physiological arousal prepares the body to fight or flee the stressor. If the alarm reaction is successful, it restores homeostasis. The alarm reaction is followed by a second stage— the stage of *resistance* (also called *adaptation*), in which defense and adaptation are sustained and optimal. If the stressor persists, the final stage, *exhaustion,* follows, and adaptive responding ceases. Illness and, in

some cases, death may follow. From the point of view of this theory, symptoms such as high blood pressure indicate that the individual is in an alarm reaction to stress. The theory postulates that psychological factors influence physical disease through the stress caused by the general adaptation syndrome (Selye, 1956, 1975; but see Mason, 1971, 1975).

With recent advances in neuroscience, the theory of stress has become more specific, and it now concentrates on the series of biological changes in the sympathetic nervous system and in the hypothalamic-pituitary-adrenal (HPA) axis that are part of the stress response. When a person is exposed to a stressor, the hypothalamus stimulates the sympathetic nervous system, which in turn causes the adrenal medulla to secrete catecholamines (adrenaline and noradrenaline). These circulate in the bloodstream and increase the heart rate, respiration, and metabolism of glucose. At the same time, the hypothalamus also releases corticotropin-releasing hormone (CRH), which travels through the bloodstream to the pituitary gland (see

Figure 12—2

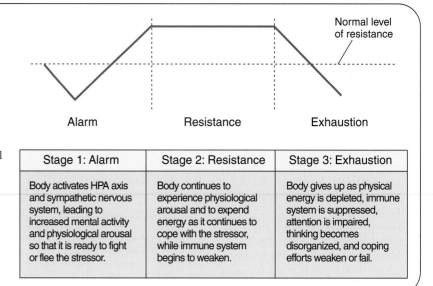

THE GENERAL ADAPTATION SYNDROME

According to Hans Selye, when the body is confronted by a stressor, it undergoes a sequence of three stages: alarm, resistance, and exhaustion. During these stages, the body goes from increased energy and physiological arousal to a depletion of energy, from increased mental activity and organized and focused efforts at coping to impaired concentration and ineffective and weakened coping efforts. (Source: Selye, 1974)

Stage 1: Alarm	Stage 2: Resistance	Stage 3: Exhaustion
Body activates HPA axis and sympathetic nervous system, leading to increased mental activity and physiological arousal so that it is ready to fight or flee the stressor.	Body continues to experience physiological arousal and to expend energy as it continues to cope with the stressor, while immune system begins to weaken.	Body gives up as physical energy is depleted, immune system is suppressed, attention is impaired, thinking becomes disorganized, and coping efforts weaken or fail.

Figure 12–3). The pituitary secretes other hormones, including ACTH (adrenocorticotropic hormone), which activates the adrenal gland, which in humans secretes cortisol (a glucocorticoid that is often referred to as a "stress hormone"). Cortisol helps the body to fight or flee, as called for by the emergency reaction (see Chapter 5).

In the short run, cortisol protects the body against the stressor. Once the stressor is gone, however, the body must shut down the stress response. It does this by reducing the release of cortisol. The brain has receptors for cortisol, particularly in the hippocampus. When these receptors are activated, a chemical message is sent that dampens the activity of the HPA axis. This helps to stop the stress response. If the stressor persists, however, and the HPA axis continues to be activated for an extended period of time, cortisol will continue to be released, and there can be major negative effects on the body and mind. Increased levels of cortisol due to chronic stress may kill cells and reduce the number of receptors in the hippocampus, which may lead to deficient problem solving and susceptibility to, and poor recovery from, disease. For example, rodents who experience the repeated stressor of periodic isolation are more susceptible to disease (Popovic, Popovic, Eric-Jovicic, and Jovanova-Nesic, 2000). It is by this path that the stunted growth of the children in the German orphanages (discussed at the beginning of the chapter) likely occurred: the H (hypothalamus) of the HPA

axis controls growth hormone release, and stress probably inhibited its release, perhaps through the actions of cortisol (Sapolsky, 1998). Remember that these negative effects of cortisol are the result of chronic, long-term stress. When cortisol is released only for a short time, however, it is protective rather than damaging to the body.

The modern theory of stress revolves around the difference between "homeostasis" and "allostasis." In Selye's classic theory, the system strives to maintain a single, ideal setpoint for each bodily state, such as blood pressure or ACTH level, so that a stable, internal balance known as **homeostasis** is maintained. So, for example, after a stressful event our body will always seek to return us to an ideal blood pressure, say 120/80. But there are three inadequacies of the classic homeostatic theory of stress:

1. The ideal setpoint is very different, depending on what activity we engage in: sleeping and pole-vaulting require vastly different blood pressures.
2. Maintaining any particular setpoint requires far-flung changes through the rest of the body—for example, to get to the ideal blood pressure for pole vaulting, changes in stomach acidity, ACTH level, and immune activity are produced.
3. Our body regulates its internal states, not only based on present events, but also based on the *expectation of future events*—for example, we are stressed not only when we are actually attacked

Figure 12—3

THE STRESS RESPONSE

When the body experiences stress, a series of biological changes occurs. There is activation of the sympathetic nervous system, which in turn activates the adrenal medulla, which secretes adrenaline and noradrenaline, leading to increased physiological arousal. There is also activation of the HPA (hypothalamic-pituitary-adrenal) axis. Activation of the hypothalamus leads to the release of hormones that travel through the bloodstream to the pituitary gland, which in turn secretes other hormones and activates the adrenal gland, which release the stress hormone, cortisol.

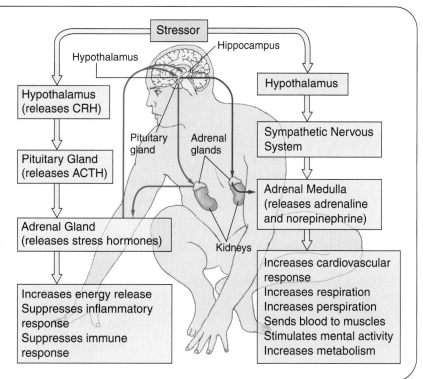

Stressor

Hypothalamus · Hippocampus

Hypothalamus (releases CRH)

Pituitary gland · Adrenal glands

Hypothalamus

Sympathetic Nervous System

Pituitary Gland (releases ACTH)

Adrenal Medulla (releases adrenaline and norepinephrine)

Adrenal Gland (releases stress hormones)

Kidneys

Increases energy release
Suppresses inflammatory response
Suppresses immune response

Increases cardiovascular response
Increases respiration
Increases perspiration
Sends blood to muscles
Stimulates mental activity
Increases metabolism

by muggers, but also when we merely think about next year's income tax.

Allostasis, in contrast, refers to the adaptation of many bodily states simultaneously across many different life circumstances. This process takes place through the expenditure of energy and production of stress mediators like the glucocorticoids and the catecholamines, which produce adaptation in the short run but can exacerbate disease over long time periods. This modern theory recognizes that much of internal regulation is in anticipation of the future and that stress mediators are produced as a result of anticipatory anxiety, which can lead to wear and tear on the body if this activated state is sustained over long periods of time. *Allostatic load* is the hidden price the body pays for this complex set of trade-offs among different systems and for the overproduction of the stress mediators (McEwen, 1998a). High allostatic load happens when there is frequent stress, repeated stress, or the inability to shut off the stress mediators efficiently in response to stress when they are aroused.

According to this view, the allostatic load is very high for a person who has a job that has little decision latitude but high demands. Lack of control on the job produces high blood pressure not only at work but also at home because the body cannot easily dampen blood pressure in the evening. This example of allostatic load takes place slowly, silently, and gradually over many years, eventually producing an enlarged left ventricle in the heart and progressive atherosclerosis. The result is coronary heart disease (CHD) (McEwen, 1998b; Sapolsky, 1998; Schulkin, McEwen, and Gold, 1994). Among the mediators of allostatic load are the very same mediators of the stress response, the glucocorticoids and catecholamines, which are routinely so useful in triggering the alarm response and promoting adaptation.

In the new terminology of allostasis, Selye's alarm response is reinterpreted as the process of adaptation in which glucocorticoids and catecholamines promote adaptation to the stressor. Selye's stage of resistance reflects the protective effects of the adaptation to the stressor. But if the alarm response is sustained and the glucocorticoids and catecholamines are repeatedly elevated over many days, allostatic load results, which is akin to Selye's phase of exhaustion. There is an important distinction, however, in that Selye's exhaustion phase implies a depletion of the protective effects,

Figure 12–4

ALLOSTASIS AND ALLOSTATIC LOAD

Allostasis is the process of maintaining homeostasis, coping with stress and life's challenges. To maintain homeostasis, the body must simultaneously regulate many bodily states, including body temperature, respiration, blood pressure, immune response, and hippocampal function in the brain. Allostatic load is the continued wear and tear on the body in response to continuous or frequent stress and the production of catecholamines (adrenaline and noradrenaline) and gluco-corticoids (cortisol). With continuing stress, high allostatic load occurs, and disease states like coronary heart disease may result. (Source: Adapted from McEwen, 1998a, p. 172)

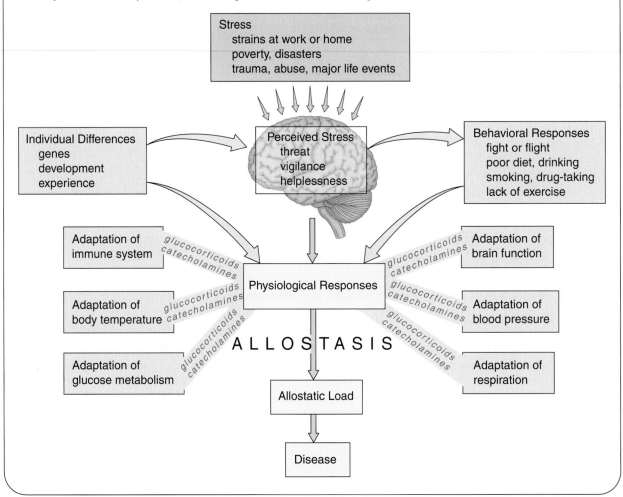

whereas allostatic load recognizes the wear and tear produced by repeated exposure; that is, too much of a good thing (see Figure 12–4). Examples of allostatic load include the acceleration of atherosclerosis, abdominal obesity, as well as loss of minerals from bone, and immunosuppression (the inactivation of the body's protective immune system), as well as atrophy (wasting away) and damage to regions of the brain, especially the hippocampus (Sapolsky, 1996; McEwen, 1998a).

In this chapter, we will look at several examples of psychological stressors aggravating physical dis-

eases, such as cardiovascular disorders and peptic ulcers, with allostatic load due to the chronic activation of glucocorticoids and catecholamines as the possible mechanism.

THE IMMUNE SYSTEM AND PSYCHONEUROIMMUNOLOGY

Psychological factors can increase the risk of infectious diseases, of allergy, of autoimmune diseases, and cancer. Besides the changes in the HPA axis, changes

High allostatic load happens when there is frequent or repeated stress, as in *(left)* these refugees from East Timor who fled their homes when fighting broke out after a vote in favor of East Timor's independence from Indonesia, or *(right)* this harried stockbroker, who must deal with the unpredictable rise and fall of stocks and constant buy and sell orders from his clients.

in the immune system brought about by psychological factors are the likely mechanisms of these psychological influences. Researchers in a field called **psychoneuroimmunology (PNI)** study how psychological factors change neural activity and the immune system, ultimately increasing the risk for such diseases. The basic findings in this field are that personality, emotion, and cognition all alter the body's immune response, and thereby alter risk for these diseases. The overriding hope of PNI is that psychological treatments can be used to prevent, and perhaps even to cure, such physical illnesses. Now we will examine how the immune system works under optimal conditions. Later in this chapter, we will go into the mechanisms whereby the immune system breaks down under psychological influences and exacerbates cancer, AIDS, and other illnesses.

The immune system has two basic tasks. First it must recognize **antigens,** foreign invaders such as bacteria and viruses, as well as internal enemies such as malignant tumors and cancer cells. Second, it must inactivate them and remove them from the body (Borysenko, 1987; Gold and Matsuuch, 1995; Maier and Watkins, 1998). The immune system detects and destroys antigens with **macrophages** (white blood cells) and **lymphocytes.** There are two main types of lymphocytes: B cells (which come from bone marrow) and T cells (which come from the thymus gland). B cells and T cells have receptors on their surface that recognize the invaders. This recognition is very specific, and any given lymphocyte recognizes only a small number of antigens, so that at any time

there are a large number of different lymphocytes surveying the body for different invaders.

What happens when antigens are spotted? They are destroyed in four main ways (see Figure 12–5). First, macrophages (literally "big eaters") surround and digest the antibodies, spitting them out onto their surface and summoning Helper T cells, which either directly destroy the processed antigen or send out cytokines (soluble protein messengers) that signal B cells and Cytotoxic T cells (also known as killer T cells) to take action. Second, B cells that are specific to that antigen multiply and produce antibodies that bind to and neutralize the antigens. Third, Cytotoxic T cells bind to a target cell containing an antigen and directly kill the antigen by "lysing" (breaking down) its cell membrane with chemicals. Fourth, when the invader is a cancerous cell, or a virus-infected

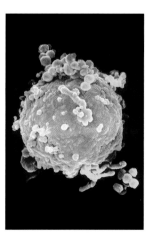

B cells are lymphocytes that are specific to a particular antigen and that can make antibodies only against that antigen. Pictured here is a B lymphocyte (the large round body) and clamydia bacteria (the clusters of small, round bodies). The photograph has a magnification of 14,000 times the actual size.

Figure 12—5

SCHEMA OF THE IMMUNE RESPONSE

The immune system works to destroy both foreign bodies, called antigens, and internal enemies like cancerous cells and virus-infected cells. To inactivate and remove antigens, (1) macrophages surround antigens, which Helper T cells inactivate, then Helper T cells send out cytokines to signal B cells and Cytotoxic T cells to take action, (2) B cells that are specific to the antigen multiply and produce antibodies to neutralize the antigen, and (3) Cytotoxic T cells multiply and directly kill the antigen with chemicals. Memory T cells and B cells are created to quickly recognize and take action against the same antigen if it appears again. Suppressor T cells regulate T-cell activity once the antigen has been destroyed. (4) To eliminate cancerous cells or virus-infected cells, NK cells take action, using surface molecules to attract and destroy the target cell.

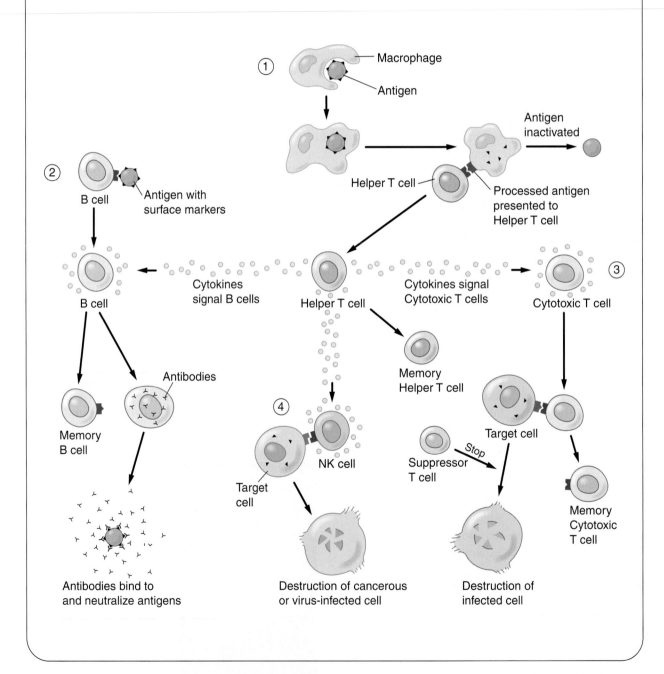

cell, Natural Killer (NK) cells rapidly lyse the cell. Suppressor T cells stop the production of antibodies and the action of Cytotoxic T cells once the antigen has been destroyed.

The second time the body is challenged by a specific invader it has seen before, the immune system does a better job of destroying it than it did the first time. This is called *immunologic "memory."* Memory T cells and B cells recognize the antigen so that the immune system can take action more rapidly the second time it is spotted. Such memory is responsible for the phenomenon of *immunocompetence,* the degree to which these events protect the organism, which can be measured in several ways:

- assessing the amount of immunoglobulin (antibodies formed by B cells) in the blood or saliva,
- assessing the amount of T-cell multiplication when antigens are challenged,
- assessing the ability of Natural Killer (NK) cells to destroy cancerous or virus-infected cells,
- measuring how much the skin reddens and swells when injected with an antigen (the greater the reaction, the better the immune system is working) using the "delayed hypersensitivity" test.

Psychological Moderating Factors

We will be taking a detailed look at a range of physical disorders that are influenced by psychological factors: coronary heart disease, peptic ulcer, infectious illness, cancer, AIDS, and asthma. In addition to these, many other physical diseases have psychosomatic components. These include migraine headache, arthritis, chronic pain, irritable bowel syndrome, and diabetes. Rather than reviewing the parallel findings on each, however, we will look here at some general principles concerning moderating factors that recur through psychological explanations of the cause and the alleviation of all the physical diseases: the role of life events and poverty, of Pavlovian conditioning, and of voluntary behavior.

LIFE EVENTS

Stress theory relies on modern neuroscience for its mechanisms and on the older construct of "life events" for its external stressors. In the early pioneering research on life events, Thomas Holmes and Richard Rahe devised a scale, the Social Readjustment Rating Scale, by having individuals rank the amount of stress different life events would cause them. Based on these rankings, Holmes and Rahe assigned a number to each stressful event (see Table 12–1). Death of a spouse was the most stressful life event; divorce and separation were near the top; taking a new job in the middle of the rankings; holidays, vacations, minor violations of the law were considered the least stressful. Some of the life events are positive entrances, such as item 25, outstanding personal achievement, while others are negative exits, like item 1, the death of a spouse. Losses or

Stressful life events such as *(left)* the death of this boy's father, or *(right)* a stock market crash, may lead to illness.

TABLE 12–1

SOCIAL READJUSTMENT RATING SCALE

Rank	Life Event	Rank	Life Event
1	Death of spouse	22	Change in responsibilities at work
2	Divorce	23	Son or daughter leaving home
3	Marital separation	24	Trouble with in-laws
4	Jail term	25	Outstanding personal achievement
5	Death of close family member	26	Wife begins or stops work
6	Personal injury or illness	27	Begin or end school
7	Marriage	28	Change in living conditions
8	Fired at work	29	Revision of personal habits
9	Marital reconciliation	30	Trouble with boss
10	Retirement	31	Change in work hours or conditions
11	Change in health of family member	32	Change in residence
12	Pregnancy	33	Change in schools
13	Sex difficulties	34	Change in recreation
14	Gain of new family member	35	Change in church activities
15	Business readjustment	36	Change in social activities
16	Change in financial state	37	Small mortgage
17	Death of close friend	38	Change in sleeping habits
18	Change to different line of work	39	Change in family get-togethers
19	Change in number of arguments with spouse	40	Change in eating habits
20	Large mortgage	41	Vacation
21	Foreclosure of mortgage or loan	42	Christmas
		43	Minor violations of the law

SOURCE: Adapted from Holmes and Rahe, 1967.

exits seem to produce more problems than do entrances (Paykel, 1974a, 1974b).

The basic idea is that the more life events an individual experiences, the more likely he or she is to get sick from a variety of disorders. For example, individuals who had heart attacks had had more total significant life events in the six months prior to their heart attack than in the year before that. Similarly, individuals who became depressed had had a larger number of life events, particularly losses, than those who did not (Holmes and Rahe, 1967; Paykel et al., 1969; Theorell and Rahe, 1971).

Stress theorists have gathered a dismaying body of data on the effects of hard life events on physical illness:

- Following the collapse of communism in Russia, the death rate among men increased by 40 percent, with blood pressure increases, atherosclerosis, and subsequent CHD as likely causes (Bobak and Marmot, 1996; McEwen, 1998a).
- Among 5,700 British civil servants, men in the lower-ranked jobs had twice the risk of serious diseases like CHD and much worse physical

functioning than men with higher-ranked jobs (Hemingway, Nicholson, Stafford, Roberts, Marmot, 1997).
- Two hundred and seventy-six volunteers were exposed to controlled amounts of a common cold virus. Severe stressors, one month or longer in duration—typically unemployment or interpersonal difficulties—were associated with a substantial increase in getting colds (Cohen et al., 1995).
- Low-income Americans are considerably more likely to suffer physical difficulties, disease, and early death than richer Americans (Lynch, Kaplan, and Shema, 1997). These health discrepancies still remain even when age, race, sex, education, and healthy behaviors are taken into account (Lantz et al., 1998).

The life events idea has spawned some refinements: First, and curiously, it may be that the *repetitive, daily hassles* of life are better predictors of illness than major life events. Losing your wallet, a price rise in the weekly food bill, and the breaking of a window may ultimately negatively affect health more

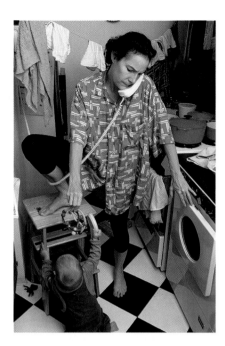

The daily hassles of life may wear a person down even more than major life events. This mother deals with a crisis at work while watching her child and doing her laundry and may feel constant stress that leaves her vulnerable to illness.

than deaths, divorces, and pregnancies (Dohrenwend and Shrout, 1985; Kanner, Coyne, Schaefer, and Lazarus, 1981). The gradual chipping away at an individual by daily annoyances may wear him down to a point where susceptibility to illness jumps dramatically (Depue and Monroe, 1986).

Second, it might not be life events themselves but *uncontrollable life events* that precede heart attacks. Death of a close family member, death of a best friend, and being laid off from work are considered uncontrollable losses, but divorce, separation, and changes in eating habits are believed to be controllable life events (Dohrenwend and Martin, 1978). David Glass identified three groups of patients who had experienced the same total number of life events in the preceding year. Those who had had heart attacks and those who had been hospitalized for noncoronary illnesses experienced more helplessness-inducing life events than did the healthy controls. This suggests that experiencing uncontrollable life events—as opposed to a large number of life events per se—may be a formula for heart attack (Glass, 1977).

Third, it might be a person's *hardiness or optimism,* and not the number of the life events, that most creates resistance to physical disease. Personality can modify the response to life events. In one study, two groups of executives had comparable numbers of life events over the previous three years, but only one group tended to become ill. The "hardy" group, characterized by a strong sense of self, a strong sense of meaning, and vigor, resisted illness (Garrity, Somes, and Marx, 1977; Kobasa, 1979). Similarly, people who are pessimists tend to suffer more illness (Buchanan, 1994; Peterson, Seligman, and Vaillant, 1988).

Stress theorizing used to be quite loose, almost to the point of emptiness. It traditionally relied on three basic nonbiological concepts—life events, coping, and social support—to explain findings such as hard lives producing more physical illness. Yet, each of these concepts has proven to be too global. So, for example, "life events" can produce good effects as well as the expected bad effects. Life events, even bad ones, can produce illness as expected, but they can also produce spurts of growth and insight. Lack of social support and a feeling of isolation can lead to illness. For example, people who feel lonely have poorer lymphocyte response than those who do not feel lonely (Kiecolt-Glaser et al., 1984). While social support sometimes bolsters health, social interaction can also undermine adaptive functioning—for example, a spouse who is psychologically disturbed can exacerbate stress (Veiel, 1993; Yager, Grant, and Bolus, 1984). Modern stress theorists now attempt to decompose these global notions into their constituent parts and look for the underlying cognitive and biological mechanisms. So, for example, Andrew Baum has proposed that one mechanism by which stressful life events produce illness is by setting off intrusive thoughts—rumination, automatic thoughts, and traumatic memories. Baum and his colleagues followed the residents of Three Mile Island, who lived near the site of a nuclear power plant where a radioactive accident occurred in March 1979. They found that the more intrusive memories an individual had, the greater the number of symptoms of somatic distress (Baum, Cohen, and Hall, 1993). When coupled to advances in neuroscience, with its hi-tech search for mechanisms, stress theory is once again showing promise of illuminating the psychological influences on physical disorders.

PAVLOVIAN CONDITIONING

Classical conditioning likely plays some role in psychosomatic disorders, with evidence that some symptoms are a conditioned response acquired when a neutral stimulus is paired with an unconditioned stimulus that produces the disorder. In one experiment with healthy adult women, red and blue colors were repeatedly paired with an arithmetic task that produced stress-related airway resistance. When presented without the task later, red and blue caused a greater level of muscle tightening in the throats of participants than did a control color, suggesting that classical conditioning had occurred (Miller and Kotses, 1995). Another example of asthma conditioned in the laboratory is the following:

> A thirty-seven-year-old shop assistant suffered from severe bronchial asthma that could be reliably set off by house dust. In the laboratory, she was sprayed with an aerosol having a neutral solvent; the aerosol was to be the conditioned stimulus. Following being sprayed with the aerosol, she inhaled house dust (unconditioned stimulus), and an asthma attack (unconditioned response) followed. Thereafter, upon inhaling from the aerosol, asthma attacks ensued. (Dekker, Pelse, and Groen, 1957)

Since individuals who suffer from asthma sometimes have attacks following exposure to highly specific events, such as experiencing a family argument or other emotional conflicts, this is an appealing model of psychosomatic illness. It has, however, only been demonstrated under limited laboratory conditions and only some patients can be so conditioned.

VOLUNTARY BEHAVIOR

Most of the work on psychosomatic disorders focuses on behaviors over which we have little or no voluntary control. Glucocorticoid secretion and negative life events seem to happen to us; for the most part, we do not choose them. But much of disease and mortality stems from poor human choices. In 1990, 2.15 million Americans died. Listed on their death certificates was the primary physical pathology: coronary heart disease, 720,000; cancer, 505,000; stroke, 144,000; accident, 92,000. But the root causes of these deaths is a deeper matter. A good estimate is that almost half of these deaths stemmed from poor choices about voluntary behavior. By factoring attributable risk into these 2.15 million deaths, McGinnis and Foege (1993) estimated that tobacco accounted for 400,000 of them; poor diet and exercise, 300,000; alcohol, 100,000; poisons, 90,000; firearms, 35,000; sexual behavior,

30,000; motor vehicles, 25,000; illicit drugs, 20,000. This implies that there is a great deal that we can do to save lives, including our own. We can quit smoking, drink alcohol only in moderation, wear safety belts, follow sound medical advice, and exercise frequently. As professional psychologists, we can encourage and support these life-saving choices. Indeed, one of the newest and most promising specialties in psychology has just this mission. It is called "health psychology" (Matarazzo, 1980). This discipline emphasizes that we choose lifestyles and particular actions that can produce illness, and that by knowing this we can choose to lead healthier lives. Health psychology studies the causes, the cure, and the prevention of physical illnesses that involve behaviors we can choose. In our discussion of coronary heart disease, we will emphasize that some causes are behavioral: lack of exercise, eating cholesterol-laden foods, and smoking. We can choose not to engage in these behaviors. We will see that other causes, like the hostility component of the Type A personality, can be changed with counseling.

Health psychology creates and evaluates treatments to change poor choices that lead to bad health. Smoking cessation, for example, is a behavior that can be facilitated by treatment. Treatments that work might combine nicotine gum with information on the consequences of smoking, might encourage the client to remove ashtrays from home and office, might contract with the client for a specific date of quitting, and might role-play not smoking in high-risk situations. In a study that used such treatments, 32 percent of inveterate smokers in the treatment group were abstinent a year later, but only 10 percent in the control group remained abstinent (Hill, Rigdon, and Johnson, 1993). Efficacious behavioral treatments are also now appearing for chronic back pain, irritable bowel syndrome, and eating disorders (Compas, Haaga, Keefe, Leitenberg, and Williams, 1998).

We now turn to an examination of coronary heart disease and peptic ulcer, two clear cases of psychological influences on physical disorders, in which stress and the HPA axis are likely mechanisms.

Coronary Heart Disease

In the last century, Sir William Osler, a famous Canadian physician, prefigured what was to be learned in the twentieth century about personality and heart attacks:

A man who has early risen and late taken rest, who has eaten the bread of carefulness, striving for success in commercial, professional, or political life, after twenty-five or thirty years of incessant toil, reaches the point where he can say, perhaps with just satisfaction, "Soul, thou has much goods laid up for many years; take thine ease," all unconscious that the fell sergeant has already issued the warrant. (Osler, 1897)

Coronary heart disease (CHD) kills more people than any other disease in the Western world. In the United States, more than half the deaths of individuals over forty-five are caused by some form of heart or circulatory problem (Eriksson, 1995; Gillum, 1994; Weiner, 1977). An underlying condition in most instances of heart attack and sudden death is *atherosclerosis,* a building up of fat on the inner walls of the coronary arteries. Such clogging blocks blood from reaching the heart muscle; heart attack and sudden death can result (Diamond, 1982; Sapolsky, 1998).

Epidemiologists have thoroughly studied risk factors for CHD. There are seven major physical risk factors: (1) growing old, (2) being male, (3) smoking cigarettes, (4) having high blood pressure (hypertension), (5) having high serum cholesterol, (6) physical inactivity, and (7) genetics. A psychological risk factor is on the list: the Type A personality, which we will consider here. We will then turn to the emotional states—hostility, helplessness, hopelessness, depression, and "stress"—all of which are implicated in CHD.

tics may begin when a person is as young as three or four years old (Steinberg, 1986).

Classifying individuals into Type A's and Type B's is done either by a standard stress interview or by a self-administered questionnaire (Bryant and Yarnold, 1995; Glass, 1977; Jenkins, Rosenman, and Friedman, 1967; Yarnold and Bryant, 1994). Typical questions are:

1. "Has your spouse or friend ever told you that you eat too fast?" Type A's say, "yes, often." Type B's say, "yes, once or twice" or "no."
2. "How would your spouse (or best friend) rate your general level of activity?" Type A's say, "too active, need to slow down." Type B's say, "too slow, should be more active."
3. "Do you ever set deadlines or quotas for yourself at work or at home?" Type A's say, "yes, once a week or more often." Type B's say, "no" or "only occasionally."
4. "When you are in the midst of doing a job and someone (not your boss) interrupts you, how do you feel inside?" Type A's say, "I really feel irritated because most such interruptions are unnecessary." Type B's say, "I feel OK because I work better after an occasional break."

Several excellent prospective studies exist of the Type A personality as a risk factor for CHD in the population at large:

The Type A Personality

An upholsterer discovered the *Type A personality.* When he came to reupholster the chairs in the office of Dr. Meyer Friedman, a physician who specialized in seeing heart attack patients, the upholsterer noticed that the chairs in the waiting rooms were worn in the front of the seat, not the back. The Type A's were sitting on the edge of their chairs, sitting forward anxiously as they awaited the doctor. In general, Type A's are defined by: (1) an exaggerated sense of time urgency, (2) competitiveness and ambition, and (3) aggressiveness and hostility, particularly when things get in their way. They contrast to *Type B personalities,* who are relaxed, serene, and have no sense of time urgency. When Type A's miss a bus, they become upset. When Type B's miss a bus, they say to themselves, "Why worry? There will always be another bus coming along." The Type A sees the environment as threatening, and seems to be engaged in prolonged emergency reactions. Type A characteris-

Type A personalities are time urgent, competitive, aggressive, and hostile. The person in the car shows signs of being such a personality.

- *The Western Collaborative Study.* Beginning in 1960, 3,200 working men who had no history of CHD were followed in a longitudinal study. Men who had been judged Type A by the structured interview had 2.2 times as much CHD as Type B's. When the physical risk factors were statistically controlled, Type A's still had double the risk for CHD (Carmelli, Dame, Swan, and Rosenman, 1991; Hecker, Chesney, Black, and Frautschi, 1988; Rosenman et al., 1975).

- *The Framingham Heart Study.* More than 1,600 men and women who were classified Type A or B by a questionnaire and who were free of any CHD were followed for eight years. White-collar Type A men had almost three times the risk of CHD as white-collar Type B's (Eaker, Haynes, and Feinleib, 1983; Haynes, Feinleib, and Kannel, 1980).

- *The Belgian Heart Disease Prevention Trial.* Two thousand men, having demonstrated good health by passing a strenuous exercise test, were rated along the Type A–B continuum and followed for

five years. The upper third (those nearer to the Type A part of the continuum) had 1.9 times the risk for CHD as the lower third (Kittel, Kornitzer, de Backer, and Dramaix, 1982).

- *The Cardiovascular Risk in Young Finns Study.* Lifestyle risk factors for CHD were studied in 3,596 Finnish children and young adults over six years. Male adolescents classified as Type A's were shown to have a high level of aggressiveness, which was significantly associated with the presence of multiple risk habits such as smoking, alcohol use, and physical inactivity. High aggressiveness also predicted an increase in metabolic factors that contribute to heart disease, including obesity and hypertension (Raitakari et al., 1995; Ravaja, Keltikangas-Järvinen, and Keskivaara, 1996).

Although the idea has not gone unchallenged (Cohen and Reed, 1985; Shekelle et al., 1985), many studies conclude that Type A confers extra risk for CHD in the general population (see Figure 12–6).

Figure 12—6

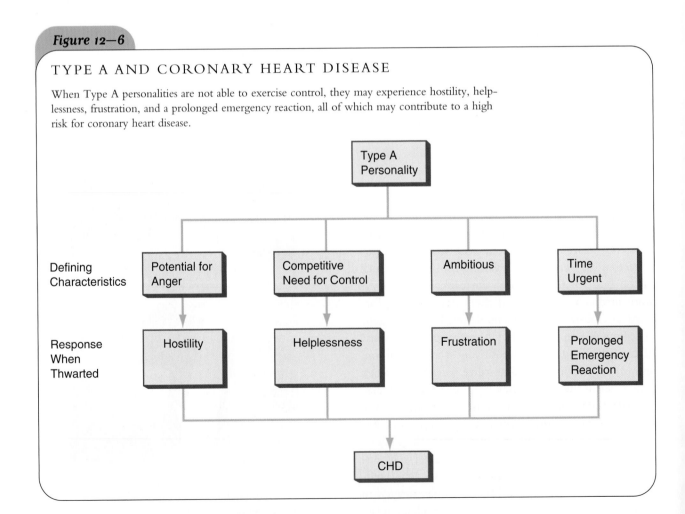

TYPE A AND CORONARY HEART DISEASE

When Type A personalities are not able to exercise control, they may experience hostility, helplessness, frustration, and a prolonged emergency reaction, all of which may contribute to a high risk for coronary heart disease.

Hostility and anger may lead to hypertension, although the opportunity to vent hostility may lower blood pressure, as in these fighting soccer players *(left),* or in this man who has just been fired from his job *(right).*

Emotional States and CHD

What is it about Type A personalities that puts them at risk for CHD? Emotional states are implicated in Type A personality and coronary heart disease. These states include feelings of hostility, helplessness, hopelessness, depression, and stress.

HOSTILITY

There are several lines of evidence that hostility may be the crucial ingredient of the Type A's susceptibility to CHD:

- In the two hours following an episode of anger, the risk of a heart attack doubles among people over fifty years old (Mittelman et al., 1995).
- People with high blood pressure are particularly sensitive to hostility and respond with even higher blood pressure and anger when they are threatened (Diamond, 1982; Kaplan, Gottschalk, Magliocco, Rohobit, and Ross, 1960; Miller, Smith, Turner, Guijarro, and Hallet, 1996; Suls, Wan, and Costa, 1995; Wolf, Cardon, Shepard, and Wolff, 1955).
- The opportunity to vent hostility lowers blood pressure; the failure to release hostility may keep blood pressure high (Dimsdale et al., 1986; Hokanson, 1961; Hokanson and Burgess, 1962; Hokanson, Willers, and Koropsak, 1968; Scheier and Bridges, 1995).
- Two hundred and fifty-five physicians were given the MMPI in medical school and were followed

for twenty-five years (see Figure 12–7). One component of the MMPI is the Cook-Medley hostility score (Cook and Medley, 1954). High hostility scores strongly predicted CHD (Barefoot, Dahlstrom, and Williams, 1983; Barefoot, Larsen, Von der Lieth, and Schroll, 1995; Williams, Barefoot, and Shekelle, 1985). This relationship was replicated in the Western Electric Study of 1,877 men followed for ten years. The high-hostility men had five times the incidence of CHD (Shekelle, Gale, Ostfeld, and Paul, 1983).

In an exploration of the biological mechanism by which hostility might damage the heart, eighteen men angrily recounted incidents from their lives that had annoyed them. As they spoke, the pumping efficiency of their heart dropped by 5 percent on average, suggesting a drop in blood flow to the heart itself. Pumping efficiency was not changed by other stressors (Ironson et al., 1992; see also Krantz et al., 1991). Researchers have speculated that hormonal changes during anger may provide a link from anger to CHD. To test this, they monitored the blood of ninety newlywed couples for hormonal changes during arguments. Hostile behavior was associated with significant changes in five different hormones (Malarkey, Kiecolt-Glaser, Pearl, and Glaser, 1994; Williams et al., 1982). Whether it is expressing anger, damming up anger, or just underlying, pervasive anger that produces CHD, and how the link from anger to hormonal changes to coronary changes actually works remain

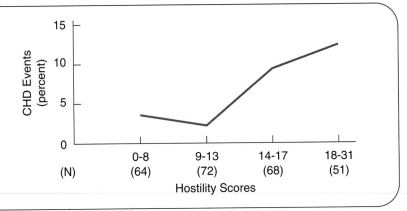

Figure 12—7

HOSTILITY AND CHD

Hostility and coronary heart disease incidence (myocardial infarction or cardiac death) over a twenty-five-year follow-up period in 255 physicians who took the MMPI during medical school. (Source: Barefoot, Dahlstrom, and Williams, 1983)

two of the most intriguing questions in psychosomatics today.

HELPLESSNESS, DEPRESSION, AND HOPELESSNESS

Hostility is not the only emotional state that is implicated in CHD. Helplessness and depression may also play a major role in heart disease. Helplessness—the state in which nothing one does makes any difference—may be part and parcel of the Type A personality. People who are ambitious, competitive, and time urgent may get themselves into, and react more strongly to, situations that produce more frustration, failure, and helplessness. Type A individuals seem to be engaged in a lifelong struggle to control a world they see as threatening. David Glass suggests that it is this struggle for control that crucially distinguishes a Type A from a Type B personality. Glass postulates that a cycle of desperate efforts to control the environment, alternating with profound giving up when the environment proves uncontrollable, is repeated over and over again during the lifetime of the Type A individual. This struggle may result in high blood pressure and other physiological changes that in turn cause heart attacks.

A second line of evidence comes from a study of the "inhibited need for power" and hypertension. Seventy-eight Harvard juniors were tested in the late 1930s and early 1940s for high blood pressure and various personality characteristics. Ten years later, these individuals were given a projective test in which they told stories about five pictures from the TAT (see Chapter 2). The themes of the stories they told were used as indications of what their personalities were like. Twenty years later, in the early 1970s, these men were tested for high blood pressure. The findings were remarkable.

Men who had a high need for power (which was greater than their need for affiliation), but who showed high inhibition, were more likely to develop high blood pressure. Twenty-three of the men fell into this group at approximately age thirty. By the time these men were in their fifties, 61 percent had shown definite signs of hypertensive pathology, whereas only 23 percent of the remaining forty-seven men showed hypertensive pathology. These findings become even more remarkable when we realize that they are unrelated to the blood pressure of these men when they were in their thirties. In other words, at age thirty the need for power combined with its inhibition predicted that individuals would be at risk for severe high blood pressure at age fifty, irrespective of what their blood pressure was when they were thirty years old (McClelland, 1979). We can view the inhibited need for power as a sign of the repeated helplessness in these individuals' lives.

Hopelessness, which is the belief that one's present helplessness will continue into the far future and undermine all one's endeavors, may also be a substantial risk factor for CHD. For four years, researchers followed almost one thousand Finnish middle-aged men who had received a baseline ultrasound scan of their heart for atherosclerosis. Those who reported high hopelessness at the time of the baseline scan had faster progression of atherosclerosis, and those with the highest hopelessness, both at baseline and four years later, had the fastest progression of all (Everson, Kaplan, Goldberg, Salonen, and Salonen, 1997). A

People who lose what is most important to them, as this man from Bosnia, often experience feelings of hopelessness and depression that may make them more susceptible to coronary heart disease.

study that looked at heart attack as the outcome among 2,428 middle-aged men found that greater hopelessness predicted a greater likelihood of heart attack (Everson et al., 1996). In another study, 303 patients had angioplasty (surgery that opens arteries from the heart), and were followed for six months afterwards. Controlling for cardiac status, the investigators tried to predict who would do well and who badly. Of the third of the patients who had the most positive expectations of the future and had the most positive view of themselves, 9.9 percent went on to have further coronary problems. Of the least positive third, 29.5 percent had further coronary problems (Helgeson and Fritz, 1999).

As we saw in Chapter 7, helplessness and hopelessness are intimately related to depression, and mounting evidence now suggests that depression puts people at risk for CHD. Two hundred and twenty-two men who had heart attacks and survived were interviewed and then followed for six months during which twelve died as a result of another heart attack. Depressive disorder during the interview predicted death, even after controlling for damage to the heart and the usual physical and psychological risk factors (Frasure-Smith, Lesperance, and Talajic, 1995). Depression produced a fivefold increase in death among these patients, over and above physical factors. In another prospective study, 2,832 people aged forty-five to seventy-seven were followed for twelve years. None had signs of heart disease at the outset, but about a quarter had at least mild symptoms of de-

pression. The rate of CHD and death was 150 percent higher among the depressed people. Those who felt the most hopeless at the start of the study had about double the rate of those who were not depressed (Anda et al., 1993).

STRESS AND CHD

Depression, helplessness, and hopelessness are usually thought of as "downers," states that demobilize the body. Stress, in contrast, is thought of as the great mobilizer of our bodily resources against attack and threat. The emergency reaction and HPA activity are well-defined mobilizing mechanisms of stress. Evolution may have actually favored the development of stress disorders. In a generally threatening environment, individuals who tended to perceive the world as hostile and responded crisply with elevation of blood pressure, muscle tension, and the like, would be those most likely to survive and reproduce. Only under modern conditions, in which the level of physical threat has been reduced from the days of the cave and the jungle, is hypertension now the symptom of a disorder rather than an evolutionary advantage. Notice that hypertension does not kill young persons; it is only deadly to individuals who are many years past the prime age of reproduction. This seems to suggest that susceptibility to various disorders may be inherited because at one time in history these "diseases" actually favored survival and reproduction.

People who work on the stock exchange may constantly experience the emergency reaction as they encounter the stress of bidding on stocks, as shown here. They may be especially prone to hypertension and coronary heart disease.

There are numerous reports that implicate the sudden mobilization of the emergency reaction in sudden coronary death. For example, during the SCUD missile attacks on Israel by Iraq in 1991, researchers reported that there were more cardiac deaths among frightened elderly Israelis than deaths from any other cause (Meisel et al., 1991). Similarly, during the 1992 Los Angeles earthquake, the rate of heart attacks jumped (Leor, Poole, and Kloner, 1996).

If one strong emergency reaction can bring on cardiac death, what happens to an individual who spends a lot of his time engaged in a lower level emergency reaction? Continuing threat leads to a continual emergency reaction. Consider the heart as a glorified pump. As a pump breaks after some fixed number of uses, so the heart fails after it has exceeded its genetically allotted number of beats. The more beats you use up, the earlier your heart will fail (see discussion of allostatic load, p. 507). Being a Type A, continually viewing the world as a hostile and threatening place, will lead to the beats being used up earlier. As we saw in Chapter 5, when we are threatened we go into an emergency reaction that involves increased heart rate and increased blood pressure (Bystritsky, Craske, Maidenberg, Vapnik, and

Shapiro, 1995; Southard, Coates, Kolodner, Parker, Padgett, and Kennedy, 1986). As such, those who view the world as threatening may experience a sustained emergency reaction, which on average will use up their allotted beats more quickly.

Data on overload at work are compatible with this simple hypothesis (Jenkins, 1982; Steptoe, Roy, Evans, and Snashall, 1995). In the Western Collaborative Study, men who carried two jobs were at greater risk for CHD. In a particularly elegant analysis, job demand and decision latitude (that is, choice) were related to CHD (Karasek, Baker, Marxer, Ahlbom, and Theorell, 1981; see also Alterman, Shekelle, Vernon, and Burau, 1994). Among over 1,500 Swedish workers, a hectic and demanding job increased the risk for CHD, as did low amount of choice (see Figure 12–8). We might infer from this that workers whose jobs create the most frequent emergency reactions (high demand, low choice) use up their beats faster than those with other kinds of jobs, and that such workers are at greater risk for coronary heart disease.

Further evidence for the possibility that people who have prolonged emergency reactions are at greater risk for CHD comes from a prospective, longitudinal study of 126 alumni from the Harvard

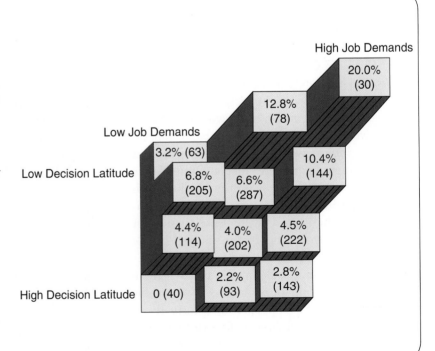

Figure 12–8

PREVALENCE OF CORONARY HEART DISEASE

The risk for coronary heart disease increases where job characteristics include high demands and low decision latitude. The vertical bars indicate the percent of people developing CHD according to whether their job characteristics include high, medium, or low job demands and high, medium, or low decision latitude. There was a grand total of 1,621 men who at the beginning of the study in 1968 did not have CHD. The numbers in parentheses are the number of people in each subgroup, and the percentage is the percent of those people in the subgroup who developed symptoms of CHD over the six-year course of the study. (Source: Adapted from Karasek, Baker, Marxer, Ahlbom, and Theorell, 1981)

Science and Practice

Box 12—2

Prevention of Death from Coronary Heart Disease and Cancer

One of the most controversial findings of the 1990s concerned the long-term prediction of death from CHD and cancer and its massive prevention by psychotherapy. Roland Grossart-Maticek began the work in the former Yugoslavia, then expanded it when he moved to Heidelberg, Germany. Largely ignored at first, it caught the fancy of Hans Eysenck, the eminent British researcher who died in 1998. Eysenck brought the work to the attention of English-speaking psychologists (Eysenck, 1991).

The first part of the project was predictive and used an interview and questionnaire that attempted to isolate "CHD-prone" individuals. The procedure also picked out "cancer-prone" individuals and contrasted both to "healthy-autonomous" individuals. According to this theory, CHD-prone individuals have issues centered on anger and aggression, whereas cancer-prone individuals tend toward helplessness and hopelessness. Ten years (or longer) later, deaths and causes of death were traced. The follow-up of 872 individuals showed consistent prediction of cause of death: among the 194 cancer-prone people, 9.8 percent had died of cancer, 1.3 percent from CHD, and 82.5 percent were still alive. Among the 227 CHD-prone people 10.1 percent had died of CHD, 4.4 percent of cancer, and 72.7 percent were still alive. Among the 261 people in the autonomous-healthy group, only 1 person had died of CHD and 1 from other causes.

Thirty-five "extremes" on each scale were followed from a different sample. Among the 35 cancer-prone extremes, 21 had died of cancer and 4 from CHD. Among the 35 CHD-prone extremes, 18 had died from CHD and 3 from cancer. Among 35 matched autonomous-healthy people, 1 person had died of CHD and cancer.

These findings are remarkable, but even more remarkable are the findings on prevention. Twelve hundred high scorers on either CHD or cancer-proneness were selected. Five hundred of them were untreated controls, and 100 were treated with psychoanalytic principles (assumed to be an inert placebo). The remaining 600 were given short-term behavior therapy and material to read, all of which emphasized autonomy and the avoidance of stress. Thirteen years later, deaths and the causes of death were traced.

Overall, more than 80 percent of those in the control group died in the course of the thirteen-year follow-up, mostly from CHD and cancer. In sharp contrast, less than one-third of those in the group that received behavior therapy died. Aside from very dramatic effects on death itself, the therapy was very cost effective since it was done in groups for about five hours total and supplemented only with reading material.

The results were greeted with a barrage of methodological criticisms. Critics charged that there were poorly specified treatment details, unrepresentative samples, poorly specified selection and matching criteria, and suspiciously low dropout rates. Nonetheless, despite the flaws in the study, results of this magnitude and lifesaving importance deserve further study to see if the results can be replicated without the methodological flaws of the initial study.

---

classes of 1952–1954. As students, these men were given an experimental stress test in which there was persistent criticism and harassment from the experimenter. Thirty-five years later, the amount of CHD was 2.5 times greater in those who had experienced severe anxiety during the stress test than in those who had not (Russek, King, Russek, and Russek, 1990).

Physical activity and exercise lower the risk for CHD, in that they reduce stress. In a review of forty-three studies, inactivity presented a consistent risk for CHD of about the same size as high blood pressure, smoking, or high cholesterol (Powell, Thompson, Caspersen, and Kendrick, 1987). The practical importance of this study is that in prevention programs, regular exercise should be promoted strongly. The theoretical importance concerns the emergency reaction: While vigorous exercise increases heart rate and blood pressure when you are engaged in it, its long-term consequences are to lower resting heart rate and blood pressure, thereby conserving the pump. Even better news concerns the possibility of prevention of CHD by psychological techniques that dampen hostility, depression, and stress (see Box 12–2).

Peptic Ulcers

Another physical disease that is clearly stress-related is peptic ulcer. An ulcer is a hole, or erosion, in the wall of an organ, and a **peptic ulcer** is an erosion of the mucous membrane of the stomach or of the duodenum, the upper portion of the small intestine. Such ulcers are called "peptic" because it is commonly thought that they are at least partially caused by pepsin, which is contained in the acidic juices normally secreted by

Pictured between the bottom dotted lines is a human stomach ulcer, which lies at the border of the exit to the small intestine and the duodenum.

the stomach. There are two sorts of peptic ulcers that derive their names from their location: stomach (gastric) ulcers and duodenal ulcers.

Roughly 25 million people in the United States today have a peptic ulcer (Center for Disease Control, 1994). Each year there are 500,000 to 850,000 new cases of peptic ulcer disease and more than one million ulcer-related hospitalizations. Peptic ulcers are the physical disorder most commonly believed by laymen to be caused by stress. The psychological influence story is complicated, however, and more is known, both about the physical pathology underlying ulcers and about psychological influence on their development and course, than for any other physical disorder. Carlos's gastrointestinal problems illustrate some ways in which stress influences peptic ulcers:

Carlos has had an ulcer for the last seventeen years. Until recently he had it under control; for whenever he experienced gastric pain, drinking a quart of milk or eating eggs would relieve it. Three years ago he was promoted to manager of a major department store and moved from his home town to a distant city. Since he took on this increased responsibility, he has experienced severe ulcer pain.

He had been born and raised in a small New England town. His father was wealthy and the head of a chain of department stores. Although his father was in general domineering and intolerant (and also had an ulcer), he was kind and generous to Carlos. After graduation from college Carlos entered the department store business and even now, at age forty-one, he feels incapable of holding a job without his father's intervention, influence, and support.

As soon as Carlos took over the management of the store, he became tense and anxious and began to brood over trivial details. He was afraid the store would

catch fire; he was afraid that there would be bookkeeping errors that he might not catch; he was afraid the store would not make a big profit. Convinced he was a complete failure, and plagued with severe pains from his duodenal ulcer, he entered psychotherapy. During these sessions, Carlos and his therapist learned how much the psychological factors in his life contributed to the worsening of the ulcer. The following three incidents particularly illustrate this.

First, on a day when the store was full of people a large ventilating fan broke. The store began to shake as the customers rushed to the street, and Carlos went into a panic. As soon as the excitement subsided and his panic diminished, severe ulcer pains started.

Second, Carlos's mother had for many years complained of a "heart condition." While his mother's physician had never isolated a physical cause, Carlos nevertheless worried about it. One day Carlos saw a hearse pass in front of the store. Immediately he thought that his mother had died and in panic ran several miles to her home, finding her quite alive. As he started to run, the stomach pains broke out, and these pains remained until he saw his mother was not ill.

Third, one night Carlos's store burned to the ground. He was highly anxious that he would be found negligent during the ensuing insurance investigation. As he awaited the results of the inquiry, his wife called and told him that his daughter had broken a leg. He ran home and found his wife in tears, and he immediately developed severe stomach pains.

Before he had become manager of the store he had occasionally had stomach pains while on the job, but he had found a technique for reliably and immediately alleviating them: he would go to an older person for comfort. Upon being reassured by an authority figure, his ulcer pain would disappear. In his new job, however, he was the authority figure, there was no one to turn to, and his ulcer pains persisted, unrelieved. (Adapted from Weisman, 1956)

Symptoms and Development of Ulcers

Carlos suffered the main symptom of peptic ulcer: abdominal pain. Such abdominal pain can vary from mild discomfort to severe and penetrating, extreme pain. Pain may be steady, aching, and gnawing, or it may be sharp and cramp-like. Pain is usually not present before breakfast; it generally starts from one to four hours after meals. Bland foods and antacids usually alleviate the pain, while peppery food, alcohol, and aspirin usually intensify it (Weiner, 1977). Peptic ulcers that become very serious sometimes perforate or bleed. Without well-timed surgery, a perforated ulcer can lead to death from internal bleeding.

In order to understand how these symptoms come to be, we must first take a brief look at the actions of the digestive system. Digestion breaks down food in the stomach so that when the food passes through the intestines, the appropriate materials can be absorbed for use by the body. In order to digest food, the stomach secretes two highly corrosive juices: hydrochloric acid, which breaks food down, and pepsin, which decomposes protein. Why, you might wonder, does the stomach not digest itself? Fortunately, the stomach and the small intestine are lined with a mucous membrane that protects them from corrosion by the hydrochloric acid the stomach secretes. In addition, gastric juices are normally secreted only when there is food in the stomach to absorb most of the corrosive acid.

But sometimes the system develops a problem. The trigger of the problem is almost always a common bacterium called *Helicobacter pylori* (*h. pylori*) which, remarkably, can survive in the acidic gastrointestinal tract by coating itself in protective bicarbonate (Blaser, 1999). This bacterium is found in more than 90 percent of people with peptic ulcers, and it apparently can create or enlarge a break in the mucous coating of the stomach or duodenum. If a break occurs in the absence of too much gastric juice, it will repair itself and no ulcer will form, since cell growth completely renews the stomach lining every three days (Davenport, 1972). If bacteria remain and an excess of hydrochloric acid or pepsin is around, however, the abrasion will worsen and an ulcer will form.

Killing the bacteria works well. When ulcer patients were treated with antibiotics, duodenal ulcers recurred in only 8 percent, but recurred in 86 percent of untreated controls (Alper, 1993; Center for Disease Control, 1989; Graham et al., 1992; Hentschel et al., 1993). Nonetheless, the bacterium cannot be the whole story, because 10 percent of people who have ulcers don't have the bacterium, and 90 percent of people infected with the bacterium don't get ulcers. And here is where stress enters the picture.

Who Is Susceptible to Ulcers?

The way an ulcer develops gives us clues about what diathesis, or constitutional weakness, makes ulcers more likely. Individuals who secrete excess hydrochloric acid or pepsin, individuals with an especially weak mucous defense against acid, and individuals whose stomach lining regenerates slowly may generally be more susceptible to ulcers. Moreover, individuals who are vulnerable to *h. pylori* may have reduced immune defense. Such vulnerabilities may be genetically inherited. If one of a pair of identical twins has a peptic ulcer, the chances are 54 out of 100 that the co-twin will also have a peptic ulcer; whereas if one of a pair of fraternal twins has a peptic ulcer, there is only a 17 percent chance that the co-twin will also have a peptic ulcer (Eberhard, 1968).

The prevalence of peptic ulcer varies widely from country to country, and from decade to decade. Today, approximately 10 percent of the adult American population has had an ulcer, and more than 500,000 Americans are hospitalized yearly for peptic ulcers. The susceptibility of women versus men seems to have undergone a major change over the past 100 years. Before 1900, peptic ulcers occurred more frequently in women than in men, but in the beginning of the twentieth century a shift occurred, with men becoming considerably more ulcer-prone. By the late 1950s, men had 3.5 times as many duodenal ulcers as women (Watkins, 1960). Nonetheless, the male/female ratio changed again in the last twenty-five years (Elashoff and Grossman, 1980). By 1978, men had only 1.2 times as many peptic ulcers as women in America. Ulcers in men had become less frequent, and ulcers in women had either stayed the same or slightly increased (Sturdevant, 1976). Social class also influences the incidence of ulcers. For a time it was commonly believed that highly pressured, upwardly mobile, and professionally successful individuals develop the most ulcers. But in fact many patients with peptic ulcer are poor and wholly unsuccessful, and those presently at highest risk for peptic ulcer are in the lower socioeconomic classes (Langman, 1974; Susser, 1967).

Psychological Factors Influencing Peptic Ulcers

To what extent does stress influence the development or worsening of peptic ulcers? When individuals who are infected with *h. pylori* or who otherwise have a constitutional weakness of the intestinal system encounter certain kinds of stress, peptic ulcers may result. What is the evidence that stress can influence peptic ulcer?

GASTRIC SECRETION, PEPTIC ULCER, AND EMOTIONAL STATES

Before the discovery of the massive influence of *h. pylori* on peptic ulcer in 1983, there was considerable research on the effects of stress. Once the bacterium was found, the amount of research on stress and ulcer plummeted because of the belief that the bacterium was the whole story. But much of the pre-1983 research was well done, and it still stands as evidence for the contribution of stress, particularly when we recall that the vast majority of people infected with *h. pylori* do not get peptic ulcers.

Let us now take a look at the evidence that emotional states affect gastric secretion. Researchers were afforded a rare opportunity to directly study the effects of anxiety and depression on digestion when they discovered a man who, because of a childhood experience, was forced to feed himself through a hole in his stomach.

> Tom was a fifty-seven-year-old workman who at the age of seven swallowed some very hot soup which burnt a hole in his esophagus so severe that it had to be surgically sealed off. Tom had to resort to feeding himself by chewing his food (to satisfy his taste) and then depositing it directly into his stomach using a funnel and a rubber tube. In his fifties, Tom allowed himself to be experimented upon. Investigators directly examined his gastric secretions under different emotional conditions. When he was anxious or angry or resentful, his gastric secretions increased. When he was sad, they decreased. (Wolff, 1965)

In another study, thirteen patients with ulcers and thirteen normal subjects were interviewed under emotion-provoking conditions. The patients with ulcers showed a greater secretion of hydrochloric acid in the stomach and more stomach motility than the patients without ulcers (Mittelmann, Wolff, and Scharf, 1942). Findings with normal individuals under hypnosis also confirmed that gastric secretions are influenced by emotion. Hypnotically induced thoughts of anger and anxiety produced high gastric secretion, while thoughts of depression, helplessness, and hopelessness produced low secretion (Kehoe and Ironside, 1963).

 High rates of peptic ulcers were found in people in occupations that produce high anxiety. For example, air traffic controllers have twice the ulcer rate of people in matched control groups, and those controllers who work at towers with much traffic have

Air traffic controllers have a high incidence of peptic ulcers, as they are responsible for the safety of thousands of people. This can create high anxiety, which can be seen in the face of John Cusack in the 1999 film *Pushing Tin.*

twice the ulcer rate of those who work at towers with less traffic (Cobb and Rose, 1973). We must be cautious, however, about this correlation between occupation and ulcers. It could be that ulcer-prone individuals for some reason choose anxiety-provoking jobs. If this is the case, the anxiety of the job may not be the cause of the ulcer.

Emotional states like anxiety and anger cause excess stomach acid; this, in turn, may contribute to the development of peptic ulcers in 10 percent of those who have *h. pylori,* as well as in the 10 percent of individuals with peptic ulcer who do not have *h. pylori.* Further, the absence of such stress in most infected individuals may help account for the fact that 90 percent of people infected with *h. pylori* do not get peptic ulcers. This must mean that something else brings on ulcers, and stress may well be the precipitating factor (Köhler, Kuhnt, and Richter, 1998).

ANIMAL MODELS OF STRESS AND PEPTIC ULCER

An elegant series of studies with animals isolated the contributions of stress on the development of peptic ulcers over and above the influence of *h. pylori.* We will look at the findings of these studies by examining three stressful situations that heighten emotionality—particularly anxiety—in animals: conflict, unpredictability, and uncontrollability.

Conflict   Can "conflict" be aroused in a rat in order to find out whether or not conflict produces ulcers? One way to bring about conflict is to make a hungry rat obtain food only after it has first run through an area in which it receives electric shock. This is called an ***avoidance-approach conflict.*** In one experiment, researchers required one group of rats to cross a shock grid in order to obtain food and water for forty-seven out of forty-eight hour cycles. During one hour, the grid was not electrified so that the animals could have sufficient water and food. Six of nine rats in this group developed ulcers, whereas none of the rats in the comparison group did. Control groups with shock alone, food and water deprivation alone, or nothing got fewer ulcers. So avoidance-approach conflict is more likely to produce stomach ulcers than is electric shock, hunger, or thirst without conflict (Sawrey, Conger, and Turrell, 1956; Sawrey and Weiss, 1956). Conflict, a psychological state that produces anxiety, can thus engender ulcers in rats.

Unpredictability and Uncontrollability When noxious events are experienced by an individual, they can either be signaled, and therefore predictable, or unsignaled, and therefore unpredictable. For example, the rockets that fell on London during World War II were signaled by an air raid siren. But when a concentration camp guard arbitrarily singled out a prisoner for a beating, this was entirely unsignaled. There is considerable evidence, both in rats and humans, that when noxious events are signaled, individuals are terrified during the signal. But they also learn that when the signal is not on, the noxious event does not occur, so they are safe and can relax. Also, if something can be done, a signal allows a person to prepare for the bad event. In contrast, when the identical noxious event occurs without a signal, individuals are afraid all the time because they have no signal of safety that tells them they can relax (Seligman and Binik, 1977).

When noxious events occur, sometimes you can do something about them, but at other times you are helpless. So, for example, being a victim of lung cancer is at least partly controllable; you can take action to avoid lung cancer by not smoking cigarettes. Losing your job during a national depression, however, is quite uncontrollable. There is very little you can do to protect your job once economic panic has set in and most of your colleagues are being fired. More precisely, an event is uncontrollable when no response an individual can make will change the probability of the event. An event is controllable when at least one response the individual has in his repertoire

These Muslim worshippers pray outside a mosque in Adapazari, Turkey, in August 1999, after a massive earthquake destroyed their homes and claimed the lives of half a million people. People who live on fault lines never know when the next earthquake will strike. They may feel that no response they make can change the probability of an earthquake, and as such, they may be susceptible to peptic ulcers.

can change the probability of the event. Which produces more ulcers, predictable or unpredictable dangers, controllable or uncontrollable dangers?

Rats were divided into six groups. Rats in two of the groups received escapable shock, shock they could turn off by rotating a wheel in front of them. Rats in two other groups were "yoked." In this condition, an "executive" rat who could turn off the shock was attached to a "partner" rat who could not do anything to control the shock. The partner rat received exactly the same pattern of shock as the executive rat, but the shock was inescapable—no response the partner rat made affected the shock; it went on and off for the partner rat at the same time as for the executive rat. Rats in two other groups received no shock. Within each of these conditions, shock was either signaled or unsignaled. In this experiment, then, both the controllability and predictability of the shock were varied (Seligman, 1968; Weiss, 1968, 1971).

As can be seen from Table 12–2, two basic findings emerged. First, unpredictability leads to ulcers—the rats developed more ulcers when they were subjected to unsignaled than to signaled shock, whether or not they could escape it. Second, uncontrollability leads to ulcers—rats who received inescapable shock developed more ulcers than the rats who could escape shock, whether or not the shock was signaled.

TABLE 12–2

MEDIAN NUMBER OF ULCERS AND WHEEL TURNS

	Ulcers	Wheel Turns
Escape Groups		
Signaled	2.0	3,717
Unsignaled	3.5	13,992
Yoked, Inescapable Groups		
Signaled	3.5	1,404
Unsignaled	6.0	4,357
No Shock Groups		
Signaled	1.0	60
Unsignaled	1.0	51

SOURCE: Adapted from Weiss, 1971.

What are we to conclude from this and other animal studies? First of all, it seems clear that the executive rats were less likely to develop ulcers. Second, this and other studies set up three conditions—conflict, unpredictability, and uncontrollability—that produce anxiety, and eventually a greater number of ulcers.

How do these rat studies relate to *h. pylori?* Studies of rats show that stress, in the absence of *h. pylori,* does not seem to produce ulcers, but it does in the presence of *h. pylori* (Levenstein et al., 1995; Pare, Burken, Allen, and Klucyznski, 1993; Sapolsky, 1998). We can infer from these studies that people (or rats) who are susceptible to ulcers because they are infected with *h. pylori* are additionally made vulnerable by conflict, unpredictability, and uncontrollability. The more such stress-inducing factors are present, the more likely that the person or rat will develop peptic ulcers.

Treatment of Peptic Ulcers

Thirty years ago, physicians treated peptic ulcers primarily by giving patients antacid drugs in an attempt to lower stomach acidity. In addition, doctors recommended that patients follow bland diets that restricted intake of foods that stimulate hydrochloric acid secretion. Smoking, drinking alcohol, and drinking coffee or tea were also restricted. About half of the ulcers usually healed under such a regimen, but relapse was frequent. In the late 1970s, cimetidine, a drug that reduces stomach acid by about two-thirds, became popular and produced healing in 70 to 95 percent of patients in a few months. The relapse rate was still high, however, with 50 percent recurrence in six months. Now antibiotics that kill *h. pylori* are used in addition, and recurrence is reduced to between 8 and 15 percent (Alper, 1993; Bardhan, 1980; Graham et al., 1992; Hentschel et al., 1993).

Psychological treatments of ulcers are less well charted. Rest, relaxation, anxiety management, and removal from the external sources of psychological stress are often prescribed for ulcer patients, and there is at least strong clinical evidence that these are effective. Nonetheless, with the discovery of *h. pylori,* progress on how to reduce the stress that exacerbates the disorder has unfortunately lagged.

To summarize, peptic ulcers are best viewed as a physical disorder that is exacerbated by psychological factors. A bacterium, *h. pylori,* infects most people who develop peptic ulcers. Once an individual is so infected, emotional states, particularly anxiety caused by conflict, unpredictability, and uncontrollability, increase vulnerability. If the bacterial load is very high, the ulcer may develop in the absence of such stress. If the bacterial load is lower, stress or its absence may tip the balance.

Immune System Disorders

Psychological factors, especially hostility, helplessness, depression, and stress, increase the risk of coronary heart disease. Do psychological factors also increase the risk of infectious diseases, AIDS, cancer, and asthma, in which the immune system plays such an important role? We have already examined how the immune system optimally works to fight off antigens. Now we will discuss how psychological influences play a role in the breakdown of the immune system (see Box 12–3).

Lowered Immunocompetence and Infectious Illness

Evidence is accumulating that psychological states produce immune and disease changes in humans (Maier and Watkins, 1998). There are several examples that have shown that depression, helplessness, hopelessness, and stressful life events are linked to immune changes in people. Infectious illnesses and number of doctor visits were counted for undergraduates who had either an optimistic or pessimistic explanatory style. Researchers first tested the subjects to determine their explanatory style. Remember that individuals who habitually see the causes of bad events as internal, stable, and global ("it's me," "it's going to last forever," "it's going to undermine everything") are said to have

---

Levels of Analysis

Box 12–3

Discovering the Pathway from Psychological Events to Disease

All the studies on the immune system and psychological states converge and suggest that pessimism, depression, helplessness, hopelessness, and stressful life events can lower immunocompetence. By what means might this occur? Consider, for example, a hypothetical chain of events that might explain how loss could bring about cancer: (1) A bereaved widow perceives that with the death of her husband she has lost someone who is irreplaceable. (2) She believes she is helpless to do anything about it and, if she has a pessimistic explanatory style, she becomes severely depressed. (3) Depression and helplessness, as we saw in Chapter 7, are accompanied by depletion of certain neurotransmitters in the brain, as well as by an increase in endorphins (internal morphine-like substances that block pain). (4) The immune system has receptors for endorphins that can then lower immunocompetence. (5) If there are pathogens in the body, say the beginnings of a tumor in the uterus, NK cells and T cells may be too inactivated to kill it. (6) A tumor that would ordinarily have been killed in its early stages can now grow to life-threatening size.

This schema is a speculation, but there is now evidence for each stage of this chain (Evans et al., 1995; Kiecolt-Glaser and Glaser, 1995; Maier, Watkins, and Fleshner, 1994). If such a chain indeed illuminates how tragedy can make us physically ill, there are important implications for prevention and therapy. Procedures that intervene at each of the steps might prevent or even reverse such illnesses. So, for example, cognitive therapy might be used to prevent the perception of helplessness or the depressive response, thereby interrupting the chain. Or drug therapy that breaks the catecholamine-endorphin link or blocks the immune receptors to endorphin stimulation might also interrupt the chain. We look forward to major advances in this area soon.

Gregory Buchanan of Beloit College has pinned down one part of this hypothetical chain of events—the pessimism-poor health link. In all the research on pessimism and ill health in humans, pessimism correlates with and predicts a variety of illnesses. But in any correlational study, no matter how well controlled, it is always possible that some third variable, which itself correlates with pessimism (for example, lots of failures in life), is the real cause of the ill health, and not the pessimism. The only way to sort this out is by taking a group of pessimists and randomly assigning some to a group that learns how to change their explanatory style from pessimism to optimism, and assigning the other pessimists to a control group, and then following the subsequent health of those in both groups. Two hundred and thirty-one pessimistic freshmen at the University of Pennsylvania were so assigned: half to a group that learned techniques for changing their pessimism into optimism, and half to a control group. Over the next three years, researchers recorded the number of visits the subjects made to doctors because of illness, and they measured the physical symptoms in the subjects. The group that learned optimism had fewer visits to doctors because of illness; fewer symptoms of physical illness, and made more preventive maintenance visits to student health centers (Buchanan, Gardenswartz, and Seligman, 1999). This study shows that it is the optimism-pessimism difference that causes health differences, and not some other third variable.

In one of the most intriguing tests of another part of the chain that ultimately links psychological events to a physical disease outcome, Janice Kiecolt-Glaser and Ronald Glaser, a psychologist-immunologist team at Ohio State University, are investigating fighting in married couples. Immune activity affects how rapidly small wounds heal, and at the outset of the study both members of the couple have a small, uniform wound inflicted on their forearms. The couples, who all claim to be happily married as a precondition of being in the study, are asked to discuss a contentious issue for thirty minutes. The researchers measure the level of emotion and, for the next twenty-four hours, they monitor the elements of the chain of hormonal events that lead to wound healing. The hypothesis is that there will be slower wound healing following high negative emotion, and that the parts of the chain that are disrupted by emotional stress can be isolated (Nagourney, 2000). It is bold experiments of just this sort that are likely to unravel the details of the effects of emotion on physical disease.

a "pessimistic explanatory style," while those who see the causes of bad events as external, unstable, and specific have an "optimistic explanatory style" (see Chapter 3). In the year following the test for explanatory style, pessimists had about twice as many infectious illnesses and made about twice as many visits to doctors as optimists (Peterson and Seligman, 1987). In another study, twenty-six spouses whose mates had died were followed for six weeks after the death of their spouses; the bereaved group showed depressed T-cell multiplication to antigens (Bartrop, Luckhurst, Lazarus, Kiloh, and Penny, 1977). In a different study of senior citizens, blood was drawn after explanatory style had been measured. Antigens were placed in the blood samples, and the efficiency of the immune reaction was measured. Pessimists had poorer T-cell function than optimists (Kamen-Siegel, Rodin, Seligman, and Dwyer, 1991). Researchers confirmed these results in a study of healthy male college students: those with a more pessimistic explanatory style for bad events showed lower T-cell responses to antigens placed in their blood samples (Zorrilla, Redei, and DeRubeis, 1994). Moreover, depressed individuals also showed lower T-cell responses (Schleifer, Keller, Bartlett, Eckholdt, and Delaney, 1996).

Natural Killer (NK) cell activity was found to be lower in women who had recently experienced major life events like the death of their spouse; the more depressed the woman, the more both NK and T-cell functions were impaired (Irwin, Daniels, Bloom, Smith, and Weiner, 1987). In a similar sample of widows, women who were diagnosed with major depression had lower NK-cell activity than did those who did not meet the criteria for major depression (Zisook et al., 1994). In another study, investigators drew blood twice from seventy-five first-year medical students, one month before and then on the day of final exams. They found that NK activity was lower at finals time, and the more loneliness and the more stressful life events reported, the lower the NK activity. Other researchers timed wound healing either during summer vacation or right before the first major examination and found that it took 40 percent longer for wounds to heal before the exam (Kiecolt-Glaser et al., 1984; Kiecolt-Glaser and Glaser, 1987; Marucha, Kiecolt-Glaser, and Favagehi, 1998).

The common cold, an immune-mediated infectious illness familiar to us all, has been linked with negative psychological states. Colds can be induced in the laboratory and susceptibility measured. In one study, 394 healthy volunteers were given controlled amounts of cold virus in a nasal spray, and the severity of the ensuing cold was measured. Subjects who had recently had more negative events in their lives, who had felt more negative affect, and who had had more perceived stress came down with worse colds (Cohen et al., 1995; Cohen et al., 1998; Cohen, Tyrrell, and Smith, 1993; Stone et al., 1994).

AIDS

Related findings are now emerging with HIV infection and AIDS. Eighty-six HIV-positive gay men were interviewed, and their explanatory style was extracted and coded. T-cell activity declined significantly over eighteen months following the interview in those men who had explained bad events as caused by the self, controlling for psychological, behavioral, social, and health confounds such as depression and health behavior. These HIV-positive subjects did not develop clinical symptoms of AIDS, however, during the study period (Segerstrom et al., 1996). In a parallel study, those HIV-positive gay men who were most depressed and stressed showed the greatest decline in Natural Killer cells and Helper T cells over a two-year follow-up (Leserman et al., 1997).

To counter the anxiety and depression felt by so many HIV-positive gay men, Neil Schneiderman and his colleagues at the University of Miami administered a ten-week cognitive-behavioral stress management course. The content focused on understanding stress, identifying catastrophic thoughts and disputing them, assertiveness, and anger management. Compared to the eighteen controls, the twenty-two men who took the stress management course had better cognitive and emotional coping. They accepted the fact of their HIV infection more and had markedly lower anxiety and depression. They also achieved more social support from friends and family (Lutgendorf et al., 1998). Improved immune functioning was also seen (Lutgendorf et al., 1997).

Not only do psychological factors influence HIV infection and AIDS, but AIDS and HIV infection can bring about major psychological changes. It is now recognized that clinically observable neurological disorders occur in about 40 percent of adult AIDS patients, and pathological changes in the nervous system have been noted in 80 to 90 percent of cases that have come to autopsy (Snyder et al., 1983; Trillo-Pazos and Everall, 1997). Some of the changes may be caused by the tumors or bacterial infections that can accompany AIDS. In a significant number of cases,

The AIDS Memorial Quilt is displayed in front of the Rose Bowl in Pasadena, California, in September 1995. The quilt is composed of three-by-six foot panels created by friends and relatives to commemorate the lives of those who have died of AIDS. Such a show of caring and support may help HIV-positive subjects to counter depression and anxiety and to have better immune functioning.

however, there is a syndrome of acquired dementia, called AIDS dementia, which cannot be explained as resulting from tumor growth or bacterial infection.

The early symptoms of AIDS dementia include word-finding difficulty, verbal memory deficits, psychomotor slowing, impaired problem-solving ability, and poor fine-motor control. AIDS was first recognized as a syndrome in 1981, and the dementia that

sometimes accompanies it was not noted until a few years later. Researchers still don't know exactly which brain regions are affected. But consistent with the behavioral symptoms, the affected region is initially subcortical; later, there is cortical involvement, particularly in the region of the frontal lobes (Brew, Rosenblum, Cronin, and Price, 1995; Gray et al., 1991; Power et al., 1998; Price, 1996; Price et al., 1988).

More controversial is whether there are any cognitive deficits in individuals who are HIV positive but who show no clinical symptoms of AIDS. Early reports of extensive deficits have been disconfirmed (Horter, 1989; Janssen et al., 1989; Law et al., 1994; McArthur et al., 1989). The consensus now is that these individuals are normal except for some psychomotor slowing on reaction-time tests, which may indicate subtle central nervous system damage (Martin, Heyes, Salazar, Law, and Williams, 1993). There is a bit of good news, however, since new treatments are now being used that seem to reverse AIDS dementia (Baldeweg, Catalan, and Gazzard, 1998; Skolnick, 1998).

Dementia caused by AIDS or by old age produces sweeping psychological changes, not only in the sufferer, but also among caregivers. Taking care of such a patient can be a helplessness-inducing, full-time task. In a longitudinal study of the consequences of taking care of such relatives, sixty-nine spouses of Alzheimer's patients were followed for thirteen months. They were compared to a matched control group of non-caregivers. Caregivers had more days of infectious illness, primarily colds. They had more depression, and the functioning of their immune system, as measured by multiplication of

DSM-IV Criteria

Dementia Due to HIV Disease

A. The development of multiple cognitive deficits manifested by both: (1) memory impairment (impaired ability to learn new information or to recall previously learned information), and (2) one (or more) of the following cognitive disturbances: (a) aphasia (language disturbance); (b) apraxia (impaired ability to carry out motor activities despite intact motor function); (c) agnosia (failure to recognize or identify objects despite intact sensory function); (d) disturbance in executive functioning (i.e., planning, organizing, sequencing, abstracting).

B. The cognitive deficits in Critera A1 and A2 each cause significant impairment in social or occupational functioning and represent a significant decline from a previous level of functioning.

C. There is evidence from the history, physical examination, or laboratory findings that the disturbance is the direct physiological consequence of HIV disease.

D. The deficits do not occur exclusively during the course of a delirium.

SOURCE: APA, DSM-IV, 1994.

cells to antigen challenge, was poorer than that of controls (Castle, Wilkins, Heck, Tanzy, and Fahey, 1995; Esterling, Kiecolt-Glaser, and Glaser, 1996; Kiecolt-Glaser, Dura, Speicher, Trask, and Glaser, 1991). We assume that similar symptoms arise among caregivers of patients with AIDS dementia.

Cancer

One of the most insidious of all illnesses influenced by psychological factors is cancer. There is mounting evidence that hopelessness may play a role in susceptibility to cancer. Fifty-one women who had previously been shown to have possibly cancerous cells in the cervix entered a clinic for a cancer test. Upon their arrival, they were interviewed by investigators, who found that eighteen of these fifty-one women had experienced significant losses in the last six months to which they reacted with feelings of hopelessness and helplessness. The others had experienced no such life event. Of the eighteen who had experienced hopelessness, eleven were found to have cancer. Of the thirty-three in the other group, only eight had cancer. The difference between the two groups was statistically significant (Schmale and Iker, 1966). In a German study of lung cancer, 103 patients were tested for their level of depression and distress before they began treatment. They were then followed for eight years. During this time, ninety-two of the patients died. Those patients who were most depressed and most distressed at the time of diagnosis survived a shorter time than the least upset patients. So, for example, the patients in the most distressed half of the sample lived an average of nine months, while the patients in the least distressed half lived an average of fifteen months. These differences in survival acted above and beyond such physical measures of prognosis as tumor stage (Faller, Bülzebruck, Drings, and Lang, 1999).

Lack of meaning in one's life, job instability, and a lack of plans for the future are better predictors of who has lung cancer better than is the amount of smoking (Horne and Picard, 1979). Conversely, breast cancer patients who responded with a fighting spirit rather than stoic acceptance had a better chance of recurrence-free survival five years later (Greer, Morris, and Pettingale, 1979).

Psychological distress may increase the rate of negative outcomes among women at risk for breast cancer by interfering with their personal health decisions. Distressed women may be less likely to seek predictive genetic testing, to volunteer for prevention trials, or to obtain regular breast examinations. The results of one randomized trial indicate that breast-cancer-risk counseling can significantly reduce breast-cancer-specific stress and improve health-related behavior (Lerman et al., 1996). It is also possible that talking about one's troubles, rather than locking them inside, may increase immunocompetence. In one dramatic study, individuals who opened up and wrote about emotionally troubling topics showed an increase in immune activity compared to those who kept their thoughts to themselves (Kelley, Lumley, and Leisen, 1997; Petrie, Booth, and Pennebaker, 1998).

David Spiegel and his colleagues followed a group of eighty-six women for ten years who had been referred to them for psychotherapy after the diagnosis of metastatic breast cancer (Spiegel, Bloom, Kraemer, and Gottheil, 1989). The women were randomly assigned either to therapy or to be controls without psychotherapy. Psychotherapy lasted for a year, while routine physical treatment for breast cancer continued. Therapy focused on encouraging the women to express their feelings about their illness and to talk about the effect of the illness on their lives. Self-hypnosis for pain control was also taught. At no time were patients led to expect that psychotherapy would affect the course of the illness.

Ten years later, Spiegel looked at survival rates of the women in the two groups. On average, women in the psychotherapy group lived twice as long as women in the control group, who developed more lung and bone metastases (Kogon, Biswas, Pearl, Carlson, and Spiegel, 1997). Figure 12–9 shows the survival curves for the two groups of women.

Similar results have also been found in better-controlled studies (Fawzy, Fawzy, and Hyun, 1994). Malignant melanoma patients received a six-week group intervention consisting of relaxation, guided imagery, stress management, and social problem solving. The control group received just routine medical care. At six-year follow-up, three of the thirty-four patients in the treatment group had died (compared to ten of the thirty-four patients in the control group) and another seven patients in the treatment group had suffered a recurrence of melanoma (compared to thirteen patients in the control group).

Although the mechanism by which psychotherapy prolongs survival is a matter of sheer speculation, we hope that the next decade will see the development of psychological interventions to treat and even prevent such illnesses as cancer and heart attack (Fawzy, Fawzy, Arndt, and Pasnau, 1995; McDaniel, Musselman, Porter, Reed, and Nemeroff, 1995).

Figure 12—9

PSYCHOTHERAPY AND CANCER SURVIVAL

Women with breast cancer were randomly assigned to either a control group that received only chemotherapy or a treatment group that received both chemotherapy and psychotherapy, which helped them learn deal with their feelings about the cancer and its effects on their lives and taught them self-hypnosis for pain control. Women in the treatment group lived significantly longer than did women in the control group. (Source: Spiegel, Bloom, Kraemer, and Gottheil, 1989)

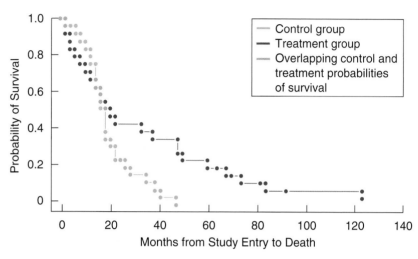

Asthma

Asthma is a condition in which the air passages of the bronchia narrow, swell, and secrete excess fluid to a variety of stimuli. This results in wheezing, which in its worst form can be severe and can produce a convulsive struggle for breath. Asthma is the most common childhood disease, with more than 4.8 million children suffering from it (Adams and Marano, 1995). Asthma can be caused by infection, by allergy, or by psychological factors. At the low end, it has been estimated that each of these plays the dominant role in about a third of the cases (Kotses et al., 1991; Weiner, 1977). At the high end, it has been estimated that 70 percent of all cases involve psychosocial factors, such as anxiety, dependency needs, and troubled relations between the parent and the asthmatic child.

Anecdotes indicate that when European children with asthma were sent off by their parents to spas "to take the waters" they cheerfully ignored their parents' long lists of instructions, showed few signs of asthma, and seemed to be psychologically improved as well. To test the possibility that separation from parents might alleviate asthma, Dennis Purcell and his colleagues chose twenty-five chronically asthmatic schoolchildren who lived with their families (Purcell

et al., 1969). They divided these children into two groups—those in whom emotional factors had usually preceded past attacks of asthma at home, and those in whom emotional factors seemed irrelevant to the onset of past attacks. The first group was expected to benefit from separation, but not the second.

The parents and siblings of the child were removed from the home and sent to a motel for two weeks, while the child continued to live in his home environment. A surrogate parent was provided, and the child continued normal attendance at school and normal play activities. After two weeks of not seeing their child, the parents returned to the home and life went on as usual.

As predicted, the effects were beneficial for the group suspected of emotionally induced asthma. Their medication during separation could be reduced by half, and on top of this the number of asthma attacks and amount of wheezing were reduced by half as well. When the parents returned, wheezing, number of attacks, and amount of necessary medication all increased. Beneficial effects of separation on asthma did not appear for the group in which emotional factors had been judged unimportant.

While emotional factors may be irrelevant to asthma in some children, in others family stresses may set off or worsen asthmatic attacks. In a prospective study of 100 infants with a family history of allergy, the researchers examined the relationship between family-related emotional distress and asthma. Researchers found that children who came from families with low cohesiveness and a poor ability to adapt to stress were no more likely to develop wheezing problems than children from more functional family environments. Nonetheless, once the child developed wheezing problems, there was a significantly greater chance for the initiation or maintenance of dysfunctional interaction patterns. Thus, asthma in children may be a cause, rather than a result, of family-related stress (Gartland and Day, 1999; Gustafsson and Kjellman, 1986; Gustafsson, Bjorksten, and Kjellman, 1994).

In cases in which emotional factors are related to asthmatic attacks, if the family members learn more effective and less stressful ways of dealing with each other, the child's asthma may get better.

Putting It All Together

For decades there has been a battle in medicine over the very existence of psychological influences on physical disorders. In an understandable desire not to admit spiritual entities (mind or emotion) into a materialistic science, many "tough-minded" medical scientists greeted the mounting tide of data on psychological influence with skepticism, and even derision. As the measurement of the psychological variables grew more reliable, however, and as the data moved from anecdotal case histories to longitudinal studies to replicated experimental demonstrations, the existence of psychological influences on physical disorders is now undeniable. Among many other examples, it is a fact that:

- hostility increases the likelihood of heart attacks,
- pessimists have a more illness-ridden middle age,
- depression and stressful life events lower Natural Killer cell activity,
- psychotherapy prolongs survival of people who have certain cancers,
- family turmoil exacerbates asthma,
- jobs with high demand and low decision latitude increase the risk of coronary problems.

How to explain these facts is still an issue, however. The mechanisms, psychological and biological,

remain shrouded in mystery and confusion. At the psychological level, in spite of the almost ritual invocation of "stress," we must acknowledge that this is a very incomplete explanation. Stressors refer to the negative events that upset an individual's balance, but there are two very different, indeed opposite, reactions to stressors. Sometimes the reaction is mobilizing: the emergency reaction and other bodily defenses go into high gear, and anxiety, fear, and hostility are seen. Hypertension and sudden heart attacks are associated with such "up" reactions. On the other hand, sometimes the reaction to stressors is demobilization: depression, giving up, helplessness, and hopelessness. The biological emergency mechanisms are inhibited in these "down" states. Yet, coronary heart disease, cancer, and peptic ulcers are associated with these bodily reactions as well. Better theories and evidence are needed to break down the overly global notion of stress into different psychological components and then to isolate the neural and immunological pathways that follow the different psychological reactions to bad events.

Another side of this problem concerns the temporal relations between stressful events and physical disorders. When a stressful event occurs, the long-term bodily reaction is often the opposite of the short-term reaction. So, for example, sudden activa-

"I'D SAY THE SALES CHART IS THE ULCER, THE PHONE IS THE HYPERTENSION, THE PAPERWORK IS THE MIGRAINE..."

tion of the HPA axis and the emergency reaction follow immediately upon a terrifying event. But soon thereafter, a compensatory reaction that inhibits and attempts to restore HPA homeostasis occurs. If a physical disorder, like heart disease, eventually develops, we cannot tell if it results from the short-term emergency reaction, or the long-term, opposite, compensatory reaction, or the sequence of the two.

It must also be said that the biological chain of events from personality types like Type A to psychological reactions to bad events are still matters of speculation. While we know that neurotransmitter changes, hormonal changes, and immunological changes all are involved in the disease process that follows, how these changes are knitted together is one of the most important scientific puzzles that the next decade of research promises to illuminate.

So, the mechanisms by which personality types, psychological events, and the ensuing emotional reactions influence physical disorders remain unclear, and the biological chain of events that follows has also not yet been pinned down. This means that the psychological "treatment of choice" for these conditions also remains unclear. To the extent that mobilizing reactions to stress are responsible for a given disorder, treatments that reduce anxiety and anger should be appropriate. So, relaxation, biofeedback, and meditation have all been used to treat a variety of psychosomatic disorders that are thought to be stress related. But to the extent that the demobilizing emotional reactions, such as hopelessness and depression, are responsible for a given disorder, other therapeutic techniques, such as cognitive therapy or antidepressant medication, should be more effective.

Summary

1. Psychological factors can influence the course, and even the beginning of, a physical illness. The criteria for a "Psychological Factor Affecting a General Medical Condition" are: (1) the existance of a disorder of known physical pathology, and (2) psychologically meaningful events preceded, and are judged to have contributed to, the onset or worsening of the disorder.

2. Such a process can be viewed within a *diathesis-stress model*. According to this view, a physical disorder occurs when an individual is both vulnerable to the particular physical problem and experiences life stress.

3. Stress may influence physical illness through the process of *allostasis,* which is the regulation of many bodily states simultaneously across many different life circumstances. Too much stress, or inefficiency of allostasis in response to stress, produce *allostatic load.*

4. The immune system recognizes and destroys *antigens,* and its activity can be influenced by psychological states. *Psychoneuroimmunology,* a field that studies this process, has shown that depression, stressful life events, hopelessness, and helplessness decrease immunocompetence and increase immune-related diseases. Yet, acute stress enhances immune function.

5. Adverse *life events* contribute to the causation of physical disorders, with hard living conditions, such as poverty, high job demand but low control, and social turmoil adding to risk.

6. Our own *voluntary behavior* plays a major role in susceptibility to physical illness, with half the deaths in the United States partly caused by unwise human choices. The field of *health psychology* studies the effect of behavior on physical health.

7. *Coronary heart disease (CHD)* is the leading cause of death in the Western world. Having the *Type A personality*—characterized by aggressiveness, time urgency, and competitiveness—is a risk factor for CHD. Hostility may be the crucial component of Type A. *Helplessness* and *hopelessness* in the face of *uncontrollable* events may be other insidious components of the Type A personality. Frequent engagement in the emergency reaction may be the process by which Type A's, hostile people, and overloaded people are at greater risk for CHD.

8. A bacterium, *h. pylori,* is almost always found in cases of *peptic ulcer.* But over and above the bacterial infection, stress, uncontrollability, unpredictability, and conflict influence whether or not peptic ulcers occur.

9. Death from lung cancer and breast cancer may be hastened by depression, hopelessness, and distress. Psychological treatments that alleviate these emotions may increase life expectancy for cancer patients.

10. The entire gamut of treatment techniques, including relaxation, biofeedback, cognitive therapy, insight, hypnosis, and medications, has been used to treat physical disorders influenced by psychological factors. But until the psychological and biological pathways are better understood, recommendations for treatment of choice cannot be made.

13

Sexual Disorders

Chapter Outline

Dora Holzhandler, *Lovers in Spring.*

Learning Objectives

→ Be able to describe the five layers of erotic life: gender identity, sexual orientation, sexual preference, sex role, and sexual performance.

→ Learn about the role of hormones in determining gender identity, why it is virtually impossible to change gender identity, and why transsexuals are willing to undergo sex-reassignment surgery to change their bodies.

→ Familiarize yourself with some theories about the origins of sexual orientation, including neuroanatomical evidence and twin data on homosexuality.

→ Be able to describe what distinguishes normal sexual interest from disordered sexual interest, and learn about three categories of paraphilias and some treatments used to change sexual preferences.

→ Understand why young children categorize the world according to sex and are likely to exhibit and believe in sex-role stereotypes, but why these stereotypes weaken as children grow older.

→ Be able to describe the physiology of the human sexual response in males and females and different ways in which sexual performance can be impaired, leading to sexual dysfunction.

→ Learn about biomedical and psychological causes and treatments of sexual dysfunction.

Notions of what is sexually abnormal and what is sexually normal change with time and place. What one society labels as "deviant" may well be labeled as "normal" by another society. Although premarital sex, masturbation, oral sex, and homosexuality were all condemned by our puritanical society in the past, most people today are tolerant of these behaviors and do not consider them to be deviant. Sex pervades our culture, and our society has become vastly more open about its sexual practices in the last half century. Emblematic of this openness are the Viagra ads featuring Robert Dole, a former senator from Kansas and the conservative Republican presidential candidate in 1996. Surveys of American and European adults all point to a marked increase in the number of sex partners in a lifetime (although the majority of people still report only one partner in the preceding year), the frequency of oral sex (around 75 percent), the frequency of premarital intercourse, and the infrequency of celibacy. The fear of AIDS and other sexually transmitted diseases, however, may be leading to more "safe" sex and less promiscuity (Billy, Tanfer, Grady, and Klepinger, 1993; Johnson, Wadsworth, Wellings, Bradshaw, and Field, 1992; Seidman and Rieder, 1994; Spira et al., 1992).

In the past, what constituted "normal sexual activity" and "normal sexual function" was clearer than it is today. Ordinary sexual practices among men and women in our society are now more diverse than they once were (Laumann, Gagnon, Michael, and Michaels, 1994). And so, our concept of sexual order has broadened, and our concept of sexual disorder and dysfunction has narrowed. This chapter narrates the story of how problems of sexuality have come to be quite well understood and how many of them can now be treated successfully. This is an area rife with controversy, and the first question is what to call sexual problems. Some call them "variations" and "preferences"; others label them "deviations," or even "diseases." We use the term "dysfunction" to refer to sexual inability. We use the term "disorder" to refer to the paraphilias and transsexualism. Open attitudes and more permissiveness in our society have not eliminated problems of sexual functioning, and we still find many instances of sexual "disorder" and sexual "dysfunction." The main disorder of gender identity is transsexualism, in which a man believes he is a woman trapped in the body of a man, or a woman believes she is a man trapped in the body of a woman. Disorders of sexual interest manifest themselves through sexual arousal to the unusual or bizarre. These are called the "paraphilias." The sexual "dysfunctions" are low desire, low arousal, pain, or problems with orgasm. Overall, our criterion for "abnormality" in the sexual realm is the gross impairment of affectionate, erotic relations between human beings, and as such, these sexual dysfunctions and sexual disorders qualify. We begin with a case in which sexual problems were indeed undermining the relationship of a married couple:

> When they first came to therapy, Carol, age twenty-nine, and Ed, age thirty-eight, had been married for three and a half years and had one child. When they were first married, Carol had achieved orgasm almost every time they made love, but now orgasm was rare for her. She was feeling more and more reluctant to have intercourse with Ed. Ed had a strong sex drive and wanted to have intercourse every day. But Carol had made rules about sex, stating what Ed could and could not do.
>
> As time went on, Carol found it more and more difficult to keep her part of the bargain. Carol's headaches, fatigue, and quarrels deterred Ed's effective initiation of lovemaking. When he did make love to her, Carol would complain about his lovemaking technique. This effectively ended the encounter.
>
> When they first sought out sexual therapy, they were having intercourse once every two weeks, but Carol was becoming progressively more reluctant and intercourse was becoming even more of a dreaded ordeal for her. (Adapted from Kaplan, 1974, case 22)

Forty years ago it could be said with near certainty that Carol and Ed's sexual relationship was doomed. Once a couple's lovemaking had reached this point, it could only go downhill toward frustration and anger, mutual recrimination, and emotional isolation. They might stay married, but they would never be erotic mates again. Today Carol and Ed's problem can usually be reversed by sexual therapy.

Five Layers of Erotic Life

To understand how to treat problems of sexuality, like that of Carol's and Ed's, we must first understand the structure of normal human sexuality. To

this end, we organize the structure of erotic life into five layers, each built over the layer beneath it. Sexual problems can occur at each layer. At the base is *gender identity,* our awareness of being male or female. The next layer is sexual orientation, followed by sexual interest, sex role, and, at the surface, sexual performance.

Gender identity almost coincides with genitals. If we have a penis, we feel ourselves to be male; if we have a vagina, we feel ourselves to be female. Scientists know that gender identity has a separate existence of its own because of a rare and astonishing dissociation of gender identity and sexual organs in some people. Some men (we call them men because they have penises and a pair of XY chromosomes) feel that they are women trapped in men's bodies. Some women (who have vaginas and a pair of XX chromosomes) feel that they are men trapped in women's bodies. These individuals, who have the gender identity disorder commonly called "transsexualism," provide the key to understanding normal gender identity.

The layer directly over gender identity is our basic *sexual orientation.* Do you fall in love with men or women or both? Are you heterosexual, homosexual, or bisexual? Our erotic fantasies tell us our sexual orientation. If you have had erotic fantasies only about the opposite sex, you are exclusively heterosexual. If you have had erotic fantasies only about members of your own sex, you are exclusively homosexual. If your erotic fantasies involve both sexes and you have often masturbated to both kinds of fantasies, you should consider yourself bisexual. The only problem that can occur at this level is when your orientation causes you distress and confusion that you want to get rid of. (In DSM-III this was known as "ego-dystonic homosexuality," but this category was eliminated in DSM-IV.)

The third layer is *sexual preference* or *sexual interest:* the types of persons, parts of the body, and situations that are the objects of your sexual fantasies and arousal. What parts of the body turn you on? What scenes do you masturbate about? What is on your mind at the moment of orgasm? For most men, the female face, breasts, buttocks, and legs are most arousing. For most women, the male chest and shoulders, arms, buttocks, and face are most arousing. But women do not commonly focus on a body part as men do; rather whole scenes, generally romantic ones, are the usual subjects of women's fantasies.

But these are not universal sexual interests by any means. Many people crave nonstandard objects, such as feet, hair, ears, belly buttons; silk or rubbery textures; panties, stockings, or jeans; or unusual situations such as peeping, flashing, and receiving or inflicting pain. When these or other more bizarre objects get in the way of an affectionate, erotic relationship with another consenting human being, the line has been crossed into sexual disorder.

The fourth layer, the one next to the surface, is our **sex role.** This is the public expression of gender identity, what an individual says or does to indicate that he is a man or she is a woman. Most people who feel that they are male adopt male sex roles, and most females adopt female sex roles. But we know of the separate existence of sex roles because men and women do not always adopt the usual male and female sex roles; some women behave aggressively and like to dominate, and some men are passive and submissive. There are no defined categories of "disorder" at this level.

The surface layer is **sexual performance** or "functioning"—how adequately you perform when you are with a suitable person in a suitable erotic setting. Do desire, arousal, and orgasm occur? There is a set of problems common to this stage, and these are called the sexual "dysfunctions."

We have organized erotic life into these five layers with one basic aim in mind—to explain how easily problems at each layer will change in the natural course of life and in therapy. The deeper the layer, the harder it is to change. This view of erotic life tells us that transsexualism is a problem at the core level and simply will not change. Sexual orientation, the next deepest layer, will strongly resist change. Sexual interests, once acquired, are strong, but some change may be wrought. Sex roles can change quite a bit. And sexual performance problems are at the surface layer, so they can be treated quite effectively.

Gender Identity: Layer I

Few things are more basic to who we are than our sense of what sex we are, and this is what has gone awry in **gender identity disorder,** also called **transsexualism.** The therapy for most sexual disorders is psychologically based, but the therapy for transsexualism does not consist of changing the identity. So deep and unchangeable is gender identity that the therapy of choice actually changes the body to conform to the disordered identity.

Characteristics of Transsexuals

A **male-to-female transsexual** is a man who feels that he is a woman trapped in a man's body. He wants to be rid of his genitals, wants female sexual characteristics, and wants to live as a woman. A **female-to-male transsexual** is a woman who feels that she is a man trapped in a woman's body. She wants to acquire male characteristics and to live as a man. From early in life, transsexuals feel that they got stuck with the wrong body. This body often disgusts them, and the prospect of having to remain in it all their days makes them feel hopeless, depressed, and possibly suicidal. They will sometimes mutilate their genitals. By their early twenties, many transsexuals will cross-dress, that is, masquerade in the clothes of the opposite sex. In effect, transsexuals often do everything they can to pass for members of the opposite sex. Unlike transvestites, transsexuals do not view such actions, particularly the cross-dressing, as sexually exciting. Rather, they are the means of leading the life compatible with their gender identity. Transvestites are decidedly not transsexual and would be horrified at the idea of changing their sex.

Before this century, transsexuals were doomed to live out their lives in a body they hated. But in the last thirty years, medical procedures have been developed—but not yet perfected—which allow transsexuals to acquire the anatomy they want. The case of Allen-Allison shows the transsexual's problems with gender identity:

For the last four years, Allen has been passing as a female, but he is in reality an anatomically normal twenty-three-year-old male. He takes female hormones, and has had his facial and chest hair removed. Six months ago, he had his first operation: plastic surgery to enlarge his breasts. He expects in the next two years to undergo sex-reassignment surgery to construct a vagina from his penis and scrotum.

Allen says that "As early as I can recall I never had any boyish interests and always wanted to become a girl and change my name to Allison." He loved to dress in his mother's clothes and always preferred to play with "feminine" things. On one occasion, when he was given a fire engine, he threw a tantrum, insisting that he wanted a doll. From about kindergarten on, he demanded acceptance from his parents as a girl and this made for constant conflict. Finally, in the

DSM-IV Criteria

Gender Identity Disorder (formerly Transsexualism)

A. A strong and persistent cross-gender identification (not merely a desire for any perceived cultural advantages of being the other sex). In children, the disturbance is manifested by four (or more) of the following: (1) repeatedly stated desire to be, or insistence that he or she is, the other sex; (2) in boys, preference for cross-dressing or simulating female attire; in girls, insistence on wearing only stereotypical masculine clothing; (3) strong and persistent preferences for cross-sex roles in make-believe play or persistent fantasies of being the other sex; (4) intense desire to participate in the stereotypical games and pastimes of the other sex; (5) strong preference for playmates of the other sex. In adolescents and adults, the disturbance is manifested by symptoms such as a stated desire to be the other sex, frequent passing as the other sex, desire to live or be treated as the other sex, or the conviction that he or she has the typical feelings and reactions of the other sex.

B. Persistent discomfort with his or her sex or sense of inappropriateness in the gender role of that sex. In children, the disturbance is manifested by any of the following: in

boys, assertion that his penis or testes are disgusting or will disappear or assertion that it would be better not to have a penis, or aversion toward rough-and-tumble play and rejection of male stereotypical toys, games, and activities; in girls, rejection of urinating in a sitting position, assertion that she has or will grow a penis, or assertion that she does not want to grow breasts or menstruate, or marked aversion toward normative feminine clothing. In adolescents and adults, the disturbance is manifested by symptoms such as preoccupation with getting rid of primary and secondary sex characteristics (e.g., request for hormones, surgery, or other procedures to physically alter sexual characteristics to simulate the other sex) or belief that he or she was born the wrong sex.

C. The disturbance is not concurrent with a physical intersex condition.

D. The disturbance causes clinically significant distress or impairment in social, occupational, or other important areas of functioning.

SOURCE: APA, DSM-IV, 1994.

fourth grade, he persuaded his parents to allow him to "be" a girl at home, except that he had to wear boys' clothes to school. For the next few years he led a double life, attending school dressed as a boy and then returning home to dress and live as a girl. By eighth grade, he began to feel very uncomfortable around people. He began to avoid school and spent a great deal of time alone.

At fifteen, both school life and family life had become unbearable, and he ran away to San Francisco, where he experimented with homosexuality. He found he could not tolerate homosexual males and left after only a month. While he was attracted to men as sexual partners, only those normal heterosexual men who had accepted him as a female aroused him sexually. Soon thereafter, he began the odyssey of physical transformation.

Allen is now becoming Allison. (Adapted from Pauly, 1969)

Allen-Allison is a male-to-female transsexual. By age three or four, his identity as a female was well on

its way to being fixed. Before puberty, most transsexual boys will play almost exclusively with girls, will act like girls, prefer to play with dolls, sew and embroider, and help their mothers with housework. They refuse to climb trees, play cowboys and Indians, or roughhouse. By puberty, they feel completely like females, and they want to be accepted by society as females (Zucker and Bradley, 1995).

Transsexualism is chronic: once it has developed, it does not spontaneously disappear. When transsexuals learn that sex-reassignment operations exist, they desperately want one (Doorn, Poortinga, and Verschoor, 1994; Money and Ehrhardt, 1972; Tiefer and Kring, 1995).

Transsexualism is rare. Perhaps somewhat more than 1 in 100,000 people is transsexual. In the overall population of transsexuals, there are many more male-to-female transsexuals, with estimates of the male-to-female ratio ranging from 2.5 to 1 up to 6.6 to 1 (Bakker, Van Kesteren, Gooren, and Bezemer, 1993; Bradley and Zucker, 1997; Zucker, Bradley, and Sanikhani, 1997).

The Etiology of Transsexualism

Where does such a deep disorder come from?★ What sorts of events must conspire in order for a physically unremarkable girl to feel that she is really a boy, or a boy to feel that he is a girl? We speculate that most of gender identity—both normal and transsexual—comes from a hypothesized hormonal process in the second to fourth month of pregnancy.

We begin with a simplified version of how a fetus becomes a normal male or female. The embryo has the potential to develop either male or female internal organs. For eight weeks after conception, however, all fetuses have undifferentiated genitals (gonads) that can develop into either testes or ovaries. The fetus will by default become female unless the next crucial step occurs: the secretion of masculinizing hormones (androgens). When these hormones are secreted, the male internal organs grow, and the male external organs develop. All this happens roughly at the end of the first three months of pregnancy (Ellis and Ames, 1987; Pillard and Weinrich, 1987).

We believe that the level of the masculinizing hormones at this stage not only determines the genitals, but also determines gender identity. The masculinizing hormones produce male gender identity. If they are insufficient, female gender identity results. So, under our theory, gender identity is present in the fetus. But there is no way of asking a fetus if he feels like a male or a female, so this is not an easy theory to test. Nonetheless, there are four startling "experiments of nature" in which gender identity is dissociated from sexual organs—all of which point toward the integrative theory we now detail.

You already know about two of the experiments of nature: male-to-female transsexuals and female-to-male transsexuals. In our theory, a massive dose of the masculinizing hormone for a chromosomal male (XY) produces both male sexual organs and male gender identity. An insufficient dose produces male sexual organs, but a female gender identity—the male-to-female transsexual. Conversely for a chromosomal female (XX), an insufficient dose of the masculinizing hormone produces both female sexual organs and female gender identity. But if more

★There is no comprehensive theory of the etiology of gender identity disorder. Here we present our own integrative view, which derives from M. Seligman, *What you can change and what you can't,* Chapter 11 (New York: Knopf, 1994).

This scene from the 1999 film *Boys Don't Cry* shows Hilary Swank (on the right), dressed and acting as a man, and Chloë Sevigny (on the left). The film was based on the true story of Teena Brandon, who was born female, but saw herself as a male. Calling herself Brandon Teena, she was living as a man in preparation for an eventual sex-change operation. Brandon was raped and murdered after her secret was discovered.

masculinizing hormone intrudes, female sexual organs develop, but a male gender identity is produced—the female-to-male transsexual.

There are two mirror-image conditions that show remarkable parallels to the two mirror-image gender identity disorders, but these are much better understood—"Adrenogenital Syndrome" (AGS) and "Androgen Insensitivity Syndrome" (AIS). These two syndromes may be the key to understanding how transsexualism comes about. AIS is the extreme version of male-to-female transsexuality, and AGS is the extreme version of female-to-male transsexuality. But unlike the transsexualisms, these both have happy endings.

People who have AIS are chromosomally male: 46XY. Their Y chromosome contains the gene that produces masculinizing hormones. It functions normally, inhibiting the development of female internal organs and causing the formation of male internal organs. But their X chromosome, which would normally contain the gene that enables their bodies to recognize and react to masculinizing hormones, does not function normally. This leads to an insensitivity to masculinizing hormones (androgens) and the corresponding inability to use the hormones produced by the internal testes to form male external genitals. Instead, female external genitals are formed. So, people with AIS are born with male internal organs (which differentiate before the ineffective masculinizing bath) but with a vagina as well. The vagina is actually a dead-end. All people with AIS are declared girls and raised as girls. They all grow up feeling female, they pursue men, and they have intercourse as women. When puberty arrives, they grow breasts under the influence of the normal male amount of estrogen, secreted by the testes (which they have deep inside), and so they look like women as well (Lewis and Money, 1983).

In our theory, a male-to-female transsexual is a less extreme version of a person with AIS. Both are 46XY fetuses with male internal organs. According to our theory, a person with AIS is insensitive to masculinizing hormones, and so both female external sexual organs and a female gender identity develop. In contrast, the male-to-female transsexual is sensitive to masculinizing hormones, such that male external organs are produced. But the level of the hormones is not sufficient to produce male gender identity. He is therefore psychologically female but is born with a working penis and so is declared and raised as a boy. He is miserable ever after—or until he loses his penis surgically. His AIS cousin is psychologically female. Because her body is insensitive to masculinizing hormones, she is born with the appearance of a vagina and is declared a girl. Her life works out because everyone thinks she is (by virtue of her vagina and later her breasts) the same sex she thinks she is—a woman.

AGS has a profound effect on the 46XX fetus (a chromosomally normal female): it bathes her in masculinizing hormones. As a result, she is born with the internal organs of a female (since they were differentiated before the bath), but she is also born with what seem to be a penis and scrotum. The penis and scrotum look convincing, but they are actually an enormously enlarged and penile-shaped clitoris (foreskin and all). The scrotum contains no testicles. Many people with AGS are declared boys and raised as boys. Since the hormonal bath continues, their voice deepens, and face and body hair sprout at puberty. These people with AGS grow up as normal men. They feel like they are male, they pursue women romantically, they have intercourse as men, and they become good husbands and fathers (by adoption or artificial insemination). There is a complete absence of bisexual fantasy or action. In contrast, when a person with AGS is surgically feminized and then reared as a girl, as sometimes happens, major problems often ensue: she may feel and act like a man, and bisexual fantasy and action are common (Imperato-McGinley, Peterson, Gautier, and Sturla, 1979; Money and Dalery, 1976; Money, Schwartz, and Lewis, 1984; Money, 1987).

In our theory, a female-to-male transsexual is a less extreme version of a person with AGS. Both are 46XX fetuses who are mistakenly exposed to too much masculinizing hormone. The person with AGS receives a massive dose, and so both male sexual organs and a male gender identity ensue. The female-to-male transsexual gets a smaller dose, so only the male gender identity ensues, but no male sexual organs appear. The person with AGS is psychologically male, and is fortunate enough also to be born with the appearance of a penis and scrotum and so is declared a boy. His life works out because what everyone thinks he is (by virtue of the appearance of a penis at birth and later by his deep voice and facial hair) is the same as he thinks he is—a man. In contrast, because of a smaller masculinizing hormonal error, the female-to-male transsexual is born psychologically male, but with a vagina, and so is declared and raised as a girl. Her life is a constant misery thereafter. It gets even worse after puberty, because unlike an AGS, she sprouts breasts and has periods.

We thus speculate that gender identity—both normal and abnormal—is so very deep because it has its origin in a fundamental hormonal process that occurs around the end of the first trimester of fetal development. The presence of sufficient masculinizing hormones at this stage produces male gender identity. Insufficient masculinizing hormones at this stage produces female gender identity. If by error sufficient masculinizing hormones at this stage are imposed on a chromosomal female, we believe a male gender identity results (the female-to-male transsexual), and if even more masculinizing hormone occurs, AGS follows. If by error insufficient masculinizing hormone occurs at this stage for a chromosomal male, we believe that a female gender identity results (the male-to-female transsexual), and if there is an insensitivity to masculinizing hormones, the AIS syndrome results. One recent study found that the hypothalamus of six male-to-female transsexuals was the same smaller size as that found in females, supporting the hypothesis that hormones interact with the developing brain to determine gender identity (Zhou, Hofman, Gooren, and Swaab, 1995). Fetal hormones are the largest, but not the only influence on gender identity. Rearing, pubertal hormones, sex organs, and stigmatization also play a role. But, at most, these later influences can reinforce, or disturb, the core identity that we have from well before the moment of our birth (see Box 13–1). This is what makes psychotherapy for gender identity disorder useless.

The Boy Who Was Raised as a Girl

What would happen to a male child who was given a girl's name, dressed as a girl, and introduced to friends, relatives, and other children as a girl? The accidental loss of a penis by one of two identical twins in early childhood led to one of the most celebrated case histories in the field of sexuality. This is a case history with a surprising ending, an ending that was kept secret from the public and from researchers until recently. Here is how the early rearing of this child was initially described:

A terrible accident took place in 1966 in the life of one of two identical twins when he was seven months old. As Bruce Reimer was being circumcised by a general practitioner in St. Boniface's Hospital in Winnipeg, Canada, his entire penis was burned off by an electrical device. Brian, his twin brother, was not circumcised. After medical and psychological advice, the parents decided to rear Bruce as a girl, starting at seventeen months of age. But would his gender identity change? Would he, in spite of his male internal organs, male hormones in utero, and seventeen months of being treated as a boy, ever come to feel, act, and have the sexual desires of a girl? After consultation with surgeons, psychiatrists, and especially with Dr. John Money, perhaps the leading expert on gender identity in the world at the time, the Reimers decided to rear Bruce in the most female-stereotyped way: clothes and hairdo were feminized, and the child was given pink shirts, frilly blouses, bracelets, and hair ribbons. Bruce was renamed Brenda, and at twenty-one months, plastic surgery was undertaken, and the appearance of a vagina constructed.

Within a year, Brenda clearly preferred dresses over slacks, and was proud of her long hair. She became much neater and daintier than her twin brother. Her mother taught her to squat while urinating, unlike her brother who stood. For the next few years, Mrs. Reimer began to prepare Brenda to become a wife and housekeeper, and Brenda began to imitate her mother in the housekeeping role. She now preferred dolls and mother roles in play, while her male identical twin preferred toy cars and father roles in play.

By the time the twins were almost six, they had a different vision of their future. "I found that my son chose very masculine things, like a fireman or policeman, or something like that. He wanted to do what Daddy does, work where Daddy does, and carry a lunch kit, and drive a car. And she didn't want any of those things. I asked her, and she said she wanted to be a doctor or a teacher. And I asked her, 'Well, did she have any plans that maybe someday she'd get married, like Mommy?' She'll get married someday—she wasn't too worried about that. She didn't think about that too much, but she wants to be a doctor. But none of the things that she ever wanted to be were like a policeman or a fireman, and that sort of thing never appealed to her" (Money and Ehrhardt, 1972).

This case was widely celebrated by advocates of nurture as demonstrating that gender identity was heavily influenced by parental rearing and the environment, rather than fixed in utero by hormones and genes. Feminists of the time, committed against a biological basis for sex differences, used the case to bolster their claims strongly. In the 1980s the twins were in adolescence, and the published indication was still that the female twin, in spite of being genetically a male—showed some, but not all, the aspects of female role and identity (Williams and Smith, 1980). While preparing the third edition of this textbook in 1987, Martin Seligman spoke with Dr. Money, the primary adviser to the family throughout the child rearing, to inquire about how the twins were doing. Dr. Money said that the twins had been lost to follow-up because of media intrusiveness (Money, personal communication, July 15, 1987).

But this was far from the whole story. John Colapinto (2000), after extensive interviews with all the relevant people (except an unwilling John Money), takes issue with the description that Money presented to the world. Here is the contrary portrait that Colapinto paints:

At the same time as the press, based on Money's description, was rhapsodizing that Brenda "has been sailing contentedly through childhood as a genuine girl," Brenda was not displaying feminine traits. Brian, her twin, says, "When I say there was nothing feminine about Brenda, I mean there was nothing feminine. She walked like a guy. Sat with her legs apart. She talked about guy things, didn't give a crap about cleaning house, getting married, wearing makeup."

In sixth grade, Brenda was given estrogen pills to make her breasts grow. Her reaction was furious. "I don't want to wear a bra! I threw a fit." When Dr. Money attempted to convince her to have vaginal surgery, Brenda told her mother that if she were ever forced to see Money again, she'd kill herself.

When Brenda was fifteen and totally rejecting of the female role, her father finally told her the truth that had been concealed from her—that she had been born a boy and was the victim of a circumcision accident. She immediately decided to revert to her born gender, changed her name to David, underwent penile reconstruction, and is now apparently happily married—to a woman.

SOURCE: Based on Colapinto, 2000; Money and Ehrhardt, 1972.

People who wish to have sex-reassignment surgery must live for several years as the other gender, as has Norbert Lindner *(left),* the mayor of Quellendorf, Germany. If the person still wants surgery after passing for and being treated as the other gender, he or she can have the sex-change operation, as did Israeli singer Dana International *(right),* who was once a man.

Therapy for Transsexualism: Sex Reassignment

Conventional psychotherapies have only very rarely, if ever, been able to reverse transsexualism. Nevertheless, there is hope for transsexuals today (see Table 13–1). Sex-change surgery (now called "sex reassignment") gives transsexuals the opportunity to acquire the sexual characteristics they desire. Once a headline-making novelty, these operations are now routine, and tens of thousands have been performed. Once the patient convinces the diagnosticians that the transgender identity is unshakable, the long process of changing the body begins.

Therapy for transsexuals consists of changing the physical characteristics of the person's sex through surgery and hormones. This biological transformation is then supported by social, vocational, domestic, and secondary bodily changes in an attempt to shore up the new gender status. Often, therapists treating a transsexual who is a candidate for sex-reassignment surgery require that the person first live for two years as the other gender, changing his or her name, dress, and mannerisms. If after two years of passing for and being treated as a female or male, the individual still wants surgery, the psychological hazards of the surgery are probably lowered. Those who have schizophrenic or delusional symp-

TABLE 13–1

Treatment

GENDER IDENTITY DISORDER

	Psychosocial Treatments	*Sex-Reassignment Surgery*
Improvement	almost none	60–90% markedly improved
Relapse★	high relapse	low to moderate relapse
Side Effects	none	moderate
Cost	inexpensive	expensive
Time Scale	weeks/months	years
Overall	**almost useless**	**very good**

★ Relapse after discontinuation of treatment.

SOURCE: Based on Seligman, 1994, Chapter 11; revised using Cohen-Kettenis and Van Goozen, 1997; Green and Fleming, 1990; Pfafflin, 1992.

toms, or who are otherwise emotionally disordered, should probably not undertake it (Money and Ambinder, 1978; Petersen and Dickey, 1995).

Bodily changes are a prerequisite for sex-reassignment surgery. In male-to-female sex changes, there is a combination of hormonal treatment to make the breasts grow, electrolysis to remove facial hair, and surgery to transform the penis into a vagina. Because the skin of the penis is used to line the vagina, sexual intercourse—when the surgery is successful—is erotically pleasurable. Orgasm is a warm, sometimes spasmodic, glow through the body.

In female-to-male sex-reassignment operations, the surgery is much more complicated. It involves multiple operations that take place over several years. First, hormonal treatment suppresses menstruation, deepens the voice, and causes growth of facial and body hair. Then surgery is performed to remove the breasts, the ovaries, and, rarely, to construct a penis. The capacity of orgasm is always retained, but such a penis cannot become erect, and a prosthesis has to be used for intercourse.

Follow-up of patients who have undergone sex-reassignment surgery shows better and better results across the three decades in which the surgeries have been performed. The early surgeries revealed mixed results: in a follow-up of fourteen patients operated on at UCLA, almost all of the patients had surgical complications (Stoller, 1976). In a six- to twenty-five-year follow-up of thirteen male-to-female transsexuals, only one-third remained sexually active after surgery, and only one-third had fair to good sexual "adjustment." Only half could reach orgasm. Four regretted having had the surgery (Lindemalm, Korlin, and Uddenberg, 1986).

In contrast to these early reports, the most recent reviews show very good long-term results: Green and Fleming (1990) found that of 130 female-to-male sex reassignments, 97 percent have had a "satisfactory" outcome; of 220 male-to-female reassignments, 87 percent report a "satisfactory" outcome. Following up on 141 sex reassignments in Holland, researchers found that the large majority were happy or very happy, were confident in their new gender role, and were satisfied or very satisfied with the surgical results (Kuiper and Cohen-Kettens, 1988; Pfafflin, 1992; Snaith, Tarsh, and Reid, 1993). In 1997, Cohen-Kettenis and Van Goozen followed 22 adolescent sex reassignments for one to five years. As a group, they were no longer dysphoric about their gender, they were functioning

quite well socially, and not a single one expressed regrets about the sex reassignment. So as radical as sex-reassignment surgery is, long-term follow-up of hundreds of patients now suggests that it is the treatment of choice for transsexuals. Although the transsexual must cope with problems of adjustment, the operation has become more satisfactory as surgical techniques have improved. Most patients are much happier and adapt fairly well to their new lives, living comfortably in their new bodies, dating, having intercourse, and marrying.

Sexual Orientation: Layer II

Sex researchers use the word "object choice" to denote how we come to love what we love. Some gay activist groups, on the other hand, say we have no choice at all. The truth is most probably in between, although much closer to the gay activists than to those who believe we freely "choose" what we love. We therefore label this layer sexual "orientation," rather than sexual "object choice." The basic sexual orientation is homosexual or heterosexual, with a continuum of bisexuality in between. We will focus on male homosexuality as an example of human sexual orientation as a whole. We emphasize that we do

These male homosexuals are at their commitment ceremony. Comfortable with their sexual orientation, they wish to publicly acknowledge their commitment. Nonetheless, such ceremonies remain controversial, and most states (with the exception of New Hampshire) still do not recognize marriage between people of the same sex.

not view homosexuality as a disorder. Rather we discuss it here because its origins shed light on the deep roots of all human sexual orientation—homosexual and heterosexual.

Origins of Sexual Orientation

When does a male become heterosexual or homosexual? How does it happen? Once sexually active, can he change if he wants to? We must distinguish between "exclusive" or "non-optional" homosexuals on the one hand and bisexuals on the other, since most men who have sex with other men are bisexuals. For as far back as they can remember, men who are exclusively homosexual have been erotically interested only in males. They have sexual fantasies only about males. They fall in love only with males. When they masturbate or have wet dreams, the objects are always males. The orientation of the exclusive male homosexual—and of the exclusive heterosexual—is firmly made. How is sexual orientation laid down?

FETAL HORMONES

A major theory of the origin of homosexuality holds that the tendency is laid down before birth by a combination of genetic, hormonal, and neurological processes, and that this orientation is activated by hormonal changes at the onset of puberty (Bancroft, 1994; Ellis and Ames, 1987; McClintock and Herdt, 1996). Learning only alters how, when, and where homosexuality will be expressed. According to the Ellis-Ames fetal disruption theory, the crucial neurochemical events that control masculinization occur during the second to fourth months of pregnancy. This sequence of events is delicate and exquisitely timed and, if it is disrupted, incomplete masculinization of the fetus will occur. The fetus is partly masculinized, however, with a male gender identity and male external organs. The main effect of fetal disruption is to change in utero just one aspect of his erotic life: sexual attraction to men rather than to women (Gladue, Green, and Hellman, 1984).

This view does not say that sexual orientation is determined in the womb. Rearing, role models, pubertal hormones, genes, the content of late childhood play, fantasies and dreams, and early sexual experiences all probably also play a role (Bailey and Zucker, 1995). In fact, Bem (1996) acknowledges the role

fetal hormones and other biological influences play; he theorizes, however, that these merely create a temperament that is attracted to exotic, rather than sex-typical, activities. In contrast, the fetal hormone view asserts that hormonal events in the womb create a strong predisposition to homosexuality or heterosexuality, leaving the later pathways to be discovered.

ANATOMICAL BASIS FOR SEXUAL ORIENTATION

Human sexual orientation may even have a basis in the anatomy of the brain (Allen and Gorshi, 1992; Reite et al., 1995; Swaab, Gooren, and Hofman, 1995; Swaab and Hofman, 1995). Brain researcher Simon LeVay (1991) examined the brains of dead homosexual men, heterosexual men, and heterosexual women. Most were AIDS victims. He focused his autopsy on one small area, the medial anterior hypothalamus. This area is implicated in male sexual behavior, and men usually have more tissue here than women. He found a remarkably large difference in the amount of tissue: heterosexual men have twice as much as homosexual men, who have about the same amount of tissue as women. Moreover, the anterior hypothalamus is just the area that controls male sexual behavior in rats, and this area develops when the brains of male rats are hormonally masculinized before birth. So it seems possible that hormonal disruption during early pregnancy may result in a smaller medial anterior hypothalamus, which may in turn affect sexual orientation.

Too little research has been done on lesbians to know if the same theories might apply to female homosexuals. It is unknown if a slight masculinization of a female fetus (chromosomally XX) produces lesbians. It is possible, but still controversial, that lesbianism is the mirror image of male homosexuality. Lesbians, unlike exclusive male homosexuals, however, commonly report choosing homosexuality after adolescence (Bailey, Kim, Hills, and Linsenmeier, 1997; Seidman and Rieder, 1994).

TWIN DATA AND THE GENETICS OF SEXUAL ORIENTATION

Identical twins are more concordant for homosexuality than are fraternal twins, and fraternal twins are more concordant than non-twin brothers are. In one study of fifty-six pairs of identical twins in which one twin was homosexual, the co-twin was also found to be homosexual in 52 percent of the identical twins, as opposed to 22 percent of the fraternal twins. Only 9 percent of non-twin brothers were concordant for homosexuality (Bailey and Pillard, 1991). Heritability seems to increase the probability of male homosexuality by a factor between three and four (Bailey, Dunne, and Martin, 2000; Bailey et al., 1999). The difference between the identical twins and the fraternal twins suggests a genetic component to homosexuality. But non-twin brothers and male fraternal twins share on average just the same percentage (50 percent) of genes. The fact that fraternal twins, who share the same uterine world, are more concordant than ordinary brothers, points to fetal hormones as an additional cause of homosexuality. They might even be concordant for a small medial anterior hypothalamus (Ellis and Ames, 1987; Haynes, 1995; Turner, 1995).

There is evidence for a sizable genetic contribution to female homosexuality as well. Out of a sample of over 100 twins, one of whom was lesbian, the co-twin was homosexual in 51 percent of the identical twins, but only in 10 percent of the fraternal twins (Bailey, Pillard, and Agyei, 1993; Pillard and Bailey, 1995).

It is possible that particular genes may be related to homosexuality. Researchers found that gay brothers were more likely than chance to share the chromosomal area, Xq28 (Hamer, Hu, Magnusson, Hu, and Patatucci, 1993; Turner, 1995). While this suggests that some gene lying within that region might influence male sexual orientation, such work must be replicated.

Change of Sexual Orientation

Up until the 1980s, the topic of homosexuality was listed in textbooks as a paraphilia or a "sexual deviation." Sexual "disorders" used to be defined as conditions that grossly impaired affectionate sexual relations between a man and a woman, and so homosexuality was, by definition, a disorder. Now there is good reason not to classify homosexuality as a disorder. DSM-IV, in fact, does not consider homosexuality a disorder. Nor do we. Our own view is that sexual disorders are conditions that grossly impair affectionate sexual relations between two human beings. Homosexuality, while it may impair such relations between men and

women, does not, of course, impair them between a man and a man, or a woman and a woman.

Occasionally, homosexuals and bisexuals who are very unhappy about their sexual orientation will enter therapy to become heterosexual. The patients used to be called "ego-dystonic homosexuals." This category has been dropped from DSM-IV, but much has been learned about the implasticity of sexual orientation from the research and therapy done to assist these individuals to change.

Traditional psychotherapy does not seem to change sexual orientation, but behavior therapy occasionally does. In two controlled studies involving seventy-one male homosexuals, a group of British behavior therapists found that sexual orientation could be changed in nearly 60 percent of the cases by using aversion therapy of the sort described below for the paraphilias (Feldman and MacCulloch, 1971; McConaghy, Armstrong, and Blaszczynski, 1981). They defined "change" as the absence of homosexual behavior, plus only occasional homosexual fantasy, plus strong heterosexual fantasy, and some overt heterosexual behavior one year after treatment. It is unlikely that these men were exclusively homosexual, however.

The fetal disruption theory (Ellis and Ames, 1987) claims that exclusive homosexuality should be almost unchangeable by therapy, since it has its origins before birth. The data are consistent with this view, since individuals who had had some heterosexual experience before therapy showed more change than exclusive homosexuals who had had no prior pleasurable heterosexual history (Haldeman, 1994; Marciano, 1982; Mendelsohn and Ross, 1959; Schwartz and Masters, 1984). When treatment concentrates on additional targets, such as intimacy and social skills, more change occurs (Adams and Sturgis, 1977). So, the behavior of homosexual men who have had some pleasurable heterosexual experience can be affected by behavior therapy, but it is unlikely that exclusively homosexual men can be changed in sexual orientation.

Sexual Preference: Layer III

Sometime in the first fifteen years of life, you acquired your sexual preferences or interests, the objects of their erotic interest, and these objects and situations are likely to be sexually arousing to you for the rest of your life. Most men are aroused by the female body, and most women are aroused by the male body. There is a very large range of situations that men and women find sexually arousing: seductive conversation, holding a member of the opposite sex in their arms, or seeing the person naked. But other more unusual objects or situations may also be sources of sexual arousal. They are called the paraphilias, and it is to these that we now turn.

Types of Paraphilias

When sexual interest is so disordered that it impairs the capacity for affectionate erotic relations between human beings, it is called a *paraphilia* (from the Greek "love of [philia] what is beyond [para]"). The paraphilias comprise an array of unusual objects and situations that are sexually arousing to some individuals. Among the common paraphilias are female underwear, shoes, inflicting or receiving pain, and "peeping." Among the rare paraphilias are dead bodies (necrophilia)—with murdering victims to obtain the corpse at the most extreme—and receiving enemas (klismaphilia).

The paraphilias divide into three categories: (1) sexual arousal and preference for nonhuman objects, including fetishes and transvestism; (2) sexual arousal and preference for situations that involve suffering and humiliation, including sadism and masochism; and (3) sexual arousal and preference for nonconsenting partners, including exhibitionism, voyeurism, telephone scatologia, and child molesting.

For some people with paraphilias, fantasies or the object itself is always included in sexual activity. For others, the paraphilia occurs only episodically, for ex-

ample, during stormy periods of life. Paraphilic fantasies are common in people who do not have a paraphila. Panties, peeping, and spanking, for example, are sexually exciting fantasies for many men. The hallmarks of crossing the line from normal fantasy to paraphilia are when the person acts on it, or when the object becomes necessary for arousal, or when the person is markedly distressed by his actions, or when the object displaces the human partner.

Often people with paraphilias are happy with their sex lives, and their only problem is the reaction of others to their sexual preferences. Many other people with paraphilias are guilt-ridden, laid low by shame, and depressed by their actions, which they regard as disgusting and immoral. Sexual dysfunctions frequently accompany paraphilias, particularly when the object is absent.

FETISHES

To have a *fetish* (from the Portuguese, *fetico*, the worship of carved wooden or stone figures) is to be sexually aroused by a nonliving object—for example, underwear, shoes, feet, hair, rubber, or silk. In many cases, the fetish is harmless. For example, women's panties are sexually arousing to many men. When a man fantasizes and talks erotically about panties during sexual intercourse with a mutually consenting partner, the paraphilia may be playful and lead to heightened arousal. More typically, however, his partner will start to feel excluded; when the underwear a woman wears displaces the woman, and her partner cannot be sexually aroused unless she is wearing it, the object is no longer a means to arousal but the end of arousal. Here is a classic example of a foot fetish:

DSM-IV Criteria

Fetishism

A. Over a period of at least 6 months, recurrent, intense sexually arousing fantasies, sexual urges, or behaviors involving the use of nonliving objects (e.g., female undergarments).

B. The fantasies, sexual urges, or behaviors cause clinically significant distress or impairment in social, occupational, or other important areas of functioning.

C. The fetish objects are not limited to articles of female clothing used in cross-dressing (as in Transvestic Fetishism) or devices designed for the purpose of tactile genital stimulation (e.g., a vibrator).

SOURCE: APA, DSM-IV, 1994.

A person with a foot fetish can only become aroused when in the presence of the paraphilic object, and will fantasize, masturbate, or have his partner hold or wear the object while having sex.

> At the age of seven Leo was taught to masturbate by his older half sister. In the course of the lesson she accidentally touched his penis with her slipper. From that time on, the mere sight of a woman's shoe was enough to induce sexual excitement and erection. Now twenty-four, virtually all his masturbation occurred while looking at women's shoes or fantasizing about them. When he was at school he was unable to keep himself from grasping his teacher's shoes and in spite of punishment continued to attack her shoes. He found an acceptable way of adapting his life to his fetish. When he was eighteen, he took a job in a shop that sold ladies' shoes and was excited sexually by fitting shoes onto his customers. He was absolutely unable to have intercourse with his pretty wife unless he was looking at, touching, or thinking about her shoes at the same time. (Krafft-Ebing, 1931, case 114)

As in Leo's case, it is typical that a fetish is acquired during childhood. The object that will become the fetish accompanies early erotic play. The fetish grows in strength when it is repeatedly fantasized about and rehearsed, especially during masturbation. The fetishist often masturbates while holding, rubbing, or smelling the object, or may ask his partner to wear or hold the object during sex. A fetish may reveal itself when adult interpersonal relationships are unsatisfactory, not uncommon among fetishists whose social skills are often minimal. At this point, the person's childhood experience may take over, and the person with the fetish may seek comfort in the simpler sexual pleasures of childhood instead of dealing with the complexity of another human being (Mason, 1997).

Interestingly, almost all cases of fetishes and the vast majority of all paraphilias occur among men. Such a man is usually full of shame and guilt about his fetish, which isolates him from sexual activity with other people. Erectile dysfunction is the regular consequence of fetishism when the fetish is absent. Depression, anxiety, and loneliness often accompany the fetish. In addition to such individual problems, people who have fetishes are occasionally in trouble with the law. They may steal objects of the fetish, lunge for the objects in public, and may masturbate on the objects. Some will frequently acquire a collection of the objects. One young shoe fetishist was discovered with a collection of 15,000 to 20,000 pictures of shoes.

TRANSVESTISM (CROSS-DRESSING)

Transvestism, or **transvestic fetishism,** occurs when a man persistently dresses in women's clothes to achieve sexual arousal. He usually has a collection of women's clothes, and while masturbating he frequently imagines that he is done up as a woman and wearing women's clothes. Transvestism is usually carried on in secret, although a transvestite's wife may share the secret and cooperate by having intercourse with him when he is dressed as a woman. The secrecy of the act makes its prevalence difficult to estimate, but it is probably rare—occurring in fewer than 1 percent of adult men. There have been virtually no reports of transvestism in women.

Transvestism usually begins with cross-dressing in childhood and among unremarkably masculine boys, as here:

> At about the age of fourteen, I discovered in my dad's photo album a photo he had taken of me at five and a half just before having my long (bobbed) hair cut off. My mother had dressed me in girls' clothes to see what I would have looked like if I had been a daughter, which is what she had wanted first. When I saw the photo I recalled the incident clearly and the sight of the photo thoroughly "shook" me, for it appeared to be a rather pretty young girl.
>
> The emotional result was twofold. It aroused my first interest in girls and also an interest in girls' clothes. I found myself compelled to go back to look at the photo again and again.
>
> One winter my wife and I were living alone. Our marital relations were good. We were spending New Year's Eve entirely alone and for some reason

DSM-IV Criteria

Transvestic Fetishism (Transvestism)

A. Over a period of at least 6 months, in a heterosexual male, recurrent, intense sexually arousing fantasies, sexual urges, or behaviors involving cross-dressing.

B. The fantasies, sexual urges, or behaviors cause clinically significant distress or impairment in social, occupational, or other important areas of functioning.

SOURCE: APA, DSM-IV, 1994.

my wife, not knowing of my mere leanings (at the time) toward transvestism (a word I did not know then), decided to put one of her dresses on me and make up my face just as a sort of New Year's Eve prank. When she finished we sat around for a while and she asked me how I liked it. When I answered in the affirmative she became resentful and very anxious for me to take off the clothes she had put on me voluntarily. (Adapted from Stoller, 1969)

When cross-dressing starts, only one or two items of clothing, such as panties, may be used. This item of clothing may become a fetish habitually used in masturbation and in intercourse with a co-operating partner. Except for the object, fetishism and transvestism are otherwise indistinguishable (Freund, Seto, and Kuban, 1996). A transvestite may wear these panties under his daily masculine garb. Cross-dressing sometimes progresses from a single

item to a total costume. It may include other "feminine" activities, such as fantasies of knitting in the presence of other women (Zucker and Blanchard, 1997). It may be done alone or as part of a whole group of transvestites. When dressed as a woman, the transvestite feels considerable pleasure and relaxation; he is intensely frustrated if circumstances block his cross-dressing. Sometimes sexual arousal by wearing women's clothes disappears, but the transvestite continues to dress up to relieve anxiety and depression.

A transvestite may believe he has two personalities: one male, which dominates his daily life, and the other female, which comes out when he is dressed up. In other respects, the transvestite is unremarkably masculine in appearance and conventional in his behavior.

Transvestism is often mistakenly confused with homosexuality on the one hand and with transsexualism on the other. Transvestites are decidedly not homosexual: almost three-quarters of them are married and have children, and on average, they have had less homosexual experience than the average American man (Adshead, 1997; Benjamin, 1966). Further, a transvestite is aroused by cross-dressing, whereas a homosexual is obviously aroused by another person. While a male homosexual will occasionally dress in female clothes in order to attract another man, a homosexual, unlike a transvestite, is not sexually aroused by the fact that he is in "drag."

Since most transvestites merely want to be left alone in order to pursue their habit secretly, we must ask why it is considered a problem. Depression, anxiety, shame, and guilt often occur in transvestites; and while sexual arousal is intense during cross-dressing, affectionate sexuality is sometimes impaired by transvestism. A transvestite will commonly be impotent

Transvestites become aroused by dressing in women's clothing. Pictured here are men at a cross-dressing festival.

unless he is wearing some female clothing, and this is often not possible when his partner objects. But overall, using the criteria of distress and disability, it has been argued that transvestitism is at most only marginally a mental disorder (Zucker and Blanchard, 1997).

SADISM AND MASOCHISM

The second class of paraphilias involves inflicting or receiving suffering as a means of sexual excitement, and it consists of two distinct disorders that complement each other. The *sadist* becomes sexually aroused by inflicting suffering or humiliation on another human being. The *masochist* becomes sexually aroused by having suffering or humiliation inflicted on him. These terms are greatly overused in ordinary language. We often hear individuals who cheerfully put up with suffering or hardship called masochists, and individuals who are aggressive and domineering called sadists. Much more than this is required for sadism or masochism. A sadist *repeatedly* and *intentionally* inflicts suffering on his partner, sometimes a nonconsenting partner, in order to produce sexual excitement (for a discussion of when sadism crosses the line to criminal behavior, see Box 13–2). And a masochist repeatedly and intentionally participates in activities in which he is

---

Society and Mental Health

Box 13—2

Sex and Crime

Where do we draw the line between sexual deviation and crime? Whereas "minor" sadism and masochism are considered paraphilias, dangerous, predatory sadism is considered a crime. These kinds of "major" sadisms range from stabbing victims—usually in the breast or buttocks—and then escaping, through vampirism—drawing and drinking the blood of victims—through necrophilia, through the extreme of lust murder. The FBI analyzed thirty cases of sexual torturers (Dietz, Hazelwood, and Warren, 1990; see also Mullen, Pathe, Purcell and Stuart, 1999, on stalkers). Half were married, 43 percent had had homosexual experience, and 20 percent cross-dressed. Nearly all carefully planned their crimes, and all offenses by definition involved torture. They typically kidnapped their victims and held them for more than a day, bound them, raped them anally and orally, and murdered 73 percent of their victims. They usually tape-recorded and photographed their crimes, keeping some momento. In one-third of the crimes they were assisted by a partner, often a woman. Importantly, none of these men were psychotic. In spite of this, these predatory sadists were usually acquitted by reason of insanity (Hucker, 1997). These seem to us like a sad failure of juries to distinguish what is insane from what is evil, and this leads us directly to comment on why we believe rape should not be labeled a mental disorder.

The heinous crime of rape—the sexual violation of one person by another—should not be considered a paraphilia for two reasons: First, to be a paraphilia, the act must be the individual's exclusive, or vastly preferred, mode of sexual release. The shoe fetishist does not become erect or have an orgasm unless he is fantasizing about, seeing, or touching shoes. In contrast, the vast majority of rapists, most of the time, can and do become sexually aroused and achieve sexual release in activities other than rape. For some rapists, physical force during sex is more arousing than consensual sex, but they are still aroused by consensual sex (Hudson and Ward, 1997; Lohr, Adams, and Davis, 1997). Second, although rapists often have major psychological problems (substance abuse, antisocial personality disorders, and depression), they have these disorders at roughly the same rate as the rest of men in prison. Third, unlike people with paraphilias, who feel distress because of their paraphilia, rapists are not much distressed by raping. There are, however, some rapists who are sadistic as well, and who are sexually aroused by brutality. In an experimental setting, these sadistic rapists become sexually aroused to aggression with sexual content in audiotapes as well as to audiotapes describing brutal rapes (Abel, Barlow, Blanchard, and Guild, 1977).

Most crucially, rape is a major crime, an act for which it is imperative that society hold the individual responsible, punishing him accordingly. If we were to include rape as a paraphilia, there would be more of a tendency to excuse the act and lighten the burden of the rapist's responsibility—even if there was not a shred of evidence other than the rape itself that indicated psychological abnormality. The acts of murder, assault, and theft are not automatically thought of as psychological disorders unless there is additional evidence of abnormality, nor should rape be thought of as a disorder. The expression "only a crazy man could have done that," when applied to lust murder or rape, seems to us deeply and insidiously confused. We must not blur the distinction between evil and crazy any further.

DSM-IV Criteria

Sexual Sadism

A. Over a period of at least 6 months, recurrent, intense sexually arousing fantasies, sexual urges, or behaviors involving acts (real, not simulated) in which the psychological or physical suffering (including humiliation) of the victim is sexually exciting to the person.

B. The fantasies, sexual urges, or behaviors cause clinically significant distress or impairment in social, occupational, or other important areas of functioning.

SOURCE: APA, DSM-IV, 1994.

physically harmed, his life is threatened, or he is otherwise made to suffer in order to feel sexual excitement. Not uncommonly, the masochist and sadist will seek each other out and marry in order to engage in mutually desirable sadomasochism. Both disorders are accompanied by persistent and insistent fantasies in which torture, beating, binding, and raping are common themes producing high sexual arousal. Consider this case:

> Thomas, a masochist, and his wife enact a periodic sadomasochistic ritual, in which about once every six weeks Thomas has himself beaten by his wife. She punishes him for his "weak" and "feminine" behavior. In his daily life he is an aggressive and controlling executive, but underneath he deeply longs to be controlled. He feels he should be punished because it is wrong for him to have feelings of needing to be dominated, and so he has his wife tie him to a rack in their cellar and beat him. (Adapted from Gagnon, 1977)

Many individuals who are neither sadists nor masochists have occasional sexual fantasies about humiliation and suffering. But such fantasies are not necessary for sexual arousal or orgasm in the great majority of individuals, and this differentiates them from sadomasochists (Gagnon, 1977; McCary, 1978). In addition to fantasies, overt acts involving suffering and humiliation in order to produce arousal must occur for sadism or masochism to be diagnosed. Nor are all overt acts that produce pain during sex play considered sadomasochistic: lightly biting a partner's earlobe or leaving scratch marks or bruises on a partner's back are common elements of sex play. The true sadist or masochist both has the relevant fantasies and engages in acts that sexually arouse him, causing more than minimal pain.

There has been debate in the recent literature about whether masochism is quite harmless, "deviance without pathology" (Baumeister and Butler, 1997). Masochists usually want the pain to be kept within well-defined limits, and partners who violate this script come to be seen as undesirable. Masochism from this perspective is a desire to surrender control and to escape from the self benignly. On the other hand, masochism may lead to reduced emotional intimacy and is associated with emotional loneliness (Thornton and Mann, 1997).

Sadists become sexually aroused by inflicting pain or humiliation on their partners, as this woman with the whip. Masochists become sexually aroused by having humiliation or pain inflicted upon them, as the man who is being dominated by the woman and the other men who wear collars and are ready to be whipped and humiliated by the women.

DSM-IV Criteria

Sexual Masochism

A. Over a period of at least 6 months, recurrent, intense sexually arousing fantasies, sexual urges, or behaviors involving acts (real, not simulated) of being humiliated, beaten, bound, or otherwise made to suffer.

B. The fantasies, sexual urges, or behaviors cause clinically significant distress or impairment in social, occupational, or other important areas of functioning.

SOURCE: APA, DSM-IV, 1994.

EXHIBITIONISM, VOYEURISM, AND PEDOPHILIA

The final category of paraphilias involves sexual arousal with nonconsenting partners. These paraphilias are crimes in our society. The criminal aspect derives from the fact that they violate the freedom of others to make their own sexual decisions. *Exhibitionism* involves exposing the genitals to unwitting, and usually unwilling, strangers. *Voyeurism* involves observing the naked body, the disrobing, or the sexual activity of an unsuspecting victim. *Telephone scatologia* consists of recurrent and intense sexual urges to make obscene calls to a nonconsenting individual. *Frotteurism* involves touching and rubbing against a nonconsenting person, usually in crowded places. *Pedophilia* involves sexual relations with children below the age of puberty, the age at which we consider it reasonable for a person to be able to give mature consent.

Exhibitionism Exhibitionism consists of exposing the genitals to an unwitting stranger, on repeated occasions, in order to produce sexual excitement. The exposure itself is the final sexual act, and the exhibi-

tionist does not go on to attempt sexual relations with his victim after exhibiting himself.

> A nineteen-year-old college student would wait near the entrance to a sorority house, hiding behind a nearby sign. When an attractive female walked by, he would masturbate. Occasionally the girl noticed him and he gradually began to enjoy the victim's fright. He began to expose himself from his car in a dimly lit park nearby. (After Maletzky, 1998)

A "flasher," or "flagwaver," as he is called in prison slang, typically approaches an adult woman or frequently a child with his genitals exposed. He usually has an erection, but sometimes he is flaccid. Sometimes he will ejaculate while exhibiting himself or, more commonly, he will masturbate when he is alone afterwards (Murphy, 1997).

Exhibitionism is the most common sexual crime in the United States, with roughly one-third of sexual offenders arrested for it (Gebhard, Gagnon, Pomeroy, and Christenson, 1965). Surprisingly enough, exhibitionism is very rare outside the United States and Europe and nonexistent in cultures such as India and Burma.

DSM-IV Criteria

Exhibitionism

A. Over a period of at least 6 months, recurrent, intense sexually arousing fantasies, sexual urges, or behaviors involving the exposure of one's genitals to an unsuspecting stranger.

B. The fantasies, sexual urges, or behaviors cause clinically significant distress or impairment in social, occupational, or other important areas of functioning.

SOURCE: APA, DSM-IV, 1994.

Exhibitionists are usually not dangerous, although they wish to shock and horrify their victims, and this is essential for the act to be gratifying. The act usually takes place six to sixty feet from the victim; very rarely is the victim touched or molested. The exhibitionist is more of a nuisance than a menace (Gagnon, 1977; McCary, 1978). But the data are flawed because the sample consists only of the men who were caught, so caution suggests that it is not unlikely that some of those who expose themselves to children will also become child molesters (Murphy, 1997).

The settings in which exhibitionists expose themselves vary. The most common are in front of girls' schools or churches, in crowds, and in parks; and in these settings, the exhibitionist may pretend he is urinating. Among the more imaginative scenarios are wearing only a raincoat in a department store, taking out a whistle and blowing it, and as the female shoppers look in the direction of the whistler, opening the raincoat; rapping on the window of a sorority house with one's erect penis; sitting down near women in darkened movie theaters and masturbating.

All these situations have one important element in common: they are public and it is very unlikely that sexual intercourse could possibly take place. The risk itself can be an important and thrilling part of the exhibitionist's preferred scenario. These points provide clues to the dynamics of an exhibitionist. The exhibitionist needs to display his masculinity without the threat of having to perform in an adequate sexual role (Kaplan, 1974). A related view is that exhibitionism is a "courtship disorder" (Freund, 1990). According to this theory, courtship has four stages, each of which can be abnormal: (1) location of a partner, (2) pretactile interactions, (3) tactile interactions, (4) intercourse. The exhibitionist has a disorder at stage 2.

Voyeurs become sexually aroused while watching people disrobing or having sexual intercourse, as in this scene showing Sharon Stone looking through a telescope in the 1993 film *Sliver.*

Voyeurism Voyeurs are individuals who repeatedly seek out situations in which they can look at unsuspecting women who are naked, disrobing, or engaged in sexual activity. In the eleventh century Leofric, the Lord of Coventry, agreed to lower taxes if his wife, Lady Godiva, would ride unclothed on a white horse through the town. As a friend of the poor, Lady Godiva consented, and everyone in town shuttered their windows and hid their eyes out of respect and gratitude. Only Tom, the tailor, peeked, and he went blind, becoming our legendary Peeping Tom, the "original" voyeur.

The acts of a Peeping Tom are secret. The voyeur will masturbate during these acts or while fantasizing about the memory of these encounters. Watching an unsuspecting stranger is the final act, and the voyeur almost never approaches his victim for sexual contact. Visual stimulation is commonly erotic both to

DSM-IV Criteria

Voyeurism

A. Over a period of at least 6 months, recurrent, intense sexually arousing fantasies, sexual urges, or behaviors involving the act of observing an unsuspecting person who is naked, in the process of disrobing, or engaging in sexual activity.

B. The fantasies, sexual urges, or behaviors cause clinically significant distress or impairment in social, occupational, or other important areas of functioning.

SOURCE: APA, DSM-IV, 1994.

men and women, but merely being aroused by seeing a naked woman or a sexual act is not equivalent to voyeurism. In normal individuals, visual stimulation is usually a prelude to further sexual activity. In contrast to voyeurs, normal men do not need to watch an unsuspecting stranger in order to become aroused. The illegal, secretive nature of his peeping is itself arousing to the voyeur.

Almost all information about voyeurs comes from those cases in which they are caught. The act is a crime, and many of the problems—such as shame and danger to reputation—that it produces come only in the aftermath of the arrest and exposure. Like exhibitionism, it can be thought of as a "courtship disorder" (Freund, 1991). In this case, however, the problem is located at stage 1, the selection of a partner. Besides shame, this disordered selection produces other dangers: voyeurs sometimes fall off window ledges, are shot as burglars, and are assaulted by couples who catch them peeping. Voyeurism is a repetitive pattern and should be distinguished from innocent sexual exploration in early adolescence, such as a twelve-year-old peeping into the girls' locker room once. Most voyeurs do not go on to more serious sex crimes, but Ted Bundy, a notorious serial killer-rapist, began his career at age nine with peeping (Holmes, 1991).

Pedophilia   The pedophile, sometimes called the child molester, prefers sexual activity with prepubescent children and acts out his preference repeatedly. The child molester may just undress the child and look, exposing himself, masturbating in front of the child, or gently touching and fondling the child. Some go further and have oral, anal, or vaginal sex with the child, sometimes using force. Penetration probably occurs in only about 10 percent of the cases of child molestation. Society feels a special sense of horror and reserves special fury for the child molester. Other than lust murder, pedophilia is the most heavily punished crime of the paraphilias. About 30 percent of all convictions for sex offenses are for child molesting, but it is probably even more common than generally supposed. Between one-quarter and one-third of all adults report that when they were children they had been approached sexually by an adult, and at least 7 percent of females and 3 percent of males report having experienced some form of sexual abuse as children (Erickson, Walbek, and Seely, 1988; Finkelhor, 1994; Kinsey, Pomeroy, and Martin, 1948; McConaghy, 1969).

There are probably two reasons society consigns pedophiles to a special hell. First, we do not consider a child capable of consenting to sexual activity in the same way a mature adult can, and so the child's freedom is seen as being grossly violated in such circumstances. Second, there is a common, but unsubstantiated belief in sexual imprinting; the child's attitude toward future sexuality may be warped by these early sexual contacts.

Society's image of the child molester as a dirty stranger lurking in the shadows is far from the truth. Most acts of convicted pedophiles take place between the child and a family acquaintance, neighbor, or relative. The acts usually occur in the child's own home or during a voluntary visit of the child to the home of the pedophile. The relationship is not usually particularly intimate, nor is it prolonged. It typically ends when the child begins to protest or reports it to the parents.

DSM-IV Criteria

Pedophilia

A. Over a period of at least 6 months, recurrent, intense sexually arousing fantasies, sexual urges, or behaviors involving sexual activity with a prepubescent child or children (generally age 13 years or younger).

B. The fantasies, sexual urges, or behaviors cause clinically significant distress or impairment in social, occupational, or other important areas of functioning.

C. The person is at least age 16 years and at least 5 years older than the child or children in Criterion A. *Note:* Do not include an individual in late adolescence involved in an ongoing sexual relationship with a 12- or 13-year-old.

SOURCE: APA, DSM-IV, 1994.

The 1998 film *Lolita* is based on Vladimir Nabokov's novel about the middle-aged Humbert Humbert (played by Jeremy Irons), a pedophile who is sexually attracted to, and obsessed by, prepubescent girls, particularly his landlady's young daughter (played by Dominique Swain).

Molesters are often beset with conflicts about religious piety versus sexuality, are guilt-ridden, and feel doomed. They typically abuse alcohol and often lack ordinary adult social skills, lack confidence, and may be uneasy in adult social and sexual relations (Overholser and Beck, 1986). They feel more comfortable with children than with adults (Levin and Stava, 1987). The disorder is usually chronic, especially in those attracted to boys. For habitual child molesters, the frequency of paraphilic behavior often fluctuates with psychosocial stress. Occasionally, isolated acts of sexual behavior with children by nonpedophilic individuals will be precipitated by a stressor, most commonly upon discovering that one's wife or girlfriend has been unfaithful. In other cases, child molesters may be substituting child contact for adult contacts that they have been unable to get (Gagnon, 1977; Barbaree and Seto, 1997).

The Causes of the Paraphilias

What does our passion attach itself to? Two schools of thought, the psychodynamic and the behavioral, have wrestled with the problem of where paraphilias come from. While neither has been completely successful, both have contributed to our understanding.

THE PSYCHODYNAMIC VIEW

According to Freud, the concepts of "fixation," "object-cathexis," and "sexual object choice" are at-

tempts to describe and explain how specific objects become imbued with erotic attraction for certain individuals as they grow up. *Cathexis* refers to the charging of a neutral object with psychical energy, either positive or negative. (Freud's more colorful word for cathexis is "besetzt" or besieged.) In the case of a "positive cathexis," the libido, or the sexual drive, attaches to the object, and it becomes loved. In the case of a "negative cathexis," the object becomes feared. Cathected paraphilias have three properties: (1) they have their beginnings in childhood experience; (2) they resist change, particularly rational change; and (3) they last and last—usually remaining for a lifetime.

Freud described the case of the typical foot fetishist who recalled that when he was six, his governess, wearing a velvet slipper, stretched her foot out on a cushion. Although it was decently concealed, this kind of foot, thin and scraggly, though it was, thereafter became his only sexual interest (Freud, 1917/1976, p. 348). The fetishist had cathected onto a thin, scraggly foot. Freud considered this cathexis to be a concentration of very high psychical energy, bounded and protected by a shield of dead layers. This protection against external stimuli allowed the cathected object to retain its erotic power through life, and only traumatic experiences could breach its protective gates.

While the concept of cathexis is useful descriptively, it is not a satisfying explanation, for as Freud acknowledged, it is unknown why it strikes one person rather than another. And this is the main question that concerns us here. The psychodynamic view posits acquired cathexis as the origin of passion for the fetishist, the transvestite, the sadist, the masochist, the exhibitionist, the voyeur, and the pedophile. But this only describes the fact that for all of these individuals their sexual object choice is not a means to an end but an end in itself, that it is persistent, and that it does not yield to reason. Cathexis does not explain how this happens.

THE BEHAVIORAL VIEW

The learning theories, too, have wrestled with the problem of erotic attachment. The most common account is Pavlovian. Recall the case of Leo, whose foot fetish began when, as a seven-year-old, his half sister's slipper touched his penis. The conditioned stimulus (CS) here is the sight of the slipper. It is paired with the unconditioned stimulus (US) of genital stimulation and the unconditioned response (UR) of sexual pleasure. As a result, slippers come to produce the conditioned response (CR) of sexual arousal. Such an account explains how cathexis might occur to odd objects in childhood, and it supplements the Freudian account by providing a mechanism.

Why do paraphilias persist, once they are conditioned? Once the fetishistic object has been paired with erotic stimulation and the person with a paraphilia masturbates to the fantasy of the object or in the presence of the very object itself, he provides himself with additional Pavlovian acquisition trials. This greatly strengthens the connection between the object and the unconditioned response of sexual pleasure. So an adolescent who experienced the sight of panties originally paired with sexual teasing by the girl next door may greatly strengthen his attachment to panties when he masturbates to orgasm while fantasizing about panties (McGuire, Carlisle, and Young, 1965; Storms, 1981).

There is another factor, **preparedness,** which was brought up in explaining phobias (see Chapter 5) and which might also help to account for the irrationality and resistance to extinction of fetishes. As for phobias, there is a limited set of objects that actually become paraphilic. Why are paraphilias about parts of the body and about dominance and submission common, but paraphilias about windows, pillows, or flannel pajamas nonexistent, despite the fact that such objects are often paired with sexual stimulation in childhood? If there is a special class of objects that are prepared to take on an erotic character

once the objects have been paired with unconditioned sexual stimuli, then the other properties of preparedness should follow. Such objects, once conditioned, should be irrational, robust, and easily learned. These facts describe both the paraphilias and phobias.

Changing Sexual Preferences

Sexual preferences rarely die of their own accord. But they can—with explicit therapy—sometimes be altered. There are extensive studies of therapy to change sexual interest, but they come mostly from atypical men: sex offenders. An exhibitionist (flasher) or a pedophile (child molester) may be arrested and then have therapy mandated in addition to, or instead of, jail. So, our knowledge of therapy outcomes for changing sexual interest, unlike most areas of therapy, comes only from people who are under strong external pressure to change (see Table 13–2).

Combined cognitive and behavioral treatment produces favorable results in changing the paraphilias, but the success rate is far from perfect (Blair and Lanyon, 1981; Laws and O'Donohue, 1997; Maletzky, 1998; Rooth and Marks, 1974). If paraphilias arise by conditioning during fantasy and masturbation, it might be sufficient for **aversion therapy** to concentrate on fantasy. The use of imagined sexual stimuli followed by aversive US's is called **covert sensitization** (Cautela, 1967; LaMontagne and LeSage, 1986; Maletzky, 1998). The treatment of exhibitionists is typical, and all of the following are used extensively, alone or in combination:

TABLE 13–2

Treatment

PARAPHILIAS

	Psychosocial Treatments *	*Chemical Castration*[†]
Improvement	more than 50% markedly improved	more than 90% markedly improved
Relapse[‡]	low to moderate relapse	high relapse
Side Effects	none	moderate to severe
Cost	inexpensive	inexpensive
Time scale	weeks/months	weeks
Overall	**good**	**very good**

*These are treatments for the entire range of paraphilias.
[†]This is a treatment for brutal rape and pedophilia only.
[‡]Relapse after discontinuation of treatment.
SOURCE: Based on Seligman, 1994, Chapter 11, and a conservative reading of Maletzky, 1998, whose conclusions await widespread replication.

1. Electric shock or chemical nauseants—The patient reads aloud, in the first person, an exciting sequence of vignettes about flashing. When he gets to the climax of exposing his erect penis, painful shock or chemical nauseants are delivered. Covert sensitization combines the aversive stimulus with the appropriate directed fantasy.

> As you hide in the bushes you see a woman walking her dog. You see her face and her body—she is really well built. You are jerking off as she comes closer. She sees you and doesn't know what to do—she is paralyzed, just staring. As you move toward her [foul odor is introduced], you step in some dog crap; it's smeared on your shoes and socks. It's slimy and smelly and it's making you sick. You go soft and try to get out of there, but you slip on it and more crap gets on you. (Maletzky, 1998)

2. Orgasmic reconditioning—The man masturbates, narrating his fantasies aloud. As he reaches climax, he substitutes a more acceptable scene for the flashing fantasy.
3. Masturbatory satiation—He continues to masturbate for half an hour after ejaculation—a deadly task—while rehearsing every variation of flashing aloud.
4. Alternative behavior completion. He rehearses a successful exit from the tempting situation.

> As you drive home one night you notice an attractive woman driver on your right in a van. She can see right into your car. You slow down and drive parallel with her as you begin to get aroused. You want to rub your penis and take it out to show her. However, the urge this time is weaker than before and you drive past her without exposing. You feel good about yourself for being able to exert control. (Maletzky, 1998)

Maletzky (1998) has reported promising results using cognitive-behavioral techniques. In a study of 4,000 offenders who were followed over an average of nine years, reoffense rates dropped to 4 percent for molesters of little girls, 4 percent for exhibitionists, 6 percent for voyeurs, 6 percent for fetishists, 22 percent for transvestites, and 25 per-cent for rapists. If these findings are replicated widely, they will provide new hope for those suffering from the paraphilias.

What is changing here? Patients report changes both in their overt behavior and in their desire to flash as well. What they do is substantially changed. We believe, however, that what they want—the preference itself—is largely unchanged. It is very much in the interest of the offender to tell the therapist, the judge, the probation officer, and the world that he no longer wants to flash, and so his reports about desire are not completely reliable. Nevertheless, the behavioral record documents that he actually does flash less. We suspect the offender learns in therapy to restrain himself from acting on his desires, which are unchanged. While not a cure, this is all to the good. It also suggests that some change—perhaps not in desire but in action—can occur with sexual interests (Hall, 1995).

There is a substantially more effective way to curtail brutal sex offenders: chemical castration. It is used in Europe for very serious offenses—brutal rape and child molestation. Castration can be done surgically by removing the testicles, where approximately 95 percent of the testosterone is produced, but more commonly it is accomplished with drugs that neutralize the hormone that the testicles produce. In four studies of over 2,000 offenders followed for many years, the reoffense rate dropped from around 70 percent to around 3 percent. Chemical suppression of the androgens, which unlike surgery is reversible, works about as well as surgical castration (Bradford, 1990, 1995, 1997; Kravitz et al., 1995). Cyproterone acetate (Androcur) and medroxyprogesterone (Depo Provera) are derivatives of the hormone progesterone and are the best-researched of the anti-androgens. They reduce testosterone levels and have a follow-up recidivism rate of less than 5 percent across all the paraphilias (Bradford, 1995). Triptorelin is a long-acting gonadotropin-releasing drug that also reduces testosterone levels. For all of these drugs to work, of course, the offender must keep taking them voluntarily. In a recent Israeli study that combined Triptorelin with psychotherapy, reoffense rate dropped to zero among thirty offenders, twenty-five of whom were intense pedophiles (Rosler and Witztum, 1998; see Figure 13–1). Twenty-one of the men experienced progressive erectile problems. Preliminary but promising re-

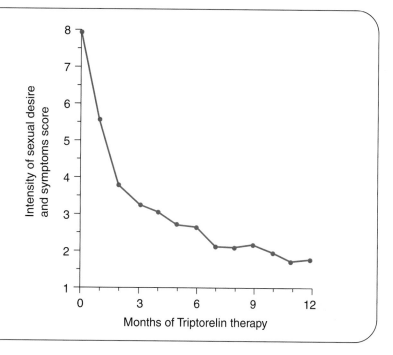

Figure 13—1

DRUG TREATMENT FOR SEVERE PARAPHILIA

The intensity of sexual desire among severe paraphilic offenders declined markedly with twelve months of the testosterone suppressant, Triptorelin, and supportive psychotherapy. The graph shows the decline in the monthly mean scores of sexual desire and symptoms in men treated with Triptorelin to reduce the intensity and frequency of their deviant sexual fantasies, sexual desire, and abnormal sexual behavior. (Source: Rosler and Witztum, 1998, p. 418)

sults have been reported for the ability of SSRI's to decrease paraphilic sexual interests without reducing non-paraphilic sexual interests, but these findings await controlled study (Federoff, 1993, Stein et al., 1992).

In America, castration is considered "cruel and unusual punishment," and is thus not performed. When we consider all the wasted years in prison, the high likelihood of repeated offenses, and the special hell that other prisoners reserve for child molesters, however, chemical castration seem to us less cruel than the "usual" punishment.

Sex Role: Layer IV

Sex role is the public expression of gender identity—what one says and what one does to indicate being a man or a woman. In today's gentler and more tolerant world, there are no "disorders" of sex role. Compassionate men and tough women, male nurses and female construction workers are not deemed to suffer from any sexual problem. We discuss the issue of sex role now—in spite of there being no sex role disorders—because sex role fills out and illuminates the layers of our sexual existence. What role we adopt is elaborated around our gender identity, our sexual orientation, and our sexual preferences.

The word "role" is misleading. As a term of the theater, it makes it sound as if sex role is a costume we can take off or put on at will—an arbitrary convention of how we are socialized. While sex role is partly learned and is more plastic or changeable than sexual interest, which is in turn more plastic than orientation and identity, it is not arbitrary.

There are huge sex-role dissimilarities between very young boys and girls (Maccoby and Jacklin, 1974; Martin, Eisenbud, and Rose, 1995; Zucker, Wilson-Smith, Kurita, and Stern, 1995):

- By age 2 boys want to play with trucks and girls want to play with dolls.
- By age 3 children know the sex stereotypes for dress, toys, jobs, games, tools, and interests.
- By age 3 children want to play with peers of their own sex.
- By age 4 most girls want to be teachers, nurses, secretaries, and mothers, while most boys want to have "masculine" jobs.

In most cultures, young children categorize the world according to sex and organize their lives

Young children categorize the world according to sex and organize their lives around these categories. No one has to force girls to play with girls *(left)* or boys to play with boys *(right)*, and they spontaneously invent sex-role stereotypes.

around these categories. No one has to teach them sex-role stereotypes: they spontaneously invent them. The usual explanation is that they learn sex roles from their parents. After all, parents decorate the rooms of girls in pink and put dolls in their cribs, while boys get blue cribs and toy guns.

What is surprising is that children reared "androgynously" (from the Greek for "both male and female") display their stereotypes as strongly as children not so reared. Young children's stereotypes bear no relationship to their parents' attitudes or to their parents' education, class, employment, or sexual politics. Children's play is strongly sex-stereotyped, even when their parents are androgynous in politics and behavior.

It is not that boys are merely indifferent to lessons about "androgyny." Boys don't merely ignore being told it's okay to play with dolls; they actively resist. Having a teacher try to persuade a child to give up a "sex-appropriate" toy produces resistance, anxiety, and backlash, particularly among boys. Watching videotapes of other kids playing joyfully with sex-inappropriate toys doesn't work either. Intensive home programs incorporating androgynous toys, songs, and books with mother as the teacher produce no changes. Extensive classroom intervention produces no changes in androgyny—outside the classroom (Huston, 1985; Sedney, 1987).

These findings seem to disprove the belief that social pressure creates sex roles in the first place. If social pressure creates it, intense social pressure by commit-

ted parents and teachers should diminish it. But it does not.

Since social pressure does not play a measurable role in creating sex roles, one determinant could, at least in part, be fetal hormones. There are two lines of evidence for this: In one study, seventy-four mothers had taken prescription drugs to prevent miscarriage during their pregnancies in the 1970s. These drugs had the common property of disrupting the masculinizing hormone (androgen). When the children were ten years old, the games they liked to play were compared to the games enjoyed by matched controls. The boys' games were less masculine, and the girls' games were more feminine (Meyer-Bahlburg, Feldman, Cohen, and Ehrhardt, 1988).

A second line of evidence is a disease (Congenital Adrenal Hyperplasia, or CAH) that bathes female fetuses with extra androgen. As young children, CAH girls like male-stereotyped toys and rough-and-tumble play, and they are more tomboyish than matched controls. These findings suggest that one source of boys' wanting to play with guns and girls' wanting to play house originates in the womb (Berenbaum and Hines, 1992; Kuhnle, Bullinger, and Schwarz, 1995; Money and Ehrhardt, 1972). These two lines of evidence are in line with the fetal hormone findings for gender identity and for sexual orientation. Our overall speculation is that at the deepest layer (gender identity), the influence of fetal hormones is enormous, virtually determining gender identity. At the next deepest layer (sexual orientation), fetal hormones play a strong, but somewhat less overpowering, role. At the next layer (sexual preference), fetal hormones are influential, but experience plays a strong role as well. At the fourth layer (sex role), there is some, but a more minor, influence of fetal hormones and increasing influence of experience.

So, the conclusion that sex roles are biologically deep and unchangeable is untenable. As children grow up, the stereotypes get weaker and easier to defy. In late childhood, children begin to have stereotypes about crying, dominance, independence, and kindness, but they are much weaker than the toy and job stereotypes of early childhood.

Although pressuring kids to become androgynous does not work immediately, it may have a "sleeper" effect. As children mature into adults, sex-role stereotypes start to melt away. When children grow up, those who were raised by androgynous parents tend to become androgynous themselves. Supporting intellectual interests for daughters and warmth and compassion for sons, exposing children to a range of roles, may work after all—but only in the long run (Reinisch, 1992).

This is important, and it makes sense. Young children see the world in black and white terms. "I'm either a boy or a girl. There's nothing in between. If I like dolls, I'm a sissy." These are deeply held convictions. Young children seem to have a drive to conform that may have its roots in the fetal brain. As a child matures, however, considerations of morality, of justice, and of fairness enter. Tolerance starts to displace blind conformity. He or she now chooses how to behave. Decisions about androgyny, about unconventionality, about rebellion are conscious choices based on a sense of what is right and what the adolescent individual wants for his or her own future. As such, the choice of androgyny requires a mature mind and a conscience; it is not a product of mechanical childhood socialization.

Sexual Performance: Layer V

Let us say that the first four layers of your sexuality are in good order. You have a clear gender identity and a clear sexual orientation, you have clear sexual preferences, and a well-entrenched sex role. You are alone with an appropriate, consenting partner. What can now go wrong? In what ways can the surface layer of erotic life—sexual performance—be impaired? Much can go wrong, but to understand what can affect sexual performance, we need to first describe the adequate sexual response.

The Physiology of the Human Sexual Response

In both men and women, the sexual response consists of four phases: The first is *erotic desire,* fantasies about sexual activity and the desire to engage in it. The second phase is *physical excitement,* which consists of the sense of sexual pleasure accompanied by penile erection in the male and vaginal lubrication and swelling in the female. The third phase is *orgasm,* in which sexual pleasure climaxes, with the male ejaculating and the female experiencing contractions in the muscles of the vaginal walls. The fourth phase is *resolution,* in which a sense of muscular relaxation and well-being takes hold. Males are refractory (unresponsive to a stimulus) for a time, but females can usually become excited again almost immediately.

MALE SEXUAL RESPONSE

In men, erotic desire and arousal result from a wide variety of events and lead to excitement. Being touched on the genitals or looking at and touching a sexually responsive partner are probably the most compelling stimuli. In addition, visual stimuli, smells, a seductive voice, and erotic fantasies, among many others, all produce arousal.

The second phase of excitement consists of penile erection. Sexual excitement stimulates parasympathetic nerves in the spinal cord, and these nerves control the blood vessels of the penis. These blood vessels widen dramatically and highly oxygen-rich blood streams in, producing erection (see discussion of Viagra below). The blood is prevented from leaving by a system of valves in the veins. When the parasympathetic fibers are inhibited, the blood vessels empty, and rapid loss of erection occurs.

Orgasm in men consists of two stages that follow each other very rapidly—emission and ejaculation. Unlike arousal and erection, orgasm is controlled by the sympathetic nervous system, as opposed to the parasympathetic nervous system. When sufficient rhythmic pressure on the head and shaft of the penis occurs, a plateau of orgasmic inevitability is reached, and orgasm arrives. Orgasm is engineered to deposit sperm deep into the vagina near the head of the uterus, maximizing the likelihood of fertilization. Emission (the discharge of semen) occurs when the male reproductive organs contract. This is followed very rapidly by ejaculation, in which powerful muscles at the base of the penis contract vigorously, ejecting sperm from the penis. During ejaculation, these muscles contract at intervals of 0.8 seconds. This phase of orgasm is accompanied by intense pleasure. After orgasm has occurred, a man, unlike a woman, is "refractory," or unresponsive to further sexual stimulation for some interval. This interval varies from a few minutes to a few hours, and it lengthens as the man gets older.

FEMALE SEXUAL RESPONSE

The sexual response of a woman transforms her normally tight and dry vagina into a lubricated, perfectly fitting receptacle for the erect penis. The stimuli that produce desire and arousal in women are similar to those that produce desire and arousal in men. Kissing and caressing, visual stimuli, and a whole host of subtle cues are usually effective as sexually arousing stimuli. There appear to be some sex differences in what is arousing, with romantic situations and gentle touch more initially arousing to women, and direct touch and body parts more arousing to men.

Once a woman is aroused, the excitement or "lubrication-swelling" phase begins. When at rest, the vagina is collapsed, pale in color, and rather dry. When arousal occurs, the vagina balloons exactly enough to "glove" an erect penis, regardless of its size. At the same time, the clitoris, a small knob of tissue located forward of the vagina, swells. Lubrication occurs on the walls of the vagina, making penile insertion easier. As excitement continues, the walls of the uterus fill with blood, and the uterus enlarges. This engorgement of blood and swelling greatly add to erotic pleasure and set the stage for orgasm.

Orgasm in women consists of a series of reflexive contractions of the muscles surrounding the vagina. These contract rhythmically at intervals of 0.8 seconds against the engorged tissue around the vagina, producing the ecstatic sensation of orgasm. Both the clitoris and the vagina itself play a role: orgasm is triggered by stimulation of the clitoris, and then expressed by contraction of the vagina.

Thus, arousal in both men and women consists of parallel events. Blood flow under the control of the parasympathetic nervous system produces physical excitement and penile erection in the male and both the lubrication and swelling phases of the vagina in the female. Orgasm consists of powerful muscular contractions at 0.8 second intervals, produced by rhythmic pressure on the head and shaft of the penis in the man and on the clitoris of the woman. These parallels are lovely and deep. Before they were known, it was easy to fall prey to the belief that chasms separated the experience of sex between a man and a woman. To learn that one's partner is probably experiencing the same kind of joys that you are is powerful and binding knowledge.

Impairment of Sexual Performance

When desire, or arousal, or orgasm go awry, we say an individual suffers a **sexual dysfunction** (see Table 13–3). Dysfunction can occur in three areas of sexual response: (1) Desire. Erotic desire may be low or nonexistent. (2) Excitement. When in an appropriate sexual situation, failure to have or maintain an erection in men and lack of vaginal lubrication and genital swelling in women may occur. (3) Orgasm. In women, orgasm may fail to occur altogether; in men, ejaculation may be premature, occurring with minimal sexual stimulation, or retarded, occurring only after prolonged, continual stimulation, if at all.

Impairment may occur in only one of these three areas of sexuality, or in all three in the same individual. The impairment may be lifelong or an acquired loss after sexual response has been normal, it may be limited to only one situation (usually with one specific partner) or occur in all situations, and it may occur infrequently and intermittently or all the time. For example, the failure to maintain an erection can develop after years of satisfactory intercourse, or it can occur from the very first attempt at sexual intercourse. It can occur only with one partner or with all women. It can occur only once in a while or it can occur every time the individual tries to have intercourse. It may be psychological in ori-

TABLE 13–3

CATEGORIES OF SEXUAL DYSFUNCTIONS

Sexual Dysfunction	*Description*
Sexual Desire Disorders	
Hypoactive sexual desire disorder	Little or no interest in sexual activity.
Sexual aversion disorder	Persistent aversion to sexual contact.
Sexual Arousal Disorders	
Male erectile disorder	Persistent inability to achieve or maintain an erection (formerly called "impotence").
Female sexual arousal disorder	Persistent inability to achieve or maintain vaginal lubrication and swelling (formerly called "frigidity").
Sexual Orgasmic Disorders	
Premature ejaculation	Ejaculation after brief stimulation, and *before* the person wishes it.
Retarded ejaculation	Delayed ejaculation after prolonged stimulation, and *after* the person wishes it.
Female orgasmic disorder	Persistent absence of orgasm after stimulation, despite desire and arousal.
Sexual Pain Disorders	
Dyspareunia	Extreme pain (in males or females) associated with intercourse.
Vaginismus	Involuntary muscle spasms at the entrance to the vagina that prevent intercourse.

gin, or it may be a side effect of a general medical condition.

SEXUAL UNRESPONSIVENESS IN WOMEN

Because erotic desire and physical excitement are so intertwined, we will treat them together. In women, lack of sexual desire and impairment of physical excitement in appropriate situations used to be called sexual "unresponsiveness" (and before that "frigidity"). Now low or absent desire is called ***sexual aversion disorder*** by DSM-IV. The symptoms are subjective: she may feel disgust, fear, or revulsion when sex becomes a possibility. She may not have sexual fantasies (Beck, 1995). Revulsion may occur to all aspects of sex (for example, kissing, touching, and intercourse), or just to one aspect (for example, vaginal penetration). The aversion can be mild, or it can range all the way to extreme distress.

Female sexual arousal disorder is a dysfunction at the excitement phase. When a woman with this disorder is sexually stimulated, her vagina does not lubricate, her clitoris may not enlarge, her uterus may not swell, and her nipples may not become erect. She may not enjoy sexual intercourse or stimulation, or she may consider sex an ordeal. Frequently, she becomes a spectator rather than losing

DSM-IV Criteria

Sexual Aversion Disorder

A. Persistent or recurrent extreme aversion to, and avoidance of, all (or almost all) genital sexual contact with a sexual partner.

B. The disturbance causes marked distress or interpersonal difficulty.

C. The sexual dysfunction is not better accounted for by another Axis I disorder (except another Sexual Dysfunction).

Specify type:
   Lifelong Type
   Acquired Type

Specify type:
   Generalized Type
   Situational Type

Specify:
   Due to Psychological Factors
   Due to Combined Factors

SOURCE: APA, DSM-IV, 1994.

DSM-IV Criteria

Female Sexual Arousal Disorder

A. Persistent or recurrent inability to attain, or to maintain until completion of the sexual activity, an adequate lubrication-swelling response of sexual excitement.

B. The disturbance causes marked distress or interpersonal difficulty.

C. The sexual dysfunction is not better accounted for by another Axis I disorder (except another Sexual Dysfunction) and is not due exclusively to the direct physiological effects of a substance (e.g., a drug of abuse, a medication) or a general medical condition.

SOURCE: APA, DSM-IV, 1994.

---

herself in the erotic act. The woman may be unresponsive in all situations or only in specific ones. For example, if the problem is situational, she may be enraged or nauseated by the sexual advances of her husband, but she may feel instantly aroused and may lubricate when an attractive, unavailable man touches her hand. Such a woman may have problems with orgasm as well (Andersen and Cyranowski, 1995), but it is not uncommon for a "sexually unresponsive" woman—whose excitement is impaired—to have an orgasm easily once intercourse takes place.

Women's reactions to this problem vary. Some women patiently endure unexciting sexual intercourse, using their bodies mechanically and hoping that their partner will ejaculate quickly. But this is often a formula for resentment and recrimination. Watching her husband derive great pleasure from sex over and over while she feels little pleasure may be frustrating and alienating for a woman. And eventually some women may attempt to avoid sex, pleading illness or deliberately provoking a quarrel before bedtime (Kaplan, 1974).

There are two female *sexual pain disorders: vaginismus,* in which the muscles of the vagina spasm involuntarily when intercourse is attempted, or even during the insertion of a tampon, and *dyspareunia,* in which severe pain occurs during intercourse, even though desire, excitement, and orgasm are all intact.

ERECTILE DYSFUNCTION IN MEN

In men, global impairment of desire (DSM-IV calls it *hypoactive sexual desire* or *sexual aversion*) does occur, but it is much rarer than in women. Rather, the most common dysfunction in men is one of excitement, called *male erectile disorder* (formerly "impotence"). It is defined as a recurrent inability to have or maintain an erection for intercourse. This condition can be humiliating, frustrating, and devastating since male self-esteem across most cultures involves good sexual performance. When erection fails, feelings of worthlessness and depression often ensue, as in the following case:

> Sheldon was nineteen when his teammates from the freshman football team dragged him along to visit a prostitute. The prostitute's bedroom was squalid; she seemed to be in her mid-fifties, and had an unattractive face, a fat body, and foul-smelling breath. He was to be the last of a group of five friends scheduled to perform with her. Sheldon had never had intercourse before and had been anxious to begin with. When his turn arrived, the other four decided to watch and cheer him on, and Sheldon could not get an erection. His teammates shouted that he should hurry up and the prostitute was obviously impatient. He was pressured beyond any ability to perform and ran out of the room. After this incident, he avoided all erotic contact with women for five years, fearing that he would fail again.
>
> At age thirty-four, he married Suzanne. Their first attempts at sexual intercourse succeeded. But after the honeymoon, Sheldon could rarely sustain an erection hard enough for intercourse. When Suzanne pressured him to have sex, he felt overwhelmed with fears that he would fail, remembering his humiliating failure with the prostitute. Sheldon had become impotent.

Erectile dysfunction in the male can be either primary or secondary, situation specific or global. Men who have had *primary erectile dysfunction* have never been able to achieve or maintain an erec-

DSM-IV Criteria

Male Erectile Disorder

A. Persistent or recurrent inability to attain, or to maintain until completion of the sexual activity, an adequate erection.

B. The disturbance causes marked distress or interpersonal difficulty.

C. The erectile dysfunction is not better accounted for by another Axis I disorder (other than a Sexual Dysfunction) and is not due exclusively to the direct physiological effects of a substance (e.g., a drug of abuse, a medication) or a general medical condition.

SOURCE: APA, DSM-IV, 1994.

tion sufficient for intercourse; whereas men who have ***secondary erectile dysfunction*** have lost this ability. When the dysfunction is situation specific, a man may be able to maintain an erection with one partner, but not with another. Some men may become erect during foreplay, but not during intercourse. When the dysfunction is global, a man cannot achieve an erection with any partner under any circumstances. It is important and reassuring for a man to know that a single failure in no way implies "erectile dysfunction," which is, by definition, recurrent. Virtually every man on one occasion or another—particularly when upset or fatigued—cannot get an erection or keep it long enough for intercourse.

Erectile disorder can also result from medical problems. Clinicians can determine whether or not erections are occurring during the night to distinguish medical problems that prevent erections altogether from psychologically induced erectile problems. During an eight-hour sleep, most people will have four bouts of rapid-eye movement (REM) sleep, during which dreaming usually occurs. REM sleep in men is almost invariably accompanied by penile erection, even though the content of the dream need not be erotic. By using a strain gauge to measure such nocturnal erections, clinicians can determine if erections are absent during sleep. If nocturnal erections do occur, this points away from a global medical or physical cause of the erectile disorder (Carey, Wincze, and Meisler, 1993; Sakheim, Barlow, Abrahamson, and Beck, 1987).

FEMALE ORGASMIC DISORDER

Some women do not achieve the third phase of sexual response: orgasm. How easily different women can achieve orgasm lies on a continuum. At one extreme are the rare women who can have an orgasm merely by having an intense erotic fantasy, without any physical stimulation at all. Then there are women who climax merely from intense foreplay, women who regularly have orgasm during intercourse,

DSM-IV Criteria

Female Orgasmic Disorder

A. Persistent or recurrent delay in, or absence of, orgasm following a normal sexual excitement phase. Women exhibit wide variability in the type or intensity of stimulation that triggers orgasm. The diagnosis of Female Orgasmic Disorder should be based on the clinician's judgment that the woman's orgasmic capacity is less than would be reasonable for her age, sexual experience, and the adequacy of sexual stimulation she receives.

B. The disturbance causes marked distress or interpersonal difficulty.

C. The orgasmic dysfunction is not better accounted for by another Axis I disorder (except another Sexual Dysfunction) and is not due exclusively to the direct physiological effects of a substance (e.g., a drug of abuse, a medication) or a general medical condition.

SOURCE: APA, DSM-IV, 1994.

women who occasionally have orgasms during intercourse, and women who need long and intense clitoral stimulation in order to climax. At the other extreme are the approximately 10 to 25 percent of adult women who have never had an orgasm in spite of having been exposed to a reasonable amount of stimulation; this is the most common sexual dysfunction in women (Laumann, Gagnon, Michael, and Michaels, 1994).

Nonorgasmic women may nonetheless have a strong sexual drive (Andersen, 1983). They may enjoy foreplay, lubricate copiously, and love the sensation of phallic penetration. But as the couple approaches climax, the woman may become self-conscious; she may stand apart and judge herself. She may ask herself, "I wonder if I'll climax." "This is taking too long; he's getting sick of it." Frustration, resentment, and the persistent erosion of a couple's erotic and affectionate relationship bring nonorgasmic women into therapy (Kaplan, 1974; McCary, 1978).

Failure to have an orgasm may be primary, with orgasm never having occurred, or secondary, with loss of orgasm. It may be situation specific, with orgasm occurring, for example, in masturbation when alone, but not in intercourse, or it may be global.

MALE ORGASMIC DISORDERS

There are two kinds of **male orgasmic disorders,** and they reflect opposite problems: premature ejaculation and retarded ejaculation.

Premature Ejaculation   Most men have occasionally ejaculated more quickly than their partner would like, but this is not equivalent to premature ejaculation. **Premature ejaculation** is the recurrent inability to exert any control over ejaculation, such that once sexually aroused, the man reaches orgasm very quickly. This is probably the most common of male sexual problems (Metz et al., 1997).

Premature ejaculation can wreak havoc with a couple's sex life. A man who is worrying about ejaculating as soon as he becomes aroused may have trouble being sensitive and responsive to his lover. He may be self-conscious, and his partner may feel rejected and perceive him as cold and insensitive. Not uncommonly, secondary erectile dysfunction often follows untreated premature ejaculation.

Retarded Ejaculation   **Retarded ejaculation,** which is less common than premature ejaculation, consists of great difficulty reaching orgasm during sexual intercourse. Frequently, the man may be able to ejaculate easily during masturbation or foreplay, but intercourse may last for thirty minutes or longer with no ejaculation. Contrary to popular myth, the staying power of the retarded ejaculator does not place him in an enviable position. His partner may feel rejected and clumsy. He may feign orgasm, and he may have high anxiety accompanied by self-conscious thoughts like, "She must think something is wrong with me." The retarded ejaculator finds his own touch most arousing, and he may be numb to his partner's touch on his penis. His psychological arousal does not keep pace with his physiological arousal (Apfelbaum, 1980). Secondary erectile dysfunction sometimes follows.

It is unwise to attach numbers to either retarded ejaculation or premature ejaculation, saying, for example, that premature ejaculation occurs whenever ejaculation persistently takes less than thirty seconds or fewer than eight thrusts and retarded ejaculation occurs whenever ejaculation persistently takes more

DSM-IV Criteria

Premature Ejaculation

A. Persistent or recurrent ejaculation with minimal sexual stimulation before, on, or shortly after penetration and before the person wishes it. The clinician must take into account factors that affect duration of the excitement phase, such as age, novelty of the sexual partner or situation, and recent frequency of sexual activity.

B. The disturbance causes marked distress or interpersonal difficulty.
C. The premature ejaculation is not due exclusively to the direct effects of a substance (e.g., withdrawal from opioids).

SOURCE: APA, DSM-IV, 1994.

Male Orgasmic Disorder (Retarded Ejaculation)

A. Persistent or recurrent delay in, or absence of, orgasm following a normal sexual excitement phase during sexual activity that the clinician, taking into account the person's age, judges to be adequate in focus, intensity, and duration.

B. The disturbance causes marked distress or interpersonal difficulty.

C. The orgasmic dysfunction is not better accounted for by another Axis I disorder (except another Sexual Dysfunction) and is not due exclusively to the direct physiological effects of a substance (e.g., a drug of abuse, a medication) or a general medical condition.

SOURCE: APA, DSM-IV, 1994.

---

than half an hour. This misses the important point that the definition of the sexual problem, both orgasmic and arousal, is always relative to your own and your partner's expectations. Many couples are able to work out quite satisfactory erotic relationships even when one partner climaxes very quickly or very slowly, and it would be inappropriate to label these individuals as having sexual dysfunction.

The Causes of Sexual Dysfunction

There are two causes of sexual dysfunction—biomedical and psychological—and the two kinds of effective treatment—medication and direct sexual therapy—follow from the causes. Until the 1990s, it was believed that the majority of sexual problems were psychological, rather than biomedical in origin. This belief came from the stunning findings of Masters and Johnson who successfully treated the great majority of sexual dysfunctions with "direct sexual therapy," which you will read about below. But in 1998 a stunning medication, Viagra, was found to markedly relieve impotence and today much research is underway on the biological aspects of sexual dysfunction (Rosen and Leiblum, 1995).

BIOLOGICAL CAUSES

Loss of sexual desire in both men and women can stem from using drugs like alcohol, cocaine, heroin, and marijuana, all of which impair sexual hormones. Similarly, medications such as antihypertensives (especially beta-blockers), major and minor tranquilizers, tricyclic antidepressants, and antihistamines also diminish sexual desire (Gitlin, 1994; Segraves and Al-

thof, 1998; Schiavi et al., 1984; Schiavi and Rehman, 1995). In one study of 596 patients receiving selective serotonin reuptake inhibitors (SSRI's) such as Prozac, 16 percent showed sexual dysfunction side effects, side effects that could be reversed in many cases by another medication, yohimbine (Ashton, Hamer, and Rosen, 1997). But the single most important clue to the importance of organic factors comes from aging. In one large study of forty- to seventy-year-old men, 52 percent reported some impotence, with three times as many of the oldest men having serious erectile problems (Feldman, Goldstein, Hatzichristou, Krane, and McKunlay, 1994; Rosen, 1996).

Poor circulation resulting in insufficient oxygen in the blood in the penis (as for example in vascular disease) and low testosterone may be responsible for some erectile dysfunction problems (Benet and Melman, 1995). Constricted arteries may make it difficult for sufficient blood to flow to the penis, and leaky veins may cause blood to flow out of the penis too quickly to maintain an erection. Out of 105 patients, 35 percent had disorders of the pituitary-hypothalamic-gonadal axis, and 90 percent of these had potency restored with biological therapy (Spark, White, and Connelly, 1980). Moreover, neurological diseases and other diseases that affect the CNS, such as diabetes and kidney disease, may also reduce sensitivity in the genital area.

There is much less evidence for the role of organic factors in female sexual dysfunctions, although the widespread use of lubricants may mask some of the biological causes of arousal problems in women. Nevertheless, a woman's capacity for sexual arousal can be impaired by injuries, physical anomalies of the genitals, hormonal imbalances, neurological disorders, and inflammations. Female sexual dysfunction can also follow surgeries such as a lumpectomy or a hysterectomy (Kaplan, 1974; McCary, 1978; Rosen and Leiblum, 1995).

PSYCHOLOGICAL CAUSES

Psychological factors markedly affect sexual desire and excitement, and psychological problems probably cause many of the sexual dysfunctions (see Table 13–4). One pathway is clear: negative emotional states directly impair sexual responsiveness. Earlier, we spoke of the sensitive interplay of physiological and psychological factors. The physiological part of the sexual response is autonomic and visceral; essentially it is produced by increased blood flow to the genitals under the control of the autonomic nervous system. But certain autonomic responses, sexual arousal among them, are inhibited by negative emotions. If a woman is frightened or sad during sex, autonomic responding may be impaired. Similarly, if a man is frightened or feeling pressured during sex, there may not be sufficient blood flow to cause erection. What are the sources of the anxiety and sadness that might cause sexual unresponsiveness in women or men?

Psychodynamic theorists emphasize unconscious conflicts: A woman may fear that she will not reach orgasm, or she may feel helpless or exploited. Some men and women feel unconscious shame or guilt. They may believe that sex is a sin; they may have grown up in situations where sex was seen as dirty and bad, and they may have trouble ridding themselves of feelings of shame and guilt even in the shelter of marriage. Some women may expect physical pain in intercourse and therefore dread it. And often there is the fear of pregnancy.

Negative emotions arising in relationships must not be overlooked. Relationships do not always progress well. People change, sometimes developing different living habits and preferences. Their partner may not change accordingly, and conflict may then ensue, bringing about negative feelings between the couple. Understandably, it is often difficult to discard these feelings when the couple enters the bedroom. Many men and women fear rejection and become self-conscious, thereby inhibiting an otherwise normal sexual response. In such cases, one or both partners may develop a sexual dysfunction, often specific to that partner.

Behavioral psychologists offer an explanation of the causes of sexual dysfunction based on learning theory. For men, erectile dysfunction may result from an early sexual experience. A particularly traumatic first sexual experience may condition strong fear to sexual encounters in either women or men. Recall Sheldon's first and formative sexual encounter, in which his teammates watched his failure to perform with a prostitute. Heterosexual activity was the conditioned stimulus (CS), paired with a humiliating, public failure to have an erection (US) and an unconditioned response (UR) of ensuing shame and anxiety. Future exposures to the CS of pressured sexual encounter in his marriage to Suzanne produced the conditioned response (CR) of anxiety, which in

TABLE 13–4

VIEWS OF ERECTILE AND ORGASMIC DYSFUNCTION

	Psychodynamic View	*Behavioral View*	*Cognitive View*	*Biological View*
Origin	Unconscious conflict, shame, or guilt about sex	Traumatic early sexual experience	Traumatic sexual experience in someone with a certain cognitive style	Insufficient blood flow to genitals.
Process	Unconscious conflict produces anxiety during sex	Conditioned fear of failure produces anxiety during sex	Person observes and judges him- or herself during sex, interfering with enjoyment and producing anxiety	Lack of blood flow blocks full erection by a simple mechanical insufficiency.
Result	Anxiety leads to sexual unresponsiveness	Anxiety blocks erection or orgasm	Anxiety blocks erection or orgasm	Adequate and prolonged erection cannot occur; hence, orgasm cannot occur.

turn blocked erections. This formulation fits many of the instances in which there is an early traumatic experience (Tsai, Feldman-Summers, and Edgar, 1979; Rosen and Leiblum, 1995), and it also explains the success of direct sexual therapy with erectile dysfunction. It fails to account for those cases in which no traumatic experience can be discovered, and it also does not account for why certain individuals are more susceptible to sexually traumatic experiences than others. For every individual who undergoes an initial sexual experience like Sheldon's that is a failure, and who develops erectile dysfunctions, there are many who encounter similar initial failures but do not develop such dysfunctions.

Cognitive theorists suggest other important considerations. For both the orgasmic and the arousal dysfunctions, what an individual thinks can greatly interfere with performance. Men and women with orgasm difficulties become "orgasm watchers." They may think, "I wonder if I'll climax this time." "This is taking much too long; he must think I'm frigid." Individuals who have arousal dysfunctions may think, "If I don't get an erection, she'll laugh at me." "I'm not going to get aroused this time either." These thoughts produce anxiety, which in turn blocks the parasympathetic responding that is the basis of the human sexual response. Such thoughts get in the way of abandoning oneself to erotic feelings. Distraction is another cognitive state that directly inhibits arousal (Abrahamson, Barlow, Beck, and Sakheim, 1985), as does transient negative mood, as induced by sad music (Mitchell, DiBartolo, Brown, and Barlow, 1998). Thus, therapy for sexual dysfunctions can deal with problems at four levels: biomedical, psychodynamic, behavioral, and cognitive, for difficulties at any of these levels can produce human sexual dysfunction.

Treatment of Sexual Dysfunction

It has been estimated that half of American marriages are flawed by some kind of sexual problem (Frank, Anderson, and Rubenstein, 1978; Masters and Johnson, 1970; Oggins, Leber, and Veroff, 1993). Sexual problems in couples occur in the nexus of a relationship between two human beings. When sex goes badly, many other aspects of the relationship may go badly, and vice versa. Sex—often, but not always—mirrors the way two people feel about and act toward each other overall. Sex therapists often find that underneath the

William Masters and Virginia Johnson brought the study of sexual behavior into the laboratory and created direct sexual therapy with sexually dysfunctional patients.

sexual problems are more basic problems of a relationship—problems with love, tenderness, respect, honesty—and that when these are overcome, a fuller sexual relationship may follow (Baucom, Shoham, Mueser, Daiuto, and Stickle, 1998; Jacobson, 1992; Speckens, Hengeveld, Lycklama a Nijeholt, Van Hemert, and Hawton, 1995). This chapter opened with such a case: Carol and Ed's relationship deteriorated in lockstep with Carol's loss of orgasm in intercourse. Carol's headaches and complaints about Ed's lovemaking technique led to heated arguments, and intercourse was now a dreaded ordeal for Carol. They then sought out therapy with Masters and Johnson.

DIRECT SEXUAL THERAPY

William Masters and Virginia Johnson, researchers who brought the study of sexual behavior into the laboratory and who have worked to discover the nature and treatment of sexual dysfunction, created ***direct sexual therapy*** with sexually dysfunctional patients like Ed and Carol. Direct sexual therapy differs in three important ways from previous sexual therapy. First, it defines the problem differently: sexual problems are not labeled as "neuroses" or "diseases" but rather as "limited dysfunctions." Direct sexual therapy formulates the problem as local rather than global. A woman like Carol is not labeled as "hysterical," defending against deep intrapsychic conflicts by "freezing" her sexual response, as psychodynamic therapists claim. Rather, she is said to suffer merely from "inhibition of arousal." Second, and most dramatic, through direct sexual therapy, the clients explicitly practice sexual behavior after systematic discussions with the therapists. A couple like Carol and Ed first receives education and instruction about their problem, then an authoritative prescription from Masters and Johnson about how to solve it, and most importantly, sexual practice sessions for the couple. Their third major departure is that people are treated not as individual patients but as couples. In treating individuals, Masters and Johnson had often found that sexual problems do not reside in one individual, but in the interaction of the couple. Carol's lack of interest in sex is not only her problem. Her husband's increasing demands, rage, and frustration contribute to her waning interest in sex. By treating the couple together, Ed and Carol's deteriorating sexual interaction was reversed.

Sensate focus is the major strategy of direct sexual therapy for impaired excitement in females and erectile dysfunction in males. The basic premise of sensate focus is that anxiety occurring during intercourse blocks sexual excitement and pleasure. In the female, anxiety blocks the lubrication and swelling phase; in the male, it blocks erection. The overriding objectives of treatment are to reduce this anxiety and to restore confidence. The immediate goal is to bring about one successful experience with intercourse. This is accomplished, however, in a way in which the demands associated with arousal and orgasm are minimized. Sensate focus has three phases: "pleasuring," genital stimulation, and nondemand intercourse (Masters and Johnson, 1970; see also Kaplan, 1974; Rosen and Leiblum, 1995). Let us look at the sensate focus treatment for Carol and Ed.

> In the "pleasuring" phase, Carol and Ed were instructed not to have sexual intercourse and not to have orgasm during these exercises. Erotic activity was limited to gently touching and caressing each other's body. Carol was instructed to caress Ed first, and then the roles were to be reversed and Ed was to stroke Carol. This was done to permit Carol to concentrate on the sensations later evoked by Ed's caresses, without being distracted by guilt over her own selfishness. It also allowed her to relax knowing that intercourse was not going to be demanded of her.
>
> After three sessions of pleasuring, Carol's response was quite dramatic. She felt freed from pressure to have an orgasm and to serve her husband, and she experienced deeply erotic sensations for the first

time in her life. Further, she felt that she had taken responsibility for her own pleasure, and she discovered that her husband did not reject her when she asserted herself. They then went on to phase two of sensate focus—"genital stimulation." In this phase, light and teasing genital play is added to pleasuring, but the husband is cautioned not to make orgasm-oriented caresses. Orgasm and intercourse are still forbidden. The woman sets the pace of the exercises and directs the husband both verbally and nonverbally, and then the roles are reversed.

> The couple's response was also very positive here. Both felt deep pleasure and were aroused and eager to go on to the next step, "nondemand intercourse." In this final phase, after Carol had reached high arousal through pleasuring and genital stimulation, she was instructed to initiate intercourse. Ed and Carol were further instructed that there was to be no pressure for Carol to have an orgasm.
>
> In spite of—or because of—the instruction, Carol had her first orgasm in months. At this point, Ed and Carol were able to work out a mutually arousing and satisfactory style of lovemaking.

Carol and Ed's improvement was typical: only about 25 percent of patients fail to improve with sensate focus for female sexual unresponsiveness (Masters and Johnson, 1970; see also Kaplan, 1974; McCary, 1978; Segraves and Althof, 1998). Carol's problem was "secondary:" She had lost the capacity for orgasm that she used to have. When a woman has never had an orgasm (primary anorgasmia), guided masturbation using a vibrator and muscle training is the treatment of choice with an overall success rate of 90 percent (LoPiccolo and Stock, 1986; Segraves and Althof, 1998).

The well-publicized successes of Masters and Johnson changed the thinking of an entire generation of sex therapists in two ways. Therapeutic optimism replaced the pessimism that sexual problems could not be cured, and researchers came to believe that sexual dysfunctions were learned rather than organic. Sensate focus became the mainstay for treatment of erectile dysfunction in the 1970s, and it was soon supplemented by other purely psychological therapies, including anxiety reduction, fantasy training, assertiveness, and couple communication skills during sex. Results of these psychological treatments, however, did not live up to the initial promise of Masters and Johnson.

BIOLOGICAL TREATMENTS AND VIAGRA

While researchers continued to acknowledge the importance of psychological factors in sexual dysfunction, they also began to look for biological treatments as well. A panoply of organic treatments was tried (Rosen, 1996). These included rigid or inflatable penile implants, surgery to increase penile blood flow, local injections of muscle relaxants, injections of vasodilating drugs into the penis, topical creams, and a variety of oral medications. Some of these seemed promising, but in 1998 Pfizer introduced a new drug, Viagra (sildenafil), which eclipsed the other organic treatments.

Viagra is a pill that works by increasing the blood supply to the penis within an hour after being swallowed. It aids erections, but only with sexual stimulation. In ten double-blind, placebo-controlled studies, sponsored by Pfizer, involving 3,361 patients with erectile dysfunction, 73 percent of the men taking Viagra benefited compared to half as many given a placebo. Only about 2 percent discontinued use because of adverse side effects, such as dyspepsia, headache, and flushing. Figure 13–2 shows the number of successful attempts at intercourse in 157 men with Viagra contrasted to 154 men with a placebo (Goldstein et al., 1998; Licht, 1998; Rosen, 1998). At about $7 to $10 a dose, it is a fairly expensive pill. In spite of its price, its sales are unprecedented, and women are experimenting with it as well. Several deaths were soon reported, all probably related to the unaccustomed exertion of in-

tercourse in formerly impotent older men (Siegel-Itzkovich, 1998). Approximately 3 percent of the men taking Viagra have experienced transient visual disturbances such as a blue-green ring or blurriness, and 17 percent have reported experiencing headaches after taking the drug (Stein, 1999). Yet, the reactions of most men taking Viagra have been very positive, as shown in the following case:

> Earl Macklin, a fifty-nine-year-old security guard in Chicago, has suffered from impotence on and off for ten years as a result of diabetes. The first two times he tried Viagra, it produced minimal results; the third time he was able to have intercourse with his girlfriend for the first time in their four-month relationship. "I've been using it every day since then," he says (four days later) with a conspiratorial chuckle. "It makes me feel like I'm in my 30s again." Macklin's insurance company has notified him that it won't be reimbursing him, so, he says, "I'll limit myself to 20 pills a month." (*Time Magazine*, May 4, 1998)

EVALUATION OF SEXUAL THERAPY

Direct sexual therapy seems to be quite effective in alleviating the dysfunctions of arousal and orgasm in both men and women (Marks, 1981; Heiman and LoPiccolo, 1983). There is more than 75 percent marked improvement in cases of premature ejaculation, and more than 75 percent marked improvement in cases of female orgasmic dysfunction

Figure 13–2

TREATMENT OF MALE ORGASMIC DYSFUNCTION

In a twelve-week study, sexual function was compared in men treated with Viagra (sildenafil) and men given a placebo. Those treated with Viagra were markedly more successful in their attempts at sexual intercourse than were those given a placebo. (Source: Goldstein et al., 1998, p. 1402)

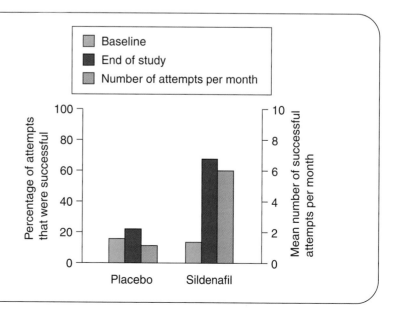

TABLE 13–5

Treatment

SEXUAL DYSFUNCTIONS

	Direct Sexual Therapy		Viagra
	Female Arousal and Desire Disorders	Male Erectile Disorder	
Improvement	more than 65% markedly improved	more than 60% markedly improved	more than 70% markedly improved
Relapse*	moderate to high relapse	moderate relapse	unknown; probably high relapse
Side Effects	none	none	mild to moderate
Cost	inexpensive	inexpensive	moderately expensive ($10 per pill)
Time Scale	weeks	weeks	minutes
Overall	**good**	**good**	**very good/excellent**

	Direct Sexual Therapy	
	Female Orgasmic Dysfunction	Male Premature Ejaculation
Improvement	more than 75% markedly improved	more than 75% markedly improved
Relapse*	low to moderate relapse	moderate to high relapse
Side Effects	none	none
Cost	inexpensive	inexpensive
Time Scale	weeks	weeks
Overall	**very good**	**good**

*Relapse after discontinuation of treatment.

SOURCE: Based on Seligman, 1994, Chapter 11; revised using Segraves and Althof, 1998.

(Segraves and Althof, 1998; see Table 13–5). Moreover, systematic desensitization may also be effective in enhancing desire and orgasm, particularly in women with sexual anxiety (Andersen, 1983). Caution is required in two respects, however. First, the Masters and Johnson reports of success are not as well documented as many would like, and there have been woefully few controlled outcome studies in the thirty years that have passed. Masters and Johnson did not report percentages of successes, but rather they reported percentages of failures. So, for example, they reported that only 24 percent of females "failed to improve" following sensate focus training for arousal dysfunction. This is not equivalent to a 75 percent cure rate. What "failure to improve" means is not well defined. Moreover, the percentage of patients showing only mild improvement, great improvement, or complete cure was not reported. While direct sex therapy techniques are far superior to what preceded them, well-controlled replications

with explicit criteria for sampling and for improvement are still needed.

In contrast, Viagra's effects appear robust and have been well documented from the outset (see Box 13–3). As a drug, rather than a kind of psychotherapy, Viagra required Federal Drug Administration approval and so was tested in large-scale controlled studies before it came on the market. Its manufacturer, Pfizer, however, sponsored almost all the initial studies. While some more recent, unbiased studies have now been published (for example, Pallas, Levine, Althof, and Risen, 2000), we await further replication, as well as long-term follow-up. Moreover, Viagra is not a cure for erectile dysfunction in the same sense that direct sexual therapy is a cure for sexual aversion disorder in women. Viagra is a palliative: once you stop taking it, erectile dysfunction will presumably return. Given this first breakthrough, however, we expect that the near future will see the testing of a host of medications for all the sexual dysfunctions.

Science and Practice

Box 13—3

The Viagra Phenomenon

While the initial studies of Viagra were sponsored by Pfizer, independent confirmation of Viagra's beneficial effects are now being published in the peer-reviewed literature. In one study (Pallas, Levine, Althof, and Risen, 2000), fifty-eight men were tracked through a two-visit follow-up. Forty-three percent had "ideal" outcomes; they were cured of erectile dysfunction. Fifty percent could have intercourse, and 63 percent had better erections. Seventeen percent were unimproved, and 21 percent were lost to follow-up. While these results are not quite as good as those reported by Pfizer, they are still impressive, and they suggest that treatment with Viagra is now the treatment of choice for male erectile disorders.

The "Viagra Craze" was the cover story of *Time Magazine* in May 1998, and prescriptions quintupled in a short period of time. Robert Dole, conservative Republican presidential candidate in 1996, was featured in advertisements for Viagra. General Sani Abacha of Nigeria died in the middle of a Viagra orgy with two women (Hitt, 2000). With all the publicity that Viagra received, it is not surprising that groups, other than those Viagra had been tested on, would try it to alleviate sexual problems or just to enhance otherwise satisfactory sex lives.

One of the first groups to discover unexpected benefits consisted of women taking antidepressant drugs. Sexual dysfunction is a common side effect of antidepressant treatment with SSRI's and tricyclics, and some women give up their medications in order to preserve their sex lives. In one uncontrolled study, Viagra was prescribed for nine such women. They took the drug one hour before sex. All nine, who had reported orgasmic problems while on antidepressants, now reported improvement in sexual function, usually with the first dose of Viagra (Nurnberg, Hensley, Lauriello, Parker, and Keith, 1999). There is still no other published research on Viagra for female sexual dysfunctions, but women as well as men may now be using Viagra both to treat sexual dysfunctions and to enhance their sex lives.

In the past, there were misconceptions that erectile dysfunction (ED) affected only older men. But it has been found that half of the men between ages forty and seventy experience some degree of erectile problems. Viagra has helped men throughout this age range. But it is occasionally being used as a recreational drug by men who are not suffering from erectile dysfunction problems. The original Pfizer advertisements were pitched to older men: a white-haired sixty-year-old man hugging his wife in a meadow, with the slogan "Let the dance begin." A more recent ad features a man and woman who appear to be in their thirties, with the slogan "Take the first step," and a new disorder "mild ED" is invoked.

While we do not wish to pass judgment on the use of a therapeutic medication that was intended initially to help suffering individuals but that is now finding a large niche as a recreational drug, we do urge caution against the use of the drug for recreational purposes. Viagra has been shown to be an effective treatment for erectile difficulties, but it cannot solve all the problems in a relationship. There may be demands for more sex in a relationship that has adjusted to a reduction in sexual activity, and perhaps as a result, an increase in extramarital affairs. To avoid such problems, communication is essential. The couple should discuss their sexual desires and expectations, and try to arrive at a mutual understanding of each other's needs. We believe that the most satisfactory sexual relations are best imbedded in loving personal relationships. Treatment for sexual dysfunctions works best in the context of such an ongoing love relationship. While Viagra makes it clear that some aspects of sexual dysfunction can be viewed as a mechanical, engineering problem, one in which the central issue is blood flow to the genitals, there is a danger that this success will deform our view of sexual therapy. A healthy erotic life, we believe, fuses a working body with overflowing positive emotion and with long-term commitment to a relationship.

Putting It All Together

We can see that the idea of increasingly deep layers organizes our erotic life and how changeable it is. Gender identity and sexual orientation are very deep and don't change much, if at all. Lack of change in therapy, lifelong fantasies of one sex only, small anterior hypothalamus, high concordance for homosexuality of identical twins, and fetal development all point to an almost inflexible process. Yet, homosexuality is not quite as unchangeable as transsexualism. Male transsexuals never lose the feeling that they are women. They rarely marry and have natural children, whereas homosexual men sometimes marry and have children. They manage this feat by a trick of fantasy. During sex with their wives, they manage to stay aroused and climax by having fantasies about homosexual sex (just as heterosexual men restricted to homosexual release in prison do). Some measure of flexibility is thus available to exclusively homosexual men—they can choose whom they perform with sexually, but they cannot choose whom they *want* to perform with.

Sexual preference and sex role are of middling depth, and accordingly, they change somewhat. Once identity and orientation are dictated largely by biology, the sexual preferences are elaborated around them largely by environmental stimuli: breasts or bottoms, peeping, lace panties, calves or feet, rubber textures, the missionary position or oral sex, sadism, blond hair, bisexuality, spanking, or high-heeled shoes. These preferences are not easily shelved once acquired. Unlike exclusive heterosexuality or homosexuality, however, they surely do not arise in the womb. Rather, our sexual preferences have their beginnings in late childhood as the first hormones of puberty awaken the dormant brain structures that were laid down in the womb and the child has encounters with potential sexual objects. With repeated masturbation and fantasy, these biologically prepared sexual objects become strong preferences, but not wholly unchangeable life goals.

Finally, sexual dysfunction is a surface problem, and with proper treatment—either direct sexual therapy or medications—it will improve quite readily. The strong beneficial effects of treatment with Viagra tell us that we can change the "plumbing" by increasing blood flow to the genitals and thereby cure a major sexual dysfunction in many cases. We can expect burgeoning research on similar mechanical, biological treatments for the entire range of sexual disorders and dysfunctions. Some of these will work and some will fail; but we must not let the enthusiasm for engineering solutions to sexual dysfunctions blind us to the fact that sexual health transcends the merely mechanical and is imbedded in affectionate, erotic relationships between two people.

Summary

1. Human sexuality is composed of five layers, each grown on top of the layer beneath it. This five-layer organization corresponds to depth. The deeper the layer, the harder it is to change.
2. The first and deepest layer of erotic life is *gender identity,* the awareness of being male or female. This layer has its origin in fetal hormones. *Transsexualism,* a disorder of gender identity, occurs in men who believe they are really women trapped in men's bodies and in women who feel that they are really men trapped in women's bodies. These individuals seek to get rid of their genitals and live in the opposite sex role. *Sex-reassignment operations* provide some relief for this most distressing condition.
3. The second deepest layer is *sexual orientation,* that is, whether you are sexually attracted to men or women. One's erotic and masturbatory fantasies reveal one's sexual orientation.
4. *Sexual preference* is the next layer of human sexuality, dealing with the persons, parts of the body, and situations that are the objects of sexual fantasy and arousal. When the object impairs an affectionate erotic relationship with another consenting human being, the line between normal and disordered sexual preference has been crossed.
5. The *paraphilias* consist of sexual desire for unusual and bizarre objects. Three categories are: sexual arousal to nonhuman objects—most commonly *fetishes* and *transvestism;* sexual arousal in situations that produce suffering and humiliation—*sadomasochism;* and sexual arousal with nonconsenting partners—*exhibitionism, voyeurism, telephone scatologia, frotteurism,* and *pedophilia.* The paraphilias are often lifelong, and they may have their origin in *cathexes,* or emotional bonding, which is then reinforced and potentiated by masturbatory fantasies about the object. It is difficult to change the paraphilias in therapy, but recent behavior therapy techniques have had moderate success.
6. *Sex role* comprises the fourth layer. This is the public expression of gender identity, what an individual does to indicate that he is a man or she is a woman. There are no disorders of sex role. Although sex-role stereotypes are rigid in young children, they become more flexible as they mature.
7. The layer closest to the surface is *sexual performance,* how adequately an individual performs with a suitable person in a suitable erotic setting. The human sexual response is similar in both men and women and consists of three phases: *erotic desire and arousal; excitement,* which consists of penile erection or vaginal lubrication; and *orgasm.*

8. The *sexual dysfunctions* consist of impairment of desire, excitement, or orgasm. In women, these are manifested by insufficient desire, lack of excitement in sexual intercourse, and infrequent or absent orgasm. In men, there is lack of erection, premature ejaculation, and retarded ejaculation. All these conditions are quite treatable. The *direct sexual therapy* of Masters and Johnson, which uses *sensate focus* to treat couples, suggests that many of these sexual dysfunctions may be markedly improved in a short period of time. *Viagra,* a new medication, increases blood supply to the penis and thereby aids erection. It is is the treatment of choice for erectile dysfunction.

14

Substance-Use Disorders

Chapter Outline

Melissa Miller, *Smokey Spirits*, 1986.

Learning Objectives

→ Learn how substance use and abuse are affected by a society's attitudes, and how substance dependence is currently defined by both DSM-IV and WHO.

→ Be able to describe the basic effects of drugs, including the route of administration, how the drug reaches the brain, and drug-receptor-neurotransmitter interactions.

→ Be able to discuss the theoretical models of drug dependence, including the personality and psychodynamic models, genetic vulnerability, opponent-process theory, and learning models.

→ Learn about the psychological effects of alcohol, the stimulants, the opiates, the hallucinogens, marijuana, nicotine, and the sedative-hypnotics, and be able to describe various treatments for ending dependence on these drugs.

→ Begin to understand the biological effects of drugs, particularly the reinforcing effects, the neurophysiological changes caused by repeated drug use, and why this may contribute to the difficulty in ending substance dependence and the likelihood of relapse even after a period of abstinence.

→ Familiarize yourself with the social and medical complications connected with substance abuse.

→ Be able to discuss the pros and cons of the various proposals to combat drug abuse.

More than any class of disorders in DSM-IV, the abuse of substances is viewed as a social and legal problem, as well as a behavioral disorder. The federal government and every state in the Union have laws governing the use of alcohol and certain mind-altering drugs. Many believe substance abuse is one of the most serious problems facing our society. But the role of psychoactive drugs in contemporary society is very complex and often associated with highly charged, emotional debates. Are substance-use disorders "diseases"? Or, are they simply unhealthy habits that are a matter of free choice? In this chapter, we will consider several viewpoints on these controversial questions.

In discussing the substance-use disorders, we should keep in mind that drug use is not a new problem. Humans have used drugs for thousands of years to cure illness, alleviate pain, and relieve mental suffering. People have often sought, in the words of Shakespeare, "some sweet oblivious antidote" to the hardships of living (*Macbeth*). People use psychoactive drugs to alter their mental states; for example, such drugs can improve mood, cause euphoria, alter perception, or reduce anxiety.

It is also important to keep in mind that people with substance-use disorders frequently have other mental disorders as well. Substance abuse shows a high rate of comorbidity with personality disorders, depression, anxiety, and schizophrenia. There is often a developmental progression, with children who have conduct disorder beginning experimentation with drugs, then progressing to antisocial personality disorder and drug addiction. Although this developmental trajectory is more common among males, it can also occur in females. The following case history of Brenda illustrates the childhood origins of substance abuse:

Brenda was the second of three children born into a middle-class family. Her father was a sales representative for a furniture company and her mother worked part-time as a hair stylist. Brenda was a happy, energetic child who did well in school and had a broad circle of friends. At the age of nine, she won a state award for her skills in jazz dance. Her family and friends attended her performance and celebrated her award. When Brenda was twelve, she traveled with a group of girls to participate in a dance competition in another state. Her group came in second place. At a party following the competition, Brenda met preteens from many areas of the country. After she returned home, Brenda began to correspond with a boy named Randy, whom she had met at the party. Brenda's parents had some apprehension about her new friend, primarily because he was fourteen years old. But, they decided not to express their reservations. One year later, when Brenda was thirteen, Randy came to visit friends in her hometown. He phoned Brenda and invited her to a party. Her parents said she could not go, and Brenda became furious. She sneaked out of the house that evening to attend the party, and didn't return until 2:00 A.M.

That evening marked the beginning of a series of behavior problems. At fourteen, Brenda began to wear makeup and clothes that made her look much older than she was. She repeatedly violated her curfew, and her grades began to drop. One night she came home at 12:00 A.M. with alcohol on her breath. Her parents grounded her and limited her privileges, but nothing seemed to affect Brenda's behavior. When she was fifteen, Brenda stole money from her parents, and she began smoking marijuana.

Brenda's first experience with an illegal drug, marijuana, was preceded by use of a legal drug, alcohol. During this transitional period, there was an increase in her noncompliance. This is a very typical developmental pattern. But for most youngsters, the behavior problems begin to subside in late adolescence, and there is no progression to adult substance abuse. It is only a minority of teens who progress to drug addiction.

Drug Use and Abuse

In most societies, the moderate use of certain psychoactive substances, such as coffee or alcohol, is considered normal and appropriate behavior. At the other end of the continuum, addiction that leads to an inability to function in society is not considered normal. But at what point on the continuum does drug taking become inappropriate and maladaptive? How do we actually define drug abuse? These are difficult questions that have posed a considerable challenge to mental health professionals, and the definitions and diagnoses have changed over the decades. Like many psychiatric disorders for which there is no obvious physical abnormality or laboratory diagnostic test, what actually constitutes depen-

In American society today, drinking at a bar is considered normal and appropriate behavior for relaxing and socializing. Nonetheless, drinking alcohol becomes inappropriate and maladaptive when it leads to clinically significant impairment or distress and comes to dominate the person's life.

dence is somewhat a matter of opinion, and often controversial.

Identifying the signs of vulnerability to addiction has been a major goal of researchers. Theories and research on drug abuse have emerged from many fields of study, including medicine, psychiatry, psychology, law, and biology (Babor, 1990). Yet, there are many key aspects of drug-taking behavior that we do not understand, and many paradoxes in terms of the way our society views drugs. For example, it is generally accepted that nicotine is highly addictive, yet we probably would refrain from calling a smoker a drug addict. Alcoholism is one of the clearest examples of drug dependence, yet many people drink alcohol throughout their lives with no dependence problem.

There is no doubt that substance abuse is *the* major health problem in the United States. The costs to society in terms of death, disease, and injury are enormous, and the emotional toll on the lives of abusers and their families is immeasurable. Consider these staggering numbers: It is estimated that 11 million Americans binge drink (five or more drinks on one occasion) at least once a week; 62 million smoke cigarettes; about 7 million use smokeless tobacco; over 10 million smoke marijuana; 3 million abuse psychotherapeutic drugs such as tranquilizers, amphetamines, or sleeping pills; about 1.5 million use cocaine; 1 million use hallucinogens such as PCP or LSD; and almost 1 million, many of them teenagers, use inhalants (U.S. Department of Health and

Human Services, 1997c; National Institute on Drug Abuse, 2000b). So why do people risk their lives to abuse these substances? We will begin our exploration of this issue by briefly reviewing the historical background.

Historical Aspects of Drug Use and Dependence

Consideration of the historical and cultural aspects of drug use provides a useful framework for understanding current viewpoints on substance-use disorders. How a society views use of a particular drug has an important influence on how we might attempt to define addiction or dependence. As we mentioned, people have used mind-altering drugs for centuries for social, religious, medicinal, and recreational purposes. For example, opium has been used in various societies for over 3,000 years. In the nineteenth century in this country and in England, various opium preparations were widely available, and even used for "treating" children. Middle-class consumption of opium was very common, and its use was not considered a major social problem or an "addiction." It was only later in this century that use of opiates came to be associated with addiction, crime, and moral degeneration.

Hallucinogenic drugs have also been viewed in different ways, depending on the social context. Plants containing powerful hallucinogens have been used for religious, ritual, or ceremonial purposes by many societies (Schultes, 1987). Alcohol has also had mixed reviews, depending on the culture or the historical period. During Prohibition in this country, in the 1920s, manufacture and sale of alcohol was illegal. It was widely believed at that time that alcohol was associated with debauchery and weak moral character. Today, alcohol is not only legal and widely available, but it is also portrayed in the media as being associated with glamour, romance, and recreational pleasures. Addiction researcher Norman Zinberg emphasizes that drug-taking behavior can best be understood in terms of "drugs, set, and setting," meaning that it is the interactions between the chemical substance, personality or individual characteristics, and social setting that determine controlled use or compulsive, destructive use of a drug (Zinberg, 1984).

The concept of addiction has undergone considerable evolution throughout recent history (Marlatt,

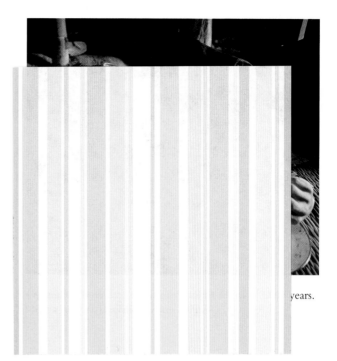

years.

1998). Central to the development of this notion has been the role of volition or "will" of the addicted individual and personal responsibility. Before the nineteenth century, addictions were generally considered as vice, sin, or moral failings. For example, people believed that excessive drinking was an undesirable "habit" over which the individual had final control and that drinking to excess was an individual choice.

In this century, the medical disease model of alcoholism and other drug addictions has been most influential (Kosten, 1998). The addict is viewed as a victim or patient with a disease, in need of medical or psychiatric treatment. Nonetheless, the disease theory of dependence has its detractors (Marlatt, 1998). For example, Stanton Peele has argued that the disease concept has actually caused addictive behavior to increase because it excuses uncontrolled behaviors and allows people to interpret their lack of control as the expression of a disease they can do nothing about (Peele, 1985).

DSM-IV Criteria

Traditionally, therapists determined if someone was "addicted" to a substance based on whether he experienced a physical withdrawal syndrome in the absence of the drug. For example, some years ago researchers believed that cocaine was not addictive because users experienced no apparent withdrawal syndrome when they stopped using the drug. Today,

DSM-IV Criteria

Substance Dependence

A maladaptive pattern of substance use, leading to clinically significant impairment or distress, as manifested by three (or more) of the following, occurring at any time in the same twelve-month period:

(1) tolerance, as defined by either of the following: (a) a need for markedly increased amounts of the substance to achieve intoxication or desired effect; (b) markedly diminished effect with continued use of the same amount of the substance;

(2) withdrawal, as manifested by either: (a) the characteristic withdrawal syndrome for the substance (refer to Criteria A and B or the criteria sets for withdrawal from the specific substances); (b) the same (or a closely related) substance is taken to relieve or avoid withdrawal symptoms;

(3) the substance is often taken in larger amounts or over a longer period than was intended;

(4) there is a persistent desire or unsuccessful efforts to cut down or control substance use;

(5) a great deal of time is spent in activities necessary to obtain the substance (e.g., visiting multiple doctors or driving long distances), use the substance (e.g., chain-smoking), or recover from its effects;

(6) important social, occupational, or recreational activities are given up or reduced because of substance use;

(7) the substance use is continued despite knowledge of having a persistent or recurrent physical or psychological problem that is likely to have been caused or exacerbated by the substance (e.g., current cocaine use despite recognition of cocaine-induced depression, or continued drinking despite recognition that an ulcer was made worse by alcohol consumption).

SOURCE: APA, DSM-IV, 1994.

---

physical signs of addiction are still important but not necessary for diagnosis. The DSM-IV criteria for psychoactive ***substance dependence*** emphasize clusters of symptoms or behavioral manifestations that clearly indicate distress or disability. These criteria reflect behavioral changes that would be considered as extremely undesirable in all cultures. There are three basic characteristics to this set of criteria: (1) loss of control over the use of the substance; (2) impairment in daily functioning and continued use of substance despite adverse consequences; and (3) physical or emotional adaptation to the drug, such as in the development of tolerance or a withdrawal syndrome. Thus, drug dependence can be defined by the "three C's": loss of **C**ontrol regarding drug use, **C**ontinued use in the face of adverse consequences, and **C**om-

DSM-IV Criteria

Substance Abuse

A. A maladaptive pattern of substance use leading to clinically significant impairment or distress, as manifested by one (or more) of the following, occurring within a twelve-month period:

(1) recurrent substance use resulting in a failure to fulfill major role obligations at work, school, or home (e.g., repeated absences or poor work performance related to substance use; substance-related absences, suspensions, or expulsions from school; neglect of children or household);

(2) recurrent substance use in situations in which it is physically hazardous (e.g., driving an automobile or operating a machine when impaired by substance use);

(3) recurrent substance-related legal problems (e.g., arrests for substance-related disorderly conduct);

(4) continued substance use despite having persistent or recurrent social or interpersonal problems caused or exacerbated by the effects of the substance (e.g., arguments with spouse about consequences of intoxication, physical fights).

B. The symptoms have never met the criteria for Substance Dependence for this class of substance.

SOURCE: APA, DSM-IV, 1994.

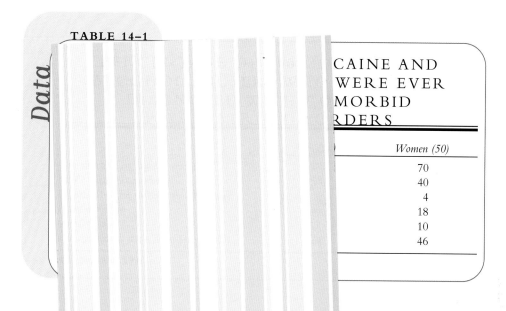

TABLE 14-1

Data...

...CAINE AND ...WERE EVER ...MORBID ...RDERS

	Women (50)
	70
	40
	4
	18
	10
	46

pulsion (or need) to use the drug (Shaffer and Jones, 1985). The criteria for *substance abuse* reflect a maladaptive, harmful pattern of drug use but do not include physical dependence.

As we have already noted, people who use psychoactive substances often have other disorders as well. Thus, substance abuse is comorbid with other psychiatric disorders (see Table 14-1). Depression and anxiety and substance abuse frequently occur in the same person. Moreover, most people who use street drugs also tend to abuse alcohol. Further, there is an increasing trend for several substances to be used simultaneously. For example, drug users may mix heroin and cocaine to make "speedballs," which produce a more intense sensation than either drug alone.

WHO Definition

The problem of defining drug abuse has also been considered by the World Health Organization (WHO) from the point of view of public health policy (World Health Organization Expert Committee on Drug Dependence, 1993). The WHO model was instrumental in formulating the "dependence syndrome" concept, which has gradually come to replace the terms "drug addiction" and "drug abuse." In 1981, the WHO committee defined the *dependence syndrome* as "a cluster of physiological, behavioral, and cognitive phenomena in which the use of a substance or a class of substances takes on a much higher priority for a given individual than other behaviors that once had higher value. A central descriptive characteristic of the dependence syndrome is the

desire (often strong, sometimes overpowering) to take drugs, alcohol or tobacco" (Edwards, Arif, and Hodgson, 1981). This model also emphasizes the high frequency of maladaptive behaviors, loss of control, and neglect of alternative pleasures or interests in favor of substance use. Incorporated into the WHO definition is the concept of *neuroadaptation,* in which the constant presence of the drug somehow induces long-lasting changes in the brain.

As is clear from both the DSM-IV and WHO criteria, modern concepts of drug dependence tend to emphasize the behavior of the individual and the adverse consequences of such behavior; they do not attempt to explain the dependence. These definitions fall within the framework of psychiatry and public health, and they reflect the current view of drug dependence as a medical problem or disease.

Basic Effects of Drugs

Many people have experimented with psychoactive drugs, yet only a small proportion goes on to become drug abusers. What are the factors that determine or contribute to the development of addiction? Why is relapse to drug use so pervasive, despite months or years of abstinence? Many individuals undergo detoxification and stop using drugs for an extended period of time, and yet they revert to drug use at some future point (Marlatt et al., 1997; Ott et al., 1999). Recidivism rates are high even among people who are motivated and have the resources to get treatment. Noted alcoholism researcher George Vaillant stated, ". . . to a remarkable degree, relapse to drugs is independent of

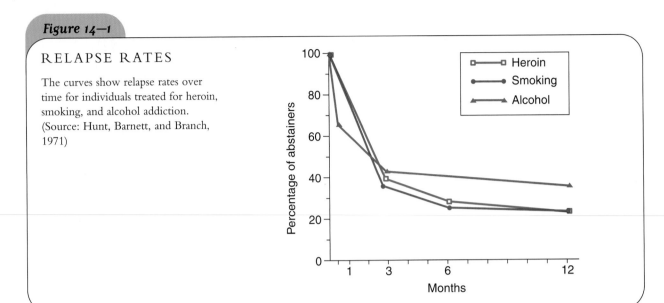

Figure 14–1

RELAPSE RATES

The curves show relapse rates over time for individuals treated for heroin, smoking, and alcohol addiction. (Source: Hunt, Barnett, and Branch, 1971)

conscious free will and motivation" (Vaillant, 1992). Figure 14–1 shows a remarkably similar pattern across a spectrum of addictive behaviors. Nearly 80 percent of people relapse following treatment, a rather discouraging figure. We will first discuss the basic effects of drugs, and then go on to an examination of theoretical models of drug dependence.

It is important to clarify exactly what we mean by the term "drug." A **drug** is any chemical substance that has the ability to alter a biological system. The drugs we discuss in this chapter are **psychoactive drugs,** which affect brain function, mood, and behavior. Although psychoactive drugs vary in their effects on the brain, they all share certain common properties and characteristics. Thus, the effectiveness and **potency** (the amount of a drug that must be given in order to obtain a particular response) of all drugs are influenced by: (1) the route of administration, (2) the ability of the drug to enter the brain, (3) how well a drug interacts with receptors in the brain, and (4) how quickly the body and brain adapt to the drug.

ROUTE OF ADMINISTRATION

For a drug to affect mental states, it must first reach the brain. All drugs are carried into the brain via the circulatory system, or blood supply to the brain. There are different ways that people take drugs to achieve this purpose (see Table 14–2). Understanding these different ways is important because very often the route of administration (how the drug is taken)

determines how much of the drug reaches the brain, how quickly a drug effect occurs, and in some cases, the actual subjective response to the drug. For example, in smokers, nicotine enters the body through inhalation. The surface area of the lungs is great and in close contact with the circulatory system. Thus, relatively large amounts of nicotine enter the blood, and hence the brain, rather quickly. In smokers trying to quit, nicotine gum is often ineffective in reducing the "craving" because oral delivery of nicotine does not produce the same subjective or physiological effects as smoking nicotine.

If a drug is taken orally, it must first pass through

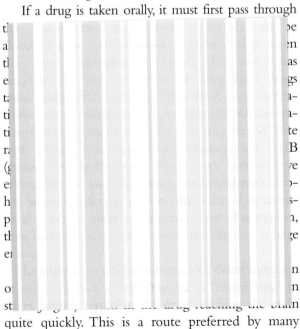

quite quickly. This is a route preferred by many

TABLE 14–2

COMMONLY ABUSED DRUGS AND ROUTE OF ADMINISTRATION

Substance	Trade or Street Names	Medical Uses	Route of Administration
Stimulants			
Amphetamine	Biphetamine, Dexedrine; Black Beauties, Crosses, Hearts	ADHD, obesity, narcolepsy	Injected, oral, smoked, sniffed
Cocaine	Coke, Crack, Flake, Rocks, Snow	Local anesthetic, vasoconstrictor	Injected, smoked, sniffed
Methamphetamine	Desoxyn; Crank, Crystal, Glass, Ice, Speed	ADHD, obesity, narcolepsy	Injected, oral, smoked, sniffed
Methylphenidate	Ritalin	ADHD, narcolepsy	Injected, oral
Nicotine	Habitrol patch, Nicorette gum, Nicotrol spray, Prostep patch; Cigars, Cigarettes, Smokeless tobacco, Snuff, Spit tobacco	Treatment for nicotine dependence	Smoked, sniffed, oral, transdermal
Hallucinogens and Other Compounds			
LSD	Acid, Microdot	None	Oral
Mescaline	Buttons, Cactus, Mesc, Peyote	None	Oral
Phencyclidine & Analogs	PCP; Angel Dust, Boat, Hog, Love Boat	Anesthetic (veterinary)	Injected, oral, smoked
Psilocybin	Magic Mushroom, Purple Passion, Shrooms	None	Oral
Amphetamine variants	DOB, DOM, MDA, MDMA; Adam, Ecstasy, STP, XTC	None	Oral
Marijuana	Blunt, Grass, Herb, Reefer, Sinsemilla, Smoke, Weed	None	Oral, smoked
Hashish	Hash	None	Oral, smoked
Tetrahydrocannabinol	Marinol, THC	Antiemetic	Oral, smoked
Anabolic Steroids	Testosterone (T/E ratio), Stanazolol, Nadrolene	Hormone Replacement Therapy	Oral, injected
Opioids and Morphine Derivatives			
Codeine	Tylenol w/codeine, Robitussin A-C, Empirin or Fiorinal with codeine	Analgesic, antitussive	Injected, oral
Heroin	Diacetylmorphine; Horse, Smack	None	Injected, smoked, sniffed
Methadone	Amidone, Dolophine, Methadose	Analgesic, treatment for opiate dependence	Injected, oral
Morphine	Roxanol, Duramorph	Analgesic	Injected, oral, smoked
Opium	Laudanum, Paregoric; Dover's Powder	Analgesic, antidiarrheal	Oral, smoked
Depressants			
Alcohol	Beer, Wine, Liquor	Antidote for methanol poisoning	Oral
Barbiturates	Amytal, Nembutal, Seconal, Phenobarbital; Barbs	Anesthetic, anticonvulsant, hypnotic, sedative	Injected, oral
Benzodiazepines	Ativan, Halcion, Librium, Rohypnol, Valium; Roofies, Tranks, Xanax	Antianxiety, anticonvulsant, hypnotic, sedative	Injected, oral
Methaqualone	Quaaludes, Ludes	None	Oral

SOURCE: Adapted from National Institute of Drug Abuse, 2000a.

heroin addicts. Other routes of administration include intranasal and intraoral delivery, in which the drug is absorbed through the lining of these tissues into the circulatory system. Chewing tobacco is an example of intraoral drug delivery.

REACHING THE BRAIN

All psychoactive drugs must cross several biological membranes before reaching their target, the brain. These biological membranes might include the stomach lining, nasal membranes, or capillaries in the lungs, depending on the route of administration. *Lipid (fat) solubility* is an important factor in whether and how fast a drug reaches the brain. Since cell membranes are composed primarily of fatty substances, a relatively more lipid soluble drug will be absorbed more quickly. For example, a small chemical modification of morphine results in heroin, which is considerably more lipid soluble than morphine. Heroin is preferred to morphine by opiate addicts because it reaches the brain more quickly and in higher concentrations. Certain general anesthetics are highly lipid soluble, reaching the brain and causing loss of consciousness within a matter of seconds.

The most important membrane or "barrier" that a drug must cross to exert a psychoactive effect is the *blood-brain barrier.* This barrier is composed of specialized cells that prevent particular compounds in the circulatory system from entering the brain. It allows certain drugs to pass through and affect brain cells, and excludes others, depending on the size and chemical characteristics of the drug molecule.

DRUG-RECEPTOR-NEUROTRANSMITTER INTERACTIONS

All psychoactive drugs have various effects upon neurotransmitter systems, the brain's chemical signaling mechanisms. One principal way for a drug to have a psychoactive effect is to mimic neurotransmitters and interact with neurotransmitter receptors. Receptors are complex protein molecules embedded in the membranes of neurons. Normally they help to conduct messages by recognizing a specific neurotransmitter much the way a lock fits a certain key (see Chapter 4). The neurotransmitter molecule activates the receptor and causes a biological response, either stimulating or inhibiting the neuron.

A neurotransmitter must be synthesized from building blocks such as amino acids. It then is stored in vesicles within the nerve terminal. When the neuron fires, it releases the neurotransmitter into the synaptic gap, where it can affect receptors on the postsynaptic neuron. After the neurotransmitter has its effect, it is removed from the synapse via two mechanisms: reuptake, which involves the neurotransmitter molecule being taken back up by the presynaptic terminal, and deactivation, which involves the breakdown of the neurotransmitter by enzymes. Psychoactive drugs affect the chemistry and activity of the brain by interacting with these mechanisms (see Figure 14–2), although different drugs have different effects. One way that a drug can influence neurotransmission is by interfering with the synthesis, or production, of the neurotransmitter in the nerve cell. Alternatively, the drug might interfere with the release of a neurotransmitter, or block the receptors on the postsynaptic neuron. Many drugs act by disrupting the reuptake or breakdown processes. For example, they can block the presynaptic receptor, leading to excessive amounts of a neurotransmitter remaining in the synaptic gap. Others can inhibit the enzymes that are responsible for eliminating excess neurotransmitter. In both cases, the end result is an "overactivation" of the neurotransmitter system.

NEUROADAPTATION: TOLERANCE AND PHYSICAL DEPENDENCE

Neuroadaptation refers to the complex biological changes that occur in the brain with repeated or chronic exposure to a drug (Crabbe, Belknap, and Buck, 1994; Self and Nestler, 1998). By their very definition, drugs induce some change in the neurochemical environment of the brain; one exposure to a particular drug will cause a specific effect (for example, increased levels of a particular neurotransmitter). However, with repeated exposure, the body and brain often adapt to the presence of the drug. Through homeostatic or "self-corrective" mechanisms, the nervous system attempts to compensate for the effects of the drug. *Tolerance* is one form of this adaptation. Tolerance refers to a state of decreased response to a drug following prior or repeated exposure to that drug. Progressively more drug is needed in order to obtain the same effect. Compared with inexperienced drinkers, people who regularly consume alcohol often show a high degree of tolerance to its behavioral effects.

Tolerance may be accompanied (although not necessarily) by *physical dependence.* Physical depen-

Figure 14—2

SYNAPTIC SITES OF ACTION OF PSYCHOACTIVE DRUGS

Drugs can cause neurotransmitter molecules to leak out of vesicles (A); crowd neurotransmitters out of storage vesicles (B); block release of neurotransmitter into the synapse (C); inhibit enzymes that synthesize the neurotransmitter (D); block neurotransmitter reuptake (E); block enzymes that degrade neurotransmitters (F); bind to postsynaptic receptors and either mimic or block the action of the neurotransmitter (G). (Source: Snyder, 1986, p. 15)

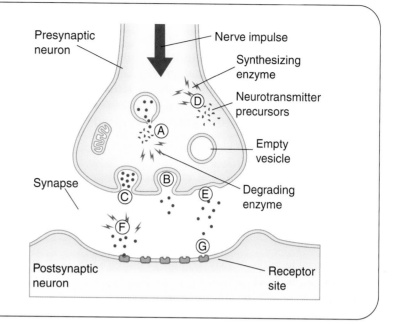

dence is characterized by the need for the presence of the drug in order to function normally, and by the appearance of a withdrawal syndrome upon cessation of the drug. The **withdrawal syndrome** (also called the abstinence syndrome) is usually characterized by observable, physical signs such as marked changes in body temperature or heart rate, seizures, tremors, or vomiting. Such a syndrome may occur, for example, following abrupt cessation of chronic heavy drinking. It is important to note that in some forms of dependence, such as that associated with cocaine or nicotine, the so-called withdrawal syndrome may not be easily observable; it may take the form of severe depression, irritability, or craving.

Brenda's early experience with marijuana provides an example of acquired tolerance to a drug:

Brenda's first experiences with marijuana were in social contexts, usually parties. After inhaling just a few times, she felt high and giddy, and she couldn't concentrate on anything. One day she smoked some marijuana when she was home alone, and within a few weeks she was smoking regularly at night before she went to bed. The effect wasn't as pronounced as it had been at first. Brenda felt relaxed, but she didn't lose her ability to concentrate. She decided to try it one morning before she went to school. The first time was a problem. Other students on the school bus noticed something was different about her, and they

asked her if she had had trouble sleeping the night before. But after a few more morning "highs," nobody seemed to notice. Brenda was confident that she could now smoke marijuana without having it affect her concentration. She had a sense of pride in "fooling" her parents and teachers.

Theoretical Models of Drug Dependence

There are many approaches, ideas, and theories pertaining to drug addiction, and in this small space we could not possibly discuss them all. But an overview of several theories or models that have been influential can provide a useful framework for understanding drug dependence. The most important point to keep in mind is that drug dependence is a complex phenomenon that results from an interaction of many factors. The goal is not to develop a single theory of dependence, but rather to understand as much as possible the psychological, social, and biological conditions that contribute to substance-use disorders.

PERSONALITY AND PSYCHOLOGICAL MODELS

For many years, it was believed that a so-called "addictive" personality existed. It was thought that substance abusers had some personality flaw that made them vulnerable to use and become addicted to drugs. Attempts to demonstrate an addictive personality empirically have not been successful. But considerable research has examined the comorbidity among substance-use disorders, as well as comorbidity of substance abuse with other disorders. Abuse of one substance is associated with an increased risk of abusing another substance (Kessler et al., 1997). Research findings are also very consistent in showing that virtually all of the other disorders in DSM-IV, including depression and schizophrenia, are associated with an elevation in the rate of substance abuse; about 35 percent of patients with a serious mental illness also suffer from substance abuse (Berry et al., 1995). But the most common coexisting disorder among male substance abusers is antisocial personality disorder (Hesselbrock, Meyer, and Hesselbrock, 1992; Myers, Stewart, and Brown, 1998). As described in Chapter 9, antisocial personality disorder is characterized by a pattern of irresponsible, destructive, antisocial behaviors beginning in childhood or early adolescence and continuing to adulthood. While the prevalence of this diagnosis is 2 to 3 percent in the general population, it ranges from 16 to 49 percent in studies of alcoholics and cocaine and heroin addicts (Gerstley, Alterman, McLellan, and Woody, 1990). Research has revealed a common developmental course in which conduct disorder frequently progresses to adult antisocial personality disorder in teenage boys who abuse drugs (Myers, Stewart, and Brown, 1998). It is clear that antisocial personality disorder is a risk factor for the development of alcoholism and other addictive disorders. It may be that such individuals are more likely to be exposed to drugs, to experiment with drugs, and to ignore their adverse consequences.

Psychodynamic views have also contributed to psychological perspectives on drug dependence. The general notion here is that drug use is seen as a means to compensate for defective ego functions (Khantzian, 1994). Early views tended to focus on "oral dependency" and libidinal drives, but more modern notions view addictions as an attempt to compensate for major deficits in ego development and affect. Thus, drugs are used to reduce painful emotional states or as a defense mechanism in relation to an internal conflict. According to one user's view, "Cocaine was a way of numbing out feelings. . . . Being stoned is like having a layer between me and reality, like doing things with gloves on. I dealt with emotions by avoiding them" (Shaffer and Jones, 1985).

Disruption of early life development, particularly regarding relationships to others, may increase vulnerability. The drug may help to dull the pain of loneliness. Need for drugs is also seen as reflecting "object deficits"; in other words, a lack of gratifying relationships with others. According to this view, the drug functions as an external aid or transitional object in order for the person to maintain a sense of well-being. If the person had little experience in developing positive relationships while growing up, relating intimately during adulthood can be particularly stressful. The use of drugs to cope with the anxiety associated with intimacy, especially during adolescence, has been noted by several theorists (Hendin, 1974).

GENETIC VULNERABILITY

People may be at risk for developing substance dependence because of biological factors that are inherited (Yates, Cadoret, and Troughton, 1999). Most of the evidence for this viewpoint comes from research on alcoholics (Guze, 1997). Children of alcoholics are four times more likely to become alcohol-dependent than people in the general population. This is true even for children who were adopted away from the alcoholic family into families with no alcoholism, suggesting that some genetic predisposition may be at work. Further, it appears that a generalized risk for substance abuse can run in families (Bierut et al., 1998). The biological relatives of alcoholics are at heightened risk for developing marijuana dependence, cocaine dependence, and habitual smoking, as well as alcohol dependence. Twin studies have also shown that substance abuse has genetic determinants (Vanyukov, 1999).

Of course, these findings do not mean that there are "drug genes" but rather that certain complex genetic factors may determine a person's biological response to drugs. A study of cocaine use in twins illustrated this; genetic factors had relatively little to do with whether the twins tried the drug, but genetic factors were predictive of who became an abuser or cocaine-dependent (Kendler and Prescott, 1998).

We do not yet know what genes lead to vulnerability for drug abuse, but it is likely that the vulnerability involves abnormalities in certain neurotransmitter systems. In fact, one view of substance abuse is that it is a form of "self-medication": people take drugs to correct (unknowingly) some predisposing biochemical imbalance in the brain. Certain psychoactive drugs might alleviate the emotional distress associated with such states.

Within the past few years, researchers have begun to use molecular genetic techniques in studies of humans who are drug dependent. These techniques allow scientists to examine specific genes in humans or animals. To date, they have examined some genes that play a role in two neurotransmitters, dopamine and GABA (Franke et al., 1999; Gelernter and Kranzler, 1999; Sander et al., 1999). Thus far, the findings provide no evidence that these genes are involved in drug dependence. This area of research is in its infancy, however, and we can expect to see more studies conducted in the future. Further, we must keep in mind that behavior genetic studies of substance abuse indicate that environmental factors play a major role as well.

OPPONENT-PROCESS THEORY

The **opponent-process theory** of acquired motivation has strongly influenced notions of addictive behavior (Koob, Caine, Parsons, Markou, and Weiss, 1997; Solomon and Corbit, 1974). The idea of opponent process is based on the theory that systems react and adapt to stimuli by opposing their initial effects. Although the theory was meant to explain many types of acquired motives such as love, social attachments, thrill seeking, and food craving, it is particularly relevant to drug addictions. The theory is best introduced with an example—that of eating a potato chip. As we all know, it's difficult to "eat just one." After consuming one chip, the motivation to eat more increases. If the bag is taken away, the craving for more chips remains for a period of time and gradually dissipates. It is as though the pleasurable experience with one chip sensitizes feelings or needs that were not there before tasting the chip. The same phenomenon is true for psychoactive drugs. A desire or craving for a drug, which clearly did not exist before experience with the substance, increases with exposure to it.

The opponent-process theory attempts to explain this increased motivation to continue drug use. It is based on three important phenomena that are common to all drugs that produce dependence. First, the pharmacological effect of drugs following initial use results in a hedonic (emotional) state known as **affective pleasure.** Different drugs arouse different subjective states, but overall these states are associated with positive affect. For example, alcohol may provide a sense of relaxation and relief from stress, while cocaine may produce feelings of arousal and energy.

Second, with repeated exposure, **affective tolerance** develops. As we saw earlier, tolerance refers to the lessening of a drug effect with repeated exposure. Tolerance will develop to the affective, euphoric effects of the drug. With continuing drug use, the rush or pleasurable feelings will not be as intense as they were the first time. In order to achieve the same subjective effect, the user will need to take progressively higher doses of the drug. The third phenomenon, which is related to tolerance, is known as **affective withdrawal.** This state, which occurs when the drug is not taken, is the hedonic opposite of affective pleasure. For example, heroin produces feelings of euphoria and calmness, while withdrawal from heroin is associated with dysphoria (discomfort), panic, and anxiety.

The opponent-process theory is represented schematically in Figure 14–3. The positive emotions that are caused by initial drug use are termed Process A. The duration and intensity of Process A depend on several factors, such as dose, duration of action, and route of administration. Process A also stimulates a compensatory reaction or "after-effect," which is opposite to Process A, called Process B. There are many examples of compensatory reactions in biological systems. A neuron that is initially inhibited by a drug may increase its baseline firing rate with repeated exposures in order to overcome or neutralize the effects of the drug. When the drug is removed, the cell continues to fire at an abnormally high rate. In any case, the model assumes that the intensity of Process A diminishes over time and with repeated drug exposure, and that Process B grows in strength with repeated stimulation. The subjective experience of these two states produces what is called **affective contrast.** With continuing drug exposures, the negative, unpleasant state comes to dominate and contrasts sharply with the memory of the positive state. Despite the fact that little pleasure is now derived from the drug, the cycle of addictive behavior continues in order to achieve at least a steady-state or neutral level. This may explain why adolescents who try drugs at such an early age use drugs more frequently, escalate to higher levels more quickly, are less likely to stop using them, and are more likely to move on from marijuana to drugs like cocaine and heroin (Johnson and Gerstein, 1998).

The opponent-process theory is primarily based on the notion of negative reinforcement. It says that people continue to take drugs and become addicted to relieve the withdrawal craving associated with B

Figure 14—3

THE OPPONENT-PROCESS THEORY

This figure shows the standard pattern of affective dynamics, based on opponent-process theory. (A) The graph shows what happens after the first few stimulations; this is the standard pattern produced by a relatively novel unconditioned stimulus. (B) This graph shows what happens after many stimulations; this is the standard pattern produced by a familiar, frequently repeated stimulus. (Source: Solomon and Corbit, 1974)

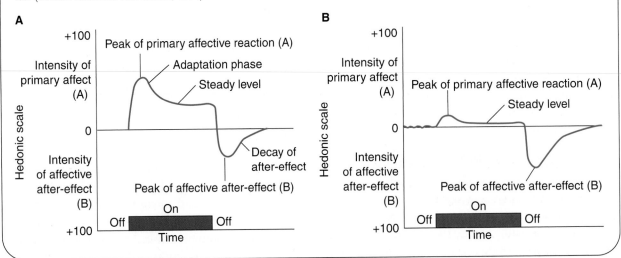

states. While the B state may be produced by fundamental biological changes that take place in the brain with repeated drug exposure, this theory does not explain the motivation to initiate drug use when no B state is present, or why many people (and animals) engage in controlled drug use.

POSITIVE REINFORCEMENT MODELS

The positive reinforcement models focus on the pleasurable, euphoric feelings induced by drugs and posit that these powerful rewarding effects are the primary explanation for drug use (Carroll and Bickel, 1998; Wise, 1998). These models were developed in the tradition of behaviorism and operant psychology. Many years ago, it was found that animals would make an operant response, such as lever pressing, to obtain an intravenous injection of a drug. In 1964, two researchers used this "self-administration" procedure and found that monkeys would reliably give themselves morphine (Thompson and Schuster, 1964). This was a landmark experiment because until that time researchers thought that drug taking was a uniquely human behavior, indicative of psychological or social stress. Soon after, it was observed that monkeys would

self-administer many of the drugs abused by humans: morphine, codeine, cocaine, amphetamine, pentobarbital, ethanol, and caffeine (Deneau, Yanagita, and Seevers, 1969). Most importantly, in that experiment it was shown that physical dependence was not a necessary condition for the animals to self-administer drugs. In the nearly thirty years that have passed since those experiments, a large body of research has confirmed that animals will self-administer nearly all of the drugs abused by humans, with the exception of hallucinogens. When given continuous access, the pattern of drug-taking behavior is remarkably similar for humans and animals. When given limited access, animals show stable self-administration without developing signs of toxicity or dependence. Such observations suggest that drugs are powerful reinforcers, even in the absence of physical dependence, and that a preexisting psychopathology or addictive vulnerability is not necessary for initial or continued drug taking (Jaffe, 1985; White, 1996). The self-administration model has been extremely useful for learning about the neurochemical systems involved in drug reinforcement.

The fact that many psychoactive drugs are powerful positive reinforcers raises the question of which brain systems are involved in their behavioral effects. For many years, behavioral neuroscientists have studied specific brain regions and neurotransmitters that may be involved in both natural (food, sex) and artificial (drugs, electrical brain stimulation) rewards. Perhaps not surprisingly, many of the systems that are known to mediate natural rewards are also those affected by reinforcing drugs (Caine, 1998; Koob and Bloom, 1988; Self and Nestler, 1998). In particular, a brain region called the nucleus accumbens and the pathways connected to it have received a great deal of attention (see Figure 14–4). This group of cells, located deep in the basal forebrain, receives input from limbic areas that process information relating to emotion and mood. One of the inputs contains the neurotransmitter dopamine. Drugs that cause strong euphoria, such as cocaine and amphetamine, induce a large increase in the amount of synaptic dopamine. This occurs in a number of brain regions, but the increase in the nucleus accumbens appears to be critical for the reinforcing effects. Several hypotheses emphasize the primary importance of dopamine in the nucleus accumbens, not only in the effect of the psychostimulants, but also in the effects of a wide range of addictive substances, including alcohol, opiates, nicotine, and barbiturates (Wise, 1998; Di Chiara and Imperato, 1988). In fact, it appears that alcohol, nicotine, marijuana, cocaine, and heroin all affect dopamine levels in the brain through a common pathway (Rodriguez de Fonseca, Carrera, Navarro, Koob, and Weiss, 1997; Tanda, Pontieri, and Di Chiara, 1997).

Wise (1998) proposes that all biological reinforcers (including many drugs) activate a common neural mechanism associated with approach, or appetitive, behaviors. Di Chiara and Imperato (1988) implanted a probe in a rat's brain that can measure the amount of neurotransmitter released from nerve terminals, while the rat is awake and freely moving. All the drugs of abuse they tested, despite belonging to differing chemical classes, were able to activate the nucleus accumbens's dopamine system. Other drugs did not produce such effects.

Although activation of dopamine may be a common property of many psychoactive drugs, other neurochemical systems may also play a role. For example, the brain contains its own "morphine-like" substances, termed **endogenous opioids.** There are several types of opioid compounds, such as enkephalins, endorphins, and dynorphins, which are found in various networks throughout the brain. These compounds are released from neurons and activate opiate receptors. Researchers believe that the opioid system also plays a fundamental role in biological reinforcement and affect. For example, opioids may regulate food intake and the affective response to sweet taste, and they are also believed to mediate the response to emotional and physical stress (Cooper and Kirkham, 1993; Jammer and Leigh, 1999; Kalin, Shelton, and Barksdale, 1988). Opiate (narcotic) drugs such as morphine and heroin undoubtedly produce their psychoactive

Figure 14–4

DRUG REWARD PATHWAYS IN THE BRAIN

The drug reward pathways (indicated in blue) are closely associated with the limbic system. The nucleus accumbens and the pathways connected to it mediate natural rewards and are affected by reinforcing drugs. (Source: Based on Bloom, Lazerson, and Hofstadter, 1985, p. 148, and Barnes, 1988, p. 416)

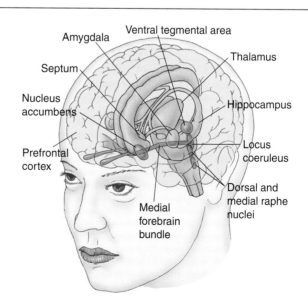

effects by acting on central opiate receptors, and alcohol may also involve the opioid system. It is interesting that opiate receptors in the nucleus accumbens may be particularly involved in the opiate "high." In animals trained to self-administer opiates, the reinforcing signal can be reduced or blocked by infusion of the opiate antagonist naloxone directly into this structure (Vaccarino, Bloom, and Koob, 1985). Although dopamine and opioids are leading candidates for modulating the reinforcing effects of drugs, it is important to realize that psychoactive drugs have complex effects on many neurotransmitter systems.

CONDITIONING AND LEARNING MODELS

Drugs bring pleasure and relieve the negative feelings that are produced by withdrawal. As a result, it is not surprising that the greatest problem in substance abuse treatment is keeping the individual abstinent. Weeks, months, or even years following successful detoxification, the patient may yield to uncontrollable drug cravings and may relapse. The conditioning and learning models provide a framework for understanding this aspect of substance dependence. These models embrace the notion that a drug is an unconditioned stimulus that becomes associated with many signals in the user's environment: sights, sounds, feelings, situations. These signals become powerful conditioned stimuli through their repeated pairing with the drug state, and they may contribute to the reinstatement of drug-seeking behavior.

The acknowledged father of conditioning models is Abraham Wikler (1973). At the Public Health Service Hospital in Lexington, Kentucky, Wikler was observing opiate addicts in a group therapy session. These particular patients had been free of drugs for several months, and there were certainly no signs of opiate withdrawal. But when the patients began talking about drugs, Wikler noticed that some of them began to show signs of withdrawal, such as tearing eyes, runny nose, sweating, and yawning. He labeled this phenomenon "conditioned withdrawal" and also noted its occurrence when the former addicts returned to neighborhoods where they had previously used drugs. Wikler suggested that through classical conditioning, environmental stimuli acquire the ability to elicit the signs of withdrawal. Moreover, these **drug cues,** or drug "reminders," induced craving for the drug as well and played an important role in triggering relapse.

There is much evidence, both from human studies and animal research, to support Wikler's theories. Charles O'Brien and his colleagues at the Addiction Research Center at the University of Pennsylvania have shown in the laboratory setting that presentation of drug-related stimuli to patients in treatment induces strong signs of physiological arousal and self-reports of drug craving (O'Brien, Childress, McLellan, and Ehrman, 1992). Their research suggests that conditioned cues elicit "drug-opposite" responses (perhaps similar to the B state in the opponent-process theory) that reinstate the overwhelming need for the drug. This may be true for a variety of psychoactive substances and situations. For example, passing a bar or arriving at a cocktail party may induce a strong desire for a drink (even in a social, moderate drinker), and the smell of smoke or sight of cigarettes can induce a strong craving for a cigarette in smokers trying to quit.

Learning processes may also govern animal drug-seeking behavior. Many years ago, Davis and Smith (1976) did an experiment in which rats were trained to lever-press for intravenous morphine. In some groups, the morphine delivery was associated with a stimulus (a buzzer). These animals continued to lever-press vigorously even when the morphine was no longer available, as long as their responses resulted in presentation of the buzzer. The conditioned stimulus was controlling the drug-seeking behavior. Physiological conditioned responses have been shown in many studies by Shepard Siegel and colleagues, in which the usual drug administration ritual is presented in the absence of the drug (Poulos, Hinson, and Siegel, 1981; Siegel and Allan, 1998). This work has demonstrated conditioned responses that are opposite in direction to the acute effects of the drug. For example, animals that have experienced repeated morphine injections, with their analgesic effects, show a conditioned hyperalgesic reaction (increased response to pain) during placebo testing. Animals that have repeatedly experienced alcohol-induced hypothermia display conditioned hyperthermia when given saline in place of alcohol. Siegel has labeled such phenomena drug-compensatory conditioned responses, and they have been shown to occur for many drug effects and many types of drugs. Such responses develop, as a kind of adaptation, in order to neutralize the pharmacologically induced homeostatic imbalance experienced in the presence of the drug. Cues that signal impending drug delivery can trigger these mechanisms. Drug-induced compensatory responses in animals may model conditioned withdrawal and craving in humans. Siegel also suggests that such mechanisms can explain drug tolerance, since the physiological effects of the drug would become progressively less.

Alcohol

Alcohol is a psychoactive drug with many of the characteristics of other drugs of abuse; it causes effects on the brain and behavior, and it has considerable potential for addiction and adverse consequences. In fact, if one excludes cigarette smoking, alcoholism is by far the most serious drug problem in the United States. For reasons that are probably social or cultural, we often do not classify alcohol as a drug. Our society accepts and even condones its controlled use. Alcohol has a long history of this "love-hate" relationship with human society (Ray and Ksir, 1987).

While in some societies, moderate alcohol drinking is considered by many as a pleasurable activity and an important part of certain social rituals, other societies or groups (such as certain religions) look upon it as an evil substance and ban its use. In American culture, odds are that fifteen of twenty adults drink moderately or occasionally, and two or three of those twenty drink to the point where their drinking is a problem or compulsive (Grilly, 1989; U. S. Department of Health and Human Services, 1997b). Since the use of alcohol products is so pervasive, it is important to take a close look at this substance.

Alcohol Use and Abuse

Most people who consume alcohol do so in moderation. They have one or two glasses, usually on social occasions. A minority engages in binge drinking. These are individuals who usually drink in moderation, but sometimes consume large amounts of alcohol. Binge drinking is often associated with special holidays, such as New Year's Eve, or events, such as fraternity parties. Although some people view this as harmless, binge drinking is, in fact, very dangerous. What begins as a festive occasion can end in the loss of life due to alcohol overdose and automobile accidents.

But the overwhelming majority of those who drink, even those who occasionally binge drink, do not become alcoholics. Who becomes an alcoholic? Well over half the adult U. S. population uses alcohol

Binge drinking is often associated with frat parties, as pictured here.

regularly, but only a small fraction of those people become dependent. In fact, half of all the alcohol drunk in this country is consumed by 10 percent of the population (Cloninger, 1987). The highest risk period for the onset of drinking that eventually leads to alcoholism is in the ten- to twenty-four-year-old age range. There is a significant sex difference, with higher rates among males than females. It appears that alcohol abuse has increased in the United States during the past four decades (Nelson, Heath, and Kessler, 1998). Yet, the gender gap is narrowing, due largely to a convergence in initial onset of drinking among young men and women, ages ten to twenty-four.

In the United States, there are significant differences among ethnic groups in the rates of alcohol use (Wallace, 1999). Overall, whites are more likely than blacks or Hispanics to use alcohol and report binge drinking. Ethnic group differences begin early. For example, among twelfth graders, 55 percent of white students, 49 percent of Hispanic students, and 35 percent of black students report having used alcohol in the last thirty days. For adults, thirty-five years of age and older, the figures for use in the past thirty days are 52 percent for whites, 47 percent for Hispanics, and 36 percent for blacks. In addition, there are sex differences in alcohol use for all ethnic groups: 28 percent of white men, 35 percent of black men, and 22 percent of Hispanic men report that they did not drink any alcohol in the year before the survey. In contrast, 36 percent of white women, compared with 48 percent of Hispanic women and 51 percent of black women report no alcohol use in the last year. Thus, in the United States, black women have the lowest rate of alcohol consumption of any subgroup. Although blacks and Hispanics also show a somewhat lower rate of alcoholism than whites, the differences are not as dramatic as they are for alcohol use.

The lower rates of alcohol use in black and Hispanic communities run counter to predictions that would be made based on known risk factors. In the United States, these two ethnic groups have higher poverty rates and are more likely to be exposed to various stressors than are whites. Poverty and stress have been shown to be associated with alcohol use. Moreover, there are proportionately more liquor stores in black and Hispanic communities, and liquor manufacturers direct a disproportionate amount of their advertising dollars at minority communities; black and Hispanic communities have significantly more billboards that feature liquor ads than white communities. So why is the rate of alcohol use lower in these communities, despite the forces compelling them to consume more alcohol? No one knows the answer to this question, but it is likely that subcultural traditions and institutions, such as the church, are playing a role in enhancing resilience in these communities.

The effects of alcohol differ in comparison to the effects of many other psychoactive drugs. Alcohol is not very potent, requiring several grams to exert measurable effects (most psychoactive drugs are effective in milligram quantities). A blood alcohol concentration (BAC) of approximately 20 to 50 mg of ethanol per 100 milliliters of blood is necessary for alcohol to have noticeable effects in most individu-

als. This would be equivalent to a BAC of 0.025 to 0.05 percent. A BAC of 0.1 percent is considered to be legally intoxicating in most states. Alcohol is consumed as a beverage and is absorbed through the stomach and small intestine into the bloodstream. The concentration of the alcohol is the primary factor in determining the rate of absorption, but other factors can influence the rate, such as food in the stomach or whether the alcohol is dissolved in a carbonated beverage. Food slows absorption of alcohol, and carbonation increases it. The amount of alcohol required to reach a particular blood alcohol concentration very much depends on the weight of the person and proportion of body fat. Alcohol is excreted in very small amounts in breath, urine, sweat, and feces, but the liver metabolizes over 90 percent. Chronic users often suffer from liver damage, because the liver spends so much time trying to metabolize the alcohol.

BEHAVIORAL EFFECTS

Most of us are quite familiar with the behavioral and subjective effects of alcohol. People have used it for millennia to stimulate feelings of pleasure and relaxation, to quell anxieties and worries, and to increase their sense of self-confidence and power. From the psychopharmacological point of view, the effects of alcohol on human behavior and performance are complex and depend on a number of factors, such as dose and previous experience with alcohol. At low to moderate doses of alcohol, most people experience a sense of relaxation and mild euphoria. Although alcohol is classified as a sedative-hypnotic drug, because of its obvious depressant properties, in low doses it can act as a stimulant. People become more talkative, more outgoing, and less constrained by social inhibitions. These effects are in large part due to disinhibition. When applied to behavior, the term "disinhibition" refers to a state in which people do things they wouldn't normally do for fear of adverse consequences. The behaviors that are released from inhibition depend on the history or personality of the individual. For example, a shy, reserved person may become gregarious, or a normally passive person may become aggressive or belligerent. As some of us unfortunately might know from experience, people may do or say things under the influence of alcohol that they would never do when sober. There is a close relationship between the blood alcohol level and the nature of

There are significantly more liquor stores and billboards advertising liquor in black and Hispanic neighborhoods than in white neighborhoods, as can be seen in this photo of an Hispanic neighborhood in Los Angeles, despite a lower rate of alcohol use in black and Hispanic communities.

When people drink alcohol, they often experience disinhibition of impulses they might normally control. *(Left)* This man who is drinking beer is wearing the box in which the beer was packaged. *(Right)* People may pass out and heavy drinkers may experience "blackouts" after periods of high consumption of alcohol.

the behavioral effects of alcohol. A colorful description of this relationship is provided by Bogen (as cited in Ray and Ksir, 1987):

At less than 0.03%, the individual is dull and dignified.
At 0.05%, he is dashing and debonair.
At 0.1%, he may become dangerous and devilish.
At 0.2%, he is likely to be dizzy and disturbing.
At 0.25%, he may be disgusting and disheveled.
At 0.3%, he is delirious and disoriented and surely drunk.
At 0.35%, he is dead drunk.
At 0.6%, the chances are that he is dead.

Higher doses of alcohol are associated with depressant effects and considerable impairment of sensory and motor functions. There are decreases in visual acuity and in sensitivity to taste and smell. Reflexes are slowed, and movement and speech may be sluggish. Reaction time is slowed by blood alcohol levels of 0.08 to 0.1 percent; complex reaction time tests, which require the subject to integrate information from several sources before responding, show that even at lower doses, both speed and accuracy are decreased (McKim, 1986). Memory processes are also disrupted by alcohol. Attention to stimuli, ability to encode new information, and short-term memory are all decreased. In heavy drinkers, "blackouts" may occur during periods of high consumption. As the name suggests, these are periods where the individual has no recollection of events surrounding the drinking episode.

DSM-IV Criteria

Alcohol Intoxication

A. Recent ingestion of alcohol.
B. Clinically significant maladaptive behavioral or psychological changes (e.g., inappropriate sexual or aggressive behavior, mood lability, impaired judgment, impaired social or occupational functioning) that developed during, or shortly after, alcohol ingestion.
C. One (or more) of the following signs, developing during, or shortly after, alcohol use: (1) slurred speech; (2) incoordination; (3) unsteady gait; (4) nystagmus; (5) impairment in attention or memory; (6) stupor or coma.
D. The symptoms are not due to a general medical condition and are not better accounted for by another mental disorder.

SOURCE: APA, DSM-IV, 1994.

CENTRAL NERVOUS SYSTEM EFFECTS

Alcohol produces a variety of complex effects on brain function. In contrast to most psychoactive drugs that have relatively specific effects at the synapse, alcohol affects many neurotransmitter systems and many aspects of neuronal function. It has long been known that alcohol has an effect on neuronal membranes (Goldstein, 1996). Its direct action on membrane proteins sets off a chain of metabolic events inside the cell that causes an inhibitory effect on neuronal activity by interfering with the ability of the neuron to conduct action potentials, thus reducing neuronal activity. The debilitating effects of high doses of alcohol on sensory and motor functions are largely due to this general depressant action. However, alcohol also affects a number of neurotransmitter systems, in particular, the biogenic amines (norepinephrine, dopamine, and serotonin) and gamma-aminobutyric acid (GABA). Alcohol's influence on these systems may be related to its mood-altering, reinforcing, and anxiety-reducing effects. For example, alcohol enhances the inhibitory actions of GABA, which is the most important inhibitory transmitter in the brain (Nestoros, 1980; Suzdak, Schwartz, Skolnick, and Paul, 1986). Alcohol acts at the same GABA receptor complex as the benzodiazepine anti-anxiety drugs, and it is believed that this action is responsible for the anxiety-relieving properties of alcohol (Larkin, 1998). Dopamine may also be involved in the rewarding and stimulant effects of low doses of alcohol. Dopamine levels in the nucleus accumbens are greatly increased in animals who have orally self-administered alcohol; moreover, in rats genetically selected for alcohol preference, this increase is much greater than in rats that do not like alcohol (Weiss, Lorang, Bloom, and Koob, 1993).

ALCOHOL TOLERANCE AND PHYSICAL DEPENDENCE

Tolerance develops to many of the effects of alcohol. In colloquial terms, someone who is able to "hold his liquor" is displaying tolerance to alcohol. There are several phenomena associated with tolerance to alcohol. The first is *metabolic tolerance,* in which the liver produces more metabolizing enzymes and breaks down alcohol at a faster rate. This mechanism does not account for most of the tolerance observed with chronic alcohol use, although it certainly contributes to liver damage. *Behavioral tolerance* and *cellular tolerance* are probably more important. Behavioral tolerance occurs when the individual learns to function under the influence of the drug. For example, there are some alcoholics who appear to work and perform activities normally at blood alcohol levels that would seriously impair most individuals. Behavioral tolerance can be demonstrated in laboratory rats. When given a motor coordination task (running a treadmill) under the influence of alcohol, rats quickly learned to overcome the disruptive effects of the drug. Yet, a group of rats given the same amount of alcohol after, rather than during, the treadmill sessions did not show any tolerance when tested under the influence of alcohol (Wenger, Tiffany, Bombardier, Nicholls, and Woods, 1981). Cellular tolerance, in which neurons adapt to the presence of the drug, can also be demonstrated. In the cerebellum, a region implicated in the motor-intoxicating effects of alcohol, neurons respond to intravenous alcohol by increasing their firing rate. But this pattern of activation returns to normal after long-term exposure to alcohol ends (Rogers, Siggins, Schulman, and Bloom, 1980). During withdrawal from alcohol, there is a marked decrease in the firing rate.

Physical reactions to alcohol develop quite rapidly. Anyone who has experienced a hangover after a bout of binge drinking is aware of this. True physical dependence, however, develops with prolonged heavy use of alcohol, and the severity of the withdrawal syndrome varies with the level and duration of drinking. As is true with most depressant drugs, the withdrawal syndrome can be quite severe and sometimes life-threatening if not treated. Symptoms usually appear eight to twelve hours following the last drinking bout. Early symptoms may include nausea, weakness, anxiety, tremors, rapid heartbeat, and disturbed sleep. In severe cases, the syndrome progresses to include hallucinations, disorientation, confusion, and agitation. In the worst cases, tremors, seizures, and severe delirium—known as **delirium tremens,** or the **D.T.'s**—may develop within two to four days. The highly aversive physical and emotional aspects of withdrawal are strong motivation for the dependent individual to resume drinking, thus setting in motion the addictive cycle. If left untreated, the syndrome will subside in about seven to ten days. But, in most cases, people undergoing alcohol withdrawal are given drugs to reduce the mortality rate and ease the symptoms. Several treatments, most prominently with the benzodiazepine drugs, are very

DSM-IV Criteria

Alcohol Withdrawal

A. Cessation of (or reduction in) alcohol use that has been heavy and prolonged.

B. Two (or more) of the following, developing within several hours to a few days after Criterion A: (1) autonomic hyperactivity (e.g., sweating or pulse rate greater than 100); (2) increased hand tremor; (3) insomnia; (4) nausea or vomiting; (5) transient visual, tactile, or auditory hallucinations or illusions; (6) psychomotor agitation; (7) anxiety; (8) grand mal seizures.

C. The symptoms in Criterion B cause clinically significant distress or impairment in social, occupational, or other important areas of functioning.

D. The symptoms are not due to a general medical condition and are not better accounted for by another mental disorder.

SOURCE: APA, DSM-IV, 1994.

---

successful in this regard (Holbrook, Crowther, Lotter, Cheng, and King, 1999; Mayo-Smith, 1997). Alcohol, paraldehyde, and barbiturates also relieve the withdrawal state at any stage (Hersh, Kranzler, and Meyer, 1997).

Defining Alcoholism

It is well recognized that alcoholism is a leading public health problem in the United States and in many parts of the world. But defining alcoholism is not easy. Excessive alcohol intake follows many different patterns. We would all agree that the man who drinks to drunkenness every day, loses his job, suffers from liver problems, and experiences delirium tremens if he does not drink is an alcoholic. But what about the high-powered, successful executive who has several martinis at business lunches and several more in the evening? Or the student who binge drinks every weekend but abstains during the week? Although there is no perfect definition of alcoholism, clinicians and researchers have tried to develop objective diagnostic criteria that attempt to encompass these different patterns of behavior.

The diagnosis for alcoholism is based on the DSM-IV criteria for substance dependence. In general, the individual diagnosed as an alcoholic has been drinking heavily over an extended period of time, and has consequently suffered from major multiple life problems. There is often compulsive drinking and an inability to stop, despite repeated efforts. Consumption is high and can exceed a fifth of liquor or its equivalent in wine or beer. Alcohol dependence can range from mild to severe.

If there is recurrent drinking with adverse consequences, but the symptoms have not met the criteria for dependence (for example, no evidence of withdrawal or compulsive use), a diagnosis of alcohol abuse may be given. Lillian Roth's personal account illustrates the pervasive loss of control and physical dependence that characterize excessive drinking (cited in Orford, 1985):

> Although beer by day and liquor by night satisfied me while I [had been] busy . . . , now my nerves demanded more. I switched from morning beer to a jigger of liquor first thing after I awoke. It seemed a good formula. I improved upon it by pouring two ounces of bourbon into my breakfast orange juice so [my husband] was none the wiser. . . . I realized that I could never go out of the house again without liquor. Orange juice and bourbon in the morning was not enough. The physical demand was growing. I would need liquor most often—not because I wanted it, but because my nerves required it. Soon I was slipping down doorways, vanishing into ladies rooms, anywhere I could gain privacy, to take a swift drink . . . the two-ounce bottles graduated to six-ounce, and then to a pint, and in the last years of my marriage . . . wherever I went, I carried a fifth of liquor in my bag. (Source: Roth, 1954)

Etiology of Alcoholism

There are many theories about the etiology of alcoholism. We can begin with the caveat that there is no one environment, upbringing, personality, or gene that causes alcoholism. Alcoholism is found in all socioeconomic classes and in all walks of life. As in all substance dependence, the development of pathological alcohol-related behavior is the result of the interaction of many factors. Research focuses on vulnerability factors that predispose an individual to alcoholism.

BIOLOGICAL VULNERABILITY TO ALCOHOLISM

There is strong evidence that alcoholism is a genetically influenced disorder (Guze, 1997). It has been known since the nineteenth century that alcoholism runs in families. In this century, over 100 studies have shown that alcoholism is three to five times as frequent in the parents, siblings, and children of alcoholics as in the general population (Cotton, 1979). In addition, the risk for other forms of substance abuse, including marijuana and cocaine, are much higher in the biological relatives of alcoholics (Bierut et al., 1998).

Research using other behavioral genetic methods suggests that the risk factor is a heritable trait. Twin studies provide evidence of the concordance rate being much higher in identical twins than in fraternal twins, although it never approaches 100 percent, suggesting that the heritability factor cannot be explained by simple genetic mechanisms (Prescott and Kendler, 1999). Adoption studies put any genetic hypothesis to the most stringent test, and here too the evidence is quite convincing. A study of Danish adopted-away sons of alcoholics revealed a rate of alcoholism at the age of thirty of 18 percent, compared with a rate of 5 percent in adopted-away control subjects, and the amount of alcoholism in the adopted children of alcoholics did not vary based on whether the adoptive parent was alcoholic or not (Goodwin, 1990; Goodwin, Schulsinger, Moller, Hermansen, and Winokur, 1974). A fourfold higher rate of alcoholism was shown in adopted-away daughters of alcoholic mothers (10.3 percent) than in controls (2.8 percent) (Bohman and Sigvardsson, 1981).

In view of the evidence for a genetic influence on alcoholism, researchers have attempted to identify a trait marker, or some observable indication of the genetic predisposition. For many years, Marc Schuckit and his colleagues at the University of California at San Diego have studied populations at high risk for alcoholism (Schuckit, 1987, 1998). This work is particularly compelling because the studies are of individuals who are at risk but who have not yet become alcoholic. The researchers analyzed reactivity to alcohol on a number of measures in two groups of subjects: those with a positive family history of alcoholism and those with a negative family history (no alcoholism). The subjects were carefully matched for other demographic, socioeconomic, and physical factors. The subjects were college-age, drinking but not yet alcoholic males, who were either sons of alcoholics or sons of nonalcoholics. The subjects were given alcohol at various intervals and were asked to rate the intensity of different aspects of intoxication, such as overall drug effect, dizziness, "high." Although both groups developed similar patterns of blood alcohol level over time, the sons of alcoholics rated themselves as significantly less intoxicated following drinking a moderate dose of alcohol than the men with no alcoholism in the family. Moreover, when alcohol was given to subjects before they took a psychomotor test, the alcohol produced fewer bodily effects in the sons of alcoholics than in the sons of nonalcoholics. When subjects are asked to stand still, with hands at sides and feet together, the amount of upper body sway is normally increased by alcohol. Men with the positive family history showed much less body sway changes induced by alcohol (see Figure 14–5). These results suggest that people at risk for developing alcoholism may need to drink more alcohol to experience the same subjective effects as people who are not at risk. A decreased sensitivity to low doses might make it more difficult for individuals to discern they are becoming drunk (Pollock, 1992; Schuckit, 1987).

To test the validity of these markers for alcoholism, it is important to show an association between the identified marker and the subsequent development of alcoholism. Utilizing a longitudinal design, Schuckit followed up the young men he had studied ten years previously (Schuckit, 1994, 1998). The men were now at the age of peak risk for alcohol dependence and abuse (average age thirty-two). Remarkably, it was found that a low level of response to alcohol at age twenty was associated with a fourfold higher likelihood of alcoholism in both the sons of alcoholics and the comparison group. For example, 56 percent of the sons of alcoholics with the low level of response developed alcoholism, compared to 14 percent of the men in this group who had highly sensitive alcohol responses. These results seem to indicate that a relatively low physiological and subjective response to alcohol may be a powerful predictor of future alcoholism.

More recently, Marc Schuckit and his colleagues have begun to search for specific genes that might be

Figure 14—5

REACTIVITY TO ALCOHOL

The curves show the responses to a low dose of alcohol (0.75 ml/kg of ethanol; indicated in dark red and blue) and to a placebo (indicated in light red and blue) for twenty-three matched pairs of sons of alcoholics and controls (sons of nonalcoholics). Both groups developed similar patterns of blood alcohol level over time, but (A) the sons of alcoholics rated themselves on a scale of 0 (none) to 36 (great) as feeling less intoxicated following alcohol consumption than did the controls, and (B) alcohol produced less body sway changes in sons of alcoholics than in sons of nonalcoholics. (Source: Schuckit, 1984)

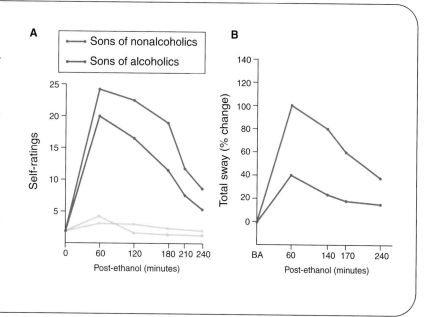

involved in risk for alcoholism (Schuckit et al., 1999). Using data from participants in their longitudinal study, they examined the genotypes of the sons of alcoholics. The young men who showed a "low level of response" to alcohol at age twenty and who later developed alcoholism differed from the others in their genotypes. These men showed a different combination of genes for two neurotransmitter systems: serotonin and GABA. This may indicate that the genetic vulnerability to alcoholism involves some abnormality in these neurotransmitter systems.

In fact, other evidence also suggests that serotonin plays a role in the effect of alcohol on the brain (Lappalainen et al., 1998; Lovinger, 1997). Serotonin may contribute to alcohol's intoxicating and rewarding effects, as abnormalities in the brain's serotonin system seem to be involved in the brain processes underlying alcohol abuse. Alcoholic humans and experimental animals that consume large quantities of alcohol show evidence of lower serotonin activity in the brain compared with nonalcoholics. They may unconsciously attempt to compensate for low levels of serotonin by consuming alcohol and thereby increasing the serotonin in their brain. Alcohol consumption affects the receptors that convert the chemical message from serotonin into changes in the neuron. Some of the rewarding effects of alcohol may result from the increase in serotonin activity that it produces. Moreover, drugs that act on serotonin

receptors affect alcohol consumption in both humans and animals.

Recent research with rhesus monkeys indicates that stress early in life may increase the biological risk for alcoholism; in monkeys who experienced early separation from their mother, there was evidence of low serotonin and behavior characteristics similar to those observed in humans with early-onset alcoholism (Heinz et al., 1998). These behavioral tendencies included greater aggressiveness and less sensitivity to alcohol-induced intoxication.

There is also increasing evidence that alcoholism is associated with an abnormality in the activity of the endogenous opioids (Ulm, Volpicelli, and Volpicelli, 1995). One of the effects of consuming alcohol is an increase in the release of endogenous opioids, which often leads to an improvement in mood, and this is believed to contribute to its appeal. People may consume alcohol to make up for a low level of endogenous opioids. In one study of people from families that had a high rate of alcoholism, researchers found evidence suggesting lower levels of endogenous opioid activity (Wand, Mangold, El Deiry, McCaul, and Hoover, 1998). This low level of endogenous opioids may be genetically determined. But, as the authors of this study point out, exposure to stress can also reduce brain opioid release. It is certainly reasonable to assume that people who grow up in families with a high rate of alcoholism are exposed to more stress. So, the similarities among family members may be increased by environmental factors.

People who are at risk for alcoholism may show subtle physical signs of nervous system abnormality before they even begin drinking. EEG irregularities have been found in sons of alcoholics, even preadolescent boys, before they have ever had a drink (Begleiter, Porjesz, Bihari, and Kissen, 1984; Ehlers and Schuckit, 1990; Finn and Justus, 1999). Similarly, children of alcoholic fathers show a more persistent physiological response to a startling stimulus than do children of nonalcoholic fathers (Grillon, Dierker, and Merikangas, 1997). It is possible that these markers are also indicators of risk for other forms of substance abuse. As mentioned previously, the family studies of alcoholism indicate that there is a generalized risk for substance abuse. Brenda's family history provides clinical evidence of this.

> In addition to being a daily user of marijuana, Brenda also drank alcohol on a regular basis. Most of the time when she drank, she was with other people. On rare occasions Brenda drank when she was alone. She also had friends who drank a lot at parties and sometimes got drunk. When she was seventeen, Brenda was stopped by the police one evening while driving a friend's car home from a party. She had been drinking and smoking marijuana. The police officers tested her blood alcohol level and discovered she was over the legal limit. Both Brenda and the officers were surprised, because she didn't seem drunk, although there was a noticeable smell of alcohol on her breath. She was given a citation for driving under the influence. Brenda's parents picked her up from the police station. They grounded her. She was required to attend classes on drinking and driving in order to get her license back.
>
> Brenda's parents were social drinkers, but neither of them ever had a drinking problem. However, they knew a lot about alcoholism because several paternal relatives had serious drinking problems. Brenda's grandfather suffered from alcoholism, and it led to a divorce from his wife. One of her uncles also abused alcohol; his drinking problem resulted in job losses and convictions for driving under the influence. The family history of alcoholism made Brenda's parents all the more concerned about her drinking. Their worry, as well as their disagreements about how to handle Brenda, put a strain on their marriage. They separated when Brenda was a senior in high school.

PERSONALITY AND PSYCHOLOGICAL FACTORS

Psychological studies of alcoholism focus on associations between psychological or environmental variables and the development of alcoholism. One major problem with evaluating psychological differences between alcoholics and controls is that many of the differences observed could be due to the effects of years of drinking, rather than the cause of alcoholism. Therefore, investigators have attempted to study what factors predate the onset of heavy drinking and may predispose the individual to alcoholism.

As is true for substance abuse in general, a diagnosis of antisocial personality disorder is a risk factor for the development of alcoholism, independent of having a family history of the disorder (Cadoret, O'Gorman, Troughton, and Heywood, 1985; Hesselbrock, Meyer, and Hesselbrock, 1992; Verheul, van den Brink, and Koeter, 1998). In addition, antisocial personality affects the age of onset, the course, treatment response, and relapse in alcoholism. In a large sample of alcoholics, individuals with antisocial personality were found to have had an earlier onset of drinking and a more rapid development of alcoholism once drinking began (Hesselbrock, Meyer, and Hesselbrock, 1992). The relapse rate is higher in these subjects compared with treated alcoholics without antisocial personality disorder.

Tension reduction has also been suggested to account for alcoholism. Some people drink to reduce anxiety or stress, and this can progress to abuse or dependence. Perhaps people who drink to excess suffer from high levels of anxiety or stress. Since alcohol

A diagnosis of antisocial personality disorder is a risk factor for developing alcoholism. This man may be comorbid both for alcohol and drug abuse and for antisocial personality disorder.

has clear anti-anxiety effects, this hypothesis has much intuitive appeal. For example, clinical observations reveal a strong association between anxiety and alcoholism, and patients with phobias report that they use alcohol to cope with the phobias (Mullaney and Trippett, 1982).

There is, in fact, mounting evidence that stress may contribute to, or trigger, the vulnerability to alcoholism. Stressful life events are associated with alcohol-use disorders in adolescents (Clark, Lesnick, and Hegedus, 1997). Among adults, work stress may be especially important (Schuckit, 1998). As mentioned above, research with rhesus monkeys suggests that early adverse life experiences may be associated with increased alcohol intake (Higley, Hasert, Suomi, and Linnoila, 1991). Monkeys who were reared in the absence of their mother (peer-reared) showed much higher levels of alcohol consumption later in life than monkeys who were reared by their mother. The peer-reared monkeys showed higher signs of stress such as increased plasma cortisol and increased fear-related behaviors. Moreover, acute stress (via social separation) in normal (mother-reared) monkeys increased their alcohol intake levels as well. This could represent a promising model to explore the environmental antecedents of alcohol abuse, including such antecedents in humans:

> Brenda took her parents' separation very hard. Even though she didn't get along with them, she had always felt that her parents were dependable and loving. Brenda believed they had misguided rules about drugs and were too strict, but she also believed they were there for her when she needed them. Now she wasn't so sure. Her mother was clearly somewhat depressed and didn't seem to have much energy. Her father had rented an apartment and only came around to visit with her on the weekends.
>
> Brenda relied on her friends for emotional support. She started to spend more time with Randy, who had moved to her hometown. She confided in him about her family problems. Most of the time, get-togethers with her friends involved smoking marijuana and drinking. When she was eighteen, a senior in high school, Brenda had her first experience with cocaine. Randy hosted a "pre-graduation" party in his apartment. By 1:00 A.M. some people were starting to leave, and Randy chided them about not having enough stamina to stay up late. He offered them some "coke" to help them "wake up." Everyone at the party, including Brenda, snorted cocaine. Brenda remained awake the rest of the night.

Clinical Subgroups of Alcoholics

Researchers have attempted to define clinical subtypes of alcoholics based on genetics, personality, development and family history, and clinical course of the disorder. Many years ago, Jellenek (1960) proposed multidimensional typologies of alcoholics, based on differences in drinking patterns and socioeconomic and cultural factors. Later theories of alcoholic typologies developed these early notions and incorporated the interactive effects of personality, genetic predisposition, psychopathology, and drinking patterns (Bohn and Meyer, 1994; Cloninger, 1987).

Cloninger reviewed studies of alcoholics that examined personality traits, antisocial behavior, criminality, and self-perception about alcoholics, and proposed two prototypic groups of alcoholics. Type 1 alcoholism affects both males and females (although women develop Type 1 predominantly), has an age of onset after twenty-five, and is associated with personality traits characteristic of persons with passive-dependent personality: high reward dependence, high harm avoidance, and low novelty seeking. This individual would typically be emotionally dependent, sensitive to social cues, apprehensive and inhibited, and not likely to engage in dangerous or disorderly behavior. Type 1 alcoholics can abstain from drinking, but they develop loss of control once drinking has resumed and feel guilty about their dependence. Analysis of adoption studies indicates that Type 1 alcoholism is "milieu-limited"; that is, its expression depends on both genetic predisposition and a family environment marked by heavy recreational drinking. Type 2 alcoholism is hypothesized to occur only in males, and is typified by personality traits opposite to those of Type 1: low reward dependence, low harm avoidance, and high novelty seeking. This individual would be impulsive, excitable, confident, and uninhibited, and would tend to be socially detached and tough-minded. The Type 2 alcoholic has problems with alcohol before the age of twenty-five, drinks heavily and cannot abstain, and typically has experienced physical conflicts, arrests, auto accidents, and other problems while drinking. The risk of Type 2 alcoholism is presumed to be high in adopted-away sons of Type 2 alcoholics, regardless of environmental background.

Recent research suggests that the majority of alcoholics do not fit these strict typologies. Although each person with alcoholism may show a predominance of Type 1 or Type 2 characteristics, there is overlap between the features of each subtype in many alcoholics (Sannibale and Hall, 1998). Moreover, there may be other subgroups with differing features; for example, developmentally limited alcoholism can occur in socially stable individuals during young adulthood, and alcoholism with depression can occur in women with a family history of mood disorder (Zucker, 1987). Although current subtyping schemes may have limitations, however, the acceptance of alcoholism as a disorder with multiple etiologies may contribute to better research on its causes and improved treatment (Bohn and Meyer, 1994).

Treatment

The goal of treatment for any drug addiction is prevention of relapse. Most alcoholics have tried to stop drinking and have remained abstinent for periods of time, but eventually relapse. **Detoxification** (the reduction and removal of alcohol from the body) is an important first step in the treatment process. This is usually done in a hospital or drug treatment center under medical supervision. Following detoxification, there is an active treatment phase. In general, rehabilitation for alcoholism utilizes the strategies employed to treat other behavioral or psychological disorders. These techniques may include psychotherapy, counseling, or behavioral therapy, often carried out in groups. Many programs emphasize the development of coping skills, enhancement of self-esteem, behavior change, and finding strategies to cope with the possibility of relapse (Friedmann, Saitz, Samet, and Glass, 1998; Grabowski and Schmitz, 1998).

COGNITIVE-BEHAVIORAL TREATMENT

The cognitive-behavioral model of treatment emphasizes three main strategies (Marlatt, 1996): skill training, cognitive restructuring, and lifestyle intervention (see Figure 14–6). Skill-training techniques include teaching the patient to identify and cope effectively with "high-risk" situations in which the loss of control or threat of relapse is increased. Examples of such situations are negative emotional states (depression, frustration, anxiety), social pressure, or interpersonal conflict. The therapist's aim is to instill a

Figure 14–6

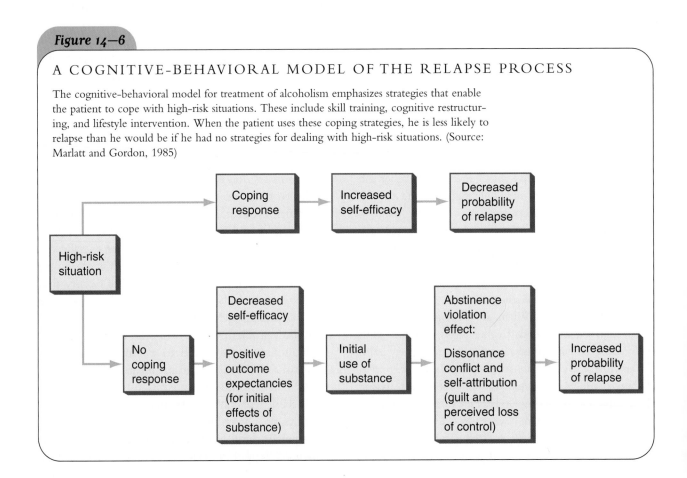

A COGNITIVE-BEHAVIORAL MODEL OF THE RELAPSE PROCESS

The cognitive-behavioral model for treatment of alcoholism emphasizes strategies that enable the patient to cope with high-risk situations. These include skill training, cognitive restructuring, and lifestyle intervention. When the patient uses these coping strategies, he is less likely to relapse than he would be if he had no strategies for dealing with high-risk situations. (Source: Marlatt and Gordon, 1985)

sense of mastery or perception of self-control in these situations. This notion of self-efficacy is described as a kind of "I know I can handle it" feeling. Cognitive restructuring involves changing the individual's perception of violation of abstinence, or a "slip." If a relapse does occur, instead of reacting to the lapse as a personal failure characterized by guilt and internal attributions, the individual is taught "to reconceptualize the episode as a single, independent event and to see it as a mistake rather than a disaster that can never be undone" (Marlatt and Gordon, 1985, p. 59). The principal goal of lifestyle intervention is to develop activities that offset sources of stress in daily life, or to replace negative addictions with "positive addictions," such as exercise, relaxation, or meditation.

Some alcoholics seek the support of the organization known as Alcoholics Anonymous (AA). AA is a self-help program that was started in 1936 by two recovering alcoholic men, and it has grown to be the world's largest self-help network. Throughout the world, alcoholics attend meetings of 36,000 groups in ninety countries (DuPont and McGovern, 1994). Its philosophy is based on experience gained through extensive work with alcoholics. AA views alcoholism as a progressive disease that cannot be controlled without the help of a higher being and the support of fellow members, and it believes that complete abstinence is required to deal with the disease. Education about alcohol and its consequences is provided, and testimonials of individuals with alcohol problems are shared.

DRUG TREATMENT

Another approach to the treatment of alcoholism is to use therapeutic drugs. Disulfiram (Antabuse) is a drug that inhibits the enzyme that aids the metabolism of alcohol. If alcohol is drunk in the presence of this drug, there is a buildup of acetaldehyde in the body and the person will feel very sick. The rationale underlying this treatment is that the fear of or prior experience with this unpleasant result will deter the individual from drinking further. It is frequently prescribed in treatment programs as an adjunct to therapy. Recent studies indicate that disulfiram can be helpful when it is used in conjunction with other forms of treatment under close supervision (Bonn, 1999; Tinsley, Finlayson, and Morse, 1998). But, it may only reduce drinking episodes, not increase abstinence (Garbutt, West, Carey, Lohr, and Crews, 1999).

Naltrexone is another medication that is effective in reducing craving and preventing relapse. Naltrexone is an opiate antagonist that blocks or reduces opioid transmission in the brain. When compared with other drug treatments, naltrexone is much more effective in reducing relapse and self-reports of alcohol craving (Garbutt, West, Carey, Lohr, and Crews, 1999; Volpicelli, Alterman, Hayashida, and O'Brien, 1992; Volpicelli, Clay, Watson, and O'Brien, 1995). The drug may actually reduce the motivation to drink, since it is even effective with recovering alcoholics who have one "slip-up," an occurrence that often leads to the resumption of binge drinking in placebo-treated subjects. These promising results suggest that endogenous opioids may play a role in alcohol-seeking behavior (Bohn, 1993). Moreover, they support experiments showing that opiate receptor blocking drugs reduce alcohol consumption in animals (Volpicelli, Davis, and Olgin, 1986).

In the past, lithium, a drug that is used to treat certain kinds of mood disorders, was also used to treat alcoholism. But recent findings indicate that it is not effective for most people who primarily have drinking problems (Garbutt, West, Carey, Lohr, and Crews, 1999). The same holds for the SSRI antidepressants, such as Prozac; although they are helpful for patients who suffer from both mood disorder and substance abuse, they do not appear to be effective in treating substance abuse alone. Of course, given the high rate of depression among alcoholics, there is often justification for prescribing the SSRI's for these people.

PROGNOSIS AND THE EFFECTS OF TREATMENT

What are the chances of recovering from alcoholism? The most extensive studies of alcoholism and its course throughout the life cycle have been conducted by George Vaillant, a Harvard researcher who has followed a group of over 700 individuals over fifty years (Vaillant, 1992, 1996). He has found, as have other researchers, that about one-third of alcoholics recover. He states a "one-third" rule for alcoholism: by age sixty-five, one-third are dead or in awful shape, one-third are abstinent or drinking socially, and one-third are still trying to quit. But Vaillant has also found that certain factors are strongly predictive of a positive outcome and recovery from alcoholism. These four factors are: (1) experiencing a strongly aversive experience related to drinking (for example, having a serious medical emergency or condition), (2) finding a substitute dependency to compete with alcohol use (for example, meditation, overeating, exercise), (3) obtaining new social supports (for example, an appreciative employer or new marriage), and (4) joining an inspirational group (for example, a religious group or AA). Vaillant finds a strong association between these factors and relapse prevention.

No specific psychosocial or drug treatment has been shown to be superior to all others, nor does any treatment "cure" alcoholism. Among patients who receive psychological therapies on an inpatient or outpatient basis, 40 to 70 percent resume drinking within a year after the treatment (Finney, Hahn, and Moos, 1996).

In the early 1990s, a group of researchers began to conduct a study of the effectiveness of several forms of psychological treatment for alcoholism. It was referred to as Project MATCH (Matching Alcoholism Treatments to Client Heterogeneity) (Project MATCH Research Group, 1998). In this study, three treatments were compared: cognitive-behavioral therapy; Twelve-Step Facilitation, a program similar to that used in AA; and motivational enhancement therapy, which focuses on changing internal motivations. All three of these therapies proved to be more effective than no treatment. Researchers also conducted studies to determine the effectiveness of various drug treatments. Several studies showed that naltrexone is much more effective than a placebo in reducing relapse to alcoholism (Garbutt, West, Carey, Lohr, and Crews, 1999).

Medical and Social Complications

The medical and social complications of alcohol use and alcoholism are extensive. Alcohol abuse is associated with a range of physical and mental health problems (O'Connor and Schottenfeld, 1998). There are about 100,000 deaths annually that are traced to alcohol abuse. The annual cost, in terms of treatment and lost productivity, is estimated to be about $100 billion in the United States. Drunken driving accounts for many motor vehicle deaths and injuries in this country. Alcohol intoxication is present in nearly half of all suicides, homicides, and accidents, and about 40 percent of all hospital admissions are alcohol related (U.S. Department of Health and Human Services, 1997b). Binge drinking, for example, seriously impairs functioning and can result in alcohol toxicity and even death. Cirrhosis of the liver, dam-

age to the nervous system, heart, and digestive system, and cancer are all associated with chronic alcohol use. Moreover, chronic use of alcohol in pregnancy can result in **fetal alcohol syndrome** in which the offspring has distinct physical and mental abnormalities. Sadly, fetal alcohol syndrome carries the costs of alcohol abuse to the next generation.

Stimulants

Although the **stimulants** amphetamine and cocaine are illegal drugs, stimulating drugs are also found in coffee, tea, soft drinks, cigarettes, chocolate, and in many nonprescription medicines. If one includes all of these sources, stimulants are by far the most widely used psychoactive drugs.

In recent years, even more over-the-counter medications have contained stimulants, including nasal decongestants, bronchodilators, appetite suppressants, and energy pills. The stimulants most often contained in these medications are ephedrine, pseudoephedrine, and phenylpropanolamine (PPA). Ephedrine and pseudoephedrine can be found in the Ephedra plant. Chinese physicians were among the first to discover the medicinal use of this plant, and its derivatives are common ingredients in sinus and asthma treatments.

Most legal, "over-the-counter" stimulants are alpha- and beta-adrenergic agonists; they stimulate receptors for norepinephrine. In doing so, they also increase heart rate and blood pressure, elevate mood, and decrease appetite. In the past, these drugs were also used to treat hypotension, asthma, heart block, depression, and narcolepsy, but they no longer are used to treat these problems. The following case illustrates the medical and psychological problems that can ensue from abuse of over-the-counter stimulants:

A thirty-three-year-old woman was admitted for inpatient treatment of stimulant dependence after an eighteen-month history of ephedrine use was discovered. She began taking two 25-mg capsules per day for appetite suppression. During the next year, her dosage escalated to approximately 60 capsules per day. She maintained her supply by purchasing ephedrine over the counter and by stealing it from work, which eventually led to her termination. Her numerous attempts to discontinue use of ephedrine failed because of rebound somnolence and fatigue. This interfered with her ability to complete household and childcare duties. Her symptoms included insomnia and irritability, increased tolerance to the drug, and an inability to abstain from using the drug. She hid her stimulant supply and was preoccupied with using the drug. She smoked one pack of cigarettes per week, rarely drank alcohol, and had experimented with cocaine and cannabis on two remote occasions. Both her psychiatric and medical histories were otherwise unremarkable. On admission, she appeared disheveled and slowed; she was emotionally labile but somnolent. Her blood pressure was 130/45 mm Hg. Her pulse was 135 beats/min and remained higher than 100 beats/min during the first 2 days of hospitalization. Findings on her physical and mental status examinations were otherwise unremarkable. Laboratory data, including a urine drug screen, were negative. (Tinsley and Watkins, 1998)

The most commonly used stimulants are amphetamine and methamphetamine. *Amphetamine* is a synthetic drug that was developed in the early part of this century as a treatment for asthma. In fact, it was a synthetic substitute for ephedrine. It was available for many years under the brand name of Benzedrine, in inhalant form for asthma. It was not until 1959 that the FDA banned the use of amphetamine in inhalants. By that time, however, the stimulant and euphoriant properties of the drug had become widely known. Various forms of amphetamines, known as "speed" in street jargon, became very popular in the 1960s hippie drug culture. With the rising popularity of cocaine as the preferred "upper" among drug abusers in the 1970s and 1980s, amphetamine use decreased. Amphetamine use increased again between 1992 and 1995 (Baberg, Nelesen, and Dimsdale, 1996).

Use of Methamphetamine

Methamphetamine is a synthetic, central nervous system stimulant of the amphetamine family. Known on the street as "meth," "crank," and "ice," methamphetamine is sold in a powder or rock form and is either injected, smoked, or inhaled. Methamphetamine is legally prescribed to treat attention deficit hyperactivity disorder and obesity due to the drug's ability to increase alertness, decrease appetite, and increase physical activity. Illegal consumers of this drug want to experience the effects of this drug on the central nervous system. Common to most amphetamine use, feelings of euphoria and exhilaration accompany

methamphetamine use. Side effects of methamphetamine include insomnia, hyperthermia, paranoia, depression, anxiety, and elevated blood pressure. Long-term abuse of the drug can lead to heart failure, stroke, and brain damage. In addition, prolonged use of the drug can also lead to symptoms that resemble symptoms of schizophrenia, such as auditory and visual hallucinations, repetitive behavior patterns, and anger and paranoia. Such psychological experiences can result in homicidal and suicidal thoughts. At the level of biology, there may also be changes; in rodents, repeated administration of amphetamines can alter the shape of neurons in the nucleus accumbens and frontal cortex (Robinson and Kolb, 1997). In particular, researchers found a long-lasting increase in the length of dendrites on neurons in the nucleus accumbens.

Law enforcement and treatment providers report that high school and college students, white blue-collar workers, and unemployed twenty- and thirty-year-olds are typical methamphetamine users (National Institute on Drug Abuse, 2000a; Koch Crime Institute, 2000). Methamphetamine use is prevalent in both urban and rural communities and is equally divided among males and females. Accounting for up to 90 percent of all drug cases in the Midwest, and coined the "poor man's cocaine," methamphetamine is less expensive and more readily accessible than cocaine. Over-the-counter cold and asthma medications, battery acid, antifreeze, and lantern fuel are a few of the ingredients used to illicitly manufacture methamphetamine in clandestine labs. Recipes for making the drug are easily accessed on the Internet. The initial investment in materials is small in comparison to the profits reaped through production and sale of the drug on the streets. Though less expensive than cocaine, methamphetamine's effects are longer lasting. Many methamphetamine binges may last up to a week, and many disturbances in mood and thought may be sustained for even longer periods of time. But like the high, the crash is also more prolonged. The devastating effects of addiction to methamphetamine are revealed in this poignant letter:

I am a current "ice" user. I had a loving marriage, beautiful son, great job and loving parents. I lost all but the job. My wife and I would smoke the rock together. Our son sleeping in the next room. At first, the thrill of being "high" together was the best. Sex would last for hours, awareness was increased and arousal was heightened. As time wore on our interest in each other decreased. My wife lost her job and refused to get another. She would rather stay home and smoke. I would spend my entire paycheck on drugs that wouldn't even last the whole pay period. I began sneaking some out of the baggie just for myself and she did the same. We came to the point that we would take turns watching the baby so the other could smoke in the bathroom. I lost 50 pounds in 4 months and my wife 40. People asked us what was our secret, like we were on an exclusive diet. We came up with a story that both could remember and stuck by that. We never communicated with our friends, lost interest in activities and mostly our son paid. He was the one who sat day in and day out in the house. I worked all day, high of course, and my wife smoked all day, did crossword puzzles, word finds etc., but never cleaned the house, washed clothes, fixed beds. I would have to call when everyone at work was eating lunch to remind her to feed our son. She lost total track of time. In the end, when all the dope was gone, the fights began. Who was going to sleep, who would cook, who spent all the money, who smoked all the shit. On holidays and birthdays we would not give presents, we would give each other a $50 paper (baggie). Fights became so intense that our neighbors looked at us funny and eventually steered clear. Our rent was way behind and the landlord started eviction papers. The car payment was due from five months prior. We had to hide the car so the repo-man couldn't take it. My wife is now gone, my son, I hardly ever see, the police was looking for me, I am broke, nearly living on the streets, and how this all started? Nine months ago a "friend" of mine offered me (and I can't handle marijuana) a couple of hits one day at work. With friends like that, you don't need enemies. Look what happened in nine months! D.P. Nov. 1999. (Source: Koch Crime Institute, 1999)

Use of Cocaine

Cocaine is prepared from the leaves of the coca plant, which grows wild and has been cultivated in South America for thousands of years. The custom of chewing the leaves by the native peoples of the Peruvian Andes dates back at least 5,000 years. The plant played an integral role in the Incan religious and social system, where it was considered a divine and highly prized plant. Incan corpses would have their cheeks stuffed with leaves, to "ease their journey to the next world" (Grinspoon and Bakalar, 1976). Cocaine was introduced into mainstream Western society in the last two decades of the nineteenth century, in various tonics, patent medicines, and remedies. In 1886, a Georgia pharmacist introduced what was to become the most famous drink of all time, Coca-Cola, which had extract of coca leaves. Cocaine's most famous proponent was Freud, who wrote extensively of its supposed virtues. He actually believed it could cure morphine and alcohol addiction! Not surprisingly, Freud struggled with a severe addiction to cocaine.

Since cocaine is the drug associated with the most medical problems and addiction, it will be the main focus of our discussion of stimulants. In the mid-1980s, the National Institute on Drug Abuse declared it was the greatest drug problem facing this country. From 1976 to 1986, there was a fifteenfold increase in the number of emergency room visits attributed to cocaine, in cocaine-related deaths, and in the number of people seeking treatment for cocaine addiction (Gawin and Ellinwood, 1988). In 1985, it was estimated that nearly 5.7 million people used cocaine. The number of people who had tried cocaine at least once in their lifetime rose from 5 million in 1974 to 22 million in 1985 and to 23 million in 1993. More recently, the estimate is that about 1.5 million people use cocaine regularly, suggesting a significant decrease in use between 1985 and 1996 (U.S. Department of Health and Human Services, 1997c). Nonetheless, the rate of cocaine use among young men is especially alarming, with 6 percent of boys between fifteen and nineteen years of age reporting cocaine use in the past year (Turner et al., 1998).

The Effects of Cocaine

Cocaine induces profound changes in behavior and psychological state as well as alterations in bodily physiology. It is administered in a variety of ways, but most commonly it is injected intravenously, snorted intranasally, or smoked in its free-base form ("crack"). Cocaine activates the sympathetic nervous system. It is a potent vasoconstrictor and increases heart rate and blood pressure. Cocaine may cause cardiac arrhythmias, which may have been the cause of sudden death in such cases as Len Bias, the basketball star who died of an overdose the day after he was drafted by the Boston Celtics. Cocaine also induces changes in mood and emotional state. In general, cocaine produces feelings of stimulation, well-being, vigor, and euphoria. Enhanced alertness, increased sexuality, heightened

DSM-IV Criteria

Cocaine Intoxication

A. Recent use of cocaine.

B. Clinically significant maladaptive behavioral or psychological changes (e.g., euphoria or affective blunting; changes in sociability; hypervigilance; interpersonal sensitivity; anxiety, tension, or anger; stereotyped behaviors; impaired judgment; or impaired social or occupational functioning) that developed during, or shortly after, use of cocaine.

C. Two (or more) of the following, developing during, or shortly after, cocaine use: (1) tachycardia or bradycardia; (2) pupillary dilation; (3) elevated or lowered blood pressure; (4) perspiration or chills; (5) nausea or vomiting; (6) evidence of weight loss; (7) psychomotor agitation or retardation; (8) muscular weakness, respiratory depression, chest pain, or cardiac arrhythmias; (9) confusion, seizures, dyskinesias, dystonias, or coma.

D. The symptoms are not due to a general medical condition and are not better accounted for by another mental disorder.

SOURCE: APA, DSM-IV, 1994.

energy, and deepening of emotions may accompany the cocaine high. In contrast to some drugs, cocaine does not appear to alter perceptual processes or distort reality. It has been said that cocaine and other stimulants produce a neurochemical magnification of the pleasure experienced in most activities (Gawin and Ellinwood, 1988). In his autobiography Malcolm X wrote that ". . . cocaine produces . . . an illusion of supreme well-being, and a soaring over-confidence in both physical and mental ability. . . ."

There have been some attempts to quantify the subjective effects of cocaine in a laboratory setting. These investigations allow careful observation and quantification of drug effects in a controlled clinical laboratory setting, while minimizing the medical risks of cocaine. Sherer (1988) studied addicts after they had taken an initial intravenous dose of cocaine, followed by a four-hour continuous infusion. The subjects conducted self-ratings of two mood states, "rush" and "high," throughout the session. This study found that ratings of "rush" and "high" were markedly increased by the cocaine infusion. But "rush" was associated only with the first dose of cocaine, reflecting perhaps the initial, rapid change in brain concentrations of cocaine. "High" was associated with feeling good and energetic, as can be seen in Brenda's case:

Brenda found her experience with cocaine to be exhilarating. She couldn't wait to go to Randy's and try it again. A few days later she went to Randy's apartment and snorted some more cocaine. When Brenda was high on cocaine, she forgot about her parents' separation, her problems at school, and her worries about the future. Nothing seemed to upset her. In fact she felt like she ruled the world. Brenda had never felt like this before. Cocaine became a part of Brenda's life at that point. During the summer after she graduated from high school she snorted cocaine at least once a week.

It is clearly the positive properties that attract people to cocaine and underlie its addictive properties. But cocaine can also induce negative emotional states and severe disruptions of behavior. High doses of stimulants can cause dysphoria and intense anxiety, and chronic use can result in hyperaggressiveness, complete insomnia, irritability, impulsiveness, and panic. Paranoid psychosis and violent behavior characterize cocaine intoxication in extreme cases. In the study by Sherer described above, nurses blind to experimental treatment made brief psychiatric evaluations of these subjects following cocaine injection and found increased paranoia and suspiciousness.

COCAINE AND REINFORCEMENT

Cocaine is a potently reinforcing drug. In fact, of all the drugs that are self-administered by animals and humans, it may well be the most reinforcing. The cocaine addict will engage in behavior that entails extraordinary risks to health and social stability. The extreme desire to obtain the drug has been shown in animal studies of cocaine use. Rats and monkeys rapidly acquire self-administration behavior when given access to intravenous cocaine via a lever-press

Figure 14—7

COCAINE SELF-ADMINISTRATION

The curve shows the pattern of cocaine self-administration in a monkey. The monkey self-administered the cocaine for a period of 21 days. The graph shows the intake for four-hour periods for days 14 through 21. Note the periods of intake and abstinence. Also note that the bingeing and crashing pattern is similar to the pattern of cocaine intake in humans. (Source: Deneau, Yaganita, and Seevers, 1969)

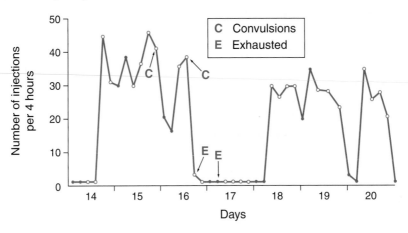

(see Figure 14–7). In fact, the pattern of drug taking strongly resembles the bingeing behavior in human cocaine addicts. In a classic study by Aigner and Balster (1978), monkeys who had previously self-injected cocaine were given a choice between food and cocaine every fifteen minutes for eight days. The animals almost exclusively chose cocaine, resulting in weight loss and other signs of toxicity. A similar result was found by Bozarth and Wise (1985) in rats; those given unlimited access to cocaine lost 47 percent of their body weight, ceased grooming, and exhibited a marked deterioration in health. By thirty days, 90 percent of the animals had died. (Rats given unlimited access to heroin, in contrast, administered the drug but did not show signs of deterioration.) Such unlimited access studies are no longer conducted for ethical reasons, but they clearly demonstrate the strong motivation that cocaine can induce.

In what is known as a "progressive ratio paradigm," an animal must make progressively more responses in order to obtain intravenous cocaine reinforcement. Researchers have shown that a monkey will make up to 6,000 lever-presses to obtain one infusion of cocaine (Yaganita, 1976). Thus, many animal studies have demonstrated that the rewarding effects produced by cocaine are indeed a powerful motivator of drug-seeking behavior. Moreover, past

studies with human volunteers have indicated that people consistently prefer to press a lever that delivers intravenous cocaine rather than placebo (Fischman and Schuster, 1982).

BIOLOGICAL MECHANISMS

Since the peak of cocaine use in the 1980s, researchers have confronted a fundamental question: What is it about cocaine's effects on the brain that makes it so rewarding and so addictive? Research suggests that cocaine and amphetamine are powerful activators of the brain's central reinforcement system. As we noted earlier, it seems that all drugs of abuse that are self-administered by humans and animals share an ability to activate dopaminergic synapses. While most of these drugs, such as alcohol, nicotine, and opiates, have many other significant pharmacological effects, with psychostimulants, activation of the dopamine system is the primary pharmacological effect. Moreover, release of dopamine in the nucleus accumbens appears to be directly linked to the rewarding properties of these drugs (Caine, 1998). For example, animals that have undergone lesions of the dopamine projection to the nucleus accumbens are not interested in self-administering cocaine or amphetamine. In view of the hypothesis that the nucleus accumbens may be critical for "natural" rewards (for example, food, sex, positive emotions), the notion that cocaine amplifies pleasure may actually have a neurochemical basis (Wise, 1998).

In an important study, Volkow and her colleagues used PET scans to determine what effect cocaine had on dopamine activity in the human brain, and how much of a change in dopamine was required to produce a subjective "high." The participants were healthy volunteers who regularly abused cocaine (Volkow et al., 1997). The researchers administered cocaine at doses commonly taken by people who abuse cocaine. They found that the cocaine significantly increased the amount of dopamine activity. Further, the intensity of the self-reported "high" was correlated with the degree of dopamine change. The time course for the psychological high paralleled the presence of cocaine within the brain regions associated with natural rewards.

The process of becoming addicted to cocaine as well as the persistent behavioral effects of cocaine appear to involve changes in the brain (Hope, 1999). Most experts in the field have long believed that the difficulty people have in overcoming addiction is much more complicated than a simple lack of willpower. Even young adults who are chronic cocaine users show reductions in mental and motor abilities over time, including impairments in motor speed and coordination (Bola, Rothman, and Cadet, 1999). These impairments persist for at least a month after the drug is last taken.

It is now known that repeated use of stimulants, particularly cocaine, can influence the expression of genes in neurons. Cocaine may turn certain genes on and others off. In doing so, cocaine can change the physical structure of the neurons and the way the brain transmits chemical signals. For example, research with animals has shown that cocaine increases the production of a certain protein, "delta-FosB," in the brain, and that this, in turn, makes the animal more sensitive to cocaine (Kelz et al., 1999). The limbic system, described in Chapter 4, may be especially susceptible to these disruptive effects of cocaine.

Cocaine Dependence

Before the 1980s, cocaine was considered to be a safe, nonaddicting drug. This belief existed for a number of reasons. First, cocaine was very expensive and its use was relatively infrequent. Second, there was very little research on cocaine abuse, and there appeared to be no overt physical symptoms that would constitute a withdrawal syndrome. The spread of "crack" cocaine in the 1980s changed this perception. Crack (solid, free-base cocaine) was much cheaper than powdered cocaine and became widely available, particularly to the poor. The smoking of the drug leads to a rapid, short-lasting but profound euphoria that is extremely addictive. It soon became clear that the criteria for substance-abuse disorder were easily met by users of cocaine. Compulsive use, loss of control, and a withdrawal syndrome began to be clearly recognized. Although cocaine dependence can occur with intravenous and (less frequently) with intranasal administration, it was the widespread practice of smoking crack that led to the cocaine epidemic of the 1980s. Further, although crack cocaine use was most widespread in low income, inner-city communities, it also devastated some middle-class families.

Gawin and Ellinwood (1988, 1989) have described distinct phases of cocaine use and dependence in detail. Early experiences with the drug result in increased pleasure in many daily activities, with heightened energy and alertness, increased self-esteem, and more positive social interactions. The upbeat affective state induced by cocaine, combined with the relative lack of negative consequences, makes such early cocaine experiences extremely seductive, as can be seen in Brenda's case:

Brenda was admitted to a four-year liberal arts college near her home. Her parents had wanted her to apply to colleges outside of the state, in part because they were worried that Randy was continuing to be a bad influence on her. But Brenda refused to even consider attending any out-of-state college; she didn't want to be separated from Randy, or from her supply of cocaine.

For the first two to three weeks, Brenda loved college. She found her classes stimulating and enjoyed meeting new people. As the work piled up, however, it became more stressful. She looked forward to the weekends when she knew she would see Randy and get high. One Saturday night some new friends invited Brenda to a party. The party was in a high-rise apartment building in the center of the city. Initially, most of the people at the party were college students, but as the evening progressed some residents from other apartments in the building began to drift in. Brenda started a conversation with a young man who lived in the apartment next door. His name was Matt. He invited Brenda to his place.

Brenda and Matt talked and drank wine alone for a while, then some friends of Matt's joined them. Matt's friends were very casual about the fact that they smoked crack cocaine. Brenda was shocked, although she tried not to show it. When they asked her if she wanted to try some, she said no. She had heard so much about how addictive crack was. In truth, she really did want to try it. Brenda loved snorting cocaine, but there wasn't any powder cocaine available. Brenda decided to smoke crack just once that evening, as a substitute for snorting.

It was the best high Brenda had ever experienced. All of her worries seemed to disappear. It was very intense. She felt almost giddy. She smoked crack two times that night, then returned home at 3:00 A.M. She kept thinking about the experience all day on Sunday. On Monday she went back to visit Matt. She had a lot of homework to do, but forgot about it after she smoked some crack.

With repeated use, the dose of cocaine is often increased, and the drug experience is intensified (Woolverton and Weiss, 1998). Eventually, the user focuses on the intense, euphoric, physical sensations produced by cocaine intoxication, rather than on the enhancement of normal, external activities. Pursuit of this state becomes so dominant that the user begins to ignore signs of mounting personal problems. The pattern of use at this stage is most often characterized by continuous bingeing, in which the individual repeatedly administers high doses of cocaine, followed by several days of abstinence. There is a complete preoccupation with the cocaine high and with obtaining more cocaine; ". . . nourishment, sleep, survival, money, loved ones, and responsibility all lose significance" (Gawin and Ellinwood, 1989).

A "triphasic" abstinence pattern generally follows a cocaine binge (Gawin and Ellinwood, 1988). The first phase is termed the "crash," which lasts from hours to days. The crash is characterized by a sharp decrease in mood and energy, agitation, anxiety, depression, and craving for cocaine. There is an extreme need for sleep, which is usually met by the ingestion of sedatives, alcohol, or opiates. The next phase, "withdrawal," can last for many weeks and is characterized primarily by an intense dysphoric syndrome in which the person experiences depression and anhedonia (inability to experience pleasure). These feelings contrast with memories of stimulant-induced euphoria and often lead to a repetition of the bingeing cycle. If the user continues to be abstinent, the third phase, "extinction," emerges. During this phase, normal mood and energy are restored. Nonetheless, the user may experience occasional cravings for cocaine for months or even years after the last binge. The cravings are usually invoked by stimuli or memories associated with the cocaine experience. If the user does not continue to be abstinent, a downward spiral usually ensues, and both the person's family and work life deteriorate, as can be seen in Brenda's case:

It didn't take very long for Brenda to become addicted to crack. Brenda started visiting Matt's apartment more often, and got physically involved with him. She was there at least four nights a week. She withdrew from all but one of the courses she was taking, in order to avoid getting failing grades. Brenda's mother asked to see her report card, but Brenda refused. She had earned three withdrawals and one "C." Brenda's mother sent for a copy of the tran-

---

DSM-IV Criteria

Cocaine Withdrawal

A. Cessation of (or reduction in) cocaine use that has been heavy and prolonged.

B. Dysphoric mood and two (or more) of the following physiological changes, developing within a few hours to several days after Criterion A: (1) fatigue; (2) vivid, unpleasant dreams; (3) insomnia or hypersomnia; (4) increased appetite; (5) psychomotor retardation or agitation.

C. The symptoms in Criterion B cause clinically significant distress or impairment in social, occupational, or other important areas of functioning.

D. The symptoms are not due to a general medical condition and are not better accounted for by another mental disorder.

SOURCE: APA, DSM-IV, 1994.

script. She was shocked to see the withdrawals and called Brenda's father. Brenda's parents decided that she would have to start working, at least part-time, in order to pay some of her living expenses.

After her dismal first semester, Brenda dropped out of school and got a job waiting tables at a pizza restaurant. When she got off work, she would go to Matt's apartment and smoke crack. Brenda would return to her mother's home early in the morning and sleep until she went back to work in the afternoon. Her mother tried to impose a curfew, but Brenda ignored it. In July, Brenda announced she was moving in with Matt. In hindsight Brenda views this move as the first step into a downward spiral. She and Matt started smoking crack during the day. Matt had already lost his job. Within a week, Brenda lost hers for not showing up on time. They lived off of a series of part-time jobs, and the money Matt made selling cocaine. Brenda's relationship with Matt grew more conflictual. He criticized her for not making enough money. When Brenda's parents came by Matt's apartment to try to find her, Matt pushed them out the door. Brenda was angry with Matt, but she didn't leave him.

Three months after moving in with Matt, Brenda started having sex with one of his friends for money. She felt ashamed at first, but gradually became desensitized. Matt didn't seem to care. He had become distant from her. In October, Brenda started working for an escort service. She smoked crack before going on a "date." When she returned late at night, she smoked some more. Her life had become a cycle of crack highs, depression, and more highs. In November Brenda was found badly beaten and unconscious on the street in front of Matt's apartment. She regained consciousness in the hospital with her parents at her bedside. Brenda was severely depressed and confused, and complained of severe stomach pains. She didn't know who beat her up, although her parents suspected it was Matt.

Tests revealed that Brenda tested positive for cocaine, had gonorrhea, and was undernourished. She was also pregnant.

Treatment

The obstacles to successful treatment of cocaine dependence are similar to those for other drug addictions. Although motivation to quit cocaine may be very high initially, relapse is a major problem, particularly in the period when depression and anhedonia are present. A number of different strategies have been tried in treatment programs, with varying outcomes. These strategies include pharmacotherapies as well as a range of psychotherapeutic techniques.

Many drugs have been used to treat patients who are addicted to cocaine, but none has been shown to have a significant beneficial effect for most abusers (Mendelson and Mello, 1996). Researchers have examined the effects of antidepressants, anticonvulsants, opioid antagonists (for example, naltrexone), and drugs that block or enhance dopamine activity. Although these medications have not proven to be effective in maintaining long-term abstinence, the antidepressants may enhance treatment compliance in abusers who are also depressed (Gawin et al., 1989). But there are a number of new drugs on the horizon that may prove to be effective in blocking the pleasure produced by cocaine, and thereby dramatically reducing relapse. One such drug is BP 897, which blocks the D3 subtype of the dopamine receptor (Pilla et al., 1999). In rats who are trained to self-administer cocaine, BP 897 dramatically reduces drug-seeking behavior. Another drug, ecopipam, blocks the D1 subtype of dopamine receptor. In a recent study, humans suffering from cocaine dependence were given either ecopipam or a placebo prior to receiving intravenous cocaine (Romach et al., 1999). Those pretreated with ecopipam reported less euphoria and stimulation from the cocaine, as well as less desire for more cocaine. Clinicians who work with cocaine addicts are eagerly awaiting the results of further research on these new medications.

Pharmacological strategies may eventually be helpful in achieving cocaine abstinence. In the meantime, counseling and intensive behavioral therapies are the mainstays for long-term success. Several approaches have met with success, including cognitive-behavioral therapy and group therapy (Crits-Christoph and Siqueland, 1996). One especially effective behavioral therapy involves contingency management (Higgins and Silverman, 1999). These programs emphasize behavioral contracting and incentives for involvement. They are supplemented with training in relapse prevention skills; counseling in alternative recreational activities; and counseling for employment, housing, financial, and legal problems. Researchers have found that cocaine abstinence is significantly improved when a friend or family member of the abuser also takes part in the contingency management.

In some contingency management programs, participants are given vouchers, contingent on cocaine-negative urine samples. The vouchers are exchangeable for retail items, or in some programs for doses of drugs that reduce craving. Research has shown that the use of vouchers enhances participation in treatment programs. In one study, cocaine-dependent outpatients were divided into two groups and studied over a twenty-four-week period (Higgins et al., 1993). One group received behavioral therapy based on the contingency-management approach. The other patients were the control group. Several times a week, patients' urine was screened for cocaine metabolites. If the urine was negative, the subject received points that were recorded as vouchers for future purchase of retail items in the community. The number of points increased with each consecutive negative urine specimen, or decreased if a positive specimen was noted. Individuals who remained abstinent for a twelve-week period could obtain nearly $1,000 worth of retail goods. This system was supplemented with the community reinforcement approach, in which a spouse, friend, or family member participates in counseling. The control group received standard drug abuse counseling based on the disease model of dependence. There was a marked difference in cocaine abstinence in the two groups (see Figure 14–8). The percentages of subjects in the behavioral and stan-

dard counseling groups who achieved at least eight and sixteen weeks of continuous abstinence, respectively, were 68 percent versus 11 percent, and 42 percent versus 5 percent. These results suggest that availability and emphasis of alternative rewards can increase the motivation of the user to abstain from cocaine.

Another treatment approach is based on the learning model of addiction. As discussed earlier, exposure to drug-related cues in the environment can trigger cravings and induce relapse even in long-abstinent individuals. These powerful drug-associated stimuli can elicit clear changes in physiological responses, such as in heart rate or skin conductance. When recovering addicts were exposed to cocaine-associated stimuli, an involuntary physiological response (lowered skin temperature) was induced. The aim of the treatment based on the learning model is to eliminate these conditioned responses through repeated exposure to drug-related stimuli in a safe, controlled setting. By repeatedly exposing the patient to cocaine "reminders" without cocaine, it should be possible to extinguish the conditioned responses (arousal, craving) that could lead to relapse (O'Brien, Childress, McLellan, and Ehrman, 1992).

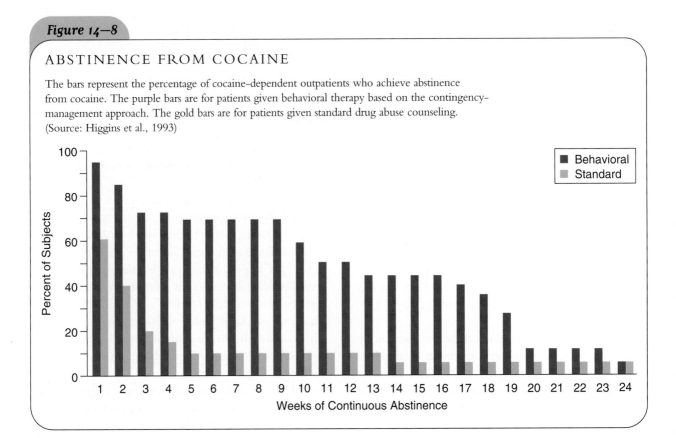

Figure 14–8

ABSTINENCE FROM COCAINE

The bars represent the percentage of cocaine-dependent outpatients who achieve abstinence from cocaine. The purple bars are for patients given behavioral therapy based on the contingency-management approach. The gold bars are for patients given standard drug abuse counseling. (Source: Higgins et al., 1993)

These researchers treated patients in the course of fifteen extinction sessions in which the subjects were exposed to audiotapes and videotapes of cocaine-related stimuli (for example, drug paraphernalia, someone shooting up) and engaged in a simulated cocaine ritual (for example, preparation of drug, handling of syringe). Over the course of the extinction sessions, the craving for cocaine was reduced. Although the physiological responses were also somewhat reduced by the last session, they were surprisingly resistant to extinction. There was a higher number of patients continuing with outpatient treatment and higher proportion of clean urines in the extinction group compared with the control groups (standard psychotherapy or drug abuse counseling).

For successful treatment of cocaine addiction, the cycle of dependence must first be broken. During the withdrawal phase, antidepressants or dopamine agonists may aid relief of depression. Behavioral therapeutic approaches may increase the motivation of the patient to stay abstinent. Extinction of the conditioned craving and physical responses elicited by drug reminders is also very important for avoidance of relapse. The treatment of Brenda's crack addiction involved all of these components.

> After being released from the hospital, Brenda returned to her mother's home and began a day treatment program. She was prescribed an antidepressant to deal with her deep depression and saw a drug counselor on a regular basis to help sustain her motivation. Brenda felt she could not cope with the prospect of having a child, so she decided to have an abortion.
>
> Brenda's parents and her counselor encouraged her to avoid all contact with Matt and their former circle of friends. Although Matt had been cleared of any involvement in Brenda's beating, the counselor was convinced that even brief contact with Matt would jeopardize Brenda's recovery. This was difficult at first, because Brenda's social life had revolved around Matt and his friends. Gradually Brenda reestablished connections with some of her former friends from high school.
>
> Reflecting back on her involvement with cocaine was very painful to Brenda. In hindsight it seemed like a bad dream, one in which she did things that ran counter to her basic moral principles. At the age of twenty she was searching for a way to rebuild her life.

Social and Medical Complications

Addiction to cocaine has had some far-reaching social consequences. A cocaine habit can cost up to $500 a day, and many addicts resort to illegal activities and crime to enable procurement. The crack epidemic of the 1980s was associated with a substantial rise in violent crimes, arrests, and family disruptions (see Box 14-1).

Many women addicted to crack become pregnant, often by exchanging sex for drugs, and they often abandon their babies in the hospital or leave them in the care of their grandmothers (Kenner and D'Apolito, 1997). There has been an increasing trend toward prosecuting women who use drugs, especially crack cocaine, during pregnancy. In July 1996, the Supreme Court of the state of South Carolina became the first to uphold the criminal prosecution of women for child abuse if they use illegal drugs while pregnant. But what if the woman is an addict? If drug addiction is viewed as a disease, then it might be argued that prosecuting pregnant women who are addicted is like punishing people for being ill. Yet, if

Crack cocaine's low price and easy availability have contributed to a range of social problems, including affecting the fetuses of pregnant women who continue to smoke crack while pregnant. This woman gave birth to twins, who were taken into a state agency's custody because the addicted mother was unable to care for them.

Box 14—1

Social Class and the Consequences of Cocaine Possession: Punish or Treat?

In April 1997, the U.S. Sentencing Commission issued its second report on federal policies for sentencing cocaine offenders (U.S. Sentencing Commission, 1997). The main focus of the report was the contrast in the severity of the penalties associated with the distribution or possession of the two forms of cocaine, powder versus crack. At the time, there was a five-year mandatory sentence for selling 500 or more grams of powder cocaine or 5 or more grams of crack cocaine. In other words, it took 100 times more powder cocaine as crack cocaine to result in the same penalty. While the simple possession of 5 grams of crack cocaine was punishable by a minimum of five years in prison, possession of any quantity of powder cocaine by first-time offenders was a misdemeanor punishable by no more than one year in prison. Why the difference?

When these guidelines were developed, lawmakers were convinced that crack cocaine was a much more dangerous drug than powder cocaine. Smoking crack cocaine has a more intense effect than snorting powder cocaine. Crack is, therefore, more addictive. In addition, there is ample evidence that crack cocaine distribution is associated with more crime and violence than powder cocaine trafficking. It seemed reasonable to implement harsher sentences for crack cocaine.

But there were significant social consequences to this policy. As would be expected, there are many more people in jail for selling or possessing crack cocaine than powder cocaine. Further, because crack cocaine is much cheaper than powder cocaine, it is the most common form of cocaine abused in low-income, minority communities. As a result,

almost 90 percent of those convicted for crack cocaine distribution are African Americans compared to less than 30 percent of those convicted for possessing powder cocaine. This has resulted in a dramatic increase in the proportion of African-American men in prisons. In addition, there was a difference in the treatment of crack addiction and powder cocaine addiction, creating great social class and ethnic disparities in the provision of treatment. Powder cocaine addicts were more likely to end up receiving treatment for their addiction, as opposed to punishment for their crime. The opposite was true of crack cocaine addicts. Thus, the form of the abused drug determined whether the person was viewed as a criminal or a person in need of treatment.

In its 1997 report, the U.S. Sentencing Commission proposed a change in the sentencing laws to reduce the difference between sentencing for possession of crack and powder cocaine. The members of the commission believed that maintaining different penalties was not fair or reasonable. In a concurring opinion issued with the report, the commission vice chairman, Michael Gelacak, suggested the following analogy: "It is a little like punishing vehicular homicide while under the influence of alcohol more severely if the defendant had become intoxicated by ingesting cheap wine rather than Scotch whiskey. That suggestion is absurd on its face and ought to be no less so when the abused substance is cocaine rather than alcohol."

The issue of differential sentencing for crack and powder cocaine continues to be the subject of heated debate. Changes in the federal laws are currently under consideration.

---

drug abuse is viewed as a bad habit that is under the individual's control, then the abuser should be held accountable for any damage she does to others, including her unborn child.

In large part, the negative social impact of cocaine is a consequence of its devastating effects on the user's sense of values. Access to the cocaine high becomes the central motivating force in the user's life; responsibilities and social commitments become meaningless. This may explain how addicts can abandon or abuse their children, engage in prostitution, or steal from family members.

The medical complications of cocaine use are considerable. Of course, the most serious adverse health consequence of intravenous cocaine use is the acquired immunodeficiency syndrome (AIDS). Shared needles contribute to the spread of the virus that causes AIDS.

This is a critical public health issue, because AIDS contracted in this manner accounts for the highest proportion of AIDS-related deaths in the heterosexual population. Cocaine addicts, especially those who use crack, often engage in sex to get money for drugs, thereby increasing risk for AIDS and all other sexually transmitted diseases. Should a crack addict who has HIV and engages in prostitution to support his or her habit be subject to criminal charges? It is certainly reasonable to argue that she is endangering the lives of others by putting them at risk of contracting a fatal disease. On the other hand, it can be argued that the individual who takes the risk of buying sex from a stranger should bear the responsibility for the potential health consequences.

Cocaine has numerous adverse effects on the mind and body. Heavy use can result in episodes of psychosis and paranoid behavior, profound irritability, and attention and concentration problems. As mentioned earlier, there is a decrease in cognitive and motor functions among chronic users. Sleeping and eating patterns may be disturbed, and weight loss is common. Panic attacks have been shown to be precipitated with cocaine (Aronson and Craig, 1986; Cowley, 1992). Because cocaine can have toxic effects on the heart, it can cause sudden death. Death may also occur by cerebral hemorrhage. This is particularly dangerous because the lethal dose varies considerably among individuals; some people may be very sensitive to the toxic effects of cocaine. Most of these mental and physical effects of cocaine can also occur with chronic use of any stimulant. Heavy use of stimulants by pregnant women may have negative consequences for the health of the fetus, although the long-term effects of stimulant use on offspring are not yet known.

The Opiates

The **opiate** drugs consist of a class of compounds that are extracted from the poppy plant *(Papaver somniferum),* including opium, morphine, and codeine, as well as synthetic derivatives such as heroin and meperidine (Demerol). Traditionally, this group of drugs has also been called **narcotics,** after the Greek word for stupor. This term was originally meant to distinguish narcotic analgesics, drugs that relieve pain and cause sleepiness, from non-narcotic analgesics such as aspirin. This term is somewhat misleading,

however, since many laypeople and law enforcement officials refer to all addicting, illegal substances as narcotics. For the present purposes, we will use the term opiate, which refers to any compound that interacts with opiate receptors in the brain.

Like many of the psychoactive compounds, opiates have long been used in human society. In fact, use of the extracts of the poppy plant for its psychological and medicinal properties may date back over 5,000 years. These substances have been known for their ability to relieve pain and suffering, and they have played an important role in many ancient cultures. References to opium use are found in the writings of early Egyptian, Greek, Roman, Arabic, and Chinese cultures. In the nineteenth century, opium became an important part of the pharmacopoeia in England and America. The primary active ingredient of opium is morphine, named after the Greek god Morpheus, the god of dreams. Morphine is still widely used for pain relief in medicine. Heroin is a semi-synthetic opiate made by adding two acetyl groups to the morphine molecule.

While the pain-relieving effects of opiates were much appreciated, the dangers and addictive properties only became clear as its use spread throughout society. As a result, in the early part of this century in the United States, opiate drugs became illegal except through prescription. **Heroin,** the most commonly used illicit opiate, is not available even by prescription in this country (it is in Britain in certain circumstances).

Heroin use is less common than marijuana or cocaine use, but there has been an increase in its use since 1992 (U.S. Department of Health and Human

Celebrities who died young as a result of heroin overdose: *(left)* Jimi Hendrix, *(center)* Janis Joplin, and *(right)* River Phoenix.

DSM-IV Criteria

Opioid Intoxication

A. Recent use of opioid.
B. Clinically significant maladaptive behavioral or psychological changes (e.g., initial euphoria followed by apathy, dysphoria, psychomotor agitation or retardation, impaired judgment, or impaired social or occupational functioning) that developed during, or shortly after, opioid use.
C. Pupillary constriction (or pupillary dilation due to anoxia from severe overdose) and one (or more) of the fol-

lowing signs, developing during, or shortly after, opioid use: (1) drowsiness or coma; (2) slurred speech; (3) impairment in attention or memory.
D. The symptoms are not due to a general medical condition and are not better accounted for by another mental disorder.

SOURCE: APA, DSM-IV, 1994.

Services, 1997a). The estimated number of people who report using heroin in the past month has increased from 68,000 (less than 0.1 percent of the population) in 1993 to 325,000 (0.2 percent of the population) in 1997. Heroin-related emergency room visits doubled from 33,900 in 1990 to 70,500 in 1996 (Greenblatt, 1997). In 1996, an estimated 171,000 persons used heroin for the first time. The number of new users, especially among youth, was at the highest level in thirty years.

Data collected by the Substance Abuse and Mental Health Services Administration in 1998 indicated that the use of heroin was increasing among middle-class suburban whites. Similarly, it has been documented that highly pure, smokable heroin is making its way through certain middle- and upper-class circles associated with the film, rock, and fashion industries (Gabriel, 1994). It has been suggested that heroin is now the "chic" drug among such people, much as cocaine was the cocktail of choice for the affluent in the early 1980s. Snorting heroin, as opposed to injecting it, is an increasingly common method of ingestion. It appears that young people erroneously believe there is a lower risk of addiction with snorting. This is problematic, however, because it may be increasing the rate of use. Nonetheless, injection is still the most prevalent means of taking heroin.

Effects of Opiates

Heroin was first made and promoted by Bayer Laboratories (the same company that makes Bayer aspirin) in 1898. It originally was marketed as a nonaddictive substitute for codeine. As use spread, however, it soon became apparent that heroin was the most addictive

of all the opiates. The minor chemical modification makes heroin much more potent than morphine, because it is more lipid soluble and therefore reaches the brain more quickly and in higher concentrations. Among the opiate addict population, heroin is the drug of choice. It is usually injected into the veins (intravenously), although it is also injected beneath the skin (which is known as "skin-popping"). When injected intravenously, heroin is absorbed very rapidly and reaches the brain in a matter of seconds. Subjective accounts by addicts of the heroin high or "rush" describe a warm flushing of the skin and intense sensations that feel like a "whole-body orgasm" (Jaffe, 1985). This initial effect lasts for less than a minute. Tolerance often develops to this euphoric effect of the drug. Opiates also can induce general feelings of well-being, calmness, and a sleepy dream-like state known as "twilight sleep." Feelings of anxiety, hostility, and aggression are reduced by opiates. Indeed, in addition to the pleasurable feelings they induce, the ability to blunt psychological pain may be an important motivation for taking these drugs.

PHYSIOLOGICAL EFFECTS

In contrast to certain other psychoactive substances, such as alcohol or cocaine, there are surprisingly few medical complications or toxic effects from long-term use of opiates per se. Death from overdose, which can cause respiratory depression, can occur from opiates, but this is actually relatively rare. In fact, most deaths among opiate addicts can be attributed to drug interactions or reactions to impurities or adulterants.

A number of physiological symptoms result from opiate administration, which is a consequence of the drug acting in several brain regions. The main physical effects these drugs have is to reduce pain perception. Opiates commonly cause nausea and vomiting, particularly with initial use. They also cause a marked constriction of the pupil, known as "pinpoint pupil." This sign is commonly seen in heroin addicts. Opiates slow the movement of food through the digestive tract and thus cause constipation. In fact, opiates have been used for thousands of years to treat diarrhea and dysentery, and they are still used for that purpose. Effects on the autonomic nervous system are more subtle than the effects of the stimulant drugs; there is not much effect on the heart, but the drugs do lower blood pressure and cause sweating. Although the initial subjective effect of heroin is likened to sexual orgasm, chronic use is associated with decreased sexual drive and sexual dysfunction. The most serious physiological effect is respiratory depression; although rare, respiratory arrest from an overdose may lead to death.

PHARMACOLOGICAL EFFECTS

The diverse effects of the opiate drugs on psychological and physiological functions are likely due to direct stimulation of opiate receptors in many areas of the brain. (Stinus, 1995). High levels of naturally occurring opiates, *enkephalins* and *endorphins,* are found in the forebrain regions mediating emotion and mood, as well as in lower brain stem centers controlling autonomic functions and pain transmission. The subjective, pleasurable effects of opiates may be caused by stimulation of opiate receptors in such limbic regions as the amygdala, nucleus accumbens, and hypothalamus (see Figure 14–9; Chang, Zhang, Janak, and Woodward, 1997). For example, researchers hypothesize that the reason animals readily learn to self-administer opiates via intravenous injection is because of reinforcing effects that are at least partially due to activation of opiate receptors in the nucleus accumbens. There is also evidence that the *endogenous* (naturally occurring) *opioids* modulate a variety of emotional experiences, in particular the response to stress. For example, exposure to stress increases the likelihood that rodents will self-administer heroin (Shaham and Stewart, 1995). Administration of opiates to infant monkeys suppresses the signs of distress observed when they are separated from their mothers (Kalin, Shelton, and Barksdale, 1988). But the desire for heroin is reduced by the administration of oxytocin, a brain neuropeptide that is typically released in animals when they have physical contact (Kovacs,

Figure 14—9

ENKEPHALINS AND ENDORPHINS

Distribution of enkephalin-containing neurons and opiate receptors in the human brain. (Source: Snyder, 1986, p. 57)

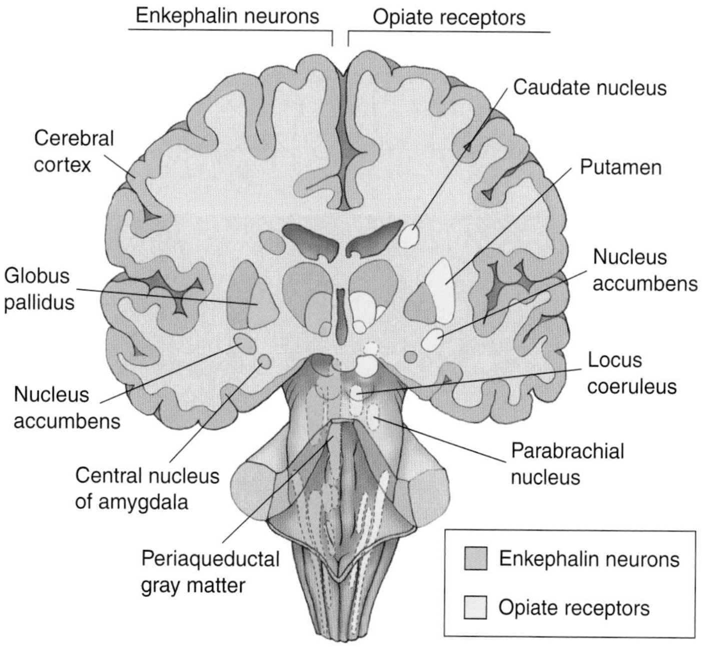

Sarnyai, and Szabo, 1998; Sarnyai and Kovacs, 1994). Thus, taking opiates may help to alleviate stressful psychological states by acting on the brain's own "coping" system.

Opiate Dependence

Opiate dependence may develop in susceptible individuals in a number of situations. One pattern of drug use begins with recreational or experimental use, usually with intravenous heroin. First use is often introduced or encouraged by a drug-using friend, and with continued use a compulsive habit may develop. In this case, the addict may need three to four injections per day, and obviously must obtain the heroin from illegal sources. Consequently, a great deal of time is spent trying to procure the drug. By far the most common group of users in this category are young males in poor, urban environments. Philippe Bourgois spent several years directly observing the culture of a group of homeless heroin addicts in a park in downtown San Francisco (Bourgois, 1998). He discovered an alarmingly high rate of risky behaviors, including daily sharing of drug paraphernalia, and illegal activity to generate income. The main focus of the lives of these addicts was on how to get more heroin. Yet, they had a code of conduct, and they showed a sense of loyalty to each other.

There are other patterns of use that are less common. For example, there is a small subgroup of addicts whose dependence began with medically prescribed oral painkillers, and who continue to obtain them somehow. Moreover, the incidence of opiate dependence among physicians, nurses, and other health professionals is higher than in people of similar background in other occupations (Jaffe, 1985; Trinkoff and Storr, 1998). These groups have easier access to the drugs and may start using them for a variety of reasons, such as relief of a physical ailment or to alleviate depression.

TOLERANCE AND WITHDRAWAL SYNDROME

Opiate dependence may be associated with a high degree of tolerance and physical dependence. With repeated use, the user needs to take a higher dose to feel the same effects. After continued use of fairly high doses, some users can administer doses up to fifty times what would kill a nontolerant individual (Grilly, 1989). But, tolerance develops to some effects of opiates and not to others. For example, a remarkable degree of tolerance may be exhibited to the respiratory depressant, sedative, analgesic, nauseating, and euphoric effects, while little tolerance is seen to the constipating and pupil-decreasing effects. Physical dependence is also classically associated with opiate addiction, and a withdrawal syndrome results when dependent individuals stop taking the drug. The degree of severity of this syndrome, however, very much depends on the type and amount of opiate taken.

There are several stages that characterize heroin withdrawal, which consists of clearly observable signs and symptoms that are generally opposite to

---

DSM-IV Criteria

Opioid Withdrawal

A. Either of the following: (1) cessation of (or reduction in) opioid use that has been heavy and prolonged (several weeks or longer); (2) administration of an opioid antagonist after a period of opioid use.

B. Three (or more) of the following, developing within minutes to several days after Criterion A: (1) dysphoric mood; (2) nausea or vomiting; (3) muscle aches; (4) lacrimation or rhinorrhea; (5) pupillary dilation, piloerection, or sweating; (6) diarrhea; (7) yawning; (8) fever; (9) insomnia.

C. The symptoms in Criterion B cause clinically significant distress or impairment in social, occupational, or other important areas of functioning.

D. The symptoms are not due to a general medical condition and are not better accounted for by another mental disorder.

SOURCE: APA, DSM-IV, 1994.

those that are produced by the drug. It starts approximately eight to twelve hours after the last dose, reaches its peak at about forty-eight to seventy-two hours, and completely subsides in seven to ten days. At first, the addict experiences restless sleep, followed by dilated pupils, irritability, loss of appetite, and tremor. At peak intensity, the individual experiences insomnia, violent yawning, excessive tearing, and sneezing. Muscle weakness and depression may be pronounced. Piloerection, resulting in "goosebumps," gives the skin the appearance of a plucked turkey; hence the expression "cold turkey" given to signify abrupt withdrawal. Gastrointestinal distress, characterized by cramps and diarrhea, is also apparent. Dehydration and weight loss may result from the failure to take food and fluids and from vomiting, sweating, and diarrhea. The syndrome can be immediately reversed at any stage by readministration of an opiate. Gradually, the acute phase subsides, although mild physiological alterations may be present for weeks. A common misperception is that the syndrome is always very severe and aversive; in fact, in most cases it is rarely life-threatening and seldom more disruptive than a bad case of the flu. Nevertheless, avoidance of the dysphoria that accompanies this state is an important motivating factor for continuing opiate use, although it cannot account for initial use or for relapse long after the syndrome has subsided.

DETERMINANTS OF OPIATE ADDICTION

It is not known what particular factors determine whether a person, once exposed to opiates, will become dependent. Nonetheless, heroin abusers do tend to come from families that are characterized by a low level of cohesiveness and support and by high levels of conflict (Knight, Broome, Cross, and Simpson, 1998). These familial tendencies are associated with an increased risk for antisocial behavior which, in turn, may eventually lead to heroin use and dependence.

As is true with all drugs with abuse potential, some people can experiment or be exposed to opiates and not develop a habit, while others become addicted. Many factors, including social environment, drug availability, and psychological state, may determine the pattern of drug use. Lee Robins conducted one of the most well-known studies of opiate addiction in the early 1970s among returning Vietnam veterans (Robins, Helzer, Hesselbrock, and Wish, 1977). Heroin was easily available, cheap, and 95 percent pure in Vietnam during the war years (compared with 5 percent purity in the United States). It was estimated that up to 15 percent of the American troops were addicted to heroin. When the servicemen returned home, however, the vast majority stopped using heroin. Researchers found that only 1 to 2 percent were using opiates eight to twelve months after returning. This study was very surprising because at the time it was believed that once exposed to heroin, compulsive use was inevitable. This was clearly not true. Opiate use may have relieved the anxiety, boredom, or unhappiness associated with the war situation; the need for the drug decreased, however, when the person was removed from that environment. Another example of controlled opiate use exists, termed "chipping" in drug jargon. Heroin "chippers" engage in occasional heroin use, much as one might occasionally smoke marijuana or drink alcohol (Zinberg, Harding, and Winkeller, 1977). These people may have stable lives, jobs, and families, but they may use heroin on weekends or with certain groups of friends.

Treatment

The problem of treatment for opiate addiction has challenged researchers and clinicians for many years (Brewer, Catalano, Haggerty, Gainey, and Fleming, 1998). Although some compulsive opiate users eventually stop drug use on their own, most chronic users need some form of treatment or therapy in order to overcome dependence. For the past thirty years, the primary treatment for opiate addiction has been pharmacological. This approach has involved substituting an oral synthetic opiate, usually methadone, for the intravenous heroin (see Box 14–2). Methadone maintenance was first described in 1966 by clinicians at Rockefeller University (Dole, Nyswander, and Kreek, 1966). These researchers found that following rather high doses of methadone, heroin addicts reported a notable decrease in their craving for narcotics. There was also a marked decrease in heroin use and in drug-related crimes, and an increase in their general social functioning. Follow-up studies have supported these findings (Murray, 1998; Strang et al., 1997).

Methadone: Addiction or Cure?

Methadone is a highly potent synthetic narcotic drug, which first became available at the end of World War II. It is similar to morphine in its analgesic effect, so it was originally used to alleviate severe pain. It is now used as a form of treatment for addiction to heroin and other narcotics. In methadone maintenance therapy (MMT), the person usually remains on methadone for several years, and sometimes for the rest of her life. The theory behind methadone maintenance is that some heroin addicts undergo an irreversible change in their brain biochemistry. Thus, they can't function "normally" in the absence of narcotics. Because it is slow acting, methadone does not cause the euphoria of heroin or the painful symptoms of drug withdrawal. Moreover, addicts maintained on sufficient doses of methadone don't feel as much of the euphoric effect of heroin, so they are less likely to relapse.

Despite strong evidence that methadone maintenance therapy is a very effective treatment for opioid dependence, it remains quite controversial. This is because people become very dependent on methadone, and in MMT they are provided with it for an indefinite amount of time. So one addiction may simply be traded for another. Furthermore, MMT does not address the person's psychological vulnerability to drug abuse and addiction.

Although methadone may get users off heroin, researchers have found that addicts enrolled in MMT may actually increase their use of other drugs. In one study, researchers found a significant increase in the frequency of crack cocaine and cannabis use among those enrolled in the program (Best et al., 2000). The same study found that the heroin addicts also increased their use of nonprescribed methadone; 21 percent who did not take "extra" methadone at the first interview reported that they used nonprescribed methadone six months later. Even more disturbing, the amount of nonprescribed methadone use at the follow-up interview was greater for those who were prescribed larger doses of methadone. Thus, higher doses of methadone may increase risk for dependence.

Is detoxification a better alternative? In practice, detoxification usually means the initial administration of methadone

to overcome withdrawal from heroin, then gradual tapering and elimination of the drug within about a year. On the surface, this would seem to be a better approach than MMT. But when MMT is compared to detoxification, there are actually some advantages to MMT. One study showed that MMT resulted in greater treatment retention (438.5 versus 174.0 days) and lower heroin use rates than did detoxification (Sees et al., 2000). MMT also produced a lower rate of drug-related HIV risk behaviors, such as needle sharing, although it did not reduce sex-related HIV risk behaviors. Also, there were no differences between groups in rates of employment, family functioning, or alcohol use. The investigators concluded that the results did not provide support for diverting money from MMT into long-term detoxification. In another comparison of an MMT program to an intensive day treatment program, the outcomes were similar, but the cost of day treatment involving intensive psychosocial intervention was *much* higher (Avants et al., 2000).

Of all the currently available approaches for treating opioid addiction, many experts in the field of addiction believe that MMT is the most "cost effective"—at least in the short run (Des Jarlais, Paone, Friedman, Peyser, Newman, 1995; Dole, 1995). Thus, based on the empirical, scientific findings, MMT is the best approach. But practitioners must face certain basic questions about their treatment goals (Robertson and Macleod, 1996). What about the long-term welfare of the addict, and his or her prospects for a full, productive life? Is trading one addiction for another in his or her best interest? Is it in society's best interest? Does the ease and low cost of MMT create complacency and reduce society's motivation to find treatments that truly eliminate the person's addiction? We may eventually discover that, even though comprehensive psychosocial interventions are much more expensive, they are worth the cost. The changes in brain biochemistry produced by heroin addiction may be reversible.

SOURCE: Avants et al., 1999; Best et al., 2000; Des Jarlais, Paone, Friedman, Peyser, and Newman, 1995; Dole, 1995; Robertson and Macleod, 1996; Sees et al., 2000.

There are a number of reasons why methadone is preferable to heroin (see Table 14–3). First, it can be taken orally, and thus intravenous injection is avoided. Second, methadone is longer acting than heroin and prevents the onset of withdrawal symptoms for up to twenty-four hours. Third, little or no euphoria is produced by methadone. Although there is an abstinence syndrome that results from with-

drawal from methadone, it is less severe in intensity than withdrawal from heroin. Moreover, methadone seems to block the effects of heroin. Several studies both in the laboratory and in street settings have shown that the heroin addict does not experience the same rush or euphoria if he does take heroin while on methadone, probably because methadone is already occupying the opiate receptors (Kreek, 1992).

TABLE 14-3

Data

HEROIN VERSUS METHADONE

	Heroin	*Methadone*
Route of administration	Intravenous	Oral
Onset of action	Immediate	30 minutes
Duration of action	3–6 hours	24–36 hours
Euphoria	First 1–2 hours	None (with appropriate dose)
Withdrawal symptoms	After 3–4 hours	After 24 hours

SOURCE: Kreek, 1992.

Since the reinforcing effects of heroin are diminished and the unpleasant withdrawal state is avoided, methadone therapy is sometimes successful in getting users off heroin.

There are several other advantages to methadone treatment. To obtain methadone, patients must come to the local clinic daily and receive the methadone drink. Thus, the clinic provides social support and structure to the addict's daily life, and helps in limiting or removing drug-related, illegal activities. Kreek (1992) has noted some of the factors that are important for a favorable outcome in methadone maintenance. A well-trained, supportive staff providing diverse services tailored to individual patients increases the retention rate (the percentage of people remaining in treatment), as does use of an adequate dose of methadone (60 mg per day).

The theory underlying methadone treatment is that once the individual is stabilized, he or she can be "weaned" from methadone with very little discomfort. Nonetheless, the relapse to illicit opiate use among methadone patients is high (Ward, Hall, and Mattick, 1999). About half of those who enter methadone treatment leave within one year, and some of those who stay continue to use heroin and other illicit drugs, although less frequently than before they entered treatment. Further, once methadone is stopped, the chances of long-term abstinence are very low (Zanis, McClellan, Alterman, and Cnaan, 1996). These rather dismal figures once again underscore the extreme difficulty in remaining completely drug-free. Many methadone patients choose to remain on methadone indefinitely, which is certainly medically possible.

As mentioned earlier, naltrexone, an opioid antagonist that is often used to treat alcohol dependence, has also been shown to be effective in treating heroin addicts, especially during the withdrawal phase. But naltrexone alone is not as effective as methadone in treating heroin addiction.

Medical and Social Complications

The most serious health consequences of heroin dependence are those produced by the behavior of the addict. In an effort to get more of the drug, addicts engage in dangerous and risky behaviors. Of course, the use of needles is associated with a whole host of dangers, including the transmission of the AIDS virus. The risk of AIDS is also increased among addicts because many engage in sexual activity in order to obtain money for drugs. This results in an increased rate of other sexually transmitted diseases among heroin addicts. Moreover, the preoccupation with obtaining drugs results in a tendency to neglect one's physical health; heroin addicts have poor diets and do not seek out preventive medical care.

Social complications are another matter. It may cost over $100 a day to support a heroin habit. Although the drug itself does not increase aggressive or criminal behavior, many addicts must engage in crimes such as robbery or prostitution in order to procure their drugs. Moreover, women who continue to use heroin while pregnant run substantial risks to the health of the unborn fetus. Such babies may undergo physical withdrawal signs when born.

Hallucinogens

Hallucinogens include a number of different drugs with varying chemical structures and behavioral effects. The feature that distinguishes these drugs from

Native Americans use peyote as part of their religious rituals as they seek spiritual renewal.

other classes of drugs is their marked ability to alter sensory perception, awareness, and thoughts. In 1931, Lewin wrote about a class of drugs he called phantasticants, that is, drugs that could produce a world of fantasy. Other terms that have been used to describe these drugs are psychedelic (mind-expanding), and psychotomimetic (inducing a psychotic state). All of these terms refer to the ability of the drugs to distort reality and affect self-perception. Today, the most common term for these drugs is hallucinogens, since they all have the ability to produce vivid and unusual sensory experiences. Drugs such as LSD, mescaline, and psilocybin are examples of such compounds.

Use of hallucinogens is relatively low according to the National Household Survey. In 1996, about 8 percent of people over the age of twelve in the United States reported ever having used LSD (U.S. Department of Health and Human Services, 1997c). In 1999, the National Institute on Drug Abuse reported that approximately 8 percent of high school seniors that were surveyed reported having used LSD in the past year (U.S. Department of Health and Human Services, 2000). There is no evidence of a significant increase in the use of hallucinogens since the 1970s. In fact, the average dose consumed by users has declined significantly.

Effects of Hallucinogens

Most of the hallucinogens are derived from plant substances and are very similar in chemical structure to the biogenic amines in the brain (serotonin, norepinephrine, and dopamine). Because of their remarkable effects upon the mind, these substances were used in religious ceremonies and folk medicine by the early cultures that discovered them. Mescaline is derived from the cactus plant peyote, and has been used for centuries in the mystical religious practices of the Mexican Indians; the Aztecs regarded the plant as sacred. Psilocybin is found in several species of mushroom, popularly known as the "magic mushroom." Stone sculptures of psychoactive mushrooms found in Central America date well before 500 B.C. (Snyder, 1986). Its Indian name meant "food of the gods," and it was used in secret religious rituals among the Indians. R. Gordon Wasson, a New York banker who became interested in the mushroom in the 1950s, established a rapport with a native group and partook in one of their ceremonies. He wrote, ". . . it permits you to travel backwards and forward in time, to enter other planes of existence, even (as the Indians say), to know God. . . ." (Wasson, 1979).

LSD also has an interesting history, although much more recent. LSD (D-lysergic acid diethylamide) is a synthetic drug, but it is related chemically to a number of compounds found in the ergot fungus that infects grains, especially rye. One of these compounds, ergotamine, causes contractions of blood vessels and other smooth muscles such as the uterus. (It had been used for centuries in obstetrics.) In the 1940s, the chemist Albert Hofmann at Sandoz Drug Company in Basel, Switzerland, was experimenting with various derivatives of ergot compounds in hopes of finding new medicines. He synthesized a series of compounds, one of which was LSD. At the time, he had no idea he was dealing with a potent hallucinogenic drug. In 1943, after conducting several experiments, he was forced to stop work because of peculiar sensations. He recorded these impressions in his laboratory notebook and suspected they were due to accidental ingestion of LSD. Several days later, he deliberately tested his theory by ingesting 0.25 mg of the substance (we know now that this is a massive dose, since LSD is an extremely potent drug). His impressions were duly recorded in his notebook:

> I had a great difficulty in speaking coherently, my field of vision swayed before me, and objects appeared distorted like images in curved mirrors. I had the impression of being unable to move from the spot, although my assistant told me afterwards that we had cycled at a good pace. . . .
>
> By the time the doctor arrived, the peak of the crisis had already passed. As far as I remember, the following were the most outstanding symptoms: vertigo, visual disturbances; the faces of those around me appeared as grotesque, colored masks; marked motor unrest, alternating with paresis; an intermittent heavy feeling in the head, limbs, and the entire body, as if they were filled with metal; cramps in the legs, coldness, and loss of feeling in the hands; a metallic taste on the tongue; dry, constricted sensation in the throat; feeling of choking; confusion alternating between clear recognition of my condition, in which state I sometimes observed, in the manner of an independent, neutral observer, that I shouted half insanely or babbled incoherent words. Occasionally I felt as if I were out of my

body. The doctor found a rather weak pulse but an otherwise normal circulation. Six hours after ingestion of the LSD-25 my condition had already improved considerably. Only the visual disturbances were still pronounced. Everything seemed to sway and the proportions were distorted like the reflections in the surface of moving water. Moreover, all objects appeared in unpleasant, constantly changing colors, the predominant shades being sickly green and blue. When I closed my eyes, an unending series of colorful, very realistic and fantastic images surged in upon me. A remarkable feature was the manner in which all acoustic perceptions (e.g., the noise of a passing car) were transformed into optical effects, every sound causing a corresponding colored hallucination constantly changing in shape and color like pictures in a kaleidoscope. At about 1 o'clock I fell asleep and awakened the next morning somewhat tired but otherwise feeling perfectly well. (Hofmann, 1968, pp. 185–86)

Reports on LSD began to appear in the scientific literature in the 1950s. Although pharmacologists and psychologists were very interested in its effects, research indicated that there was little therapeutic value to the compound. In the early 1960s, the drug became illegal, although soon after, in the late 1960s and early 1970s, its use in the "hippie" subculture reached its peak.

PSYCHOLOGICAL EFFECTS

The psychological effects of the hallucinogenic drugs vary from one person to the next. The effects also change as a function of the person's expectations and experience with the drug. As described above,

---

DSM-IV Criteria

Hallucinogen Intoxication

A. Recent use of a hallucinogen.

B. Clinically significant maladaptive behavioral or psychological changes (e.g., marked anxiety or depression, ideas of reference, fear of losing one's mind, paranoid ideation, impaired judgment, or impaired social or occupational functioning) that developed during, or shortly after, hallucinogen use.

C. Perceptual changes occurring in a state of full wakefulness and alertness (e.g., subjective intensification of perceptions, depersonalization, derealization, illusions, hallucina-

tions, synesthesias) that developed during, or shortly after, hallucinogen use.

D. Two (or more) of the following signs, developing during, or shortly after, hallucinogen use: (1) pupillary dilation; (2) tachycardia; (3) sweating; (4) palpitations; (5) blurring of vision; (6) tremors; (7) incoordination.

E. The symptoms are not due to a general medical condition and are not better accounted for by another mental disorder.

SOURCE: APA, DSM-IV, 1994.

one of most common reports is that of strange sensory perceptions, including visual, tactile, or auditory distortions. Images and sounds may be remarkably vivid or bizarre. Aesthetic experiences, such as viewing art or listening to music, can be enhanced. The sense of time is also extremely altered. The neuropharmacologist Solomon Snyder, upon having ingested LSD, noted that "two hours after having taken the drug, I felt as if I had been under its influence for thousands of years. The remainder of my life on the planet Earth seemed to stretch ahead into infinity, and at the same time I felt infinitely old" (Snyder, 1986). Sensations may be transposed from one mode to another, a phenomenon known as synesthesia. Snyder wrote: "I clapped my hands and saw sound waves passing before my eyes." Emotions and the sense of self are often affected, with a feeling of depersonalization or loss of ego boundaries. In many cases, users report that they develop special insights into themselves or the world. In some instances, this feeling is experienced as positive; for others, it can be quite disturbing and result in profound dysphoria.

There are a number of important differences between hallucinogens and other drugs of abuse. Unlike drugs such as cocaine, amphetamine, or heroin, hallucinogens do not cause a rush or strong feeling of pleasure. People seem to desire these drugs uniquely for their complex effects on the mind, rather than for euphoriant or relaxing properties. It is possible that the hallucinogens do not affect the brain reward system the way most other drugs of abuse do. Animals cannot be taught to self-administer these compounds; they seem to lack true reinforcing effects in both animals and humans. Use of hallucinogens is not continual or chronic; people generally take these compounds on infrequent occasions. Moreover, people do not develop physical dependence or become addicted to them. Although they are illegal, hallucinogens do not induce cravings or compulsions.

NEUROPHYSIOLOGICAL MECHANISMS

Because of their very unusual psychological and sensory effects, researchers have long been interested in how hallucinogenic substances affect the brain. In fact, although there has been much research conducted, the neurophysiological mechanisms associated with these drugs are not well understood. The chemical structures of most of the compounds in this class are remarkably similar to the neurotransmitters serotonin and norepinephrine, and it is likely that they have potent effects on these neural systems.

Research on animals as well as PET scan studies of humans have shown that many neurotransmitter systems are involved in the mental changes produced by LSD and other hallucinogens, such as psilocybin (Vollenweider, 1998). Similar neurotransmitter changes may contribute to naturally occurring psychoses. It appears that LSD produces an imbalance among three neurotransmitter systems: serotonin, glutamate, and dopamine. Serotonin activity is markedly reduced by

Hallucinogens have complex effects on the mind and may cause people to have hallucinations, such as the one depicted in this painting by Guillaume Pujolle.

DSM-IV Criteria

Hallucinogen Persisting Perception Disorder (Flashbacks)

A. The reexperiencing, following cessation of use of a hallucinogen, of one or more of the perceptual symptoms that were experienced while intoxicated with the hallucinogen (e.g., geometric hallucinations, false perceptions of movement in the peripheral visual fields, flashes of color, intensified colors, trails of images of moving objects, positive afterimages, halos around objects, macropsia, and micropsia).

B. The symptoms in Criterion A cause clinically significant distress or impairment in social, occupational, or other important areas of functioning.

C. The symptoms are not due to a general medical condition (e.g., anatomical lesions and infections of the brain, visual epilepsies) and are not better accounted for by another mental disorder (e.g., delirium, dementia, schizophrenia) or hypnopompic hallucinations.

SOURCE: APA, DSM-IV, 1994.

hallucinogens (Marek and Aghajanian, 1998). PET scan studies of humans who have taken LSD have revealed pronounced changes in the limbic circuits of the brain—the same circuitry that is believed to be involved in the development of psychotic symptoms.

Medical and Social Complications

The hallucinogens have not received a great deal of attention as a medical or public health problem because of their low rates of use; moreover, since they are not injected intravenously, there is little risk of AIDS transmission. The most commonly used hallucinogens, such as LSD, mescaline, and psilocybin have very few toxic effects. Deaths attributed to direct effects of LSD are unknown. Nonetheless, consumption of hallucinogens does have potential adverse consequences. Most common is an acute psychotic reaction or "bad trip," in which the user experiences a severe panic reaction due to the feeling that he or she is going insane (Hemsley and Ward, 1985). In rare but tragic cases, the perceptual alterations may cause suicide; in the 1960s, stories appeared about young LSD users jumping out of windows because they believed they could fly. Another serious side effect of LSD is a phenomenon known as "flashbacks," brief episodes of drug effects that occur long after the last exposure. No one knows what causes flashbacks, which happen in approximately 15 percent of users, but they can be quite disturbing and recur intermittently even for years after LSD exposure. People who score high on "neuroticism," a personality trait that involves tendencies to worry and become anxious, are more likely to have bad trips on hallucinogens.

PCP and MDMA

Several other drugs that have hallucinogenic effects have been used for recreational purposes. **PCP** (phencyclidine, known on the street as "angel dust," "wack," or "rocket fuel") and the related drug ketamine were originally developed in the 1950s as anesthetics. People anesthetized with these drugs were awake but appeared disconnected from their environment. For this reason, these drugs were classified as dissociative anesthetics. But it was soon discovered that they had similar properties to hallucinogens, and their use was discontinued in humans.

PCP was synthesized illicitly in the 1970s, when its use as a recreational drug was popular. The drug is smoked, snorted, or injected intravenously. Ingestion results in subjective feelings of intoxication, warmth, a tingling feeling, and sense of numbness in the extremities. Unlike the visual hallucinations that characterize LSD intoxication, distortions in body image and feelings of extreme depersonalization are typical of the PCP state. With increasing doses, confused, excited intoxication may develop or there may be stupor or coma. In some people, a schizophrenia-like psychosis appears, which may persist for weeks or months. Often PCP is combined with marijuana to produce "killer joints." The use of PCP has declined sharply in recent years; in 1979, about 13 percent of twelfth graders reported having used it, but in 1997, the rate fell to 4 percent. This decrease is probably due to the bad reputation that PCP has attained. Nonetheless, there is still cause for concern because PCP has been linked to violence and aggressive behavior, suicides, and depression (Johnson and Jones, 1990).

DSM-IV Criteria

Phencyclidine Intoxication

A. Recent use of a phencyclidine (or a related substance).

B. Clinically significant maladaptive behavioral changes (e.g., belligerence, assaultiveness, impulsiveness, unpredictability, psychomotor agitation, impaired judgment, or impaired social or occupational functioning) that developed during, or shortly after, phencyclidine use.

C. Within an hour (less when smoked, "snorted," or used intravenously), two (or more) of the following signs: (1) vertical or horizontal nystagmus; (2) hypertension or tachycardia; (3) numbness or diminished responsiveness to pain; (4) ataxia; (5) dysarthria; (6) muscle rigidity; (7) seizures or coma; (8) hyperacusis.

D. The symptoms are not due to a general medical condition and are not better accounted for by another mental disorder.

SOURCE: APA, DSM-IV, 1994.

MDMA (3,4-methylenedioxymethamphetamine), known as "Ecstasy" or "XTC" in street language, is a drug chemically related to amphetamine. It is principally classified as a hallucinogen, however, and not as a stimulant because it causes changes in perceptual awareness. Recreational users say that MDMA causes feelings of euphoria, tingling, and a sense of increased sociability. Users claim that even after the acute effects of the drug have subsided, they feel more insightful, empathetic, and aware. In the early 1980s, before it became illegal, a number of psychiatrists claimed they had been discretely using it to aid the therapeutic process and claimed it facilitated communication and expression of emotions (Greer and Tolbert, 1986; Grinspoon and Bakalar, 1986). Some people who used MDMA for recreational purposes believed that it made people feel more trusting in each other, and broke down barriers between family members and friends. These claims proved to have little substance.

In fact, it is now known that MDMA can produce serious brain damage. It has neurotoxic effects on the brain, most notably on the serotonin neurons (Morris, 1998; Stone, Merchant, Hanson, and Gibb, 1987). One dose can be enough to damage a significant number of serotonin neurons. It is fortunate that use of MDMA is not widespread; estimates for 1997 are that around 6 percent of youth have ever tried the drug. As information about its effects on the brain become more widely known, its use is expected to decline.

Marijuana

Marijuana is a preparation of the leaves from the hemp plant, or *Cannabis sativa*. It is not known where the plant originated, but it is likely that it was somewhere in central Asia. It is now cultivated in many areas of the world. Use of cannabis in human societies predates recorded history. It was used in China as an intoxicant as early as 6,000 years ago. In the Western world, the hemp plant was grown for its medicinal properties and fiber (for making rope), without its intoxicating effects being widely recognized. In the nineteenth century, European physicians expounded the usefulness of hemp as an appetite stimulant and anticonvulsant, and in treating a wide variety of ills such as migraine, asthma, and painful menstruation. It is believed that marijuana smoking for recreational purposes was introduced into this country by Mexican laborers in the early twentieth century (McKim, 1986). Use spread slowly and eventually stirred the concerns of people who thought that its use was associated with moral degeneration and violent crime. By the end of the 1930s, marijuana was illegal in most states.

In contrast to the hallucinogens, marijuana continues to be the most commonly used illicit drug in the United States (U.S. Department of Health and Human Services, 1997c). As of 1996, about one-third of the target population in the National Household survey reported that they had used marijuana one or more times in their lifetime; about 9 percent had used it within the last year. These figures translate into nearly 70 million people who have used marijuana at least once. Among teenagers, use is more prevalent (see Figure 14–10); nearly 40 percent of twelfth graders reported having used it within the past year and 50 percent reported use at some time in their life. As is true for most other illicit drugs, however, use is markedly down from the late 1970s, when 60 percent of twelfth graders reported having used marijuana.

Figure 14–10

TRENDS IN ADOLESCENTS' USE OF MARIJUANA

The figure shows the use of marijuana in the past year for eighth, tenth, and twelfth graders. Only twelfth graders were surveyed between 1985 and 1990; since 1991, adolescents in three grades have been surveyed. While marijuana use declined between 1985 and 1992, it started to increase again in 1992, although it remained below the all-time high of 50.8 percent in 1979. Rates of use remained fairly stable between 1998 and 1999. (Source: Mathias, 1996; National Institute of Drug Abuse, 2000c)

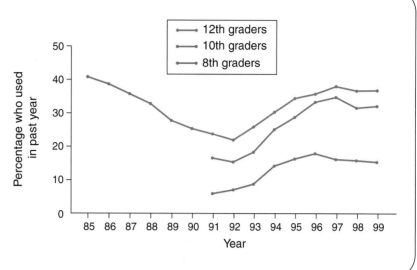

Effects of Marijuana

The psychoactive ingredient in cannabis is delta-9-tetrahydrocannabinol (THC), which is concentrated in the resin of the plant. The concentration of this substance varies (from 0.5 to 11 percent) with different preparations of the plant. Marijuana is a preparation of the leaves and buds; hashish is almost pure resin and therefore much more potent. Marijuana and hashish are usually smoked, and as we know, this is a very efficient way of delivering the drug to the brain. Psychoactive effects begin after a few minutes and reach their peak after about thirty minutes. People sometimes take this drug orally, baked in cookies or brownies. Since absorption through the GI tract is much slower, effects are not felt before two to three hours. THC is highly lipid soluble. It is taken up and stored in the fatty tissues of the body. This characteristic results in THC remaining in the body for long periods of time, for as long as one month following one dose of THC.

PSYCHOLOGICAL EFFECTS

Knowledge of the behavioral and cognitive effects of marijuana is based on both reports of users and a considerable amount of laboratory research in both animals and humans. It is difficult to describe precisely the psychological changes caused by marijuana because individuals may have differing reactions, depending on dose, experience with drug, expectations, and so on. In an experienced user, marijuana typically elicits feelings of well-being and mild euphoria, usually referred to as "being high." An initial stimulating effect may be replaced by feelings of tranquillity and dreaminess. Rapid mood changes or exaggerated emotions may occur. Often, when marijuana is consumed socially, there is frequent laughter and hilarity. Perceptual and sensory changes may occur, but generally these are mild exaggerations of pleasurable experiences. For example, music or tastes may be enhanced. But following very high doses of THC, hallucinations and feelings of paranoia may occur.

About half of teenagers and young adults, as of 1991, reported that they had tried marijuana at least once.

The cognitive deficits induced by smoking marijuana are also variable, but it is well established that there are rather striking deficits in short-term memory, so that it is more difficult to hold information in consciousness for short periods (Miller, 1999). Also, following cannabis intoxication, users may show what has been called temporal disintegration; that is, they may lose the ability to retain and coordinate information for a purpose (McKim, 1986). It is common, for example, for people to start a sentence and fail to finish it because they forgot what they started to say. This may be due to the intrusion of irrelevant associations (Hooker and Jones, 1987). Moreover, as with hallucinogens, there is a distortion in the sense of time, which seems to pass much more slowly.

Are the psychological changes produced by marijuana temporary or permanent? We do not know for sure. But recent studies of animals raise concerns about the neurotoxicity of THC. In one study, researchers examined the effects of THC on brain cells from animals (Chan, Hinds, Impey, and Storm, 1998). The application of THC to cultured neurons or hippocampal tissue caused shrinkage of neuronal cell bodies and cell nuclei. You may recall that the hippocampus plays an important role in memory. These findings suggest that some of the memory deficits caused by cannabinoids may be the result of neurotoxicity. But even more troubling, the THC produced breaks in the DNA strands contained in the nucleus. So THC may actually cause genetic damage.

TOLERANCE AND DEPENDENCE

Tolerance occurs to some of the effects of marijuana, although users often claim that there is a reverse tolerance, or sensitization to the drug. In one laboratory study in which subjects were given oral doses of THC every four hours for several weeks, tolerance developed to the effects on heart rate, to the subjective effects, and to the disruptive effects on cognitive and motor performance (Jones and Benowitz, 1976). It is likely that high, chronic doses of marijuana are needed for tolerance to develop. The impression of sensitization in experienced users may result primarily from learning to inhale and thus to increase more effectively blood concentrations of THC, as well as from learning what to expect from the drug-induced subjective state.

Physical dependence is very unlikely with marijuana (Nahas et al., 1999). The majority of social users smoke it occasionally, not daily. Ceasing to smoke marijuana after having smoked one marijuana cigarette a day for twenty-eight days does not lead to withdrawal symptoms (Frank, Lessin, Tyrrell, Hahn, and Szara, 1976). But following abrupt cessation of chronic high doses of THC, an abstinence syndrome can occur. This syndrome is characterized by irritability, restlessness, weight loss, insomnia, tremor, and increased body temperature. Psychological dependence is more common with marijuana, although even here most experts would agree that compulsive use and craving is considerably less than that associated with other drugs such as cocaine, opiates, and alcohol. Nevertheless, certain individuals may meet the DSM-IV criteria for Cannabis Dependence, in which they use very potent cannabis for months or years and spend considerable time acquiring and using the substance.

PHYSIOLOGICAL AND NEUROCHEMICAL EFFECTS

Researchers have been very interested in investigating the pharmacological and neurochemical effects of the cannabinoids, but in contrast to other drugs of abuse, less is understood about the neural basis of

DSM-IV Criteria

Cannabis Intoxication

A. Recent use of cannabis.

B. Clinically significant maladaptive behavioral or psychological changes (e.g., impaired motor coordination, euphoria, anxiety, sensation of slowed time, impaired judgment, social withdrawal) that developed during, or shortly after, cannabis use.

C. Two (or more) of the following signs, developing within 2 hours of cannabis use: (1) conjunctival (eye) infection; (2) increased appetite; (3) dry mouth; (4) tachycardia.

D. The symptoms are not due to a general medical condition and are not better accounted for by another mental disorder.

SOURCE: APA, DSM-IV, 1994.

THC's psychoactive effects. Part of the lack of understanding is due to THC's unusual characteristics as a drug (Nahas et al., 1999). THC is extremely lipid soluble and is absorbed by all tissues. It affects nearly all biological systems and has a "fluidizing" effect on biomembranes (similar to the effects of alcohol). Therefore, for many years, it was thought to be "nonspecific" pharmacologically. But over a decade ago, a unique receptor that binds cannabinoids was characterized and localized in specific brain structures, particularly the nucleus accumbens and regions in the limbic system that play a role in pleasurable sensations (Herkenham et al., 1990). Researchers have recently begun to use PET scans to study the effects of marijuana on the system of cannabinoid receptors in the human brain (Gatley, Volkow, and Makriyannis, 1999).

There is also evidence that THC has anticholinergic activity (disrupting functions of the neurotransmitter acetylcholine), which may underlie the memory deficits induced by the drug, and some of the physiological effects such as dry mouth (Domino, 1999). Acetylcholine is a very important neurotransmitter in the hippocampus, where it seems to be necessary for memory formation. Altered activity in the hippocampus may partially explain the short–term memory problems associated with the drug (Molina-Holgado, Gonzalez, and Leret, 1995).

Medical and Social Complications

There are a number of potential hazards associated with chronic marijuana use. Perhaps most important are the effects on the lungs, which are not due to THC itself but rather to inhalation of tars and other substances found in the smoke of the marijuana cigarette (Hollister, 1986). Bronchitis and asthma have long been known to be associated with marijuana smoking. Cannabinoids are also known to suppress immune responses, although the clinical significance of this result is unclear (Friedman, Klein, and Specter, 1991). Over the years, many other adverse health effects have been attributed to heavy marijuana use, none of which have been definitively proved.

Occasionally, when a young person starts smoking marijuana regularly, there may be quite marked changes in the person's lifestyle, personality, and ambitions. Chronic marijuana users may exhibit dullness, apathy, cognitive and memory impairments, and loss of interest in personal appearance and pursuit of conventional goals (Bailes, 1998;

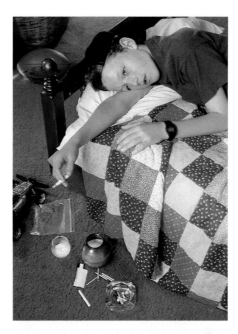

Regular use of marijuana may lead to a sense of tranquillity and dreaminess but also to dullness and apathy, as can be seen in this teenager who is smoking marijuana.

McGlothin and West, 1968). These changes have collectively been called the "amotivational syndrome." Although this syndrome is clearly a cause for concern, it is not apparent whether use of marijuana is the causal factor or whether the psychological and motivational changes precede drug use. As is true for alcohol, it is exceedingly difficult to separate the psychological effects of the drug from the psychological factors that led to its use to begin with. The syndrome does not develop in all heavy users of marijuana. Cessation of heavy use may lead to gradual improvement over several weeks or months. Although there is no evidence of permanent brain damage from heavy use of marijuana by humans, the animal studies, described above, suggest that marijuana may be neurotoxic.

Tobacco

Tobacco has been used by humans for several thousand years. Native peoples in North and South America were the first to grow the tobacco plant and smoked its leaves for its psychoactive effects. New World explorers first observed tobacco smoking in the time of Columbus, and it was introduced into Western cultures and other parts of the world in the

Roy Carruthers' *Three Smokers*.

sixteenth century. The plant was named *Nicotiana tabacum* after the French ambassador Jean Nicot, who promoted its development and believed that it had medicinal values. In colonial times, tobacco was smoked in pipes, chewed, or ground into a powder and used as snuff. In the mid-nineteenth century, the cigarette was developed, which produced a smoke so mild (compared to cigars or pipes) that it could be inhaled.

In our present society, smoking is a common and legal form of psychoactive drug consumption. Although there are over 3,000 chemical components in cigarette smoke, we believe that **nicotine** is the active and addictive ingredient. Thus, nicotine is one of the most widely consumed psychoactive drugs in the world. A one-pack-per-day smoker will administer hundreds of nicotine doses to himself daily (about 200 puffs), which amounts to over 70,000 doses of nicotine per year. Levels of smoking in the population have declined in recent years; the National Household Survey reports that smoking has decreased from about 40 percent of the target population to about 30 percent over the past twenty-five years (U.S. Department of Health and Human Services, 1997c). Although these are encouraging figures, people continue to smoke despite current widespread knowledge of the adverse health consequences of smoking. In fact, there was an increase in cigarette smoking among twelve-

to-thirteen-year-old youth between 1996 and 1997; the rate rose from 7.3 percent to 9.7 percent. This led to national programs aimed at reducing teen smoking. Strategies included educational efforts as well as pressuring the tobacco industry to stop marketing to youth. As of 1999, there was a decline in smoking rates among this population. Among thirteen-to-fourteen-year-olds, 17.5 percent reported in 1999 that they had smoked one or more cigarettes in the past thirty days, in contrast to the peak of 21 percent in 1996 (U.S. Department of Health and Human Services, 2000).

It is paradoxical that in a society that condemns drug use, nicotine consumption is a legal activity. Worldwide it is a $400 billion industry. But it is important to realize that a major difference between cigarette smoking and taking other drugs such as cocaine or alcohol is that chronic use of nicotine, even in high quantities, does not result in impairment of mental functioning. Although nicotine is certainly a "psychoactive" drug, its effects on the brain and behavior are subtle. Ironically, however, smoking kills nearly twenty times as many people per year as all illegal drugs combined.

Effects of Nicotine

Nicotine can be administered in a variety of ways, but smoking is by far the most common route of administration. As smoke is drawn into the lungs via particles of "tar" (condensate), nicotine is absorbed rapidly into the circulatory system. Blood concentrations rise rapidly, and nicotine enters the brain in approximately seven seconds. Ingestion of nicotine via oral routes (chewing tobacco, nicotine gum, oral snuff) results in a much slower rise in blood nicotine concentrations, and levels persist for longer periods. Nicotine has a variety of complex effects on the peripheral and central nervous systems. It can act as both a stimulant and a depressant. In studies of subjective effects of smoking, people say that they smoke for both its arousing and relaxation effects. The two principal actions of nicotine on neurotransmitters involve effects at cholinergic and aminergic synapses. Nicotine stimulates cholinergic receptors in the autonomic nervous system, and at the neuromuscular junction. Nicotine also induces the release of catecholamines, which results in cardiovascular activation (accelerated heart rate, increased blood pressure and cardiac output, and vasoconstriction). In the central nervous system, exposure to nicotine results in activation of several central nervous system pathways, leading to the release of acetylcholine, norepinephrine, serotonin, dopamine, and in effects on the endocrine system (Benowitz, 1988). The release of acetylcholine is largely responsible for the increase in alertness or arousal produced by nicotine. Elevations in serotonin may enhance the sense of relaxation.

Nicotine appears to have a generalized activating effect on the human brain. In one study, functional magnetic resonance imaging (functional MRI) was used to observe the immediate effects of intravenous nicotine on brain activity in cigarette smokers (Stein et al., 1998). The research participants reported that the nicotine induced feelings of a "rush" or "high." Nicotine also caused an increase in the activity of neurons in several brain regions, including the frontal lobes, nucleus accumbens, and amygdala. Studies of the effects of cocaine and some other abused drugs have indicated that the nucleus accumbens and amygdala are also involved in their reinforcing effects. Thus, the action of nicotine on these brain regions may be responsible for its reinforcing properties.

There are evidently some long-term changes in the brains of smokers. This is assumed because tolerance develops to many of the effects of nicotine. The first smoke one experiences as a teenager often produces nausea, vomiting, pallor, and dizziness. Tolerance rapidly occurs to these aversive effects with continued smoking. A certain degree of tolerance also develops to the arousing and subjective effects of nicotine. Presumably, at least in susceptible individuals, the positive effects of smoking outweigh the unpleasant side effects, such that smoking behavior is repeated. Physical dependence may then develop, which is discussed below.

Nicotine Dependence

As recently as 1994, executives of tobacco companies claimed that smoking and nicotine were not addictive (Hilts, 1994a). But a vast amount of scientific evidence suggested otherwise, and in 1997 some tobacco companies publicly acknowledged the addictive and dangerous effects of smoking. In fact, the scientific evidence suggests that nicotine may be among the most addictive of drugs. Two of the leading experts in drug research compared nicotine to five other drugs; both ranked nicotine low as far as the level of intoxication it produces, but highest as far as dependence (see Table 14–4). Of those smokers trying to quit, approximately 70 percent relapse within three months. Figure 14–1 (see p. 580) shows that relapse to smoking follows a similar pattern to relapse to other drugs such as heroin and alcohol. The surgeon general has proclaimed nicotine to be as addictive as heroin, which might seem shocking given that nicotine is a legal drug. But it comes as no surprise to people who have tried numerous times to quit. As Mark Twain quipped, "I could quit smoking if I tried; I've done it a thousand times" (cited in Volpicelli, 1989). What is nicotine dependence, and why is it so difficult to give up smoking, often despite high levels of motivation to quit?

If we review some of the major criteria for drug dependence disorder, we find that cigarette smoking meets these criteria in most individuals who smoke: compulsive drug use, overwhelming involvement with the use of the drug, concern with the securing of its supply, and a high tendency to relapse after its withdrawal. Of course, some people smoke very little or only occasionally, but that situation is relatively

---

DSM-IV Criteria

Nicotine Withdrawal

A. Daily use of nicotine for at least several weeks.

B. Abrupt cessation of nicotine use, or reduction in the amount of nicotine used, followed within 24 hours by four (or more) of the following signs: (1) dysphoric or depressed mood; (2) insomnia; (3) irritability, frustration, or anger; (4) anxiety; (5) difficulty concentrating; (6) restlessness; (7) decreased heart rate; (8) increased appetite or weight gain.

C. The symptoms in Criterion B cause clinically significant distress or impairment in social, occupational, or other important areas of functioning.

D. The symptoms are not due to a general medical condition and are not better accounted for by another mental disorder.

SOURCE: APA, DSM-IV, 1994.

TABLE 14-4

NICOTINE COMPARED TO OTHER DRUGS

Dr. Jack E. Henningfield of the National Institute on Drug Abuse and Dr. Neal L. Benowitz of the University of California at San Francisco ranked six substances based on five problem areas.

1 = Most Serious   6 = Least Serious

HENNINGFIELD RATINGS

Substance	Withdrawal	Reinforcement	Tolerance	Dependence	Intoxication
Nicotine	3	4	2	1	5
Heroin	2	2	1	2	2
Cocaine	4	1	4	3	3
Alcohol	1	3	3	4	1
Caffeine	5	6	5	5	6
Marijuana	6	5	6	6	4

BENOWITZ RATINGS

Substance	Withdrawal	Reinforcement	Tolerance	Dependence	Intoxication
Nicotine	3★	4	4	1	6
Heroin	2	2	2	2	2
Cocaine	3★	1	1	3	3
Alcohol	1	3	4	4	1
Caffeine	4	5	3	5	5
Marijuana	5	6	5	6	4

★Equal ratings
SOURCE: Hilts, 1994b, p. C3.

Withdrawal Presence and severity of characteristic withdrawal symptoms.

Reinforcement A measure of the substance's ability, in human and animal tests, to get users to take it again and again, and in preference to other substances.

Tolerance How much of the substance is needed to satisfy increasing cravings for it, and the level of stable need that is eventually reached.

Dependence How difficult it is for the user to quit, the relapse rate, the percentage of people who eventually become dependent, the rating users give their own need for the substance, and the degree to which the substance will be used in the face of evidence that is causes harm.

Intoxication Though not usually counted as a measure of addiction in itself, the level of intoxication is associated with addiction and increases the personal and social damage a substance may do.

rare. Smoking cessation often results in a distinct withdrawal syndrome, although it may vary from person to person in its intensity and specific symptoms. The most common signs and symptoms are irritability, anxiety, restlessness, impaired concentration, and a strong craving for tobacco. Headaches, drowsiness, insomnia, and gastrointestinal complaints are also common. Neuropsychological tests in smokers undergoing withdrawal show decreases in vigilance, attention, psychomotor performance, and increases in hostility. The syndrome gradually subsides within days or weeks, but the craving and desire for a cigarette often far outlast the physical complaints. Increased appetite and weight gain are extremely common problems associated with smoking cessation. (Smokers as a group weigh less than non-

smokers.) Research on animals and humans has shown this to be due to a number of metabolic changes, although the strong desire for a "substitute" oral behavior may also contribute. The fear of gaining weight after stopping smoking may contribute to a lowered motivation to quit, particularly among women.

THEORIES OF NICOTINE DEPENDENCE

Why do people smoke? *Social factors* are probably very important in the teenage years, when smoking dependence most often develops. Peer pressure, parental modeling, and experimentation may contribute to initiation of the behavior. When the habit is well es-

Peer pressure, parental modeling, and experimentation may contribute to the initiation of smoking. These eight-year-old boys in Kiev, Ukraine, light their cigarettes despite the anti-smoking poster in the background.

tablished, it is likely that other factors related to the biological effects of nicotine contribute to the maintenance of the behavior. Perhaps most important of these are nicotine's *positive reinforcing effects*. Like all drugs of abuse, nicotine affects mood, emotion, and cognitive functions. Self-administration tests in animals have shown that rats and monkeys will press a lever to deliver intravenous nicotine (Corrigall and Coen, 1991; Henningfield and Goldberg, 1983). Nicotine presumably has pleasurable properties for people who smoke; laboratory studies in humans have shown this to be the case (Henningfield and Jasinski, 1983). One study in England found that subjects rated smoking as an activity with both "pleasurable-relaxation" and "pleasurable-stimulation" effects (Warburton, 1988). But nicotine does not produce the powerful euphoria or "rush" that is experienced with other drugs that are smoked or delivered intravenously, such as heroin or cocaine.

A further important model of smoking behavior is the *coping model*. This notion is related to the idea that people take drugs to relieve distress, or to help them cope with stresses or challenges of daily life. Many studies have found that people smoke more when worried, nervous, or anxious, and that they find smoking helps to relieve these feelings. For example, a study of students found that they smoked more and inhaled more strongly during examination periods (Warburton, 1988). Other work has found that autonomic responsivity, such as skin conductance, is blunted by smoking, thus providing evidence that smoking is able to reduce some aspects of the stress response (Gilbert and Hagen, 1980).

The *functional model* focuses on nicotine's ability to improve performance, and emphasizes that people smoke to control their psychological state and to gain optimal mental functioning. It appears that the mild stimulant properties of nicotine indeed can improve performance. In tests of vigilance, attention, memory, or information processing, smoking or ingesting oral nicotine results in improved scores. These effects are present even in nonsmokers given oral nicotine (Sahakian, Jones, Levy, Gray, and Warburton, 1989; Wesnes and Warburton, 1984a, 1984b). Thus, people may smoke because of the beneficial effects nicotine provides when performing the many tasks of everyday life.

Other research has shown that nicotine also has beneficial effects on patients with Alzheimer's disease and other forms of dementia (Nordberg, 1996). Patients who receive nicotine manifest an improvement in memory and concentration. Further, persons with a history of smoking may be less likely to develop Alzheimer's disease. These effects are presumed to be due to the long-term impact of nicotine on certain neurotransmitter receptors in the brain. There is also evidence that nicotine has some benefits for patients with schizophrenia, in that it may reduce their confusion and distractibility (Adler et al., 1998). Patients with schizophrenia smoke at a much higher rate than other people. Researchers have suggested that this may be due to the fact that the vulnerability to schizophrenia involves an abnormality in the neurotransmitter receptors. They therefore hypothesize that smoking cigarettes may help patients with schizophrenia compensate for a brain abnormality (see Box 14–3). Thus, paradoxically, it appears that nicotine has some potential health benefits, despite the fact that smoking also has many health risks (Le Houezec, 1998).

It is likely that all three of the models discussed above are relevant for most smokers. Thus, the models should not be viewed as mutually exclusive. Many people smoke for a combination of factors: because of the mild pleasurable effects produced by nicotine, the alleviation of negative psychological states, and the improvement in daily functioning.

Treatment

Most smokers who successfully quit do so without assistance from counseling programs, groups, or pharmacotherapies (Fiore et. al., 1990). About two-thirds of smokers make serious attempts to quit each year, but most relapse within weeks or months. Although behavioral therapy, group counseling, or physician advice may be helpful in some cases, these strategies work much better when combined with nicotine replacement therapy (Tsoh et al., 1997). Nicotine replacement, via nicotine gum or a transdermal patch (a patch placed on the skin that slowly releases nicotine, which is then absorbed by the skin into the body), has been shown to be effective in smokers unable to quit by alternative methods. The rationale underlying this approach is similar to that used in treating opiate addiction with methadone. The aim is to eliminate smoking behavior while still making nicotine available for a limited period of time. Nicotine delivered this way does not result in the same blood levels or psychoactive effects of smoking, but it does reduce the severity of the withdrawal symptoms and craving. The transdermal nicotine patch is easier to use and causes fewer side effects than nicotine gum. A meta-analysis of seventeen studies involving more than 5,000 smokers showed that about 25 percent of smokers who used transdermal patches were abstinent six months later, compared with only 10 percent of smokers who were given dummy patches (Fiore, Smith, Jorenby, and Baker, 1994). This study, conducted at the Center for Tobacco Research and Intervention at the University of Wisconsin, also found that counseling made little difference in the rate at which patch users stopped smoking. Moreover, the patch was just as effective when worn for six to eight weeks as for the recommended ten to eighteen weeks.

Levels of Analysis   Box 14—3

Nicotine and Schizophrenia

Cigarette smoking is more common among patients with mental illnesses than it is among healthy people. But for patients who suffer from schizophrenia, the rate of smoking is extraordinarily high, with estimates ranging from 50 to 85 percent (Dalack, Healy, and Meador-Woodruff, 1998). Why is smoking so common among those diagnosed with schizophrenia? This question has captured the attention of investigators in recent years, because many believe that the elevated rate of nicotine use among patients with schizophrenia may be telling us something about the cause of their illness.

In their study of the psychology of why people smoke, Glynn and Sussman (1990) began by asking people why they do so and found that patients with schizophrenia gave answers similar to those offered by healthy people. The patients said that smoking made them feel more relaxed and calm, and that it had become a habit. In addition, many patients said that they believed that smoking reduced their symptoms. There is limited evidence that this may indeed be true. Some case studies suggest that the symptoms of schizophrenia increase in severity upon cessation of smoking (Dalack, Healy, and Meador-Woodruff, 1998). Further, nicotine consumption, either through smoking or nicotine patches, has been found to improve the cognitive functions of patients with schizophrenia.

In general, the findings on the psychological consequences of smoking by patients with schizophrenia fit with what is known about the biology of nicotine in the brain.

Receptors for nicotine are distributed in many regions of the brain. Some researchers have hypothesized that patients with schizophrenia have a defect in the "nicotinergic" system in the brain, and that this leads to problems with the ability to ignore or "gate out" irrelevant sensory input. Smoking may be reducing symptoms because it improves the patient's ability to focus attention. Also, nicotine seems to change the activity of an important neurotransmitter that is believed to be involved in schizophrenia, namely, dopamine (see Chapter 10). By smoking, patients with schizophrenia may be normalizing dopamine activity in their brains, especially in a system called the "mesolimbic dopamine system."

Taken together, all of this suggests that patients are engaging in "self-medication" when they smoke cigarettes. So what is the best approach to dealing with nicotine addiction in people with serious mental illnesses? Should we strongly encourage patients to quit smoking, even if they insist that it is helping them cope with their psychological symptoms? Or should the clinician give first priority to the psychological benefits that smoking seems to give to the patients, despite the negative physical health consequences? This is a complex question for which there is no simple answer. The best approach must be determined, individually, for each patient.

SOURCE: Dalack, Healy, and Meador-Woodroff, 1998; Glynn and Sussman, 1990.

Smoking during pregnancy may have adverse effects on the unborn fetus, a point made by this anti-smoking billboard.

Medical and Social Complications

According to the World Health Organization, smoking is the most avoidable cause of death and the most important public health issue of our time (World Health Organization Expert Committee on Drug Dependence, 1993). The statistics indeed are overwhelming. It has been estimated that there are 450,000 smoking-related deaths per year in the United States. (For purposes of comparison, there are approximately 100,000 alcohol-related deaths, and 35,000 deaths due to AIDS annually.) Disease and death due to smoking results in over $70 billion in annual smoking-related costs to society, including health-care costs and lost productivity. There are a number of diseases causally linked to smoking, including lung cancer, coronary heart disease, hypertension, and chronic lung diseases such as emphysema. The likelihood of developing these disorders increases with the amount of exposure; chronic smoking shortens the life span. Smoking contributes to approximately 30 percent of all cancer deaths and to 30 percent of all deaths due to cardiovascular disease. Although nicotine is the addictive component in smoke, these serious diseases are primarily caused by exposure to carbon monoxide and the many known carcinogens in smoke. But nicotine itself, particularly with long-term exposure, may aggravate a number of cardiovascular conditions because of its stimulatory effects. Smoking during pregnancy also has adverse effects on the unborn fetus. Babies born to smokers have lower birth weights than babies born to nonsmokers (see Chapter 8 for a discussion of evidence that smoking during pregnancy may also increase the risk of behavioral disorders in offspring).

Barbiturates and Benzodiazepines

Barbiturates and *benzodiazepines* are sedative-hypnotic drugs ("downers"); that is, their principal effect is to depress the activity of the central nervous system. In this way, they are similar to alcohol, which is also a sedative-hypnotic, but there are some important differences as well. In contrast to many of the abused drugs that have been used for thousands of years, barbiturates and benzodiazepines are drugs that were developed in this century for therapeutic purposes. The barbiturates were first synthesized in Germany in the early 1900s, and many of them are still prescribed today for anesthesia, sedation, and control of seizure disorders. Examples of barbiturates are pentobarbital (Nembutal), secobarbital (Seconal), amobarbital (Amytal), and phenobarbital (Luminal). These compounds differ slightly in chemical structure and duration of action. Benzodiazepines were introduced in the 1960s as safer alternatives to the barbiturates, particularly in the treatment of anxiety states and insomnia. Well-known benzodiazepines include alprazalam (Xanax), diazepam (Valium), chlordiazepoxide (Librium), triazolam (Halcion), and oxazepam (Tranxene). Valium is one of the most commonly prescribed drugs in the U.S. Although both the barbiturates and benzodiazepines have important medical uses, they are also abused drugs.

Effects of Sedatives

The psychological and physical effects of barbiturates are very similar to the effects of alcohol. At low or moderate doses, barbiturates cause mild euphoria, lightheadedness, and loss of motor coordination. Higher doses may cause severe intoxication characterized by difficulty in thinking, slurred speech, poor comprehension and memory, emotionality, and aggressive behavior. Loss of consciousness may occur, and breathing is slowed. With large enough doses, as in accidental or intentional overdose, breathing ceases altogether. Indeed, barbiturates are the favored drug for committing suicide. More than 15,000 deaths per year result from overdose, and the majority of these are suicides. Unintentional deaths may result from combining alcohol with barbiturates or benzodiazepines, since the effects of these drugs are additive.

Psychological and physical effects of benzodiazepines share some characteristics with the effects of barbiturates, but in general they have milder effects and much lower toxicity. In therapeutic doses they have anxiolytic (anxiety-relieving) effects, although at these doses there are few discernible effects in nonanxious individuals. At moderate doses, they can cause mild pleasurable feelings and paradoxical stimulant effects, similar to low doses of alcohol. Both benzodiazepines and barbiturates are self-administered by animals, indicating their reinforcing effects. Higher doses of benzodiazepines cause sedation and sleep, but respiration rate is not nearly as affected as with the barbiturates. Since the margin of safety is very high with these drugs, these are the preferred drugs for treatment of anxiety and insomnia. Death from overdose of benzodiazepines is virtually unheard of, although the combination of these drugs with alcohol is dangerous.

Several potential side effects of the benzodiazepines are of considerable concern, however. Memory deficits may be associated with benzodiazepine use, and cases of complete amnesia induced by the short-acting benzodiazepines such as triazolam have been reported (Lister, 1985). Increased hostility or aggression can occur in chronic users of these drugs.

NEUROCHEMICAL MECHANISMS

Researchers have made considerable progress in understanding the neural mechanisms underlying the psychoactive effects of barbiturates and benzodiazepines (Leonard, 1999). These studies are particularly interesting because they provide insight into the neural basis of anxiety and anxiety disorders. Although these compounds interact with many neurotransmitter systems, the one most affected is GABA. As mentioned earlier, GABA is an inhibitory neurotransmitter found in many parts of the brain. Barbiturates, benzodiazepines, and alcohol all interact with GABA receptors. The GABA receptor is actually a molecular complex of several binding sites, including

---

DSM-IV Criteria

Sedative, Hypnotic, or Anxiolytic Intoxication

A. Recent use of a sedative, hypnotic, or anxiolytic.

B. Clinically significant maladaptive behavioral or psychological changes (e.g., inappropriate sexual or aggressive behavior, mood lability, impaired judgment, impaired social or occupational functioning) that developed during, or shortly after, sedative, hypnotic, or anxiolytic use.

C. One (or more) of the following signs, developing during, or shortly after, sedative, hypnotic, or anxiolytic use:

(1) slurred speech; (2) incoordination; (3) unsteady gait; (4) nystagmus; (5) impairment in attention or memory; (6) stupor or coma.

D. The symptoms are not due to a general medical condition and are not better accounted for by another mental disorder.

SOURCE: APA, DSM-IV, 1994.

one for GABA, one for benzodiazepines, and one for barbiturates and alcohol. GABA normally causes inhibition of the neuron it affects. In the presence of sedative-hypnotics, GABA becomes even more effective, and the inhibitory action is enhanced. It is thought that the anxiety-relieving effects of these drugs are due to direct effects on the GABA receptor complex. Moreover, abnormal activity of GABA and the systems that it modulates may be involved in anxiety states (Ninan et al., 1982).

Sedative Dependence

While abuse and dependence on sedatives have decreased in recent years, they are nevertheless a problem. In 1997, about 1 percent of the population reported nonmedical use of sedatives or tranquilizers at some point in their lives. People dependent on other drugs, such as opiates or alcohol, sometimes use sedatives as well. Although sedatives can be obtained through illicit sources, often the first contact is through a physician's prescription. In these individuals, the development of the problem may be gradual, beginning with habitual use for insomnia or anxiety, and progressing to increased dosage several times a day (Jaffe, 1985).

Tolerance and dependence develop with both classes of sedatives. Barbiturate dependence and its corresponding withdrawal syndrome have been problems since the drugs were first developed. The symptoms are similar to alcohol withdrawal and can be life-threatening in extreme cases. Tremors, anxiety, insomnia, delirium, and seizures can occur following cessation of chronic use of barbiturates. After the benzodiazepines were developed, it was thought for many years that chronic use of these compounds, at least in therapeutic doses, was not associated with a withdrawal syndrome. All the benzodiazepines have less addiction potential than the barbiturates, but in recent years it has been recognized that a withdrawal syndrome can result when chronic use of the drugs stops, and that benzodiazepine withdrawal is associated with increases in anxiety and sleep disturbances, heightened sensitivity to stimuli, and EEG changes (Petursson and Lader, 1981; Lader, 1988). Treatment of barbiturate or benzodiazepine dependence consists primarily of management of the withdrawal syndrome, usually through a gradual reduction of dosage over a period of weeks or months, combined with supportive psychotherapy.

Reducing Drug Abuse

Herbert Kleber, an expert on drug abuse and treatment, observes that most people are poor judges of their own susceptibility to addiction (Kleber, 1994). In the thirty years he has treated drug addicts, he notes that few anticipated addiction when they started using drugs. Most believed they had the will power to use drugs occasionally or casually. Although many people do use drugs or alcohol in a controlled or socially acceptable manner, many others become entrapped in a destructive cycle of dependence that has widespread social implications. We will now consider several approaches to the problem of drug abuse.

Legalize Drugs?

Perhaps we should begin with the most controversial of all the proposals for dealing with substance abuse—legalizing all drugs. Various proposals for decriminalizing drug use have been put forth. The broadest proposal is to legalize all drugs, removing all restrictions on drug possession, use, and distribution. No one knows for sure what consequences legalization of drugs might have. Proponents are very optimistic. They predict that legalization will reduce crime and other social ills linked with drug abuse. Benson Roe, a professor at the University of California at San Francisco, argues that it is hypocritical to shun the use of drugs and ignore the health risks and hazards of other legal addictive substances, such as alcohol and tobacco (Roe, 1999). In addition, Roe claims that the legalization of illicit drugs would allow for (1) purity assurance under Food and Drug Administration regulation, (2) labeled concentration of the product (to avoid overdose), (3) obliteration of vigorous marketing ("pushers"), (4) reduction of drug crime and reduction of theft crime, (5) savings in law enforcement, and (6) significant tax revenues.

The legalization of drugs is not incompatible with the disease model of dependence. In fact, legalization would place all of the responsibility for dealing with the problems of drug abuse in the hands of health-care providers. The disease model has fostered a sense of social obligation to help dependent individuals, so it is likely that medical and psychological treatments for abusers would continue, perhaps on a larger scale.

Opponents of legalization make dire predictions. They claim that legalization would lead to a significant increase in drug use. The Partnership for a Drug-Free America maintains that legalizing drugs would send a message that drug use is tolerable and a social norm, and that there are no significant risks or potential harm associated with use (Abrams, 1999; Partnership for a Drug Free America, 1994). Barry McCaffrey, head of the Office of National Drug Control Policy, believes that those who support drug legalization "want drugs made widely available, in chewing gums and sodas, over the Internet and at the corner store, even though this would be tantamount to putting drugs in the hands of children." McCaffrey also cites the drug-tolerant Netherlands as having an increasing rate of crime and drug abuse and claims that the anti-drug campaigns and policies of the United States have helped to curb such rates in this country.

Some have argued for a more limited approach to the legalization of drugs—for example, in situations where the use of illegal drugs can serve medicinal purposes, such as pain relief or symptom reduction (Gurley, Aranow, and Katz, 1998). Marijuana is a case

in point. Some believe that marijuana is helpful in the treatment of certain illnesses, such as glaucoma, as well as in the reduction of pain. The San Francisco Cannabis Club was established for this purpose. But the club was raided and temporarily closed by state authorities in 1996. Shortly afterwards, Harvey Feldman and Jerry Mandel conducted interviews with former members of the cannabis club to find out how they felt about the club and the medicinal benefits of marijuana (Feldman and Mandel, 1998). The former members reported very positive health benefits from smoking marijuana, and they mentioned even greater benefits from the social and emotional support they received at the club. Thus, it seems that cannabis clubs can provide an excellent therapeutic setting for medical use of cannabis. On the other side of the debate, some professionals see no unique medical benefits to marijuana and view cannabis clubs as excuses for recreational drug use.

We do not know how the legalization of drugs would affect drug use in the United States. But experiences in other countries, most notably in the Netherlands, offer some basis for speculation (MacCoun and Reuter, 1997). The Dutch legalized the use of marijuana by adults in 1976. (The possession or distribution of large quantities was not legalized.) This was followed by a gradual increase in the reported use of marijuana. Currently the use of marijuana is higher in the Netherlands than in the United States and in other European countries where data are available. Judging from these results, it might be predicted that the legalization of marijuana would result in a slight increase in use in the United States. But can we generalize from the experiences of the Dutch? The social structure and culture of the United States differ from those in other countries. The effect in the United States, where there is greater economic disparity and a greater emphasis on competition, might be very different. This is the risk that any experiment with legalization will have to confront.

Limit Drug Availability?

Putting more stringent limits on drug availability is an alternative approach to combating drug dependence. If there were no drugs, there would be no drug dependence. If there were no alcohol, as is true in some Islamic societies, there would be no alcoholism. Use of legal drugs—alcohol, nicotine, caffeine—is by far

John Entwistle, co-founder of the San Francisco Cannabis club, smokes a marijuana joint while at a celebration of the first anniversary of the passing of the law that gives Californians the right to cultivate, use, and possess marijuana on a doctor's recommendation for a medical condition.

greater than use of illicit drugs. In general, as availability of a substance increases, so does the substance-use disorder. When the legal drinking age was lowered in some states to eighteen in the 1970s, drinking and alcohol-related traffic fatalities among youth increased greatly. When the legal limit was raised again, fatalities dropped. The period of lowest alcohol consumption in this country was during Prohibition (1920–1933).

At the present time, law enforcement agencies do devote considerable effort to limiting the availability of illicit drugs. Highways, post offices, and airports are monitored to reduce the flow of illegal substances. Materials for cultivating or manufacturing illegal substances are confiscated by officials. These efforts are probably reducing the availability of drugs to potential users. Nonetheless, drug abuse continues to be a problem. Would more stringent law enforcement solve the problem? Some have attributed the decline in substance abuse that we have witnessed over the past two decades to more stringent penalties for distribution. But others believe these changes are due to public education about the dangers of drugs.

Drug Education and Prevention

It is now recognized that one of the most effective deterrents to drug use is education and dissemination of knowledge about drugs, alcohol, and their effects. This is particularly important for children and adolescents. Broad-based community programs, in schools or in youth services or in religious organizations, as well as media campaigns and parent programs are critical for providing this information. For example, many public schools, even at the elementary level, have drug education programs, and many have the "drug-free zone" symbol posted on the school property. Such initiatives increase awareness of the drug problem at a very young age.

But warning about the dangers of drug use is a necessary, but not sufficient, component of prevention (Kleber, 1994). Teaching adolescents decision-making skills and techniques for confronting peer pressure to use drugs are also thought to be very important (Ellickson, 1994). The success of the anti-smoking and anti-drunk driving campaigns gives cause for optimism. Overall rates of smoking cigarettes have declined in the past twenty years from 40 to 30 percent of the adult population. Over the past fifteen years, the incidence of driver intoxication in

A policeman discusses the dangers of drugs with fourth graders in a drug awareness program aimed at deterring drug use among children.

fatal crashes has been cut by almost a third (Ayres, 1994). In the 1980s, the government's "Be Smart! Don't Start! Just Say No!" advertising campaign may have contributed to the substantial decline in illicit drug use. Thus, although progress is slow, aggressive and widespread, education campaigns can be effective in reducing drug abuse.

Improve Treatment and Research

There is a critical need for more effective and expanded treatment programs. Both the number of treatment programs and their effectiveness remain woefully inadequate. Thus, more funding is needed from federal and state governments to expand resources and the number of treatment centers. If this need is incorporated into the current agenda for health-care reform, billions of dollars may be saved in medical and economic costs. Treatment methods and research on improving treatment must also be expanded. We need much more research about the determinants of successful treatment and the factors involved in relapse. Basic biological research, for example, may lead to development of better drug therapies for reducing craving in the recovering addict. Further research into behavioral and cognitive treatment methods could result in improved long-term outcome. Some have proposed that a restructuring of priorities (for example, less money for drug law enforcement, more for research and treatment) would significantly enhance prevention efforts.

Putting It All Together

Drug dependence, as defined by the DSM-IV, entails serious impairments in the ability of a person to function. The vulnerability to addiction seems to be a consequence of both constitutional factors and exposure to environments that are stressful. Scientific research has shown us that at least some drugs have the potential to produce addiction by changing the way the brain functions. For this reason, many believe that it is reasonable to consider addiction a disease—one that involves a physical disability and requires treatment. But another perspective views addiction as a pattern of learned behaviors. Thus, rather than treating the person with drugs that alter biochemistry, the best approach to treating drug dependence is to change the behavioral contingencies.

Alcohol and nicotine are widely used addictive substances. Both contribute to health problems, and alcohol abuse and addiction can also have pervasive effects on the person's daily functioning. But many view the illegal drugs as the most serious threat. The stimulants, especially cocaine, have attracted the attention of the media because their addictive potential seems so devastating. Users of crack cocaine can undergo dramatic changes in personality and lifestyle. Similarly, the opiates, particularly heroin, can produce a powerful addiction that results in a seeming metamorphosis in the individual's personality and behavior. The use of hallucinogens, which became popular in the 1960s, produces altered sensory experiences, which are usually pleasurable. Dependence on hallucinogens is less widespread than addiction to stimulants and opioids. By far, however, the most widely used illicit drug is marijuana. Its primary active ingredient, THC, has the potential to produce euphoria and a sense of well-being. Despite the fact that a large portion of the population has tried marijuana, its use continues to raise concerns because it is viewed as a prelude to other, more serious drugs.

It is fortunate that there has been a substantial decline in use of drugs in the United States in the last fifteen years. Nonetheless, adolescent drug use continues at unacceptably high levels. Further, drug abuse remains one of the most critical public health problems facing our society. Each year, drug abuse kills hundreds of thousands of Americans and costs taxpayers over $270 billion in unnecessary health-care costs, extra law enforcement, auto accidents, crime, and lost productivity. Drug abuse is linked to neglect of children, family violence, homelessness,

Drug abuse kills hundreds of thousands of Americans and costs taxpayers billions of dollars in extra law enforcement. Here officers of the Drug Enforcement Administration prepare to pack money seized in a drug bust in Miami.

AIDS, urban decay, and many other social problems (Kleber, 1994). There is no solution to the problem in sight, and experts in the field differ in their views on the direction we should take. Some believe legalization is the solution, others believe legalization would be a social disaster. What is certain, however, is that research on the causes and treatments for drug dependence will continue. The stakes are too high to ignore the problem.

Summary

1. *Substance abuse* is a major health problem in the United States. The costs to society are enormous, and yet our society continues to have ambivalent attitudes about psychoactive drugs.
2. The diagnosis of *drug dependence* is made if the person exhibits: (1) loss of control over the use of the substance, (2) impairment in psychological and social functioning, and (3) physical or emotional adaptation to the drug.
3. The greatest problem in substance-abuse treatment is prevention of *relapse*. Even after very long periods of abstinence, most patients yield to uncontrollable drug cravings and revert to drug use.
4. The effectiveness of psychoactive drugs depends on several important factors, such as the route of administration, the ability of the drug to enter the brain, how well the drug interacts with the brain's receptors, and how quickly the drug is deactivated.

5. Psychological, social, and biological factors contribute to the development of substance-use disorders. A diagnosis of antisocial personality disorder is a risk factor for drug and alcohol addiction. Genetic factors may also influence vulnerability to addiction.

6. The *opponent-process theory* suggests that drugs may produce *affective pleasure,* which diminishes with *tolerance* (lessened response to the drug). *Affective withdrawal,* the opposite of affective pleasure, results when the drug is removed, and avoidance of this negative state may explain continued drug taking.

7. *Positive reinforcement models* of addiction posit that the powerful rewarding effects of drugs are the primary explanation for their use. Animals self-administer many of the drugs abused by humans. There are several brain systems and brain areas thought to play a critical role in drug reinforcement: the dopamine and opioid systems, and the nucleus accumbens.

8. The *conditioning and learning models* of addiction postulate that a drug state is an unconditioned stimulus that becomes associated with many signals in the user's environment. These signals become powerful conditioned stimuli and may contribute to the reinstatement of drug-seeking behavior.

9. *Alcohol dependence* is a very common disorder. Chronic use of alcohol results in impaired mental functioning and physical damage to organs. Physical dependence develops rapidly with excessive alcohol use. There is convincing evidence that alcoholism is a genetically influenced disorder. Many alcoholics do not recover; however, certain factors such as social stability, a substitute dependency, and membership in a supportive group have positive influences on outcome.

10. *Amphetamine* and *cocaine* are the most commonly used illegal stimulants, and cocaine dependence is a serious problem in the United States. Cocaine, and particularly its more potent form, *crack,* produces profound euphoria and is extremely addictive. Cocaine use is associated with many medical and social problems. Chronic use can cause psychosis and paranoia, and withdrawal from cocaine is accompanied by dysphoria and depression.

11. *Opiate drugs* produce their pharmacological effects by binding to opiate receptors in the brain. Most opiate addicts are intravenous heroin users, and therefore at risk for being infected with the HIV virus. Opiate use is associated with a high degree of tolerance and physical dependence. Maintenance therapy with a synthetic opiate, *methadone,* is the primary treatment for opiate addiction.

12. *Hallucinogens* distort reality and alter self-perception. *LSD* is the prototypical hallucinogen. People take hallucinogens for their complex sensory and perceptual effects, rather than for euphoric or relaxing properties. Physical dependence does not develop with hallucinogens.

13. *Marijuana* is a commonly used illicit drug and causes mild perceptual changes and feelings of well-being.

14. People smoke cigarettes for the mild pleasurable effects produced by *nicotine,* for stress reduction, and for improvement in cognitive functioning. The use of nicotine as a drug to treat cognitive deficits, such as those associated with schizophrenia and Alzheimer's disease, is being explored by researchers. On the negative side, nicotine has been found to be highly addictive, and the majority of smokers are not able to stop smoking permanently. The costs of cigarette smoking to personal health and to society are staggering.

15. *Barbiturates* and *benzodiazepines* are depressants of the central nervous system. People take them to relieve anxiety and insomnia. Abuse of barbiturates has decreased in recent years, but benzodiazepine abuse and dependence have been increasingly recognized as problems. The benzodiazepines increase the effectiveness of GABA, the principal inhibitory neurotransmitter in the brain.

16. There is considerable controversy about the best approach to *reducing drug abuse.* Some have taken the position that drugs should be legalized. Others advocate stronger legal penalties. It is likely that drug education, prevention programs, expanded treatment programs, and more research can all contribute to reducing drug abuse in our society. Limiting drug availability can also lower rates of drug use and dependence.

15

Social and Legal Perspectives

Painting by Marshall Arisman.

Learning Objectives

→ Be able to describe the impact of mental illness on the individual with mental illness, on his or her family, and on society at large.

→ Familiarize yourself with involuntary (civil) commitment procedures, including the criteria and standards of proof used to commit individuals to psychiatric facilities.

→ Describe restrictions that some states impose on the individual rights of psychiatric patients, as well as some of the rights advocated by the "Patients' Bill of Rights," including the patients' right to treatment.

→ Be able to explain what criminal commitment is, including the concepts of *mens rea* and competency to stand trial.

→ Learn what the insanity defense is and the tests for determining sanity.

→ Be able to describe the problems for the legal system of dissociative identity disorder and recovered memories.

→ Learn about the potential for abuse of mental health care, including clinical malpractice, governments' use of involuntary hospitalization and drug treatment to stifle dissent, and society's stigmatizing of individuals who have had mental disorders.

In the past twenty years, the emphasis in mental health care has shifted away from institutionalization and toward community treatment. This has largely solved the problem of overcrowded mental hospitals that have neglected patients who have no freedom. Rarely do we now see news stories about state hospitals where psychiatric patients are overdrugged and forgotten. Instead, we are more likely to read newspaper accounts about former patients who are homeless or live in squalid conditions in the community. Sometimes, as in the case of Thomas Kolt, the situation involves a tragic outcome:

Thomas Kolt shot and killed his wife Diane, and then committed suicide, on New Year's Day, 1992. One of their children discovered their bodies. His family considered the tragedy to be due, in part, to the negligence of the doctors at the Veterans Administration Medical Center (VAMC), where Kolt had received treatment for his mental illness.

Thomas Kolt had served in the army and was later employed as a laboratory technician. He was married in 1971 and had four children. His psychological problems began early in his marriage. Kolt was diagnosed with bipolar disorder and also had problems with alcohol and recurring suicidal thoughts. He was cited for driving while intoxicated on several occasions. Once in 1982, and again in September 1990, Kolt discharged a gun in his home, and the police were called by relatives. On both occasions, he agreed to a voluntary psychiatric hospitalization. When Kolt's family opposed his release from the hospital in 1990, his mother reluctantly agreed to let him stay with her. Between 1990 and 1992, Kolt's condition deteriorated, with increasing suicidal thoughts and preoccupation with weapons. His wife's threats of divorce also increased. The murder and suicide occurred within days of a discussion about divorce with his wife.

Thomas Kolt's family accused doctors at the VAMC of negligent mental health care. They believed Kolt's therapists should have further probed into his obsession with guns and his feelings about his wife's interest in divorce. More specifically, they faulted the doctors for failing to ask Kolt about the availability of weapons or about his plans if his wife did divorce him. Based on the responses they believe Kolt would have given, the family cited malpractice for failure to hospitalize. They believe Kolt should have been asked to voluntarily commit himself to a psychiatric facility. If he had refused, they believed he should have been involuntarily committed.

The case was closed in 1998, after a New York court ruled in favor of the U.S. government and the VAMC. The court held that the VAMC doctors did not have sufficient reason to involuntarily commit Kolt, and that their treatment of him did not depart from accepted standards of care. *(Kolt v. U.S. and the Veterans Administration Medical Center)**

As you may have guessed, Thomas Kolt was diagnosed with major depression. He received some treatment for his mood disorder, but it was not enough to prevent him from losing control and taking his spouse's life. In preceding chapters, you learned about the signs and potential causes of depression and other mental disorders. Our focus was on the behavior and personal experiences of individuals. In this chapter, the focus is broadened. We move from the symptoms and syndromes to the larger context. We begin by exploring social factors: the effects of society on the patient *and* the effects of mental illness on society. Next, we examine some political and economic issues, including the funding of mental health care. Then we discuss legal ramifications of abnormal behavior, including the criteria for involuntary commitment, commitment procedures, the right of the patient to treatment, and the insanity defense. We also discuss the challenges of dissociative identity disorder and recovered memories in the courtroom. Finally, we examine the potential for abuses of mental health care.

The Impact of Mental Illness

Today, more than 17 percent of Americans experience an episode of major depression at some point in their life, about 1 percent are diagnosed with schizophrenia, and about 2 percent with bipolar disorder (Kessler et al., 1994). If we add up the risk rates for these and other disorders, it becomes quite obvious that mental illness continues to be a significant problem for many individuals, their families, and the communities in which they live.

Of course, most problems brought to the attention of mental health practitioners are mild and tran-

*Estate of Thomas and Diane Kolt v. United States of America and the Veterans Administration Medical Center, April 24, 1998.

sient. For example, a person may experience an episode of anxiety or depression in coping with the loss of a loved one. Friends and family members may find it challenging to deal with the individual's symptoms, but the disruption is usually temporary. In contrast, severe and chronic mental illnesses pose a more formidable challenge to everyone involved, placing a burden on the individual, and having an impact on the family of the patient, as well as on society at large.

The Burden on the Individual

Most of us have never experienced a depression so severe that we attempt to take our own life. Nor have most of us experienced a psychotic episode in which we hear threatening voices and see frightening images not seen by others. The despair and terror associated with some mental disorders is beyond our comprehension. The psychological burden of mental illness certainly falls most heavily on the patient.

One especially burdensome aspect of mental illness is *stigma* (Fink and Tasman, 1992). Among the general public, some view the symptoms of mental disorders as willful, offensive behaviors (Angermeyer and Matschinger, 1996a). Others view mental illness as a sign of weakness or depravity—something that should be hidden from public view. The stigma of mental illness is fueled by the perception that psychiatric patients are dangerous (Angermeyer and Matschinger, 1996b). This view is undoubtedly strengthened by media depictions of the mentally ill (see Box 15–1). Research has revealed that individuals with serious mental illnesses are two to three times more likely to show aggression than nonpatients (Monahan, 1992; Torrey, 1994). Nonetheless, most individuals (90 percent) with mental illnesses never show aggressive behavior. And it is likely that even fewer patients would manifest aggressive behavior if treatment were more readily accessible.

Stigma can hamper effective treatment. It keeps some people from seeking mental health services from which they could benefit. Also, stigmatizing attitudes often interfere with community services for the mentally ill. For example, it is not uncommon for citizens to protest the location of new treatment facilities for the mentally ill in their neighborhood (Ahrens, 1993). In contrast, it is rare for citizens to protest the location of a new facility for treating individuals with physical disabilities.

Hollywood Depictions of the Mentally Ill

Many films that have dealt with abnormal behavior have depicted the mentally ill as depraved and dangerous individuals. A classic in this genre is *Psycho*. In this popular film, originally made in the 1960s, a young man who manifests delusional and eccentric behavior murders an innocent young woman. The brutality of the murder is so extreme that the scene, along with its accompanying soundtrack, has become an exemplar of American horror films. The 1998 remake of this film involved even more graphic violence than the original. Of course, taken in isolation this would not be a problem. The problem is that so many of the films that deal with the subject of mental illness emphasize propensities toward violent behavior. Included among these are *Silence of the Lambs, ConAir, Butcher Boy, Dr. Strangelove,* and *Twelve Monkeys*. Given the influence of Hollywood on American culture, there is every reason to believe that such films contribute to the stereotype of the mentally ill as "mad men" who are a threat to the welfare of the community. These negative stereotypes can then fuel the flames of community resistance to group homes or treatment programs for the mentally ill in residential areas. Further, negative depictions of the mentally ill might contribute to the trend toward incarcerating, rather than treating, those suffering from mental illness.

Should advocacy groups and mental health professionals try to influence media depictions of the mentally ill? Some believe that they should. On the other hand, some would argue that this is a form of censorship. Attempts to influence the media may also infringe on "artistic freedom."

Perhaps the best solution is to encourage the media to focus more attention on the plight of the mentally ill. Some films have done this by depicting the struggles and bravery of persons with severe mental illness. Examples of such films are *Girl, Interrupted, I Never Promised You a Rose Garden, Benny and Joon,* and *Awakenings*. By portraying the everyday lives of people with mental illness, the motion picture industry can help to educate the general public and increase community support for mental health programs.

(Left) The 1960 film *Psycho* emphasized the tendency toward violence of the mentally ill Norman Bates (played by Anthony Perkins), while *(right)* the 1999 film *Girl, Interrupted,* with Angelina Jolie and Winona Ryder, depicts the struggles of hospitalized patients to deal with their mental disorders.

Finally, stigmatizing attitudes also complicate the everyday lives of patients. For many, dealing with negative attitudes toward the mentally ill is just one more stressor in an already overwhelming situation. It contributes to feelings of dehumanization. Stigma can be an obstacle in dealing with family, friends, and the workplace. Some individuals with a history of mental disorder feel compelled to conceal it from employers in order to avoid discrimination. Research has shown that property owners are more likely to refuse to rent apartments to persons they suspect of having a psychiatric disorder (Page, 1977).

It is fortunate that many organizations and individuals have devoted a great deal of effort to the elimination of stigma against the mentally ill. The media have played a positive role in some of these efforts. In the past decade, there have been more television documentaries and films aimed at educating

Rod Steiger *(left),* Patty Duke *(center),* and Mike Wallace *(right)* have all suffered from clinical depression or bipolar disorder and have publicly discussed their battles with the disorder.

the public about mental health issues. Celebrities who have suffered from mental illness have come forward to talk about their personal experiences. For example, Rod Steiger, an accomplished actor, has publicly discussed his personal battle with depression. Patty Duke has also come forward to describe her struggle with bipolar disorder.

Not only are stigma and the depiction of the mentally ill by the media primary concerns, but in recent years homelessness among the mentally ill has also become a major issue. It is a tragedy that so many of the mentally ill have entered the ranks of the homeless, especially in urban areas (Culhane, Avery, and Hadley, 1998; Vazquez, Munoz, and Sanz, 1997). Estimates of the proportion of the homeless with a DSM-IV mental illness or substance abuse disorder range between 45 and 72 percent (Dennis, Buckner, Lipton, and Levine, 1991; Zima, Wells, Benjamin, and Duan, 1996). During 1992 and 1993, over 19,000 homeless people were admitted to public hospitals in New York City; 23 percent had a mental illness and 28 percent a substance abuse disorder (Salit, Kuhn, Hartz, Vu, and Mosso, 1998). The homeless mentally ill live chaotic lives, and they are often the victims of exploitation and criminal behavior (Lam and Rosencheck, 1998). Some become inmates in jail (Green, 1997). This is usually due to bizarre or disorderly public behavior, rather than serious criminal offenses. Because of this problem, police departments are making greater efforts to educate officers about the symptoms of mental illness.

The burden on the individual with mental illness increases the longer the illness goes untreated. For example, in the case of psychoses, the longer the du-

ration of the illness episode before antipsychotic medication is taken, the more severe the course of the illness (Wyatt and Henter, 1998). Thus, the failure to provide prompt, effective treatment can worsen illness prognosis and thereby increase both the personal and social costs.

Patients often also experience economic consequences of their illness. Many are unable to obtain or keep a job, and they must depend on others for financial support throughout their adult lives. The lack of income adds further to the difficulty of getting quality mental health care. The situation has become even more complex as deinstitutionalization has left more patients to fend for themselves in the community (Lamb, 1998).

The Cost to the Family

There are some similarities between serious physical illnesses and serious mental illnesses from the standpoint of their impact on the family. The similarities include the family's psychological pain at seeing a loved one suffer and their worry about his or her future well-being. But there are often extra burdens for the families of patients with mental disorders (Lamb, Bachrach, and Kase, 1992).

Let us begin by considering the situation from the perspective of parents who have a child with a mental illness. Of course, like virtually all parents, they have a deep emotional commitment to their child's well-being and success in life. When a child is first diagnosed with a mental illness, they must confront the possibility that their hopes may not be realized. If the disorder is severe and chronic, they may eventually have to come to terms with the fact that their child will never be fully independent and self-supporting. In many cases, there were no noticeable signs of abnormality in childhood. In fact, some who are diagnosed with schizophrenia or debilitating mood disorders in adulthood were above-average children who excelled in academics or extracurricular activities. The parents of these individuals must dramatically lower their expectations for their child. They often find that their mentally ill child remains financially dependent on them even as an adult. The case below is one such example of how parents must change their perspective on their child's future:

Our daughter was diagnosed as having a mental disorder when she was twenty-three. This did not come as a surprise to us because she had started a period of decline two years earlier. When she was twenty-one, Jane became very depressed and withdrawn. This lasted over a month. After she came out of the depression, she became very energetic. She cooked up a business scheme that involved buying rental property in the city. She tried to get her brother and several friends involved. She must have convinced some of them, because her brother and at least two friends loaned her money. She was convinced she and her "associates" were going to "get rich." Nothing ever came of this, and to the best of our knowledge Jane squandered all the money. She also took one of our credit cards and charged over $10,000 worth of merchandise that she gave to her friends as gifts.

Jane dropped out of college during her junior year to get a full-time job. She needed a job because she owed several people a lot of money, and one of them was taking her to court. It was easy for Jane to get hired. She is very pretty and she can be so charming and enthusiastic—when she is in a good mood. Jane went from one job to another that year. Sometimes she quit over an argument with her supervisor. She was fired three times for being unreliable. Then she went into another depression. This time it was worse, and she became suicidal. My husband and I urged Jane to see a doctor about her problems, but she would not accept that she had a problem.

Around the time she turned twenty-three, Jane began to have trouble sleeping. At this point, she entered another high-energy period. She would get up late at night and go out, then come home drunk the next morning. After sleeping most of the day, she woke up with outlandish stories about what she had done the previous night. But, as before, Jane's good mood gave way to another depression. This time she was very irritable. Sometimes she would beat on our bedroom door when we were asleep and yell at us for refusing to give her money. This depression went on for over a month. We finally convinced her that she needed to see a doctor, and the doctor was able to convince her that she needed to be hospitalized. We were relieved to have verification that she had a mental illness.

Jane's illness changed our outlook and our lives. In high school Jane was very popular and had the lead role in several theatrical productions. She was a good student and there seemed to be no limits on her potential. It was not surprising to anyone that she received a partial scholarship to college. We expected her to have a very successful career in the arts. But now it seems like her world, and our lives, have been turned upside down. I have cried myself to sleep on more nights than I care to remember.

Jane spends most of her time at home, so I cut back on my hours at work to be there with her. One weekend my husband and I went to visit friends. Jane invited some of her "friends" over and they stole several valuable items from our home. She was so upset when she discovered this that she called her brother at 3:00 A.M. in the morning. She woke him, his wife, and their baby. Of course now we worry about leaving Jane alone for extended periods of time, so we don't go on vacations.

Research has shown that caring for a chronically mentally ill family member can be a significant emotional burden (Webb et al., 1998). Parents sometimes carry this burden into late adulthood, and they worry about what will happen to their child when they are no longer around to provide care. They fear that their loved one could become homeless or be put in prison.

Certain aspects of the severe mental illnesses can make the task of caregiving more difficult. Many patients with severe mental illnesses lack insight and refuse to accept any kind of treatment. This is illustrated by Jane's case. During manic phases of her illness, no one could convince Jane that she needed help. This "denial" of illness is especially common among those suffering from bipolar disorder or schizophrenia. As a result, compared with physical illnesses, the effective treatment of mental disorders typically requires more intense and extensive support services. When these services are unavailable, many in need of treatment do not receive it. We will return to the case of Jane later when we take a look at the current mental health care system in the United States.

In the past, parents were also burdened by theories that attributed serious mental illnesses to poor child rearing. For example, the theory of the "schizophrenogenic mother" posited that schizophrenia was caused by mothers who were cold and uncaring. So, in addition to dealing with the devastation of their child's illness, the parents were also forced to cope with mental health professionals who held them responsible for it. It is fortunate that research has now clarified that schizophrenia and other major mental illnesses are biologically based. Nonetheless, the after-affects of past theories cause many parents to wonder whether there was something they could have done to prevent their child's illness.

Siblings of patients with serious mental illnesses face another set of challenges. If they grew up with an older sibling with a mental illness, they may have had to confront curiosity or even ridicule from peers. The younger brothers and sisters of people with mental disorders sometimes report that they felt awkward bringing friends home because they didn't want them to be aware of their sibling's illness. As adults, siblings of patients often worry about the caregiving burden faced by their parents. But perhaps the greatest worry for siblings is that they too may develop a mental illness or have a child with a mental illness. Genetic counselors are trained to address this concern.

The rate of marriage among patients with serious mental illnesses is much lower than it is among the general population (see Chapter 10). But some individuals marry prior to the onset of their illness. In these situations, the spouse sometimes finds that he or she must take on most household, financial, and child-rearing responsibilities.

Finally, we must consider the experiences of children who have a parent with a mental disorder. Very young children may find their parent's behavior confusing and unpredictable. They may be forced to function independently long before they are equipped to do so. For older children who have acquired an understanding of the illness, the experience may foster greater empathy. Nonetheless, like the siblings of patients, most children of mentally ill parents deal with worries about their parent's well-being, as well as their own vulnerability. It is important to mention, however, that some patients are excellent parents, despite otherwise debilitating symptoms of mental illness.

The Costs to Society

We have described some of the challenges encountered by families when they attempt to cope with mental illness in a relative. We now address the costs paid by society. In the case of Jane, whom we described earlier, her parents worried that without treatment she would end up on the streets or in jail or a state hospital at the taxpayers' expense:

> For us, the most upsetting times have been when Jane has disappeared for days—without her medication. The first time she stayed at a friend's apartment for several days, then left after an argument and ended up roaming the streets. She didn't want to come home because she knew we would try to convince her to take her medication. We didn't want to call the police, because we were afraid she would resist them and end up in jail or the state hospital. And the state law will only allow involuntary hospitalizations to last two days, so Jane would quickly end up on the street again. It is unfortunate that the state just closed the psychiatric hospital that was closest to our home. If Jane ever has to be committed again she will be sent to a public hospital that is forty miles away. We don't want this to happen, so when Jane leaves home, we just anxiously wait for her to return on her own.

COST-BENEFIT ANALYSIS

At the social level, a cost-benefit analysis of mental health care might involve weighing the costs to society of providing more treatment (for example, commitment of professional and staff time, facilities, medication) against the benefits derived from reduced costs in other sectors (for example, the workplace, criminal justice system, general medical care) and increased well-being for the community (for example, reductions in family discord, homelessness).

One obvious cost of mental illness is economic: the loss in worker productivity. This applies not only to the person who is afflicted with an illness, but also to family members who are involved in providing care. Family members spend time and resources on the care of their loved one. Often this involves lost workdays or reduced levels of work productivity.

Of course, the costs to society are greatest when mental disorders are untreated or "undertreated" by our health-care system (Gabbard, 1998). The result of this failure is a shift of responsibility from the mental-health-care system to other sectors of our society. For example, the criminal justice system bears a substantial burden in caring for individuals with mental illnesses (Booth et al., 1997; Lamb and Weinberger, 1998). This is because those with untreated mental illnesses sometimes engage in aberrant public behavior that results in their incarceration. Some have referred to this as the *criminalization* of mental illness. It is estimated that between 10 and 20 percent of prisoners in American jails currently suffer from a serious Axis I mental disorder, such as schizophrenia or bipolar disorder (Lamb and Weinberger, 1998; Wettstein, 1998). Since the costs of housing someone in prison are far greater than the costs of effectively treating mental illness, the criminalization of the mentally ill results in a waste of tax dollars, and also contributes further to the suffering of the individual.

Untreated mental illnesses also increase the demand for general medical services. For example, it has been shown that depressed individuals utilize more health services for physical problems than do nondepressed persons (Gabbard, 1998). Thus, the effective treatment of depression can result in a reduction in costs for general medical care.

MANAGED CARE AND MENTAL HEALTH

When compared to the treatment of general medical disorders, the treatment of mental illness poses some unique challenges to our health-care system. Some of the cognitive symptoms of mental illnesses can interfere with the individual's involvement in the treatment process. Complications also stem from negative societal attitudes toward the afflicted. But in addition to these factors, changes in the U.S. health-care system are fueling greater concerns about the quality of mental health care. In the present discussion, we will emphasize the treatment of the more serious mental illnesses, because these disorders constitute the largest portion of mental-health-care expenditures (Bazelon Center for Mental Health Law, 1994).

During the 1990s, we witnessed sweeping changes in the U.S. health-care system. Early in the Clinton administration, Bill Clinton and Hillary Rodham Clinton attempted to make systematic reforms in the health-care system. These efforts did not meet with success, but they did contribute to an already growing trend toward change. Private insurance companies and the *fee-for-service* system, in which doctors charge patients directly, gave way to managed health care, specifically *health maintenance organizations (HMOs)*.

In order to understand the evolution of this situation, we must briefly return to the mid-twentieth century. As we described in Chapter 10, from 1930 to 1960, most individuals with serious mental disorders received treatment in hospitals supported by the government. In fact, at that time, some mental health professionals were worried about the rapid increase in the number of state psychiatric hospitals (Bateman, 1945; Einbinder and Robinson, 1946). They feared that individuals who remained in state hospitals for extended periods of time would lose their independent living skills and their social connections with the larger community. In other words, they would become *institutionalized*. Thus, it was argued that patients with mental illnesses should be kept in the community whenever possible.

The introduction of psychotropic medications in the 1950s improved the prognosis for people suffering from serious mental illnesses. New antipsychotic and antidepressant drugs made it possible for more patients to live outside the hospital. Also, during the 1960s and 1970s, the "community mental health movement" gained momentum, with the intent of improving the functioning of patients by keeping them in community settings. Both of these trends contributed to the larger social movement toward the ***deinstitutionalization*** of mental patients. State legislatures closed public mental hospitals across the country, but the monies saved were not directed toward the development of community resources for treatment, support, and rehabilitation (Lamb, 1998).

The second half of the twentieth century witnessed a dramatic increase in the number of mental health practitioners and the number of persons utilizing mental health services (Klerman, 1983; Mechanic, 1989, 1993). Researchers have attributed this to greater public awareness about psychological treatment, rather than to an increase in psychological problems. Also, during the 1970s and 1980s, as public inpatient facilities closed, private for-profit psychiatric hospitals expanded. The private facilities were primarily supported through insurance reimbursements. It became common practice for families of psychiatric patients to exhaust their hospitalization coverage in a private facility, then, if further inpatient treatment was needed, to move the patient into a public setting. A "revolving door" phenomenon developed in which patients experienced repeated brief hospitalizations with the goal of stabilizing symptoms rather than rehabilitation.

In the beginning of the 1990s, with the expansion of managed care, there was a significant decrease in the reimbursements provided for both inpatient and outpatient psychiatric services. In fact, some HMOs and insurance companies offer no mental health services. This is because they feel they will lose money if they cover the costs of treating the mentally ill. People with mental illnesses, especially the major mental disorders, tend to be less independent, have more physical health problems, and have fewer financial resources (Frank, Huskamp, McGuire, and Newhouse, 1996). Even those patients who come from families with average or above financial resources find that these dwindle if the illness becomes chronic.

As a result of cutbacks in the mental health coverage offered by HMOs and insurance companies, many private psychiatric hospitals have closed. Others have changed their specialty to serve populations that were expected to grow, such as the geriatric patient population. At the same time, public psychiatric hospital beds have continued to decline in number. In 1960, 239 of every 100,000 people in the United States were in psychiatric hospitals. In 1990, only 41 out of every 100,000 people were hospitalized. This is a dramatic change.

Today in the United States there are three major sources of mental health treatment support: public money (state and federal, including Medicaid and Medicare), managed care organizations (HMOs), and private insurance companies (for example, Blue Cross/Blue Shield) (Frank, Goldman, and McGuire, 1994). Although government support of inpatient mental health services has declined since 1950, the government still provides the lion's share of the funding for inpatient treatment. Thus, throughout the century, mental health care has been distinguished from general medical care by the proportion of costs covered by government funds.

It was hoped that the expansion of managed care would bring spiraling health-care costs under some control. This is a noteworthy goal because, up to the 1990s, U.S. health-care costs were skyrocketing far beyond those of other industrialized nations. But most of us are familiar with the problems that have ensued. Health-care providers complain that their efforts to provide optimal care are thwarted by HMO representatives who do not understand medical needs. Many physicians believe that the new system undermines the traditional doctor–patient relationship. Similarly, patients complain that they are unable to see the physician of their choice. In several recent legal cases, patients have sued HMOs for failing to provide adequate treatment.

In many respects, the problems in the contemporary health-care system are amplified when it comes to mental health. For example, concerns about the privacy of the relationship between the patient and the health-care provider are especially salient when it comes to mental health. This is because of the stigma associated with mental illness. Yet, typical managed care procedures require that the treatment provider submit detailed information about the individual's life history, symptoms, and treatment. Further, clinicians are only reimbursed for their services if the nature and duration of the treatment conforms to the HMO guidelines. Patients worry that information about their mental illness might get into the wrong hands and jeopardize their employment opportunities, personal relationships, or future eligibility for insurance.

There is also widespread concern about the availability and quality of treatment, and many people claim that mental health care has declined with the expansion of HMOs. In the past few years, a substantial number of HMOs and insurance companies have eliminated coverage for mental health services (Frank, Koyanagi, and McGuire, 1997; Hennessey and Stephens, 1997). Others offer optional and/or partial coverage. Recent reports indicate that some HMOs and insurance companies have raised copayments and deductibles in order to restrict use of mental health services (Mental Health News Alert, July 20, 1998). In Massachusetts, where private HMOs are now operating some public mental health facilities, there have been reports of substandard care and deterioration in patient welfare, including a rise in the number of patient suicides (*Boston Globe,* September 23, 1995).

There is no doubt that cutbacks in access to mental health services from private and public sources have had negative consequences for patients and their families. Because the average age at onset of major mental illness is in young adulthood, parents of patients are usually middle-aged when their child is diagnosed. Once insurance or HMO benefits are exhausted, parents are left to either pay treatment costs out-of-pocket or to seek disability status for their child to obtain Medicaid. Under these circumstances, recurrences of the illness are especially problematic, as can be seen in Jane's case:

When Jane first became ill, we had private insurance that covered her treatment. She was hospitalized in a private hospital that had all the comforts of home and plenty of attentive staff members. But the insurance policy only covered about thirty hospital days per year, and we eventually had to have Jane transferred to a public hospital. She hated being there, and we couldn't wait for her release. When my husband changed jobs, we transferred to an HMO. It was hard to find one that would take Jane because of her medical history. The original plan we took was supposed to provide for outpatient and inpatient treatment. But as it turned out, their definition of outpatient services only included a maximum of ten psychotherapy sessions a year. That meant Jane could not continue to have regular sessions with the psychologist who had helped her through recoveries from illness episodes. We simply could not afford to pay for it ourselves.

The HMO also limited hospital days. They would only allow two or three days. Jane went through one especially bad period where she kept threatening suicide. The HMO representatives stuck to the three-day limit, because they said Jane could be under "suicide watch" at home. When she returned from the hospital she was still depressed. It was so stressful for my husband and me. After four days of this, Jane's psychiatrist increased her medication. This did help to lift Jane's mood, but it also caused her to sleep most of the day.

Limits on HMO and insurance coverage, in conjunction with the shrinkage of public sector mental health services, have frustrated patients and their families. In response, many advocacy groups (for example, the National Alliance for the Mentally Ill, the Fairness Coalition, and the American Psychological Association) have spearheaded legislation aimed at regulating insurance companies and managed care organizations. Specifically, they have sought *parity* for the treatment of mental illnesses. The intent of parity legislation is to enact legal requirements for equal coverage of mental illness and general medical illnesses by HMOs and insurance companies (Frank, Koyanagi, and McGuire, 1997).

In 1997, the efforts for parity legislation met with limited success in the form of the Domenici-Wellstone amendment. This amendment mandates that benefits for mental illness be provided with the same treatment limitations and financial requirements that are imposed on other medical conditions. Thus, no specific coverage requirement is specified,

but parity is required. Nonetheless, there are significant limits to the amendment. The amendment only applies to plans that already have mental health benefits; it does not mandate the provision of mental health coverage, and it does not prohibit the termination of mental health coverage by any plan. It also permits the application of higher levels of cost-sharing (copayments and deductibles) to mental health services. All of the limitations reflect the compromises required of the amendment's proponents in order to overcome objections from some in the health-care industry.

Despite the shortcomings of the Domenici-Wellstone amendment, it represents a big success from the standpoint of public education. In advocating for the bill, many legislators came forward to talk about their personal experiences with mental illness. Their eloquent statements went down on record and undoubtedly helped in the fight to reduce stigma.

Patient and Family Activism

The deinstitutionalization movement has contributed to the formation of community-based patient groups. In many communities, former psychiatric patients have established self-help groups that, in addition to providing social networks and employment opportunities, have also given the mentally ill a political base. A Presidential Commission on Mental Health, appointed by President Jimmy Carter in 1978, led to the passage of Section 501 of the Mental Health Systems Act of 1980, otherwise known as the Patients' Bill of Rights (see Table 15–1). While this law is only advisory in nature, most states provide at least some of those rights, and some states provide all of them.

To promote the welfare of the mentally ill, former patients, their families, and others have come together to form advocacy organizations, such as the National Mental Health Association, the Federation of Families for Children's Mental Health, and the National Alliance for the Mentally Ill (NAMI). These groups work for changes in state laws, monitor mental health treatment facilities, and, in some cases, provide legal representation for patients. In addition, these organizations have played a major role in public education aimed at disseminating scientific information about the causes of mental illness. In the process, they have helped to reduce the stigma associated with mental illness. The benefits of such groups can be seen in Jane's case:

TABLE 15–1

THE PATIENTS' BILL OF RIGHTS

Treatment	*Environment*	*Records and Grievances*
The right to appropriate treatment and related services in a setting which is most supportive and least restrictive of a person's liberty.	The right to be free from restraint or seclusion except in an emergency situation pursuant to a contemporaneous written order by a responsible mental health professional.	The right to confidentiality of personal records.
The right to an individualized, written treatment or service plan.	The right to a humane treatment environment that affords reasonable protection from harm and appropriate privacy.	The right to have access to personal mental health records and have a lawyer or legal representative have reasonable access to records if the patient provides written authorization.
The right, consistent with one's capabilities, to participate in and receive a reasonable explanation of the care and treatment process.	The right to private conversations, to reasonable access to telephones and mail, and to visitation during regular visiting hours.	The right to assert grievances with regard to the infringement of rights.
The right not to receive treatment without informed, voluntary, written consent, except in a documented emergency or as permitted under applicable law for someone who has been civilly committed.	The right to timely and meaningful information about one's rights at the time of and after admission.	The right to have a fair, timely, and impartial grievance procedure provided.
The right not to participate in experimentation in the absence of informed, voluntary, written consent.	The right of access to, including private communications with, any available rights protection service or qualified advocate.	The right to confidentiality of and access to records continues following one's discharge.
The right to referral as appropriate to other providers of mental health services upon discharge.		The patient has a right that his attorney or legal representative has reasonable access to the patient/client, the facility at which the patient resides, and, with written authorization, the patient's medical and service records.
The right to exercise other rights without reprisal, including denial of appropriate treatment.		

SOURCE: Adapted from the Mental Health Systems Act, 1980.

Despite Jane's illness, she has never lost her sense of pride and self-determination. Several years ago she got involved with a patients' rights group. At first she only attended meetings and helped send out newsletters. Then she agreed to serve as the vice president. Two years ago Jane got more involved, and she helped to start a theatrical group for former patients. Since that time we have really seen her blossom. She has found a way to use her talents in pursuing a worthy goal. Jane played the lead role in a recent production and won an award from the Metropolitan Arts Association. When my husband and I watched her walk up on the stage to get her award we were in tears. This was a dream I always had for Jane.

Another major concern of advocacy groups is the support of research on the causes of mental illness. The amount of federal money provided to support research on mental illnesses is much smaller than that allocated for studies of physical illnesses. NAMI and other organizations have worked hard to get the federal government to spend more money on mental health research. In addition, several private foundations have been established to fund scientific research on mental illness. These include the National Alliance for Research on Schizophrenia and Depression (NARSAD) and the Stanley Foundation. Many of the research findings discussed in previous chapters have come from studies funded by these private foundations.

Involuntary Commitment

In our society, few would disagree with the notion that government has a responsibility to protect both the rights and the safety of its citizens. This, of course, includes those with mental disorders. But

Mental illness may compromise the person's judgment and capacity for insight. This man who thinks he is a soldier in the Foreign Legion may not realize that he is mentally ill and needs treatment.

these illnesses sometimes compromise the person's judgment and capacity for insight. In fact, many patients with chronic psychotic disorders say they do not believe they are mentally ill (about 19 percent) or say they are not sure they are mentally ill (25 percent) (Walker and Rossiter, 1989). Ironically, it is those with the most severe symptoms who are the most likely to deny their mental illness. Instead, they attribute their situation to bad luck, personal vendettas, or conspiracies against them. As a result, some who would benefit from treatment either fail to seek help or resist the efforts of mental health professionals (Cohen, 1997).

The fact that many persons who have a mental illness do not believe they are ill poses significant problems. Should these persons be compelled to receive treatment? Should they be subject to **involuntary commitment,** or **civil commitment,** that is, commitment to a psychiatric facility without their consent? The proper course of action is not always clear-cut. The civil rights of the mentally ill must be balanced against the rights of others and the rights of society. Sometimes the civil rights of patients have to be compromised in order to insure their physical safety or the safety of the community.

For most people, violence against self or others is a compelling argument for involuntary hospitalization. Where there is danger to human life, most people would agree that some intervention is necessary. But many cases are not nearly so clear-cut. Indeed, these borderline cases test the very meaning of normality and abnormality (see Chapter 1). Abnormal

by whose standard? Some people believe themselves depressed for good reason, but society finds them mentally ill and in need of treatment. Others enjoy the relaxation and "highs" conferred by recreational drugs, yet society views them as addicts who require medical attention. Still others radically alter their lifestyles on discovering "the ultimate truth," but society may designate that discovery as psychotic and commit the person to a psychiatric facility. In the past, most controversies about involuntary treatment involved allegations of unnecessary hospitalizations. *Mayock* v. *Martin*★ illustrates this point:

Mr. Mayock was hospitalized in July 1944 after he had removed his right eye. He was subsequently diagnosed as having paranoid schizophrenia, eventually released on probation, and finally discharged three years later. Three days after discharge, Mayock removed his right hand, and was committed once again to the state hospital. At the time of trial, some twenty years later, Mayock was still confined involuntarily to the state hospital with the diagnosis of paranoid schizophrenia.

At his trial, Mayock insisted that there was nothing mysterious or crazy about his self-maiming. Rather, he is a deeply religious man who believes that society's attempts to establish peace by force are entirely misguided. God's way, he says, is to encourage peace through love. If society continues on its present path, many lives will be lost through war. Mayock believes that one man has been chosen to make a peace offering to God: that he, Mayock, is that man, and that it is better for one person to accept a message from God to sacrifice an eye or a hand than it is for society to suffer a great loss of human life.

During the twenty years that he had been hospitalized, Mayock had had complete freedom of the hospital grounds. He had not once maimed himself. Yet, he acknowledged that he would gladly do so again either as a significant freewill offering or in response to divine revelation.

Beyond this single symptom, there was no further evidence that Mayock was disturbed. He had risen to a position of considerable responsibility in the hospital, running the recreation center for parole-privileged patients, as well as the hospital newsstand. There was ample evidence that he could handle financial matters and take care of himself in all other respects.

★Mayock v. Martin, 157 Conn. 56, 245A. 2d (1968).

Psychiatrists at the hospital contended that his prophetic view of himself was "grandiose," that his religious beliefs were "grossly false," and that the diagnosis of paranoid schizophrenia was entirely warranted by the facts. Mayock contended that he is religious, not mentally ill, and that his First Amendment constitutional rights ("Congress shall make no law respecting an establishment of religion or prohibiting the free exercise thereof. . . .") had been violated.

The court found that Mayock should continue to be hospitalized. Some will feel that this decision was correct, for only those with severe mental illness would gouge out their eyes and chop off their arms. Others will feel that this was a tragedy, for Mayock was acting with courage upon deeply held religious beliefs and harming no one but himself. Perhaps the tragedy lies in that ambiguity, for Mayock can be seen as quite abnormal by some standards, and not abnormal by others.

In general, the use of involuntary hospitalization of people who are believed to be dangerous to themselves ought to be guided by the "thank you" test (Stone, 1975). This test asks: Will the person, once recovered, be grateful for that hospitalization, however much it was protested? The test would likely be passed by people who are severely depressed and suicidal and who, once the depression lifted, would be grateful to be alive. But what about those who are a danger to others, as in the following case:

On July 24, 1998, forty-one-year-old Russell Eugene Weston, Jr., walked into the U.S. Capitol building in Washington, D.C., with a .38 caliber handgun. When confronted by a police officer, Weston opened fire and began a rapid shooting spree that left two police officers dead and injured some tourists. Weston also sustained injuries.

Weston's family described him as odd but harmless as a child and somewhat of a loner. In 1984, Weston was diagnosed with paranoid schizophrenia and received treatment for the illness. He was involuntarily admitted to a psychiatric hospital in 1996 after sending a letter to President Clinton accusing him of sending CIA agents to try to kill him. He was released two months later on the condition that he continue treatment at an outpatient clinic. But Weston did not pursue treatment and discontinued his antipsychotic medication. "We couldn't get him to a doctor," said

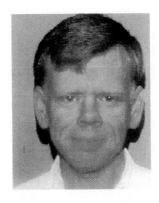

Russell Eugene Weston, Jr.

Weston's father. "Most of the time we would try to say to him, 'Rusty, you know that's not true' and he would say, 'You're the one that's sick.'" His mother said, "I kept hoping that maybe he would get picked up for something minor and the sheriff would make him go and get the help he needed." That never happened. Days before the Capitol shooting, Russell Weston shot two of the family's pet cats in the head with a shotgun. (Based on the *Washington Post,* July 27, 1998)

Today, there are many more controversial cases about failure to hospitalize. These are situations where involuntary commitment may have been appropriate, but was not used. Why has failure to hospitalize become a more salient issue in recent years? Some believe this is due to the declining number of public inpatient facilities and decreased availability of treatment. Others attribute it to a greater emphasis on patient rights than on patient safety. Whatever the cause, some family members have sued practitioners and mental health agencies on the grounds that they failed to provide adequate treatment. One such example is the case of Thomas Kolt, described at the beginning of this chapter. Imagine yourself in the position of the doctors who treated Kolt. Would you have made efforts to hospitalize him? What if you were a family member? Would you support your loved one's involuntary hospitalization?

In most countries, legal factors play a major role in determining who is hospitalized against their will. In order to understand the legal aspects of involuntary hospitalization, we need to know something about the laws that regulate commitment procedures. Our focus will be on laws in the United States, but it is worth noting that many other countries have similar laws.

Civil Commitment Procedures

The practice of civil commitment has been surrounded by intense controversy for many years. Commitment procedures have varied over time and from state to state. In recent years, the laws governing involuntary commitment have become more stringent, so that fewer patients are hospitalized against their will (Appelbaum, 1997). Also, the duration of civil commitments is shorter. Data from Philadelphia in 1991 and 1992 showed that there were 2,200 involuntary civil commitments in psychiatric hospitals during this period (Sanguineti, Samuel, Schwartz, and Robeson, 1996). The majority received a diagnosis of schizophrenia. The mean length of hospitalization was six and a half days. In contrast, national data from 1980 indicated that the mean length of stay for involuntary patients was about twenty-five days (Rosenstein, Steadman, MacAskill, and Mandersheid, 1986).

As mentioned earlier, some believe that the laws governing commitment have become too strict, and that the restrictions are endangering both society and the patient. The ranks of the homeless and imprisoned mentally ill have grown dramatically in recent years. Have the scales tipped so far in the direction of protecting patients' civil rights that some are being deprived of good treatment or exposed to unnecessary danger? We will examine several viewpoints on this issue.

There are several ways that a person can end up being civilly committed for mental illness. In some cases, family members seek civil commitment for a relative who they believe is unable to care for himself because of mental illness. This can be a very lengthy process. More often, mental health professionals licensed by the state seek civil commitment for their patient. For example, in the state of Georgia, a person can be involuntarily hospitalized for a period of twenty-four hours if a licensed psychologist or psychiatrist formally authorizes the police to do so.

The majority of civil commitments occur when the person is brought to an emergency room by family members or the police. In fact, police officers are often the first authorities to initiate the process of civil commitment (Green, 1997). As a result, most metropolitan police departments provide their officers with rudimentary training in the detection of mental illness. This prepares them to deal with the homeless mentally ill who often engage in behavior that brings them to the attention of the police. Usu-

ally, the behavior involves a violation of local ordinances governing public conduct, such as "disturbing the peace." When this occurs, police officers must make a judgment as to whether the individual should be taken to a jail or to a psychiatric facility. Although in a perfect world this decision should be based on a thorough psychological evaluation, such is rarely the case. In fact, in the real world the decision is often based on pragmatic considerations, such as: How far is the nearest mental health facility that will take indigent patients? Do we have sufficient personnel to transport the individual?

When a person is brought in for emergency evaluation, he is usually suicidal, disoriented, and/or agitated. The first challenge is to calm him, and then to obtain information that will assist in diagnosis. If the clinician believes the individual meets the state's criteria for civil commitment, the subject may be kept at the hospital. In many states, two doctoral level (M.D. or Ph.D.) mental health professionals must sign a certificate indicating that it is their opinion that the person is in need of commitment. But this is a temporary measure for emergency commitments. If a judge's order for an extended period of commitment is not obtained within a matter of hours, the patient must be released. The judge makes this decision after a formal hearing. The criteria for commitment and the specified length of involuntary hospitalization vary among the states.

COMMITMENT CRITERIA

The procedures and criteria for civil commitment vary among states because each jurisdiction has made its own attempts to clarify and improve commitment procedures. But three elements are included in all statutes: (1) the presence of mental disorder, (2) dangerousness to self or others, and (3) grave disability. In addition, the American Psychiatric Association has proposed a fourth criterion, "likely to suffer substantial mental or physical deterioration," and it has attempted to convince state legislatures to include such a criterion in their commitment procedures (American Psychiatric Association, 1983; Monahan and Shah, 1989). This criterion is fundamentally a predictive one that encourages civil commitment when, as evidenced by recent behavior, if not treated, a person will "suffer or continue to suffer severe and abnormal mental, emotional, or physical distress [which] . . . is associated with significant impairment of judgment, reason, or behavior causing a substantial deterioration of his previous ability to function on his own" (American Psychiatric Association, 1983, p. 673). To date, this criterion has not been routinely implemented.

Defining "Mental Disorder"

All states require that an individual be suffering from a psychological disability, variously termed "mental illness," "mental disease," "mental disorder" or "mental disability." But often these phrases are not specifically defined, leaving unclear which disabilities qualify and which do not. Definitions of mental disorder vary widely across the states. Perhaps the most thoughtful is that offered by the American Psychiatric Association, which would restrict civil commitment only to those with severe mental disorders. It defines a severe mental disorder as "an illness, disease, organic brain disorder, or other condition that (1) substantially impairs the person's thought, perception of reality, emotional process, or judgment, or (2) substantially impairs behavior as manifested by recent disturbed behavior." In general, a severe mental disorder corresponds to a psychotic disorder or severe depression.

Dangerousness to Self or Others

Most states require that there be some evidence that the individual is dangerous, either to himself or to others. And indeed, more involuntary hospitalizations are justified on these grounds than on any others. A study of civil commitment in California found that roughly 60 percent of those committed were held to be dangerous to themselves (suicidal), 49 percent were dangerous to others, and 32 percent were "gravely disabled" (Segal, Watson, Goldfinger, and Averbuck, 1988). As you might well imagine, substantial proportions of mentally disordered people are committed because they meet more than one criterion. Jane was involuntarily hospitalized when she threatened to kill herself:

> There were several times when we were tempted to have Jane hospitalized against her will. Friends of ours from NAMI told us about the state laws, so we knew that we might be able to get her hospitalized if we told her doctor that she was suicidal. The problem was that Jane would be so furious at us she might never speak to us again. One time she was involuntarily admitted by a psychologist, Dr. Naylor. Jane had told Dr. Naylor she was going to kill herself, so Dr. Naylor had an ethical duty to hospitalize her. But as a result, Jane vowed to never speak to the doctor again, and she stuck to that promise.

In some state statutes, the definition of dangerousness is vague. Alabama, for example, provides for commitment when a person "poses a real and present threat of substantial harm"(Code of Alabama 22-52-37, 1998). Massachusetts law states that individuals can be involuntarily committed by a qualified clinician if "failure to hospitalize would create a likelihood of serious harm by reason of mental illness" (Massachusetts General Law, Chapter 123). Florida law specifies that a mentally disordered individual can be hospitalized if "[t]here is substantial likelihood that in the near future he will inflict serious bodily harm on himself or another person, as evidenced by recent behavior causing, attempting, or threatening such harm."

But regardless of how carefully or vaguely dangerousness is defined, two problems arise, one legal and the other scientific. The legal problem is straightforward. Hospitalizing people because they are expected to be dangerous creates a dilemma. This is because Western legal traditions generally mandate the deprivation of liberty only after a crime has been committed, not before. Some would argue that the mere fact that someone is expected to violate the law is not sufficient reason for limiting their freedom.

The scientific problem is whether dangerousness can ever be predicted so precisely that only the dangerous will be hospitalized. Clearly, the ability to predict dangerous behavior lies at the very heart of civilized and rational civil commitment procedures. Over the past two decades, researchers have sought to identify the predictors of violent behavior. One of the most interesting early studies arose out of the case of *Baxstrom v. Herold*★ (Steadman and Keveles, 1972, 1978):

> After serving more than two years for second-degree assault, Johnnie K. Baxstrom was certified as insane by a prison physician and transferred to a prison hospital. Baxstrom's sentence was about to end, however, but because he was still in need of psychiatric care, the director of the prison hospital petitioned that Baxstrom be committed involuntarily to an ordinary psychiatric hospital. That petition was denied for administrative reasons. Baxstrom, therefore, was forced to remain where he was.
>
> Baxstrom went to court with the following contention: If he was sane, he deserved to be discharged as soon as he completed his sentence. And if he was not sane, he should be transferred to an ordinary psychi-

★Baxstrom v. Herold, 383 U.S. 107 (1966).

atric hospital. Thus, he argued, his constitutional rights were being violated insofar as he was required to remain in prison beyond the termination of his sentence.

The United States Supreme Court agreed. As a result, "Operation Baxstrom," which was designed to effect the rapid release of 967 similarly confined patients from New York State's prison-hospitals, was launched. It was feared that the released patients would act violently upon their release. They were considered to be criminally insane. They had been violent in the past and were expected to be violent in the future. Would those predictions hold up?

In fact, there were abundant false positives—individuals who did not act out violently—as well as false negatives—individuals released as nonviolent who later committed violent crimes. After four years, Steadman and Keveles (1972) reported that only 2.7 percent of the released patients had behaved dangerously and were either in a correctional facility or back in a hospital for the criminally insane. Careful examination of the patients who were later rehospitalized or imprisoned revealed no "set of factors that could have selected these returnees from all the Baxstrom patients without a very large number of false positives" (Steadman, 1973, p. 318).

More recently, there have been some improvements in our ability to predict violent behavior. For example, there is evidence that a subgroup of the mentally ill who are experiencing psychotic symptoms, abuse drugs, and fail to take their medication are more likely to be violent (Link, Andrews and Cullen, 1992; Mona-han, 1992). One current controversy surrounds the relative superiority of *clinical* prediction versus *actuarial* prediction (Harris and Rice, 1997; Lidz, Mulvey, and Gardner, 1993; Swartz et al., 1998). Clinical prediction of violence draws on the professional's experience with varied cases, whereas actuarial prediction is based upon mathematical formulas and specific, objective data on the patient. It is possible that future research will reveal that a combination of both clinical expertise and actuarial data yields the best prediction. In the meantime, there is evidence that experts in the field can offer predictions that are significantly better than chance.

Grave Disability   A few states permit commitment of distressed individuals when, as a result of their mental state (and for no other reason), they are unable to provide for their basic needs for food, shelter, clothing, health, and safety. Thus incapacitated, they become "passively dangerous," that is, dangerous to themselves, not because they might actively attempt suicide or mutilation, but because they will not do those things that seem necessary to stay alive and healthy. California defines "grave disability" as "a condition in which a person, as a result of mental disorder, is unable to provide for his basic personal needs for food, clothes, or shelter."

DUE PROCESS OF LAW

Prior to the 1970s, the rights of patients with mental disorder received relatively little attention. This situation changed gradually, and today we have reached a

Patients who have been released from mental hospitals may remain unable to take care of themselves and end up homeless and sleeping on the streets like the man pictured here.

point where some believe the balance has shifted too far in the opposite direction. Has the pendulum swung so far so that the rights of family members and society are not given enough consideration? Are we sacrificing the safety and welfare of some patients in the name of preserving their civil rights?

From the perspective of preserving civil rights, it would seem reasonable to provide the psychologically distressed with the same privileges that are afforded to anyone whose liberty is threatened by state action—to criminal defendants, for example. These rights and privileges are collectively called "due process of law" and include:

- the right to be notified of trial in a timely manner,
- the right to trial by jury,
- the right to be present at one's own trial,
- the right to legal counsel and the appointment of counsel in a timely manner,
- the right to exclude unreliable evidence, such as hearsay evidence, from the testimony,
- the right to challenge witnesses.
- the privilege against self-incrimination,
- the right to counsel at all interviews, including psychiatric interviews,
- the right to know, with considerable precision, which laws one has violated and under which laws one stands accused.

Commitment to a psychiatric hospital involves a serious restriction of individual rights. For example, in some states those judged to be mentally ill are unable to vote and may not serve on a jury. Their right to practice certain professions is restricted, as are their rights to make contracts, to sue, and to be sued. These restrictions distinguish psychiatric from other kinds of medical disorders, and require that special attention be paid to due process issues. As we mentioned, patients' rights' activists successfully lobbied Congress to pass a "Patients' Bill of Rights," which advises states to safeguard the rights of those who are committed to psychiatric facilities (see Table 15–1).

STANDARD OF PROOF

Involuntary hospitalization involves a significant deprivation of liberty. In order to so restrict a person's freedom, it must be proved that, in accord with the law, he belongs in a psychiatric hospital. Mere allegation is insufficient. What standard of proof should be required? Generally speaking, three standards of

proof are available in law: preponderance of evidence, beyond a reasonable doubt, and clear and convincing proof.

Often called the "51 percent standard," the **preponderance of evidence** standard requires just enough proof to shift the weight of evidence to one side. This is the standard used in civil cases, where penalties are often monetary and do not involve deprivation of liberty.

Beyond a reasonable doubt is the most severe standard of proof and requires that the evidence be so compelling as to convince a reasonable listener beyond a reasonable doubt. This standard is used in criminal law, where the presumption of a defendant's innocence is very strong, and the cost of wrongful incarceration of an innocent person high indeed. It is often termed the 90 percent or 99 percent standard, implying that the weight of evidence must be such that people would be willing to stake high odds on the guilt of the defendant.

Clear and convincing proof is an intermediate standard that is not quite so severe as that requiring proof beyond a reasonable doubt, but not as lenient as the 51 percent standard that requires the mere preponderance of evidence. Consider it the 75 percent standard.

Recalling what you have read here regarding the validity of predictions of dangerousness, and what you have learned about the reliability and validity of psychiatric diagnoses generally, what standard of proof should be invoked in order to commit a person involuntarily? In 1979, the matter was taken up by the Supreme Court in *Addington* v. *Texas*.★

Frank O'Neal Addington had been hospitalized seven times between 1967 and 1975. His mother now petitioned the court to have him involuntarily committed because he was both dangerous to himself and dangerous to others. In accord with Texas law, a jury trial was held to determine if he required hospitalization. The judge instructed the jury to determine whether there was "clear, unequivocal and convincing evidence"— the 75 percent standard—that Addington was mentally ill and required hospitalization for his protection and for the safety of others. The jury so found, but Addington appealed the decision to the U.S. Supreme Court on the grounds that the appropriate standard of proof should have been a tougher one—beyond a reasonable doubt—the 90 percent standard.

★Addington v. Texas, 99 S. Ct. 1804 (1979).

The Supreme Court held that the 90 percent standard was simply too severe. Given the uncertainties of psychiatric diagnosis and prediction, requiring proof beyond a reasonable doubt would render the state unable to commit many truly distressed people who were much in need of treatment. The preponderance of evidence standard, on the other hand, was much too lenient. If the state wanted to deprive a person of liberty, it needed to bear a greater burden of proof than that implied in the 51 percent standard. The Supreme Court therefore upheld the original decision, maintaining that the presentation of clear and convincing evidence—roughly 75 percent certainty—is the minimum standard for involuntary commitment and that states may not commit below this minimum standard (though they are free to fix standards that are higher than this required minimum).

The Right to Treatment

The *Addington* case dealt with the standard of proof that is required before someone could be involuntarily committed. What about after he or she has been committed? Is there a "right to treatment" for those who have been deprived of their liberty, presumably because they required psychiatric treatment? Oddly, and with few exceptions, the courts have been very cautious on this matter. They are understandably reluctant to invent new "rights." Yet, deprivation of liberty is a serious matter in a democratic society, and the courts have occasionally been responsive to cases in which hospitalization has occurred without the person receiving adequate treatment. Thus, in *Rouse* v. *Cameron*,★ Judge David Bazelon clearly enunciated a right to treatment that was rooted in federal statute. He wrote: "The purpose of involuntary hospitalization is treatment, not punishment . . . absent treatment, the hospital is transform[ed] . . . into a penitentiary where one could be held indefinitely for no convicted offense" (*Rouse* v. *Cameron,* 1966, p. 453). Not all "treatments" count as treatment, however. Bazelon wrote:

> The hospital need not show that the treatment will cure or improve him but only that there is a bona fide effort to do so. This requires the hospital to show that

initial and periodic inquiries are made into the needs and conditions of the patient with a view to providing suitable treatment for him. . . . Treatment that has therapeutic value for some may not have such value for others. For example, it may not be assumed that confinement in a hospital is beneficial "environment therapy" for all." (*Rouse* v. *Cameron,* 1966, p. 456)

In a later opinion, Judge Frank Johnson (*Wyatt* v. *Stickney*★) stipulated minimal objective standards of care, which were far below those recommended by the American Psychiatric Association. He also made clear that patients have a right to privacy and dignity, to the least restrictive regimen necessary to achieve the purposes of commitment, and to freedom from unnecessary or excessive medication. He affirmed their right to send sealed mail and to use the telephone—privileges that are often denied patients on the grounds that they might say things that they would later have cause to regret. Finally, Johnson said that each patient was entitled to an individual treatment plan, and to periodic review of his or her plan and progress.

Opinions written in such cases as *Rouse* v. *Cameron* and *Wyatt* v. *Stickney* alerted people to the plight of psychiatric patients, and held promise for improving their fate. But, unfortunately, they also had a major unintended consequence. Faced with the prospect of pouring more money into psychiatric care, many states took the least expensive route and simply discharged patients from psychiatric hospitals, and closed the hospitals. During the 1970s, for example, California closed a majority of its psychiatric hospitals and cut back severely on funding of mental health programs. Other states followed suit. As a result, thousands of people who were formerly housed in psychiatric hospitals were shunted to "board and care" homes in local communities.

But community placements were no panacea. The new visibility of these former inpatients, combined with the stigma associated with those labeled mentally ill, frequently created a harsh community reaction. Many found employment difficult to obtain, and social relationships difficult to establish. Some ended up on the streets, homeless and untreated. Given these facts, a policy that establishes community-based treatment and provides support is clearly called for.

★Rouse v. Cameron, 373 F. 2d 451 (D.C. Cir. 1966).

★Wyatt v. Stickney, 344 F. Supp. 343 (M.D. Ala. 1972).

A new approach that has recently been adopted by some states is "outpatient commitment." In these programs, the court orders the patient to cooperate with a course of treatment. This usually includes taking antipsychotic medication and being supervised by a designated professional. If the patient fails to take the prescribed medication or to keep appointments, he or she can be hospitalized against his or her will. This approach is only used with patients who have not cooperated with treatment and are found to be dangerous to themselves or others (see Box 15–2).

Several states, including Iowa, North Carolina, and Ohio, have implemented such laws with good success. In all of these states involuntary hospital admissions were reduced by about one-half!

Abolish or Expand Involuntary Hospitalization?

Some critics of involuntary commitment have argued that it should be abolished. During the 1960s and 1970s, Thomas Szasz, a psychiatrist, was especially

---

Ensuring Adequate Treatment

In a recent letter published on the Op-Ed page of the *Philadelphia Inquirer,* E. Fuller Torrey, a noted scientist who studies schizophrenia, and Mary Zdanowicz, of the Treatment Advocacy Center in Arlington, Virginia, expressed their opinions about the standards for involuntary treatment. These authors take the position that the laws governing involuntary hospitalization are too strict, and that they ultimately do a disservice to society and those afflicted with mental illness. They propose changing the criteria for involuntary treatment from "danger to self or others" to "inability to help oneself." Clearly this would represent a major departure from current policy. Is their proposal reasonable? How would their proposal be reconciled with patient civil rights?

Following are excerpts from their letter:

Theodore Kaczynski [the "Unabomber"; see p. 666], Michael Laudor [a mentally ill man who killed his pregnant fiancée; see p. 659], Russell Weston [see p. 650]. Three tragic figures inextricably linked in our nation's headlines this year—each symbolizing the woeful failure of deinstitutionalization. All three have schizophrenia, and none was taking the medication needed to control his delusions and hallucinations when he committed fatal acts of violence.

Ironically, nearly half of those who have schizophrenia or manic-depressive illness do not realize they are sick and in need of treatment. Because they do not believe they are sick, they refuse to take their medication, which is perfectly acceptable in the eyes of the law.

Conversely, studies have shown that people receiving proper treatment are no more prone to violence than the general public. A study released earlier this year by the MacArthur Foundation, in fact, showed that violence among people being treated for their psychiatric illnesses was reduced by half.

Because of the lack of community supports, deinstitutionalization has not only contributed to the nation's rate of violence, but also has affected our quality of life. We see it especially clearly in our bigger cities—the deterioration of

public transportation facilities, loss of use of public parks, and disruption of public libraries are a few examples. The presence of even nonviolent mentally ill homeless in the streets and parks creates an inescapable sense of squalor and degradation. These people often end up victimized, in jail for misdemeanors, or prematurely dead from accidents, suicide, or untreated illnesses.

What can we do to insure adequate treatment for these patients?

Change the standard. The legal standard for assisted treatment should be the inability to help oneself, not, as it is now, "danger to self or others." Society has an obligation to save people from degradation, not just death.

Require compliance. Most individuals with severe mental illnesses can live in the community. But that must be conditioned on continued medication compliance. Outpatient commitments, conservatorships, and conditional hospital releases should be used widely to ensure that discharged patients comply with the requirement that they take their medication.

Build supports in the community. For assisted treatment to work, states must build a network of outreach services in their communities to ensure compliance and to provide the supports needed for daily living and to prevent relapse. It means building the services that were promised to replace the closed psychiatric hospitals.

The case of the seriously mentally ill in twentieth-century America has been a public disgrace. More than 150 years of warehousing patients in inhumane state hospitals has been followed by almost 40 years of dumping them into bleak boarding homes or onto streets. As we enter the new millennium, it is time to help individuals with severe mental illness become life's victors and not remain its victims.

SOURCE: *The Philadelphia Inquirer,* December 3, 1998.

vocal in this regard. Szasz argued that mental illness is different from physical illness, in that the criteria for mental disorders are less precise and specific. "[L]ooking for evidence of such illness is like searching for evidence of heresy: Once the investigator gets into the proper frame of mind, anything may seem to her to be a symptom of mental illness" (Szasz, 1963, p. 225). Szasz continues to believe that psychiatry has a great potential for social abuse, particularly as it lends itself, through involuntary commitment, to ridding society of all manner of deviants and eccentrics, all in the name of treating mental illness (Szasz, 1994, 1998). Szasz is not opposed to voluntary hospitalization, provided patients are frankly told whether or not they will receive the best treatment.

Some critics, including Szasz, not only oppose involuntary hospitalization, but involuntary treatment as well. Citing the adverse side effects of certain antipsychotic drugs, there have been lawsuits by patients to assert the right to refuse medications. Szasz (1998) has recently argued that true parity for the mentally ill will only be achieved when they are free to refuse *all* treatments. In other words, like patients with cancer or heart disease, the mentally ill should have the option of foregoing medication and hospitalization.

On the other side of the debate, many believe attempts to protect patients against involuntary hospitalization and treatment are not really helping the patients (see Box 15–2). They argue that the current guidelines on involuntary treatment are too restrictive and deprive many patients of needed care. For example, they point out that concerns about medication for mental disorders have diminished as new drugs with fewer side effects have become available. These medications can make the difference between a life of dependency and suffering versus one of self-sufficiency and personal fulfillment. In addition, family members of patients object to the requirement that "dangerousness" be demonstrated in order to obtain inpatient treatment for their loved one. The situation places an especially great burden on elderly parents who worry about the welfare of their mentally ill child when they are no longer able to care for him or her. The case of Russell Weston illustrates the plight of parents whose severely disturbed son easily avoided treatment in the current health-care climate. It is interesting to consider whether the outcome might have been different if Weston had received periodic home visits from a mental health specialist who delivered his medication.

Criminal Commitment

Involuntary commitment is called civil commitment because it involves a person who is *not* suspected of having committed a crime. **Criminal commitment,** on the other hand, refers to the psychiatric hospitalization of people who have been accused of committing a felony, but who are not legally responsible because they lack a "guilty mind" or *mens rea.* "Where there is no *mens* (mind) there can be no *mens rea*" the legal maxim goes (Fingarette and Hasse, 1979, p. 200). In the eyes of the law, such people are "insane," and the legal defense used in their cases is called the **insanity defense.**

Competency to Stand Trial

In order to stand trial for any felony, an individual must be viewed as "competent." What does "incompetent to stand trial" mean? Most statutory definitions are similar to New York's, which defines an "incompetent person" as one "who as a result of mental disease or defect lacks capacity to understand the proceedings against him or to assist in his own defense."[*] The intent of the statute is noble, growing out of the English common law tradition that forbids a trial in absentia. While the defendant may be physically present, when he is judged incompetent to stand trial, he is believed to be psychologically absent, and the trial is delayed until he can participate in his own defense.

In most states, competency to stand trial is assumed if the defendant is aware of his or her personal identity, is oriented to time and space (that is, knows the year and his/her physical location), and can understand the roles of the judge, jury, and attorneys. Needless to say, these are very simple criteria, and most people meet them. That is precisely as intended. A trial by jury is considered a basic right of all defendants; thus the criteria are written so that very few people will be deprived of this right. As you might expect, many people with serious mental illnesses can pass competency exams (Neumann, Walker, Weinstein, and Cutshaw, 1996). This sometimes results in trials of mentally ill defendants whose symptoms are readily apparent to all in the courtroom.

[*]New York Criminal Code S730.10(1) (1993).

Junius Wilson after his release from a locked psychiatric ward at age 96.

Defendants found incompetent to stand trial are sent to institutions until they are able to be tried. Because of current legal guidelines, efforts are made to keep the period of confinement to a minimum. Yet, in the past some people alleged to be incompetent to stand trial, such as Mr. Junius Wilson, were remanded to institutions for the criminally insane for decades:

Junius Wilson is now a free man. He was ninety-six years old when, in 1994, he was released from the locked ward of Cherry Hospital, a psychiatric institution located in Goldsboro, North Carolina. Black and deaf, he had been on the locked ward of that hospital for sixty-eight years, ever since 1925 when he was twenty-eight years old and was charged with assault with the intent to commit rape. He was never convicted of that (or any other) criminal offense. In fact, the charge was eventually dropped. Moreover, there is no evidence that he was ever insane. Nevertheless, he was declared insane and committed to what was then the state insane asylum for black people. Before he entered the hospital, the state had him castrated.

In 1970, hospital authorities realized that Mr. Wilson was perfectly sane and that he did not belong in the hospital. But by then, he had lived in Cherry Hospital for more than forty years. His family could not be found. And it was by no means clear that freeing him then would have improved his life. Living in a psychiatric hospital is not ideal preparation for living outside of it. So he remained on the locked ward, although he was given "privileges."

In 1991, John Wasson was appointed Wilson's legal guardian and social worker. Once he learned that Wilson was not insane, Wasson worked to get Wilson out of the locked ward of the hospital. Wasson threatened to sue the state for Wilson's release. It took three years, but in February 1994, North Car-

olina renovated a cottage on hospital grounds, and Wilson occupied it. A free man at last, Wilson could pass the rest of his life outside the locked psychiatric ward.

A study conducted prior to the deinstitutionalization movement revealed that one institution had three people who were able to stand trial, but who had been "overlooked" for many years. They had been incarcerated for forty-two, thirty-nine, and seventeen years respectively—this, before any determination of their guilt had been made (McGarry and Bendt, 1969). Until 1972, there were no limits on how long people could be committed until judged competent to stand trial. What if they would never be competent to stand trial? Such a dilemma arose tragically in *Jackson v. Indiana*.★

Theon Jackson was a mentally defective deaf-mute. He could not read, write, or otherwise communicate except through limited sign language. In May, 1968, at the age of twenty-seven, Jackson was charged with separate robberies of two women, both of which robberies were alleged to have occurred in the previous July. The first robbery involved a purse and its contents; the total value was four dollars. The second concerned five dollars in cash. Jackson entered a plea of not guilty through his attorney.

Had he been convicted, Jackson would likely have received a sentence of sixty days. But he could not be tried because, in accord with Indiana law, Jackson was examined by two psychiatrists who found that he lacked the intellectual and communicative skills to participate in his own defense, and that the prognosis for acquiring them was dim indeed. Moreover, Jackson's interpreter testified that Indiana had no facilities that could help someone as badly off as Jackson to learn minimal communication skills. The trial court, therefore, found that Jackson "lack[ed] comprehension sufficient to make his defense," and ordered him committed until the Indiana Department of Mental Health certified that the "defendant is sane."

Jackson's attorney filed for a new trial, contending that Jackson was not insane, but that because his mental retardation was so severe, he could never attain competence to stand trial. Jackson's commitment under these circumstances amounted to a life sentence without his ever having been convicted of a crime! By

★*Jackson v. Indiana*, 406 U.S. 715 (1972).

the time the case reached the U.S. Supreme Court, Jackson had already been "hospitalized" for three and a half years. Justice Blackmun, writing for a unanimous court, concurred with Jackson's attorney that Indiana's rule was unconstitutional. Jackson was freed.

Theon Jackson's case resolved one issue—that a person who would never be competent to stand trial could not be detained indefinitely. Many others are still unresolved. What of a person who might some day be competent to stand trial? How long may he or she be held? Some states set no limits. Other states limit the duration of hospitalization to the time of the maximum sentence the individual would have received if he had been competent to stand trial and found guilty. Federal courts require release after eighteen months. But do even those limited periods violate a person's right to bail and to a speedy trial? And should they count against time served if convicted? Can a person be required to take medications against his or her will in order to be competent to stand trial? Practices in these matters vary enormously across states and are unlikely to be systematically resolved in the near future because such defendants, by definition, often lack the resources to press their claims vigorously.

As a result, some have urged that the notion of incompetence to stand trial be abolished on the grounds that even if impaired, the defendant is better off tried. "Withholding trial often results in an endless prolongation of the incompetent defendant's accused status, and his virtually automatic civil commitment. This is a cruelly ironic way by which to ensure that the permanently incompetent defendant is fairly treated" (Burt and Morris, 1972, p. 75). This view, however, violates the Supreme Court's dictum in *Pate* v. *Robinson* that "the conviction of an accused person while he is legally incompetent violated due process . . .".★

The Insanity Defense

Once it is established that the defendant is competent to stand trial, a plea (guilty, not guilty, or the insanity plea) must be entered. The **insanity defense** requires that the defendant was wholly or partially irrational when the crime took place, and that this state of mind affected his or her behavior. The psychologist or psychiatrist who serves as an expert witness in this

★Pate v. Robinson, 383 U.S. 375, 378 (1966).

The insanity defense requires that the defendant was wholly or partially insane when he committed the crime, and that his state of mind affected his behavior. Despite a long and well-documented history of severe mental illness, the jury rejected the not guilty by reason of insanity plea of Andrew Goldstein *(left)*, who pushed a young woman to her death in front of a Manhattan subway train in 1999. In July 2000, a judge ruled that Michael Laudor *(right)*, who had previously been treated for schizophrenia and had stabbed to death his pregnant fiancée in 1998, was not competent to stand trial because of his mental disorder, and he remanded Laudor to a psychiatric facility for treatment.

matter attempts to reconstruct the defendant's state of mind as it was before and during the crime. This is not a simple task. If diagnostic opinions are sometimes unreliable for present behavior, how much more unreliable are they for speculative reconstructions of the past? No wonder, then, that experts for the defense are often contradicted by equally capable experts for the prosecution, and that judges and jurors will disagree on the defendant's state of mind when he committed the crime (Low, Jeffries, and Bonnie, 1986).

Popular opinion notwithstanding, the insanity defense is not widely used. It is invoked in fewer than 1 out of 400 homicide cases that come to trial, even more rarely in nonhomicide trials. And it is successful in many fewer cases than that. Even when successful, the defense usually leads to long-term incarceration in an institution for the criminally insane, a fate sometimes worse than jail because the length of stay is determined by a panel of experts rather than a judge. Nevertheless, the role and meaning of the insanity defense is one of the most hotly debated issues in criminal law. Why should that be?

While the insanity defense is something of a bother in the criminal law, "we must put up with [it] . . . because to exclude it is to deprive the criminal law of its chief paradigm of free will" (Packer, 1968). Thus, the insanity defense is the exception that proves the rule: the notion that each of us is responsible for his or her behavior is strengthened by the recognition that some of us patently are not (Rosenhan, 1983; Stone, 1975). Below are three cases in which the insanity defense has been used (adapted from Livermore and Meehl, 1967). Is there *mens rea* in each of these defendants?★

Case 1: The Pigtail Snipper. Victor Weiner, a hair fetishist, was charged with assault for snipping off a girl's pigtail while standing on a crowded bus. His experience before cutting off the pigtail (which was corroborated by psychiatric testimony and by an acquaintance with whom he had discussed this problem several days earlier) was one of mounting tension, accompanied by a feeling that was close to anxiety and erotic excitement. He made various efforts to distract himself and place himself in situations where he would be safe from performing this act, but finally he gave in to the impulse and boarded the bus with a pair of scissors in his pocket. Victor was diagnosed "sociopathic personality disturbance, sexual deviation, fetishism."

Case 2: The Axe-handle Murderer. Arthur Wolff, a fifteen-year-old, was charged with murdering his mother.★ During the year preceding the crime, Wolff "spent a lot of time thinking about sex." He made a list of the names and addresses of seven girls in his community whom he planned to anesthetize and then either rape or photograph nude. One night, about three weeks before the murder, he took a container of ether and attempted to enter the house of one of these girls through the chimney. But he became wedged in and had to be rescued. In the ensuing weeks, Wolff apparently decided that he would have to bring the girls to his house to achieve his sexual purposes, and that it would therefore be necessary to get his mother (and possibly his brother) out of the way first.

On the Friday or Saturday before he murdered his mother, Wolff obtained an axe handle from the family garage and hid it under the mattress of his bed. On Sunday, he took the axe handle from its hiding place and approached his mother from behind, raising the weapon to strike her. She sensed his presence and asked him what he was doing; he answered that it was "nothing," and returned to his room and hid the axe handle under his mattress again. The following morning, Wolff ate the breakfast that his mother had prepared, went to his room, and took the axe handle from its hiding place. He returned to the kitchen, approached his mother from behind, and struck her on the back of the head. She turned around screaming. He hit her several more times, and they fell to the floor fighting. He got up to turn off the water running in the sink, and she fled through the dining room. He gave chase, caught her in the front room, and choked her to death with his hands.

Wolff then took off his shirt and hung it by the fire, washed the blood off his face and hands, read a few lines from the Bible or prayer book lying upon the dining room table, and walked down to the police station to turn himself in. He told the desk officer, "I have something I wish to report . . . I just killed my mother with an axe handle." The officer testified that Wolff spoke in a quiet voice and that "his conversation was quite coherent in what he was saying and he answered everything I asked him right to a T."

★51 Minn L. Rev. 789, 833–55 (1967).

★People v. Wolff, 61 Cal. 2d 795, 800.

At his trial, four expert witnesses testified that Arthur Wolff had been suffering from schizophrenia when he murdered his mother.

Case 3: The Delusional Informer. Calvin Ellery suffered from paranoid schizophrenia and experienced delusions and hallucinations. He believed that the Masons were plotting to take over the government. He believed, moreover, that the Masons had learned that he was aware of their intentions, and that because he was a potential informer, the Masons had determined to do away with him.

As a result of delusional misinterpretation of certain things he had heard on a news broadcast, Ellery believed that "today is the day for his execution." When a salesman with a Masonic button on his lapel came to the front door, he was sure that the salesman had been sent to kill him. When the salesman reached into his pocket for his business card, Ellery was convinced that he was reaching for a revolver. Ellery drew his own weapon and shot first in self-defense.

What determines if the insanity defense can be used? Is it when is a person is considered to be so insane in the eyes of the law that the ordinary canons of criminal law do not apply? Because the answer to these questions is crucial to the very meaning of criminal law, the questions themselves have generated hot dispute. Historically, there have been three views of the insanity defense: the M'Naghten rule, the Durham test, and the American Law Institute rule. And more recently, under the Insanity Defense Reform Act (IDRA), another standard has been introduced (see Figure 15–1).

Figure 15—1

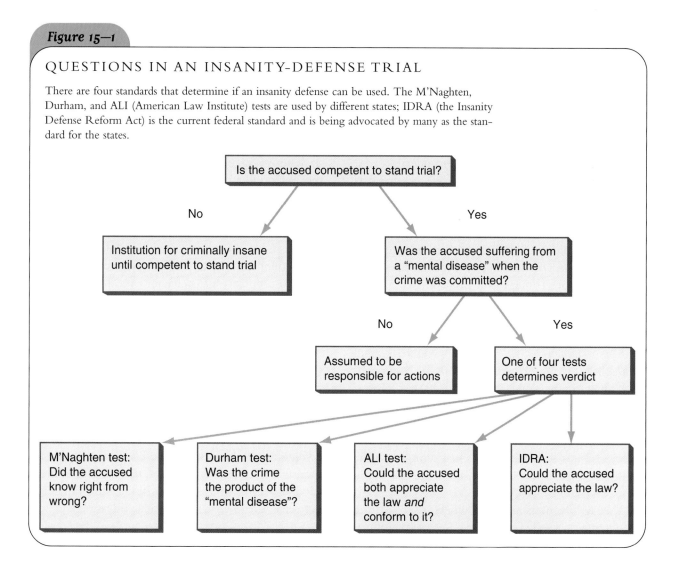

QUESTIONS IN AN INSANITY-DEFENSE TRIAL

There are four standards that determine if an insanity defense can be used. The M'Naghten, Durham, and ALI (American Law Institute) tests are used by different states; IDRA (the Insanity Defense Reform Act) is the current federal standard and is being advocated by many as the standard for the states.

M'NAGHTEN: THE "COGNITIVE" FORMULA

In 1843, Daniel M'Naghten came to London for the purpose of killing Sir Robert Peel, the British prime minister. In so doing, M'Naghten was responding to a "voice of God," which had instructed him to kill the prime minister. Peel, however, was traveling with Queen Victoria on that day, and Edward Drummond, Peel's secretary, was in the prime minister's carriage. Drummond caught M'Naghten's bullet and was killed. M'Naghten testified that:

> The tories in my native city have compelled me to do this. They follow and persecute me wherever I go and have entirely destroyed my peace of mind. . . . I cannot sleep at night in consequent of the course they pursue towards me. . . . They have accused me of crimes of which I am not guilty; they do everything in their power to harass and persecute me; in fact they wish to murder me.

The trial was remarkable in that M'Naghten's defense counsel relied heavily on *Medical Jurisprudence of Insanity* (1838), a published work by Dr. Isaac Ray. The defense counsel argued that the defendant was clearly deranged, in that he suffered delusions of persecution (and, in modern terms, command hallucinations). It was one of the first times that psychiatric testimony had been permitted in a murder trial, and the judges were so impressed that the lord chief justice practically directed a verdict for M'Naghten. But subsequently, Queen Victoria, who had been subject to attempted assassination three times in the preceding two years, called in the lord chief justice, as well as the other fourteen justices, and reproved them. They buckled quickly and wrote what has since been known as the **M'Naghten rule,** under which Daniel M'Naghten would clearly have been convicted! According to that rule, it must be clearly proved that, at the time of the committing of the act, "the party accused was laboring under such a defect of reason, from disease of the mind, as not to know the nature and quality of the act he was doing; or, if he did know it, that he did not know he was doing what was wrong."

The M'Naghten rule is widely used in the United States. Nearly half of the states use it alone as the yardstick for insanity, while other states use the M'Naghten rule in conjunction with other rules. It is a relatively narrow test, which relies merely on whether the accused suffered "a disease of the mind," what he understood about the nature of his actions, and whether he understood that those actions were wrong. But while the test is narrow, it brings into question everything we have learned about abnormal psychology. What, for example, are diseases of the mind? Do they really exist, or are they simply metaphoric? And how do we know whether someone understood his actions when he attempted murder, and whether he knew that murder was "wrong"?

Under the M'Naghten rule, only Calvin Ellery, the delusional informer, would be acquitted, for only he clearly did not "know the nature and quality of the act he was doing," believing that he was acting in justifiable self-defense. The axe-handle murderer's behavior was clearly bizarre, yet because there was no evidence that he failed to distinguish right from wrong, he could not be acquitted according to the M'Naghten rule. Similarly, Weiner, the pigtail snipper, though clearly disturbed and seemingly caught up in an impulse that ultimately overcame his best efforts at suppression, could not be acquitted under the M'Naghten rule. He, too, knew right from wrong (see Table 15-2).

The M'Naghten standard focused exclusively on the individual's cognitions: knowledge of right and wrong. Feelings and impulses were not considered relevant in this test of "sanity." Some legal experts of the time believed this standard was too narrow. They argued that a defendant might have fully understood the wrongfulness of an act, but was nonetheless unable to control his behavior. In 1896 Alabama adopted the **irresistible impulse rule,** which stated that mental disease may impair self-control even when reasoning ability remains intact.

DURHAM: "THE PRODUCT OF MENTAL DISEASE"

In a case that was tried in 1954, *Durham v. United States,*★ Judge David Bazelon broadened the insanity defense to state that "an accused is not criminally responsible if his unlawful act was the product of mental disease or mental defect." Notice the difference between the Durham "mental disease" and the

---

★Durham v. United States, 214 F. 2d 862 (D.C. Cir. 1954).

TABLE 15–2

ACQUITTAL UNDER THE VARIOUS INSANITY DEFENSES

Case	Diagnosis	M'Naghten "right-wrong" test	Durham "product of mental disease" test	American Law Institute (ALI) "appreciate and conform" test	Guilty but mentally ill	Insanity Defense Reform Act
Victor Weiner (Pigtail snipper)	Fetishism	Guilty—he knew it was wrong.	Not guilty—fetishism is a mental disease according to DSM-IV.	Maybe—depends on court's assessment of his ability to conform his conduct to law.	Guilty	Guilty
Arthur Wolff (Axe-handle murderer)	Schizophrenia	Guilty—he knew it was wrong.	Probably acquitted—if he were not schizophrenic, he probably would not have murdered.	Probably guilty if *affectively*, he knew murder was wrong.	Guilty	Guilty
Calvin Ellery (Delusional informer)	Paranoid schizophrenia	Not guilty—he thought he was shooting in self-defense.	Not guilty—the killing was clearly the product of his delusions.	Not guilty—he could not appreciate the criminality of his conduct.	Guilty	Not guilty

M'Naghten "right-wrong" test. In the Durham test, incapacitating conditions, such as the inability to tell right from wrong, are not specified. One goes directly from "mental disease" to the act (Brooks, 1974), leaving it to advanced knowledge in psychiatry and psychology to determine whether the act was or was not a product of mental disease or mental defect. Under the Durham rule, the axe-handle murderer would probably have been acquitted on the grounds that, absent his schizophrenic condition, he would not have murdered his mother. Likewise, defining fetishism as a "mental disease," the pigtail snipper, too, would have been acquitted on the grounds that if he did not have a fetish, he would not have had such a prurient interest in little girls' pigtails. And, of course, Calvin Ellery, the delusional informer, would also have been acquitted under the "mental disease" test (he suffered from paranoid schizophrenia), as well as under the M'Naghten "right-wrong" test.

As Justice Bazelon maintained, the Durham rule was an experiment, one that extended for some eighteen years, from 1954 until 1972. During that time, a view of criminal responsibility and nonresponsibility was developed. Fundamentally, the Durham rule was withdrawn for two reasons: (1) it relied too heavily on the expert testimony of psychiatrists, rendering judge and jury wholly dependent upon psychiatric testimony for the determination of criminal responsibility, and (2) it was as difficult then as it is now to know and attain agreement about what constitutes a "mental disease." The metaphor itself left much to be desired, implying a distinct and verifiable organic state. Moreover, one could never be sure which of the disorders listed in the Diagnostic and Statistical Manual of Mental Disorders qualified. Should stuttering, tobacco dependence, and antisocial personality disorder all be considered mental diseases that can produce unlawful acts? The seeming breadth of the Durham rule created problems that were difficult to adjudicate and that ultimately led to its near demise. Only one state, New Hampshire, still uses the Durham test.

THE AMERICAN LAW INSTITUTE (ALI) RULE: "APPRECIATE AND CONFORM"

In *United States* v. *Brawner,*★ Archie Brawner, Jr., was accused of murdering a man after becoming involved in a physical confrontation at a party. All expert witnesses called to provide opinions agreed that Brawner was suffering from a psychiatric or neurological abnormality, although they did not agree on the nature of the disorder. Brawner's attorney provided evidence that the defendant was suffering from a mental condition produced by epilepsy. The judge ruled that there was insufficient evidence to take the case to a jury, thus a verdict of acquittal was ruled on the first-degree murder charge. As a result of the judge's 1972 ruling in the *Brawner* case, the Durham mental disease test was modified. The modification was one that had earlier been advocated by the American Law Institute. That rule is considerably more specific than the Durham rule, and yet not so narrow as the M'Naghten rule. It states:

1. A person is not responsible for criminal conduct if, at the time of such conduct, as a result of mental disease or defect, he lacks substantial capacity either to appreciate the criminality (wrongfulness) of his conduct or to conform his conduct to the requirements of law.
2. As used in the Article, the terms "mental disease or defect" do not include an abnormality manifested only by repeated criminal or otherwise antisocial conduct. (American Law Institute, 1985, p. 62).

In the *Brawner* case, the court tried to further narrow the meaning of "mental disease." Citing an earlier case,† it wrote:

[A] mental disease or defect includes any abnormal condition of the mind which substantially affects mental or emotional processes and substantially impairs behavior controls.

The ALI rule, as modified in the *Brawner* case, is used in twenty-one state courts. Under that standard, Calvin Ellery would, of course, be acquitted. Convinced that the Masons were both plotting to take over the government and assassinate him, Ellery

clearly lacked "substantial capacity . . . to appreciate the criminality (wrongfulness) of his conduct." The verdict with regard to Victor Weiner, the pigtail snipper, would depend on whether the court was willing and able to assess the strength of Weiner's desire and, therefore, his ability "to conform his conduct to the requirements of law."

The outcome of the case of Arthur Wolff, who murdered his mother because she seemed in the way of his sexual schemes, depends wholly on how a jury would interpret the word "appreciate" in the section of the ALI rule that says ". . . he lacks substantial capacity . . . to appreciate the criminality (wrongfulness) of his conduct. . . ." Wolff "knew" he did wrong in killing his mother, as he confessed immediately at the police station. But did he really appreciate that this was wrong? Did he "feel it in his heart" affectively, or did he merely "know" cognitively? If the latter, he would be acquitted under the ALI rule. If the former, he would be convicted of murdering his mother.

THE INSANITY DEFENSE REFORM ACT

On June 21, 1982, a federal jury found John W. Hinckley, Jr., not guilty by reason of insanity in his attempted assassination of President Ronald Reagan. The jury's verdict was based on its perception that Hinckley was unable "to conform his conduct to the requirements of the law," which is the "volitional" standard of the ALI rule. But the public was outraged with that verdict. Only three days after the jury acquitted Hinckley, the Subcommittee on Criminal Law of the Committee of the Judiciary of the United States Senate began hearings on limiting the insanity defense. And over the next two and a half years, similar hearings were conducted in the legislative hearing rooms of many states.

At issue was the volitional prong (whether the criminal impulse could be resisted) of the ALI standard. Was it truly an irresistible impulse, or simply an impulse not resisted? Whether volition itself was a useful notion was a matter about which psychologists and psychiatrists could not agree, raising serious questions about whether the law should even include it. Ultimately, in 1984, President Reagan signed the *Insanity Defense Reform Act (IDRA),* which eliminated the volitional prong of the insanity defense in federal courts. The new federal standard states that:

★United States v. Brawner, 471 F. 2d 969 (D.C. Cir. 1972).
†McDonald v. United States, 312 F. 3d 847 (D.C. Cir. 1962).

 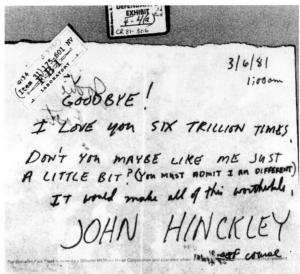

John Hinckley, Jr. *(left)* and the letter *(right)* he sent to Jodie Foster, the actress with whom he was obsessed, before attempting to assassinate former President Ronald Reagan.

It is an affirmative defense to a prosecution under any federal statute that, at the time of the commission of the acts constituting the offense, the defendant, as a result of a severe mental disease or defect, was unable to appreciate the nature and quality or the wrongfulness of his acts. Mental disease or defect does not otherwise constitute a defense.

It had previously been the task of the prosecution to prove sanity, and sanity is very difficult to prove. With the new federal standard, the burden of proving that the defendant was insane, and hence not responsible for his actions, was placed on the defendant. Thus, by making insanity an affirmative defense, the defendant was required to play an active role in his or her own defense. This requirement created some new problems (stemming from the nature of psychotic symptoms) that had not been anticipated.

REFUSING THE INSANITY DEFENSE

Delusions and lack of insight are among the defining features of psychosis. So what happens if a mentally ill defendant refuses the insanity defense on the grounds that he or she is *not* insane? This has happened in numerous criminal cases documented in the literature. Although the attorney is required to provide the client with sound legal advice, the attorney cannot impose a defense on a client. In many of these cases, the defendant has a long history of treatment for mental illness and readily admits to committing a serious crime. If the defendant passes a

competency exam, he or she must be tried for the crime. It is not uncommon for a defendant with a serious mental illness, such as paranoid schizophrenia, to insist that that he is sane and, in fact, motivated by a higher purpose.

An example of this is the case of the *People* v. *McDowell*.★ The defendant was accused of killing an elderly man who managed the boarding house where she lived after being released from the state hospital. The defendant admitted the murder, but despite her attorney's advice, she resisted the insanity plea. Instead, she insisted that she was not mentally ill, but rather divinely inspired. A higher power had commanded her to commit the murder. She claimed she was "Jezreal, Lord God woman" and that her acts were justified because they were based on supreme wisdom. She was convicted and sentenced to prison.

In another case that received attention from the national media, a young man was accused of murdering several people on a subway train in New York City. The man had been treated for paranoid schizophrenia prior to the murders. He not only refused the insanity defense, but he also insisted on representing himself. He entered a plea of not guilty on his own behalf. Despite the fact that numerous witnesses testified that they had observed him committing the murders, he engaged in a rambling defense in which he maintained that he was not at the scene

★People v. McDowell, N.Y. S. Ct., No. 86-46 (July 3, 1986).

of the crime. He was also convicted. But in recent years the most widely publicized case involving a mentally ill defendant who refused to use the insanity defense was that of the "Unabomber," Ted Kaczynski:

> After decades of eluding authorities, Ted Kaczynski, a former mathematics professor, was arrested. As the "Unabomber" he had made numerous terrorist threats and sent a series of mail bombs that killed three and wounded many others. In 1995, he sent a 35,000 word "manifesto" describing his philosophy to the *New York Times* and the *Washington Post*. Both papers agreed to publish the statement with the hope that it would aid police in finding the Unabomber. It did! The letter was read by David Kaczynski, Ted's brother, who recognized the paranoid political beliefs as those of his brother. David alerted police to the possibility that the Unabomber might be Ted, who was living in a primitive shack in the Montana wilderness. In 1996, authorities located the shack and arrested Ted Kaczynski. They found extensive incriminating evidence in the shack, and Ted confessed to the mail bombings.
>
> David soon became the spokesperson for the Kaczynski family. He described his brother as an intelligent, but disturbed man. Ted was a bright student who had skipped two years of high school and had a passion for mathematics. He graduated from Harvard University and received both a master's degree and a doctoral degree from the University of Michigan.

Ted Kaczynski was judged competent to stand trial and was convicted as the "Unabomber" after refusing to use the insanity defense.

After leaving a position as a professor of mathematics at the University of California, Berkeley, Kaczynski moved to Montana and lived as a hermit for a number of years. His family acknowledged Ted's abnormal behavior, including grandiose and paranoid thoughts and delusional rage. He was obsessed with government and technological conspiracies and saw himself as a potential savior of the world. He had withdrawn completely from all social contact.

Kaczynski was judged competent to stand trial in that he was capable of understanding the case and could assist in his own defense. Given Ted's history of psychiatric symptoms, it was expected that his defense attorneys would put forward an insanity defense. Indeed, they strongly encouraged Ted to plea "not guilty by reason of insanity," but Ted refused. He steadfastly refused to accept any plea that implied a mental disorder. The judge called Kaczynski's refusal to allow his lawyers to use a mental health defense "completely unreasonable" and was angry that the trial was delayed by the conflicts between Kaczynski and his attorneys. At one point, Kaczynski requested that he be allowed to defend himself, but the judge denied his request. Three psychiatrists who evaluated Kaczynski concluded that he was suffering from paranoid schizophrenia.

As part of a plea bargain, Ted Kaczynski was spared the death penalty, but he was sentenced to life in prison without the possibility of parole. Throughout the hearings, he showed no signs of sadness, anger or regret. He occasionally joked. (Based on the *Washington Post,* January 1998).

GUILTY BUT MENTALLY ILL (GBMI) OR DIMINISHED CAPACITY

Partially as a result of public perceptions that defendants are "beating the rap" by entering insanity pleas, some states have abolished the "not guilty by reason of insanity" verdict, replacing it with the verdict of "guilty but mentally ill" (GBMI). A finding that a defendant is guilty but mentally ill results in commitment to a mental institution rather than to a prison.★

The GBMI verdict is an instance of a legislative rush to action, and it is mistaken on at least two counts. In the first place, the insanity defense is rarely invoked and much more rarely successful. The public impression of its usefulness arises nearly

★Thirteen states had adopted this standard by 1985.

wholly from sensational news stories, not from accurate estimates of incidence. Moreover, the GBMI verdict is a contradiction in its own terms. In order to be found guilty, one needs to have been able to form a morally coherent intent to harm (*mens rea*—see p. 657). But mental illness exonerates one precisely because one is held to be unable to form such an intent. How then can one be simultaneously guilty and mentally ill?

In the 1950s, the plea of "guilty but with diminished capacity" was introduced. This plea is based on the assumption that some people are incapable of possessing the mental state to intentionally commit a crime because they suffer from mental impairment or disease. In other words, the individual's moral responsibility for the act is presumed to be lessened by her mental illness. If the diminished capacity plea is successful, the defendant is convicted of a lesser offense. For example, in a murder case the conviction may be for manslaughter, rather than for first-degree murder. This defense was used in *California* v. *White* and caused an uproar (Cornell Law, 2000). In this case, Dan White, a former city supervisor of the city of San Francisco, shot and killed the mayor, George Moscone, and another city supervisor, Harvey Milk. Although there was extensive evidence of premeditation, White's attorney argued that he had "diminished capacity" because his diet consisted primarily of junk food, such as "Twinkies," that this created a chemical imbalance in his brain, and that he was therefore unable to premeditate murder. (Premeditation was necessary for a verdict of first-degree murder.) The jury was swayed by this argument, and White was convicted of voluntary manslaughter instead of homicide. This verdict unleashed a public outcry, and the diminished capacity defense was overturned in California in 1982.

Clearly, enormous effort has gone into defining the legal meaning of insanity. But that effort has not yet paid off in terms of outcome. Regardless of which definition of insanity is used, people seem to convict and acquit in pretty much the same proportions (Finkel, 1989; James, 1959; Steadman et al., 1993). One possible reason for this outcome is that the law typically gives jurors only two choices: guilty (for whatever reason) or not guilty (for whatever reason). But when jurors in simulated trials were permitted to distinguish among several shades and types of insanity, they were better able to tailor their verdicts to the requirements of law (Finkel, 1990, 1991).

New Challenges to the Legal System

Insanity and its various defenses are not the only psychological issues that confront our contemporary legal system. There are two phenomena that have captured a great deal of attention in recent years because they raise important questions about responsibility and about evidence. They are dissociative identity disorder (formerly "multiple personality") and recovered memories. These two issues are interrelated because some theorists believe that dissociation and recovered memories have the same childhood origins.

Dissociative Identity Disorder and Legal Responsibility

Ordinarily, when someone is accused of a crime, at issue is whether the person committed the crime or not. But consider the following case:

James Carlson stood trial for rape, theft, forgery and kidnapping. He claimed that he had eleven different personalities and was suffering from a multiple personality disorder. Among those personalities were Jim, who committed the rape; Woofie, a fifteen-year-old boy; Jimmy, a seven-year-old; and Laurie Burke, a seventeen-year-old lesbian prostitute. In fact, at one point during the trial, Carlson took the witness stand as Laurie, wearing a skirt, black tights, pink sweater, high-heel shoes, press-on nails, and a wedding band.

In her summation, Carlson's lawyer put the issue to the jury as follows. "James Carlson's body committed the crimes. But James was not in control of the body when any of the acts occurred." The prosecutor put the matter differently. "Your Honor, the statements [Carlson's confession] were made by a human being, sitting here today. The charges are not brought against any one [personality]. They are brought against the human being."

As is commonly the case in such trials, there was a battle of experts. One psychologist testified that Carlson suffered from a multiple personality disorder

James Carlson took the witness stand dressed as a woman during his 1994 trial in Arizona. He pleaded not guilty on the grounds that he suffered from multiple personality disorder (dissociative identity disorder) and could therefore not be held responsible for the crimes committed by one of his alters. He was later found to be faking the disorder.

that developed after Carlson had been molested in kindergarten. Another psychologist thought Carlson was faking, and faking badly.

The jury convicted Carlson. After the trial, Carlson acknowledged that he had read about multiple personalities in a psychology textbook and faked his performance, both because he wanted to avoid prison, and because he had fallen in love with his attorney. She "would see more of me when I was a multiple than if I was just myself." (*Arizona Republic,* 1994)

Carlson's case raises some very dramatic questions. First, does the dissociative identity (multiple personality) disorder really exist? In other words, is it possible for separate personalities to exist within the same skin, and not know each other? Second, if multiple personalities do exist, how do we distinguish real from faked personalities? And third, assuming the defendant is convicted, how can we punish the whole person for the acts of only one of his personalities? None of these questions was answered in Carlson's case, and they remain highly controversial among legal scholars (Kenny, 1998).

The DSM-IV criteria for dissociative identity disorder (DID) state that it involves "two or more distinct personality states" and that "at least two of these identities or personality states recurrently take control of the person's behavior" (DSM-IV, p. 487).

The terms used to define this disorder clearly imply that individuals suffering from it are, from a psychological standpoint, more than one "person." One of the "alters" might be law-abiding, sensitive, and responsible, while the other is crass, aggressive, and lacking in concern for others. And most important from a legal perspective, the individual's behavior is controlled by the personality that is currently in charge. Thus, according to the theory, there is one physical body, but two or more identities or personalities.

If all of this is accurate, then it presents a thorny problem for the legal system. Punishment for criminal acts is intended to make the guilty individual physically and emotionally uncomfortable. In addition, the criminal justice system attempts to rehabilitate the offender by changing his attitudes and behavior. If a convicted person has DID, then both the guilty and the innocent personalities will be punished and rehabilitated. This is not consistent with the Judeo-Christian moral tradition that has guided the development of our legal codes.

In Chapter 6, we discussed the controversies surrounding the diagnosis of dissociative disorders, especially DID. Some believe the diagnosis is a product of cultural trends, and that the DID syndrome is most likely to be adopted by individuals who are highly suggestible and are reinforced by others for their behavior. If this is true, then the "diagnosis" should be eliminated from the DSM, and certainly should not be allowed to play a role in legal proceedings. But how will we ever determine whether DID, or any other dissociative disorder for that matter, is valid? Some believe the answer will come from research. Others believe the controversy shows that psychiatric diagnoses should not be allowed to influence legal proceedings.

Accuracy of Recovered Memories

Memories for events have always played a key role in criminal law. Witnesses are called into the courtroom and asked to swear on a Bible that they will tell the truth. A witness's memory can be the deciding factor in a trial outcome, so the defendant's fate hinges on whether the memory is accurate or inaccurate. The "common sense" assumption is that memories are relatively stable and accessible to the witness. But this is not always the case.

The idea of repressed memories is central to many views of personality, and especially the psychodynamic theories. Despite criticism from some memory researchers (Loftus, 1993, 1994), a substantial number of clinicians continue to believe that repression is a real phenomenon. The theory of repression assumes that experiences and memories that evoke shame, guilt, humiliation, or self-deprecation are often unconscious, especially when those experiences conflict with one's self-image. But when a memory is repressed, it does not disappear. Instead, it continues to exist and is simply inaccessible to consciousness, at least for the present. When psychological conditions change, the memory may reappear and the individual may become aware again of experiences long forgotten.

The renewed awareness, however, is quite problematic. First, when you recover the memory of an event that transpired, say, twenty years ago, how can you be sure that what you are recalling actually occurred? For some memories, that's hardly a problem. If you suddenly remember that you were lost in a department store when you were five years old, you can often find confirmation (or disconfirmation) by turning to your parents or siblings. But what if the event recalled occurred privately and involved misconduct? What if the event concerned sexual molestation, for which there was no witness? How, then, do we determine whether what is "recalled" occurred? The conviction with which the belief is held is, unfortunately, no sure guide. A person who now vividly "recalls" having been sexually abused by her father may well have a father who, just as vividly, has absolutely no recollection of the alleged events. That person may confuse an event that was only imagined or suggested with a true one, incorporating elements of the truth, such that this imagined memory has the feeling of authenticity.

Second, the recovery of long-buried memories creates significant problems for the statute of limitations, which requires that claims for injuries must be instituted promptly. That requirement insures that memories remain fresh, and that witnesses can be examined. But where the incidents have been forgotten, how can legal proceedings be initiated if one can't remember the harmful events?

The other side of the coin is the impact on the alleged perpetrator. It is not surprising that many of those who are accused of past abuse deny it. But is it possible that an innocent person would admit to past crimes that he did not commit? The case of Paul Ingram is an example of a defendant who came to the conclusion that he must have been guilty of abuse if his loved ones accused him of it:

> Paul Ingram had been widely respected in Olympia, Washington, and not without reason. He was chairman of the local Republican party, chief civil deputy in the sheriff's department, and an active member of his church. His personnel file was filled with commendations from ordinary citizens who thanked him for his courtesy. Across seventeen years, no letter of complaint had ever been received about him. His wife Sandy operated a day-care center out of their home. Neighbors described them as strict but loving parents to their children.
>
> But on November 28, 1988, fifteen minutes after he arrived at work, Sheriff Gary Edwards summoned Ingram to his office and relieved him of his automatic pistol. Ericka and Julie Ingram, then twenty-two and eighteen respectively, had accused their father of sexual molestation. While Ingram could not remember ever having molested his daughters, he added, "there may be a dark side of me that I don't know about." By the end of the day, Ingram confessed. "I really believe that the allegations did occur and that I did violate them and abuse them and probably for a long period of time. I've repressed it." Asked why he was confessing if he couldn't remember the violations, Ingram replied, "Well, number one, my daughters know me. They wouldn't lie about something like this."
>
> Ingram's daughters' allegations had first surfaced some three months earlier. They were at a religious retreat when the leader told the sixty girls in attendance that she had a vision of someone in the audience who had been molested by a relative. There are a number of conflicting stories concerning how this occurred, but according to the leader, she simply prayed over Ericka and felt herself prompted by the Lord to say "You have been abused as a child, sexually abused." Ericka wept quietly. The leader received another divine prompting, and said, "It's by her father, and it's been happening for years." Ericka then began to sob hysterically. The leader urged her to obtain counseling in order to work through the memories that were causing her so much pain. Later, Ericka's memories included her brothers, as well as her father's friends among those who had molested her. Later still, her mother and brothers were included, not only in sexual abuse, but in satanic rituals that involved, among other things, sacrificing a baby.

After each of these allegations, Paul Ingram would go into a trancelike state, and would retrieve vivid recollections of these events. Encouraged by his pastor and detectives in his own department, Ingram found more and more to confess to. Nearly everyone, except his accused friends and one social psychologist, seemed convinced that Ingram was precisely as his children had described him: utterly corrupt.

The psychologist, Dr. Richard Ofshe, was intrigued by Ingram's ability to imagine scenes of abuse, and then come to feel, with great confidence, that they had actually occurred. This seemed to Ofshe more like suggestibility than anything else, and that hypothesis was worth testing. Ofshe told Ingram that one of his sons and one of his daughters had reported that Ingram had made them have sex together. At first, Ingram, quite correctly, couldn't remember having done that. Then he closed his eyes and acknowledged that he could see his son and daughter. The next time Ofshe visited, Ingram said he now had clear memories of his children having sex. And at their third meeting, Ingram proudly produced a three-page confession that described how he had directed his children to have sex with each other, and what they had done.

Of course, none of this was true. By the time Mr. Ingram realized that his visualizations had been fantasies, not real memories, he obtained a new lawyer and filed to retract his confessions on the grounds that they had been coerced by his investigators. But it was too late to stop the legal process, and Ingram was convicted. And in a sad footnote to a painful case, Ericka Ingram appeared at her father's leniency hearing to demand that the judge give him the most severe sentence possible. Paul Ingram was sentenced to twenty years.

Because there has been a rise in the incidence of recovered memories where the alleged crime consists of physical and sexual abuse, a substantial number of states have made an exception to the statute of limitations for such cases, much as they do for certain medical malpractice cases. If, for example, a surgeon left a roll of tape in a patient's stomach, but the tape was not discovered until many years later when the patient had a physical examination, the doctor can nevertheless be sued for malpractice under the delayed discovery doctrine, which holds that the statute of limitations does not begin to toll until all the facts that are essential to the complaint

have been discovered. Similarly, when memories of sexual abuse have been repressed, no cause of action can be filed until they are recovered. The statute of limitations begins to toll from that point. It is clear that recovered memories are not merely a personal problem, but rather touch on many lives and raise important questions about the nature of psychological treatment.

The Abuse of Mental Health Care

The chief goal in the practice of clinical psychology and psychiatry is to help humankind. But in various societies at various times, mental health practitioners have failed to act in the best interests of society and/or the individual. In some cases, this is due to incompetent or unethical practice on the part of the clinician. In other cases, social forces play a role.

Clinical Malpractice

Potential for abuse arises in part from the fact that society endows psychologists and psychiatrists with enormous power. Perry London (1986) says they constitute a "secular priesthood." Any reservations we might have about psychiatry and psychology often dissolve when our own lives are touched by psychological distress. At these times, we tend to accept the views of "experts." Our personal reliance on a practitioner and our vulnerability to the practitioner's judgments and recommendations make us particularly vulnerable to abuse.

Mental health practitioners are expected to subscribe to high standards of ethical conduct (Corey, Corey, and Callahan, 1998). The American Psychological Association publishes a lengthy and detailed set of guidelines entitled "Ethical Principles for Psychologists." All psychologists, both practitioners and those in academic settings, are expected to conform to these guidelines. Similar ethical codes are endorsed by professional organizations in social work, psychiatry, and psychiatric nursing. Nonetheless, violations sometimes occur, and these often involve the exploitation or mistreatment of clients.

In the 1991 film *Prince of Tides,* a therapist (played by Barbra Streisand) and her patient (played by Nick Nolte) have a sexual affair. Such a relationship between patient and therapist constitutes an ethical violation on the part of the mental health practitioner that breaks the trust of the patient and prevents effective treatment.

One example is the sexual exploitation of individuals in treatment. Having a sexual relationship with a client is considered an ethical violation. Nonetheless, the evidence suggests that it is the most frequently occurring of all ethics violations by mental health practitioners (Report of the Ethics Committee, 1997). When this occurs, the critical bond of trust is broken, and effective treatment is no longer possible. Nonetheless, some practitioners have violated this guideline. When their "malpractice" is discovered, they are required to relinquish their license to practice and they are barred from membership in most professional organizations.

Within the past decade, several popular films have depicted therapists who are involved in sexual relationships with clients (for example, *Prince of Tides*). What is usually missing from these films is any reference to the real-world consequences; namely, the sanctions that are applied to professionals who engage in this conduct. Because there are serious consequences to ethical violations, the American Psychological Association has a special committee whose sole function is the investigation of allegations. In addition, some cases end up in the legal system; the client accuses the practitioner of malpractice or violation of a local statute, and the case goes to court.

Many cases of sexual misconduct by professionals are ambiguous. The case of *Palazzolo* v. *Ruggiano*★ is one example :

> Donna Palazzolo was a client of Dr. John Ruggiano for three years, from 1992 to 1995. However, she later sued him in court on the grounds that he inappropriately touched her in a sexual manner on three separate occasions. The first incident allegedly occurred two years into therapy when Dr. Ruggiano placed his arms around the client's waist. A second incident occurred when Dr. Ruggiano touched her shoulders and allegedly pressed himself against the back of her body. Contact lasted for a few seconds, and then the therapy session continued as scheduled. On the third occasion, Ruggiano asked Palazzolo if there was "anything in her file indicating that she did not need a kiss and a hug." Palazzolo answered "no," and then stood up. According to the court records, Ruggiano then approached her, wrapped his arms around her shoulders, and pressed himself against the front of her body. The client pushed him away and then left the session.
>
> When the case was brought before the Rhode Island court, Palazzolo accused Ruggiano of unwelcome sexual advances, as well as violating the "Violence Against Women Act." (This act was established to protect the civil rights of victims of gender-motivated violence.) However the court ruled in favor of Ruggiano, citing a lack of sufficient evidence to establish that his actions were threatening. In addition, because Ms. Palazzolo acknowledged that Ruggiano had never used force or coercion, accusations of second-degree sexual assault were also dismissed.

Was Palazzolo justified in taking her psychiatrist to court? Some might argue that the psychiatrist's actions were clearly outside the boundaries of professional practice, and the lawsuit served the purpose of drawing attention to sexual abuse of clients. Others might contend that the psychiatrist's behavior, while unethical, was not illegal and should not be addressed in a court of law.

In the recent controversy surrounding recovered memories, some practitioners have been accused of "encouraging" patients to recover memories of

★Palazzolo v. Ruggiano, U. S. S. Ct. for the District of Rhode Island (February 24, 1998).

abuse by subtly planting the idea (Read et al., 1997). The practitioner's motives are not always clear; some have been accused of intentionally attempting to cultivate the client's dependency, whereas other practitioners have been viewed as naïve and poorly trained. Whatever the case, when a client is encouraged by a mental health practitioner to adopt false beliefs, this constitutes malpractice. Not only is the individual misled, but innocent people, including family members, may also suffer. The worst consequence is the potential loss of credibility for victims of abuse who have suffered deep psychological trauma.

The case of Holly Ramona is one of a number of highly publicized lawsuits by clients and/or their families who believe "false memories" were planted by a therapist:

> Holly Ramona was nineteen years old when she consulted Marche Isabella for treatment. Holly's problem was bulimia and depression. Ms. Isabella suggested that bulimia might be rooted in childhood sexual abuse. Soon, Holly had terrifying flashbacks in which she recalled her father repeatedly molesting her between the ages of five and sixteen. In order to confirm her own memory, she undertook a "truth serum" interview. Reassured of the accuracy of her memory, she instituted legal proceedings against her father.
>
> Holly's father, Gary, was just as convinced that the sexual abuse had never occurred, but was rather suggested to Holly by her therapist. He sued the therapist, contending that Holly's allegation had caused his wife to seek a divorce, alienated him from his other children, and led directly to the loss of his job as an executive. The jury returned a verdict in his favor.
>
> According to the jury's foreman, the jury had not explored the efficacy of recovered memories, but had concentrated on the therapist's alleged negligence. Holly Ramona, however, remains convinced of the truth of her memories and feels that she benefited greatly from her therapy. And Gary Ramona remains equally convinced that "Holly's supposed memories are the result of the [therapist's] drugs and quackery, not anything I did." (*The New York Times,* 1994)

No one knows how often psychotherapists actually encourage false memories, but some are convinced that it has become quite common. In response, an organization called the "False Memory Foundation" was founded in the United States. The goal of this organization is to educate the general public so that they adopt a healthy skepticism about claims of recovered memories of abuse. The organization has reported over 17,000 inquiries since 1993.

Finally, we may see some new ethical challenges and abuses stemming from managed care procedures (Bilynsky and Vernaglia, 1998). For example, what happens when professional ethical principles about confidentiality conflict with HMO guidelines for reviewing case material? What is the responsibility of a practitioner if she observes a failure on the part of an HMO to cover the costs of providing an "acceptable" standard of treatment? Professional organizations, such as the American Psychological Association, have established committees to address these questions.

Abuse by Society

Attitudes toward work, sexuality, manners, marriage, and clothing—indeed, toward most of the significant aspects of social life—have changed over the decades and will continue to change. Canons of appropriate behavior and attitude are fundamental to judgments of normality and abnormality. As these canons change, so will our notions of what is normal, and what is abnormal.

Some social stereotypes have had negative influences on the practice of psychology and psychiatry. The most salient example is the effect of social stereotypes on diagnostic practices. For example, in DSM-II, which was approved by the American Psychiatric Association in 1968, homosexuality was listed as a mental disorder. But subsequent research showed that about 20 percent of adult men have had homosexual contact at some point in their life, and 2 to 3 percent are exclusively homosexual (Friedman and Downey, 1994). Among women, it is estimated that about 3 percent have had homosexual relationships after adolescence. Furthermore, the overwhelming majority of homosexual men and women do not meet criteria for any mental disorder. Homosexual behavior, therefore, is no longer as unconventional as it had once seemed, nor does it violate community standards as intensely as it once did. Consequently, in 1976, by a vote of its membership, the association

Pyotr Grigorenko.

decided that homosexuality was no longer a mental disorder.

At times, governments have abused the mental-health-care system in order to control individuals who hold dissident views. In large part, the potential for this form of abuse arises from the very definition of abnormality that was discussed in Chapter 1. Among the behaviors or elements of abnormality are: whether the person produces discomfort in others, the degree to which his or her behavior is unconventional, and the degree to which the behavior violates idealized standards. If an individual's behavior triggers these criteria, he or she may be labeled abnormal, even though other criteria for abnormality, such as intense suffering, are absent. People who hold different views from those of a society's leaders might be seen (or made to be seen) as unconventional, or in violation of idealized standards.

Psychiatric diagnoses, involuntary hospitalization, and treatment with antipsychotic drugs have been used in some countries to stifle political dissent. Political psychiatry was heavily relied upon in the former Soviet Union. Anatoli Koryagin, a Soviet psychiatrist who emigrated to the West, described the Soviet use of psychiatric hospitals and drugs to punish political activists. At least 210 sane people—others claim higher figures (Podrabenek, in Fireside, 1979)—were interned in Soviet prison-hospitals for political reasons (Bloch and Reddaway, 1977). Pyotr Grigorenko, a distinguished general who had served in the Red Army for thirty-five years, provides a case in point:

At the age of fifty-four, he began to question the policies of the Communist party of which he was a member. Ultimately, he was remanded for psychiatric examination at Moscow's Serbsky Institute, where his diagnosis read "paranoid development of the personality, with reformist ideas arising in the personality, with psychopathic features of the character and the presence of symptoms of arteriosclerosis of the brain." Shortly thereafter, he underwent an examination by a second group of psychiatrists who found him admirably sane and vigorous. But a third commission overruled the second and, as a result, Grigorenko spent six years in three of the most difficult Soviet "psychoprisons" before he was permitted to emigrate to the United States. (Fireside, 1979)

While such abuses were especially well documented in the former Soviet Union, which had developed a psychiatric nomenclature especially for political dissidents (Medvedev and Medvedev, 1971; Fireside, 1979), they also once existed in the United States, as shown in the case of Ezra Pound:

When the Second World War was over, Ezra Pound, the eminent poet, was taken into custody by the American troops in Italy, returned to the United States, and charged with treason. Pound had lived in fascist Italy during the war and had supported Mussolini. It was alleged that the broadcasts that Pound made from Rome were treasonous. Pound denied the charge, but he never came to trial. Instead, the government and his attorneys agreed that he was incompetent to stand trial. He was therefore remanded to St. Elizabeth's Hospital in Washington, D.C., and effectively imprisoned without trial. Thirteen years later, in 1958, he was still considered "insane," incurably so, but not dangerous to others. He was therefore released.

Ezra Pound.

All his life, Pound had been an eccentric: enormously conceited, flamboyant, sometimes downright outrageous. But he had never had a brush with the law, nor had he received psychiatric care. But because his politics were aversive, his eccentricities were invoked to indicate that he was not of sound mind and therefore that he could not stand trial (Torrey, 1983). In this case, eccentric behaviors changed meaning when observed in a diagnostic context. Conceit and flamboyance became "grandiosity of ideas and beliefs," contributing to the impression that he was mentally ill.

It has occasionally been argued that Pound was protected by psychiatry, without which he would have faced a worse fate: prison. That may well have been the case, though without a trial, there is no way to know whether, or for how long, Pound would have been imprisoned. But even if one grants that Pound was protected from prison by psychiatric intervention, his case remains an example of the political use of psychiatry in the United States. His case also illustrates the complicated relationship between psychiatry and the law.

Society has also abused ordinary individuals with mental disorders. It has often stigmatized ordinary people who have sought psychiatric care, often to the disadvantage of both the individual and society, as the following case indicates:

> Myra Grossman had had a difficult childhood and adolescence. Yet she managed to survive well enough to graduate high school, enter college, and be at the very top of her class during her first two years. Conflicts with her parents, however, and a nagging depression continued unabated and, during her third year, she left school to seek treatment. She began seeing a psychotherapist and subsequently entered a private psychiatric hospital. During that year, Myra developed considerable ability to deal with her own distress and her family conflicts. She returned to college, continued to major in both chemistry and psychology, earned membership in Phi Beta Kappa in her junior year, and graduated magna cum laude.
>
> During her senior year, she applied to medical school. Her Medical College Aptitude Test (MCAT) scores were extraordinarily high, and she had won a New York State Regent's Medical Scholarship. But she was rejected by all thirteen schools to which she had applied.

> She consulted an attorney, and they jointly decided to concentrate on the "easiest" school that had rejected her. During the trial, it became known that fewer than 8 percent of those admitted to this school had won the Regent's Medical Scholarship, that none had been admitted to Phi Beta Kappa, and that she possibly had the highest MCAT scores of any applicant. She was an attractive person, obviously well motivated, clearly bright. Why then had she been rejected? Clearly, it was because of her prior psychiatric hospitalization.
>
> Ms. Grossman and her attorney marshaled clear evidence that she was quite well integrated psychologically. Five psychiatrists and a psychologist testified in effect that she was the better for her prior troubles, and that they had no doubt that she could successfully complete medical school and become a first-rate doctor. She and her attorney successfully demolished the contention that she might still suffer from her prior "illness." But still, the judge ruled against her. Ms. Grossman might have appealed that decision, and might well have won her appeal had not a far better medical school admitted her when the ruling came down. (Ennis, 1972)

Social stigma about treatment for psychological disorders has also played a negative role in political campaigns. During the 1972 presidential campaign, George McGovern, the front-running Democratic nominee, proposed Senator Thomas Eagleton as his vice-presidential running mate. Eagleton apparently neglected to tell McGovern that he had been treated for depression, either because he viewed that as a private matter or because the stigma of such treatment might deprive him of the candidacy. Once the press learned that Eagleton had undergone treatment, it became a national story. After much pressure, McGovern took Eagleton off the ticket. There was no question of Eagleton's effectiveness: he had served splendidly as a senator from Missouri. Rather, there was considerable fear that he would weaken the ticket. He was, after all, stigmatized (Reich, 1986; Rosenhan, 1975).

More recent events, however, indicate that the stigma associated with mental illness has decreased. Former U.S. senator Lawton Chiles ran for governor of Florida in 1990 and publicly acknowledged that he had been diagnosed with depression and treated with Prozac. Throughout his campaign, Chiles openly answered questions about his treat-

The stigma associated with mental illness seems to have decreased, as shown by attitudes toward Thomas Eagleton *(left)*, who in 1972 was taken off the ticket for vice president because of his treatment for depression, and Lawton Chiles *(right)*, who successfully ran for governor of Florida in 1990, even though he openly acknowledged that he too had been treated for depression.

ment for depression and released his medical records. Chiles refuted claims by his opponent that he had suicidal tendencies. He won the gubernatorial race. This political outcome, and others like it, have been lauded by those who have fought to reduce stigma.

Putting It All Together

In this chapter, we have explored the delicate balance between the welfare of society and the rights and needs of the mentally ill. Mental illness is a burden for the individual, the family, the community, and the nation. Like all illnesses that can result in disability, mental illnesses deserve attention from health-care providers and all sectors of society. It is clear that the deinstitutionalization movement gave rise to a dramatic shift in mental health care in the United States. Past concerns about excessively restrictive care have given way to concerns that the mentally ill are being abandoned. Front-page stories about patients confined to institutions have been replaced by headlines about criminalization and homelessness of the mentally ill. Rather than

being concerned about excessive restraint and forced treatment, patients worry about being abandoned by an increasingly fragmented mental-health-care system.

In addition to problems with access to quality care, the mentally ill are forced to contend with stigmatizing social attitudes which, at best, hold them responsible for their illness and, at worst, depict them as sinister and dangerous. These negative views are a major impediment to community programs aimed at easing the recovering patients' transition back into the community.

Solving these problems will not be easy. It will be necessary for society to devote more resources to mental health care and rehabilitation. We will have to find ways of assuring adequate treatment in a health-care system that is undergoing rapid change. The problems are daunting, but there is reason for optimism. Advocacy groups have devoted a great deal of effort to the elimination of stigmatizing social attitudes, and it appears that these efforts are beginning to pay off. Many prominent individuals who have suffered from mental illness now discuss their experiences in public forums. There is greater confidence in the efficacy of treatments for mental disorders, including both psychological and pharmacological treatments. We believe there is reason to be optimistic about the quality of mental health care in the future.

Summary

1. When patients with mental disorders do not receive adequate treatment, they may end up homeless or in jail. This represents a shift of responsibility from our mental-health-care system to other sectors of society. A positive result of *deinstitutionalization,* however, has been the growth of the *patients' rights movement,* including self-help organizations and patients' rights advocates.

2. Serious mental illnesses are not only a tragedy for the patient, but also for family members. They are distressed at seeing their loved one suffer and must often play a major role in caregiving.

3. *Stigma* against the mentally ill is a major social problem that places an extra burden on patients and their families.

4. The expansion of managed health care in the United States, combined with the decrease in public hospitals, has posed special problems for the treatment of mental disorders. Many individuals with serious mental illnesses are finding it increasingly difficult to get good treatment. This situation has given rise to efforts to gain *parity* for the treatment of mental illness.

5. Serious mental illnesses often diminish the individual's capacity for insight. Many do not view themselves as having an illness that would benefit from treatment. When individuals with mental disorders refuse treatment, the legal system is sometimes called upon to resolve the conflict.

6. There is no one federal standard for *involuntary commitment,* but all state statutes require that individuals who are committed must be mentally disordered, dangerous to themselves or others, or suffering from a "grave disability." The notion of dangerousness, especially, is rife with scientific, legal, and moral problems.

7. Because involuntary commitment deprives a person of liberty, there must be clear and convincing evidence that the person requires hospitalization.

8. Several significant court decisions have held that those committed to psychiatric hospitals have a right to treatment that includes individual diagnosis and the preparation of a treatment plan that is periodically reviewed. One negative consequence of right-to-treatment decisions has been the decline in support for mental health programs, as the states often prefer to cut back their support for these programs rather than incurring the additional costs of implementing proper treatment.

9. *Criminal commitment* can occur either because a person was "insane" at the time of the crime, or because he or she is presently psychologically incompetent to stand trial.

10. The notion of *competency to stand trial* is rooted in the right of every person to defend himself against accusations. A person judged incompetent to stand trial is sent to an institution for the criminally insane until he is able to be tried, which often means a long period of restriction. The courts have decided that people who can never become competent to stand trial need not be "hospitalized" forever. But there is still no uniform practice regarding how long those who are treatable but incompetent may be committed, and whether the time spent in such commitment is later to be subtracted from the defendant's sentence.

11. The *insanity defense* requires that the defendant was wholly or partially irrational when the crime took place, and that this irrationality affected his or her behavior. While the insanity defense seemingly protects those who commit crimes while distressed, such people are commonly sent to prison-hospitals, where care is worse than in prisons themselves, and incarceration is longer. Because being indefinitely committed to a psychiatric hospital is often worse than going to prison, the insanity defense is rarely used.

12. There have been several legal guidelines for the insanity defense, most notably the *M'Naghten "right-wrong" test,* the *Durham "product of mental disease" test,* and the *American Law Institute (ALI) "appreciate and conform" rule.* The modern standard, which is now used in all federal courts, was instituted in 1984 under the *Insanity Defense Reform Act (IDRA).* It requires only that the defendant "was unable to appreciate the na-

ture and quality or the wrongfulness of his acts."

13. Abuses of mental health treatment are sometimes a consequence of professional malpractice and sometimes due to social factors. When mental health professionals violate ethical guidelines they are subject to revocation of their license as well as expulsion from professional organizations.

16

Future Directions

Chapter Outline

Helen Kossoff, *Panel of Faces.*

Learning Objectives

→ Be able to give some possible explanations for why, although the rate of violent crime overall is down, there have been some highly visible rampage killings in recent years.

→ Learn how both biology and psychology can contribute to violent behavior, and why it is so difficult to predict in advance when a rampage killing is likely to occur.

→ Describe the difference between efficacy and effectiveness studies, and why each kind of study is valuable but has flaws in determining outcomes of therapy.

→ Be able to explain what is meant by the "tactics" and "nonspecifics" of therapy, and how they can account for the lack of big, specific effects of particular therapies as well as for the placebo effect.

→ Familiarize yourself with the economics of psychotherapy and how Managed Care is affecting the practice of psychotherapy.

→ Learn about the importance of prevention, and be able to describe some programs to prevent at-risk children from becoming depressed, anxious, or violent.

→ Explain what is meant by "positive psychology" and what its aims and methods of treatment are.

There are two psychological epidemics in the United States today. One is the epidemic of depression, and we have discussed it at length in Chapter 7. The other is an epidemic of violence among young people. In the late 1980s and early 1990s, arrests of juveniles for violent crimes were 67 percent greater than in 1986. While such arrests have decreased in recent years and school violence overall is declining, the rate of gun violence has increased. Moreover, some shocking rampage killings at schools have shaken society to its very core. There were thirteen rampage murders in 1999, and the schoolyard shootings, almost unknown forty years ago, were the most horrific. In the last three years of the millennium, there were twenty such rampage murders in American schools, including the one described here:

> On a warm Monday morning, December 1, 1997, fourteen-year-old Michael Carneal walked into a prayer meeting at Heath High School in West Paducah, Kentucky, carrying a blanket. He unwrapped several firearms from it and opened fire. He first shot and killed Nicole Hadley. He then murdered two more girls, and wounded five more people. Nicole had been his best friend, a sympathetic girl he had called almost every night in the two months before the shootings. (Based on Belkin, 1999)

A discussion of such events is usually considered outside the realm of Abnormal Psychology, since murderous violence, and even disproportionate aggression, is not a category of mental illness in DSM-IV. Nonetheless, such violence may sometimes have its roots in mental health problems. So we ask here: Can Michael's rampage be seen as an instance of mental disorder and could his behavior have been foreseen?

> Michael's family life seemed banal. His parents were involved in the community: one of them was always at every school event that involved one of their children. Dad was a lawyer, a Boy Scout troop leader, and a church elder. His older sister was valedictorian of her high school class. Ann Carneal, his Mom, had been an English major in college but had stopped working when Michael was born. She says "It's hard to focus on time, because, you see before this happened, everything . . . was so ordinary." (Based on Belkin, 1999)

But looked at more closely, everything was not so ordinary.

> In the spring of 1997, Michael showed his mother a copy of the gossip column, *Rumor Has It,* in his school newspaper. It said that Michael and a male classmate had "feelings for each other." Ann wanted to complain to the school, but Michael calmly told her that that would "really not be a good idea because then people would think it was true." Ann felt that Michael had handled it "diplomatically and maturely."
>
> "During the fall of 1997," Dad says, "Mike's grades were good. He was happy in band. And, to our knowledge, he was happy at Heath High School." After the murders, Michael was interviewed intensively by a psychologist and a psychiatrist, and a very different picture emerges from their notes.
>
> "People picked on me, and I'd never do anything about it," Michael says. His grades began to drop precipitously, and other kids called him "gay" or "faggot" several times a day during ninth grade. (Based on Belkin, 1999)

The usual explanation of school shootings has been external: centered on poor parental supervision and on easy availability of guns. Neither of these is true of Michael, since his parents seemed highly involved with their children, and Michael had to steal the murder weapons he used. Rather, the explanation here seems much more internal to Michael's psychological makeup.

We have built this book around the four great themes that we believe capture the most significant currents in Abnormal Psychology in the year 2000. We close the book by discussing a single pressing issue from each of the four themes that we believe will be central to progress in Abnormal Psychology during the first decade of our new century. Michael Carneal's rampage in West Paducah illustrates each of the themes.

The first theme is "Levels of Analysis: Biology and Psychology." This theme is about the either/or mentality in which the cause, treatment, and prevention of abnormality are seen as either psychological or biological. Our view is that this dichotomy, although widely held, is usually not helpful. In the case of rampage murders, important clues, both psychological and biological, are beginning to emerge. While this jigsaw puzzle is far away from being able to predict such "needle-in-the-haystack" events, an explanation that uses both levels of analysis can be cogently given, but only after the fact. Our view is that if disproportionate aggression and violence were to become a legitimate category of DSM and a routine topic for study, progress toward prediction and prevention would follow, and lives would be saved. The issue we will discuss around our first theme is the biopsychology of murder.

The second theme of the book is "Science and Practice." This theme is in essence the daily problems that therapists face in trying to use the very best scientific information when they confront the real troubles patients present in the clinician's consulting rooms. Therapists often feel frustrated when they try to apply the scientific literature to their patients, and once having determined what treatment the literature suggests is best to do, they are often checkmated by the economics of health care. So we will round this theme off by discussing the effectiveness and the economics of psychotherapy.

The third theme of the book is "Development," the clues that the growing and changing human being offer to understand the cause and treatment of abnormality. We believe that great strides will occur in the next decade in the prevention of abnormality by interventions delivered to young people at risk but before abnormality has taken hold. The twin epidemics of depression and violence will likely be ameliorated more by prevention efforts than by treatment after the fact. So we will discuss the most promising programs of prevention.

The final theme of the book is the search for the "Treatment of Choice." Almost all forms of psychotherapy proceed by finding out what is wrong and then trying to heal what is broken. We will discuss a different way of proceeding, which takes its clue from prevention. This approach rejects the disease model and is called "positive psychology." Positive psychology seeks to buffer human strength rather than to repair damage. It operates on the belief that this is central to both effective prevention and successful treatment. To prevent violence, substance abuse, anxiety, and depression, it focuses on interventions that lead to moral, exemplary young people and that emphasize optimism and future-mindedness.

Levels of Analysis: The Biopsychology of Murder

Some of the residents of West Paducah have dismissed Michael Carneal as a "monster," as evil. Indeed, we have argued when discussing rape that the distinction between crazy and evil should not be blurred and that the subject matter of Abnormal Psychology is the former, not the latter. A classification system that excludes violence bolsters this distinction. And yet, when we examine the thoughts and feelings and biology of particular killers, we realize that in some cases psychopathology may have affected their actions, as has been suggested in Michael Carneal's case:

> Michael began to think about shooting himself, but he didn't because of his family. He reports that he was hearing voices calling his name in empty rooms and thought that people were looking in his windows at night or were under his bed. He wrote a school essay called "The Halloween Surprise" in which a character named Michael kills his fellow students, and he graphically described their deaths. Michael drifted toward an older group of alienated students. He stole a gun from the garage of a friend and waved it around in the band room on the day before Thanksgiving. The kids were impressed.
>
> The day after Thanksgiving, Michael stole a cache of guns. A friend slept over the next night, and Michael told him that "something big was gonna happen." On Monday morning, it did. (Based on Belkin, 1999)

While the act of mass murder by a fourteen-year-old boy is surely evil, a closer look at the circumstances and at Michael's thoughts and feelings makes Michael's rampage look very much in form like the cases of depression and schizophrenia that have been a central focus of the book. Michael was the object

of harassment, probably unfounded. He reacted calmly on the surface, but he saw himself as a deeply wronged victim, and his anger and despair underneath are clear, at least in retrospect. When he took a gun to school, he felt he had impressed his fellow classmates. He had suicidal thoughts. He heard voices. He felt spied upon.

So Michael displayed an array of worrisome, abnormal symptoms. Why did his parents and his close friends not see all this? One possibility is these symptoms were largely made up only after the murders to bolster Michael's "not guilty by reason of insanity" plea. (Michael was sentenced to twenty-five years in prison without the possibility of parole.) More likely, it is because Michael kept them to himself, fearing the stigma that he and most of the citizens of West Paducah attach to mental illness. The Surgeon General's Report on Mental Health shows how large a role stigma plays in preventing people from opening up to others about symptoms of abnormality. The report states:

> The stigma that envelops mental illness deters people from seeking treatment. Stigma assumes many forms, both subtle and overt. It appears as prejudice and discrimination, fear, distrust, and stereotyping. It prompts many people to avoid working, socializing, and living with people who have a mental disorder. Stigma impedes people from seeking help for fear that the confidentiality of their diagnosis or treatment will be breached. It gives insurers—in the public sector as well as the private—tacit permission to restrict coverage for mental health services that would not be tolerated for other illnesses. (The Surgeon General's Report on Mental Health, 1999, Chapter 8)

Michael Carneal, shown here being led to the circuit courthouse after his arrest for the rampage killings at his school, had displayed symptoms of abnormality before the killings.

So we believe that Michael's rampage is a proper subject for the study of Abnormal Psychology, and that some categories of violence are proper categories for the future DSM-V. Michael's case is teeming with psychological factors, some of which were harbingers of violence, and some of which might have been treated and even prevented. Overcoming the stigma of mental illness is one important factor. Several other factors need to be considered to begin to understand—and prevent—similar rampages. Access to guns, media-borne contagion, and the breakdown of the family are the obvious external changes. But the psychological changes in America among children are even more frightening, with many children feeling they have no one to talk to and no moral compass or sense of responsibility for their actions.

Many children today have a need for instant gratification, and they display an impulsivity and a present-mindedness that may be undermining society. Moreover, many children are imbued with a sense of victimology. What started as a useful way of getting alcoholics to believe they were victims of a disease, rather than hopelessly sinful, and then evolved into the nobility of the civil rights movement, has gone overboard. Victimology has become the American way of blame. It is routine for adults and their kids to now explain all their problems as victimization. When a boy in trouble sees himself as a victim, this view festers into seething anger. With the availability of guns, it can explode as murder.

In an excellent piece of journalism, the *New York Times* looked at the 102 killers in 100 cases of rampage killing in the United States over the last fifty years (Fessenden, 2000). In contrast to murders in the heat of passion or in an armed robbery or in gang warfare, which seem to make some "sense," these hundred episodes seem "senseless." But they have a pattern. In rampage murders, the perpetrator does not flee. Eighty-nine of the 102 rampage killers didn't even leave the scene of the crime. Michael Carneal simply put down his gun and said, "I'm sorry."

Forty-six of the rampage killers killed themselves, or let themselves be killed, in what is known as "suicide by cop." The rampage killers were better educated, less "deprived," and more likely to be white than were other killers. Most strikingly, at least half of them had histories of serious mental disorders. Forty-eight had a formal diagnosis, usually schizophrenia, and half of these diagnoses were on the books before the crimes. We have been at pains throughout this book to emphasize that only a tiny percentage of mentally disordered people are violent. Advocates for the mentally ill rightly bristle at any mention of an association between mental illness and violence, lest this troubled population become even more stigmatized and mistreated. But these sentiments, which we share, should not blind us to the likelihood that this particular phenomenon—rampage killing—is tied to mental illness.

So the disposition to rampage murder yields clues of mental disorder, and the immediate path to the acts does as well (Goodstein and Glaberson, 2000). These are decidedly not quiet and mild-mannered people who mysteriously snap. They often have nicknames like "Crazy Joe" or "Crazy Pat" that their intimates hang on them. Most of the workplace shooters had already been fired or disciplined for violence or for threats of violence. Michael Carneal told his schoolmates that "it would be cool" to shoot into a student prayer group. Other rampage murderers describe precisely who, where, and when they are going to kill. But friends, family, teachers and co-workers who see all this are often unable or unwilling to take the signs seriously. Kip Kinkel, another schoolyard rampage killer, yelled out loud in his literature class, "God damn this voice inside my head." His teacher wrote up a disciplinary note right away. It asked, "What could you do differently to prevent this problem?" Kinkel dutifully filled out, "Not to say 'damn.'" The teacher signed it. His mother signed it. No one, however, seemed to notice the part about the voice inside his head (Goodstein and Glaberson, 2000).

On the road to a rampage killing, there are plenty of psychological warnings: explicit threats, a violent and bizarre history, diagnosis of mental illness, all set against the background of a ragged health-care system that more and more lets severe mental disorders slip through the cracks. In addition, there may be a deep biology to murder. Adrian Raine is a UCLA psychologist who emigrated from England to California partly because there were more murderers in California who could be studied in systematic psychobiological research (Raine, 1999). Raine has studied the living brains of forty-one convicted murderers using PET scans. His forty-one control subjects are matched on age, sex, handedness, history of head injury, diagnosis of mental illness (six of each of the forty-one are diagnosed with schizophrenia), medications, and drug use. The brain-scan differences are striking.

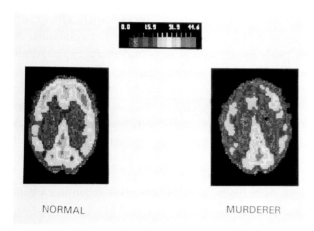

NORMAL   MURDERER

PET scans of a normal control and a convicted murderer show differences in activation of the prefrontal area of the brain. The prefrontal area is at the top of the scan, and the occipital area is at the bottom of the scan. Normal patients show more activation (as indicated by the red and yellow colors on the scan) of the prefrontal cortex than do convicted murderers. The low activation of the prefrontal cortex of the murderer is indicated by the blue and green colors on the scan. Activation of the occipital area is the same in both the normal control and the convicted murderer.

First, normal controls show more activation of the prefrontal cortex than the murderers do. This deficit is specific to the prefrontal areas. The temporal and occipital cortex areas do not differ in activation. Reduced prefrontal activity is implicated in loss of control over aggressive feelings, in greater risk taking and rule breaking, in aggressive outbursts, in loss of self-control, in poor reasoning ability, and in present-mindedness.

Additional brain differences appear. The corpus callosum, which is the band of nerve fibers linking the two hemispheres, has reduced activation. Raine speculates that this may mean a poor connection between the right hemisphere, which generates much of negative emotion, and the inhibitory and controlling processes of the dominant left hemisphere. Further, the left amygdala, hippocampus, and thalamus of the murderers show lower activation, and the right, higher activation than those of the normal controls. Raine speculates that since the amygdala is tightly implicated in aggression, this may explain the antisocial behavior and misinterpretation of ambiguous stimuli in social situations (the murderer's belief that some accidental slight was done on purpose) that have the potential to explode into violence.

Raine's findings may also illuminate the difference between impulsive murderers and cold-blooded killers who plan their actions. Of the forty-one murderers studied by Raine, fifteen fit the cold-blooded pattern, and nine fit the impulsive pattern of murder. How do their brains differ? The cold-blooded killers had better prefrontal activity than the impulsive murderers, but both groups had higher activation of the right amygdala, hippocampus, thalamus, and midbrain than their matched controls. Raine speculates that this higher subcortical activity predisposes aggression in both groups of murderers, while the good prefrontal activity allows the cold-blooded murderers to be able to plan and regulate their aggressive outbursts, rather than just exploding instantly when provoked.

When we recall that Michael Carneal and many of the rampage killers came from "good" homes, and were decidedly not children of poverty, we see yet another intriguing finding in Raine's data. Twelve of his sample came from poverty and twenty-six from minimal deprivation. The brains of the murderers from good homes had a 14.2 percent reduction in activity of the right orbitofrontal cortex. Other adults who acquire this pattern of damage (from strokes or head injuries) show personality and emotional changes that look like sociopathy (Damasio, 1994). This makes it plausible that when a murderer comes from a "bad" home, upbringing may be a major cause, but when a murderer comes from a "good" home, biological deficits may be a major factor.

So rampage killings may have psychobiological underpinnings. The brain activation of murderers differs from that of nonviolent controls. The brain

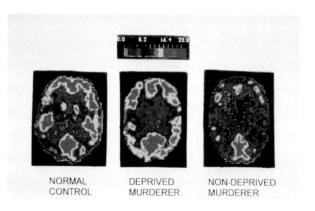

NORMAL   DEPRIVED   NON-DEPRIVED
CONTROL   MURDERER   MURDERER

PET scans showing a normal control, a deprived murderer (someone from a "bad home"), and a nondeprived murderer (someone from a "good home"). The nondeprived murderer shows reduced activation in the frontal cortex (as shown by the blue and green colors at the top of the scan) compared to the normal control and the deprived murderer.

activation of cold-blooded murderers and murderers from "good homes" can be distinguished from the brain activity of both impulsive murderers and controls. In addition, rampage killers show a substantial amount of prediagnosed mental disorder. They usually leave a trail of explicit hints about whom they are going to kill and when they are going to kill. They worry their family and friends a great deal, but usually not enough for effective prevention to occur. And they slip through our tattered system of health care.

Before we conclude that rampage killers (and disproportionate aggression more generally) should take a rightful place in diagnostic systems of mental illness and in the Abnormal Psychology textbooks of the future, two cautions are in order to prevent us from further stigmatizing and maltreating the mentally ill. First, only a minute percentage of those with mental disorders are violent. Second, while violence is frequent in our society, rampage killing is rare. Attempts to predict it are like attempts to predict airplane crashes or suicide: weak statistical predictions can be made, but particular crashes can almost never be predicted. The false alarm rate of predicting rampage killings would be so high as to be totally unacceptable to a free society. Our society only apprehends and punishes those who commit actual crimes, not those who are more "likely" than those in control groups to commit crimes or those who merely intend to commit crimes. With these caveats explicit, we believe that making rampage killing and more generally, violence, a legitimate object of study in Abnormal Psychology will save many lives and will prevent the ruination of even more lives. With scrupulous regard for the rights of the mentally ill and for the protection of the innocent, a science and a practice built around the prevention and treatment of violence is long overdue.

Science and Practice: Effectiveness and Economics of Psychotherapy

Given the existence of rampage killers, as well as people who are depressed or anxious or who suffer from schizophrenia, we need to find ways to treat troubled individuals when their problems overwhelm them and society at large. Much research is being conducted as to both psychological and biological explanations and treatments of mental disorders. But it is not always clear how to apply research findings to people with multiple problems in the real world. Diagnosis is not always clear-cut. Therapists are not always aware of the full extent of a patient's problems and may miss signs of trouble. Scientific findings may be too general or may offer several plausible explanations that may not be relevant to overcoming a particular, troubled individual's abnormal thoughts or behaviors. Translating science into practice is not always an easy task.

Throughout this book, we have presented a great deal of information on the efficacy of different kinds of drugs and psychotherapy for each disorder, and we have synthesized all this into summary tables in every chapter. So you will remember, for example, that Viagra works well for male erectile dysfunction, and is more efficacious than direct sexual therapy, and that exposure therapy is probably more efficacious than antidepressant drugs for obsessive-compulsive disorder. You would think, therefore, that clinicians would be firmly guided by these scientific findings in choosing what treatment to offer, and that this would translate directly into practice. You would also think that health insurance would reimburse patients most readily for being treated in the ways that outcome studies find work best. But neither of these suppositions is true, as we will see.

The Effectiveness of Psychotherapy★

Why is actual psychotherapy not always, or even usually, guided by the scientific literature on outcomes that you have read about all this semester? Why do practitioners have trouble translating research into practice? Why have psychological organizations, like the American Psychological Association, not created standards for practice that mandate the use of scientifically proven treatments for each disorder? These questions boil down to the tension between efficacy studies (controlled laboratory studies

★This section is based on Seligman, M.E.P. (1998). Afterword: A plea. In P. Nathan and J. Gorman (Eds), *Treatments that work.* New York: Oxford.

of therapy) and effectiveness studies (studies of psychotherapy as it is actually done in the real world).

Almost all of the outcome information on psychological disorders comes from efficacy studies, but efficacy studies in the laboratory differ from effectiveness studies with real patients in a clinician's office. Results vary for efficacy and effectiveness studies for several reasons: First, the kinds of problems they examine differ. Clinicians see patients who have many problems, while patients in efficacy studies usually only have a single disorder. Researchers in efficacy studies examine a well-defined DSM disorder. In contrast, although many patients may go to a therapist because they have a DSM disorder that they want cured, most often they will go to a therapist because they are unhappy, because they are doing badly at work or love, because they are languishing and have lost their zest for living, or because they want to grow. Second, therapy differs in efficacy studies and in effectiveness studies. In an efficacy study, patients are randomly assigned to therapists. In real life, patients choose to work with a particular therapist because they believe in her; they choose the kind of therapy she does because they believe it will help them. Therapy in efficacy studies is short term; therapy with a clinician is often long term. Efficacy studies test well-defined therapy. Therapy by clinicians, however, is often eclectic, with the therapist borrowing techniques as needed from several schools. If one of the techniques fails, she drops it and switches to another. Sometimes, the therapist switches modalities altogether. She generally does not use a manual. Moreover, treatment in real life may be derived from psychodynamic thinking and from family systems, and none of these modalities has been tested in efficacy studies (Lipsey and Wilson, 1993; Luborsky, Singer, and Luborsky, 1975; Shapiro and Shapiro, 1982).

In November 1995, *Consumer Reports* published the largest effectiveness study of psychotherapy and medication ever done (Consumer Reports, 1995). It was a study of treatment as it is actually administered in the field, in contrast to treatment as distilled into controlled efficacy studies. Because the study was based on a survey of its readers, it had quite a number of methodological flaws, including self-report, retrospection (looking back at past problems and therapy), and lack of external control groups (Seligman, 1995, 1996). But there were three robust results of substantial relevance to the gap between treatment in the office and efficacy studies.

1. Treatment worked very well. Most respondents got a lot better. Of the 426 people who were feeling "very poor" when they began therapy, 87 percent were feeling very good, good, or at least so-so by the time of the survey. Of the 786 people who were feeling "fairly poor" at the outset, 92 percent were feeling very good, good, or at least so-so by the time of the survey. These findings converge with meta-analyses of efficacy, but contrast dramatically with the 50 to 65 percent improvement reports that typify the efficacy studies we have relied on throughout this book (Lipsey and Wilson, 1993; Smith, Glass, and Miller, 1980; Shapiro and Shapiro, 1982).

2. Long-term therapy produced much more improvement than short-term therapy. Roughly double the number of people in treatment over six months, compared to people in treatment for less than six months, reported major improvement in their presenting problem.

3. No specific modality of psychotherapy did any better than any other for any problem. These results confirm the "dodo bird" hypothesis, which holds that all forms of psychotherapy do about equally well (Luborsky, Singer, and Luborsky, 1975).

These findings present a contrast to almost all the efficacy studies relied on in the first fifteen chapters of this book. Efficacy studies show high specificity of technique, only modest patient gains, and they do not endorse long-term treatment. Why such a difference in the results from the two kinds of studies? There are two possibilities. The first is that the *Consumer Reports* study and other similar effectiveness studies are methodologically flawed and should be ignored. The second is that the efficacy studies are methodologically flawed. We think that both methods are flawed and that creating a new method that has the virtues of both without the flaws is an urgent and promising project, which will occupy clinical scientists over the next decade.

The flaws of the effectiveness design generally and the *Consumer Reports* study in particular are flaws of "internal validity": they involve insufficiently tight control, including possible sampling bias, lack of external control groups, lack of rigorous diagnosis, self-report inaccuracy, retrospective distortions, and the need for a fuller battery of tests. The flaws of the efficacy design are flaws of "external validity": the therapy is carried out under conditions so different from those of actual therapy as to make generalizing to actual therapy very hazardous. Or to put it another way, the laboratory nature of the efficacy design omits so many crucial elements of real therapy and introduces others so alien to real therapy that it masks, minimizes, and distorts the results that actual therapy produces. In particular, five properties listed below characterize psychotherapy as it is done in the field. Each of these properties is absent from an efficacy study done under controlled conditions. If these properties are important to patients' getting better, efficacy studies will underestimate or even miss altogether the value of psychotherapy done in the field.

1. Psychotherapy in the field is *not of fixed duration.* It usually keeps going until the patient is markedly improved or until he quits. In contrast, the intervention in efficacy studies stops after a limited number of sessions—usually between eight and twelve—regardless of how well or poorly the patient is doing.

2. Psychotherapy in the field is *self-correcting.* If one technique is not working, the therapist usually tries another technique or even another approach. In contrast, the intervention in efficacy studies is confined to a small number of techniques, all within one approach and following a fixed order according to a treatment manual.

3. Patients in psychotherapy in the field use *active* shopping to find a specific kind of treatment and a therapist whom they screen and decide to work with. In contrast, patients enter efficacy studies by the *passive* process of random assignment to treatment, agreeing to work with whatever therapist and to undergo whatever therapy is offered in the study. Moreover, the patients willing to be guinea pigs in an efficacy study may be quite different from those who enter actual therapy.

4. Patients in psychotherapy in the field usually have *multiple problems,* and psychotherapy is geared to relieve parallel and interacting difficulties. Patients in efficacy studies are usually selected to study one problem, and their diagnosis is determined by a set of exclusion and inclusion criteria.

5. Psychotherapy in the field is almost always concerned with *improvement in the general functioning* of patients, as well as relief of specific, presenting symptoms of a particular disorder. Efficacy studies usually focus only on specific symptom reduction and whether the disorder ends.

Most generally, efficacy studies minimize the role of clinical judgment on outcome, while effectiveness studies maximize the role of clinical judgment. In the *Consumer Reports* study, individual therapy did not differ from group therapy for any outcome variable. Does this mean that we should rush in and assign people to group therapy all the time? It is much cheaper. If the *Consumer Reports* study had been an efficacy study and had assigned people at random to group versus individual therapy, this would have implied that on average individuals would benefit equally from either. But people were not assigned randomly in the *Consumer Reports* study. Therapists, in conjunction with their patients, presumably used a great deal of clinical judgment to decide if the patients would do better in individual or group therapy. (Does she respond well to authority? Does she change markedly when criticized by others?) So the results mean that once clinical judgment filters who gets individual therapy and who gets group therapy, *then* the two modalities do equally well.

Much of the success of therapy may depend on "nonspecifics" that all good therapists do, and this may account for why *Consumer Reports* found that no therapy or drug did better than any other for any disorder. There are specific curative ingredients in psychotherapy. Among those that we documented in the first fifteen chapters are:

- applied tension for blood and injury phobia,
- penile squeeze for premature ejaculation,
- cognitive therapy for panic,
- relaxation for phobia,
- exposure for OCD,
- behavior therapy for bed-wetting.

In spite of this, when one active treatment is compared to another active treatment, as in the *Consumer Reports* study, specificity tends to disappear or becomes quite a small effect. Lester Luborsky's work on the "dodo bird effect" (Luborsky, Singer, and Luborsky, 1975) and the National Collaborative Study of Depression (Elkin et al., 1989) both show this. The lack of robust specificity is also apparent in much of the drug literature as well. Methodologists argue endlessly over flaws in such effectiveness studies, but they cannot overlook the problem of the general lack of specificity of these studies. The fact is that almost no psychotherapy technique (with the exceptions above) shows big, specific effects when it is compared to another form of psychotherapy or drug, adequately administered. Finally, the seriously large "placebo effect" (see Chapter 12) found in al-most all studies of psychotherapy and of drugs, also affects outcomes, with at least 40 percent of clients often responding well to inert procedures.

Why is there such little robust specificity and such a large placebo effect with medications and with psychotherapy? Much of the explanation can be found under the derogatory misnomer "non-specifics of therapy." We believe that there are two classes of nonspecifics: tactics and deep strategies. Among the **tactics** of all good therapy are:

- attention,
- authority figure,
- rapport,
- tricks of the trade (for example, saying "Let's pause here," rather than "Let's stop here"),
- paying for services,
- trust,
- opening up,
- naming the problem.

The **deep strategies** are not mysteries. Rather, we believe they can be the subjects of large-scale science and of new techniques, which maximize them. One strategy is instilling hope (see Chapter 7). The other is "building buffering strengths." Assume for a mo-ment that the buffering effects of strength-building strategies have a larger effect than the specific "heal-ing" ingredients that we have reviewed throughout this book. If this is true, it would explain the small specificity found when different active therapies and

This therapist counsels a patient who has been raped. Some tactics of good therapy that the therapist may be using include developing trust and rapport with the patient so that the patient is able to open up, name the problem, and talk about it, as well as helping the patient to develop deep strategies that will buffer her against further traumas.

different drugs are compared as well as the massive placebo effects that often occur. Among the strengths built in psychotherapy are:

- courage,
- interpersonal skill,
- rationality,
- insight,
- optimism,
- honesty,
- perseverance,
- realism,
- capacity for pleasure,
- putting troubles into perspective,
- future-mindedness,
- finding purpose and meaning.

The efficacy method cannot answer questions about variables, which are omitted from its design—such as deploying clinical judgment and building strengths—and these may play a large role in out-come. Efficacy methodology cannot test long and complicated psychotherapy. Manuals cannot be writ-ten for long or complicated treatment. Patients can-not be randomly assigned, ethically, to a placebo condition for the many months or years that long-term treatment takes. A control group of patients who have equally severe symptoms, but who are willing to eschew therapy in favor of talking to sym-pathetic friends, ministers, or doing nothing, cannot be found. We believe that the next decade holds the promise of studies that will answer the questions of the effectiveness of real psychotherapy, studies that real practitioners can put to use. The strengths of the two methods can be combined to do compelling studies of complex treatments—treatments that in-volve a good deal of clinical judgment, that have variable duration, that have self-correcting improvi-sations, that are aimed at improved quality of life as well as symptom relief, and that are carried out with patients who choose the treatment, are not randomly assigned, and have multiple problems. Such studies would be *total sample* studies, in which all the patients from a wide and representative range of modalities of treatment would be included. Such studies would be *longitudinal,* with patients looked at before, during, and long after treatment. They would have *four per-spectives on outcome,* including the patient's self-report, the therapist's view, blind diagnosis, and a full battery of tests, and they would be *externally valid,* with patients choosing the modality they wanted, with duration of treatment the joint decision of patient and therapist, with self-correction of techniques, but without manuals and without exclusion of any patients based on multiple diagnoses.

The Economics of Psychotherapy

Until the early 1990s, most psychotherapy was paid for at the "point of service." Patients directly paid their therapists the going rate for treatment received. Many patients were then reimbursed for some percentage of their payment by health insurance. A patient could choose which therapist he wanted to see from virtually the entire community of therapists. The patient and therapist together decided what the goals of therapy would be, and they decided when those goals had been reached. There were limits on duration of treatment and limits on percent of reimbursement, but these tended to be adequate.

The advent of Managed Care (MC) changed all this. In MC schemes, which now cover more than half of the people in the United States, the medical claims of an entire company (or institution) are bundled together. Here's a simplified version of how it works:

A large organization, like General Motors or the city government of Erie or the University of Colorado, contracts with a Managed Care company to provide all the health care (physical and mental) to its employees. General Motors pays a fixed amount in advance to the MC, based on the number of its employees and their predicted illnesses. The MC is publicly owned and wants to make a profit for its shareholders, and it also wants to compete successfully against other MC's by attracting new companies based on low premiums as well as high level of health care. Low premiums are of course easier to document than high levels of care. The MC establishes a "panel" of providers (physicians, psychotherapists, and other health-care experts) and standards for treating each disorder. These standards are enforced by a "case reviewer," who tells the therapist what kind of treatment is allowed and for how long it will be allowed. The patient can only see an approved panel member, and the therapist must negotiate with the case reviewer, usually not a trained therapist, if he believes longer or different or more expensive treatment is warranted. It is obvious that allowing long and expensive treatments and allowing a patient to see any therapist he wants will seriously weaken profits. As a consequence, the individual no longer has much choice about what therapist or what treatment he will have, and the therapist no longer has much choice about what treatment to give and for how long.

As Karen Shore, the president of the National Coalition of Mental Health Professionals and Consumers, puts it: "Managed Care has eliminated true psychotherapy as a covered service, and replaced it with their own model of crisis intervention and brief, problem-focused treatment. The aim is to reduce the most obvious symptoms without exploring the causes of the problems or looking at other problems in the patient's life. Many plans openly state that they 'do not cover chronic or ongoing problems,' a standard that would never be acceptable in medical/surgical care. Many plans allow no more than four to ten sessions. Case managers are told not to allow more than a few sessions, and clinicians who average more than a handful of sessions are refused referrals. The more seriously impaired consumers are left without treatment" (Personal communication, Karen Shore, November 22, 1999). The consequences of such a lack of treatment can be seen in the following case:

> A thirty-four-year-old man had repeatedly sought treatment for extreme depression, suicidal tendencies, delusions, and sexual abnormalities. He believed his boss was the Archangel Michael, and that his colleagues were out to kill him. Twice, the MC's reviewers overruled emergency room doctors who recommended hospitalization. The reviewers instead recommended a drop-in therapy group and telephone help. As the patient worsened, the patient's family called the MC several times, but the company did not return the calls. After two days of trying to call the company, the patient rammed his car into a highway stanchion, killing himself and his wife. (Personal communication, Karen Shore, November 22, 1999)

The upshot of the new economics of therapy is to widen the gulf between what therapists believe they should do and what they are allowed to do. It is common for therapists to believe that a patient needs medium- or long-term treatment (fifteen to thirty sessions), and effectiveness evidence supports this belief. But it is just as common for the therapist to be told by the case reviewer that she can have only two sessions. It is common for a psychiatrist to believe that a specific medication in combination with psychotherapy is the best treatment for his patient, only to be told by the case reviewer that another, less expensive, drug should be prescribed and no psychotherapy will be forthcoming. It is against this background of a tattered system that individuals like Michael Carneal slip through.

The new economics also widens the gulf between good science and good practice. Efficacy studies of brief, by-the-manual psychotherapy are in the interest of profit-driven Managed Care, because fewer sessions cost less than more, and because less qualified and less experienced therapists can use manuals easily. Effectiveness studies involving longer treatment, highly skilled therapists, and clinical judgments would push toward much more expensive treatment. So there is pressure for MC's to rely on efficacy information and to set standards of care based on less expensive, short-term, by-the-manual therapy. The ultimate result may be a health-care system that systematically undertreats the mentally ill for short-term profit, resulting in the huge long-term losses—both in suffering and dollars—that result from increased relapse and recurrence of the mental disorders. Our vision for the future is of a health-care system that provides the highest quality care for mental disorders, that looks at mental health in the widest and longest terms, and that when it errs, errs on the side of adequate treatment and prevention.

Workshops in which children are taught skills for coping with depression, anxiety, or violent impulses may help to prevent the children from developing mental disorders. The children are taught cognitive and problem-solving skills through the use of drawings and cartoons, skits, and role playing.

Development: The Prevention Frontier

Taking into account the need to find real-life therapies that are both effective and economically viable, we turn to development and prevention. As we have discussed throughout the book, humans grow and develop throughout their entire life span. This suggests that prevention, carried out early in life, may enable an at-risk individual to avoid mental illness later in life, and that this may save much more suffering than therapy for a full-blown mental illness and may lead to cost savings as well as treatments that have quantifiable results. The vast bulk of improved human health in the twentieth century came not from treatment, but from preventive, public health measures—like inoculation for polio—that took place before any disorder had set in. Prevention is likely to be optimally carried out, yielding the maximum payoff, when just the right developmental period is targeted. For example, much of the contribution to the epidemic of depression begins when youngsters

reach puberty. Michael Carneal was fourteen and troubled by teasing about his sexuality. A developmentally sensitive intervention right at this period might have helped him to cope better with both the teasing and his confusion about his thoughts and his feelings. Along these lines, we predict that the vast bulk of progress in treating abnormality will result from effective prevention programs administered to young people. There are promising results already in three areas: depression, anxiety, and aggression.

Depression

Since depression is recurrent and episodic, usually lasting just a few months, prevention is a major concern. Medications have not been documented as preventive, but the techniques of cognitive therapy have proven to be preventive. There are five substantial studies with uniform results showing that cognitive therapy used in an educative, rather than a therapy mode can prevent depression in young, vulnerable individuals.

The APEX project at the University of Pennsylvania teaches college students at risk for depression the basic skills of cognitive therapy in a workshop setting. "At risk" is defined as being in the most pessimistic quarter of explanatory style. Two hundred and thirty-one students were randomly assigned to either an eight-week-long prevention workshop that met in groups of ten, once a week for two hours, or into an assessment-only control group. Participants were followed for three years. Those in the workshop group had significantly fewer episodes of generalized anxiety disorder than did those in the control group, and they had fewer major depressive episodes. Second, participants in the workshop group had significantly fewer depressive symptoms and anxiety symptoms than did those in the control group, as measured by self-report. Third, students in the workshop group had significantly greater improvements in explanatory style, less hopelessness, and fewer dysfunctional attitudes than did those in the control group, and these improvements helped to prevent depression in the students in the workshop group (Seligman, Schulman, DeRubeis, and Hollon, 1999). Very similar results using group cognitive therapy with high school students at risk for depression were found in two other studies (Clarke, Hawkins, Murphy, and Sheeber, 1993; Clarke et al., 1995). The researchers found that, over the twelve-month follow-up, the incidence of mood disorders was 14.5 percent for the teenagers in the prevention program compared to 25.7 percent for those in the control group.

Parallel results occur with preadolescent children who are at risk for depression. The Pennsylvania Prevention Project determined that the children were at risk for depression by one of two criteria: either they had mild symptoms of depression already, or their parents were fighting. Researchers in the program taught cognitive techniques to the at-risk children to see if depressive symptoms could be prevented in advance (Jaycox, Reivich, Gillham, and Seligman, 1994; Gillham, Reivich, Jaycox, and Seligman, 1995). They taught at-risk ten- to thirteen-year-olds the cognitive and problem-solving skills that patients are taught during cognitive therapy. A child manual with cartoons, skits, and role playing was used as a guide for teaching children these skills (see Figure 16-1). The results showed that depressive symptoms were markedly reduced in the children in the prevention groups as compared to those in the control groups, that those in the prevention groups had been "inoculated" against depression. Two-year follow-up showed fewer symptoms of depression in the treated children versus the controls.

The most surprising findings appeared in the one-year follow-up. It is a universal finding in therapy outcome studies that even "successful" effects wane. Surprisingly, the Pennsylvania Prevention Project found that the prevention effects got larger over the first two years. One-year, eighteen-month, and two-year follow-ups showed increasing gains and increasing separation between the treated groups and control groups on depressive symptoms. At the twenty-four-month point, 44 percent of the control children had moderate or severe depressive symptoms, but only 22 percent of the treated children showed such symptoms. In addition, prevention was most effective in the children who were most at risk. By three-year follow-up, when the project ended, the differences between the control group and the "inoculated" group were no longer significant, with the inoculated group showing almost as much depression as the control group (Gillham and Reivich, 1999). We do not know why the effect disappears, but we believe that booster sessions given about two years after the initial skills are learned may maintain the prevention effect.

These researchers may have found a critical age to teach skills to guard against depression. The skills become incorporated into the child's repertoire. As the child goes into puberty, and depression becomes more commonplace, he or she can use these skills repeatedly and increasingly to navigate the shoals of adolescence. Nonetheless, these skills may wane, and booster sessions are presently being designed to produce permanent immunization against depression.

Anxiety

Promising prevention results are emerging from the Queensland, Australia, Early Intervention and Prevention of Anxiety Project conducted by Mark Dadds and Sue Spence in Brisbane, Australia (Dadds et al., 1999). In the study, one hundred and twenty-eight children, ranging in age from nine to fourteen, were designated as at risk for anxiety disorders because their teachers had identified them as being particularly anxious, and because, when tested, they had scored high on anxiety symptoms. The children, who were predominantly white and middle class, were randomly assigned to either a control group or a group that used the "Coping Koala" prevention training from the manual that is an adaptation of Kendall's (1994) "Coping Cat" anxiety program for children. Clinical psychologists, with assistance by clinical graduate students, led the ten one- to two-hour sessions, and parents participated in three sessions as well. In essence, this program teaches children cognitive, behavioral, and physiological strategies to cope with events they are particularly afraid of.

Figure 16–1

TEACHING COGNITIVE AND PROBLEM-SOLVING SKILLS

In the Pennsylvania Prevention Project, preadolescent children at risk for depression are taught cognitive techniques to prevent them from developing depression. This bubble cartoon is one of a series of cartoons, skits, and role-playing tasks contained in a manual for teaching such cognitive skills. The aim of the cartoon pictured here is to teach an optimistic explananatory style. The child in the cartoon is confronted with the adversity of being called a "chicken" for not smoking. The pessimistic child has a pessimistic thought in which a permanent, characterological and unchangeable cause is invoked: "I'm not cool." To learn to substitute more optimistic explanations, the child must now think up and fill in a temporary cause, for example: "These kids are acting like swaggering idiots." The temporary explanation leads to a better mood state than the permanent one. (Source: Gillham, Reivich, Seligman, and Silver, Penn Optimism Program: Depression Prevention for School Children, 1996)

The children have been followed for two years, and researchers have measured the occurrence of anxiety disorders and symptoms of anxiety. At six-month follow-up, only 16 percent of the children in the Coping Koala group had an anxiety disorder as compared to 54 percent in the control group. These preventive effects disappeared at one-year follow-up, but they resurfaced at two-year follow-up. At two years, both parents' reports and clinicians' ratings suggested less anxiety in the children in the Coping Koala group. Researchers do not know why prevention effects wax and wane over time, but this seems to be a regular finding across different studies, and one that warrants future investigation.

Aggression and Violence

As we have said, the two mental health epidemics in the United States today are depression and violence. We have already discussed the tenfold increase in depression and its possible causes (see Chapter 7). Earlier in the chapter, we introduced the problem of violence and the term "rampage killers." Although schoolyard murders like those committed by

Michael Carneal are not a new phenomenon, and rampage killings make up only one-tenth of 1 percent of all homicides, the number of such killings increased significantly between 1990 and 1997. Between 1976 and 1989, there was an average of twenty-three such killings a year; between 1990 and 1997, the average number rose to thirty-four a year (Fessenden, 2000). Moreover, at the end of the 1990s, there were around twenty large-scale schoolyard murders in which children and teenagers killed their schoolmates with guns. Can such incidents be prevented and, more generally, can children at risk for becoming violent offenders be immunized against disproportionate aggression and violence by psychological prevention programs?

There are more than a dozen such programs now being tested. Most take a multifaceted approach to treatment and prevention, seeking to deal with the self, family, peers, the school, and the community through multisystemic therapy. The largest and best known is the Fast-Track Program (Conduct Problems Prevention Research Group, 1999). The Fast-Track program's rationale is that there is a combination of risk factors that interact to produce conduct disorder, aggression, and violence: poverty, living in a high-crime neighborhood, individual traits of hyperactivity and poor attention span, violent and unstable families. Problems at home then spill over to the school. Children who experience these risk factors may have difficulty coping with the social and emotional demands of school. Parental indifference to school and high-crime neighborhoods further exacerbate the problem. So Fast-Track intervenes at the school, at home, and with peers, and does so beginning in the first grade. The program is designed to continue into the fifth grade. At present, the intervention has been completed for children in first, second, and third grades.

The intervention consists of a curriculum that stresses self-control, emotional understanding, self-esteem, and interpersonal skills (Greenberg, Kusche, Cook, and Quamma, 1995). In addition, there are parent training groups designed to increase the parents' involvement in the schools, home visits to enhance problem-solving skills, child social skills training groups, literacy training, and friendship enhancement activities. This is an expensive, long-term, and global program. It has been carried out on 898 high-risk children, of whom 66 percent are boys, and 51 percent are African Americans. The children were randomly assigned to intervention or control conditions.

The results are preliminary, but positive. Parents report less aggression among the children in the intervention group. Teachers report fewer conduct problems, and the children in the intervention group needed 26 percent fewer special education services than the children in the control group. While these results are encouraging, we will await the results as the children approach the older ages at which violence and crime, not mere classroom misbehavior, begin to occur. Could Michael's rampage killings have been prevented? Right now the answer is probably "no." Our hope is that ten years from now our answer will be "probably, yes."

Treatment of Choice: Positive Psychology

In searching for the treatment of choice for each disorder, the final theme of this book, we found that all our strategies had something in common: they were framed within the disease model. They all implicitly held that abnormality was a disorder that could be treated by repairing something broken, by healing damage in the mind, in the brain, or in behavior. There is another way of looking at the treatment of abnormality. One can identify the unique strengths that an individual with problems has, and amplify those strengths, helping the patient to use his strengths as buffers against the troubles that beset him.

We will now explore this notion of building human strength rather than repairing pathology, and discuss its implications for psychotherapy. We call this approach "positive psychology." At the subjective level, the field of positive psychology is about positive subjective experiences: well-being, contentment, and satisfaction (past); hope, faith, and optimism (future); and flow and happiness (present). At the individual level, positive psychology is about positive individual traits: the capacity for love and vocation, courage, interpersonal skill, aesthetic sensibility, perseverance, forgiveness, originality, future-mindedness, spirituality, high talent, and wisdom. At the group level, it is about civic virtues and the institutions that move individuals toward better citizenship: responsibility, nurturance, altruism, civility, moderation, tolerance, and work ethic.

For the first author of this book, the idea of positive psychology began at a moment in time a few

Positive psychology aims to build strengths that will buffer people against loss and trauma. This includes building hope, courage, optimism, perseverance, and happiness on a personal level, and responsibility, altruism, and tolerance on a group level. These people who are building a home as part of a project for Habitat for Humanity are making active efforts that are helping others as well as themselves.

months after he had been elected president of the American Psychological Association.

I was weeding in my garden with my five-year-old daughter, Nikki. I have to confess that even though I write books about children, I'm really not all that good with children. I am goal-oriented and time-urgent, and when I'm weeding in the garden, I'm actually trying to get the weeding done. Nikki, however, was throwing weeds into the air, singing, and dancing around. I yelled at her. She walked away, came back, and said,

"Daddy, I want to talk to you."

"Yes, Nikki?"

"Daddy, do you remember before my fifth birthday? From the time I was three to the time I was five, I was a whiner. I whined every day. When I turned five, I decided not to whine anymore. That was the hardest thing I've ever done. And if I can stop whining, you can stop being such a grouch."

This was for me an epiphany. I learned something about Nikki, about raising kids, about myself, and a great deal about my profession. First, I realized that raising Nikki is not about correcting whining. Nikki was able to do that herself. Rather, I realized that raising Nikki is about taking this marvelous strength—which could be found in each individual by "seeing into the soul"—and amplifying it, nurturing it, helping her to lead her life around it so that it can buffer her against her weaknesses and the storms of life. Raising children, I realized, is vastly more than fixing what is wrong with them. It is about identify-

ing and nurturing their strongest qualities, what they own and are best at, and helping them find niches in which they can best live out these strengths.

As for my own life, Nikki hit the nail right on the head. I was a grouch. I had spent fifty years mostly enduring wet weather in my soul, and the last ten years being a nimbus cloud in a household full of sunshine. Any good fortune I had was probably not due to my grumpiness, but in spite of it. In that moment, I resolved to change.

The broadest implication of identifying and nurturing people's strengths, however, applies to the science and profession of psychology. Before World War II, psychology had three distinct missions: (1) curing mental illness, (2) making the lives of all people more productive and fulfilling, and (3) identifying and nurturing high talent. The early focus on positive psychology is exemplified by such work as Terman's studies of giftedness (Terman, 1939) and marital happiness (Terman, Buttenweiser, Johnson, and Wilson, 1938), Watson's writings on effective parenting (Watson, 1928), and Jung's work concerning the search and discovery of meaning in life (Jung, 1933). Right after the war, two events—both economic—changed the face of psychology: (1) in 1946, the Veteran's Administration was founded, and (2) thousands of psychologists found out that they could make a living treating mental illness. In 1947, the National Institute of Mental Health (which, in spite of its charter, has always been based on the disease model, and should now more appropriately be renamed the National Institute of Mental Illness) was founded, and academics found out that they could get grants if their research was about pathology.

Psychology's empirical focus shifted to assessing and curing individual suffering. Research emphasized psychological disorders and the negative effects of environmental stressors such as parental divorce, death, and physical and sexual abuse. Practitioners went about treating the mental illness of patients within a disease framework by repairing damage: damaged habits, damaged drives, damaged childhoods, and damaged brains.

This emphasis on the disease framework did bring huge strides in the understanding and therapy for mental illness. As this book testifies, at least fourteen previously untreatable disorders have yielded their secrets to science and can now be either cured or considerably relieved. But the downside was that the other two fundamental missions of psychology—making the lives of all people better and nurturing genius—were all but forgotten. It wasn't only the subject matter that was altered by funding, but the currency of the theories underpinning how we viewed ourselves. We came to see ourselves as a mere subfield of the health professions, and we became a victimology. We saw human beings as passive foci: "stimuli" came on and elicited "responses" (what an extraordinarily passive word!). External reinforcements weakened or strengthened responses. Drives, tissue needs, instincts, and conflicts from childhood pushed each of us around.

Our discussion of prevention is the foreground of a different approach. Rather than emphasizing stimuli and responses, it emphasizes active interventions. Rather than asking how we repair damage, we ask how we can prevent it. Our questions include: How can we prevent problems like depression or substance abuse or schizophrenia in young people who are genetically vulnerable or who live in worlds that nurture these problems? How can we prevent murderous schoolyard violence in children who have access to weapons, poor parental supervision, overactive right amygdalas, and a mean streak? We have learned over fifty years that the disease model does not move us closer to the prevention of these serious problems. Indeed, the major strides in prevention that we saw in the last section have largely come from a perspective focused on systematically building competency, not correcting weakness.

As we have stated already, prevention researchers have discovered that there are human strengths that act as buffers against mental illness: courage, future-mindedness, optimism, interpersonal skill, faith, work ethic, hope, honesty, perseverance, the capacity for flow and insight, to name several. Much of the task of prevention in this new century will be to create a science of human strength whose mission will be to understand and learn how to foster these virtues in young people.

Working exclusively on personal weakness and on damaged brains, however, has rendered science poorly equipped to do effective prevention. We now need massive research on human strength and virtue. We need to encourage psychologists to work with families, schools, religious communities, and corporations to develop climates that foster these strengths. We need to ask practitioners to recognize that much of the best work they already do in their offices is to amplify strengths rather than repair the weaknesses of their clients.

All good therapy involves "narration." Perhaps telling the stories of our lives, making sense of what otherwise seems chaotic, distilling and discovering a trajectory in our lives, viewing our lives with a sense of agency rather than victimhood is powerfully positive and healing (Csikszentmihalyi, 1993). Perhaps all competent psychotherapy forces such narration, and this buffers against mental disorder in the same way hope does. Despite our intuition that narration is such an important part of therapy, it is still not a subject of research as a therapeutic technique, there are not categories of narration, clinicians are not trained to better facilitate narration, and practitioners are not reimbursed for using this technique.

The search for empirically validated therapies has, in its present form, handcuffed Abnormal Psychology by focusing only on validating the specific techniques that repair damage and that map uniquely into DSM-IV categories, rather than using positive psychology techniques. The parallel emphasis among Managed Care Organizations on delivering only brief treatments directed solely at healing damage may rob patients of the very best weapons in the arsenal of therapy—making patients stronger human beings through psychotherapy. By working in the disease model of abnormality and looking solely for the salves to heal the wounds, we have misplaced much of our science, our practice, and our training. We now need to also address the other side of psychology—the positive side that identifies buffering strengths. When we do so, we will be reclaiming the birthright of psychology and psychotherapy—a birthright that embraces both healing what is weak as well as nurturing what is strong.

Putting It All Together

Both biological and psychological factors interact to make people what they are, both those who are good workers, good parents, and good citizens, as well as those who become rampage killers. Chemicals and neurons and brain structures affect what a person becomes, just as do psychological factors like optimism and depression, and societal variables like friends and family. Moreover, biology and psychology continue to interact and to affect gene expression and physical and mental health. We need to study both biology and psychology, seeking to determine the role of each on behavior, as well as how their interplay affects both social and antisocial thoughts and actions.

Psychologists seek not only to understand what makes people who they are, but also to treat those who present with psychological problems. To date, effectiveness and efficacy studies have been conducted in an effort to determine which therapies work best for which disorders, but both kinds of studies have drawbacks. Efficacy studies narrow down what is evaluated to determine whether a particular treatment relieves a particular disorder, while effectiveness studies evaluate real-life treatments by clinicians in the field who deal with patients who have more than one problem. We need to learn how to evaluate outcomes by creating and using new methods that can combine the strengths of each of the old methods.

With the advent of Managed Care, therapists and patients have found that economic considerations can not only limit the duration of treatment, but also how a disorder can be treated. We must find an economically viable means of restoring decision making about treatment to practitioners and their patients so that high-quality care can continue to ease the suffering of those with mental health problems.

Not only do we need to find treatments for mental illness, however, we also need to devote our resources to prevention of mental illness. By devoting resources to programs that use the techniques of positive psychology to build buffering strengths in young children, and to maintain these strengths in adolescents and adults, we hope to create happier, more creative, and more fulfilled individuals.

With this end in mind, we envision a day in which Abnormal Psychology textbooks will be not only about repairing what is broken, but also about assessing and building the panoply of human strengths. It is possible that by creating a science of positive psychology and with it creating a replicable way of building strengths, we will be able to improve the effectiveness of psychotherapy. A nosology of strengths, reliable means of assessing strength, and reliable ways of building strength may turn out to be the very best weapons in the arsenal of the treatments of abnormality.

Summary

1. Both psychology and biology can lead to rampage killings.

2. *Efficacy studies* are controlled laboratory studies of therapy. They show high specificity of technique, are based on random assignment of participants to therapists and treatments, are short term, and produce only modest treatment gains.

3. *Effectiveness studies* are studies of psychotherapy as it is actually done in the real world. They study eclectic therapy by real clinicians chosen by the patients themselves. They show that most respondents get better, that long-term therapy leads to more improvement than short-term therapy, and that in many cases no specific modality of therapy works much better than any other.

4. The *nonspecifics* of therapy may lead to positive outcomes as well as the placebo effect. The two classes of nonspecifics are: *tactics* and *deep strategies*. Tactics include paying attention, trust, rapport, and opening up. Deep strategies include building buffering strengths such as courage, interpersonal skill, optimism, perseverance, honesty, realism, and future-mindedness.

5. Managed Care has widened the gulf between what therapists believe they should do and what they are allowed to do.

6. Because humans develop and grow throughout their lives, it makes sense to find techniques that will prevent at-risk children from becoming depressed, anxious, or violent.

7. *Positive psychology* seeks to identify positive subjective experiences and to encourage individuals to develop strengths that will make them feel content, hopeful, and happy, and that will help them to cope with negative experiences and to buffer them against mental illness.

Glossary

acquisition   In Pavlovian conditioning, the learning of a response based on the contingency between a conditioned stimulus and an unconditioned stimulus.

acute schizophrenia   A condition characterized by the rapid and sudden onset of very florid symptoms of schizophrenia.

acute stress disorder   Anxiety, numbness, and disinterest, occurring during the first month after having experienced, witnessed, or been confronted by an event that involved the threat of death, injury, or threat to the physical integrity of self or others. If symptoms continue after the first month, it is called post-traumatic stress disorder.

addiction   *See* dependence syndrome.

adoption study   The study of offspring and biological and adoptive parents to see whether the occurrence of a trait is related to genes or environment. This method is one of two widely used methods (the other is the twin study) for quantifying the relative contribution of genetic to non-genetic determinants of psychological traits.

affective contrast   The subjective experience of positive and negative emotions based on drug exposure and withdrawal.

affective disorders   *See* mood disorders.

affective pleasure   An effect of drug use in the opponent-process model of addiction. Affective pleasure is the pleasant emotional state that is the initial pharmacological effect produced by the drug.

affective tolerance   An effect of drug use in the opponent-process model of addiction. With continued use, the addictive drug tends to lose its affective pleasure.

affective withdrawal   An effect of drug use in the opponent-process model of addiction. The sudden termination of narcotic use often produces the opposite affective state of the initial pleasant one.

agnosia   The failure to identify familiar objects or people.

agonists   Drugs that increase activity in particular neurotransmitter systems.

agoraphobia   An anxiety disorder characterized by fear of situations in which one might be trapped and unable to acquire help, especially in the event of a panic attack. People with agoraphobia will avoid crowds, enclosed spaces (such as elevators and buses), or large open spaces. From the Greek "fear of the marketplace."

akathisia   A side effect of chlorpromazine in which an itchiness in the muscles occurs and results in an inability to sit still.

alarm reaction   The first stage of a person's reaction to stress, according to Selye's theory of a general adaptation syndrome. The physiological arousal prepares the body to fight or flee the stressor.

alexithymia   The word literally means "no words for feelings" and is used to describe people who have difficulty expressing their feelings.

allele   One of the forms of a gene pair.

allostasis   The adaptation of many bodily states simultaneously across many different life circumstances.

allostatic load   The hidden price the body pays for its mediation of stress in the short run. High allostatic stress happens when there is frequent stress, repeated stress, or the inability to shut off stress mediators when they have been aroused.

altruistic suicide   Suicide required by the society (as defined by Durkheim; for example, hari-kari).

Alzheimer's disease   Degenerative disease of late middle or old age, in which mental functions deteriorate. An amnesic syndrome is often the major feature of this disorder. Its initial symptoms include loss of initiative, extreme forgetfulness, memory disability, and spatial disorders. It progresses to severe deteriorations of intellect and basic maintenance functions that lead to death.

amenorrhea   Loss of the menstrual period. A common occurrence in women who have anorexia.

American Law Institute (ALI) rule   A legal test for insanity that holds that a person is not responsible for his criminal conduct if, at the time of the crime and as a result of mental disease or defect, he lacks substantial capacity to appreciate the criminality of the conduct or to conform his conduct to the law.

amnesia   A dissociative disorder characterized by loss of memory of happenings during a certain time period, or loss of memory of personal identity. Includes generalized amnesia, retrograde amnesia, post-traumatic amnesia, anterograde amnesia, and selective amnesia.

amphetamine A stimulant that causes agitation, increase in energy and activity, hyper-responsiveness to the environment, euphoria, and a number of physiological signs of hyperactivation.

anaclitic depression A depression experienced by some infants between the ages of six and eighteen months who have been separated from their mothers for prolonged periods. This disorder is characterized by apathy, listlessness, weight loss, susceptibility to illness, and sometimes death.

androgen A hormone that is principally responsible for the morphological development of the external genitals of the male.

androgen insensitivity syndrome A syndrome in which a chromosomally male fetus lacks the gene that enables its body to recognize and react to masculinizing hormones, leading to an insensitivity to masculinizing hormones and the formation of female external genitals, rather than male external genitals.

animal phobias Specific phobias in which an individual has a fear of a particular animal, usually cats, dogs, birds, rats, snakes, and insects.

animism The belief in premodern societies that everyone and everything has a "soul" and that mental disturbance was due to animistic causes, e.g., an evil spirit had taken control of an individual and was controlling that individual's behavior.

anomic suicide Suicide precipitated by a shattering break in an individual's relationship to his society (as defined by Durkheim).

anorexia nervosa A disorder in which the individual has an intense fear of becoming fat, eats far too little to sustain herself, and has a distorted body image.

antagonists Drugs that reduce the activity of a particular neurotransmitter by interfering with synthesis or blocking postsynaptic uptake of the neurotransmitter.

anterograde amnesia Difficulty learning new material after a traumatic event.

antigens Invaders of the immune system.

antisocial personality disorder (or psychopathy, sociopathy) A personality disorder in which the individual has a rapacious attitude toward others and a chronic insensitivity and indifference to the rights of other people. The behavior must be long-standing and must be manifested in at least three classes of behavior, among which are: repeated aggressiveness; recklessness that endangers others; deceitfulness, lack of remorse, and consistent irresponsibility; failure to honor financial obligations.

anxiety Fear characterized by the expectation of an unspecified danger, dread, terror, or apprehension, often leading to an emergency reaction and "flight or fight" behavior. As used in psychoanalytic theory, the psychic pain that results from conflicts among the various personality processes.

anxiety disorders A class of mental disorders characterized by chronic and debilitating anxiety. These include agoraphobia, generalized anxiety disorder, panic disorder, phobias, post-traumatic stress disorder and obsessive-compulsive disorder.

aphasia Disorders of language resulting from damage to certain areas of the cerebral cortex.

applied tension A technique in which, upon seeing blood, people with a blood phobia tense the muscles of their arms, legs, and chest, thereby raising their blood pressure and heart rate, which prevents them from fainting at the sight of blood.

appraisal Evaluation of short-term mental events, a target of cognitive therapy.

apraxia A disorder of movement in the absence of muscle weakness or inability to perform any specific movement.

arbitrary inference Reaching a conclusion for which there is little or no evidence. According to Beck, people who are depressed are prone to making arbitrary inferences.

archetypes As used by Jung, universal ideas about which we are knowledgeable even at birth.

Asperger's disorder A pervasive development disorder that is usually not detected until the preschool period or later. It involves social impairment and repetitive patterns of behavior and limited interests.

association areas Sectors of the brain that serve to integrate information from diverse sources.

attention deficit hyperactivity disorder A disorder characterized by marked impulsivity, inattention, and hyperactivity.

attribution An assignment of cause for an event; a short-term mental event, and a target of cognitive therapy.

autism A childhood disorder whose central feature is the failure to develop the ability to respond to others within the first thirty months of life.

automatic thoughts Discrete sentences, negative in character, that a person says to himself, quickly and habitually. According to Beck, people who are depressed typically engage in automatic thoughts.

aversion therapy A behavior therapy that seeks to rid a client of undesired behavior by pairing that behavior with aversive consequences.

avoidance-approach conflict A conflict between a desire to approach an object or situation that has some positive value, and a desire to avoid that object or situation because it has been associated with harm. According to traditional learning theory, this conflict is a root of anxiety.

avoidance responding The act of getting out of a situation that has been previously associated with an aversive event, thereby preventing the aversive event. Differs from escape responding, which is getting out of the aversive event itself.

avoidant personality disorder A disorder whose central feature is social withdrawal combined with hypersensitivity to rejection.

Babinski reflex A reflex reaction, normally shown only by infants, in which the big toe turns upward and the toes fan out when stroked.

barbiturates A class of drugs depressing the central nervous system, decreasing anxiety and blunting sensitivity to the environment. Includes phenobarbital, pentobarbital, secobarbital, and benzodiapines.

B cells Lymphocytes that come from bone marrow and that have receptors on their surface for specific antigens.

behavioral activation system (BAS) A circuit connecting subcortical and cortical regions of the brain. It has been proposed that this system, which is sensitive to signs of pleasure and reward, inhibits the activity of the BIS.

behavioral assessment   A record of behaviors and thoughts one wishes to change, including their time of occurrence, duration, and intensity.

behavioral disorder   A disorder in which something behavioral, rather than emotional, is amiss, such as hyperactivity, attentional problems, and aggressive, destructive, and dishonest behaviors.

behavioral inhibition system (BIS)   A circuit connecting subcortical and cortical regions of the brain. It is believed to play an important role in the experience of anxiety.

behavioral model   The school of abnormal psychology that claims that behavior is shaped by the environment, and that behavior can be changed by changing the environment. According to the behavioral theorists, the symptomatic behavior of a mental disorder is the disorder, and is that which should be treated.

behavioral therapy   A therapy that is rooted in the view that psychological distress results from learned behavior that can be unlearned; the therapy seeks to replace the distressing behavior with more constructive modes of coping and adaptation.

behaviorism   A movement in academic psychology from the 1920s to the mid-1960s that sought to discover in the laboratory the general laws of learning and to apply these laws to society as a whole.

benzodiazepines   A group of mild tranquilizers producing muscle relaxation, decreased anxiety, and sedation. Includes Librium, Valium, and Dalmane.

biofeedback   Therapeutic technique in which the individual is given electronically amplified information on certain (somewhat) controllable physiological systems (such as heart rate and blood pressure) and trained to control that response system.

biogenic amines   Neurochemicals that facilitate neural transmission, including catecholamines and indoleamines.

biomedical model of abnormality   The school of abnormal psychology that claims that mental disorders are illnesses of the body resulting from an underlying physiological pathology such as a virus, disordered biochemistry or genes, or a dysfunctional organ.

bipolar disorder (or manic-depressive)   An affective disorder characterized by alternating periods of depression and mania.

bisexuality   Desire for sexual relations with members of both sexes.

blitz rape   Sudden and unexpected rape, as contrasted to acquaintance rape, often leading to PTSD.

blood-brain barrier   A barrier in the brain composed of specialized cells that prevent certain compounds in the circulatory system from entering the brain.

blood phobia   A specific phobia in which the individual becomes highly anxious in situations involving the sight of blood, injections, and injuries.

body dysmorphic disorder (BDD)   The exaggeration of a slight bodily defect into the perception of wholesale ugliness, the preoccupation with which comes to dominate the person's life.

borderline personality disorder   A broad Axis-II diagnostic category that designates people whose salient characteristic is instability in a variety of personality areas, including interpersonal relationships, behavior, mood, and self-image.

brain imaging   Techniques such as PET scans and CAT scans that capture the way that the brain looks and functions.

breakdown   One of the ways in which norepinephrine is reduced during neural transmission; the enzyme monoamine oxidase (MAO) and other enzymes chemically break down the norepinephrine in the synaptic gap and render it inactive.

Briquet's syndrome   *See* somatization disorder.

bulimia   A disorder in which people alternately gorge themselves with enormous quantities of food, and then purge themselves of that food by vomiting, or using laxatives or diuretics.

caffeine   A drug that stimulates the central nervous system and the skeletal muscles, lengthening the time it takes to fall asleep, decreasing fatigue, and aiding the individual in doing physical work.

catatonic schizophrenia   A subtype of schizophrenia that involves motor behavior that is either enormously excited or strikingly frozen.

catecholamines   Hormones involved in neural transmission in the brain. Includes norepinephrine, epinephrine, and dopamine.

categorical amnesia   *See* selective amnesia.

categorical approach   An approach to diagnosis (and diagnostic manuals), in which the person either meets the behavioral criteria and falls in the category, or fails to meet the criteria and is deemed not to have that particular disorder.

catharsis   In psychoanalytic theory, the uncovering and reliving of early traumatic conflicts.

cathexis   The charging of a neutral object with psychic energy, either positive or negative.

CAT scan   *See* computerized axial tomography.

central nervous system (CNS)   That part of the nervous system that coordinates all of the activity of the nervous system. In vertebrates, the CNS is made up of the brain and the spinal cord. All sensory inputs are transmitted to the CNS and all motor impulses are transmitted from the CNS.

cerebral cortex   The outermost layer (gray matter) of the cerebral hemispheres.

childhood disintegrative disorder   A pervasive development disorder that resembles autism. Symptoms do not appear until the child reaches at least two years of age, at which time he or she begins to show a loss of skills in two of three areas: language, social, and motor.

chromosomes   The DNA-containing bodies that contain the individual's genes.

chronic depression   A depressive state in which the individual has both a chronic depression and an episodic depression on top of that. *See also* double depression.

chronic schizophrenia   A condition characterized by a prolonged and gradual period of decline in which no specific crisis or stressor can be identified.

civil commitment   The process used to hospitalize mentally disordered people who have committed no crime.

clang associations   Associations produced by the rhyme of words. Commonly found in people who have schizophrenia.

classical conditioning   *See* Pavlovian conditioning.

clinical case history   The record of part of the life of an individual seen in therapy.

clinical interview   The most common method of assessment. Clinicians use this approach to get information about a patient's psychological state by listening to what the patient says and how he or she says it.

cocaine   The psychoactive agent in the coca plant. Cocaine increases energy, combats fatigue and boredom, and enhances the individual's responsiveness to things in his environment.

cognitions   Beliefs, thoughts, attitudes, expectations, and other mental events.

cognitive-behavioral therapy   A therapeutic technique in which therapists attempt to alter both the maladaptive thoughts and maladaptive behaviors of a client through restructuring of maladaptive belief systems and re-training behavior.

cognitive (or **selective**) **filter**   A mechanism for sorting out stimuli to determine which ones will be admitted and which ones barred; something seems wrong with this filter in people who have schizophrenia.

cognitive model   The school of abnormal psychology that claims that many disorders result from maladaptive beliefs or thought styles.

cognitive rehabilitation   A treatment focussing on attention, memory, and executive functions.

cognitive restructuring   Treatments that are predicated on the assumption that irrational thoughts create irrational behaviors, which can be eliminated by changing the underlying thoughts.

cognitive therapy   Used primarily in the treatment of depression, this therapy seeks to change the cognitive triad of (a) self-devaluation, (b) a negative view of life experience, and (c) the pessimistic view of the future, as the determining cognitions for depression.

cognitive triad   According to Beck, a group of cognitions characterizing people diagnosed with depression. These cognitions include (a) negative thoughts about the self, (b) negative thoughts about ongoing experience, and (c) negative thoughts about the future.

collective unconscious   As used by Jung, the memory traces of the experience of past generations.

comorbidity   The co-occurrence of two or more diagnoses.

comparative studies   A type of study that contrasts two or more groups in order to find out how people with a particular symptom or disorder differ from people without the symptom or disorder.

compulsion   A repetitive, stereotyped, and unwanted action that can be resisted only with difficulty. It is usually associated with obsessions.

computerized-axial tomography (**CAT** or **CT scan**)   An X-ray technique, used in neurological diagnosis, for constructing three-dimensional representations of the X-ray density of different areas of the brain.

concordant   When both of two twins have a disorder such as schizophrenia, they are called concordant for that disorder. *See also* discordant.

conditioned response (**CR**)   A response that is evoked by a certain stimulus (conditioned stimulus) once that stimulus has become associated with some other stimulus (uncondi-

tioned stimulus) that naturally evokes the unconditioned response. *See also* Pavlovian conditioning.

conditioned stimulus (**CS**)   A stimulus that, because of its having been paired with another stimulus (unconditioned stimulus) that naturally provokes an unconditioned response, is eventually able to evoke that response. *See also* Pavlovian conditioning.

conduct disorders   A cluster of children's behavioral disorders consisting mainly of aggressive and rule-breaking behaviors.

confound   A factor other than the experimentally controlled independent variable that might produce an experimental effect.

congenital adrenal hyperplasia (**CAH**)   A disease that bathes female fetuses with extra androgen. As young children, CAH girls like male-stereotyped toys, rough and tumble play, and are more tomboyish than matched controls.

construct validity   The extent to which diagnostic tests facilitate communication by describing and categorizing patients.

contingency   A conditional relationship between two objects or events, describable by the probability of event A given event B, along with the probability of event A in the absence of event B. A positive contingency between A and B obtains when A is more likely in the presence of B than in the absence of B. *See also* Pavlovian conditioning.

control group   A group of subjects similar to those in an experimental group, who experience everything the experimental group does, except the independent variable.

conversion   A somatoform disorder characterized by the loss of functioning of some part of the body not due to any physical disorder, but apparently due to psychological conflicts. The loss is not under voluntary control.

coping strategies   As used by psychoanalytic theorists, the process by which people alter the meaning and significance of troublesome drives and impulses in order to eliminate anxiety.

coprolalia   The repetition of socially unacceptable words sometimes manifested by people with Tourette's disorder.

core self   The self that develops first, between the second and sixth month of an infant's life. It embraces the infant's awareness that she and her caregiver are physically separate.

coronary heart disease (**CHD**)   Heart or circulatory problems often caused by arteriosclerosis; it can often lead to heart attack and sudden death.

correlation   Pure observation without manipulation to determine the relationship between two classes of events.

correlational studies   A type of study in which experimenters observe the relationship between two or more factors as they exist in the real world.

correlation coefficient   A statistic indicating the degree of contingency between two variables.

co-twin   As used in psychological research, one of a pair of twins whose sibling is seen at a psychiatric clinic in order to diagnose a psychological problem.

counterconditioning   A therapeutic technique for phobias in which a patient with a phobia is helped to relax while imagining fear-provoking situations (usually the least fear-provoking situation first, then gradually more and more fear-provoking situations). The relaxation response to the imagined situation is incompatible with the fear the patient has previously associated with the situation, and the fear is thus extinguished.

covert sensitization   A behavioral therapy for changing sexual interest; it uses imaged sexual stimuli followed by aversive US's to treat such paraphilias as exhibitionism.

criminal commitment   The coerced psychiatric hospitalization of mentally disordered people who have acted harmfully but are not legally responsible because they lack *mens rea,* or a "guilty mind."

cross tolerance   When tolerance to one drug produces tolerance to other drugs.

cultural-familial mental retardation   A condition in which there is no identified biological basis for the retardation. Many researchers believe that this form of retardation is caused by insufficient intellectual stimulation from the child's environment.

cyclothymic disorder   A mild but chronic form of bipolar disorder in which the patient experiences depressive and hypomanic symptoms for at least two years.

deep strategies of psychotherapy   One of the "nonspecifics of therapy" used by all good therapists. They include such techniques as instilling hope and building buffering strengths in patients.

defense mechanisms   *See* coping strategies.

degradation   A mechanism that clears the synapse by eliminating excess neurotransmitter through the action of enzymes.

deinstitutionalization   A mass movement that released patients from psychiatric hospitals into the community at large.

delayed auditory feedback   A method of treatment for stuttering that involves hearing one's own speech played back at about a .1 second delay.

delirium   A cognitive disturbance that has a rapid onset, fluctuates over time, and usually responds to treatment.

delirium tremens   A dangerous syndrome of withdrawal from alcohol, which is characterized by psychomotor agitation, hyperactivity of the autonomic nervous system, anxiety, loss of appetite, delusions, amnesia, and convulsions.

delusional disorder   A psychotic disorder in which the person experiences nonbizarre delusions for at least one month in duration.

delusions   False beliefs that resist all argument and are sustained in the face of evidence that normally would be sufficient to destroy them.

delusions of control   Beliefs that one's thoughts or behaviors are being controlled from without.

delusions of grandeur   Unsubstantiable convictions that one is especially important.

delusions of persecution   Groundless fears that individuals, groups, or the government has malevolent intentions and is "out to get me."

delusions of reference   Incorrect beliefs that the casual remarks or behaviors of others apply to oneself.

demand characteristics   Aspects of the experimental setting that induce the subject to invent and act on a hypothesis about how one should behave.

dementia   A more or less general deterioration of mental function, found most commonly in old people. Alzheimer's disease is a common form of dementia.

denial   As used in psychoanalytic theory, the process by which distressing external facts are eliminated.

dependence syndrome   A cluster of physiological, behavioral, and cognitive phenomena in which the use of a substance or a class of substances takes on a much higher priority for a given individual than other behaviors that once had higher value.

dependent personality disorder   A disorder wherein people allow others to make major decisions, to initiate important actions, and to assume responsibility for the significant areas of their life.

dependent variable   The factor that the experimenter expects will be affected by changes in the independent variable.

depersonalization   Feeling detachment from oneself; just going through the motions or looking at oneself from the outside.

depression   A mood disorder characterized by (a) sad affect and loss of interest in usually satisfying activities, (b) a negative view of the self and hopelessness, (c) passivity, indecisiveness, and suicidal intentions, and (d) loss of appetite, weight loss, sleep disturbances, and other physical symptoms.

derealization   Feeling as if the world, not the self, seems unreal.

detoxification   The reduction and removal of alcohol from the body.

developmental disorders   A cluster of disorders of childhood that may consist of deficits in language comprehension, speech, and responses to others that can result in such serious disorders as autism.

diathesis   Physical vulnerability or predisposition to a particular disorder.

diathesis-stress model   A general model of disorders that postulates that an individual develops a disorder when he both has some constitutional vulnerability (diathesis) and when he experiences psychological disturbance (stress).

diffusion   A mechanism that clears the synapse by reducing concentrations of neurotransmitter through an intermingling with other substances outside the neuron.

dimensional approach   An approach to diagnosis (and diagnostic manuals), in which the behaviors and traits that define personality disorders are believed to fall on a continuum.

direct sexual therapy   A therapeutic method developed by Masters and Johnson, in which (a) sexual dysfunctions are clearly and simply defined, (b) clients explicitly practice sexual behavior under the systematic guidance of therapists, and (c) clients are treated as couples, not as individuals.

discordant   When only one of two twins has a disorder such as schizophrenia, they are called discordant for that disorder. *See also* concordant.

discriminative stimulus   A signal that means reinforcement is available if the operant is made.

disinhibition   An increase in some reaction resulting from release of inhibition.

disorganized schizophrenia   A schizophrenic disorder whose most striking behavioral characteristic is apparent silliness and incoherence. Behavior is jovial but quite bizarre and absurd, suggesting extreme sensitivity to internal cues and extreme insensitivity to external ones, but without systematic delusions or hallucinations.

displacement   A cognitive alteration of reality that involves replacing the true object of one's emotions with one that is more innocent and less threatening.

disruptive behavior disorders   A cluster of disorders characterized by symptoms such as hyperactivity, inattention, aggressiveness, destructiveness, and defiance of authority.

dissociation   A situation in which two or more mental processes co-exist or alternate without being connected or influencing each other, with some area of memory split off or dissociated from conscious awareness.

dissociative amnesia   A loss of personal memory caused by severe trauma such as the death of a child or the dashing of a career. (Formerly known as psychogenic amnesia.)

dissociative disorders   A group of mental disorders characterized by fragmentation of an individual's identity. Dissociative disorders include amnesia, fugue, dissociative identity disorder, and depersonalization disorder.

dissociative identity disorder (or multiple personality disorder)   The occurrence of two or more identities in the same individual, each of which is sufficiently integrated to have a relatively stable life of its own and recurrently to take full control of the person's behavior.

dizygotic twins   Fraternal twins, or twins who developed from separate eggs, and whose genes are no more alike than are those of any pair of non-identical-twin siblings.

DNA (deoxyribonucleic acid)   The double helix molecule that contains the genes and serves as the blueprint for the synthesis of RNA, and the production of proteins and amino acids. The entwined strands of DNA are made up of phosphates, sugars, and four nucleotide bases.

dominant gene   Genes that can, on their own, produce a specific trait.

dopamine   A catecholamine that facilitates neural transmission.

dopamine hypothesis   The theory that schizophrenia results from an excess of the neurotransmitter dopamine.

double-blind experiment   An experiment in which both the subject and experimenter do not know whether the subject has received an experimental treatment or a placebo.

double depression   A major depressive episode superimposed on an underlying chronic depression.

Down syndrome   A disorder that results from the fact that an individual has forty-seven rather than the usual forty-six chromosomes in his or her cells.

drug cues   Drug reminders, such as settings in which drugs were taken, that induce craving for the drug and can trigger relapse in those who have been free of drugs.

drug dependence   The regular use of drugs acting on the brain that leads to maladaptive behavioral changes that would be seen as maladaptive in any culture. Three criteria characterize the disorder: (a) a pattern of pathological use of a drug, (b) impairment in occupational, social, physical, or emotional functioning, and (c) evidence of affective or physical adaptation to the drug.

drug tolerance   The need to use increased amounts of the drug to get the desired effect.

drug withdrawal   Characteristic affective and physical symptoms that follow drug use after the drug is discontinued.

DSM-IV   Published in 1994, this is the fourth edition of the *Diagnostic and Statistical Manual of Mental Disorders* of the American Psychiatric Association.

Durham test   A legal test for insanity which provides that an accused is not criminally responsible if his unlawful act was the product of mental disease or mental defect.

dysfunction   Impairment of functioning.

dyslexia   A learning disorder that leads to a difficulty in learning to read.

dyspareunia   *See* sexual pain disorders.

dysphoria   An unpleasant emotional state experienced during drug withdrawal; the opposite of euphoria.

dysthymic disorder   Chronic depression in which the individual has been depressed for at least two years without having had a remission to normality that lasted more than two months.

eating disorders   A disruption in the individual's pattern of eating. This disorder can occur at either extreme: excessive consumption of food or dramatic reductions in food intake. *See also* anorexia nervosa, bulimia.

effectiveness studies   Research studies in which the outcome of therapy is tested as it is delivered in the field.

efficacy expectation   According to Bandura, a person's belief that he can successfully execute the behavior that will produce a desired outcome.

efficacy studies   Research studies in which a therapy is tested under laboratory conditions.

ego   The self.

ego-dystonic homosexuality   Homosexuality that is incongruent with the individual's desire for sexual preference, and which the individual wants to change.

egoistic suicide   Suicide resulting when the individual has too few ties to his fellow humans (as defined by Durkheim).

ego-syntonic homosexuality   Homosexuality that is congruent with the individual's desire for sexual preference, and which the individual does not want to change.

electroconvulsive shock treatment (ECT)   A therapeutic treatment for depression, in which metal electrodes are taped to either side of the patient's head, and the patient is anesthetized. A high current is passed through the brain for a half second, followed by convulsions lasting almost one minute.

electroencephalogram (EEG)   A record of the electrical activity of cells in the brain (primarily the cortex) obtained from wires placed on the skull, and used in neurological diagnosis.

EMDR (Eye Movement Desensitization and Reprocessing)   A therapy used to treat patients with post-traumatic stress disorder in which the patient follows the rapidly moving finger of the therapist while concentrating on a disturbing image or memory; patients come to replace negative thoughts with positive thoughts and to experience less distress.

emergency reaction   A reaction to threat in which the sympathetic nervous system mobilizes the body for action. The blood pressure rises, heart rate increases, breathing becomes deeper, perspiration increases, and the liver releases sugar for use by the muscles.

emotional disorders   A cluster of disorders in which symptoms of fear, anxiety, inhibition, shyness, and overattachment predominate.

encopresis The failure to control bowel movements.

endogenous opoids Naturally occurring "morphine-like" compounds in the brain that modulate a variety of emotional experiences, in particular the response to stress.

endorphins Endogenous morphine-like substances.

enkephalins Small amino acid compounds that are endogenous opioids.

enuresis (or bed-wetting) A disorder that is manifested by regular and involuntary voiding of urine.

environmentalism The first assumption of behaviorism; it states that all organisms, including humans, are shaped by the environment.

epidemiological evidence Evidence from many individuals.

episodic depression Depression that has a clear onset and that lasts less than two years.

erectile disorder (or impotence) In males, recurrent inability to have or to maintain an erection for intercourse.

errors in logic The second mechanism of depression, according to Beck. A person who suffers from depression makes five errors in logic: arbitrary inference, selective abstraction, overgeneralization, magnification/minimization, and personalization.

escape responding The act of getting out of an ongoing harmful situation. *See also* avoidance responding.

etiology Causal description of the development of a disorder.

excitatory receptor A receptor in the brain that, when triggered by a particular neurotransmitter, will increase activity in the postsynaptic neuron.

exhaustion The third (final) stage of a person's reaction to stress, according to Selye, in which adaptive responding ceases. Illness, and in some cases, death may follow.

exhibitionism A psychosexual disorder in which the individual is sexually aroused primarily by exposing his genitals to unwitting strangers.

exhortative will The will whereby we force ourselves to work.

existential theory A theory that holds that mental disorders result when an individual fails to confront the basic questions of life successfully. Three issues are particularly important: fear of dying, personal responsibility, and will.

existential therapy A therapy that encourages clients to view their psychological problems as being of their own making.

expectations Cognitions that extrapolate the present to the anticipation of future events.

experiment A procedure in which a hypothesized cause (independent variable) is manipulated and the occurrence of an effect (dependent variable) is measured.

experimental effect The change in the dependent variable as a result of the manipulation of the independent variable.

experimental group A group of subjects who are given experience with an independent variable.

experimentalism The behaviorist view that experiments can reveal what aspects of the environment cause behavior.

experimenter bias The exertion of subtle influences by the experimenter on subjects' responses in an experiment.

experimenter-blind design An experiment in which the experimenter, but not the subject, is blind as to whether a subject is receiving a drug or placebo.

experiments of nature Studies in which the experimenter observes the effects of an unusual natural event.

explicit memory Stored knowledge about objects, people, and events.

exposure A behavioral form of treatment for phobia and PTSD in which the patient repeatedly endures the phobic object or original trauma in vivo or in imagination. *See also* extinction, response prevention.

expressed emotion Characteristics of interpersonal communication that seem to bear a relationship to the course of schizophrenia. They include cynical, hostile comments toward the patient and marked emotional overinvolvement by a relative or other care provider.

expression of genes The actual appearance, or manifestation, of the genes. The cell's ultimate qualities, such as its form and function, are determined according to whether or not certain genes are expressed.

external attribution An assignment of cause for an event to a factor that is outside oneself (i.e., other people or circumstances).

extinction In Pavlovian conditioning, cessation of a previously conditioned response to a conditioned stimulus, due to having learned that the conditioned stimulus no longer signals the onset of an aversive or desirable event. In instrumental learning, cessation of acquired operant responses due to reinforcement being discontinued. Modern theorists believe that extinction occurs when there is a negative contingency between the conditioned stimulus and the unconditioned stimulus. *See also* contingency.

factitious disorder (or Munchhausen syndrome) A mental disorder characterized by multiple hospitalizations and operations precipitated by the individual's having self-inflicted signs of illness.

false alarm In experimental analysis, accepting the hypothesis that independent and dependent variables are related, when they really are not. *See also* miss.

family resemblance approach Assessing abnormality based on the match between an individual's characteristics and the seven elements of abnormality: suffering, maladaptiveness, incomprehensibility and irrationality, unpredictability and loss of control, vividness, observer discomfort, and violation of moral and ideal standards.

family study method Documents the occurrence of characteristics or disorders in individuals who vary in their genetic relatedness.

family therapy A group of diverse psychotherapies that treat the couple or family, rather than the individual alone.

fat solubility *See* lipid solubility.

fear Characterized by distress about specific, dangerous objects.

fetal alcohol syndrome (FAS) A condition involving a variety of physical defects and deformities and mental retardation in fetuses exposed to alcohol through the mother's drinking during pregnancy.

fetish A psychosexual disorder characterized by a need to have an inanimate object close by in order to become sexually aroused.

fight/flight response An emergency reaction in which intense arousal of the sympathetic branch of the autonomic nervous system prompts attempts to either flee or resist threat.

flooding   A method used by behavioral therapists to treat phobias. The phobic individual is exposed to the situations or objects most feared for an extended length of time without the opportunity to escape. *See also* exposure, response prevention.

fluoxetine (Prozac)   A serotonin reuptake inhibitor prescribed for depression.

free association   A psychoanalytic instruction to say whatever comes to mind, regardless of how ridiculous or embarrassing it is, and without attempting to censor.

frequency distribution   The number of observations in each given class observed.

frontal lobe   A lobe in each cerebral hemisphere that includes control and organization of motor function.

frontal lobe dementia (Pick's disease)   A disorder in which patients show variable, often mild memory deficits and little or no visuo-spatial impairment in early stages. They may present symptoms such as changes in personality, disinhibition of language and behavior, and language problems. In later stages of the disease, they may show memory problems and apraxia.

frotteurism   A disorder that involves touching and rubbing of genitals against a nonconsenting person, usually in crowded places.

fugue state   A dissociative disorder in which an individual, in an amnesic state, travels away from home and assumes a new identity.

functional MRI (fMRI)   A neuroimaging technique that allows researchers to observe and measure the metabolic activity of the brain.

fusion   Protecting oneself against the fear of death or non-being by fusing with others such that one becomes attached to and indistinguishable from the others.

gender identity   Awareness of being male or being female.

gender identity disorder   A class of mental disorders in which the essential feature is an incongruence between anatomic sex and gender identity. Includes transsexualism.

gender role   Public expression of gender identity; what an individual does and says to indicate that he is a man or she is a woman.

general adaptation syndrome   According to Selye, a sequence of three stages that ensues when an individual is stressed: (a) the somatic emergency reaction is initiated, (b) the individual engages in defensive behaviors, and (c) eventually the individual's adaptive actions are exhausted.

generalizability   The quality whereby several randomly chosen individuals show a certain effect, increasing the chance that any other person would also show the effect.

generalized anxiety disorder   An anxiety disorder characterized by chronic tenseness and vigilance, beliefs that something bad will happen, mild emergency reactions, and feelings of wanting to run away.

genes   The basic functional units of heredity that contain the code or "program" for our inherited traits.

genetic linkage analysis   An approach in which researchers locate a family with a prevalence of a certain disorder. They then look for genetic markers in all the family members. If the gene or genes for the specific disorder are near the marker gene, there will be a linkage between the marker and the disorder in family members.

genotype   The specific genes inherited by an individual.

global amnesia   A state causing a complete loss of one's memory.

global attribution   An individual's assignment of cause for an event to a factor that will affect a number of different areas of his life.

goal-directed will   The will that develops out of hope, expectation, and competence, wherein we are able to work toward future goals.

grave disability   A legal phrase that describes an individual's psychological inability to provide food or shelter for herself, which places her in imminent danger.

group residences   Group homes for patients discharged from psychiatric hospitals in which the patients live together and run the household, shop, and work.

habit disorders   A collection of childhood disorders in which the prominent symptoms include difficulties associated with eating, movement disorders, or tics. These disorders consist of a diverse group of problems with physical manifestations such as bed-wetting, stuttering, sleepwalking and epilepsy.

half-life   The length of time it takes for the level of a drug in the blood to be decreased by 50 percent.

hallucination   A perception that occurs in the absence of an identifiable stimulus.

hallucinogens   Chemicals that cause perceptual disorientation, depersonalization, illusions, hallucinations, and physiological symptoms such as tachycardia, palpitations, and tremors. Includes LSD, PCP, and MDMA.

health psychology   The field that deals with disorders that stand at the border of psychology and medicine.

hebephrenic schizophrenia   *See* disorganized schizophrenia.

heroin   The most commonly used illicit opiate.

heterosexuality   Preference for sexual partners of the opposite sex.

histrionic personality disorder   A personality disorder in which people are shallow, egocentric, and self-absorbed and have long histories of drawing attention to themselves and engaging in excited emotional displays caused by insignificant events.

homosexuality   Preference for sexual partners of one's own sex.

hopelessness model of depression   A theory that emphasizes the stable and global dimensions for negative events as determinants of hopelessness.

hormones   Genes that modulate physical growth, bodily differentiation, and psychological growth.

hyperactivity   A disorder that is marked by developmentally inappropriate impulsiveness, inattentiveness, and excessive motor behavior. *See also* attention deficit hyperactivity disorder.

hypertension   High blood pressure.

hypoactive sexual desire   *See* sexual aversion disorder.

hypochondriasis   The sustained conviction, in the absence of medical evidence, that one is ill or about to become ill.

hypomanic personality   A chronic form of mania involving an unbroken two-year-long manic state. *See also* mania.

hypothalamic-pituitary-adrenal (HPA) axis   One of the primary systems mediating the biological response to stress.

hypothesis   A tentative explanation that can be scientifically tested.

hysteria   One of the first psychological disorders thought to have arisen from physical causes. From the Greek word for "womb."

hysterical conversion   *See* conversion.

id   In psychoanalytic theory, the mental representation of biological drives.

ideas of reference   The belief that certain events and people have special significance for the patient (e.g., that newscasters are speaking to him or that strangers in the street are looking at him).

identity alteration   A dissociative experience in which one displays a skill that one did not know one had.

identity confusion   A dissociative state in which one is confused or uncertain about who one is.

illness and injury phobias (or **nosophobias**)   Specific phobias in which an individual fears having one specific illness or injury or death.

immunocompetence   The degree to which the immune system is able to protect the organism efficiently.

immunologic memory   The factor that enables those T cells and B cells that initially combated an antigen to multiply more rapidly the second time the antigen is spotted, such that the immune system is able to do a better job of destroying the antigen than it did the first time.

implicit memory   Stored knowledge about perceptual and motor skills and various procedures and principles, such as grammar and emotions.

incidence   The rate of new cases of a disorder in a given time period.

independent variable   The hypothesized cause of some effect, manipulated by the experimenter in an experiment.

index case (or **proband**)   In psychological research, one of a pair of twins who is first seen at a psychiatric clinic.

inferential statistics   The mathematical procedures used to decide whether research findings are meaningful or due to chance.

inhibition   An active process through which the excitability of a particular neuron or center (group of neurons) is decreased.

inhibitory receptor   A receptor in the brain that, when triggered by a particular neurotransmitter, decreases activity in the postsynaptic neuron.

insanity defense   A defense for a crime that requires that the individual was wholly or partially irrational when the crime took place, and that this irrationality affected his or her behavior.

Insanity Defense Reform Act (IDRA)   A federal standard for determining whether the insanity defense can be used; it eliminates the volitional prong of the ALI standard and states that the insanity defense can be used if at the time of the crime the defendant, as a result of severe mental disease or defect, was unable to appreciate the nature and quality or wrongfulness of his act.

instrumental conditioning   A technique in which an organism must learn to perform some voluntary behavior in order to acquire a desired outcome, or to stop an undesirable event.

instrumental response   A response whose probability can be modified by reinforcement; a response that an organism has learned will bring about a desired outcome, or will stop an undesired event. *See also* operant.

intelligence quotient (IQ)   A numerical score that represents a person's level of intelligence, based on the person's performance on standardized tests.

inter-judge reliability   *See* inter-rater reliability.

internal attribution   An individual's assignment of cause for an event to a factor that is an aspect of himself.

interpersonal therapy (IPT)   A therapy that deals with depression as it results from interpersonal difficulties.

inter-rater reliability   The extent to which two or more psychologists will arrive at the same conclusion based on psychological tests, diagnostic interviews, and observational procedures.

intoxication   An acute, maladaptive psychological change, such as impaired thinking or judgment, that develops after ingestion of alcohol or a drug and that goes away in time.

involuntary commitment   The process whereby the state hospitalizes people for their own good, and even over their vigorous protest.

irresistible impulse rule   States that mental disease may impair self-control even when reasoning ability remains intact.

knockout procedures   Procedures by which researchers eliminate, or "knock out" specific genes in embryos.

Korsakoff's syndrome   A particular form of the amnesic syndrome caused by alcoholism.

laboratory model   The production, under controlled conditions, of phenomena analogous to naturally occurring mental disorders.

late-onset schizophrenia (paraphrenia)   Schizophrenia that first appears after the age of sixty-five.

law of effect   A principle that states that, in a given stimulus situation, when a response is followed by positive consequences, it will tend to be repeated; when the response is followed by negative consequences, it will tend not to be repeated.

learned helplessness   A condition characterized by an expectation that bad events will occur, and that there is nothing one can do to prevent their occurrence. Results in passivity, cognitive deficits, and other symptoms that resemble depression.

learning disorders   Difficulties that reflect enormous developmental tardiness and mainly affect the development of language and academic skills, including reading difficulties.

lifetime prevalence   The proportion of people in a sample who have ever experienced a particular disorder.

limbic system   Comprised of the middle areas of the frontal, temporal, and parietal lobes.

lipid (or **fat**) **solubility**   Ability of a drug to be stored in fat cells; this is an important factor in whether or how fast a drug reaches the brain; more lipid soluble drugs will be absorbed more quickly.

long-term potentiation (LTP)   The cellular process by which relatively permanent changes in the firing patterns of groups of neurons (ensembles) are made. This is believed to play an important role in memory formation.

LSD (lysergic acid diethylamide)   An hallucinogenic drug that causes changes in body sensations (dizziness, weakness, nausea), perception (distorted time sense), emotion, and cognitive processes.

lymphocytes   Cells in the immune system that recognize foreign cells.

macrophages   Cells in the immune system that "eat" antigens.

magnetic resonance imaging (MRI)   A brain-imaging technique in which each type of atom behaves like a tiny spinning magnet, wobbling at a characteristic frequency in the magnetic field. An MRI shows the elemental composition of cells and surrounding tissue. Damaged areas of the brain have a different concentration of elements than normal areas and appear differently on an MRI.

magnetoencephalography (MEG)   A relatively new technique that allows researchers to detect and measure weak magnetic fields produced by electrical activity in the brain.

magnification   Overestimating the impact of a small bad event; error of logic made by those who are depressed.

major depression   A depressive state, in which the individual suffers symptoms such as sadness, hopelessness, and passivity, but does not experience mania. *See also* unipolar depression.

malingering   A disorder in which the individual reports somatic symptoms, but these symptoms are under the individual's control, and the individual has an obvious motive for the somatic complaints. *See also* conversion.

mania   An affective disorder characterized by excessive elation, expansiveness, irritability, talkativeness, inflated self-esteem, and flight of ideas.

manic-depression   *See* bipolar disorder.

manic episode   A diagnosis for an individual who is in a manic state (euphoric thoughts, frenetic acts, insomnia), but who has never had a depressive episode.

MAO (monoamine oxidase)   An enzyme that helps to break down catecholamines and indoleamines. MAO inhibitors are used to treat depression.

marijuana   A psychoactive drug that, when used chronically and heavily, causes impairment of ability to focus on a task, impulsive and compulsive behavior, delusions, sensory-perceptual distortions, and sometimes panic reactions.

masochism   A psychosexual disorder in which the individual prefers to become sexually aroused by having suffering or humiliation inflicted upon him.

MDMA (Ecstasy)   A hallucinogenic drug chemically related to amphetamine; it causes changes in perceptual awareness.

mean   Average value of a set of values.

medical model   An approach to abnormality that treats it as a physical illness.

meditation   A relaxation technique in which one closes one's eyes and silently repeats a mantra; it works by blocking thoughts that produce anxiety.

melancholia   Depression characterized chiefly by loss of pleasure in most activities and by somatic symptoms, including sleep loss and loss of appetite.

mental disorder   In DSM-IV, a behavioral or psychological pattern that is genuinely dysfunctional and that either distresses or disables the individual in one or more significant areas of functioning.

mental retardation   Substantial limitations in present functioning; characterized by significantly subaverage intellectual functioning and limitations in two or more skill areas such as communication, self-care, home living, social skills, community use, self-direction, health and safety, functional academics, leisure, and work.

mesmerism   A treatment proposed by Franz Anton Mesmer that attempted to correct an imbalance in magnetic fluid in the body by treating the patient with iron filings and suggestion.

methadone   A narcotic used in heroin treatment programs. Methadone acts as a substitute for heroin, and prevents the heroin addict from experiencing withdrawal.

methamphetamine   A synthetic, central nervous system stimulant of the amphetamine family.

milieu therapy   Therapy in which patients are provided with training in social communication, work, and recreation.

minimization   Downplaying good events; an error of logic in depression.

Minnesota Multiphasic Personality Inventory (MMPI)   A widely used personality inventory consisting of 550 test items that inquire into a wide array of behaviors, thoughts, and feelings.

miss   Rejecting a hypothesis that the independent variable and dependent variable are related, when they really are.

M'Naghten test   A legal test for insanity which provides that a person cannot be found guilty of a crime if, at the time of committing the offense, due to "disease of the mind," the individual did not know the nature and quality of the act or that the act was wrong.

modeling   The observation and gradual imitation of a model who exhibits behavior that the client seeks to adopt in place of an undesirable behavior.

monozygotic (MZ) twins   Identical twins, or twins who developed from a single egg fertilized by a single sperm, which divided and produced two individuals who have identical genes and chromosomes.

mood disorders   Serious disturbance of a person's mood.

moral treatment   The humane, nonthreatening treatment of the insane.

MRI   *See* magnetic resonance imaging.

multimodal therapy   The combination of treatment techniques.

multiple personality disorder (or dissociative identity disorder)   A dissociative disorder in which more than one distinct identity exists in the same individual, and each identity is relatively stable and recurrently takes full control of the person's behavior.

multisystemic therapy (MST)   A family-based method of treatment for conduct disorder that intervenes in all aspects of the child's daily life: home, school, and peer groups.

myelination   The formation of a myelin sheath around the neurons of an embryo, beginning in the spinal cord in the first trimester and in the neurons of the brain in the second trimester.

Munchhausen syndrome   *See* factitious disorder.

narcissistic personality disorder   A personality disorder whose salient characteristics are an outlandish sense of self-importance, continual self-absorption, fantasies of unlimited success, power and/or beauty, and need for constant admiration.

narcotics   A class of psychoactive drugs blocking emotional response to pain and producing euphoria, dysphoria, apathy, psychomotor retardation, drowsiness, slurred speech, and maladaptive behavior. Includes opium, morphine, heroin, and methadone.

natural environment phobias   Irrational fear of heights, storms, dirt, darkness, running water, or wind.

Natural Killer cells   Cells in the immune system that lyse cells of a tumor.

negative affect   A general level of distress, comprised of both anxiety and depression.

negative correlation   A relationship between two classes of events wherein as one increases, the other decreases.

negative reinforcer   An event whose removal increases the probability of a response that precedes it. *See also* punishment.

negative symptoms of schizophrenia   Symptoms that entail a reduction in normal behavior.

Neo-Freudians   Psychodynamic theorists who modified and expanded upon Freud's views.

neuroadaptation   The complex biological changes that occur in the brain with repeated or chronic exposure to a drug.

neurodevelopment   The development of the nervous system. It extends from the embryonic stages through old age.

neuroimaging   Techniques for imaging the living human brain.

neurons   Nerve cells, the building blocks of the nervous system.

neurosis   Formerly, a category for disorders in which the individual experienced (a) emotionally distressing symptoms, (b) an unwelcome psychological state, (c) reasonably good reality testing, and (d) behavior that was reasonably within social norms. A neurotic disorder was not considered a transient reaction to stress or the result of organic brain damage.

neurotoxic   Destructive to nerves or nervous tissue.

neurotransmitter   A chemical that facilitates the transmission of electrical impulses among nerve endings in the brain.

nicotine   The active ingredient in tobacco that produces psychoactive effects.

norepinephrine   A neurochemical involved in neural transmission. Disturbances of the availability of norepinephrine in the brain have been associated with affective disorders.

nosophobias   *See* illness and injury phobias.

obsessions   Repetitive thoughts, images, or impulses that invade consciousness, are abhorrent, and are very difficult to dismiss or control; usually associated with compulsions.

obsessive-compulsive disorder   An anxiety disorder in which the individual is plagued with uncontrollable, repulsive thoughts (obsessions) and engages in seemingly senseless rituals (compulsive behaviors).

obsessive-compulsive personality disorder   A personality disorder characterized by a pervasive pattern of striving for perfection in oneself and others.

operant   A response whose probability can be increased by positive reinforcement, or decreased by negative reinforcement.

operant conditioning   Training the organism to perform some instrumental response in order to escape punishment or gain reward.

operational definition   A set of observable and measurable conditions under which a phenomenon is defined to occur.

opiates (or **narcotics**)   Drugs that produce euphoria or dysphoria, apathy, psychomotor retardation, pupillary constriction, drowsiness, slurred speech, and impairment in attention and memory. Includes codeine, opium, morphine, heroin, and methadone.

opponent-process model of addiction   A model developed by Richard Solomon which explains the increased motivation to use a drug that occurs with continued use of that drug. According to the model, all drugs that produce dependence have three properties: affective pleasure, affective tolerance, and affective withdrawal.

oppositional defiant disorder   A disruptive behavior disorder in which children show a pattern of negativistic, hostile, and defiant behavior, but do not show the more serious violations of others' rights as do children with conduct disorders.

orgasmic disorder   Disorders with the orgasic phase of sexual functioning. There are two male orgasmic disorders: premature ejaculation and retarded ejaculation.

outcome expectation   A person's estimate that a given behavior will lead to the desired outcome. *See also* efficacy expectation.

outcome studies   Research studies in which the effects of a therapy are observed as it attempts to alleviate a disorder. Therapy outcome studies can be either efficacy studies or effectiveness studies. *See also* effectiveness studies, efficacy studies.

overgeneralization   Drawing global conclusions on the basis of a single fact; an error of logic made by those who are depressed.

overinclusiveness   The tendency to form concepts from both relevant and irrelevant information; this thought defect, which is generally present in people with schizophrenia, arises from an impaired capacity to resist distracting information.

pain disorder (or **psychalgia**)   A somatoform disorder in which the individual experiences pain, not attributable to a physical cause, but to psychological conflict.

panic disorder   An anxiety disorder characterized by severe attacks of panic, in which the person (a) is overwhelmed with intense apprehension, dread, or terror, (b) experiences an acute emergency reaction, (c) thinks he might go crazy or die, and (d) engages in fight or flight behavior.

paranoid personality disorder   A personality disorder in which the person has a pervasive and long-standing distrust and suspiciousness of others; hypersensitivity to slight; and a tendency to look for hidden motives for innocuous behavior.

paranoid schizophrenia   A form of schizophrenia in which delusions of persecution or grandeur are systematized and complex.

paraphilias   A group of psychosexual disorders in which bizarre sexual acts or imagery are needed to produce sexual arousal. Includes fetishes, masochism, exhibitionism, voyeurism, transvestism, sadism, zoophilia, and pedophilia.

paraphrenia   *See* late-onset schizophrenia.

Parkinson's disease   A disorder that results in a degeneration of dopamine neurons in subcortical regions of the brain. The signs of Parkinson's disease are movement abnormalities, tremors in the limbs and head, muscle rigidity, and a generalized inability to initiate movement. Cognitive symptoms include memory loss and deficits in executive functions, such as planning. Between 20 and 60 percent of patients also show dementia.

Pavlovian conditioning (or **classical conditioning**)   Training in which an organism is exposed to one neutral stimulus (conditioned stimulus) and a stimulus (unconditioned stimulus) that naturally provokes a certain response (unconditioned response). Through the learned association between the conditioned stimulus and the unconditioned stimulus, the conditioned stimulus is able to evoke the conditioned response. Modern theorists believe that acquisition occurs when there is a positive contingency between the conditioned stimulus and the unconditioned stimulus. *See also* contingency.

PCP (phencyclidine)   An hallucinogen that causes sensitization to all sensory inputs, depersonalization, diminished awareness of self and the environment, disorientation, muddled thinking, and impaired attention and memory.

pedophilia   A psychosexual disorder in which the individual needs to engage in sexual relations with children below the age of mature consent in order to be sexually aroused.

penetrance   The likelihood that a particular gene or genotype will be expressed.

peptic ulcer   An erosion of the mucous membrane of the stomach or of the duodenum (the upper part of the small intestine).

peripheral nervous system   Comprised of the neural pathways located outside the central nervous system. It sends messages to glands, organs, and muscles.

perseveration   A difficulty in making transitions between one action and the next, or a difficulty in simply stopping a behavior or response.

personality disorders   Disorders in which characteristic ways of perceiving and thinking about oneself and one's environment are inflexible and a source of social and occupational maladjustment. *See also* antisocial personality disorder, avoidant personality disorder, dependent personality disorder, histrionic personality disorder, narcissistic personality disorder, obsessive-compulsive personality disorder, paranoid personality disorder, schizoid personality disorder, schizotypal personality disorder.

personalization   Incorrectly taking responsibility for bad events; an error of logic in those who are depressed.

pervasive development disorders   Disorders involving noticeable abnormalities in a child's social adjustment. These disorders include autism, Rett's disorder, childhood disintegrative disorder, and Asperger's disorder.

PET scan   *See* positron emission tomography.

phenotype   The specific physical or behavioral characteristics associated with a particular genotype.

phenylalanine   An amino acid that is an essential component of proteins. Children with phenylketonuria cannot metabolize phenylalanine.

phenylketonuria (PKU)   A rare metabolic disease that prevents digestion of an essential amino acid called phenylalanine. As a result of this disease, phenopyruvic acid, a derivative of phenylalanine, builds up in and poisons the nervous system, causing irreversible damage.

phobia   An anxiety disorder characterized by (a) persistent fear of a specific situation out of proportion to the reality of the danger, (b) compelling desire to avoid and escape the situation, (c) recognition that the fear is unreasonably excessive, and (d) the fact that it is not due to any other disorder.

physical dependence   The need for the presence of a drug to function normally, and the appearance of the withdrawal syndrome upon cessation of the drug.

Pick's disease   *See* frontal lobe dementia.

placebo   A neutral stimulus that produces some response because the subject believes it should produce that response.

placebo effect   A positive treatment outcome that results from the administration of placebos.

pleasure principle   As used in psychodynamic theory, biological drives that clamor for immediate gratification.

polygenic characteristics   Characteristics that are influenced by multiple genes.

population   The entire set of potential observations.

positive correlation   A relationship between two classes of events wherein when one increases so does the other.

positive reinforcer   An event that increases the probability of a response when made contingent upon it. *See also* instrumental learning, operant.

positive symptoms of schizophrenia   Symptoms, such as hallucinations and delusions, that involve an excess in sensory perceptions and ideas.

positron emission tomography (PET) scan   A brain-imaging technique that produces a three-dimensional image of the brain. A radioactive substance, usually glucose or oxygen, is incorporated directly into the neuron in proportion to the metabolic rate. With the aid of a computer, a representation of metabolic rate in different brain regions can be shown.

post-traumatic amnesia   The inability to recall events *after* the traumatic episode

post-traumatic stress disorder (PTSD)   An anxiety disorder resulting from having witnessed or been confronted by the threat of death, injury, or threat to the physical integrity of self or others, including rape, mugging, watching a bloody accident, or watching or committing an atrocity; the three symptoms defining the disorder are: (a) numbness to the world, (b) reliving of the trauma in dreams, flashbacks, and memories, and (c) symptoms of anxiety and arousal not present before the trauma.

potency   The amount of a drug that must be given in order to obtain a particular response.

predictive (or **outcome**) **validity**   The ability of the diagnostic categories in a system of diagnosis to predict the course and outcome of treatment.

premature ejaculation   The recurrent inability to exert any control over ejaculation, resulting in rapid ejaculation after penetration.

prementrual dysphoric disorder   A tentative DSM-IV classification of prementrual symptoms into a disorder characterized by a combination of some or all of the following symptoms: emotional lability, anger, tension, depression, low interest, fatigue, a feeling of being overwhelmed, difficulty concentrating, oversensitivity to rejection, and appetite and sleep changes.

prepared classical conditioning   In learning theory, the concept of the organism as being biologically predisposed to learning about relationships between certain stimuli, and therefore learning the relationship very easily.

prevalence   The percentage of a population having a certain disorder at a given time.

primary erectile dysfunction   A disorder in which the male has never been able to achieve or maintain an erection sufficient for intercourse.

proband   *See* index case.

prognosis   Outlook for the future of a disorder.

progressive relaxation   A technique for reducing anxiety in which one tightens and then turns off each of the major muscle groups of one's body, until the muscles are wholly flaccid; the resulting relaxation engages a response system that competes with anxious arousal.

projection   Attributing private understandings and meanings to others; substituting "you" for "I."

projective tests   Psychological assessment tests that allow people to impose their own psychological tendencies onto ambiguous stimuli, such as inkblots or pictures.

psychalgia   *See* pain disorder.

psychic energy   The energies that fuel psychological life.

psychoactive drugs   Drugs that affect consciousness, mood, and behavior.

psychoanalysis   The psychological theory that claims that disorders are the result of intrapsychic conflicts, usually sexual or aggressive in nature, stemming from childhood fixations. Psychoanalysis is also a therapeutic method in which the therapist helps the patient gain insight into those intrapsychic conflicts behind his or her symptoms.

psychodynamic   Dealing with the psychological forces that influence mind and behavior.

psychodynamic approach   An approach whose theorists believe that abnormality is driven by hidden conflicts within the personality.

psychogenic   "Originating in the soul." This approach to abnormality, practiced by the ancient Greeks and Romans, was a forerunner of the psychological level of analysis.

psychogenic amnesia   *See* dissociative amnesia.

psychological assessment   An evaluation of a person's mental functions and psychological health.

psychological inventory   A highly structured test containing a variety of statements that the client can answer true or false as to whether or not they apply to her; used for vocational guidance, personal counseling, or in connection with a job.

psychomotor retardation   Slowing down of movement and speech; prominent in severe depression.

psychoneuroimmunology (PNI)   The study of how mental state and behavior influence the immune system.

psychophysiological assessment   The measurement of one or more physiological processes that reflect autonomic nervous system activity (heart rate, brain electrical activity, body temperature).

psychosis   A mental state characterized by profound disturbances in reality testing, thought, and emotion. *See also* schizophrenia.

psychosomatic disorders   A group of disorders in which actual physical illness is caused or influenced by psychological factors. The diagnosis of a psychosomatic disorder requires that the physical symptoms represent a known physical pathology and that psychologically meaningful events preceded and are judged to have contributed to the onset or worsening of the physical disorder.

punishers   Events whose onset will decrease the probability of recurrence of a response that precedes it.

punishment   In psychology experiments, inflicting aversive stimuli on an organism, which reduces the probability of recurrence of certain behaviors by that organism. *See also* negative reinforcement.

purgers   People with anorexia who are thin because they often refuse to eat, and when they do eat, they use vomiting and laxatives to purge what they have eaten.

quantitative genetic methods   Procedures, including mathematical equations, statistics, and data about large samples of people, that researchers use to try to estimate how much a person's genotype contributes to a particular trait or disorder.

random assignment   Assigning subjects to groups in an experiment such that each subject has an equal chance of being assigned to each group.

random sample   A nonbiased selection of subjects.

rape   The sexual violation of one person by another.

rape trauma syndrome   A woman's reaction to rape in which symptoms similar to those of post-traumatic stress disorder occur.

rational-emotive therapy   A therapy in which the therapist challenges the irrational beliefs of the client, and encourages the client to engage in behavior that will counteract his irrational beliefs.

rationalization   The process of assigning to behavior socially desirable motives, which an impartial analysis would not substantiate.

reaction formation   The process of substituting an opposite reaction for a given impulse.

reactive attachment disorder   A marked disturbance in a child's ability to relate to other people.

reactive schizophrenia   A schizophrenic condition precipitated by a severe social or emotional upset from which the individual perceives no escape.

reality principle   In psychodynamic theory, the way in which the ego expresses and gratifies the desires of the id in accordance with the requirements of reality.

reality testing   *See* exposure.

recessive gene   Genes that can produce a specific trait only when paired with another copy of the same recessive gene.

recovered memories   Memories that were repressed because of shame, guilt, humiliation, or self-deprecation but that reappear and become accessible to consciousness years later.

recurrence   The return of depressive symptoms following at least six months without significant symptoms of depression.

reinforcement   An event that, when made contingent on a response, increases its probability. A reward or punishment.

relapse   The return of depressive symptoms after drugs or psychotherapy have relieved the depression for less than six months.

relaxation response   Physiological response regulated by the parasympathetic nervous system (PNS), which counteracts the emergency reaction to threat. In the relaxation response, the PNS inhibits heart action, constricts respiratory passages, and causes secretion of digestive fluids.

reliability   The characteristic whereby an assessment device generates the same findings on repeated use.

repeatability   The chance that, if an experimental manipulation is repeated, it will produce similar results.

replication   The repetition of a study, using the same or similar methods.

repression   A coping strategy by which the individual forces unwanted thoughts or prohibited desires out of consciousness and into the unconscious mind.

residual schizophrenia   A form of schizophrenia characterized by the absence of such prominent symptoms as delusions, hallucinations, incoherence or grossly disorganized behavior, but in which there is continuing evidence of the presence of two or more relatively minor but distressing symptoms.

resistance   Momentary blocking in dealing with a particular issue. This is the second stage of a person's reaction to stress, according to Selye, in which defense and adaptation are sustained and optimal.

response prevention   A therapeutic technique in which a therapist prevents the individual from engaging in a behavior that the therapist wishes to extinguish. *See also* flooding.

restricters   People with anorexia who are thin primarily because they refuse to eat.

retarded ejaculation   In men, great difficulty reaching orgasm during sexual intercourse.

retrograde amnesia   Loss of memory of events predating some disease or trauma. The loss is often confined to a period seconds or minutes prior to a trauma.

Rett's disorder   A rare pervasive developmental disorder with an onset between five and forty-eight months of age that occurs only in females. It involves a slowing down in head growth and a persistent and progressive decline in motor and communication skills.

reuptake   One of the ways in which a neurotransmitter is inactivated during neural transmission, wherein the presynaptic neuron reabsorbs the neurotransmitter in the synaptic gap, thereby decreasing the amount of neurotransmitter at the receptors of the postsynaptic neuron.

reward   In psychology experiments, giving the organism positive stimuli, which increases the probability of recurrence of certain behaviors by the organism. *See also* positive reinforcer.

RNA (ribonucleic acid)   A molecule that acts as a messenger, carrying a copy of the genetic code to the cell's cytoplasm and translating it by telling the ribosome to add amino acids to the protein it is synthesizing.

Rorschach test   A personality test consisting of ten bilaterally symmetrical "inkblots," some in color, some in black, gray, and white, each on an individual card. The respondent is shown each card separately and asked to name everything the inkblot could resemble. The test is supposed to elicit unconscious conflicts, latent fears, sexual and aggressive impulses, and hidden anxieties.

sadism   A psychosexual disorder in which the individual becomes sexually aroused only by inflicting physical and psychological suffering and humiliation on another human being.

sample   A selection of items or people, from the entire population of similar items or people.

schizoid personality disorder   A disorder that is characterized by the inability to form social relationships, the absence of desire for social involvements, indifference to both praise and criticism, insensitivity to feelings of others, and by lack of social skills.

schizophrenia   A group of disorders characterized by incoherence of speech and thought, hallucinations, delusions, blunted or inappropriate emotion, deterioration in social and occupational functioning, and lack of self-care.

schizotypal personality disorder   A personality disorder characterized by long-standing oddities in thinking, perceiving, communicating, and behaving.

school phobia   A persistent and irrational fear of going to school.

seasonal affective disorder (SAD)   Characterized by depression beginning each year in the fall and remitting or switching to mania in the spring.

secondary erectile dysfunction   Loss of the ability in a male to achieve or maintain an erection.

secondary gains   Deriving benefits from one's environment as a result of having abnormal symptoms.

sedative-hypnotic drugs   Also known as "downers," these drugs depress the activity of the central nervous system.

selective abstraction   Focusing on one insignificant detail while ignoring the more important features of a situation; an error of logic in those who are depressed.

selective amnesia (or categorical amnesia)   Loss of memory of all events related to a particular theme.

selective positive reinforcement   Therapeutic technique in which the therapist delivers positive reinforcement contingent on the occurrence of one particular behavior.

selective punishment   Therapeutic technique in which the therapist negatively reinforces a certain target event, causing it to decrease in probability.

self-fulfilling prophesies   The tendency for experimenters to observe only what they already expect to find in an experiment or to unconsciously influence the results to conform with their predictions.

selfobject   Those people and things that are critically significant for personality cohesiveness.

sensate focus   A strategy of direct sexual therapy that involves (a) a "pleasuring" phase during which the couple engages in nongenital erotic activity, but restrains from intercourse, then (b) a phase of "genital stimulation" in which the couple engages in genital play, but without intercourse, then (c) the phase of "nondemand intercourse" in which the couple engages in intercourse, but without making demands on each other.

separation anxiety disorder A disorder characterized by a very strong fear of being separated from one's family. Children with this disorder become panicked if they must separate from loved ones, and they often show continual physical symptoms of anxiety.

sex role The public expression of sexual identity, what an individual says or does to indicate that he is a man or she is a woman.

sexual arousal disorder A dysfunction at the excitement phase of the sexual response.

sexual aversion disorder Low or absent sexual desire.

sexual dysfunction Disorders in which adequate sexual arousal, desire, or orgasm are inhibited.

sexual interest The types of persons, parts of the body, and situations that are the objects of sexual fantasies, arousal, and preferences.

sexual orientation Attraction to and erotic fantasies about men, women, or both.

sexual pain disorders Disorders in which a woman feels severe pain when intercourse is attempted.

sexual performance How adequately a person performs sexually when he or she is with a suitable person in a suitable erotic setting.

shadowing A method of treatment for stuttering in which the therapist reads from a book, and the stutterer repeats the therapist's words shortly after the latter has spoken them (and without reading the words).

single-blind experiment An experiment in which the subject, but not the experimenter, does not know whether the subject has received an experimental treatment or a placebo.

situational phobias Irrational fear of flying airplanes, bridges, tunnels, enclosed spaces, public transportation, elevators.

social causation hypothesis of schizophrenia The notion that adversity and stress cause schizophrenia.

social drift hypothesis The view that constitutionally predisposed people develop schizophrenia and then drift down into lower social classes.

social phobias Unreasonable fear of and desire to avoid situations in which one might be humiliated in front of other people.

somatic Having to do with the body.

somatization disorder (or Briquet's syndrome) A somatoform disorder characterized by the experience of a large number and variety of physical symptoms for which there are no medical explanations. These symptoms are not under the voluntary control of the individual.

somatoform disorders A group of mental disorders characterized by (a) loss or alteration in physical functioning, for which there is no physiological explanation, (b) evidence that psychological factors have caused the physical symptoms, (c) lack of voluntary control over physical symptoms, and (d) indifference by the patient to the physical loss. Includes conversion, pain disorder, somatization disorder.

specific attribution An individual's assignment of cause for an event to a factor that is relevant only to that situation.

specific phobias There are four classes of specific phobias: animal phobias are unreasonable fears of and desires to avoid or escape specific animals. Natural environment phobias are irrational fears of heights, storms, dirt, darkness, running water, or wind. Situational phobias are irrational fears of flying in airplanes, bridges, public transportation, tunnels, enclosed spaces, and elevators. Blood-injection-injury phobias are unreasonable fears at the sight of blood, injections, and injuries.

stable attribution An individual's assignment of cause for an event to a factor that persists in time.

statistical inferences Procedures used to decide whether a sample or a set of observations is truly representative of the population.

statistically significant effect An effect that is highly unlikely (typically less than one time in twenty) to occur solely by chance.

stimulants A class of psychoactive drugs that induces psychomotor agitation, physiological hyperactivity, elation, grandiosity, loquacity, and hypervigilance. Includes amphetamines and cocaine.

stuttering A marked disorder in speech rhythm.

subclinical The property of being symptomatic, but more mild than a full-blown disorder.

subject bias The influence of a subject's beliefs about what he is expected to do in an experiment on his responses in the experiment.

subjective self The second sense of self, which develops between the age of seven and nine months. It gives rise to the sense that we understand each others' feelings and intentions.

sublimation In psychoanalytic theory, the transfer of libidinal energies from relatively narcissistic gratifications to those which gratify others and are highly socialized. More generally, the process of rechanneling psychic energy from socially undesirable goals to constructive and socially desirable ones.

substance abuse A maladaptive, harmful pattern of drug use.

substance dependence Condition involving loss of control regarding drug use, continued use in the face of adverse consequences, and compulsion (or need) to use the drug.

superego Those psychological processes that are "above the self," i.e., conscience, ideals, and morals.

syllable-timed speech A method of treatment for stuttering that requires stutterers to speak in time to a metronome or beeper that sounds in an earpiece.

symptom A sign of disorder.

synaptic pruning The process by which connections among neurons are eliminated throughout development.

syndrome A set of symptoms that tend to co-occur.

systematic desensitization A behavior therapy primarily used to treat phobias and specific anxieties. The phobic is first given training in deep muscle relaxation and is then progressively exposed to increasingly anxiety-evoking situations (real or imagined). Because relaxation and fear are mutually exclusive, stimuli that formerly induced panic are now greeted calmly.

tactics of psychotherapy One of the classes of "nonspecifics of therapy" that all good therapists do. Among the tactics of all good therapy are the following elements: attention, authority figure, rapport, tricks of the trade, paying for services, trust, opening up, and naming the problem.

tardive dyskinesia   A nonreversible neurological side effect of antipsychotic drug treatment, whose symptoms consist of sucking, lip smacking, and peculiar tongue movements.

T cells   Cells in the immune system that are produced in the thymus gland. They have receptors on their surfaces for specific antigens.

telephone scatologia   A paraphilia that consists of recurrent and intense sexual urges to make obscene telephone calls to a nonconsenting individual.

temporal lobe   A lobe in each cerebral hemisphere that includes the auditory projection area and is particularly involved in memory.

tension reduction hypothesis   A hypothesis that states that people drink alcohol to reduce tension.

test-retest reliability   The extent to which a test will yield the same result in repeated trials.

test stability   *See* test-retest reliability.

Thematic Apperception Test (TAT)   A personality test that consists of a series of pictures that are not as ambiguous as Rorschach cards, but not as clear as photographs either. Respondents look at each picture and make up a story about it. The test is supposed to elicit underlying psychological dynamics.

tic   A repetitive, involuntary movement or vocalization that has a very sudden onset.

tolerance   The state of drug addiction in which, after repeated use of a drug, the addict needs more and more of the drug to produce the desired reaction, and there is great diminution of the effect of a given dose.

Tourette's disorder   A disorder characterized by motor tics and uncontrollable verbal outbursts, usually beginning in childhood.

transcription   The process by which RNA is constructed, using DNA as a template.

transference   A patient's redirection of emotions, conflicts, and expectations onto his or her therapist.

transgenic   An animal with artificially combined genes.

transsexualism   A psychosexual disorder characterized by the belief that one is a woman trapped in the body of a man, or a man trapped in the body of a woman.

transvestism (or **transvestic fetishism**)   A psychosexual disorder in which a man often dresses in the clothes of a woman in order to achieve sexual arousal.

tricyclic antidepressants   Antidepressant drugs that block uptake of norepinephrine, thus increasing the availability of norepinephrine.

tumor   An abnormal tissue that grows by cell multiplication more rapidly than is normal.

twin study   The study of the degree of concordance of a trait in identical versus fraternal twins. This method allows the quantification of the heritability of psychological traits. *See also* adoption study.

Type A behavior pattern   A personality type characterized by (a) an exaggerated sense of time urgency, (b) competitive-

ness and ambition, and (c) aggressiveness and hostility when thwarted.

Type I schizophrenia   A type of schizophrenia proposed by Crow that entails mostly negative symptoms, such as flat affect, poverty of speech, social withdrawal, etc.

Type II schizophrenia   A type of schizophrenia proposed by Crow that entails mostly positive symptoms, such as delusions, hallucinations, and forms of thought disorder.

unconditioned stimulus (US)   A stimulus that will provoke an unconditioned response without training. For example, a loud noise will naturally provoke a startle response in humans.

unconscious   In psychoanalytic theory, the large mass of hidden memories, experiences, and impulses.

uncorrelated   Unrelated.

undifferentiated schizophrenia   A category of schizophrenia used to describe disturbed individuals who present evidence of thought disorder, as well as behavioral and affective anomalies, but who are not classifiable under the other subtypes.

unipolar depression   A disorder characterized by depression, in the absence of a history of mania.

unstable attribution   An individual's assignment of cause for an event to a factor that is transient.

vaginismus   *See* sexual pain disorders.

validity   The extent to which a test of something is actually measuring that something.

vascular dementia   The leading cause of irreversible dementia, it is often caused by a stroke and the resulting loss of oxygen to the brain kills brain tissue. The cognitive signs parallel those of Alzheimer's disease, but the patient often shows unusual reflexes and movement abnormalities.

ventricles   Cavities in the brain, containing cerebral spinal fluid.

verbal self   The third sense of self, which develops between fifteen and eighteen months of age. It is the verbal and symbolic storehouse of experience and knowledge.

voyeurism   A psychosexual disorder in which the individual habitually becomes sexually aroused only by observing the naked body, the disrobing, or the sexual activity of an unsuspecting victim.

withdrawal syndrome (or **abstinence syndrome**)   A substance-specific syndrome that follows cessation of the intake of a substance that has been regularly used by the individual to induce intoxication; usually characterized by observable, physical signs such as marked changes in body temperature or heart rate, seizures, tremors, or vomiting.

yoking   An experimental procedure in which both experimental and control groups receive exactly the same physical events, but only the experimental group influences these events by its responding.

zygote   A cell formed from the union of the egg and the sperm.

References

Abe, K., Oda, N., Ikenaga, K., & Yamada, T. (1993). Twin study on night terrors, fears and some physiological and behavioural characteristics in childhood. *Psychiatric Genetics, 3,* 39–43.

Abel, G. G., Barlow, D. H., Blanchard, E. B., & Guild, D. (1977). The components of rapists' sexual arousal. *Archives of General Psychiatry, 34,* 895–903.

Abi-Dargham, A., Gil, R., Krystal, J., Baldwin, R. M., Seibyl, J. P., Bowers, M., van Dyck, C. H., Charney, D. S., Innis, R. B., & Laruelle, M. (1998). Increased striatal dopamine transmission in schizophrenia: Confirmation in a second cohort. *American Journal of Psychiatry, 155,* 761–67.

Abi-Dargham, A., Laruelle, M., Aghajanian, G. K., Charney, D., & Krystal, J. (1997). The role of serotonin in the pathophysiology and treatment of schizophrenia. *Journal of Neuropsychiatry and Clinical Neurosciences, 9,* 1–7.

Abraham, K. (1911). Notes on psychoanalytic investigation and treatment of manic-depressive insanity and applied conditions. In *Selected papers of Karl Abraham, M.D.* (D. Bryan & A. Strachey, Trans.). London: Hogarth Press, 1948.

Abrahamson, D., Barlow, Beck, G., & D., & Sakheim, D., (1985). Effects of distraction on sexual responding in functional and dysfunctional men. *Behavior Therapy, 16,* 503–15.

Abramowitz, J. S. (1998). Does cognitive-behavioral therapy cure obsessive-compulsive disorder? A meta-analytic evaluation of clinical significance. *Behavior Therapy, 29* (2): 339–55.

Abramowitz, L. (1996). The Jerusalem syndrome. *The Israel Review of Arts and Letter, 102.*

Abrams, J. (1999). Drug chief discourages legalization. *Washington Post,* June 16. http://search.washingtonpost.com/wp-srv/WAPO/19990616/V000899-061699-idx.html

Abrams, R., Taylor, M., Faber, R., Ts'o, T., Williams, R., & Almy, G. (1983). Bilateral vs. unilateral electroconvulsive therapy: Efficacy and melancholia. *American Journal of Psychiatry, 140,* 463–65.

Abrams, R., & Vedak, C. (1991). Prediction of ECT response in melancholia. *Convulsive Therapy, 7,* 81–84.

Abramson, L. Y. (1978). *Universal versus personal helplessness.* Unpublished doctoral dissertation, University of Pennsylvania.

Abramson, L. Y., Garber, J., Edwards, N., & Seligman, M. E. P. (1978). Expectancy change in depression and schizophrenia. *Journal of Abnormal Psychology, 87,* 165–79.

Abramson, L., Metalsky, G., & Alloy, L. (1989). Hopelessness depression: A theory-based subtype of depression. *Psychological Review, 96,* 358–72.

Abramson, L. Y., Seligman, M. E. P., & Teasdale, J. (1978). Learned helplessness in humans: Critique and reformulation. *Journal of Abnormal Psychology, 87,* 32–48.

ACNP-FDA Task Force. (1973). Medical intelligence—drug therapy. *New England Journal of Medicine, 130,* 20–24.

Adams, H. E., & Sturgis, E. T. (1977). Status of behavioral reorientation techniques in the modification of homosexuality: A review. *Psychological Bulletin, 84,* 1171–88.

Adams, P., & Marano, M. (1995). Current estimates from the National Interview Survey, 1994. *Vital and Health Statistics, 5,* 95–114.

Adams, R. D. (1989). *Principles of neurology* (3rd ed.). New York: McGraw-Hill.

Adams, W. L., Barry, K. L., & Fleming, M. F. (1996). Screening for problem drinking in older primary care patients. *Journal of the American Medical Association, 276*(24): 1964–67.

Adams, W. L., Garry, P. J., Rhyne, R., Hunt, W. C., & Goodwin, J. S. (1990). Alcohol intake in the healthy elderly. Changes with age in a cross-sectional and longitudinal study. *Journal of the American Geriatrics Society, 38* (3): 211–16.

Addington, J., McCleary, L., & Munroe-Blum, H. (1998). Relationship between cognitive and social dysfunction in schizophrenia. *Schizophrenia Research, 34,* 59–66.

Adler, L. E., Oliney, A., Waldo, M., Harris, J. G., Griffith, J., Stevens, K., Flach, K., Nagamoto, H., Bickford, P., Leanord, S., & Freedman, R. (1998). Schizophrenia, sensory gating and nicotinic receptors. *Schizophrenia Bulletin, 24,* 189–202.

Adler, T. (1989). Integrity test popularity prompts close scrutiny. *APA Monitor, 7.*

Adolphs, R., Russell, J. A., & Tranel, D. (1999). A role for the human amygdala in recognizing emotional arousal from unpleasant stimuli. *Psychological Science, 10* (2), 167–71.

Adolphs, R., Tranel, D., Damasio, H., & Damasio, A. R. (1994). Impaired recognition of emotion in facial expressions following bilateral damage to the human amygdala. *Nature, 372,* 669–72.

Adolphs, R., Tranel, D., & Damasio, A. R. (1998). The human amygdala in social judgment. *Nature, 393,* 470–74.

Adshead, G. (1997). Transvestic fetishism: Assessment and treatment. In D. R. Laws & W. O'Donohue (Eds.), *Sexual deviance: Theory, assessment, and treatment* (pp. 280–96). New York: Guilford Press.

Agras, S., Sylvester, D., & Oliveau, D. (1969). The epidemiology of common fears and phobia. *Comprehensive Psychiatry, 10* (2): 151–56.

Agras, W. S. (1993). Short-term psychological treatments for binge eating. In C. G. Fairburn & G. T. Wilson (Eds.), *Binge eating: Nature, assessment, and treatment.* New York: Guilford Press.

Agras, W. S., & Kirkley, B. G. (1986). Bulimia: Theories of etiology. In K. D. Brownell & J. P. Foreyt (Eds.), *Handbook of eating disorders: Physiology, psychology and treatment of obesity, anorexia, and bulimia.* New York: Basic Books.

Agras, W. S., Rossiter, E. M., Arnow, B., Schneider, J. A., Telch, C. F., Raeburn, S. D., Bruce, B., Perl, M., & Koran, L. M. (1992). Pharmacologic and cognitive-behavioral treatment for bulimia nervosa: A controlled comparison. *American Journal of Psychiatry, 149,* 82–87.

Agras, W. S., Schneider, J. A., Arnow, B., Raeburn, S. D., & Telch, C. F. (1989a). Cognitive-behavioral and response-prevention treatments for bulimia nervosa. *Journal of Consulting and Clinical Psychology, 57*(2): 215–21.

Agras, W. S., Schneider, J. A., Arnow, B., Raeburn, S. D., & Telch, C. F. (1989b). Cognitive-behavioral treatment with and without exposure plus response prevention in the treatment of bulimia nervosa. *Journal of Consulting and Clinical Psychology, 57*(2): 778–79.

Agronin, M. E. (1994). Personality disorders in the elderly: An overview. *Journal of Geriatric Psychiatry, 27*(2): 151–91.

Ahrens, D. (1993). What do the neighbours think now? Community residences on Long Island, New York. *Community Mental Health Journal, 29,* 235–45.

Aigner, T. G., & Balster, R. L. (1978). Choice behavior in rhesus monkeys: Cocaine versus food. *Science, 201,* 534–35.

Alaghband-Rad, J., Hamburger, S. D., Giedd, J. N., Frazier, J. A., et al. (1997). Childhood-onset of schizophrenia: Biological markers in relation to clinical characteristics. *American Journal of Psychiatry, 154,* 64–68.

Albertini, R. S., & Phillips, K. A. (1999). Thirty-three cases of body dysmorphic disorder in children and adolescents. *Journal of the American Academy of Child and Adolescent Psychiatry, 38* (4): 453–59.

Alden, L. E., & Capreol, M. J. (1993). Avoidant personality disorder: Interpersonal problems as predictors of treatment response. *Behavior Therapy, 24* (3): 357–76.

Alden, L. E., & Wallace, S. T. (1995). Social phobia and social appraisal in successful and unsuccessful social interactions. *Behaviour Research and Therapy, 33* (5): 497–505.

Alexander, F. (1950). *Psychosomatic medicine.* New York: Norton.

Allen, A. J., Leonard, H. L., & Swedo, S. E. (1995). Case study: A new infection-triggered, autoimmune subtype of pediatric OCD and Tourette syndrome. *Journal of the American Academy of Child and Adolescent Psychiatry, 34,* 307–11.

Allen, K. D., & Shriver, M. D. (1998). Role of parent-mediated pain behavior management strategies in biofeedback treatment of childhood migraines. *Behavior Therapy, 29* (3), 477–90.

Allen, K. W. (1996). Chronic nailbiting: A controlled comparison of competing response and mild aversion treatments. *Behaviour Research and Therapy, 34* (3): 269–72.

Allen, L., & Gorski, R. (1992). Sexual orientation and the size of the anterior commissure in the human brain. *Proceedings of the National Academy of Sciences, 89,* 7199–7202.

Allen, M. G. (1976). Twin studies of affective illness. *Archives of General Psychiatry, 33,* 1476–78.

Allnut, S., & Links, P. S. (1996). Diagnosing specific personality disorders and the optimal criteria. In P. S. Links (Ed.), *Clinical assessment and management of severe personality disorders.* Washington, DC: American Psychiatric Press.

Alloy, L. B., & Abramson, L. Y. (1997). *The Temple-Wisconsin cognitive vulnerability to depression project: Lifetime prevalence and prospective incidence of Axis I psychopathology.* Paper presented at the Midwestern Psychological Association, Chicago.

Alloy, L. B., Kelly, K. A., Mineka, S., & Clements, C. M. (1990). Comorbidity of anxiety and depressive disorders: A helplessness/hopelessness perspective. In J. D. Maser & C. R. Cloninger (Eds.), *Comorbidy in anxiety and mood disorders* (pp. 499–543). Washington, DC: American Psychiatric Press.

Alloy, L. B., Lipman, A. J., & Abramson, L. Y. (1992). Attributional style as a vulnerability factor for depression: Validation by past history of mood disorders. *Cognitive Therapy and Research, 16* (4): 391–407.

Almeida, O. P., Howard, R. J., Levy, R., & David, A. S. (1995). Psychotic states arising in late life (late paraphrenia): The role of risk factors. *British Journal of Psychiatry, 166,* 215–28.

Alper, J. (1993). Ulcers as an infectious disease. *Science, 260,* 159–60.

Alterman, T., Shekelle, R. B., Vernon, S. W., & Burau, K. D. (1994). Decision latitude, psychologic demand, job strain, and coronary heart disease in the Western Electric Study. *American Journal of Epidemiology, 139* (6): 620–27.

Amanzio, M., & Benedetti, F. (1999). Neuropharmacological dissection of placebo analgesia: Expectation-activated opioid systems versus conditioning-activated specific subsystems. *Journal of Neuroscience, 19,* 484–94.

Amara, A., & Cerrato, P. L. (1996). Eating disorders: Still a threat. *Registered Nurse, 59,* 30–35.

Ambrose, N., Yairi, E., & Cox, N. (1993). Genetic aspects of early childhood stuttering. *Journal of Speech and Hearing Research, 36* (4), 701–706.

American Academy of Pediatrics (1996). Newborn screening fact sheets. *Pediatrics, 98,* 473–501.

American Academy of Pediatrics. (1998). Auditory integration training and facilitated communication for autism. *Pediatrics, 102,* 431–33.

American Psychiatric Association. (1980). *Diagnostic and statistical manual of mental disorders* (3rd ed.) (DSM-III). Washington, DC: Author.

American Psychiatric Association. (1983). Guidelines for legislation on the psychiatric hospitalization of adults. *American Journal of Psychiatry, 140,* 672–79.

American Psychiatric Association. (1987). *Diagnostic and statistical manual of mental disorders* (3rd ed., revised) (DSM-III-R). Washington, DC: Author.

American Psychiatric Association. (1993). Practice guidelines for major depressive disorder in adults. *American Journal of Psychiatry, 150* (Suppl. 4).

American Psychiatric Association. (1994). *Diagnostic and statistical manual of mental disorders* (4th ed.) (DSM-IV). Washington, DC: Author.

Amir, R. E., Van den Veyver, I. B., Wan M, Tran, C. Q., Francke, U. & Zoghbi, H. Y. (1999). Rett syndrome is caused by mutations in X-linked MECP2, encoding methyl-CpG-binding protein 2. *Nature Genetics, 23,* 185–88.

Anda, R., Williamson D., Jones, D., Macera, C., Eaker, E., Glassman, A., & Marks, J. (1993). Depressed affect, hopelessness, and the risk of ischemic heart disease in a cohort of U.S. adults. *Epidemiology, 4* (4):285–94.

Andersen, B. L. (1983). Primary orgasmic dysfunction: Diagnostic conditions and review of treatment. *Psychological Bulletin, 93,* 105–36.

Andersen, B. L., & Cyranowski, J. M. (1995). Women's sexuality: Behaviors, responses, and individual differences. *Journal of Consulting and Clinical Psychology, 63* (6): 891–906.

Anderson, J. C., Williams, S., McGee, R., & Silva, P. A. (1987). DSM-III: Disorders in preadolescent children. *Archives of General Psychiatry, 44,* 69–76.

Anderson, J. R., & Bower, G. H. (1973). *Human associative memory.* Washington, DC: Winston.

Andreasen, N. C. (1978). Creativity and psychiatric illness. *Psychiatric Annals, 8,* 23–45.

Andreasen, N. C., Nasrallah, H. A., Dunn, V., Olson, S. C., Grove, W. M., Ehrhardt, J. C., Coffman, J. A., & Crossett, J. H. (1986). Structural abnormalities in the frontal system in schizophrenia: A magnetic resonance imaging study. *Archives of General Psychiatry, 43* (2): 136–44.

Angermeyer, M. C., & Matschinger, H. (1996a). The effects of personal experience with mental illness on attitudes towards individuals suffering from mental disorders. *Social Psychiatry and Psychiatric Epidemiology, 31,* 321–26.

Angermeyer, M. C. & Matschinger, H. (1996b). The effect of violent attacks by schizophrenic persons on the attitude of the public towards the mentally ill. *Social Science and Medicine, 43,* 1721–28.

Angold, A. (1994). Unpublished data. Presentation to NIMH Workshop on Emergence of Sex Differences in Depression, Bethesda, MD, March 1994.

Angst, J. (1992). Epidemiology of depression. 2nd International Symposium on Moclobemide: RIMA (Reversible Inhibitor of Monoamine Oxidase Type A): A new concept in the treatment of depression. *Psychopharmacology, 106* (Suppl): 71–74.

Angst, J., Baastrup, P., Grof, P., Hippius, H., Poldinger, W., & Weis, P. (1973). The course of monopolar depression and bipolar psychoses. *Psykiotrika, Neurologika and Neurochirurgia, 76,* 489–500.

Angst, J., & Wicki, W. (1991). The Zurich Study: XI. Is dysthymia a separate form of depression? Results of the Zurich Cohort Study. *European Archives of Psychiatry and Clinical Neuroscience, 240* (6): 349–54.

Anisman, H. (1978). Aversively motivated behavior as a tool in psychopharmacological analysis. In H. Anisman & G. Binami (Eds.), *Psychopharmacology of aversively motivated behavior.* New York: Plenum.

Annas, G. J. (1995). The health of the president and presidential candidates—The public's right to know. *New England Journal of Medicine, 333,* 945–49.

Annas, P. (1997). *Fears, phobias, and the inheritance of learning.* Uppsala: Uppsala University Press.

Annau, Z., & Kamin, L. J. (1961). The conditional emotional response as a function of intensity of the US. *Journal of Comparative and Physiological Psychology, 54,* 428–32.

Ansbacher, H. L., & Ansbacher, R. (1956). *The individual psychology of Alfred Adler.* New York: Basic Books.

Anthony, W. A., Cohen, M. R., & Danley, K. S. (1988). The psychiatric rehabilitation model as applied to vocational rehabilitation. In J. A. Cardiello & M. D. Bell (Eds.), *Vocational rehabilitation of persons with prolonged psychiatric disorders.* Baltimore: Johns Hopkins University Press.

Antoni, M. H., Cruess, D. G., Cruess, S., Lutgendorf, S., Kumar, M., Ironson, G., Klimas, N., Fletcher, M., & Schneiderman, N. (2000). Cognitive-behavioral stress management intervention effects on anxiety, 24-hr urinary norepinephrine output, and T-cytotoxic/suppressor cells over time among symptomatic HIV-infected gay men. *Journal of Consulting and Clinical Psychology, 68*(1).

Antonuccio, D. (1995). Psychotherapy for depression: No stronger medicine. *American Psychologist, 50*(6): 450–52.

Antonuccio, D. O., Danton, W. G., DeNelsky, G. Y., Greenberg, R. P., & Gordon, J. S. (1999). Raising questions about antidepressants. *Psychotherapy and Psychosomatics, 68*(1): 3–14.

Antonuccio, D. O., Thomas, M., & Danton, W. G. (1997). A cost-effectiveness analysis of cognitive behavior therapy and fluoxetine (Prozac) in the treatment of depression. *Behavior Therapy, 28* (2): 187–210.

Anvret, M., & Clarke, A. (1997). Genetics and Rett syndrome. *European Child and Adolescent Psychiatry, 6,* 89–90.

Apfelbaum, B. (1980). The diagnosis and treatment of retarded ejaculation. In S. A. Leiblum & L. A. Pervin (Eds.), *Principles and practice of sex therapy* (pp. 236–96). New York: Guilford Press.

Appelbaum, P. S. (1997). Almost a revolution: An international perspective on the law of involuntary commitment. *Journal of the American Academy of Psychiatry and Law, 25,* 135–47.

Arajaervi, T., Kivalo, A., & Nyberg, P. (1977). Effect of antidepressants on enuretic school children. *Psychiatria Fennica,* 83–87.

Arango, V., & Underwood, M. D. (1997). Serotonin chemistry in the brain of suicide victims. In R. W. Maris, M. M. Silverman, & S. S. Canetton (Eds.), *Review of Suicidology, 1997* (pp. 237–50). New York: Guilford Press.

Arborelius, L., Owens, M. J., Plotsky, P. M., & Nemeroff, C. B. (1999). The role of corticotropin-releasing factor in depression and anxiety disorders. *Journal of Endocrinology, 160,* 1–12.

Archibald, H. C., & Tuddenham, R. D. (1965). Persistent stress reaction after combat. *Archives of General Psychiatry, 12,* 475–81.

Arendt, H. (1978). *The life of the mind*. New York: Harcourt Brace Jovanovich.

Arieti, S. (1974). *Interpretation of schizophrenia*. New York: Basic Books.

Arieti, S., & Bemporad, J. (1978). *Severe and mild depression*. New York: Basic Books.

Arizona Republic. (1994). Liar in drag: Rapist admits faking multiple personalities. *Arizona Republic*, April 20.

Arnold, S. E., Ruscheinsky, D. D., & Han, L. (1997). Further evidence of abnormal cytoarchitecture of the entorhinal cortex in schizophrenia using spatial point pattern analysis. *Biological Psychiatry, 42*, 639–47.

Arntz, A. (1999). Do personality disorders exist? On the validity of the concept and its cognitive-behavioral formulation and treatment. *Behaviour Research and Therapy, 37*.

Arntz, A., Dietzel, R., & Dreessen, L. (1999). Assumptions in borderline personality disorder: Specificity, stability and relationship with etiological factors. *Behaviour Research and Therapy, 37*, 545–57.

Aro, S., Aro, H., & Keskimaki, I. (1995). Socio-economic mobility among patients with schizophrenia or major affective disorder: A 17-year restrospective follow-up. *British Journal of Psychiatry, 166(6)*: 1759–67.

Aronow, E., & Reznikoff, M. (1976). *Rorschach content interpretation*. New York: Grune & Stratton.

Aronson, T. A., & Craig, T. J. (1986). Cocaine precipitation of panic disorder. *American Journal of Psychiatry, 143*, 643–45.

Ary, D. V., Duncan, T. E., Duncan, S. C., & Hops, H. (1999). Adolescent problem behavior: The influence of parents and peers. *Behaviour Research and Therapy, 37* (3): 217–30.

Asarnow, J. R., Goldstein, M. J., & Ben-Meir, S. (1988a). Children with schizophrenia spectrum and depressive disorders. *Journal of Child Psychology and Psychiatry and Allied Disciplines, 29*, 477–88.

Asarnow, J. R., Goldstein, M. J., & Ben-Meir, S. (1988b). Parental communication deviance in childhood onset schizophrenia spectrum and depressive disorders. *Journal of Child Psychology and Psychiatry and Allied Disciplines, 29*, 825–38.

Asberg, M., Traskman, L., & Thoren, P. (1976). 5–HIAA in the cerebrospinal fluid. *Archives of General Psychiatry, 33*, 1193–97.

Asch, S. E. (1951). Effects of group pressure on the modification and distortion of judgments. In H. Guetzkow (Ed.), *Groups, leadership and men: Research in human relations*. Pittsburgh, PA: Carnegie Press.

Ashton, A. K., Hamer, R., & Rosen, R. C. (1997). Serotonin reuptake inhibitor-induced sexual dysfunction and its treatment: A large-scale retrospective study of 596 psychiatric outpatients. *Journal of Sex and Marital Therapy, 23* (3): 165–75.

Assad, G., & Shapiro, B. (1986). Hallucinations: Theoretical and clinical overview. *American Journal of Psychiatry, 143* (9): 1088–97.

Atkinson, J. W. (1992). Motivational determinants of thematic apperception. In C. P. Smith, J. W. Atkinson, & J. Veroff (Eds.), *Motivation and personality: Handbook of thematic content analysis* (pp. 21–48). New York: Cambridge University Press.

Avants, S. K., Margolin, A., Sindelar, J. L., Rounsaville, B. J., Schottenfeld, R., Stine, S., Cooney, N. L., Rosenheck, R. A., Li, S., & Kosten, T. R. (1999). Day treatment versus enhanced standard methadone services for opioid-dependent patients: A comparison of clinical efficacy and cost. *American Journal of Psychiatry, 156*(1): 27–33.

Ayd, F. J. (1994). Prescribing anxiolytics and hypnotics for the elderly. *Psychiatric Annals, 24* (2): 91–97.

Ayllon, T., & Michael, J. (1959). The psychiatric nurse as a behavioral engineer. *Journal of the Experimental Analysis of Behavior, 2*, 323–34.

Aylward, E., Walker, E., & Bettes, B. (1984). Intelligence in schizophrenia: A review and meta-analysis of the literature. *Schizophrenia Bulletin, 10*, 430–59.

Ayres, B. D., Jr. (1994). Big gains are seen in battle to stem drunken driving. *New York Times*, May 22, p. A1.

Baberg, H. T., Nelesen, R. A., & Dimsdale, J. E. (1996). Amphetamine use: Return of an old scourge in a consultation psychiatry setting. *American Journal of Psychiatry, 153*, 789–93.

Babor, T. F. (1990). Social, scientific and medical issues in the definition of alcohol and drug dependence. In A. Edwards & M. Lader (Eds.), *The nature of drug dependence* (pp. 19–40). New York: Oxford University Press.

Bach, M., & Bach, D. (1995). Predictive value of alexithymia: A prospective study in somatizing patients. *Psychotherapy and Psychosomatics, 64* (1): 43–48.

Bacon, D. L. (1969). Incompetency to stand trial: Commitment to an inclusive test. *Southern California Law Review, 42*, 444.

Baer, D. M., & Guess, D. (1971). Receptive training of adjectival inflections in mental retardates. *Journal of Applied Behavior Analysis, 4*, 129–39.

Bahrick, L., Fraser, J., Fivush, R., & Levitt, M. (1998). The effects of stress on young children's memory for a natural disaster. *Journal of Experimental Psychology: Applied, 4* (4): 308–31.

Bailes, B. K. (1998). What perioperative nurses need to know about substance abuse. *AORN Journal, 68*, 611–26.

Bailey, A., Le Couteur, A., Gottesman, I., & Bolton, P. (1995). Autism as a strongly genetic disorder: Evidence from a British twin study. *Psychological Medicine, 25*, 63–77.

Bailey, J. M., Dunne, M., & Martin, N. (2000). Genetic and environmental influences on sexual orientation and its correlates in an Australian twin sample. *Journal of Personality and Social Psychology, 78*, 524–36.

Bailey, J. M., Kim, P., Hills, A., & Linsenmeier, J. (1997). Butch, femme, or straight action: Partner preferences of gay men and lesbians. *Journal of Personality and Social Psychology, 73*, 960–73.

Bailey, J. M., & Pillard, R. (1991). A genetic study of male sexual orientation. *Archives of General Psychiatry, 48*, 1089–96.

Bailey, J. M., Pillard, R., & Agyei, Y. (1993). A genetic study of female sexual orientation. *Archives of General Psychiatry, 50*, 217–23.

Bailey, J. M., Pillard, R., Dawood, K., et al. (1999). A family history study of male sexual orientation using three independent samples. *Behavior Genetics, 29*, 79–86.

Bailey, J. M., & Shriver, A. (1999). Does childhood sexual abuse cause borderline personality disorder? *Journal of Sex and Marital Therapy, 25*, 45–57.

Bailey, J. M., & Zucker, K. J. (1995). Childhood sex-typed behavior and sexual orientation: A conceptual analysis and quantitative review. *Developmental Psychology, 31*, 43–55.

Baillie, A. J., & Lampe, L. A. (1998). Avoidant personality disorder: Empirical support for DSM-IV revisions. *Journal of Personality Disorders, 12,* 23–30.

Baker, L. A., Mack, W., Moffitt, T. E., & Mednick, S. (1989). Sex differences in property crime in a Danish adoption cohort. *Behavior Genetics, 19* (3).

Bakker, A., Van Kesteren, P., Gooren, L., & Bezemer, P. (1993). The prevalence of transsexualism in the Netherlands. *Acta Psychiatrica Scandinavica, 87,* 237–38.

Baldeweg, T., Catalan, J., & Gazzard, B. G. (1998). Risk of HIV dementia and opportunistic brain disease in AIDS and zidovudine therapy. *Journal of Neurology, Neurosurgery and Psychiatry, 65* (1): 34–41.

Balk, J., et al. (1995). Parkinson-like locomotor impairment in mice lacking dopamine D2 receptors. *Nature, 377,* 242–48.

Ball, J. C., & Ross, A. (1991). *The effectiveness of methadone maintenance treatment: Patients, programs, services, and outcome.* New York: Springer-Verlag.

Ball, S. G., Baer, L., & Otto, M. W. (1996). Symptoms subtypes of obsessive-compulsive disorder in behavioral treatment studies: A quantitative review. *Behaviour Research and Therapy, 34* (1): 47–51.

Ballaban-Gil, K., Rapin, I., Tuchman, R., & Shinnar S. (1996). Longitudinal examination of the behavioral, language, and social changes in a population of adolescents and young adults with autistic disorder. *Pediatric Neurology, 15,* 217–23.

Ballenger, J. C. (1986). Pharmacotherapy of the panic disorders. *Journal of Clinical Psychiatry, 47* (Suppl): 27–32.

Ballenger, J. C., McDonald, S., Noyes, R., Rickels, K., et al. (1991). The first double-blind, placebo-controlled trial of a partial benzodiazepine agonist abecarnil (ZK 112–119) in generalized anxiety disorder. *Psychopharmacology Bulletin, 27* (2): 171–79.

Baltes, P. B., Reese, H. W., & Lipsitt, L. P. (1980). Life-span developmental psychology. *Annual Review of Psychology, 31,* 65–110.

Bancroft, J. (1994). Homosexual orientation: The search for a biological basis. *British Journal of Psychology, 64,* 437–40.

Bandura, A. (1969). *Principles of behavior modification.* New York: Holt, Rinehart & Winston.

Bandura, A. (1977). Self efficacy: Toward a unifying theory of behavioral change. *Psychological Review, 84,* 191–215.

Bandura, A. (1982). Self-efficacy mechanism in human agency. *American Psychologist, 37,* 122–47.

Bandura, A. (1986). Fearful expectations and avoidant actions as coeffects of personal self-inefficacy. *American Psychologist, 41* (12): 1389–91.

Bandura, A. (1993). Perceived self-efficacy in cognitive development and functioning. *Educational Psychologist, 28,* 117–48.

Bandura, A., & Adams, N. E. (1977). Analysis of self-efficacy theory of behavioral changes. *Cognitive Therapy and Research, 1,* 287–310.

Bandura, A., Adams, N. E., & Beyer, J. (1977). Cognitive processes mediating behavioral change. *Journal of Personality and Social Psychology, 35,* 125–39.

Barak, Y., Kimhi, R., Stein, D., Gutman, J., & Weizman, A. (1999). Autistic subjects with comorbid epilepsy: A possible association with viral infections. *Child Psychiatry and Human Development, 29,* 245–51.

Barbaree, H. E., & Seto, M. C. (1997). Pedophilia: Assessment and treatment. In D. R. Laws & W. O'Donohue (Eds.), *Sexual deviance: Theory, assessment, and treatment* (pp. 175–93). New York: Guilford Press.

Barbazanges, A., Vallee, M., Mayo, W., Day, J., et al. (1996). Early and later adoptions have different long-term effects on male rat offspring. *Journal of Neuroscience, 16,* 7783–90.

Barber, J. P., Morse, J. Q., Krakauer, I. D., Chittams, J., & Crits-Christoph, K. (1997). Change in obsessive-compulsive and avoidant personality disorders following time-limited supportive-expressive therapy. *Psychotherapy, 34,* 133–43.

Barbour, V. (2000). The balance of risk and benefit in gene therapy trials. *The Lancet, 355*(9201): 384.

Bardhan, K. D. (1980). Cimetidinea in duodenal ulcer: The present position. In A. Torsoli, P. E. Lucchelli, & R. W. Brimbelcombe (Eds), *H2 antagonists.* Amsterdam: Excerpta Medica.

Barefoot, J. C., Dahlstrom, W. G., & Williams, R. B. (1983). Hostility, CHD incidence, and total mortality: A 25-year follow-up study of 255 physicians. *Psychosomatic Medicine, 45* (1): 59–63.

Barefoot, J. C., Larsen, S., Von der Lieth, & Schroll, M. (1995). Hostility, incidence of acute myocardial infarction, and mortality in a sample of older Danish men and women. *American Journal of Epidemiology, 142* (5): 477–84.

Barker, S. E., & O'Neil, P. M. (1999). Anorexia and bulimia nervosa. In A. J. Goreczny & M. Hersen (Eds.), *Handbook of pediatric and adolescent health psychology* (pp. 71–86). Boston: Allyn & Bacon.

Barkley, R. A. (1997). Behavioral inhibition, sustained attention, and executive functions: Constructing a unifying theory of ADHD. *Psychological Bulletin, 121,* 65–94.

Barkley, R. A. (1998a). ADHD, Ritalin, and conspiracies: Talking back to Peter Breggin. Available: http://www.chadd.org/news/russ-review.html.

Barkley, R. A. (1998b). *Attention-deficit hyperactivity disorder: A handbook for diagnosis and treatment* (2nd ed.). New York: Guilford Press.

Barkley, R. A., Edwards, G. H., & Robin, A. L. (1999). *Defiant teens: A clinician's manual for assessment and family intervention.* New York: Guilford Press.

Barkley, R. A., Fischer, M., Edelbrock, C. S., & Smallish, L. (1990). The adolescent outcome of hyperactive children diagnosed by research criteria. I. An 8-year prospective follow-up. *Journal of the American Academy of Child and Adolescent Psychiatry, 29* (4): 546–57.

Barlow, D. H. (1986). The classification of anxiety disorders. In G. L. Tischler (Ed.), *Diagnoses and classification in psychiatry: A critical appraisal of DSM-III* (pp. 223–42). Cambridge: Cambridge University Press.

Barlow, D. H. (1988). *Anxiety and its disorders: The nature and treatment of anxiety and panic.* New York: Guilford Press.

Barlow, D. (2000). *Anxiety and its disorders: The nature and treatment of anxiety and panic* (2nd ed.). New York: Guilford Press.

Barlow, D. H., Abel, G. G., & Blanchard, E. B. (1979). Gender identity change in transsexuals. *Archives of General Psychiatry, 36,* 1001–1007.

Barlow, D. H., Chorpita, B. F., & Turovsky, J. (1996). Fear, panic, anxiety, and disorders of emotion. In D. A. Hope (Ed.), *Nebraska Symposium on Motivation, 1995: Perspectives on anxiety, panic, and fear. Current Theory and Research in Motivation* (Vol. 43, pp. 251–328). Lincoln, NE: University of Nebraska Press.

Barlow, D. H., Esler, J. L., & Vitali, A. E. (1998). Psychosocial treatments for panic disorders, phobias, and generalized anxiety disorder. In P. E. Nathan & J. M. Gorman (Eds.), *A guide to treatments that work* (pp. 288–318). New York: Oxford University Press.

Barnes, D. M. (1988). The biological tangle of drug addiction. *Science, 241,* 415–17.

Barnes, G. E., & Prosin, H. (1985). Parental death and depression. *Journal of Abnormal Psychology, 94,* 64–69.

Barnes, T. R. E., & Braude, W. M. (1985). Akathisia variants and tardive dyskinesia. *Archives of General Psychiatry, 42,* 874–78.

Baron, M., Gruen, R., Kane, J., & Amis, L. (1985). Modern research criteria and the genetics of schizophrenia. *American Journal of Psychiatry, 142,* 697–701.

Baron-Cohen, S. (1995). *Mindblindness: An essay on autism and theory of mind.* Cambridge, MA: MIT Press.

Baron-Cohen, S. (Ed.). (1997). *The maladapted mind: Classic readings in evolutionary psychopathology.* Hove, England: Psychology Press/Erlbaum (UK) Taylor & Francis.

Barr, C. E., Mednick, S. A., & Munk-Jorgensen, P. (1990). Exposure to influenza epidemics during gestation and adult schizophrenia: A 40-year study. *Archives of General Psychiatry, 47,* 869–74.

Barrett, P. M. (1998). Evaluation of cognitive-behavioral group treatments for childhood anxiety disorders. *Journal of Clinical Child Psychology, 27,* 459–68.

Barsky, A., Wyshak, G., Klerman, G., & Latham, K. (1990). The prevalence of hypochondriasis in medical outpatients. *Social Psychiatry and Psychiatric Epidemiology, 25,* 89–94.

Bartak, L., & Rutter, M. (1974). Use of personal pronouns by autistic children. *Journal of Autistic Children and Schizophrenia, 4,* 217–22.

Bartrop, R. W., Luckhurst, E., Lazarus, L., Kiloh, L. G., & Penny, R. (1977). Depressed lymphocyte function after bereavement. *Lancet, I,* April 16, 834–36.

Basoglu, M., Mineka, S., Paker, M., Aker, T., Livanou, M., & Goek, S. (1997). Psychological preparedness for trauma as a protective factor in survivors of torture. *Psychological Medicine, 27*(6): 1421–33.

Bassett, A. S., Bury, A., Hodgkinson, K. A., & Honer, W. G. (1996). Reproductive fitness in familial schizophrenia. *Schizophrenia Research, 21,* 151–60.

Bateman, J. F. (1945). Curb postwar construction of hospitals for mental care? *Hospitals,* February, 55–57.

Bateson, G., Jackson, D. D., Haley, J., & Weakland, J. (1956). Toward a theory of schizophrenia. *Behavioral Science, 1,* 251–64.

Bath, R., Morton, R., Uing, A., & Williams, C. (1996). Nocturnal enuresis and the use of desmopressin: Is it helpful? *Child: Care, Health and Development, 22,* 73–84.

Battaglia, M., & Bellodi, L. (1996). Familial risks and reproductive fitness in schizophrenia. *Schizophrenia Bulletin, 22,* 191–95.

Battaglia, M., Bernardeschi, L., Franchini, L., Bellodi, L., et al. (1995) A family study of schizotypal disorder. *Schizophrenia Bulletin, 21*(1): 33–45.

Baucom, D. H., Shoham, V., Mueser, K. T., Daiuto, A. D., & Stickle, T. R. (1998). Empirically supported couple and family interventions for marital distress and adult mental health problems. *Journal of Consulting and Clinical Psychology, 66* (1): 53–88.

Baum, A. (1990). Stress, intrusive imagery, and chronic distress. *Health Psychology, 9,* 653–75.

Baum, A., Cohen, L., & Hall, M. (1993). Control and intrusive memories as possible determinants of chronic stress. *Psychosomatic Medicine, 55,* 274–86.

Baum, M. (1969). Extinction of an avoidance response following response prevention: Some parametric investigations. *Canadian Journal of Psychology, 23,* 1–10.

Baumeister, R. F. (1997). Esteem threat, self-regulatory breakdown, and emotional distress as factors in self-defeating behavior. *Review of General Psychology, 1* (2): 145–74.

Baumeister, R. F., & Butler, J. L. (1997). Sexual masochism: Deviance without pathology. In D. R. Laws & W. O'Donohue (Eds.), *Sexual deviance: Theory, assessment, and treatment* (pp. 225–239). New York: Guilford Press.

Baxter, L., Schwartz, J., Bergman, K., Szuba, M., et al. (1992). Caudate glucose metabolic rate changes with both drug and behavior therapy for obsessive-compulsive disorder. *Archives of General Psychiatry, 49,* 681–89.

Bazelon Center for Mental Health Law. (1994). *Health care reform fact sheet #1: The prevalence and costs of mental illness and substance abuse and current funding sources for mental health care.* Washington, DC: Author.

Bear, D. M., & Fedio, P.(1977). Quantitative analysis of interictal behavior in temporal lobe epilepsy. *Archives of Neurology, 34,* 454–67.

Beasley, C .M., Dornseif, B.E., Bosomworth, J. C., Sayler, M. E., Rampey, A. H., Heiligenstein, J. H., Thompson, V. L., Murphy, D. J., & Masica, D. N. (1991). Fluoxetine and suicide: A meta-analysis of controlled trials of treatment for depression. *British Medical Journal, 303* (6804): 685–92.

Beasley, C., Dornseif, B., Bosomworth, J., et al. (1992). Fluoxetine and suicide: A meta-analysis of controlled trials of treatment for depression. *International Clinical Psychopharmacology, 6* (Suppl. 6): 35–57.

Beaumont, G. (1990). Adverse effects of antidepressants. *International Clinical Psychopharmacology, 5,* 61–66.

Beauvais, M. F., & Derouesne, J. (1979). Phonological alexia: The dissociations. *Journal of Neurology, Neurosurgery, and Psychiatry, 42,* 1115–24.

Beck, A. T. (1967). *Depression: Clinical, experimental, and theoretical aspects.* New York: Hoeber.

Beck, A. T. (1973). *The diagnosis and management of depression.* Philadelphia: University of Pennsylvania Press.

Beck, A. T. (1976). *Cognitive therapy and the emotional disorders.* New York: International Universities Press.

Beck, A. T. (1999). *Prisoners of hate: The cognitive basis of anger, hostility, and violence.* New York: HarperCollins.

Beck, A. T., & Emery, G. (1985). *Anxiety disorders and phobias: A cognitive perspective.* New York: Basic Books.

Beck, A. T., & Freeman, A.M. (1990). *Cognitive therapy of personality disorders.* New York: Guilford.

Beck, A. T., Rush, A. J., Shaw, B. F., & Emery, G. (1979). *Cognitive therapy of depression.* New York: Guilford Press.

Beck, A. T., Sokol, L., Clark, D., Berchick, B., & Wright, F. (1991). *Focussed cognitive therapy of panic disorder: A crossover design and one-year follow-up.* Manuscript.

Beck, A. T., Steer R. A., & Epstein, N. (1992). Self-concept dimensions of clinically depressed and anxious outpatients. *Journal of Clinical Psychology, 48,* 423–32.

Beck, A. T., Ward, C. H., Mendelson, M., Mock, J. E., & Erbaugh, J. K. (1962). Reliability of psychiatric diagnoses II: A study of consistency of clinical judgments and ratings. *American Journal of Psychiatry, 119,* 351–57.

Beck, J. G. (1995). Hypoactive sexual desire disorder: An overview. *Journal of Consulting and Clinical Psychology, 63* (6): 919–27.

Becker, A. E., Grinspoon, S. K., Klibanski, A., & Herzog, D. B. (1999). Eating disorders *New England Journal of Medicine, 340,*1092–98.

Becker, R. E., Meisler, N., Stormer, G., & Brondino, M. J. (1999). Employment outcomes for clients with severe mental illness in a PACT model replication. *Psychiatric Services, 50,* 104–106.

Beech, H. R., & Vaughan, M. (1979). *Behavioural treatment of obsessional states.* Chichester: Wiley.

Beecher, H. K. (1955). The powerful placebo. *Journal of the American Dental Association, 159,* 1602–1606.

Beecher, H. K. (1959). *Measurement of subjective responses: Quantitative effects of drugs.* New York: Oxford University Press.

Beekman, A., de Beurs, E., van Balkom, A., et al. (2000). Anxiety and depression in later life: Co-occurrence and commonality of risk factors. *American Journal of Psychiatry, 157,* 89–95.

Beers, D. R., Henkel, J. S., Kesner, R. P., & Stroop, W. G. (1995). Spatial recognition memory deficits without notable CNS pathology in rats following herpes simplex encephalitis. *Journal of the Neurological Sciences, 131,* 119–27.

Begleiter, H., Porjesz, B., Bihari, & Kissen, B. (1984). Event-related brain potentials in children at risk for alcoholism. *Science, 227,* 1493–96.

Bejjani,B.-P., Damier, P., Arnulf, I., Thivard, L., Bonnet, A.-M., Dormont, D., Cornu, P., Pidoux, B., Samson, Y., & Agid, Y. (1999). Transient acute depression induced by high-frequency deep-brain stimulation. *New England Journal of Medicine, 340.*

Belkin, L. (1999). Parents blaming parents. *New York Times Magazine,* October 31, pp. 61–101.

Bell, I. R. (1999). A guide to current psychopharmacological treatments for affective disorders in older adults: Anxiety, agitation, and depression. In M. Duffy (Ed.), *Handbook of counseling and psychotherapy with older adults* (pp. 561–76). New York: Wiley.

Bellack, A. S. (1992). Cognitive rehabilitation for schizophrenia: Is it really possible? Is it necessary? *Schizophrenia Bulletin, 18* (1): 43–50.

Bellack, A. S., Blanchard, J. J., Murphy, P., & Podell, K. (1996). Generalization effects of training on the Wisconsin Card Sorting Test for schizophrenia patients. *Schizophrenia Research, 19,* 189–94.

Bellack, A. S., & Hersen, M. (1998). *Behavioral assessment: A practical handbook* (4th ed.). Boston: Allyn & Bacon, Inc.

Bellak, L., & Abrams, D. (1997). *The Thematic Apperception Test, the Children's Apperception Test, and the Senior Apperception Technique in clinical use* (6th ed.). Boston: Allyn & Bacon, Inc.

Bell-Dolan, D., & Brazeal, T. J. (1993). Separation anxiety disorder, overanxious disorder, and school refusal. *Child and Adolescent Psychiatric Clinics of North America, 2,* 563–80.

Belson, R. (1975). The importance of the second interview in marriage counseling. *Counseling Psychologist, 5* (3): 27–31.

Bem, D. J. (1996). Exotic becomes erotic: A developmental theory of sexual orientation. *Psychological Review, 103,* 320–35.

Bench, C. J., Frackowiak, R. S. J., & Dolan, R. J. (1995). Changes in regional cerebral blood flow on recovery from depression. *Psychological Medicine, 25,* 247–51.

Bench, C. J., Friston, K. J., Brown, R. G., Frackowiak, R. S. J., & Dolan, R. J. (1993). Regional cerebral blood flow in depression measured by positron emission tomography: The relationship with clinical dimensions. *Psychological Medicine, 23,* 579–90.

Bendetti, F., Sforzini, L., Colombo, C., Marrei, C., & Smeraldi, E. (1998). Low-dose clozapine in acute and continuation treatment of severe borderline personality disorder. *Journal of Clinical Psychiatry, 59* (3): 103–107.

Benedict, R. H., Dobraski, M., & Goldstein, M. Z. (1999). A preliminary study of the association between changes in mood and cognition in a mixed geriatric psychiatry sample. *Journals of Gerontology, Series B-Psychological Sciences and Social Sciences, 54B,* P94–P99.

Benes, F. M. (1994). Development of the corticolimbic system. In G. Dawson, K. W. Fischer, et al. (Eds.), *Human behavior and the developing brain* (pp. 176–206). New York: Guilford Press.

Benes, F. M. (1997). The role of stress and dopamine-GABA interactions in the vulnerability for schizophrenia. *Journal of Psychiatric Research, 31,* 257–75.

Benes, F. M. (1998). Model generation and testing to probe neural circuitry in the cingulate cortex of postmortem schizophrenic brain. *Schizophrenia Bulletin, 24,* 219–30.

Benes, F. M., Davidson, J., & Bird, E. D. (1986). Quantitative cytoarchitectural studies of the cerebral cortex of schizophrenics. *Archives of General Psychiatry, 42,* 874–78.

Benes, F. M., Kwok, E. W., Vincent, S. L., & Todtenkopf, M. S. (1998). A reduction of nonpyramidal cells in sector CA2 of schizophrenics and manic depressives. *Biological Psychiatry, 44,* 88–97.

Benet, A. E., & Melman, A. (1995). The epidemiology of erectile dysfunction. *Urologic Clinics of North America, 22* (4): 699–709.

Benight, C. C., Antoni, M. H., Kilbourn, K., Ironson, G., et al. (1997). Coping self-efficacy buffers psychological and physiological disturbances in HIV-infected men following a natural disaster. *Health Psychology, 16* (3): 248–255.

Benjamin, H. (1966). *The transsexual phenomenon.* New York: Julian Press.

Benjamin, L. S. (1987). The use of the SASB dimensional model to develop treatment plans for personality disorders. I: Narcissism. *Journal of Personality Disorders, 1* (1): 43–70.

Benjamin, L. S. (1996). Interpersonal diagnosis and treatment of personality disorders. In W. J. Livesley (Ed.), *The DSM-IV personality disorders: Diagnosis and treatment of mental disorders* (2nd ed.). New York: Guilford Press.

Bennett, K. J., Lipman, E. L., Racine, Y., & Offord, D. R. (1998). Do measures of externalising behaviour in normal populations predict later outcome?: Implications for targeted interventions to prevent conduct disorder. *Journal of Child Psychology and Psychiatry and Allied Disciplines, 39,* 1059–70.

Benowitz, N. L. (1988). Pharmacologic aspects of cigarette smoking and nicotine adiction. *New England Journal of Medicine, 17,* 1318–30.

Ben-Shakhar, G., Bar-Hillel, M., Bilu, Y., & Shefler, G. (1998). Seek and ye shall find: Test results are what you hypothesize they are. *Journal of Behavioral Decision Making, 11*(4), 235–49.

Benson, H., & Friedman, R. (1976). Harnessing the power of the placebo effect and renaming it "remembered wellness." *Annual Review of Medicine, 47,* 193–99.

Benton, M. K., & Schroeder, H. E. (1990). Social skills training with schizophrenics: A meta-analytic evaluation. *Journal of Consulting and Clinical Psychology, 58,* 741–47.

Bentsen, H., Munkvold, O. G., Notland, T. H., Boye, B., Oskarsson, K. H., Uren, G., Lersbryggen, A. B., Bjorge, H., Berg-Larsen, R., Lingjaerde, O., & Malt, U. F. (1998). Relatives' emotional warmth towards patients with schizophrenia or related psychoses: Demographic and clinical predictors. *Acta Psychiatrica Scandinavica, 97,* 86–92.

Berenbaum, S. A. (1998). How hormones affect behavioral and neural development: Introduction to the special issue on "Gonadal hormones and sex differences in behavior." *Developmental Neuropsychology, 14,* 175–96.

Berenbaum, S., & Hines, M. (1992). Early androgens are related to childhood sex-typed toy preferences. *Psychological Science, 3,* 203–206.

Berg, S., & Dellasega, C. (1996). The use of psychoactive medications and cognitive function in older adults. *Journal of Aging and Health, 8* (1): 136–49.

Bergem, A. L. M., Engedal, K., & Kringlen, E. (1997). The role of heredity in late-onset Alzheimer disease and vascular dementia: A twin study. *Archives of General Psychiatry, 54,* 264–70.

Berger, F. (1970). Anxiety and the discovery of tranquilizers. In F. J. Ayd & H. Blackwell (Eds.), *Discoveries in biological psychiatry.* Philadelphia: Lippincott.

Berger, P. (1977). Antidepressant medications and the treatment of depression. In J. Barchas, P. Berger, R. Ciaranello, & G. Elliot (Eds.), *Psychopharmacology.* New York: Oxford University Press.

Bergman, A. J., Harvey, P. D., Roitman, S. L., Mohs, R. C., Marder, D., Silverman, J. M., & Siever, L. J. (1998). Verbal learning and memory in schizotypal personality disorder. *Schizophrenia Bulletin, 24,* 635–41.

Berkman, L. F. (1984). Assessing the physical health effects of social networks and social support. *Annual Review of Public Health, 5,* 413–32.

Berkman, L. F. (1986). Social networks, support, and health: Taking the next step forward. *American Journal of Epidemiology, 123,* 559–62.

Berkman, L. F. (1999). Social networks and disability transitions across eight intervals of yearly data in the New Haven EPESE. *Journals of Gerontology. Series B, Psychological Sciences and Social Sciences, 54B* (3): S162–172.

Berkowitz, L. (1994). Guns and youth. In L. D. Eron & J. H. Gentry (Eds.), *Reason to hope: A psychosocial perspective on violence and youth* (pp. 251–79). Washington, DC: American Psychological Association.

Bernheim (1886). In J. E. Gordon (Ed.), *Handbook of clinical and experimental hypnosis.* New York: Macmillan, 1967.

Bernstein, D. P., Cohen, P., Velez, C. N., Schwab-Stone, M., et al. (1993). Prevalence and stability of the DSM-III-R personality disorders in a community-based survey of adolescents. *American Journal of Psychiatry, 150* (8): 1237–43.

Bernstein, D. P., Useda, D., & Siever, L. J. (1993). Paranoid personality disorder: Review of the literature and recommendations for DSM-IV. *Journal of Personality Disorders, 7,* 53–62.

Bernstein, D. P., Useda, D., & Siever, L. J. (1995). Paranoid personality disorder. In W. J. Livesley, (Ed.), *The DSM-IV personality disorders: Diagnosis and treatment of mental disorders* (pp. 45–57). New York: Guilford Press.

Bernstein, G. A., & Borchardt, C. M. (1991). Anxiety disorders of childhood and adolescence: A critical review. *Journal of the American Academy of Child and Adolescent Psychiatry, 30* (4): 519–32.

Berridge, V. (1990). Dependence: Historical concepts and constructs. In A. Edwards & M. Lader (Eds.), *The nature of drug dependence* (pp. 1–18). New York: Oxford University Press.

Berrettini, W. H., Ferraro, T. N., Goldin, L. R., Detera-Wadleigh, S. D., et al. (1997). A linkage study of bipolar illness. *Archives of General Psychiatry, 54* (1): 27–35.

Berridge, V. (1990). Dependence: Historical concepts and constructs. In A. Edwards & M. Lader (Eds.), *The nature of drug dependence* (pp. 1–18). New York: Oxford University Press.

Berry, K. L., Fleming, M. F., Greenlay, J., Widlak, P., Kropp, S., & Mckee, D. (1995). Assessment of alcohol and other drug disorders in the seriously mentally ill. *Schizophrenia Bulletin, 21,* 313–21.

Bertelsen, A. (1999). Reflections on the clinical utility of the ICD-10 and DSM-IV classifications and their diagnostic criteria. *Australian and New Zealand Journal of Psychiatry, 33* (2): 166–73.

Berthier, M. L., Kulisevsky, J., Gironell, A., & Heras, J. A. (1996). Obsessive-compulsive disorder associated with brain lesions: Clinical phenomenology, cognitive function, and anatomic correlates. *Neurology, 47* (2): 353–61.

Best, D., Harris, J., Gossop, M., Farrell, M., Finch, E., Noble, A., & Strang, J. (2000). Use of non-prescribed methadone and other illicit drugs during methadone maintenance treatment. *Drug and Alcohol Review, 19* (1): 9–16.

Bettelheim, B. (1967). *The empty fortress.* New York: The Free Press.

Beutler, L.E. (1996). The clinical interview. In L. E. Beutler & M.R. Berren (Eds.), *Integrative assessment of adult personality* (pp. 94–120). New York: Guilford Press.

Bexton, W. H., Heron, W., & Scott, T. H. (1954). Effects of decreased variation in the sensory environment. *Canadian Journal of Psychology, 8,* 70–76.

Bhugra, D., Leff, J., Mallett, R., Der, G., et al. (1997). Incidence and outcome of schizophrenia in Whites, African-Caribbeans and Asians in London. *Psychological Medicine, 27,* 791–98.

Bibring, E. (1953). The mechanism of depression. In P. Greenacre (Ed.), *Affective disorders.* New York: International Universities Press.

Bierut, L. J., Dinwiddie, S. H. Begleiter, H., Crowe, R. R., Hesselbrock, V., Nurnberger, J. I., Porjesz, B., Schuckit, M. A., & Reich, T. (1998). Familial transmission of substance dependence: Alcohol, marijuana, cocaine, and habitual smoking: A report from the collaborative study on the genetics of alcoholism. *Archives of General Psychiatry, 55,* 982–88.

Bigler, E. D., & Clement, P. F. (1997). *Diagnostic clinical neuropsychology* (3rd ed.). Austin, TX: University of Texas Press.

Bigler, E. D., Lowry, C. M., & Porter, S. S. (1997). Neuroimaging in clinical neuropsychology. In A. M. Horton & D. Wedding (Eds.), *The neuropsychology handbook, Vol. 1: Foundations and assessment* (2nd ed., pp. 199–220). New York: Springer.

Billett, E. A., Richter, M. A., & Kennedy, J. L. (1998). Genetics of obsessive-compulsive disorder. In R. P. Swinson & M. M. Antony (Eds.), *Obsessive-compulsive disorder: Theory, research, and treatment* (pp. 181–206). New York: Guilford Press.

Billy, J., Tanfer, K., Grady, W., & Klepinger, D. (1993). The sexual behavior of men in the United States. *Family Planning Perspectives, 25,* 52–60.

Bilynsky, N. S., & Vernaglia, E. R. (1998). The ethical practice of psychology in a managed-care framework. *Psychotherapy: Theory, Research and Practice, 35,* 54–68.

Binzer, M., & Kullgren, G. (1998). Motor conversion disorder: A prospective 2- to 5-year follow-up study. *Psychosomatics, 39* (6): 519–27.

Biran, M., & Wilson, G. T. (1981). Treatment of phobic disorders using cognitive and exposure methods: A self-efficacy analysis. *Journal of Consulting and Clinical Psychology, 48,* 886–87.

Bird, H. (1996). Epidemiology of childhood disorders in a cross-cultural context. *Journal of Child Psychology and Psychiatry, 37,* 35–49.

Bird J. (1979). The behavioural treatment of hysteria. *British Journal of Psychiatry, 134,* 129–37.

Birenbaum, A., & Rei, M. A. (1979). Resettling mentally retarded adults in the community—almost 4 years later. *American Journal of Mental Deficiency, 83,* 323–29.

Birmaher, B., & Brent, D. (1998). Practice parameters for the assessment and treatment of children and adolescents with depressive disorders. *Journal of the American Academy of Child and Adolescent Psychiatry, 37,* 63S–83S.

Birmaher, B., Ryan, N. D., Williamson, D. E., Brent, D. A., et al. (1996a). Childhood and adolescent depression: A review of the past 10 years, Part I. *Journal of the American Academy of Child and Adolescent Psychiatry, 35,* 1427–39.

Birmaher, B., Ryan, N. D., Williamson, D. E., Brent, D. A., et al. (1996b). Childhood and adolescent depression: A review of the past 10 years, Part II. *Journal of the American Academy of Child and Adolescent Psychiatry, 35,* 1575–83.

Biver, F., Goldman, S., Delvenne, V., Luxen, A., De Maertelaer, V., Hubain, P., Mendlewicz, J., & Lotstra, F. (1994). Frontal and parietal metabolic disturbances in unipolar depression. *Biological Psychiatry, 36,* 381–88.

Black, D. W; Monahan, P., Wesner, R., Gabel, J., & Bowers, W. (1996). The effect of fluvoxamine, cognitive therapy, and placebo on abnormal personality traits in 44 patients with panic disorder. *Journal of Personality Disorders, 10,* 185–94.

Black, D. W., Noyes, R., Goldstein, R. B., & Blum, N. (1992). A family study of obsessive-compulsive disorder. *Archives of General Psychiatry, 49,* 362–68.

Blagg, N., & Yule, W. (1994). School phobia. In T. H. Ollendick & N. J. King (Eds.), *International handbook of phobic and anxiety disorders in children and adolescents: Issues in clinical child psychology.* New York: Plenum.

Blair, C. D., & Lanyon, R. I. (1981). Exhibitionism: A critical review of the etiology and treatment. *Psychological Bulletin, 89,* 439–63.

Blair, R. J. R., Jones, L., Clark, F., & Smith, M. (1997). The psychopathic individual: A lack of responsiveness to distress cues? *Psychophysiology, 34,* 192–98.

Blakemore, C. (1998). How the environment helps to build the brain. In B. Cartledge et al. (Eds.), *Mind, brain, and the environment: The Linacre Lectures 1995–1996* (pp. 28–56). Oxford, England: Oxford University Press.

Blaser, M. J. (1999). Hypothesis: the changing relationships of Helicobacter pylori and humans: implications for health and disease. *Journal of Infectious Diseases, 179* (6):1523–30.

Blashfield, R. K., & Draguns, J. G. (1976). Evaluative criteria for psychiatric classification. *Journal of Abnormal Psychology, 85,* 40–150.

Blashfield, R. K., & Livesley, W. J. (1991). Metaphorical analysis of psychiatric classification as a psychological test. *Journal of Abnormal Psychology, 100* (3): 262–70.

Blashfield, R., & Livesley, W. J. (1999) Classification. In T. Millon, P. Blaney, & R. Davis (Eds.), *Oxford textbook of psychopathology.* Oxford: Oxford University Press.

Blazer, D., Hughes, D., & George, L. (1987). Stressful life events and the onset of generalized anxiety syndrome. *American Journal of Psychiatry, 144,* 1178–83.

Blazer, D.G., Hughes, D., George, L.K., Swartz, M., & Boyer, R. (1991). Generalized anxiety disorder. In L. N. Robins & D. A. Regier (Eds.), *Psychiatric disorders in America* (pp. 180–203). New York: Free Press.

Bleuler, E. (1924). *Textbook of psychiatry.* New York: Macmillan.

Bliss, E. L. (1980). Multiple personalities: Report of fourteen cases with implications for schizophrenia and hysteria. *Archives of General Psychiatry, 37,* 1388–97.

Bliss, E. L., & Jeppsen, A. (1985). Prevalence of multiple personality among inpatients and outpatients. *American Journal of Psychiatry, 142,* 250–51.

Bloch, S., & Reddaway, P. (1977). *Psychiatric terror: How Soviet psychiatry is used to suppress dissent.* New York: Basic Books.

Bloom, F. E., Lazerson, A., & Hofstadter, L. (1985). *Brain, mind, and behavior.* New York: Freeman.

Blumberg, S. H., & Izard, C. E. (1985). Affective and cognitive characteristics of depression in 10- and 11-year-old children. *Journal of Personality and Social Psychology, 49,* 194–202.

Bobak, M., & Marmot, M. (1996). East-West mortality divide and its potential explanations: Proposed research agenda. *British Medical Journal, 312* (7028):421–25.

Bobinski, M., de Leon, M. J., Tarnawski, M., Wegiel, J., Bobinski, M., Reisberg, B., Miller, D. C., & Wisniewski, H. M. (1998). Neuronal and volume loss in CA1 of the hippocampal formation uniquely predicts duration and severity of Alzheimer disease. *Brain Research, 805,* 267–69.

Bodlund, O., & Kullgren, G. (1996). Transsexualism—General outcome and prognostic factors: A five-year follow-up study of nineteen transsexuals in the process of changing sex. *Archives of Sexual Behavior, 25*(3): 303–16.

Boerlin, H. L., Gitlin, M. J., Zoellner, L. A., & Hammen, C. L. (1998). Bipolar depression and antidepressant-induced mania: A naturalistic study. *Journal of Clinical Psychiatry 59* (7): 374–79.

Bogerts, B. (1993). Recent advances in the neuropathology of schizophrenia. *Schizophrenia Bulletin, 19,* 431–45.

Bohman, M., Cloninger, R., Sigvardsson, S., & von Knorring, A. L. (1987). The genetics of alcoholism and related disorders. *Journal of Psychiatric Research, 21,* 447–52.

Bohman, M., Cloninger, C. R., von Knorring, A. L., & Sigvardsson, S. (1984). An adoption study of somatoform disorders. III. Cross-fostering analysis and genetic relationship to alcoholism and criminality. *Archives of General Psychiatry, 41,* 872–78.

Bohman, M., & Sigvardsson, S. C. (1981). Maternal inheritance of alcohol abuse: Cross-fostering analysis of adopted women. *Archives of General Psychiatry, 38,* 965–69.

Bohn, M. J. (1993). Pharmacotherapy: Alcoholism. In D. Dunner (Ed.), *Psychopharmacology. Volume 2: Psychiatric Clinics of North America.* New York: W. B. Saunders.

Bohn, M. J., & Meyer, R. E. (1994). Typologies of addiction. In M. Galanter & H. Kleber (Eds.), *Treatment of substance abuse.* Washington, DC: American Psychiatric Press.

Bola, K. J., Rothman, R., & Cadet, J. L. (1999). Dose-related neurobehavioral effects of chronic cocaine use. *Journal of Neuropsychiatry and Clinical Neuroscience, 11,* 361–69.

Boller, F., Ganansia-Ganem, A., Lebert, F., & Pasquier, F. (1999). Neuropsychiatric afflictions of modern French presidents: Marechal Henri-Philippe Petain and Paul Deschanel. *European Journal of Neurology, 6,* 133–36.

Boney-McCoy, S., & Finkelhor, D. (1995). Psychosocial sequelae of violent victimization in a national youth sample. *Journal of Consulting and Clinical Psychology, 63* (5): 726–36.

Bonn, D. (1999). New treatments for alcohol dependency better than old. *Lancet, 353,* 213.

Booker, J. M., & Hellekson, C. J. (1992). Prevalence of seasonal affective disorder in Alaska. *American Journal of Psychiatry, 149* (9): 1176–82.

Booth, B. M., Mingliang, Z., Rost, K. M., Vlardy, J. A., Smith, L. G., & Smith, R. G. (1997). Measuring outcomes and costs for major depression. *Psychopharmacology Bulletin, 33,* 653–58.

Borduin, C. M. (1999). Multisystemic treatment of criminality and violence in adolescents. *Journal of the American Academy of Child and Adolescent Psychiatry, 38,* 242–49.

Borduin, C. M., Mann, B. J., Cone, L. T., Henggeler, S. W., Fucci, B. R., Blaske, D. M., & Williams, R. A. (1995). Multisystemic treatment of adolescent sexual offenders. *International Journal of Offender Therapy and Comparative Criminology, 34,* 105–13.

Borkovec, T., & Costello, E. (1993). Efficacy of applied relaxation and cognitive-behavioral therapy in the treatment of generalized anxiety disorder. *Journal of Consulting and Clinical Psychology, 61,* 611–19.

Borkovec, T. D., & Inz, J. (1990). The nature of worry in generalized anxiety disorder: A predominance of thought activity. *Behaviour Research and Therapy, 28* (2): 153–58.

Bornstein, R. F. (1992). The dependent personality: Developmental, social, and clinical perspectives. *Psychological Bulletin, 112* (1): 3–23.

Bornstein, R. F. (1996). Sex differences in dependent personality disorder prevalence rates. *Clinical Psychology—Science and Practice, 3,* 1–12.

Bornstein, R. F. (1999). Dependent and histrionic personality disorders. In T. Millon & P. Blaney (Eds.), *Oxford textbook of psychopathology. Oxford textbooks in clinical psychology* (Vol. 4). New York: Oxford University Press.

Borysenko, M. (1987). The immune system: An overview. *Annals of Behavioral Medicine, 9,* 3–10.

Boscarino, J. A. (1995). Post-traumatic stress and associated disorders among Vietnam veterans: The significance of combat exposure and social support. *Journal of Traumatic Stress, 8* (2): 317–36.

Boseley, S. (1999). They said it was safe. *The Guardian,* October 30.

Bouchard, T. J. (1994). Genes, environment, and personality. *Science, 264,* 1700–1701.

Bouchard, T. J. (1996). The genetics of personality. In K. Blum & E. P. Noble (Eds.), *Handbook of psychiatric genetics.* Boca Raton, FL: CRC Press.

Bouchard, T. J. (1997). IQ similarity in twins reared apart: Findings and responses to critics. In R. J. Sternberg & E. L. Grigorenko (Eds.), *Intelligence, heredity, and environment.* New York: Cambridge University Press.

Bouchard, S., Gauthier, J., Benoit, L., French, D., Pelletier, M., & Godbout, C. (1996). Exposure versus cognitive restructuring in the treatment of panic disorder with agoraphobia. *Behaviour Research and Therapy, 34* (3): 213–24.

Bouchard, T., Lykken, D., McGue, M., Segal, N., & Tellegen, A. (1990). Sources of human psychological differences: The Minnesota study of twins reared apart. *Science, 250,* 223–28.

Boulos, C., Kutcher, S., Gardner, D., & Young, E. (1992). An open naturalistic trial of fluoxetine in adolescents and young adults with treatment-resistant major depression. *Journal of Child and Adolescent Psychopharmacology, 2,* 103–11.

Bouras, N., & Szymanski, L. (1997) Services for people with mental retardation and psychiatric disorders: US-UK comparative overview. *International Journal of Social Psychiatry, 43* (1): 64–71.

Bourdon, K., Boyd, J., Rae, D., & Burns, B. (1988). Gender differences in phobias: Results of the ECA community survey. *Journal of Anxiety Disorders, 2,* 227–41.

Bourgeois, M. (1991). Serotonin, impulsivity, and suicide. *Human Psychopharmacology: Clinical and Experimental, 6,* 31–36.

Bourgois, P. (1998). The moral economies of homeless heroin addicts: Confronting ethnography, HIV risk, and everyday violence in San Francisco shooting encampments. *Substance Use and Misuse, 33,* 2323–51.

Bouwer, C., & Stein, D. J. (1997). Association of panic disorder with a history of traumatic suffocation. *American Journal of Psychiatry, 154* (11): 1566–70.

Bowden, C. L. (1996). Role of newer medications for bipolar disorder. *Journal of Clinical Psychopharmacology, 16* (Suppl. 2): 48–55.

Bowlby, J. (1988). Developmental psychiatry comes of age. *American Journal of Psychiatry, 145,* 1–10.

Bowlby, J. (1989). The role of attachment in personality development and psychopathology. In S. I. Greenspan & G. H. Pollock (Eds.), *The course of life, Vol. 1: Infancy* (pp. 229–70). Madison, CT: International Universities Press.

Boyd, J., Rae, D., Thompson, J., & Burns, B. (1990). Phobia: Prevalence and risk factors. *Social Psychiatry and Psychiatric Epidemiology, 25,* 314–23.

Bozarth, M. A., & Wise, R. A. (1985). Toxicity associated with long-term intravenous heroin and cocaine self-administration in the rat. *Journal of the American Medical Association, 254,* 81–83.

Bracha, H. S., Lange, B., Gill, P. S., Gilger, J. W., et al. (1995). Subclinical microcrania, subclinical, macrocrania, and fifth-month fetal markers (of growth retardation or edema) in schizophrenia: A co-twin control study of discordant monozygotic twins. *Neuropsychiatry, Neuropsychology, and Behavioral Neurology, 8,* 44–52.

Bracha, H. S., Torrey, E. F., Gottesman, I. I., Bigelow, L. B., et al. (1992). Second-trimester markers of fetal size in schizophrenia: A study of monozygotic twins. *American Journal of Psychiatry, 149,* 1355–61.

Bradbury, T. N., & Miller, G. A. (1985). Season of birth in schizophrenia: A review of evidence, methodology, and etiology. *Psychological Bulletin, 98,* 569–94.

Bradford, J. (1988). Organic treatment for the male sexual offender. *Annals of the New York Academy of Sciences, 528,* 193–202.

Bradford, J. M. (1990). The antiandrogen and hormal treatment of sex offenders. In W. L. Marshall, D. R. Laws, & H. E. Barbaree (Eds.), *Handbook of sexual assault: Issues, theories, and treatment of the offender* (pp. 363–85). New York: Plenum.

Bradford, J. M. (1995). Pharmacological treatment of the paraphilias. In J. M. Oldham & M. B. Reba (Eds.), *American Psychiatric Press Review of Psychiatry* (Vol. 14). Washington, DC: American Psychiatric Press.

Bradford, J. M. (1997). Medical interventions in sexual deviance. In D. R. Laws & W. O'Donohue (Eds.), *Sexual deviance: Theory, assessment, and treatment* (pp. 449–64). New York: Guilford Press.

Bradley, S. J., & Zucker, K. J. (1997). Gender identity disorder: A review of the past 10 years. *Journal of the American Academy of Child and Adolescent Psychiatry, 36,* 872–80.

Bradshaw, J. (1990). *Homecoming: Reclaiming and championing your inner child.* New York: Bantam.

Brady, J. P., & Lind D. L. (1961). Experimental analysis of hysterical blindness: Operant conditioning techniques. *Archives of General Psychiatry, 4,* 331–39.

Braff, D. L., & Saccuzzo, D. P. (1985). The time course of information-processing deficits in schizophrenia. *American Journal of Psychiatry, 142* (2): 170–74.

Brandenburg N. A., Friedman, R. M., & Silver, S. E. (1990). The epidemiology of childhood psychiatric disorders: Prevalence findings from recent studies. *Journal of the American Academy of Child and Adolescent Psychiatry, 29* (1): 76–83.

Brebion, G., Smith, M. J., Gorman, J. M., & Amador, X. (1997). Discrimination accuracy and decision biases in different types of reality monitoring in schizophrenia. *Journal of Nervous and Mental Disease, 185,* 247–53.

Breedlove, S. M. (1994). Sexual differentiation of the human nervous system. *Annual Review of Psychology, 45,* 389–418.

Breggin, P. R. (1998). *Talking back to Ritalin: What doctors aren't telling you about stimulants for children.* Monroe, ME: Common Courage Press.

Breier, A., Albus, M., Pickar, D., Zahn, T.P. et al. (1987). Controllable and controllable stress in humans: Alterations in mood and neuroendocrine and psychophysiological function. *American Journal of Psychiatry, 144* (11): 1419–25.

Breier, A., Charney, D. S., & Heninger, G. R. (1986). Agoraphobia with panic attacks: Development, diagnostic stability, and course of illness. *Archives of General Psychiatry, 43,* 1029–36.

Bremner, J. D., Licinio, J., Darnell, A., Krystal, A. H., Owens, M. J., Southwick, S. M., Nemeroff, C. B., & Charney, D. S. (1997). Elevated CSF corticotropin-releasing factor concentrations in posttraumatic stress disorder. *American Journal of Psychiatry, 154,* 624–29.

Bremner, J. D., Randall, P., Vermetten, E., Staib, L., et al. (1997). Magnetic resonance imaging-based measurement of hippocampal volume in posttraumatic stress disorder related to childhood physical and sexual abuse: A preliminary report. *Biological Psychiatry, 41,* 23–32.

Brennan, P. A., Grekin, E. R., & Mednick, S. A. (1999). Maternal smoking during pregnancy and adult male criminal outcomes. *Archives of General Psychiatry, 56,* 215–19.

Brennan, P., Mednick, S., & Kandel, E. (1991). Congenital determinants of violent and property offending. In D. J. Pepler & K. H. Rubin (Eds.), *The development and treatment of childhood aggression* (pp. 81–92). Hillsdale, NJ: Lawrence Erlbaum.

Brennan, P. A., Raine, A., Schulsinger, F., Kirkegaard-Sorensen, L., Knop, J., Hutchings, B., Rosenberg, R., & Mednick, S. A. (1997). Psychophysiological protective factors for male subjects at high risk for criminal behavior. *American Journal of Psychiatry, 154,* 853–55.

Brenner, H. D., Hirsbrunner, A., & Heimberg, D. (1996). Integrated psychological therapy program: Training in cognitive and social skills for schizophrenic patients. In P. W. Corrigan & S. C. Yudofsky (Eds.), *Cognitive rehabilitation for neuropsychiatric disorders* (pp. 329–48). Washington, DC: Ameican Psychiatric Press.

Brenner, H. D., Hodel, B., Roder, V., & Corrigan, P. (1992). Treatment of cognitive dysfunctions and behavioral deficits in schizophrenia. *Schizophrenia Bulletin, 18* (1): 21–26.

Brenner, H. D., Roder, V., Hodel, B., Kienzle, N., Reed, D., & Liberman, R. P. (1994). *Integrated psychological therapy for schizophrenic patients (IPT).* Goettingen, Germany: Hogrefe & Huber.

Brent, D. A., & Perper, J. A. (1995). Research in adolescent suicide: Implications for training, service delivery and public policy. *Suicide and Life-Threatening Behavior, 25,* 222–30.

Breslau, N. & Davis, G. C. (1986). Chronic stress and major depression. *Archives of General Psychiatry, 43,* 309–14.

Breslau, N., & Davis, G. C. (1987). Posttraumatic stress disorder: The etiologic specificity of wartime stressors. *American Journal of Psychiatry, 144,* 578–83.

Breslin, F. C., Hayward, M., & Baum, A. (1994). Effect of stress on perceived intoxication and the Blood Alcohol Curve in men and women. *Health Psychology, 13* (6): 479–87.

Breslin, N. H. (1992). Treatment of schizophrenia: Current practice and future promise. *Hospital and Community Psychiatry, 43,* 877–85.

Brestan, E. V., & Eyberg, S. M. (1998). Effective psychosocial treatments of conduct-disordered children and adolescents: 29 years, 82 studies, and 5,272 kids. *Journal of Clinical Child Psychology, 27,* 180–89.

Brett, C. W., Burling, T. A., & Pavlik, W. B. (1981). Electroconvulsive shock and learned helplessness in rats. *Animal Learning and Behavior, 9,* 38–44.

Brett, D., Kirkby, K., Hay, D., Mowry, B., & Jones, I. (1998). Predictability of hospitalization over 5 years for schizophrenia, bipolar disorder and depression. *Australian and New Zealand Journal of Psychiatry, 32,* 281–86.

Brew, B. J., Rosenblum, M., Cronin, K., & Price, R. W. (1995). AIDS Dementia Complex and HIV-1 brain infection: Clinical-virological correlations. *Annals of Neurology, 38* (4): 563–70.

Brewer, D. D., Catalano, R. F., Haggerty, K., Gainey, R. R., & Fleming, C. B. (1998). A meta-analysis of predictors of continued drug use during and after treatment for opiate addiction. *Addiction, 93,* 73–92.

Brickman, A. S., McManus, M., Grapentine, W. L., & Alessi, N. (1984). Neuropsychological assessment of seriously delinquent adolescents. *Journal of the American Academy of Child Psychiatry, 23,* 453–57.

Broadbent, D. E. (1958). *Perception of communication.* London: Pergamon.

Brodie, H. K. H., & Leff, M. J. (1971). Bipolar depression: A comparative study of patient characteristics. *American Journal of Psychiatry, 127,* 1086–90.

Broman, S. H. & Michel, M. E. (Eds.). (1995). *Traumatic head injury in children.* New York: Oxford.

Bromfield, R. (1996). Is Ritalin overprescribed? — Yes. *Priorities, 8,* (on-line). http://www.acsh.org/publications/priorities/0803/pcyes.html

Brooks, A. D. (1974). *Law, psychiatry and the mental health system.* Boston: Little, Brown.

Brooks, N., & McKinlay, W. (1992). Mental health consequences of the Lockerbie disaster. *Journal of Traumatic Stress, 5,* 527–43

Brooks-Gunn, J. (1988). Antecedents and consequences of variations in girls' maturational timing. *Journal of Adolescent Health Care, 90* (5):365–73.

Broome, K. M., Knight, K., Joe, G. W., & Simpson, D. (1996). Evaluating the drug-abusing probationer: Clinical interview versus self-administered assessment. *Criminal Justice and Behavior, 23* (4): 593–606.

Brown, G. W., & Harris, T. (1978). *Social origins of depression.* London: Tavistock.

Brown, R., Colter, N., Corsellis, J. A., Crow, T. J., Frith, C. D., Jagoe, R., Johnstone, E. C., & Marsh, L. (1986). Post-mortem evidence of structural brain changes in schizophrenia. Differences in brain weight, temporal horn area, and parahippocampal gyrus compared with affective disorder. *Archives of General Psychiatry, 43* (1): 36–42.

Brown, T. A., Barlow, D. H., & Liebowitz, M. R. (1994). The empirical basis of generalized anxiety disorder. *American Journal of Psychiatry 151*(9): 1272–80.

Bruch, H. (1982). Anorexia nervosa: Therapy and theory. *American Journal of Psychiatry, 139,* 1531–38.

Bruininks, R. H., Woodcock, R. W., Weatherman, R. E., & Hill, B. K. (1984). *Scales of independent behavior: Woodcock-Johnson Psycho-Educational Battery: Part IV.* Allen, TX: DLM Teaching Resources.

Brumberg, J. (1998). *The body project: An intimate history of American girls.* New York: Random House.

Brunner, D., & Hen, R. (1997). Insights into the neurobiology of impulsive behavior from serotonin receptor knockout mice. In D. M. Stoff & J. J. Mann (Eds.), *The neurobiology of suicide: From the bench to the clinic* (Annals of The New York Academy of Sciences, Vol. 836; pp. 81–105). New York: New York Academy of Sciences.

Bryant, F. B., & Yarnold, P. R. (1995). Comparing five alternative factor-models of the Student Jenkins Activity Survey: Separating the wheat from the chaff. *Journal of Personality Assessment, 64* (1): 145–58.

Bryant, R. N., & McConkey, K. M. (1989). Visual conversion disorder: A case analysis of the influence of visual information. *Journal of Abnormal Psychology, 98,* 326–29.

Bryson, G., Bell, M. D., Kaplan, E., & Greig, T. (1998). The functional consequences of memory impairments on initial work performance in people with schizophrenia. *Journal of Nervous and Mental Disease, 186,* 610–15.

Brzustowicz, L. M., Hodgkinson, K. A., Chow, E. W., Honer, W. G., & Bassett, A. S. (2000). Location of a major susceptibility locus for familial schizophrenia on chromosome 1q21-q22. *Science, 288* (5466): 678–82.

Buchanan, G. (1994). Explanatory style and coronary heart disease. In G. Buchanan & M. Seligman (Eds.), *Explanatory style.* Hillsdale, NJ: Erlbaum.

Buchanan, G., Gardenswartz, C., & Seligman, M. (1999). Physical health following a cognitive-behavioral intervention. *Prevention and Treatment, 2.*

Buchanan, R. W. (1995). Clozapine: Efficacy and safety. *Schizophrenia Bulletin, 21* (4): 579–91.

Buchsbaum, M. S. (1990). The frontal lobes, basal ganglia, and temporal lobes as sites for schizophrenia. *Schizophrenia Bulletin, 16* (3): 379–89.

Buchsbaum, M. S., & Heier, R. J. (1987). Functional and anatomical brain imaging: Impact on schizophrenia research. *Schizophrenia Bulletin, 13,* 115–32.

Buchsbaum, M. S., Someya, T., Teng, C. Y., Abel, L., Chin, S., Najafi, A., Heier, R. J., Wu, J., and Bunney, W. E., Jr. (1996). PET and MRI of the thalamus in never-medicated patients with schizophrenia. *American Journal of Psychiatry, 151* (3): 343–50.

Buchwald, A. M., Coyne, J. C., & Cole, C. S. (1978). A critical evaluation of the learned helplessness model of depression. *Journal of Abnormal Psychology, 87,* 180–93.

Buck, C., Simpson, H., & Wanklin, J. M. (1977). Survival of nieces and nephews of schizophrenic patients. *British Journal of Psychiatry, 130,* 506–508.

Buckley, P. F. (1997). New dimensions in the pharmacologic treatment of schizophrenia and related psychoses. *Journal of Clinical Pharmacology, 37* (5): 363–78.

Buckley, P. F., Sajatovic, M., & Meltzer, H. Y. (1994). Clozapine treatment of delusional disorders. *American Journal of Psychiatry, 151,* 1394–95.

Budzynski, T. H., Stoyva, J. M., Adler, C. S., & Mullaney, D. M. (1973). EMG biofeedback and tension headache: A controlled outcome study. *Psychosomatic Medicine, 35,* 484–96.

Bulik, C. M., Sullivan, P. F., & Weltzin, T. E. (1995). Temperance in eating disorders. *International Journal of Eating Disorders, 17,* 251–61.

Bunney, W. E., & Murphy, D. L. (1974). Switch processes in psychiatric illness. In S. S. Kline (Ed.), *Factors in depression.* New York: Raven Press.

Burgess, A., & Holmstrom, L. (1979). Adaptive strategies and recovery from rape. *American Journal of Psychiatry, 136,* 1278–82.

Burke, A. E., & Silverman, W. K. (1987). The prescriptive treatment of school refusal. *Clinical Psychology Review, 7,* 353–62.

Burman, A. M. (1988). Sexual assault and mental disorders in a community population. *Journal of Consulting and Clinical Psychology, 56* (6): 843–50.

Burns, B., & Reyher, J. (1976). Activating posthypnotic conflict: Emergent, uncovering, psychopathology, repression and psychopathology. *Journal of Personality Assessment, 40,* 492–501.

Burns, B. J., Costello, E. J., Angold, A., Tweed, D., Stangl, D., Farmer, E. M., & Erkanli, A. (1995). Children's mental health service use across service sectors. *Health Affairs, 14* (3): 147–59.

Burt, R. A., & Morris, N. (1972). A proposal for the abolition of the incompetency plea. *Chicago Law Review, 40,* 66–80.

Bushman, B. J., & Baumeister, R. F. (1998).Threatened egotism, narcissism, self-esteem, and direct and displaced aggression: Does self-love or self-hate lead to violence? *Journal of Personality and Social Psychology, 75* (1): 219–29.

Butcher, J. N. (1969). *MMPI: Research developments and clinical applications.* New York: McGraw-Hill.

Butcher, J. N. (Ed.), et al. (1996). *International adaptations of the MMPI-2: Research and clinical applications.* (pp. 26–43). Minneapolis: University of Minnesota Press.

Butcher, J. N. (1999). *A beginner's guide to the MMPI-2.* Washington, DC: American Psychological Association.

Butcher, J. N., Dahlstrom, W. G., Graham, J. R., Tellegen, A., & Kraemer, B. (1989). *Minnesota Multiphasic Personality Inventory-2: Manual for administration and scoring.* Minneapolis: University of Minnesota Press.

Butcher, J. N., Dahlstrom, W. G., Graham, J. R., Tellegen, A., & Kraemer, B. (1994). *Minnesota Multiphasic Personality Inventory—2 (MMPI-2).* Minneapolis: NCS Assessments.

Butcher, J. N., & Rouse, S. V. (1996). Personality: Individual differences and clinical assessment. *Annual Review of Psychology, 47,* 87–111.

Butler, G., Fennell, M., Robson, P., & Gelder, M. (1991). Comparison of behavior therapy and cognitive behavior therapy in the treatment of generalized anxiety disorder. *Journal of Consulting and Clinical Psychology, 59,* 167–75.

Butler, R. N. (1997). Population aging and health. *British Medical Journal, 315,* 1082–84.

Butler, S. M., & Snowdon, D. A. (1996). Trends in mortality in older women: Findings from the Nun Study. *Journals of Gerontology, Series B, Psychological Sciences and Social Sciences, 51B,* S201–S208.

Butzlaff, R. L., & Hooley, J. M. (1998). Expressed emotion and psychiatric relapse: A meta-analysis. *Archives of General Psychiatry, 55,* 547–52.

Buysse, D. J., Reynolds, C. F., Hauri, P. J., Roth, T., Stepanski, E. J., Thorpy, M. J., Bixler, E.O., Kales, A., Manfredi, R. L., Vgontsas, A. N., Stapf, D. M., Houck, P. R., & Kupfer, D. J. (1994). Diagnostic concordance for DSM-IV Sleep Disorders: A report from the APA/NIMH DSM-IV field trial. *American Journal of Psychiatry, 151* (9): 1351–60.

Bynum, W. F. (Jr.). (1981). Rationales for therapy in British psychiatry, 1780–1835. In A. Scull (Ed.), *Madhouses, mad-doctors, and madmen: The social history of psychiatry in the Victorian era* (pp. 35–57). Philadelphia: University of Pennsylvania Press.

Bystritsky, A., Craske, M., Maidenberg, E., Vapnik, T., & Shapiro, D. (1995). Ambulatory monitoring of panic patients during regular activity: A preliminary report. *Biological Psychiatry, 38,* 684–89.

Cade, W. (1970). The story of lithium. In F. J. Ayd & H. Blackwell (Eds.), *Discoveries in biological psychiatry.* Philadelphia: Lippincott.

Cadoret, R. (1986). Epidemiology of antisocial personality. In W. H. Reid, D. Dorr, J. I. Walker, & J. W. Bonner, III (Eds.), *Unmasking the psychopath: Antisocial personality and related syndromes* (pp. 28–44). New York: Norton.

Cadoret, R. J., O'Gorman, T. W., Troughton, E., & Heywood, E. (1985). Alcoholism and antisocial personality. *Archives of General Psychiatry, 42,* 161–67.

Cadoret, R. J. & Stewart, M. A. (1991). An adoption study of attention deficit/hyperactivity/aggression and their relationship to adult antisocial personality. *Comprehensive Psychiatry, 32,* 73–82.

Cadoret, R. J., Yates, W. R., Troughton, E., Woodworth, G., & Stewart, M. A. (1995a). Adoption study demonstrating two genetic pathways to drug abuse. *Archives of General Psychiatry, 52,* 42–52.

Cadoret, R. J., Yates, W. R., Troughton, E., Woodworth, G., & Stewart, M. A. (1995b). Genetic-environmental interaction in the genesis of aggressivity and conduct disorders. *Archives of General Psychiatry, 52,* 916–24.

Cadoret, R. J., Yates, W. R., Troughton, E., Woodworth, G., & Stewart, M. A. (1996). An adoption study of drug abuse/dependency in females. *Comprehensive Psychiatry, 37* (2): 88–94.

Caine, S. B. (1998). Neuroanatomical bases of the reinforcing stimulus effects of cocaine. In S. T. Higgins & J. L. Katz (Eds.), *Cocaine abuse: Behavior, pharmacology, and clinical applications* (pp. 21–50). San Diego: Academic Press.

Calabrese, J. R., Bowden, C. L., Sachs, G. S., Ascher, J. A., Monaghan, E., & Rudd, G. D. (1999). A double-blind placebo-controlled study of lamotrigine monotherapy in outpatients with bipolar I depression. *Journal of Clinical Psychiatry, 60* (2): 79–88.

Caldwell, C. B., & Gottesman, I. I. (1990). Schizophrenics kill themselves too: A review of risk factors for suicide. *Schizophrenia Bulletin, 16* (4): 571–89.

Caldwell, C. B., & Gottesman, I. I. (1992). Schizophrenia–a high risk factor for suicide: Clues to risk reduction. *Suicide and Life-Threatening Behavior, 2,* 479–93.

Calingasan, N. Y., Gandy, S. E., Baker, H., Sheu, K. R., Kim, K., Wisniewski, H. M., & Gibson, G. E. (1995). Accumulation of amyloid precursor protein-like immunoreactivity in rat brain in response to thiamine deficiency. *Brain Research, 677,* 50–60.

Callahan, R. (1996). Why is 100% cure rate unattainable in psychotherapy? July, 30, 1996, personal communication.

Cameron, N. (1938). Reasoning, regression and communication in schizophrenia. *Psychological Monographs, 50* (Whole No. 221).

Cameron, N. (1947). *The psychology of behavior disorders.* Boston: Houghton Mifflin.

Campbell, M., & Cueva, J. (1995). Psychopharmacology in child and adolescent psychiatry: A review of the past seven years. Part 2. *Journal of the American Academy of Child and Adolescent Psychiatry, 34* (10).

Canetto, S., & Lester, D. (1995). Gender and the primary prevention of suicide mortality. *Suicide and Life Threatening Behavior, 25,* 58–69.

Cannon, M., Jones, P., Gilvarry, C., Rifkin, L., McKenzie, K., Foerster, A., & Murray, R. M. (1997). Premorbid social functioning in schizophrenia and bipolar disorder: Similarities and differences. *American Journal of Psychiatry, 154,* 1544–50.

Cannon, T. D. (1997). On the nature and mechanisms of obstetric influences in schizophrenia: A review and synthesis of epidemiologic studies. *International Review of Psychiatry, 9,* 387–97.

Cannon, T. D., Kaprio, J., Lonnqvist, J., Huttunen, M., & Koshenvuo, M. (1998). The genetic epidemiology of schizophrenia in a Finnish twin cohort: A population based modeling study. *Archives of General Psychiatry, 55,* 67–74.

Cannon, T. D., & Mednick, S. A. (1993). The schizophrenia high-risk project in Copenhagen: Three decades of progress. *Acta Psychiatrica Scandinavica, 87* (Suppl. 370): 33–47.

Cantwell, D. P. (1998). ADHD through the life span: The role of bupropion in treatment. *Journal of Clinical Psychiatry, 59,* 92–94.

Cantwell, D. P., Baker, L., & Rutter, M. (1978). Family factors in the syndrome of infantile autism. In M. Rutter & E. Schopler (Eds.), *Autism: A reappraisal of concepts and treatment.* New York: Plenum.

Cardno, A. G., Marshall, E. G., Coid, B., Macdonald, A. M., Ribchester, T. R., Davies, N. J., Venturi, P., Jones, L. A., Lewis, S. W., Sham, P. C., Gottesman, I. I., Farmer, A. E., McGuffin, P., Reveley, A. M., & Murray, R. M. (1999). Heritability estimates for psychotic disorders: The Maudsley twin psychosis series. *Archives of General Psychiatry, 56,* 162–68.

Carey, G., & Gottesman, I. I. (1981). Twin and family studies of anxiety, phobic, and obsessive disorders. In D. F. Klein & J. Rabkin (Eds.), *Anxiety: New research and changing concepts* (pp. 117–36). New York: Raven Press.

Carey, M., Wincze, J., & Meisler, A. (1993). Sexual dysfunction: Male erectile disorder. In D. Barlow (Ed.), *Clinical handbook of psychological disorders* (2nd ed., pp. 442–80). New York: Guilford Press.

Carlson, G. A., Kotin, J., Davenport, Y. B., & Adland, M. (1974). Follow-up of 53 bipolar manic depressive patients. *British Journal of Psychiatry, 124,* 134–39.

Carlson, L. (1999). *A fever in Salem: A new interpretation of the New England witch trials.* Ivan Dee.

Carmagnat-Dubois, F., Desombre, H., Perrot, A., Roux, S., Le Noir, P., Sauvage, D., & Garreau, B. (1997). Autism and Rett syndrome: A comparison study during infancy using family home movies. *Encephale, 23,* 273–79.

Carmelli, D., Dame, A., Swan, G., & Rosenman, R. (1991). Long-term changes in Type A behavior: A 27-year follow-up of the Western Collaborative Group Study. *Journal of Behavioral Medicine, 14,* 593–606.

Carnahan, H., Aguilar, O., Malla, A., & Norman, R. (1997). An investigation into movement planning and execution deficits in individuals with schizophrenia. *Schizophrenia Research, 23,* 213–21.

Carney, R., Freedland, K., & Jaffe, A. (1990). Insomnia and depression prior to myocardial infarction. *Psychosomatic Medicine, 52,* 603–609.

Carpenter, W. T., Jr. (1992). The negative symptom challenge [comment]. *Archives of General Psychiatry, 49* (3): 236–37.

Carpenter, W. T., Jr., & Buchanan, R.(1994). Medical progress: Schizophrenia. *New England Journal of Medicine, 330* (10): 681–90.

Carroll, A., Fattah, S., Clyde, Z., Coffey, I., Owens, D. G., & Johnstone, E. C. (1999). Correlates of insight and insight change in schizophrenia. *Schizophrenia Research, 35,* 247–54.

Carroll, B. J. (1994). Brain mechanisms in manic depression. *Clinical Chemistry, 40* (2): 303–308.

Carroll, M. E., & Bickel, W. K. (1998). Behavioral-environmental determinants of the reinforcing functions of cocaine. In S. T. Higgins & J. L. Katz (Eds.), *Cocaine abuse: Behavior, pharmacology, and clinical applications* (pp. 81–106). San Diego: Academic Press.

Carter, A. B. (1949). The prognosis of certain hysterical symptoms. *British Medical Journal, 1,* 1076–80.

Carter, C. H. (1970). *Handbook of mental retardation syndromes.* Springfield, IL: Charles C. Thomas.

Carter, J. D., Joyce, P. R., Mulder, R. T., Sullivan, P. F., & Luty, S. E. (1999). Gender differences in the frequency of personality disorders in depressed outpatients. *Journal of Personality Disorders, 13,* 67–74.

Carter, J. R., & Neufeld, R. W. J. (1998). Cultural aspects of understanding people with schizophrenic disorders. In S. S. Kazarian & D. R. Evans (Eds.), *Cultural clinical psychology: Theory, research, and practice* (pp. 246–66). New York: Oxford University Press.

Carter, J. W., Parnas, J., Cannon, T. D., Schulsinger, F., & Mednick, S. A. (1999). MMPI variables predictive of schizophrenia in the Copenhagen High-Risk Project: A 25-year follow-up. *Acta Psychiatrica Scandinavica, 99* (6): 432–40.

Castle, D., & Murray, R. (1993). The epidemiology of late-onset schizophrenia. *Schizophrenia Bulletin, 19* (4): 691–700.

Castle, D. J., Wessely, S., & Murray, R. M. (1993). Sex and schizophrenia: Effects of diagnostic stringency, and associations with premorbid variables. *British Journal of Psychiatry, 162,* 658–64.

Castle, J., Groothues, C., Bredenkamp, D., Beckett, C., O'Connor, T., & Rutter, M. E.R.A. Study Team. (1999). Effects of qualities of early institutional care on cognitive attainment. *American Journal of Orthopsychiatry, 69* (4): 424–37.

Castle, S., Wilkins, S., Heck, E., Tanzy, K., & Fahey, J. (1995). Depression in caregivers of demented patients is associated with altered immunity: Impaired proliferative capacity, increased CD8+, and a decline in lymphocytes with surface signal transduction molecules (CD38+) and a cytotoxicity marker (CD56+ CD8+). *Clinical and Experimental Immunology, 101,* 487–93.

Cautela, J. R. (1967). Covert sensitization. *Psychological Reports, 20,* 459–68.

Cegelka, W. J., & Tyler, J. L. (1970). The efficacy of special class placement for the mentally retarded in proper perspective. *Training School Bulletin, 67,* 33–68.

Ceniceros, S. (1998). Alzheimer's disease and depression. *Psychiatric Services, 49,* 389.

Center for Disease Control. (1989*). CDC morbidity and mortality weekly report (MMWR).* http://www2.cdc.gov/mmwr

Center for Disease Control. (1994). *Helicobacter pylori and peptic ulcer disease.* http://www.cdc.gov/ncidod/dbmd/hpylori.htm

Centrella, M. (1994). Physician addiction and impairment—Current thinking: A review. *Journal of Addictive Diseases, 13* (1): 91–105.

Chakraborty, R., Little, M. P., & Sankaranarayanan, K. (1998). Cancer predisposition, radiosensitivity and the risk of radiation-induced cancers. IV. Prediction of risks in relatives of cancer-predisposed individuals. *Radiation Research, 149,* 493–507.

Chamberlain, P., & Rosicky, J. G. (1995). The effectiveness of family therapy in the treatment of adolescents with conduct disorders and delinquency. *Journal of Marital and Family Therapy, 21,* 441–59.

Chambers, D. L. (1972). Alternatives to civil commitment of the mentally ill: Practical guides and constitutional imperatives. *Michigan Law Review, 70B,* 1107–1200.

Chan, G. C., Hinds, T. R., Impey, S., & Storm, D. R. (1998). Hippocampal neurotoxicity of Delta-sup-9-tetrahydrocannabinol. *Journal of Neuroscience, 18,* 5322–32.

Chandler, J., & Winokur, G. (1989). How antipsychotic are antipsychotics? A clinical study of the subjective antipsychotic effect of the antipsychotics in chronic schizophrenia. *Annals of Clinical Psychiatry, 1,* 215–20.

Chang, J., Zhang, L., Janak, P. H., & Woodward, D. J. (1997). Neuronal responses in prefrontal cortex and nucleus accumbens during heroin self-administration in freely moving rats. *Brain Research, 754,* 12–20.

Chapin, K. J., Rosenbaum, G., Fields, R. B., & Wightman, L. H. (1996). Multiple deficit theory of schizophrenia: Incidence of markers vs. symptoms. *Journal of Clinical Psychology, 52,* 109–23.

Chapman, L. J., & Chapman, D. T. (1969). Illusory correlations as an obstacle to the use of valid psychodiagnostic signs. *Journal of Abnormal Psychology, 74,* 271–80.

Chapman, L. J., & Chapman, J. P. (1973). *Disordered thought in schizophrenia.* New York: Appleton-Century-Crofts.

Chapman, L. J., & Taylor, J. A. (1957). Breadth of deviate concepts used by schizophrenics. *Journal of Abnormal Social Psychology, 54,* 118–23.

Charman, T., Swettenham, J., Baron-Cohen, S., Cox, A., Baird, G., & Drew, A. (1998). An experimental investigation of social-cognitive abilities in infants with autism: Clinical implications. *Infant Mental Health Journal, 19,* 260–75.

Charney, D. S., & Heninger, G. R. (1985). Noradrenergic function and the mechanism of action of antianxiety treatment: The effect of long-term imipramine treatment. *Archives of General Psychiatry, 42,* 473–81.

Charney, D. S., & Heninger, G. R. (1986). Abnormal regulation of noradrenergic function in panic disorders: Effects of clonidine in healthy subjects and patients with agoraphobia and panic disorder. *Archives of General Psychiatry, 43* (11): 1042–54.

Chengappa, K. N., Ebeling, T., Kang, J., Levine, J., & Parepally, H. (1999). Clozapine reduces severe self-mutilation and aggression in psychotic patients with borderline personality disorder. *Journal of Clinical Psychiatry, 60,* 477–84.

Cherry, C., & Sayers, B. McA. (1956). Experiments upon the total inhibition of stammering by external control and some clinical results. *Journal of Psychosomatic Research, 1,* 233.

Cheseldine, S., & McConkey, R. (1979). Parental speech to young Down's syndrome children: An intervention study. *American Journal of Mental Deficiency, 83,* 612–20.

Chin, J. H., & Goldstein, D. B. (1977). Drug tolerance in biomembranes: A spin label study of the effects of ethanol. *Science, 196,* 684–85.

Chinn, P. C., Drew, C. J., & Logan, D. R. (1979). *Mental retardation: A life cycle approach* (2nd ed.). St. Louis: Mosby.

Chodoff, P. (1974). The diagnosis of hysteria: An overview. *American Journal of Psychiatry, 131,* 1073–78.

Christensen, H., Jorm, A. F., Mackinnon, A. J., Korten, A. E., Jacomb, P. A., Henderson, A. S., & Rodgers, B. (1999). Age differences in depression and anxiety symptoms: A structural Equation modelling analysis of data from a general population sample. *Psychological Medicine, 29,* 325–39.

Christiansen, K. (1977). A review of studies of criminality among twins. In S. Mednick and K. Christiansen (Eds.), *Biosocial bases of criminal behavior.* New York: Gardner.

Christophersen, E. R., & Finney, J. W. (1999). Oppositional defiant disorder. In R. T. Ammerman & M. Hersen (Eds.), *Handbook of prescriptive treatments for children and adolescents* (2nd ed., pp. 102–13). Boston: Allyn & Bacon.

Chrousos, G. P., McCarty, R., Pecak, K., Cizza, G., Sternberg, E., Gold, P. W., & Kvetnansky, R. (Eds.). (1995). *Stress: Basic mechanisms and clinical implications* (Annals of the New York Academy of Sciences, Vol. 771). New York: New York Academy of Sciences.

Chugani, D. C., Muzik, O., Rothermel, R., Behen, M., Chakraborty, P., Mangner, T., da Silva, E. A., & Chugani, H. T. (1997). Altered serotonin synthesis in the dentatothalamocortical pathway in autistic boys. *Annals of Neurology, 42,* 666–69.

Chugani, H. T. (1994). Development of brain glucose metabolism in relation to behavior and plasticity. In G. Dawson, K. W. Fischer, et al. (Eds.), *Human behavior and the developing brain* (pp. 176–206). New York: Guilford Press.

Ciaranello, A. L., & Ciaranello, R. D. (1995). The neurobiology of infantile autism. *Annual Review of Neuroscience, 18,* 101–28.

Cicchetti, D., & Rogosch, F. A. (1999). Psychopathology as risk for adolescent substance use disorders: A developmental psychopathology perspective. *Journal of Clinical Child Psychology, 28* (3): 355–65.

Clark, D. A., Beck, A. T., & Beck, J. S. (1994). Symptom differences in major depression, dysthymia, panic disorder, and generalized anxiety disorder. *American Journal of Psychiatry, 151* (2): 205–209.

Clark, D. B., Lesnick, L., & Hegedus, A. M. (1997). Traumas and other adverse life events in adolescents with alcohol use and dependence. *Journal of the American Academy of Child and Adolescent Psychiatry, 36,* 1744–51.

Clark, D. M. (1988). A cognitive model of panic attacks. In S. Rachman & J. D. Maser (Eds.), *Panic: Psychological perspectives.* Hillsdale, NJ: Erlbaum.

Clark, D. (1989). Anxiety states: Panic and generalized anxiety. In K. Hawton, P. Salkovskis, J. Kirk, & D. Clark (Eds.), *Cognitive behaviour therapy for psychiatric problems: A practical guide.* Oxford, England: Oxford University Press.

Clark, D. M. (1999). Anxiety disorders: Why they persist and how to treat them. *Behaviour Research and Therapy, 37* (Suppl 1): S5–S27.

Clark, D., Gelder, M., Salkovskis, P., Hackman, A., Middleton, H., & Anatasiades, A. (1990). *Cognitive therapy for panic: Comparative efficacy.* Presented at the annual meeting of the American Psychiatric Association, New York, May 15, 1990.

Clark, L. A. (1999). Dimensional approaches to personality disorder assessment and diagnosis. In C. Cloninger (Ed.), *Personality and psychopathology.* Washington, DC: American Psychiatric Press.

Clark, L. A., Livesley, W. J., & Morey, L. (1997). Personality disorder assessment: The challenge of construct validity. *Journal of Personality Disorders, 11* (3): 205–31.

Clark, L. A., Livesley, W. J., Schroeder, M. L., & Irish, S. L. (1996). Convergence of two systems for assessing specific traits of personality disorder. *Psychological Assessment, 8*(3): 294–303.

Clark, R. E. (1948). The relationship of schizophrenia to occupational income and occupational prestige. *American Sociological Review, 13,* 325–30.

Clarke, G. N., Hawkins, W., Murphy, M. & Sheeber, L. (1993). School-based primary prevention of depressive symptomatology in adolescents: Findings from two studies. *Journal of Adolescent Research, 8*(2): 183–204.

Clarke, G. N., Hawkins, W., Murphy, M., Sheeber, L. B., et al. (1995). Targeted prevention of unipolar depressive disorder in an at-risk sample of high school adolescents: A randomized trial of group cognitive intervention. *Journal of the American Academy of Child and Adolescent Psychiatry, 34* (3): 312–21.

Clarkin, J. F., Yeomans, F. E., & Kernberg, O. F. (1999). Psychotherapy for borderline personality. New York: Wiley.

Clausen, J. A., & Kohn, M. L. (1959). Relation of schizophrenia to the social structure of a small city. In B. Pasamanick (Ed.), *Epidemiology of mental disorder.* Washington, DC: American Association for the Advancement of Science.

Cleckley, H. (1964). *The mask of sanity.* St. Louis: Mosby.

Clementz, B. A., Sweeney, J. A., Hirt, M., & Haas, G. (1990). Pursuit gain and saccadic intrusions in first-degree relatives of probands with schizophrenia. *Journal of Abnormal Psychology, 99*(4): 327–35.

Clomipramine Collaborative Study Group. (1991). Clomipramine in the treatment of obsessive-compulsive disorder. *Archives of General Psychiatry, 48,* 730–38.

Cloninger, C. R. (1987). Neurogenic adaptive mechanisms in alcoholism. *Science, 236.*

Cloninger, C. R. (1998). The genetics and psychobiology of the seven-factor model of personality. In K. R. Silk (Ed.), *Biology of personality disorders: Review of psychiatry series* (pp. 63–92). Washington, DC: American Psychiatric Press.

Cloninger, C. R. (1999). *Personality and psychopathology.* Washington, DC: American Psychiatric Press.

Cloninger, C. R., Bayon, C., & Przybeck, T. R. (1997). Epidemiology and Axis I comorbidity of antisocial personality. In D. M. Stoff, J. Breiling, & J. D. Maser (Eds.), *Handbook of antisocial behavior* (pp. 12–21). New York: Wiley.

Cloninger, C. R., & Gottesman, I. I. (1987). Genetic and environmental factors in antisocial behavior disorders. In S. A. Mednick, T. E. Moffitt, & S. A. Strack (Eds.), *The causes of crime: New biological approaches.* Cambridge: Cambridge University Press.

Cloninger, C. R., Martin, R. L., Guze, S. B., & Clayton, P. J. (1986). A prospective follow-up and family study of somatization in men and women. *American Journal of Psychiatry, 143,* 873–78.

Cloninger, C. R., Reich, T., & Guze, S. B. (1975). The multifactorial model of disease transmission. II. Sex differences in familial transmission of sociopathy (antisocial personality). *British Journal of Psychiatry, 127,* 11–22.

Cloninger, C. R., Sigvardsson, S., von Knorring, A., & Bohman, M. (1984). An adoption study of somatoform disorders: II. Identification of two discrete somatoform disorders. *Archives of General Psychiatry, 41,* 863–71.

Cloninger, C. R., von Knorring, A. L., Sigvardsson, S., & Bohman, M. (1986). Symptom patterns and causes of somatization in men: II. Genetic and environmental independence from somatization in women. *Genetic Epidemiology, 3,* 171–85.

Cobb, L. A., Thomas, G. I., Dillard, D. H., Merendino, K. A., & Bruce, R. A. (1959). An evaluation of internal-mammary-artery ligation by a double-blind technic. *New England Journal of Medicine, 260,* 1115–18.

Cobb, S., & Rose, R. M. (1973). Hypertension, peptic ulcer and diabetes and the traffic controllers. *Journal of the American Medical Association, 224,* 489–92.

Coccaro, E. F. (1998). Clinical outcome of psychopharmacologic treatment of borderline and schizotypal personality disordered subjects. *Journal of Clinical Psychiatry, 59,* 30–35.

Coccaro E. F., Silverman, J. M., Klar, H. M., Horvath, T. B., & Siever, L. J. (1994). Familial correlates of reduced central serotonergic system function in patients with personality disorders. *Archives of General Psychiatry, 51,* 318–24.

Cohen, C. I. (1993). Poverty and the course of schizophrenia: Implications for research and policy. *Hospital and Community Psychiatry, 44,* 951–58.

Cohen, D., & Strayer, J. (1996). Empathy in conduct-disordered and comparison youth. *Developmental Psychology, 32,* 988–98.

Cohen, D. J., & Volkmar, F. R. (Eds.). (1997). *Autism and pervasive developmental disorders: A handbook.* New York: Wiley.

Cohen, I. (1970). The benzodiazepines. In F. J. Ayd & H. Blackwell (Eds.), *Discoveries in biological psychiatry.* Philadelphia: Lippincott.

Cohen, J. B., & Reed, D. (1985). The Type A behavior pattern and coronary heart disease among Japanese men in Hawaii. *Journal of Behavioral Medicine, 8* (4): 343–52.

Cohen, N. (1997). Treatment compliance in schizophrenia: Issues for the therapeutic alliance and public mental health. In B. Blackwell et al. (Eds.), *Treatment compliance and the therapeutic alliance.* (Chronic mental illness, Vol. 5; pp. 239–50). Singapore: Harwood.

Cohen, P., & Hesselbart, C.S. (1993). Demographic factors in the use of children's mental health services. *American Journal of Public Health, 83* (1): 49–52.

Cohen, P., Slomkowski, C., & Robins, L. N. (1999). *Historical and geographical influences on psychopathology.* Mahwah, NJ: Lawrence Erlbaum.

Cohen, R. J., Swerdlik, M. E., & Smith, D. K. (1992). *Psychological testing and assessment: An introduction to test and measurement* (2nd ed.). Mountain View, CA: Mayfield Publishing Company.

Cohen, S., Doyle, W. J., Skoner, D. P., Fireman, P., Gwaltney Jr., J. M., & Newsom, J. T. (1995). State and trait negative affect as predictors of objective and subjective symptoms of respiratory viral infections. *Journal of Personality and Social Psychology, 68* (1): 159–69.

Cohen, S., Frank, E., Doyle, W. J., Skoner, D. P., Rabin, B. S., & Gwaltney, J. M., Jr. (1998). Types of stressors that increase susceptibility to the common cold in healthy adults. *Health Psychology, 17* (3): 214–23.

Cohen, S., Tyrrell, D., & Smith, A. (1993). Negative life events, perceived stress, negative affect, and susceptibility to the common cold. *Journal of Personality and Social Psychology, 64,* 131–40.

Cohen-Kettenis, P. T., & Van Goozen, S. H. M. (1997). Sex reassignment of adolescent transsexuals: A follow-up study. *Journal of American Academy of Child and Adolescent Psychiatry, 36*(2): 263–71.

Coie, J. D., & Kupersmidt, J. B. (1983). A behavioral analysis of emerging social status in boys' groups. *Child Development, 54,* 1400–16.

Coie, J., Terry, R., Lenox, K., & Lochman, J. (1995). Childhood peer rejection and aggression as predictors of stable patterns of adolescent disorder. *Development and Psychopathology, 7,* 697–713.

Colapinto, J. (2000). *As nature made him.* New York: Harper-Collins.

Collins, K. (2000). Gene therapy: FDA and NIH roll out new monitoring rules. *Contra Costa Times, Politics and Policy,* March 8.

Coltheart, M. (1985). Cognitive neuropsychology and the study of reading. In M. I. Posner & O. S. M. Marin (Eds.), *Attention and performance XI.* Hillsdale, NJ: Erlbaum.

Compas, B. E., Haaga, D. A. F., Keefe, F. J., Leitenberg, H., & Williams, D. A. (1998). Sampling of empirically supported psychological treatments from health psychology: Smoking, chronic pain, cancer, and bulimia nervosa. *Journal of Consulting and Clinical Psychology, 66* (1): 89–112.

Compton, W. M., Helzer, J. E., Hwu, H., Yeh, E., McEvoy, L., Tipp, J. E., & Spitznagel, E. L. (1991). New methods in cross-cultural psychiatry: Psychiatric illness in Taiwan and the United States. *American Journal of Psychiatry, 148* (12): 1697–1704.

Conduct Problems Prevention Research Group. (1999). Initial impact of the Fast-Track Prevention Trial for Conduct Problems: I. The high risk sample. *Journal of Clinical and Consulting Psychology, 67* (5): 631–47.

Consumer Reports (1995). Mental health: Does therapy help? *Consumer Reports,* November, 734–39.

Conture, E. G. (1996). Treatment efficacy: Stuttering. *Journal of Speech and Hearing Research, 39,* S18–S26.

Conway, C. R., & Steffens, D. C. (1999). Geriatric depression: Further evidence for the "vascular depression" hypothesis. *Current Opinion in Psychiatry, 12,* 463–70.

Cook, W. W., & Medley, D. M. (1954). Proposed hostility and pharisaic-virtue scales for the MMPI. *Journal of Applied Psychology, 38,* 414–18.

Coons, P. M. (1994). Confirmation of childhood abuse in child and adolescent cases of multiple personality disorder and dissociative disorder not otherwise specified. *Journal of Nervous and Mental Disease, 182* (8): 461–64.

Coons, P. M. (1998). The dissociative disorders. Rarely considered and underdiagnosed. *Psychiatric Clinics of North America, 21*(3):637–48.

Coons, P., Bowman, E., Pellow, T., & Schneider, P. (1989). Post-traumatic aspects of the treatment of victims of sexual abuse and incest. *Psychiatric Clinics of North America, 12,* 325–35.

Cooper, G. (1988). The safety of fluoxetine—An update. *British Journal of Psychiatry, 153,* 77–86.

Cooper, M. J., Todd, G., & Wells, A. (1998). Content, origins, and consequences of dysfunctional beliefs in anorexia nervosa and bulimia nervosa. *Journal of Cognitive Psychotherapy, 12,* 213–30.

Cooper, S. J., & Kirkham, T. C. (1993). Opioid mechanisms in the control of food consumption and taste preferences. In A. Herz (Ed.), *Handbook of experimental pharmacology,* 104/II (pp. 239–62). Berlin: Springer-Verlag.

Copeland, J. R. M., Dewey, M. E., Scott, A., Gilmore, C., Larkin, B. A., Cleave, N., McCracken, C. F. M., & McKibbin, P. E. (1998). Schizophrenia and delusional disorder in old age: Community prevalence, incidence, comorbidity, and outcome. *Schizophrenia Bulletin, 24,* 153–61.

Corcoran, R., Cahill, C., & Frith, C. D. (1997). The appreciation of visual jokes in people with schizophrenia: A study of "mentalizing" ability. *Schizophrenia Research, 24,* 319–27.

Corder, E. H., Saunders, A. M., Strittmatter, W. J., et al. (1993). Gene dose of apolipoprotein E type 4 allele and the risk of Alzheimer's disease in late onset families. *Science, 261,* 921–23.

Corey, G., Corey, M. S., & Callanan, P. (1998). *Issues and ethics in the helping professions.* Pacific Grove, CA: Brooks/Cole.

Cornblatt, B., & Obuchowski, M. (1997). Update of high-risk research: 1987–1997. *International Review of Psychiatry, 9,* 437–47.

Cornblatt, B., Obuchowski, M., Schnur, D. B., & O'Brien, J. (1997). Attention and clinical symptoms in schizophrenia. Schizophrenia Research, 17, 257–65.

Cornell Law. (2000). http://www.law.cornell.edu/background/insane/capacity.html

Corrigan, P. W., Hirschbeck, J. N., & Wolfe, M. (1995). Memory and vigilance training to improve social perception in schizophrenia. Schizophrenia Research, 17, 257–65.

Corrigall, W. A., & Coen, K. A. (1991). Selective dopamine antagonists reduce nicotine self-administration. *Psychopharmacology, 104,* 171–76.

Coryell, W., Scheftner, W., Keller, M., Endicott, J., et al. (1993). The enduring psychosocial consequences of mania and depression. *American Journal of Psychiatry, 150* (5): 720–27.

Costa, P., & Widiger, T. (1994). *Personality disorders and the five-factor model of personality.* Washington, DC: American Psychological Association.

Costantino, G., & Malgady, R. (1983). Verbal fluency of Hispanic, Black and White children on TAT and TEMAS, a new thematic apperception test. *Hispanic Journal of Behavioral Sciences, 5* (2), 199–206.

Costello, C. G. (1972). Depression: Loss of reinforcers or loss of reinforcer effectiveness. *Behavior Therapy, 3,* 240–47.

Costello, C. (1982). Fears and phobias in women: A community study. *Journal of Abnormal Psychology, 91,* 280–86.

Cottler, L. B., Price, R. K., Compton, W. M., & Mager, D. E. (1995). Subtypes of adult antisocial personality behavior among drug abusers. *Journal of Nervous and Mental Disease, 183* (3): 154–61.

Cotton, N. S. (1979). The familial incidence of alcoholism: A review. *Journal of Studies on Alcohol, 40,* 89–116.

Cottraux, J., & Gerard, D. (1998). Neuroimaging and neuroanatomical issues in obsessive-compulsive disorder: Toward an integrative model—perceived impulsivity. In R. P. Swinson & M. M. Antony (Eds.), *Obsessive-compulsive disorder: Theory, research, and treatment* (pp. 154–80). New York: Guilford Press.

Courchesne, E., Townsend, J., & Saitoh, O. (1994). The brain in infantile autism: Posterior fossa structures are abnormal. *Neurology, 44,* 214–23.

Cowley, D. S. (1992). Alcohol abuse, substance abuse, and panic disorders. *American Journal of Medicine, 92,* 41–48.

Cox, P., Hallam, R., O'Connor, K., & Rachman, S. (1983). An experimental analysis of fearlessness and courage. *British Journal of Psychology, 74,* 107–17.

Coyle, J. T., Price, D. L., & DeLong, M. R. (1983). Alzheimer's disease: A disorder of cortical cholinergic innervation. *Science, 219,* 1184–90.

Crabbe, J. C., Belknap, J. K., & Buck, K. J. (1994). Genetic animal models of alcohol and drug abuse. *Science, 264,* 1715–23.

Craighead, W. E., Craighead, L. W., & Ilardi, S. S. (1998). Psychosocial treatments for major depressive disorder. In P. E. Nathan & J. M. Gorman (Eds.), *A guide to treatments that work* (pp. 226–39). New York: Oxford University Press.

Craighead, W. E., Miklowitz, D., & Vajk, F. (1998). Psychosocial treatments for bipolar disorder. In P. Nathan & J. Gorman (Eds.), *A guide to treatments that work.* New York: Oxford University Press.

Cramer, P. (1999). Future directions for the Thematic Apperception Test. *Journal of Personality Assessment, 72*(1): 74–92.

Craske, M. G., Maidenberg, E., & Bystritsky, A. (1995). Brief depression: Overview, clinical efficacy, and future directions. *Clinical Psychology: Science and Practice, 2* (4): 349–69.

Crisp, A. H. (1980). *Anorexia nervosa—Let me be.* New York: Plenum.

Crits-Cristoph, P. (1992). The efficacy of brief psychotherapy: A meta-analysis. *American Journal of Psychiatry, 149* (2): 151–57.

Crits-Christoph, P. (1998). Psychosocial treatments for personality disorder. In P. Nathan & J. Gorman (Eds.), *A guide to treatments that work* (pp. 544–53). New York: Oxford University Press.

Crits-Christoph, P., & Siqueland, L. (1996). Psychosocial treatment for drug abuse: Selected review and recommendations for national health care. *Archives of General Psychiatry, 53,* 749–56.

Crittenden, P. M., & Ainsworth, M. D. S. (1989). Child maltreatment and attachment theory. In D. Chichetti & V. Carlson (Eds.), *Child maltreatment* (pp. 432–63). Cambridge: Cambridge University Press.

Cromwell, R. L. (1993). Searching for the origins of schizophrenia. *Psychological Science, 4,* 276–79.

Cross-National Collaborative Group. (1992). The changing rate of major depression. Cross-national comparisons. *Journal of the American Medical Association, 268* (21): 3098–3105.

Crow, T. J. (1980). Molecular pathology of schizophrenia: More than one disease process? *British Medical Journal, 280,* 66–68.

Crow, T. J. (1982). Two dimensions of pathology in schizophrenia: Dopaminergic and non-dopaminergic. *Psychopharmacology Bulletin, 18,* 22–29.

Crow, T. J. (1985). The two-syndrome concept: Origins and current status. *Schizophrenia Bulletin, 11* (3): 471–85.

Crow, T. J. (1997). Schizophrenia as a failure of hemispheric dominance for language. *Trends in Neurosciences, 20,* 339–43.

Crow, Y. J., & Tolmie, J. L. (1998). Recurrence risks in mental retardation. *Journal of Medical Genetics, 35,* 177–82.

Crowe, M. J., Marks, I. M., Agras, W. S., & Leitenberg, H. (1972). Time limited desensitization, implosion and shaping for phobic patients: A crossover study. *Behaviour Research and Therapy, 10*(4): 319–28.

Crowe, R. (1990). Panic disorder: Genetic considerations. *Journal of Psychiatric Researchers, 24,* 129–34.

Crowe, R. R., Noyes, R., Samuelson, S., Wesner, R. B, et al. (1990). Close linkage between panic disorder and !a-haptoglobin excluded in 10 families. *Archives of General Psychiatry, 47* (4): 377–80.

Csikszentmihalyi, M. (1990). *Flow: The psychology of optimal experience.* New York: Harper & Row.

Csikszentmihalyi, M. (1993). *The evolving self.* New York: HarperCollins.

Cui, X. J., & Vaillant G. E. (1996). Antecedents and consequences of negative life events in adulthood: A longitudinal study. *American Journal of Psychiatry, 153* (1): 21–26.

Culhane, D. P., Avery, J. M., & Hadley, T. R. (1998). Prevalence of treated behavioral disorders among adult shelter users: A longitudinal study. *American Journal of Orthopsychiatry, 68,* 63–72.

Cunningham, J. D. (1989). *Human biology,* (2nd ed.). New York: Harper & Row.

Cureton, E. E., Cronbach, L. J., Meehl, P. E., Ebel, R. L. et al. (1996). Validity. In A.W. Ward & H.W. Stoker (Eds.), *Educational measurement: Origins, theories, and explications, Vol. 1: Basic concepts and theories* (pp. 125–243). Lanham, MD,: University Press of America.

Curran, H. V. (1994). Forgetting your troubles? Effects of anti-anxiety treatments upon human memory. In L. J. Fitten (Ed.), *Facts and research in gerontology: Dementia and cognitive impairments.* (Facts and research in gerontology, Supplement; pp. 111–19). New York: Springer.

Curtis, B. A., Jacobson, S., & Marcus, E. M. (1972). *An introduction to the neurosciences.* Philadelphia: Saunders.

Cutler, S., & Nolen-Hoeksema, S. (1991). Accounting for sex differences in depression through female victimization: Childhood sexual abuse. *Sex Roles, 24,* 425–38.

Cytryn, L., & McKnew, D. H. (1972). Proposed classification of childhood depression. *American Journal of Psychiatry, 129,* 149–55.

Cytryn, L., & McKnew, D.H. (1996*). Growing up sad: Childhood depression and its treatment.* New York: Norton.

Dacey, C. M., Nelson, W. M. III, & Stoeckel, J. (1999). Reliability, criterion-related validity and qualitative comments of the Fourth Edition of the Stanford-Binet Intelligence Scale with a young adult population with intellectual disability. *Journal of Intellectual Disability Research, 43,* 179–84.

Dadds, M. R., Holland, D. E., Laurens, K. R., Mullins, M., Barrett, P. M., & Spence, S. H. (1999). Early intervention and prevention of anxiety disorders in children: Results at 2-year follow-up. *Journal of Consulting and Clinical Psychology, 67*(1): 145–50.

Dadds, M. R., Spence, S. H., Holland, D. E., Barrett, P.M., & Laurens, K. R. (1997). Prevention and early intervention for anxiety disorders: A controlled trial. *Journal of Consulting and Clinical Psychology, 65* (4): 627–35.

Dalack, G. W., Healy, D. J., & Meador-Woodruff, J. H. (1998). Nicotine dependence in schizophrenia: Clinical phenomena and laboratory findings. *American Journal of Psychiatry, 155,* 1490–1501.

Dale, L. C., Hurt, R. D., Offord, K. P., Lawson, G. M., Croghan, I. T., & Schroeder, D. R. (1995). High-dose nicotine patch therapy: Percentage of replacement and smoking cessation. *Journal of the American Medical Association, 274* (17): 1353–58.

Damasio, A. (1994). Descartes' error: Emotion, reason, and the human brain. New York: Grosset/Putnam.

Damasio, A. R., Tranel, D., & Damasio, H. C. (1990). Individuals with sociopathic behavior caused by frontal damage fail to respond autonomically to social stimuli. *Behavioral Brain Research, 41,* 81–94.

Damasio, H., Grabowski, T., Frank, R., Galaburda, A. M., & Damasio, A. R. (1994). The return of Phineas Gage: Clues about the brain from the skull of a famous patient. *Science, 264,* 1102–1105.

Daryanani, H. E., Santolaria, F. J., Reimers, E. G., Jorge, J. A., Lopez, N. B., Hernandez, F. M., Riera, A. M., & Rodriguez, E. R. Alcoholic withdrawal syndrome and seizures. *Alcohol and Alcoholism, 29* (3): 323–28.

Das, M. K., Kulhara, P. L., & Verma, S. K. (1997). Life events preceding relapse of schizophrenia. *International Journal of Social Psychiatry, 43,* 56–63.

Da Silva, P., & Marks, M. (1999). The role of traumatic experience in the genesis of obsessive-compulsive disorder. *Behaviour Research and Therapy, 37,* 941–52.

Davenport, H. W. (1972). Why the stomach does not digest itself. *Scientific American, 226,* 86–92.

Davidoff, S. A., Forester, B. P., Ghaemi, S. N., & Bodkin, J. A. (1998). Effect of video self-observation on development of insight on psychotic disorders. *Journal of Nervous and Mental Disease, 186,* 697–700.

Davidson, J., Kudler, H., Smith, R., et al. (1990). Treatment of PTSD with amitriptyline and placebo. *Archives of General Psychiatry, 47,* 250–60.

Davidson, R. J. (1998). Affective style and affective disorders: Perspectives from affective neuroscience. *Cognition and Emotion, 12* (5): 307–30.

Davidson, R. J. (1999). Biological bases of personality. In V. J. Derlega, B. A. Winstead, et al. (Eds.), *Personality: Contemporary theory and research.* (Nelson-Hall series in psychology, 2nd ed.; pp. 101–25). Chicago: Nelson-Hall.

Davidson, R. J., Schaffer, C. E., & Saron, C. (1985). Effects of lateralized presentations of faces on self-reports of emotion and EEG assymmetry in depressed and non-depressed subjects. *Psychophysiology, 22* (30): 353–64.

Davies, J. C. V., & Maliphant, R. (1971). Autonomic responses of male adolescents exhibiting refractory behavior in school. *Journal of Child Psychology and Psychiatry, 12,* 115–27.

Davis, J. O., & Bracha, H. S. (1996). Prenatal growth markers in schizophrenia: A monozygotic co-twin control study. *American Journal of Psychiatry, 153,* 1166–72.

Davis, P. H., & Osherson, A. (1977). The current treatment of a multiple-personality woman and her son. *American Journal of Psychotherapy, 31,* 504–15.

Davis, J. O., & Phelps, J. A. (1995). Twins with schizophrenia: Genes or germs? *Schizophrenia Bulletin, 21,* 13–18.

Davis, P. J., & Schwartz, G. E. (1987). Repression and the inaccessibility of affective memories. *Journal of Personality and Social Psychology, 51* (1): 155–62.

Davis, W. M., & Smith, S. G. (1976). Role of conditioned reinforcers in the initiation, maintenance and extinction of drug-seeking behavior. *Pavlovian Journal of Biological Sciences, 11,* 222–36.

Davison, G. C. (1976). Homosexuality: The ethical challenge. *Journal of Counseling and Clinical Psychology, 44,* 157–62.

Davison, G. C. (1978). Not can but ought: The treatment of homosexuality. *Journal of Consulting and Clinical Psychology, 46,* 170–72.

DeAngelis, T. (1990). Cambodians' sight loss tied to seeing atrocities. *APA Monitor,* July, pp. 36–37.

Deadwyler, S. A., & Hampson, R. E. (1997). The significance of neural ensemble codes during behavior and cognition. *Annual Review of Neuroscience, 20,* 217–44.

Deb, S., & Thompson, B. (1998). Neuroimaging in autism. *British Journal of Psychiatry, 173,* 299–302.

De Beurs, E., Beekman, A.T., Van Balkom, A. J., Deeg, D. J., Van Dyck, R., & Van Tilburg, W. (1999). Consequences of anxiety in older persons: Its effect on disability, well-being and use of health services. *Psychological Medicine 29* (3): 583–93.

De Beurs, E., Van Balkom, A. J., Anton, J. L. M., Lange, A., Koele, P., & Van Dyck, R. (1995). Treatment of panic disorder with agoraphobia: Comparison of fluvoxamine placebo, and psychological panic management combined with exposure and exposure in vivo alone. *American Journal of Psychiatry, 152* (5): 673–82.

De Beurs, E., Van Balkom, A. J., Lange, A., Koele, P., & Van Dyck, R. (1995). Treatment of panic disorder with agora-phobia: Comparison of fluvoxamine placebo, and psychologi-cal panic management combined with exposure and exposure in vivo alone. *American Journal of Psychiatry, 152* (5): 683–91.

de Bonis, M., Epelbaum, C., & Feline, A. (1992). Cognitive processing of contradictory statements: An experimental study of reasoning on proverbs in schizophrenia. *Psychopathology, 25,* 100–108.

de Craen, A. J., Moerman, D. E., Heisterkamp, S. H., Tytgat, G. N., Tijssen, J. G., & Kleijnen, J. (1999). Placebo effect in the treatment of duodenal ulcer. *British Journal of Clinical Pharmacology, 48,* 853–60.

de Craen, A. J., Tijssen, J. G., de Gans, J., & Kleijnen, J. (2000). Placebo effect in the acute treatment of migraine: Subcutaneous placebos are better than oral placebos. *Journal of Neurology, 247,* 183–88.

Deckel, A. W., Hesselbrock, V., & Bauer, L. (1996). Antisocial personality disorder, childhood delinquency, and frontal brain functioning: EEG and neuropsychological findings. *Journal of Clinical Psychology, 52,* 639–50.

DeGrandpre R. (1999). *Ritalin nation.* New York: Norton.

Dekker, E., Pelse, H., & Groen, J. (1957). Conditioning as a cause of asthmatic attacks: A laboratory study. *Journal of Psychosomatic Research, 2,* 97–108.

DeLisi, L. E. (1997). The genetics of schizophrenia: Past, pre-sent, and future concepts. *Schizophrenia Research, 28,* 163–75.

DeMartino, R., Mollica, R. F., & Wilk, V. (1995). Monoamine oxidase inhibitors in posttraumatic stress disor-der: Promise and problems in Indochinese survivors of trauma. *Journal of Nervous and Mental Disease, 183* (8): 510–15.

DeMeyer, M. K., Barton, S., Alpern, G. D., Kimberlin, C., Allen, J., Yang, E., & Steel, R. (1974). The measured intel-ligence of autistic children. *Journal of Autistic Children and Schizophrenia, 4,* 42–60.

Deneau, G., Yanagita, T., & Seevers, M. H. (1969). Self-administration of psychoactive substances by the monkey. *Psychopharmacologia (Berl.), 16,* 30–48.

Dennis, D. L., Buckner, J. C., Lipton, F. R., & Levine, I. S. (1991). A decade of research and services for homeless mentally ill persons: Where do we stand? *American Psychologist, 46,* 1129–38.

Department of Health and Human Services. (1999). *Mental health: A report of the Surgeon General.* Rockville, MD: U.S. Department of Health and Human Services, Substance Abuse and Mental Health Services Administration, Center for Mental Health Services, National Institute of Health, National Institute of Mental Health.

Department of International Economic and Social Affairs. (1985). *Demographic yearbook* (37th ed.). New York: United Nations.

Depue, R. H. (1979). *The psychobiology of the depressive disorders: Implications for the effect of stress.* New York: Academic Press.

Depue, R. H., & Monroe, S. (1978). The unipolar-bipolar distinction in depressive disorders. *Psychological Bulletin, 85,* 1001–29.

Depue, R. A., & Monroe, S. M. (1986). Conceptualization and measurement of human disorder in life stress research: The problem of chronic disturbance. *Psychological Bulletin, 99,* 36–51.

Dershowitz, A. M. (1968). Psychiatry in the legal process: "A knife that cuts both ways." *Trial, 4,* 29.

DeRubeis, R. J., Evans, M. D., Hollon, S. D., & Garvey, M. J. (1990). How does cognitive therapy work? Cognitive change and symptom change in cognitive therapy and phar-macotherapy for depression. *Journal of Consulting and Clinical Psychology, 58* (6): 862–69.

DeRubeis, R. J., Gelfand, L. A., Tang, T. Z., & Simons, A. D. (1999). Medications versus cognitive behavior therapy for severely depressed outpatients: Mega-analysis of four ran-domized comparisons. *American Journal of Psychiatry, 156* (7): 1007–13.

Des Jarlais, D. C., Paone, D., Friedman, S. R., Peyser, N., & Newman, R. G. (1995). Regulating controversial programs for unpopular people: Methadone maintenance and syringe exchange programs. American Journal of Public Health, 85(11):1577–84.

De Silva, P., Rachman, S., & Seligman, M. E. P. (1977). Prepared phobias and obsessions: Therapeutic outcome. *Behaviour Research and Therapy, 15* (1): 65–77.

Deutsch, A. (1949). *The mentally ill in America.* New York: Columbia University Press.

Devanand, D. P., Fitzsimons, L., Prudic, J., & Sackheim, H. A. (1995). Subjective side effects during electroconvulsive ther-apy. *Convulsive Therapy, 11* (4): 232–40.

Devanand, D. P., Sackheim, H., & Prudic, J. (1991). Electro-convulsive therapy in the treatment-resistant patient. *Electro-convulsive Therapy, 14,* 905–23.

Deveson, A. (1992). Tell me I'm here: One family's experi-ence of schizophrenia. New York: Penguin.

Diamond, B. L. (1974). Psychiatric prediction of dangerous-ness. *University of Pennsylvania Law Review, 123,* 439–52.

Diamond, E. L. (1982). The role of anger and hostility in essential hypertension and coronary heart disease. *Psychological Bulletin, 92,* 410–33.

Diamond, R. G., & Rozin, P. (1984). Activation of existing memories in anterograde amnesia. *Journal of Abnormal Psychology, 93,* 98–105.

DiChiara, G., & Imperato, A. (1988). Drugs abused by humans preferentially increase synaptic dopamine concen-tration in the mesolimbic system of freely moving rats. *Proceedings of the National Academy of Sciences, 85,* 5274–78.

Dick, L. P., Gallagher-Thompson, D., & Thompson, L. W. (1996). Cognitive-behavioral therapy. In R. T. Woods (Ed.), *Handbook of the clinical psychology of aging* (pp. 509–44). New York: Wiley.

Dickerson, F. B. (2000). Cognitive behavioral psychotherapy for schizophrenia: A review of recent empirical studies. *Schizophrenia Research, 43,* 71–90.

Dickey, C. C., McCarley, R. W., Voglmaier, M. M., Niznikiewicz, M. A., Seidman, L. J., Hirayasu, Y., Fischer, I., Teh, E. K., Van Rhoads, R., Jakab, M., Kikinis, R., Jolesz, F. A., & Shenton, M. E. (1999). Schizotypal personality disorder and MRI abnormalities of temporal lobe gray matter. *Biological Psychiatry, 45,* 1392–1402.

Diekstra, R. (1992). The prevention of suicidal behavior: Evidence for the efficacy of clinical and community-based programs. *International Journal of Mental Health, 21,* 69–87.

Dietz, P. E., Hazelwood, R. R., & Warren, J. (1990). The sexually sadistic criminal and his offenses. *Bulletin of the American Academy of Psychiatry and the Law, 18* (2): 163–78.

Dikmen, S. S., Heaton, R. K., Grant, I., & Temkin, N. R. (1999). Test-retest reliability and practice effects of Expanded Halstead-Reitan Neuropsychological Test Battery. *Journal of the International Neuropsychological Society, 5* (4): 346–56.

Dilip, J. V., Caligiuri, M. P., Paulsen, J. S., Heaton, R. K., Lacro, J. P., Harris, M. J., Bailey, A., Fell, R. L., & McAdams, L. A. (1995). Risk of tardive dyskinesia in older patients. *Archives of General Psychiatry, 52,* 756–65.

Dimeff, L. A., McDavid, J., & Linehan, M. M. (1999). Pharmacotherapy for borderline personality disorder: A review of the literature and recommendations for treatment. *Journal of Clinical Psychology in Medical Settings, 6,* 113–38.

Dimsdale, J. E., Pierce, C., Schoenfeld, D., Brown, A., Zusman, R., & Graham, R. (1986). Suppressed anger and blood pressure: The effects of race, sex, social class, obesity, and age. *Psychosomatic Medicine, 48,* 430–36.

Dishion, T. J., & Andrews, D. W. (1995). Preventing escalation in problem behaviors with high-risk young adolescents: Immediate and 1-year outcomes. *Journal of Consulting and Clinical Psychology, 63,* 538–48.

Dixon, L. B., Lehman, A. F., & Levine, J. (1995). Conventional antipsychotic medications for schizophrenia. *Schizophrenia Bulletin, 21*(4): 567–77.

Doane, J. A., Falloon, I. R. H., Goldstein, M. J., & Mintz, J. (1985). Parental affective style and the treatment of schizophrenia: Predicting the course of illness and social functioning. *Archives of General Psychiatry, 42,* 34–42.

Dodge, K. A. (1983). Behavioral antecedents of peer social status. *Child Development, 54,* 1386–99.

Dodge, K. A., & Schwartz, D. (1997). Social information processing mechanisms in aggressive behavior. In D. M. Stoff & J. Breiling (Eds.), *Handbook of antisocial behavior* (pp. 171–80). New York: Wiley.

Doering, S., Mueller, E., Koepcke, W., Pietzcker, A., Gaebel, W., Linden, M., Mueller, P., Mueller-Spahn, F., Tegeler, J., & Schuessler, G. (1998). Predictors of relapse and rehospitalization in schizophrenia and schizoaffective disorder. *Schizophrenia Bulletin, 24,* 87–98.

Dohrenwend, B. P., Levav, I., Shrout, P. E., Schwartz, S., Naveh, G., Link, B. G., Skodol, A. E., & Stueve, A. (1992). Socio-economic status and psychiatric disorders: The causation-selection issue. *Science, 255,* 946–52.

Dohrenwend, B. P., Levav, I., Shrout, P. E., Schwartz, S., Naveh, G., Link, B. G., Skodol, A. E., & Stueve, A. (1998). Ethnicity, socioeconomic status, and psychiatric disorders: A test of the social causation-social selection issue. In B. P. Dohrenwend et al. (Eds.), *Adversity, stress, and psychopathology* (pp. 285–318). New York: Oxford University Press.

Dohrenwend, B. S., & Martin, J. L. (1978, February). *Personal vs. situational determination of anticipation and control of the occurrence of stressful life events.* Paper presented at the annual meeting of AAAS, Washington, DC.

Dohrenwend, B. P., & Shrout, P. E. (1985). "Hassles" in the conceptualization and measurement of life stress variables. *American Psychologist, 40,* 780–85.

Dohrenwend, B. P., et al. (Eds.). (1998). *Adversity, stress, and psychopathology.* New York: Oxford University Press.

Dolberg, O. T., Iancu, I., Sasson, Y., & Zohar, J. (1996). The pathogenesis and treatment of obsessive-compulsive disorder. *Clinical Neuropharmacology, 19* (2): 129–47.

Dole, V. P. (1995). On federal regulation of methadone treatment. *Journal of the American Medical Association, 274* (16): 1307.

Dole, V. P., Nyswander, M. E., & Kreek, M. J. (1966). Narcotic blockade. *Archives of Internal Medicine, 118,* 304–309.

Doleys, D. M. (1979). Assessment and treatment of childhood enuresis. In A. J. Finch, Jr., & P. C. Kendall (Eds.), *Clinical treatment and research in child psychopathology* (pp. 207–33). New York: Spectrum.

Dollinger, S. J. (1985). Lightning-strike disaster among children. *British Journal of Medical Psychology, 58* (4): 375–83.

Dominguez, R. A., & Mestre, S. M. (1994). Management of treatment-refractory obsessive-compulsive patients. *Journal of Clinical Psychiatry, 55 (10):* 86–92.

Domino, E. F. (1999). Cannabonoids and the cholinergic system. In G. G. Nahas, K. M. Sutin, et al. (Eds.), *Marihuana and medicine* (pp. 223–26). Clifton, NJ: Humana.

Donaldson, D. (1976). *Insanity inside out.* New York: Crown.

Donaldson, S. I., Graham, J. W., Piccinin, A. M., & Hansen, W.B. (1995). Resistance-skills training and onset of alcohol use: Evidence for beneficial and potentially harmful effects in public schools and in private Catholic schools. *Health Psychology, 14* (4): 291–300.

Doorn, C. D., Poortinga, J., & Verschoor, A. M. (1994). Cross-gender identity in transvestites and male transsexuals. *Archives of Sexual Behavior, 23* (2): 185–201.

Dorsey, M. F., Iwata, B. A., Ong, P., & McSween, T. (1980). Treatment of self-injurious behavior using a water mist: Initial response suppression and generalization. *Journal of Applied Behavior Analysis, 13,* 343–53.

Douglas, M. (Ed.). (1970). *Witchcraft: Confessions and accusations.* London: Tavistock.

Douglas, V. I. (1983). Attentional and cognitive problems. In M. Rutter (Ed.), *Developmental neuropsychiatry* (pp. 280–329). New York: Guilford Press.

Drachman, D. A. (1997). Aging and the brain: a new frontier. Annals of Neurology, 42(6): 819–28.

Drake, R., & Vaillant, G. E. (1988). Predicting alcoholism and personality disorder in a 30-year longitudinal study of children of alcoholics. *British Journal of Addiction, 83,* 799–807.

Drewnowski, A., Hopkins, S. A., & Kessler, R. C. (1988). The prevalence of bulimia nervosa in the U.S. college student population. *American Journal of Public Health, 78* (10): 1322–25.

Driscoll, P., Escorihuela, R. M., Fernandez-Teruel, A., Giorgi, O., Schwegler, H., Steimer, T., Wiersma, A., Corda, M. G., Flint, J., Koolhaas, J. M., Langhans, W., Schulz, P. E., Siegel, J., & Tobena, A. (1998). Genetic selection and differential stress responses: The Roman lines/strains of rats. In P. Csermely et al. (Ed.), *Stress of life: From molecules to man* (Annals of the New York Academy of Sciences, Vol. 851; pp. 501–10). New York: New York Academy of Sciences.

Drossman, D. A. (1982). Patients with psychogenic abdominal pain: Six years' observation in the medical setting. *American Journal of Psychiatry, 139,* 1549–57.

Droungas, A., Ehrman, R. N., Childress, A. R., & O'Brien, C. P. (1995). Effect of smoking cues and cigarette availability on craving and smoking behavior. *Addictive Behaviors, 20* (5): 657–73.

DuBois, D. L., Felner, R. D., Bartels, C. L., & Silverman, M. M. (1995). Stability of self-reported depressive symptoms in a community sample of children and adolescents. *Journal of Clinical Child Psychology, 24* (4): 386–96.

Duchan, J. F. (1999). Views of facilitated communication: What's the point? *Language, Speech and Hearing Services in the Schools, 30*(4): 401–407.

Dulawa, S. C., Hen, R., Scearce-Levie, K., & Geyer, M. A. (1997). Serotonin-sub(1B) receptor modulation of startle reactivity, habituation, and prepulse inhibition in wild-type and serotonin-sub(1B) knockout mice. *Psychopharmacology, 132,* 125–34.

Dunmore, E., Clark, D. M., & Ehlers, A. (1999). Cognitive factors involved in the onset and maintenance of posttraumatic stress disorder (PTSD) after physical or sexual assault. *Behaviour Research and Therapy, 37*(9): 809–29.

Dunner, D. L., Gershom, E. S., & Goodwin, F. K. (1976). Heritable factors in the severity of affective illness. *Biological Psychiatry, 11,* 31–42.

DuPaul, G. J., & Barkley, R. A. (1993). Behavioral contributions to pharmacotherapy: The utility of behavioral methodology in medication treatment of children with attention deficit hyperactivity disorder. *Behavior Therapy, 24,* 47–65.

DuPont, R. L., & McGovern J. P. (1994). *A bridge to recovery: An introduction to 12-step programs.* Washington, DC: American Psychiatric Press.

Dupree, L. W., & Schonfeld, L. (1999). Management of alcohol abuse in older adults. In M. Duffy (Ed.), *Handbook of counseling and psychotherapy with older adults* (pp. 632–49). New York: Wiley.

Durand, V. M., & Mapstone, E. (1999). Pervasive developmental disorders. In W. K. Silverman & T. H. Ollendick (Eds.), *Developmental issues in the clinical treatment of children* (pp. 307–17). Boston: Allyn & Bacon.

Durham, R. C., Murphy, T., Allan, T., Richard, K., et al. (1994). Cognitive therapy, analytic psychotherapy and anxiety management training for generalised anxiety disorder. *British Journal of Psychiatry, 165* (3): 315–23.

Eaker, E., Haynes, S., & Feinleib, M. (1983). Spouse behavior and coronary heart disease. *Activitas Nervosa Superior, 25,* 81–90.

Eaton, W. W., Neufeld, K., Chen, L. S., & Cai G. (2000). A comparison of self-report and clinical diagnostic interviews for depression: Diagnostic interview schedule and schedules for clinical assessment in neuropsychiatry in the Baltimore epidemiologic catchment area follow-up. *Archives of General Psychiatry, 57* (3): 217–22.

Eaves, L. J., Silberg, J. L., Maes, H. H., Simonoff, E., Pickles, A., Rutter, M., Neale, M. C., Reynolds, C. A., Erikson, M. T., Heath, A. C., Loeber, R., Truett, K. R., & Hewitt, J. K. (1997). Genetics and developmental psychopathology: 2. The main effects of genes and environment on behavioral problems in the Virginia Twin Study of Adolescent Behavioral Development. *Journal of Child Psychology and Psychiatry and Allied Disciplines, 38,* 965–80.

Eberhard, G. (1968). Personality in peptic ulcer: Preliminary report of a twin study. *Acta Psychiatrica Scandinavia, 203,* 131.

Edelbrock, C., Rende, R., Plomin, R., & Thompson, L. A. (1995). A twin study of competence and problem behavior in childhood and early adolescence. *Journal of Child Psychology and Psychiatry, 36* (5): 775–85.

Edelmann, R. J. (1992). *Anxiety: Theory, research, and intervention in clinical and health psychology.* Chinchester, England: Wiley.

Edwards, G., Arif, A., & Hodgson, R. (1981). Nomenclature and classification of drug- and alcohol-related problems: A WHO memorandum. *Bulletin of the World Health Organization, 59,* 225–42.

Edwards-Hewitt, T., & Gray, J. J. (1993). The prevalence of disordered eating attitudes and behaviours in Black-American and White-American college women: Ethnic, regional, class, and media differences. *European Eating Disorders Review, 1,* 41–54.

Egeland, J. A., & Hostetter, A. M. (1983). Amish study: I. Affective disorders among the Amish, 1976–1980. *American Journal of Psychiatry, 140* (1), 56–61.

Egeland, J. A., & Sussex, J. N. (1985). Suicide and family loading for affective disorders. *Journal of the American Medical Association, 254,* 915–18.

Ehlers, A., & Breuer, P. (1992). Increased cardiac awareness in panic disorder. *Journal of Abnormal Psychology, 101* (3): 371–82.

Ehlers, A., & Clark, D. (2000). A cognitive model of posttraumatic stress disorder. *Behaviour Research and Therapy, 38,* 319–46.

Ehlers, C. L., & Schuckit, M. A. (1990). EEG fast frequency activity in the sons of alcoholics. *Biological Psychiatry, 27,* 631–41.

Eidelson, J. I. (1977). *Perceived control and psychopathology.* Unpublished doctoral dissertation, Duke University.

Einbinder, Z., & Robinson, M. (1946). Psychiatric care: Missing link in the community. *Hospitals, 20,* 73–74.

Eisen, A. R., Engler, L. B., & Geyer, B. (1998). Parent training for separation anxiety disorder. In J. M. Briesmeister & C. E. Schaefer (Eds.), *Handbook of parent training: Parents as co-therapists for children's behavior problems* (2nd ed.; pp. 205–24). New York: Wiley.

Eisenberg, V. H., & Schenker, J. G. (1997). Genetic engineering: Moral aspects and control of practice. *Journal of Assisted Reproduction and Genetics, 14* (6): 297–316.

Eisenmajer, R., Prior, M., Leekam, S., Wing, L., Ong, B., Gould, J., & Welham, M. (1998). Delayed language onset as a predictor of clinical symptoms in pervasive developmental disorders. *Journal of Autism and Developmental Disorders, 28,* 527–33.

Ekman, P., Friesen, W. V., & Ellsworth, P. (1972). *Emotion in the human face.* New York: Pergamon.

Ekselius, L., & von Knorring, L. (1999). Changes in personality traits during treatment with sertraline or citalopram. *British Journal of Psychiatry, 174,* 444–48.

Elashoff, J. D., & Grossman, M. I. (1980). Trends in hospital admissions and death rates for peptic ulcer in the United States from 1970 to 1978. *Gastroenterology, 78,* 280–85.

Elia, J., Ambrosini, P. J., & Rapoport, J. L. (1999). Drug therapy: Treatment of attention-deficit-hyperactivity disorder. *New England Journal of Medicine, 340,* 780–88.

Elkin, I., Parloff, M. B., Hadley, S. W., & Autry, J. H. (1985). NIMH Treatment of Depression Collaborative Research Program. *Archives of General Psychiatry, 42,* 305–16.

Elkin, I., Shea, T., Imber, S., Pilkonis, P., Sotsky, S., Glass, D., Watkins, J., Leber, W., & Collins, J. (1986). *NIMH Treatment of Depression Collaborative Research Program: Initial outcome findings.* Paper presented at meetings of the American Association for the Advancement of Science, May 1986.

Elkin, I., Shea, M. T., Watkins, J. T., Imber, S. D., Sotsky, S. M., Collins, J. F., Glass, D. R., Pilkonis, P. A., Leber, W. R., Docherty, J. P., Fiester, S. J., & Parloff, M. B. (1989). National Institutes of Mental Health Treatment of Depression Collaboration Research Program: General effectiveness of treatments. *Archives of General Psychiatry, 46* (11): 971–82.

Ellason, J. W., & Ross, C. A. (1997). Two-year follow-up of inpatients with dissociative disorder. *American Journal of Psychiatry, 154* (6): 832–39.

Ellenberger, H. F. (1970). *The discovery of the unconscious: The history and evolution of dynamic psychiatry.* New York: Basic Books.

Ellenbroek, B. A., van den Kroonenberg, P. T. J. M., & Cools, A. R. (1998). The effects of an early stressful life event on sensorimotor gating in adult rats. *Schizophrenia Research, 30,* 251–60.

Ellgring, J. H. (1999). Depression, psychosis, and dementia: Impact on the family. *Neurology, 52* (Supp. 3): S17–S20.

Ellickson, P. L. (1994). School-based drug prevention: What should it do? What has been done? In R. Coombs & D. Ziedonis (Eds.), *Handbook on drug abuse prevention.* Englewood Cliffs, NJ: Prentice-Hall.

Elliott, D. S., Hulzinga, D., & Ageton, S. S. (1985). *Explaining delinquency and drug use.* Beverly Hills, CA: Sage.

Elliott, S. N., & Gresham, F. M. (1993). Social skills interventions for children. *Behavior Modification, 17* (3): 287–313.

Ellis, A (1962). *Reason and emotion in psychotherapy.* New York: Lyle Stuart.

Ellis, L., & Ames, M. A. (1987). Neurohormonal functioning and sexual orientation: A theory of homosexuality-heterosexuality. *Psychological Bulletin, 101* (2): 233–58.

Ellsworth, P. C., & Carlsmith, M. J. (1968). Effects of eye contact and verbal content on affective response to dyadic interactions. *Journal of Personality and Social Psychology, 10,* 15–20.

Elmhorn, K. (1965). Study in self-reported delinquency among school children. In *Scandinavian studies in criminology.* London: Tavistock.

Emmelkamp, P., Hoekstra, R., & Visser, S. (1985). The behavioral treatment of obsessive-compulsive disorder: Prediction of outcome at 3.5 years follow-up. In P. Pichot, A. Brenner, R. Wolf, & K. Thau (Eds.), *Psychiatry: The state of the art* (Vol. 4). New York: Plenum.

Emmelkamp, P., & Kuipers, A. (1979). Agoraphobia: A follow-up study four years after treatment. *British Journal of Psychiatry, 134,* 352–55.

Emrick, D. C. (1982). Evaluation of alcoholism therapy methods. In E. M. Pattison & E. Kaufman (Eds.), *Encyclopedic handbook of alcoholism.* New York: Gardner Press.

Engdahl, B., Dikel, T. N., Eberly, R., & Blank, A., Jr. (1997). Posttraumatic stress disorder in a community group of former prisoners of war: A normative response to severe trauma. *American Journal of Psychiatry, 154* (11): 1576–81.

Enkelmann, R. (1991). Alprazolam versus busiprone in the treatment of outpatients with generalized anxiety disorder. *Psychophamacology, 105,* 428–32.

Ennis, B. J. (1972). *Prisoners of psychiatry: Mental patients, psychiatrists, and the law.* New York: Harcourt Brace Jovanovich.

Ennis, B. J., & Litwack, T. R. (1974). Psychiatry and the presumption of expertise: Flipping coins in the courtroom. *California Law Review, 62,* 693.

Epperson, C. N., Wisner, K. L., & Yamamoto, B. (1999). Gonadal steroids in the treatment of mood disorders. *Psychosomatic Medicine, 61,* 676–97.

Eppley, K., Abrams, A., & Shear, J. (1989). Differential effects of relaxation techniques on trait anxiety: A meta-analysis. *Journal of Clinical Psychology, 45,* 957–74.

Epstein, J. A., Botvin, G. J., Diaz, T., Toth, V., & Schinke, S. P. (1995). Social and personal factors in marijuana use and intentions to use drugs among inner city minority youth. *Developmental and Behavioral Pediatrics, 16* (1): 14–20.

Erickson, W. D., Walbek, N. H., & Seely, R. K. (1988). Behavior patterns of child molesters. *Archives of Sexual Behavior, 17*(1): 77–86.

Erikkson, H. (1995). Heart failure: A growing public health problem. *Journal of Internal Medicine, 237,* 135–41.

Erikson, K. (1976). *Everything in its path: Destruction and community in the Buffalo Creek flood.* New York: Simon & Schuster.

Erlenmeyer-Kimling, L., Squires-Wheeler, E., Adamo, U. H., Bassett, A. S., et al. (1995). The New York High-Risk Project. *Archives of General Psychiatry, 52,* 857–65.

Eslinger, P. J., & Damasio, A. R. (1985). Severe disturbance of higher cognition after bilateral frontal lobe ablation: Patient E.V.R. *Neurology, 35,* 1731–41.

Essen-Moller, E. (1970). Twenty-one psychiatric cases and their MZ cotwins: A thirty year follow-up. *Acta Geneticae Medicae et Gemelloligiae, 19,* 315–17.

Esterling, B. A., Kiecolt-Glaser, J. K., & Glaser, R. (1996). Psychosocial modulation of cytokine-induced natural killer cell activity in older adults. *Psychosomatic Medicine, 58,* 264–72.

Esteves, F., Parra, C., Dimberg, U., & Oehman, A. (1994). Nonconscious associative learning: Pavlovian conditioning of skin conductance responses to masked fear relevant facial stimuli. *Psychophysiology, 31* (4): 375–85.

Evans, D. L., Leserman, J., Perkins, D. O., Stern, R. A., Murphy, C., Tamul, K., Liao, D., Van der Horst, C. M.,

Hall, C. D., Folds, J. D., Golden, R. N., & Petitto, J. M. (1995). Stress-associated reductions of cytotoxic T lymphocytes and natural killer cells in asymptomatic HIV infection. *American Journal of Psychiatry, 152* (4): 543–50.

Evans, M. D., Hollon, S. D., DeRubeis, R. J., Piasecki, J. M., et al. (1992). Differential relapse following cognitive therapy and pharmacotherapy for depression. *Archives of General Psychiatry, 49* (10): 802–808.

Everson, S. A., Goldberg, D. E., Kaplan, G. A., Cohen, R. D., et al. (1996). Hopelessness and risk of mortality and incidence of myocardial infarction and cancer. *Psychosomatic Medicine, 58* (2): 113–21.

Everson, S. A., Kaplan, G. A., Goldberg, D. E., Salonen, R., & Salonen, J. T. (1997). Hopelessness and 4-year progression of carotid atherosclerosis. *Arteriosclerosis, Thrombosis, and Vascular Biology, 17* (8): 2–7.

Exline, R., & Winters, L. C. (1965). Affective relations and mutual glances in dyads. In S. Tomkins & C. E. Izard (Eds.), *Affect, cognition and personality.* New York: Springer.

Exner, J. E. (1978). *The Rorschach: A comprehensive system: Vol. 2. Current research and advanced interpretation.* New York: Wiley.

Exner, J. E. (1993). *The Rorschach: A comprehensive system. Vol. 3: Assessment of children and adolescents.* New York: Wiley.

Exner, J. E., Jr. (1999). The Rorschach: Measurement concepts and issues of validity. In S. E. Embretson & S. L. Hershberger (Eds.), *The new rules of measurement: What every psychologist and educator should know* (pp. 159–83). Mahwah, NJ: Lawrence Erlbaum.

Exner, J. E., & Weiner, I. B. (1994). *The Rorschach: A comprehensive system. Vol. 3: Assessment of children and adolescents.* New York: Wiley.

Eysenck, H. J. (1979). The conditioning model of neurosis. *Communications in Behavioral Biology, 2,* 155–99.

Eysenck, H. J. (1991). Personality, stress, and disease: An interactionist perspective. *Psychological Inquiry, 2* (3): 221–32.

Fabrega, H., Ulrich, R., Pilkonis, P., & Mezzich, J. (1991). On the homogeneity of personality disorder clusters. *Comprehensive Psychiatry, 32* (5): 373–86.

Fairburn, C. G., Shafran, R., & Cooper, Z. (1999). A cognitive behavioural theory of anorexia nervosa. *Behaviour Research and Therapy, 37,* 1–13.

Fairburn, C. G., Welch, S. L., & Hay, P. J. (1993). The classification of recurrent overeating. The "binge eating disorder" proposal. *International Journal of Eating Disorders, 13* (2): 155–59.

Fairburn, C. G., & Wilson, G. T. (1993). Binge eating: Definition and classification. In C. G. Fairburn & G. T. Wilson (Eds.), *Binge eating: Nature, assessment, and treatment.* New York: Guilford Press.

Faller, H., Bnlzebruck, H., Drings, P., & Lang, H. (1999). Coping, distress, and survival among patients with lung cancer. *Archives of General Psychiatry, 56* (8): 756–62.

Falloon, I. R. H. (1988). Editorial: Expressed emotion: Current status. *Psychological Medicine, 18,* 269–74.

Faraone, S. V., & Biederman, J. (1998). Neurobiology of attention-deficit hyperactivity disorder. *Biological Psychiatry, 44,* 951–58.

Faraone, S., Chen, W., Goldstein, J., & Tsuang, M. (1994). Gender differences in age at onset of schizophrenia. *British Journal of Psychiatry, 164,* 625–29.

Faraone, S. V., Matise, T., Svrakic, D., Pepple, J., Malaspina, D., Suarez, B,. Hampe, C., Zambuto, C. T., Schmitt, K., Meyer, J., Markel, P., Lee, H., Harkavy, Friedman, J., Kaufmann, C., Cloninger, C. R. & Tsuang, M. T. (1998). Genome scan of European-American schizophrenia pedigrees: Results of the NIMH Genetics Initiative and Millennium Consortium. *American Journal of Medical Genetics, 81:* 290–95.

Farde, L. (1997). Brain imaging of schizophrenia: The dopamine hypothesis. *Schizophrenia Research, 28,* 157–62.

Faris, R. E. L., & Dunham, H. W. (1939*). Mental disorders in urban areas.* Chicago: University of Chicago Press.

Farmer, A. E., McGuffin, P., & Gottesman, I. I. (1987). Twin concordance for DSM-III schizophrenia: Scrutinizing the validity of the definition. *Archives of General Psychiatry, 44,* 634–41.

Farrington, D. P. (1978). The family background of aggressive youths. In L. A. Hersov & D. Shaffer (Eds.), *Aggression and antisocial behavior in childhood and adolescence.* New York: Pergamon.

Farrington, D. P., Loeber, R., & Van Kammen. (1990). Long-term outcomes of hyperactivity-impulsivity-attention deficit and conduct problems in childhood. In L. N. Robbins & M. Rutter (Eds.), *Straight and devious pathways from childhood to adulthood* (pp. 62–81). Cambridge, England: Cambridge University Press.

Fava, G. A., Grandi, S., Zielezny, M., & Rafanelli, C. (1996). Four-year outcome for cognitive behavioral treatment of residual symptoms in major depression. *American Journal of Psychiatry, 153* (7): 945–47.

Fava, G. A., Rafanelli, C., Grandi, S., Canestrari, R., & Morphy, M. A. (1998). Six-year outcome for cognitive behavioral treatment of residual symptoms in major depression. *American Journal of Psychiatry, 155* (10): 1443–45.

Fava, G. A., Zielezny, M., Savron, G., & Grandi, S. (1995). Long-term effects of behavioural treatment for panic disorder with agoraphobia. *British Journal of Psychiatry, 166,* 87–92.

Fava, M., Rankin, M. A., Wright, E. C., Alpert, J. E., Nierenberg, A. A., Pava, J., & Rosenbaum, J. F. (2000). Anxiety disorders in major depression. *Comprehensive Psychiatry, 41,* 97–102.

Fawzy, F. I., Fawzy, N. W., Arndt, L. A., & Pasnau, R. O. (1995). Critical review of psychosocial interventions in cancer care. *Archives of General Psychiatry, 52,* 100–13.

Fawzy, F., Fawzy, N., Hyun, C., et al. (1993). Malignant melanoma: Effects of an early structured psychiatric intervention, coping, and affective state on recurrence and survival 6 years later. *Archives of General Psychiatry, 50,* 681–89.

Fawzy, F., Fawzy, N., & Hyun, C. (1994). *Short-term psychiatric intervention with malignant melanoma. The psychoimmunology of cancer* (pp. 292–319). New York Oxford University Press.

Federoff, J. (1993). Serotonergic drug treatment of deviant sexual interests. *Annals of Sex Research, 6,* 105–21.

Feinberg, T. E., Rifkin, A., Schaffer, C., & Walker, E. (1986). Facial discrimination and emotional recognition in schizophrenia and affective disorders. *Archives of General Psychiatry, 43,* 276–79.

Feinstein, R. E. (1999). Psychiatric symptoms due to medical illness. In R. E. Feinstein & A. A. Brewer (Eds.), *Primary care psychiatry and behavioral medicine: Brief office treatment and management pathways* (pp. 113–45). New York: Springer.

Feldman, H. A., Goldstein, I., Hatzichristou, D. G., Krane, R. J., & McKunlay, J. B. (1994). Impotence and its medical and psychosocial correlates: Results of the Massachusetts Male Aging Study. *Journal of Urology, 151,* 54–61.

Feldman, H. W., & Mandel, J. (1998). Providing medical marijuana: The importance of cannabis clubs. *Journal of Psychoactive Drugs, 30,* 179–86.

Feldman, M. P., & MacCulloch, M. J. (1971). *Homosexual behaviour: Theory and assessment.* Oxford: Pergamon.

Felthous, A. R., & Kellert, S. R. (1986). Violence against animals and people: Is aggression against living creatures generalized? *Bulletin of the American Academy of Psychiatry and the Law, 14,* 55–69.

Fenichel, O. (1945). *The psychoanalytic theory of neurosis.* New York: Norton.

Fenton, W. S., & McGlashan, T. H. (1991). Natural history of schizophrenia subtypes. I. Longitudinal study of paranoid, hebephrenic, and undifferentiated schizophrenia. *Archives of General Psychiatry, 48* (11): 969–77.

Fenton, W., & McGlashan, T. (1997). We can talk: individual psychotherapy for schizophrenia. *American Journal of Psychiatry, 154,* 1493–95.

Fergusson, D. M., Horwood, L. J., & Lynskey, M. T. (1993). Early dentine lead levels and subsequent cognitive and behavioural development. *Journal of Child Psychology and Psychiatry, 34,* 215–27.

Fernandez, E., & McDowell, J. J. (1995). Response-reinforcement relationships in chronic pain syndrome: Applicability of Herrnstein's law. *Behaviour Research and Therapy, 33* (7): 855–63.

Ferster, C. B. (1961). Positive reinforcement and the behavioral deficits of autistic children. *Child Development, 32,* 437–56.

Fessenden, F. (2000). They threaten, seethe and unhinge, then kill in quantity. *New York Times, 149* (April 9).

Fieve, R. R. (1975). *Mood swing.* New York: Morrow.

Fine, C. G. (1991). Treatment stabilization and crisis prevention. Pacing the therapy of the multiple personality disorder patient. *Psychiatric Clinics of North America, 14,* 661–75.

Fingarette, H., & Hasse, A. (1979). *Mental disabilities and criminal responsibility.* Berkeley: University of California Press.

Fingerhut, L. A. (1993). *Firearm mortality among children, youth, and young adults 1–34 years of age, trends and current status: United States, 1985–1990.* (Advance Data From Vital and Health Statistics, No. 231). Hyattsville, MD: National Center for Health Statistics.

Fink, G., Sumner, B., Rosie, R., Wilson, H., & McQueen, J. (1999). Androgen actions on central serotonin neurotransmission: Relevance for mood, mental state and memory. *Behavioral Brain Research, 105,* 53–68.

Fink, M. (1979). *Convulsive therapy: Therapy and practice.* New York: Raven Press.

Fink, P. J., & Tasman, A. (Eds.). (1992). *Stigma and mental illness.* Washington, DC: American Psychiatric Press.

Finkel, N. J. (1989). The Insanity Defense Reform Act of 1984: Much ado about nothing. *Behavioral Sciences and the Law, 7,* 403–19.

Finkel, N. J. (1990). De facto departures from insanity instructions: Toward the remaking of common law. *Law and Human Behavior, 14,* 105–22.

Finkel, N. J. (1991). The insanity defense: A comparison between verdict schemas. *Law and Human Behavior, 15,* 533–55.

Finkelhor, D. (1994). Current information on the scope and nature of child sexual abuse. *Future of Children, 4* (2): 31–53.

Finn, P. R., & Justus, A. (1999). Reduced EEG alpha power in the male and female offspring of alcoholics. *Alcoholism, Clinical and Experimental Research, 23,* 256–62.

Finney, J. W., Hahn, A. C., & Moos, R. H. (1996). The effectiveness of inpatient and outpatient treatment for alcohol abuse: The need to focus on mediators and moderators of setting effects. *Addiction, 91,* 1773–96.

Fiore, M. C., Novotny, T. E., Pierce, J. P., Giovino, G. A., Hatziandrev, G. A., Newcomb, E. J., Surawicz, T. S., & Davis, R. M. (1990). Methods used to quit smoking in the United States: Do cessation programs help? *Journal of the American Medical Association, 263,* 2760–65.

Fiore, M. C., Smith, S., Jorenby, D., & Baker, T. B. (1994). The effectiveness of the nicotine patch for smoking cessation: A meta-analysis. *Journal of the American Medical Association, 271* (24): 1940–47.

Fireside, H. (1979). *Soviet psychoprisons.* New York: Norton.

First, M. B., Spitzer, R. L., Gibbons, M., & Williams, J. B. (1995). *Structured Clinical Interview for DSM-IV Axis I Disorders, Patient Edition (SCID-P), version 2.* New York: New York State Psychiatric Institute Biometrics Research.

Fischer, D. J., Himle, J. A., & Thyer, B. A. (1999). Separation anxiety disorder. In R. T. Ammerman & M. Hersen (Eds.), *Handbook of prescriptive treatments for children and adolescents* (2nd ed.; pp. 141–54). Boston: Allyn & Bacon.

Fischer, M. (1973). Genetic and environmental factors in schizophrenia. *Acta Psychiatrica Scandinavica, 115,* 981–90.

Fischer, M., Barkley, R. A., Fletcher, K. E., & Smallish, L. (1993). The adolescent outcome of hyperactive children: Predictors of psychiatric, academic, social, and emotional adjustment. *Journal of the American Academy of Child and Adolescent Psychiatry, 32,* 324–32.

Fischman, M. W., & Schuster, C. R. (1982). Cocaine self-administration in humans. *Federation Proceedings, 41* (2): 241–46.

Fish, B. (1977). Neurobiological antecedents of schizophrenia in children: Evidence for an inherited, congenital, neurointegrative defect. *Archives of General Psychiatry, 34,* 197–313.

Fish, B. (1987). Infant predictors of the longitudinal course of schizophrenic development. *Schizophrenia Bulletin, 13,* 395–410.

Fish, B., Marcus, J., Hans, S. L., Auerbach, J. G., & Perdue, S. (1992). Infants at risk for schizophrenia: Sequelae of a genetic neurointegrative defect: A review and repliction analysis of pandysmuturation in the Jerusalem Infant Development Study. *Archives of General Psychiatry, 49* (3): 321–35.

Fishbain, D. A., Cutler, R. B., Rosomoff, H. L., & Rosomoff, R. S. (1998). Do antidepressants have an analgesic effect in psychogenic pain and somatoform pain disorder? A meta-analysis. *Psychosomatic Medicine, 60* (4): 503–509.

Fisher, J., Epstein, L. J., & Harris, M. R. (1967). Validity of the psychiatric interview: Predicting the effectiveness of the first Peace Corps volunteers in Ghana. *Archives of General Psychiatry, 17,* 744–50.

Fleming, J. E., & Offord, D. R. (1990). Epidemiology of childhood depressive disorders: A critical review. *Journal of the American Academy of Child and Adolescent Psychiatry, 29* (4): 571–80.

Fletcher, P. C., McKenna, P. J., Frith, C., Grasby, P. M., Friston, K. J., & Dolan, R. J. (1998). Brain activations in schizophrenia during a graded memory task studies with functional neuroimaging. *Archives of General Psychiatry, 55,* 1001–1008.

Flett, G., Vredenburg, K., & Krames, L. (1997). The continuity of depression in clinical and nonclinical samples. *Psychological Bulletin, 121,* 395–416.

Flood, R., & Seager, C. (1968). A retrospective examination of psychiatric case records of patients who subsequently commit suicide. *British Journal of Psychiatry, 114,* 443–50.

Flynn, J. R. (1998). WAIS-III and WISC-III gains in the United States from 1972 to 1995: How to compensate for obsolete norms. *Perceptual and Motor Skills, 86* (3): 1231–39.

Flynn, J. R. (1999). Searching for justice: The discovery of IQ gains over time. *American Psychologist, 54* (1): 5–20.

Foa, E. B., Dancu, C. V., Hembree, E. A., Jaycox, L. H., Meadows, E. A., & Street, G. P. (1999a). A comparison of exposure therapy, stress inoculation training, and their combination for reducing posttraumatic stress disorder in female assault victims. *Journal of Consulting and Clinical Psychology, 67* (2): 194–200.

Foa, E. B., Davidson, J. R. T., Frances, A., Culpepper, L., Ross, R., & Ross, D. (Eds.). (1999b). The expert consensus guideline series: Treatment of posttraumatic stress disorder. *Journal of Clinical Psychiatry, 60* (Suppl 16): 4–76.

Foa, E. B., & Franklin, M. E. (1998). Cognitive-behavioral treatment of obsessive-compulsive disorder. In D. K. Routh & R. J. DeRubeis (Eds.), *The science of clinical psychology: Accomplishments and future directions* (pp. 235–63). Washington, DC: American Psychological Association.

Foa, E. B., Hearst-Ikeda, D., & Perry, K. J. (1995). Evaluation of a brief cognitive-behavioral program for the prevention of chronic PTSD in recent assault victims. *Journal of Consulting and Clinical Psychology, 63* (6): 948–55.

Foa, E. B., & Kozak, M. J. (1986). Emotional processing of fear: Exposure to corrective information. *Psychological Bulletin, 99,* 20–35.

Foa, E. B., & Kozak, M. (1993). Obsessive-compulsive disorder: Long-term outcome of psychological treatment. In M. Mavissakalian & R. Prien (Eds.), *Long-term treatments of anxiety disorders*. Washington, DC: American Psychiatric Press.

Foa, E. B., & Meadows, E. A. (1997). Psychosocial treatments for posttraumatic stress disorder: A critical review. *Annual Review of Psychology, 48,* 449–80.

Foa, E. B., & Riggs, D. S. (1995). Post-traumatic stress disorder following assault: Theoretical considerations and empirical findings. *Current Directions in Psychological Science, 4* (2): 61–65.

Foa, E. F., Riggs, D. S., Massie, E. D., & Yarczower, M. (1995). The impact of fear activation and anger on the efficacy of exposure treatment for posttraumatic stress disorder. *Behavior Therapy, 26* (3): 487–99.

Foa, E. B., & Rothbaum, B. O. (1998). *Treating the trauma of rape: Cognitive-behavioral therapy for PTSD*. New York: Guilford Press.

Foa, E. F., Rothbaum, B. O., Riggs, D., & Murdock, T. (1991). Treatment of post-traumatic stress disorder in rape victims: A comparison between cognitive-behavioral procedures and counseling. *Journal of Consulting and Clinical Psychology, 59,* 715–23.

Fogarty, F., Russell, J. M., Newman, S. C., & Bland, R. C. (1994). Mania. *Acta Psychiatrica ScandInivica, 89* (Suppl. 376): 16–23.

Folks, D. G. (1995). Munchausen's syndrome and other factitious disorders. *Neurologic Clinics, 13* (2): 267–81.

Fombonne, E. (1998). Epidemiological surveys of autism. In F. R. Volkmar (Ed.), Autism and pervasive developmental disorders. *Cambridge Monographs in Child and Adolescent Psychiatry* (pp. 32–63). New York: Cambridge University Press.

Fonagy, P., Leigh, T., Steele, M., Steele, H., Kennedy, R., Mattoon, G., Target, M., & Gerber, A. (1996). The relation of attachment status, psychiatric classification, and response to psychotherapy. *Journal of Consulting and Clinical Psychology, 64* (1): 22–31.

Ford, M. R., & Widiger, T. A. (1989). Sex bias in the diagnosis of histrionic and antisocial personality disorders. *Journal of Consulting and Clinical Psychology, 57* (2): 301–305.

Fortner, B. V., & Neimeyer, R. A. (1999). Death anxiety in older adults: A quantitative review. *Death Studies, 23* (5): 387–411.

Foucault, M. (1965). *Madness and civilization: A history of insanity in the age of reason*. New York: Random House.

Fowles, D. C., & Furuseth, A. M. (1994). Electrodermal hyporeactivity and antisocial behavior. In D. K. Routh (Ed.), *Disruptive behavior disorders in childhood* (pp. 181–205). New York: Plenum.

Fowles, D. C., & Gersh, F. (1979). Neurotic depression: The endogenous neurotic distinction. In R. A. Depue (Ed.), *The psychobiology of the depressive disorders: Implications for the effects of stress*. New York: Academic Press.

Frances, A. J., & Egger, H. L. (1999). Whither psychiatric diagnosis. *Australian and New Zealand Journal of Psychiatry, 33* (2): 161–65.

Francis, G., & Ollendick, T. (1990). Behavioral treatment of social anxiety. In E. L. Feindler & G. R. Kalfus (Eds.), *Adolescent behavior therapy handbook*. New York: Springer Publishing Company.

Frank, E., Anderson, C., & Rubinstein, D. (1978). Frequency of sexual dysfunction in "normal" couples. *New England Journal of Medicine, 299,* 111–15.

Frank, E., & Spanier, C. (1995). Interpersonal psychotherapy for depression: Overview, clinical efficacy, and future directions. *Clinical Psychology—Science and Practice, 2* (4): 349–69.

Frank, E., Kupfer, D. J., Perel, J. M., Cornes, C., et al. (1990). Three-year outcomes for maintenance therapies in recurrent depression. *Archives of General Psychiatry, 47* (12): 1093–99.

Frank, G., Goldman, H., & McGuire, T. G. (1994). Who will pay for health care reform? *Hospital and Community Psychiatry, 45,* 906–10.

Frank, H., & Hoffman, N. (1986). Borderline empathy: An empirical investigation. *Comprehensive Psychiatry, 2,* 387–95.

Frank, I. M., Lessin, P. J., Tyrrell, E. D., Hahn, P. M., & Szara, S. (1976). Acute and cumulative effects of marihuana smoking on hospitalized subjects: A 36–day study. In M. C. Braude & S. Szara (Eds.), *Pharmacology of marihuana* (Vol. 2; pp. 673–80). New York: Academic Press.

Frank, J., Kosten, T., Giller, E., & Dan, E. (1988). A randomized clinical trial of phenelzine and imipramine for posttraumatic stress disorder. *American Journal of Psychiatry, 145,* 1289–91.

Frank, R. G., Huskamp, H. A., McGuire, T. G., & Newhouse, J. P. (1996). Some economics of mental health carve-outs. *Archives of General Psychiatry, 53* (10): 933–37.

Frank, R. G., Koyanagi, C., & McGuire, T. G. (1997). The politics and economics of mental health parity laws. *Health Affairs, 16,* 108–19.

Franke, P., Schwab, S. G., Knapp, M., Gaensicke, M., Delmo, C., Zill, P., Trixler, M., Lichtermann, D., Hallmayer, J., Wildenauer, D. B., & Maier, W. (1999). DAT1 gene polymorphism in alcoholism: A family-based association study. *Biological Psychiatry, 45,* 652–54.

Franklin, M., & Foa, E. (1998). Cognitive-behavioral treatments for obsessive-compulsive disorder. In P. Nathan & J. Gorman (Eds.), *A guide to treatments that work* (pp. 339–57). New York: Oxford University Press.

Franzen, G. (1971). Serum cortisol in chronic schizophrenia: Changes in the diurnal rhythm and psychiatric mental status on withdrawal of drugs. *Psychiatrica Clinica, 4,* 237–46.

Frasure-Smith, N., Lesperance, F., & Talajic, M. (1995). The impact of negative emotions on prognosis following myocardial infarction: Is it more than depression? *Health Psychology, 14* (5): 388–98.

Frederick, C. J. (1978). Current trends in suicidal behavior in the United States. *American Journal of Psychotherapy, 32,* 172–200.

Fredrikson, M., Annas, P., Fischer, H., & Wik, G. (1996). Gender and age differences in the prevalence of specific fears and phobias. *Behaviour Research and Therapy, 34*(1): 33–39.

Fredrikson, M., Annas, P., & Wik, G. (1997). Parental history, aversive exposure and the development of snake and spider phobia in women. *Behaviour Research and Therapy, 35* (1): 23–28.

Freeman, B. J. (1997). Guidelines for evaluating intervention programs for children with autism. *Journal of Autism and Developmental Disorders, 27,* 641–51.

Freeman, B. J., Ritvo, E. R., Mason-Brothers, A., Pingree, C., et al. (1989). Psychometric assessment of first-degree relatives of 62 autistic probands in Utah. *American Journal of Psychiatry, 146,* 361–64.

Freeman, E. W., Schweizer, E., & Rickels, K. (1995). Personality factors in women with premenstrual syndrome. *Psychosomatic Medicine, 57,* 453–59.

Freeman, H. (1994). Schizophrenia and city residence. *British Journal of Psychiatry, 164* (Supp. 23): 39–50.

Freud, A. (1936). *The ego and mechanisms of defense* (rev. ed.). New York: International Universities Press, 1967.

Freud, S. (1894). The neuro-psychoses of defense. In J. Strachey (Ed. and Trans.), *The complete psychological works* (Vol. 3). New York: Norton, 1976.

Freud, S. (1917a). Introductory lectures on psychoanalysis, Part III. In J. Strachey (Ed. and Trans.), *The complete psychological works* (Vol. 16). New York: Norton, 1976.

Freud, S. (1917b). Mourning and melancholia. In J. Strachey (Ed. and Trans.), *The complete psychological works* (Vol. 16). New York: Norton, 1976.

Freund, K. (1990). Courtship disorder. In W. L. Marshall & D. R. Laws (Eds.), *Handbook of sexual assault: Issues, theories, and treatment of the offender. Applied Clinical Psychology* (pp. 195–207). New York: Plenum.

Freund, K. (1991). Reflections on the development of the phallometric method of assessing erotic preferences. *Annals of Sex Research, 4* (3–4): 221–28.

Freund, K., Seto, M. C., & Kuban, M. (1996). Two types of fetishism. *Behaviour Research and Therapy, 34* (9): 687–94.

Frick, P. J. (1994). Family dysfunction and the disruptive behavior disorders: A review of recent empirical findings. *Advances in Clinical Child Psychology, 16,* 203–26.

Frick, P. J. (1998). Conduct disorders and severe antisocial behavior. *Clinical Child Psychology Library.* New York: Plenum.

Frick, P. J., Christian, R. E., & Wooton, J. M. (1999). Age trends in association between parenting practices and conduct problems. *Behavior Modification, 23,* 106–28.

Friedman, H., Klein, T., & Specter, S. (1991). Immunosuppression by marijuana and components. In R. Ader, D. L. Felten, et al. (Eds.), *Psychoneuroimmunology* (2nd ed.; pp. 931–53). San Diego: Academic Press.

Friedman, M. (1988). Toward rational pharmacotherapy for post-traumatic stress disorder: An interim report. *American Journal of Psychiatry, 145,* 281–85.

Friedmann, P. D., Saitz, R., Samet, J. H., & Glass, R. M. (Eds.). (1998). Management of adults recovering from alcohol or other drug problems: Relapse prevention in primary care. *Journal of the American Medical Association, 279,* 1227–31.

Friedman, R. C. & Downey, J. I. (1994). Homosexuality. *New England Journal of Medicine, 331,* 923–30.

Friman, P. C., & Warzak, W. J. (1990). Nocturnal enuresis: A prevalent, persistent, yet curable parasomnia. *Pediatrician, 17,* 38–45.

Fritz, G. K., Fritsch, S., & Hagino, O. (1997). Somatoform disorders in children and adolescents: A review of the past 10 years. *Journal of the American Academy of Child and Adolescent Psychiatry, 36* (10): 1329–38.

Frueh, B. C., Turner, S. M., & Beidel, D. C. (1995). Exposure therapy for combat-related posttraumatic stress disorder: A critical review. *Clinical Psychology Review, 15* (8): 799–817.

Fuchs, J. L., Montemayor, M., & Greenough, W. (1990). Effect of environmental complexity on size of the superior colliculus. *Behavioral and Neural Biology, 54,* 198–203.

Funtowicz, M. N., & Widiger, T. A. (1999). Sex bias in the diagnosis of personality disorders: An evaluation of DSM-IV criteria. *Journal of Abnormal Psychology, 108* (2): 195–201.

Fyer, A. J., Mannuzza, S., Gallops, M. S., Martin, L. Y., Aaronson, G., Gorman, J. M., Liebowitz, M. R., & Klein, D. F. (1990). Familial transmission of simple phobias and fears: A preliminary report. *Archives of General Psychiatry, 47,* 252–56.

Gabbard, G. O. (1992). Psychodynamic psychiatry in the "Decade of the Brain." *American Journal of Psychiatry, 149* (8): 991–98.

Gabbard, G. O. (1998). The cost effectiveness of treating depression. *Psychiatric Annals, 28,* 98–101.

Gabbard, G. O., & Lazar, S. G. (1999). Efficacy and cost offset of psychotherapy for borderline personality disorder. In D. Spiegel (Ed.), *Efficacy and cost-effectiveness of psychotherapy: Clinical practice* (Vol. 45; pp. 111–23). Washington, DC: American Psychiatric Association.

Gabbard, G. O., Lazar, S. G., Hornberger, J., & Spiegel, D. (1997). The economic impact of psychotherapy: A review. *American Journal of Psychiatry, 154,* 147–55.

Gabriel, T. (1994). Heroin finds a new market along the cutting edge of style. *New York Times,* May 8, p. A1.

Gagnon, J. H. (1977*). Human sexuality*. Chicago: Scott, Foresman.

Galani, R., Jarrard, L. E., Will, B. E., & Kelche, C. (1997). Effects of postoperative housing conditions on functional recovery in rats with lesions of the hippocampus, subiculum, or entorhinal cortex. *Neurobiology of Learning and Memory, 67,* 43–56.

Galen. In Veith, I., *Hysteria: The history of a disease*. Chicago: University of Chicago Press, 1965.

Gallo, J. J., Rabins, P. V., & Anthony, J. C. (1999). Sadness in older persons: 13-year follow-up of a community sample in Baltimore, Maryland. *Psychological Medicine, 29,* 341–50.

Ganaway, G. K. (1989). Historical versus narrative truth: Clarifying the role of exogenous trauma in the etiology of MPD and its variants. *Dissociation: Progress in the Dissociative Disorders, 2,* 205–20.

Gao, S., Hendrie, H. C., Hall, K. S., & Hui, S. (1998). The relationships between age, sex, and the incidence of dementia and Alzheimer disease: A meta-analysis. *Archives of General Psychiatry, 55,* 809–15.

Garb, H. N. (1998a). *Studying the clinician: Judgment research and psychological assessment*. Washington, DC: American Psychological Association.

Garb, H. N. (1998b). Recommendations for training in the use of the Thematic Appereception Test (TAT). *Professional Psychology—Research and Practice, 29* (6): 621–22.

Garb, H. N., Florio, C. M., & Grove, W. M. (1998). The validity of the Rorschach and the Minnesota Multiphasic Personality Inventory: Results from meta-analyses. *Psychological Science, 9* (5): 402–404.

Garbutt, J. C., West, S. L., Carey, T. S., Lohr, K. N., & Crews, F. T. (1999). Pharmacological treatment of alcohol dependence: A review of the evidence. *Journal of the American Medical Association, 281,* 1318–25.

Garcia, E., Guess, D., & Brynes, J. (1973). Development of syntax in a retarded girl using procedures of imitation, reinforcement, and modelling. *Journal of Applied Behavior Analysis, 6,* 299–310.

Gardner, D., & Cowdry, R. (1985). Suicidal and parasuicidal behavior in borderline personality disorder. *Psychiatric Clinics of North America, 8,* 389–402.

Garfield, S. (2000). The Rorschach test in clinical diagnosis—A brief commentary. *Journal of Clinical Psychology, 56,* 431–34.

Garfinkel, P. E., & Garner, D. M. (1982). *Anorexia nervosa: A multidimensional perspective*. New York: Brunner/Mazel.

Garmezy, N. (1977a). DSM-III: Never mind the psychologists—Is it good for the children? *Clinical Psychologist, 31,* 3–4.

Garmezy, N. (1977b). The psychology and psychopathology of Allenhead. *Schizophrenia Bulletin, 3,* 360–69.

Garner, D. M. (1993). Binge eating: Definition and classification. In C. G. Fairburn, G. T. Wilson, C. G. Fairburn, & G. T. Wilson (Eds.), *Binge eating: Nature, assessment, and treatment*. New York: Guilford Press.

Garner, D. M., & Garfinkel, P. E. (Eds). (1997). *Handbook of treatment for eating disorders* (2nd ed.). New York: Guilford Press.

Garner, D., & Wooley, S. (1991). Confronting the failure of behavioral and dietary treatments for obesity. *Clinical Psychology Review, 11,* 729–80.

Garrison, C. Z., Addy, C. L., Jackson, K. L., McKeown, R. E., & Waller, J. L. (1992). Major depressive disorder and dysthymia in young adolescents. *American Journal of Epidemiology, 135* (7): 792–802.

Garrity, T. F., Somes, G. W., & Marx, M. B. (1977). Personality factors in resistance to illness after recent life changes. *Journal of Psychosomatic Research, 21,* 23–32.

Gartland, H. J., & Day, H. D. (1999). Family predictors of the incidence of children's asthma symptoms: Expressed emotion, medication, parent contact, and life events. *Journal of Clinical Psychology, 55* (5):573–84.

Garven, S., Wood, J. M., Malpass, R. S., & Shaw, J. S. III. (1998). More than suggestion: The effect of interviewing techniques from the McMartin Preschool case. *Journal of Applied Psychology, 83* (3): 347–59.

Gatley, S. J., Volkow, N. D., & Makriyannis, A. (1999). Studies of the brain cannabinoid system using positron and single-photon emission tomography. In G. G. Nahas, K. M. Sutin, et al. (Eds.), *Marihuana and medicine* (pp. 163–76). Clifton, NJ: Humana.

Gatz, M., Kasl-Godley, J. E., & Karel, M. J. (1996). Aging and mental disorders. In J. E. Birren, K. W. Schaie, R. P. Abeles, M. Gatz, & T. A. Salthouse (Eds.), *Handbook of the psychology of aging. The handbooks of aging* (4th ed.; pp. 365–82). San Diego: Academic Press.

Gawin, F. H., & Ellinwood, E. H. (1988). Cocaine and other stimulants. *New England Journal of Medicine, 318,* 1173–82.

Gawin, F. H., & Ellinwood, E. H. (1989). Cocaine dependence. *Annual Review of Medicine, 40,* 149–61.

Gawin, F. H., Kleber, H. D., Byck, R., Rounsaville, B. J., Kosten, T. R., Jatlow, P. I., & Morgan, C. (1989). Desipramine facilitation of initial cocaine abstinence. *Archives of General Psychiatry, 46,* 117–21.

Ge, X., Conger, R., Cadoret, R., & Neiderhiser, J. (1996). The developmental interface between nature and nurture: A mutual influence model of child antisocial behavior and parent behaviors. *Developmental Psychology, 32* (4): 574–89.

Gebhard, P. H., Gagnon, J. H., Pomeroy, W. B., & Christenson, C. V. (1965). *Sex offenders*. New York: Harper & Row.

Geffken, G. R., & Monaco, L. (1996). Assessment and treatment of encopresis. *Journal of Psychological Practice, 2* (3): 22–30.

Gehring, W., Himle, J., & Nisenson, L. (2000). Action-monitoring dysfunction in obsessive-compulsive disorder. *Psychological Science, 11,* 7–12.

Geist, R., Heinman, M., Stephens, D., Davis, R., & Katzman, D. K. (2000). Comparison of family therapy and family group psychoeducation in adolescents with anorexia nervosa. *Canadian Journal of Psychiatry, 45,* 173–78.

Gelb, D. J., Oliver, E., & Gilman, S. (1999). Diagnostic criteria for Parkinson disease. *Archives of Neurology, 56,* 33–39.

Gelenberg, A. J., & Klerman, G. L. (1978). Maintenance drug therapy in long-term treatment of depression. In J. P. Brady & H. K. H. Brodie (Eds.), *Controversy in psychiatry.* Philadelphia: Saunders.

Gelernter, J., & Kranzler, H. (1999). D-sub-2 dopamine receptor gene (DRD2) allele and haplotype frequencies in alcohol dependent and control subjects: No association with phenotype or severity of phenotype. *Neuropsychopharmacology, 20,* 640–49.

Gelfand, D. M. (1978). Social withdrawal and negative emotional states: Behavioral treatment. In B. B. Wolman, J. Egan, & A. O. Ross (Eds.), *Handbook of treatment of mental disorders in childhood and adolescence.* Englewood Cliffs, NJ: Prentice-Hall.

Gendreau, P. L., Petitto, J. M., Gariepy, J., & Lewis, M. H. (1997). D-sub-1 dopamine receptor mediation of social and nonsocial emotional reactivity in mice: Effects of housing and strain difference in motor activity. *Behavioral Neuroscience, 111,* 424–34.

George, M., Trimble, M., Ring, H., et al. (1993). Obsessions in obsessive-compulsive disorder with and without Gilles de la Tourette's syndrome. *American Journal of Psychiatry, 150,* 93–97.

George, M. S., Wasserman, E. M., Williams, W. A., Callahan, A., Ketter, T. A., Basser, P., Hallet, M., & Post, R. M. (1995). Daily repetitive transcranial magnetic stimulation (rTMS) improves mood in depression. *Neuroreport, 6,* 1853–56.

Gergen, K. J. (1982). *Toward transformation in social knowledge.* New York: Springer Verlag.

Gerstley, L. J., Alterman, A. I., McLellan, A. T., & Woody, G. E. (1990). Antisocial personality disorder in patients with substance abuse disorders. *American Journal of Psychiatry, 147,* 481–87.

Geschwind, N. (1975). The apraxias: Neural mechanisms of disorders of learned movement. *American Scientist, 188,* 188–95.

Ghuman, H. S., Ghuman, J. K., & Ford, L. W. (1998). Pervasive developmental disorders and learning disorders. In H. S. Ghuman & R. M. Sarles (Eds.), *Handbook of child and adolescent outpatient, day treatment and community psychiatry* (pp. 197–212). Philadelphia: Brunner/Mazel.

Gianoulakis, C. (1996). Implications of endogenous opioids and dopamine in alcoholism: Human and basic science studies. *Alcohol and Alcoholism, 31* (Suppl. 1): 33–42.

Gibbs, N. A. (1996). Nonclinical populations in research in obsessive-compulsive disorder: A critical review. *Clinical Psychology Review, 16* (8): 729–73.

Gilberg, C. (1991). Outcome in autism and autistic-like conditions. *Journal of the American Academy of Child and Adolescent Psychiatry, 30* (3): 375–82.

Gilberg, C., & Svennerholm, L. (1987). CSF monoamines in autistic syndromes and other pervasive developmental disorders in childhood. *British Journal of Psychiatry, 151,* 89–94.

Gilbert, D. G., & Hagen, R. L. (1980). The effects of nicotine and extraversion on self-report, skin conductance, electromyographic, and heart responses to emotional stimuli. *Addictive Behavior, 5,* 247–57.

Gilberstadt, H., & Duker, J. (1965). *A handbook for clinical and actuarial MMPI interpretations.* Philadelphia: Saunders.

Gillham, J., & Reivich, K. (1999). Prevention of depressive symptoms in schoolchildren: A research update. *Psychological Science, 10,* 461–62.

Gillham, J., Reivich, K., Jaycox, L., & Seligman, M. (1995). Prevention of depressive symptoms in schoolchildren: Two-year follow-up. *Psychological Science, 6* (6): 343–51.

Gillum, R. F. (1994). Trends in acute myocardial infarction and coronary heart disease death in the United States. *Journal of the American College of Cardiology, 23* (6): 1273–77.

Girelli, S., Resick, P., Marhoefer-Dvorak, S., & Hutter, C. (1986). Subjective distress and violence during rape: The effects on long-term fear. *Violence and Victims, 1,* 35–46.

Gitlin, M. J. (1993). Pharmacotherapy of personality disorders: Conceptual framework and clinical strategies. *Journal of Clinical Psychopharmacology, 13* (5): 343–53.

Gitlin, M. J. (1994). Psychotropic medications and their effects on sexual function: Diagnosis, biology, and treatment approaches. *Journal of Clinical Psychiatry, 55* (9): 406–13.

Gittelman, R., & Klein, D. F. (1984). Relationship between separation anxiety and panic and agoraphobic disorders. *Psychopathology, 17,* 56–65.

Gittleman, M., & Birch, H. G. (1967). Childhood schizophrenia: Intellect, neurologic status, perinatal risk, prognosis and family pathology. *Archives of General Psychiatry, 17,* 16–25.

Gittleson, N. L. (1966). Depressive psychosis in the obsessional neurotic. *British Journal of Psychiatry, 122,* 883–87.

Gladue, B. A., Green, R., & Hellman, R. E. (1984). Neuroendocrine response to estrogen and sexual orientation. *Science, 225,* 496–99.

Glaser, W. (1993). Is personality disorder a mental illness? Garry David and the lessons of history. *International Journal of Mental Health, 22,* 61–70.

Glass, D. C. (1977). *Behavior pattern stress in coronary disease.* Hillsdale, NJ: Erlbaum.

Glazer, H. I., & Weiss, J. M. (1976). Long-term interference effect: An alternative to "learned helplessness." *Journal of Experimental Psychology: Animal Behavior Processes, 2,* 202–13.

Gleitman, H. (1981). *Psychology.* New York: Norton.

Gleitman, H. (1991). *Psychology* (3rd ed.). New York: Norton.

Glynn, S. M., & Sussman, S. (1990). Why patients smoke (letter). *Hospital and Community Psychiatry, 41,* 1027–28.

Gobert, A., Rivet, J. M., Cistarelli, L., Melon, C., & Millan, M. J. (1999). Buspirone modulates basal and fluoxetine-stimulated dialysate levels of dopamine, noradrenaline and serotonin in the frontal cortex of freely moving rats: Activation of serotonin1A receptors and blockade of alpha2-adrenergic receptors underlie its actions. *Neuroscience, 93,* 1251–62.

Goddard, A. W., Woods, S. W., & Charney, D. S. (1996). A critical review of the role of norepinephrine in panic disorder: Focus on its interaction with serotonin. In H. G. Westenberg, J. A. Den Boer, & D. L. Murphy (Eds.), *Advances in the neurobiology of anxiety disorders* (pp. 107–37). Chicester, England: Wiley.

Goenjian, A. K., Karayan, I., Pynoos, R. S., Minassian, D., et al. (1997). Outcome of psychotherapy among early adolescents after trauma. *American Journal of Psychiatry, 154* (4): 536–42.

Goin, R. P. (1998). Nocturnal enuresis in children. *Child: Care, Health and Development, 24,* 277–88.

Gold, J. M., Randolph, C., Carpenter, C. J., Goldberg, T. E., & Weinberger, D. R. (1992). Forms of memory failure in schizophrenia. *Journal of Abnormal Psychology, 101* (3): 487–94.

Gold, M. R., & Matsuuch, L. (1995). Signal transduction by the antigen receptors of B and T lymphocytes. *International Review of Cytology, 157,* 181–276.

Gold, M. S., Miller, N. S., Stennie, K., & Populla-Vardi, C. (1995). Abraham, K. (1911). Notes on psychoanalytic investigation and treatment of manic-depressive insanity and applied conditions. In *Selected papers of Karl Abraham, M.D.* (D. Bryan & A. Strachey, Trans.). London: Hogarth Press, 1948.

Golden, C. J. (1981). The Luria-Nebraska Children's Battery: Theory and formulation. In G. W. Hynd & J. E. Obrzut (Eds.), *Neuropsychological assessment and the school-age child: Issues and procedures.* New York: Grune & Stratton.

Golden, C. J., Hammeke, T. A., & Puriosch, A. D. (1980). *Manual for the Luria-Nebraska Neuropsychological Battery.* Los Angeles: Western Psychological Services.

Golding, J. M., Rost, K., Kashner, T. M., & Smith, G. R., Jr. (1992). Family psychiatric history of patients with somatization disorder. *Psychiatric Medicine, 10,* 33–47.

Goldman, D. (1995). Identifying alcoholism vulnerability alleles. *Alcoholism: Clinical and Experimental Research, 19* (4): 824–31.

Goldman-Rakic, P. S. (1987). Circuitry of primate prefrontal cortex and regulation of behavior by representational memory. In F. Plum (Ed.), *Handbook of physiology: The nervous system* (Vol. 5; pp. 373–417). Bethesda, MD: American Physiological Society.

Goldstein, D. B. (1996). Effects of alcohol on membrane lipids. In H. Begleiter & B. Kissin (Eds.), *The pharmacology of alcohol and alcohol dependence: Alcohol and alcoholism* (No. 2; pp. 309–34). New York: Oxford University Press.

Goldstein, D. J., Wilson, M. C., Ashcroft, R. C., & Al-Banna, M. (1999). Effectiveness of fluoxetine therapy in bulimia nervosa regardless of comorbid depression. *International Journal of Eating Disorders, 25* (1): 19–27.

Goldstein, G. (1998). Neuropsychological assessment of adults. In G. Goldstein (Ed.), *Neuropsychology. Human brain function: Assessment and rehabilitation* (pp. 63–81). New York: Plenum Press.

Goldstein, I., Lue, T. F., Padma-Nathan, H., Rosen, R. C., Steers, W. D., & Wicker, P. A. (1998). Oral sildenafil in the treatment of erectile dysfunction. Sildenafil Study Group. *New England Journal of Medicine, 338* (20):1397–1404.

Goldstein, J. M. (1988). Gender differences in the course of schizophrenia. *American Journal of Psychiatry, 145,* 684–89.

Goldstein, J. M. (1997). Sex differences in schizophrenia: Epidemiology, genetics and the brain. *International Review of Psychiatry, 9,* 399–408.

Goldstein, M. J., Strachan, A. M., & Wynne, L. C. (1994). DSM-IV literature review: Relational problems with high expressed emotion. In T. A. Widiger, A. J. Frances, H. A. Pincus, W. Davis, & M. First (Eds.), *DSM-IV sourcebook.* Washington, DC: American Psychiatric Association.

Gomberg, E. S., & Zucker, R. A. (1998). Substance use and abuse in old age. In I. H. Nordhus & G. R. Van den Bos (Eds.), *Clinical geropsychology* (pp. 189–204). Washington, DC: American Psychological Association.

Goodman, R. (1990). Technical note: Are perinatal complications causes or consequences of autism? *Journal of Child Psychology and Psychiatry, 31* (5): 809–12.

Goodstein, L., & Glaberson, W. (2000). The well-marked road to homicidal rage. *New York Times, 149* (April 10).

Goodwin, D. W. (1988). Alcoholism: Who gets better and who does not. In R. M. Rose & J. Barrett (Eds.), *Alcoholism: Origins and outcomes* (pp. 281–92). New York: Raven Press.

Goodwin, D. W. (1990). The genetics of alcoholism. In P. R. McHugh & V. A. McKusick (Eds.), *Genes, brain and behavior* (pp. 219–26). New York: Raven Press.

Goodwin, D. W., Schulsinger, F., Hermansen, L., Guze, S. B., & Winokur, G. (1973). Alcohol problems in adoptees raised apart from alcoholic biological parents. *Archives of General Psychiatry, 28,* 238–43.

Goodwin, D. W., Schulsinger, F., Moller, N., Hermansen, L., & Winokur, G. (1974). Drinking problems in adopted and non-adopted sons of alcoholics. *Archives of General Psychiatry, 31,* 164–69.

Gordon, D. A., Arbuthnot, J., Gustafson, K. E., & McGreen, P. (1988). Home-based behavioral systems family therapy with disadvantaged juvenile delinquents. *Journal of Family Therapy, 16,* 243–55.

Gorelick, P. B., Freels, S., Harris, Y., Dollear, T., et al. (1994). Epidemiology of vascular and Alzheimer's dementia among African Americans in Chicago, IL: Baseline frequency and comparison of risk factors. *Neurology, 44,* 1391–96.

Gorelick, P. B., Roman, G., & Mangone, C. A. (1994). Vascular dementia. In P. B. Gorelick & M. A. Alter (Eds.), *Handbook of neuroepidemiology* (pp. 197–214). New York: Marcel Dekker.

Gorenstein, E. E., & Newman, J. P. (1980). Disinhibitory psychopathology: A new perspective and a model for research. *Psychological Review, 87,* 301–15.

Gorman, J., Kent, J., Sullivan. G., & Coplan, J. (2000). Neuroanatomical hypothesis of panic disorder. *American Journal of Psychiatry, 157,* 493–505.

Gorman, J. M., Liebowitz, M. R., Fyer, A. J., & Stein, J. A. (1989). Neuroanatomical hypothesis for panic disorder. *American Journal of Psychiatry, 146,* 148–61.

Gorman, J. M., Nemeroff, C. B., & Charney, D. S. (1999). The role of norepinephrine in the treatment of depression. *Journal of Clinical Psychiatry, 60* (9): 623–31.

Gorman, J., & Shear, K. (1998). Practice guideline for the treatment of patients with panic disorder. *American Journal of Psychiatry* (Supp.): *155,* 1–34.

Gottesman, I. I. (1991). *Schizophrenia genesis: The origins of madness.* New York: W. H. Freeman.

Gottesman, I. I. (1993). Origins of schizophrenia: Past as prologue. In R. Plomin & G. E. McClearn (Eds.), *Nature, nurture, and psychology* (pp. 231–44). Washington, DC: American Psychological Association.

Gottesman, I. I., McGuffin, P., & Farmer, A. E. (1987). Clinical genetics as clues to the "real" genetics of schizophrenia (a decade of modest gains while playing for time). *Schizophrenia Bulletin, 13,* 23–47.

Gottesman, I. I., & Shields, J. (1972). *Schizophrenia and genetics: A twin study vantage point.* New York: Academic Press.

Gould, S. J. (1981). *The mismeasure of man.* New York: Norton.

Grabowski, J., & Schmitz, J. M. (1998). Psychologic treatment of substance abuse. *Current Opinion in Psychiatry, 11,* 289–93.

Grace, W. J., & Graham, D. T. (1952). Relationship of specific attitudes and emotions to certain bodily disease. *Psychosomatic Medicine, 14,* 243–51.

Graham, D. Y., Lew, G. M., Klein, P. D., Evans, D. G., Evans, D. J., Jr., Saeed, Z. A., & Malaty, H. M. (1992). Effect of treatment of Helicobacter pylori infection on the long-term recurrence of gastric or duodenal ulcer: A randomized, controlled study. *Annals of Internal Medicine, 116* (9):705–708.

Graham, P. J., et al. (Eds.). (1998). *Cognitive-behaviour therapy for children and families.* New York: Cambridge University Press.

Gram, L. F. (1994). Fluoxetine. *New England Journal of Medicine, 331* (20): 1354–61.

Gray, F., Huag, H., Chimelli, L., et al. (1991). Prominent cortical atrophy with neuronal loss as correlate of human immunodeficiency virus encephalopathy. *Acta Neuropathologica, 82,* 229–33.

Gray, J. A. (1982). *The neurobiology of anxiety.* New York: Oxford University Press.

Gray, J. A. (1985). Issues in the neuropsychology of anxiety. In A. H. Tuma & J.D. Maser (Eds.), *Anxiety and the anxiety disorders* (pp. 5–25). Hillsdale, NJ: Lawrence Erlbaum.

Gray, J. A. (1987). Perspectives on anxiety and impulsivity: A commentary. *Journal of Research in Personality, 21* (4): 493–509.

Gray, J., & McNaughton, N. (1996). The neuropsychology of anxiety. In D. Hope (Ed.), *Perspectives on anxiety, panic, and fear* (pp. 61–134). Lincoln, NE: Nebraska University Press.

Greco, A. (1995). Structural neuroimaging: Magnetic resonance. In M. M. Robertson, V. Eapen, et al. (Eds.), *Movement and allied disorders in childhood* (pp. 279–92). Chichester, England: Wiley.

Green, A. R., Cross, A. J., & Goodwin, G.M. (1995). Review of the pharmacology and clinical pharmacology of 3,4- methylenedioxymethamphetamine (MDMA or "Ecstasy"). *Psychopharmacology, 119,* 247–60.

Green, B. L., Gleser, G. C., Lindy, J. D., Grace, M. C., & Leonard, A. (1996). Age-related reactions to the Buffalo Creek dam collapse: Effects in the second decade. In P. E. Ruskin & J. A. Talbott (Eds.), *Aging and post-traumatic stress disorder* (pp. 101–25). Washington, DC: American Psychiatric Press.

Green, B., Lindy, J., Grace, M., & Leonard, A. (1992). Chronic post-traumatic stress disorder and diagnostic comorbidity in a disaster sample. *Journal of Nervous and Mental Diseases, 180,* 760–66.

Green, M. F. (1993). Cognitive remediation in schizophrenia: Is it time yet? *American Journal of Psychiatry, 150,* 178–87.

Green, M. F. (1996). What are the functional consequences of neurocognitive deficits in schizophrenia? *American Journal of Psychiatry, 153,* 321–30.

Green, M. F., Nuechterlein, K. H., & Breitmeyer, B. (1997). Backward masking performance in unaffected siblings of schizophrenic patients: Evidence for a vulnerability indicator. *Archives of General Psychiatry, 54,* 465–72.

Green, M. F., Nuechterlein, K. H., & Mintz, J. (1994a). Backward masking in schizophrenia and mania: I. Specifying a mechanism. *Archives of General Psychiatry, 51,* 939–44.

Green, M. F., Nuechterlein, K. H., & Mintz, J. (1994b). Backward masking in schizophrenia and mania: II. Specifying the visual channels. *Archives of General Psychiatry, 51,* 945–51.

Green, R., & Fleming, D. T. (1990). Transsexual surgery follow-up: Status in the 1990s. *Annual Review of Sex Research, 1,* 163–74.

Green, T. M. (1997). Police as frontline mental health workers: The decision to arrest or refer to mental health agencies. *International Journal of Law and Psychiatry, 20,* 469–86.

Greenberg, M., Kusche, C., Cook, E., & Quamma, J. (1995). Promoting emotional competence in school-aged deaf children: The effects of the PATH curriculum. *Development and Psychopathology, 7,* 117–36.

Greenberg, R. P., Bornstein, R. G., Zborowski, M. J., Fisher, S., & Greenberg, M. D. (1994). A meta-analysis of fluoxetine outcome in the treatment of depression. *Journal of Nervous and Mental Disease, 182* (10): 547–51.

Greenblatt, J. (1997). *Year-end preliminary estimates from the 1996 Drug Abuse Warning Network (Office of Applied Studies).* Rockville, MD: U.S. Department of Health and Human Services.

Greene, R. L. (1991). *The MMPI-2/MMPI: An interpretive manual.* Boston: Allyn & Bacon.

Greenhill, L. (1998). Childhood attention deficit hyperactivity disorder: Pharmacological treatment. In P. Nathan & J. Gorman (Eds.), *A guide to treatments that work* (pp. 42–64). New York: Oxford University Press.

Greer, G., & Tolbert, R. (1986). Subjective reports of the effects of MDMA in a clinical setting. *Journal of Psychiatric Drugs, 18,* 319–27.

Greer, S. (1964). Study of parental loss in neurotics and sociopaths. *Archives of General Psychiatry, 11,* 177–80.

Greer, S., Morris, T., & Pettingale, K. W. (1979). Psychological response to breast cancer: Effect on outcome. *Lancet, II,* October 13, 785–87.

Gregoire, A. J., Kumar, R., Everitt, B., Henderson, A. F., & Studd, J. W. (1996). Transdermal estrogen for treatment of severe postnatal depression. *Lancet, 347,* 930–33.

Gregory, I. (1958). Studies on parental deprivation in psychiatric patients. *American Journal of Psychiatry, 115,* 432–42.

Gregory, R. (Ed.). (1987). *Oxford companion to the mind.* Oxford, England: Oxford University Press.

Greist, J. (1990). Treating the anxiety: Therapeutic options in obsessive-compulsive disorder. *Journal of Clinical Psychology, 51,* 29–34.

Greyson, B. (1997). Near-death narratives. In S. Krippner and S. Powers (Eds.), *Broken images, broken selves* (pp. 163–80). Washington, DC: Brunner/Mazel.

Griest, J. H. (1994). Behavior therapy for obsessive-compulsive disorder. *Journal of Clinical Psychiatry, 55* (10): 60–68.

Griest, J. H., Jefferson, J. W., Kobak, K. A., Katzelnick, D. J., & Serlin, R. C. (1995). Efficacy and tolerability of serotonin transport inhibitors in obsessive-compulsive disorder: A meta-analysis. *Archives of General Psychiatry, 52* (1): 53–60.

Grillon, C., Dierker, L., & Merikangas, K. R. (1997). Startle modulation in children at risk for anxiety disorders and/or alcoholism. *Journal of the American Academy of Child and Adolescent Psychiatry, 36,* 925–32.

Grilly, D. M. (1989). *Drugs and human behavior.* Boston: Allyn & Bacon.

Grinspoon, L., & Bakalar, J. B. (1976). *Cocaine.* New York: Basic Books.

Grinspoon, L., & Bakalar, J. B. (1986). Can drugs be used to enhance the psychotherapeutic process? *American Journal of Psychotherapy, 40,* 393–404.

Gross, H. J., & Zimmerman, J. (1965). Experimental analysis of hysterical blindness: A follow-up report and new experimental data. *Archives of General Psychiatry, 13,* 255–60.

Gross, R., Sasson, Y., Chopra, I., & Zohar, J. (1998). Biological models of obsessive-compulsive disorder: The serotonin hypothesis. In R. Swinson, M. Antony, S. Rachman, & M. Richter (Eds.), *Obsessive-compulsive disorder: Theory, research, and treatment* (pp. 141–53). New York: Guilford Press.

Grossman, H. J. (1983a). *Classification in mental retardation.* Washington, DC: American Association of Mental Deficiency.

Grossman, H. J. (Ed.). (1983b). *Manual on terminology and classification in mental retardation.* Washington, DC: American Association of Mental Deficiency.

Grove, W. M., & Andreasen, N. C. (1985). Language and thinking in psychosis. *Archives of General Psychiatry, 42,* 26–32.

Grueneich, R. (1992). The borderline personality disorder diagnosis: Reliability, diagnostic efficiency, and covariation with other personality disorder diagnoses. *Journal of Personality Disorders, 6* (3): 197–212.

Gualtieri, C. (1991). *Neuropsychiatry and behavioral pharmacology.* New York: Springer-Verlag.

Guarnaccia, P., & Rogler, L. (1999). Research on culture-bound syndromes: New directions. *American Journal of Psychiatry, 156* (9): 1322–27.

Gun, R. T., Korten, A. E., Jorm, A. F., Henderson, A. S., et al. (1997). Occupational risk factors for Alzheimer disease: A case-control study. *Alzheimer Disease and Associated Disorders, 11* (1): 21–27.

Gunderson, J. G., & Mosher, L. R. (1975). The cost of schizophrenia. *American Journal of Psychiatry, 132,* 901–906.

Gur, R. E., Mozley, P. D., Shtasel, D. L., Cannon, T. D., Gallacher, F., Turetsky, B., Grossman, R., & Gur, R. C. (1994). Clinical subtypes of schizophrenia: Differences in brain and CSF volume. *American Journal of Psychiatry, 151* (3): 343–50.

Gureje, O., Simon, G., Ustun, T., & Goldberg, D. P. (1997). Somatization in cross-cultural perspective: A World Health Organization study in primary care. *American Journal of Psychiatry, 154* (7): 989–95.

Gurley, R. J. , Aranow, R., & Katz, M. (1998). Medicinal marijuana: A comprehensive review. *Journal of Psychoactive Drugs, 30,* 137–47.

Gurvits, T. V., Shenton, M. E., Hokama, H., & Ohta, H. (1996). Magnetic resonance imaging study of hippocampal volume in chronic, combat-related posttraumatic stress disorder. *Biological Psychiatry, 40,* 1091–99.

Gurvits, T., Gilbertson, M., Lasko, N., et al. (2000). Neurological soft signs in chronic posttraumatic stress disorder. *American Journal of Psychiatry, 157,* 181–86.

Gustafsson, P. A., Bjorksten, B., & Kjellman, N.-I. (1994). Family dysfunction in asthma: A prospective study of illness development. *Journal of Pediatrics, 125* (3): 493–98.

Gustafsson, P. A., & Kjellman, N.-I. (1986). Family therapy in the treatment of severe childhood asthma. *Journal of Psychosomatic Research, 30* (3): 369–74.

Guze, S. B. (1993). Genetics of Briquet's syndrome and somatization disorder. A review of family, adoption, and twin studies. *Annals of Clinical Psychiatry, 5,* 225–30.

Guze, S. B. (1997). The genetics of alcoholism: 1997. *Clinical Genetics, 52,* 398–403.

Haas, G. L., & Sweeney, J. A. (1992). Premorbid and onset features of first-episode schizophrenia. *Schizophrenia Bulletin, 18,* 373–86.

Hackmann, A., & McLean, C. (1975). A comparison of flooding and thought-stopping treatment. *Behaviour Research and Therapy, 13,* 263–69.

Haldeman, D. C. (1994). The practice and ethics of sexual orientation conversion therapy. *Journal of Consulting and Clinical Psychology, 62* (2): 221–27.

Hall, G. C. (1995). Sexual offender recidivism revisited: A meta-analysis of recent treatment studies. *Journal of Consulting and Clinical Psychology, 63* (5): 802–809.

Hall, J. (1988). Fluoxetine: Efficacy against placebo and by dose—An overview. *British Journal of Psychiatry,* 59–63.

Hall, R. V., Fox, R., Willard, D., Goldsmith, L., Emerson, M., Owen, M., Davis, T., & Porcia, E. (1971). The teacher as observer and experimenter in the modification of disputing and talking-out behaviors. *Journal of Applied Behavior Analysis, 4,* 141–49.

Halpern, J. (1977). Projection: A test of the psychoanalytic hypothesis. *Journal of Abnormal Psychology, 86,* 536–42.

Hamburger, M. E., Lilienfeld, S. O., & Hogben, M. (1996). Psychopathy, gender, and gender roles: Implications for antisocial and histrionic personality disorders. *Journal of Personality Disorders, 10,* 41–55.

Hamer, D. H., Hu, S., Magnusson, V. L., Hu, N., & Patatucci, A. M. L. (1993). A linkage between DNA markers on the X chromosome and male sexual orientation. *Science, 261,* 321–27.

Hameury, L., Roux, S., Barthelemy, C., Adrien, J. L., et al. (1995). Quantified multidimensional assessment of autism and other pervasive developmental disorders: Application for bioclinical research. *European Child and Adolescent Psychiatry, 4,* 123–35.

Hamilton, M. (1967). Development of a rating scale for primary depressive illness. *British Journal of Social and Clinical Psychology, 6,* 278–96.

Hammen, C. (1991). *Depression runs in families: The social context of risk and resilience in children of depressed mothers.* New York: Springer Verlag.

Hammen, C. L., & Glass, D. R. (1975). Expression, activity, and evaluation of reinforcement. *Journal of Abnormal Psychology, 84,* 718–21.

Hammen, D. L., & Padesky, C. A. (1977). Sex differences in the expression of depressive responses on the Beck Depression Inventory. *Journal of Abnormal Psychology, 86,* 609–14.

Han, L., Schmaling, K., & Dunner, D. (1995). Descriptive validity and stability of diagnostic criteria for dysthymic disorder. *Comprehensive Psychiatry, 36* (5): 338–43.

Hankin, B. L., Abramson, L. Y., Moffitt, T. E., Silva, P. A., McGee, R., & Angell, K. E. (1998). Development of depression from preadolescence to young adulthood: Emerging gender differences in a 10-year longitudinal study. *Journal of Abnormal Psychology, 107,* 128–40.

Hanley, J. R., & Gard, F. (1995). A dissociation between developmental surface and phonological dyslexia in two undergraduate students. *Neuropsychologia, 33* (7): 909–14.

Hannum, R. D., Rosellini, R. A., & Seligman, M. E. P. (1976). Retention of learned helplessness and immunization in the rat from weaning to adulthood. *Developmental Psychology, 12,* 449–54.

Hardi, S. S., Craighead, W. E., & Evans, D. D. (1997). Modeling relapse in unipolar depression: The effects of dysfunctional cognitions and personality disorders. *Journal of Consulting and Clinical Psychology, 65* (3): 381–91.

Harding, C. M., & Keller, A. B. (1998). Long-term outcome of social functioning. In K. T. Mueser & N. Tarrier (Eds.), *Handbook of social functioning in schizophrenia* (pp. 134–48). Boston: Allyn & Bacon.

Hardy, J. A., & Higgins, G. A. (1992). Alzheimer's disease: The amyloid cascade hypothesis. *Science, 256,* 184.

Hardy, M. S., Armstrong, F. D., Martin, B. L., & Strawn, K. N. (1996). A firearm safety program for children: They just can't say no. *Journal of Developmental and Behavioral Pediatrics, 17,* 216–21.

Hare, R. D. (1965). Temporal gradient of fear arousal in psychopaths. *Journal of Abnormal Psychology, 70,* 442–45.

Hare, R. D. (1978). Electrodermal and cardiovascular correlates of sociopathy. In R. D. Hare & D. Schalling (Eds.), *Psychopathic behavior: Approaches to research.* New York: Wiley.

Hare, R. D. (1980). A research scale for the assessment of psychopathy in criminal populations. *Personality and Individual Differences, 1,* 111–19.

Hare, R. D. (1996). Psychopathy: A clinical construct whose time has come. *Criminal Justice and Behavior, 23,* 25–54.

Hare, R. D. (1998). Psychopaths and their nature: Implications for the mental health and criminal justice systems. In T. Millon, E. Simonsen, M. Birket-Smith, & R. D. Davis (Eds.), *Psychopathy: Antisocial, criminal, and violent behavior* (pp. 188–212). New York: Guilford Press.

Hare, R. D., & McPherson, L. M. (1984). Violent and aggressive behavior by criminal psychopaths. *International Journal of Law and Psychiatry, 7,* 329–37.

Hare, R. D., Williamson, S. E., & Harpur, T. J. (1988). Psychopathy and language. In T. E. Moffitt & S. A.

Mednick (Eds.), *Biological contributions to crime causation* (pp. 68–92). Dordecht, The Netherlands: Martinuus Nijhoff.

Hare, R. D., Harpur, T. J., Hakstian, A. R., & Forth, A. E. (1990). The revised psychopathy checklist: Reliability and factor structure. *Psychological Assessment, 2* (3): 338–41.

Harkness, K., Monroe, D., Simons, A., & Thase, M. (1999). The generation of life events in recurrent and non-recurrent depression. *Psychological Medicine, 29,* 135–44.

Harlow, J. M. (1868). Recovery from the passage of an iron bar through the head. *Publications of the Massachusetts Medical Society, 2,* 327.

Harrington, A. (Ed.) (1999). *The placebo effect.* Cambridge, MA: Harvard University Press.

Harrington, R. (1992). Annotation: The natural history and treatment of child and adolescent affective disorders. *Journal of Child Psychology and Psychiatry, 33* (8): 1287–1302.

Harris, C., & Goetsch, V. (1990). Multicomponent flooding treatment of adolescent phobia . In Feindler, E.L., & Kalfus, G. R. (1990). *Adolescent behavior therapy handbook* (pp. 147–65). New York: Springer Publishing Company.

Harris, E. L., Noyes, R., Crowe, R. R., & Chaudry, D. R. (1983). Family study of agoraphobia. *Archives of General Psychiatry, 40,* 1061–64.

Harris, G. J., Lewis, R. F., Satlin, A., English, C. D., Scott, T. M., Yurgelun-Todd, D. A., & Renshaw, P. F. (1996). Dynamic susceptibility contrast MRI of regional cerebral blood volume in Alzheimer's disease. *American Journal of Psychiatry, 153* (5): 721–24.

Harris, G. T., & Rice, M. E. (1997). Risk appraisal and management of violent behavior. *Psychiatric Services, 48,* 1168–76.

Harrison, R. (1965). Thematic apperceptive methods. In B. B. Wolman (Ed.), *Handbook of clinical psychology.* New York: Wiley.

Hart, K., & Kenny, M. E. (1997). Adherence to the Super Woman ideal and eating disorder symptoms among college women. *Sex Roles, 36,* 461–78.

Hartlage, L., Asken, M., & Hornsby, J. (1987). *Essentials of neuropsychological assessment.* New York: Springer.

Harvard Mental Health Letter. (1996a). Suicide, Part I. *The Harvard Mental Health Letter.* 13 (5): 1–5.

Harvard Mental Health Letter (1996b). Suicide, Part II. *The Harvard Mental Health Letter.* 13 (6): 1–5.

Haslam, N., & Beck, A. T. (1994). Subtyping major depression: A taxometric analysis. *Journal of Abnormal Psychology, 103* (4):686–92.

Hathaway, S. R., & McKinley, J. C. (1943). *MMPI manual.* New York: Psychological Corporation.

Hatton, C. (1998). Intellectual disabilities—Epidemiology and causes. In E. Emerson & C. Hatton (Eds.), *Clinical psychology and people with intellectual disabilities. The Wiley Series in Clinical Psychology* (pp. 20–38). Chichester, England: American Ethnological Press.

Hatzichristou, D. G., Bertero, E. B., & Goldstein, I. (1994). Decision making in the evaluation of impotence: The patient profile-oriented algorithm. *Sexuality and Disability, 12* (1): 29–37.

Haynes, J. D. (1995). A critique of the possibility of genetic inheritance of homosexual orientation. *Journal of Homosexuality, 28* (1–2): 91–113.

Haynes, S. G., Feinleib, M., & Kannel, W. B. (1980). The relationship of psychosocial factors to coronary heart disease in the Framingham study: III. Eight years incidence in coronary heart disease. *American Journal of Epidemiology, 3*, 37–85.

Hawley, G. A. (1988). *Measures of psychosocial development: Professional manual.* Odessa, FL: Psychological Assessment Resources.

Hazell, P., & Lewin, T. (1993). An evaluation of postvention following adolescent suicide. *Suicide and Life-Threatening Behavior, 23*, 101–109.

Hazlett, R. L., Falkin, S., Lawhorn, W., Friedman, E., & Haynes, S. N. (1997). Cardiovascular reactivity to a naturally occurring stressor: Development and psychometric evaluation of a psychophysiological assessment procedure. *Journal of Behavioral Medicine, 20* (6): 551–70.

Healy, D. (1994) The fluoxetine and suicide controversy: A review of the evidence. *Consumer Drugs, 1* (3): 223–31.

Healy, D., Langmaak, C., & Savage, M. (1999). Suicide in the course of the treatment of depression. *Journal of Psychopharmacology, 13*(1): 94–99.

Heatherton, T. F., & Baumeister, R. F. (1991). Binge eating as escape from self-awareness. *Psychological Bulletin, 101* (3): 428–42.

Heatherton, T. F., & Baumeister, R. F. (1991). Binge eating as escape from self-awareness. *Psychological Bulletin 110* (1): 86–108.

Heavey, L., Pring, L., & Hermelin, B. (1999). A date to remember: The nature of memory in savant calendrical calculators. *Psychological Medicine, 29*, 145–60.

Hecker, M., Chesney, M., Black, G., & Frautschi, N. (1988). Coronary-prone behaviors in the Western Collaborative Group Study. *Psychosomatic Medicine, 50*, 153–64.

Heebink, D. M., Sunday, S. R., & Halmi, K. A. (1995). Anorexia nervosa and bulimia nervosa in adolescence: Effects of age and menstrual status on psychological variables. *Journal of the American Academy of Child and Adolescent Psychiatry, 34* (3): 378–82.

Heider, F. (1958). *The psychology of interpersonal relationships.* New York: Wiley.

Heilbrun, A. B., Jr. (1993). Hallucinations. In C. G. Costello (Ed.), *Symptoms of schizophrenia* (pp. 56–91). New York: Wiley.

Heim, C., Owens, M.J., Plotsky, P.M., & Nemeroff, C.B. (1997). Persistent changes in corticotropin-releasing factor systems due to early life stress: Relationship to the pathophysiology of major depression and post-traumatic stress disorder. *Psychopharmacology Bulletin, 33*, 185–92.

Heiman, J. R., & LoPiccolo, J. (1983). Clinical outcome of sex therapy. *Archives of General Psychiatry, 40*, 443–49.

Heimberg, R. G., Liebowitz, M. R., Hope, D. A., Schneier, F. R., Holt, C. S., Welkowitz, L. A., Juster, H. R., Campeas, R., Bruch, M. A., Cloitre, M., Fallon, B., & Klein, D. F. (1998). Cognitive behavioral group therapy vs phenelzine therapy for social phobia: 12-week outcome. *Archives of General Psychiatry, 55* (12): 1133–41.

Heinrichs, R. W., & Zakzanis, K. K. (1998). Neurocognitive deficit in schizophrenia: A quantitative review of the evidence. *Neuropsychology, 12*, 426–45.

Heinz, A., Higley, J. D., Gorey, J. G., Saunders, R. C., Jones, D. W., Hommer, D., Zajicek, K., Suomi, S. J., Lesch, K.,

Weinberger, D. R., & Linnoila, M. (1998). In vivo association between alcohol intoxication, aggression, serotonin transporter availability in nonhuman primates. *American Journal of Psychiatry, 155*, 1023–28.

Heinz, A. Knable, M. B., Wolf, S. S., Jones, D. W., Gorey, J. G., Hyde, T. M., & Weinberger, D. R. (1998). Tourette's syndrome: [I-123]beta-CIT SPECT correlates of vocal tic severity. *Neurology, 51*, 1069–74.

Heinz, A., Schmidt, L. G., & Reischies, F. M. (1994). Anhedonia in schizophrenic, depressed, or alcohol-dependent patients: Neurobiological correlates. *Pharmacopsychiatry, 27* (Suppl. 1): 7–10.

Helderman-van den Enden, A. T. J. M., Maaswinkel-Mooij, P. D., Hoogendoorn, E., Willemsen, R., Maat-Kievit, J. A., Losekoot, M., & Oostra, B. A. (1999). Monozygotic twin brothers with the fragile X syndrome: Different CGG repeats and different mental capacities. *Journal of Medical Genetics, 36*, 253–57.

Helgeson, V. S., & Fritz, H. L. (1999).Cognitive adaptation as a predictor of new coronary events after percutaneous transluminal coronary angioplasty. *Psychosomatic Medicine, 61* (4): 488–95.

Hellekson, C. J., Kline, J. A., & Rosenthal, N. E. (1986). Phototherapy for seasonal affective disorder in Alaska. *American Journal of Psychiatry, 143*, 1035–37.

Hellewell, J. S. E., Connell, J., & Deakin, J. F. W. (1994). Affect judgement and facial recognition memory in schizophrenia. *Psychopathology, 27*, 255–61.

Hellman, S. G., Kern, R. S., Neilson, L. M., & Green, M. F. (1998). Monetary reinforcement and Wisconsin Card Sorting performance in schizophrenia: Why show me the money? *Schizophrenia Research, 34*, 67–75.

Hellström, K., Fellenius, J., & Ost, L-G. (1996). One versus five sessions of applied tension in the treatment of blood phobia. *Behaviour Research and Therapy, 34* (2): 101–12.

Helmes, E., & Reddon, J. R. (1993) A perspective on developments in assessing psychopathology: A critical review of the MMPI and MMPI-2. *Psychological Bulletin. 113* (3): 453–71.

Hemingway, H., Nicholson, A., Stafford, M., Roberts, R., & Marmot, M. (1997). The impact of socioeconomic status on health functioning as assessed by the SF-36 questionnaire: the Whitehall II Study. *American Journal of Public Health, 87*(9):1484–90.

Hemphill, J. F., Hare, R. D., & Wong, S. (1998). Psychopathy and recidivism: A review. *Legal and Criminological Psychology, 3*, 139–70.

Hemsley, D. R., & Ward, E. S. (1985). Individual differences in reaction to the abuse of LSD. *Personality and Individual Differences, 6*, 515–17.

Hemsley, R., Howlin, P., Berger, M., Hersov, L., Holbrook, D., Rutter, M., & Yule, W. (1978). Treating autistic children in a family context. In M. Rutter & E. Schopler (Eds.), *Autism: A reappraisal of concepts and treatment.* New York: Plenum.

Henderson, A. S., & Hasegawa, K. (1992). The epidemiology of dementia and depression in later life. In M. Bergener, K. Hasegawa, S. Finkel, & T. Nishimura (Eds.), *Aging and mental disorders* (pp. 65–79). New York: Springer.

Henderson, A. S., Jorm, A. F., Korten, A. E., Jacomb, P., Christensen, H. & Rodgers, B. (1998). Symptoms of anxiety and depression during adult life: Evidence for a decline in prevalence with age. *Psychological Medicine, 28,* 1321–28.

Henderson, A. S., & Kay, D. W. K. (1997). The epidemiology of functional psychoses of late onset. *European Archives of Psychiatry and Clinical Neuroscience, 247,* 176–89.

Henderson, A. S., Korten, A. E, Levings, C., Jorm, A. F., Christensen, H., Jacomb, P. A., & Rodgers, B. (1998). Psychotic symptoms in the elderly: A prospective study in a population sample. *International Journal of Geriatric Psychiatry, 13* (7): 484–92.

Hendin, H. (1969). Black suicide. *Archives of General Psychiatry, 21,* 407–22.

Hendin, H. (1974). Students on heroin. *Journal of Nervous Mental Disorders, 156,* 240–55.

Henker, B., & Whalen, C. K. (1989). Hyperactivity and attention deficits. *American Psychologist, 44* (2): 216–23.

Hennessy, K. D., & Stephens, S. (1997). Mental health parity: Clarifying our objectives. Psychiatric Services, 48, 161–64.

Henningfield, J. E., & Goldberg, S. R. (1983). Nicotine as a reinforcer in human subjects and laboratory animals. *Pharmacology, Biochemistry and Behavior, 19,* 989–92.

Henningfield, J. E., & Jasinski, D. R. (1983). Human pharmacology of nicotine. *Psychopharmacological Bulletin, 19,* 413–15.

Henry, C., Gilles, G., Cador, M., Arnauld, E., Arsaut, J., LeMoal, M., & Demotes-Mainard, J. (1995). Prenatal stress in rats facilitates amphetamine induced sensitization and induces long-lasting changes in dopamine receptors in the nucleus accumbens. *Brain Research, 685,* 179–86.

Henry, J. (1992). Toxicity of antidepressants: Comparison with fluoxetine. *International Clinical Psychopharmacology, 6* (Suppl. 6): 22–27.

Henry, J. P. (1992). Biological basis of the stress response. *Integrative Physiological and Behavioral Science, 27,* 66–83.

Hentschel, E., Brandstatter, G., Dragosics, B., Hirschl, A. M., Nemec, H., Schutze, K., Taufer, M., & Wurzer, H. (1993). Effect of ranitidine and amoxicillin plus metronidazole on the eradication of Helicobacter pylori and the recurrence of duodenal ulcer. *New England Journal of Medicine, 328*(5):308–12.

Herbert, J. D., Hope, D. A., & Bellack, A. S. (1992). Validity of the distinction between generalized social phobia and avoidance personality disorder. *Journal of Abnormal Psychology, 101* (2): 332–39.

Herkenham, M., Lynn, A. B., Little, M. D., Johnson, M. R., Melvin, L. S., de Costa, B., & Rice, K. C. (1990). Cannabinoid receptor localization in brain. *Proceedings of the National Academy of Sciences U.S.A., 87,* 1932–36.

Herman, C. P., & Mack, D. (1975). Restrained and unrestrained eating. *Journal of Personality, 43,* 647–60.

Hermann, C., Blanchard, E.B., & Flor, H. (1997). Biofeedback treatment for pediatric migraine: Prediction of treatment outcome. *Journal of Consulting and Clinical Psychology, 65* (4): 611–16.

Hermann, R. C., Dorwart, R. A., Hoover, C. W., & Brody, J. (1995).Variation in ECT use in the United States. *American Journal of Psychiatry, 152* (6): 869–75.

Hermelin, B., & O'Connor, N. (1970). *Psychological experiments with autistic children.* Oxford, England: Pergamon.

Herrmann, M., Bartels, C., Schumacher, M., & Wallesch, C. (1995). Poststroke depression: Is there a pathoanatomic correlate for depression in the postacute stage of stroke? *Stroke, 26* (5): 850–56.

Hersen, M., & Turner, S. M. (1994). *Diagnostic interviewing* (2nd ed.). New York: Plenum Press.

Hersh, D., Kranzler, H. R., & Meyer, R. E. (1997). Persistent delirium following cessation of heavy alcohol consumption: Diagnostic treatment implications. *American Journal of Psychiatry, 154,* 846–55.

Hesselbrock, V., Meyer, R., & Hesselbrock, M. (1992). Psychopathology and addictive disorders: The specific case of antisocial personality disorder. In C. P. O'Brien & J. H. Jaffe (Eds.), *Addictive states.* New York: Raven Press.

Heston, L. L. (1966). Psychiatric disorders in foster home reared children of schizophrenic mothers. *British Journal of Psychiatry, 112,* 819–25.

Heston, L. L., & Denney, D. (1968). Interactions between early life experience and biological factors in schizophrenia. In D. Rosenthal & S. S. Kety (Eds.), *The transmission of schizophrenia* (pp. 363–76). New York: Pergamon.

Hetherington, E. M., & Martin, B. (1979). Family interaction. In H. C. Quay & J. S. Werry (Eds.), *Psychopathological disorders of childhood.* New York: Wiley.

Heumann, K. A., & Morey, L. C. (1990). Reliability of categorical and dimensional judgments of personality disorder. *American Journal of Psychiatry, 147* (4): 498–500.

Heun, R., & Maier, W. (1995). Risk of Alzheimer's disease in first-degree relatives. [Letter to the Editor]. *Archives of General Psychiatry, 52.*

Hewitt, J. K., Silberg, J. L., Rutter, M., Simonoff, E., Meyer, J. M., Maes, H., Pickles, A., Neale, M. C., Loeber, R., Erickson, M. T., Kendler, K. S., Heath, A. C., Truett, K. R., Reynolds, C. A., & Eaves, L. J. (1997). Genetics and developmental psychopathology: 1. Phenotypic assessment in the Virginia Twin Study of Adolescent Behavioral Development. *Journal of Child Psychology and Psychiatry and Allied Disciplines, 38,* 943–63.

Higgins, S. T., Budney, A. J., Bickel, W. K., Hughes, J. R., Foerg, F., & Badger, G. (1993). Achieving cocaine abstinence with a behavioral approach. *American Journal of Psychiatry, 150* (5): 763–69.

Higgins, S. T., & Silverman, K. (Eds.). (1999). *Motivating behavior change among illicit-drug abusers: Research on contingency management interventions.* Washington, DC: American Psychological Association.

Higley, J. D., Hasert, M. F., Suomi, S. J., & Linnoila, M. (1991). Non-human primate model of alcohol abuse: Effects of early experience, personality and stress on alcohol consumption. *Proceedings of the National Academy of Sciences U.S.A., 88,* 7261–65.

Higley, J. D., King, S. T., Hasert, M. F., Champoux, M., Suomi, S. J., & Linnoila, M. (1996). Stability of interindividual differences in serotonin function and its relationship to severe aggression and competent social behavior in rhesus macaque females. *Neuropsychopharmacology, 14,* 67–76.

Higley, J. D., Mehlman, P. T., Taub, D. M., Higley, S. B., et al. (1992). Cerebrospinal fluid monoamine and adrenal correlates of aggression in free-ranging rhesus monkeys. *Archives of General Psychiatry, 49,* 436–41.

Higley, J. D., Suomi, S. J., & Linnoila, M. (1990). Parallels in aggression and serotonin: Consideration of development, rearing history, and sex differences. In H. M. van Praag & R. Plutchik (Eds.), *Violence and suicidality: Perspectives in clinical and psychobiological research. Clinical and experimental psychiatry* (Vol. 3; pp. 245–56). New York: Brunner/Mazel.

Hilgard, E. R. (1977). *Divided consciousness: Multiple controls in human thought and action.* New York: Wiley.

Hill, P. O. (1972). Latent aggression and drug-abuse: An investigation of adolescent personality factors using an original cartoon-o-graphic aggressive tendencies test. *Dissertation Abstracts International, 33,* 1765.

Hill, R., Rigdon, M., & Johnson, S. (1993). Behavioral smoking cessation treatment for older chronic smokers. *Behavior Therapy, 24,* 321–29.

Hiller, W., Rief, W., & Fichter, M. M. (1997). How disabled are patients with somatoform disorders? *General Hospital Psychiatry, 19* (6): 432–38.

Hilsenroth, M. J., Holdwick, D. J., Castlebury, F. D., & Blais, M. A. (1998). The effects of DSM-IV cluster B personality disorder symptoms on the termination and continuation of psychotherapy. *Psychotherapy, 35,* 163–76.

Hilsman, R., & Garber, J. (1995). A test of the cognitive diathesis-stress model of depression in children: Academic stressors, attributional style, perceived competence, and control. *Journal of Personality and Social Psychology, 69* (2): 370–80.

Hilton, G. (1994). Behavioral and cognitive sequelae of head trauma. *Orthopaedic Nursing, 13* (4): 25–32.

Hilts, P. J. (1994a). Cigarette makers dispute reports on addictiveness. *New York Times,* April 15, p. A1.

Hilts, P. J. (1994b). Is nicotine addictive? It depends on whose criteria you use. *New York Times,* August 2, pp. C1, C3.

Hinshaw, S. P., Klein, R. G., & Abikoff, H. (1998). Childhood attention deficit hyperactivity disorder: Nonpharmacological and combination treatments. In P. E. Nathan & J. M. Gorman (Eds.), *A guide to treatments that work* (pp. 26–41). New York: Oxford University Press.

Hinshaw, S. P., & Melnick, S. M. (1995). Peer relationships in boys with attention-deficit hyperactivity disorder with and without comorbid aggression. *Development and Psychopathology, 7*(4): 627–47.

Hirayasu, Y., Shenton, M., Salisbury, D. F., Dickey, C. C., Fischer, I. A., Mazzoni, P., Kisler, T., Arakaki, H., Kwon, J. S., Anderson, J. E., Yurgelun-Todd, D., Tohen, M., & McCarley, R. (1998). Lower left temporal lobe MRI volumes in patients with first-episode schizophrenia compared with psychotic patients with first-episode affective disorder and normal subjects. *American Journal of Psychiatry, 155,* 1384–91.

Hiroto, D. S. (1974). Locus of control and learned helplessness. *Journal of Experimental Psychology, 102,* 187–93.

Hiroto, D. S., & Seligman, M. E. P. (1975). Generality of learned helplessness in man. *Journal of Personality and Social Psychology, 31,* 311–27.

Hirschfeld, R. (1997). Pharmacotherapy of borderline personality disorder. *Journal of Clinical Psychiatry, 58* (Suppl 14): 48–52.

Hirschfeld, R. M. A. (1999). Efficacy of SSRIs and newer antidepressants in severe depression: Comparison with TCAs. *Journal of Clinical Psychiatry, 60* (5): 326–35.

Hirst, W. (1982). The amnesic syndrome: Descriptions and explanations. *Psychology Bulletin, 91,* 1480–83.

Hitt, J. (2000). The second sexual revolution. *New York Times Magazine,* February 20.

Hobbs, F., & Damon, B. (1996). 65 + in the United States. In *U. S. Bureau of the Census, Current Population Reports* (pp. 23–190). Washington, DC: US Bureau of the Census.

Hobson, R. P. (1986). The autistic child's appraisal of expressions of emotion. *Journal of Childhood Psychology and Psychiatry, 27,* 321–42.

Hodel, B., & Brenner, H. D. (1997). A new development in integrated psychological therapy for schizophrenic patients (IPT): First results of emotional management training. In H. D. Brenner & W. Boeker (Eds.), *Towards a comprehensive therapy for schizophrenia* (pp. 118–34). Goettingen, Germany: Hogrefe & Huber.

Hodgson, R., Rachman, S., & Marks, I. (1972). The treatment of chronic obsessive-compulsive neurosis. *Behaviour Research and Therapy, 10,* 181–89.

Hofmann, A. (1968). Psychotomimetic agents. In A. Burger (Ed.), *Drugs affecting the central nervous system* (Vol. 2). New York: Marcel Dekker.

Hogan, R. (1969). Development of an empathy scale. *Journal of Consulting and Clinical Psychology, 33,* 307–16.

Hogarty, G. E., Anderson, C. M., Reiss, D. J., Kornblith, S. J., Greenwald, D. P., Javna, C. D., & Madonia, M. J. (1986). Family psychoeducation, social skills training and maintenance chemotherapy in the aftercare treatment of schizophrenia: I. One-year effects of a controlled study on relapse and expressed emotion. *Archives of General Psychiatry, 43,* 633–42.

Hogarty, G. E., Greenwald, D., Ulrich, R. F., Kornblith, S. J., DiBarry, A. L., Cooley, S., Carter, M., & Flesher, S. (1997). Three-year trials of personal therapy among schizophrenic patients living with or independent of family, II: Effects on adjustment of patients. *American Journal of Psychiatry, 154* (11): 1514–24.

Hogarty, G. E., Kornblith, S. J., Greenwald, D., DiBarry, A. L., Cooley, S., Ulrich, R. F., Carter, M., & Flesher, S. (1997). Three-year trials of personal therapy among schizophrenic patients living with or independent of family: I. Description of study and effects of relapse rates. *American Journal of Psychiatry, 154* (11): 1504–13.

Hokanson, J. E. (1961). The effects of frustration and anxiety on aggression. *Journal of Abnormal and Social Psychology, 62,* 346.

Hokanson, J. E., & Burgess, M. (1962). The effects of three types of aggression on vascular processes. *Journal of Abnormal and Social Psychology, 65,* 446–49.

Hokanson, J. E., Willers, K. R., & Koropsak, E. (1968). Modification of autonomic responses during aggressive interchange. *Journal of Personality, 36,* 386–404.

Holahan, C. J., Valentiner, D. P., & Moos, R. H. (1995). Parental support, coping strategies, and psychological adjustment: An integrative model with late adolescents. *Journal of Youth and Adolescence, 24* (6): 633–48.

Holahan, C. J., Holahan, C. K., Moos, R. H., & Brennan, P. L. (1997). Psychosocial adjustment in patients reporting cardiac illness. *Psychology and Health, 12* (3): 345–59.

Holbrook, A. M., Crowther, R., Lotter, A., Cheng, C., & King, D. (1999). Diagnosis and management of acute alcohol withdrawal. *Canadian Medical Association Journal, 160,* 675–80.

Holcomb, H. H., Ritzl, E. K., Medoff, D. R., Nevitt, J., et al. (1995). Tone discrimination performance in schizophrenic patients and normal volunteers: Impact of stimulus presentation levels and frequency differences. *Psychiatry Research, 57,* 75–82.

Holden, C. (1986). Youth suicide: New research focuses on a growing social problem. *Science, 233,* 839–41.

Holden, C. (2000). Global survey examines impact of depression. *Science, 288,* 39–40.

Hollander, E., & Aronowitz, B. R. (1999). Comorbid social anxiety and body dysmorphic disorder: Managing the complicated patient. *Journal of Clinical Psychiatry, 60* (Suppl 9): 27–31.

Hollander, E., Schiffman, E., Cohen, B., et al. (1990). Signs of central nervous system dysfunction in obsessive-compulsive disorder. *Archives of General Psychiatry, 47,* 27–32.

Hollingshead, A. B., & Redlich, F. C. (1958). *Social class and mental illness: A community study.* New York: Wiley.

Hollister, L. E. (1986). Health aspects of cannabis. *Pharmacological Reviews, 38,* 1–20.

Hollon, S. D., & Kendall, P. C. (1980). Cognitive self-statements in depression: Development of an automatic thoughts questionnaire. *Cognitive Therapy and Research, 4,* 383–95.

Hollon, S. D., Kendall, P. C., & Lumry, A. (1986). Specificity of depressotypic cognitions in clinical depression. *Journal of Abnormal Psychology, 95,* 52–59.

Holmes, D. (1990). The evidence for repression: An example of sixty years of research. In J. Singer (Ed.), *Repression and dissociation: Implications for personality theory, psychopathology, and health* (pp. 85–102). Chicago: University of Chicago Press.

Holmes, R. M. (1991). *Sex crimes.* Newbury Park, CA: Sage Publications.

Holmes, T. H., & Rahe, R. H. (1967). The social readjustment ratings scale. *Journal of Psychosomatic Research, 11,* 213–18.

Holster, S. L. (1996). Facilitated communication. *Pediatrics, 97,* 584–86.

Holt, C. S., Heimberg, R. G., & Hope, D. A. (1992). Avoidant personality disorder and the generalized subtype in social phobia. *Journal of Abnormal Psychology, 102,* 318–25.

Holtzman, W. H. (1961). *Inkblot perception and personality: Holtzman Inkblot Technique.* Austin: University of Texas Press.

Hooker, W. D., & Jones, R. T. (1987). Increased susceptibility to memory intrusions and the Stroop interference effect during acute marijuana intoxication. *Psychopharmacology, 91,* 20–24.

Hooley, J. M. (1998). Expressed emotion and locus of control. *Journal of Nervous and Mental Disease, 186,* 374–78.

Hope, B. T. (1999). Cocaine and a mechanism for long-term changes in gene expression. In G. G. Nahas & K. M. Sutin (Eds.), *Marihuana and medicine* (pp. 213–22). Clifton, NJ: Humana.

Horne, R. L., & Picard, R. S. (1979). Psychosocial risk factors for lung cancer. *Psychosomatic Medicine, 41,* 503–14.

Horney, K. (1945). *Our inner conflicts: A constructive theory of neurosis.* New York: Norton.

Horowitz, M. (1975). Intrusive and repetitive thoughts after experimental stress. *Archives of General Psychiatry, 32,* 1457–63.

Horowitz, M. J. (1997). Psychotherapy of histrionic personality disorder. *Journal of Psychotherapy Practice and Research, 6*(2): 93–107.

Horowitz, M., Stinson, C., Curtis, D., et al. (1993). Topic and signs: Defensive control of emotional expression. *Journal of Consulting and Clinical Psychology, 61,* 421–30.

Horter, D. H. (1989). Neuropsychological status of asymptomatic individuals seropositive to HIV-1. *Annals of Neurology, 26,* 589–91.

Horton, A.M., Jr. (1997). The Halstead-Reitan Neuropsychological Test Battery: Problems and prospects. In A.M. Horton Jr. & D. Wedding (Eds.), *The neuropsychology handbook, Vol. 1: Foundations and assessment* (2nd ed.; pp. 221–54). New York: Springer.

Houghton, G., & Tipper, S. P. (1998). A model of selective attention as a mechanism of cognitive control. In J. Grainger & A. M. Jacobs (Eds.), *Localist connectionist approaches to human cognition. Scientific psychology series* (pp. 39–74). Mahwah, NJ: Lawrence Erlbaum.

Houts, A. C. (1991). Nocturnal enuresis as a biobehavioral problem. *Behavior Therapy, 22,* 133–51.

Howard, K. I., Kopta, S. M., Krause, M. K., & Orlinsky, D. E. (1986). The dose effect relationship of psychotherapy. *American Psychologist, 41,* 159–64.

Howard, R., Castle, D., Wessely, S., & Murray, R. (1993). A comparative study of 470 cases of early-onset and late-onset schizophrenia. *British Journal of Psychiatry, 163,* 352–57.

Hrubec, Z., & Omenn, G. S. (1981). Evidence of genetic predisposition to alcohol cirrhosis and psychosis: Twin concordances for alcoholism and its biological end points by zygosity among male veterans. *Alcoholism: Clinical and Experimental Research, 5,* 207–12.

Hsu, L. K. G. (1980). Outcomes of anorexia nervosa: A review of the literature (1954–1979). *Archives of General Psychiatry, 37,* 1041–45.

Hu, T., & Jerrell, J. M. (1998). Estimating the cost of impact of three case management programmes for treating people with severe mental illness. *British Journal of Psychiatry, 173* (Supp. 36): 26–32.

Hubel, D. H. (1995). *Eye, brain, and vision. Scientific American library series* (No. 22). New York: Scientific American Library/Scientific American Books.

Hucker, S. J. (1997). Sexual sadism: Psychopathology and theory. In D. R. Laws & W. O'Donohue (Eds.), *Sexual deviance: Theory, assessment, and treatment* (pp. 194–209). New York: Guilford Press.

Hudson, J. I., Pope, H. G., Jonas, J. M., & Yurgelun-Todd, D. (1987). A controlled family history study of bulimia. *Psychological Medicine, 17* (4): 883–90.

Hudson, S. M., & Ward, T. (1997). Rape: Psychopathology and theory. In D. R. Laws & W. O'Donohue (Eds.), *Sexual deviance: Theory, assessment, and treatment* (pp. 332–55). New York: Guilford Press.

Huesmann, L. R., Eron, L. D., Lefkowitz, M. M., & Walder, L. O. (1984). Stability of aggression over time and generations. *Developmental Psychology, 20,* 1120–34.

Hugdahl, K., & Ohman, A. (1977). Effects of instruction on acquisition and extinction of electrodermal response to fear-relevant stimuli. *Journal of Experimental Psychology: Human Learning and Memory, 3* (5): 608–18.

Hulstaert, F., Blennow, K., Ivanoiu, A., Schoonderwaldt, H. C., Riemenschneider, M., De Deyn, P. P., Bancher, C., Cras, P., Wiltfang, J., Mehta, P. D., Iqbal, K., Pottel, H., Vanmechelen, E., & Vanderstichele, H. (1999). Improved discrimination of AD patients using beta-amyloid-sub (1-42) and tau levels in CSF. *Neurology, 52,* 1555–62.

Hultman, C. M., Wieselgren, I., & Oehman, A. (1997). Relationships between social support, social coping and life events in the relapse of schizophrenic patients. *Scandinavian Journal of Psychology, 38,* 3–13.

Hung, D. W., Rotman, Z., Consentino, A., & MacMillan, M. (1983). Cost and effectiveness of an educational program for autistic children using a systems approach. *Education and Treatment of Children, 6* (1): 47–68.

Hunt, C., & Andrews, G. (1995). Comorbidity in the anxiety disorders: The use of a life-chart approach. *Journal of Psychiatric Research, 29,* 467–80.

Hunt, C., & Singh, M. (1991). Generalized anxiety disorder. *International Review of Psychiatry, 3,* 215–29.

Hunt, E., Browning, P., & Nave, G. (1982). A behavioral exploration of dependent and independent mildly mentally retarded adolescents and their mothers. *Applied Research in Mental Retardation, 3,* 141–50.

Hunt, M. G. (1998). The only way out is through: Emotional processing and recovery after a depressing life event. *Behaviour Research and Therapy, 36* (4): 361–84.

Hunt, W. A., Barnett, L. W., & Branch, L. G. (1971). Relapse rates in addiction programs. *Journal of Clinical Psychology, 27,* 455–56.

Hur, Y., & Bouchard, T. J. (1995). Genetic influences on perceptions of childhood family environment: A reared apart twin study. *Child Development, 66,* 330–45.

Husain, S. A., Nair, J., Holcomb, W., Reid, J. C., Vargas, V., & Nair, S. S. (1998). Stress reactions of children and adolescents in war and siege conditions. *American Journal of Psychiatry, 155* (12): 1718–19.

Huston, A. (1985). The development of sex typing: Themes from recent research. *Developmental Review, 5,* 1–17.

Hutchings, B., & Mednick, S. A. (1977). Criminality in adoptees and their adoptive and biological parents: A pilot study. In S. A. Mednick & K. O. Christiansen (Eds.), *Biosocial bases of criminal behavior* (pp. 127–41). New York: Gardner Press.

Huttenlocher, P. R. (1990). Morphometric study of human cerebral cortex development. *Neuropsychologia 28* (6): 517–27.

Huttunen, M. (1989). Maternal stress during pregnancy and the behavior of the offspring. In S. Doxiadis & S. Stewert (Eds.), *Early influences shaping the individual. NATO Advanced Science Institute Series: Life Sciences* (Vol. 160). New York: Plenum Press.

Huttunen, M. O., Machon, R. A., & Mednick, S. A. (1994). Prenatal factors in the pathogenesis of schizophrenia. *British Journal of Psychiatry, 164* (Suppl. 23): 15–19.

Hyde, T. M., Aaronson, B. A., Randolph, C., Rickler, K. C., & Weinberger, D. R. (1992). Relationship of birth weight to the phenotypic expression of Gilles de la Tourette's syndrome in monozygotic twins. *Neurology, 42,* 652–58.

Hyler, S. E., & Spitzer, R. T. (1978). Hysteria split asunder. *American Journal of Psychiatry, 135,* 1500–1504.

Hyman, B. M. & Pedrick, C. (1999). *The OCD Workbook: Your guide to breaking free from obsessive-compulsive disorder.* Oakland, CA: New Harbinger Publications.

Hyman, S. E. (2000). The millennium of mind, brain, and behavior. *Archives of General Psychiatry, 57* (1): 88–89.

Iacono, W. G., Moreau, M., Beiser, M., Fleming, J. A. E., & Lin, R. Y. (1992). Smooth-pursuit eye tracking in first-episode psychotic patients and their relatives. *Journal of Abnormal Psychology, 101,* 104–16.

Ilardi, S. S., Craighead, W. E., & Evans, D. D. (1997). Modeling relapse in unipolar depression: The effects of dysfunctional cognitions and personality disorders. *Journal of Consulting and Clinical Psychology, 65*(3): 381–91.

Imber, S. D., Pilkonis, P. A., Sotsky, S. M., & Elkin, I. (1990). Mode-specific effects among three treatments for depression. *Journal of Consulting and Clinical Psychology 58*(3): 352–59.

Imboden, J. B., Cantor, A., & Cluff, L. E. (1961). Convalescence from influenza: The study of the psychological and clinical determinants. *Archives of Internal Medicine, 108,* 393–99.

Imperato-McGinley, J., Peterson, R. E., Gautier, T., & Sturla, E. (1979). Androgens and the evolution of male-gender identity among male pseudohermaphrodites with 5-(-reductase deficiency. *New England Journal of Medicine, 300,* 1233–39.

Ingham, R. J., Andrews, G., & Winkler, R. (1972). Stuttering: A comparative evaluation of the short-term effectiveness of four treatment techniques. *Journal of Communicative Disorders, 5,* 91–117.

Inouye, E. (1972). A search for a research framework of schizophrenia in twins and chromosomes. In A. R. Kaplan (Ed.), *Genetic factors in schizophrenia* (pp. 495–503). Springfield, IL: Thomas.

Insel, T. R. (1992). Toward a neuroanatomy of obsessive-compulsive disorder. *Archives of General Psychiatry, 49,* 739–44.

Insel, T. R. (1997). A neurobiological basis of social attachment. *American Journal of Psychiatry, 154,* 726–35.

Intrator, J., Hare, R., Stritzke, P., Brichtswein, K., Dorfman, D., Harpur, T., Bernstein, D., Handelsman, L., Schaefer, C., Keilp, J., Rosen, J., & Machac, J. (1997). A brain imaging (single photon emission computerized tomography) study of semantic and affective processing in psychopaths. *Biological Psychiatry, 42,* 96–103.

Ironson, M., Taylor, F., Boltwood, M., et al. (1992). Effects of anger on left ventricle rejection fraction in coronary artery disease. *American Journal of Cardiology, 70,* 281–85.

Irwin, M., Daniels, M., Bloom, E. T., Smith, T. L., & Weiner, H. (1987). Life events, depressive symptoms, and immune function. *American Journal of Psychiatry, 144,* 437–41.

Ivarsson, T., Larsson, B., & Gillberg, C. (1998). A 2–4 year follow-up of depressive symptoms, suicidal ideation, and suicide attempts among adolescent psychiatric inpatients. *European Child and Adolescent Psychiatry, 7,* 96–104.

Jablensky, A. (1997). The 100-year epidemiology of schizophrenia. *Schizophrenia Research, 28,* 111–25.

Jablensky, A., Sartorius, N., Ernberg, G., Anker, M., Korten, A., Cooper, J. E., Day, R., & Bertelsen, A. (1992). Schizophrenia: Manifestations, incidence, and course in different cultures. A World Health Organization ten-country study. *Psychological Medicine* (Monograph Supplement 20): 1–97.

Jackson, D. D. (Ed). (1960). *The etiology of schizophrenia.* New York: Basic Books.

Jackson, I. M. (1998). The thyroid axis and depression. *Thyroid, 8,* 951–56.

Jacobsen, F. M. (1995). Can psychotropic medications change ethnoculturally determined behavior? *Cultural Diversity and Mental Health, 1,* 67–72.

Jacobsen, L. K., Giedd, J. N., Castellanos, F. X., Vaituzis, A. C., Hamburger, S. D., Kumra, S., Lenane, M. C., & Rapoport, J. L. (1998). Progressive reduction of temporal lobe structures in childhood-onset schizophrenia. *American Journal of Psychiatry, 155,* 678–85.

Jacobson, N. (1992). Behavior couple therapy: A new beginning. *Behavior Therapy, 23,* 493–506.

Jacobson, N., & Gortner, E. (2000). Can depression be demedicalized in the 21st century: Scientific revolutions, counter-revolutions and the magnetic field of normal science. *Behaviour Research and Therapy, 38,* 103–18.

Jacobson, N. S., Dobson, K. S., Truax, P. A., Addis, M. E., Koerner, K., Gollan, J. K., Gortner, E. & Prince, S. E. (1996). A component analysis of cognitive-behavioral treatment for depression. *Journal of Consulting and Clinical Psychology, 64* (2): 295–304.

Jacobson, N. S., & Hollon, S. D. (1996a). Cognitive-behavior therapy versus pharmacotherapy: Now that the jury's returned its verdict, it's time to present the rest of the evidence. *Journal of Consulting and Clinical Psychology, 64* (1): 74–80.

Jacobson, N. S., & Hollon, S. D. (1996b). Prospects for future comparisons between drugs and psychotherapy: Lessons from the CBT-versus-pharmacotherapy exchange. *Journal of Consulting and Clinical Psychology, 64* (1): 104–8.

Jaffe, J. H. (1985). Drug addiction and drug abuse. In A. J. Goodman & L. S. Gilman (Eds.), *The pharmacological basis of therapeutics.* New York: Macmillan.

James, B. (1997). *Handbook of treatment of attachment—trauma problems in children.* New York: Free Press.

James, R. M. (1959). Jurors' assessment of criminal responsibility. *Social Problems, 7,* 58–67.

Jammer, L. D., & Leigh, H. (1999). Repressive/defensive coping, endogenous opioids, and health: How a life so perfect can make you sick. *Psychiatry Research, 85,* 17–31.

Janssen, R. S., Saykin, A. J., Cannon, L., et al. (1989). Neurological and neuropsychological manifestation of HIV-1 infection: Association with AIDS-related complex but not asymptomatic HIV-1 infection. *Annals of Neurology, 26,* 592–600.

Jarrett, R. B., Basco, M. R., Risser, R., Ramanan, J., Marwill, M., Kraft, D., & Rush, A. J. (1998). Is there a role for continuation phase cognitive therapy for depressed outpatients? *Journal of Consulting and Clinical Psychology, 66* (6): 1036–40.

Jaycox, L., Reivich, K., Gillham, J., & Seligman, M. (1994). Prevention of depressive symptoms in schoolchildren. *Behaviour Research and Therapy, 32* (8):801–16.

Jefferson, J. (1990). Lithium: The present and the future. *Journal of Clinical Psychiatry, 5,* 4–8.

Jefferson, J. W., & Griest, J. H. (1996). The pharmacotherapy of obsessive-compulsive disorder. *Psychiatric Annals, 26* (4): 202–209.

Jeffrey, R., Adlis, S., & Forster, J. (1991). Prevalence of dieting among working men and women: The healthy worker project. *Health Psychology, 10,* 274–81.

Jellenek, E. (1960). *The disease concept of alcoholism.* Highland Park, NJ: Hillhouse.

Jenike, M., Baer, L., Ballantine, T., et al. (1991). Cingulotomy for refractory obsessive-compulsive disorder. *Archives of General Psychiatry, 48,* 548–55.

Jenike, M., Baer, L., Summergrad, P., et al. (1989). Obsessive-compulsive disorder: A double-blind, placebo-controlled trial of clomipramine in 27 patients. *American Journal of Psychiatry, 146,* 1328–30.

Jenkins, C. D. (1982). Psychosocial risk factors for coronary heart disease. *Acta Medica Scandinavia Supplimentum, 660,* 123–36.

Jenkins, C. D., Rosenman, R. H., & Friedman, M. (1967). Development of an objective psychological test for the determination of the coronary prone behavior pattern in employed men. *Journal of Chronic Disease, 20,* 371–79.

Jens, K. S., & Evans, H. I. (1983). *The diagnosis and treatment of multiple personality clients.* Workshop presented at the Rocky Mountain Psychological Association, Snowbird, Utah, April 1983.

Jerome, J. (1880). Intern's syndrome. In *Three men in a boat, not to mention the dog.*

Jerome, J. (1979). Catching them before suicide. *New York Times Magazine,* January 14.

Jeste, D. V., & Caligiuri, M. P. (1993). Tardive dyskinesia. *Schizophrenia Bulletin, 19,* 303–15.

Jeste, D. V., Alexopoulos, G. S., Bartels, S. J., Cummings, J. L., Gallo, J. J., Gottlieb, G. L. Halpain, M. C., Palmer, B. W., Patterson, T. L., Reynolds, C. F., & Lebowitz, B. D. (1999). Consensus statement on the upcoming crisis in geriatric mental health: Research agenda for the next 2 decades. *Archives of General Psychiatry, 56* (9): 848–53.

Johnson, A. M., Wadsworth, J., Wellings, K., Bradshaw, S., & Field, J. (1992). Sexual lifestyles and the HIV risk. *Nature, 360,* 410–12.

Johnson, D. A. (1981). Studies of depressive symptoms in schizophrenia: I The prevalence of depression and its possible causes. *British Journal of Psychiatry, 139,* 89–101.

Johnson, H., Olafsson, K., Andersen, J., Plenge, P., et al. (1989). Lithium every second day. *American Journal of Psychiatry, 146,* 557.

Johnson, K. M., & Jones, S. M. (1990). Neuropharmacology of phencyclidine: Basic mechanisms and therapeutic potential. *Annual Review of Pharmacology and Toxicology, 30,* 707–50.

Johnson, R. A., & Gerstein, D. R. (1998). Initiation of use of alchohol, cigarettes, marijuana, cocaine, and other substances in U.S. birth cohorts since 1919. *American Journal of Public Health, 88,* 27–33.

Johnson, S., & Jacob, T. (2000). Sequential interactions in the marital communication of depressed men and women. *Journal of Consulting and Clinical Psychology, 68,* 4–12.

Johnston, C., & Ohan, J. L. (1999). Externalizing disorders. In W. K. Silverman & T. H. Ollendick (Eds.), *Developmental issues in the clinical treatment of children* (pp. 279–94). Boston: Allyn & Bacon.

Joiner, T. E., Catanzaro, S. J., & Laurent, J. (1996) Tripartite structure of positive and negative affect, depression, and anxiety in child and adolescent psychiatric patients. *Journal of Abnormal Psychology 105* (3): 401–409.

Jones, B. C., Hou, X., & Cook, M. N. (1996). Effect of exposure to novelty on brain monoamines in C57BL/6 and DBA/2 mice. *Physiology and Behavior, 59,* 361–67.

Jones, K. M., & Friman, P. C. (1999). A case study of behavioral assessment and treatment of insect phobia. *Journal of Applied Behavior Analysis, 32* (1): 95–98.

Jones, P. (1995). Childhood motor milestones and IQ prior to adult schizophrenia: Results from a 43-year-old British birth cohort. *Psychiatria Fennica, 26,* 63–80.

Jones, P. B., Bebbington, P., Foerster, A., Lewis, S. W., et al. (1993). Premorbid social underachievement in schizophrenia: Results from the Camberwell Collaborative Psychosis Study. *British Journal of Psychiatry, 162,* 65–71.

Jones, P. B., Rantakallio, P., Hartikainen, A., Isohanni, M., & Sipila, P. (1998). Schizophrenia as a long-term outcome of pregnancy, delivery, and perinatal complications: A 28-year follow-up of the 1966 North Finland general population birth cohort. *American Journal of Psychiatry, 155,* 355–64.

Jones, R. T., & Benowitz, N. (1976). The 30–day trip: Clinical studies of cannabis tolerance and dependence. In M. C. Braude & S. Szara (Eds.), *Pharmacology of marihuana* (Vol. 2; pp. 627–42). New York: Academic Press.

Jordan, R., & Powell, S. (1995). *Understanding and teaching children with autism.* Chichester, England: Wiley.

Jorm, A. F. (1995). The epidemiology of depressive states in the elderly: Implications for recognition, intervention, and prevention. *Social Psychiatry and Psychiatric Epidemiology, 30,* 53–59.

Josefson, D. (1999). Scientists raise possibility of vaccine for Alzheimer's disease. *British Medical Journal, 319*:145.

Joseph, S. (1997). *Personality disorders: New symptom-focused drug therapy.* New York: Haworth Medical Press/Haworth Press.

Jourard, S. M. (1974). *Healthy personality: An approach from the viewpoint of humanistic psychology.* New York: Macmillan.

Joyce, P., Bushnell, J., Oakley-Browne, M., & Wells, J. (1989). The epidemiology of panic symptomatology and agoraphobic avoidance. *Comprehensive Psychiatry, 30,* 303–12.

Judd, L., Paulus, M., Wells, K., & Rapaport, M. (1996). Functional impairment associated with subsyndromal depression. *American Journal of Psychiatry, 153,* 1411–17.

Jung, C. (1933). *Modern man in search of a soul.* New York: Harcourt, Brace.

Junginger, J., Barker, S., & Coe, D. (1992). Mood themes and bizarreness of delusions in schizophrenia and mood psychosis. *Journal of Abnormal Psychology, 101* (2): 287–92.

Kabat-Zinn, J., Massion, A., Kristeller, J., et al. (1992). Effectiveness of meditation-based stress reduction program in the treatment of anxiety disorders. *American Journal of Psychiatry, 149,* 937–43.

Kaij, L. (1960). *Studies on the etiology and sequels of abuse and alcohol.* Lund, Sweden: University of Lund.

Kalin, N. H., Shelton, S. E., & Barksdale, C. M. (1988). Opiate modulation of separation-induced distress in nonhuman primates. *Brain Research, 40,* 285–92.

Kamen-Siegel, L., Rodin, J., Seligman, M., & Dwyer, J. (1991). Explanatory style and cell-mediated immunity in elderly men and women. *Health Psychology, 10,* 229–35.

Kamin, L. J. (1974). *The science and politics of IQ.* Potomac, MD: Erlbaum.

Kamphaus, R. W. (1993). *Clinical assessment of children's intellligence.* Boston: Allyn & Bacon.

Kandel, E. R., Schwartz, J. H., & Jessell, T. M. (1991). *Principles of neural science* (3rd ed.). Norwalk, CT: Appleton & Lange.

Kandel, E. R., Schwarz, J. H., & Jessel, T. M. (1995). *Essentials of neuroscience.* Norwalk, CT: Appleton & Lang.

Kane, J. M., & Marder, S. R. (1993). Psychopharmacologic treatment of schizophrenia. *Schizophrenia Bulletin, 19,* 287–302.

Kanfer, F. H., & Karoly, P. (1972). Self-control. A behavioristic excursion into the lion's den. *Behavior Therapy, 3,* 398–416.

Kaniasty, K., & Norris, F. H. (1995). Mobilization and deterioration of social support following natural disasters. *Current Directions in Psychological Science, 4* (3): 94–98.

Kanner, A. D., Coyne, J. C., Schaefer, C., & Lazarus, R. S. (1981). Comparison of two modes of stress measurement: Minor daily hassles and uplifts vs. major life events. *Journal of Behavioral Medicine, 4,* 1–39.

Kanner, L. (1943). Autistic disturbances of affective contact. *Nervous Child, 2,* 217–50.

Kanter, R. A., Williams, B. E., & Cummings, C. (1992). Personal and parental alcohol abuse, and victimization in obese binge eaters and nonbingeing obese. *Addictive Behaviors, 17* (5): 439–45.

Kaplan, C. A. & Hussain, S. (1995). Use of drugs in child and adolescent psychiatry. *British Journal of Psychiatry, 166* (3): 291–98.

Kaplan, H. S. (1974). *The new sex therapy.* New York: Brunner/Mazel.

Kaplan, S. M., Gottschalk, L. A., Magliocco, D., Rohobit, D., & Ross, W. D. (1960). Hostility in hypnotic "dreams" of hypertensive patients. (Comparisons between hypertensive and normotensive groups and within hypertensive individuals.) *Psychosomatic Medicine, 22,* 320.

Kapur, S., & Remington, G. (1996). Serotonin-dopamine interaction and its relevance to schizophrenia. *American Journal of Psychiatry, 153* (4): 466–76.

Karasek, R., Baker, D., Marxer, F., Ahlbom, A., & Theorell, T. (1981). Job decision latitude, job demand, and cardiovascular disease: A prospective study of Swedish men. *American Journal of Public Health, 71,* 694–705.

Karbe, H., Kessler, J., Herholz, K., Fink, G.R., & Heiss, W.-D. (1995). Long-term prognosis of poststroke aphasia studied with positron emission tomography. *Archives of Neurology, 52,* 186–90.

Karlsson, J. L. (1972). An Icelandic family study of schizophrenia. In A. R. Kaplan (Ed.), *Genetic factors in schizophrenia* (pp. 246–55). Springfield, Il: Charles C. Thomas.

Karlsson, J. L. (1991). *Genetics of human mentality.* New York: Praeger.

Karno, M., Golding, J. M., Sorenson, S. B., & Burnam, M. A. (1988). The epidemiology of obsessive-compulsive disorder in five U.S. communities. *Archives of General Psychiatry, 45* (12): 1094–99.

Karon, B. P. (1999). The tragedy of schizophrenia. *General Psychologist, 35,* 1–12.

Karp, D. A. (1996). *Speaking of sadness: Depression, disconnection, and the meaning of illness.* New York: Oxford University Press.

Kasen, S., Cohen, P., Skodol, A. E., Johnson, J. G., & Brook, J. S. (1999). Influence of child and adolescent psychiatric disorders on young adult personality disorder. *American Journal of Psychiatry, 156* (10): 1529–35.

Kaslow, N. J., Tannenbaum, R. L., Abramson, L. Y., Peterson, C., & Seligman, M. E. P. (1983). Problem solving deficits and depressive symptoms among children. *Journal of Abnormal Child Psychology, 11* (4):497–502.

Kass, F., Spitzer, R. L., & Williams, J. B. W. (1983). An empirical study of the issue of sex bias in the diagnostic criteria of DSM-III axis II personality disorders. *American Psychologist, 38,* 799–801.

Katchadourian, H. A., & Lunde, D. T. (1972). *Fundamentals of human sexuality.* New York: Holt, Rinehart & Winston.

Katula, J. A., Blissmer, B. J., & McAuley, E. (1999). Exercise and self-efficacy effects on anxiety reduction in healthy, older adults. *Journal of Behavioral Medicine, 22* (3): 233–47.

Katz, H. B., Davies, C. A., & Dobbing, J. (1980). The effect of environmental stimulation on brain weight in previously undernourished rats. *Behavioural Brain Research, 1* (5): 445–49.

Katz, R. J., DeVeaugh-Geiss, J., & Landau, P. (1990a). Clinical predictors of treatment response in obsessive-compulsive disorder: Explanatory analyses from multicenter trials of clomipramine. *Psychopharmacology Bulletin, 26,* 54–59.

Katz, R. J., DeVeaugh-Geiss, J., & Landau, P. (1990b). Clomipramine in obsessive-compulsive disorder. *Biological Psychiatry, 28,* 401–14.

Kazdin, A. E. (1993). Treatment of conduct disorder: Progress and directions in psychotherapy research. *Development and Psychopathology, 5,* 277–310.

Kazdin, A. E. (1997). Practitioner review: Psychosocial treatments for conduct disorder in children. *Journal of Child Psychology and Psychiatry, 38,* 161–78.

Kazdin, A. E. (1998a). Conduct disorder. In R. J. Morris & T. R. Kratochwill (Eds.), *The practice of child therapy* (3rd ed.; pp. 199–230). Boston: Allyn & Bacon.

Kazdin, A. E. (1998b). *Methodological issues and strategies in clinical research* (2nd ed.). Washington, DC: American Psychological Association.

Kazdin, A. E. (1998c). Psychosocial treatments of conduct disorder in children. In P. Nathan & J. Gorman (Eds.), *A guide to treatments that work* (pp. 65–89). New York: Oxford University Press.

Kazdin, A. E., & Wilcoxon, L. A. (1976). Systematic desensitization and nonspecific treatment effects: A methodological evaluation. *Psychological Bulletin, 83* (5): 729–58.

Kazes, M., Berthet, L., Danion, J., Amado, I., Willard, D., Robert, P., & Poirer, M. (1999). Impairment of consciously controlled use of memory in schizophrenia. *Neuropsychology, 13,* 54–61.

Keane, T. M., Kolb, L. C., Kaloupek, D. G., Orr, S. P., Blanchard, E. B., Thomas, R. G., Hsieh, F. Y., & Lavori, P. W. (1998). Utility of psychophysiology measurement in the diagnosis of posttraumatic stress disorder: Results from a department of Veteran's Affairs cooperative study. *Journal of Consulting and Clinical Psychology, 66* (6): 914–23.

Keane, T. M. (1998). Psychological and behavioral treatments of post-traumatic stress disorder. In P. E. Nathan & J. M. Gorman (Eds.), *A guide to treatments that work* (pp. 398–407). New York: Oxford University Press.

Keaney, J. C., & Farley, M. (1996). Dissociation in an outpatient sample of women reporting childhood sexual abuse. *Psychological Reports, 78,* 59–65.

Keck, P., Cohen, B., Baldessarini, R., & McElroy, S. (1989). Time course of antipsychotic effects of neuroleptic drugs. *American Journal of Psychiatry, 146,* 1289–92.

Keck, P., & McElroy, S. (1998). Bipolar disorders. In P. Nathan & J. Gorman (Eds.), *A guide to treatments that work.* New York: Oxford University Press.

Kegan, R. (1986), Pathology in moral development. In W. H. Reid, D. Dor, J. I. Walker, & J. W. Bonner, III (Eds.), *Unmasking the psychopath: Antisocial personality and related syndromes.* New York: Norton.

Kehoe, M., & Ironside, W. (1963). Studies on the experimental evocation of depressive responses using hypnosis: II. The influence upon the secretion of gastric acid. *Psychosomatic Medicine, 25,* 403–19.

Keinan, G. & Hobfoll, S. E. (1989). Stress, dependency and social support: Who benefits from husbands' presence in delivery? *Journal of Social and Clinical Psychology, 8,* 32–44.

Keith, S. J., Gunderson, J. G., Reifman, A., Buchsbaum, S., & Mosher, L. R. (1976). Special report: Schizophrenia, 1976. *Schizophrenia Bulletin, 2,* 510–65.

Keller, J., Nitschke, J., Bhargava, T., et al. (2000). Neuropsychological differentiation of depression and anxiety. *Journal of Abnormal Psychology, 109,* 3–10.

Keller, M. B., & Baker, C. A. (1991). Bipolar disorder: Epidemiology, course, diagnosis, and treatment. *Bulletin of the Menninger Clinic, 55* (2): 172–81.

Keller, M. B., Beardslee, W. R., Dorer, D. J., Lavori, P. W., Samuelson, H., & Klerman, G. R. (1986). Impact of severity and chronicity of parental affective illness on adaptive functioning and psychopathology in children. *Archives of General Psychiatry, 43,* 930–37.

Keller, M. B., Klein, D. N., Hirschfeld, R. M. A., Kocsis, J. H., McCullough, J. P., Miller, I., First, M. B., Holzer, C. P., Keitner, G. I., Marin, D. N., and Shea, T. (1995). Results of the DSM-IV mood disorders field trial. *American Journal of Psychiatry, 152* (6): 843–49.

Keller, M. B., Lavori, P. W., Mueller, T. I., & Endicott, J. (1992). Time to recovery, chronicity, and levels of psychopathology in major depression: A 5-year prospective follow-up of 431 subjects. *Archives of General Psychiatry, 49* (10): 809–16.

Keller, M., McCullough, P., Klein, D. et al. (2000). A comparison of Nefazodone, the cognitive behavioral-analysis system of psychotherapy, and their combination for the treatment of chronic depression. *New England Journal of Medicine, 342.*

Keller, M., & Shapiro, R. (1982). "Double depression": Superimposition of acute depressive episodes on chronic depressive disorders. *American Journal of Psychiatry, 139,* 438–42.

Kelley, H. H. (1967). Attribution theory in social psychology. In D. Levine (Ed.), *Nebraska symposium on motivation* (pp. 192–240). Lincoln: Dot Nebraska Press.

Kelley, J. E., Lumley, M. A., & Leisen, J. C. C. (1997). Health effects of emotional disclosure in rheumatoid arthritis patients. *Health Psychology, 16* (4): 331–40.

Kellner, R. (1986). Somatization and hypochondriasis. New York: Praeger-Greenwood.

Kelsoe, J. R., Ginns, E. I., Egeland, J. A., Gerhard, D. S., Goldstein, A. M., Bale, S. J., Pauls, D. L., Long, R. T., Kidd, K. K., Conte, G., Housman, D. E., & Paul, S. M. (1989). Re-evaluation of the linkage relationship between chromosome 11p loci and the gene for bipolar affective disorder in the Old Order Amish. *Nature, 342* (6247):238–43.

Kelz, M. B., Chen, J., Carlezon, W. A., Whisler, K., Gilden, L., Beckman, A. M., Steffan, C., Zhang, Y., Marotti, L., Self, D. W., Tkatch, T., Baranauskas, G., Surmeier, D. J., Neve, R. L., Duman, R. S., Picciotto, M. R., & Nestler, E. (1999). Expression of the transcription factor DeltaFosB in the brain controls sensitivity to cocaine. *Nature, 401:* 272–76.

Kendall, P. C. (1994). Treating anxiety disorders in children: Results of a randomized clinical trial. *Journal of Consulting and Clinical Psychology, 62* (1): 100–10.

Kendall, P. C., Haaga, D. A. F., Ellis, A., & Bernard, M. (1995). Rational-emotive therapy in the 1990's and beyond: Current status, recent revisions, and research questions. *Clinical Psychology Review, 15* (3): 169–85.

Kendler, K. S. (1997).The diagnostic validity of melancholic major depression in a population-based sample of female twins. *Archives of General Psychiatry, 54* (4): 299–304.

Kendler, K. S., & Diehl, S. R. (1993). The genetics of schizophrenia. *Schizophrenia Bulletin, 19,* 261–86.

Kendler, K. S., & Gruenberg, A. M. (1982). Genetic relationship between paranoid personality disorder and the "schizophrenic spectrum" disorders. *American Journal of Psychiatry, 139,* 1185–86.

Kendler, K. S., & Gruenberg, A. M. (1984). An independent analysis of the Danish adoption study of schizophrenia: VI. The relationship between psychiatric disorders as defined by DSM-III in the relatives and adoptees. *Archives of General Psychiatry, 41,* 555–64.

Kendler, K. S., & Hays, P. (1981). Paranoid psychosis (delusional disorder) and schizophrenia: A family history study. *Archives of General Psychiatry, 38* (5): 547–51.

Kendler, K. S., Kessler, R. C., Walters, E. E., MacLean, C., Neale, M. C., Heath, A. C., & Eaves, L. J. (1995). Stressful life events, genetic liability, and onset of an episode of major depression in women. *American Journal of Psychiatry, 152* (6): 833–42.

Kendler, K. S., MacLean, C., Neale, M., et al. (1991). The genetic epidemiology of bulimia nervosa. *American Journal of Psychiatry, 148,* 1627.

Kendler, K. S., Neale, M. C., Heath, A. C., Kessler, R. C., & Eaves, L. J. (1994). A twin-family study of alcoholism in women. *American Journal of Psychiatry, 151* (5): 707–15.

Kendler, K., Neale, M., Kessler, R., & Heath, A. (1992). Generalized anxiety disorder in women: A population-based twin study. *Archives of General Psychiatry, 49,* 267–72.

Kendler, K. S., Neale, M. C., Kessler, R. C., Heath, A. C., & Eaves, L. J. (1992a). Major depression and generalized anxiety disorder: Same genes, (partly) different environments? *Archives of General Psychiatry, 49* (9): 716–25.

Kendler, K. S., Neale, M. C., Kessler, R. C., Heath, A. C., & Eaves, L. J. (1992b). The genetic epidemiology of phobias in women: The interrelationship of agoraphobia, social phobia, situational phobia, and simple phobia. *Archives of General Psychiatry, 49,* 273–81.

Kendler, K. S., Pederson, N., Johnson, L., Neale, M. C., & Mathe, A. A. (1993). A pilot Swedish twin study of affective illness, including hospital- and population-ascertained subsamples. *Archives of General Psychiatry, 50,* 699–706.

Kendler, K. S., & Prescott, C. A. (1998). Cocaine use, abuse and dependence in a population-based sample of female twins. *British Journal of Psychiatry, 173,* 345–50.

Kendler, K. S., & Robinette, D. (1983). Schizophrenia in the National Academy of Sciences National Research Council Twin Registry: A 16-year update. *American Journal of Psychiatry, 140,* 1551–63.

Kendler, K. S., Walters, E. E., Neale, M. C., Kessler, R. C., et al. (1995). The structure of the genetic and environmental risk factors for six major psychiatric disorders in women: Phobia, generalized anxiety disorder, panic disorder, bulimia, major depression, and alcoholism. *Archives of General Psychiatry, 52* (5): 374–83.

Kenner, C., & D'Apolito, K. (1997). Outcomes for children exposed to drugs in utero. *Journal of Obstetric, Gynecologic, and Neonatal Nursing, 26,* 595–603.

Kenny, M. G. (1998). Disease process or social phenomenon?: Reflections on the future of multiple personality. *Journal of Nervous and Mental Disease, 186,* 449–54.

Kern, R. S., & Green, M. F. (1998). Cognitive remediation in schizophrenia. In K. T. Mueser, N. Tarrier, et al. (Eds.), *Handbook of social functioning in schizophrenia* (pp. 342–54). Boston: Allyn & Bacon.

Kernberg, O. F. (1975). *Borderline conditions and pathological narcissism.* New York: Jason Aronson.

Kernberg, O. F. (1992). *Aggression in personality disorders and perversions.* New Haven: Yale University Press.

Kerr, S. L., & Neale, J. M. (1993). Emotion perception in schizophrenia: Specific deficit or further evidence of generalized poor performance? *Journal of Abnormal Psychology, 102,* 312–18.

Kerr, T. A., Roth, M., Schapira, K., & Gurney, C. (1972). The assessment and prediction of outcome in affective disorders. *British Journal of Psychiatry, 121,* 167.

Kertesz, A. (1982). Two case studies: Broca's brain and Wernicke's aphasia. In M. A. Arbib, D. Caplan, & J. C. Marshall (Eds.), *Neural models of language processes.* New York: Academic Press.

Kessler, R. C. (1997). The effects of stressful life events on depression. *Annual Review of Psychology, 48,* 191–214.

Kessler, R. C., Crum, R. M., Warner, L. A., Nelson, C. B., Schulenberg, J., & Anthony, J. C. (1997). Lifetime co-occurrence of DSM-III-R alcohol abuse and dependence with other psychiatric disorders in the National Comorbidity Survey. *Archives of General Psychiatry, 54,* 313–21.

Kessler, R. C., McGonagle, K. A., Swartz, M., Blazer, D. G., et al. (1993). Sex and depression in the National Comorbidity Survey I: Lifetime prevalence, chronicity, and recurrence. *Journal of Affective Disorders, 29,* 85–96.

Kessler, R. C., McGonagle, K. A., Zhao, S., Nelson, C. B., et al. (1994). Lifetime and 12-month prevalence of DSM-III—R psychiatric disorders in the United States: Results from the National Comorbidity Study. *Archives of General Psychiatry, 51* (1): 8–19.

Kessler, R. C., Sonnega, A., Bromet, E., Hughes, M., et al. (1995). Posttraumatic stress disorder in the National Comorbidity Survey. *Archives of General Psychiatry, 52* (12):1048–60.

Kertesz, A. (1982). Two case studies: Broca's brain and Wernicke's aphasia. In M. A. Arbib, D. Caplan, & J. C. Marshall (Eds.), *Neural models of language processes.* New York: Academic Press.

Kety, J. (1974). Biochemical and neurochemical effects of electroconvulsive shock. In M. Fink, S. Kety, & J. McGough (Eds.), *Psychology of convulsive therapy.* Washington, DC: Winston.

Kety, S., Rosenthal, D., Wender, P. H., & Schulsinger, F. (1968). The types and prevalence of mental illness in the biological and adoptive families of adopted schizophrenics. In D. Rosenthal & S. S. Kety (Eds.), *The transmission of schizophrenia.* New York: Pergamon Press.

Khan, A., Warner, H., & Brown, W. (2000). Symptom reduction and suicide risk in patients treated with placebo in antidepressant clinical trials. *Archives of General Psychiatry, 57,* 311–17.

Khantzian, E. J. (1994). Some treatment implications of the ego and self disturbances in alcoholism. (1994). In J. D. Levin & R. H. Weiss (Eds.), *The dynamics and treatment of alcoholism: Essential papers* (pp. 232–55). Northvale, NJ: Jason Aronson.

Kiecolt-Glaser, J., Dura, J., Speicher, C., Trask, J., & Glaser, R. (1991). Spousal caregivers of dementia victims: Longitudinal changes in immunity and health. *Psychosomatic Medicine, 53,* 345–62.

Kiecolt-Glaser, J. K., Garner, W., Speicher, C., Penn, G. M., Holliday, J., & Glaser, R. (1984). Psychosocial modifiers of immunocompetence in medical students. *Psychosomatic Medicine, 46,* 7–14.

Kiecolt-Glaser, J. K., & Glaser, R. (1987). Psychosocial moderators of immune function. *Annals of Behavioral Medicine, 9,* 16–20.

Kiecolt-Glaser, J. K., & Glaser, R. (1995). Psychoneuroimmunology and health consequences: Data and shared mechanisms. *Psychosomatic Medicine, 57,* 269–74.

Kiecolt-Glaser, J. K., Page, G. G., Marucha, P. T., MacCallum, R. C., & Glaser, R. (1998). Psychological influences on surgical recovery: Perspectives from psychoneuroimmunology. *American Psychologist, 53,* 1209–18.

Kiely, J. L., Paneth, N., & Susser, M. (1981). Low birthweight, neonatal care and cerebral palsy: An epidemiological review. In P. J. Mittler & J. M. deJong (Eds.), *Frontiers in mental retardation: II: Biomedical aspects.* Baltimore, MD: University Park Press.

Kienle, G. S., & Kiene, H. (1997). The powerful placebo effect: Fact or fiction? *Journal of Clinical Epidemiology, 50,* 1311–18.

Kiessling, L. S., Marcotte, A. C., & Culpepper, L. (1993). Antineuronal antibodies in movement disorder. *Pediatrics, 92* (1): 39–43.

Kilpatrick, D., Resnick, P., & Veronen, L. (1981). Effects of a rape experience: A longitudinal study. *Journal of Social Issues, 37,* 105–22.

Kilpatrick, D., Saunders, B., Amick-McMullan, A., et al. (1989). Victim and crime factors associated with the development of crime-related post-traumatic stress disorder. *Behavior Therapy, 20,* 199–214.

Kilpatrick, D., Saunders, B., Veronen, L., Best, C., & Von, J. (1987). Criminal victimization: Lifetime prevalence, reporting to police, and psychological impact. *Crime and Delinquency, 33,* 479–89.

Kindermann, S. S., Karimi, A., Symonds, L., Brown, G. G., & Jeste, D. V. (1997). Review of functional magnetic resonance imaging in schizophrenia. *Schizophrenia Research, 27,* 143–56.

King, A. C., Taylor, C., & Haskell, W. L. (1993). Effects of differing intensities and formats of 12 months of exercise training on psychological outcomes in older adults. *Health Psychology, 12* (4): 292–300.

King, N. J., Eleonora, G., & Ollendick, T. H. (1998). Etiology of childhood phobias: Current status of Rachman's three pathways theory. *Behaviour Research and Therapy, 36* (3): 297–309.

King, R. A., Scahill, L., Findley, D., & Cohen, D. J. (1999). Psychosocial and behavioral treatments. In J. F. Leckman & D. J. Cohen (Eds.), *Tourette's syndrome—Tics, obsessions, compulsions: Developmental psychopathology and clinical care* (pp. 338–59). New York: Wiley.

King, S., Barr, R., duFort, G., Meaney, M., Zelazo, P. LaPlante, D., & Saucier, J. (1999). *The 1998 Quebec ice storm: Perinatal and infant outcomes.* Paper presented at the annual Meeting of the Society for Research in Psychopathology, Montreal, Canada, November 20, 1999.

Kinney, D. K., Levy, D. L., Yurgelun-Todd, D. A., Tramer, S. J., & Holzman, P. S. (1998). Inverse relationship of perinatal complications and eye tracking dysfunction in relatives of patients with schizophrenia: Evidence for a two-factor model. *American Journal of Psychiatry, 155,* 976–78.

Kinsey, A. C., Pomeroy, W. D., & Martin, C. E. (1948). *Sexual behavior in the human male.* Philadelphia: Saunders.

Kirigin, K. A., & Wolf, M. M. (1998). Application of the teaching-family model to children and adolescents with conduct disorder. In V. B. Van Hasselt & M. Hersen (Eds.), *Handbook of psychological treatment protocols for children and adolescents. The LEA Series in Personality and Clinical Psychology* (pp. 359–80). Mahwah, NJ: Lawrence Erlbaum.

Kirigin, K. A., Braukmann, C. J., Atwater, J. D., & Wolf, M. M. (1982). An evaluation of teaching-family (Achievement Place) group homes for juvenile offenders. *Journal of Applied Behavior Analysis, 15* (1): 1–16.

Kirigin, K., Wolf, M. M., Braukman, C. J., Fixsen, D. L., & Phillips, E. L. (1979). Achievement Place: A preliminary outcome evaluation. In J. S. Stumphauzer (Ed.), *Progress in behavior therapy with delinquents.* Springfield, IL: Charles C. Thomas.

Kirk, S. A., & Kutchins, H. (1992). *The selling of DSM: The rhetoric of science in psychiatry.* New York: Aldine de Gruyter.

Kirmayer, L. J., & Corin, E. (1998). Inside knowledge: Cultural constructions of insight in psychosis. In X. F. Amador & A. S. David (Eds.), *Insight and psychosis* (pp. 193–220). New York: Oxford University Press.

Kirsch, I., & Saperstein, G. (1998). Listening to Prozac but hearing placebo: A meta-analysis of antidepressant medication. *Prevention and Treatment, 1.*

Kirschbaum, C., Wust, S., Faig, H. G., & Hellhammer, D. H. (1992). Heritability of cortisol responses to human corticotropin-releasing hormone, ergometry, and psychological stress in humans. *Journal of Clinical Endocrinology and Metabolism, 75,* 1526–30.

Kittel, F., Kornitzer, M., de Backer, G., & Dramaix, M. (1982). Metrological study of psychological questionnaires with reference to social variables: The Belgian Heart Disease Prevention Project (BHDPP). *Journal of Behavioral Medicine, 5* (1): 9–35.

Klar, H., & Siever, L. (1984). The psychopharmacologic treatment of personality disorders. *Psychiatric Clinics of North America, 7,* 791–800.

Kleber, H. D. (1994). Our current approach to drug abuse: Progress, problems, proposals. *New England Journal of Medicine, 330* (5): 361–64.

Klein, D. F. (1996a). Discussion of "methodological controversies in the treatment of panic disorder." *Behaviour Research and Therapy, 34* (11–12): 849–53.

Klein, D. F. (1996b). Preventing hung juries about therapy studies. *Journal of Consulting and Clinical Psychology, 64* (1): 81–87.

Klein, D. F. (1999). Harmful dysfunction, disorder, disease, illness, and evolution. *Journal of Abnormal Psychology, 108*(3): 421–29.

Klein, D. F., & Gittelman-Klein, R. (1975). Are behavioral and psychometric changes related in methylphenidate treated, hyperactive children? *International Journal of Mental Health, 14* (1–2): 182–98.

Klein, D. F., Ross, D. C., & Cohen, P. (1987). Panic and avoidance in agoraphobia, application of path analysis to treatment studies. *Archives of General Psychiatry, 44,* 377–85.

Klein, R. G. & Abikoff, H. (1997). Behavior therapy and methylphenidate in the treatment of children with ADHD. *Journal of Attention Disorders, 2,* 89–114.

Kleinknecht, R. A. (1994). Acquisition of blood, injury, and needle fears and phobias. *Behaviour Research and Therapy, 32* (8): 817–23.

Kleinknecht, R. A., Dinnel, D. L., Kleinknecht, E. E., Hiruma, N., et al. (1997). Cultural factors in social anxiety: A comparison of social phobia symptoms and Taijin Kyofusho. *Journal of Anxiety Disorders, 11*(2): 157–77.

Kleinknecht, R., & Lenz, J. (1989). Blood/injury fear, fainting and avoidance of medically related situations: A family correspondence study. *Behaviour Research and Therapy, 27,* 537–47.

Kleinman, A. M. (1986). *Social origins of distress and disease: Depression, neurasthenia and pain in modern China.* New Haven, CT: Yale University Press.

Klerman, G. (1983). The psychiatric revolution of the past 25 years. In W. Gove (Ed.), *Deviance and mental illness.* Newbury Park, PA: Sage.

Klerman, G. L., Lavori, P. W., & Rice, J., et al. (1985). Birth cohort trends in rates of major depressive disorder among relatives of patients with affective disorder. *Archives of General Psychiatry, 42* (7): 689–93.

Klerman, G. L., Weissman, M. M., Rounsaville, N. B., & Chevron, E. (1984). *Interpersonal psychotherapy of depression.* New York: Basic Books.

Kline, N. (1970). Monoamine oxidase inhibitors: An unfinished picaresque tale. In F. J. Ayd & H. Blackwell (Eds.), *Discoveries in biological psychiatry.* Philadelphia: Lippincott.

Klinkman, M. S., Schwenk, T. L., & Coyne, J. C. (1997). Depression in primary care—More like asthma than appendicitis: The Michigan Depression Project. *Canadian Journal of Psychiatry, 42* (9): 966–73.

Klosko, J., Barlow, D., Tassarini, R., & Cerny, J. (1988). Comparison of alprazolam and cognitive behavior therapy in the treatment of panic disorder: A preliminary report. In I. Hand & H. Wittchen (Eds.), *Treatment of panic and phobias: Modes of application and variables affecting outcome.* Berlin: Springer-Verlag.

Kluft, R. (1984). Treatment of multiple personality. *Psychiatric Clinics of North America, 7,* 9–29.

Kluft, R. P. (1987). An update on multiple personality disorder. *Hospital and Community Psychiatry, 38,* 363–73.

Kluft, R. P. (1991). Multiple personality disorder. In Tasman, A., & Goldfinger, S. M. (Eds.), *American Psychiatric Press Review of Psychiatry, 10,* 161–88.

Klykylo, W. M., Kay, J., & Rube, D. (1998). *Clinical child psychiatry.* Philadelphia: Saunders.

Knight, D. K., Broome, K. M., Cross, D. R., & Simpson, D. D. (1998). Antisocial tendency among drug-addicted adults: Potential long-term effects of parental absence, support and conflict during childhood. *American Journal of Drug and Alcohol Abuse, 24,* 361–75.

Kobasa, S. C. (1979). Stressful life events, personality, and health: An inquiry into hardiness. *Journal of Personality and Social Psychology, 37,* 1–11.

Koch Crime Institute. (1999). http://www.kci.org/meth_info/letters/1999/nov2.htm

Koch Crime Institute. (2000). http://www.kci.org/meth_info/links.htm

Kocsis, J. H., Friedman, R.A., Markowitz, J. C., Leon, A. C., Miller, N. L., Gniwesch, L., & Parides, M. (1996). Maintenance therapy for chronic depression: A controlled clinical trial of desipramine. *Archives of General Psychiatry, 53* (9): 769–74.

Koerner, K., & Dimeff, L. A. (2000). Further data on dialectical behavior therapy. *Clinical Psychology—Science and Practice, 7* (1), online journal.

Kogon, M. M., Biswas, A., Pearl, D., Carlson, R. W., & Spiegel, D. (1997). Psychotherapy improves cancer survival. *Clinician's Research Digest, 15* (10): 4.

Köhler, T., Kuhnt, K., & Richter, R. (1998). The role of life event stress in the pathogenesis of duodenal ulcer. *Stress Medicine, 14* (2): 121–24.

Kohut, H. (1971). *The analysis of the self.* New York: International Universities Press.

Kohut, H. (1977). *The restoration of the self*. New York: International Universities Press.

Kohut, H. (1978). *The search for self*. New York: International Universities Press.

Kokkevi, A., & Stefanis, C. (1995). Drug abuse and psychiatric comorbidity. *Comprehensive Psychiatry, 36* (5): 329–37.

Kolata, G. (2000). Scientists Report the First Success of Gene Therapy. *New York Times,* April 28.

Kondas, O. (1997). Cognitive and behavior psychotherapy in Slovakia: A historical overview. *Studia Psychologica, 39,* 247–55.

Koob, G. F., & Bloom, F. E. (1988). Cellular and molecular mechanisms of drug dependence. *Science, 242,* 715–23.

Koob, G. F., Caine, S. B., Parsons, L., Markou, A., & Weiss, F. (1997). Opponent process model and psychostimulant addiction. *Pharmacology, Biochemistry and Behavior, 57,* 513–21.

Kopelowicz, A., & Liberman, R. P. (1998). Psychosocial treatments for schizophrenia. In P. Nathan & J. Gorman (Eds.), *A guide to treatments that work* (pp. 190–211). New York: Oxford University Press.

Korchin, S. J. (1976). *Modern clinical psychology: Principles of intervention in the clinic and the community*. New York: Basic Books.

Koren, D., Seidman, L. J., Harrison, R. H., Lyons, M. J., Kremem, W. S., Caplan, B., Goldstein, J. M., Faraone, S. V., & Tsuang, M. T. (1998). Factor structure of the Wisconsin Card Sorting Test: Dimensions of deficit in schizophrenia. *Neuropsychology, 12,* 289–302.

Koren, D., Arnon, I., & Klein, E. (1999). Acute stress response and posttraumatic stress disorder in traffic accident victims: A one-year prospective, follow-up study. *American Journal of Psychiatry, 156* (3): 367–73.

Kornstein, S.G. (1997). Gender differences in depression: Implications for treatment. *Journal of Clinical Psychiatry, 58* (Suppl 15): 12–18.

Kosten, T. R. (1998). Addiction as a brain disease. *American Journal of Psychiatry, 155,* 711–13.

Kotses, H., Harver, A., Segreto, J., Glaus, K. D., et al. (1991). Long-term effects of biofeedback-induced facial relaxation on measures of asthma severity in children. *Biofeedback and Self Regulation, 16* (1): 1–21.

Kotsopoulos, S., & Snow, B. (1986). Conversion disorders in children: A study of clinical outcome. *Psychiatric Journal of the University of Ottawa, 11,* 134–39.

Kovacs, G. L., Sarnyai, Z., & Szabo, G. (1998). Oxytocin and addiction: A review. *Psychoneuroendocrinology, 23,* 945–62.

Kovacs, M., & Beck, A. T. (1977). An empirical-clinical approach towards a definition of childhood depression. In J. G. Schulterbrand & A. Raven (Eds.), *Depression in childhood: Diagnosis, treatment, and conceptual models*. New York: Raven Press.

Kovacs, M., Gatsonis, C., Paulauskas, S. L., & Richards, C. (1989). Depressive disorders in childhood: I V. A longitudinal study of comorbidity with and risk for anxiety disorders. *Archives of General Psychiatry, 46* (9): 776–82.

Kovacs, M., Rush, A. J., Beck, A. T., & Hollon, S. D. (1981). Depressed outpatient treatment with cognitive therapy or pharmaco therapy: A one year follow-up. *Archives of General Psychiatry, 38,* 33–39.

Kraepelin, E. (1919). *Dementia praecox and paraphrenia*. New York: Robert E. Krieger.

Krafft-Ebing, R. von. (1931). *Psychopathia sexualis*. New York: Physicians and Surgeons Book Co.

Kramer, P. D. (1994). *Listening to Prozac*. London: Fourth Estate.

Krantz, D., Helmers, K., Bairey, N., et al. (1991). Cardiovascular reactivity and mental stress-induced myocardial ischemia in patients with coronary artery disease. *Psychosomatic Medicine, 53,* 1–12.

Kravitz, H. M., Haywood, T. W., Kelly, J., Wahlstrom, C., Liles, S., & Cavanaugh, J. L. (1995). Medroxyprogesterone treatment for paraphiliacs. *Bulletin of the American Academy of Psychiatry and the Law, 23* (1): 19–33.

Kreek, M. J. (1992). Rationale for maintenance pharmacotherapy of opiate dependence. In C. P. O'Brien & J. H. Jaffe (Eds.), *Addictive states* (pp. 205–30). New York: Raven Press.

Kremen, W. S., Buka, S. L., Seidman, L. J., Goldstein, J. M., Koren, D., & Tsuang, M. T. (1998). IQ decline during childhood and adult psychotic symptoms in a community sample: A 19-year longitudinal study. *American Journal of Psychiatry, 155,* 672–77.

Krieckhaus, E., Donahoe, J., & Morgan, M. (1992). Paranoid schizophrenia may be caused by dopamine hyperactivity of CA1 hippocampus. *Biological Psychiatry, 31,* 560–70.

Kringlen, E. (1968). An epidemiological-clinical twin study of schizophrenia. In D. Rosenthal and S. S. Kety (Eds.), *The transmission of schizophrenia* (pp. 49–63). Oxford, England: Pergamon.

Krischer, C. C., Coenen, R., Heckner, M., & Hoeppner, D. (1994). Gliding text: A new aid to improve the reading performance of poor readers by subconscious gaze control. *Educational Research, 36* (3): 271–83.

Kroenke, K., Spitzer, R. L., deGruy, F. V., & Swindle, R. (1998). A symptom checklist to screen for somatoform disorders in primary care. *Psychosomatics, 39* (3): 263–72.

Krug, E. G., Kresnow, M., Peddicord, J. P., Dahlberg, L. L., Powell, K. E., Crosby, A. E., Annest, J. L. (1998). Suicide after natural disasters. *New England Journal of Medicine, 338* (6), 373–78.

Kruger, S., Cooke, R. G., Hasey, G. M., Jorna, T., & Persad, E. (1995). Comorbidity of obsessive-compulsive disorder in bipolar disorder. *Journal of Affective Disorders, 34,* 117–20.

Krystal, H. (1968). *Massive psychic trauma*. New York: International Universities Press.

Kuch, K., & Cox, B. (1992). Symptoms of PTSD in 124 survivors of the Holocaust. *American Journal of Psychiatry, 149,* 337–40.

Kuhnle, U., Bullinger, M., & Schwarz, H.P. (1995). The quality of life in adult female patients with congenital adrenal hyperplasia: A comprehensive study of the impact of genital malformations and chronic disease on female patients' life. *European Journal of Pediatrics, 154,* 708–16.

Kuiper, B., & Cohen-Kettenis, P. (1988). Sex reassignment surgery: A study of 141 Dutch transsexuals. *Archives of Sexual Behaviour, 17,* 439–57.

Kupfer, D., Frank, E., Perel, J., et al. (1992). Five-year outcome for maintenance therapies in recurrent depression. *Archives of General Psychiatry, 49,* 769–73.

Kurland, H. D., Yeager, C. T., & Arthur, R. J. (1963). Psychophysiologic aspects of severe behavior disorders. *Archives of General Psychiatry, 8,* 599–604.

Kuruoglu, A. C., Arikan, Z., Vural, G., Karatas, M., Arac, M., & Isik, E. (1996). Single photon emission computerised tomography in chronic alcoholism. Antisocial personality disorder may be associated with decreased frontal perfusion. *British Journal of Psychiatry, 169,* 348–54.

Kyrios, M. (1998). A cognitive-behavioral approach to the understanding and management of obsessive-compulsive personality disorder. In C. Perris & P. D. McGorry (Eds.), *Cognitive psychotherapy of psychotic and personality disorders: Handbook of theory and practice* (pp. 351–78). Chichester, England: American Ethnological Press.

Lacey, J. I. (1950). Individual differences in somatic response patterns. *Journal of Comparative and Physiological Psychology, 43,* 338–50.

Lachman, H. M., Papolos, D. F., Boyle, A., Sheftel, G., et al. (1993). Alterations in glucocorticoid inducible RNAs in the limbic system of learned helpless rats. *Brain Research, 609* (1–2): 110–16.

Lachman, S. J. (1972). *Psychosomatic disorders: Behavioristic interpretations.* New York: Wiley.

Ladd, C.O., Huot, R. L., Thrivikraman, K. V., Nemeroff, C. B., Meaney, M. J., & Plotsky, P. M. (2000). Long-term behavioral and neuroendocrine adaptations to adverse early experience. *Progress in Brain Research, 122,* 81–103.

Lader, M. (1988). The psychopharmacology of addiction: Benzodiazepine tolerance and dependence. In M. Lader (Ed.), *The psychopharmacology of addiction.* New York: Oxford University Press.

Ladisich, W., & Feil, W. B. (1988). Empathy in psychiatric patients. *British Journal of Medical Psychology, 61,* 155–62.

La Greca, A. M., Silverman, W. K., & Wasserstein, S. B. (1998). Children's predisaster functioning as a predictor of posttraumatic stress following Hurricane Andrew. *Journal of Consulting and Clinical Psychology, 66*(6): 883–92.

Lahey, B. B., Loeber, R., Hart, E. L., Frick, P. J., Applegate, B., Zhang, Q., Green, S. M., and Russo, M. F. (1995). Four-year longitudinal study of conduct disorder in boys: Patterns and predictors of persistence. *Journal of Abnormal Psychology, 104* (1): 83–93.

Lahey, B. B., Piacentini, J. C., McBurnett, K., Stone, P., Hartdagen, S., & Hynd, G. (1988). Psychopathology in the parents of children with conduct disorder and hyperactivity. *Journal of the American Academy of Child and Adolescent Psychiatry, 27,* 163–70.

Lam, J. A., & Rosencheck, R. (1998). The effect of victimization on clinical outcomes of homeless persons with serious mental illness. *Psychiatric Services, 49,* 678–83.

Lam, R. W., Peters, R., Sladen-Dew, M., & Altman, S. (1998). A community-based clinic survey of antidepressant use in persons with schizophrenia. *Canadian Journal of Psychiatry, 43,* 513–16.

Lamb, R. H. (1998). Deinstitutionalization at the beginning of the new millennium. *Harvard Review of Psychiatry, 6,* 1–10.

Lamb, R. H., Bachrach, L. L., & Kase, F. I. (Eds.). (1992). *The homeless mentally ill: A task force report of the American Psychiatric Association.* Washington, DC: American Psychiatric Association.

Lamb, R. H. & Weinberger, L. E. (1998). Persons with severe mental illness in jails and prisons: A review. *Psychiatric Services, 49,* 483–92.

Lambert, M., Weisz, J., Knight, F., et al. (1992). Jamaican and American adult perspectives on child psychopathology. *Journal of Consulting and Clinical Psychology, 60,* 146–49.

Lamberts, S. W., van den Beld, A. W., & van der Lely, A. (1997). The endocrinology of aging. *Science, 278* (5337): 419–24.

LaMontagne, Y., & LeSage, A. (1986). Private exposure and covert sensitization in the treatment of exhibitionism. *Journal of Behavior Therapy and Experimental Psychiatry, 17* (3): 197–201.

Lang, H. (1997). Obsessive-compulsive disorders in neurosis and psychosis. *Journal of the American Academy of Psychoanalysis, 25* (1): 143–50.

Lang, P. (1967). Fear reduction and fear behavior. In J. Schlein (Ed.), *Research in psychotherapy.* Washington DC: American Psychological Association.

Lang, P. J. (1979). A bio-informational theory of emotional imagery. *Psychophysiology, 92* (3): 276–306.

Langbehn, D. R., Cadoret, R. J., Yates, W. R., Troughton, E. P., & Stewart, M. A. (1998). Distinct contributions of conduct and oppositional defiant symptoms to adult antisocial behavior: Evidence from an adoption study. *Archives of General Psychiatry, 55,* 821–29.

Langer, E. J., & Abelson, R. P. (1974). A patient by any other name. . . : Clinician group difference in labelling bias. *Journal of Consulting and Clinical Psychology, 42,* 4–9.

Langman, M. (1974). The changing nature of the duodenal ulcer diathesis. In C. Waspell (Ed.), *Westminster Hospital Symposium on chronic duodenal ulcer* (pp. 3–12). London: Butterworth.

Langs, G., Quehenberger, F., Fabisch, K., Klug, G., Fabisch, H., & Zapotoczky, H. G. (2000). The development of agoraphobia in panic disorder: A predictable process? *Journal of Affective Disorders, 58,* 43–50.

Lantz, P. M., House, J. S., Lepkowski, J. M., Williams, D. R., Mero, R. P., & Chen, J. (1998). Socioeconomic factors, health behaviors, and mortality: Results from a nationally representative prospective study of U.S. adults. *Journal of the American Medical Association, 279* (21): 1703–1708.

Laor, N., Wolmer, L., Wiener, Z., Sharon, O., Weizman, R., Toren, P., & Ron, S. (1999). Image vividness as a psychophysiological regulator in posttraumaatic stress disorder. *Journal of Clinical and Experimental Neuropsychology, 21* (1): 39–48.

Lappalainen, J., Long, J. C., Eggert, M., Ozaki, N., Robing, R. W., Brown, G. L., Naukkarinen, H., Virkkunen, M., Linnoila, M., & Goldman, D. (1998). Linkage of antisocial alcoholism to the serotonin 5-HT1B receptor gene in 2 populations. *Archives of General Psychiatry, 55,* 989–94.

Larkin, M. (1998). Festive drinking's slippery slope beckons. *Lancet, 352,* 19–26.

Lasser, R.A., & Baldessarini, R. J. (1997). Thyroid hormones in depressive disorders: A reappraisal of clinical utility. *Harvard Review of Psychiatry, 4,* 291–305.

Last, C. (1992). Anxiety disorders in childhood and adolescence. In W. Reynolds (Ed.), *Internalizing disorders in children and adolescents* (pp. 61–106). New York: Wiley.

Laughlin, H. P. (1967). *The neuroses.* Washington, DC: Butterworth.

Laumann, E., Gagnon, J., Michael, R., & Michaels, S. (1994). *The social organization of sexuality: Sexual practices in the United States.* Chicago: University of Chicago Press.

Lauriello, J., Bustillo, J., & Keith, S. J. (1999). A critical review of research on psychosocial treatment of schizophrenia. *Biological Psychiatry, 46* (10): 1409–17.

Lavigne, J. V., Arend, R., Rosenbaum, D., Sinacore, J., Cicchetti, C., Binns, H. J., Christoffel, K. K., Hayford, J. R., & McGuire, P. (1994). Interrater reliability of the DSM-IIIR with preschool children. *Journal of Abnormal Child Psychology, 22* (6): 679–90.

Law, W. A., Martin, A., Mapou, R. L., Roller, T. L., Salazar, A. M., Temoshack, L. R., & Rundell, J. R. (1994). Working memory in individuals with HIV infection. *Journal of Clinical and Experimental Neuropsychology, 16,* 173–82.

Lawrie, S. M., & Abukmeil, S. S. (1998). Brain abnormality in schizophrenia. A systematic and quantitative review of volumetric magnetic resonance imaging studies. *British Journal of Psychiatry, 172,* 110–20.

Lawrie, S. M., Whalley, H., Kestelman, J. N., Abukmeil, S. S., Byrne, M., Hodges, A., Rimmington, J. E., Best, J. J. K., Owens, D. G. C., & Johnstone, E. C. (1999). Magnetic resonance imaging of brain in people at high risk of developing schizophrenia. *Lancet, 353,* 30–33.

Laws, D. R., & O'Donohue, W. T. (Eds.). (1997). *Sexual deviance: Theory, assessment, and treatment.* New York: Guilford Press.

Laws, K. R., & McKenna, P. J. (1997). Psychotic symptoms and cognitive deficits: What relationship? *Neurocase, 3,* 41–49.

Lazarus, A. A. (1976). *Multimodal behavior therapy.* New York: Springer.

Lazarus, A. A. (1993). Tailoring the therapeutic relationship, or being an authentic chameleon. *Psychotherapy, 30* (3): 404–407.

Lazarus, A. A., & Beutler, L. E. (1993). On technical eclecticism. *Journal of Counseling and Development, 71* (4): 381–85.

LeDoux, J. E. (1992). Emotion and the amygdala. In J. P. Aggleton et al. (Eds.), *The amygdala: Neurobiological aspects of emotion, memory, and mental dysfunction* (pp. 339–51). New York: Wiley-Liss.

LeDoux, J. (1996). *The emotional brain: The mysterious underpinnings of emotional life.* New York: Simon and Schuster.

Ledoux, J. (1998). Fear and the brain: Where have we been, and where are we going? *Biological Psychiatry, 44,* 1229–38.

Lee, A., Hobson, R. P., & Chiat, S. (1994). I, you, me, and autism: An experimental study. *Journal of Autism and Developmental Disorders, 24,* 155–76.

Lee, D. J., Gomez-Marin, O., & Prineas, R. J. (1996). Type A behavior pattern and change in blood pressure from childhood to adolescence. *American Journal of Epidemiology, 143* (1):63–72.

Leff, J. P. (1976). Schizophrenia and sensitivity to the family environment. *Schizophrenia Bulletin, 2,* 566–74.

Leff, M. J., Roatch, J. F., & Bunney, W. E. (1970). Environmental factors preceding the onset of severe depressions. *Psychiatry, 33,* 293–311.

Lehman, D. R., Wortman, C. B., & Williams, A. F. (1987). Long-term effects of losing a spouse or child in a motor vehicle crash. *Journal of Personality and Social Psychology, 52,* 218–31.

Lehmkuhl, G., Blanz, B., Lehmkuhl, U., & Braun-Scharm, H. (1989). Conversion disorder (DSM-III 300.11): Symptomatology and course in childhood and adolescence. *European Archives of Psychiatry and Neurological Sciences, 238,* 155–60.

Le Houezec, J. (1998). Nicotine: Abused substance and therapeutic agent. *Journal of Psychiatry and Neuroscience, 23,* 95–108.

Leon, A., Keller, M. B., Warshaw, M. G., Mueller, T. I., Solomon, D. A., Coryell, W., & Endicott, J. (1999). Prospective study of fluoxetine treatment and suicidal behavior in affectively III subjects. *American Journal of Psychiatry, 156* (2): 195–201.

Leon, G. (1990). *Case histories in psychopathology.* Boston: Allyn & Bacon.

Leonard, B. E. (1999). Therapeutic applications of benzodiazepine receptor ligands in anxiety. *Human Psychopharmacology, 14,* 125–35.

Leonard, H. L. (1997). New developments in the treatment of obsessive-compulsive disorder. *Journal of Clinical Psychiatry, 58* (Suppl 14): 39–45.

Leonard, H., Lenane, M., Swedo, S., et al. (1992). Tics and Tourette's disorder: A 2- to 7-year follow-up of 54 obsessive-compulsive children. *American Journal of Psychiatry, 149,* 1244–51.

Leonard, H. L. & Rapoport, J. L. (1991). Separation anxiety, overanxious, and avoidant disorders. In J. M. Weiner (Ed.), *Textbook of child and adolescent psychiatry.* Washington, DC: American Psychiatric Press.

Leonard, H. L., Swedo, S., Lenane, M., et al. (1991). A double-blind desipramine substitution during long-term clomipramine treatment in children and adolescents with obsessive-compulsive disorder. *Archives of General Psychiatry, 48,* 922–27.

Leonard, H., Swedo, S., Lenane, M., et al. (1993). A 2- to 7-year follow-up study of 54 obsessive-compulsive children and adolescents. *Archives of General Psychiatry, 50,* 429–39.

Leor, J., Poole, W. K., & Kloner, R. A. (1996). Sudden cardiac death triggered by an earthquake. *New England Journal of Medicine, 334*(7):413–19.

Lerman, C., Schwartz, M. D., Miller, S. M., Daly, M., Sands, C., & Rimer, B. K. (1996). A randomized trial of breast cancer risk counseling: Interacting effects of counseling, educational level, and coping style. *Health Psychology, 15* (2): 75–83.

Leserman, J., Petitto, J. M., Perkins, D. O., Folds, J. D., et al. (1997). Severe stress, depressive symptoms, and changes in lymphocyte subsets in human immunodeficiency virus-infected men. A 2-year follow-up study. *Archives of General Psychiatry, 54* (3): 279–85.

Lesser, I. M. (1985). Current concepts in psychiatry: Alexithymia. *New England Journal of Medicine, 312,* 690–92.

Lester, D. (1977). Multiple personality: A review. *Psychology, 14,* 54–59.

Lester, D. (1993). The effectiveness of suicide prevention centers. *Suicide and Life-Threatening Behavior, 23,* 263–67.

Lester, D., & Wilson, C. (1988). Suicide in Zimbabwe. *Central African Journal of Medicine, 34,* 147–49.

Leung, P., Luk, S., Ho, T., Taylor, E., Mak, F., & Bacon-Shone, J. (1996). The diagnosis and prevalence of hyperactivity in Chinese schoolboys. *British Journal of Psychiatry, 168* (4): 486–96.

LeVay, S. (1991). A difference in the hypothalamic structure between heterosexual and homosexual men. *Science, 253,* 1034–37.

Levendosky, A. A., Okun, A., & Parker, J. G. (1995). Depression and maltreatment as predictors of social competence and social problem-solving skills in school-age children. *Child Abuse and Neglect, 19* (10): 1183–95.

Levenstein, S., Prantera, C., Varvo, V., et al. (1995). Patterns of biologic and psychologic risk factors in duodenal ulcer patients. *Journal of Clinical Gastroenterology, 21,* 110.

Levin, A., Scheier, F., & Liebowitz, M. (1989). Social phobia: Biology and pharmacology. *Clinical Psychology Review, 9,* 129–40.

Levin, S., & Stava, L. (1987). Personality characteristics of sex offenders: A review. *Archives of Sexual Behavior, 16,* 57–79.

Levinson, D., Mahtani, M., Nancarrow, D., Brown, D., Kruglyak, L., Kirby, A., Hayward, N., Crowe, R., Andreasen, N., Black, D., Silverman, J., Endicott, J., Sharpe, L., Mohs, R., Siever, L., Walters, M., Lennon, D., Jones, H., Nertney, D., Daly, M., Gladis, M., & Mowry, B. (1998). Genome scan in schizophrenia. *American Journal of Psychiatry, 155,* 741–50.

Levitan, R. D., Parikh, S. V., Lesage, A. D., Hegadoren, K. M., Adams, M., Kennedy, S. H., & Goering, P. N. (1998). Major depression in individuals with a history of childhood physical or sexual abuse: Relationship to neurovegetative features, mania, and gender. *American Journal of Psychiatry, 155* (12): 1746–52.

Levy, G. D. (1995). Recall of related and unrelated gender-typed item pairs by young children. *Sex Roles, 32* (5–6): 393–406.

Levy, J. (1972). Lateral specialization of the human brain: Behavioral manifestations and possible evolutionary basis. In J. A. Krieger, Jr. (Ed.), *The biology of behavior* (pp. 159–80). Corvallis, OR: Oregon State University Press.

Lewine, R. R. J. (1981). Sex differences in schizophrenia: Timing or subtypes. *Psychological Bulletin, 90,* 432–44.

Lewinsohn, P. M. (1975). Engagement in pleasant activities and depression level. *Journal of Abnormal Psychology, 84,* 718–21.

Lewinsohn, P. M., & Clarke, G. N. (1999). Psychosocial treatments for adolescent depression. *Clinical Psychology Review, 19* (3): 329–42.

Lewinsohn, P. M., Clarke, G. N., Hops, H., & Andrews, J. (1990). Cognitive-behavioural treatment for depressed adolescents. *Behaviour Therapy, 21,* 385–401.

Lewinsohn, P. M., Gotlib, I. H., & Seeley, J. R. (1995). Adolescent psychopathology: IV: Specificity of psychosocial risk factors for depression and substance abuse in older adolescents. *American Academy of Child and Adolescent Psychiatry, 34* (9): 1221–1229.

Lewinsohn, P. M., Klein, D. N., & Seeley, J. R. (1995). Bipolar disorders in a community sample of older adolescents: Prevalence, phenomenology, comorbidity, and course. *Journal of the American Academy of Child and Adolescent Psychiatry, 34*(4): 454–63.

Lewinsohn, P. M., Rohde, P., Seeley, J. R., & Fischer, S. A. (1993). Age cohort changes in the lifetime occurrence of depression and other mental disorders. *Journal of Abnormal Psychology, 102* (1): 110–20.

Lewis, D. O., Yeager, C. A., Swica, Y., Pincus, J. H., & Lewis, M. (1997). Objective documentation of child abuse and dissociation in 12 murderers with dissociative identity disorder. *American Journal of Psychiatry, 154* (12): 1703–10.

Lewis, J. M., Rodnick, E. H., & Goldstein, M. J. (1981). Interfamilial interactive behavior, parental communication deviance, and risk for schizophrenia. *Journal of Abnormal Psychology, 90,* 448–57.

Lewis, R., Kapur, S., Jones, C., DaSilva, J., Brown, G. M., Wilson, A. A., Houle, S., & Zipursky, R. B. (1999). Serotonin 5-HT-sub-2 receptors in schizophrenia: A PET study using [-sup-1-sup-8F] setoperone in neuroleptic-naive patients and normal subjects. *American Journal of Psychiatry, 156,* 72–78.

Lewis, V., & Money, J. (1983). Gender identity/role: GI/R Part A: XY (androgen-insensitivity) syndrome and XX (Rokitansky) syndrome of vaginal atresia compared. In L. Dennerstein & G. Burrows (Eds.), *Handbook of psychosomatic obstetrics and gynecology* (pp. 51–60). New York: Elsevier.

Lewy, A. J., Bauer, V. K., Cutler, N. L., Sack, R. L., Ahmed, S., Thomas, K. H., Blood, M. L., & Jackson, J. M. L. (1998). Morning vs. evening light treatment of patients with winter depression. *Archives of General Psychiatry, 55* (10): 890–96.

Lewy, A. J., Sack, L., Miller, S., & Hoban, T. M. (1987). Antidepressant and circadian phase-shifting effects of light. *Science, 235,* 352–54.

Leys, D., & Pasquier, F. (1998). Subcortical vascular dementia: Epidemiology and risk factors. *Archives of Gerontology and Geriatrics* (Supp. 6): 281–94.

Lezak, M. (1983). *Neuropsychological assessment.* New York: Oxford University Press.

Liberman, R., & Green, M. (1992). Whither cognitive-behavioral therapy for schizophrenia? *Schizophrenia Bulletin, 18,* 27–33.

Liberman, R. P., Mueser, K. T., & Wallace, C. J. (1986). Social skills training for schizophrenic individuals at risk for relapse. *American Journal of Psychiatry, 143*(4): 523–26.

Liberman, R. P., Neuchterlein, K. H., & Wallace, C. J. (1982). Social skills training and the nature of schizophrenia. In J. P. Curran & P. M. Monti (Eds.), *Social skills training: A practical handbook* (pp. 5–56). New York: Guilford Press.

Licht, M. R. (1998). Sildenafil (Viagra) for treating male erectile dysfunction. *Cleveland Clinic Journal of Medicine, 65* (6):301–304.

Lichtenburg, P. A. (1999). *Handbook of assessment in clinical gerontology.* New York: Wiley.

Licinio, J., Wong, M., & Gold, P. W. (1996). The hypothalamic-pituitary-adrenal axis in anorexia nervosa. *Psychiatry Research, 62,* 75–83.

Lidz, C. W., Mulvey, E. P., & Gardner, W. (1993). The accuracy of predictions of violence to others. *Journal of the American Medical Association, 269*(8): 1007–11.

Liebowitz, M. R., Fyer, A. J., Gorman, J. M., Dillon, D., Davies, S., Stein, J. M., Cohen, B. S., & Klein, D. F. (1985). Specificity of lactate infusions in social phobia versus panic disorders. *American Journal of Psychiatry, 142,* 947–50.

Liebowitz, M. R. , Gorman, J. M., Fyer, A. J., Levitt, M., Dillon, D., Levy, G., Appleby, I. L., Anderson, S., Palij, M., Davies, S. O., & Klein, D. F. (1985). Lactate provocation of panic attacks: II. Biochemical and physiological findings. *Archives of General Psychiatry, 42,* 709–19.

Liese, B. S., & Larson, M. W. (1995). Coping with life threatening illness: A cognitive therapy perspective. *Journal of Cognitive Psychotherapy, 9*(1): 19–34.

Lilenfield, L. R., Kaye, W. H., Greeno, C. G., Merikangas, K. R., Plotnicov, K., Pollice, C., Rao, R., Strober, M., Bulik, C. M., & Nagy, L. (1998). A controlled family study of anorexia nervosa and bulimia nervosa: Psychiatric disorders in first-degree relatives and effects of proband comorbidity. *Archives of General Psychiatry, 55,* 603–10.

Lilienfeld, S. O., Lynn, S., Kirsch, et al. (1999). Dissociative identity disorder and the sociocognitive model: Recalling lessons from the past. *Psychological Bulletin, 125,* 507–23.

Lilienfeld, S. O., & Marino, L. (1999). Essentialism revisited: Evolutionary theory and the concept of mental disorder. *Journal of Abnormal Psychology, 108* (3): 400–411.

Lilienfeld, S. O., Purcell, C., & Jones-Alexander, J. (1997). Assessment of antisocial behavior in adults. In D. M. Stoff, J. Breiling, & J. D. Maser (Eds.), *Handbook of antisocial behavior* (pp. 60–74). New York: Wiley.

Lilienfeld, S. O., Van Valkenburg, C., Larntz, K., & Akiskal, H. S. (1986). The relationship of histrionic personality disorder to antisocial personality and somatization disorders. *American Journal of Psychiatry, 143,* 718–22.

Lilienfeld, S., Waldman, I., & Israel, A. (1994). A critical examination of the use of the term and concept of comorbidity in psychopathology research. *Clinical Psychology— Science and Practice, 1* (1): 71–83.

Lindamer, L. A., Lohr, J. B., Harris, M. J., & Jeste, D. V. (1997). Gender, estrogen, and schizophrenia. *Psychopharmacology Bulletin, 33,* 221–28.

Lindemalm, G., Korlin, D., & Uddenberg, N. (1986). Long-term follow-up of "sex change" in 13 male-to-female transsexuals. *Archives of Sexual Behavior, 15,* 187–210.

Lindemann, E. (1944). The symptomatology and management of acute grief. *American Journal of Psychiatry, 101,* 141–48.

Linden, L. L., & Breed, W. (1976). The demographic epidemiology of suicide. In E. S. Shneidman (Ed.), *Suicidology: Contemporary developments.* New York: Grune & Stratton.

Lindstroem, E., Widerloev, B., & von Knorring, L. (1997). The ICD-10 and DSM-IV diagnostic criteria and the prevalence of schizophrenia. *European Psychiatry, 12,* 217–23.

Lindy, J. D., Green, B. L., Grace, M. C., MacLeod, J. A., & Spitz, L. (1988). *Vietnam: A casebook.* New York: Brunner/Mazel.

Linehan, M. M. (1997). Behavioral treatments of suicidal behavior: Definitional obfuscation and treatment outcomes. In D. M. Stoff, & J. J. Mann (Eds.), *The neurobiology of suicide: From the bench to the clinic. Annals of The New York Academy of Sciences* (Vol. 836; pp. 302–28). New York: New York Academy of Sciences.

Linehan, M. M., Heard, H. L., & Armstrong, H. E. (1993). Naturalistic follow-up of a behavioral treatment for chronically parasuicidal borderline patients. *Archives of General Psychiatry, 50* (12): 971–74.

Link, B. G., Andrews, H., & Cullen, F. T. (1992). The violent and illegal behavior of mental patients reconsidered. *American Sociological Review, 57,* 275–92.

Linkowski, P., Van Onderbergen, A., Kerkhofs, M., Bosson, D., Mendlewicz, J. & Van Cauter, E. (1993). Twin study of the 24-h cortisol profile: Evidence for genetic control of the human circadian clock. *American Journal of Physiology, 264,* E173–E181.

Linsky, A. S., Straus, M. A., & Colby, J. P. (1985). Stressful events, stressful conditions, and alcohol problems in the United States, a partial test of Bale's Theory. *Journal of Studies on Alcohol, 33,* 979–89.

Lipman, E. L., Bennett, K. J., Racine, Y. A., Mazumdar, R., & Offord, D. R. (1998). What does early antisocial behaviour predict? A follow-up of 4- and 5-year-olds from the Ontario Child Health Study. *Canadian Journal of Psychiatry, 43,* 605–13.

Lipowski, Z. J. (1990). Chronic idiopathic pain syndrome. *Annals of Medicine, 22,* 213–17.

Lippold, S., & Claiborn, J. M. (1983). Comparison of the Wechsler Adult Intelligence Scale and the Wechsler Adult Intelligence Scale-Revised. *Journal of Consulting and Clinical Psychology, 51,* 315.

Lipschitz, D. S., Rasmusson, A. M., & Southwick, S. M. (1998). Childhood posttraumatic stress disorder: A review of neurobiologic sequelae. *Psychiatric Annals, 28* (8): 452–57.

Lipsey, M. W., & Derzon, J. H. (1998). Predictors of violent or serious delinquency in adolescence and early adulthood: A synthesis of longitudinal research. In R. Loeber & D. P. Farrington (Eds.), *Serious and violent juvenile offenders: Risk factors and successful interventions* (pp. 86–105). Thousand Oaks, CA: Sage.

Lipsey, M., & Wilson, D. (1993). The efficacy of psychological, educational, and behavioral treatment: Confirmation from meta-analysis. *American Psychologist, 48,* 1181–1209.

Lister, R. G. (1985). The amnesic action of benzodiazepines in man. *Neuroscience and Biobehavioral Reviews, 9,* 87–94.

Littlefield, C. H., & Rushton, J. P. (1986). When a child dies: The sociobiology of bereavement. *Journal of Personality and Social Psychology, 51,* 797–802.

Liu, D., Diorio, J., Tannenbaum, B., Caldji, C., Francis, D., Freedman, A., Sharma, S., Pearson, D., Plotsky, P. M., & Meaney, M. J. (1997). Maternal care, hippocampal glucocorticoid receptors and hypothalamic-pituitary-adrenal axis activity. *Science, 277,* 1659–62.

Livermore, J. M., & Meehl, P. E. (1967). The virtues of M'Naghten. *Minnesota Law Review, 51,* 789–856.

Livesley, W. J. (1995). *The DSM-IV personality disorders: Diagnosis and treatment of mental disorders.* New York: Guilford Press.

Livingston, H., Livingston, M., Brooks, D., & McKinlay, W. (1992). Elderly survivors of the Lockerbie air disaster. *International Journal of Geriatric Psychiatry, 7,* 725–29.

Lloyd, K. (1998). Ethnicity, social inequality, and mental illness: In a community setting the picture is complex. *British Medical Journal, 316,* 7147–63.

Lochman, J. E., White, K. J., & Wayland, K. K. (1991). Cognitive-behavioral assessment and treatment with aggressive children. In P. C. Kendall (Ed.), *Child and adolescent therapy*. New York: Guilford Press.

Lockyer, L., & Rutter, M. (1969). A five- to fifteen-year follow-up study of infantile psychosis. *British Journal of Psychiatry, 115,* 865–82.

Loeber, R. (1990). Development and risk factors of juvenile antisocial behavior and delinquency. *Clinical Psychology Review, 10,* 1–41.

Loeber, R., & Dishion, T. J. (1983). Early predictors of male delinquency: A review. *Psychological Bulletin, 94,* 68–99.

Loeber, R., Farrington, D. P., Stouthamer-Loeber, M., & Van Kammen, W. B. (1998). Multiple risk factors for multiproblem boys: Co-occurrence of delinquency, substance use, attention deficit, conduct problems, physical aggression, covert behavior, depressed mood, and shy/withdrawn behavior. In R. Jessor (Ed.), *New perspectives on adolescent risk behavior* (pp. 90–149). New York: Cambridge University Press.

Loewenstein, R. J., & Ross, D. R. (1992). Multiple personality and psychoanalysis: An introduction. *Psychoanalytic Inquiry, 12,* 3–48.

Loftus, E. (1993). The reality of repressed memories. *American Psychologist, 48,* 518–37.

Loftus, E. (1994). The repressed memory controversy. *American Psychologist, 49,* 443–45.

Loftus, E. F. (1997). Repressed memory accusations: Devastated families and devastated patients. *Applied Cognitive Psychology, 11,* 25–30.

Loftus, E., Grant, B., Franklin, G., Parr, L., & Brown, R. (1996). Crime victims' compensation and repressed memory. Submitted to *New England Journal of Medicine*.

Lohr, B. A., Adams, H. E., & Davis J. M. (1997). Sexual arousal to erotic and aggressive stimuli in sexually coercive and noncoercive men. *Journal of Abnormal Psychology, 106* (2):230–42.

Lohr, J. M., Kleinknecht, R. A., Tolin, D. F., & Barrett, R. H. (1995). The empirical status of the clinical application of eye movement desensitization and reprocessing. *Journal of Behavior Therapy and Experimental Psychiatry, 26* (4): 285–302.

Lomborso, P. J. (2000). Genetics of childhood disorders: XIV. A gene for Rett Syndrome: News flash. *Journal of the American Academy of Child and Adolescent Psychiatry, 39,* 671–74.

London, P. (1986). *The modes and morals of psychotherapy*. New York: Hemisphere.

Long, P. W. (1990). *Delusional disorder treatment*. Internet Mental Health. Online: http://www.mentalhealth.com/rx/p23-ps02.html

Lonnquist, J., Shihvo, S., Syvalahti, E., Sintonen, H., Kiviruusu, O., & Piktkanen, H. (1995). Moclobemide and fluoxetine in the prevention of relapses following acute treatment of depression. *Acta Psychiatrica Scandinavica, 91,* 189–94.

Looney, J. G., Lipp, M. G., & Spitzer R. L. (1978). A new method of classification for psychophysiological disorders. *American Journal of Psychiatry, 135,* 304–308.

LoPiccolo, J., & Stock, W. E. (1986). Treatment of sexual dysfunction. *Journal of Consulting and Clinical Psychology, 54,* 158–67.

Loranger, A. W. (1996). Dependent personality disorder: Age, sex, and Axis I comorbidity. *Journal of Nervous and Mental Disease, 184,* 17–21.

Loranger, A., & Levine, P. (1978). Age of onset of bipolar affective illness. *Archives of General Psychiatry, 35,* 1345–48.

Loranger, A. W., Susman, V. L., Oldham, J. M., & Russakoff, L. M. (1987). The personality disorder examination: A preliminary report. *Journal of Personality Disorders, 1*(1): 1–13.

Losonczy, M. F., Song, I. S., Mohs, R. C., Mathe, A. A., Davidson, M., Davis, B. M., & Davis, K. L. (1986). Correlates of lateral ventricular size in chronic schizophrenia: II. Biological measures. *American Journal of Psychiatry, 143* (9): 1113–17.

Lovaas, O. I. (1966). A program for the establishment of speech in psychotic children. In J. K. Wing (Ed.), *Early childhood autism*. New York: Pergamon.

Lovaas, O. I. (1973). *Behavioral treatment of autistic children*. Morristown, NJ: General Learning Press.

Lovaas, O. I. (1987). Behavioral treatment and abnormal education and intellectual functioning in young autistic children. *Journal of Consulting and Clinical Psychology, 55,* 3–9.

Lovaas, O. I., & Buch, G. (1997). Intensive behavioral intervention with young children with autism. In N. N. Singh (Ed.), *Prevention and treatment of severe behavior problems: Models and methods in developmental disabilities* (pp. 61–86). Pacific Grove, CA: Brooks/Cole.

Lovaas, O. I., & Simmons, J. Q. (1969). Manipulation of self-destruction in three retarded children. *Journal of Applied Behavior Analysis, 2,* 143–57.

Lovibond, S. H., & Coote, M. A. (1970). Enuresis. In C. G. Costello (Ed.), *Symptoms of psychopathology*. New York: Wiley.

Lovinger, D. M. (1997). Serotonin's role in alcohol's effects on the brain. Alcohol Health and Research World, 21, 114–20.

Low, P. W., Jeffries, Jr., J. C. , & Bonnie, R. J. (1986). *The trial of John W. Hinckley, Jr.: A case study in the insanity defense*. Mineola, NY: Foundation Press.

Lowenstein, L. F. (1996). The diagnosis and treatment of young psychopaths: Part two. Criminologist, 20, 207–17.

Luborsky, L. (1984). *Principles of psychoanalytic theory: A manual for supportive expressive treatment*. New York: Basic Books.

Luborsky, L., Diguer, L., Seligman, D. A., Rosenthal, R., Krause, E. D., Johnson, S., Halperin, G., Bishop, M., Berman, J. S., Schweizer, E. (1999). The researcher's own therapy allegiances: A "wild card" in comparisons of treatment efficacy. *Clinical Psychology-Science & Practice, 6*(1): 95–106.

Luborsky, L., Popp, C., Luborsky, E., & Mark, D. (1994). The core conflictual relationship theme. *Psychotherapy Research, 4* (3–4): 172–83.

Luborsky, L., Singer, B., & Luborsky, E. (1975). Comparative studies of psychotherapies. *Archives of General Psychiatry, 32,* 995–1008.

Lucas, A. R., Beard, C. M., O'Fallon, W. M., & Kurlan, L. T. (1991). Fifty-year trends in the incidence of anorexia nervosa in Rochester, Minnesota: A population-based study. *American Journal of Psychiatry, 148,* 917.

Luckasson, R., Coulter, D. L., Polloway, E. A., Reiss, S., Schalock, R. L., Snell, M. E., Spitalnik, D. M., & Stark,

J. A. (1992). *Mental retardation: Definition, classification, and systems of support*. Washington, DC: American Association on Mental Retardation.

Ludlow, C. L. (1999). A conceptual framework for investigating the neurobiology of stuttering. In N.B. Ratner & E.C. Healey (Eds.), *Stuttering research and practice: Bridging the gap*. Mahwah, NJ: Lawrence Erlbaum.

Luria, A. (1973). *The working brain*. New York: Basic Books.

Lutgendorf, S. K., Antoni, M. H., Ironson, G., Klimas, N., et al. (1997). Cognitive-behavioral stress management decreases dysphoric mood and herpes simplex virus-Type 2 antibody titers in symptomatic HIV-seropositive gay men. *Journal of Consulting and Clinical Psychology, 65*(1): 31–43.

Lutgendorf, S. K., Antoni, M. H., Ironson, G., Starr, K., Costello, N., Zuckerman, M., Klimas, N., Fletcher, M. A., & Schneiderman, N. (1998). Changes in cognitive coping skills and social support during cognitive behavioral stress management intervention and distress outcomes in symptomatic human immunodeficiency virus (HIV)-seropositive gay men. *Psychosomatic Medicine, 60*(2): 204–14.

Lydiard, R. B., Ballenger, J. C., & Rickels, K. (1997). A double-blind evaluation of the safety and efficacy of abecarnil, alprazolam, and placebo in outpatients with generalized anxiety disorder. *Journal of Clinical Psychiatry, 58*(Suppl 11): 11–18.

Lykken, D. T. (1957). A study of anxiety in the sociopathic personality. *Journal of Abnormal and Social Psychology, 55,* 6–10.

Lykken, D. T. (1997). Incompetent parenting: Its causes and cures. *Child Psychiatry and Human Development, 27,* 129–37.

Lykken, D. (1998). The case for parental licensure. In T. Millon, E. Simonsen, M. Birket-Smith, & R. D. Davis (Eds.), *Psychopathy: Antisocial, criminal, and violent behavior* (pp. 122–43). New York: Guilford Press.

Lykken, D. (1999). *Happiness*. New York: Golden Books.

Lynam, D. R. (1998). Early identification of the fledgling psychopath: Locating the psychopathic child in the current nomenclature. *Journal of Abnormal Psychology, 107,* 566–75.

Lynch, J. W., Kaplan, G. A., & Shema, S. J. (1997). Cumulative impact of sustained economic hardship on physical, cognitive, psychological, and social functioning. *New England Journal of Medicine, 337* (26): 1889–95.

Lyon, G. R. (1996). Learning disabilities. In E. J. Mash & R. A. Barkley (Eds.), *Child psychopathology* (pp. 390–435). New York: Guilford Press.

Lyon, G. R., et al. (Eds.). (1994). *Frames of reference for the assessment of learning disabilities: New views on measurement issues* (pp. 185–200). Baltimore: Paul H. Brookes.

Lyons, M. J., True, W. R., Eisen, S. A., Goldberg, J., Meyer, J. M., Faraone, S. V., Eaves, L. J., & Tsuang, M. T. (1995). Differential heritability of adult and juvenile antisocial traits. *Archives of General Psychiatry, 52,* 906–15.

Lyoo, I. K., Han, M. H., & Cho, D. Y. (1998). A brain MRI study in subjects with borderline personality disorder. *Journal of Affective Disorders, 50,* 235–43.

Maas, J. W. (1975). Biogenic amines and depression. *Archives of General Psychiatry, 32,* 1357–61.

MacCoun, R., & Reuter, P. (1997). Interpreting Dutch cannabis policy: Reasoning by analogy in the legalization debate. *Science, 278,* 47–52.

Maccoby, E., & Jacklin, C. (1974). *The psychology of sex differences*. Stanford: Stanford University Press.

MacCrimmon, D. J., Cleghorn, J. M., Asarnow, R. F., & Steffy, R. A. (1980). Children at risk for schizophrenia: Clinical and attentional characteristics. *Archives of General Psychiatry, 37,* 671–74.

Macdonald, A. J. D. (1997). ABC of mental health: Mental health in old age. *British Medical Journal, 315,* 413–17.

MacDonald, N. (1960). Living with schizophrenia. *Canadian Medical Association Journal, 82,* 218–21.

Mace, F. C., Vollmer, T. R., Progar, P. R. & Mace, A. B. (1998). Assessment and treatment of self-injury. In Watson, T. S. and Gresham, F. M. (Eds), *Handbook of child behavior therapy. Issues in clinical child psychology*. (pp. 413–30). New York: Plenum.

Mace, N., & Robins, P. V. (1981). *The thirty-six hour day*. Baltimore: Johns Hopkins Press.

Machlin, G. (1996). Some causes of genotypic and phenotypic discordance in monozygotic twin pairs. *American Journal of Medical Genetics, 61,* 216–28.

Mackay, A. V. P. (1980). Positive and negative schizophrenic symptoms and the role of dopamine. *British Journal of Psychiatry, 137,* 379–86.

MacLeod, A. K., & Cropley, M. L. (1995). Depressive future-thinking: The role of valence and specificity. *Cognitive Therapy and Research, 19* (1): 35–50.

MacLeod, C., & McLaughlin, K. (1995). Implicit and explicit memory bias in anxiety: A conceptual replication. *Behaviour Research and Therapy, 33* (1): 1–14.

MacMillan, D. L., & Semmel, M. I. (1977). Evaluation of mainstreaming programs. *Focus on Exceptional Children, 6* (4): 8–14.

Madakasira, S., & O'Brien, K. (1987). Acute post-traumatic stress disorder in victims of a natural disaster. *Journal of Nervous and Mental Disease, 175,* 286–90.

Maffei, C., Fossati, A., Agostoni, I., Barraco, A., Bagnato, M., Deborah, D. Namia, C., Novella, L., & Petrachi, M. (1997). Interrater reliability and internal consistency of the Structured Clinical Interview for DSM-IV Axis II Personality Disorders (SCID-II), version 2.0. *Journal of Personality Disorders, 11*(3), 279–84.

Magaro, P. A. (1981). The paranoid and the schizophrenic: The case for distinct cognitive style. *Schizophrenia Bulletin, 7,* 632–61.

Magee, W.J., Eaton, W.W., Wittchen, H.-U., McGonagle, K. A., & Kessler, R. C. (1996). Agoraphobia, simple phobia, and social phobia in the national comorbidity survey. *Archives of General Psychiatry, 53* (2): 159–68.

Magid, K., McKelvey, C. A., & Schroeder, P. (1989). *High risk: Children without a conscience*. New York: Bantam.

Magnusson, D. (1988). *Individual development from an interactional perspective: A longitudinal study*. Hillsdale, NJ: Erlbaum.

Magnusson, A., Axelsson, J., Karlsson, M., & Oskarsson, H. (2000). Lack of seasonal mood change in the Icelandic population. *American Journal of Psychiatry, 157,* 234–38.

Maher, B. (1992). Delusions: Contemporary etiological hypotheses. *Psychiatric Annals, 22* (5): 260–68.

Maher, B. A. (1966). *Principles of psychopathology: An experimental approach*. New York: McGraw-Hill.

Mahler, M. (1979). *The selected papers of Margaret Mahler* (Vol. 1, 2, 3). New York: Jason Aronson.

Mahoney, M. J. (1971). The self-management of covert behavior: A case study. *Behavior Therapy, 2,* 575–78.

Mahoney, M. J. (1974). *Cognition and behavior modification.* Cambridge, MA.: Ballinger.

Mahoney, M. J., & Thoresen, C. E. (1974). *Self-control: Power to the person.* Belmont, CA: Brooks/Cole.

Maier, S. F., Laudenslager, M., & Ryan, S. M. (1985). Stressor controllability, immune function, and endogenous opiates. In F. Bush & J. B. Overmier (Eds.), *Affect, conditioning, and cognition.* Hillside, NJ: Erlbaum.

Maier, S. F., & Seligman, M. E. P. (1976). Learned helplessness: Theory and evidence. *Journal of Experimental Psychology, 105* (1): 3–46.

Maier, S. F., Seligman, M. E. P., & Solomon, R. L. (1969). Pavlovian fear conditioning and learned helplessness: Effects on escape and avoidance behavior of (a) the CS-US contingency and (b) the independence of the US and voluntary responding. In Campbell & Church (Eds.), *Punishment and aversive behavior.* New York: Appleton.

Maier, S. F., & Watkins, L. R. (1998). Cytokines for psychologists: Implications of bidirectional immune-to-brain communication for understanding behavior, mood, and cognition. *Psychological Review, 105* (1): 83–107.

Maier, S. F., Watkins, L. R., & Fleshner, M. (1994). Psychoneuroimmunology: The interface between behavior, brain, and immunity. *American Psychologist, 49* (2): 1004–17.

Maier, W., Lichtermann, D., Minges, J., Delmo, C., & Heun, R. (1995). The relationship between bipolar disorder and alcoholism: A controlled family study. *Psychological Medicine, 25,* 787–96.

Mailleux, P., Verslype, M., Preud'homme, X., & Vanderhaeghen, J. J. (1994). Activation of multiple transcription factor genes by tetrahydrocannabinol in rat forebrain. *NeuroReport, 5,* 1265–68.

Main, M. (1991). Metacognitive knowledge, metacognitive monitoring, and singular (coherent) vs. Multiple (incoherent) models of attachment: Findings and directions for future research. In P. Harris, J. Stevenson-Hinde & C. Parkes (Eds.), *Attachment across the lifecycle* (pp. 127–59). New York: Routledge-Kegan Paul.

Maki, P. M. Zonderman, A. B., & Weingartner, H. (1999). Age differences in implicit memory: Fragmented object identification and category exemplar generation. *Psychology and Aging, 14* (2): 284–94.

Malarkey, W., Kiecolt-Glaser, J., Pearl, D., & Glaser, R. (1994). Hostile behavior during marital conflict alters pituitary and adrenal hormones. *Psychosomatic Medicine, 56,* 41–51.

Malaspina, D., Perera, G. M., Lignelli, A., Marshall, R. S., Esser, P. D., Storer, S., Furman, V., Wray, A. D., Coleman, E., Gorman, J. M., & Van Heertum, R. L. (1998). SPECT imaging of odor identification in schizophrenia. *Psychiatry Research: Neuroimaging, 82,* 53–61.

Malenka, R. C., & Nicoli, R. A. (1997). Learning and memory: Never fear, LTP is here. *Nature, 390* (6660): 552–53.

Maletzky, B. M. (1974). "Assisted" covert sensitization in the treatment of exhibitionism. *Journal of Consulting and Clinical Psychology, 42,* 34–40.

Maletzky, B. M. (1998). The paraphilias: Research and treatment. In P. E. Nathan & J. M. Gorman (Eds.), *A guide to treatments that work* (pp. 472–500). New York: Oxford University Press.

Malitz, S., et al. (1984). Low dosage ECT: Electrode placement and acute physiological and cognitive effects. Special Issue: Electroconvulsive therapy. *American Journal of Social Psychiatry, 4* (4): 47–53.

Malmo, R. B., & Shagass, C. (1949). Physiological study of symptom mechanism in psychiatric patients under stress. *Psychosomatic Medicine, 11,* 25–29.

Malt, U., & Weisaeth, L. (1989). Disaster psychiatry and traumatic stress studies in Norway. *Acta Psychiatrica Scandinavica, 80,* 7–12.

Maltsberger, J. T., & Lovett, C. G. (1992). Suicide in borderline personality disorder. In D. Silver & M. Rossenbluth (Eds.), *Handbook of borderline disorders* (pp. 335–87). Madison, CT: International Universities Press.

Mancini, F., Gragnani, A., Orazi, F., & Pietrangeli, M. G. (1999). Obsessions and compulsions: Normative data on the Padua Inventory from an Italian non-clinical adolescent sample. *Behaviour Research and Therapy, 37* (10): 919–25.

Manji, H. K., Potter, W. Z., & Lenox, R. H. (1995). Signal transduction pathways: Molecular targets for lithium's actions. *Archives of General Psychiatry, 52,* 531–43.

Mann, J., Arango, V., & Underwood, M. (1990). Serotonin and suicidal behavior. *Annals of the New York Academy of Sciences, 600,* 476–85.

Mannuzza, S., Fyer, A. J., Martin, L. Y., Gallops, M., S., Endicott, J., Gorman, J., Liebowitz, M. R., and Klein, D. F. (1989). Reliability of anxiety assessment. *Archives of General Psychiatry, 46,* 1093–1101.

Marchevsky, D. (1999). Selective serotonin reuptake inhibitors and personality change. *British Journal of Psychiatry, 175,* 589–90.

Marciano, T. D. (1982). Four marriage and family texts: A brief (but telling) array. *Contemporary Sociology, 11,* 150–53.

Marcus, J., Hans, S. L., Auerbach, J. G., & Auerbach, A. G. (1993). Children at risk for schizophrenia: The Jerusalem Infant Development Study: II. Neurobehavioral deficits at school age. *Archives of General Psychiatry, 50,* 797–809.

Marder, K., Tang, M. X., Alfaro, B., Mejia, H., Cote, L., Louis, E., Stern, Y., & Mayeux, R. (1999). Risk of Alzheimer's disease in relatives of Parkinson's disease patients with and without dementia. *Neurology, 52,* 719–24.

Marek, G. J., & Aghajanian, G. K. (1998). Indoleamine and the phenethylamine hallucinogens: Mechanisms of psychotomimetic action. *Drug and Alcohol Dependence, 51,* 189–98.

Marengo, J. T., Harrow, M., & Edell, W. S. (1993). Thought disorder. In C. G. Costello (Ed.), *Symptoms of schizophrenia* (pp. 27–55). New York: Wiley.

Margraf, J., Barlow, D., Clark, D., & Telch, M. (1993). Psychological treatment of panic: Work in progress on outcome, active ingredients, and follow-up. *Behaviour Research and Therapy, 31* (1): 1–8.

Margraf, J., & Schneider, S. (1991). *Outcome and active ingredients of cognitive-behavioural treatments for panic disorder.* Paper presented at the annual meeting of the Association for the Advancement of Behavior Therapy, New York, November 26, 1991.

Marin, D., De Meo, M., Frances, A., Kocsis, J., & Mann, J. (1989). Biological models and treatments for personality disorders. *Psychiatric Annals, 19,* 143–46.

Mariotto, M., Paul, G. L., & Licht, M. H. (1995). Assessing the chronically mentally ill patient. In J. N. Butcher (Ed.), *Clinical personality assessment: Practical considerations.* New York: Oxford University Press.

Markovitch, S., Goldberg, S., Gold., A., & Washington, J. (1997). Determinants of behavioral problems in Romanian children adopted in Ontario. *International Journal of Behavioral Development, 20,* 17–31.

Marks, I. M. (1969). *Fears and phobias.* New York: Academic Press.

Marks, I. (1977). Phobias and obsessions: Clinical phenomena in search of laboratory models. In J. Maser & M. E. P. Seligman (Eds.), *Psychopathology: Experimental models.* San Francisco: Freeman.

Marks, I. M. (1981). Review of behavioral psychotherapy: II. Sexual disorders. *American Journal of Psychiatry, 138,* 750–56.

Marks, I. M. (1986). Epidemiology of anxiety. *Social Psychiatry, 21,* 167–71.

Marks, I., Boulougouris, J., & Marset, P. (1971). Flooding versus desensitization in the treatment of phobic patients: A crossover study. *British Journal of Psychiatry, 119,* 353–75.

Marks, I. M., Gray, S., Cohen, D., Hill, R., Mawson, D., Ramm, E., & Stern, R. S. (1983). Imipramine and brief therapist-aided exposure in agoraphobics having self-exposure homework. *Archives of General Psychiatry, 40,* 153–62.

Marks, I., Lovell, K., Noshirvani, H., Livanou, M., & Thrasher, S. (1998). Treatment of posttraumatic stress disorder by exposure and/or cognitive restructuring: A controlled study. *Archives of General Psychiatry, 55* (4): 317–25.

Marks, I. M., & Rachman, S. J. (1978). *Interim report to the Medical Research Council.*

Marks, I., & Tobena, A. (1990). Learning and unlearning fear: A clinical and evolutionary perspective. *Neuroscience and Biobehavioral Reviews, 14,* 365–84.

Marlatt, G. A. (1996). Section I. Theoretical perspectives on relapse: Taxonomy of high-risk situations for alcohol relapse: Evolution and development of a cognitive-behavioral model. *Addiction, 91,* S37–S49.

Marlatt, G. A. (Ed.). (1998). *Harm reduction: Pragmatic strategies for managing high-risk behaviors.* New York: Guilford Press.

Marlatt, G. A., & Gordon, J. R. (1985). *Relapse prevention.* New York: Guilford Press.

Marlatt, G. A., VandenBos, G. R., et al. (Eds.). (1997). *Addictive behaviors: Readings on etiology, prevention, and treatment.* Washington, DC: American Psychological Association.

Marshall, R. D., Stein, D. J., Liebowitz, M. R., & Yehuda, R. (1996). A pharmacotherapy algorithm in the treatment of posttraumatic stress disorder. *Psychiatric Annals, 26* (4): 217–26.

Marshall, W., Eccles, A., & Barbaree, H. (1991). The treatment of exhibitionists: A focus on sexual deviance versus cognitive and relationship features. *Behaviour Research and Therapy, 29,* 129–35.

Martin, A. (1987). Representation of semantic and spatial knowledge in Alzheimer's patients: Implications for models of preserved learning in amnesia. *Journal of Clinical and Experimental Neuropsychology, 9,* 191–224.

Martin, A., Heyes, M. P., Salazar, A. M., Law, W. A., & Williams, J. (1993). Impaired motor-skill learning, slowed reaction time, and elevated cerebro-spinal fluid guinolinic acid in a subgroup of HIV-infected individuals. *Neuropsychology, 7,* 149–57.

Martin, B. (1977). *Abnormal psychology.* New York: Holt, Rinehart & Winston.

Martin, C. L., Eisenbud, L., & Rose, H. (1995). Children's gender-based reasoning about toys. *Child Development, 66,* 1453–71.

Martin, J. (1999). Mechanisms of disease: Molecular basis of the neurodegenerative disorders. *New England Journal of Medicine, 340* (25): 1970–80.

Marucha, P., Kiecolt-Glaser, J., & Favagehi, M. (1998). Mucosal wound healing is impaired by examination stress. *Psychosomatic Medicine, 60,* 362–65.

Mason, F. L. (1997). Fetishism: Psychopathology and theory. In D. R. Laws & W. O'Donohue (Eds.), *Sexual deviance: Theory, assessment, and treatment* (pp. 75–91). New York: Guilford Press.

Mason, J. W. (1971). A re-evaluation of the concept of "nonspecificity" in stress theory. *Journal of Psychiatric Research, 8,* 323–33.

Mason, J. W. (1975). A historical view of the stress field, Part I. *Journal of Human Stress, 1,* 6–12.

Mason, P., Harrison, G., Croudace, T., Glazebrook, C., & Medley, I. (1997). The predictive validity of a diagnosis of schizophrenia: A report from the International Study of Schizophrenia (ISoS) coordinated by the World Health Organization and the Department of Psychiatry, University of Nottingham. *British Journal of Psychiatry, 170* (4): 321–27.

Masters, W. H., & Johnson, V. E. (1970). *Human sexual inadequacy.* Boston: Little, Brown.

Matarazzo, J. (1980). Behavioral health and behavioral medicine: Frontiers for a new health psychology. *American Psychologist, 35,* 807–17.

Matarazzo, J. D. (1983). The reliability of psychiatric and psychological diagnosis. *Clinical Psychology Review, 3,* 103–45.

Mathias, R. (1996). Students' use of marijuana, other illicit drugs, and cigarettes continued to rise in 1995. *NIDA Research Advances, 11* (1).

Mattes, J. A. (1997). Risperidone: How good is the evidence for efficacy? *Schizophrenia Bulletin, 23* (1): 155–62.

Matthews, A., & MacLeod, C. (1986). Discrimination of threat cues without awareness in anxiety states. *Journal of Abnormal Psychology, 95,* 131–38.

Matthews, A., Mogg, K., Kentish, J., & Eysenck, M. (1995). Effect of psychological treatment on cognitive bias in generalized anxiety disorder. *Behaviour Research and Therapy, 33* (3): 293–303.

Matthys, W., Cuperus, J. M., & van Engeland, H. (1999). Deficient social problem-solving in boys with ODD/CD, with ADHD, and with both disorders. *Journal of the American Academy of Child and Adolescent Psychiatry, 38,* 311–21.

Matthysse, S. (1973). Antipsychotic drug actions: A clue to the neuropathology of the schizophrenias. *Federation Proceedings, 32,* 200–205.

Mattick, R., Andrews, G., Hadzi-Pavlovic, D., & Christensen, H. (1990). Treatment of panic and agoraphobia: An integrative review. *Journal of Nervous and Mental Disease, 178,* 567–78.

Mattson, S. N., Riley, E. P., Gramling, L., Delis, D. C., & Lyons-Jones, K. (1997). Heavy prenatal exposure with or without physical features of fetal alcohol syndrome leads to IQ deficits. *Journal of Pediatrics, 131,* 718–21.

Mavissakalian, M., Jones, B., Olson, S., & Perel, J. (1990). Clomipramine in obsessive-compulsive disorder: Clinical response and plasma levels. *Journal of Clinical Psychopharmacology, 10,* 261–68.

Mavissakalian, M., & Michelson, L. (1986). Two-year follow-up of exposure and imipramine treatment of agoraphobia. *American Journal of Psychiatry, 143,* 1106–12.

Mavissakalian, M. R., & Perel, J. M. (1995). Imipramine treatment of panic disorder with agoraphobia: Dose ranging and plasma level-response relationships. *American Journal of Psychiatry, 152* (5): 673–82.

Mavissakalian, M. R., & Perel, J. M. (1999). Long-term maintenance and discontinuation of imipramine therapy in panic disorder with agoraphobia. *Archives of General Psychiatry, 56* (9): 821–27.

Mavissakalian, M., Perel, J., Bowler, K., & Dealy, R. (1987). Trazodone in the treatment of panic disorder and agoraphobia with panic attacks. *American Journal of Psychiatry, 144,* 785–91.

Mayberg, H. S., Liotti, M., Brannan, S. K., McGinnis, S., Mahurin, R. K., Jerabek, P. A., Silva, J. A., Tekell, J. L., Martin, C. C., Lancaster, J. L., & Fox, P. T. (1999). Reciprocal limbic-cortical function and negative mood: Converging PET findings in depression and normal sadness. *American Journal of Psychiatry, 156* (5):675–82.

Mayer, L. E. S., & Walsh, B. T. (1998). The use of selective serotonin reuptake inhibitors in eating disorders. *Journal of Clinical Psychiatry, 59,* 28–34.

Mayeux, R., & Sano, M. (1999). Drug therapy: Treatment of Alzheimer's disease. *New England Journal of Medicine, 341,* 1670–79.

Mayo-Smith, M. F. (1997). Pharmacological management of alcohol withdrawal: A meta-analysis and evidence-based practice guideline. *Journal of the American Medical Association, 278,* 144–51.

McArthur, J. C., Cohen, B. A., Selnes, O. A., et al. (1989). Low prevalence of neurological and neuropsychological abnormalities in otherwise healthy HIV-1–infected individuals. Results from the multicenter AIDS cohort study. *Annals of Neurology, 26,* 601–10.

McBride, P. A., Anderson, G. M., Hertzig, M. E., Snow, M. E., Thompson, S. M., Khait, V. D., Shapiro, T., & Cohen, D. J. (1998). Effects of diagnosis, race, and puberty on platelet serotonin levels in autism and mental retardation. *Journal of the American Academy of Child and Adolescent Psychiatry, 37,* 767–76.

McCarthy, G. W., & Craig, K. D. (1995). Flying therapy for flying phobia. *Aviation, Space, and Environmental Medicine, 66* (12): 1179–84.

McCarthy, M. (1990). The thin ideal, depression, and eating disorders in women. *Behaviour Research and Therapy, 28* (3): 205–15.

McCary, J. L. (1978). Human sexuality: Past present and future. *Journal of Marriage and Family Counseling, 4,* 3–12.

McClelland, D. C. (1979). Inhibited power motivation and high blood pressure in men. *Journal of Abnormal Psychology, 88,* 182–90.

McClelland, D. C., Atkinson, J. W., Clark, R. A., & Lowell, E. L. (1953). *The achievement motive.* New York: Appleton.

McClintock, M. K., & Herdt, G. (1996). Rethinking puberty: The development of sexual attraction. *Psychological Science, 5* (6):178–83.

McConaghy, N. (1969). Subjective and penil plethysmograph response following aversion-relief and apomorphine aversion therapy for homosexual impulses. *British Journal of Psychiatry, 115,* 723–30.

McConaghy, N., Armstrong, M., & Blaszczynski, A. (1981). Controlled comparison of aversive therapy and covert sensitization in compulsive homosexuality. *Behaviour Research and Therapy, 19,* 425–34.

McCord, J. (1979). Some child-rearing antecedents of criminal behavior in adult men. *Journal of Personality and Social Psychology, 37,* 1477–86.

McCord, J. (1980). *Myths and realities about criminal sanctions.* Paper presented at the annual meetings of the American Society of Criminology, San Francisco, CA, November 5–8, 1980.

McCord, J., Tremblay, R. E., Vitaro, F., & Desmarais-Gervais, L. (1994). Boys' disruptive behaviour, school adjustment, and delinquency: The Montreal prevention experiment. *International Journal of Behavioral Development, 17,* 739–52.

McCrae, R. R., & Costa, P. T. (1997). Personality trait structure as a human universal. *American Psychologist, 52* (5): 509–16.

McCrae, R. R., & Costa, P. T. (1999). A five-factor theory of personality. In L. Pervin & O. John (Eds.), *Handbook of personality: Theory and research* (2nd ed.). New York: Guilford Press.

McCrae, R., Costa, P., de Lima, M., Simoes, A., Ostendorf, F., Marusic, I., Bratko, D., Caprara, G., Barbaranelli, C., Chae, J., & Piedmont, R. (1999). Age differences in personality across the adult life span: Parallels in five cultures. *Developmental Psychology, 35* (2): 466–77.

McCreery, C., & Claridge, G. (1996). A study of hallucination in normal subjects—I. Self report data. *Personality and Individual Differences, 21,* 739–47.

McDaniel, J. S., Musselman, D. L., Porter, M. R., Reed, D. A., & Nemroff, C. B. (1995). Depression in patients with cancer. *Archives of General Psychiatry, 52,* 89–99.

McDowell, F. H. (1994). Neurorehabilitation. *Western Journal of Medicine, 161,* 323–27.

McEwen, B. S. (1994a). How do sex and stress hormones affect nerve cells? In V. N. Luine & Harding, C. F. (Eds.), *Hormonal restructuring of the adult brain: Basic and clinical perspectives* (Annals of the New York Academy of Sciences, Vol. 743; pp. 1–18). New York: New York Academy of Sciences.

McEwen, B. (1998b). Protective and damaging effects of stress mediators. *New England Journal of Medicine, 338* (3): 171–79.

McEwen, B. S. (1998c). Stress, adaptation, and disease: Allostasis and allostatic load. In S. M. McCann, & J. M. Lipton (Eds.), *Neuroimmunomodulation: Molecular aspects, integrative systems, and clinical advances* (Annals of the New York Academy of Sciences, Vol. 840; pp. 33–44). New York: New York Academy of Sciences.

McEwen, B. (1994d). Steroid hormone action on the brain: When is the genome involved? *Hormones and Behavior, 28,* 396–405.

McFarlane, A. (1989). The aetiology of post-traumatic morbidity: Predisposing, precipitating, and perpetuating factors. *British Journal of Psychiatry, 154,* 1221–28.

McFarlane, A. C. (2000). Posttraumatic stress disorder: A model of the longitudinal course and the role of risk factors. *Journal of Clinical Psychiatry, 61* (Suppl 5): 15–20.

McGarry, A. L., & Bendt, R. H. (1969). Criminal vs. civil commitment of psychotic offenders: A seven year follow-up. *American Journal of Psychiatry, 125,* 1387–94.

McGhie, A., & Chapman, J. S. (1961). Disorders of attention and perception in early schizophrenia. *British Journal of Medical Psychology, 34,* 103–16.

McGinnis J. M., & Foege W. H. (1993). Actual causes of death in the United States. *Journal of the American Medical Association, 270* (18):2207–12.

McGlashan, T. H. (1986a). Predictors of shorter-, medium-, and longer-term outcome in schizophrenia. *American Journal of Psychiatry, 142* (10): 50–55.

McGlashan, T. H. (1986b). Schizotypal personality disorder. Chestnut Lodge follow-up study: VI. Long-term follow-up perspectives. *Archives of General Psychiatry, 43,* 329–34.

McGlashan, T. H. (1987). Testing DSM-III symptom criteria for schizotypal and borderline personality disorders. *Archives of General Psychiatry, 44,* 143–48.

McGlashan, T. H., & Fenton, W. S. (1992). The positive-negative distinction in schizophrenia: Review of natural history validators. *Archives of General Psychiatry, 49* (1): 63–72.

McGlothin, W. H., & West, L. J. (1968). The marihuana problem: An overview. *American Journal of Psychiatry, 125,* 370–78.

McGorry, P. D., & Jackson, H. J. (1999). *The recognition and management of early psychosis: A preventive approach.* New York: Cambridge University Press.

McGrew, K. S., & Flanagan, D. P. (1998). *The intelligence test desk reference (ITDR): Gf-Gc cross-battery assessment.* Boston, MA: Allyn & Bacon.

McGue, M. (1992). When assessing twin concordance, use the probandwise not the pairwise rate. *Schizophrenia Bulletin, 18,* 171–76.

McGue, M., Gottesman, I. I., & Rao, D. C. (1985). Resolving genetic models for the transmission of schizophrenia. *Genetic Epidemiology, 2,* 99–110.

McGuffin, P., & Katz, R. (1989). The genetics of depression and manic-depressive disorder. *British Journal of Psychiatry, 155,* 294–304.

McGuffin, P., Katz, R., Watkins, S., & Rutherford, J. (1996). A hospital-based twin register of the heritability of DSM-IV unipolar depression. *Archives of General Psychiatry, 53,* 129–36.

McGuffin, P., & Thapar, A. (1998). Genetics and antisocial personality disorder. In T. Millon & E. Simonsen (Eds.), *Psychopathy: Antisocial, criminal, and violent behavior* (pp. 215–30). New York: Guilford Press.

McGuire, P. K., Silbersweig, D. A., Wright, I., Murray, R. M., David, A. S., Frackowiak, R. S. J., & Frith, C. D. (1995). Abnormal monitoring of inner speech: A physiological basis for auditory hallucinations. *Lancet, 346,* 596–600.

McGuire, R. J., Carlisle, J. M., & Young, B. G. (1965). Sexual deviation as conditioned behavior. *Behaviour Research and Therapy, 2,* 185–90.

McHugh, P. (1997).The Kervorkian epidemic. *American Scholar,* Winter, 15–27.

McIntosh, J. (1989). Trends in racial differences in U.S. suicide statistics. *Death Studies, 13,* 275–86.

McKim, W. A. (1986). *Drugs and behavior.* Englewood Cliffs, NJ: Prentice-Hall.

McLeod, D., Hoehn-Saric, R., Zimmerli, W., & De Souza, E. (1990). Treatment effects of alprazolam and imipramine: Physiological versus subjective changes in patients with generalized anxiety disorder. *Biological Psychiatry, 28,* 849–61.

McLoughlin, D. M., Lucey, J. V., & Dinan, T. G. (1994). Central serotonergic hyperresponsivity in late-onset Alzheimer's disease. *American Journal of Psychiatry, 151* (11): 1701–1703.

McNally, R. J. (1987). Preparedness and phobias: A review. *Psychological Bulletin, 101,* 283–303.

McNally, R. J. (1994). Choking phobia: A review of the literature. *Comprehensive Psychiatry, 35* (1): 83–89.

McNally, R. (1996). Review of Eye Movement Desensitization and Reprocessing: Basic principles, protocols, and procedures. *Anxiety, 2,* 153–55.

McNally, R. J. (1999). EMDR and mesmerism: A comparative historical analysis. *Journal of Anxiety Disorders, 13* (1–2): 225–36.

McNeal, E. T., & Cimbolic, P. (1986). Antidepressants and biochemical theories of depression. *Psychological Bulletin, 99* (3): 361–74.

McNeil, T. F., Cantor-Graae, E., Torrey, E. F., Sjoestroem, K., et al. (1994). Obstetric complications in histories of monozygotic twins discordant and concordant for schizophrenia. *Acta Psychiatrica Scandinavica, 89,* 196–204.

McNitt, P. C., & Thornton, D. W. (1978). Depression and perceived reinforcement: A consideration. *Journal of Abnormal Psychology, 87,* 137–40.

Meares, R. (1994). A pathology of privacy: Towards a new theoretical approach to obsessive-compulsive disorder. *Contemporary Psychoanalysis, 30* (1): 83–100.

Mechanic, D. (1989). *Mental health and social policy* (3rd ed.). Englewood Cliffs, N.J.: Prentice-Hall.

Mechanic, D. (1993). Mental health services in the context of health insurance reform. *Milbank Quarterly, 71,* 349–64.

Mednick, B. R. (1973). Breakdown in high-risk subjects: Familial and early environmental factors. *Journal of Abnormal Psychology, 82,* 469–75.

Mednick, S. A., Brennan, P., & Kandel, E. (1988). Predisposition to violence. *Aggressive Behavior, 14,* 25–33.

Mednick, S. A., Cudeck, R., Griffith, J. J., Talovic, S. A., & Schulsinger, F. (1984). The Danish high-risk project: Recent methods and findings. In N. F. Watt, E. J. Anthony, L. C. Wynne, & J. E. Rolf (Eds.), *Children at risk for schizophrenia: A longitudinal perspective* (pp. 21–42). Cambridge: Cambridge University Press.

Mednick, S. A., Gabriella, W. F., & Hutchings, B. (1984). Genetic influences in criminal convictions: Evidence from an adoption cohort. *Science, 224,* 891–94.

Mednick, S. A., Gabriella, W. F., & Hutchings, B. (1987). Genetic factors and etiology of criminal behavior. In S. A. Mednick, T. E. Moffitt, & S. A. Stack (Eds.), *Causes of crime: New biological approaches* (pp. 74–91). New York: Cambridge University Press.

Mednick, S. A., Machon, R. A., & Huttunen, M. O. (1989). Disturbances of fetal neural development and adult schizophrenia. In S. C. Schulz & C. A. Tamminga (Eds.), *Schizophrenia: Scientific progress* (pp. 69–77). New York: Oxford University Press.

Mednick, S. A., Parnas, J., & Schulsinger, F. (1987). The Copenhagen high-risk project, 1962–1986. *Schizophrenic Bulletin, 13,* 485–95.

Mednick, S. A., Watson, J. B., Huttunen, M., Cannon, T. D., Katila, H., Machon, R., Mednick, B., Hollister, M., Parnas, J., Schulsinger, F., Sajaniemi, N., Voldsgaard, P., Pyhala, R., Gutkind, D., & Wang, X. (1998). A two-hit working model of the etiology of schizophrenia. In M. F. Lenzenweger & R. H. Dworkin (Eds.), *Origins and development of schizophrenia: Advances in experimental psychopathology* (pp. 27–66). Washington, DC: American Psychological Association.

Medvedev, Z. A., & Medvedev, R. A. (1971). *A question of madness.* New York: Knopf.

Meehl, P.E. (1996). *Clinical versus statistical prediction: A theoretical analysis and a review of the evidence.* Northvale, NJ: Jason Aronson, Inc.

Meichenbaum, D. (1977). *Cognitive-behavior modification.* New York: Plenum.

Meisel, S. R., Kutz, I., Dayan, K. I., Pauzner, H., Chetboun, I., Arbel, Y., & David, D. (1991). Effect of Iraqi missile war on incidence of acute myocardial infarction and sudden death in Israeli civilians. *Lancet, 338* (8768): 660–61.

Meloy, J. R. (1997). Predatory violence during mass murder. *Journal of Forensic Sciences, 42,* 326–29.

Melton, G. B., Petrila, J., Poythress, N. G., & Slobogin, C. (1987). *Psychological evaluations for the courts.* New York: Guilford Press.

Melton, M. A., Van Sickle, T. D., Hersen, M., Van Hasselt, V. B. (1999). Treatment of poststroke anxiety in an older adult male: A single-case analysis. *Journal of Clinical Geropsychology, 5* (3): 203–13.

Melzack, R. (1973). *The puzzle of pain.* New York: Basic Books.

Mendels, J. (1970). *Concepts of depression.* New York: Wiley.

Mendels, J., & Cochran, C. (1968). The nosology of depression: The endogenous-reactive concept. *American Journal of Psychiatry, 124,* Supplement 1–11.

Mendelsohn, F., & Ross, M. (1959). An analysis of 133 homosexuals seen at a university health service. *Diseases of the Nervous System, 20,* 246–50.

Mendelson, J. H., & Mello, N. K. (1996). Drug therapy: Management of cocaine abuse and dependence. *New England Journal of Medicine, 334,* 965–72.

Mendes de Leon, C. F., Glass, T. A., Beckett, L. A., Seeman, T. E., Evans, D. A., & Berkman, L. (1999). Social networks and disability transitions across eight intervals of yearly data in the New Haven EPESE. *Journals of Gerontology Series B-Psychological Sciences and Social Sciences. 54B* (3): S162–S172.

Menzies, R. G., & Clark, J. C. (1995). Etiology of phobias: A nonassociative account. *Psychophysiology, 32* (3): 208–14.

Menzin, J., Lang, K., & Friedman, M. (1999). The economic cost of Alzheimer's disease to a state Medicaid program. *Neurology, 52* (Supp. 2): A8–A9.

Mercer, J. R. (1979). *The system of multicultural pluralistic assessment: Conceptual and technical manual.* New York: The Psychological Corporation.

Mercer, J. R., & Lewis, J. E. (1978). *Adaptive behavior inventory for children.* New York: The Psychological Corporation.

Merckelbach, H., deJong, P.J., Muris, P., & van den Hout, M.A. (1996). The etiology of specific phobias: A review. *Clinical Psychology Review, 16,* 337–61.

Merikangas, K. R., Leckman, J. F., Prusoff, B. A., Pauls, D. L., & Weissman, M. M. (1985). Familial transmission of depression and alcoholism. *Archives of General Psychiatry, 42,* 367–72.

Metalsky, G. I., & Joiner, T. E. (1992).Vulnerability to depressive symptomatology: A prospective test of the diathesis-stress and causal mediation components of the hopelessness theory of depression. *Journal of Personality and Social Psychology, 63* (4): 667–75.

Metz, M. E., Pryor, J. L., Nesvacil, L. J., Abuzzahab, F., Sr., et al. (1997). Premature ejaculation: A psychophysiological review. *Journal of Sex and Marital Therapy, 23* (1): 3–23.

Meyer, C. B., & Taylor, S. E. (1986). Adjustment to rape. *Journal of Personality and Social Psychology, 50,* 1226–34.

Meyer, G. A., Blum, N. J., Hitchcock, W., & Fortina, P. (1998). Absence of the fragile X CGG trinucleotide repeat expansion in girls diagnosed with a pervasive developmental disorder. *Journal of Pediatrics, 133,* 363–65.

Meyer, V. (1966). Modification of expectations in cases with obsessional rituals. *Behaviour Research and Therapy, 4,* 273–80.

Meyer, V., & Mair, J. M. M. (1963). A new technique to control stammering: A preliminary report. *Behavior Research Therapy, 1,* 251–54.

Meyer-Bahlburg, H., Feldman, J., Cohen, P., & Ehrhardt, A. (1988). Perinatal factors in the development of gender-related play behavior: Sex hormones versus pregnancy complications. *Psychiatry, 51,* 260–71.

Meyers, A. W., & Craighead, W. E. (Eds.) (1984). *Cognitive behavior therapy with children.* New York: Plenum Press.

Mezzich, J., Kirmayer, L., Kleinman, A., Fabrega, H., Parron, D., Good, B., Lin, K., & Manson, S. (1999). The place of culture in DSM-IV. *Journal of Nervous and Mental Disease, 187* (18): 457–64.

Michelson, D., Lydiard, B., Pollack, M. H., Tamura, R.N., Hoog, S. L., Tepner, R., Demitrack, M. A., & Tollefson, G. D. (1998). Fluoxetine Panic Disorder Study Group. Outcome assessment and clinical improvement in panic disorder: Evidence from a randomized controlled trial of fluoxetine and placebo. *American Journal of Psychiatry, 155* (11): 1570–77.

Michelson, D., Pollack, M., Lydiard, R. B., Tamura, R., Tepner, R., & Tollefson, G. (1999). Continuing treatment of panic disorder after acute response: Randomised, placebo-controlled trial with fluoxetine. The Fluoxetine Panic Disorder Study Group. *British Journal of Psychiatry, 174,* 213–18.

Michelson, L., & Marchione, K. (1989). *Cognitive, behavioral, and physiologically based treatments of agoraphobia: A comparative outcome study.* Paper presented at the annual meeting of the American Association for the Advancement of Behavior Therapy, Washington, DC, November 1989.

Michelson, L. K., Marchione, K. E., Greenwald, M., Testa, S., & Marchione, N. J. (1996). A comparative outcome and follow-up investigation of panic disorder with agoraphobia: The relative and combined efficacy of cognitive therapy, relaxation training, and therapist-assisted exposure. *Journal of Anxiety Disorders, 10* (5): 297–330.

Miech, R. A., Caspi, A., Moffitt, T. E., Wright, B. R. E., & Silva, P. A. (1999). Low socioeconomic status and mental disorders: A longitudinal study of selection and causation during young adulthood. *American Journal of Sociology, 104,* 1096–1131.

Miklowitz, D. J. (1994). Family risk indicators in schizophrenia. *Schizophrenia Bulletin, 20,* 137–49.

Miller, B. L., & Cummings, J. L. (Eds.). (1999). *The human frontal lobes: Functions and disorders.* The Science and Practice of Neuropsychology Series. New York: Guilford Press.

Miller, D. J., & Kotses, H. (1995). Classical conditioning of total respiratory resistance in humans. *Psychosomatic Medicine, 57,* 148–53.

Miller, L. L. (1999). Marihuana: Acute effects on human memory. In G. G. Nahas & K. M. Sutin (Eds.), *Marihuana and medicine* (pp. 227–31). Clifton, NJ: Humana.

Miller, L. L., & Branconnier, R. J. (1983). Cannabis: Effects on memory and the cholinergic system. *Psychological Bulletin, 93,* 441–56.

Miller, N. E. (1985). The value of behavioral research on animals. *American Psychologist, 40,* 423–40.

Miller, N. S. (1995). Pharmacotherapy in alcoholism. *Journal of Addictive Diseases, 14* (1): 23–46.

Miller, N. S., Gold, M. S., & Stennie, K. (1995). Benzodiazepines: The dissociation of addiction from pharmacological dependence/withdrawal. *Psychiatric Annals, 25* (3): 149–52.

Miller, T. Q., Smith, T. W., Turner, C. W., Guijarro, M. L., & Hallet, A. J. (1996). A meta-analytic review of research on hostility and physical health. *Psychological Bulletin, 119* (2): 322–48.

Miller, W. R., & Seligman, M. E. P. (1975). Depression and learned helplessness in man. *Journal of Abnormal Psychology, 84,* 228–38.

Miller, W. R., & Seligman, M. E. P. (1976). Learned helplessness, depression, and the perception of reinforcement. *Behaviour Research and Therapy, 14,* 7–17.

Millon, T., & Davis, R. D. (1995). The development of personality disorders. In D. Cicchetti & D. Cohen (Eds.), *Developmental psychopathology, Vol. 2: Risk, disorder, and adaptation.* (Wiley Series on Personality Processes.) New York: Wiley.

Millon, T., & Martinez, A. (1995). Avoidant personality disorder. In W. J. Livesley (Ed.), *The DSM-IV personality disorders: Diagnosis and treatment of mental disorders* (pp. 218–33). New York: Guilford Press.

Millon, T. (1996). The relationship of depression to disorders of personality. In T. Millon (Ed.), *Personality and psychopathology: Building a clinical science.* New York: Wiley.

Millon, T., & Davis, R. (1996). *Disorders of personality: DSM-IV and beyond.* New York: Wiley.

Millon, T., Davis, R., Millon, C., Escovar, L., & Meagher, S. (2000). *Personality disorders in modern life.* New York: Wiley.

Mills, P. E., Cole, K. N., Jenkins, J. R., & Dale, P. S. (1998). Effects of differing levels of inclusion on preschoolers with disabilities. *Exceptional Children, 65,* 79–90.

Milner, B. (1970). Memory and the medial temporal regions of the brain. In K. H. Pribram & D. E. Broadbent (Eds.), *Biology of memory.* New York: Academic Press.

Milner, B. (1972). Disorders of learning and memory after temporal lobe lesions in man. *Clinical Neurosurgery, 19,* 421–46.

Min, S. K., & Lee, B. O. (1997). Laterality in somatization. *Psychosomatic Medicine, 59* (3): 236–40.

Mineka, S., Davidson, M., Cook, M., & Keir, R. (1984). Observational conditioning of snake fear in rhesus monkeys. *Journal of Abnormal Psychology, 93* (4): 355–72.

Mineka, S., & Zinbarg, R. (1996). Conditioning and ethological models of anxiety disorders: Stress in dynamic context anxiety models. In D. Hope (Ed.), *Perspectives on anxiety, panic, and fear: Nebraska Symposium on Motivation.* Lincoln, NE: University of Nebraska Press.

Minuchin, S., Rosman, B. L., & Baker, L. (1980). *Psychosomatic families: Anorexia nervosa in context.* Cambridge: Harvard University Press.

Mischel, W. (1973). Toward a cognitive social learning reconceptualization of personality. *Psychological Review, 80,* 252–83.

Mischel, W. (1976). *Introduction to personality* (2nd ed.). New York: Holt, Rinehart & Winston.

Mischel, W., & Peake, P. K. (1982). Beyond deja vu in the search for cross-situational consistency. *Psychological Review, 89,* 730–55.

Mishkin, M., & Appenzeller, T. (1987). The anatomy of memory. *Scientific American, 256* (6): 80–89.

Mishra, S. P., & Brown, K. H. (1983). The comparability of WAIS and WAIS-R IQs and subtest scores. *Journal of Clinical Psychology, 39,* 754–57.

Mitchell, A. J. (1998). The role of corticotropin-releasing factor in depressive illness: A critical review. *Neuroscience and Biobehavorial Review, 22,* 635–51.

Mitchell, J. E. (1986). Anorexia nervosa: Medical and psychological aspects. In K. D. Brownell & J. P. Foreyt (Eds.), *Handbook of eating disorders: Physiology, psychology, and treatment of obesity, anorexia, and bulimia.* New York: Basic Books.

Mitchell, J. E., & de Zwaan, M. (1993). Pharmacological treatments of binge eating. In C. G. Fairburn & G. T. Wilson (Eds.), *Binge eating: Nature, assessment, and treatment.* New York: Guilford Press.

Mitchell, J., Pyle, R., Eckert, E., et al. (1990). A comparison study of antidepressants and structured intensive group psychotherapy in the treatment of bulimia nervosa. *Archives of General Psychiatry, 47,* 149–57.

Mitchell, J. E., Raymond, N., & Specker, S. (1993). A review of the controlled trials of pharmacotherapy and psychotherapy in the treatment of bulimia nervosa. *International Journal of Eating Disorders, 14* (3): 229–47.

Mitchell, W. B., DiBartolo, P. M., Brown, T. A., & Barlow, D. H. (1998). Effects of positive and negative mood on sexual arousal in sexually functional males. *Archives of Sexual Behavior, 27* (2): 197–207.

Mitrushina, M., Abara, J., & Blumenfeld, A. (1996). A comparison of cognitive profiles in schizophrenia and other psychiatric disorders. *Journal of Clinical Psychology, 52,* 177–90.

Mittelmann, B., Wolff, H. G., & Scharf, M. (1942). Emotions in gastroduodenal functions. *Psychosomatic Medicine, 4,* 5–61.

Mittelman, M. S., Ferris, S. H., Shulman, E., Steinberg, G., & Levin, B. (1996). A family intervention to delay nursing home placement of patients with Alzheimer disease: A randomized controlled trial. *Journal of the American Medical Association, 276,* 1725–31.

Mittelman, M., Maclure, M., Sherwood, J., et al. (1995). Triggering of acute myocardial infarction onset by episodes of anger. *Circulation, 92,* 1720–25.

Mittler, P., Gillies, S., & Jukes, E. (1966). Prognosis in psychotic children. Report of follow-up study. *Journal of Mental Deficiency Research, 10,* 73–83.

Mjoberg, B., Hellquist, E., Mallmin, H., & Lindh, U. (1997). Aluminum, Alzheimer's disease and bone fragility. *Acta Orthopaedica Scandinavica, 68,* 511–14.

Moffitt, T. E. (1990). Juvenile delinquency and attention-deficit disorder: Boys' developmental trajectories from age 3 to age 15. *Child Development, 61,* 893–910.

Moffitt, T. E. (1997a). Adolescence-limited and life-course-persistent offending: A complementary pair of developmental theories. In T. P. Thornberry (Ed.), *Developmental theories of crime and delinquency: Advances in criminological theory* (Vol. 7; pp. 11–54). New Brunswick, NJ: Transaction.

Moffitt, T. E. (1997b). Nocturnal enuresis: A review of the efficacy of treatments and practical advice for clinicians. *Developmental and Behavioral Pediatrics, 18* (1): 49–56.

Moffitt, T. E., Brammer, G. L., Caspi, A., Fawcett, J. P., Raleigh, M., Yuwiler, A., & Silva, P. (1998). Whole blood serotonin relates to violence in an epidemiological study. *Biological Psychiatry, 43,* 446–57.

Moffitt, T. E., & Silva, P. A. (1988). Self-reported delinquency, neuropsychological assessment, and history of attention deficit disorder. *Journal of Abnormal Child Psychlogy, 16,* 553–69.

Mohs, R. D., Breitner, J. C. S., Silverman, J. M., & Davis, K. L. (1987). Alzheimer's disease: Morbid risk among first-degree relatives approximates fifty percent by ninety years of age. *Archives of General Psychiatry, 44,* 405–408.

Molin, J., Mellerup, E., Bolwig, T., Scheike, T., & Dam, H. (1996). The influence of climate on winter depression. *Journal of Affective Disorders, 37,* 151–55.

Molina-Holgado, F., Gonzalez, M. I., & Leret, M. L. (1995). Effect of delta 9-tetrahydrocannabinol on short-term memory in the rat. *Physiology and Behavior, 57* (1):177–79.

Molinari, V., Kunik, M. E., Snow-Turek, A. L., Deleon, H., & Williams, W. (1999). Age-related personality differences in inpatients with personality disorder: A cross-sectional study. *Journal of Clinical Geropsychology, 5* (3): 191–202.

Monahan, J. (1992). Mental disorder and violent behavior. *American Psychologist, 47,* 511–21.

Monahan, J., & Shah, S. A. (1989). Dangerousness and commitment of the mentally disordered in the United States. *Schizophrenia Bulletin, 15* (4): 541–53.

Money, J. (1987). "Sin, sickness, or status?" *American Psychologist, 42,* 384–99.

Money, J., & Ambinder, R. (1978). Two-year, real-life diagnostic test: Rehabilitation vs. cure. In J. P. Brady & H. K. H. Brodie (Eds.), *Controversy in psychiatry.* Philadelphia: Saunders.

Money, J., & Dalery, J. (1976). Iatrogenic homosexuality: gender identity in seven 46XX chromosomal females with hyperadrenocortical hermaphroditism born with a penis, three reared as boys, four reared as girls. *Journal of Homosexuality, 1,* 357–71.

Money, J., & Ehrhardt, A. A. (1972). *Man and woman, boy and girl.* Baltimore: John Hopkins University Press.

Money, J., Schwartz, M., & Lewis, V. (1984). Adult erotosexual status and fetal hormonal masculinization and demasculinization: 46XX congenital virilizing adrenal hyperplasia and 46XY androgen-insensitivity syndrome compared. *Psychoneuroendocrinology, 9,* 405–14.

Monroe, S., Rohde, P., Seeley, J., & Lewinsohn, P. (1999). Life events and depression in adolescence. Relationship loss as a prospective risk factor for first onset of major depressive disorder. *Journal of Abnormal Psychology, 108,* 606–14.

Montgomery, S. A. (1994). Antidepressants in long-term treatment. *Annual Review of Medicine, 45,* 447–57.

Monthly Vital Statistic Report. (1996). Vol. 46.

Montoya, I. D., Chenier, E. E., & Richard, A. J. (1996). Drug abuse, AIDS, and the coming crisis in long-term care. *Journal of Nursing Management, 4* (3): 151–62.

Moody, R. L. (1946). Bodily changes during abreaction. *Lancet, 2,* 934–35.

Moore, K. E., Geffken, G. R., & Royal, G. P. (1995). Behavioral interventions to reduce child distress during self-injection. *Clinical Pediatrics, 34* (10): 530–34.

Morgan, A. E., & Hynd, G. W. (1998). Dyslexia, neurolinguistic ability, and anatomical variation of the planum temporale. *Neuropsychology Review, 8,* 79–93.

Morris, K. (1998). Ecstasy users face consequences of neurotoxicity. *Lancet, 352,* 1913.

Morrison, R. L., & Bellack, A. (1984). Social skills training. In A. S. Bellack (Ed.), *Schizophrenia: Treatment, management, and rehabilitation* (pp. 247–79). Orlando, FL: Grune & Stratton.

Morrison-Stewart, S. L., Williamson, P. C., Corning, W. C., Kutcher, S. P., & Merskey, H. (1991). Coherence on electroencephalography and aberrant functional organisation of the brain in schizophrenic patients during activation tasks. *British Journal of Psychiatry, 159,* 636–44.

Moscovitch, M. (1982a). Multiple dissociations of function in amnesia. In L. S. Cermak (Ed.), *Human memory and amnesia.* Hillsdale, NJ: Erlbaum.

Moscovitch, M. (1982b). A neuropsychological approach to perception and memory in normal and pathological aging. In F. I. M. Craik & S. Trehub (Eds.), *Aging and cognitive processes.* New York: Plenum.

Moscovitch, M. (1992). Memory and working-with-memory: A component process model based on modules and central systems. *Journal of Cognitive Neuroscience, 4,* 257–67.

Moscovitch, M., Vriezen, E., & Goshen-Gottstein, Y. (1994). Implicit trots of memory in patients with focal lesions and degenerative brain disorders. In F. Boller & J. Grafman (Eds.), *Handbook of neuropsychology.* Amsterdam: Elsevier.

Moscovitch, M., & Winokur, G. (1992). The neuropsychology of memory and aging. In F. I. M. Craik & T. A. Salthouse (Eds.), *The handbook of aging and cognition.* Hillsdale, NJ: Erlbaum.

Mottron, L., Belleville, S., Stip, E., & Morasse, K. (1998). Atypical memory performance in an autistic savant. *Memory, 6,* 593–607.

Mowbray, C. T., Collins, M .E., Plum, T. B., Masterton, T., Mulder, R., & Harbinger, I. (1997). The development and evaluation of the first PACT replication. *Administration and Policy in Mental Health, 25,* 105–23.

Mowrer, O. H. (1948). Learning theory and the neurotic paradox. *American Journal of Orthopsychiatry, 18,* 571–610.

Mowrer, O. H., & Mowrer, W. M. (1938). Enuresis: A method for its study and treatment. *American Journal of Orthopsychiatry, 8,* 436–59.

MTA Cooperative Group. (1999a). Moderators and mediators of treatment response for children with attention-deficit/hyperactivity disorder: The multimodal treatment study of children with Attention-deficit/hyperactivity disorder. *Archives of General Psychiatry, 56* (12): 1088–96.

MTA Cooperative Group. (1999b). A 14-month randomized clinical trial of treatment strategies for attention-deficit/hyperactivity disorder. The multimodal treatment study of children with ADHD. *Archives of General Psychiatry, 56* (12): 1073–86.

Mueller, T. I., Keller, M. B., Leon, A. C., Solomon, D. A., Shea, M. T., Coryell, W., & Endicott, J. (1996). Recovery after 5 years of unremitting major depressive disorder. *Archives of General Psychiatry, 53* (9): 794–99.

Mueller, T. I., Leon, A. C., Keller, M. B., Solomon, D. A., Endicott, J., Coryell, W., Warshaw, M., & Maser, J. D. (1999). Recurrence after recovery from major depressive disorder during 15 years of observational follow-up. *American Journal of Psychiatry, 156* (7): 1000–1006.

Mueser, K. T., Bellack, A. S., Morrison, R. L., & Wade, J. H. (1990). Gender, social competence, and symptomatology in schizophrenia: A longitudinal analysis. *Journal of Abnormal Psychology, 99* (2): 138–47.

Mueser, K. T., Penn, D. L., Blanchard, J. J., & Bellack, A. S. (1997). Affect recognition in schizophrenia: A synthesis of findings across three studies. *Psychiatry: Interpersonal and Biological Processes, 60,* 301–308.

Mueser, K. T., Valentiner, D. P., & Agresta, J. (1998). Coping with negative symptoms of schizophrenia: Patient and family perspectives. *Year Book of Psychiatry and Applied Mental Health, 4,* 110–11.

Mufson, L., Weissman, M. M., Moreau, D., & Garfinkel, R. (1999). Efficacy of interpersonal psychotherapy for depressed adolescents. *Archives of General Psychiatry, 57* (6): 573–79.

Muir, J. L. (1997). Acetylcholine, aging, and Alzheimer's disease. *Pharmacology, Biochemistry and Behavior, 56* (4): 687–96.

Mullaney, J. A., & Trippett, C. J. (1982). Alcohol dependence and phobias: Clinical description and relevance. *British Journal of Psychiatry, 135,* 565–73.

Mullen, P., Pathe, M., Purcell, R., & Stuart, G. (1999). Study of stalkers. *American Journal of Psychiatry, 156,* 1244–49.

Mulrow, C. D., Williams, J. W. Jr., Trivedi, M., Chiquette, E., Aguilar, C., Cornell, J. E., Badgett, R., Noeel, P. H., Lawrence, V., Lee, S., Luther, M., Ramirez, G. Richardson, W. S., & Stamm, K. (1998). Evidence report: Treatment of depression—New pharmacotherapies. *Psychopharmacology Bulletin, 34* (4): 409–795.

Munoz, R. F., Hollon, S. D., McGrath, E., Rehm, L. P., & VandenBas, G. R. (1994). On the AHCPR depression in primary care guidelines: Further considerations for practitioners. *American Psychologist, 49* (1): 42–61.

Munro, A. (1992). Psychiatric disorders characterized by delusions: Treatment in relation to specific types. *Psychiatric Annals, 22,* 232–40.

Munro, A. (1995). The classification of delusional disorders. In M. J. Sedler (Ed.), *Delusional disorders. Psychiatric Clinics of North America, 18* (pp. 199–212). Philadelphia: Saunders.

Munzinger, H. (1975). The adopted child's IQ: A critical review. *Psychological Bulletin, 80,* 623–29.

Muris, P., Merckelbach, H., Mayer, B., & Prins, E. (2000). How serious are childhood fears? *Behaviour Research and Therapy, 38* (3): 217–28.

Muris, P., Merckelbach, H., Meesters, C., & Van Lier, P. (1997). What do children fear most often? *Journal of Behavior Therapy and Experimental Psychiatry, 28,* 263–67.

Murphy, D. L., Greenburg, B., Altemus, M., Benjamin, J., Grady, T., & Pigott, T. (1996). The neuropharmacology and neurobiology of obsessive-compulsive disorder: An update on the serotonin hypothesis. In H. G. Westenberg, J. A. Den Boer, & D. L. Murphy (Eds.), *Advances in the neurobiology of anxiety disorders* (pp. 279–97). Chichester, England: Wiley.

Murphy, J., Laird, N., & Monson, R. (2000). A 40-year perspective on the prevalence of depression. *Archives of General Psychiatry, 57,* 209–15.

Murphy, W. D. (1997). Exhibitionism: Psychopathology and theory. In D. R. Laws & W. O'Donohue (Eds.), *Sexual deviance: Theory, assessment, and treatment* (pp. 22–39). New York: Guilford Press.

Murray, H. A. (1951). Forward. In H. H. Anderson & G. L. Anderson (Eds.), *An introduction to projective techniques.* Englewood Cliffs, NJ: Prentice-Hall.

Murray, J. B. (1998). Effectiveness of methadone maintenance for heroin addiction. *Psychological Reports, 83,* 295–302.

Murray, K. T., & Sines, J. O. (1996). Parsing the genetic and nongenetic variance in children's depressive behavior. *Journal of Affective Disorders, 38,* 23–34.

Murray, R. M., Jones, P. B., O'Callaghan, E., Takei, N., et al. (1992). Genes, viruses and neurodevelopmental schizophrenia. *Journal of Psychiatric Research, 26,* 225–35.

Murstein, B. I. (1965). New thoughts about ambiguity and the TAT. *Journal of Projective Techniques and Personality Assessment, 29,* 219–25.

Muscari, M. (1998). Screening for anorexia and bulimia. *American Journal of Nursing, 98,* 22–24.

Myers, J. K., Weissman, M. M., Tischler, G. L., Holzer, C. E., Leaf, P. J., Orvaschel, H., Anthony, J. C., Boyd, J. H., Burke, J. D., Kramer, M., & Stolzman, R. (1984). Six-month prevalence of psychiatric disorders in three communities: 1980 to 1982. *Archives of General Psychiatry, 41,* 959–67.

Myers, M. G., Stewart, D. G., & Brown, S. A. (1998). Progression from conduct disorder to antisocial personality disorder following treatment for adolescent substance abuse. *American Journal of Psychiatry, 155,* 479–85.

Nadel, L. (1999). Down syndrome in cognitive neuroscience perspective. In H. Tager-Flusberg (Ed.), *Neurodevelopmental disorders. Developmental cognitive neuroscience.* Cambridge, MA: MIT Press.

Nagourney, E. (2000). When it pays to argue with a spouse. *New York Times,* Week in Review, Feb. 20, p. 2.

Nagy, A. (1987). Possible reasons for a negative attitude to benzodiazepines as antianxiety drugs. *Nordisk Psykiatrisk Tidsskrift, 4,* 27–30.

Nahas, G. G., Sutin, K. M., et. al. (Eds.). (1999). *Marihuana and medicine.* Clifton, N.J.: Humana.

Nathan, P. E., & Lagenbucher, J. W. (1999). Psychopathology: Description and classification. *Annual Review of Psychology, 50,* 79–107.

National Institute of Drug Abuse. (2000a). http://www.nida.nih.gov http://www.nida.nih.gov

National Institute of Drug Abuse. (2000b). http://www.nida.nih.gov/researchreports/nicotine/nicotine2.html

National Institute of Drug Abuse (2000c). *Infofax: High school and youth trends.* Washington, D. C.: National Institute of Drug Abuse.

National Institute of Mental Health. (1989a). *Delusional disorders.* DHHS Publication Number: (ADM) 89–1495. Washington, DC: U. S. Department of Health and Human Services.

National Institute of Mental Health. (1989b). *Depression among the aged. From depressive illnesses: Treatments bringing new hope.* Bethesda, MD: Author.

Neale, M. C., Walters, E. E., Eaves, L. J., Kessler, R. C., Heath, A. C., & Kendler, K. S. (1994). Genetics of blood-injury fears and phobias: A population twin-based study. *American Journal of Medical Genetics, 54* (4): 326–34.

Neary, D., Snowden, J. S., Northern, B., & Goulding, P. (1988). Dementia of frontal lobe type. *Journal of Neurology, Neurosurgery, and Psychiatry, 51,* 353–61.

Neisser, U. (1998). *The rising curve: Long-term gains in IQ and related measures.* Washington, DC, USA: American Psychological Association.

Nelissen, I., Muris, P., & Merckelbach, H. (1995). Computerized exposure and in vivo exposure treatments of spider fear in children: Two case reports. *Journal of Behavior Therapy and Experimental Psychiatry, 26,* 153–56.

Nelson, C. B., Heath, A. C., & Kessler, R. C. (1998). Temporal progression of alcohol dependence symptoms in the U. S. household population: Results from the National Comorbidity Survey. *Journal of Consulting and Clinical Psychology, 66,* 474–83.

Nelson, C., Mazure, C., & Jatlow, P. (1990). Does melancholia predict response in major depression? *Journal of Affective Disorders, 18,* 157–65.

Nelson, D., & Weiss, R. (2000), Earlier gene test deaths not reported; NIH was unaware of "adverse events." *Washington Post,* January 31.

Nelson, M. D., Saykin, A. J., Flashman, L. A., & Riordan, H. J. (1998). Hippocampal volume reduction in schizophrenia as assessed by magnetic resonance imaging: A meta-analytic study. *Archives of General Psychiatry, 55,* 433–40.

Nemeroff, C. B. (1996). The corticotropin-releasing factor (CRF) hypothesis of depression: New findings and new directions. *Molecular Psychiatry, 1,* 336–42.

Nemeroff, C. B., & Schatzberg, A. F. (1998). Pharmacological treatment of unipolar depression. In P. E. Nathan & J. M. Gorman (Eds.), *A guide to treatments that work* (pp. 212–25). New York: Oxford University Press.

Neri, M., De Vreese, L. P., Finelli, C., & Iacono, S. (1998). Subcortical vascular dementia: A review on care and management. *Archives of Gerontology and Geriatrics* (Supp. 6): 355–62.

Nesse, F. M., Cameron, O. G., Curtis, G. C., McCann, D. S., & Huber-Smith, M. J. (1984). Adrenergic function in patients with panic anxiety. *Archives of General Psychiatry, 41,* 771–76.

Nestadt, G., et al. (1990). An epidemiological study of histrionic personality disorder. *Psychological Medicine, 29,* 413–22.

Nestadt, G., et al. (1991). DSM-III compulsive personality disorder: An epidemiological survey. *Psychological Medicine, 21* (2): 461–71.

Nestoros, J. N. (1980). Ethanol specifically potentiates GABA-mediated neurotransmission in the feline cerebral cortex. *Science, 209,* 708–10.

Neumann, C., & Walker, E. (1995). Developmental pathways to schizophrenia: Behavioral subtypes. *Journal of Abnormal Psychology, 104,* 1–9.

Neumann, C., Walker, E., Weinstein, J., & Cutshaw, C. (1996). Psychotic patients' awareness of mental illness: Implications for legal defense proceedings. *Journal of Psychiatry and Law, 24* (3): 421–42.

Newman, J. P. (1997). Conceptual models of the nervous system: Implications for antisocial behavior. In D. M. Stoff & J. Breiling (Eds.), *Handbook of antisocial behavior* (pp. 324–35). New York: Wiley.

Newman, J. P., & Schmitt, W. A. (1998). Passive avoidance in psychopathic offenders: A replication and extension. *Journal of Abnormal Psychology, 107,* 527–32.

Newman, J. P., Schmitt, W. A., & Voss, W. D. (1997). The impact of motivationally neutral cues on psychopathic individuals: Assessing the generality of the response modulation hypothesis. *Journal of Abnormal Psychology, 106,* 563–75.

Newman, S. C. (1999). The prevalence of depression in Alzheimer's disease and vascular dementia in a population sample. *Journal of Affective Disorders, 52,* 169–76.

Newmark, C. S. (1996). *Major psychological assessment instruments* (2nd ed.). Boston: Allyn & Bacon.

New York Times. (1994a). Albany plans house calls to monitor the mentally ill, April 24, 1994.

New York Times. (1994b). Father who fought "memory therapy" wins damage suit, May 14, 1994.

Nicolson, N., Storms, C., Ponds, R., & Sulon, J. (1997). Salivary cortisol levels and stress reactivity in human aging. *Journals of Gerontology. Series A, Biological Sciences and Medical Sciences, 52A,* M68-M75.

Nigg, J. T., & Goldsmith, H. (1994). Genetics of personality disorders: Perspectives from personality and psychopathology research. *Psychological Bulletin, 115* (3): 346–80.

Nihira, K., Foster, R., Shellhaas, M., Leland, H., Lambert, N., & Windmiller, M. (1981). *AAMD adaptive behavior scale* (school edition). Monterey, CA: Publisher's Test Service.

Nimgaonkar, V. L. (1998). Reduced fertility in schizophrenia: Here to stay? *Acta Psychiatrica Scandinavica, 98,* 348–53.

Ninan, P. T. (1999). The functional anatomy, neurochemistry, and pharmacology of anxiety. *Journal of Clinical Psychiatry, 60* (Suppl 22): 12–17.

Ninan, P., Insel, T., Cohen, R., Cook, J., Skolnick, P., & Paul, S. (1982). Benzodiazepine receptor-mediated experimental "anxiety" in primates. *Science, 218,* 1332–34.

Ninan, P. T. (1999). The functional anatomy, neurochemistry, and pharmacology of anxiety. *Journal of Clinical Psychiatry, 60* (Suppl 22): 12–17.

Nisbett, R., & Ross, L. (1980). *Human inference: Strategies and shortcomings of social judgment.* Englewood Cliffs, NJ: Prentice-Hall.

Nolen-Hoeksema, S. (1987). Sex differences in unipolar depression: Evidence and theory. *Psychological Bulletin, 101* (2): 259–82.

Nolen-Hoeksema, S. (1988). Life-span views on depression. In P. B. Baltes, D. L. Featherman, & R. M. Lerner (Eds.), *Life span development and behavior* (Vol. 9). New York: Erlbaum.

Nolen-Hoeksema, S. (1990). *Sex differences in depression.* Stanford: Stanford University Press.

Nolen-Hoeksema, S. (1991). Responses to depression and their effects on the duration of depressive episodes. *Journal of Abnormal Psychology, 102,* 569–82.

Nolen-Hoeksema, S. (1998). *Abnormal psychology.* New York: McGraw-Hill.

Nolen-Hoeksema, S., & Girgus, J. S. (1994). The emergence of gender differences in depression during adolescence. *Psychological Bulletin, 115* (3): 424–43.

Nolen-Hoeksema, S., Girgus, J., & Seligman, M. E. P. (1986). Learned helplessness in children: A longitudinal study of depression, achievement, and explanatory style. *Journal of Personality and Social Psychology, 51,* 435–42.

Nolen-Hoeksema, S., Girgus, J., & Seligman, M. (1992). Predictors and consequences of childhood depressive symptoms: A 5-year longitudinal study. *Journal of Abnormal Psychology, 101* (3): 405–22.

Nolen-Hoeksema, S., Mumme, D., Wolfson, A., & Guskin, K. (1995). Helplessness in children of depressed and nondepressed mothers. *Developmental Psychology, 31* (3): 377–87.

Nopoulos, P., Torres, I., Flaum, M., Andreasen, N. C., Ehrhardt, J. C., & Yuh, W. T. C. (1995). Brain morphology in first-episode schizophrenia. *American Journal of Psychiatry, 152* (12): 1721–23.

Nordahl, H. M., & Stiles, T. C. (1997). Perceptions of parental bonding in patients with various personality disorders, lifetime depressive disorders, and healthy controls. *Journal of Personality Disorders, 11,* 391–402.

Nordberg, A. (1996). Pharmacological treatment of cognitive dysfunction in dementia disorders. *Acta Neurologica Scandinavica Supplementum, 168,* 87–92.

Norman, R. M., & Malla, A. K. (1993a). Stressful life events and schizophrenia: I. A review of the research. *British Journal of Psychiatry, 162,* 161–66.

Norman, R. M., & Malla, A. K. (1993b). Stressful life events and schizophrenia: II. Conceptual and methodological issues. *British Journal of Psychiatry, 162,* 166–74.

Norton, D. E. (1998). Counseling substance-abusing older clients. *Educational Gerontology, 24*(4): 373–89.

Nowicki, S., & Duke, M. P. (1994) Individual differences in the nonverbal communication of affect: The Diagnostic Analysis of Nonverbal Accuracy Scale. *Journal of Nonverbal Behavior, 18* (1): 9–35.

Noyes, R., Chaudry, D., & Domingo, D. (1986). Pharmacologic treatment of phobic disorders. *Journal of Clinical Psychiatry, 47,* 445–52.

Noyes, R., Clarkson, C., Crowe, R., & Yates, W. (1987). A family study of generalized anxiety disorder. *American Journal of Psychiatry, 144,* 1019–24.

Noyes, R., & Kletti, R. (1977). Depersonalization in response to life-threatening danger. *Comprehensive Psychiatry, 18,* 375–84.

Nuechterlein, K. H., Asarnow, R. F., Subotnik, K. L., Fogelson, D. L., Ventura, J., Torquato, R. D., & Dawson, M. E. (1998). Neurocognitive vulnerability factors for schizophrenia: Convergence across genetic risk studies and longitudinal trait-state studies. In M. F. Lenzenweger & R. H. Dworkin (Eds.), *Origins and development of schizophrenia: Advances in experimental psychopathology* (pp. 99–327). Washington, DC: American Psychological Association.

Nugter, M. A., Dingemans, P. M. A. J., Linszen, D. H., Van der Does, A. J. W., & Gersons, B. P. R. (1997). The relationships between expressed emotion, affective style and communication deviance in recent-onset schizophrenia. *Acta Psychiatrica Scandinavica, 96,* 445–51.

Nurnberg, H. G., Hensley, P. L., Lauriello, J., Parker, L. M., & Keith, S. J. (1999). Sildenafil for women patients with antidepressant-induced sexual dysfunction. *Psychiatric Services, 50* (8): 1076–78.

Nyenhuis, D. L., & Gorelick, P. B. (1998). Vascular dementia: A contemporary review of epidemiology, diagnosis, prevention, and treatment. *Journal of the American Geriatrics Society, 46,* 1437–48.

Nyman, A. K., & Jonsson, H. (1983). Differential evaluation of outcome in schizophrenia. *Acta Psychiatrica Scandinavica, 68,* 458–75.

O'Brien, C. P. (1994). Overview: The treatment of drug dependence. *Addiction, 89,* 1565–69.

O'Brien, C. P., Childress, A. R., McLellan, A. T., & Ehrman, R. (1992). A learning model of addiction. In C. P. O'Brien & J. H. Jaffe (Eds.), *Addictive states* (pp. 157–78). New York: Raven Press.

O'Connor, P. G., & Schottenfeld, R. S. (1998). Medical progress: Patients with alcohol problems. *New England Journal of Medicine, 338,* 592–602.

Offord, D., & Bennet, K. (1994). Conduct disorder: Long-term outcomes and intervention effectiveness. *Journal of the American Academy of Child and Adolescent Psychiatry, 33*(8).

Offord, D. R., Boyle, M. D., Racine, Y. A., Fleming, J. E., Cadman, D. T., Blum, H. M., Byrne, C., Links, P. S., Lipman, E. L., MacMillan, H. L., Grant, N. I., Rae, D., Sanford, M. N., Szatmari, P., Thomas, H., & Woodward, C. A. (1992). Outcome, prognosis, and risk in a longitudinal follow-up study. *Journal of the Academy for Child and Adolescent Psychiatry, 31*(5): 916–23.

Oggins, J., Leber, D., & Veroff, J. (1993). Race and gender differences in Black and White newlyweds' perceptions of sexual and marital relations. *Journal of Sex Research, 30* (2): 152–60.

Ogloff, J., Wong, S. & Greenwood, A. (1990). Treating criminal psychopaths in a therapeutic community program. *Behavioral Sciences and the Law, 8,* 181–90.

Ohara, K., Xu, H., Matsunaga, T., Xu, D., Huang, X., Gu, G., Ohara, K., & Wang, Z. (1998). Cerebral ventricle-brain ratio in monozygotic twins discordant and concordant for schizophrenia. *Progress in Neuro-Psychopharmacology and Biological Psychiatry, 22,* 1043–50.

Ohman, A., Fredrikson, M., Hugdahl, K., & Rimmo, P. (1976). The premise of equipotentiality in human classical conditioning: Conditioned electrodermal responses to potentially phobic stimuli. *Journal of Experimental Psychology-General, 105* (4): 313–37.

Ohman, A., Nordby, H., & d'Elia, G. (1986). Orienting and schizophrenia: Stimulus significance, attention, and distraction in a signaled reaction time task. *Journal of Abnormal Psychology, 95* (4): 326–34.

Ohwaki, S., & Stayton, S. E. (1978). The relation of length of institutionalization to the intellectual functioning of the profoundly retarded. *Child Development, 49,* 105–109.

Olds, D., Henderson, C. R., Cole, R., Eckenrode, J., Kitzman, H., Luckey, D., Pettitt, L., Sidora, K., Morris, P., & Powers, J. (1998). Long-term effects of nurse home visitation on children's criminal and antisocial behavior: 15-year follow-up of a randomized controlled trial. *Journal of the American Medical Association, 280,* 1238–44.

Olin, S. S., & Mednick, S. (1996). Risk factors of psychosis: Identifying vulnerable populations premorbidly. *Schizophrenia Bulletin, 22,* 223–40.

Olivieri, S., Cantopher, T., & Edwards, J. (1986). Two hundred years of anxiolytic drug dependence. *Neuropharmacology, 25,* 669–70.

Ollendick, T. H. (1983). Reliability and validity of the Fear Survey Schedule for Children-Revised (FSSC-R). *Behavior Research and Therapy, 21,* 685–92.

Ollendick, T. H. (1996). Violence in youth: Where do we go from here? Behavior therapy's response. *Behavior Therapy, 27* (4): 485–514.

Ollendick, T. H., & King, N. J. (1994). Fears and their level of interference in adolescents. *Behaviour Research and Therapy, 32,* 635–38.

Ollendick, T. H., & Ollendick, D. G. (1990). Tics and Tourette syndrome. In A. M. Gross & R. S. Drabman (Eds.), *Handbook of clinical behavioral pediatrics* (pp. 243–52). New York: Plenum.

Ollendick, T. H., Yang, B., Dong, Q., Xia, Y., et al. (1995). Perceptions of fear in other children and adolescents: The role of gender and friendship status. *Journal of Abnormal Child Psychology, 23,* 439–52.

Ollendick, T. H., Yang, B., King, N. J., Dong, Q., et al. (1996). Fears in American, Australian, Chinese, and Nigerian children and adolescents: A cross-cultural study. *Journal of Child Psychology and Psychiatry and Allied Disciplines, 37,* 213–20.

Oltman, J., & Friedman, S. (1967). Parental deprivation in psychiatric conditions. *Diseases of the Nervous System, 28,* 298–303.

Olweus, D. (1979). Stability of aggressive reaction patterns in males: A review. *Psychological Bulletin, 86,* 852–75.

Orengo, C. A., Kunik, M. E., Molinari, V., & Workman, R. H. (1996). The use and tolerability of fluoxetine in geropsychiatric inpatients. *Journal of Clinical Psychiatry, 57*(1): 12–16.

Orford, J. (1985). *Excessive appetites: A psychological view of addictions.* Chicester, England: Wiley.

Ormel, J., VonKorff, M., Ustun, T., Pini, S., et al. (1994). Common mental disorders and disability across cultures: Results from the WHO Collaborative Study on Psychological Problems in General Health Care. *Journal of the American Medical Association, 272* (22): 1741–48.

Orne, M. T. (1962). On the social psychology of the psychological experiment: With particular reference to demand characteristics and their implications. *American Psychologist, 17,* 776–83.

Osler, W. (1897). *Lectures on angina pectoris and allied states.* New York: Appleton.

Öst, L.-G. (1987). Applied relaxation: Description of a coping technique and review of controlled studies. *Behaviour Research and Therapy, 25,* 397–410.

Öst, L.-G. (1991). *Cognitive therapy versus applied relaxation in the treatment of panic disorder.* Paper presented at the annual meeting of the European Association of Behavior Therapy, Oslo, September 1991.

Öst, L.-G. (1996a). Long-term effects of behavior therapy for specific phobia. In M. R. Mavissakalian & R. F. Prien (Eds.), *Long-term treatments of anxiety disorders* (pp. 121–70). Washington, DC: American Psychiatric Press.

Öst, L.-G. (1996b). One-session group treatment of spider phobia. *Behaviour Research and Therapy, 34* (9): 707–15.

Öst, L.-G., Fellenius, J., & Sterner, U. (1991). Applied tension, exposure in vivo, and tension-only in the treatment of blood phobia. *Behaviour Research and Therapy, 29* (6): 561–74.

Öst, L.-G., Sterner, U., & Fellenius, J. (1989). Applied tension, applied relaxation, and the combination in the treatment of blood phobia. *Behaviour Research and Therapy, 27,* 109–21.

Osterlund, M. K., Overstreet, D. H., & Hurd, Y. L. (1999). The flinders sensitive line rats, a genetic model of depression, show abnormal serotonin receptor mRNA expression in the brain that is reversed by 17 beta-estradiol. *Molecular Brain Research, 74,* 158–66.

O'Sullivan, G., Noshirvani, H., Marks, I., et al. (1991). Six-year follow-up after exposure and clomipramine therapy for obsessive-compulsive disorder. *Journal of Clinical Psychiatry, 52,* 150–55.

Ott, A., van Rossum, C. T. M., van Harskamp, F., van de Mheen, H., Hofman, A., & Breteler, M. M. B. (1999). Education and the incidence of dementia in a large population-based study: The Rotterdam Study. *Neurology, 52* (3): 663–66.

Ott, P. J., Tarter, R. E., et al. (Eds.). (1999). *Sourcebook on substance abuse: Etiology, epidemiology, assessment, and treatment.* Boston: Allyn & Bacon.

Ouimette, P.C., & Klein, D.N. (1995). Test-test stability, mood-state dependence, and informant-subject concordance of the SCID-Axis II Questionnaire in a nonclinical sample. *Journal of Personality Disorders, 9* (2), 105–11.

Overholser, J. C., & Beck, S. (1986). Multimethod assessment of rapists, child molesters, and three control groups on behavioral and psychological measures. *Journal of Consulting and Clinical Psychology, 54* (5): 682–87.

Overmier, J. B., & Seligman, M. E. P. (1967). Effects of inescapable shock upon subsequent escape and avoidance learning. *Journal of Comparative and Physiological Psychology, 63,* 23–33.

Overtoom, C. C. E., Verbaten, M. N., Kemner, C., Kenemans, J. L., van Engeland, H., Buitelaar, J. K., Camfferman, G., & Koelega, H. S. (1998). Associations between event-related potentials and measures of attention and inhibition in the Continuous Performance Task in children with ADHD and normal controls. *Journal of the American Academy of Child and Adolescent Psychiatry, 37,* 977–85.

Packer, H. (1968). *The limits of the criminal sanction.* Stanford: Stanford University Press.

Page, S. (1977). Effects of the mental illness label in attempts to obtain accommodation. *Canadian Journal of Behavioural Science, 9,* 85–90.

Pallas, J., Levine, S. B., Althof, S. E., & Risen, C. B. (2000). Sildenafil for women patients with antidepressant-induced sexual dysfunction. *Journal of Sex and Marital Therapy, 26* (1): 41–50.

Palsson, S., Aevarsson, O., & Skoog, I. (1999). Depression, cerebral atrophy, cognitive performance and incidence of dementia: Population study of 85-year-olds. *British Journal of Psychiatry, 174,* 249–53.

Pandey, G. N., Pandey, S. C., Dwivedi, Y., Sharma, R. P., Janicak, P. G., & Davis, J. M. (1995). Platelet serotonin-2A receptors: A potential biological marker for suicidal behavior. *American Journal of Psychiatry, 152* (6): 850–55.

Pandya, D. N., & Barnes, C. L. (1987). Architecture and connections of the frontal lobe. In E. Perecman (Ed.), *The frontal lobes revisited* (pp. 41–72). Hillsdale, NJ: Erlbaum.

Papassotiropoulos, A., & Heun, R. (1999). Detection of subthreshold depression and subthreshold anxiety in the elderly. *International Journal of Geriatric Psychiatry, 14* (8): 643–50.

Parada, M. A., Puig de Parada, M., & Hoebel, B. G. (1995). Rats self-inject a dopamine antagonist in the lateral hypothalamus where it acts to increase extracellular dopamine in the nucleus accumbens. *Pharmacology, Biochemistry and Behavior, 22* (1): 179–87.

Pare, W., Burken, M., Allen, W., & Kluczynski, J. (1993). Reduced incidence of stress in germ-free Sprague-Dawley rats. *Life Sciences, 53,* 1099.

Paris, J. (1990). Completed suicide in borderline personality disorder. *Psychiatric Annals, 20,* 19–21.

Paris, J., & Zweig-Frank, H. (1992). A critical review of the role of childhood sexual abuse in the etiology of borderline personality disorder. *Canadian Journal of Psychiatry, 37* (2): 125–28.

Park, L. C., Imboden, J. B., Park, T. J., Hulse, S. H., & Unger, H. T. (1992). Giftedness and psychological abuse in borderline personality disorder: Their relevance to genesis and treatment. *Journal of Personality Disorders, 6,* 226–40.

Parker, G., & Hadzi-Pavlovic, D. (1993). Prediction of response to antidepressant medication by a sign-based index of melancholia. *Australian and New Zealand Journal of Psychiatry, 27,* 56–61.

Parnas, J., Cannon, T. D., Jacobsen, B., Schulsinger, H., Schulsinger, F., & Mednick, S. A. (1993). Lifetime DSM-IIIR diagnostic outcomes in the offspring of schizophrenic mothers. Results from the Copenhagen high-risk study. *Archives of General Psychiatry, 50,* 707–14.

Partnership for a Drug-Free America. (1994). *The wrong message of legalizing illicit drugs.* (The Schaffer Library of Drug Policy). http://druglibrary.org/schaffer/GOVPUBS/wrong1.htm

Pato, M. T. (1999a). Beyond depression: Citalopram for obsessive-compulsive disorder. *International Clinical Psychopharmacology, 14* (Suppl 2): S19–S26.

Pato, M. (1999b). *The expert consensus guideline series: Treatment of obsessive-compulsive disorders.* In J. March, A. Frances, D. Carpenter, & D. Kahn (Eds.), http:www.psychguides.com/ocgt.html

Pato, M., Piggott, T., Hill, J., et al. (1991). Controlled comparison of buspirone and clomipramine in obsessive-compulsive disorder. *American Journal of Psychiatry, 148,* 127–29.

Pato, M., Zohar-Kadouch, R., Zohar, J., & Murphy, D. (1988). Return of symptoms after discontinuation of clomipramine in patients with obsessive-compulsive disorder. *American Journal of Psychiatry, 145,* 1521–25.

Patrick, C. J., Bradley, M., & Cuthbert, B. N. (1990). The criminal psychopath and startle modulation. *Psychophysiology, 27* (Suppl. 4A): 87.

Patrick, C. J., Cuthbert, B. N., & Lang, P. J. (1990). Emotion in the criminal psychopath: Fear imagery. *Psychophysiology, 27* (Suppl. 4A): 55.

Patrick, M., Hobson, P., Castle, P., Howard, R., & Maughan, B. (1994). Personality disorder and the mental representation of early social experience. *Development and Psychopathology, 94,* 374–88.

Patterson, C. M., & Newman, J. P. (1993) Reflectivity and learning from aversive events: Toward a psychological mechanism for the syndrome of disinhibition. *Psychological Review, 100,* 716–36.

Patterson, G. R. (1975). *Families: Applications of social learning theory to family life* (2nd ed.). Champaign, IL: Research Press.

Patterson, G. R., DeBaryshe, B. D., & Ramsey, E. (1989). A developmental perspective on antisocial behavior. *American Psychologist, 44,* 329–35.

Patterson, G. R., Reid, J. B., & Dishion, T. J. (1998). Antisocial boys. In J. M. Jenkins & K. Oatley (Eds.), *Human emotions: A reader* (pp. 330–36). Malden, MA: Blackwell.

Patterson, T., Spohn, H. E., Bogia, D. P., & Hayes, K. (1986). Thought disorder in schizophrenia: Cognitive and neuroscience approaches. *Schizophrenia Bulletin, 12* (3): 460–72.

Patterson, T. L., & Jeste, D. V. (1999). The potential impact of the baby-boom generation on substance abuse among elderly persons. *Psychiatric Services, 50* (9): 1184–88.

Pattie, F. A. (1967). A brief history of hypnotism. In J. E. Gordon (Ed.), *Handbook of clinical and experimental hypnosis.* New York: Macmillan.

Paul, G. L. (1966). *Insight vs. desensitization in psychotherapy.* Stanford: Stanford University Press.

Paul, G. L. (1967). Insight vs. desensitization in psychotherapy two years after termination. *Journal of Consulting Psychology, 31* (4): 333–48.

Paul, G. L. (1969). Outcome of systematic desensitization. II. Controlled investigations of individual treatment, technique variations, and current status (pp. 105–59). In C. M. Franks (Ed.), *Behavior therapy: Appraisal and status.* New York: McGraw-Hill.

Pauls, D. L., Alsobrook, J. P., Gelernter, J., & Leckman, J. F. (1999). Genetic vulnerability. In J. F. Leckman & D. J. Cohen (Eds.), *Tourette's syndrome—Tics, obsessions, compulsions: Developmental psychopathology and clinical care* (pp. 194–212). New York: Wiley.

Pauly, I. B. (1969). Adult manifestation of male transsexualism. In R. Green & J. Money (Eds.), *Transsexualism and sex reassignment.* Baltimore: Johns Hopkins Press.

Pauly, I. B. (1974). Female transsexualism. *Archives of Sexual Behavior, 3,* 487–526.

Pavel, O. (1990). *How I came to know fish* (trans. J. Baclai & R. McDowell). New York: Story Line Press/New Directions.

Paykel, E. S. (1973). Life events and acute depression. In J. P. Scott & E. C. Senay (Eds.), *Separation and depression.* Washington, DC: American Association for the Advancement of Science.

Paykel, E. S. (1974a). Recent life events and clinical depression. In E. K. E. Gunderson & R. H. Rahe (Eds.), *Life stress and illness* (pp. 150–51). Springfield, IL: Charles C. Thomas.

Paykel, E. S. (1974b). Life stress and psychiatric disorder: Application of the clinical approach. In B. P. Dohrenwend & B. S. Dohrenwend (Eds.), *Stressful life events: Their nature and effects* (pp. 135–49). New York: Wiley.

Paykel, E. S., Meyers, J. K., Dienelt, M. N., Klerman, J. L., Lindenthal, J. J., & Pfeffer, M. P. (1969). Life events and depression. *Archives of General Psychiatry, 21,* 753–60.

Paykel, E. S., Scott, J., Teasdale, J. D., Johnson, A. L., Garland, A., Moore, R., Jenaway, A., Cornwall, P. L., Hayhurst, H., Abbott, R., & Pope, M. (1999). Prevention of relapse in residual depression by cognitive therapy: A controlled trial. *Archives of General Psychiatry, 56* (9): 829–35.

Payne, R. W. (1966). The measurement and significance of overinclusive thinking and retardation in schizophrenic patients. In P. H. Hoch & J. Zubin (Eds.), *Psychopathology of schizophrenia* (pp. 77–79). New York: Grune & Stratton.

Peasley-Miklus, C., & Vrana, S. (2000). Effect of worrisome and relaxing thinking on fearful emotional processing. *Behaviour Research and Therapy, 38,* 129–44.

Pecknold, J., Swinson, R., Kuch, K., & Lewis, C. (1988). Alprazolam in panic disorder and agoraphobia: Results from a multicenter trial: III. Discontinuation effects. *Archives of General Psychiatry, 45,* 429–36.

Pedersen, N. L., McClearn, G. E., Plomin, R., Nesselroade, J. R., Berg, S., & DeFaire, U. (1991). The Swedish Adoption Twin Study of Aging: An update. *Acta Geneticae Medicae et Gemellologiaie, 40,* 7–20.

Peele, S. (1985). *The meaning of addiction: Compulsive experience and its interpretation.* Lexington, MA: Lexington Books.

Pelham, W. E. (1989). Behavioral therapy, behavioral assessment, and psychostimulant medication in the treatment of attention deficit disorder: An interactive approach. In J. Swanson & I. Bloomingdale (Eds.), *Attention deficit disorder: IV. Current concepts and emerging trends in attentional and behavioral disorders of childhood* (pp. 169–95). New York: Pergamon.

Penin, F., Maheut-Bosser, A., Geradin, P., Jeandel, C., et al. (1993). Delusional disorder in a geriatric oriented internal medicine unit. A practical approach. *Psychologie Medicale, 25,* 803–807.

Penn, D., & Mueser, K. (1996). Research update on the psychological treatment of schizophrenia. *American Journal of Psychiatry, 153,* 607–17.

Pennebaker, J. W. (1985). Traumatic experience and psychosomatic disease: Exploring the roles of behavioural inhibition, obsession, and confiding. *Canadian Psychology, 26,* 82–95.

Pennebaker, J. (1990). *Opening up.* New York: Morrow.

Pennington, B. F., & Bennetto, L. (1993). Main effects of transactions in the neuropsychology of conduct disorder? Commentary on "The neuropsychology of conduct disorder." *Development and Psychopathology, 5,* 153–64.

Pennington, B. F. (1999). Dyslexia as a neurodevelopmental disorder. In H. Tager-Flusberg (Ed.), *Neurodevelopmental disorders. Developmental cognitive neuroscience.* Cambridge, MA: MIT Press.

Penninx, B. W., Guralnik, J. M., Simonsick, E. M., Kasper, J. D., Ferrucci, L., & Fried L. P. (1998). Emotional vitality among disabled older women: The women's health and aging study. *Journal of the American Geriatrics Society, 46* (7): 807–15.

Perkins, K. A., & Reyher, J. (1971). Repression, psychopathology and drive representation: An experimental hypnotic investigation of impulse inhibition. *American Journal of Clinical Hypnosis, 13,* 249–58.

Perris, C. (1968). The course of depressive psychosis. *Acta Psychiatrica Scandinavica, 44,* 238–48.

Perry, J., Banon, E., & Ianni, F. (1999). Effectiveness of psychotherapy for personality disorders. *American Journal of Psychiatry, 156* (9): 1312–21.

Persons, J. B. (1986). The advantages of studying psychological phenomena rather than psychiatric diagnoses. *American Psychologist, 41,* 1252–60.

Perugi, G., Akiskal, H. S., Pfanner, C., Presta, S., Gemignani, A., Milanfranchi, A., Lensi, P., Ravagli, S., & Cassano, G. B. (1997). The clinical impact of bipolar and unipolar affective comorbidity on obsessive-compulsive disorder. *Journal of Affective Disorders, 46,* 15–23.

Peters, M. L., Godaert, G. L., Ballieux, R. E., van Vliet, M., Willemsen, J. J., Sweep, F. C. G. J., & Heijnen, C. J. (1998). Cardiovascular and endocrine responses to experimental stress: Effects of mental effort and controllability. *Psychoneuroendocrinology, 23,* 1–17.

Peterson, B. S., Leckman, J. F., Arnsten, A., Anderson, G. M. Staib, L. H., Gore, J. C., Bronen, R. A., Malison, R., Scahill, L., & Cohen, D. J. (1999). Neuroanatomical circuitry. In J. F. Leckman & D. J. Cohen (Eds.), *Tourette's syndrome—Tics, obsessions, compulsions: Developmental psychopathology and clinical care* (pp. 230–60). New York: Wiley.

Peterson, C., Maier, S., & Seligman, M. (1993). *Learned helplessness.* New York: Oxford University Press.

Peterson, C., & Seligman, M. E. P. (1984). Causal explanations as a risk factor for depression: Theory and evidence. *Psychological Review, 91* (31):347–74.

Peterson, C., & Seligman, M. E. P. (1987). Explanatory style and illness. Special Issue: Personality and physical health. *Journal of Personality, 55* (2): 237–65.

Peterson, C., Seligman, M. E. P., & Vaillant, G. (1988). Pessimistic explanatory style as a risk factor for physical illness: A 35-year longitudinal study. *Journal of Personality and Social Psychology, 55,* 23–27.

Petersen, M. E., & Dickey, R. (1995). Surgical sex reassignment: A comparative survey of international centers. *Archives of Sexual Behavior, 24* (2): 135–56.

Petrie, K. J., Booth, R. J., & Pennebaker, J. W. (1998). The immunological effects of thought suppression. *Journal of Personality and Social Psychology, 75* (5): 1264–72.

Petronis, A. (1995). Unstable genes—unstable mind? *American Journal of Psychiatry, 152* (2): 164–72.

Petursson, H. (1994). The benzodiazepine withdrawal syndrome. *Addiction, 89,* 1455–59.

Petursson, H., & Lader, M. H. (1981). Withdrawal from long-term benzodiazepine treatment. *British Medical Journal, 283,* 643–45.

Petzel, T. P., & Johnson, J. E. (1972). Time estimation by process and reactive schizophrenics under crowded and uncrowded conditions. *Journal of Clinical Psychology, 28* (3): 345–47.

Pfafflin, F. (1992). Regrets after sex reassignment surgery. Special Issue: Gender dysphoria: Interdisciplinary approaches in clinical management. *Journal of Psychology and Human Sexuality, 5* (4): 69–85.

Pfohl, B. (1991). Histrionic personality disorder: A review of available data and recommendations for DSM-IV. *Journal of Personality Disorders, 5*(2): 150–66.

Pfohl, B. (1999). Axis I and Axis II: Comorbidity or confusion? In C. Cloninger (Ed.), *Personality and psychopathology.* Washington, DC: American Psychiatric Press.

Phahwa, R., Paolo, A., Troester, A., & Koller, W. (1998). Cognitive impairment in Parkinson's disease. *European Journal of Neurology, 5,* 431–41.

Phelps, J. A., Davis, J. O., & Schartz, K. M. (1997). Nature, nurture, and twin research strategies. *Current Directions in Psychological Science, 6,* 117–21.

Philibert, R. A., Richards, L., Lynch, C. F., & Winokur, G. (1995). Effect of ECT on mortality and clinical outcome in geriatric unipolar depression. *Journal of Clinical Psychiatry, 56* (9): 390–94.

Phillips, K. A., Gunderson, C. G., Mallya, G., McElroy, S. L., & Carter, W. (1998). A comparison study of body dysmorphic disorder and obsessive-compulsive disorder. *Journal of Clinical Psychiatry, 59* (11): 568–75.

Pickar, D. (1995). Prospects for pharmacotherapy of schizophrenia, *Lancet, 345* (8949):557–62.

Piggott, T., Pato, M., Bernstein, S., et al. (1990). Controlled comparisons of clomipramine and fluoxetine in the treatment of obsessive-compulsive disorder. *Archives of General Psychiatry, 47,* 926–32.

Pilla, M. Perachon, S., Sautel, F. Garrido, F. Mann, A., Wermuth, C.G., Schwartz, J., Everitt, B.J. & Sokoloff, P. (1999). Selective inhibition of cocaine-seeking behavior by a partial dopamine D3 receptor agonist. *Nature, 400,* 371–75.

Pillard, R. C., & Bailey, J. M. (1995). A biological perspective on sexual orientation. *Psychiatric Clinics of North America, 18* (1): 71–84.

Pillard, R., & Weinrich, J. (1987). The periodic table model of the gender transpositions: Part I. A theory based on

masculinization and defeminization of the brain. *Journal of Sex Research, 4,* 425–54.

Pine, D. S., Coplan, J. D., Wasserman, G. A., Miller, L. S., Fried, J. E., Davies, M., Cooper, T. B., Greenhill, L., Shaffer, D., & Parsons, B. (1997). Neuroendocrine response to fenfluramine challenge in boys: Associations with aggressive behavior and adverse rearing. *Archives of General Psychiatry, 54,* 839–46.

Piquero, A., & Tibbetts, S. (1999). The impact of pre/perinatal disturbances and disadvantaged familial environment in predicting criminal offending. *Studies on Crime and Crime Prevention, 8,* 52–70.

Place, E. J. S., & Gilmore, G. C. (1980). Perceptual organization in schizophrenia. *Journal of Abnormal Psychology, 89,* 409–18.

Plassman, B. L., & Breitner, J. C. S. (1996). Recent advances in the genetics of Alzheimer's disease and vascular dementia with an emphasis on gene-environment interactions. *Journal of the American Geriatric Society, 44,* 1242–50.

Plomin, R., Corley, R., DeFries, J., & Fulker, D. (1990). Individual differences in television viewing in early childhood: Nature as well as nurture. *Psychological Science, 1,* 371–77.

Plomin, R., McClearn, G. E., Pedersen, N. L., Nesselroade, J. R., et al. (1988). Genetic influence on childhood family environment perceived retrospectively from the last half of the life span. *Developmental Psychology, 24,* 738–45.

Plomin, R., Scheier, M. F., Bergeman, C. S., Pedersen, N. L., Nesselroade, J. R., & McClearn, G. (1992). Optimism, pessimism and mental health: A twin/adoption analysis. *Personality and Individual Differences, 13* (8): 921–30.

Pokorny, A. D. (1964). Suicide rates and various psychiatric disorders. *Journal of Nervous and Mental Diseases, 139,* 499–506.

Polivy, J. (1976). Perception of calories and regulation of intake in restrained and unrestrained subjects. *Addictive Behaviors, 1,* 237–44.

Pollack, J. M. (1979). Obsessive-compulsive personality: A review. *Psychological Bulletin, 86,* 225–41.

Pollard, C., Bronson, S., & Kenney, M. (1989). Prevalence of agoraphobia without panic in clinical settings. *American Journal of Psychiatry, 146,* 559.

Pollock, V. I. (1992). Meta-analysis of subjective sensitivity to alcohol in sons of alcoholicss. *American Journal of Psychiatry, 149,* 1534–38.

Pope, H. G., Jonas, J. M., & Jones, B. (1982). Factitious psychosis: Phenomenology, family history, and long-term outcome of nine patients. *American Journal of Psychiatry, 139,* 1480–83.

Pope, H. G., Jr., Hudson, J. I., Bodkin, J. A., & Oliva, P. (1998). Questionable validity of "dissociative amnesia" in trauma victims: Evidence from prospective studies. *British Journal of Psychiatry, 172,* 210–15.

Popovic, M., Popovic, N., Eric-Jovicic, M., Jovanova-Nesic, K. (2000). Immune responses in nucleus basalis magnocellularis-lesioned rats exposed to chronic isolation stress. *International Journal of Neuroscience, 100* (1–4): 125–31.

Porsolt, R. D., Anton, G., Blavet, N., & Jalfre, M. (1978). Behavioral despair in rats: A new model sensitive to antidepressant treatments. *European Journal of Pharmacology, 47,* 379–91.

Post, R. (1992). Transduction of psychological stress into the neurobiology of recurrent affective disorder. *American Journal of Psychiatry, 149,* 999–1010.

Post, R. M., Denicoff, K. D., Frye, M. A., Dunn, R. T., Leverich, G. S., Osuch, E., & Speer, A. (1998). A history of the use of anticonvulsants as mood stabilizers in the last two decades of the 20th century. *Neuropsychobiology, 38* (3): 152–66.

Post, R. M., Weiss, S. R. B., Smith, M. A., & Leverich, G. S. (1996). Impact of psychosocial stress on gene expression: Implications for PTSD and recurrent affective disorder. In T. W. Miller et al. (Eds.), *Theory and assessment of stressful life events.* International Universities Press stress and health series (pp. 37–91). Madison, CT: International Universities.

Potter, W. Z., & Manji, H. K. (1994). Catecholamines in depression: An update. *Clinical Chemistry, 40* (2): 279–87.

Poulos, C. X., Hinson, R. E., & Siegel, S. (1981). The role of Pavlovian processes in drug tolerance and dependence: Implications for treatment. *Addictive Behaviors, 6,* 205–11.

Poulton, R., & Menzies, R. (2000). Non-associative fear acquisition: A review of the evidence from retrospective and longitudinal research. *Behaviour Research and Therapy,* in press.

Pourcher, E., Baruch, P., Bouchard, R. H., Filteau, M., & Bergeron, D. (1995). Neuroleptic associated tardive dyskinesias in young people with psychoses. *British Journal of Psychiatry, 166,* 768–72.

Powell, K. E., Thompson, P. D., Caspersen, C. J., & Kendrick, J. S. (1987). Physical activity and the incidence of coronary heart disease. *Annual Review of Public Health, 8,* 253–87.

Power, C., McArthur, J. C., Nath, A., Wehrly, K., Mayne, M., Nishio, J., Langelier, T., Johnson, R. T., & Chesebro, B. (1998). Neuronal death induced by brain-derived human immunodeficiency virus type 1 envelope genes differs between demented and nondemented AIDS patients. *Journal of Virology, 72* (11): 9045–53.

Power, K., Simpson, R., Swanson, V., & Wallace, L. (1990). A controlled comparison of cognitive-behavior therapy, diazepam, and placebo, alone or in combination, for the treatment of generalized anxiety disorder. *Journal of Anxiety Disorders, 4,* 267–92.

Practice Guidelines Coalition (1999). *What is panic disorder?* Department of Psychology, University of Nevada.

Practice Guideline for the Treatment of Patients with Major Depressive Disorder (Revision). (2000). *American Journal of Psychiatry, 157* (Suppl.): 1–45.

Prasad, B. M., Sorg, B. A., Ulibarri, C., & Kalivas, P. W. (1995). Sensitization to stress and psychostimulants: Involvement of dopamine transmission versus the HPA axis. In G. P. Chrousos, R. McCarty, et al. (Eds.), *Stress: Basic mechanisms and clinical implications* (Annals of the New York Academy of Sciences, Vol. 771; pp. 617–25). New York: New York Academy of Sciences.

Premack, D. (1959). Toward empirical behavior laws: I. Positive reinforcement. *Psychological Review, 66,* 219–33.

Prescott, C. A., & Kendler, K. S. (1999). Genetic and environmental contributions to alcohol abuse and dependence in a population-based sample of male twins. *American Journal of Psychiatry, 156,* 34–40.

Preskorn, S., & Jerkovich, G. (1990). Central nervous system toxicity of tricyclic antidepressants: Phenomenology, course, risk factors, and the role of drug monitoring. *Journal of Clinical Psychopharmacology, 10,* 88–95.

Price, D. D., Milling, L. S., Kirsch, I., Duff, A., Montgomery, G. H., & Nicholls, S. S. (1999). An analysis of factors that contribute to the magnitude of placebo analgesia in an experimental paradigm. *Pain, 83,* 147–56.

Price, K. P., Tryon, W. W., & Raps, C. S. (1978). Learned helplessness and depression in a clinical population: A test of two behavioral hypotheses. *Journal of Abnormal Psychology, 87,* 113–21.

Price, R. W. (1996). Neurological complications of HIV infection. *Lancet, 348* (9025):445–52.

Price, R. W., Brew, B., Sidtis, J., et al. (1988). The brain in AIDS: Central nervous system HIV-1 infection and AIDS dementia complex. *Science, 239,* 586–92.

Prichard, J. C. (1837). *Treatise on insanity and other disorders affecting the mind.* Philadelphia: Haswell, Barrington & Haswell.

Priebe, S., Warner, R., Hubschmid, T., & Eckle, I. (1998). Employment, attitudes toward work and quality of life among people with schizophrenia in three countries. *Schizophrenia Bulletin, 24,* 469–77.

Prior, M. R. (1987). Biological and neuropsychological approaches to childhood autism. *British Journal of Psychiatry, 150,* 8–17.

Project MATCH Research Group. (1998). Matching alcoholism treatments to client heterogeneity: Project MATCH three-year drinking outcomes. *Alcoholism, Clinical and Experimental Research, 22,* 1300–1311.

Pulska, T., Pahkala, K., Laippala, P., & Kivela, S. (1999). Follow-up study of longstanding depression as predictor of mortality in elderly people living in the community. *British Medical Journal, 318,* 432–33.

Purcell, D., Brady, K., Chai, H., Muser, J., Molk, L., Gordon, N., & Means, J. (1969). The effect of asthma in children during experimental separation from the family. *Psychosomatic Medicine, 31,* 144–64.

Putnam, F. (1989). *Diagnosis and treatment of multiple personality.* New York: Guilford Press.

Putnam, F. W., Guroff, J. J., & Silberman, E. K., et al. (1986). The clinical phenomenology of multiple personality disorder: Review of 100 recent cases. *Journal of Clinical Psychiatry, 47* (6): 285–93.

Putnam, F., & Loewenstein, R. (1993). Treatment of multiple personality disorder: A survey of current practices. *American Journal of Psychiatry, 150,* 1048–52.

Putnam, F. W., Zahn, T. P., & Post, R. M. (1990). Differential autonomic nervous system activity in multiple personality disorder. *Psychiatry Research, 31,* 251–60.

Quay, H. C. (1986). Conduct disorders. In H. C. Quay & J. S. Werry (Eds.), *Psychopathological disorders of childhood* (pp. 35–62). New York: Wiley.

Quay, H. C., Routh, D. K., & Shapiro, S. K. (1987). Psychopathology of childhood: From description to validation. *Annual Review of Psychology, 38,* 491–532.

Quitkin, F., & Klein, D. (2000). What conditions are necessary to assess antidepressant efficacy. *Archives of General Psychiatry, 57,* 323–24.

Quitkin, F., Rabkin, J., Gerald, J., Davis, J., & Klein, D. (2000). Validity of clinical trials of antidepressants. *American Journal of Psychiatry, 157,* 327–37.

Rabavilos, A. D., Boulougouris, J. C., & Stefanis, C. (1976). Duration of flooding session in the treatment of obsessive-compulsive patients. *Behaviour Research and Therapy, 14,* 349–55.

Rachman, S. J. (1976). Therapeutic modeling. In M. Felman & A. Broadhurst (Eds.), *Theoretical and experimental bases of behavior therapy.* Chichester: Wiley.

Rachman, S. J. (1978). *Fear and courage.* New York: Freeman.

Rachman, S. (1990). The determinants and treatment of simple phobias. Advances *in Behaviour Research and Therapy, 12* (1): 1–30.

Rachman, S. (1994). Pollution of the mind. *Behaviour Research and Therapy, 32* (3): 311–14.

Rachman, S. (1997). *Best of behavior research and therapy.* New York: Pergamon/Elsevier Science Inc.

Rachman, S. J., Cobb, J., Grey, S., MacDonald, B., Mawson, C., Sartory, G., & Stern, R. (1979). The behavioral treatment of obsessive-compulsive disorders, with and without domipramine. *Behaviour Research and Therapy, 17,* 467–78.

Rachman, S. J., & Hodgson, R. J. (1980). *Obsessions and compulsions.* Englewood Cliffs, NJ: Prentice-Hall.

Rachman, S. J., Hodgson, R., & Marks, I. M. (1971). The treatment of chronic obsessional neurosis. *Behaviour Research and Therapy, 9,* 237–47.

Rachman, S. J., Marks, I., & Hodgson, R. (1973). The treatment of chronic obsessive-compulsive neurosis by modeling and flooding in vivo. *Behaviour Research and Therapy, 11,* 463–71.

Rachman, S., & Shafran, R. (1998). Cognitive and behavioral features of obsessive-compulsive disorder. In R. P. Swinson & M. M. Antony (Eds.), *Obsessive-compulsive disorder: Theory, research, and treatment* (pp. 51–78). New York: Guilford Press.

Radloff, L. S. (1975). Sex differences in depression: The effects of occupation and marital status. *Sex Roles, 1,* 249–65.

Rado, S. (1928). Psychodynamics of depression from the etiological point of view. In W. Galen (Ed.), *The meaning of despair.* New York: Science House.

Rafel, R., Smith, J., Krantz, J., Cohen, A., & Brennan, C. (1990). Extrageniculate vision in hemianopic humans: Saccade inhibition by signals in the blind field. *Science, 250,* 118–21.

Raine, A. (1991). The SPQ: A scale for the assessment of schizotypal personality. *Schizophrenia Bulletin, 17,* 555–64.

Raine, A. (1993). *The psychopathology of crime: Criminal behavior as a clinical disorder.* San Diego, CA: Academic Press.

Raine, A. (1996). Autonomic nervous system activity and violence. In D. M. Stoff & R. B. Cairns (Eds.), *Aggression and violence: Genetic, neurobiological, and biosocial perspectives* (pp. 145–68). Mahwah, NJ: Lawrence Erlbaum.

Raine, A. (1997). Antisocial behavior and psychophysiology: A biosocial perspective and a prefrontal dysfunction hypothesis. In D. M. Stoff, J. Breiling, & J. D. Maser (Eds.), *Handbook of antisocial behavior* (pp. 289–304). New York: Wiley.

Raine, A. (1999). Murderous minds: Can we see the mark of Cain? *Cerebrum, 1,* 15–30.

Raine, A., Brennan, P., & Mednick, S. A. (1997). Interaction between birth complications and early maternal rejection in predisposing individuals to adult violence: Specificity to serious, early-onset violence. *American Journal of Psychiatry, 154,* 1265–71.

Raine, A., & Buchsbaum, M. S. (1996). Violence, brain imaging, and neuropsychology. In D. M. Stoff, R. B. Cairns, et al. (Eds.), *Aggression and violence: Genetic, neurobiological, and biosocial perspectives* (pp. 195–217). Mahwah, NJ: Lawrence Erlbaum.

Raine, A., Lencz, T., & Mednick, S. A. (Eds.). (1995). *Schizotypal personality.* New York: Cambridge University Press.

Raitakari, O. T., Leino, M., Raikkonen, K., Porkka, K. V. K., Taimela, S., Rasanen, L., & Viikari, J. S. A. (1995). Clustering of risk habits in young adults: The Cardiovascular Risk in Young Finns Study. *American Journal of Epidemiology, 142* (1): 36–44.

Ramey, C. T., & Ramey, S. L. (1998). Early intervention and early experience. *American Psychologist, 53,* 109–20.

Rao, U., Weissman, M. M., Martin, J. A., & Hammond, R. W. (1993). Childhood depression and risk of suicide: A preliminary report of a longitudinal study. *Journal of the American Academy of Child and Adolescent Psychiatry, 32*(1): 21–27.

Rapee, R. (1991). Generalized anxiety disorder: A review of clinical features and theoretical concepts. *Clinical Psychology Review, 11,* 419–40.

Rapin, I. (1997) Current concepts: Autism. *New England Journal of Medicine, 397,* 97–104.

Rapin, I. (1999). Autism in search of a home in the brain. *Neurology, 52* (5): 902–904.

Rapin, I., & Katzman, R. (1998). Neurobiology of autism. *Annals of Neurology, 43,* 7–14.

Rapoport, J. L. (1988). The neurobiology of obsessive-compulsive disorder. *Journal of the American Medical Association, 260,* 2888–90.

Rapoport, J. L. (1990). *The boy who couldn't stop washing.* New York: Plume.

Rapport, M. D. (1987). Attention deficit disorder with hyperactivity. In M. Hersen & V. B. Van Hasselt (Eds.), *Behavior therapy with children and adolescents* (pp. 325–62). New York: Wiley.

Raps, C. S., Reinhard, K. E., & Seligman, M. E. P. (1980). Reversal of cognitive and affective deficits associated with depression and learned helplessness by mood elevation in patients. *Journal of Abnormal Psychology, 89,* 342–49.

Rattan, R. B., & Chapman, L. J. (1973). Associative intrusions in schizophrenic verbal behavior. *Journal of Abnormal Psychology, 82,* 169–73.

Rauch, S. L., & Jenike, M. A. (1998). Pharmacological treatment of obsessive compulsive disorder. In P. E. Nathan & J. M. Gorman (Eds.), *A guide to treatments that work* (pp. 358–76). New York: Oxford University Press.

Ravaglia, G., Forti, P., Maioli, F., De Ronchi, D., Boschi, F., Scali, R. C., Cavazzoni, M., Bovina, C., & Bugiardini, R. (1998). Antioxidant vitamins and dementia. *Archives of Gerontology and Geriatrics,* Suppl 6, 431–34.

Ravaja, N., Keltikangas-Jarvinen, L., & Keskivaara, P. (1996). Type A factors as predictors of changes in the metabolic syndrome precursors in adolescents and young adults—A 3-year follow-up study. *Health Psychology, 15*(1): 18–29.

Rawlings D., & MacFarlane, C. (1994). A multidimensional schizotypal traits questionnaire for young adolescents. *Personality and Individual Differences, 17,* 489–96.

Ray, O., & Ksir, C. (1987). *Drugs, society, and human behavior.* St. Louis: Times Mirror/Mosby.

Read, D. J., Lindsay, D. S., et al. (1997). *Recollections of trauma: Scientific evidence and clinical practice.* New York: Plenum.

Redmond, D. E., Jr. (1985). Neurochemical basis for anxiety and anxiety disorders: Evidence from drugs which decrease human fear of anxiety. In A. H. Tuma & J. D. Maser (Eds.), *Anxiety and the anxiety disorders.* Hillsdale, NJ: Lawrence Erlbaum.

Reed, T. E. (1993). Effect of enriched (complex) environment on nerve conduction velocity: New data and review of implications for the speed of information processing. *Intelligence, 17,* 533–540.

Reed, T., Carmelli, D., & Rosenman, R. H. (1991). Effects of placentation on selected Type A behaviors in adult males in the National Heart, Lung, and Blood Institute (NHLBI) twin study. *Behavior Genetics, 21,* 9–19.

Regan, M., & Howard, R. (1995). Fear conditioning, preparedness, and the contingent negative variation. *Clinical Psychology Review, 15* (1): 23–48.

Regier, A., Boyd, J. H., Burke, J. D., Rae, D. S., Myers, J. K., Kramer, M., Robins, L. N., George, L. K., Karno, M., & Locke, B. Z. (1988). One month prevalence of mental disorders in the United States. *Archives of General Psychiatry, 45,* 977–86.

Regier, D., Myers, J., Kramer, M., Robins, L., Blayer, D., Hough, R., Easton, W., & Locke, B. (1984). The NIMH Epidemiological Catchment Area program: Historical context, major objectives, and study population characteristics. *Archives of General Psychiatry, 41,* 934–41.

Regier, D. A., Narrow, W. E., & Rae, D. S. (1990). The epidemiology of anxiety disorders: The Epidemiological Catchment Area (ECA) experience. Symposium: Benzodiazepines: Therapeutic,biologic, and psychological issues. *Journal of Psychiatric Research, 24* (Suppl 2): 3–14.

Rehm, L. P. (1978). Mood pleasant events, and unpleasant events: Two pilot studies. *Journal of Consulting and Clinical Psychology, 46,* 854–59.

Rehyer, J., & Smyth, L. (1971). Suggestibility during the execution of a posthypnotic suggestion. *Journal of Abnormal Psychology, 78,* 258–65.

Reich, J. H. (1990). Comparisons of males and females in DSM-III dependent personality disorder. *Psychiatry Research, 23* (2): 207–14.

Reich, L. H., Davies, R. K., & Himmelhoch, J. M. (1974). Excessive alcohol use in manic-depressive illness. *American Journal of Psychiatry, 131* (1): 83–86.

Reich, W. (1986). Diagnostic ethics: The uses and limits of psychiatric explanation. In L. Tancredi (Ed.), *Ethical issues in epidemiological research.* New Brunswick, NJ: Rutgers University Press.

Reiff, H. B., Gerber, P. J., & Ginsberg, R. (1997). *Exceeding expectations: Successful adults with learning disabilities.* Austin, TX: Pro-Ed.

Reiman, E., Raichle, M., Robins, E., et al. (1986). The application of positron emission tomography to the study of panic disorder. *American Journal of Psychiatry, 143,* 469–77.

Reinecke, M. A., Ryan, N. E., & DuBois, D. L. (1998). Cognitive-behavioral therapy of depression and depressive symptoms during adolescence: A review and meta-analysis. *Journal of the American Academy of Child and Adolescent Psychiatry, 37* (1): 26–34.

Reinisch, J. (1992). Unpublished study cited in C. Gorman, Sizing up the sexes. *Time, 139,* 45–46.

Reitan, R. M., & Davison, L. A. (1974). *Clinical neuropsychology: Current status and applications.* Washington, DC: Winston and Sons.

Reite, M., Sheeder, J., Teale, P., Richardson, M., Adams, M., & Simon, J. (1995). MEG based brain laterality: Sex differences in normal adults. *Neuropsychologia, 33* (12): 1607–16.

Rende, R. (1999). Adaptive and maladaptive pathways in development: A quantitative genetic perspective. In M. C. LaBuda & E. L. Grigorenko (Eds.), *On the way to individuality: Current methodological issues in behavioral genetics* (pp. 1–21). Commack, NY: Nova Science Publishers.

Report of the Ethics Committee. (1997). *American Psychologist, 53,* 969–80.

Rescorla R. A., & Solomon, R. L. (1967). Two-process learning theory: Relationship between Pavlovian conditioning and instrumental learning. *Psychological Review, 74,* 151–82.

Resick, P., Jordan, C., Girelli, S., Hutter, C., et al. (1988). A comparative outcome study of behavioral group therapy for sexual assault victims. *Behavior Therapy, 19,* 385–401.

Ressler, K., & Nemeroff, C. B. (1999). Role of norepinephrine in the pathophysiology and treatment of mood disorders. *Biological Psychiatry, 46* (9): 1219–33.

Reynolds, C. F., Buysse, D. J., & Kupfer, D. J. (1999). Treating insomnia in older adults: Taking a long-term view. *Journal of the American Medical Association, 281* (11): 1034–35.

Reynolds, C. F., Frank, E., Perel, J. M., Imber, S. D., Cornes, C., Miller, M. D., Mazumdar, S., Houck, P. R., Dew, M. A., Stack, J. A., Pollock, B. G., & Kupfer, D. J. (1999). Nortriptyline and interpersonal psychotherapy as maintenance therapies for recurrent major depression: A randomized controlled trial in patients older than 59 years. *Journal of the American Medical Association, 281,* 39–45.

Reynolds, C. F., Kupfer, D. J., Hoch, C. C., & Sewitch, D. E. (1985). Sleeping pills for the elderly: Are they ever justified? *Journal of Clinical Psychiatry, 46,* 9–12.

Reynolds, W. M., & Coats, K. I. (1986). A comparison of cognitive-behavioral therapy and relaxation training for the treatment of depression in adolescents. *Journal of Consulting and Clinical Psychology, 54,* 653–60.

Rheaume, J., Freeston, M., Ladouceur, R., et al. (2000). Functional and dysfunctional perfectionists: Are they different on compulsive behaviors? *Behaviour Research and Therapy, 38,* 119–28.

Rhee, S. H., Waldman, I. D., Hay, D. A., & Levy, F. (1999). Sex differences in genetic and environmental influences on DSM-III-R attention-deficit/hyperactivity disorder. *Journal of Abnormal Psychology, 108,* 24–41.

Rhodewalt, F., Madrian, J. C., & Cheney, S. (1998). Narcissism, self-knowledge organization, and emotional reactivity: The effect of daily experiences on self-esteem and affect. *Personality and Social Psychology Bulletin, 24,* 75–87.

Ricciardi, J. N. (1995). Depressed mood is related to obsessions, but not to compulsions, in obsessive-compulsive disorder. *Journal of Anxiety Disorders, 9* (3): 249–56.

Rice, J., Reich, T., Andreasen, N. C., Endicott, J., Van Eerdewegh, M., Fishman, R., Hirschfeld, R. M. A., & Klerman, G. L. (1987). The familial transmission of bipolar illness. *Archives of General Psychiatry, 44,* 441–47.

Rice, M. E., Harris, G. T., & Quinsey, V. L. (1990). A follow-up study of rapists assessed in a maximum security psychiatric facility. *Journal of Interpersonal Violence, 5,* 435–40.

Richard, I. H., & Kurlan, R. (1997). A survey of antidepressant drug use in Parkinson's disease. *Neurology, 49,* 1168–70.

Richards, S. S., & Hendrie, H. C. (1999). Diagnosis, management, and treatment of Alzheimer disease: A guide for the internist. *Archives of Internal Medicine, 159,* 789–98.

Richters, M. M., & Volkmar, F. R. (1994). Reactive attachment disorder of infancy or early childhood. *Journal of the American Academy of Child and Adolescent Psychiatry, 33,* 328–32.

Rickels, K., DeMartinis, N., & Aufdembrinke, B. (2000). A double-blind, placebo-controlled trial of abecarnil and diazepam in the treatment of patients with generalized anxiety disorder. *Journal of Clinical Psychopharmacology, 20,* 12–18.

Rie, H. E. (1966). Depression in childhood: A survey of some pertinent contributions. *Journal of the American Academy of Child Psychiatry, 5,* 653–85.

Riskind, J. H., Moore, R., & Bowley, L. (1995). The looming of spiders: The fearful perceptual distortion of movement and menace. *Behaviour Research and Therapy, 33*(2): 171–78.

Risley, T., & Wolf, M. (1967). Establishing functional speech in echolalic children. *Behaviour Research and Therapy, 5,* 73–88.

Ritsner, M. S., Sherina, O., & Ginath, Y. (1992). Genetic epidemiological study of schizophrenia: Reproduction behaviour. *Acta Psychiatrica Scandinavica, 85,* 423–29.

Ritvo, E. R., Freeman, B. J., Pingree, C., Mason-Brothers, A., Jorde, L., Jenson, W. R., McMahon, W. M., Petersen, P. B., Mo, A., & Ritvo, A. (1989). The UCLA-University of Utah Epidemiology Survey of Autism: Prevalence. *American Journal of Psychiatry, 146* (2): 194–99.

Roache, J. (1990). Addiction potential of benzodiazepines and non-benzodiazepine anxiolytics. *Advances in Alcohol and Substance Abuse, 9,* 103–28.

Robbins, T. W. (1990). The case of frontostriatal dysfunction in schizophrenia. *Schizophrenia Bulletin, 16* (3): 391–402.

Roberts, R. E., Kaplan, G. A., Shema, S. J., & Strawbridge, W. J. (1997). Does growing old increase the risk for depression? *American Journal of Psychiatry, 154* (10): 1384–90.

Robertson, J. R., & Macleod, J. (1996). Methadone treatment: Methadone treatment is not the only option. *British Medical Journal, 313* (7070):1480–81.

Robertson, M., Trimble, M., & Lees, A. (1988). The psychopathology of Gilles de la Tourette syndrome. *British Journal of Psychiatry, 152,* 383–90.

Robins, E., & Guze, S. B. (1972). Classification of affective disorders: The primary-secondary, the endogenous-reactive, and the neurotic-psychotic concepts. In T. A. Williams, M. M. Katz, & J. A. Shields (Eds.), *Recent advances in the psychobiology of the depressive illnesses* (pp. 283–93). Washington, DC: U.S. Government Printing Office.

Robins, L. N. (1966). *Deviant children grow up.* Baltimore: Williams & Wilkins.

Robins, L. N. (1985). Epidemiology: Reflections on testing the validity of psychiatric interviews. *Archives of General Psychiatry, 42,* 918–24.

Robins, L. N. (1991). Conduct disorder. *Journal of Child Psychology and Psychiatry, 32,* 193–212.

Robins, L. N. (1999). A 70-year history of conduct disorder: Variations in definition, prevalence, and correlates. In P. Cohen, C. Slomkowski, & L. N. Robins (Eds.), *Historical and geographical influences on psychopathology* (pp. 37–56). Mahwah, NJ: Lawrence Erlbaum.

Robins, L. N., & Helzer, J. E. (1986). Diagnosis and clinical assessment: The current state of psychiatric diagnosis. *Annual Review of Psychology, 37,* 409–32.

Robins, L. N., Helzer, J. E., Hesselbrock, M., & Wish, E. D. (1977). Vietnam veterans three years after Vietnam: How our study changed our views of heroin. In L. Harris (Ed.), *Problems of drug dependence.* Richmond, VA: Committee on Problems of Drug Dependence.

Robins, L. N., Helzer, J. E., Weissman, M. M., Orvaschel, H., Gruenberg, E., Burke, J. D., & Regier, D. A. (1984). Lifetime prevalence of specific psychiatric disorders in three sites. *Archives of General Psychiatry, 41,* 949–58.

Robins, L. N., & Price, R. K. (1991). Adult disorders predicted by childhood conduct problems: Results from the NIMH Epidemiological Catchment Area project. *Psychiatry, 54,* 116–32.

Robinson, D. S., Davis, J., Nies, A., Ravaris, C., & Sylvester, D. (1971). Relation of sex in aging to monoamine oxidase activity in human brain, plasma, and platelets. *Archives of General Psychiatry, 24,* 536.

Robinson, D., Wu, H., Munne, R. A., Ashtari, M., Alvir, J. M. J., Lerner, G., Koreen, A., Cole, K., & Bogerts, B. (1995). Reduced caudate nucleus volume in obsessive-compulsive disorder. *Archives of General Psychiatry, 52* (5): 393–98.

Robinson, T. E., & Kolb, B. (1997) Persistent structural modifications in nucleus accumbens and prefrontal cortex neurons produced by previous experience with amphetamine. *Journal of Neuroscience, 17* (21): 8491–97.

Rodgers, W. M., & Brawley, L. R. (1996). The influence of outcome expectance and self-efficacy on the behavioral intentions of novice exercisers. *Journal of Applied Social Psychology, 26* (7): 618–34.

Rodnick, E. H., Goldstein, M. J., Lewis, J. M., & Doane, J. A. (1984). Parental communication style, affect, and role as precursors of offspring schizophrenia-spectrum disorders. In N. F. Watt, E. J. Anthony, L. C. Wynne, & J. E. Rolf (Eds.), *Children at risk for schizophrenia: A longitudinal perspective* (pp. 81–92). Cambridge: Cambridge University Press.

Rodriguez de Fonseca, F., Carrera, M. R. A., Navarro, M., Koob, G. F., & Weiss, F. (1997). Activation of corticotropin-releasing factor in the limbic system during cannabinoid withdrawal. *Science, 276,* 205–54.

Roe, B. B. (1999). *Why we should legalize drugs.* (The Schaffer Library of Drug Policy). http://druglibrary.org/schaffer/Misc/roe1.htm

Roediger, H., Weldon, M., & Challis, B. (1989). Explaining dissociations between implicit and explicit measures of retention: A processing account. In H. Roediger & F. Craik (Eds.), *Varieties of memory and consciousness: Essays in honor of Endel Tulvin,* (pp. 3–14). Hillsdale, NJ: Erlbaum.

Roeleveld, N., Zielhuis, G. A., & Gabreels, F. (1997). The prevalence of mental retardation: A critical review of recent literature. *Developmental Medical Child Neurology, 39,* 125–32.

Roff, J. D., & Knight, R. (1981). Family characteristics, childhood symptoms, and adult outcomes in schizophrenia. *Journal of Abnormal Psychology, 90,* 510–20.

Rogers, J., Siggins, G. R., Schulman, J. R., & Bloom, F. E. (1980). Physiological correlates of ethanol intoxication tolerance, and dependence in rat cerebellar Purkinje cells. *Brain Research, 196,* 183–98.

Rogers, M. P., Weinshenker, N. J., Warshaw, M. G., Goisman, R. M., Rodriguez-Villa, F. J., Fierman, E. J., & Keller, M. B. (1996). Prevalence of somatoform disorders in a large sample of patients with anxiety disorders. *Psychosomatics, 37*(1): 17–22.

Rogers, R., Johansen, J., Chang, J. J., & Salekin, R. T. (1997) Predictors of adolescent psychopathy: Oppositional and conduct-disordered symptoms. *Journal of the American Academy of Psychiatry and the Law, 25,* 261–71.

Roitman, S. E., Lees, B. S., Cornblatt, B. A., Bergman, A., Obuchowski, M., Mitropoulou, V., Keefe, R. S. E., Silverman, J. M., & Siever, L. J. (1997). Attentional functioning in schizotypal personality disorder. *American Journal of Psychiatry, 154,* 655–60.

Rolls, E. T. (1995). A theory of emotion and consciousness, and its application to understanding the neural basis of emotion. In M. Gazzaniga (Ed), *The cognitive neurosciences.* Cambridge, MA: MIT Press.

Romach, M. K., Glue, P., Kampman, K., Kaplan, H., Somer, G., Poole, S., Clarke, L., Coffin, V., Cornish, J., O'Brien, C., & Sellers, E. (1999) Attenuation of the euphoric effects of cocaine by the dopamine D1/D5 antagonist ecopipam (SCH 39166). *Archives of General Psychiatry, 56,* 1101–1106.

Romero, J., Garcia, L., Fernandez-Ruiz, J., Cebeira, M., & Ramos, J. A. (1995). Changes in rat brain cannabinoid binding sites after acute or chronic exposure to their endogenous agonist, anandamide, or to delta 9- tetrahydrocannabinol. *Pharmacology, Biochemistry and Behavior, 51* (4): 731–37.

Ronningstam, E. F. (Ed). (1998). *Disorders of narcissism: Diagnostic, clinical, and empirical implications* (pp. 375–413). Washington, DC: American Psychiatric Press.

Ronningstam, E. (1999). Narcissistic personality disorder. In T. Millon, P. Blaney, & R. Davis (Eds.), *Oxford textbook of psychopathology* (Vol. 4). New York: Oxford University Press.

Rooth, F. G., & Marks, I. M. (1974). Persistent exhibitionism: Short-term responses to aversion, self-regulation, and relaxation treatment. *Archives of Sexual Behavior, 3,* 227–48.

Roper, G., Rachman, S., & Marks, I. M. (1975). Passive and participant modeling in exposure treatment of obsessive compulsive neurotics. *Behaviour Research and Therapy, 13,* 271–79.

Rosen, A. J., Lockhart, J. J., Gants, E. S., & Westergaard, C. K. (1991). Maintenance of grip-induced muscle tension: A behavioral marker of schizophrenia. *Journal of Abnormal Psychology, 100,* 583–93.

Rosen, J. B., & Schulkin, J. (1998). From normal fear to pathological anxiety. *Psychological Review, 105* (2): 325–50.

Rosen, J. C., & Leitenberg, H. (1982). Bulimia nervosa: Treatment with exposure and response prevention. *Behavior Therapy, 13,* 117–24.

Rosen, R. C. (1996). Erectile dysfunction: The medicalization of male sexuality. *Clinical Psychology Review, 16* (6): 497–519.

Rosen, R. C. (1998). Sildenafil: Medical advance or media event? *Lancet, 351* (9116):1599–1600.

Rosen, R. C., & Leiblum, S. R. (1995). Treatment of sexual disorders in the 1990s: An integrated approach. *Journal of Consulting and Clinical Psychology, 63* (6): 877–90.

Rosenberg, D. R., & Keshavan, M. S. (1998). Toward a neurodevelopmental model of obsessive-compulsive disorder. *Biological Psychiatry, 43* (9): 623–40.

Rosenhan, D. L. (1973). On being sane in insane places. *Science, 179,* 250–58.

Rosenhan, D. L. (1975). The contextual nature of psychiatric diagnosis. *Journal of Abnormal Psychology, 84,* 462–74.

Rosenhan, D. L. (1983). Psychological abnormality and law. In C. J. Scheirer & B. L. Hammonds (Eds.), *Psychology and the law* (pp. 89–118). Washington, DC: American Psychological Association.

Rosenman, R. H., Brand, R. J., Jenkins, C. D., Friedman, M., Straus, R., & Wurm, M. (1975). Coronary heart disease in the Western Collaborative Group study: Final follow-up experience at eight-and-a-half years. *Journal of the American Medical Association, 233,* 872–77.

Rosenstein, L. D. (1998). Differential diagnosis of the major progressive dementias and depression in middle and late adulthood: A summary of the literature of the early 1990s. *Neuropsychology Review, 8,* 109–67.

Rosenstein, M. J., Milazzo-Sayre, L. J., & Manderscheid, R. W. (1990). Characteristics of persons using specialty inpatient, outpatient, and partial care programs in 1986. In R. W. Manderscheid & M. A. Sonnenschein (Eds.), *Mental health in the United States* (pp. 139–72). Washington, DC: U.S. Government Printing Office.

Rosenstein, M. J., Steadman, H. J., MacAskill, R. L., & Manderscheid, R. W. (1986). Legal status of admissions to three inpatient psychiatric settings, United States, 1980. *Mental Health Statistical Note No. 178,* October, 26.

Rosenthal, D. (1970a). Genetic research in the schizophrenic syndrome. In R. Cancro (Ed.), *The schizophrenic reactions* (pp. 245–58). New York: Brunner/Mazel.

Rosenthal, D. (1970b). *Genetic theory and abnormal behavior.* New York: McGraw-Hill.

Rosenthal, D. (1979). Was Thomas Wolfe a borderline? *Schizophrenia Bulletin, 5,* 87–94.

Rosenthal, N. E., Carpenter, C. J., James, S. P., Parry, B. L., Rogers, S. L. B., & Wehr, T. A. (1986). Seasonal affective disorder in children and adolescents. *American Journal of Psychiatry, 143,* 356–86.

Rosenthal, N. E., Moul, D. E., Hellekson, C. J., & Oren, D. A. (1993). A multicenter study of the light visor for seasonal affective disorder: No difference in efficacy found between two different intensities. *Neuropsychopharmacology, 8* (2): 151–60.

Rosenthal, N. E., Sack, D. A., Gillin, J. C., Lewy, A. J., Goodwin, F. K., Davenport, Y., Mueller, P. S., Newsome, D. A., & Wehr, T. A. (1984). Seasonal affective disorder: A description of the syndrome and preliminary findings with light therapy. *Archives of General Psychiatry, 41,* 72–80.

Rosenthal, P. A., & Rosenthal, S. (1984). Suicidal behavior by preschool children. American *Journal of Psychiatry, 141,* 520–25.

Rosenthal, T. L., & Bandura, A. (1979). Psychological modeling: Theory and practice. In A. Bergin & S. Garfield (Eds.), *Handbook of psychotherapy and behavior change.* New York: Wiley.

Rosler, A., & Witztum, E. (1998). Treatment of men with paraphilia with a long-acting analogue of gonadotropin-releasing hormone. *New England Journal of Medicine, 338* (7): 416–22.

Ross, C. A. (1991). Epidemiology of multiple personality disorder and dissociation. *Psychiatric Clinics of North America, 14,* 503–17.

Ross, C. A., Anderson, G., Fleisher, W. P., & Norton, G. R. (1991). The frequency of multiple personality disorder among psychiatric inpatients. *American Journal of Psychiatry, 148,* 1717–20.

Ross, C. A., Miller, S. D., Reagor, P., Bjornson, L., et al. (1990). Structured interview data on 102 cases of multiple personality disorder from four centers. *American Journal of Psychiatry, 147,* 596–601.

Ross, J. D., & Wirt, R. D. (1984). Childhood aggression and social adjustment as antecedents of delinquency. *Journal of Abnormal Child Psychology, 12*(1): 111–26.

Ross, L., Greene, D., & House, P. (1977). The false consensus phenomenon: An attributional bias in self perception and social perception processes. *Journal of Experimental Social Psychology, 13,* 279–301.

Rossi-Arnaud, C., Fagioli, S., & Ammassari-Teule, M. (1991). Spatial learning in two inbred strains of mice: Genotype dependent effect of amygdaloid and hippocampal lesions. *Behavioural Brain Research, 45* (1): 9–16.

Roth, L. (1954). *I'll cry tomorrow.* New York: Fell.

Rothbaum, B. O. (1997). A controlled study of eye movement desensitization and reprocessing in the treatment of posttraumatic stress disordered sexual assault victims. *Bulletin of the Menninger Clinic, 61* (3): 317–34.

Rothbaum, B. O., Foa, E., Riggs, D., Murdock, T., & Walsh, W. (1992). A prospective examination of post-traumatic stress disorder in rape victims. *Journal of Traumatic Stress, 5* (3): 455–75.

Rothbaum, B. O., Hodges, L., Alarcon, R., Ready, D., Shahar, F., Graap, K., Pair, J., Hebert, P., Gotz, D., Wills, B., & Baltzell, D. (1999). Virtual reality exposure therapy for PTSD Vietnam veterans: A case study. *Journal of Traumatic Stress, 12* (2): 263–71.

Rothbaum, B. O., Hodges, L. F., Kooper, R., Opdyke, D., Williford, J., & North, M. M. (*1995*). Effectiveness of virtual reality graded exposure in the treatment of acrophobia. *American Journal of Psychiatry, 152,* 626–28.

Rothbaum, B. O., Hodges, L., Watson, B.A., Kessler, G. D., & Opdyke, D. (1996). Virtual reality exposure therapy in the treatment of fear of flying: A case report. *Behaviour Research and Therapy, 34,* 477–81.

Rothbaum, B. O., Ninan, P. T., & Thomas, L. (1996). Sertraline in the treatment of rape victims with posttraumatic stress disorder. *Journal of Traumatic Stress, 9* (4): 865–71.

Rotter, J. B. (1966). Generalized expectancies for internal versus external control of reinforcement. *Psychological Monographs, 80* (1).

Rotton, J., Dubitsky, S. S., Milov, A., White, S. M. et al. (1997). Distress, elevated cortisol, cognitive deficits, and illness following a natural disaster. *Journal of Environmental Education, 17* (2), 85–98.

Roy, M. A., Neale, M. C., Pederson, N. L., Mathe, A. A., & Kendler, K. S. (1995). A twin study of generalized anxiety disorder and major depression. *Psychological Medicine, 25,* 1037–49.

Roy-Byrne, P., & Cowley, D. (1998). Pharmacological treatment of panic, generalized anxiety, and phobic disorders. In P. Nathan & J. Gorman (Eds.), *A guide to treatments that work.* New York: Oxford University Press.

Rozin, P. (1976). The psychobiological approach to human memory. In M. R. Rosenzweig & E. L. Bennett (Eds.), *Neural mechanisms of learning and memory* (pp. 3–46). Cambridge, MA: MIT Press.

Rubenstein, C. (1982, May). What's good. *Psychology Today, 16,* 62–72.

Rubin, R. T. (1982). Koro (Shook Yang): A culture-bound psychogenic syndrome. In. C. Friedman & R. Fauger (Eds), *Extraordinary disorders of human behavior.* (pp. 155–72). New York: Plenum.

Rubin, R., Villanueva-Meyer, J., Ananth, J., et al. (1992). Regional xenon 133 cerebral blood flow and cerebral technetium 99m HMPAO uptake in unmedicated patients with obsessive-compulsive disorder and matched normal control subjects. *Archives of General Psychiatry, 49,* 739–44.

Rubonis, A. V., & Bickman, L. (1991). Psychological impairment in the wake of disaster: The disaster-psychopathology relationship. *Psychological Bulletin, 109* (3): 384–99.

Rugg, M. D., Mark, R. E., Walla, P., Schloerscheidt, A.M., Birch, C. S., Allan, K. (1998). Dissociation of the neural correlates of implicit and explicit memory. *Nature, 392* (6676): 595–98.

Rush, A. J., & Weissenburger, J. E. (1994). Melancholic symptom features and DSM-IV. *American Journal of Psychiatry, 151* (4): 489–98.

Rush, H. A., Beck, A. T., Kovacs, M., & Hollon, S. (1977). Comparative efficacy of cognitive therapy and pharmacotherapy in the treatment of depressed outpatients. *Cognitive Research and Therapy, 1,* 17–37.

Ruskin, P. E., Reed, S., Kumar, R., Kling, M. A., Siegel, E., Rosen, M., & Hauser, P. (1998). Reliability and acceptability of psychiatric diagnosis via telecommunication and audiovisual technology. *Psychiatric Services, 49* (8): 1086–88.

Russek, L., King, S., Russek, S., & Russek, H. (1990). The Harvard mastery of stress study 35-year follow-up: Prognostic significance of patterns of psychophysiological arousal and adaptation. *Psychosomatic Medicine, 52,* 271–85.

Russell, W. R. (1959). *Brain, memory, learning: A neurologist's view.* Oxford, England: Oxford University Press.

Rutter, M. (1975). *Helping troubled children.* New York: Plenum.

Rutter, M. (1978). Prevalence and types of dyslexia. In A. L. Benton & D. Pearl, *Dyslexia: An appraisal of current knowledge.* New York: Oxford University Press.

Rutter, M. (1985). Family and school influence on behavioural development. *Journal of Child Psychology and Psychiatry, 26,* 349–68.

Rutter, M. (1989). Isle of Wight revisited: Twenty-five years of psychiatric epidemiology. *Journal of the American Academy of Child and Adolescent Psychiatry, 28* (5): 633–53.

Rutter, M. L. (1997). Nature-nurture integration: The example of antisocial behavior. *American Psychologist, 52* (4): 390–98.

Rutter, M., & Garmezy, N. (1983). Developmental psychopathology. In P. H. Mussen (Ed.), *Handbook of child psychology, Vol. 4: Socialization, personality, and social development.* New York: Wiley.

Rutter, M., Macdonald, H., Le Couteur, A., Harrington, R., Bolton, P., & Bailey, A. (1990). Genetic factors in child psychiatric disorders: II. Empirical findings. *Journal of Child Psychology and Psychiatry, 31* (1): 39–83.

Rutter, M., Quinton, D., & Hill, J. (1990). Adult outcome of institution-reared children: Males. In L. Robins & M. Rutter (Eds.), *Straight and devious pathways from childhood to adulthood* (pp. 135–57). New York: Cambridge University Press.

Saccuzzo, D. P., & Braff, D. L. (1986). Information processing abnormalities: Trait- and state-dependent components. *Schizophrenia Bulletin, 12* (3): 447–59.

Sachar, E. J., Kanter, S. S., Buie, D., Engle, R., & Mehlman, R. (1970). Psychoendocrinology of ego disintegration. *American Journal of Psychiatry, 126,* 1067–78.

Sachdev, P., & Hay, P. (1995). Does neurosurgery for obsessive-compulsive disorder produce personality change? *Journal of Nervous and Mental Disease, 183* (6): 408–13.

Sack, R., & De Fraites, E. (1977). Lithium and the treatment of mania. In J. Barchas, P. Berger, R. Ciaranello, & G. Elliot (Eds.), *Psychopharmacology.* New York: Oxford University Press.

Sack, W., Clarke, G., Him, C., & Dickason, D. (1993). A 6–year follow-up study of Cambodian refugee adolescents traumatized as children. *Journal of the American Academy of Child and Adolescent Psychiatry, 32,* 431–37.

Sackeim, H. A., Greenberg, M. S., Weiman, A. L., Gur, R. C., Hunger-Buhler, J. P., & Geschwind, N. (1982). Hemispheric asymmetry in the expression of positive and negative emotions: Neurological evidence. *Archives of Neurology, 39,* 210–18.

Sackeim, H. A., Nordlie, J. W., & Gur, R. C. (1979). A model of hysterical and hypnotic blindness: Cognitions, motivation and awareness. *Journal of Abnormal Psychology, 88,* 474–89.

Sackeim, H., Prudic, J., Devanand, D., et al. (1993). Effects of stimulus intensity and electrode placement on the efficacy and cognitive effects of electroconvulsive therapy. *New England Journal of Medicine, 328,* 839–46.

Sackeim, H., Prudic, J., Devanand, D., et al. (2000). A comparison of bilateral and right unilateral ECT. *Archives of General Psychiatry, 57,* 425–34.

Sackeim, H. A., & Rush, A. J. (1995, August). Melancholia and response to ECT [Letter to the editor]. *American Journal of Psychiatry,* p. 1243.

Sacks, O. W. (1995). *An anthropologist on Mars: Seven paradoxical tales.* New York: Knopf.

Sagvolden, T., & Sargeant, J. A. (1998). Attention deficit/hyperactivity disorder: From brain dysfunctions to behaviour. *Behavioural Brain Research, 94,* 1–10.

Sahakian, B., Jones, G., Levy, R., Gray, J., & Warburton, D. (1989). The effects of nicotine on attention, information processing, and short-term memory in patients with dementia of the Alzheimer type. *British Journal of Psychiatry, 154,* 797–800.

Saigh, P. A., Mroueh, M., Zimmerman, B. J., & Fairbank, J. A. (1996). Self-efficacy expectation among traumatized adolescents. *Behaviour Research and Therapy, 33*(6): 701–704.

Sakai, T. (1967). Clinico-genetic study on obsessive compulsive neurosis. *Bulletin of Osaka Medical School, Supplement XII,* 323–31.

Sakamoto, K., Kamo, T., Nakadaira, S., & Tamura, A. (1993). A nationwide survey of seasonal affective disorder at 53 outpatient university clinics in Japan. *Acta Psychiatrica Scandinavica, 87* (4): 258–65.

Sakheim, D. K., Barlow, D. H., Abrahamson, D. J., & Beck, J. G. (1987). Distinguishing between organogenic and psychogenic erectile dysfunction. *Behaviour Research and Therapy, 25,* 379–90.

Salamone, J. D., Kurth, P., McCullough, L. D., & Sokolowski, J. D. (1995). The effects of nucleus accumbens dopamine depletions on continuously reinforced operant responding: Contrasts with the effects of extinction. *Pharmacology, Biochemistry and Behavior, 50* (3): 437–43.

Salit, S. A., Kuhn, E. M., Hartz, A. J., Vu, J. M., & Mosso, A. L. (1998). Hospitalization costs associated with homelessness in New York City. *New England Journal of Medicine, 338,* 1734–40.

Salkovskis, P. M. (1985). Obsessional-compulsive problems: A cognitive-behavioural analysis. *Behaviour Research and Therapy, 23* (5): 571–83.

Salkovskis, P. M. (1999).Understanding and treating obsessive-compulsive disorder. *Behaviour Research and Therapy, 37* (Suppl 1): S29–S52.

Salkovskis, P. M., Clark, D. M., & Gelder, M. G. (1996). Cognition-behaviour links in the persistence of panic. *Behaviour Research and Therapy, 34* (5–6): 453–58.

Salkovskis, P. M., Forrester, E., & Richards, C. (1998). Cognitive-behavioural approach to understanding obsessional thinking. *British Journal of Psychiatry, 173* (Suppl 35): 53–63.

Salzman, C. (1993). Benzodiazepine treatment of panic and agoraphobic symptoms: Use, dependence, toxicity, abuse. *Journal of Psychiatric Research, 27,* 97–110.

Salzman, L., & Thaler, F. (1981). Obsessive-compulsive disorders: A review of the literature. *American Journal of Psychiatry, 138,* 286–96.

Sameroff, A. J., Seifer, R., & Barocas, R. (1983). Impact of parental psychopathology: Diagnosis, severity, or social status effects. *Infant Mental Health Journal, 4,* 236–49.

Sander, T., Ball, D., Murray, R., Patel, J., Samochowiec, J., Winterer, G., Rommelspacher, H., Schmidt, L. G., & Loh, E. (1999). Association analysis of sequence variants of the GABAapprox alpha6, beta2, and gamma2 gene cluster and alcohol dependence. *Alcoholism, Clinical and Experimental Research, 23,* 427–31.

Sandler, J., & Hazari, A. (1960). The "obsessional": On the psychological classification of obsessional character traits and symptoms. *British Journal of Medical Psychology, 33,* 113–22.

Sandler, R. S., Zorich, N. L., Filloon, T. G., Wiseman, H. B., Lietz, D. J., Brock, M. H., Royer, M. G., & Miday, R. K. (1999). Gastrointestinal symptoms in 3181 volunteers ingesting snack foods containing olestra or triglycerides. A 6-week randomized, placebo-controlled trial. *Annals of Internal Medicine, 130,* 253–61.

Sanguineti, V. R., Samuel, S. E., Schwartz, S. L., & Robeson, M. R. (1996). Retrospective study of 2200 involuntary psychiatric admissions and readmissions. *American Journal of Psychiatry, 153,* 392–96.

Sannibale, C., & Hall, W. (1998). An evaluation of Cloninger's typology of alcohol abuse. *Addiction, 93,* 1241–49.

Sapolsky, R. M. (1992). *Stress, the aging brain, and the mechanisms of neuron death.* Cambridge, MA: MIT Press.

Sapolsky, R. (1996). Why stress is bad for your brain. *Science, 273,* 949–50.

Sapolsky, R. M. (1998). *Why zebras don't get ulcers.* New York: Freeman.

Sapolsky, R. M., Romero, L. M., & Munck, A. U. (2000). How do glucocorticoids influence stress responses? Integrating permissive, suppressive, stimulatory, and preparative actions. *Endocrinological Review, 21,* 55–89.

Sargent, J. (1994). Brain-imaging studies of cognitive functions. Trends in *Neuroscience, 17,* 221–27.

Sartorius, N., Jablensky, A., Korten, A., Ernberg, G., Anker, M., Cooper, J. E., & Day, R. (1986). Early manifestations and first-contact incidence of schizophrenia in different cultures. *Psychological Medicine, 16,* 909–28.

Sarnyai, Z., & Kovacs, G. L. (1994). Role of oxytocin in the neuroadaptation to drugs of abuse. *Psychoneuroendocrinology, 19,* 85–117.

Sastry, P. S., Rao, K. S. (2000). Apoptosis and nervous system. *Journal of Neurochemistry, 74* (1).

Satcher, D. (1999). *Mental health: A report of the surgeon general.* http://www.mentalhealth.org/specials/surgeongeneralreport

Satterfield, J. H., Hoppe, C. & Schell, A. (1982). A prospective study of delinquency in 110 adolescent boys with attention deficit disorder and 88 normal adolescent boys. *American Journal of Psychiatry, 139,* 795–98.

Saugstad, L. F. (1989). Social class, marriage and fertility in schizophrenia. *Schizophrenia Bulletin, 15,* 9–43.

Saunders, A. M., Strittmatter, M. D., Schmechel, M. D., et al. (1993). Association of apolipoprotein E allele type 4 with late-onset familial and sporadic Alzheimer's disease. *Neurology, 43,* 1467–72.

Saunders, R. C., Kolachana, B. S., Bachevalier, J., & Weinberger, D. R.. (1998). Neonatal lesions of the medial temporal lobe disrupt prefrontal cortical regulation of striatal dopamine. *Nature, 393,* 169–71.

Saver, J. L., & Damasio, A. R. (1991). Preserved access and processing of social knowledge in a patient with acquired sociopathy due to ventromedial frontal damage. *Neuropsychologia, 29,* 1241–49.

Sawrey, W. L., Conger, J. J., & Turrell, E. S. (1956). An experimental investigation of the role of psychological factors in the production of gastric ulcers in rats. *Journal of Comparative and Physiological Psychology, 49,* 457–61.

Sawrey, W. L., & Weiss, J. D. (1956). An experimental method of producing gastric ulcers. *Journal of Comparative and Physiological Psychology, 49,* 269.

Saxena, S., Brody, A. L., Schwartz, J. M., & Baxter, L. R. (1998). Neuroimaging and frontal-subcortical circuitry in obsessive-compulsive disorder. *British Journal of Psychiatry, 173* (Suppl 35): 26–37.

Scardo, J. A., Ellings, J. M., & Newman, R. B. (1995). Prospective determination of chorionicity, amnionicity, and zygosity in twin gestations. *American Journal of Obstetrics and Gynecology, 173,* 1376–80.

Scarpa, A., & Raine, A. (1997). Biology of wickedness. *Psychiatric Annals, 27* (9): 624–29.

Scarr, S. (1975). Genetics and the development of intelligence. In F. D. Horowitz (Ed.), *Child development research* (Vol. 4). Chicago: University of Chicago Press.

Scazufca, M., & Kuipers, E. (1998). Stability of expressed emotion in relatives of those with schizophrenia and its relationship with burden of care and perception of patients' social functioning. *Psychological Medicine, 28,* 453–61.

Schacter, D. L. (1992). Priming and multiple memory systems: Perceptual mechanisms of implicit memory. *Journal of Cognitive Neuroscience, 4,* 244–56.

Schaefer, G., Thompson, J., Bodensteiner, J., & McConnell, J. M. (1996). Hypoplasia of the cerebellar vermis in neurogenetic syndromes. *Annals of Neurology, 39* (3): 382–85.

Schaeffer, L. F. (1959) The Rorschach Inkblot Test. In O. K. Buros (Ed.), *The fifth mental measurements yearbook* (pp. 285–89). Highland Park, NJ: Gryphon.

Schall, U., Schoen, A., Zerbin, D., Eggers, C., et. al. (1996). Event-related potentials during an auditory discrimination with prepulse inhibition in patients with schizophrenia, obsessive-compulsive disorder and healthy subjects. *International Journal of Neuroscience, 84,* 15–33.

Scheel, K. R. (2000) The empirical basis of dialectical behavior therapy: Summary, critique, and implications. *Clinical Psychology—Science and Practice, 7* (1): 68–86.

Scheff, T. J. (1966). *Being mentally ill: A sociological theory.* Chicago: Aldine.

Scheier, M. F., & Bridges, M. W. (1995). Person variables and health: Personality predispositions and acute psychological states as shared determinants for disease. *Psychosomatic Medicine, 57,* 255–68.

Schiavi, R. C., et al. (1984). Pituitary-gonadal function during sleep in men with erectile impotence and normal controls. *Psychosomatic Medicine, 46* (3): 239–54.

Schiavi, R. C., & Rehman, J. (1995). Sexuality and aging. *Urologic Clinics of North America, 22* (4): 711–26.

Schildkraut, J. J. (1965). The catecholamine hypothesis of affective disorders: A review of supporting evidence. *American Journal of Psychiatry, 122,* 509–22.

Schlager, D. (1995). Evolutionary perspectives on paranoid disorder. In M. J. Sedler (Ed.), *Delusional disorders* (Psychiatric Clinics of North America, Vol. 18; pp. 63–279). Philadelphia: Saunders.

Schleifer, S. J., Keller, S. E., Bartlett, J. A., Eckholdt, H. M., & Delaney, B. R. (1996). Immunity in young adults with major depressive disorder. *American Journal of Psychiatry, 153* (4): 477–82.

Schmale A., & Iker, H. (1966). The psychological setting of uterine cervical cancer. *Annals of the New York Academy of Sciences, 125,* 807–13.

Schmauk, F. J. (1970). Punishment, arousal, and avoidance learning in sociopaths. *Journal of Abnormal Psychology, 76,* 443–53.

Schneider, K. (1998). Toward a science of the heart: Romanticism and the revival of psychology. *American Psychologist, 53,* 277–89.

Schneider, M. (1992). The effect of mild stress during pregnancy on birth weight and neuromotor maturation in rhesus monkey infants. *Infant Behavior and Development, 15,* 389–403.

Schneier, F., Johnson, J., Hornig, C., et al. (1992). Social phobia: Comorbidity and morbidity in an epidemiologic sample. *Archives of General Psychiatry, 49,* 282–88.

Scholing, A., & Emmelkamp, P. M. G. (1996). Treatment of generalized social phobia: Results at long-term follow-up. *Behaviour Research and Therapy, 34* (5–6): 447–52.

Schopler, E., Mesibov, G. B., & Kunce, L. J. (Eds.). (1998). *Asperger syndrome or high-functioning autism?* New York: Plenum.

Schotte, D. E., & Stunkard, A. J. (1987). Bulimia vs. bulimic behaviors on a college campus. *Journal of the American Medical Association, 258,* 1213–15.

Schou, M. (1997). Forty years of lithium treatment. *Archives of General Psychiatry, 34,* 9–13.

Schreiber, F. R. (1974). *Sybil.* New York: Warner Books.

Schreibman, L. (1975). Effects of within-stimulus and extra-stimulus prompting on discrimination learning in autistic children. *Journal of Applied Behavioral Analysis, 8,* 91–112.

Schuckit, M. A. (1984). Subjective responses to alcohol in sons of alcoholics and controls. *Archives of General Psychiatry, 41,* 879–84.

Schuckit, M. A. (1987). Biological vulnerability to alcoholism. *Journal of Consulting and Clinical Psychology, 55,* 301–309.

Schuckit, M. A. (1994). Low level of response to alcohol as a predictor of future alcoholism. *American Journal of Psychiatry, 151,* 184–89.

Schuckit, M. A. (1998). Biological, psychological and environmental predictors of the alcoholism risk: A longitudinal study. *Journal of Studies on Alcohol, 59,* 485–94.

Schuckit, M. A., Mazzanti, C., Smith, T. L., Ahmed, U., Radel, M., Iwata, N., & Goldman, D. (1999). Selective genotyping for the role of 5-HT/2sub(A), 5-HT/2-sub(C), and GABA sub alpha/6 receptors and the serotonin transporter in the level of response to alcohol: A pilot study. *Biological Psychiatry, 45,* 647–51.

Schulberg, H., & Rush, A. J. (1994). Clinical practice guidelines for managing major depression in primary care practice. *American Psychologist, 49,* 34–41.

Schulkin, J., McEwen, B. S., & Gold, P. W. (1994). Allostasis, amygdala, and anticipatory angst. *Neuroscience and Biobehavioral Reviews, 18* (3): 385–96.

Schulman, P., Keith, D., & Seligman, M. (1993). Is optimism heritable? A study of twins. *Behaviour Research and Therapy, 6,* 569–74.

Schulsinger, F. (1972). Psychopathy, heredity and environment. *International Journal of Mental Health, 1,* 190–206.

Schulterbrand, J. G., & Raven, A. (Eds.). (1977). *Depression in childhood: Diagnosis, treatment, and conceptual models.* New York: Raven Press.

Schultes, R. E. (1987). Coca and other psychoactive plants: Magico-religious roles in primitive societies of the new world. In S. Fisher et al. (Eds.), *Cocaine: Clinical and biobehavioral aspects.* New York: Oxford University Press.

Schulz, S. C., Camlin, K. L., Berry, S. A., & Jesberger, J. A. (1999). Olanzapine safety and efficacy in patients with borderline personality disorder and comorbid dysthymia. *Biological Psychiatry, 46* (10): 1429–35.

Schuyler, D. (1974). The evaluation of the suicidal patient. In J. R. Novello (Ed.), *Practical handbook of psychiatry.* Springfield, IL: Charles C. Thomas.

Schwab, J. J., Bialow, M., Holzer, C. E., Brown, J. M., & Stevenson, B. E. (1967). Socio-cultural aspects of depression in medical inpatients. *Archives of General Psychiatry, 17,* 533–43.

Schwartz, B. (1984). *Psychology of learning and behavior* (2nd ed.). New York: Norton.

Schwartz, C. E., Snidman, N., & Kagan, J. (1999). Adolescent social anxiety as an outcome of inhibited temperament in childhood. *Journal of the American Academy of Child and Adolescent Psychiatry, 38* (8): 1008–15.

Schwartz, J. M. (1998). Neuroanatomical aspects of cognitive-behavioural therapy response in obsessive-compulsive disorder: An evolving perspective on brain and behaviour. *British Journal of Psychiatry, 173* (35): 38–44.

Schwartz, M. F., Baron, J., & Moscovitch, M. (1990). Symptomatology of Alzheimer-type dementia: Report on a survey-by-mail. In M. F. Schwartz (Ed.), *Modular deficits in Alzheimer-type dementia.* Cambridge, MA: MIT Press/Bradford.

Schwartz, M. F., & Masters, W. H. (1984). The Masters and Johnson treatment program for dissatisfied homosexual men. *American Journal of Psychiatry, 141* (2): 173–81.

Schwartz, R. C. (1998). Insight and illness in chronic schizophrenia. *Comprehensive Psychiatry, 39,* 249–54.

Schwartz, S., & Johnson J. H. (1985). *Psychopathology of childhood: A clinical-experimental approach.* New York: Pergamon.

Schwarz, T., Loewenstein, J., & Isenberg, K. E. (1995). Maintenance ECT: Indications and outcome. *Convulsive Therapy, 11* (1): 14–23.

Schweizer, E., Rickels, K., Csanalosi, I., & London, J. (1990). A placebo-controlled study of enciprazine in the treatment of generalized anxiety disorder. *Psychopharmacology Bulletin, 26,* 215–17.

Scovern, A. W., & Killman, P. R. (1980). Status of electroconvulsive therapy: Review of the outcome literature. *Psychological Bulletin, 87,* 260–303.

Scoville, W. B., & Milner, B. (1957). Loss of recent memory after bilateral hippocampal lesions. *Journal of Neurology, Neurosurgery and Psychiatry, 20,* 11–21.

Scull, A. (1981). Moral treatment reconsidered: Some sociological comments on an episode in the history of British psychiatry. In A. Scull (Ed.), *Madhouses, mad-doctors, and madmen: The social history of psychiatry in the Victorian era* (pp. 105–18). Philadelphia: University of Pennsylvania Press.

Searles, H. F. (1959). The effort to drive the other person crazy! An element in the aetiology and psychotherapy of schizophrenia. *British Journal of Medical Psychology, 32,* 1–18.

Sedney, M. (1987). Development of adrogyny: Parental influences. *Psychology of Women Quarterly, 11,* 321–26.

Seeck, M., Mainwaring, N., Ives, J., Blume, H., et al. (1993). Differential neural activity in the human temporal lobe evoked by faces of family members and friends. *Annals of Neurology, 34,* 369–75.

Sees, K. L., Delucchi, K. L., Masson, C., Rosen, A., Clark, H. W., Robillard, H., Banys, P., & Hall, S. M. (2000). Methadone maintenance versus 180-day psychosocially enriched detoxification for treatment of opioid dependence: A randomized controlled trial. *Journal of the American Medical Association, 283* (10): 1303–10.

Segal, S., Watson, M., Goldfinger, S., & Averbuck, D. (1988). Civil commitment in the psychiatric emergency room: II. Mental disorder indicators and three dangerousness criteria. *Archives of General Psychiatry, 45,* 753–58.

Segerstrom, S. C., Taylor, S. E., Kemeny, M. E., Reed, G. M., et al. (1996). Causal attributions predict rate of immune decline in HIV-seropositive gay men. *Health Psychology, 15*(6): 485–93.

Segraves, R., & Althof, S. (1998). Psychotherapy and pharmacotherapy of sexual dysfunctions. In P. Nathan & J. Gorman (Eds.), *A guide to treatments that work* (pp. 447–71). New York: Oxford University Press.

Seidman, S. N., & Rieder, R. O. (1994). A review of sexual behavior in the United States. *American Journal of Psychiatry, 151,* 330–41.

Seidman, S. N., & Walsh, B. T. (1999). Testosterone and depression in aging men. *American Journal of Geriatric Psychiatry, 7,* 18–33.

Seiffge-Krenke, I. (1993). Coping behavior in normal and clinical samples: More similarities than differences? *Journal of Adolescence, 16,* 285–303.

Self, D. W., & Nestler, E. J. (1998). Relapse to drug-seeking: Neural and molecular mechanisms. *Drug and Alcohol Dependence, 51,* 49–60.

Seligman, M. E. P. (1968). Chronic fear produced by unpredictable shock. *Journal of Comparative and Physiological Psychology, 66,* 402–11.

Seligman, M. E. P. (1970). On the generality of the laws of learning. *Psychological Review, 77,* 406–18.

Seligman, M. E. P. (1972). Learned helplessness. *Annual Review of Medicine, 23,* 207–412.

Seligman, M. E. P. (1975). *Helplessness: On depression, development, and death.* San Francisco: Freeman.

Seligman, M. E. P. (1991). *Learned optimism: The skill to conquer life's obstacles, large and small.* New York: Random House.

Seligman, M. E. P. (1994). *What you can change and what you can't: The ultimate guide to self-improvement.* New York: Knopf.

Seligman, M. (1995a). The effectiveness of psychotherapy: The *Consumer Reports* study. *American Psychologist, 50,* 965–74.

Seligman, M. E. P. (1995b). *The optimistic child.* New York: Houghton Mifflin.

Seligman, M. E. P. (1996). Science as an ally of practice. *American Psychologist, 51,* 1072–79.

Seligman, M. E. P. (1998). The president's address. *American Psychologist, 54,* 559–62.

Seligman, M. E. P., Abramson, L. Y., Semmel, A., & von Baeyer, C. (1979). Depressive attributional style. *Journal of Abnormal Psychology, 88,* 242–47.

Seligman, M. E. P., & Binik, Y. M. (1977). The safety signal hypothesis. In H. Davis & H. Hurwitz (Eds.), *Pavlovian operant interactions.* Hillsdale, NJ: Erlbaum.

Seligman, M. E. P., & Csikszentmihalyi, M. (2000). Positive psychology: An introduction. *American Psychologist, 1* (55): 5–14.

Seligman, M. E. P., & Johnston, J. C. (1973). A cognitive theory of avoidance learning. In F. J. McGuigan, & D. B. Lumsden (Eds.), *Contemporary approaches to conditioning and learning.* Washington, DC: Winston.

Seligman, M. E. P., & Maier, S. F. (1967). Failure to escape traumatic shock. *Journal of Experimental Psychology, 74,* 1–9.

Seligman, M., Reivich, K., Jaycox, L., & Gillham, J. (1995). *The optimistic child.* New York: Houghton Mifflin.

Seligman, M. E. P., Schulman, P., DeRubeis, R. J., & Hollon, S. D. (1999). The prevention of depression and anxiety. *Prevention and Treatment, 2.*

Seligman, M., & Yellin, A. (1987). What is a dream? *Behaviour Research and Therapy, 25,* 1–24.

Seltzer, B., Vasterling, J. J., & Buswell, A. (1995). Awareness of deficit in Alzheimer's disease: Association with psychiatric symptoms and other disease variables. *Journal of Clinical Geropsychology, 1,* 79–87.

Selye, H. (1956). *The stress of life.* New York: McGraw-Hill.

Selye, H. (1974). *Stress without distress.* New York: Harper Collins.

Selye, H. (1975). Confusion and controversy in the stress field. *Journal of Human Stress, 1,* 37–44.

Sensky, T., Turkington, D., Kingdon, D., Scott, J. L., Scott, J., Siddle, R., O'Carroll, M., & Barnes, T. R. E. (2000). A randomized controlled trial of cognitive-behavioral therapy for persistent symptoms in schizophrenia resistant to medication. *Archives of General Psychiatry, 57* (2): 165–72.

Serling, R. J. (1986). Curing a fear of flying. *US AIR,* 12–19.

Shaham, Y., & Stewart, J. (1995). Stress reinstates heroin-seeking in drug-free animals: An effect mimicking heroin, not withdrawal. *Psychopharmacology, 119,* 334–41.

Shaffer, D. (1976). Enuresis. In M. Rutter & L. Hersov (Eds.), *Child psychiatry: Modern approaches.* Oxford: Blackwell.

Shaffer, H. J., & Jones, S. B. (1985). *Quitting cocaine: The struggle against impulse.* Lexington, MA: Lexington Books.

Shalev, A. Y., Sahar, T., Freedman, S., Peri, T., Glick, N., Brandes, D., Orr, S. P., & Pitman, R. K. (1998). A prospective study of heart rate response following trauma and the subsequent development of posttraumatic stress disorder. *Archives of General Psychiatry, 55* (6): 553–59.

Shallice, T., & Burgess, P. W. (1991). Deficits in strategy applications following frontal-lobe damage in man. *Brain, 114,* 727–41.

Shanok, S. S., & Lewis, D. O. (1981). Medical histories of female delinquents. *Archives of General Psychiatry, 38,* 211–13.

Shapiro, D. (1965). *Neurotic styles.* New York: Basic Books.

Shapiro, D., & Shapiro, D. (1982). Meta-analysis of comparative therapy outcome studies: A replication and refinement. *Psychological Bulletin, 92,* 581–604.

Shapiro, F. (1995). *Eye Movement Desensitization and Reprocessing.* New York: Guilford Press.

Sharma, A. R., McGue, M. K., & Benson, P. L. (1996). The emotional and behavioral adjustment of United States adopted adolescents: Part II. Age at adoption. *Children and Youth Services Review, 18* (1–2): 101–14.

Sharma, R., & Markar, H. R. (1994). Mortality in affective disorder. *Journal of Affective Disorders, 31,* 91–96.

Shea, M. T., Elkin, I., Imber, S. D., & Sotsky, S. M. (1992). Course of depressive symptoms over follow-up: Findings about the National Institute of Mental Health Treatment of Depression Collaborative Research Program. *Archives of General Psychiatry, 49* (10): 782–87.

Sheitman, B., Kinon, B. J., Ridgway, B., & Liberman, J. A. (1998). Pharmacological treatments of schizophrenia. In P. Nathan & J. Gorman (Eds.), *A guide to treatments that work* (pp. 167–89). New York: Oxford University Press.

Shekelle, R. B., Gale, M., Ostfeld, A. M., & Paul, O. (1983). Hostility, risk of coronary heart disease, and mortality. *Psychosomatic Medicine, 45* (2): 109–14.

Shekelle, R. B., Hulley, S. B., Neaton, J. D., et al. (1985). The MRFIT behavior study. Type A behavior and incidence of coronary heart disease. *American Journal of Epidemiology, 122,* 559–70.

Sheldon, S. H. (1996). Sleep-related enuresis. *Child and Adolescent Psychiatric Clinics of North America, 5,* 661–72.

Sheline, Y. I., Sanghavi, M., Mintun, M. A., & Gado, M. H. (1999). Depression duration but not age predicts hippocampal volume loss in medically healthy women with recurrent major depression. *Journal of Neuroscience, 19,* 5034–43.

Sherer, M. A. (1988). Intravenous cocaine: Psychiatric effects, biological mechanisms. *Biological Psychiatry, 24,* 865–85.

Sherif, F. M., & Ahmed, S. S. (1995). Basic aspects of GABA-transaminase in neuropsychiatric disorders. *Clinical Biochemistry, 28* (2): 145–54.

Shermaan, D., McGue, M., & Iacono, W. (1997). Twin concordance for attention deficit hyperactivity disorder: A comparison of mothers and teachers reports. *American Journal of Psychiatry, 154,* 532–35.

Sherman, A. D., & Petty, F. (1980). Neurochemical basis of the action of antidepressants on learned helplessness. *Behavioral and Neurological Biology, 30,* 119–34.

Sherman, J. (1998). Effects of psychotherapeutic treatments for PTSD: A meta-analysis of controlled clinical trials. *Journal of Traumatic Stress, 11* (3): 413–35.

Shetty, N., Friedman, J. H., Kieburtz, K., Marshall, F. J., & Oakes, D. (1999). The placebo response in Parkinson's disease. Parkinson Study Group. *Clinical Neuropharmacology, 22,* 207–12.

Shimizu, M. (1992). Suicide and depression in late life. In M. Bergener, K. Hasegawa, S. I. Finkel, & T. Nishimura (Eds.), *Aging and mental disorders: International perspectives* (pp. 91–101). New York: Springer.

Shin, L. M., Kosslyn, S., McNally, R. J., Alpert, N. M., et al. (1997). Visual imagery and perception in posttraumatic stress disorder: A positron emission tomographic investigation. *Archives of General Psychiatry, 54* (3): 233–41.

Shin, R. (1997). Interaction of aluminum with paired helical filament tau is involved in neurofibriallary pathology of Alzheimer's disease. *Gerontology, 43* (Suppl 1): 16–23.

Shneidman, E. (1976). Suicide among the gifted. In E. S. Shneidman (Ed.), *Suicidology: Contemporary developments.* New York: Grune & Stratton.

Siegel, S., & Allan, L. G. (1998). Learning and homeostasis: Drug addiction and the McCollough effect. *Psychological Bulletin, 124,* 230–39.

Siegel-Itzkovich, J. (1998). Israel bans import of sildenafil citrate after six deaths in the U.S. *British Medical Journal, 316* (7145): 1625.

Siever, L. J. (1990a). Adoptive and family studies of schizophrenic probands suggest that genetic factors associated with schizophrenia are expressed as a spectrum of schizophrenia-related disorders, including schizotypal personality disorder and paranoid personality disorder. *Journal of Abnormal Psychology, 103* (1).

Siever, L. J. (1990b). Increased morbid risk for schizophrenia-related disorders in relatives of schizotypal personality disordered patients. *Archives of General Psychiatry, 47* (2): 634–40.

Siever, L., Bernstein, D., & Silverman, J. (1991). Schizotypal personality disorder: A review of its current status. *Journal of Personality Disorders, 5,* 178–93.

Siever, L. J., Bernstein, D. P., & Silverman, J. M. (1995). Schizotypal personality disorder. In W. J. Livesley (Ed.), *The DSM-IV personality disorders: Diagnosis and treatment of mental disorders* (pp. 71–90). New York: Guilford Press.

Sifneos, P. E. (1973). The prevalence of "alexithymic" characteristics in psychosomatic patients. *Psychotherapy and Psychosomatics, 22,* 255–62.

Sigman, M., Arbelle, S., & Dissanayake, C. (1995). Current research findings on childhood autism. *Canadian Journal of Psychiatry, 40* (6): 289–94.

Sigvardsson, S., von Knorring, A. L., Bohman, M., & Cloninger, C. R. (1984). An adoption study of somatoform disorders. I. The relationship of somatization to psychiatric disability. *Archives of General Psychiatry, 41,* 853–59.

Silberg, J. L., Pickles, A., Rutter, M., Hewitt, J., Simonoff, E., Maes, H., Carbonneau, R., Murrelle, L., Foley, D., & Eaves, L. (1999). The influence of genetic factors and life stress on depression among adolescent girls. *Archives of General Psychiatry, 56* (3): 225–32.

Silberstein, R. B., Farrow, M., Levy, F., Pipingas, A., Hay, D. A., & Jarman, F. C. (1998). Functional brain electrical activity mapping in boys with attention-deficit/hyperactivity disorder. *Archives of General Psychiatry, 55,* 1105–12.

Silberswieg, D. A., Stern, E., Frith, C., Cahill, C., et al. (1995). A functional neuroanatomy of hallucinations in schizophrenia. *Nature, 378,* 176–79.

Silk, K. R. (1996). Rational pharmacotherapy for patients with personality disorders. In P. S. Links (Ed), *Clinical assessment and management of severe personality disorders* (Clinical Practice, No. 35; pp. 109–42). Washington, DC: American Psychiatric Press.

Silverman, J. M., Zaccario, M. L., Smith, C. J., Schmeidler, J., Mohs, R. C., & Davis, K. L. (1994). Patterns of risk in first-degree relatives of patients with Alzheimer's disease. *Archives of General Psychiatry, 51,* 577–86.

Silverman, L. H. (1976). Psychoanalytic theory: The reports of my death are greatly exaggerated. *American Psychologist, 31* (9): 621–37.

Silverman, W., Kurtines, W., Ginsburg, G., et al. (1999). Treating anxiety disorders in children with group cognitive-behavioral therapy: A randomized clinical trial. *Journal of Consulting and Clinical Psychology, 67,* 995–1003.

Silverman, W. K., & Rabian, B. (1993). Simple phobias. *Child and Adolescent Psychiatric Clinics of North America, 2,* 603–23.

Silverstein, S. M., Matteson, S., & Knight, R. A. (1996). Reduced top-down influence in auditory perceptual organization in schizophrenia. *Journal of Abnormal Psychology, 105,* 663–67.

Simeon, D., Gross, S., Guralnik, O., et al. (1997). Thirty cases of DSM-III-R depersonalization disorder. *American Journal of Psychiatry, 154,* 11.

Simon, G. E., VonKorff, M., Piccinelli, M., Fullerton, C., & Ormel, J. (1999). An international study of the relation between somatic symptoms and depression. *New England Journal of Medicine, 341* (18): 1329–35.

Simon, N. M., Pollack, M. H., Tuby, K. S., & Stern, T. A. (1998). Dizziness and panic disorder: A review of the association between vestibular dysfunction and anxiety. *Annals of Clinical Psychiatry, 10,* 75–80.

Simonoff, E., Bolton, P., & Rutter, M. (1996) Mental retardation: Genetic findings, clinical implications and research agenda. *Journal of Child Psychology and Psychiatry, 37,* 259–80.

Simonoff, E., Pickles, A., Meyer, J. M., Silberg, J. L., Maes, H. H., Loeber, R., Rutter, M., Hewitt, J. K., & Eaves, L. J. (1997). The Virginia twin study of adolescent behavioral development: Influence of age, sex, and impairment on rates of disorder. *Archives of General Psychiatry, 54,* 801–808.

Sisoda, S. S., & Price, D. L. (1995). Role of the B-amyloid protein in Alzheimer's disease. *The PHASEB Journal, 9,* 366–70.

Skodol, A. E., Oldham, J. M., & Gallaher, P. E. (1999). Axis II comorbidity of substance use disorders among patients referred for treatment of personality disorders. *American Journal of Psychiatry, 156* (5): 733–38.

Skolnick, A. A. (1998). Protease inhibitors may reverse AIDS dementia. *Journal of American Medical Association, 279* (6): 419.

Slater, L. (1998). *Prozac diary.* New York: Random House.

Slutske, W. S., Heath, A. C., Dinwiddie, S. H., Madden, P. A., Bucholz, K. K., Dunne, M. P., Statham, D. J., & Martin, N.G. (1997). Modeling genetic and environmental influences in the etiology of conduct disorder. *Journal of Abnormal Psychology, 106,* 266–79.

Smith, C. A. (1998). Early detection of conduct disorder. *Journal of Paediatrics and Child Health, 34,* 101–103.

Smith, G. S., Reynolds, C. F., Pollock, B., Derbyshire, S., Nofzinger, E., Dew, M. A., Houck, P. R., Milko, D., Meltzer, C. C., & Kupfer, D. J. (1999). Cerebral glucose metabolic response to combined total sleep deprivation and antidepressant treatment in geriatric depression. *American Journal of Psychiatry, 156,* 683–89.

Smith, I. M., & Bryson, S. E. (1998). Gesture imitation in autism I: Nonsymbolic postures and sequences. *Cognitive Neuropsychology, 15,* 747–70.

Smith, J. C., Glass, G. V., & Miller, T. I. (1980). *The benefits of psychotherapy.* Baltimore: Johns Hopkins Press.

Smith, R. J. (1978). *The psychopath in society.* New York: Academic Press.

Smith, S. L., & Donnerstein, E. (1998). Harmful effects of exposure to media violence: Learning of aggression, emotional desensitization, and fear. In R. G. Geen & E. Donnerstein (Eds.), *Human aggression: Theories, research, and implications for social policy* (pp. 167–202). San Diego, CA: Academic Press.

Smith, T. (1999). Outcome of early intervention for children with autism. *Clinical Psychology—Science and Practice, 6,* 33–49.

Smith, T. E., Hull, J. W., & Santos, L. (1998). The relationship between symptoms and insight in schizophrenia: A longitudinal perspective. *Schizophrenia Research, 33,* 63–67.

Smythe, J. W., McCormick, C. M., Rochford, J., & Meaney, M. J. (1994). The interaction between prenatal stress and neonatal handling on nociceptive response latencies in male and female rats. *Physiology and Behavior, 55* (5): 971–74.

Snaith, P., Tarsh, M. J., & Reid, R. W. (1993). Sex reassignment surgery: A study of 141 Dutch transsexuals. *British Journal of Psychiatry, 162,* 681–85.

Snell, M. E. (1998). Characteristics of elementary school classrooms where children with moderate and severe disabilities are included: A compilation of findings. In S. J. Vitello & D. E. Mithaug (Eds.), *Inclusive schooling: National and international perspectives* (pp. 76–97). Mahwah, NJ: Lawrence Erlbaum.

Snowdon, D. A., Kemper, S. J., Mortimer, J. A., Greiner, L. H., Wekstein, D. R., & Markesbery, W. R. (1996). Linguistic ability in early life and cognitive function and Alzheimer's disease in late life. Findings from the Nun Study. *Journal of the American Medical Association, 275,* 528–32.

Snyder, K. S., Wallace, C. J., Moe, K., Ventura, J., et al. (1995). The relationship of residential care-home operators' expressed emotion and schizophrenic residents' symptoms and quality of life. *International Journal of Mental Health, 24,* 27–37.

Snyder, S. H. (1974a). Catecholamines as mediators of drug effects in schizophrenia. In F. O. Schmitt & F. G. Worden (Eds.), *The neurosciences: Third study program.* Cambridge, MA: MIT Press.

Snyder, S. H. (1974b). *Madness and the brain.* New York: McGraw-Hill.

Snyder, S. H. (1981). Dopamine receptors, neuroleptics and schizophrenia. *American Journal of Psychiatry, 138,* 460–64.

Snyder, S. H. (1986). *Drugs and the brain.* New York: Scientific American Library.

Snyder, S. H., Banerjee, S. P., Yamamura, H. I., & Greenberg, D. (1974). Neurotransmitters and schizophrenia. *Science, 184,* 1243–53.

Snyder, W. D., Simpson, D. M., Nielson, S., et al., (1983). Neurological complications of Acquired Immune Deficiency Syndrome: Analysis of 50 patients. *Annals of Neurology, 14,* 403–18.

Sokol, D. K., Moore, C. A., Rose, R. J., Williams, C. J., et al. (1995). Intrapair differences in personality and cognitive ability among young monozygotic twins distinguished by chorion type. *Behavior Genetics, 25,* 457–66.

Sokol, L., Beck, A. T., Greenberg, R. L., Wright, F. D., & Berchick, R. J. (1989). Cognitive therapy of panic disorder: A nonpharmacological alternative. *Journal of Nervous and Mental Diseases, 177* (12): 711–16.

Soloff, P. H. (1986). Progress in pharmacotherapy of borderline disorders: A double-blind study of amitriptyline, haloperidol, and placebo. *Archives of General Psychiatry, 43,* 691–97.

Soloff, P. H. (2000). Psychophamacology of borderline personality disorder. *Psychiatric Clinics of North America, 23* (1): 169–92.

Solomon, D. A., Keitner, G. I., Miller, I. W., Shea, M. T., & Keller, M. B. (1995). Course of illness and maintenance treatments for patients with bipolar disorder. *Journal of Clinical Psychiatry, 56* (1): 5–13.

Solomon, D., Keller, M., Leon, A., et al. (2000). Multiple recurrences of a major depressive disorder. *American Journal of Psychiatry, 157,* 229–33.

Solomon, R. L., & Corbit, J. D. (1974). An opponent process theory of motivation. *Psychological Reviews, 81* (2): 119–45.

Solomon, Z., Kotler, M., & Mikulincer, M. (1988). Combat-related post-traumatic stress disorder among second-generation Holocaust survivors: Preliminary findings. *American Journal of Psychiatry, 145,* 865–68.

Solomon, Z., Laor, N., Weiler, D., & Muller, U. (1993). The psychological impact of the Gulf War: A study of acute stress in Israeli evacuees. *Archives of General Psychiatry, 50,* 320–21.

Solomon, Z., Oppenheimer, B., Elizur, Y., & Waysman, M. (1990). Exposure to recurrent combat stress: Can successful coping in a second war heal combat-related PTSD from the past? *Journal of Anxiety Disorders, 4,* 141–45.

Songer, D. A., & Roman, B. (1996). Treatment of somatic delusional disorder with atypical antipsychotic agents. *American Journal of Psychiatry, 153* (4): 578–79.

Southard, D. R., Coates, T. J., Kolodner, K., Parker, F. C., Padgett, N. E., & Kennedy, H. L. (1986). Relationship between mood and blood pressure in the natural environment: An adolescent population. *Health Psychology, 5,* 469–80.

Sowell, E. R., Thompson, P. M., Holmes, C. J., Batth, R., Jernigan, T. L., & Toga A. W. (1999). Localizing age-related changes in brain structure between childhood and adolescence using statistical parametric mapping. *Neuroimage 9* (6 Pt 1): 587–97.

Spangler, D. L., Simons, A. D., Monroe, S. M., & Thase, M. E. (1997). Respond to cognitive-behavioral therapy in depression: Effects of pretreatment cognitive dysfunction and life stress. *Consulting and Clinical Psychology, 65* (4): 568–75.

Spangler, W. D. (1992). Validity of questionnaire and TAT measures of need for achievement: Two meta-analyses. *Psychological Bulletin, 112* (1): 140–54.

Spark, R. F., White, R. A., & Connelly, P. B. (1980). Impotence is not always psychogenic. *Journal of the American Medical Association, 243,* 750–55.

Sparrow, S. S., Balla, D. A., & Cicchetti, D. V. (1984). *Vineland adaptive behavior scales.* Circle Pines, MN: American Guidance Service.

Spaulding, W., Reed, D., Storzbach, D., Sullivan, M., Weiler, M., & Richardson, C. (1998). The effects of a remediational approach to cognitive therapy for schizophrenia. In T. Wykes & N. Tarrier (Eds.), *Outcome and innovation in psychological treatment of schizophrenia* (pp. 145–60). Chichester, England: Wiley.

Speckens, A. E. M., Hengeveld, M. W., Lycklama a Nijeholt, G., Van Hemert, A. M., & Hawton, K. E. (1995). Psychosexual functioning of partners of men with presumed nonorganic erectile dysfunction: Cause or consequence of the disorder? *Archives of Sexual Behavior, 24* (2): 157–72.

Spiegel, D. (1984). Multiple personality as a post-traumatic stress disorder. *Psychiatric Clinics of North America, 7,* 101–10.

Spiegel, D. (1990). Dissociating dissociation: A commentary on Dr. Garcia's article. *Dissociation: Progress in the Dissociative Disorders, 3,* 214–15.

Spiegel, D., Bloom, J., Kraemer, H., & Gottheil, E. (1989). Effect of psychosocial treatment on survival of patients with metastatic breast cancer. *Lancet,* October 14, pp. 888–91.

Spiegel, D., & Cardena, E. (1991). Disintegrated experience: The dissociative disorders revisited. *Journal of Abnormal Psychology, 100,* 366–78.

Spiegel, R. (1989). *Psychopharmacology* (2nd ed.). New York: Wiley.

Spiletz, D. M., O'Neill, G. P., Favreau, L., Dufresne, C., Gallant, M., Gareau, Y., Guay, D., Labelle, M., & Metters, K. M. (1995). Activation of the human peripheral cannabinoid receptor results in inhibition of adenylyl cyclase. *Molecular Pharmacology, 48,* 352–61.

Spira, A., Bajos, N., Bejin, A., Beltzer, N., Bozon, M., Ducot, M., Durandeau, A., Ferrand, A., Giami, A., Gilloire, A., Giraud, M., Leridon, H., Messiah, A., Ludwig, D., Moatti, J., Mounnier, L., Olomucki, H., Poplavsky, J., Riadney, B., Spencer, B., Sztalryd, J., & Touzard, H. (1992). AIDS and sexual behavior in France. *Nature, 360,* 407–409.

Spitz, R. A. (1946). Anaclitic depression. *Psychoanalytic Study of the Child, 2,* 313–47.

Spitzer, R. L. (1975). On pseudoscience in science, logic in remission and psychiatric diagnosis: A critique of Rosenhan's "On being sane in insane places." *Journal of Abnormal Psychology, 84,* 442–52.

Spitzer, R. L. (1991). An outsider-insider's views about revising the DSMs. *Journal of Abnormal Psychology, 100* (3): 294–96.

Spitzer, R. L., & Fleiss, J. L. (1974). A reanalysis of the reliability of psychiatric diagnosis. *British Journal of Psychiatry, 125,* 341–47.

Spitzer, R., Gibbon, M., Skodol, A., Williams, J., & First, M. (1989). *DSM-III-R case book.* Washington, DC: American Psychiatric Press.

Spoont, M. (1992). Modulatory role of serotonin in information processing: Implications for human psychopathology. *Psychological Bulletin, 112,* 330–50.

Spring, B., & Ravdin, L. (1992). Cognitive remediation in schizophrenia: Should we attempt it? *Schizophrenia Bulletin, 18,* 15–18.

Squire, L. R. (1986). Memory functions as affected by electroconvulsive therapy. *Annals of the New York Academy of Sciences, 462,* 307–14.

Squire, L. R., (1987). *Memory and brain.* New York: Oxford University Press.

Squire, L. R. (1992). Memory and the hippocampus: A synthesis from findings with rats, monkeys, and humans. *Psychological Review, 79,* 195–231.

Squire, L. R., & Butters, N. (Eds.). (1992). *The neuropsychology of memory* (2nd ed.). New York: Guilford Press.

Srole, L., Langner, T. S., Michael, S. T., Opler, M. K., & Rennie, T. A. (1962). *Mental health in the metropolis: The midtown Manhattan study.* New York: McGraw-Hill.

Staats, A. W. (1978). *Child learning intelligence and personality* (rev. ed.). Kalamazoo, MI: Behaviordela.

Stampfl, T. G., & Levis, D. J. (1967). Essentials of implosive therapy: A learning-theory-based psychodynamic behavioral therapy. *Journal of Abnormal Psychology, 72,* 496–503.

Stangl, D., Pfohl, B., Zimmerman, M., Bowers, W., & Corenthal, R. (1985). A structured interview for the DSM-III personality disorders: A preliminary report. *Archives of General Psychiatry, 42,* 591–96.

Stanley, M. A., & Averill, P. M. (1999). Strategies for treating generalized anxiety in the elderly. In M. Duffy (Ed.), *Handbook of counseling and psychotherapy with older adults.* New York: Wiley.

Stapleton, J. A., Russell, M. A. H., Feyerabend, C., Wiseman, S., Gustavsson, G., Sawe, U., & Wiseman, D. (1995). Dose effects and predictors of outcome in a randomized trial of transdermal nicotine patches in general practice. *Addiction, 90,* 31–42.

Stark, K. D. (1990). *Childhood depression: School-based intervention.* New York: Guilford Press.

Statistical Abstract of the United States. (1993). Washington, DC: U.S. Dept. of Commerce, Economics and Statistics Administration, Bureau of the Census, Data User Services Division, 1993–1998.

Steadman, H. J. (1973). Follow-up on Baxstrom patients returned to hospitals for the criminally insane. *American Journal of Psychiatry, 3,* 317–19.

Steadman, H. J. (1981). The statistical prediction of violent behavior: Measuring the costs of a public protectionist versus a civil libertarian model. *Law and Human Behavior, 5,* 263–74.

Steadman, H. J., & Keveles, G. (1972). The community adjustment and criminal activity of the Baxstrom patients: 1966–1970. *American Journal of Psychiatry, 129,* 304–10.

Steadman, H., & Keveles, C. (1978). The community adjustment and criminal activity of Baxstrom patients. *American Journal of Psychiatry, 135,* 1218–20.

Steadman, H. J., McGreevy, M. A., Morrissey, J. P., Callahan, L. A., Robbins, P. C., & Cirincione, C. (1993). *Before and after Hinckley: Evaluating insanity defense reform.* New York: Guilford Press.

Steadman, H. J., Monahan, J., Hartstone, E., Davis, S. K., & Robbins, P. C. (1982). Mentally disordered offenders: A national survey of patients and facilities. *Law and Human Behavior, 8* (1): 31–37.

Steffens, D. C., Helms, M. J., Krishnan, K. R., & Burke, G. L. (1999). Cerebrovascular disease and depression symptoms in the cardiovascular health study. *Stroke, 30* (10): 2159–66.

Stein, D. G. (2000). Brain injury and theories of recovery. In A. L. Christensen & B. P. Uzzell (Eds.), International handbook of neuropsychological rehabilitation. *Critical issues in neuropsychology* (pp. 9–32). New York: Kluwer Academic/Plenum Publishers.

Stein, D. J., Hollander, E., Anthony, D. T., Schneier, F. R., Fallon, B. A., Liebowitz, M. R., & Klein, D. F. (1992). Serotonergic medications for sexual obsessions, sexual addictions, and paraphilias. *Journal of Clinical Psychiatry, 53* (8): 267–71.

Stein, E. A., Pankiewicz, J., Harsch, H. H., Cho, J., Fuller, S. A., Hoffman, R. G., Hawkins, M., Rao, S. M., Bandettini, P. A., & Bloom, A. S. (1998). Nicotine-induced limbic cortical activation in the human brain: A functional MRI study. *American Journal of Psychiatry, 155,* 1009–15.

Stein, J. A., Golding, J. M., Siegel, J. M., Burnam, M. A., Sorenson, S. B., & Powell, G. J. (1988). Long-term psychological sequelae of child sexual abuse: The Los Angeles epidemiologic catchment area study. In G. E. Wyatt (Ed.), *Lasting effects of child sexual abuse.* Newbury Park, CA: Sage.

Stein, M. B. (1998). Neurobiological perspectives on social phobia: From affiliation to zoology. *Biological Psychiatry, 44,* 1277–85.

Stein, M. (1999). Viagra and cluster headache. *Headache, 39,* 58–59.

Stein, M. B., Koverola, C., Hanna, C., Torchia, M. G., et al. (1997). Hippocampal volume in women victimized by childhood sexual abuse. *Psychological Medicine, 27,* 951–59.

Stein, M. B., Liebowitz, M. R., Lydiard, R. B., Pitts, C. D., Bushnell, W., & Gergel, I. (1998). Paroxetine treatment of generalized social phobia (social anxiety disorder): A randomized controlled trial. *Journal of the American Medical Association, 280* (8): 708–13.

Steinberg, L. (1986). Stability and instability of Type A behavior from childhood to young adulthood. *Developmental Psychology, 22,* 393–401.

Steinberg, M., Rounsaville, B., & Cicchetti, D. V. (1990). The structured clinical interview for DSM-III-R dissociative disorders: Preliminary report on a new diagnostic instrument. *American Journal of Psychiatry, 147,* 76–82.

Steketee, G., Eisen, J., Dyck, I., Warshaw, M., & Rasmussen, S. (1999). Predictors of course in obsessive-compulsive disorder. *Psychiatry Research, 89,* 229–38.

Steptoe, A., Roy, M. P., Evans, O., & Snashall, D. (1995). Cardiovascular stress reactivity and job strain as determinants of ambulatory blood pressure at work. *Journal of Hypertension, 13* (2): 201–10.

Stern, D. (1985). *The interpersonal world of the infant.* New York: Basic Books.

Stern, J. (1981). Brain dysfunction in some hereditary disorders of amino acid metabolism. In P. J. Mittler, & J. M. deJong (Eds.), *Frontiers of knowledge in mental retardation: Vol II. Biomedical aspects.* Baltimore, MD: University Park Press.

Stevens, A. A., Goldman-Rakic, P. S., Gore, J. C., Fulbright, R. K., & Wexler, B. E. (1998). Cortical dysfunction in schizophrenia during auditory word and tone working memory demonstrated by functional magnetic resonance imaging. *Archives of General Psychiatry, 55,* 1097–1103.

St. George-Hyslop, P., et al., (1987). The genetic defect causing familial Alzheimer's disease maps on chromosome 21. *Science, 235,* 885–90.

St. George-Hyslop, P., Haines, J., Rogaev, E., et al. (1992). Genetic evidence for a novel familial Alzheimer's disease locus on chromosome 14. *Nature Genetics, 2,* 330–34.

Stice, E. (1994). Review of the evidence for a sociocultural model of bulimia nervosa and an exploration of the mechanisms of action. *Clinical Psychology Review, 14* (7): 633–61.

Stinnett, J. (1978). Personal communication.

Stinus, L. (1995). Neurobiological aspects of opiate tolerance and dependence. In C. N. Stefanis, H. Hippius, et al. (Eds.), *Research in addiction: An update* (Psychiatry in Progress Series, Vol. 2; pp. 1–21). Goettingen, Germany: Hogrefe and Huber.

Stip, E. (2000). Novel antipsychotics: Issues and controversies. Typicality of atypical antipsychotics. *Journal of Psychiatry and Neuroscience, 25,* 137–53.

Stirling, J. D., Hellewell, J. S. E., & Hewitt, J. (1997). Verbal memory impairment in schizophrenia: No sparing of short-term recall. *Schizophrenia Research, 25,* 85–95.

Stoeber, G., Franzek, E., & Beckmann, H. (1997). Maternal infectious illness and schizophrenia. *American Journal of Psychiatry, 154,* 292–93.

Stoff, D. M., Breiling, J., & Maser, J. D. (1997). *Handbook of antisocial behavior.* New York: Wiley.

Stoller, R. J. (1969). Parental influences in male transsexualism. In R. Green & J. Money (Eds.), *Transsexualism and sex reassignment.* Baltimore: Johns Hopkins Press.

Stoller, R. J. (1976). *Sexual gender—the transsexual experiment* (Vol. II). New York: Jason Aronson.

Stone, A. A. (1975). *Mental health and law: A system in transition.* Rockville, MD.: National Institute of Mental Health, Center for Studies of Crime and Delinquency.

Stone, A. A., Neale, J. M., Cox, D. S., Napoli, A., Valdimarsdottir, H., & Kennedy-Moore, E. (1994). Daily events are associated with a secretory immune response to an oral antigen in men. *Health Psychology, 13* (5): 440–46.

Stone, D. M., Merchant, K. M., Hanson, G. R., & Gibb, J. W. (1987). Immediate and long-term effects of 3, 4-methylenedioxymethamphetamine (MDMA) on serotonin pathways in brain of rat. *Neuropharmacology, 26,* 1677–83.

Stone, M. H. (1990). Abuse and abusiveness in borderline personality disorder. In P. S. Links (Ed.), *Family environment and borderline personality disorder* (pp. 131–48). Washington, DC: American Psychiatric Press.

Storms, M. D. (1981). A theory of erotic orientation development. *Psychological Review, 88,* 340–53.

Strang, J., Finch, E., Hankinson, L., Farrell, M., Taylor, C., & Gossop, M. (1997). Methadone treatment for opiate addiction: Benefits in the first month. *Addiction Research, 5,* 71–76.

Straus, M. A., & Mouradian, V. E. (1998). Impulsive corporal punishment by mothers and antisocial behavior and impulsiveness of children. *Behavioral Sciences and the Law, 16,* 353–74.

Strauss, M. E., Foreman, W. C., & Parwatikar, S. D. (1974). Schizophrenics' size estimations of thematic stimuli. *Journal of Abnormal Psychology, 83* (2): 117–23.

Streeter, C. C., van Reekum, R., Shorr, R. I., Bachman, D. L., et al. (1995). Prior head injury in male veterans with borderline personality disorder. *Journal of Nervous and Mental Disease, 183,* 577–81.

Streissguth, A. P., Grant, T. M., & Barr, H. M. (1991). Cocaine and the use of alcohol and other drugs during pregnancy. *American Journal of Obstetrics and Gynecology, 164,* 1239–43.

Streissguth, A., & Kanter, J. (Eds.). (1997). *The challenge of fetal alcohol syndrome: Overcoming secondary disabilities.* Seattle, WA: University of Washington Press.

Stroehle, A., Poettig, M., Barden, N., Holsboer, F., & Montkowski, A. (1998). Age- and stimulus-dependent changes in anxiety-related behaviour of transgenic mice with GR dysfunction. *Neuroreport: An International Journal for the Rapid Communication of Research in Neuroscience, 9,* 2099–2102.

Stueve, A., Dohrenwend, B. P., & Skodol, A. E. (1998). Relationships between stressful life events and episodes of major depression and nonaffective psychotic disorders: Selected results from a New York risk factor study. In B. P. Dohrenwend et al. (Eds.), *Adversity, stress, and psychopathology* (pp. 341–57). New York: Oxford University Press.

Stunkard, A. J. (1976). Anorexia nervosa. In J. P. Sanford (Ed.), *The science and practice of clinical medicine* (pp. 361–63). New York: Grune & Stratton.

Sturdevant, R. A. L. (1976). Epidemiology of peptic ulcer: Report of a conference. *American Journal of Epidemiology, 104,* 9–14.

Sturgis, E.T., & Gramling, S.E. (1998). Psychophysiological assessment. In A. S. Bellack & M. Hersen (Eds.), *Behavioral assessment: A practical handbook* (4th ed.; pp. 126–57). Boston, MA: Allyn & Bacon.

Suarez, J. M., & Pittluck, A. T. (1976). Global amnesia: Organic and functional considerations. *Bulletin of the American Academy of Psychiatric Law, 3,* 17–24.

Suddath, R. L., Christison, M. D., Torrey, E. F., Casanova, M., & Weinberger, D. R. (1990). Anatomic abnormalities in the brains of monozygotic twins discordant for schizophrenia. *New England Journal of Medicine, 322,* 789–94.

Sullivan, P. F., Bulik, C. M., & Kendler, K. S. (1998). The epidemiology and classification of bulimia nervosa. *Psychological Medicine, 28,* 599–610.

Sullivan, P. M., & Burley, S. K. (1990). Mental testing of the hearing-impaired child. In C. R. Reynolds & R. W. Kamphaus (Eds.), *Handbook of psychological and emotional assessment of children.* New York: Guilford Press.

Suls, J., Wan, C. K., & Costa, P. T. (1995). Relationship of trait anger to resting blood pressure: A meta-analysis. *Health Psychology, 14* (5): 444–56.

Summerville, M. B., Kaslow, N. J., & Doepke, K. J. (1996). Psychopathology and cognitive and family functioning in suicidal African-American adolescents. *Current Directions in Psychological Science, 5* (1): 7–11.

Susser, M. (1967). Causes of peptic ulcer: A selective epidemiological review. *Journal of Chronic Disabilities, 20,* 435–56.

Suzdak, P. P., Schwartz, R. D., Skolnick, P., & Paul, S. M. (1986). Ethanol stimulates gamma-aminobutyric acid receptor-mediated chloride transport in rat brain synaptoneurosomes. *Proceedings of National Academy of Sciences, U. S. A., 83,* 4071–75.

Svebak, S., Cameron, A., & Levander, S. (1990). Clonazepam and imipramine in the treatment of panic attacks. *Journal of Clinical Psychiatry, 51,* 14–17.

Svrakic, N. M., Svrakic, D. M., & Cloninger, C. R. (1996). A general quantitative theory of personality development: Fundamentals of a self-organizing psychobiological complex. *Development and Psychopathology, 8,* 247–72.

Swaab, D. F., & Hofman, M. A. (1995). Sexual differentiation of the human hypothalamus in relation to gender and sexual orientation. *Trends in Neuroscience, 18* (6): 264–70.

Swaab, D. F., Gooren, L. J., & Hofman, M. A. (1995). Brain research, gender and sexual orientation. *Journal of Homosexuality, 28* (3–4): 283–301.

Swan, N. (1997). Gender affects relationships between drug abuse and psychiatric disorders. *NIDA Research Advances, 12* (4): 22–23.

Swanson, W. C., & Breed, W. (1976). Black suicide in New Orleans. In E. S. Shneidman (Ed.), *Suicidology: Contemporary developments.* New York: Grune & Stratton.

Swartz, J. R. (1999). Dopamine projections and frontal systems function. In B. L. Miller & J. L. Cummings (Eds.), *The human frontal lobes: Functions and disorders* (Science and Practice of Neuropsychology Series; pp. 159–73). New York: Guilford Press.

Swartz, M., Blazer, D., George, L., & Winfield, I. (1990). Estimating the prevalence of borderline personality disorder in the community. *Journal of Personality Disorders, 4,* 257–72.

Swartz, M. S., Swanson, J. W., Hiday, V. A., Borum, R., Wagner, H. R., & Burns, B. J. (1998). Violence and severe mental illness: The effects of substance abuse and nonadherence to medication. *American Journal of Psychiatry, 155,* 226–31.

Swedo, S. E. (1994). Sydenham's Chorea: A model for childhood autoimmune neuropsychiatric disorders. *Journal of the American Medical Association, 272* (22): 1788–91.

Swedo, S. E., & Kiessling, L. S. (1994). Speculations on antineuronal antibody-mediated neuropsychiatric disorders of childhood. *Pediatrics, 93* (2): 323–26.

Swedo, S. E., Leonard, H. L., Garvey, M., Mittleman, B., Allen, A. J., Perlmutter, S., Lougee, L., Dow, S., Zamkoff, J., & Dubbert, B. K. (1998). Pediatric autoimmune neuropsychiatric disorders associated with streptococcal infections: Clinical description of the first 50 cases. *American Journal of Psychiatry, 155,* 264–71.

Swedo, S. E., Leonard, H. L., Schapiro, M. B., Casey, B. J., Mannheim, G. B., Lenane, M. C., & Rettew, D. C. (1993). Sydenham's Chorea: Physical and psychological symptoms of St. Vitus Dance. *Pediatrics, 91* (4): 706–13.

Swedo, S., Pietrini, P., Leonard, H., et al. (1992). Cerebral glucose metabolism in childhood-onset obsessive-compulsive disorder. *Archives of General Psychiatry, 49,* 690–94.

Swedo, S. E., Rapoport, J. L., Cheslow, D. L., Leonard, H. L., Ayoub, E. M., Hosier, D. M., & Wald, E. R. (1989). High prevalence of obsessive-compulsive symptoms in patients with Sydenham's Chorea. *American Journal of Psychiatry, 146* (2): 246–49.

Sweeney, J. A., Haas, G. L., & Li, S. (1992). Neuropsychological and eye movement abnormalities in first-episode and chronic schizophrenia. *Schizophrenia Bulletin, 18* (2): 283–93.

Swerdlow, N. R., Bakshi, V., Waikar, M., Taaid, N., & Geyer, M. A. (1998). Seroquel, clozapine and chlorpromazine restore sensorimotor gating in ketamine-treated rats. *Psychopharmacology, 140,* 75–80.

Swerdlow, N. R., & Geyer, M. A. (1998). Using an animal model of deficient sensorimotor gating to study the pathophysiology and new treatments of schizophrenia. *Schizophrenia Bulletin, 24,* 285–301.

Swinson, R., Antony, M., Rachman, S., & Richter, M. (1998). *Obsessive-compulsive disorder: Theory, research, and treatment.* New York: Guilford Press.

Szasz, T. S. (1963). *Law, liberty and psychiatry: An inquiry into the social uses of mental health practices.* New York: Macmillan.

Szasz, T. S. (1970). *The manufacture of madness.* New York: Dell.

Szasz, T. S. (1974). The ethics of suicide. *Bulletin of suicidology* (Vol. 9). Philadelphia: Charles Press.

Szasz, T. (1994). *Cruel compassion: Psychiatric control of society's unwanted.* New York: Wiley.

Szasz, T. (1998). Parity for mental illness, disparity for the mental patient. *Lancet, 352,* 1213–15.

Szatmari, P., Bartolucci, G., Bremner, R., Bond, S., et al. (1989). A follow-up study of high-functioning autistic children. *Journal of Autism and Developmental Disorders, 19,* 213–25.

Tagiuri, R., Bruner, J. S., & Blake, R. R. (1958). On the relation between feelings and the perception of feelings among members of small groups. In E. E. Maccoby, T. M. Newcomb, & E. L. Hartley (Eds.), *Readings in social psychology* (pp. 110–16). New York: Holt, Rinehart & Winston.

Talovic, S. A., Mednick, S. A., Schulsinger, F., & Falloon, I. R. H. (1981). Schizophrenia in high-risk subjects: Prognostic maternal characteristics. *Journal of Abnormal Psychology, 89,* 501–504.

Tamerin, J. S., & Mendelson, J. (1970). Alcoholic's expectancies and recall of experiences during intoxication. *American Journal of Psychiatry, 126,* 1697–1704.

Tamminga, C. A., Holcomb, H. H., Gao, X., & Lahti, A. C. (1995). Glutamate pharmacology and the treatment of schizophrenia: Current status and future directions. *International Clinical Psychopharmacology, 10* (Supp. 3): 29–37.

Tanda, G., Pontieri, F. E., & Di Chiara, G. (1997). Cannabinoid and heroin activation of mesolimbic dopamine transmission by a common opioid receptor mechanism. *Science, 276,* 2048–50.

Tang, T. Z., & DeRubeis, R. J. (1999). Sudden gains and critical sessions in cognitive-behavioral therapy for depression. *Journal of Consulting and Clinical Psychology, 67* (6): 894–904.

Tang, Y., Shimizu, E., Dube, G. R., Rampon, C., Kerchner, G. A., Zhuo, M., Liu, G., & Tsien, J. Z. (1999). Genetic enhancement of learning and memory in mice. *Nature, 401,* 63–69.

Tangney, J. P., Wagner, P., & Gramzow, R. (1992). Proneness to shame, proneness to guilt, and psychopathology. *Journal of Abnormal Psychology, 101* (3): 469–78.

Taub, J. M. (1996). Sociodemography of borderline personality disorder (PD): A comparison with axis II PDS and psychiatric symptom disorders convergent validation. *International Journal of Neuroscience, 88,* 27–52.

Taube, C. A. (1976). *Readmissions to inpatient services of state and county hospitals 1972. Statistical note 110.* (DHEW Publication No. ADM 76-308). Rockville, MD: National Institute of Mental Health.

Taylor, D. P., Carter, R. B., Eison, A. S., Mullins, U. L., Smith, H. L., Torrente, J. R., Wright, R. N., & Yocca, F. D. (1995). Pharmacology and neurochemistry of Nefazodone, a novel antidepressant drug. *Journal of Clinical Psychiatry, 56* (Suppl. 6): 3–11.

Taylor, R. L., & Richards, S. B. (1990). Validity of the Estimated Learning Potential and other measures of learning potential. *Perceptual and Motor Skills, 71,* 225–29.

Taylor, S. (1996). Meta-analysis of cognitive-behavioral treatment for social phobia. *Journal of Behavior Therapy and Experimental Psychiatry, 27* (1): 1–9.

Taylor, W. S., & Martin, M. F. (1944). Multiple personality. *Journal of Abnormal and Social Psychology, 39,* 281–300.

Teasdale, J. D., & Rezin, V. (1978). The effect of reducing frequency of negative thoughts on the mood of depressed patients: Test of a cognitive model of depression. *British Journal of Social and Clinical Psychology, 17,* 65–74.

Teasdale, J. D., Segal, Z., & Williams, J. M. G. (1995). How does cognitive therapy prevent depressive relapse and why should attentional control (mindfulness) training help? *Behaviour Research and Therapy, 33* (1): 25–39.

Teasdale, J., Segal, Z., Williams, M., et al. (2000). Prevention of relapse/recurrence in major depression by mindfulness-based cognitive therapy. *Journal of Consulting and Clinical Psychology,* in press.

Teicher, M., Glod, C., & Cole, J. (1990). Emergence of intense suicidal preoccupation during fluoxetine treatment. *American Journal of Psychiatry, 147,* 207–10.

Teicher, M. H., Glod, C., & Cole, J. O. (1990) Emergence of suicidal preoccupation during fluoxetine. *American Journal of Psychiatry, 147* (2): 207–10.

Telch, M., Agras, S., Taylor, C., et al. (1985). Combined pharmacological and behavioral treatment for agoraphobia. *Behaviour Research and Therapy, 23,* 325–35.

Temerlin, M. K. (1970). Diagnostic bias in community mental health. *Community Mental Health Journal, 6,* 110–17.

Teplin, L. A., Abram, K. M., McClelland, G. M. (1994). Does psychiatric disorder predict violent crime among released jail detainees? *American Psychologist, 49,* 335–42.

Terman, L. (1939). The gifted student and his academic environment. *School and Society, 49,* 65–73.

Terman, L., Buttenweiser, P., Johnson, W., & Wilson, D. (1938). *Psychological factors in marital happiness.* New York: McGraw-Hill.

ter Riet, G., de Craen, A. J., de Boer, A., & Kessels, A. G.(1998). Is placebo analgesia mediated by endogenous opioids? A systematic review. *Pain, 76,* 273–75.

Terry, R. D., & Davies, P. (1980). Dementia of the Alzheimer type. *Annual Review of Neuroscience, 3,* 77–95.

Tesar, G. (1990). High potency benzodiazepines for short-term management of panic disorder: The U.S. experience. *Journal of Clinical Psychiatry, 51,* 4–10.

Test, M. A., Knoedler, W. H., Allness, D. J., Senn Burke, S., et al. (1997). Comprehensive community care of persons with schizophrenia through the Programme of Assertive Community Treatment (PACT). In H. D. Brenner & W. Boeker (Eds.), *Towards a comprehensive therapy for schizophrenia* (pp. 167–80). Goettingen, Germany: Hogrefe & Huber.

Tharpar, A., & McGuffin, P. (1994). A twin study of depressive symptoms in childhood. *British Journal of Psychiatry, 165,* 259–65.

Thase, M., & Howland, R. (1995). Biological processes in depression: An updated review and integration. In. E. Beckham & W. Leber (Eds.), *Handbook of depression* (2nd ed.). New York: Guilford Press.

Thase, M. E., Dube, S., Bowler, K., Howland, R. H., et al. (1996). Hypothalamic-pituitary-adrenocortical activity and response to cognitive behavior therapy in unmedicated, hospitalized depressed patients. *American Journal of Psychiatry, 153* (7): 886–91.

Thatcher, R. W. (1994). Cyclic cortical reorganization: Origins of human cognitive development. In G. Dawson & K. W. Fischer (Eds.), *Human behavior and the developing brain* (pp. 176–206). New York: Guilford Press.

Thayer, J. F., Friedman, B. H., & Borkovec, T. D. (1996). Autonomic characteristics of generalized anxiety disorder and worry. *Biological Psychiatry, 39* (4): 255–66.

Theodor, L. H., & Mandelcorn, M. S. (1978). Hysterical blindness: A case report and study using a modern psychophysical technique. *Journal of Abnormal Psychology, 82,* 552–53.

Theorell, T., & Rahe, R. H. (1971). Psychosocial factors in myocardial infarction. I. An inpatient study in Sweden. *Journal of Psychosomatic Research, 15,* 25–31.

Thigpen C. H., & Cleckley, H. (1954). A case of multiple personality. *Journal of Abnormal and Social Psychology, 49,* 135–51.

Thompson, J., Burns, B., Bartko, J., et al. (1988). The use of ambulatory services by persons with and without phobias. *Medical Care, 26,* 183–98.

Thompson, P. M. (1996). Generalized anxiety disorder treatment algorithm. *Psychiatric Annals, 26* (4): 227–32.

Thompson, P. M., Giedd, J. N., Woods, R. P., MacDonald D., Evans A. C., & Toga, A. W. (2000). Growth patterns in the developing brain detected by using continuum mechanical tensor maps. *Nature, 404* (6774):190–93.

Thompson, S., & Rey, J. M. (1995). Functional enuresis: Is Desmopressin the answer? *Journal of the American Academy of Child and Adolescent Psychiatry, 34* (3): 266–71.

Thompson, T., & Schuster, C. R. (1964). Morphine in self-administration, food-reinforced, and avoidance behaviors in rhesus monkeys. *Psychopharmacologia, 5,* 87–94.

Thornton, D., & Mann, R. (1997). Sexual masochism: Assessment and treatment. In D. R. Laws & W. O'Donohue (Eds.), *Sexual deviance: Theory, assessment, and treatment* (pp. 240–52). New York: Guilford Press.

Thorpe, S. J., & Salkovskis, P. M. (1995). Phobic beliefs: Do cognitive factors play a role in specific phobias? *Behaviour Research and Therapy, 33* (7): 805–16.

Tiefer, L., & Kring, B. (1995). Gender and the organization of sexual behavior. *Psychiatric Clinics of North America, 18* (1): 25–37.

Tien, A., Pearlson, G., Machlin, S., et al. (1992). Oculomotor performance in obsessive-compulsive disorder. *American Journal of Psychiatry, 150,* 641–46.

Tienari, A. (1975). Schizophrenia in Finnish male twins. In M. H. Lader (Ed.), *Studies of schizophrenia* (pp. 29–53). Ashford, England: Headley Brothers.

Tienari, P. (1991). Interaction between genetic vulnerability and family environment: The Finnish adoptive family study of schizophrenia. *Acta Psychiatrica Scandinavica, 84,* 460–65.

Tienari, P., Wynne, L. C., Moring, J., Lahti, I., et al. (1994). The Finnish adoptive family study of schizophrenia: Implications for family research. *British Journal of Psychiatry, 164,* 20–26.

Tinklenberg, J. (1977). Anti-anxiety medications and the treatment of anxiety. In J. Barchas, P. Berger, R. Ciaranello, & G. Elliot (Eds.), *Psychopharmacology.* New York: Oxford University Press.

Tinsley, J. A., Finlayson, R. E., & Morse, R. M. (1998). Developments in the treatment of alcoholism. *Mayo Clinic Proceedings, 73,* 857–63.

Tinsley, J. A., & Watkins, D. D. (1998). Over-the-counter stimulants: Abuse and addiction. *Mayo Clinic Proceedings, 73,* 977–82.

Tisher, M., Tonge, B. J., & Horne, D. J. DeL. (1994). Childhood depression, stressors and parental depression. *Australian and New Zealand Journal of Psychiatry, 28,* 635–41.

Tollefson, G. D., Fawcett, J., Winokur, G., Beasley, C. M., Potvin, J. H., Faries, D. E., Rampey, A. H., & Sayler, M. E. (1993). Evaluation of suicidality during pharmacologic treatment of mood and nonmood disorders. *Annals of Psychiatry, 5* (4): 209–24.

Tollefson, G. D., Sanger, T. M., Lu, Y., & Thieme, M. E. (1998). Depressive signs and symptoms in schizophrenia: A prospective blinded trial of olanzapine and haloperidol. *Achives of General Psychiatry, 55* (3): 250–58.

Tomasello, M., & Camnioni, L. (1997). A comparison of the gestural communication of apes and human infants. *Human Development, 40,* 7–24.

Tomasson, K., Kent, D., & Coryell, W. (1991). Somatization and conversion disorders: Comorbity and demographics at presentation. *Acta Psychiatrica Scandinavica, 84,* 288–93.

Tonks, C. M., Paykel, E. S., & Klerman, J. L. (1970). Clinical depressions among Negroes. *American Journal of Psychiatry, 127,* 329–35.

Toole, J. F. (1999). Dementia in world leaders and its effects upon international events: The examples of Franklin D. Roosevelt and T. Woodrow Wilson. *European Journal of Neurology, 6,* 115–19.

Torasdotter, M., Metsis, M., Henriksson, B. G., Winblad, B., & Mohammed, A. H. (1998). Environmental enrichment results in higher levels of nerve growth factor mRNA in the rat visual cortex and hippocampus. *Behavioural Brain Research, 93,* 83–90.

Torgersen, S. (1983). Genetic factors in anxiety disorders. *Archives of General Psychiatry, 40,* 1085–89.

Torgersen, S. (1986a). Genetic factors in moderately severe and mild affective disorders. *Archives of General Psychiatry, 43,* 222–26.

Torgersen, S. (1986b). Genetics of somatoform disorders. *Archives of General Psychiatry, 43,* 502–505.

Torrey, E. F. (1983). *The roots of treason: Ezra Pound and the secret of St. Elizabeth's.* New York: McGraw-Hill.

Torrey, E. F. (1992). Are we overestimating the genetic contribution to schizophrenia? *Schizophrenia Bulletin, 18* (2): 159–70.

Torrey, E. F. (1994). Violent behaviour by individuals with serious mental illness. *Hospital and Community Psychiatry, 45,* 653–62.

Torrey, E. F. (1997). *Out of the shadows: Confronting America's mental illness crisis.* New York: Wiley.

Torrey, E. F., Bowler, A. E., & Taylor, E. H. (1994). *Schizophrenia and manic-depressive disorder: The biological roots of mental illness as revealed by the landmark study of identical twins.* New York: Basic Books.

Torrey, E. F., Miller, J., Rawlings, R., & Yolken, R. H. (1997). Seasonality of births in schizophrenia and bipolar disorder: A review of the literature. *Schizophrenia Research, 28,* 1–38.

Toupin, J., Dery, M., Pauze, R., Fortin, L., & Mercier, H. (1997). Social, psychological, and neuropsychological correlates of conduct disorder in children and adolescents. In A. Raine & P. A. Brennan (Eds.), *Biosocial bases of violence* (NATO ASI Series: Series A: Life Sciences, Vol. 292; pp. 309–11). New York: Plenum.

Tourette Syndrome Study Group (1999). Short-term versus longer term pimozide therapy in Tourette's syndrome: A preliminary study. *Neurology, 52,* 874–77.

Traskman-Bendz, L., Alling, C., Alsen, M., et al. (1993). The role of monoamines in suicidal behavior. *Acta Psychiatrica Scandinavica, 87,* 45–47.

Trasler, G. (1973). Criminal behavior. In H. J. Eysenck (Ed.), *Handbook of abnormal psychology.* London: Pitman Medical.

Treece, C., & Khantzian, E. J. (1986). Psychodynamic factors in the development of drug dependence. *Psychiatric Clinics of North America, 9,* 399–412.

Trillo-Pazos G., & Everall, I. P. (1997). From human immunodeficiency virus (HIV) infection of the brain to dementia. *Genitourinary Medicine, 73*(5):343–47.

Trimble, M. (1990). Worldwide use of clomipramine. *Journal of Clinical Psychiatry, 51,* 51–58.

Trinkoff, A. M., & Storr, C. L. (1998). Substance use among nurses: Differences between specialties. *American Journal of Public Health, 88,* 581–85.

True, W., Rice, J., Eisen, S., et al. (1993). A twin study of genetic and environmental contributions to liability for post-traumatic stress symptoms. *Archives of General Psychiatry, 50,* 257–64.

Trull, T. J., & Geary, D. C. (1997). Comparison of the Big-Five Factor structure across samples of Chinese and American adults. *Journal of Personality Assessment, 69* (2): 324–41.

Trull, T. J., Useda, D., Conforti, K., & Doan, B. (1997). Borderline personality disorder features in nonclinical young adults: 2. Two-year outcome. *Journal of Abnormal Psychology, 106* (2): 307–14.

Tryon, W. W. (1976). Models of behavior disorder. *American Psychologist, 31,* 509–18.

Tsai, M., Feldman-Summers, S., & Edgar, M. (1979). Childhood molestation: Variables related to differential impacts on psychosexual functioning in adult women. *Journal of Abnormal Psychology, 88* (4): 407–17.

Tsoh, J. Y., McClure, J. B., Skaar, K. L., Wetter, D. W., et al. (1997). Smoking cessation: 2. Components of effective intervention. *Behavioral Medicine, 23,* 15–27.

Tucker, D. M., Luu, P., & Pribaum, K. H. (1995). Social and emotional self-regulation. *Annals of the New York Academy of Sciences, 769,* 213–39.

Tulving, E., Markowitsch, H. J., Craik, F. I. M, Habib, R., Houle. (1996). Novelty and familiarity activations in PET studies of memory encoding and retrieval. *Cerebral Cortex, 6,* 71–79.

Tune, L. E., & Sunderland, T. (1998). New cholinergic therapies: Treatment tools for the psychiatrist. Journal of Clinical Psychiatry, 59, 31–35.

Turgay, A. (1990). Treatment outcome for children and adolescents with conversion disorder. *Canadian Journal of Psychiatry, 35,* 585–89.

Turner, C. F., Ku, L., Rogers, S. M., Lindberg, L. D., Pleck, J. H., & Sonenstein, F. L. (1998). Adolescent sexual behavior, drug use, and violence: Increased reporting with computer survey technology. *Science, 280,* 867–73.

Turner, S. M., Beidel, D. C., Dancu, C. V., & Keys, D. J. (1986). Psychopathology of social phobia and comparison to avoidant personality disorder. *Journal of Abnormal Psychology, 95,* 389–94.

Turner, S. M., Beidel, D. C., & Jacob, R. G. (1994). Social phobia: A comparison of behavior therapy and atenolol. *Journal of Consulting and Clinical Psychology, 62* (2): 350–58.

Turner, S. M., Beidel, D. C., & Townsley, R. M. (1992). Social phobia: A comparison of specific and generalized subtypes and avoidant personality disorder. *Journal of Abnormal Psychology, 101* (2): 326–31.

Turner, W. J. (1995). Homosexuality, Type 1: An Xq28 phenomenon. *Archives of Sexual Behavior, 24* (2): 109–34.

Tyrka, A. R., Cannon, T. D., Haslam, N., Mednick, S. A., Schulsinger, F., Schulsinger, H., & Parnas, J. (1995). The latent structure of schizotypy: I. Premorbid indicators of a taxon of individuals at risk for schizophrenia-spectrum disorders. *Journal of Abnormal Psychology, 104* (1): 173–83.

Uecker A., Reiman E. M., Schacter, D. L., Polster, M. R., Cooper, L. A., Yun, L. S., & Chen, K. (1997). Neuroanatomical correlates of implicit and explicit memory for structurally possible and impossible visual objects. *Learning and Memory, 4* (4): 337–55.

Ullman, L. P., & Krasner, L. (1965). *Case studies in behavior modification.* New York: Holt, Rinehart & Winston.

Ulm, R. R., Volpicelli, J. R., & Volpicelli, L. A. (1995). Opiates and alcohol self-administration in animals. *Journal of Clinical Psychiatry, 56,* 5–14.

Unis, A. S., Cook, E. H., Vincent, J. G., Gjerde, D. K., Perry, B. D., Mason, C., & Mitchell, J. (1997). Platelet serotonin measures in adolescents with conduct disorder. *Biological Psychiatry, 42,* 553–59.

United States Census Bureau. (1999a). *Resident Population Estimates of the United States by Age and Sex: April 1, 1990 to May 1, 1999.* Population Estimates Program, Population Division, U.S. Census Bureau, Washington, D.C. Online: www.blue.census.gov/population/estimates/nation/infile2-1.txt

Upham, C. W. (1867). Salem witchcraft. Cited in A. Deutsch, *The mentally ill in America.* New York: Columbia University Press, 1949.

Urbina, S. P., Golden, C. J., & Ariel, R. N. (1982). WAIS/WAIS-R: Initial comparisons. *Clinical Neuropsychology, 4,* 145–46.

U. S. Department of Health and Human Services. (1987). *Vital Statistics of the United States, 1984. Volume II: Mortality.* National Center for Health Statistics, Hyattsville, MD.

U. S. Department of Health and Human Services, Substance Abuse and Mental Health Services Administration. (1996). *Preliminary Results from the 1996 National Household Survey of Drug Abuse.* http://www.samhsa.gov/oas/nhsda/pe1996/httoc.htm

U. S. Department of Health and Human Services. (1997a). *Heroin abuse in the United States.* Rockville, MD: Author.

U. S. Department of Health and Human Services. (1997b). *Ninth Special Report to the U.S. Congress on Alcohol and Health* (NIH publication no. 97–401). Washington, DC: Government Printing Office.

U. S. Department of Health and Human Services, Substance Abuse and Mental Health Services Administration. (1997c). *Preliminary Results from the 1996 National Household Survey on Drug Abuse.* Rockville, MD: Author.

U. S. Department of Health and Human Services (2000). *The monitoring the future: National Results on Adolescent Drug Use.* Bethesda, MD: Author.

U. S. Sentencing Commission. (1997). *Cocaine and federal sentencing policy.* Washington, DC: Author.

Vaccarino, F. J., Bloom, F. E., & Koob, G. F. (1985). Block of nucleus accumbens opiate receptors attenuates intravenous heroin reward in the rat. *Psychopharmacology, 86,* 37–42.

Vaillant, G. E. (1978). Natural history of male psychological health: IV. What kinds of men do not get psychosomatic illness. *Psychosomatic Medicine, 40,* 420–31.

Vaillant, G. E. (1983). *The natural history of alcoholism.* Cambridge, MA: Harvard University Press.

Vaillant, G. E. (1992). Is there a natural history of addiction? In C. P. O'Brien & J. H. Jaffe (Eds.), *Addictive states.* New York: Raven Press.

Vaillant, G. E. (1996). A long-term follow-up of male alcohol abuse. *Archives of General Psychiatry, 53,* 243–49.

Vaillant, G. (2000). Adaptive mental mechanisms—their role in a positive psychology. *American Psychologist,* in press.

Van der Does, A., Antony, M., Ehlers, A., & Barsky, A. (2000). Heartbeat perception in panic disorder: A reanalysis. *Behaviour Research and Therapy, 38,* 47–62.

Vanderlinden, J., Van Dyck, R., Vandereycken, W., & Vertommen, H. (1991). Dissociative experiences in the general population in the Netherlands and Belgium: A study with the Dissociative Questionnaire (DIS-Q). *Dissociation: Progress in the Dissociative Disorders, 4,* 180–84.

Van Dyke, C., Zilberg, N. J., & McKinnon, J. A. (1985). Post-traumatic stress disorder: A thirty-year delay in a World War II veteran. *American Journal of Psychiatry, 142,* 1070–73.

Van Goozen, S. H. M., Cohen-Kettenis, P. T., Gooren, L. J. G., Frijda, N. H., & Van de Poll, N. E. (1995). Gender differences in behaviour: Activating effects of cross-sex hormones. *Psychoneuroendocrinology, 20* (4): 343–63.

van Goozen, S. H. M., Matthys, W., Cohen-Kettenis, P. T., Westenberg, H., & van Engeland, H. (1999). Plasma monoamine metabolites and aggression: Two studies of normal and oppositional defiant disorder children. *European Neuropsychopharmacology, 9,* 141–47.

Van Kempen, G. M., Zitman, F. G., Linssen, A. C., & Edelbroek, P. M. (1992). Biochemical measures in patients with somatoform pain disorder, before, during, and after treatment with amitriptyline with or without flupentixol. *Biological Psychiatry, 31,* 670–80.

Van Moffaert, M. (1990). Self-mutilation: diagnosis and practical treatment. International *Journal of Psychiatry in Medicine, 20,* 373–382.

van Os, J., & Selten, J. (1998). Prenatal exposure to maternal stress and subsequent schizophrenia: The May 1940 invasion of The Netherlands. *British Journal of Psychiatry, 172,* 324–26.

van Praag, H., Qu, P. M., Elliott, R. C., Wu, H., Dreyfus, C. F., & Black, I. B. (1998). Unilateral hippocampal lesions in newborn and adult rats: Effects on spatial memory and BDNF gene expression. *Behavioural Brain Research 92,* 21–30.

Vanyukov, M. M. (1999). Genetics. In P. J. Ott & R. E. Tarter (Eds.), *Sourcebook on substance abuse: Etiology, epidemiology, assessment, and treatment* (pp. 126–40). Boston: Allyn and Bacon.

Varnik, A., & Wasserman, D. (1992). Suicides in the former Soviet republics. *Acta Psychiatrica Scandinavica, 86,* 76–78.

Vaughn, C. E., Snyder, K. S., Jones, S., Freeman, W. B., & Falloon, I. R. H. (1984). Family factors in schizophrenic relapse: Replication in California of British research on expressed emotion. *Archives of General Psychiatry, 41,* 1169–77.

Vazquez, C., Munoz, M., & Sanz, J. (1997). Lifetime and 12-month prevalence of DSM-III-R mental disorders among the homeless in Madrid: A European study using the CIDI. *Acta Psychiatrica Scandinavica, 95,* 523–30.

Veiel, H. (1993). Detrimental effects of kin support networks on the course of depression. *Journal of Abnormal Psychology, 102,* 419–29.

Veith, I. (1965). *Hysteria: The history of a disease.* Chicago: University of Chicago Press.

Ventura, J., Liberman, R. P., Green, M. F., Shaner, A., & Mintz, J. (1998). Training and quality assurance with Structured Clinical Interview for DSM-IV (SCID-I/P). *Psychiatry Research, 79* (2): 163–73.

Ventura, J., Nuechterlein, K. H., Lukoff, D., & Hardesty, J. P. (1989). A prospective study of stressful life events and schizophrenic relapse. *Journal of Abnormal Psychology, 98* (4): 407–11.

Verhaak, P. F. M, Kerssens, J. J., Dekker, J., Sorbi, M. J., & Bensing, J. M. (1998). Prevalence of chronic benign pain disorder among adults: A review of the literature. *Pain, 77* (3): 231–39.

Verhaeghe, J., Loos, R., Vlietinck, R., Van Herck, E., van Bree, R., & De Schutter, A. (1996). Fetus-placenta-newborn: C-peptide, insulin-like growth factors I and II, and insulin-like growth factor binding protein-1 in cord serum of twins: Genetic versus environmental regulation. *American Journal of Obstetrics and Gynecology, 175,* 1180–88.

Verheul, R., van den Brink, W., & Koeter, M. W. J. (1998). Temporal stability of diagnostic criteria for antisocial personality disorder in male alcohol dependent patients. *Journal of Personality Disorders, 12,* 316–31.

Verhey, F. R. J., & Honig, A. (1997). Depression in the elderly. In A. Honig & H. M. van Praag (Eds.), *Depression: Neurobiological, psychopathological and therapeutic advances* (Wiley Series on Clinical and Neurobiological Advances in Psychiatry, Vol. 3; pp. 59–81). Chichester, England: Wiley.

Verhoeven, W. M. A., Marijnissen, G., Van Ooy, J. M., Tuiner, S., Van Den Berg, Y. W. M. M., Pepplinkhuizen, L., & Fekkes, D. (1999). Dysperceptions and serotonergic parameters in borderline personality disorders: Effects of treatment with risperidone. *New Trends in Experimental and Clinical Psychiatry, 15* (1): 9–16.

Versiani, M., Mundim, F., Nardi, A., et al. (1988). Tranylcypromine in social phobia. *Journal of Clinical Psychopharmacology, 8,* 279–83.

Vgontzas, A. N., Kales, A., & Bixler, E. O. (1995). Benzodiazepine side effects: Role of pharmacokinetics and pharmacodynamics. *Pharmacology, 51,* 205–23.

Victor, M., Adams, R. D., & Collins, G. H. (1971). *The Wernicke-Korsakoff syndrome. A clinical and pathological study of 245 patients, 82 with post-mortem examinations.* Philadelphia: Davis.

Videbech, P. (1997). MRI findings in patients with affective disorder: A meta-analysis. *Acta Psychiatrica Scandinavica, 96,* 157–68.

Videbech, T. (1975). A study of genetic factors, childhood bereavement, and premorbid personality traits in patients with anancastic endogenous depression. *Acta Psychiatrica Scandinavica, 52,* 178–222.

Visser, F. E, Aldenkamp, A. P., van Huffelen, A. C, & Kuilman, M. (1997). Prospective study of the prevalence of Alzheimer-type dementia in institutionalized individuals with Down syndrome. *American Journal on Mental Retardation, 101* (4): 400–412.

Vitkus, J. (1996). *Casebook in abnormal psychology.* New York: McGraw-Hill.

Vogel, G. W. (1975). A review of REM sleep deprivation. *Archives of General Psychiatry, 32,* 96–97.

Vogel, G. W., Buffenstein, A., Minter, K., & Hennessey, A. (1990). Drug effects on REM sleep and on endogenous depression. *Neuroscience and Biobehavioral Reviews, 14,* 49–63.

Volkmar, F. (1996). *Psychoses and pervasive developmental disorders in childhood and adolescence.* Washington, DC: American Psychiatric Press.

Volkmar, F. R., Carter, A., Sparrow, S. S., & Cicchetti, D. V. (1993). Quantifying social development in autism. *Journal of the American Academy of Child and Adolescent Psychiatry, 32* (3): 627–32.

Volkmar, F. R., Klin, A., Schultz, R. T., Rubin, E., & Bronen, R. (2000). Asperger's disorder. *American Journal of Psychiatry, 157* (2): 262–67.

Volkow, N. D., Wang, G. J., Fischman, M. W., Foltin, R. W., et al. (1997). Relationship between subjective effects of cocaine and dopamine transporter occupancy. *Nature, 386,* 827–30.

Vollenweider, F. X. (1998). Advances and pathophysiological models of hallucinogenic drug actions in humans: A preamble to schizophrenia research. *Pharmacopsychiatry, 31* (Supp. 2): 92–103.

Volpicelli, J. R. (1989). Psychoactive substance use disorders. In D. L. Rosenhan & M. E. P. Seligman (Eds.), *Abnormal psychology.* New York: Norton.

Volpicelli, J. R., Alterman, A. I., Hayashida, M., & O'Brien, C. P. (1992). Naltrexone in the treatment of alcohol dependence. *Archives of General Psychiatry, 49,* 876–80.

Volpicelli, J. R., Clay, K. L., Watson, N. T., & O'Brien, C. P. (1995). Naltrexone in the treatment of alcoholism: Predicting response to Naltrexone. *Journal of Clinical Psychiatry, 56* (Suppl. 7): 39–44.

Volpicelli, J. R., Davis, M. A., & Olgin, J. E. (1986). Naltrexone blocks the post-shock increase of ethanol consumption. *Life Sciences, 38,* 841–47.

Volz, H., Gaser, C., Haeger, F., Rzanny, R., Mentzel, H., Kreitschmann-Andermahr, I., Alois Kaiser, W., & Sauer, H. (1997). Brain activation during cognitive stimulation with the Wisconsin Card Sorting Test—A functional MRI study on healthy volunteers and schizophrenics. *Psychiatry Research: Neuroimaging, 75,* 145–57.

von Gontard, A., & Lehmkuhl, G. (1997). Nocturnal enuresis: A review of genetic, pathophysiologic, and psychiatric associations. *Praxis der Kinderpsychologie und Kinderpsychiatrie, 46,* 709–26.

Vrtunski, P. B., Konicki, P. E., Jaskiw, G. E., Brescan, D. W., Kwon, K. Y., & Jurjus, G. (1998). Clozapine effects on force control in schizophrenia patients. *Schizophrenia Research, 34,* 39–48.

Wacker, D. P., Berg, W. K., & Harding, J. W. (1999). Mental retardation. In R. T. Ammerman & M. Hersen (Eds.), *Handbook of prescriptive treatments for children and adolescents* (2nd ed.; pp. 31–47). Boston: Allyn & Bacon.

Wadden, T., Stunkard, A., & Smoller, J. (1986). Dieting and depression: A methodological study. *Journal of Consulting and Clinical Psychology, 54,* 869–71.

Wagner, A. W., & Linehan, M. M. (1994). Relationship between childhood sexual abuse and topography of parasuicide among women with borderline personality disorder. *Journal of Personality Disorders, 8,* 1–9.

Wagner, A. W., & Linehan, M. M. (1997). Biosocial perspective on the relationship of childhood sexual abuse, suicidal behavior, and borderline personality disorder. In M C. Zanarini, (Ed.), *Role of sexual abuse in the etiology of borderline personality disorder: Progress in psychiatry* (No. 49; pp. 203–23). Washington, DC: American Psychiatric Press.

Wahlbeck, K., Cheine, M., Essali, A., & Adams, C. (1999). Evidence of clozapine's effectiveness in schizophrenia: A systematic review and meta-analysis of randomized trials. *American Journal of Psychiatry, 156* (7): 990–99.

Wakefield, J. C. (1992a). Disorder as harmful dysfunction: A conceptual critique of DSM-III-R's definition of mental disorder. *Psychological Review, 99,* 232–47.

Wakefield, J. C. (1992b). The concept of mental disorder: On the boundary between biological facts and social values. *American Psychologist, 47,* 373–88.

Wakefield, J. C. (1993). The limits of operationalization: A critique of Spitzer and Endicott's proposed operational criteria of mental disorder. *Journal of Abnormal Psychology, 102,* 160–72.

Wakefield, J. C. (1999). Evolutionary versus prototype analyses of the concept of disorder. *Journal of Abnormal Psychology, 108* (3): 374–99.

Walker, E. F. (1994). Developmentally moderated expressions of the neuropathology underlying schizophrenia. *Schizophrenia Bulletin, 20,* 453–480.

Walker, E. F., Baum, K. M., & Diforio, D. (1998). Developmental changes in the behavioral expression of vulnerability for schizophrenia. In M. F. Lenzenweger & R. H. Dworkin (Eds.), *Origins and development of schizophrenia: Advances in experimental psychopathology* (pp. 469–91). Washington, DC: American Psychological Association.

Walker, E. F., Cudeck, R., Mednick, S. A., & Schulsinger, F. (1981). Effects of parental absence and institutionalization on the development of clinical symptoms in high-risk children. *Acta Psychiatrica Scandinavica, 63,* 95–109.

Walker, E. F., & Diforio, D. (1997). Schizophrenia: A neural diathesis-stress model. *Psychological Review, 104,* 667–85.

Walker, E., Downey, G., & Caspi, A. (1991). Twin studies of psychopathology: Why do concordance rates vary? *Schizophrenia Research, 5,* 211–21.

Walker, E., Grimes, K., Davis, D. & Smith, A. (1993). Childhood precursors of schizophrenia; Facial expressions of emotion. *American Journal of Psychiatry, 150,* 1654–60.

Walker, E. , & Lewine, R. (1990). The prediction of adult-onset schizophrenia from childhood home-movies. *American Journal of Psychiatry, 147,* 1052–56.

Walker, E., Lewine, R. J., & Neumann, C. (1996). Childhood behavioral characteristics and adult brain morphology in schizophrenia patients. *Schizophrenia Research, 22,* 93–101.

Walker, E., Lewis, N., Loewy, R., & Paylo, S. (1999). Motor functions and psychopathology. *Development and Psychopathology, 11* (3): 509–23.

Walker, E., McGuire, M., & Bettes, B. (1984). Recognition and identification of facial stimuli by schizophrenics and patients with affective disorders. *British Journal of Clinical Psychology, 23,* 37–44.

Walker, E., & Rossiter, J. (1989). Schizophrenic patient's self-perceptions: Legal and clinical implications. *Journal of Psychiatry and Law, 17,* 53–73.

Walker, E., Savoie, T. & Davis, D. (1994). Neuromotor precursors of schizophrenia. *Schizophrenia Bulletin, 20,* 441–52.

Wallace, J. M. (1999). The social ecology of addiction: Race, risk, and resilience. *Pediatrics, 103,* 1122–27.

Wallace, J., Vitale, J. E., & Newman, J. P. (1999). Response modulation deficits: Implications for the diagnosis and treatment of psychopathy. *Journal of Cognitive Psychotherapy, 13,* 55–70.

Waller, N., Kojetin, B., Bouchard, T., Lykken, D., & Tellegen, A. (1990). Genetic and environmental influences on religious interests, attitudes, and values. *Psychological Science, 1,* 138–42.

Wallerstein, J. S., & Kelly, J. B. (1980). California children of divorce. *Psychology Today, 13.*

Walinder, J. (1967). *Transsexualism.* Goteburg: Scandinavian University Books.

Wand, G. S., Mangold, D., El Deiry, S., McCaul, M. E., & Hoover, D. (1998). Family history of alcoholism and hypothalamic opioidergic activity. *Archives of General Psychiatry, 55,* 1114–19.

Warburton, D. M. (1988). The puzzle of nicotine use. In M. Lader (Ed.), *The psychopharmacology of addiction* (pp. 27–49). New York: Oxford University Press.

Warburton, D. M., & Wesnes, K. (1978). Individual differences in smoking and attentional performance. In R. E. Thornten (Ed.), *Smoking behavior: Physiological and psychological influence* (pp. 19–43). Edinburgh: Churchill-Livingstone.

Ward, J., Hall, W., & Mattick, R. P. (1999). Role of maintenance treatment in opioid dependence. *Lancet, 353,* 221–26.

Warner, R. (1978). The diagnosis of antisocial and personality disorders: An example of sex bias. *Journal of Nervous and Mental Disease, 166,* 839–45.

Warner, R., deGirolamo, G. B., Bologna, C., Fioritti, A., & Rosini, G. (1998). The quality of life of people with schizophrenia in Boulder, Colorado and Bologna, Italy. *Schizophrenia Bulletin, 24,* 559–68.

Warner, V., Mufson, L., & Weissman, M. M. (1995). Offspring at high and low risk for depression and anxiety: Mechanisms of psychiatric disorder. *Journal of the American Academy of Child and Adolescent Psychiatry, 34* (6): 786–97.

Warren, M. P., & Capponi, A. (1996). The role of culture in the development of narcissistic personality disorders in American, Japan, and Denmark. *Journal of Applied Social Sciences, 20* (1): 77–82.

Warrington, E. K., & Weiskrantz, L. (1973). An analysis of short-term and long-term memory defects in man. In J. A. Deutsch (Ed.), *The physiological basis of memory* (pp. 365–96). New York: Academic Press.

Warshaw, M.G., & Keller, M. B. (1996). The relationship between fluoxetine use and suicidal behavior in 654 subjects with anxiety disorders. *Journal of Clinical Psychiatry, 57* (4): 158–66.

Wasson, R. G. (1979). The divine mushroom of immortality. In P. T. Furst (Ed.), *Flesh of the gods* (pp. 185–200). New York: Praeger.

Watkins, G. (1960). The incidence of chronic peptic ulcer sounded necropsy: The study of 20,000 examinations performed in Leeds in 1930 to 1949 and in England and Scotland in 1956. *Gut, 1,* 14.

Watson, B. C., & Miller, S. (1994). The relationship between communication attitude, anxiety and depression in stutterers and nonstutterers. *Journal of Speech and Hearing Research, 37* (1): 92–95.

Watson, C. G., & Buranen, C. (1979). The frequency of conversion reaction. *Journal of Abnormal Psychology, 88,* 209–11.

Watson, J. (1928). *Psychological care of infant and child.* New York: Norton.

Watson, J. B., & Rayner, R. (1920). Conditioned emotional reactions. *Journal of Experimental Psychology, 3,* 1–14.

Watson, L. S., & Uzzell, R. (1981). *Handbook of behavior modification with the mentally retarded.* New York: Plenum.

Watt, N. F. (1978). Patterns of childhood social development in adult schizophrenics. *Archives of General Psychiatry, 35,* 160–65.

Watt, N. F., Anthony, E. J., Wynne, L. C., & Rolf, J. E. (Eds.). (1984). *Children at risk for schizophrenia: A longitudinal perspective.* Cambridge: Cambridge University Press.

Watt, N. F., & Lubensky, A. W. (1976). Childhood roots of schizophrenia. *Journal of Consulting and Clinical Psychology, 44,* 363–75.

Weaver, T., & Clum, G. (1993). Early family environment and traumatic experiences associated with borderline personality disorders. *Journal of Consulting and Clinical Psychology, 61,* 1068–75.

Webb, C., Pfeiffer, M., Mueser, K. T., Gladis, M., Mensch, E., DeGirolamo, J., & Levinson, D. F. (1998). Burden and well-being of caregivers for the severely mentally ill: The role of coping style and support. *Schizophrenia Research, 34,* 169–80.

Wegner, D. M., & Zanakos, S. (1994). Chronic thought suppression. *Journal of Personality, 62* (4): 615–40.

Wegner, J. T., Catalano, F., Gibralter, J., & Kane, J. M. (1985). Schizophrenics with tardive dyskinesia. *Archives of General Psychiatry, 42,* 860–65.

Weinberger, D. R. (1988). Schizophrenia and the frontal lobes. *Trends in Neuroscience, 11,* 367–70.

Weinberger, D. R., Berman, K. F., & Zec, R. F. (1986). Physiologic dysfunction of dorsolateral prefrontal cortex in schizophrenia. I. Regional cerebral blood flow evidence. *Archives of General Psychiatry, 43* (2): 114–24.

Weine, S. M., Kulenovic, A. D., Pavkovic, I., & Gibbons, R. (1998). Testimony psychotherapy in Bosnian refugees: A pilot study. *American Journal of Psychiatry, 155* (12): 1720–26.

Weiner, B. (1972). *Theories of motivation: From mechanism to cognition.* Chicago: Rand McNally.

Weiner, B. (Ed.). (1974). *Achievement motivation and attribution theory.* Morristown, NJ: General Learning Press.

Weiner, H. M. (1977). *Psychology and human disease.* New York: Elsevier.

Weiner, I. B. (1996). Some observations on the validity of the Rorschach Inkblot Method. *Psychological Assessment, 8* (2): 206–13.

Weiner, I. (2000). Using the Rorschach properly in practice and research. *Journal of Clinical Psychology, 56,* 435–38.

Weiner, J. R. (1997). *Textbook of child and adolescent psychiatry* (2nd. ed.). Washington, DC: American Psychiatric Press.

Weinstein, D. D., Diforio, D., Schiffman, J., Walker, E., & Bonsall, R. (1999). Minor physical anomalies, dermatoglyphic asymmetries, and cortisol levels in adolescents with schizotypal personality disorder. *American Journal of Psychiatry, 156,* 617–23.

Weinstock, M. (1996). Does prenatal stress impair coping and regulation of hypothalamic-pituitary-adrenal axis? *Neuroscience and Biobehavioral Reviews, 21,* 1–10.

Weisaeth, L. (1989). A study of behavioural responses to industrial disaster. *Acta Psychiatrica Scandinavica, 80,* 13–24.

Weiskrantz, L., Warrington, E. K., Sanders M. D., & Marshall, J. (1974). Visual capacity of the hemianopic field following a restricted occipital ablation. *Brain, 97,* 709–28.

Weisman, A. D. (1956). A study of the psychodynamics of duodenal ulcer exacerbations. *Psychosomatic Medicine, 18,* 2–42.

Weiss, E. L., Longhurst, J.G. and Mazure, C. M. (1999). Childhood sexual abuse as a risk factor for depression in women: Psychosocial and neurobiological correlates. *American Journal of Psychiatry, 156* (6): 816–28.

Weiss, F., Lorang, M. T., Bloom, F. E., & Koob, G. F. (1993). Oral alcohol self-administration stimulates dopamine release in the rat nucleus accumbens: Genetic and motivational determinants. *Journal of Pharmacological and Experimental Therapy, 267,* 250–58.

Weiss, F., Parsons, L. H., Schulteis, G., Hyytia, P., Lorang, M. T., Bloom, F. E., & Koob, G. F. (1996). Ethanol self-administration restores withdrawal-associated deficiencies in accumbal dopamine and 5-hydroxytryptamine release in dependent rats. *Journal of Neuroscience, 16* (10): 3474–85.

Weiss, J. M. (1968). Effects of predictable and unpredictable shock on the development of gastrointestinal lesion in rats. *Proceedings of the 76th Annual Convention of the American Psychological Association, 3,* 263–64.

Weiss, J. M. (1971). Effects of coping behavior in different warning signaled conditions on stress pathology in rats. *Journal of Comparative and Physiological Psychology, 77,* 1–13.

Weiss, J. M., Glazer, H. I., & Pohoresky, L. A. (1976). Coping behavior and neurochemical change in rats: An alternative explanation for the original "learned helplessness" experiments. In G. Serban & A. King (Eds.), *Animal models in human psychobiology.* New York: Plenum.

Weiss, J. M., Simson, P. G., Ambrose, M. J., Webster, A., & Hoffman, L. J. (1985). Neurochemical basis of behavioral depression. *Advances in Behavioral Medicine, 1,* 253–75.

Weissman, M. (1990). Panic and generalized anxiety: Are they separate disorders? *Journal of Psychiatric Research, 24,* 157–62.

Weissman, M. M. (1993). The epidemiology of personality disorders: A 1990 update. *Journal of Personality Disorders, 7* (Supp., Spring): 44–62.

Weissman, M. M., Bland, R. C., Canino, G. J., Faravelli, C., Greenwald, S., Hwu, H., Joyce, P. R., Karam, E. G., Lee, C. K., Lellouch, J., Lepine, J. P., Newman, S. C., Rubio-Stipec, M., Wells, J. E., Wickramaratne, P. J., Wittchen, H. U., & Yeh, E. K. (1996). Cross-national epidemiology of major depression and bipolar disorder. *Journal of the American Medical Association, 276* (4): 293–99.

Weissman, M. M., Bland, R. C., Canino, G. J., Faravelli, C., et al. (1997).The cross-national epidemiology of panic disorder. *Archives of General Psychiatry, 54* (4): 305–309.

Weissman, M. M., Kidd, K. K., & Prusoff, B. A. (1982). Variability in rates of affective disorders in relatives of depressed and normal probands. *Archives of General Psychiatry, 39,* 1397–1403.

Weissman, M. M., & Olfson, M. (1995). Depression in women: Implications for health care research. *Science, 269,* 799–801.

Weissman, M. M., & Paykel, E. S. (1974). *The depressed woman: A study of social relationships.* Evanston: University of Chicago Press.

Weisz, J. R. (1990). Cultural-familial mental retardation: A developmental perspective on cognitive performance and "helpless" behavior. In R. M. Hodapp & J. A. Burack (Eds.), *Issues in the developmental approach to mental retardation.* New York: Cambridge University Press.

Weisz, J. R., et al. (1995). A multimethod study of problem behavior among Thai and American children in school. *Child Development, 66,* 402–15.

Weller, R. A., Kapadia, P., Weller, E. B., Fristad, M., Lazaroff, L. B., & Preskorn, S. H. (1994). Psychopathology in families of children with major depressive disorders. *Journal of Affective Disorders, 31,* 247–52.

Wellman, C. L., Cullen, M. J., & Pelleymounter, M. A. (1998). Effects of controllability of stress on hippocampal pharmacology. *Psychobiology, 26,* 65–72.

Wells, A., & Butler, G. (1997). Generalized anxiety disorder. In D. M. Clark & C.G. Fairburn (Eds.), *Science and practice of cognitive behaviour therapy* (pp. 155–78). New York: Oxford University Press.

Wells, J. K., Howard, G. S., Nolin, W. F., & Vargas, M. J. (1986). Presurgical anxiety and postsurgical pain and adjustment: Effects of a stress inoculation procedure. *Journal of Consulting and Clinical Psychology, 54* (6): 831–35.

Wells, K., Burnam, M., Rogers, W., & Hays, R. (1992). The course of depression in adult outpatients: Results from the Medical Outcomes Study. *Archives of General Psychiatry, 49,* 788–94.

Wender, P. H., Kety, S. S., Rosenthal, D., Schulsinger, F., Ortmann, J., & Lunde, I. (1986). Psychiatric disorders in the biological and adoptive families of adopted individuals with affective disorders. *Archives of General Psychiatry, 43,* 923–29.

Wenger, J. R., Tiffany, T. M. , Bombardier, C., Nicholls, K., & Woods, S. C. (1981). Ethanol tolerance in the rat is learned. *Science, 213,* 575–76.

Wernicke, J. (1985). The side effect profile and safety of fluoxetine. *Journal of Clinical Psychiatry, 46,* 59–67.

Wesnes, K., & Warburton, D.M. (1984a). Effects of scopolamine and nicotine in human rapid information-processing and performance. *Psychopharmacology, 82,* 147–50.

Wesnes, K., & Warburton, D. M. (1984b). The effects of cigarettes of varying yield on rapid information processing performance. *Psychopharmacology, 82,* 338–42.

West, R., & Craik, F. I. M. (1999). Age-related decline in prospective memory: The roles of cue accessibility and cue sensitivity. *Psychology and Aging, 14* (2): 264–72.

Westen, D., & Shedler, J. (1999). Revising and assessing axis II, Part I: Developing a clinically and empirically valid assessment method. *American Journal of Psychiatry, 156,* 258–72.

Westermeyer, J., Bouafuely, M., Neider, J., & Callies, A. (1989). Somatization among refugees: An epidemiologic study. *Psychosomatics, 30,* 34–43.

Westling, B. E., & Ost, L. G. (1995). Cognitive bias in panic disorder patients and changes after cognitive-behavioral treatments. *Behaviour Research and Therapy, 33* (5): 585–88.

Wettstein, R. M. (Ed.). (1998). *Treatment of offenders with mental disorders.* New York: Guilford Press.

Wexler, B. E., Hawkins, K. A., Rounsaville, B., Anderson, M., Sernyak, M. J., & Green, M. F. (1997). Normal neurocognitive performance after extended practice in patients with schizophrenia. *Schizophrenia Research, 26,* 173–80.

Wexler, B. E., Stevens, A. A., Bowers, A. A., Sernyak, M. J., & Goldman-Rakic, P. S. (1998). Word and tone working memory deficits in schizophrenia. *Archives of General Psychiatry, 55,* 1093–96.

Wheeler, D., Jacobson, J., Paglieri, R. A., & Schwartz, A. (1993). An experimental assessment of facilitated communication. *Mental Retardation, 31,* 49–60.

White, K., Wykoff, W., Tynes, L., Schneider, L., et al. (1990). Fluvoxamine in the treatment of tricyclic-resistant depression. *Psychiatric Journal of the University of Ottawa, 15,* 156–58.

White, N. M. (1996). Addictive drugs as reinforcers: Multiple partial actions on memory systems. *Addiction, 91* (7): 921–49.

Whitehouse, P. J., & Kalaria, R. N. (1995). Nicotinic receptors and neurodegenerative dementing diseases: Basic research and clinical implications. *Alzheimer Disease and Associated Disorders, 9* (Supp. 2): 3–5.

Whitehouse, W. G., Dinges, D. F., Orne, E. C., Keller, S. E., Bates, B. L., Bauer, N. K., Morahan, P., Haupt, B. A., Carlin, M. M., Bloom, P. B., Zaugg, L., & Orne, M. T. (1996). Psychosocial and immune effects of self-hypnosis training for stress management throughout the first semester of medical school. *Psychosomatic Medicine, 58,* 249–63.

Whybrow, P. C. (1997). *A mood apart: Depression, mania, and other afflictions of the self.* New York: Basic Books.

Widiger, T. A. (1992). Generalized social phobia versus avoidant personality disorder: A commentary on three studies. *Journal of Abnormal Psychology, 101* (2): 340–43.

Widiger, T. A. (1998). Sex biases in the diagnosis of personality disorders. *Journal of Personality Disorders, 12,* 95–118.

Widiger, T. A., & Corbitt, E. M. (1995). Are personality disorders well-classified in DSM-IV? In W. J. Lively (Ed.), *The DSM-IV personality disorders* (pp. 103–26). New York: Guilford Press.

Widiger, T. A., Frances, A. J., Pincus, H. A., Davis, W. W., & First, M. B. (1991). Toward an empirical classification for the DSM-IV. *Journal of Abnormal Psychology, 100* (3): 280–88.

Widiger, T. A., Verheul, R., & van den Brink, W. (1999). Personality and psychopathology. In L. Pervin & O. John (Eds.), *Handbook of personality: Theory and research* (2nd ed.). New York: Guilford Press.

Widiger, T. A., & Weissman, M. M. (1991). Epidemiology of borderline personality disorder. *Hospital and Community Psychiatry, 42* (10): 1015–21.

Widom, C. S. (1997). Child abuse, neglect, and witnessing violence. In D. M. Stoff, J. Breiling, & J. D. Maser (Eds.), *Handbook of antisocial behavior* (pp. 159–70). New York: Wiley.

Widom, C. S. (1998). Child victims: Searching for opportunities to break the cycle of violence. *Applied and Preventive Psychology, 7,* 225–34.

Widdowson, E. (1951). Mental contentment and physical growth. *Lancet, 16,* 1316.

Wiener, J. (1996). *Is Ritalin overprescribed?* (No. Priorities, 8, (on-line). http://www.acsh.org/publications/priorities/0803/pcyes.html

Wikler, A. (1973). Dynamics of drug dependence. *Archives of General Psychiatry, 28,* 611–16.

Wilens, T. E., Biederman, J., Baldessarini, R. J., Geller, B., Schleifer, D., Spencer, T. J., Birmaher, B., & Goldblatt, A. (1998). Cardiovascular effects of therapeutic doses of tricyclic antidepressants in children and adolescents. In M. E. Hertzig & E. A. Farber (Eds.), *Annual progress in child psychiatry and child development: 1997* (pp. 349–64). Bristol, PA: Brunner/Mazel.

Wilens, T. E., Spencer, T. J., Frazier, J., & Biederman, J. (1998). Child and adolescent psychopharmacology. In T. H. Ollendick & M. Hersen (Eds.), *Handbook of child psychopathology* (3rd ed.; pp. 603–36). New York: Plenum.

Wilhelm, F. H., & Roth, W. T. (1998). Taking the laboratory to the skies: Ambulatory assessment of self-report, autonomic, and resipiratory responses in flying phobia. *Psychophysiology, 35* (5): 596–606.

Wilhelm, S., Keuthen, N. J., Deckersbach, T., Engelhard, I. M., Forker, A. E., Baer, L., O'Sullivan, R. L., & Jenike, M. A. (1999). Self-injurious skin picking: Clinical characteristics and comorbidity. *Journal of Clinical Psychiatry, 60* (7): 454–59.

Wilhelm, S., Otto, M. W., Lohr, B., & Deckersbach, T. (1999). Cognitive behavior group therapy for body dysmorphic disorder: A case series. *Behaviour Research and Therapy, 37* (1): 71–75.

Wilkinson, C. (1983). Aftermath of a disaster: The collapse of the Hyatt Regency Hotel skywalks. *American Journal of Psychiatry, 140,* 1134–39.

Williams, P., & Smith, M. (1980). Interview in "The First Question." London: British Broadcasting System, Sciences and Features Department Film, 1979. Cited in M. Diamond & A. Karlen (Eds.), *Sexual decisions.* Boston: Little, Brown.

Williams, R. B., Barefoot, J. C., & Shekelle, R. B. (1985). The health consequences of hostility. In M. Chesney & R. Rosenman (Eds.), *Anger and hostility in cardiovascular and behavioral disorders.* New York: McGraw-Hill/Hemisphere.

Williams, R., Lane, J., Kuhn, C., et al. (1982). Type A behavior and elevated physiological and neuroendocrine responses to cognitive tasks. *Science, 218,* 483–85.

Williamson, S., Hare, R. D., & Wong, S. (1987). Violence: Criminal psychopaths and their victims. *Canadian Journal of Behavioral Science, 19,* 454–62.

Williamson, S., Harpur, T. J., & Hare, R. D. (1990). *Sensitivity to emotional valence in psychopaths.* Paper presented at the 98th Annual Convention of the American Psychological Association, Boston, MA.

Williamson, S., Harpur, T. J., & Hare, R. D. (1991). Abnormal processing of affective words by psychopaths. *Psychophysiology, 28,* 260–73.

Willis, M. H., & Blaney, P. H. (1978). Three tests of the learned helplessness model of depression. *Journal of Abnormal Psychology, 87,* 131–36.

Wilner, A., Reich, T., Robins, I., Fishman, R., & Van Doren, T. (1976). Obsessive-compulsive neurosis. *Comprehensive Psychiatry, 17,* 527–39.

Wilson, A. L., Langley, L. K., & Monley, J. (1995). Nicotine patches in Alzheimer's disease: pilot study on learning, memory, and safety. *Pharmacology and Biochemical Behavior, 51,* 509–14.

Wilson, G. T., & Fairburn, C. G. (1998). Treatments for eating disorders. In P. Nathan & J. Gorman (Eds.), *A guide to treatments that work.* New York: Oxford University Press.

Wilson, S., Becker, L. & Tinker, R. (1996). Eye Movement Desensitization and Reprocessing (EMDR) treatment for psychologically traumatized individuals. *Journal of Consulting and Clinical Psychology, 63* (6): 928–37.

Winchel, R., & Stanley, M. (1991). Self-injurious behavior: a review of the behavior and biology of self-mutilation. *American Journal of Psychiatry, 148,* 306–17.

Winerip, M. (1994). *9 Highland Road.* New York: Pantheon.

Wing, L. (1976). *Diagnosis, clinical description and prognosis.* Oxford, England: Pergamon.

Wing, L. (1997). The autistic spectrum. *Lancet, 350,* 1761–66.

Winick, B. J. (1995). Ambiguities in the legal meaning and significance of mental illness. *Psychology, Public Policy, and Law, 1,* 534–611.

Winnicott, D. W. (1971). *Playing and reality.* New York: International Universities Press.

Winokur, G. (1972). Family history studies VIII: Secondary depression is alive and well and . . . . *Diseases of the Nervous System, 33,* 94–99.

Winokur, G., & Coryell, W. (1992). Familial subtypes of unipolar depression: A prospective study of familial pure depressive disease compared to depression spectrum disease. *Biological Psychiatry, 32* (11): 1012–18.

Winokur, G., Scharfetter, C., & Angst, J. (1985). The diagnostic value in assessing mood congruence in delusions and hallucinations and their relationship to the affective state. *European Archives of Psychiatry and Neurological Science, 234,* 299–302.

Winsberg, B. G., Sverd, J., Castells, S., Hurwic, M., & Perel, J. M. (1980). Estimation of monoamine and cyclic-AMP turnover and amino acid concentrations in the spinal fluid of autistic children. *Neuropediatrics, 11,* 250–55.

Wirz-Justice, A., Graw, P., Krauchi, K., Sarrafzadeh, A., English, J., Arendt, J., & Sand, L. (1996). "Natural" light treatment of seasonal affective disorder. *Journal of Affective Disorders, 37,* 109–20.

Wise, B. W., Olson, R. K., Ring, J., & Johnson, M. (1998). Interactive computer support for improving phonological skills. In J. L. Metsala & L. C. Ehri (Eds.), *Word recognition in beginning literacy.* Mahwah, NJ: Lawrence Erlbaum.

Wise, R. A. (1998). Drug-activation of brain reward pathways. *Drug and Alcohol Dependence, 51,* 13–22.

Wolf, M. M., Phillips, E. L., & Fixsen, D. C. (1975). *Achievement Place, phase II: Final report.* Kansas: Department of Human Development, University of Kansas.

Wolf, S., Cardon, P. V., Shepard, E. M., & Wolff, H. G. (1955). *Life stress and essential hypertension.* Baltimore: Williams & Wilkins.

Wolfe, J., Erickson, D. J., Sharkansky, E. J., King, D. W., & King, L. A. (1999). Course and predictors of posttraumatic stress disorder among Gulf War veterans: A prospective analysis. *Journal of Consulting and Clinical Psychology, 67* (4): 520–28.

Wolff, N., Helminiak, T. W., Morse, G. A., Calsyn, R. J., Klinkenberg, W. D., & Trusty, M. L. (1997). Cost-effectiveness evaluation of three approaches to case management for homeless mentally ill clients. *American Journal of Psychiatry, 154,* 341–48.

Wolff, S. (1965). *The stomach.* New York: Oxford University Press.

Wolpe, J. (1969). Basic principles and practices of behavior therapy of neuroses. *American Journal of Psychiatry, 125* (5): 1242–47.

Wolters, E. (1999). Dopaminomimetic psychosis in Parkinson's disease patients: Diagnosis and treatment. *Neurology, 52* (Supp. 3): S10–S13.

Wong, D., Horng, J., et al. (1974). A selective inhibitor of serotonin uptake: Lilly 110140, 3–(ptrifluoromethylphenoxy-N-Methyl-3-Phenylpropylamine). *Life Sciences, 15,* 471–79.

Wood, J., Lilienfeld, S., Garb, H., & Nezworski, M. (2000). The Rorschach Test in clinical diagnoses: A critical review, with a backward look at Garfield (1947). *Journal of Clinical Psychology, 56,* 395–430.

Wood, J. M., Nezworski, M. T., & Stejskal, W. J. (1996a). The comprehensive system for the Rorschach: A critical examination. *Psychological Science, 7* (1): 3–10.

Wood, J. M., Nezworski, M. T., & Stejskal, W. J. (1996b). Thinking critically about the comprehensive system for the Rorschach. A reply to Exner. *Psychological Science, 7,* 14–17.

Woodruff, R. A., Clayton, P. J., & Guze, S. B. (1971). Hysteria: Studies of diagnosis, outcome and prevalence. *Journal of the American Medical Association, 215,* 425–28.

Woods, N. S., Eyler, F. D., Conlon, M., Behnke, M., & Wobie, K. (1998). Pygmalion in the cradle: Observer bias against cocaine-exposed infants. *Journal of Developmental and Behavioral Pediatrics, 19* (4): 283–85.

Woodward, B., & Armstrong, A. (1979). *The brethren: Inside the Supreme Court.* New York: Simon & Schuster.

Woolverton, W. L., & Weiss, S. R. B. (1998). Tolerance and sensitization to cocaine: An integrated view. In S. T. Higgins & J. L. Katz (Eds.), *Cocaine abuse: Behavior, pharmacology, and clinical applications* (pp. 107–34). San Diego: Academic Press.

Woo-Ming, A., & Siever, L. P. (1998). Psychopharmacological treatment of personality disorder. In P. Nathan & J. Gorman (Eds.), *A guide to treatments that work* (pp. 554–67). New York: Oxford University Press.

World Health Organization. (1995). *The state of world health—executive summary.*

World Health Organization Expert Committee on Drug Dependence. (1993). *World Health Organization Technical Report, 836,* 1–44.

Wrangham, R. W., & Peterson, D. (1996). *Demonic males: Apes and the origins of human violence.* Boston: Houghton Mifflin.

Wrobel, T. A., & Lochar, D. (1982). Validity of the Wiener subtle and obvious scales for the MMPI: Another example of the importance of inventory-item content. *Journal of Consulting and Clinical Psychology, 50,* 469–70.

Wu, J., Kramer, G.L., Kram, M., Steciuk, M., Crawford, I.L., & Petty, F. (1999). Serotonin and learned helplessness: A regional study of 5-HT-sub(1A), 5-HT-sub(2A) receptors and the serotonin transport site in rat brain. *Journal of Psychiatric Research, 33* (1): 17–22.

Wyatt, R. J., & Henter, I. D. (1998). The effects of early and sustained intervention on the long-term morbidity of schizophrenia. *Journal of Psychiatric Research, 32,* 169–77.

Wykes, T. (1998). What are we changing with neurocognitive rehabilitation? Illustrations from two single cases of changes in neuropsychological performance and brain systems as measured by SPECT. *Schizophrenia Research, 34,* 77–86.

Wykes, T., Reeder, C., Corner, J., Williams, C., & Everitt, B. (1999). The effects of neurocognitive remediation on executive processing in patients with schizophrenia. *Schizophrenia Bulletin, 25* (2): 291–307.

Yaffe, K., Blackwell, T., Gore, R., Sands, L., Reus, V., & Browner, W. S. (1999). Depressive symptoms and cognitive decline in nondemented elderly women: A prospective study. *Archives of General Psychiatry, 56,* 425–30.

Yaganita, T. (1976). Some methodological problems in assessing dependence-producing properties of drugs in animals. *Pharmacological Reviews, 27,* 503–509.

Yager, J., Grant, I., & Bolus, R. (1984). Interaction of life events and symptoms in psychiatric patient and nonpatient married couples. *Journal of Nervous and Mental Disease, 172* (1): 21–25.

Yager, T., Laufer, R., & Gallops, M. (1984). Some problems associated with war experience in men of the Vietnam generation. *Archives of General Psychiatry, 41,* 327–33.

Yalom, I. D. (1980). *Existential psychotherapy.* New York: Basic Books.

Yalom, I. (1990). *Love's executioner, and other tales of psychotherapy.* New York: Harper-Collins.

Yargic, L. I., Sar, V., Tutkun, H., & Alyanak, B. (1998). Comparison of dissociative identity disorder with other diagnostic groups using a structured interview in Turkey. *Comprehensive Psychiatry, 39* (6): 345–51.

Yarnold, P. R., & Bryant, F. B. (1994). A measurement model for the Type A Self-rating Inventory. *Journal of Personality Assessment, 62* (1):102–15.

Yates, A. (1966). *Theory and practice in behavior therapy* (2nd ed.). New York: Wiley.

Yates, A. (1990). Current perspectives on eating disorders: 2. Treatment, outcomes and research directions. *Journal of the American Academy of Child and Adolescent Psychiatry, 29* (1).

Yates, W. R., Cadoret, R. J., & Troughton, E. P. (1999). The Iowa adoption studies: Methods and results. In M. C. LaBuda, E. L. Grigorenko, et al. (Eds.), *On the way to individuality: Current methodological issues in behavioral genetics* (pp. 95–125). Commack, NY: Nova Science.

Yeates, K. O., Taylor, H. G., Drotar, D., Wade, S. L., Klein, S., Stancin, T., & Schatschneider, C. (1997). Preinjury family environment as a determinant of recovery from traumatic brain injuries in school-age children. *Journal of the International Neuropsychological Society, 3,* 617–30.

Yehuda, R. (2000). Biology of posttraumatic stress disorder. *Journal of Clinical Psychiatry, 61* (Suppl 7): 14–21.

Yehuda, R., Marshall, R., & Giller, E. L., Jr. (1998). Psychopharmacological treatment of post-traumatic stress disorder. In P. E. Gorman and J. M. Nathan (Eds.), *A guide to treatments that work* (pp. 377–97). New York: Oxford University Press.

Yoshioka, H., Yoshida, A., Okana, S., & Yamazoe, I. (1995). Effects of early undernutrition and subsequent nutritional rehabilitation on brain development: I. The most critical period. *Developmental Brain Dysfunction, 8,* 66–72.

Yule, W., Hersov, L., & Treseder, J. (1980). Behavioral treatments of school refusal. In L. Hersov & I. Berg (Eds.), *Out of school: Modern perspectives in truancy and school refusal.* New York: Wiley.

Yule, W., & Rutter, M. (1976). Epidemiology and social implication of specific reading retardation. In R. M. Knights & D. J. Bakker (Eds.), *The neuropsychology of learning disorders.* Baltimore: University Park Press.

Zafiropoulou, M., & McPherson, F. M. (1986). "Preparedness" and the severity and outcomes of clinical phobias. *Behaviour Research and Therapy, 24,* 221–22.

Zahner, G. E., Pawelkiewicz, W., DeFrancesco, J. J., & Adnopoz, J. (1992). Children's mental health service needs and utilization patterns in an urban community: An epidemiological assessment. *Journal of the American Academy of Child and Adolescent Psychiatry, 31* (5): 951–60.

Zametkin, A. J., & Ernst, M. (1999). Current concepts: Problems in the management of attention-deficit-hyperactivity disorder. *New England Journal of Medicine, 340,* 40–46.

Zanarini, M. C., Gunderson, J. G., Marina, M. F., Schwartz, E. O., & Frankenberg, F. R. (1989). Childhood experiences of borderline patients. *Comprehensive Psychiatry, 30,* 18–25.

Zanarini, M. C., Williams, A. A., Lewis, R. E., Reich, R. B., Vera, S. C., Marino, M. F., Levin, A., Yong, L., & Frankenburg, F. R. (1997). Reported pathological childhood experiences associated with the development of borderline personality disorder. *American Journal of Psychiatry, 154,* 1101–1106.

Zanis, D. A., McLellan, T., Alterman, A. I., & Cnaan, R. A. (1996). Efficacy of enhanced outreach counseling to reenroll high-risk drug users 1 year after discharge from treatment. *American Journal of Psychiatry, 153* (8): 1095–96.

Zarit, S. H. , & Knight, B. G. (Eds.). (1996). *A guide to psychotherapy and aging: Effective clinical interventions in a life-stage context.* Washington, DC: American Psychological Association.

Zeiss, A. M., & Steffen, A. (1996). Behavioral and cognitive-behavioral treatments: An overview of social learning. In S. H. Zarit & B. G. Knight (Eds.), *A guide to psychotherapy and aging: Effective clinical interventions in a life-stage context* (pp. 35–60). Washington, DC: American Psychological Association.

Zentall, S. S., & Zentall, T. R. (1983). Optimal stimulation: A model of disordered activity and performance in normal and deviant children. *Psychological Bulletin, 94,* 446–71.

Zhang, Y., Raap, D. K., Garcia, F., Serres, F., Ma, Q., Battaglia, G., & Van de Kar, L. D. (2000). Long-term fluoxetine produces behavioral anxiolytic effects without inhibiting neuroendocrine responses to conditioned stress in rats. *Brain Research, 855,* 58–66.

Zhou, J. N., Hofman, M. A., Gooren, L. J. G., & Swaab, D. F. (1995). A sex difference in the human brain and its relation to transsexuality. [Letter to the Editor]. *Nature, 378.*

Ziegler, F. J., & Imboden, J. B. (1962). Contemporary conversion reactions: II. A conceptual model. *Archives of General Psychiatry, 6,* 279–87.

Zigler, E., & Levine, J. (1981). Age on first hospitalization of schizophrenics: A developmental approach. *Journal of Abnormal Psychology, 90,* 458–67.

Zigler, E., & Phillips, L. (1961). Psychiatric diagnosis and symptomatology. Journal of *Abnormal and Social Psychology, 63,* 69–75.

Zilbergeld, B., & Evans, M. (1980). The inadequacy of Masters and Johnson. *Psychology Today, 14,* 28–43.

Zima, B. T., Wells, K. B., Benjamin, B., & Duan, N. (1996). Mental health problems among homeless mothers: Relationship to service use and child mental health problems. *Archives of General Psychiatry, 53,* 332–38.

Zimbardo, P. G. (1977). Shy murderers. *Psychology Today, 148,* 66–76.

Zimmerberg, B., & Shartrand, A. M. (1992). Temperature-dependent effects of maternal separation on growth, activity, and amphetamine sensitivity in the rat. *Developmental Psychobiology, 25,* 213–26.

Zimmerman, M., & Mattia, J. I. (1998). Body dysmorphic disorder in psychiatric outpatients: Recognition, prevalence, comorbidity, demographic, and clinical correlates. *Comprehensive Psychiatry, 39* (5): 265–70.

Zimring, F. (1998). *American youth violence.* London: Oxford University Press.

Zinbarg, R. E., Barlow, D. H., Liebowitz, M., Street, L., Broadhead, E., Katon, W., Roy-Byrne, P., Lepine, J-P., Teharani, M., Richards, J., Brantley, P. J., & Kraemer, H. (1994). The DSM-IV field trial for mixed anxiety and depression. *American Journal of Psychiatry, 151*(8): 1153–62.

Zinberg, N. E. (1984). *Drugs, set, and setting.* New Haven, CT: Yale University Press.

Zinberg, N. E., Harding, W. M., & Winkeller, M. (1977). A study of social regulatory mechanisms in controlled illicit drug users. *Journal of Drug Issues, 7,* 117–33.

Zisook, S., Shuchter, S. R., Irwin, M., Darko, D. F., et al. (1994). Bereavement, depression, and immune function. *Psychiatry Research, 52* (1): 1–10.

Zitrin, C. M., Klein, D. F., Woerner, M. G., & Ross, D. C. (1983). Treatment of phobias. I. Comparison of imipramine hydrochloride and placebo. *Archives of General Psychiatry, 40,* 125–38.

Zlotnick, C. (1999) Antisocial personality disorder, affect dysregulation and childhood abuse among incarcerated women. *Journal of Personality Disorders, 13* (1): 90–95.

Zoccolillo, M., Pickles, A., Quinton, D., & Rutter, M. (1992). The outcome of childood conduct disorder: Implications for defining adult personality disorder and conduct disorder. *Psychological Medicine, 22,* 971–86.

Zoccolillo, M., Price, R., Ji, T., Hyun, C., & Hwu, H. (1999). Antisocial personality disorder: Comparisons of prevalence, symptoms, and correlates in four countries. In P. Cohen & C. Slomkowski (Eds.), *Historical and geographical influences on psychopathology* (pp. 249–77). Mahwah, NJ: Lawrence Erlbaum.

Zohar, A. H., Apter, A., King, R. A., Pauls, D. L., Leckman, J. F., & Cohen, D. J. (1999). Epidemiological studies. In J. F. Leckman & D. J. Cohen (Eds.), *Tourette's syndrome: Tics, obsessions, compulsions: Developmental psychopathology and clinical care* (pp. 177–93). New York: Wiley.

Zola-Morgan, S., Squire, L. R., & Amaral, D. (1986). Human amnesia and the medial temporal region: Enduring memory impairment following a bilateral lesion limited to the CA 1 field of the hippocampus. *Journal of Neuroscience, 6,* 2950–67.

Zorrilla, E. P., Redei, E., & DeRubeis, R. J. (1994). Reduced cytokine levels and T-cell function in healthy males: Relation to individual differences in subclinical anxiety. *Brain, Behavior, and Immunity, 8* (4): 293–312.

Zubin, J. E., & Spring, B. (1977). Vulnerability: A new view of schizophrenia. *Journal of Abnormal Psychology, 86,* 103–26.

Zucker, K. J., & Blanchard, R. (1997). Transvestic fetishism: Psychopathology and theory. In D. R. Laws & W. O'Donohue (Eds.), *Sexual deviance: Theory, assessment, and treatment* (pp. 253–79). New York: Guilford Press.

Zucker, K. J., & Bradley, S. J. (1995). *Gender identity disorder and psychosexual problems in children and adolescents.* New York: Guilford Press.

Zucker, K. J., Bradley, S. J., & Sanikhani, M. (1997). Sex differences in referral rates of children with gender identity disorder: Some hypotheses. *Journal of Abnormal Child Psychology, 25* (3): 217–27.

Zucker, K. J., Wilson-Smith, D. N., Kurita, J. A., & Stern, A. (1995). Children's appraisals of sex-typed behavior in their peers. *Sex Roles, 33* (11–12): 703–25.

Zucker, R. A. (1987). The four alcoholisms: A developmental account of the etiological process. In P. C. Rivers (Ed.), *Alcohol and addictive behavior* (pp. 27–83). Lincoln, NB: University of Nebraska Press.

Zuckerman, M. (1994). *Behavioral expressions and bio-social bases of sensation seeking.* New York: Cambridge University Press.

Zullow, H., & Seligman, M. E. P. (1985). *Pessimistic ruminations predict increase in depressive symptoms: A process model and longitudinal study.* Unpublished manuscript.

Acknowledgments and Copyrights

Excerpts

Front endpapers: DSM-IV classifications; adapted from the American Psychiatric Association, *Diagnostic and Statistical Manual of Mental Disorders,* Fourth edition. Washington, D.C.: American Psychiatric Association, 1994. Reprinted by permission. **Pages 23–24:** From the American Psychiatric Association, *Diagnostic and Statistical Manual of Mental Disorders,* Third edition. Washington, D.C.: American Psychiatric Association, 1981. Reprinted by permission. **Page 38:** From Harris, C., & Goetsch, V., Multi-component flooding treatment of adolescent phobia, in E. F. Feindler & G. Kalfus (Eds.), *Adolescent behavior therapy handbook.* Springer Publishing, Inc., New York, 10012. Used by permission. **Pages 66–67:** Francis, G., & Ollendick, T., Case study of Rebecca, in E. Feindler & G. Kalfus (Eds.), *Adolescent behavior therapy handbook.* Springer Publishing, Inc., New York, 10012. Used by permission. **Page 75:** Jones, K. M., & Friman, P. C., a case study of behavioral assessment and treatment of insect phobia. From *Journal of Applied Behavior Analysis,* 199, *32:* 95–98. **Page 115:** Ellis, A., *Reason and emotion in psychotherapy.* Copyright © 1962 by the Institute for Rational Living. Published by arrangement with Carol Publishing Group. **Pages 170, 171, 182:** From the American Psychiatric Association, *Diagnostic and Statistical Manual of Mental Disorders,* Fourth edition. Washington, D.C.: American Psychiatric Association, 1994. Reprinted by permission. **Page 163:** Vitkus, J., *Casebook in abnormal psychology.* New York: McGraw-Hill. Copyright © 1996 by the McGraw-Hill Companies. **Pages 183–184:** From Erikson, Kai, *Everything in its path: Destruction of community in the Buffalo Creek flood.* New York: Simon & Schuster, 1976. **Page 186:** Foa, E. B., & Rothbaum, B. O., *Treating the trauma of rape: Cognitive-behavioral therapy for PTSD.* New York: Guilford Press, 1997. **Pages 193, 202, 210:** Laughlin, H. P. *The neuroses.* Copyright © 1967 by Butterworth Publishers, Woburn, MA. Excerpted by permission. **Pages 194, 200, 203, 206:** From the American Psychiatric Association, *Diagnostic and Statistical Manual of Mental Disorders,* Fourth edition. Washington, D.C.: American Psychiatric Association, 1994. Reprinted by permission. **Pages 198–99:** Clark, D. Anxiety states: Panic and generalized anxiety, in K. Hawton, P.

Salkovskis, J. Kirk, & D. Clark (Eds.), *Cognitive behavior therapy for psychiatric problems: A practical guide.* Oxford, England: Oxford University Press, 1989. **Pages 207–208:** Rachman, S. J., & Hodgson, R. J., *Obsessions and compulsions.* Copyright © 1980 by Prentice Hall, Inc., Englewood Cliffs, N.J. **Pages 221–22:** Personal communication from Dr. James Stinnett, University of Pennsylvania Hospital, 1978. Used by permission. **Pages 224, 233:** Laughlin, H. P. *The neuroses.* Copyright © 1967 by Butterworth Publishers, Woburn, MA. Excerpted by permission. **Pages 224, 225, 226, 234, 236, 237:** From the American Psychiatric Association, *Diagnostic and Statistical Manual of Mental Disorders,* Fourth edition. Washington, D.C.: American Psychiatric Association, 1994. Reprinted by permission. **Page 236:** Greyson, B. Near-death narratives, in S. Krippner & S. Powers (Eds.), *Broken images, broken selves.* Washington, D.C.: Brunner/Mazel. **Page 238:** Davis, P. H., & Osherson, A., The current treatment of a multiple-personality woman and her son. *American Journal of Psychotherapy,* 1977, *31:* 504–15. Reprinted by permission of the Association for the Advancement of Psychotherapy. **Pages 251–52:** Karp, D. A. *Speaking of sadness: Depression, disconnection, and the meaning of illness.* New York: Oxford University Press, 1996, p. 24. **Page 252:** From the American Psychiatric Association, *Diagnostic and Statistical Manual of Mental Disorders,* Fourth edition. Washington, D.C.: American Psychiatric Association, 1994. Reprinted by permission. **Pages 254, 255, 279–80:** Beck, A. T., Rush, A. J., Shaw, B. F., & Emery, G., *Cognitive therapy of depression.* New York: Guilford Press, 1979. **Page 284:** From the American Psychiatric Association, *Diagnostic and Statistical Manual of Mental Disorders,* Fourth edition. Washington, D.C.: American Psychiatic Association, 1994. Reprinted by permission. **Pages 284–86:** Fieve, R. R., *Mood swing,* Copyright © 1975 by Ronald Fieve. Reprinted by permission of HarperCollins Publishers, Inc. **Pages 285–86:** Pavel, O., *How I came to know fish* (trans. J. Barclai & R. McDowell). New York: Story Line Press/New Directions, 1990. Reprinted by permission. **Pages 290, 307, 310, 316, 326, 327, 328, 330, 339, 340, 344, 346, 347, 350, 361, 363, 372, 376, 379, 380, 381, 384, 398, 400, 403, 407, 408, 410, 418:** From the American Psychiatric Association, *Diagnostic* and *Statistical Manual of Mental Disorders*, Fourth edition. Washington, D.C.: American Psychiatric Association, 1994. Reprinted by permission. **Page 290:** Adapted from Spitzer, R. L., Skodol, A. E., Gibbon, M., & Williams, J. B. W., *DSM-III casebook*. Washington, D.C.: American Psychiatric Association, 1989, pp. 19–21, 129–30. Reprinted by permission of the American Psychiatric Association. **Pages 295–96:** Jerome, J., Catching them before suicide, *The New York Times Magazine*, January 11, 1979. Copyright © 1979 by the New York Times Company. Reprinted by permission. **Pages 458–60:** Goode, E., With help, climbing back from schizophrenia's isolation. Copyright © 1999 by the New York Times Co. Reprinted by permission. **Pages 477, 483, 486, 487:** From the American Psychiatric Association, *Diagnostic and Statistical Manual of Mental Disorders*, Fourth edition. Washington, D.C.: American Psychiatric Association, 1994. Reprinted by permission. **Page 478:** Mace, N., & Rabins, P. V., *The thirty-six hour day: A family guide to caring for persons with Alzheimer's disease*. Baltimore: The Johns Hopkins University Press, 1981. Used with permission. **Page 485:** Neary, D., Snowden, J. S., Northern, B., & Goulding, P., Dementia of frontal lobe type. *Journal of Neurology*, Neuroscience and Psychiatry, 1988, *51:* 353–61. **Page 488:** Lichtenburg, P. A. (1999). *Handbook of clinical gerontology*. New York: Wiley. **Pages 490–92:** Dick, L. P., Gallagher-Thompson, D., & Thompson, L. W., Cognitive-behavioral therapy. In R. T. Woods (Ed.), *Handbook of the clinical psychology of aging*, pp. 509–44. New York: Wiley-Liss, 1996. **Pages 495, 504:** From the American Psychiatric Association, *Diagnostic and Statistical Manual of Mental Disorders*, Fourth edition. Washington, D.C.: American Psychiatric Association, 1994. Reprinted by permission. **Page 501:** Widdowson, E., Mental contentment and physical growth. *The Lancet*, 1951, *16:* 1316. Copyright © 1951 by the Lancet Ltd. **Page 522:** Weisman, A. D., A study of the psychosomatics of duodenal ulcer exascerbations. From *Psychosomatic Medicine*, 1956, *18:* 2–42. **Pages 529, 538, 546, 548, 550, 551, 552, 553, 561, 562, 563, 564, 565:** From the American Psychiatric Association, *Diagnostic and Statistical Manual of Mental Disorders*, Fourth edition. Washington, D.C.: American Psychiatric Association, 1994. Reprinted by permission. **Pages 537–38:** Pauly, I. B., Adult manifestations of male transsexualism, in R. Green & J. Money (Eds), *Transsexualism and sex reassignment*. Baltimore: Johns Hopkins University Press, 1969. Copyright © 1969 by the Johns Hopkins University Press. Adapted by permission. **Pages 547–48:** Stoller, R. J., Parental influence in male transsexualism, in R. Green & J. Money (Eds.); *Transsexualism and sex reassignment*. Baltimore: John Hopkins University Press, 1969. Copyright © 1969 by the Johns Hopkins University Press. Adapted by permission. **Pages 551, 556:** Maletzky, B. M. The paraphilias: Research and treatment, in P. E. Nathan & J. M. Gorman (Eds.), *A guide to treatments that work*. New York: Oxford University Press, 1998. **Page 569:** Handy. B., The Viagra craze. *Time Magazine*, May 9, 1998, *151:* 7. Copyright © Time Inc. Reprinted by permission. **Pages 578, 591, 593, 603, 606, 612, 614, 619, 621, 622, 624, 627, 632:** From the American Psychiatric Association, *Diagnostic and Statistical Manual of Mental Disorders*, Fourth edition. Washington, D.C.: American Psychiatric Associaiton, 1994. Reprinted by permission. **Pages 600–601:** Tinsley, J. A., & Watkins, D. D., Over-the-counter stimulants: Abuse and addiction. *Mayo Clinic Proceedings*, 1998, *73:* 977–82. **Page 660:** Livermore, J. M., and Meehl, P. E., from the *Minnesota Law Review*, 1967, *789:* 833–55. Reprinted by permission. **Page 674:**

Ennis, Bruce J., *Prisoners of psychiatry: Mental patients, psychiatrists, and the law*. Copyright © 1972 by Bruce J. Ennis. Reprinted by the permission of Harcourt Brace, Inc.

Figures

Figure 2–1: Rosenzweig, M. R., & Leiman, A. L., *Physiological Psychology*, 2nd ed. New York: McGraw-Hill, Copyright © 1989 by the McGraw-Hill Companies. Reprinted by permission. **Figure 2–2:** (A) Adapted from *Psychology* by Henrty Gleitman by permission of W. W. Norton and Company, Inc. Copyright © 1981 by W. W. Norton & Company, Inc. (B) Dr. James Butcher, the Minnesota report. Copyright by the University of Minnesota Press. **Figure 2–3:** Reprinted from *Psychology* by Henry Gleitman, by permission of W. W. Norton & Company, Inc. Copyright © 1981 by W. W. Norton and Company. **Figure 2–4:** Reprinted from *Psychology* by Henry Gleitman, by permission of W. W. Norton & Company, Inc. Copyright © 1981 by W. W. Norton and Company. **Figure 2–8:** Jones, K. M., & Friman, P. C., A case study of behavioral assessment and treatment of insect phobia. From *Journal of Applied Behavior Analysis*, 1999, *32:* 97. **Figure 3–2:** Adapted from Schwartz, B. *Psychology of learning and behavior*, 2nd ed. New York: W. W. Norton & Company, Inc. Reprinted by permission. **Figure 4–3:** Cunningham, J. D., figure 6.19, from *Human Biology*, 2nd ed. Copyrght © 1989 by John D. Cunningham. Reprinted by permission of Addison Wesley Longman Publishers, Inc. **Figure 4–4:** Cunningham, J. D., figure 10.7, from *Human Biology*, 2nd ed. Copyright © 1989 by John D. Cunningham. Reprinted by permission of Addison Wesley Longman Publishers, Inc. **Figure 4–6:** Nicholls, J. G., Martin, A. R., & Wallace, B. G., *From Neuron to Brain*. Copyright © 1992 by Sinauer Associates, Inc. **Figure 4–11:** Adapted from A. Luria, The functional organization of the brain. *Scientific American*, 1970, *222:* 71. **Figure 4–15:** Cunningham, J. D., figure 6.9, from *Human Biology*, 2nd ed. Copyright © 1989 by John D. Cunningham. Reprinted by permission of Addison Wesley Longman Publishers, Inc. **Figure 4–16:** Reprinted from *Neuropsychologia, 28,* P. R. Huttenlocher, Morphometric study of human cerebral cortex development. Copyright © 1990, with permission from Elsevier Science. **Figure 5–3:** Archibald, H. C., & Tuddenham, R. D. Persistent stress reaction after combat. *Archives of General Psychiatry*, 1965, *12:* 475–81. Copyright © 1965, American Medical Association. Reprinted by permission. **Figure 6–1:** Lewis, D. O., Yeager, C. A., Swica, Y., Pincus, J. H., & Lewis, M., Objective documentation of child abuse and dissociation in twelve murderers with DID. *American Journal of Psychiatry*, 1997, *154* (12): 1706. Copyright © 1997, The American Psychiatric Association. Reprinted by permission. **Figure 7–1:** Cross-National Collaborative Group, The changing rate of major depression. Cross-national comparisons. *Journal of the American Medical Association*, 1992, *268* (21): 3100–3102. Copyright © 1992, American Medical Association. Reprinted by permission. **Figure 7–2:** Modified from *Drugs and the Brain* by Solomon H. Snyder. Copyright © 1986 by Scientific American Library, Inc. Used with permission of W. H. Freeman & Company. **Figure 7–3:** Schildkraut, J., The catecholamine hypothesis, *The American Journal of Psychiatry*, 1997, *122:* 509–522. Copyright © 1997, the American Psychiatric Association. Reprinted by permission.

Figure 7–4: Adapted from Maier, S. F., Seligman, M. E. P., & Solomon, R. L., Pavlovian fear conditioning and learned helplessness: Effects on escape and avoidance behavior of (a) the CS-US contingency and (b) the independence of the US and voluntary responding, in B. A. Campbell, & R. M. Church (Eds.), *Punishment and aversive behavior*, 1969, p. 328. **Figure 7–7:** Bunney, W. E., Jr., & Murphy, D. L., The switch process in bipolar disorder, in N. S. Kline (Ed.), *Factors in depression*, 1974. Copyright © Lippincott Williams & Wilkins. **Figure 7–8:** Rosenthal, N. E., Sack, D. A., Gillin, J. C., Lewy, A. J., Goodwin, F. K., Davenport, Y., Mueller, P. S., Newsome, D. A., & Wehr, T. A., Seasonal affective disorder: A description of the syndrome and preliminary findings with light therapy. *Archives of General Psychiatry*, 1984, *41*, 72–80. Copyright © 1984, American Medical Association. Reprinted by permission. **Figure 10–1:** From *Schizophrenia genesis: The origins of madness*, by Irving I. Gottesman. Copyright © 1991 by Irving I. Gottesman. Used by permission of W. H. Freeman and Company. **Figure 10–3:** Adapted from Kandel, E. R., Schwartz, J. H., & Jessel, T. M., *Principles of neural science* (3rd ed.). Norwalk, CT: Appleton & Lange, 1991, p. 864. **Figure 10–5:** Courtesy of National Institutes of Mental Health. **Figure 11–1:** Reprinted with permission from Lamberts, S. W., van den Beld, A. W., & van der Lely, A., The endocrinology of aging. *Science*, 1997, *278* (5337): 419–24. Copyright © 1997 by the American Association for the Advancement of Science. **Figure 11–2:** Graph from Gatz, M., Kasl-Godley, J. E., & Karel, M. J., Aging and mental disorders, in *Handbook of the Psychology of Aging*, 4th ed., Birren & Schaie, (Eds.). Copyright © 1996 by Academic Press. Reproduced by permission of the publisher. **Figure 11–3:** Henderson, A. S., Jorm, A. F., Korten, A. E., Jacomb, P., Christensen, H., & Rodgers, B., Symptoms of anxiety and depression during adult life: Evidence for a decline in prevalence with age. *Psychological Medicine*, 1998, *28*, 1324. **Figure 11–4:** Howard, R., Castle, D., Wessely, S., & Murray, R., A comparative study of 470 cases of early-onset and late-onset schizophrenia. *British Journal of Psychiatry*, 1993, *163*: 354. **Figure 12–2:** Selye, H., *Stress without distress*. Copyright 1974 by HarperCollins Publishers, Inc. Reprinted by permission of HarperCollins Publishers, Inc. **Figure 12–4:** Adapted from McEwen, B., Protective and damaging effects of stress mediators. *New England Journal of Medicine*, 1998, *338*: 172. **Figure 12–7:** Barefoot, J. C., Dahlstrom, W. G., & Williams, R. B., Hostility, CHD incidence, and total mortality: A 25-year follow-up study of 255 physicians. *Psychosomatic Medicine*, 1983, *45* (1): 59–63. Copyright © 1983 by the American Psychosomatic Society, Inc. **Figure 12–8:** Karasek, R., Baker, D., Marxer, F., Ahlbom, A., & Theorell, T., Job decision latitude, job demand, and cardiovascular disease: A prospective study of Swedish men. *American Journal of Public Health*, 1981, *71*: 694–705. Reprinted by permission. **Figure 12–9:** Spiegel D., Bloom, J. R., Kraemer H. C., & Gottheil E., Effect of psychosocial treatment on survival of patients with metastatic breast cancer. *The Lancet*, October 14, 1989, pp. 888–91. Copyright © 1989 by the Lancet Ltd. **Figure 13–1:** Rosler, A., & Witzum, E., Treatment of men with paraphilia with a long-acting analogue of gonadotropin-releasing hormone, *New England Journal of Medicine*, 1998, *338*: 416–422. Copyright © 1998, by the Massachusetts Medical Society. **Figure 13–2:** Goldstein, I., Lue, T. F., Padma-Nathan, H., Rosen, R. C., Steers, W. D., & Wicker, P. A., Oral Sildenafil in the treatment of erectile dysfunction, *New England Journal of Medicine*, 1998, *338*: 1402. Copyright © 1998 by the Massachusetts Medical Society. **Figure 14–1:** Hunt, W. A., Barnett, L. W., & Branch, L. G., Relapse rates in addiction programs. *Journal of Clinical Psychology*, 1971, *27*, 455–56. **Figure 14–2:** Modified from *Drugs and the brain* by Solomon H. Snyder. Copyright © 1986 by Scientific American Books, Inc. Used with permission of W. H. Freeman and Company. **Figure 14–3:** Solomon, R. I., & Corbit, J. D. An opponent process theory of motivation, from *Psychological Reviews*, 1974, *81* (2): 119–45. Reprinted by permission. **Figure 14–5:** Schuckit, M. A. Subjective response to alcohol in sons of alcoholics and controls. *Archives of General Psychiatry*, 1984, *41*: 879–84. Copyright © 1984, American Medical Association. **Figure 14–6:** Marlatt, G. A., & Gordon, J. R. *Relapse prevention: Maintenance strategies in the treatment of addictive behaviors*, Figure 1–4. New York: Guilford Press, 1985, p. 38. **Figure 14–7:** Deneau, G., Yaganita, T., & Seevers, M. H., Self-administration of psychoactive substances by the monkey. *Psychopharmacologia* (Berlin), 1969, *16*: 30–48. Copyright © 1969 by Springer-Verlag Berlin-Heidelberg. **Figure 14–8:** Higgins, S. T., Budney, A. J., Bickel, W. K., Hughes, J. R., Foerg, F., & Badger, G., Achieving cocaine abstinence with a behavioral approach. *American Journal of Psychiatry*, 1993, *150* (5): 763–69. Copyright © 1993 by the American Psychiatric Association. Reprinted by permission. **Figure 14–9:** From *Drugs and the brain* by Solomon N. Snyder. Copyright © 1986 by Scientific American Books, Inc. Used with permission of W. H. Freeman and Company. **Figure 14–10:** Matthias, R. Students' use of marijuana, other illicit drugs, and cigarettes continued to rise in 1995. *NIDA Research Advances*, 1996, *11* (1). **Figure 16–1:** From the manual for the Penn Optimism Program, Depressive Prevention for School Children, 1996; courtesy Dr. M. E. P. Seligman.

Tables

Table 2–1: Butcher, J. N., *MMPI Research developments and clinical applications*. Copyright © 1969 by McGraw Hill, Inc., New York. Used with permission of the McGraw-Hill Book Company. **Table 2–2:** Robins, L. N., Helzer, J. E., Weissman, M. M., Orvaschel, H., Gruenberg, E., Burke, J. D., & Regier, D. A., Lifetime prevalence of specific psychiatric disorders in three sites. *Archives of General Psychiatry*, 1995, *41*: 949–58. Copyright © 1995 by the American Medical Association. **Table 2–3:** Kessler, R. C., McGonagle, K. A., Zhao, S., Nelson, C. B., Hughes, M., Eshleman, S., Wittchen, H., & Kendler, K. S., Lifetime and 12-month prevalence of DSM-III-R psychiatric disorders in the United States. *Archives of General Psychiatry*, 1994, *51*: 8–19. Copyright © 1994 by the American Medical Association. **Table 3–4:** Abramson, L. Y., Seligman, M. E. P., & Teasdale, J., Learned helplessness in humans: Critique and reformulation. *Journal of Abnormal Psychology*, 1978, *87*: 32–48. Copyright © 1978 by the American Psychological Association. Reprinted by permission. **Table 3–5:** Adapted from Lazarus, A. A., *Multimodal behavior theory*. Copyright © 1976, Springer Publishing Company, Inc., New York, 10012. **Table 5–2:** Seligman, M. E. P., *What you can change and what you can't*. New York: Knopf, 1994, p. 78–79. Adapted by permission. **Table 5–4:** Seligman, M. E. P., *What you can change and what you can't*. New York: Knopf, 1994, p. 143. Adapted by permission. **Table 5–6:** Seligman, M. E. P., *What you can change and what you can't*. New

York: Knopf, 1994, p. 67. Adapted by permission. **Table 5–7:** Seligman, M. E. P., *What you can change and what you can't.* New York: Knopf, 1994, pp. 78–79. Adapted by permission. **Table 5–10:** Seligman, M. E. P., *What you can change and what you can't.* New York: Knopf, 1994, p. 93. Adapted by permission. **Table 5–11:** Seligman, M. E. P., *What you can change and what you can't.* New York: Knopf, 1994, p. 58. Adapted by permission. **Table 6–3:** Lewis, D. O., Yeager, C. A., Swica, Y., Pincus, J. H., & Lewis, M., Objective documentation of child abuse and dissociation in 12 murderers with dissociative identity disorder. *American Journal of Psychiatry,* 1997, *154* (12): 1704. Copyright © 1997, The American Psychiatric Association. Reprinted by permission. **Table 7–1:** Robins, L. N., Helzer, J. E., Weissman, M. M., Orvaschel, H., Gruenberg, E., Burke, J. D., & Regier, D. A., Lifetime prevalence of specific psychiatric disorders in three sites. *Archives of General Psychiatry,* 1984, *41:* 949–58. Copyright © 1984, American Medical Association. **Table 7–3:** Seligman, M. E. P., *What you can change and what you can't.* New York: Knopf, 1994, p. 114. Adapted by permission. **Table 7–5:** Shneidman, E., Suicide among the gifted. In E. S. Shneidman (Ed.), *Suicidology: Contemporary developments.* New York: Grune & Stratton, 1976. Adapted by permission of Edwin Shneidman. **Table 7–6:** WHO division of Mental Health. **Table 9–2:** Lyons, M. J., True, W. R., Eisen, S. A., Goldberg, J., Meyer, J. M., Faraone, S. V., Eaves, L. J., & Tsuang, M. T., Differential heritability of adult and juvenile antisocial traits. *Archives of General Psychiatry,* 1995, *52:* 906–915. Copyright © 1995 by the American Medical Association. **Table 9–3:** Modified from Hutchings, B., & Mednick, S. A., Criminality in adoptees and their adoptive parents: A pilot study, M. S. A. Mednick & K. O. Christiansen (Eds.), *Biosocial bases of criminal behavior.* New York: Gardner Press, 1977, p. 132. **Table 10–2:** Adapted from *Schizophrenia genesis: The Origins of Madness* by Irving I. Gettesman. Copyright © 1991 by Irving I. Gottesman. **Table 11–1:** Jeste, D. V., Alexopoulos, G. S., Bartels, S. J., Cummings, J. L., Gallo, J. J., Gottlieb, G. L., Halpain, M. C., Palmer, B. W., Patterson, T. L., Reynolds, C. F. III, & Lebowitz, B. D. Consensus statement on the upcoming crisis in geriatric mental health. *Archives of General Psychiatry,* 1999, *56* (9): 848–53. Copyright © 1999 by the American Medical Association. **Table 12–1:** Holmes, T. H., & Rahe, R. H., The social readjustments ratings scale. *Journal of Psychosomatic Research,* 1967, *11:* 213–18. Elsevier Science, Ltd., Pergamon Imprint, Oxford, England. **Table 12–2:** Weiss, J. M. Effects of coping behavior in different warning signaled conditions on stress pathology in rats. *Journal of Comparative and Physiological Psychology,* 1971, *77:* 1–13. Copyright © 1971 by the American Psychological Association. Reprinted by permission of the author. **Table 13–1:** Seligman, M. E. P., *What you can change and what you can't.* New York: Knopf, 1994. Adapted by permission. **Table 14–1:** Swan, T., Gender affects relationships between drug abuse and psychiatric disorders. *NIDA Research Advances,* *12*(4): 22. **Table 14–2:** Adapted from National Institute of Drug Abuse, 2000. **Table 14–3:** Kreek, M. J. Rationale for maintenance pharmacotherapy of opiate dependence, in C. P. O'Brien & J. H. Jaffe (Eds.), *Addictive States.* New York: Raven Press, 1992. **Table 14–4:** Adapted from Philip J. Hilts, Is nicotine addictive? It depends on whose criteria you use, in *New York Times,* August 2, 1994, p. C3. Copyright © 1994 by The New York Times Company.

Boxes

Box 2–2: Adapted from the American Psychiatric Association, *The DSM-IV Casebook: A Learning Companion to the Diagnostic and Statistical Manual of Mental Disorders,* Fourth Edition. Washington, D.C.: American Psychiatric Association, 1994. Reprinted by permission. **Box 2–3:** From the American Psychiatric Association, *Diagnostic and Statistical Manual of Mental Disorders,* Fourth edition. Washington, D.C.: American Psychiatric Association, 1994. Reprinted by permission. **Box 5–3:** Rachman, S. J., & Hodgson, R. J. *Obsessions and compulsions.* Copyright © 1980 by Prentice-Hall, Inc., Englewood Cliffs, NJ. **Box 5–4:** "Self-Analysis Questionnaire," developed by Charles Spielberger in collaboration with G. Jacobs, R. Crane, S. Russell, L. Westberry, L. Barker, E. Johnson, J. Knight, & E. Marks. Adapted by permission of Dr. Charles Spielberger. **Box 6–1:** DeAngelis, T., Cambodians' sight loss tied to seeing atrocities, *APA Monitor,* July, 1990, pp. 36–37. Copyright © 1990 by the American Psychological Association. Adapted by permission. **Box 6–2:** Lewis, D. O., Yeager, C. A., Swica, Y., Pincus, J. H., & Lewis, M., Objective documentation of child abuse and dissociation in 12 murderers with dissociative identity disorder. *American Journal of Psychiatry,* 1997, *154* (12): 1708. Copyright © 1997, The American Psychiatric Association. Reprinted by permission. **Box 7–1:** Seligman, M. E. P., *What you can change and what you can't.* New York: Knopf, 1994, p. 58. Adapted by permission. **Box 7–2:** Seligman, M. E. P., Reivich, K., Jaycox, L., & Gillham, J., *The optimistic child.* New York: Houghton Mifflin, 1995. **Box 7–3:** Adapted from S. Boseley, They said it was safe, *The Guardian,* October 30, 1999. **Box 9–1:** Reprinted from Raine, A., The SPQ: A scale for the assessment of schizotypal personality. *Schizophrenia Bulletin,* 1991, *17:* 555–64. **Box 9–3:** Meloy, J. R., Predatory violence during mass murder. Extracted with permission from the *Journal of Forensic Sciences,* 1997, *42,* p. 326–29. Copyright © 1997 by the American Society for Testing and Materials, West Conshohocken, PA 19428.

Photo and Cartoon Credits

Chapter 1 Opener (p. 2): August Natterer, *The Miraculous Shepherd (II);* reproduced with permission of the Prinzhorn-Sammlung, University of Heidelberg. **p. 4:** Adolf Wölfli, *La Violette Geante;* reproduced with permission of the Art Brut Collection, Lausanne. **p. 12:** John Verano/Smithsonian Institute. **p. 13:** T. H. Matteson, *Examination of a Witch,* 1853, courtesy Peabody Essex Museum Salem, MA. **p. 14:** Jan Sanders, *The Stone of Folly,* 1530; courtesy Museo del Prado, Madrid. **p. 15:** National Library of Medicine. **p. 17:** © Bettmann/Corbis. **p. 20:** *(left)* Drawing by Paul Duhem, Art en Marge, Brussels; *(right)* "Stressé?," illustration by Genevieve Côté. **p. 21:** Painting by Jennie Maruki; reproduced with permission of Hospital Audiences, Inc. **p. 22:** © Marcia Weinstein. **p. 23:** Photofest. **p. 25:** Guillaume Pujolle, *La Chaise Electrique;* reproduced with permission of the Art Brut Collection, Lausanne. **Chapter 2 Opener (p. 30):** Gaston Duf, *Gânsthêrs Vitrês'-he;* reproduced with permission of the Art Brut Collection, Lausanne. **p. 33:** AP/Wide World Photos, Ruth Fremson. **p. 38:** © 1994, B.S.I.P./Custom Medical Stock Photos. **p. 39:** Michael Rosenfeld/Stone Images. **p. 40:** Dr. Marcus E. Raichle. **p. 41:** Courtesy Dr. Henry Wagner. **p. 45:** Laura

A114 Credits

Collection, Lausanne. **p. 416:** From Charles Bell's "Madness" from *Essays on the Anatomy of Expression in Painting* (London: Longman, 1806). **p. 419:** Carl Lange, "Holy Miracle on the Insole"; reproduced with permission of the Prinzhorn-Sammlung, University of Heidelberg. **p. 420:** Courtesy Dr. D. A. Silbersweig, Functional Neuroimaging Laboratory. **p. 421:** Renée Magritte, *Song of the Violet*, © 1995 C. Herscovici, Brussels/Artists Rights Society, New York. **p. 423:** © Barbara J. Feigles/Stock Boston. **p. 424:** *(left)* Library of Congress; *(right)* Bethlem Royal Hospital Archives Museum. **p. 426:** Pencil drawing by Edmund Monsiel; reproduced with permission of Henry Boxer Gallery, London. **p. 431:** Drawing by August Klotz (Klett); reproduced with permission of the Prinzhorn-Sammlung, University of Heidelberg. **p. 432:** Drawing by Johann Knüpfer; reproduced with permission of the Prinzhorn-Sammlung, University of Heidelberg. **p. 434:** Reproduced with permission of the Prinzhorn-Sammlung, University of Heidelberg. **p. 436:** Photo courtesy of Edna A. Morlok. **p. 444:** *(all)* Courtesy of Anne Deveson. **p. 445:** Courtesy Elaine Walker. **p. 448:** *(left)* © Science Source/Photo Researchers; *(right)* © Science Source/Photo Researchers. **p. 451:** Courtesy National Institute of Mental Health. **p. 452:** Fine Line (Courtesy Kobal). **p. 454:** AP/Wide World Photos. **p. 457:** © 1979 Jerry Cooke/Photo Researchers. **p. 460:** M. Agins/*The New York Times*. **p. 462:** © Laura Pedrick/Sygma/Corbis. **Chapter 11 Opener (p. 468):** Jean-Marie Heyligen, *Blue People*; reproduced with permission of Art en Marge, Brussels. **p. 470:** © Will and Deny McIntyre/Photo Researchers. **p. 472:** Courtesy of Dr. Gary Small, UCLA. **p. 475:** © Sidney Harris. **p. 476:** *(left)* © Corbis/Bettmann; *(center)* © Corbis/Bettmann; *(right)* H. Ruckemann/UPI. **p. 478:** © 1989 Sarah Leen/Matrix. **p. 480:** Blessed, G., Tomlinsun, B. E., & Roth, M. The association between quantitative measures of dementia and senile change in the cerebral gray matter of elderly subjects. *British Journal of Psychiatry*, 1968, *114:* 797–811. Reproduced by permission. **p. 481:** Visuals Unlimited. **p. 483:** © 1990 *The New Yorker* Collection, Jack Ziegler, from www.cartoonbank.com. **p. 485:** Damasio, H., Grabowski, T., Frank, R., Galaburda, A. M., & Damasio, A. R., The return of Phineas Gage: Clues about the brain from the skull of a famous person, *Science, 264*, © 1994 by the AAAS; courtesy Hanna Damasio. **p. 486:** *(left)* AP/Wide World Photos; *(right)* Photofest. **p. 490:** © Nathan Benn/Corbis/Bettmann. **p. 492:** © David Tunley/Corbis/Bettmann. **Chapter 12 Opener (p. 500):** Heinrich Anton Mueller, *L'Homme aux Mouches et le Serpent*; reproduced with permission of the Art Brut Collection, Lausanne. **p. 509:** *(top left)* AP/Wide World Photos; *(top right)* © 1994, Joel Gordon *(bottom)* © 1986 Lennart Nilsson/*National Geographic*; courtesy Bonniers Fakta, Sweden. **p. 511:** *(left)* © 1999 Christopher Morris/Black Star; *(right)* © 1998 Lisa Quinones/Black Star. **p. 513:** © Laura Dwight/Corbis. **p. 515:** Wartenberg/Picture Press/Corbis. **p. 517:** *(left)* Sportsphoto/Hulton Deutsch; *(right)* © Esbin-Anderson/The Image Works. **p. 519:** *(top)* AP/Wide World Photos; *(bottom)* Reuters/Bettmann. **p. 522:** Oi, M., Oshida, K., & Sugimura, A. Location of the gastric ulcer. *Gastroenterology*, 1959, *36*, 45–56. Copyright © 1959 The Williams and Wilkins Co. Reprinted by permission. **p. 524:** Photofest. **p. 525:** AP/Wide World Photos. **p. 529:** AP/Wide World Photos. **p. 532:** © Sidney Harris. **Chapter 13 Opener (p. 534):** Dora Holzhandler, *Lovers in Spring*. Reprinted with

permission of Henry Boxer Gallery, London. **p. 539:** Photofest. **p. 542:** *(left)* AP/Wide World Photos; *(right)* AP/Wide World Photos. **p. 543:** © Catherine Karnow/Corbis. **p. 547:** © Evan Agostini/Liaison Agency. **p. 548:** © Porter Gifford/Liaison Agency. **p. 550:** © Emmanuel Colombier/Liaison Agency **p. 552:** Photofest. **p. 554:** Photofest. **p. 558:** *(left)* © Ellen Senisi/The Image Works; *(right)* © Rhoda Sidney/The Image Works. **p. 567:** Courtesy Scott F. Johnson. **Chapter 14 Opener (p. 574):** Melissa Miller, *Smokey Spirits*, 1986; courtesy of Melissa Miller, Texas Gallery, Houston. **p. 576:** Roswell Angier/Stock Boston. **p. 577:** © Michael S. Yamashita/Corbis. **p. 589:** Robin Nelson/Black Star. **p. 590:** © A. Ramey/Stock Boston. **p. 591:** *(left)* © Christopher Brown/Stock Boston; *(right)* Todd Yates/Black Star. **p. 596:** Andrew Lichtenstein/Corbis Sygma. **p. 609:** Eugene Richards/Magnum. **p. 611:** *(left)* Amalie R. Rothschild; *(center)* Photofest; *(right)* Motion Picture & Television Photo Archive. **p. 618:** AP/Wide World Photos. **p. 620:** *Les Aigles-la Plume d'oie* by Guillaume Pujolle. Reproduced with permission of the Art Brut Collection, Lausanne. **p. 623:** AP/Wide World Photos. **p. 625:** David Young-Wolff/© Tony Stone Worldwide, Ltd. **p. 626:** Roy Carruthers, *Three Smokers*, courtesy Carruthers & Company/Newborn Group. **p. 629:** AP/Wide World Photos. **p. 631:** AP/Wide World Photos. **p. 634:** AP/Wide World Photos. **p. 635:** © Bob Daemmrich/Stock Boston. **p. 636:** AP/Wide World Photos. **Chapter 15 Opener (p. 639):** Painting by Marshall Arisman, © Marshall Arisman, School of Visual Arts, New York. **p. 641:** *(left)* Paramount (Courtesy Kobal); *(right)* Columbia/TriStar (Courtesy Kobal). **p. 642:** *(left)* © Hulton-Deutsch Collection/Corbis; *(center)* © Bettman/Corbis; *(right)* © Bettman/Corbis. **p. 649:** © Richard Bickel/Corbis. **p. 650:** AP/Wide World Photos. **p. 653:** AP/Wide World Photos. **p. 658:** Courtesy of John Wasson. **p. 659:** *(left)* AP/Wide World Photos; *(right)* AP/Wide World Photos. **p. 665:** *(left)* AP/Wide World Photos; *(right)* AP/Wide World Photos. **p. 666:** AP/Wide World Photos. **p. 668:** © M. Ging/*The Phoenix Gazette*. **p. 671:** Columbia (Courtesy Kobal). **p. 673:** *(left)* The Warder Collection; *(right)* United Press International Photos. **p. 675:** *(left)* Ken Hawkins/Corbis Sygma; *(right)* AP/Wide World Photos. **Chapter 16 Opener (p. 678):** Helen Kossoff, *Panel of Faces*; reproduced with permission of Hospital Audiences, Inc. **p. 681:** © Sommers/SIPA. **p. 683:** *(top and bottom)* Courtesy of Dr. Adrian Raine, University of Southern California. **p. 687:** © Gale Zucker/Stock Boston. **p. 689:** Eyewire/PhotoDisc. **p. 693:** © Raymond Gehman/Corbis.

Every effort has been made to contact the copyright holders of each of these selections. Rights holders of any selection not credited should contact W. W. Norton & Company, Inc., 500 Fifth Avenue, New York, NY 10010, in order for a correction to be made in the next reprinting of our work.

Name Index

Aaronson, B. A., 348
Abara, J., 431
Abe, K., 344
Abel, G. G., 549
Abi-Dargham, A., 449
Abikoff, H., 365, 367
Abrahamson, D. J., 563, 567
Abramowitz, J. S., 214
Abramowitz, L., 3
Abrams, A., 217
Abrams, D., 48
Abrams, J., 634
Abrams, R., 279
Abramson, L. Y., 70, 114, 259,
    271, 272, 273, 274
Abukmeil, S. S., 450
Adams, C., 459
Adams, H. E., 545, 549
Adams, N. E., 112, 178, 179
Adams, P., 531
Adams, W. L., 493
Addington, Frank O'Neal, 654-55
Addington, J., 435
Addy, C. L., 257
Adland, M., 287
Adler, Alfred, 91-92
Adler, L. E., 629
Adler, T., 44
Adlis, S., 261
Adnopoz, J., 304
Adolphs, R., 157
Adshead, G., 548
Aevarsson, O., 485
Ageton, S. S., 355
Aghajanian, G. K., 449, 621
Agras, S., 170
Agras, W. S., 340, 341
Agresta, J., 453
Agronin, M. E., 470
Aguilar, O., 435
Agyei, Y., 545
Ahlbom, A., 520

Ahrens, D., 640
Aigner, T. G., 604
Akiskal, H. S., 229
Alaghband-Rad, J., 450
Alarcon, R., 178
Al-Banna, M., 342
Albertini, R. S., 226
Alden, L. E., 113, 407
Aldenkamp, A. P., 333
Alessi, N., 53
Allan, L. G., 588
Allen, A. J., 212
Allen, K. D., 39
Allen, K. W., 109
Allen, L., 544
Allen, M. G., 265, 289
Allen, W., 526
Allnut, S., 401, 408
Alloy, L. B., 272
Almeida, O. P., 497
Alper, J., 523, 526
Alsobrook, J. P., 348
Alterman, A. I., 584, 599, 617
Alterman, T., 520
Althof, S., 565, 568, 570, 571
Altman, S., 459
Alyanak, B., 239
Amanzio, M., 503
Amara, A., 338
Ambinder, R., 543
Ambrose, M. J., 70
Ambrose, N., 345
Ambrosini, P. J., 364
Ames, M. A., 539, 544, 545
Amir, R. E., 327
Ammassari-Teule, M., 158
Anda, R., 519
Andersen, B. L., 562, 564, 570
Anderson, C., 567
Anderson, G., 237
Anderson, J. C., 353, 358
Anderson, J. R., 90

Andreasen, N. C., 430
Andrews, D. W., 358
Andrews, G., 201, 218, 346
Andrews, H., 653
Andrews, J., 315
Angermeyer, M. C., 640
Angold, A., 314
Angst, J., 256, 264, 284
Annas, P., 169, 170, 173, 175,
    476
Annau, Z., 175
Ansbacher, H. L., 92
Ansbacher, R., 92
Anthony, J. C., 489
Anthony, W. A., 460
Antoni, M. H., 139
Antonuccio, D. O., 277, 282
Antony, M., 196, 379
Anvret, M., 327
Apfelbaum, B., 564
Appelbaum, P. S., 651
Arajaervi, T., 344
Arango, V., 293
Aranow, R., 634
Arborelius, L., 268
Arbuthnot, J., 358
Archibald, H. C., 188
Arendt, Hannah, 99
Arif, A., 579
Armstrong, F. D., 354
Armstrong, Lance, 99
Armstrong, M., 545
Arndt, L. A., 530
Arnold, S. E., 451
Arnon, I., 187
Arnow, B., 342
Arntz, A., 404, 411
Aronowitz, B. R., 226
Aronson, T. A., 611
Ary, D. V., 392
Asarnow, J. R., 446
Asarnow, R. F., 443

Asberg, M., 293
Asch, Solomon E., 61
Ashcroft, R. C., 342
Ashton, A. K., 565
Assad, G., 420
Atkinson, J. W., 48
Atwater, J. D., 360
Auerbach, A. G., 443
Auerbach, J. G., 443
Aufdembrinke, B., 205
Avants, S. K., 616
Averbuck, D., 652
Averill, P. M., 493
Avery, J. M., 642
Axelsson, J. M., 290
Ayd, F. J., 493
Ayllon, T., 110
Aylward, E., 430
Ayres, B. D.,, Jr., 635

Baberg, H. T., 601
Babor, T. F., 576
Bach, D., 231
Bach, M., 231
Bachrach, L. L., 642
Bahrick, L., 77
Bailes, B. K., 625
Bailey, A., 322
Bailey, J. M., 404, 544, 545
Baillie, A. J., 407
Bakalar, J. B., 602, 622
Baker, C. A., 286
Baker, D., 520
Baker, L., 322, 342
Baker, L. A., 390
Baker, T. B., 630
Bakker, A., 538
Bakshi, V., 432
Baldessarini, R. J., 267
Baldeweg, T., 529
Ballaban-Gil, K., 325
Ballenger, J. C., 201, 202, 205

Subject Index